THREE CRITIQUES

CRITIQUE OF PURE REASON, CRITIQUE OF PRACTICAL REASON, CRITIQUE OF JUDGEMENT

IMMANUEL KANT

Translated by J.M.D. MEIKLEJOHN
Translated by THOMAS KINGSMILL ABBOTT
Translated by J.H. BERNARD

CONTENTS

CRITIQUE OF PURE REASON
Immanuel Kant

CRITIQUE OF PRACTICAL REASON
Immanuel Kant

FIRST PART — ELEMENTS OF PURE PRACTICAL REASON.

SECOND PART — METHODOLOGY OF PURE PRACTICAL REASON

CRITIQUE OF JUDGEMENT
Immanuel Kant

CRITIQUE OF PURE REASON

TRANSLATED BY J.M.D. MEIKLEJOHN

IMMANUEL KANT

PREFACE TO THE FIRST EDITION, 1781

Human reason, in one sphere of its cognition, is called upon to consider questions, which it cannot decline, as they are presented by its own nature, but which it cannot answer, as they transcend every faculty of the mind.

It falls into this difficulty without any fault of its own. It begins with principles, which cannot be dispensed with in the field of experience, and the truth and sufficiency of which are, at the same time, insured by experience. With these principles it rises, in obedience to the laws of its own nature, to ever higher and more remote conditions. But it quickly discovers that, in this way, its labours must remain ever incomplete, because new questions never cease to present themselves; and thus it finds itself compelled to have recourse to principles which transcend the region of experience, while they are regarded by common sense without distrust. It thus falls into confusion and contradictions, from which it conjectures the presence of latent errors, which, however, it is unable to discover, because the principles it employs, transcending the limits of experience, cannot be tested by that criterion. The arena of these endless contests is called *Metaphysic*.

Time was, when she was the *queen* of all the sciences; and, if we take the will for the deed, she certainly deserves, so far as regards the high importance of her object-matter, this title of honour. Now, it is the fashion of the time to heap contempt and scorn upon her; and the matron mourns, forlorn and forsaken, like Hecuba:

Modo maxima rerum,
Tot generis, natisque potens...
Nunc trahor exul, inops.

— OVID, METAMORPHOSES. XIII

At first, her government, under the administration of the *dogmatists*, was an absolute *despotism*. But, as the legislative continued to show traces of the ancient barbaric rule, her empire gradually broke up, and intestine wars introduced the reign of *anarchy*; while the *sceptics*, like nomadic tribes, who hate a permanent habitation and settled mode of living, attacked from time to time those who had organized themselves into civil communities. But their number was, very happily, small; and thus they could not entirely put a stop to the exertions of those who persisted in raising new edifices, although on no settled or uniform plan. In recent times the hope dawned upon us of seeing those disputes settled, and the legitimacy of her claims established by a kind of *physiology* of the human understanding—that of the celebrated Locke. But it was found that—although it was affirmed that this so-called queen could not refer her descent to any higher source than that of common experience, a circumstance which necessarily brought suspicion on her claims—as this *genealogy* was incorrect, she persisted in the advancement of her claims to sovereignty. Thus metaphysics necessarily fell back into the antiquated and rotten constitution of *dogmatism*, and again became obnoxious to the contempt from which efforts had been made to save it. At present, as all methods, according to the general persuasion, have been tried in vain, there reigns nought but weariness and complete *indifferentism*—the mother of chaos and night in the scientific world, but at the same time the source of, or at least the prelude to, the re-creation and reinstallation of a science, when it has fallen into confusion, obscurity, and disuse from ill directed effort.

For it is in reality vain to profess *indifference* in regard to such inquiries, the object of which cannot be indifferent to humanity. Besides, these pretended *indifferentists*, however much they may try to disguise themselves by the assumption of a popular style and by changes on the language of the schools, unavoidably fall into metaphysical declarations and propositions, which they profess to regard with so much contempt. At the same time, this indifference, which has arisen in the world of science, and which relates to that kind of knowledge which we should wish to see destroyed the last, is a phenomenon that well deserves our attention and reflection. It is plainly not the effect of the levity, but of the matured *judgement*[1] of the age, which refuses to be any longer entertained with illusory knowledge, It is, in fact, a call to reason, again to undertake the most laborious of all tasks—that of self-examination, and to establish a tribunal, which may secure it in its well-grounded claims, while it pronounces against all baseless assumptions and pretensions, not in an arbitrary manner, but according to its own eternal and unchangeable laws. This tribunal is nothing less than the *Critical Investigation of Pure Reason*.

I do not mean by this a criticism of books and systems, but a critical inquiry into the faculty of reason, with reference to the cognitions to which it strives to attain *without the aid of experience*; in other words, the solution of the question regarding the possibility or impossibility of metaphysics, and the determination of the origin, as well as of the extent and limits of this science. All this must be done on the basis of principles.

This path—the only one now remaining—has been entered upon by me; and I flatter myself that I have, in this way, discovered the cause of—and consequently the mode of removing—all the errors which have hitherto set reason at variance with itself, in the sphere of non-empirical thought. I have not returned an evasive answer to the questions of reason, by alleging the inability and limitation of the faculties of the mind; I have, on the contrary, examined them completely in the light of principles, and, after having discovered the cause of the doubts and contradictions into which reason fell, have solved them to its perfect satisfaction. It is true, these questions have not been solved as dogmatism, in its vain fancies and desires, had expected; for it can only be satisfied by the exercise of magical arts, and of these I have no knowledge. But neither do these come within the compass of our mental powers; and it was the duty of philosophy to destroy the illusions which had their origin in misconceptions, whatever darling hopes and valued expectations may be ruined by its explanations. My chief aim in this work has been thoroughness; and I make bold to say that there is not a single metaphysical problem that does not find its solution, or at least the key to its solution, here. Pure reason is a perfect unity; and therefore, if the principle presented by it prove to be insufficient for the solution of even a single one of those questions to which the very nature of reason gives birth, we must reject it, as we could not be perfectly certain of its sufficiency in the case of the others.

While I say this, I think I see upon the countenance of the reader signs of dissatisfaction mingled with contempt, when he hears declarations which sound so boastful and extravagant; and yet they are beyond comparison more moderate than those advanced by the commonest author of the commonest philosophical programme, in which the dogmatist professes to demonstrate the simple nature of the soul, or the necessity of a primal being. Such a dogmatist promises to extend human knowledge beyond the limits of possible experience; while I humbly confess that this is completely beyond my power. Instead of any such attempt, I confine myself to the examination of reason alone and its pure thought; and I do not need to seek far for the sum-total of its cognition, because it has its seat in my own mind. Besides, common logic presents me with a complete and systematic catalogue of all the simple operations of reason; and it is my task to answer the question how far reason can go, without the material presented and the aid furnished by experience.

So much for the completeness and thoroughness necessary in the execution of the present task. The aims set before us are not arbitrarily proposed, but are imposed upon us by the nature of cognition itself.

The above remarks relate to the *matter* of our critical inquiry. As regards the *form*, there are two indispensable conditions, which any one who undertakes so difficult a task as that of a critique of pure reason, is bound to fulfil. These conditions are *certitude* and *clearness*.

As regards *certitude*, I have fully convinced myself that, in this sphere of thought, *opinion* is perfectly inadmissible, and that everything which bears the least semblance of an hypothesis must be excluded, as of no value in such discussions. For it is a necessary condition of every cognition that is to be established upon *à priori* grounds that it shall be held to be absolutely necessary; much more is this the case with an attempt to determine all pure *à priori* cognition, and to furnish the standard— and consequently an example—of all apodeictic (philosophical) certitude. Whether I have succeeded in what I professed to do, it is for the reader to determine; it is the author's business merely to adduce grounds and reasons, without determining what influence these ought to have on the mind of his judges. But, lest anything he may have said may become the innocent cause of doubt in their minds, or tend to weaken the effect which his arguments might otherwise produce—he may be allowed to point out those passages which may occasion mistrust or difficulty, although these do not concern the main purpose of the present work. He does this solely with the view of removing from the mind of the reader any doubts which might affect his judgement of the work as a whole, and in regard to its ultimate aim.

I know no investigations more necessary for a full insight into the nature of the faculty which we call *understanding*, and at the same time for the determination of the rules and limits of its use, than those undertaken in the second chapter of the "Transcendental Analytic," under the title of *Deduction of the Pure Conceptions of the Understanding*; and they have also cost me by far the greatest labour—labour which, I hope, will not remain uncompensated. The view there taken, which goes somewhat deeply into the subject, has two sides. The one relates to the objects of the pure understanding, and is intended to demonstrate and to render comprehensible the objective validity of its *à priori* conceptions; and it forms for this reason an essential part of the Critique. The other considers the pure understanding itself, its possibility and its powers of cognition—that is, from a subjective point of view; and, although this exposition is of great importance, it does not belong essentially to the main purpose of the work, because the grand question is what and how much can reason and understanding, apart from experience, cognize, and not, how is the faculty of thought itself possible? As the latter is an inquiry into the cause of a given effect, and has thus in it some semblance of an hypothesis (although, as I shall show on another occasion, this is really not the fact), it would seem that, in the present instance, I had allowed myself to enounce a mere *opinion*, and that the reader must therefore be at liberty to hold a different *opinion*. But I beg to remind him that, if my subjective deduction does not produce in his mind the conviction of its certitude at which I aimed, the objective deduction, with which alone the present work is properly concerned, is in every respect satisfactory.

As regards *clearness*, the reader has a right to demand, in the first place, *discursive* or logical clearness, that is, on the basis of conceptions, and, secondly, *intuitive* or æsthetic clearness, by means of intuitions, that is, by examples or other modes of illustration *in concreto*. I have done what I could for the first kind of intelligibility. This was essential to my purpose; and it thus became the accidental cause of my inability to do complete justice to the second requirement. I have been almost always at a loss, during the progress of this work, how to settle this question. Examples and illustrations always appeared to me necessary, and, in the first sketch of the Critique, naturally fell into their proper places. But I very soon became aware of the magnitude of my task, and the numerous problems with which I should be engaged; and, as I perceived that this critical investigation would, even if delivered in the driest *scholastic* manner, be far from being brief, I found it unadvisable to enlarge it still more with examples and explanations, which are necessary only from a *popular* point of view. I was induced to take this course from the consideration also that the present work is not intended for popular use, that those devoted to science do not require such helps, although they are always acceptable, and that they would have materially interfered with my present purpose. Abbé Terrasson remarks with great justice that, if we estimate the size of a work, not from the number of its pages, but from the time which we require to make ourselves master of it, it may be said of many a book—*that it would be much shorter, if it were not so short.* On the other hand, as regards the comprehensibility of a system of speculative cognition, connected under a single principle, we may say with equal justice: many a book would have been much clearer, if it had not been intended to be so very clear. For explanations and examples, and other helps to intelligibility, aid us in the comprehension of *parts*, but they distract the attention, dissipate the mental power of the reader, and stand in the way of his forming a clear conception of the *whole*; as he cannot attain soon enough to a survey of the system, and the colouring and embellishments bestowed upon it prevent his observing its articulation or organization—which is the most important consideration with him, when he comes to judge of its unity and stability.

The reader must naturally have a strong inducement to co-operate with the present author, if he has formed the intention of erecting a complete and solid edifice of metaphysical science, according to the plan now laid before him. Metaphysics, as here represented, is the only science which admits of completion—and with little labour, if it is united, in a short time; so that nothing will be left to future generations except the task of illustrating and applying it *didactically*. For this science is nothing more than the inventory of all that is given us by *pure reason*, systematically arranged. Nothing can escape our notice; for what reason produces from itself cannot lie concealed, but must be brought to the light by reason itself, so soon as we have discovered the common principle of the ideas we seek. The perfect unity of this kind of cognitions, which are based upon pure conceptions, and uninfluenced by any empirical element, or any peculiar intuition leading to determinate experience, renders this completeness not only practicable, but also necessary.

Tecum habita, et nôris quam sit tibi curta supellex.

— PERSIUS. SATIRAE IV. 52.

Such a system of pure speculative reason I hope to be able to publish under the title of *Metaphysic of Nature*[2]. The content of this work (which will not be half so long) will be very much richer than that of the present Critique, which has to discover the sources of this cognition and expose the conditions of its possibility, and at the same time to clear and level a fit foundation for the scientific edifice. In the present work, I look for the patient hearing and the impartiality of a *judge*; in the other, for the good-will and assistance of a *co-labourer*. For, however complete the list of *principles* for this system may be in the Critique, the correctness of the system requires that no *deduced* conceptions should be absent. These cannot be presented à priori, but must be gradually discovered; and, while the *synthesis* of conceptions has been fully exhausted in the Critique, it is necessary that, in the proposed work, the same should be the case with their *analysis*. But this will be rather an amusement than a labour.

---

1. We very often hear complaints of the shallowness of the present age, and of the decay of profound science. But I do not think that those which rest upon a secure foundation, such as mathematics, physical science, etc., in the least deserve this reproach, but that they rather maintain their ancient fame, and in the latter case, indeed, far surpass it. The same would be the case with the other kinds of cognition, if their principles were but firmly established. In the absence of this security, indifference, doubt, and finally, severe criticism are rather signs of a profound habit of thought. Our age is the age of criticism, to which everything must be subjected. The sacredness of religion, and the authority of legislation, are by many regarded as grounds of exemption from the examination of this tribunal. But, if they are exempted, they become the subjects of just suspicion, and cannot lay claim to sincere respect, which reason accords only to that which has stood the test of a free and public examination.
2. In contradistinction to the Metaphysic of Ethics. This work was never published.

PREFACE TO THE SECOND EDITION, 1787

Whether the treatment of that portion of our knowledge which lies within the province of pure reason advances with that undeviating certainty which characterizes the progress of *science*, we shall be at no loss to determine. If we find those who are engaged in metaphysical pursuits, unable to come to an understanding as to the method which they ought to follow; if we find them, after the most elaborate preparations, invariably brought to a stand before the goal is reached, and compelled to retrace their steps and strike into fresh paths, we may then feel quite sure that they are far from having attained to the certainty of scientific progress and may rather be said to be merely groping about in the dark. In these circumstances we shall render an important service to reason if we succeed in simply indicating the path along which it must travel, in order to arrive at any results—even if it should be found necessary to abandon many of those aims which, without reflection, have been proposed for its attainment.

That *Logic* has advanced in this sure course, even from the earliest times, is apparent from the fact that, since Aristotle, it has been unable to advance a step and, thus, to all appearance has reached its completion. For, if some of the moderns have thought to enlarge its domain by introducing *psychological* discussions on the mental faculties, such as imagination and wit, *metaphysical*, discussions on the origin of knowledge and the different kinds of certitude, according to the difference of the objects (idealism, scepticism, and so on), or *anthropological* discussions on prejudices, their causes and remedies: this attempt, on the part of these authors, only shows their ignorance of the peculiar nature of logical science. We do not enlarge but disfigure the sciences when we lose sight of their respective limits and allow them to run into one another. Now logic is enclosed within limits which admit of perfectly clear definition; it is a science which has for its object nothing but the exposition and proof of the *formal* laws of all thought, whether it be *à priori* or empirical, whatever be its origin or its object, and whatever the difficulties—natural or accidental—which it encounters in the human mind.

The early success of logic must be attributed exclusively to the narrowness of its field, in which abstraction may, or rather must, be made of all the objects of cognition with their characteristic distinctions, and in which the understanding has only to deal with itself and with its own forms. It is, obviously, a much more difficult task for reason to strike into the sure path of science, where it has to deal not simply with itself, but with objects external to itself. Hence, logic is properly only a *propædeutic*—forms, as it were, the vestibule of the sciences; and while it is necessary to enable us to form a correct judgement with regard to the various branches of knowledge, still the acquisition of real, substantive knowledge is to be sought only in the sciences properly so called, that is, in the objective sciences.

Now these sciences, if they can be termed rational at all, must contain elements of *à priori* cognition, and this cognition may stand in a twofold relation to its object. Either it may have to *determine* the conception of the object—which must be supplied extraneously, or it may have to *establish its reality*. The former is *theoretical*, the latter *practical*, rational cognition. In both, the *pure* or *à priori* element must be treated first, and must be carefully distinguished from that which is supplied from other sources. Any other method can only lead to irremediable confusion.

Mathematics and *physics* are the two theoretical sciences which have to determine their objects *à priori*. The former is purely *à priori*, the latter is partially so, but is also dependent on other sources of cognition.

In the earliest times of which history affords us any record, *mathematics* had already entered on the sure course of science, among that wonderful nation, the Greeks. Still it is not to be supposed that it was as easy for this science to strike into, or rather to construct for itself, that royal road, as it was for logic, in which reason has only to deal with itself. On the contrary, I believe that it must have remained long—chiefly among the Egyptians—in the stage of blind groping after its true aims and destination, and that it was revolutionized by the happy idea of one man, who struck out and determined for all time the path which this science must follow, and which admits of an indefinite advancement. The history of this intellectual revolution—much more important in its results than the discovery of the passage round the celebrated Cape of Good Hope—and of its author, has not been preserved. But Diogenes Laertius, in naming the supposed discoverer of some of the simplest elements of geometrical demonstration—elements which, according to the ordinary opinion, do not even require to be proved—makes it apparent that the change introduced by the first indication of this new path, must have seemed of the utmost importance to the mathematicians of that age, and it has thus been secured against the chance of oblivion. A new light must have flashed on the mind of the first man (*Thales*, or whatever may have been his name) who demonstrated the properties of the *isosceles* triangle. For he found that it was not sufficient to meditate on the figure, as it lay before his eyes, or the conception of it, as it existed in his mind, and thus endeavour to get at the knowledge of its properties, but that it was necessary to produce these properties, as it were, by a positive *à priori construction*; and that, in order to arrive with certainty at *à priori* cognition, he must not attribute to the object any other properties than those which necessarily followed from that which he had himself, in accordance with his conception, placed in the object.

A much longer period elapsed before *Physics* entered on the highway of science. For it is only about a century and a half since the wise BACON gave a new direction to physical studies, or rather—as others were already on the right track—imparted fresh vigour to the pursuit of this new direction. Here, too, as in the case of mathematics, we find evidence of a rapid intellectual revolution. In the remarks which follow I shall confine myself to the *empirical* side of natural science.

When GALILEI experimented with balls of a definite weight on the inclined plane, when TORRICELLI caused the air to sustain a weight which he had calculated beforehand to be equal to that of a definite column of water, or when STAHL, at a later period, converted metals into lime, and reconverted lime into metal, by the addition and subtraction of certain elements;[1] a light broke upon all natural philosophers. They learned that reason only perceives that which it produces after its own design; that it must not be content to follow, as it were, in the leading-strings of nature, but must proceed in advance with principles of judgement according to unvarying laws, and compel nature to reply its questions. For accidental observations, made according to no preconceived plan, cannot be united under a necessary law. But it is this that reason seeks for and requires. It is only the principles of reason which can give to concordant phenomena the validity of laws, and it is only when experiment is directed by these rational principles that it can have any real utility. Reason must approach nature with the view, indeed, of receiving information from it, not, however, in the character of a pupil, who listens to all that his master chooses to tell him, but in that of a judge, who compels the witnesses to reply to those questions which he himself thinks fit to propose. To this single idea must the revolution be ascribed, by which, after groping in the dark for so many centuries, natural science was at length conducted into the path of certain progress.

We come now to *metaphysics*, a purely speculative science, which occupies a completely isolated position and is entirely independent of the teachings of experience. It deals with mere conceptions—not, like mathematics, with conceptions applied to intuition—and in it, reason is the pupil of itself alone. It is the oldest of the sciences, and would still survive, even if all the rest were swallowed up in the abyss of an all-destroying barbarism. But it has not yet had the good fortune to attain to the sure scientific method. This will be apparent; if we apply the tests which we proposed at the outset. We find that reason perpetually comes to a stand, when it attempts to gain *à priori* the perception even of those laws which the most common experience confirms. We find it compelled to retrace its steps in innumerable instances, and to abandon the path on which it had entered, because this does not lead to the desired result. We find, too, that those who are engaged in metaphysical pursuits are far from being able to agree among themselves, but that, on the contrary, this science appears to furnish an arena specially adapted for the display of skill or the exercise of strength in mock-contests—a field in which no combatant ever yet succeeded in gaining an inch of ground, in which, at least, no victory was ever yet crowned with permanent possession.

This leads us to inquire why it is that, in metaphysics, the sure path of science has not hitherto been found. Shall we suppose that it is impossible to discover it? Why then should nature have visited our reason with restless aspirations after it, as if it were one of our weightiest concerns? Nay, more, how little cause should we have to place confidence in our reason, if it abandons us in a matter about which, most of all, we desire to know the truth—and not only so, but even allures us to the pursuit of vain phantoms, only to betray us in the end? Or, if the path has only hitherto been missed, what indications do we possess to guide us in a renewed investigation, and to enable us to hope for greater success than has fallen to the lot of our predecessors?

It appears to me that the examples of mathematics and natural philosophy, which, as we have seen, were brought into their present condition by a sudden revolution, are sufficiently remarkable to fix our attention on the essential circumstances of the change which has proved so advantageous to them, and to induce us to make the experiment of imitating them, so far as the analogy which, as rational sciences, they bear to metaphysics may permit. It has hitherto been assumed that our cognition must conform to the objects; but all attempts to ascertain anything about these objects *à priori*, by means of conceptions, and thus to extend the range of our knowledge, have been rendered abortive by this assumption. Let us then make the experiment whether we may not be more successful in metaphysics, if we assume that the objects must conform to our cognition. This appears, at all events, to accord better with the *possibility* of our gaining the end we have in view, that is to say, of arriving at the cognition of objects *à priori*, of determining something with respect to these objects, before they are given to us. We here propose to do just what COPERNICUS did in attempting to explain the celestial movements. When he found that he could make no progress by assuming that all the heavenly bodies revolved round the spectator, he reversed the process, and tried the experiment of assuming that the spectator revolved, while the stars remained at rest. We may make the same experiment with regard to the intuition of objects. If the intuition must conform to the nature of the objects, I do not see how we can know anything of them *à priori*. If, on the other hand, the object conforms to the nature of our faculty of intuition, I can then easily conceive the possibility of such an *à priori* knowledge. Now as I cannot rest in the mere intuitions, but—if they are to become cognitions—must refer them, as *representations*, to something, as *object*, and must determine the latter by means of the former, here again there are two courses open to me. *Either*, first, I may assume that the conceptions, by which I effect this determination, conform to the object—and in this case I am reduced to the same perplexity as before; *or* secondly, I may assume that the objects, or, which is the same thing, that *experience*, in which alone as given objects they are cognized, conform to my conceptions—and then I am at no loss how to proceed. For experience itself is a mode of cognition which requires understanding. Before objects, are given to me, that is, *à priori*, I must presuppose in myself laws of the understanding which are expressed in conceptions *à priori*. To these conceptions, then, all the objects of experience must necessarily conform. Now there are objects which reason *thinks*, and that necessarily, but which cannot be given in experience, or, at least, cannot be given *so* as reason thinks them. The attempt to think these objects will hereafter furnish an excellent test of the new method of thought which we have adopted, and which is based on the principle that we only cognize in things *à priori* that which we ourselves place in them.[2]

This attempt succeeds as well as we could desire, and promises to metaphysics, in its first part—that is, where it is occupied with conceptions *à priori*, of which the corresponding objects may be given in experience—the certain course of science. For by this new method we are enabled perfectly to explain the possibility of *à priori* cognition, and, what is more, to demonstrate satisfactorily the laws which lie *à priori* at the foundation of nature, as the sum of the objects of experience—neither of which was possible according to the procedure hitherto followed. But from this deduction of the faculty of *à priori* cognition in the first part of metaphysics, we derive a surprising result, and one which, to all appearance, militates against the great end of metaphysics, as treated in the second part. For we come to the conclusion that our faculty of cognition is unable to transcend the limits of possible experience; and yet this is precisely the most essential object of this science. The estimate of our rational cognition *à priori* at which we arrive is that it has only to do with phenomena, and that things in themselves, while possessing a real existence, lie beyond its sphere. Here we are enabled to put the justice of this estimate to the test. For that which of necessity impels us to transcend the limits of experience and of all phenomena is the *unconditioned*, which reason absolutely requires in things as they are in themselves, in order to complete the series of conditions. Now, if it appears that when, on the one hand, we assume that our cognition conforms to its objects as things in themselves, *the unconditioned cannot be thought without contradiction*, and that when, on the other hand, we assume that our representation of things as they are given to us, does not conform to these things as they are in themselves, but that these objects, as phenomena, conform to our mode of representation, *the contradiction disappears:* we shall then be convinced of the truth of that which we began by assuming for the sake of experiment; we may look upon it as established that the unconditioned does not lie in things as we know them, or as they are given to us, but in things as they are in themselves, beyond the range of our cognition.[3]

But, after we have thus denied the power of speculative reason to make any progress in the sphere of the supersensible, it still remains for our consideration whether data do not exist in *practical* cognition which may enable us to determine the transcendent conception of the unconditioned, to rise beyond the limits of all possible experience from a *practical* point of view, and thus to satisfy the great ends of metaphysics. Speculative reason has thus, at least, made room for such an extension of our knowledge: and, if it must leave this space vacant, still it does not rob us of the liberty to fill it up, if we can, by means of practical data—nay, it even challenges us to make the attempt.[4]

This attempt to introduce a complete revolution in the procedure of metaphysics, after the *example* of the geometricians and natural philosophers, constitutes the aim of the Critique of Pure Speculative Reason. It is a treatise on the method to be followed, not a system of the science itself. But, at the same time, it marks out and defines both the external boundaries and the internal structure of this science. For pure speculative reason has this peculiarity, that, in choosing the various objects of thought, it is able to define the limits of its own faculties, and even to give a complete enumeration of the possible modes of proposing problems to itself, and thus to sketch out the entire system of metaphysics. For, on the one hand, in cognition *à priori*, nothing must be attributed to the objects but what the thinking subject derives from itself; and, on the other hand, reason is, in regard to the principles of cognition, a perfectly distinct, independent unity, in which, as in an organized body, every member exists for the sake of the others, and all for the sake of each, so that no principle can be viewed, with safety, in one relationship, unless it is, at the same time, viewed in relation to the total use of pure reason. Hence, too, metaphysics has this singular advantage—an advantage which falls to the lot of no other science which has to do with *objects*—that, if once it is conducted into the sure path of science, by means of this criticism, it can then take in the whole sphere of its cognitions, and can thus complete its work, and leave it for the use of posterity, as a capital which can never receive fresh accessions. For metaphysics has to deal only with principles and with the limitations of its own employment as determined by these principles. To this perfection it is, therefore, bound, as the fundamental science, to attain, and to it the maxim may justly be applied:

Nil actum reputans, si quid superesset agendum.

But, it will be asked, what kind of a treasure is this that we propose to bequeath to posterity? What is the real value of this system of metaphysics, purified by criticism, and thereby reduced to a permanent condition? A cursory view of the present work will lead to the supposition that its use is merely *negative*, that it only serves to warn us against venturing, with speculative reason, beyond the limits of experience. This is, in fact, its primary use. But this, at once, assumes a *positive* value, when we observe that the principles with which speculative reason endeavours to transcend its limits lead inevitably, not to the *extension*, but to the *contraction* of the use of reason, inasmuch as they threaten to extend the limits of sensibility, which is their proper sphere, over the entire realm of thought and, thus, to supplant the pure (practical) use of reason. So far, then, as this criticism is occupied in confining speculative reason within its proper bounds, it is only negative; but, inasmuch as it thereby, at the same time, removes an obstacle which impedes and even threatens to destroy the use of practical reason, it possesses a positive and very important value. In order to admit this, we have only to be convinced that there is an absolutely necessary use of pure reason—the moral use— in which it inevitably transcends the limits of sensibility, without the aid of speculation, requiring only to be insured against the effects of a speculation which would involve it in contradiction with itself. To deny the positive advantage of the service which this criticism renders us would be as absurd as to maintain that the system of police is productive of no positive benefit, since its main business is to prevent the violence which citizen has to apprehend from citizen, that so each may pursue his vocation in peace and security. That space and time are only forms of sensible intuition, and hence are only conditions of the existence of things as phenomena; that, moreover, we have no conceptions of the understanding, and, consequently, no elements for the cognition of things, except in so far as a corresponding intuition can be given to these conceptions; that, accordingly, we can have no cognition of an object, as a thing in itself, but only as an object of sensible intuition, that is, as phenomenon—all this is proved in the analytical part of the Critique; and from this the limitation of all possible speculative cognition to the mere objects of *experience*, follows as a necessary result. At the same time, it must be carefully borne in mind that, while we surrender the power of *cognizing*, we still reserve the power of *thinking* objects, as things in themselves.[5] For, otherwise, we should require to affirm the existence of an appearance, without something that appears —which would be absurd. Now let us suppose, for a moment, that we had not undertaken this criticism and, accordingly, had not drawn the necessary distinction between things as objects of experience and things as they are in themselves. The principle of causality, and, by consequence, the mechanism of nature as determined by causality, would then have absolute validity in relation to all things as efficient causes. I should then be unable to assert, with regard to one and the same being, e.g., the human soul, that its will is *free*, and yet, at the same time, subject to natural necessity, that is, *not free*, without falling into a palpable contradiction, for in both propositions I should take the soul in *the same signification*, as a thing in general, as a thing in itself—as, without previous criticism, I could not but take it. Suppose now, on the other hand, that we *have* undertaken this criticism, and have learnt that an object may be taken in *two senses*, first, as a phenomenon, secondly, as a thing in itself; and that, according to the deduction of the conceptions of the understanding, the principle of causality has reference only to things in the first sense. We then see how it does not involve any contradiction to assert, on the one hand, that the will, in the phenomenal sphere—in visible action—is necessarily obedient to the law of nature, and, in so far, *not free*; and, on the other hand, that, as belonging to a thing in itself, it is not subject to that law, and, accordingly, is *free*. Now, it is true that I cannot, by means of speculative reason, and still less by empirical observation, *cognize* my soul as a thing in itself and consequently, cannot cognize liberty as the property of a being to which I ascribe effects in the world of sense. For, to do so, I must cognize this being as existing, and yet not in time, which—since I cannot support my conception by any intuition—is impossible. At the same time, while I cannot *cognize*, I can quite well *think* freedom, that is to say, my representation of it involves at least no contradiction, if we bear in mind the critical distinction of the two modes of representation (the sensible and the intellectual) and the consequent limitation of the conceptions of the pure understanding and of the principles which flow from them. Suppose now that morality necessarily presupposed liberty, in the strictest sense, as a property of our will; suppose that reason contained certain practical, original principles *à priori*, which were absolutely impossible without this presupposition; and suppose, at the same time, that speculative reason had proved that liberty was incapable of being thought at all. It would then follow that the moral presupposition must give way to the speculative affirmation, the opposite of which involves an obvious contradiction, and that *liberty* and, with it, morality must yield to the *mechanism of nature*; for the negation of morality involves no contradiction, except on the presupposition of liberty. Now morality does not require the speculative cognition of liberty; it is enough that I can think it, that its conception involves no contradiction, that it does not interfere with the mechanism of nature. But even this requirement we could not satisfy, if we had not learnt the twofold sense in which things may be taken; and it is only in this way that the doctrine of morality and the doctrine of nature are confined within their proper limits. For this result, then, we are indebted to a criticism which warns us of our unavoidable ignorance with regard to things in themselves, and establishes the necessary limitation of our theoretical *cognition* to mere phenomena.

The positive value of the critical principles of pure reason in relation to the conception of *God* and of the *simple nature* of the *soul*, admits of a similar exemplification; but on this point I shall not dwell. I cannot even make the assumption—as the practical interests of morality require—of God, freedom, and immortality, if I do not deprive speculative reason of its pretensions to transcendent insight. For to arrive at these, it must make use of principles which, in fact, extend only to the objects of possible experience, and which cannot be applied to objects beyond this sphere without converting them into phenomena, and thus rendering the *practical extension* of pure reason impossible. I must, therefore, abolish *knowledge*, to make room for *belief*. The dogmatism of metaphysics, that is, the presumption that it is possible to advance in metaphysics without previous criticism, is the true source of the unbelief (always dogmatic) which militates against morality.

Thus, while it may be no very difficult task to bequeath a legacy to posterity, in the shape of a system of metaphysics constructed in accordance with the Critique of Pure Reason, still the value of such a bequest is not to be depreciated. It will render an important service to reason, by substituting the certainty of scientific method for that random groping after results without the guidance of principles, which has hitherto characterized the pursuit of metaphysical studies. It will render an important service to the inquiring mind of youth, by leading the student to apply his powers to the cultivation of genuine science, instead of wasting them, as at present, on speculations which can never lead to any result, or on the idle attempt to invent new ideas and opinions. But, above all, it will confer an inestimable benefit on morality and religion, by showing that all the objections urged against them may be silenced for ever by the *Socratic* method, that is to say, by proving the ignorance of the objector. For, as the world has never been, and, no doubt, never will be without a system of metaphysics of one kind or another, it is the highest and weightiest concern of philosophy to render it powerless for harm, by closing up the sources of error.

This important change in the field of the sciences, this loss of its fancied possessions, to which speculative reason must submit, does not prove in any way detrimental to the general interests of humanity. The advantages which the world has derived from the teachings of pure reason are not at all impaired. The loss falls, in its whole extent, on the *monopoly of the schools*, but does not in the slightest degree touch the *interests of mankind.* I appeal to the most obstinate dogmatist, whether the proof of the continued existence of the soul after death, derived from the simplicity of its substance; of the freedom of the will in opposition to the general mechanism of nature, drawn from the subtle but impotent distinction of subjective and objective practical necessity; or of the existence of God, deduced from the conception of an *ens realissimum*—the contingency of the changeable, and the necessity of a prime mover, has ever been able to pass beyond the limits of the schools, to penetrate the public mind, or to exercise the slightest influence on its convictions. It must be admitted that this has not been the case and that, owing to the unfitness of the common understanding for such subtle speculations, it can never be expected to take place. On the contrary, it is plain that *the hope of a future life* arises from the feeling, which exists in the breast of every man, that the temporal is inadequate to meet and satisfy the demands of his nature. In like manner, it cannot be doubted that the clear exhibition of duties in opposition to all the claims of inclination, gives rise to the consciousness of *freedom,* and that the glorious order, beauty, and providential care, everywhere displayed in nature, give rise to the belief in a wise and great Author of the Universe. Such is the genesis of these general convictions of mankind, so far as they depend on rational grounds; and this public property not only remains undisturbed, but is even raised to greater importance, by the doctrine that the schools have no right to arrogate to themselves a more profound insight into a matter of general human concernment than that to which the great mass of men, ever held by us in the highest estimation, can without difficulty attain, and that the schools should, therefore, confine themselves to the elaboration of these universally comprehensible and, from a moral point of view, amply satisfactory proofs. The change, therefore, affects only the arrogant pretensions of the schools, which would gladly retain, in their own exclusive possession, the key to the truths which they impart to the public.

Quod mecum nescit, solus vult scire videri.

At the same time it does not deprive the speculative philosopher of his just title to be the sole depositor of a science which benefits the public without its knowledge—I mean, the Critique of Pure Reason. This can never become popular and, indeed, has no occasion to be so; for finespun arguments in favour of useful truths make just as little impression on the public mind as the equally subtle objections brought against these truths. On the other hand, since both inevitably force themselves on every man who rises to the height of speculation, it becomes the manifest duty of the schools to enter upon a thorough investigation of the rights of speculative reason and, thus, to prevent the scandal which metaphysical controversies are sure, sooner or later, to cause even to the masses. It is only by criticism that metaphysicians (and, as such, theologians too) can be saved from these controversies and from the consequent perversion of their doctrines. Criticism alone can strike a blow at the root of materialism, fatalism, atheism, free-thinking, fanaticism, and superstition, which are universally injurious—as well as of idealism and scepticism, which are dangerous to the schools, but can scarcely pass over to the public. If governments think proper to interfere with the affairs of the learned, it would be more consistent with a wise regard for the interests of science, as well as for those of society, to favour a criticism of this kind, by which alone the labours of reason can be established on a firm basis, than to support the ridiculous despotism of the schools, which raise a loud cry of danger to the public over the destruction of cobwebs, of which the public has never taken any notice, and the loss of which, therefore, it can never feel.

This critical science is not opposed to the *dogmatic procedure* of reason in pure cognition; for pure cognition must always be dogmatic, that is, must rest on strict demonstration from sure principles à priori—but to *dogmatism*, that is, to the presumption that it is possible to make any progress with a pure cognition, derived from (philosophical) conceptions, according to the principles which reason has long been in the habit of employing—without first inquiring in what way and by what right reason has come into the possession of these principles. Dogmatism is thus the dogmatic procedure of pure reason *without previous criticism of its own powers*, and in opposing this procedure, we must not be supposed to lend any countenance to that loquacious shallowness which arrogates to itself the name of popularity, nor yet to scepticism, which makes short work with the whole science of metaphysics. On the contrary, our criticism is the necessary preparation for a thoroughly scientific system of metaphysics which must perform its task entirely à priori, to the complete satisfaction of speculative reason, and must, therefore, be treated, not popularly, but scholastically. In carrying out the plan which the Critique prescribes, that is, in the future system of metaphysics, we must have recourse to the strict method of the celebrated WOLF, the greatest of all dogmatic philosophers. He was the first to point out the necessity of establishing fixed principles, of clearly defining our conceptions, and of subjecting our demonstrations to the most severe scrutiny, instead of rashly jumping at conclusions. The example which he set served to awaken that spirit of profound and thorough investigation which is not yet extinct in Germany. He would have been peculiarly well fitted to give a truly scientific character to metaphysical studies, had it occurred to him to prepare the field by a criticism of the *organum*, that is, of pure reason itself. That he failed to perceive the necessity

of such a procedure must be ascribed to the dogmatic mode of thought which characterized his age, and on this point the philosophers of his time, as well as of all previous
times, have nothing to reproach each other with. Those who reject at once the method of
Wolf, and of the Critique of Pure Reason, can have no other aim but to shake off the
fetters of *science*, to change labour into sport, certainty into opinion, and philosophy into
philodoxy.

In this *second edition*, I have endeavoured, as far as possible, to remove the difficulties and obscurity which, without fault of mine perhaps, have given rise to many
misconceptions even among acute thinkers. In the propositions themselves, and in the
demonstrations by which they are supported, as well as in the form and the entire plan
of the work, I have found nothing to alter; which must be attributed partly to the long
examination to which I had subjected the whole before offering it to the public and
partly to the nature of the case. For pure speculative reason is an organic structure in
which there is nothing isolated or independent, but every Single part is essential to all
the rest; and hence, the slightest imperfection, whether defect or positive error, could
not fail to betray itself in use. I venture, further, to hope, that this system will maintain
the same unalterable character for the future. I am led to entertain this confidence, not
by vanity, but by the evidence which the equality of the result affords, when we
proceed, first, from the simplest elements up to the complete whole of pure reason and,
and then, backwards from the whole to each part. We find that the attempt to make the
slightest alteration, in any part, leads inevitably to contradictions, not merely in this
system, but in human reason itself. At the same time, there is still much room for
improvement in the *exposition* of the doctrines contained in this work. In the present
edition, I have endeavoured to remove misapprehensions of the æsthetical part, especially with regard to the conception of time; to clear away the obscurity which has been
found in the deduction of the conceptions of the understanding; to supply the supposed
want of sufficient evidence in the demonstration of the principles of the pure understanding; and, lastly, to obviate the misunderstanding of the paralogisms which immediately precede the Rational Psychology. Beyond this point—the end of the second main
division of the "Transcendental Dialectic"—I have not extended my alterations,[6] partly
from want of time, and partly because I am not aware that any portion of the remainder
has given rise to misconceptions among intelligent and impartial critics, whom I do not
here mention with that praise which is their due, but who will find that their
suggestions have been attended to in the work itself.

In attempting to render the exposition of my views as intelligible as possible, I have
been compelled to leave out or abridge various passages which were not essential to the
completeness of the work, but which many readers might consider useful in other
respects, and might be unwilling to miss. This trifling loss, which could not be avoided
without swelling the book beyond due limits, may be supplied, at the pleasure of the
reader, by a comparison with the first edition, and will, I hope, be more than compen-
sated for by the greater clearness of the exposition as it now stands.

I have observed, with pleasure and thankfulness, in the pages of various reviews
and treatises, that the spirit of profound and thorough investigation is not extinct in
Germany, though it may have been overborne and silenced for a time by the fashion-
able tone of a licence in thinking, which gives itself the airs of genius, and that the
difficulties which beset the paths of criticism have not prevented energetic and acute

thinkers from making themselves masters of the science of pure reason to which these paths conduct—a science which is not popular, but scholastic in its character, and which alone can hope for a lasting existence or possess an abiding value. To these deserving men, who so happily combine profundity of view with a talent for lucid exposition—a talent which I myself am not conscious of possessing—I leave the task of removing any obscurity which may still adhere to the statement of my doctrines. For, in this case, the danger is not that of being refuted, but of being misunderstood. For my own part, I must henceforward abstain from controversy, although I shall carefully attend to all suggestions, whether from friends or adversaries, which may be of use in the future elaboration of the system of this Propædeutic. As, during these labours, I have advanced pretty far in years this month I reach my sixty-fourth year—it will be necessary for me to economize time, if I am to carry out my plan of elaborating the metaphysics of nature as well as of morals, in confirmation of the correctness of the principles established in this Critique of Pure Reason, both speculative and practical; and I must, therefore, leave the task of clearing up the obscurities of the present work—inevitable, perhaps, at the outset—as well as, the defence of the whole, to those deserving men, who have made my system their own. A philosophical system cannot come forward armed at all points like a mathematical treatise, and hence it may be quite possible to take objection to particular passages, while the organic structure of the system, considered as a unity, has no danger to apprehend. But few possess the ability, and still fewer the inclination, to take a comprehensive view of a new system. By confining the view to particular passages, taking these out of their connection and comparing them with one another, it is easy to pick out apparent contradictions, especially in a work written with any freedom of style. These contradictions place the work in an unfavourable light in the eyes of those who rely on the judgement of others, but are easily reconciled by those who have mastered the idea of the whole. If a theory possesses stability in itself, the action and reaction which seemed at first to threaten its existence serve only, in the course of time, to smooth down any superficial roughness or inequality, and—if men of insight, impartiality, and truly popular gifts, turn their attention to it—to secure to it, in a short time, the requisite elegance also.

KÖNIGSBERG, *April* 1787.

---

1. I do not here follow with exactness the history of the experimental method, of which, indeed, the first steps are involved in some obscurity.
2. This method, accordingly, which we have borrowed from the natural philosopher, consists in seeking for the elements of pure reason in that *which admits of confirmation or refutation by experiment.* Now the propositions of pure reason, especially when they transcend the limits of possible experience, do not admit of our making any experiment with their *objects,* as in natural science. Hence, with regard to those *conceptions* and *principles* which we assume à priori, our only course will be to view them from two different sides. We must regard one and the same conception, *on the one hand,* in relation to experience as an object of the senses and of the understanding, *on the other hand,* in relation to reason, isolated and transcending the limits of experience, as an object of mere thought. Now if we find that, when we regard things from this double point of view, the result is in harmony with the principle of pure reason, but that, when we regard them from a single point of view, reason is involved in self-contradiction, then the experiment will establish the correctness of this distinction.
3. This experiment of pure reason has a great similarity to that of the *Chemists,* which they term the experiment of *reduction,* or, more usually, the *synthetic* process. The *analysis* of the metaphysician separates pure cognition à priori into two heterogeneous elements, viz., the cognition of things as phenomena, and of things in

themselves. *Dialectic* combines these again into harmony with the necessary rational idea of the uncondi- tioned, and finds that this harmony never results except through the above distinction, which is, therefore, concluded to be just.

4. So the central laws of the movements of the heavenly bodies established the truth of that which Copernicus, first, assumed only as a hypothesis, and, at the same time, brought to light that invisible force (Newtonian attraction) which holds the universe together. The latter would have remained forever undiscovered, if Copernicus had not ventured on the experiment—contrary to the senses but still just—of looking for the observed movements not in the heavenly bodies, but in the spectator. In this Preface I treat the new meta- physical method as a hypothesis with the view of rendering apparent the first attempts at such a change of method, which are always hypothetical. But in the Critique itself it will be demonstrated, not hypothetically, but apodeictically, from the nature of our representations of space and time, and from the elementary conceptions of the understanding.

5. In order to *cognize* an object, I must be able to prove its possibility, either from its reality as attested by expe- rience, or *à priori*, by means of reason. But I can *think* what I please, provided only I do not contradict myself; that is, provided my conception is a possible thought, though I may be unable to answer for the existence of a corresponding object in the sum of possibilities. But something more is required before I can attribute to such a conception objective validity, that is real possibility—the other possibility being merely logical. We are not, however, confined to theoretical sources of cognition for the means of satisfying this additional require- ment, but may derive them from practical sources.

6. The only addition, properly so called—and that only in the method of proof—which I have made in the present edition, consists of a new refutation of psychological *Idealism*, and a strict demonstration—the only one possible, as I believe—of the objective reality of external intuition. However harmless idealism may be considered—although in reality it is not so—in regard to the essential ends of metaphysics, it must still remain a scandal to philosophy and to the general human reason to be obliged to assume, as an article of mere belief, the existence of things external to ourselves (from which, yet, we derive the whole material of cognition for the internal sense), and not to be able to oppose a satisfactory proof to any one who may call it in question. As there is some obscurity of expression in the demonstration as it stands in the text, I propose to alter the passage in question as follows: "But this permanent cannot be an intuition in me. For all the determining grounds of my existence which can be found in me are representations and, as such, do them- selves require a permanent, distinct from them, which may determine my existence in relation to their changes, that is, my existence in time, wherein they change." It may, probably, be urged in opposition to this proof that, after all, I am only conscious immediately of that which is in me, that is, of my *representation* of external things, and that, consequently, it must always remain uncertain whether anything corresponding to this representation does or does not exist externally to me. But I am conscious, through internal *experience*, of my *existence in time* (consequently, also, of the determinability of the former in the latter), and that is more than the simple consciousness of my representation. It is, in fact, the same as the *empirical consciousness of my existence*, which can only be determined in relation to something, which, while connected with my existence, is *external to me*. This consciousness of my existence in time is, therefore, identical with the consciousness of a relation to something external to me, and it is, therefore, experience, not fiction, sense, not imagination, which inseparably connects the external with my internal sense. For the external sense is, in itself, the rela- tion of intuition to something real, external to me; and the reality of this something, as opposed to the mere imagination of it, rests solely on its inseparable connection with internal experience as the condition of its possibility. If with the *intellectual consciousness* of my existence, in the representation: *I am*, which accompa- nies all my judgements, and all the operations of my understanding, I could, at the same time, connect a determination of my existence by *intellectual intuition*, then the consciousness of a relation to something external to me would not be necessary. But the internal intuition in which alone my existence can be deter- mined, though preceded by that purely intellectual consciousness, is itself sensible and attached to the condition of time. Hence this determination of my existence, and consequently my internal experience itself, must depend on something permanent which is not in me, which can be, therefore, only in something external to me, to which I must look upon myself as being related. Thus the reality of the external sense is necessarily connected with that of the internal, in order to the possibility of experience in general; that is, I am just as certainly conscious that there are things external to me related to my sense as I am that I myself exist as determined in time. But in order to ascertain to what given intuitions objects, external me, really correspond, in other words, what intuitions belong to the external sense and not to imagination, I must have recourse, in every particular case, to those rules according to which experience in general (even internal experience) is distinguished from imagination, and which are always based on the proposition that there really is an external experience.—We may add the remark that the representation of something *permanent* in existence, is not the same thing as the *permanent representation;* for a representation may be very variable and changing—as all our representations, even that of matter, are—and yet refer to something permanent, which must, therefore, be distinct from all my representations and external to me, the existence of which is neces- sarily included in the determination of my own existence, and with it constitutes *one* experience—an experi- ence which would not even be possible internally, if it were not also at the same time, in part, external. To the question *How?* we are no more able to reply, than we are, in general, to think the stationary in time, the coex- istence of which with the variable, produces the conception of change.

INTRODUCTION

I. OF THE DIFFERENCE BETWEEN PURE AND EMPIRICAL KNOWLEDGE

THAT ALL OUR knowledge begins with experience there can be no doubt. For how is it possible that the faculty of cognition should be awakened into exercise otherwise than by means of objects which affect our senses, and partly of themselves produce representations, partly rouse our powers of understanding into activity, to compare to connect, or to separate these, and so to convert the raw material of our sensuous impressions into a knowledge of objects, which is called experience? In respect of time, therefore, no knowledge of ours is antecedent to experience, but begins with it.

But, though all our knowledge begins with experience, it by no means follows that all arises out of experience. For, on the contrary, it is quite possible that our empirical knowledge is a compound of that which we receive through impressions, and that which the faculty of cognition supplies from itself (sensuous impressions giving merely the occasion), an addition which we cannot distinguish from the original element given by sense, till long practice has made us attentive to, and skillful in separating it. It is, therefore, a question which requires close investigation, and not to be answered at first sight, whether there exists a knowledge altogether independent of experience, and even of all sensuous impressions? Knowledge of this kind is called à priori, in contradistinction to empirical knowledge, which has its sources à posteriori, that is, in experience.

But the expression, "à priori," is not as yet definite enough adequately to indicate the whole meaning of the question above started. For, in speaking of knowledge which has its sources in experience, we are wont to say, that this or that may be known à priori, because we do not derive this knowledge immediately from experience, but from a general rule, which, however, we have itself borrowed from experience. Thus, if a man undermined his house, we say, "he might know à priori that it would have fallen;" that is, he needed not to have waited for the experience that it did actually fall. But still, à priori, he could not know even this much. For, that bodies are heavy, and, consequently, that they fall when their supports are taken away, must have been known to him previously, by means of experience.

By the term "knowledge à priori," therefore, we shall in the sequel understand, not such as is independent of this or that kind of experience, but such as is absolutely so of all experience. Opposed to this is empirical knowledge, or that which is possible only à posteriori, that is, through experience. Knowledge à priori is either pure or impure. Pure knowledge à priori is that with which no empirical element is mixed up. For example, the proposition, "Every change has a cause," is a proposition à priori, but impure, because change is a conception which can only be derived from experience.

II. THE HUMAN INTELLECT, EVEN IN AN UNPHILOSOPHICAL STATE, IS IN POSSESSION OF CERTAIN COGNITIONS "À PRIORI".

The question now is as to a criterion, by which we may securely distinguish a pure from an empirical cognition. Experience no doubt teaches us that this or that object is constituted in such and such a manner, but not that it could not possibly exist otherwise. Now, in the first place, if we have a proposition which contains the idea of necessity in its very conception, it is priori. If, moreover, it is not derived from any other proposition, unless from one equally involving the idea of necessity, it is absolutely priori. Secondly, an empirical judgement never exhibits strict and absolute, but only assumed and comparative universality (by induction); therefore, the most we can say is—so far as we have hitherto observed, there is no exception to this or that rule. If, on the other hand, a judgement carries with it strict and absolute universality, that is, admits of no possible exception, it is not derived from experience, but is valid absolutely à priori.

Empirical universality is, therefore, only an arbitrary extension of validity, from that which may be predicated of a proposition valid in most cases, to that which is asserted of a proposition which holds good in all; as, for example, in the affirmation, "All bodies are heavy." When, on the contrary, strict universality characterizes a judgement, it necessarily indicates another peculiar source of knowledge, namely, a faculty of cognition à priori. Necessity and strict universality, therefore, are infallible tests for distinguishing pure from empirical knowledge, and are inseparably connected with each other. But as in the use of these criteria the empirical limitation is sometimes more easily detected than the contingency of the judgement, or the unlimited universality which we attach to a judgement is often a more convincing proof than its necessity, it may be advisable to use the criteria separately, each being by itself infallible.

Now, that in the sphere of human cognition we have judgements which are necessary, and in the strictest sense universal, consequently pure à priori, it will be an easy matter to show. If we desire an example from the sciences, we need only take any proposition in mathematics. If we cast our eyes upon the commonest operations of the understanding, the proposition, "Every change must have a cause," will amply serve our purpose. In the latter case, indeed, the conception of a cause so plainly involves the conception of a necessity of connection with an effect, and of a strict universality of the law, that the very notion of a cause would entirely disappear, were we to derive it, like Hume, from a frequent association of what happens with that which precedes; and the habit thence originating of connecting representations—the necessity inherent in the judgement being therefore merely subjective. Besides, without seeking for such exam-

ples of principles existing à priori in cognition, we might easily show that such principles are the indispensable basis of the possibility of experience itself, and consequently
prove their existence à priori. For whence could our experience itself acquire certainty, if
all the rules on which it depends were themselves empirical, and consequently fortu-
itous? No one, therefore, can admit the validity of the use of such rules as first principles. But, for the present, we may content ourselves with having established the fact,
that we do possess and exercise a faculty of pure à priori cognition; and, secondly, with
having pointed out the proper tests of such cognition, namely, universality and
necessity.

Not only in judgements, however, but even in conceptions, is an à priori origin
manifest. For example, if we take away by degrees from our conceptions of a body all
that can be referred to mere sensuous experience—colour, hardness or softness, weight,
even impenetrability—the body will then vanish; but the space which it occupied still
remains, and this it is utterly impossible to annihilate in thought. Again, if we take
away, in like manner, from our empirical conception of any object, corporeal or incorporeal, all properties which mere experience has taught us to connect with it, still we
cannot think away those through which we cogitate it as substance, or adhering to
substance, although our conception of substance is more determined than that of an
object. Compelled, therefore, by that necessity with which the conception of substance
forces itself upon us, we must confess that it has its seat in our faculty of cognition à
priori.

III. PHILOSOPHY STANDS IN NEED OF A SCIENCE WHICH SHALL DETERMINE THE POSSIBILITY, PRINCIPLES, AND EXTENT OF HUMAN KNOWLEDGE "À PRIORI"

Of far more importance than all that has been above said, is the consideration that
certain of our cognitions rise completely above the sphere of all possible experience, and
by means of conceptions, to which there exists in the whole extent of experience no
corresponding object, seem to extend the range of our judgements beyond its bounds.
And just in this transcendental or supersensible sphere, where experience affords us
neither instruction nor guidance, lie the investigations of reason, which, on account of
their importance, we consider far preferable to, and as having a far more elevated aim
than, all that the understanding can achieve within the sphere of sensuous phenomena.
So high a value do we set upon these investigations, that even at the risk of error, we
persist in following them out, and permit neither doubt nor disregard nor indifference
to restrain us from the pursuit. These unavoidable problems of mere pure reason are
God, freedom (of will), and immortality. The science which, with all its preliminaries,
has for its especial object the solution of these problems is named metaphysics—a
science which is at the very outset dogmatical, that is, it confidently takes upon itself the
execution of this task without any previous investigation of the ability or inability of
reason for such an undertaking.

Now the safe ground of experience being thus abandoned, it seems nevertheless
natural that we should hesitate to erect a building with the cognitions we possess,
without knowing whence they come, and on the strength of principles, the origin of
which is undiscovered. Instead of thus trying to build without a foundation, it is rather

to be expected that we should long ago have put the question, how the understanding can arrive at these à priori cognitions, and what is the extent, validity, and worth which they may possess? We say, "This is natural enough," meaning by the word natural, that which is consistent with a just and reasonable way of thinking; but if we understand by the term, that which usually happens, nothing indeed could be more natural and more comprehensible than that this investigation should be left long unattempted. For one part of our pure knowledge, the science of mathematics, has been long firmly established, and thus leads us to form flattering expectations with regard to others, though these may be of quite a different nature. Besides, when we get beyond the bounds of experience, we are of course safe from opposition in that quarter; and the charm of widening the range of our knowledge is so great that, unless we are brought to a standstill by some evident contradiction, we hurry on undoubtingly in our course. This, however, may be avoided, if we are sufficiently cautious in the construction of our fictions, which are not the less fictions on that account.

Mathematical science affords us a brilliant example, how far, independently of all experience, we may carry our à priori knowledge. It is true that the mathematician occupies himself with objects and cognitions only in so far as they can be represented by means of intuition. But this circumstance is easily overlooked, because the said intuition can itself be given à priori, and therefore is hardly to be distinguished from a mere pure conception. Deceived by such a proof of the power of reason, we can perceive no limits to the extension of our knowledge. The light dove cleaving in free flight the thin air, whose resistance it feels, might imagine that her movements would be far more free and rapid in airless space. Just in the same way did Plato, abandoning the world of sense because of the narrow limits it sets to the understanding, venture upon the wings of ideas beyond it, into the void space of pure intellect. He did not reflect that he made no real progress by all his efforts; for he met with no resistance which might serve him for a support, as it were, whereon to rest, and on which he might apply his powers, in order to let the intellect acquire momentum for its progress. It is, indeed, the common fate of human reason in speculation, to finish the imposing edifice of thought as rapidly as possible, and then for the first time to begin to examine whether the foundation is a solid one or no. Arrived at this point, all sorts of excuses are sought after, in order to console us for its want of stability, or rather, indeed, to enable Us to dispense altogether with so late and dangerous an investigation. But what frees us during the process of building from all apprehension or suspicion, and flatters us into the belief of its solidity, is this. A great part, perhaps the greatest part, of the business of our reason consists in the analysation of the conceptions which we already possess of objects. By this means we gain a multitude of cognitions, which although really nothing more than elucidations or explanations of that which (though in a confused manner) was already thought in our conceptions, are, at least in respect of their form, prized as new introspections; whilst, so far as regards their matter or content, we have really made no addition to our conceptions, but only disinvolved them. But as this process does furnish a real priori knowledge, which has a sure progress and useful results, reason, deceived by this, slips in, without being itself aware of it, assertions of a quite different kind; in which, to given conceptions it adds others, à priori indeed, but entirely foreign to them, without our knowing how it arrives at these, and, indeed, without such a question ever suggesting itself. I shall therefore at once proceed to examine the difference between these two modes of knowledge.

IV. OF THE DIFFERENCE BETWEEN ANALYTICAL AND SYNTHETICAL JUDGEMENTS.

In all judgements wherein the relation of a subject to the predicate is cogitated (I mention affirmative judgements only here; the application to negative will be very easy), this relation is possible in two different ways. Either the predicate B belongs to the subject A, as somewhat which is contained (though covertly) in the conception A; or the predicate B lies completely out of the conception A, although it stands in connection with it. In the first instance, I term the judgement analytical, in the second, synthetical. Analytical judgements (affirmative) are therefore those in which the connection of the predicate with the subject is cogitated through identity; those in which this connection is cogitated without identity, are called synthetical judgements. The former may be called explicative, the latter augmentative judgements; because the former add in the predicate nothing to the conception of the subject, but only analyse it into its constituent conceptions, which were thought already in the subject, although in a confused manner; the latter add to our conceptions of the subject a predicate which was not contained in it, and which no analysis could ever have discovered therein. For example, when I say, "All bodies are extended," this is an analytical judgement. For I need not go beyond the conception of body in order to find extension connected with it, but merely analyse the conception, that is, become conscious of the manifold properties which I think in that conception, in order to discover this predicate in it: it is therefore an analytical judgement. On the other hand, when I say, "All bodies are heavy," the predicate is something totally different from that which I think in the mere conception of a body. By the addition of such a predicate, therefore, it becomes a synthetical judgement.

Judgements of experience, as such, are always synthetical. For it would be absurd to think of grounding an analytical judgement on experience, because in forming such a judgement I need not go out of the sphere of my conceptions, and therefore recourse to the testimony of experience is quite unnecessary. That "bodies are extended" is not an empirical judgement, but a proposition which stands firm à priori. For before addressing myself to experience, I already have in my conception all the requisite conditions for the judgement, and I have only to extract the predicate from the conception, according to the principle of contradiction, and thereby at the same time become conscious of the necessity of the judgement, a necessity which I could never learn from experience. On the other hand, though at first I do not at all include the predicate of weight in my conception of body in general, that conception still indicates an object of experience, a part of the totality of experience, to which I can still add other parts; and this I do when I recognize by observation that bodies are heavy. I can cognize beforehand by analysis the conception of body through the characteristics of extension, impenetrability, shape, etc., all which are cogitated in this conception. But now I extend my knowledge, and looking back on experience from which I had derived this conception of body, I find weight at all times connected with the above characteristics, and therefore I synthetically add to my conceptions this as a predicate, and say, "All bodies are heavy." Thus it is experience upon which rests the possibility of the synthesis of the predicate of weight with the conception of body, because both conceptions, although the one is not contained in the other, still belong to one another (only contingently, however), as parts of a whole, namely, of experience, which is itself a synthesis of intuitions.

But to synthetical judgements à priori, such aid is entirely wanting. If I go out of and beyond the conception A, in order to recognize another B as connected with it, what foundation have I to rest on, whereby to render the synthesis possible? I have here no longer the advantage of looking out in the sphere of experience for what I want. Let us take, for example, the proposition, "Everything that happens has a cause." In the conception of "something that happens," I indeed think an existence which a certain time antecedes, and from this I can derive analytical judgements. But the conception of a cause lies quite out of the above conception, and indicates something entirely different from "that which happens," and is consequently not contained in that conception. How then am I able to assert concerning the general conception—"that which happens"— something entirely different from that conception, and to recognize the conception of cause although not contained in it, yet as belonging to it, and even necessarily? what is here the unknown = X, upon which the understanding rests when it believes it has found, out of the conception A a foreign predicate B, which it nevertheless considers to be connected with it? It cannot be experience, because the principle adduced annexes the two representations, cause and effect, to the representation existence, not only with universality, which experience cannot give, but also with the expression of necessity, therefore completely à priori and from pure conceptions. Upon such synthetical, that is augmentative propositions, depends the whole aim of our speculative knowledge à priori; for although analytical judgements are indeed highly important and necessary, they are so, only to arrive at that clearness of conceptions which is requisite for a sure and extended synthesis, and this alone is a real acquisition.

V. IN ALL THEORETICAL SCIENCES OF REASON, SYNTHETICAL JUDGEMENTS "À PRIORI" ARE CONTAINED AS PRINCIPLES.

1. Mathematical judgements are always synthetical. Hitherto this fact, though incontestably true and very important in its consequences, seems to have escaped the analysts of the human mind, nay, to be in complete opposition to all their conjectures. For as it was found that mathematical conclusions all proceed according to the principle of contradiction (which the nature of every apodeictic certainty requires), people became persuaded that the fundamental principles of the science also were recognized and admitted in the same way. But the notion is fallacious; for although a synthetical proposition can certainly be discerned by means of the principle of contradiction, this is possible only when another synthetical proposition precedes, from which the latter is deduced, but never of itself.

Before all, be it observed, that proper mathematical propositions are always judgements à priori, and not empirical, because they carry along with them the conception of necessity, which cannot be given by experience. If this be demurred to, it matters not; I will then limit my assertion to pure mathematics, the very conception of which implies that it consists of knowledge altogether non-empirical and à priori.

We might, indeed at first suppose that the proposition $7 + 5 = 12$ is a merely analytical proposition, following (according to the principle of contradiction) from the conception of a sum of seven and five. But if we regard it more narrowly, we find that our conception of the sum of seven and five contains nothing more than the uniting of both sums into one, whereby it cannot at all be cogitated what this single number is which embraces both. The conception of twelve is by no means obtained by merely cogitating the union of seven and five; and we may analyse our conception of such a possible sum as long as we will, still we shall never discover in it the notion of twelve. We must go beyond these conceptions, and have recourse to an intuition which corresponds to one of the two—our five fingers, for example, or like Segner in his Arithmetic five points, and so by degrees, add the units contained in the five given in the intuition, to the conception of seven. For I first take the number 7, and, for the conception of 5 calling in the aid of the fingers of my hand as objects of intuition, I add the units, which I before took together to make up the number 5, gradually now by means of the material image my hand, to the number 7, and by this process, I at length see the number 12 arise. That 7 should be added to 5, I have certainly cogitated in my conception of a sum = 7 + 5, but not that this sum was equal to 12. Arithmetical propositions are therefore always synthetical, of which we may become more clearly convinced by trying large numbers. For it will thus become quite evident that, turn and twist our conceptions as we may, it is impossible, without having recourse to intuition, to arrive at the sum total or product by means of the mere analysis of our conceptions. Just as little is any principle of pure geometry analytical. "A straight line between two points is the shortest," is a synthetical proposition. For my conception of straight contains no notion of quantity, but is merely qualitative. The conception of the shortest is therefore fore wholly an addition, and by no analysis can it be extracted from our conception of a straight line. Intuition must therefore here lend its aid, by means of which, and thus only, our synthesis is possible.

Some few principles preposited by geometricians are, indeed, really analytical, and depend on the principle of contradiction. They serve, however, like identical propositions, as links in the chain of method, not as principles—for example, a = a, the whole is equal to itself, or (a+b) —> a, the whole is greater than its part. And yet even these principles themselves, though they derive their validity from pure conceptions, are only admitted in mathematics because they can be presented in intuition. What causes us here commonly to believe that the predicate of such apodeictic judgements is already contained in our conception, and that the judgement is therefore analytical, is merely the equivocal nature of the expression. We must join in thought a certain predicate to a given conception, and this necessity cleaves already to the conception. But the question is, not what we must join in thought to the given conception, but what we really think therein, though only obscurely, and then it becomes manifest that the predicate pertains to these conceptions, necessarily indeed, yet not as thought in the conception itself, but by virtue of an intuition, which must be added to the conception.

2. The science of natural philosophy (physics) contains in itself synthetical judgements à priori, as principles. I shall adduce two propositions. For instance, the proposition, "In all changes of the material world, the quantity of matter remains unchanged"; or, that, "In all communication of motion, action and reaction must always be equal." In both of these, not only is the necessity, and therefore their origin à priori clear, but also that they are synthetical propositions. For in the conception of matter, I do not cogitate its permanency, but merely its presence in space, which it fills. I therefore really go out of and beyond the conception of matter, in order to think on to it something à priori,

which I did not think in it. The proposition is therefore not analytical, but synthetical, and nevertheless conceived à priori; and so it is with regard to the other propositions of the pure part of natural philosophy.

3. As to metaphysics, even if we look upon it merely as an attempted science, yet, from the nature of human reason, an indispensable one, we find that it must contain synthetical propositions à priori. It is not merely the duty of metaphysics to dissect, and thereby analytically to illustrate the conceptions which we form à priori of things; but we seek to widen the range of our à priori knowledge. For this purpose, we must avail ourselves of such principles as add something to the original conception—something not identical with, nor contained in it, and by means of synthetical judgements à priori, leave far behind us the limits of experience; for example, in the proposition, "the world must have a beginning," and such like. Thus metaphysics, according to the proper aim of the science, consists merely of synthetical propositions à priori.

VI. THE UNIVERSAL PROBLEM OF PURE REASON.

It is extremely advantageous to be able to bring a number of investigations under the formula of a single problem. For in this manner, we not only facilitate our own labour, inasmuch as we define it clearly to ourselves, but also render it more easy for others to decide whether we have done justice to our undertaking. The proper problem of pure reason, then, is contained in the question: "How are synthetical judgements à priori possible?"

That metaphysical science has hitherto remained in so vacillating a state of uncertainty and contradiction, is only to be attributed to the fact that this great problem, and perhaps even the difference between analytical and synthetical judgements, did not sooner suggest itself to philosophers. Upon the solution of this problem, or upon sufficient proof of the impossibility of synthetical knowledge à priori, depends the existence or downfall of the science of metaphysics. Among philosophers, David Hume came the nearest of all to this problem; yet it never acquired in his mind sufficient precision, nor did he regard the question in its universality. On the contrary, he stopped short at the synthetical proposition of the connection of an effect with its cause (principium causalitatis), insisting that such proposition à priori was impossible. According to his conclusions, then, all that we term metaphysical science is a mere delusion, arising from the fancied insight of reason into that which is in truth borrowed from experience, and to which habit has given the appearance of necessity. Against this assertion, destructive to all pure philosophy, he would have been guarded, had he had our problem before his eyes in its universality. For he would then have perceived that, according to his own argument, there likewise could not be any pure mathematical science, which assuredly cannot exist without synthetical propositions à priori—an absurdity from which his good understanding must have saved him.

In the solution of the above problem is at the same time comprehended the possibility of the use of pure reason in the foundation and construction of all sciences which contain theoretical knowledge à priori of objects, that is to say, the answer to the following questions:

How is pure mathematical science possible?

How is pure natural science possible?

Respecting these sciences, as they do certainly exist, it may with propriety be asked, how they are possible?—for that they must be possible is shown by the fact of their really existing.[1] But as to metaphysics, the miserable progress it has hitherto made, and the fact that of no one system yet brought forward, far as regards its true aim, can it be said that this science really exists, leaves any one at liberty to doubt with reason the very possibility of its existence.

Yet, in a certain sense, this kind of knowledge must unquestionably be looked upon as given; in other words, metaphysics must be considered as really existing, if not as a science, nevertheless as a natural disposition of the human mind (metaphysica naturalis). For human reason, without any instigations imputable to the mere vanity of great knowledge, unceasingly progresses, urged on by its own feeling of need, towards such questions as cannot be answered by any empirical application of reason, or principles derived therefrom; and so there has ever really existed in every man some system of metaphysics. It will always exist, so soon as reason awakes to the exercise of its power of speculation. And now the question arises: "How is metaphysics, as a natural disposition, possible?" In other words, how, from the nature of universal human reason, do those questions arise which pure reason proposes to itself, and which it is impelled by its own feeling of need to answer as well as it can?

But as in all the attempts hitherto made to answer the questions which reason is prompted by its very nature to propose to itself, for example, whether the world had a beginning, or has existed from eternity, it has always met with unavoidable contradictions, we must not rest satisfied with the mere natural disposition of the mind to metaphysics, that is, with the existence of the faculty of pure reason, whence, indeed, some sort of metaphysical system always arises; but it must be possible to arrive at certainty in regard to the question whether we know or do not know the things of which metaphysics treats. We must be able to arrive at a decision on the subjects of its questions, or on the ability or inability of reason to form any judgement respecting them; and therefore either to extend with confidence the bounds of our pure reason, or to set strictly defined and safe limits to its action. This last question, which arises out of the above universal problem, would properly run thus: "How is metaphysics possible as a science?"

Thus, the critique of reason leads at last, naturally and necessarily, to science; and, on the other hand, the dogmatical use of reason without criticism leads to groundless assertions, against which others equally specious can always be set, thus ending unavoidably in scepticism.

Besides, this science cannot be of great and formidable prolixity, because it has not to do with objects of reason, the variety of which is inexhaustible, but merely with Reason herself and her problems; problems which arise out of her own bosom, and are not proposed to her by the nature of outward things, but by her own nature. And when once Reason has previously become able completely to understand her own power in regard to objects which she meets with in experience, it will be easy to determine securely the extent and limits of her attempted application to objects beyond the confines of experience.

We may and must, therefore, regard the attempts hitherto made to establish metaphysical science dogmatically as non-existent. For what of analysis, that is, mere dissection of conceptions, is contained in one or other, is not the aim of, but only a preparation for metaphysics proper, which has for its object the extension, by means of synthesis, of our à priori knowledge. And for this purpose, mere analysis is of course useless, because it only shows what is contained in these conceptions, but not how we arrive, à priori, at them; and this it is her duty to show, in order to be able afterwards to determine their valid use in regard to all objects of experience, to all knowledge in general. But little self-denial, indeed, is needed to give up these pretensions, seeing the undeniable, and in the dogmatic mode of procedure, inevitable contradictions of Reason with herself, have long since ruined the reputation of every system of metaphysics that has appeared up to this time. It will require more firmness to remain undeterred by difficulty from within, and opposition from without, from endeavouring, by a method quite opposed to all those hitherto followed, to further the growth and fruitfulness of a science indispensable to human reason—a science from which every branch it has borne may be cut away, but whose roots remain indestructible.

VII. IDEA AND DIVISION OF A PARTICULAR SCIENCE, UNDER THE NAME OF A CRITIQUE OF PURE REASON.

From all that has been said, there results the idea of a particular science, which may be called the Critique of Pure Reason. For reason is the faculty which furnishes us with the principles of knowledge à priori. Hence, pure reason is the faculty which contains the principles of cognizing anything absolutely à priori. An organon of pure reason would be a compendium of those principles according to which alone all pure cognitions à priori can be obtained. The completely extended application of such an organon would afford us a system of pure reason. As this, however, is demanding a great deal, and it is yet doubtful whether any extension of our knowledge be here possible, or, if so, in what cases; we can regard a science of the mere criticism of pure reason, its sources and limits, as the propædeutic to a system of pure reason. Such a science must not be called a doctrine, but only a critique of pure reason; and its use, in regard to speculation, would be only negative, not to enlarge the bounds of, but to purify, our reason, and to shield it against error—which alone is no little gain. I apply the term transcendental to all knowledge which is not so much occupied with objects as with the mode of our cognition of these objects, so far as this mode of cognition is possible à priori. A system of such conceptions would be called transcendental philosophy. But this, again, is still beyond the bounds of our present essay. For as such a science must contain a complete exposition not only of our synthetical à priori, but of our analytical à priori knowledge, it is of too wide a range for our present purpose, because we do not require to carry our analysis any farther than is necessary to understand, in their full extent, the principles of synthesis à priori, with which alone we have to do. This investigation, which we cannot properly call a doctrine, but only a transcendental critique, because it aims not at the enlargement, but at the correction and guidance, of our knowledge, and is to serve as a touchstone of the worth or worthlessness of all knowledge à priori, is the sole object of our present essay. Such a critique is consequently, as far as possible, a preparation for an organon; and if this new organon should be found to fail, at least for a canon of pure reason, according to which the complete system of the philosophy of pure reason, whether it extend or limit the bounds of that reason, might one day be set forth both analytically and synthetically. For that this is possible, nay, that such a system is not of so great extent as to preclude the hope of its ever being completed, is evident. For we have not here to do with the nature of outward objects, which is infinite, but solely with the mind, which judges of the nature of objects, and, again, with the mind only in respect of its cognition à priori. And the object of our investigations, as it is not to be sought without, but, altogether within, ourselves, cannot remain concealed, and in all probability is limited enough to be completely surveyed and fairly estimated, according to its worth or worthlessness. Still less let the reader here expect a critique of books and systems of pure reason; our present object is exclusively a critique of the faculty of pure reason itself. Only when we make this critique our foundation, do we possess a pure touchstone for estimating the philosophical value of ancient and modern writings on this subject; and without this criterion, the incompetent historian or judge decides upon and corrects the groundless assertions of others with his own, which have themselves just as little foundation.

Transcendental philosophy is the idea of a science, for which the Critique of Pure Reason must sketch the whole plan architectonically, that is, from principles, with a full guarantee for the validity and stability of all the parts which enter into the building. It is the system of all the principles of pure reason. If this Critique itself does not assume the title of transcendental philosophy, it is only because, to be a complete system, it ought to contain a full analysis of all human knowledge à priori. Our critique must, indeed, lay before us a complete enumeration of all the radical conceptions which constitute the said pure knowledge. But from the complete analysis of these conceptions themselves, as also from a complete investigation of those derived from them, it abstains with reason; partly because it would be deviating from the end in view to occupy itself with this analysis, since this process is not attended with the difficulty and insecurity to be found in the synthesis, to which our critique is entirely devoted, and partly because it would be inconsistent with the unity of our plan to burden this essay with the vindication of the completeness of such an analysis and deduction, with which, after all, we have at present nothing to do. This completeness of the analysis of these radical conceptions, as well as of the deduction from the conceptions à priori which may be given by the analysis, we can, however, easily attain, provided only that we are in possession of all these radical conceptions, which are to serve as principles of the synthesis, and that in respect of this main purpose nothing is wanting.

To the Critique of Pure Reason, therefore, belongs all that constitutes transcendental philosophy; and it is the complete idea of transcendental philosophy, but still not the science itself; because it only proceeds so far with the analysis as is necessary to the power of judging completely of our synthetical knowledge à priori.

The principal thing we must attend to, in the division of the parts of a science like this, is that no conceptions must enter it which contain aught empirical; in other words, that the knowledge à priori must be completely pure. Hence, although the highest principles and fundamental conceptions of morality are certainly cognitions à priori, yet they do not belong to transcendental philosophy; because, though they certainly do not lay the conceptions of pain, pleasure, desires, inclinations, etc. (which are all of empirical origin), at the foundation of its precepts, yet still into the conception of duty—as an obstacle to be overcome, or as an incitement which should not be made into a motive— these empirical conceptions must necessarily enter, in the construction of a system of pure morality. Transcendental philosophy is consequently a philosophy of the pure and merely speculative reason. For all that is practical, so far as it contains motives, relates to feelings, and these belong to empirical sources of cognition.

If we wish to divide this science from the universal point of view of a science in general, it ought to comprehend, first, a Doctrine of the Elements, and, secondly, a Doctrine of the Method of pure reason. Each of these main divisions will have its subdivisions, the separate reasons for which we cannot here particularize. Only so much seems necessary, by way of introduction of premonition, that there are two sources of human knowledge (which probably spring from a common, but to us unknown root), namely, sense and understanding. By the former, objects are given to us; by the latter, thought. So far as the faculty of sense may contain representations à priori, which form the conditions under which objects are given, in so far it belongs to transcendental philosophy. The transcendental doctrine of sense must form the first part of our science of elements, because the conditions under which alone the objects of human knowledge are given must precede those under which they are thought.

---

1. As to the existence of pure natural science, or physics, perhaps many may still express doubts. But we have only to look at the different propositions which are commonly treated of at the commencement of proper (empirical) physical science—those, for example, relating to the permanence of the same quantity of matter, the vis inertiae, the equality of action and reaction, etc.—to be soon convinced that they form a science of pure physics (physica pura, or rationalis), which well deserves to be separately exposed as a special science, in its whole extent, whether that be great or confined.

I. TRANSCENDENTAL DOCTRINE OF
ELEMENTS

FIRST PART—TRANSCENDENTAL ÆSTHETIC

§ I. INTRODUCTORY.

IN WHATSOEVER MODE, or by whatsoever means, our knowledge may relate to objects, it is at least quite clear that the only manner in which it immediately relates to them is by means of an intuition. To this as the indispensable groundwork, all thought points. But an intuition can take place only in so far as the object is given to us. This, again, is only possible, to man at least, on condition that the object affect the mind in a certain manner. The capacity for receiving representations (receptivity) through the mode in which we are affected by objects, objects, is called sensibility. By means of sensibility, therefore, objects are given to us, and it alone furnishes us with intuitions; by the understanding they are thought, and from it arise conceptions. But an thought must directly, or indirectly, by means of certain signs, relate ultimately to intuitions; consequently, with us, to sensibility, because in no other way can an object be given to us.

The effect of an object upon the faculty of representation, so far as we are affected by the said object, is sensation. That sort of intuition which relates to an object by means of sensation is called an empirical intuition. The undetermined object of an empirical intuition is called phenomenon. That which in the phenomenon corresponds to the sensation, I term its matter; but that which effects that the content of the phenomenon can be arranged under certain relations, I call its form. But that in which our sensations are merely arranged, and by which they are susceptible of assuming a certain form, cannot be itself sensation. It is, then, the matter of all phenomena that is given to us à posteriori; the form must lie ready à priori for them in the mind, and consequently can be regarded separately from all sensation.

I call all representations pure, in the transcendental meaning of the word, wherein nothing is met with that belongs to sensation. And accordingly we find existing in the mind à priori, the pure form of sensuous intuitions in general, in which all the manifold content of the phenomenal world is arranged and viewed under certain relations. This pure form of sensibility I shall call pure intuition. Thus, if I take away from our representation of a body all that the understanding thinks as belonging to it, as substance, force, divisibility, etc., and also whatever belongs to sensation, as impenetrability, hardness, colour, etc.; yet there is still something left us from this empirical intuition, namely, extension and shape. These belong to pure intuition, which exists à priori in the mind, as a mere form of sensibility, and without any real object of the senses or any sensation.

The science of all the principles of sensibility à priori, I call transcendental æsthetic.[1] There must, then, be such a science forming the first part of the transcendental doctrine of elements, in contradistinction to that part which contains the principles of pure thought, and which is called transcendental logic.

In the science of transcendental æsthetic accordingly, we shall first isolate sensibility or the sensuous faculty, by separating from it all that is annexed to its perceptions by the conceptions of understanding, so that nothing be left but empirical intuition. In the next place we shall take away from this intuition all that belongs to sensation, so that nothing may remain but pure intuition, and the mere form of phenomena, which is all that the sensibility can afford à priori. From this investigation it will be found that there are two pure forms of sensuous intuition, as principles of knowledge à priori, namely, space and time. To the consideration of these we shall now proceed.

SECTION I. OF SPACE.

§ 2. METAPHYSICAL EXPOSITION OF THIS CONCEPTION.

By means of the external sense (a property of the mind), we represent to ourselves objects as without us, and these all in space. Herein alone are their shape, dimensions, and relations to each other determined or determinable. The internal sense, by means of which the mind contemplates itself or its internal state, gives, indeed, no intuition of the soul as an object; yet there is nevertheless a determinate form, under which alone the contemplation of our internal state is possible, so that all which relates to the inward determinations of the mind is represented in relations of time. Of time we cannot have any external intuition, any more than we can have an internal intuition of space. What then are time and space? Are they real existences? Or, are they merely relations or determinations of things, such, however, as would equally belong to these things in themselves, though they should never become objects of intuition; or, are they such as belong only to the form of intuition, and consequently to the subjective constitution of the mind, without which these predicates of time and space could not be attached to any object? In order to become informed on these points, we shall first give an exposition of the conception of space. By exposition, I mean the clear, though not detailed, representation of that which belongs to a conception; and an exposition is metaphysical when it contains that which represents the conception as given à priori.

1. Space is not a conception which has been derived from outward experiences. For, in order that certain sensations may relate to something without me (that is, to some-

thing which occupies a different part of space from that in which I am); in like manner, in order that I may represent them not merely as without, of, and near to each other, but also in separate places, the representation of space must already exist as a foundation. Consequently, the representation of space cannot be borrowed from the relations of external phenomena through experience; but, on the contrary, this external experience is itself only possible through the said antecedent representation.

2. Space then is a necessary representation à priori, which serves for the foundation of all external intuitions. We never can imagine or make a representation to ourselves of the non-existence of space, though we may easily enough think that no objects are found in it. It must, therefore, be considered as the condition of the possibility of phenomena, and by no means as a determination dependent on them, and is a representation à priori, which necessarily supplies the basis for external phenomena.

3. Space is no discursive, or as we say, general conception of the relations of things, but a pure intuition. For, in the first place, we can only represent to ourselves one space, and, when we talk of divers spaces, we mean only parts of one and the same space. Moreover, these parts cannot antecede this one all-embracing space, as the component parts from which the aggregate can be made up, but can be cogitated only as existing in it. Space is essentially one, and multiplicity in it, consequently the general notion of spaces, of this or that space, depends solely upon limitations. Hence it follows that an à priori intuition (which is not empirical) lies at the root of all our conceptions of space. Thus, moreover, the principles of geometry—for example, that "in a triangle, two sides together are greater than the third," are never deduced from general conceptions of line and triangle, but from intuition, and this à priori, with apodeictic certainty.

4. Space is represented as an infinite given quantity. Now every conception must indeed be considered as a representation which is contained in an infinite multitude of different possible representations, which, therefore, comprises these under itself; but no conception, as such, can be so conceived, as if it contained within itself an infinite multitude of representations. Nevertheless, space is so conceived of, for all parts of space are equally capable of being produced to infinity. Consequently, the original representation of space is an intuition à priori, and not a conception.

§ 3. TRANSCENDENTAL EXPOSITION OF THE CONCEPTION OF SPACE.

By a transcendental exposition, I mean the explanation of a conception, as a principle, whence can be discerned the possibility of other synthetical à priori cognitions. For this purpose, it is requisite, firstly, that such cognitions do really flow from the given conception; and, secondly, that the said cognitions are only possible under the presupposition of a given mode of explaining this conception.

Geometry is a science which determines the properties of space synthetically, and yet à priori. What, then, must be our representation of space, in order that such a cognition of it may be possible? It must be originally intuition, for from a mere conception, no propositions can be deduced which go out beyond the conception, and yet this happens in geometry. (Introd. V.) But this intuition must be found in the mind à priori, that is, before any perception of objects, consequently must be pure, not empirical, intuition. For geometrical principles are always apodeictic, that is, united with the consciousness of their necessity, as: "Space has only three dimensions." But propositions of this kind cannot be empirical judgements, nor conclusions from them. (Introd. II.) Now, how can an external intuition anterior to objects themselves, and in which our conception of objects can be determined à priori, exist in the human mind? Obviously not otherwise than in so far as it has its seat in the subject only, as the formal capacity of the subject's being affected by objects, and thereby of obtaining immediate representation, that is, intuition; consequently, only as the form of the external sense in general.

Thus it is only by means of our explanation that the possibility of geometry, as a synthetical science à priori, becomes comprehensible. Every mode of explanation which does not show us this possibility, although in appearance it may be similar to ours, can with the utmost certainty be distinguished from it by these marks.

§ 4. CONCLUSIONS FROM THE FOREGOING CONCEPTIONS.

(a) Space does not represent any property of objects as things in themselves, nor does it represent them in their relations to each other; in other words, space does not represent to us any determination of objects such as attaches to the objects themselves, and would remain, even though all subjective conditions of the intuition were abstracted. For neither absolute nor relative determinations of objects can be intuited prior to the existence of the things to which they belong, and therefore not à priori.

(b) Space is nothing else than the form of all phenomena of the external sense, that is, the subjective condition of the sensibility, under which alone external intuition is possible. Now, because the receptivity or capacity of the subject to be affected by objects necessarily antecedes all intuitions of these objects, it is easily understood how the form of all phenomena can be given in the mind previous to all actual perceptions, therefore à priori, and how it, as a pure intuition, in which all objects must be determined, can contain principles of the relations of these objects prior to all experience.

It is therefore from the human point of view only that we can speak of space, extended objects, etc. If we depart from the subjective condition, under which alone we can obtain external intuition, or, in other words, by means of which we are affected by objects, the representation of space has no meaning whatsoever. This predicate is only applicable to things in so far as they appear to us, that is, are objects of sensibility. The constant form of this receptivity, which we call sensibility, is a necessary condition of all relations in which objects can be intuited as existing without us, and when abstraction of these objects is made, is a pure intuition, to which we give the name of space. It is clear that we cannot make the special conditions of sensibility into conditions of the possibility of things, but only of the possibility of their existence as far as they are phenomena. And so we may correctly say that space contains all which can appear to us externally, but not all things considered as things in themselves, be they intuited or not, or by whatsoever subject one will. As to the intuitions of other thinking beings, we cannot judge whether they are or are not bound by the same conditions which limit our own intuition, and which for us are universally valid. If we join the limitation of a judgement to the conception of the subject, then the judgement will possess unconditioned validity. For example, the proposition, "All objects are beside each other in space," is valid only under the limitation that these things are taken as objects of our sensuous intuition. But if I join the condition to the conception and say, "All things, as external phenomena, are beside each other in space," then the rule is valid universally, and without any limitation. Our expositions, consequently, teach the reality (i.e., the objective validity) of space in regard of all which can be presented to us externally as object, and at the same time also the ideality of space in regard to objects when they are considered by means of reason as things in themselves, that is, without reference to the constitution of our sensibility. We maintain, therefore, the empirical reality of space in regard to all possible external experience, although we must admit its transcendental ideality; in other words, that it is nothing, so soon as we withdraw the condition upon which the possibility of all experience depends and look upon space as something that belongs to things in themselves.

But, with the exception of space, there is no representation, subjective and referring to something external to us, which could be called objective à priori. For there are no other subjective representations from which we can deduce synthetical propositions à priori, as we can from the intuition of space. (See § 3.) Therefore, to speak accurately, no ideality whatever belongs to these, although they agree in this respect with the representation of space, that they belong merely to the subjective nature of the mode of sensuous perception; such a mode, for example, as that of sight, of hearing, and of feeling, by means of the sensations of colour, sound, and heat, but which, because they are only sensations and not intuitions, do not of themselves give us the cognition of any object, least of all, an à priori cognition. My purpose, in the above remark, is merely this: to guard any one against illustrating the asserted ideality of space by examples quite insufficient, for example, by colour, taste, etc.; for these must be contemplated not as properties of things, but only as changes in the subject, changes which may be different in different men. For, in such a case, that which is originally a mere phenomenon, a rose, for example, is taken by the empirical understanding for a thing in itself, though to every different eye, in respect of its colour, it may appear different. On the contrary, the transcendental conception of phenomena in space is a critical admonition, that, in general, nothing which is intuited in space is a thing in itself, and that space is not a form which belongs as a property to things; but that objects are quite unknown to us in themselves, and what we call outward objects, are nothing else but mere representations of our sensibility, whose form is space, but whose real correlate, the thing in itself, is not known by means of these representations, nor ever can be, but respecting which, in experience, no inquiry is ever made.

SECTION II. OF TIME.

§ 5. METAPHYSICAL EXPOSITION OF THIS CONCEPTION.

1. Time is not an empirical conception. For neither coexistence nor succession would be perceived by us, if the representation of time did not exist as a foundation à priori. Without this presupposition we could not represent to ourselves that things exist together at one and the same time, or at different times, that is, contemporaneously, or in succession.

2. Time is a necessary representation, lying at the foundation of all our intuitions. With regard to phenomena in general, we cannot think away time from them, and represent them to ourselves as out of and unconnected with time, but we can quite well

represent to ourselves time void of phenomena. Time is therefore given à priori. In it alone is all reality of phenomena possible. These may all be annihilated in thought, but time itself, as the universal condition of their possibility, cannot be so annulled.

3. On this necessity à priori is also founded the possibility of apodeictic principles of the relations of time, or axioms of time in general, such as: "Time has only one dimension," "Different times are not coexistent but successive" (as different spaces are not successive but coexistent). These principles cannot be derived from experience, for it would give neither strict universality, nor apodeictic certainty. We should only be able to say, "so common experience teaches us," but not "it must be so." They are valid as rules, through which, in general, experience is possible; and they instruct us respecting experience, and not by means of it.

4. Time is not a discursive, or as it is called, general conception, but a pure form of the sensuous intuition. Different times are merely parts of one and the same time. But the representation which can only be given by a single object is an intuition. Besides, the proposition that different times cannot be coexistent could not be derived from a general conception. For this proposition is synthetical, and therefore cannot spring out of conceptions alone. It is therefore contained immediately in the intuition and representation of time.

5. The infinity of time signifies nothing more than that every determined quantity of time is possible only through limitations of one time lying at the foundation. Consequently, the original representation, time, must be given as unlimited. But as the determinate representation of the parts of time and of every quantity of an object can only be obtained by limitation, the complete representation of time must not be furnished by means of conceptions, for these contain only partial representations. Conceptions, on the contrary, must have immediate intuition for their basis.

§ 6 TRANSCENDENTAL EXPOSITION OF THE CONCEPTION OF TIME.

I may here refer to what is said above (§ 5, 3), where, for or sake of brevity, I have placed under the head of metaphysical exposition, that which is properly transcendental. Here I shall add that the conception of change, and with it the conception of motion, as change of place, is possible only through and in the representation of time; that if this representation were not an intuition (internal) à priori, no conception, of whatever kind, could render comprehensible the possibility of change, in other words, of a conjunction of contradictorily opposed predicates in one and the same object, for example, the presence of a thing in a place and the non-presence of the same thing in the same place. It is only in time that it is possible to meet with two contradictorily opposed determinations in one thing, that is, after each other. Thus our conception of time explains the possibility of so much synthetical knowledge à priori, as is exhibited in the general doctrine of motion, which is not a little fruitful.

§ 7. CONCLUSIONS FROM THE ABOVE CONCEPTIONS.

(a) Time is not something which subsists of itself, or which inheres in things as an objective determination, and therefore remains, when abstraction is made of the subjective conditions of the intuition of things. For in the former case, it would be something real, yet without presenting to any power of perception any real object. In the latter case, as an order or determination inherent in things themselves, it could not be antecedent to things, as their condition, nor discerned or intuited by means of synthetical propositions à priori. But all this is quite possible when we regard time as merely the subjective condition under which all our intuitions take place. For in that case, this form of the inward intuition can be represented prior to the objects, and consequently à priori.

(b) Time is nothing else than the form of the internal sense, that is, of the intuitions of self and of our internal state. For time cannot be any determination of outward phenomena. It has to do neither with shape nor position; on the contrary, it determines the relation of representations in our internal state. And precisely because this internal intuition presents to us no shape or form, we endeavour to supply this want by analogies, and represent the course of time by a line progressing to infinity, the content of which constitutes a series which is only of one dimension; and we conclude from the properties of this line as to all the properties of time, with this single exception, that the parts of the line are coexistent, whilst those of time are successive. From this it is clear also that the representation of time is itself an intuition, because all its relations can be expressed in an external intuition.

(c) Time is the formal condition à priori of all phenomena whatsoever. Space, as the pure form of external intuition, is limited as a condition à priori to external phenomena alone. On the other hand, because all representations, whether they have or have not external things for their objects, still in themselves, as determinations of the mind, belong to our internal state; and because this internal state is subject to the formal condition of the internal intuition, that is, to time—time is a condition à priori of all phenomena whatsoever—the immediate condition of all internal, and thereby the mediate condition of all external phenomena. If I can say à priori, "All outward phenomena are in space, and determined à priori according to the relations of space," I can also, from the principle of the internal sense, affirm universally, "All phenomena in general, that is, all objects of the senses, are in time and stand necessarily in relations of time."

If we abstract our internal intuition of ourselves and all external intuitions, possible only by virtue of this internal intuition and presented to us by our faculty of representation, and consequently take objects as they are in themselves, then time is nothing. It is only of objective validity in regard to phenomena, because these are things which we regard as objects of our senses. It no longer objective we, make abstraction of the sensuousness of our intuition, in other words, of that mode of representation which is peculiar to us, and speak of things in general. Time is therefore merely a subjective condition of our (human) intuition (which is always sensuous, that is, so far as we are affected by objects), and in itself, independently of the mind or subject, is nothing. Nevertheless, in respect of all phenomena, consequently of all things which come within the sphere of our experience, it is necessarily objective. We cannot say, "All things are in time," because in this conception of things in general, we abstract and make no mention of any sort of intuition of things. But this is the proper condition under which time belongs to our representation of objects. If we add the condition to the conception, and say, "All things, as phenomena, that is, objects of sensuous intuition, are in time," then the proposition has its sound objective validity and universality à priori.

What we have now set forth teaches, therefore, the empirical reality of time; that is, its objective validity in reference to all objects which can ever be presented to our senses. And as our intuition is always sensuous, no object ever can be presented to us in experience, which does not come under the conditions of time. On the other hand, we deny to time all claim to absolute reality; that is, we deny that it, without having regard to the form of our sensuous intuition, absolutely inheres in things as a condition or property. Such properties as belong to objects as things in themselves never can be presented to us through the medium of the senses. Herein consists, therefore, the transcendental ideality of time, according to which, if we abstract the subjective conditions of sensuous intuition, it is nothing, and cannot be reckoned as subsisting or inhering in objects as things in themselves, independently of its relation to our intuition. This ideality, like that of space, is not to be proved or illustrated by fallacious analogies with sensations, for this reason—that in such arguments or illustrations, we make the presupposition that the phenomenon, in which such and such predicates inhere, has objective reality, while in this case we can only find such an objective reality as is itself empirical, that is, regards the object as a mere phenomenon. In reference to this subject, see the remark in Section I (§ 4)

§ 8. ELUCIDATION.

Against this theory, which grants empirical reality to time, but denies to it absolute and transcendental reality, I have heard from intelligent men an objection so unanimously urged that I conclude that it must naturally present itself to every reader to whom these considerations are novel. It runs thus: "Changes are real" (this the continual change in our own representations demonstrates, even though the existence of all external phenomena, together with their changes, is denied). Now, changes are only possible in time, and therefore time must be something real. But there is no difficulty in answering this. I grant the whole argument. Time, no doubt, is something real, that is, it is the real form of our internal intuition. It therefore has subjective reality, in reference to our internal experience, that is, I have really the representation of time and of my determinations therein. Time, therefore, is not to be regarded as an object, but as the mode of representation of myself as an object. But if I could intuite myself, or be intuited by another being, without this condition of sensibility, then those very determinations which we now represent to ourselves as changes, would present to us a knowledge in which the representation of time, and consequently of change, would not appear. The empirical reality of time, therefore, remains, as the condition of all our experience. But absolute reality, according to what has been said above, cannot be granted it. Time is nothing but the form of our internal intuition.[2] If we take away from it the special condition of our sensibility, the conception of time also vanishes; and it inheres not in the objects themselves, but solely in the subject (or mind) which intuites them.

But the reason why this objection is so unanimously brought against our doctrine of time, and that too by disputants who cannot start any intelligible arguments against the doctrine of the ideality of space, is this—they have no hope of demonstrating apodeictically the absolute reality of space, because the doctrine of idealism is against them, according to which the reality of external objects is not capable of any strict proof. On the other hand, the reality of the object of our internal sense (that is, myself and my internal state) is clear immediately through consciousness. The former—external objects in space—might be a mere delusion, but the latter—the object of my internal perception —is undeniably real. They do not, however, reflect that both, without question of their reality as representations, belong only to the genus phenomenon, which has always two aspects, the one, the object considered as a thing in itself, without regard to the mode of intuiting it, and the nature of which remains for this very reason problematical, the other, the form of our intuition of the object, which must be sought not in the object as a thing in itself, but in the subject to which it appears—which form of intuition nevertheless belongs really and necessarily to the phenomenal object.

Time and space are, therefore, two sources of knowledge, from which, à priori, various synthetical cognitions can be drawn. Of this we find a striking example in the cognitions of space and its relations, which form the foundation of pure mathematics. They are the two pure forms of all intuitions, and thereby make synthetical propositions à priori possible. But these sources of knowledge being merely conditions of our sensibility, do therefore, and as such, strictly determine their own range and purpose, in that they do not and cannot present objects as things in themselves, but are applicable to them solely in so far as they are considered as sensuous phenomena. The sphere of phenomena is the only sphere of their validity, and if we venture out of this, no further objective use can be made of them. For the rest, this formal reality of time and space leaves the validity of our empirical knowledge unshaken; for our certainty in that respect is equally firm, whether these forms necessarily inhere in the things themselves, or only in our intuitions of them. On the other hand, those who maintain the absolute reality of time and space, whether as essentially subsisting, or only inhering, as modifications, in things, must find themselves at utter variance with the principles of experience itself. For, if they decide for the first view, and make space and time into substances, this being the side taken by mathematical natural philosophers, they must admit two self-subsisting nonentities, infinite and eternal, which exist (yet without there being anything real) for the purpose of containing in themselves everything that is real. If they adopt the second view of inherence, which is preferred by some metaphysical natural philosophers, and regard space and time as relations (contiguity in space or succession in time), abstracted from experience, though represented confusedly in this state of separation, they find themselves in that case necessitated to deny the validity of mathematical doctrines à priori in reference to real things (for example, in space)—at all events their apodeictic certainty. For such certainty cannot be found in an à posteriori proposition; and the conceptions à priori of space and time are, according to this opinion, mere creations of the imagination, having their source really in experience, inasmuch as, out of relations abstracted from experience, imagination has made up something which contains, indeed, general statements of these relations, yet of which no application can be made without the restrictions attached thereto by nature. The former of these parties gains this advantage, that they keep the sphere of phenomena free for mathematical science. On the other hand, these very conditions (space and time) embarrass them greatly, when the understanding endeavours to pass the limits of that sphere. The latter has, indeed, this advantage, that the representations of space and time do not come in their way when they wish to judge of objects, not as phenomena, but merely in their relation to the understanding. Devoid, however, of a true and objectively valid à priori intuition, they can neither furnish any basis for the possibility of mathematical cognitions à priori, nor bring the propositions of experience into necessary accordance with those of mathematics. In our theory of the true nature of these two original forms of the sensibility, both difficulties are surmounted.

In conclusion, that transcendental æsthetic cannot contain any more than these two elements—space and time, is sufficiently obvious from the fact that all other conceptions appertaining to sensibility, even that of motion, which unites in itself both elements, presuppose something empirical. Motion, for example, presupposes the perception of something movable. But space considered in itself contains nothing movable, consequently motion must be something which is found in space only through experience—in other words, an empirical datum. In like manner, transcendental æsthetic cannot number the conception of change among its data à priori; for time itself does not change, but only something which is in time. To acquire the conception of change, therefore, the perception of some existing object and of the succession of its determinations, in one word, experience, is necessary.

§ 9. GENERAL REMARKS ON TRANSCENDENTAL ÆSTHETIC.

I. In order to prevent any misunderstanding, it will be requisite, in the first place, to recapitulate, as clearly as possible, what our opinion is with respect to the fundamental nature of our sensuous cognition in general. We have intended, then, to say that all our intuition is nothing but the representation of phenomena; that the things which we intuite, are not in themselves the same as our representations of them in intuition, nor are their relations in themselves so constituted as they appear to us; and that if we take away the subject, or even only the subjective constitution of our senses in general, then not only the nature and relations of objects in space and time, but even space and time themselves disappear; and that these, as phenomena, cannot exist in themselves, but only in us. What may be the nature of objects considered as things in themselves and without reference to the receptivity of our sensibility is quite unknown to us. We know nothing more than our mode of perceiving them, which is peculiar to us, and which, though not of necessity pertaining to every animated being, is so to the whole human race. With this alone we have to do. Space and time are the pure forms thereof; sensation the matter. The former alone can we cognize à priori, that is, antecedent to all actual perception; and for this reason such cognition is called pure intuition. The latter is that in our cognition which is called cognition à posteriori, that is, empirical intuition. The former appertain absolutely and necessarily to our sensibility, of whatsoever kind our sensations may be; the latter may be of very diversified character. Supposing that we should carry our empirical intuition even to the very highest degree of clearness, we should not thereby advance one step nearer to a knowledge of the constitution of objects as things in themselves. For we could only, at best, arrive at a complete cognition of our own mode of intuition, that is of our sensibility, and this always under the conditions originally attaching to the subject, namely, the conditions of space and time; while the question: "What are objects considered as things in themselves?" remains unanswerable even after the most thorough examination of the phenomenal world.

To say, then, that all our sensibility is nothing but the confused representation of things containing exclusively that which belongs to them as things in themselves, and this under an accumulation of characteristic marks and partial representations which we cannot distinguish in consciousness, is a falsification of the conception of sensibility and phenomenization, which renders our whole doctrine thereof empty and useless. The difference between a confused and a clear representation is merely logical and has nothing to do with content. No doubt the conception of right, as employed by a sound understanding, contains all that the most subtle investigation could unfold from it, although, in the ordinary practical use of the word, we are not conscious of the manifold representations comprised in the conception. But we cannot for this reason assert that the ordinary conception is a sensuous one, containing a mere phenomenon, for right cannot appear as a phenomenon; but the conception of it lies in the understanding, and represents a property (the moral property) of actions, which belongs to them in themselves. On the other hand, the representation in intuition of a body contains nothing which could belong to an object considered as a thing in itself, but merely the phenomenon or appearance of something, and the mode in which we are affected by that appearance; and this receptivity of our faculty of cognition is called sensibility, and remains toto caelo different from the cognition of an object in itself, even though we should examine the content of the phenomenon to the very bottom.

It must be admitted that the Leibnitz-Wolfian philosophy has assigned an entirely erroneous point of view to all investigations into the nature and origin of our cognitions, inasmuch as it regards the distinction between the sensuous and the intellectual as merely logical, whereas it is plainly transcendental, and concerns not merely the clearness or obscurity, but the content and origin of both. For the faculty of sensibility not only does not present us with an indistinct and confused cognition of objects as things in themselves, but, in fact, gives us no knowledge of these at all. On the contrary, so soon as we abstract in thought our own subjective nature, the object represented, with the properties ascribed to it by sensuous intuition, entirely disappears, because it was only this subjective nature that determined the form of the object as a phenomenon.

In phenomena, we commonly, indeed, distinguish that which essentially belongs to the intuition of them, and is valid for the sensuous faculty of every human being, from that which belongs to the same intuition accidentally, as valid not for the sensuous faculty in general, but for a particular state or organization of this or that sense. Accordingly, we are accustomed to say that the former is a cognition which represents the object itself, whilst the latter presents only a particular appearance or phenomenon thereof. This distinction, however, is only empirical. If we stop here (as is usual), and do not regard the empirical intuition as itself a mere phenomenon (as we ought to do), in which nothing that can appertain to a thing in itself is to be found, our transcendental distinction is lost, and we believe that we cognize objects as things in themselves, although in the whole range of the sensuous world, investigate the nature of its objects as profoundly as we may, we have to do with nothing but phenomena. Thus, we call the rainbow a mere appearance of phenomenon in a sunny shower, and the rain, the reality or thing in itself; and this is right enough, if we understand the latter conception in a merely physical sense, that is, as that which in universal experience, and under whatever conditions of sensuous perception, is known in intuition to be so and so determined, and not otherwise. But if we consider this empirical datum generally, and inquire, without reference to its accordance with all our senses, whether there can be discovered in it aught which represents an object as a thing in itself (the raindrops of course are not such, for they are, as phenomena, empirical objects), the question of the relation of the representation to the object is transcendental; and not only are the raindrops mere phenomena, but even their circular form, nay, the space itself through which they fall, is nothing in itself, but both are mere modifications or fundamental dispositions of our sensuous intuition, whilst the transcendental object remains for us utterly unknown.

The second important concern of our æsthetic is that it does not obtain favour merely as a plausible hypothesis, but possess as undoubted a character of certainty as can be demanded of any theory which is to serve for an organon. In order fully to convince the reader of this certainty, we shall select a case which will serve to make its validity apparent, and also to illustrate what has been said in § 3.

Suppose, then, that space and time are in themselves objective, and conditions of the —possibility of objects as things in themselves. In the first place, it is evident that both present us, with very many apodeictic and synthetic propositions à priori, but especially space—and for this reason we shall prefer it for investigation at present. As the propositions of geometry are cognized synthetically à priori, and with apodeictic certainty, I inquire: Whence do you obtain propositions of this kind, and on what basis does the understanding rest, in order to arrive at such absolutely necessary and universally valid truths?

There is no other way than through intuitions or conceptions, as such; and these are given either à priori or à posteriori. The latter, namely, empirical conceptions, together with the empirical intuition on which they are founded, cannot afford any synthetical proposition, except such as is itself also empirical, that is, a proposition of experience. But an empirical proposition cannot possess the qualities of necessity and absolute universality, which, nevertheless, are the characteristics of all geometrical propositions. As to the first and only means to arrive at such cognitions, namely, through mere conceptions or intuitions à priori, it is quite clear that from mere conceptions no synthetical cognitions, but only analytical ones, can be obtained. Take, for example, the proposition: "Two straight lines cannot enclose a space, and with these alone no figure is possible," and try to deduce it from the conception of a straight line and the number two; or take the proposition: "It is possible to construct a figure with three straight lines," and endeavour, in like manner, to deduce it from the mere conception of a straight line and the number three. All your endeavours are in vain, and you find yourself forced to have recourse to intuition, as, in fact, geometry always does. You therefore give yourself an object in intuition. But of what kind is this intuition? Is it a pure à priori, or is it an empirical intuition? If the latter, then neither an universally valid, much less an apodeictic proposition can arise from it, for experience never can give us any such proposition. You must, therefore, give yourself an object à priori in intuition, and upon that ground your synthetical proposition. Now if there did not exist within you a faculty of intuition à priori; if this subjective condition were not in respect to its form also the universal condition à priori under which alone the object of this external intuition is itself possible; if the object (that is, the triangle) were something in itself, without relation to you the subject; how could you affirm that that which lies necessarily in your subjective conditions in order to construct a triangle, must also necessarily belong to the triangle in itself? For to your conceptions of three lines, you could not add anything new (that is, the figure); which, therefore, must necessarily be found in the object, because the object is given before your cognition, and not by means of it. If, therefore, space (and time also) were not a mere form of your intuition, which contains conditions à priori, under which alone things can become external objects for you, and without which subjective conditions the objects are in themselves nothing, you could not construct any synthetical proposition whatsoever regarding external objects. It is therefore not merely possible or probable, but indubitably certain, that space and time, as the necessary conditions of all our external and internal experience, are merely subjective conditions of all our intuitions, in relation to which all objects are therefore mere phenomena, and not things in themselves, presented to us in this particular manner. And for this reason, in respect to the form of phenomena, much may be said à priori, whilst of the thing in itself, which may lie at the foundation of these phenomena, it is impossible to say anything.

II. In confirmation of this theory of the ideality of the external as well as internal sense, consequently of all objects of sense, as mere phenomena, we may especially remark that all in our cognition that belongs to intuition contains nothing more than mere relations. (The feelings of pain and pleasure, and the will, which are not cognitions, are excepted.) The relations, to wit, of place in an intuition (extension), change of place (motion), and laws according to which this change is determined (moving forces). That, however, which is present in this or that place, or any operation going on, or result taking place in the things themselves, with the exception of change of place, is not given to us by intuition. Now by means of mere relations, a thing cannot be known in itself; and it may therefore be fairly concluded, that, as through the external sense nothing but mere representations of relations are given us, the said external sense in its representation can contain only the relation of the object to the subject, but not the essential nature of the object as a thing in itself.

The same is the case with the internal intuition, not only because, in the internal intuition, the representation of the external senses constitutes the material with which the mind is occupied; but because time, in which we place, and which itself antecedes the consciousness of, these representations in experience, and which, as the formal condition of the mode according to which objects are placed in the mind, lies at the foundation of them, contains relations of the successive, the coexistent, and of that which always must be coexistent with succession, the permanent. Now that which, as representation, can antecede every exercise of thought (of an object), is intuition; and when it contains nothing but relations, it is the form of the intuition, which, as it presents us with no representation, except in so far as something is placed in the mind, can be nothing else than the mode in which the mind is affected by its own activity, to wit—its presenting to itself representations, consequently the mode in which the mind is affected by itself; that is, it can be nothing but an internal sense in respect to its form. Everything that is represented through the medium of sense is so far phenomenal; consequently, we must either refuse altogether to admit an internal sense, or the subject, which is the object of that sense, could only be represented by it as phenomenon, and not as it would judge of itself, if its intuition were pure spontaneous activity, that is, were intellectual. The difficulty here lies wholly in the question: How can the subject have an internal intuition of itself? But this difficulty is common to every theory. The consciousness of self (apperception) is the simple representation of the "ego"; and if by means of that representation alone, all the manifold representations in the subject were spontaneously given, then our internal intuition would be intellectual. This consciousness in man requires an internal perception of the manifold representations which are previously given in the subject; and the manner in which these representations are given in the mind without spontaneity, must, on account of this difference (the want of spontaneity), be called sensibility. If the faculty of self-consciousness is to apprehend what lies in the mind, it must all act that and can in this way alone produce an intuition of self. But the form of this intuition, which lies in the original constitution of the mind, determines, in the representation of time, the manner in which the manifold representations are to combine themselves in the mind; since the subject intuites itself, not as it would represent itself immediately and spontaneously, but according to the manner in which the mind is internally affected, consequently, as it appears, and not as it is.

III. When we say that the intuition of external objects, and also the self-intuition of the subject, represent both, objects and subject, in space and time, as they affect our senses, that is, as they appear—this is by no means equivalent to asserting that these objects are mere illusory appearances. For when we speak of things as phenomena, the objects, nay, even the properties which we ascribe to them, are looked upon as really given; only that, in so far as this or that property depends upon the mode of intuition of the subject, in the relation of the given object to the subject, the object as phenomenon is to be distinguished from the object as a thing in itself. Thus I do not say that bodies seem or appear to be external to me, or that my soul seems merely to be given in my self-consciousness, although I maintain that the properties of space and time, in conformity to which I set both, as the condition of their existence, abide in my mode of intuition, and not in the objects in themselves. It would be my own fault, if out of that which I should reckon as phenomenon, I made mere illusory appearance.[3] But this will not happen, because of our principle of the ideality of all sensuous intuitions. On the contrary, if we ascribe objective reality to these forms of representation, it becomes impossible to avoid changing everything into mere appearance. For if we regard space and time as properties, which must be found in objects as things in themselves, as sine quibus non of the possibility of their existence, and reflect on the absurdities in which we then find ourselves involved, inasmuch as we are compelled to admit the existence of two infinite things, which are nevertheless not substances, nor anything really inhering in substances, nay, to admit that they are the necessary conditions of the existence of all things, and moreover, that they must continue to exist, although all existing things were annihilated—we cannot blame the good Berkeley for degrading bodies to mere illusory appearances. Nay, even our own existence, which would in this case depend upon the self-existent reality of such a mere nonentity as time, would necessarily be changed with it into mere appearance—an absurdity which no one has as yet been guilty of.

IV. In natural theology, where we think of an object—God—which never can be an object of intuition to us, and even to himself can never be an object of sensuous intuition, we carefully avoid attributing to his intuition the conditions of space and time—and intuition all his cognition must be, and not thought, which always includes limitation. But with what right can we do this if we make them forms of objects as things in themselves, and such, moreover, as would continue to exist as à priori conditions of the existence of things, even though the things themselves were annihilated? For as conditions of all existence in general, space and time must be conditions of the existence of the Supreme Being also. But if we do not thus make them objective forms of all things, there is no other way left than to make them subjective forms of our mode of intuition—

external and internal; which is called sensuous, because it is not primitive, that is, is not such as gives in itself the existence of the object of the intuition (a mode of intuition which, so far as we can judge, can belong only to the Creator), but is dependent on the existence of the object, is possible, therefore, only on condition that the representative faculty of the subject is affected by the object.

It is, moreover, not necessary that we should limit the mode of intuition in space and time to the sensuous faculty of man. It may well be that all finite thinking beings must necessarily in this respect agree with man (though as to this we cannot decide), but sensibility does not on account of this universality cease to be sensibility, for this very reason, that it is a deduced (intuitus derivativus), and not an original (intuitus originarius), consequently not an intellectual intuition, and this intuition, as such, for reasons above mentioned, seems to belong solely to the Supreme Being, but never to a being dependent, quoad its existence, as well as its intuition (which its existence determines and limits relatively to given objects). This latter remark, however, must be taken only as an illustration, and not as any proof of the truth of our æsthetical theory.

§ 10. CONCLUSION OF THE TRANSCENDENTAL ÆSTHETIC.

We have now completely before us one part of the solution of the grand general problem of transcendental philosophy, namely, the question: "How are synthetical propositions à priori possible?" That is to say, we have shown that we are in possession of pure à priori intuitions, namely, space and time, in which we find, when in a judgement à priori we pass out beyond the given conception, something which is not discoverable in that conception, but is certainly found à priori in the intuition which corresponds to the conception, and can be united synthetically with it. But the judgements which these pure intuitions enable us to make, never reach farther than to objects of the senses, and are valid only for objects of possible experience.

SECOND PART—TRANSCENDENTAL LOGIC

INTRODUCTION. IDEA OF A TRANSCENDENTAL LOGIC.

I. OF LOGIC IN GENERAL.

Our knowledge springs from two main sources in the mind, first of which is the faculty or power of receiving representations (receptivity for impressions); the second is the power of cognizing by means of these representations (spontaneity in the production of conceptions). Through the first an object is given to us; through the second, it is, in relation to the representation (which is a mere determination of the mind), thought. Intuition and conceptions constitute, therefore, the elements of all our knowledge, so that neither conceptions without an intuition in some way corresponding to them, nor intuition without conceptions, can afford us a cognition. Both are either pure or empirical. They are empirical, when sensation (which presupposes the actual presence of the object) is contained in them; and pure, when no sensation is mixed with the representation. Sensations we may call the matter of sensuous cognition. Pure intuition consequently contains merely the form under which something is intuited, and pure conception only the form of the thought of an object. Only pure intuitions and pure conceptions are possible à priori; the empirical only à posteriori.

We apply the term sensibility to the receptivity of the mind for impressions, in so far as it is in some way affected; and, on the other hand, we call the faculty of spontaneously producing representations, or the spontaneity of cognition, understanding. Our nature is so constituted that intuition with us never can be other than sensuous, that is, it contains only the mode in which we are affected by objects. On the other hand, the faculty of thinking the object of sensuous intuition is the understanding. Neither of these faculties has a preference over the other. Without the sensuous faculty no object would be given to us, and without the understanding no object would be thought. Thoughts without content are void; intuitions without conceptions, blind. Hence it is as necessary for the mind to make its conceptions sensuous (that is, to join to them the object in intuition), as to make its intuitions intelligible (that is, to bring them under conceptions). Neither of these faculties can exchange its proper function. Understanding cannot intuite, and the sensuous faculty cannot think. In no other way than from the united operation of both, can knowledge arise. But no one ought, on this account, to overlook the difference of the elements contributed by each; we have rather great reason carefully to separate and distinguish them. We therefore distinguish the science of the laws of sensibility, that is, æsthetic, from the science of the laws of the understanding, that is, logic.

Now, logic in its turn may be considered as twofold—namely, as logic of the general, or of the particular use of the understanding. The first contains the absolutely necessary laws of thought, without which no use whatsoever of the understanding is possible, and gives laws therefore to the understanding, without regard to the difference of objects on which it may be employed. The logic of the particular use of the understanding contains the laws of correct thinking upon a particular class of objects. The former may be called elemental logic—the latter, the organon of this or that particular science. The latter is for the most part employed in the schools, as a propædeutic to the sciences, although, indeed, according to the course of human reason, it is the last thing we arrive at, when the science has been already matured, and needs only the finishing touches towards its correction and completion; for our knowledge of the objects of our attempted science must be tolerably extensive and complete before we can indicate the laws by which a science of these objects can be established.

General logic is again either pure or applied. In the former, we abstract all the empirical conditions under which the understanding is exercised; for example, the influence of the senses, the play of the fantasy or imagination, the laws of the memory, the force of habit, of inclination, etc., consequently also, the sources of prejudice—in a word, we abstract all causes from which particular cognitions arise, because these causes regard the understanding under certain circumstances of its application, and, to the knowledge of them experience is required. Pure general logic has to do, therefore, merely with pure à priori principles, and is a canon of understanding and reason, but only in respect of the formal part of their use, be the content what it may, empirical or transcendental. General logic is called applied, when it is directed to the laws of the use of the understanding, under the subjective empirical conditions which psychology teaches us. It has therefore empirical principles, although, at the same time, it is in so far general, that it applies to the exercise of the understanding, without regard to the difference of objects. On this account, moreover, it is neither a canon of the understanding in general, nor an organon of a particular science, but merely a cathartic of the human understanding.

In general logic, therefore, that part which constitutes pure logic must be carefully distinguished from that which constitutes applied (though still general) logic. The former alone is properly science, although short and dry, as the methodical exposition of an elemental doctrine of the understanding ought to be. In this, therefore, logicians must always bear in mind two rules:

1. As general logic, it makes abstraction of all content of the cognition of the understanding, and of the difference of objects, and has to do with nothing but the mere form of thought.

2. As pure logic, it has no empirical principles, and consequently draws nothing (contrary to the common persuasion) from psychology, which therefore has no influence on the canon of the understanding. It is a demonstrated doctrine, and everything in it must be certain completely à priori.

What I called applied logic (contrary to the common acceptation of this term, according to which it should contain certain exercises for the scholar, for which pure logic gives the rules), is a representation of the understanding, and of the rules of its necessary employment in concreto, that is to say, under the accidental conditions of the subject, which may either hinder or promote this employment, and which are all given only empirically. Thus applied logic treats of attention, its impediments and consequences, of the origin of error, of the state of doubt, hesitation, conviction, etc., and to it is related pure general logic in the same way that pure morality, which contains only the necessary moral laws of a free will, is related to practical ethics, which considers these laws under all the impediments of feelings, inclinations, and passions to which men are more or less subjected, and which never can furnish us with a true and demonstrated science, because it, as well as applied logic, requires empirical and psychological principles.

II. OF TRANSCENDENTAL LOGIC.

General logic, as we have seen, makes abstraction of all content of cognition, that is, of all relation of cognition to its object, and regards only the logical form in the relation of cognitions to each other, that is, the form of thought in general. But as we have both pure and empirical intuitions (as transcendental æsthetic proves), in like manner a distinction might be drawn between pure and empirical thought (of objects). In this case, there would exist a kind of logic, in which we should not make abstraction of all content of cognition; for or logic which should comprise merely the laws of pure thought (of an object), would of course exclude all those cognitions which were of empirical content. This kind of logic would also examine the origin of our cognitions of objects, so far as that origin cannot be ascribed to the objects themselves; while, on the contrary, general logic has nothing to do with the origin of our cognitions, but contemplates our representations, be they given primitively à priori in ourselves, or be they only of empirical origin, solely according to the laws which the understanding observes in employing them in the process of thought, in relation to each other. Consequently, general logic treats of the form of the understanding only, which can be applied to representations, from whatever source they may have arisen.

And here I shall make a remark, which the reader must bear well in mind in the course of the following considerations, to wit, that not every cognition à priori, but only those through which we cognize that and how certain representations (intuitions or conceptions) are applied or are possible only à priori; that is to say, the à priori possibility of cognition and the à priori use of it are transcendental. Therefore neither is space, nor any à priori geometrical determination of space, a transcendental Representation, but only the knowledge that such a representation is not of empirical origin, and the possibility of its relating to objects of experience, although itself à priori, can be called transcendental. So also, the application of space to objects in general would be transcendental; but if it be limited to objects of sense it is empirical. Thus, the distinction of the transcendental and empirical belongs only to the critique of cognitions, and does not concern the relation of these to their object.

Accordingly, in the expectation that there may perhaps be conceptions which relate à priori to objects, not as pure or sensuous intuitions, but merely as acts of pure thought (which are therefore conceptions, but neither of empirical nor æsthetical origin)—in this expectation, I say, we form to ourselves, by anticipation, the idea of a science of pure understanding and rational cognition, by means of which we may cogitate objects entirely à priori. A science of this kind, which should determine the origin, the extent, and the objective validity of such cognitions, must be called transcendental logic, because it has not, like general logic, to do with the laws of understanding and reason in relation to empirical as well as pure rational cognitions without distinction, but concerns itself with these only in an à priori relation to objects.

III. OF THE DIVISION OF GENERAL LOGIC INTO ANALYTIC AND DIALECTIC.

The old question with which people sought to push logicians into a corner, so that they must either have recourse to pitiful sophisms or confess their ignorance, and consequently the vanity of their whole art, is this: "What is truth?" The definition of the word truth, to wit, "the accordance of the cognition with its object," is presupposed in the question; but we desire to be told, in the answer to it, what is the universal and secure criterion of the truth of every cognition.

To know what questions we may reasonably propose is in itself a strong evidence of sagacity and intelligence. For if a question be in itself absurd and unsusceptible of a rational answer, it is attended with the danger—not to mention the shame that falls upon the person who proposes it—of seducing the unguarded listener into making absurd answers, and we are presented with the ridiculous spectacle of one (as the ancients said) "milking the he-goat, and the other holding a sieve."

If truth consists in the accordance of a cognition with its object, this object must be, ipso facto, distinguished from all others; for a cognition is false if it does not accord with the object to which it relates, although it contains something which may be affirmed of other objects. Now an universal criterion of truth would be that which is valid for all cognitions, without distinction of their objects. But it is evident that since, in the case of such a criterion, we make abstraction of all the content of a cognition (that is, of all relation to its object), and truth relates precisely to this content, it must be utterly absurd to ask for a mark of the truth of this content of cognition; and that, accordingly, a sufficient, and at the same time universal, test of truth cannot possibly be found. As we have already termed the content of a cognition its matter, we shall say: "Of the truth of our cognitions in respect of their matter, no universal test can be demanded, because such a demand is self-contradictory."

On the other hand, with regard to our cognition in respect of its mere form (excluding all content), it is equally manifest that logic, in so far as it exhibits the universal and necessary laws of the understanding, must in these very laws present us with criteria of truth. Whatever contradicts these rules is false, because thereby the understanding is made to contradict its own universal laws of thought; that is, to contradict itself. These criteria, however, apply solely to the form of truth, that is, of thought in general, and in so far they are perfectly accurate, yet not sufficient. For although a cognition may be perfectly accurate as to logical form, that is, not self-contradictory, it is notwithstanding quite possible that it may not stand in agreement with its object. Consequently, the merely logical criterion of truth, namely, the accordance of a cognition with the universal and formal laws of understanding and reason, is nothing more than the conditio sine qua non, or negative condition of all truth. Farther than this logic cannot go, and the error which depends not on the form, but on the content of the cognition, it has no test to discover.

General logic, then, resolves the whole formal business of understanding and reason into its elements, and exhibits them as principles of all logical judging of our cognitions. This part of logic may, therefore, be called analytic, and is at least the negative test of truth, because all cognitions must first of an be estimated and tried according to these laws before we proceed to investigate them in respect of their content, in order to discover whether they contain positive truth in regard to their object. Because, however, the mere form of a cognition, accurately as it may accord with logical laws, is insufficient to supply us with material (objective) truth, no one, by means of logic alone, can venture to predicate anything of or decide concerning objects, unless he has obtained, independently of logic, well-grounded information about them, in order afterwards to examine, according to logical laws, into the use and connection, in a cohering whole, of that information, or, what is still better, merely to test it by them. Notwithstanding, there lies so seductive a charm in the possession of a specious art like this—an art which gives to all our cognitions the form of the understanding, although with respect to the content thereof we may be sadly deficient—that general logic, which is merely a canon of judgement, has been employed as an organon for the actual production, or rather for the semblance of production, of objective assertions, and has thus been grossly misapplied. Now general logic, in its assumed character of organon, is called dialectic.

Different as are the significations in which the ancients used this term for a science or an art, we may safely infer, from their actual employment of it, that with them it was nothing else than a logic of illusion—a sophistical art for giving ignorance, nay, even intentional sophistries, the colouring of truth, in which the thoroughness of procedure which logic requires was imitated, and their topic employed to cloak the empty pretensions. Now it may be taken as a safe and useful warning, that general logic, considered as an organon, must always be a logic of illusion, that is, be dialectical, for, as it teaches us nothing whatever respecting the content of our cognitions, but merely the formal conditions of their accordance with the understanding, which do not relate to and are quite indifferent in respect of objects, any attempt to employ it as an instrument (organon) in order to extend and enlarge the range of our knowledge must end in mere prating; any one being able to maintain or oppose, with some appearance of truth, any single assertion whatever.

Such instruction is quite unbecoming the dignity of philosophy. For these reasons we have chosen to denominate this part of logic dialectic, in the sense of a critique of dialectical illusion, and we wish the term to be so understood in this place.

IV. OF THE DIVISION OF TRANSCENDENTAL LOGIC INTO TRANSCENDENTAL ANALYTIC AND DIALECTIC.

In transcendental logic we isolate the understanding (as in transcendental æsthetic the sensibility) and select from our cognition merely that part of thought which has its origin in the understanding alone. The exercise of this pure cognition, however, depends upon this as its condition, that objects to which it may be applied be given to us in intuition, for without intuition the whole of our cognition is without objects, and is therefore quite void. That part of transcendental logic, then, which treats of the elements of pure cognition of the understanding, and of the principles without which no object at all can be thought, is transcendental analytic, and at the same time a logic of truth. For no cognition can contradict it, without losing at the same time all content, that is, losing all reference to an object, and therefore all truth. But because we are very easily seduced into employing these pure cognitions and principles of the understanding by themselves, and that even beyond the boundaries of experience, which yet is the only source whence we can obtain matter (objects) on which those pure conceptions may be employed—understanding runs the risk of making, by means of empty sophisms, a material and objective use of the mere formal principles of the pure understanding, and of passing judgements on objects without distinction—objects which are not given to us, nay, perhaps cannot be given to us in any way. Now, as it ought properly to be only a canon for judging of the empirical use of the understanding, this kind of logic is misused when we seek to employ it as an organon of the universal and unlimited exercise of the understanding, and attempt with the pure understanding alone to judge synthetically, affirm, and determine respecting objects in general. In this case the exercise of the pure understanding becomes dialectical. The second part of our transcendental logic must therefore be a critique of dialectical illusion, and this critique we shall term transcendental dialectic—not meaning it as an art of producing dogmatically such illusion (an art which is unfortunately too current among the practitioners of metaphysical juggling), but as a critique of understanding and reason in regard to their hyperphysical use. This critique will expose the groundless nature of the pretensions of these two faculties, and invalidate their claims to the discovery and enlargement of our cognitions merely by means of transcendental principles, and show that the proper employment of these faculties is to test the judgements made by the pure understanding, and to guard it from sophistical delusion.

FIRST DIVISION. TRANSCENDENTAL LOGIC. TRANSCENDENTAL ANALYTIC. § 1

Transcendental analytic is the dissection of the whole of our à priori knowledge into the elements of the pure cognition of the understanding. In order to effect our purpose, it is necessary: (1) That the conceptions be pure and not empirical; (2) That they belong not to intuition and sensibility, but to thought and understanding; (3) That they be elementary conceptions, and as such, quite different from deduced or compound conceptions; (4) That our table of these elementary conceptions be complete, and fill up the whole sphere of the pure understanding. Now this completeness of a science cannot be accepted with confidence on the guarantee of a mere estimate of its existence in an aggregate formed only by means of repeated experiments and attempts. The completeness which we require is possible only by means of an idea of the totality of the à priori cognition of the understanding, and through the thereby determined division of the conceptions which form the said whole; consequently, only by means of their connection in a system. Pure understanding distinguishes itself not merely from everything empirical, but also completely from all sensibility. It is a unity self-subsistent, self-sufficient, and not to be enlarged by any additions from without. Hence the sum of its cognition constitutes a system to be determined by and comprised under an idea; and the completeness and articulation of this system can at the same time serve as a test of the correctness and genuineness of all the parts of cognition that belong to it. The whole of this part of transcendental logic consists of two books, of which the one contains the conceptions, and the other the principles of pure understanding.

BOOK I. ANALYTIC OF CONCEPTIONS. § 2

By the term Analytic of Conceptions, I do not understand the analysis of these, or the usual process in philosophical investigations of dissecting the conceptions which present themselves, according to their content, and so making them clear; but I mean the hitherto little attempted dissection of the faculty of understanding itself, in order to investigate the possibility of conceptions à priori, by looking for them in the understanding alone, as their birthplace, and analysing the pure use of this faculty. For this is the proper duty of a transcendental philosophy; what remains is the logical treatment of the conceptions in philosophy in general. We shall therefore follow up the pure conceptions even to their germs and beginnings in the human understanding, in which they lie, until they are developed on occasions presented by experience, and, freed by the same understanding from the empirical conditions attaching to them, are set forth in their unalloyed purity.

CHAPTER I. OF THE TRANSCENDENTAL CLUE TO THE DISCOVERY OF ALL PURE CONCEPTIONS OF THE UNDERSTANDING

INTRODUCTORY § 3

When we call into play a faculty of cognition, different conceptions manifest themselves according to the different circumstances, and make known this faculty, and assemble themselves into a more or less extensive collection, according to the time or penetration that has been applied to the consideration of them. Where this process, conducted as it is mechanically, so to speak, will end, cannot be determined with certainty. Besides, the conceptions which we discover in this haphazard manner present themselves by no means in order and systematic unity, but are at last coupled together only according to resemblances to each other, and arranged in series, according to the quantity of their content, from the simpler to the more complex—series which are anything but systematic, though not altogether without a certain kind of method in their construction.

Transcendental philosophy has the advantage, and moreover the duty, of searching for its conceptions according to a principle; because these conceptions spring pure and unmixed out of the understanding as an absolute unity, and therefore must be connected with each other according to one conception or idea. A connection of this kind, however, furnishes us with a ready prepared rule, by which its proper place may be assigned to every pure conception of the understanding, and the completeness of the system of all be determined à priori—both which would otherwise have been dependent on mere choice or chance.

SECTION I. OF THE LOGICAL USE OF THE UNDERSTANDING IN GENERAL § 4

The understanding was defined above only negatively, as a non-sensuous faculty of cognition. Now, independently of sensibility, we cannot possibly have any intuition; consequently, the understanding is no faculty of intuition. But besides intuition there is no other mode of cognition, except through conceptions; consequently, the cognition of every, at least of every human, understanding is a cognition through conceptions—not intuitive, but discursive. All intuitions, as sensuous, depend on affections; conceptions, therefore, upon functions. By the word function I understand the unity of the act of arranging diverse representations under one common representation. Conceptions, then, are based on the spontaneity of thought, as sensuous intuitions are on the receptivity of impressions. Now, the understanding cannot make any other use of these conceptions than to judge by means of them. As no representation, except an intuition, relates immediately to its object, a conception never relates immediately to an object, but only to some other representation thereof, be that an intuition or itself a conception. A judgement, therefore, is the mediate cognition of an object, consequently the representation of a representation of it. In every judgement there is a conception which applies to, and is valid for many other conceptions, and which among these comprehends also a given representation, this last being immediately connected with an object. For example, in the judgement—"All bodies are divisible," our conception of divisible applies to various other conceptions; among these, however, it is here particularly applied to the conception of body, and this conception of body relates to certain phenomena which occur to us. These objects, therefore, are mediately represented by the conception of divisibility. All judgements, accordingly, are functions of unity in our representations, inasmuch as, instead of an immediate, a higher representation, which comprises this and various others, is used for our cognition of the object, and thereby many possible cognitions are collected into one. But we can reduce all acts of the understanding to judgements, so that understanding may be represented as the faculty of judging. For it is, according to what has been said above, a faculty of thought. Now thought is cognition by means of conceptions. But conceptions, as predicates of possible judgements, relate to some representation of a yet undetermined object. Thus the conception of body indicates something—for example, metal—which can be cognized by means of that conception. It is therefore a conception, for the reason alone that other representations are contained under it, by means of which it can relate to objects. It is therefore the predicate to a possible judgement; for example: "Every metal is a body." All the functions of the understanding therefore can be discovered, when we can completely exhibit the functions of unity in judgements. And that this may be effected very easily, the following section will show.

SECTION II. OF THE LOGICAL FUNCTION OF THE UNDERSTANDING IN JUDGEMENTS § 5

If we abstract all the content of a judgement, and consider only the intellectual form thereof, we find that the function of thought in a judgement can be brought under four heads, of which each contains three momenta. These may be conveniently represented in the following table:

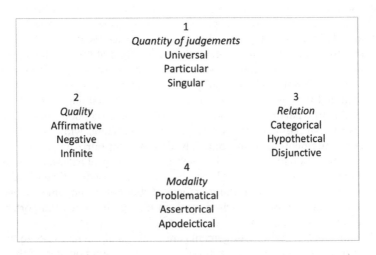

	1	
	Quantity of judgements	
	Universal	
	Particular	
	Singular	
2		3
Quality		*Relation*
Affirmative		Categorical
Negative		Hypothetical
Infinite		Disjunctive
	4	
	Modality	
	Problematical	
	Assertorical	
	Apodeictical	

As THIS DIVISION appears to differ in some, though not essential points, from the usual technique of logicians, the following observations, for the prevention of otherwise possible misunderstanding, will not be without their use.

1. Logicians say, with justice, that in the use of judgements in syllogisms, singular judgements may be treated like universal ones. For, precisely because a singular judgement has no extent at all, its predicate cannot refer to a part of that which is contained in the conception of the subject and be excluded from the rest. The predicate is valid for the whole conception just as if it were a general conception, and had extent, to the whole of which the predicate applied. On the other hand, let us compare a singular with a general judgement, merely as a cognition, in regard to quantity. The singular judgement relates to the general one, as unity to infinity, and is therefore in itself essentially different. Thus, if we estimate a singular judgement (*judicium singulare*) not merely according to its intrinsic validity as a judgement, but also as a cognition generally, according to its quantity in comparison with that of other cognitions, it is then entirely different from a general judgement (*judicium commune*), and in a complete table of the momenta of thought deserves a separate place—though, indeed, this would not be necessary in a logic limited merely to the consideration of the use of judgements in reference to each other.

2. In like manner, in transcendental logic, infinite must be distinguished from affirmative judgements, although in general logic they are rightly enough classed under affirmative. General logic abstracts all content of the predicate (though it be negative), and only considers whether the said predicate be affirmed or denied of the subject. But transcendental logic considers also the worth or content of this logical affirmation—an affirmation by means of a merely negative predicate, and inquires how much the sum total of our cognition gains by this affirmation. For example, if I say of the soul, "It is not mortal"—by this negative judgement I should at least ward off error. Now, by the proposition, "The soul is not mortal," I have, in respect of the logical form, really affirmed, inasmuch as I thereby place the soul in the unlimited sphere of immortal beings. Now, because of the whole sphere of possible existences, the mortal occupies one part, and the immortal the other, neither more nor less is affirmed by the proposition than that the soul is one among the infinite multitude of things which remain over, when I take away the whole mortal part. But by this proceeding we accomplish only this much, that the infinite sphere of all possible existences is in so far limited that the mortal is excluded from it, and the soul is placed in the remaining part of the extent of this sphere. But this part remains, notwithstanding this exception, infinite, and more and more parts may be taken away from the whole sphere, without in the slightest degree thereby augmenting or affirmatively determining our conception of the soul. These judgements, therefore, infinite in respect of their logical extent, are, in respect of the content of their cognition, merely limitative; and are consequently entitled to a place in our transcendental table of all the momenta of thought in judgements, because the function of the understanding exercised by them may perhaps be of importance in the field of its pure à priori cognition.

3. All relations of thought in judgements are those (a) of the predicate to the subject; (b) of the principle to its consequence; (c) of the divided cognition and all the members of the division to each other. In the first of these three classes, we consider only two conceptions; in the second, two judgements; in the third, several judgements in relation

to each other. The hypothetical proposition, "If perfect justice exists, the obstinately wicked are punished," contains properly the relation to each other of two propositions, namely, "Perfect justice exists," and "The obstinately wicked are punished." Whether these propositions are in themselves true is a question not here decided. Nothing is cogitated by means of this judgement except a certain consequence. Finally, the disjunctive judgement contains a relation of two or more propositions to each other—a relation not of consequence, but of logical opposition, in so far as the sphere of the one proposition excludes that of the other. But it contains at the same time a relation of community, in so far as all the propositions taken together fill up the sphere of the cognition. The disjunctive judgement contains, therefore, the relation of the parts of the whole sphere of a cognition, since the sphere of each part is a complemental part of the sphere of the other, each contributing to form the sum total of the divided cognition. Take, for example, the proposition, "The world exists either through blind chance, or through internal necessity, or through an external cause." Each of these propositions embraces a part of the sphere of our possible cognition as to the existence of a world; all of them taken together, the whole sphere. To take the cognition out of one of these spheres, is equivalent to placing it in one of the others; and, on the other hand, to place it in one sphere is equivalent to taking it out of the rest. There is, therefore, in a disjunctive judgement a certain community of cognitions, which consists in this, that they mutually exclude each other, yet thereby determine, as a whole, the true cognition, inasmuch as, taken together, they make up the complete content of a particular given cognition. And this is all that I find necessary, for the sake of what follows, to remark in this place.

4. The modality of judgements is a quite peculiar function, with this distinguishing characteristic, that it contributes nothing to the content of a judgement (for besides quantity, quality, and relation, there is nothing more that constitutes the content of a judgement), but concerns itself only with the value of the copula in relation to thought in general. Problematical judgements are those in which the affirmation or negation is accepted as merely possible (ad libitum). In the assertorical, we regard the proposition as real (true); in the apodeictical, we look on it as necessary.[4] Thus the two judgements (antecedens et consequens), the relation of which constitutes a hypothetical judgement, likewise those (the members of the division) in whose reciprocity the disjunctive consists, are only problematical. In the example above given the proposition, "There exists perfect justice," is not stated assertorically, but as an ad libitum judgement, which someone may choose to adopt, and the consequence alone is assertorical. Hence such judgements may be obviously false, and yet, taken problematically, be conditions of our cognition of the truth. Thus the proposition, "The world exists only by blind chance," is in the disjunctive judgement of problematical import only: that is to say, one may accept it for the moment, and it helps us (like the indication of the wrong road among all the roads that one can take) to find out the true proposition. The problematical proposition is, therefore, that which expresses only logical possibility (which is not objective); that is, it expresses a free choice to admit the validity of such a proposition—a merely arbitrary reception of it into the understanding. The assertorical speaks of logical reality or truth; as, for example, in a hypothetical syllogism, the antecedens presents itself in a problematical form in the major, in an assertorical form in the minor, and it shows that the proposition is in harmony with the laws of the understanding. The apodeictical proposition cogitates the assertorical as determined by these very laws of the under-

standing, consequently as affirming à priori, and in this manner it expresses logical necessity. Now because all is here gradually incorporated with the understanding—inasmuch as in the first place we judge problematically; then accept assertorically our judgement as true; lastly, affirm it as inseparably united with the understanding, that is, as necessary and apodeictical—we may safely reckon these three functions of modality as so many momenta of thought.

SECTION III. OF THE PURE CONCEPTIONS OF THE UNDERSTANDING, OR CATEGORIES § 6

General logic, as has been repeatedly said, makes abstraction of all content of cognition, and expects to receive representations from some other quarter, in order, by means of analysis, to convert them into conceptions. On the contrary, transcendental logic has lying before it the manifold content of à priori sensibility, which transcendental æsthetic presents to it in order to give matter to the pure conceptions of the understanding, without which transcendental logic would have no content, and be therefore utterly void. Now space and time contain an infinite diversity of determinations of pure à priori intuition, but are nevertheless the condition of the mind's receptivity, under which alone it can obtain representations of objects, and which, consequently, must always affect the conception of these objects. But the spontaneity of thought requires that this diversity be examined after a certain manner, received into the mind, and connected, in order afterwards to form a cognition out of it. This Process I call synthesis.

By the word synthesis, in its most general signification, I understand the process of joining different representations to each other and of comprehending their diversity in one cognition. This synthesis is pure when the diversity is not given empirically but à priori (as that in space and time). Our representations must be given previously to any analysis of them; and no conceptions can arise, quoad their content, analytically. But the synthesis of a diversity (be it given à priori or empirically) is the first requisite for the production of a cognition, which in its beginning, indeed, may be crude and confused, and therefore in need of analysis—still, synthesis is that by which alone the elements of our cognitions are collected and united into a certain content, consequently it is the first thing on which we must fix our attention, if we wish to investigate the origin of our knowledge.

Synthesis, generally speaking, is, as we shall afterwards see, the mere operation of the imagination—a blind but indispensable function of the soul, without which we should have no cognition whatever, but of the working of which we are seldom even conscious. But to reduce this synthesis to conceptions is a function of the understanding, by means of which we attain to cognition, in the proper meaning of the term.

Pure synthesis, represented generally, gives us the pure conception of the understanding. But by this pure synthesis, I mean that which rests upon a basis of à priori synthetical unity. Thus, our numeration (and this is more observable in large numbers) is a synthesis according to conceptions, because it takes place according to a common basis of unity (for example, the decade). By means of this conception, therefore, the unity in the synthesis of the manifold becomes necessary.

By means of analysis different representations are brought under one conception—an operation of which general logic treats. On the other hand, the duty of transcendental logic is to reduce to conceptions, not representations, but the pure synthesis of representations. The first thing which must be given to us for the sake of the à priori cognition of all objects, is the diversity of the pure intuition; the synthesis of this diversity by means of the imagination is the second; but this gives, as yet, no cognition. The conceptions which give unity to this pure synthesis, and which consist solely in the representation of this necessary synthetical unity, furnish the third requisite for the cognition of an object, and these conceptions are given by the understanding.

The same function which gives unity to the different representation in a judgement, gives also unity to the mere synthesis of different representations in an intuition; and this unity we call the pure conception of the understanding. Thus, the same understanding, and by the same operations, whereby in conceptions, by means of analytical unity, it produced the logical form of a judgement, introduces, by means of the synthetical unity of the manifold in intuition, a transcendental content into its representations, on which account they are called pure conceptions of the understanding, and they apply à priori to objects, a result not within the power of general logic.

In this manner, there arise exactly so many pure conceptions of the understanding, applying à priori to objects of intuition in general, as there are logical functions in all possible judgements. For there is no other function or faculty existing in the understanding besides those enumerated in that table. These conceptions we shall, with Aristotle, call categories, our purpose being originally identical with his, notwithstanding the great difference in the execution.

Table of the Categories

1 *Of Quantity* Unity Plurality Totality	2 *Of Quality* Reality Negation Limitation

3
Of Relation
Of Inherence and Subsistence (substantia et accidens)
Of Causality and Dependence (cause and effect)
Of Community (reciprocity between the agent and patient)

4
Of Modality
Possibility—Impossibility
Existence—Non-existence
Necessity—Contingence

This, then, is a catalogue of all the originally pure conceptions of the synthesis which the understanding contains à priori, and these conceptions alone entitle it to be called a pure understanding; inasmuch as only by them it can render the manifold of intuition conceivable, in other words, think an object of intuition. This division is made systematically from a common principle, namely the faculty of judgement (which is just the same as the power of thought), and has not arisen rhapsodically from a search at haphazard after pure conceptions, respecting the full number of which we never could be certain, inasmuch as we employ induction alone in our search, without considering that in this way we can never understand wherefore precisely these conceptions, and none others, abide in the pure understanding. It was a design worthy of an acute thinker like Aristotle, to search for these fundamental conceptions. Destitute, however, of any guiding principle, he picked them up just as they occurred to him, and at first hunted out ten, which he called categories (predicaments). Afterwards be believed that he had discovered five others, which were added under the name of post predicaments. But his catalogue still remained defective. Besides, there are to be found among them some of the modes of pure sensibility (quando, ubi, situs, also prius, simul), and likewise an empirical conception (motus)—which can by no means belong to this genealogical register of the pure understanding. Moreover, there are deduced conceptions (actio, passio) enumerated among the original conceptions, and, of the latter, some are entirely wanting.

With regard to these, it is to be remarked, that the categories, as the true primitive conceptions of the pure understanding, have also their pure deduced conceptions, which, in a complete system of transcendental philosophy, must by no means be passed over; though in a merely critical essay we must be contented with the simple mention of the fact.

Let it be allowed me to call these pure, but deduced conceptions of the understanding, the predicables of the pure understanding, in contradistinction to predicaments. If we are in possession of the original and primitive, the deduced and subsidiary conceptions can easily be added, and the genealogical tree of the understanding completely delineated. As my present aim is not to set forth a complete system, but merely the principles of one, I reserve this task for another time. It may be easily executed by any one who will refer to the ontological manuals, and subordinate to the category of causality, for example, the predicables of force, action, passion; to that of community, those of presence and resistance; to the categories of modality, those of origination, extinction, change; and so with the rest. The categories combined with the modes of pure sensibility, or with one another, afford a great number of deduced à priori conceptions; a complete enumeration of which would be a useful and not unpleasant, but in this place a perfectly dispensable, occupation.

I purposely omit the definitions of the categories in this treatise. I shall analyse these conceptions only so far as is necessary for the doctrine of method, which is to form a part of this critique. In a system of pure reason, definitions of them would be with justice demanded of me, but to give them here would only bide from our view the main aim of our investigation, at the same time raising doubts and objections, the consideration of which, without injustice to our main purpose, may be very well postponed till another opportunity. Meanwhile, it ought to be sufficiently clear, from the little we have already said on this subject, that the formation of a complete vocabulary of pure conceptions, accompanied by all the requisite explanations, is not only a possible, but an easy undertaking. The compartments already exist; it is only necessary to fill them up; and a systematic topic like the present, indicates with perfect precision the proper place to which each conception belongs, while it readily points out any that have not yet been filled up.

§ 7

Our table of the categories suggests considerations of some importance, which may perhaps have significant results in regard to the scientific form of all rational cognitions. For, that this table is useful in the theoretical part of philosophy, nay, indispensable for the sketching of the complete plan of a science, so far as that science rests upon conceptions à priori, and for dividing it mathematically, according to fixed principles, is most manifest from the fact that it contains all the elementary conceptions of the understanding, nay, even the form of a system of these in the understanding itself, and consequently indicates all the momenta, and also the internal arrangement of a projected speculative science, as I have elsewhere shown.[5] Here follow some of these observations.

I. This table, which contains four classes of conceptions of the understanding, may, in the first instance, be divided into two classes, the first of which relates to objects of intuition—pure as well as empirical; the second, to the existence of these objects, either in relation to one another, or to the understanding.

The former of these classes of categories I would entitle the mathematical, and the latter the dynamical categories. The former, as we see, has no correlates; these are only to be found in the second class. This difference must have a ground in the nature of the human understanding.

II. The number of the categories in each class is always the same, namely, three—a fact which also demands some consideration, because in all other cases division à priori through conceptions is necessarily dichotomy. It is to be added, that the third category in each triad always arises from the combination of the second with the first.

Thus totality is nothing else but plurality contemplated as unity; limitation is merely reality conjoined with negation; community is the causality of a substance, reciprocally determining, and determined by other substances; and finally, necessity is nothing but existence, which is given through the possibility itself. Let it not be supposed, however, that the third category is merely a deduced, and not a primitive conception of the pure understanding. For the conjunction of the first and second, in order to produce the third conception, requires a particular function of the understanding, which is by no means identical with those which are exercised in the first and second. Thus, the conception of a number (which belongs to the category of totality) is not always possible, where the conceptions of multitude and unity exist (for example, in the representation of the infinite). Or, if I conjoin the conception of a cause with that of a substance, it does not follow that the conception of influence, that is, how one substance can be the cause of something in another substance, will be understood from that. Thus it is evident that a particular act of the understanding is here necessary; and so in the other instances.

III. With respect to one category, namely, that of community, which is found in the third class, it is not so easy as with the others to detect its accordance with the form of the disjunctive judgement which corresponds to it in the table of the logical functions.

In order to assure ourselves of this accordance, we must observe that in every disjunctive judgement, the sphere of the judgement (that is, the complex of all that is contained in it) is represented as a whole divided into parts; and, since one part cannot be contained in the other, they are cogitated as co-ordinated with, not subordinated to each other, so that they do not determine each other unilaterally, as in a linear series, but reciprocally, as in an aggregate—(if one member of the division is posited, all the rest are excluded; and conversely).

Now a like connection is cogitated in a whole of things; for one thing is not subordinated, as effect, to another as cause of its existence, but, on the contrary, is co-ordinated contemporaneously and reciprocally, as a cause in relation to the determination of the others (for example, in a body—the parts of which mutually attract and repel each other). And this is an entirely different kind of connection from that which we find in the mere relation of the cause to the effect (the principle to the consequence), for in such a connection the consequence does not in its turn determine the principle, and therefore does not constitute, with the latter, a whole—just as the Creator does not with the world make up a whole. The process of understanding by which it represents to itself the sphere of a divided conception, is employed also when we think of a thing as divisible; and in the same manner as the members of the division in the former exclude one another, and yet are connected in one sphere, so the understanding represents to itself the parts of the latter, as having—each of them—an existence (as substances), independently of the others, and yet as united in one whole.

§ 8

In the transcendental philosophy of the ancients there exists one more leading division, which contains pure conceptions of the understanding, and which, although not numbered among the categories, ought, according to them, as conceptions à priori, to be valid of objects. But in this case they would augment the number of the categories; which cannot be. These are set forth in the proposition, so renowned among the schoolmen—'*Quodlibet ens est UNUM, VERUM, BONUM.*' Now, though the inferences from this principle were mere tautological propositions, and though it is allowed only by courtesy to retain a place in modern metaphysics, yet a thought which maintained itself for such a length of time, however empty it seems to be, deserves an investigation of its origin, and justifies the conjecture that it must be grounded in some law of the understanding, which, as is often the case, has only been erroneously interpreted. These pretended transcendental predicates are, in fact, nothing but logical requisites and criteria of all cognition of objects, and they employ, as the basis for this cognition, the categories of quantity, namely, unity, plurality, and totality. But these, which must be taken as material conditions, that is, as belonging to the possibility of things themselves, they employed merely in a formal signification, as belonging to the logical requisites of all cognition, and yet most unguardedly changed these criteria of thought into properties of objects, as things in themselves. Now, in every cognition of an object, there is unity of conception, which may be called qualitative unity, so far as by this term we understand only the unity in our connection of the manifold; for example, unity of the theme in a play, an oration, or a story. Secondly, there is truth in respect of the deductions from it. The more true deductions we have from a given conception, the more criteria of its objective reality. This we might call the qualitative plurality of characteristic marks, which belong to a conception as to a common foundation, but are not cogitated as a quantity in it. Thirdly, there is perfection—which consists in this, that the plurality falls back upon the unity of the conception, and accords completely with that conception and with no other. This we may denominate qualitative completeness.

Hence it is evident that these logical criteria of the possibility of cognition are merely the three categories of quantity modified and transformed to suit an unauthorized manner of applying them. That is to say, the three categories, in which the unity in the production of the quantum must be homogeneous throughout, are transformed solely with a view to the connection of heterogeneous parts of cognition in one act of consciousness, by means of the quality of the cognition, which is the principle of that connection. Thus the criterion of the possibility of a conception (not of its object) is the definition of it, in which the unity of the conception, the truth of all that may be immediately deduced from it, and finally, the completeness of what has been thus deduced, constitute the requisites for the reproduction of the whole conception. Thus also, the criterion or test of an hypothesis is the intelligibility of the received principle of explanation, or its unity (without help from any subsidiary hypothesis)—the truth of our deductions from it (consistency with each other and with experience)—and lastly, the completeness of the principle of the explanation of these deductions, which refer to neither more nor less than what was admitted in the hypothesis, restoring analytically and à posteriori, what was cogitated synthetically and à priori. By the conceptions, therefore, of unity, truth, and perfection, we have made no addition to the transcendental table of the categories, which is complete without them. We have, on the contrary, merely employed the three categories of quantity, setting aside their application to objects of experience, as general logical laws of the consistency of cognition with itself.

CHAPTER II. OF THE DEDUCTION OF THE PURE CONCEPTIONS OF THE UNDERSTANDING

SECTION I. OF THE PRINCIPLES OF A TRANSCENDENTAL DEDUCTION IN GENERAL § 9

Teachers of jurisprudence, when speaking of rights and claims, distinguish in a cause the question of right (quid juris) from the question of fact (quid facti), and while they demand proof of both, they give to the proof of the former, which goes to establish right or claim in law, the name of deduction. Now we make use of a great number of empirical conceptions, without opposition from any one; and consider ourselves, even without any attempt at deduction, justified in attaching to them a sense, and a supposititious signification, because we have always experience at hand to demonstrate their objective reality. There exist also, however, usurped conceptions, such as fortune, fate, which circulate with almost universal indulgence, and yet are occasionally challenged by the question, "quid juris?" In such cases, we have great difficulty in discovering any deduction for these terms, inasmuch as we cannot produce any manifest ground of right, either from experience or from reason, on which the claim to employ them can be founded.

Among the many conceptions, which make up the very variegated web of human cognition, some are destined for pure use à priori, independent of all experience; and their title to be so employed always requires a deduction, inasmuch as, to justify such use of them, proofs from experience are not sufficient; but it is necessary to know how these conceptions can apply to objects without being derived from experience. I term, therefore, an examination of the manner in which conceptions can apply à priori to objects, the transcendental deduction of conceptions, and I distinguish it from the empirical deduction, which indicates the mode in which conception is obtained through experience and reflection thereon; consequently, does not concern itself with the right, but only with the fact of our obtaining conceptions in such and such a manner. We have already seen that we are in possession of two perfectly different kinds of conceptions, which nevertheless agree with each other in this, that they both apply to objects completely à priori. These are the conceptions of space and time as forms of sensibility, and the categories as pure conceptions of the understanding. To attempt an empirical deduction of either of these classes would be labour in vain, because the distinguishing characteristic of their nature consists in this, that they apply to their objects, without having borrowed anything from experience towards the representation of them. Consequently, if a deduction of these conceptions is necessary, it must always be transcendental.

Meanwhile, with respect to these conceptions, as with respect to all our cognition, we certainly may discover in experience, if not the principle of their possibility, yet the occasioning causes of their production. It will be found that the impressions of sense give the first occasion for bringing into action the whole faculty of cognition, and for the production of experience, which contains two very dissimilar elements, namely, a matter for cognition, given by the senses, and a certain form for the arrangement of this matter, arising out of the inner fountain of pure intuition and thought; and these, on occasion given by sensuous impressions, are called into exercise and produce conceptions. Such an investigation into the first efforts of our faculty of cognition to mount from particular perceptions to general conceptions is undoubtedly of great utility; and we have to thank the celebrated Locke for having first opened the way for this inquiry. But a deduction of the pure à priori conceptions of course never can be made in this way, seeing that, in regard to their future employment, which must be entirely independent of experience, they must have a far different certificate of birth to show from that of a descent from experience. This attempted physiological derivation, which cannot properly be called deduction, because it relates merely to a quaestio facti, I shall entitle an explanation of the possession of a pure cognition. It is therefore manifest that there can only be a transcendental deduction of these conceptions and by no means an empirical one; also, that all attempts at an empirical deduction, in regard to pure à priori conceptions, are vain, and can only be made by one who does not understand the altogether peculiar nature of these cognitions.

But although it is admitted that the only possible deduction of pure à priori cognition is a transcendental deduction, it is not, for that reason, perfectly manifest that such a deduction is absolutely necessary. We have already traced to their sources the conceptions of space and time, by means of a transcendental deduction, and we have explained and determined their objective validity à priori. Geometry, nevertheless, advances steadily and securely in the province of pure à priori cognitions, without needing to ask from philosophy any certificate as to the pure and legitimate origin of its fundamental conception of space. But the use of the conception in this science extends only to the external world of sense, the pure form of the intuition of which is space; and in this world, therefore, all geometrical cognition, because it is founded upon à priori intuition, possesses immediate evidence, and the objects of this cognition are given à priori (as regards their form) in intuition by and through the cognition itself. With the pure conceptions of understanding, on the contrary, commences the absolute necessity of seeking a transcendental deduction, not only of these conceptions themselves, but likewise of space, because, inasmuch as they make affirmations concerning objects not by means of the predicates of intuition and sensibility, but of pure thought à priori, they apply to objects without any of the conditions of sensibility. Besides, not being founded on experience, they are not presented with any object in à priori intuition upon which, antecedently to experience, they might base their synthesis. Hence results, not only doubt as to the objective validity and proper limits of their use, but that even our conception of space is rendered equivocal; inasmuch as we are very ready with the aid of the categories, to carry the use of this conception beyond the conditions of sensuous intuition—and, for this reason, we have already found a transcendental deduction of it needful. The reader, then, must be quite convinced of the absolute necessity of a transcendental deduction, before taking a single step in the field of pure reason; because otherwise he goes to work blindly, and after he has wondered about in all directions, returns to the state of utter ignorance from which he started. He ought, moreover, clearly to recognize beforehand the unavoidable difficulties in his undertaking, so that he may not afterwards complain of the obscurity in which the subject itself is deeply involved, or become too soon impatient of the obstacles in his path; because we have a choice of only two things—either at once to give up all pretensions to knowledge beyond the limits of possible experience, or to bring this critical investigation to completion.

We have been able, with very little trouble, to make it comprehensible how the conceptions of space and time, although à priori cognitions, must necessarily apply to external objects, and render a synthetical cognition of these possible, independently of all experience. For inasmuch as only by means of such pure form of sensibility an object can appear to us, that is, be an object of empirical intuition, space and time are pure intuitions, which contain à priori the condition of the possibility of objects as phenomena, and an à priori synthesis in these intuitions possesses objective validity.

On the other hand, the categories of the understanding do not represent the conditions under which objects are given to us in intuition; objects can consequently appear to us without necessarily connecting themselves with these, and consequently without any necessity binding on the understanding to contain à priori the conditions of these objects. Thus we find ourselves involved in a difficulty which did not present itself in the sphere of sensibility, that is to say, we cannot discover how the subjective conditions of thought can have objective validity, in other words, can become conditions of the possibility of all cognition of objects; for phenomena may certainly be given to us in intuition without any help from the functions of the understanding. Let us take, for example, the conception of cause, which indicates a peculiar kind of synthesis, namely, that with something, A, something entirely different, B, is connected according to a law. It is not à priori manifest why phenomena should contain anything of this kind (we are of course debarred from appealing for proof to experience, for the objective validity of this conception must be demonstrated à priori), and it hence remains doubtful à priori, whether such a conception be not quite void and without any corresponding object among phenomena. For that objects of sensuous intuition must correspond to the formal conditions of sensibility existing à priori in the mind is quite evident, from the fact that without these they could not be objects for us; but that they must also correspond to the conditions which understanding requires for the synthetical unity of thought is an assertion, the grounds for which are not so easily to be discovered. For phenomena might be so constituted as not to correspond to the conditions of the unity of thought; and all things might lie in such confusion that, for example, nothing could be met with in the sphere of phenomena to suggest a law of synthesis, and so correspond to the conception of cause and effect; so that this conception would be quite void, null, and without significance. Phenomena would nevertheless continue to present objects to our intuition; for mere intuition does not in any respect stand in need of the functions of thought.

If we thought to free ourselves from the labour of these investigations by saying: "Experience is constantly offering us examples of the relation of cause and effect in phenomena, and presents us with abundant opportunity of abstracting the conception of cause, and so at the same time of corroborating the objective validity of this conception"; we should in this case be overlooking the fact, that the conception of cause cannot arise in this way at all; that, on the contrary, it must either have an à priori basis in the understanding, or be rejected as a mere chimera. For this conception demands that something, A, should be of such a nature that something else, B, should follow from it necessarily, and according to an absolutely universal law. We may certainly collect from phenomena a law, according to which this or that usually happens, but the element of necessity is not to be found in it. Hence it is evident that to the synthesis of cause and effect belongs a dignity, which is utterly wanting in any empirical synthesis; for it is no mere mechanical synthesis, by means of addition, but a dynamical one; that is to say, the effect is not to be cogitated as merely annexed to the cause, but as posited by and through the cause, and resulting from it. The strict universality of this law never can be a characteristic of empirical laws, which obtain through induction only a comparative universality, that is, an extended range of practical application. But the pure conceptions of the understanding would entirely lose all their peculiar character, if we treated them merely as the productions of experience.

TRANSITION TO THE TRANSCENDENTAL DEDUCTION OF THE CATEGORIES § 10

There are only two possible ways in which synthetical representation and its objects can coincide with and relate necessarily to each other, and, as it were, meet together. Either the object alone makes the representation possible, or the representation alone makes the object possible. In the former case, the relation between them is only empirical, and an à priori representation is impossible. And this is the case with phenomena, as regards that in them which is referable to mere sensation. In the latter case—although representation alone (for of its causality, by means of the will, we do not here speak) does not produce the object as to its existence, it must nevertheless be à priori determinative in regard to the object, if it is only by means of the representation that we can cognize anything as an object. Now there are only two conditions of the possibility of a cognition of objects; firstly, intuition, by means of which the object, though only as phenomenon, is given; secondly, conception, by means of which the object which corresponds to this intuition is thought. But it is evident from what has been said on æsthetic that the first condition, under which alone objects can be intuited, must in fact exist, as a formal basis for them, à priori in the mind. With this formal condition of sensibility, therefore, all phenomena necessarily correspond, because it is only through it that they can be phenomena at all; that is, can be empirically intuited and given. Now the question is whether there do not exist, à priori in the mind, conceptions of understanding also, as conditions under which alone something, if not intuited, is yet thought as object. If this question be answered in the affirmative, it follows that all empirical cognition of objects is necessarily conformable to such conceptions, since, if they are not presupposed, it is impossible that anything can be an object of experience. Now all experience contains, besides the intuition of the senses through which an object is given, a conception also of an object that is given in intuition. Accordingly, conceptions of objects in general must lie as à priori conditions at the foundation of all empirical cognition; and consequently, the objective validity of the categories, as à priori conceptions, will rest upon this, that experience (as far as regards the form of thought) is possible only by their means. For in that case they apply necessarily and à priori to objects of experience, because only through them can an object of experience be thought.

The whole aim of the transcendental deduction of all à priori conceptions is to show that these conceptions are à priori conditions of the possibility of all experience. Conceptions which afford us the objective foundation of the possibility of experience are for that very reason necessary. But the analysis of the experiences in which they are met with is not deduction, but only an illustration of them, because from experience they could never derive the attribute of necessity. Without their original applicability and relation to all possible experience, in which all objects of cognition present themselves, the relation of the categories to objects, of whatever nature, would be quite incomprehensible.

The celebrated Locke, for want of due reflection on these points, and because he met with pure conceptions of the understanding in experience, sought also to deduce them from experience, and yet proceeded so inconsequently as to attempt, with their aid, to arrive it cognitions which lie far beyond the limits of all experience. David Hume perceived that, to render this possible, it was necessary that the conceptions should have an à priori origin. But as he could not explain how it was possible that conceptions which are not connected with each other in the understanding must nevertheless be thought as necessarily connected in the object—and it never occurred to him that the understanding itself might, perhaps, by means of these conceptions, be the author of the experience in which its objects were presented to it—he was forced to drive these conceptions from experience, that is, from a subjective necessity arising from repeated association of experiences erroneously considered to be objective—in one word, from habit. But he proceeded with perfect consequence and declared it to be impossible, with such conceptions and the principles arising from them, to overstep the limits of experience. The empirical derivation, however, which both of these philosophers attributed to these conceptions, cannot possibly be reconciled with the fact that we do possess scientific à priori cognitions, namely, those of pure mathematics and general physics.

The former of these two celebrated men opened a wide door to extravagance—(for if reason has once undoubted right on its side, it will not allow itself to be confined to set limits, by vague recommendations of moderation); the latter gave himself up entirely to scepticism—a natural consequence, after having discovered, as he thought, that the faculty of cognition was not trustworthy. We now intend to make a trial whether it be not possible safely to conduct reason between these two rocks, to assign her determinate limits, and yet leave open for her the entire sphere of her legitimate activity.

I shall merely premise an explanation of what the categories are. They are conceptions of an object in general, by means of which its intuition is contemplated as determined in relation to one of the logical functions of judgement. The following will make this plain. The function of the categorical judgement is that of the relation of subject to predicate; for example, in the proposition: "All bodies are divisible." But in regard to the merely logical use of the understanding, it still remains undetermined to which Of these two conceptions belongs the function Of subject and to which that of predicate. For we could also say: "Some divisible is a body." But the category of substance, when the conception of a body is brought under it, determines that; and its empirical intuition in experience must be contemplated always as subject and never as mere predicate. And so with all the other categories.

SECTION II. TRANSCENDENTAL DEDUCTION OF THE PURE CONCEPTIONS OF THE UNDERSTANDING

OF THE POSSIBILITY OF A CONJUNCTION OF THE MANIFOLD REPRESENTATIONS GIVEN BY SENSE § 11.

The manifold content in our representations can be given in an intuition which is merely sensuous—in other words, is nothing but susceptibility; and the form of this intuition can exist à priori in our faculty of representation, without being anything else but the mode in which the subject is affected. But the conjunction (conjunctio) of a manifold in intuition never can be given us by the senses; it cannot therefore be contained in the pure form of sensuous intuition, for it is a spontaneous act of the faculty of representation. And as we must, to distinguish it from sensibility, entitle this faculty understanding; so all conjunction whether conscious or unconscious, be it of the manifold in intuition, sensuous or non-sensuous, or of several conceptions—is an act of the understanding. To this act we shall give the general appellation of synthesis, thereby to indicate, at the same time, that we cannot represent anything as conjoined in the object without having previously conjoined it ourselves. Of all mental notions, that of conjunction is the only one which cannot be given through objects, but can be originated only by the subject itself, because it is an act of its purely spontaneous activity. The reader will easily enough perceive that the possibility of conjunction must be grounded in the very nature of this act, and that it must be equally valid for all conjunction, and that analysis, which appears to be its contrary, must, nevertheless, always presuppose it; for where the understanding has not previously conjoined, it cannot dissect or analyse, because only as conjoined by it, must that which is to be analysed have been given to our faculty of representation.

But the conception of conjunction includes, besides the conception of the manifold and of the synthesis of it, that of the unity of it also. Conjunction is the representation of the synthetical unity of the manifold.[6] This idea of unity, therefore, cannot arise out of that of conjunction; much rather does that idea, by combining itself with the representation of the manifold, render the conception of conjunction possible. This unity, which à priori precedes all conceptions of conjunction, is not the category of unity (§ 6); for all the categories are based upon logical functions of judgement, and in these functions we already have conjunction, and consequently unity of given conceptions. It is therefore evident that the category of unity presupposes conjunction. We must therefore look still higher for this unity (as qualitative, § 8), in that, namely, which contains the ground of the unity of diverse conceptions in judgements, the ground, consequently, of the possibility of the existence of the understanding, even in regard to its logical use.

OF THE ORIGINALLY SYNTHETICAL UNITY OF APPERCEPTION § 12

The "I think" must accompany all my representations, for otherwise something would be represented in me which could not be thought; in other words, the representation would either be impossible, or at least be, in relation to me, nothing. That representation which can be given previously to all thought is called intuition. All the diversity or manifold content of intuition, has, therefore, a necessary relation to the "I think," in the subject in which this diversity is found. But this representation, "I think," is an act of spontaneity; that is to say, it cannot be regarded as belonging to mere sensibility. I call it pure apperception, in order to distinguish it from empirical; or primitive apperception, because it is self-consciousness which, whilst it gives birth to the representation "I think," must necessarily be capable of accompanying all our representations. It is in all acts of consciousness one and the same, and unaccompanied by it, no representation can exist for me. The unity of this apperception I call the transcendental unity of self-consciousness, in order to indicate the possibility of à priori cognition arising from it. For the manifold representations which are given in an intuition would not all of them be my representations, if they did not all belong to one self-consciousness, that is, as my representations (even although I am not conscious of them as such), they must conform to the condition under which alone they can exist together in a common self-consciousness, because otherwise they would not all without exception belong to me. From this primitive conjunction follow many important results.

For example, this universal identity of the apperception of the manifold given in intuition contains a synthesis of representations and is possible only by means of the consciousness of this synthesis. For the empirical consciousness which accompanies different representations is in itself fragmentary and disunited, and without relation to the identity of the subject. This relation, then, does not exist because I accompany every representation with consciousness, but because I join one representation to another, and am conscious of the synthesis of them. Consequently, only because I can connect a variety of given representations in one consciousness, is it possible that I can represent to myself the identity of consciousness in these representations; in other words, the analytical unity of apperception is possible only under the presupposition of a synthetical unity.[7] The thought, "These representations given in intuition belong all of them to me," is accordingly just the same as, "I unite them in one self-consciousness, or can at least so unite them"; and although this thought is not itself the consciousness of the synthesis of representations, it presupposes the possibility of it; that is to say, for the reason alone that I can comprehend the variety of my representations in one consciousness, do I call them my representations, for otherwise I must have as many-coloured and various a self as are the representations of which I am conscious. Synthetical unity of the manifold in intuitions, as given à priori, is therefore the foundation of the identity of apperception itself, which antecedes à priori all determinate thought. But the conjunction of representations into a conception is not to be found in objects themselves, nor can it be, as it were, borrowed from them and taken up into the understanding by perception, but it is on the contrary an operation of the understanding itself, which is nothing more than the faculty of conjoining à priori and of bringing the variety of given representations under the unity of apperception. This principle is the highest in all human cognition.

This fundamental principle of the necessary unity of apperception is indeed an identical, and therefore analytical, proposition; but it nevertheless explains the necessity for a synthesis of the manifold given in an intuition, without which the identity of self-consciousness would be incogitable. For the ego, as a simple representation, presents us with no manifold content; only in intuition, which is quite different from the representation ego, can it be given us, and by means of conjunction it is cogitated in one self-consciousness. An understanding, in which all the manifold should be given by means of consciousness itself, would be intuitive; our understanding can only think and must look for its intuition to sense. I am, therefore, conscious of my identical self, in relation to all the variety of representations given to me in an intuition, because I call all of them my representations. In other words, I am conscious myself of a necessary à priori synthesis of my representations, which is called the original synthetical unity of apperception, under which rank all the representations presented to me, but that only by means of a synthesis.

THE PRINCIPLE OF THE SYNTHETICAL UNITY OF APPERCEPTION IS THE HIGHEST PRINCIPLE OF ALL EXERCISE OF THE UNDERSTANDING § 13

The supreme principle of the possibility of all intuition in relation to sensibility was, according to our transcendental æsthetic, that all the manifold in intuition be subject to the formal conditions of space and time. The supreme principle of the possibility of it in relation to the understanding is that all the manifold in it be subject to conditions of the originally synthetical unity or apperception.[8] To the former of these two principles are subject all the various representations of intuition, in so far as they are given to us; to the latter, in so far as they must be capable of conjunction in one consciousness; for without this nothing can be thought or cognized, because the given representations would not have in common the act Of the apperception "I think" and therefore could not be connected in one self-consciousness.

Understanding is, to speak generally, the faculty Of cognitions. These consist in the determined relation of given representation to an object. But an object is that, in the conception of which the manifold in a given intuition is united. Now all union of representations requires unity of consciousness in the synthesis of them. Consequently, it is the unity of consciousness alone that constitutes the possibility of representations relating to an object, and therefore of their objective validity, and of their becoming cognitions, and consequently, the possibility of the existence of the understanding itself.

The first pure cognition of understanding, then, upon which is founded all its other exercise, and which is at the same time perfectly independent of all conditions of mere sensuous intuition, is the principle of the original synthetical unity of apperception. Thus the mere form of external sensuous intuition, namely, space, affords us, per se, no cognition; it merely contributes the manifold in à priori intuition to a possible cognition. But, in order to cognize something in space (for example, a line), I must draw it, and thus produce synthetically a determined conjunction of the given manifold, so that the unity of this act is at the same time the unity of consciousness (in the conception of a line), and by this means alone is an object (a determinate space) cognized. The synthetical unity of consciousness is, therefore, an objective condition of all cognition, which I do not merely require in order to cognize an object, but to which every intuition must necessarily be subject, in order to become an object for me; because in any other way, and without this synthesis, the manifold in intuition could not be united in one consciousness.

This proposition is, as already said, itself analytical, although it constitutes the synthetical unity, the condition of all thought; for it states nothing more than that all my representations in any given intuition must be subject to the condition which alone enables me to connect them, as my representation with the identical self, and so to unite them synthetically in one apperception, by means of the general expression, "I think."

But this principle is not to be regarded as a principle for every possible understanding, but only for the understanding by means of whose pure apperception in the thought I am, no manifold content is given. The understanding or mind which contained the manifold in intuition, in and through the act itself of its own self-consciousness, in other words, an understanding by and in the representation of which the objects of the representation should at the same time exist, would not require a special act of synthesis of the manifold as the condition of the unity of its consciousness, an act of which the human understanding, which thinks only and cannot intuite, has absolute need. But this principle is the first principle of all the operations of our understanding, so that we cannot form the least conception of any other possible understanding, either of one such as should be itself intuition, or possess a sensuous intuition, but with forms different from those of space and time.

WHAT OBJECTIVE UNITY OF SELF-CONSCIOUSNESS IS § 14

It is by means of the transcendental unity of apperception that all the manifold, given in an intuition is united into a conception of the object. On this account it is called objective, and must be distinguished from the subjective unity of consciousness, which is a determination of the internal sense, by means of which the said manifold in intuition is given empirically to be so united. Whether I can be empirically conscious of the manifold as coexistent or as successive, depends upon circumstances, or empirical conditions. Hence the empirical unity of consciousness by means of association of representations, itself relates to a phenomenal world and is wholly contingent. On the contrary, the pure form of intuition in time, merely as an intuition, which contains a given manifold, is subject to the original unity of consciousness, and that solely by means of the necessary relation of the manifold in intuition to the "I think," consequently by means of the pure synthesis of the understanding, which lies à priori at the foundation of all empirical synthesis. The transcendental unity of apperception is alone objectively valid; the empirical which we do not consider in this essay, and which is merely a unity deduced from the former under given conditions in concreto, possesses only subjective validity. One person connects the notion conveyed in a word with one thing, another with another thing; and the unity of consciousness in that which is empirical, is, in relation to that which is given by experience, not necessarily and universally valid.

THE LOGICAL FORM OF ALL JUDGEMENTS CONSISTS IN THE OBJECTIVE UNITY OF APPERCEPTION OF THE CONCEPTIONS CONTAINED THEREIN § 15

I could never satisfy myself with the definition which logicians give of a judgement. It is, according to them, the representation of a relation between two conceptions. I shall not dwell here on the faultiness of this definition, in that it suits only for categorical and not for hypothetical or disjunctive judgements, these latter containing a relation not of conceptions but of judgements themselves—a blunder from which many evil results have followed.[9] It is more important for our present purpose to observe, that this definition does not determine in what the said relation consists.

But if I investigate more closely the relation of given cognitions in every judgement, and distinguish it, as belonging to the understanding, from the relation which is produced according to laws of the reproductive imagination (which has only subjective validity), I find that judgement is nothing but the mode of bringing given cognitions under the objective unit of apperception. This is plain from our use of the term of relation is in judgements, in order to distinguish the objective unity of given representations from the subjective unity. For this term indicates the relation of these representations to the original apperception, and also their necessary unity, even although the judgement is empirical, therefore contingent, as in the judgement: "All bodies are heavy." I do not mean by this, that these representations do necessarily belong to each other in empirical intuition, but that by means of the necessary unity of appreciation they belong to each other in the synthesis of intuitions, that is to say, they belong to each other according to principles of the objective determination of all our representations, in so far as cognition can arise from them, these principles being all deduced from the main principle of the transcendental unity of apperception. In this way alone can there arise from this relation a judgement, that is, a relation which has objective validity, and is perfectly distinct from that relation of the very same representations which has only subjective validity— a relation, to wit, which is produced according to laws of association. According to these laws, I could only say: "When I hold in my hand or carry a body, I feel an impression of weight"; but I could not say: "It, the body, is heavy"; for this is tantamount to saying both these representations are conjoined in the object, that is, without distinction as to the condition of the subject, and do not merely stand together in my perception, however frequently the perceptive act may be repeated.

ALL SENSUOUS INTUITIONS ARE SUBJECT TO THE CATEGORIES, AS CONDITIONS UNDER WHICH ALONE THE MANIFOLD CONTENT OF THEM CAN BE UNITED IN ONE CONSCIOUSNESS § 16

The manifold content given in a sensuous intuition comes necessarily under the original synthetical unity of apperception, because thereby alone is the unity of intuition possible (§ 13). But that act of the understanding, by which the manifold content of given representations (whether intuitions or conceptions) is brought under one apperception, is the logical function of judgements (§ 15). All the manifold, therefore, in so far as it is given in one empirical intuition, is determined in relation to one of the logical functions of judgement, by means of which it is brought into union in one consciousness. Now the categories are nothing else than these functions of judgement so far as the manifold in a given intuition is determined in relation to them (§ 9). Consequently, the manifold in a given intuition is necessarily subject to the categories of the understanding.

OBSERVATION § 17

The manifold in an intuition, which I call mine, is represented by means of the synthesis of the understanding, as belonging to the necessary unity of self-consciousness, and this takes place by means of the category.[10] The category indicates accordingly that the empirical consciousness of a given manifold in an intuition is subject to a pure self-consciousness à priori, in the same manner as an empirical intuition is subject to a pure sensuous intuition, which is also à priori. In the above proposition, then, lies the beginning of a deduction of the pure conceptions of the understanding. Now, as the categories have their origin in the understanding alone, independently of sensibility, I must in my deduction make abstraction of the mode in which the manifold of an empirical intuition is given, in order to fix my attention exclusively on the unity which is brought by the understanding into the intuition by means of the category. In what follows (§ 22), it will be shown, from the mode in which the empirical intuition is given in the faculty of sensibility, that the unity which belongs to it is no other than that which the category (according to § 16) imposes on the manifold in a given intuition, and thus, its à priori validity in regard to all objects of sense being established, the purpose of our deduction will be fully attained.

But there is one thing in the above demonstration of which I could not make abstraction, namely, that the manifold to be intuited must be given previously to the synthesis of the understanding, and independently of it. How this takes place remains here undetermined. For if I cogitate an understanding which was itself intuitive (as, for example, a divine understanding which should not represent given objects, but by whose representation the objects themselves should be given or produced), the categories would possess no significance in relation to such a faculty of cognition. They are merely rules for an understanding, whose whole power consists in thought, that is, in the act of submitting the synthesis of the manifold which is presented to it in intuition from a very different quarter, to the unity of apperception; a faculty, therefore, which cognizes nothing per se, but only connects and arranges the material of cognition, the intuition, namely, which must be presented to it by means of the object. But to show reasons for this peculiar character of our understandings, that it produces unity of apperception à priori only by means of categories, and a certain kind and number thereof, is as impossible as to explain why we are endowed with precisely so many functions of judgement and no more, or why time and space are the only forms of our intuition.

IN COGNITION, ITS APPLICATION TO OBJECTS OF EXPERIENCE IS THE ONLY LEGITIMATE USE OF THE CATEGORY § 18

To think an object and to cognize an object are by no means the same thing. In cognition there are two elements: firstly, the conception, whereby an object is cogitated (the category); and, secondly, the intuition, whereby the object is given. For supposing that to the conception a corresponding intuition could not be given, it would still be a thought as regards its form, but without any object, and no cognition of anything would be possible by means of it, inasmuch as, so far as I knew, there existed and could exist nothing to which my thought could be applied. Now all intuition possible to us is sensuous; consequently, our thought of an object by means of a pure conception of the understanding, can become cognition for us only in so far as this conception is applied to objects of the senses. Sensuous intuition is either pure intuition (space and time) or empirical intuition—of that which is immediately represented in space and time by means of sensation as real. Through the determination of pure intuition we obtain à priori cognitions of objects, as in mathematics, but only as regards their form as phenomena; whether there can exist things which must be intuited in this form is not thereby established. All mathematical conceptions, therefore, are not per se cognition, except in so far as we presuppose that there exist things which can only be represented conformably to the form of our pure sensuous intuition. But things in space and time are given only in so far as they are perceptions (representations accompanied with sensation), therefore only by empirical representation. Consequently the pure conceptions of the understanding, even when they are applied to intuitions à priori (as in mathematics), produce cognition only in so far as these (and therefore the conceptions of the understanding by means of them) can be applied to empirical intuitions. Consequently the categories do not, even by means of pure intuition afford us any cognition of things; they can only do so in so far as they can be applied to empirical intuition. That is to say, the categories serve only to render empirical cognition possible. But this is what we call experience. Consequently, in cognition, their application to objects of experience is the only legitimate use of the categories.

§ 19

The foregoing proposition is of the utmost importance, for it determines the limits of the exercise of the pure conceptions of the understanding in regard to objects, just as transcendental æsthetic determined the limits of the exercise of the pure form of our sensuous intuition. Space and time, as conditions of the possibility of the presentation of objects to us, are valid no further than for objects of sense, consequently, only for experience. Beyond these limits they represent to us nothing, for they belong only to sense, and have no reality apart from it. The pure conceptions of the understanding are free from this limitation, and extend to objects of intuition in general, be the intuition like or unlike to ours, provided only it be sensuous, and not intellectual. But this extension of conceptions beyond the range of our intuition is of no advantage; for they are then mere empty conceptions of objects, as to the possibility or impossibility of the existence of which they furnish us with no means of discovery. They are mere forms of thought, without objective reality, because we have no intuition to which the synthetical unity of apperception, which alone the categories contain, could be applied, for the purpose of determining an object. Our sensuous and empirical intuition can alone give them significance and meaning.

If, then, we suppose an object of a non-sensuous intuition to be given we can in that case represent it by all those predicates which are implied in the presupposition that nothing appertaining to sensuous intuition belongs to it; for example, that it is not extended, or in space; that its duration is not time; that in it no change (the effect of the determinations in time) is to be met with, and so on. But it is no proper knowledge if I merely indicate what the intuition of the object is not, without being able to say what is contained in it, for I have not shown the possibility of an object to which my pure conception of understanding could be applicable, because I have not been able to furnish any intuition corresponding to it, but am only able to say that our intuition is not valid for it. But the most important point is this, that to a something of this kind not one category can be found applicable. Take, for example, the conception of substance, that is, something that can exist as subject, but never as mere predicate; in regard to this conception I am quite ignorant whether there can really be anything to correspond to such a determination of thought, if empirical intuition did not afford me the occasion for its application. But of this more in the sequel.

OF THE APPLICATION OF THE CATEGORIES TO OBJECTS OF THE SENSES IN GENERAL § 20

The pure conceptions of the understanding apply to objects of intuition in general, through the understanding alone, whether the intuition be our own or some other, provided only it be sensuous, but are, for this very reason, mere forms of thought, by means of which alone no determined object can be cognized. The synthesis or conjunction of the manifold in these conceptions relates, we have said, only to the unity of apperception, and is for this reason the ground of the possibility of à priori cognition, in so far as this cognition is dependent on the understanding. This synthesis is, therefore, not merely transcendental, but also purely intellectual. But because a certain form of sensuous intuition exists in the mind à priori which rests on the receptivity of the representative faculty (sensibility), the understanding, as a spontaneity, is able to determine the internal sense by means of the diversity of given representations, conformably to the synthetical unity of apperception, and thus to cogitate the synthetical unity of the apperception of the manifold of sensuous intuition à priori, as the condition to which must necessarily be submitted all objects of human intuition. And in this manner the categories as mere forms of thought receive objective reality, that is, application to objects which are given to us in intuition, but that only as phenomena, for it is only of phenomena that we are capable of à priori intuition.

This synthesis of the manifold of sensuous intuition, which is possible and necessary à priori, may be called figurative (synthesis speciosa), in contradistinction to that which is cogitated in the mere category in regard to the manifold of an intuition in general, and is called connection or conjunction of the understanding (synthesis intellectualis). Both are transcendental, not merely because they themselves precede à priori all experience, but also because they form the basis for the possibility of other cognition à priori.

But the figurative synthesis, when it has relation only to the originally synthetical unity of apperception, that is to the transcendental unity cogitated in the categories, must, to be distinguished from the purely intellectual conjunction, be entitled the transcendental synthesis of imagination. Imagination is the faculty of representing an object even without its presence in intuition. Now, as all our intuition is sensuous, imagination, by reason of the subjective condition under which alone it can give a corresponding intuition to the conceptions of the understanding, belongs to sensibility. But in so far as the synthesis of the imagination is an act of spontaneity, which is determinative, and not, like sense, merely determinable, and which is consequently able to determine sense à priori, according to its form, conformably to the unity of apperception, in so far is the imagination a faculty of determining sensibility à priori, and its synthesis of intuitions according to the categories must be the transcendental synthesis of the imagination. It is an operation of the understanding on sensibility, and the first application of the understanding to objects of possible intuition, and at the same time the basis for the exercise of the other functions of that faculty. As figurative, it is distinguished from the merely intellectual synthesis, which is produced by the understanding alone, without the aid of imagination. Now, in so far as imagination is spontaneity, I sometimes call it also the productive imagination, and distinguish it from the reproductive, the synthesis of which is subject entirely to empirical laws, those of association, namely, and which, therefore, contributes nothing to the explanation of the possibility of à priori cognition, and for this reason belongs not to transcendental philosophy, but to psychology.

We have now arrived at the proper place for explaining the paradox which must have struck every one in our exposition of the internal sense (§ 6), namely—how this sense represents us to our own consciousness, only as we appear to ourselves, not as we are in ourselves, because, to wit, we intuite ourselves only as we are inwardly affected. Now this appears to be contradictory, inasmuch as we thus stand in a passive relation to ourselves; and therefore in the systems of psychology, the internal sense is commonly held to be one with the faculty of apperception, while we, on the contrary, carefully distinguish them.

That which determines the internal sense is the understanding, and its original power of conjoining the manifold of intuition, that is, of bringing this under an apperception (upon which rests the possibility of the understanding itself). Now, as the human understanding is not in itself a faculty of intuition, and is unable to exercise such a power, in order to conjoin, as it were, the manifold of its own intuition, the synthesis of understanding is, considered per se, nothing but the unity of action, of which, as such, it is self-conscious, even apart from sensibility, by which, moreover, it is able to determine our internal sense in respect of the manifold which may be presented to it according to the form of sensuous intuition. Thus, under the name of a transcendental synthesis of imagination, the understanding exercises an activity upon the passive subject, whose faculty it is; and so we are right in saying that the internal sense is affected thereby. Apperception and its synthetical unity are by no means one and the same with the internal sense. The former, as the source of all our synthetical conjunction, applies, under the name of the categories, to the manifold of intuition in general, prior to all sensuous intuition of objects. The internal sense, on the contrary, contains merely the form of intuition, but without any synthetical conjunction of the manifold therein, and consequently does not contain any determined intuition, which is possible only through consciousness of the determination of the manifold by the transcendental act of the imagination (synthetical influence of the understanding on the internal sense), which I have named figurative synthesis.

This we can indeed always perceive in ourselves. We cannot cogitate a geometrical line without drawing it in thought, nor a circle without describing it, nor represent the three dimensions of space without drawing three lines from the same point perpendicular to one another. We cannot even cogitate time, unless, in drawing a straight line (which is to serve as the external figurative representation of time), we fix our attention on the act of the synthesis of the manifold, whereby we determine successively the internal sense, and thus attend also to the succession of this determination. Motion as an act of the subject (not as a determination of an object),[11] consequently the synthesis of the manifold in space, if we make abstraction of space and attend merely to the act by which we determine the internal sense according to its form, is that which produces the conception of succession. The understanding, therefore, does by no means find in the internal sense any such synthesis of the manifold, but produces it, in that it affects this sense. At the same time, how "I who think" is distinct from the "i" which intuites itself (other modes of intuition being cogitable as at least possible), and yet one and the same with this latter as the same subject; how, therefore, I am able to say: "I, as an intelligence and thinking subject, cognize myself as an object thought, so far as I am, moreover, given to myself in intuition—only, like other phenomena, not as I am in myself, and as considered by the understanding, but merely as I appear"—is a question that has in it neither more nor less difficulty than the question—"How can I be an object to myself?" or this—"How I can be an object of my own intuition and internal perceptions?" But that such must be the fact, if we admit that space is merely a pure form of the phenomena of external sense, can be clearly proved by the consideration that we cannot represent time, which is not an object of external intuition, in any other way than under the image of a line, which we draw in thought, a mode of representation without which we could not cognize the unity of its dimension, and also that we are necessitated to take our determination of periods of time, or of points of time, for all our internal perceptions from the changes which we perceive in outward things. It follows that we must arrange the determinations of the internal sense, as phenomena in time, exactly in the same manner as we arrange those of the external senses in space. And consequently, if we grant, respecting this latter, that by means of them we know objects only in so far as we are affected externally, we must also confess, with regard to the internal sense, that by means of it we intuite ourselves only as we are internally affected by ourselves; in other words, as regards internal intuition, we cognize our own subject only as phenomenon, and not as it is in itself.[12]

§ 21

On the other hand, in the transcendental synthesis of the manifold content of representations, consequently in the synthetical unity of apperception, I am conscious of myself, not as I appear to myself, nor as I am in myself, but only that "I am." This representation is a thought, not an intuition. Now, as in order to cognize ourselves, in addition to the act of thinking, which subjects the manifold of every possible intuition to the unity of apperception, there is necessary a determinate mode of intuition, whereby this manifold is given; although my own existence is certainly not mere phenomenon (much less mere illusion), the determination of my existence[13] Can only take place conformably to the form of the internal sense, according to the particular mode in which the manifold which I conjoin is given in internal intuition, and I have therefore no knowledge of myself as I am, but merely as I appear to myself. The consciousness of self is thus very far from a knowledge of self, in which I do not use the categories, whereby I cogitate an object, by means of the conjunction of the manifold in one apperception. In the same way as I require, for the sake of the cognition of an object distinct from myself, not only the thought of an object in general (in the category), but also an intuition by which to determine that general conception, in the same way do I require, in order to the cognition of myself, not only the consciousness of myself or the thought that I think myself, but in addition an intuition of the manifold in myself, by which to determine this thought. It is true that I exist as an intelligence which is conscious only of its faculty of conjunction or synthesis, but subjected in relation to the manifold which this intelligence has to conjoin to a limitative conjunction called the internal sense. My intelligence (that is, I) can render that conjunction or synthesis perceptible only according to the relations of time, which are quite beyond the proper sphere of the conceptions of the understanding and consequently cognize itself in respect to an intuition (which cannot possibly be intellectual, nor given by the understanding), only as it appears to itself, and not as it would cognize itself, if its intuition were intellectual.

TRANSCENDENTAL DEDUCTION OF THE UNIVERSALLY POSSIBLE EMPLOYMENT IN EXPERIENCE OF THE PURE CONCEPTIONS OF THE UNDERSTANDING § 22

In the metaphysical deduction, the à priori origin of categories was proved by their complete accordance with the general logical of thought; in the transcendental deduction was exhibited the possibility of the categories as à priori cognitions of objects of an intuition in general (§ 16 and 17).At present we are about to explain the possibility of cognizing, à priori, by means of the categories, all objects which can possibly be presented to our senses, not, indeed, according to the form of their intuition, but according to the laws of their conjunction or synthesis, and thus, as it were, of prescribing laws to nature and even of rendering nature possible. For if the categories were inadequate to this task, it would not be evident to us why everything that is presented to our senses must be subject to those laws which have an à priori origin in the understanding itself.

I premise that by the term synthesis of apprehension I understand the combination of the manifold in an empirical intuition, whereby perception, that is, empirical consciousness of the intuition (as phenomenon), is possible.

We have à priori forms of the external and internal sensuous intuition in the representations of space and time, and to these must the synthesis of apprehension of the manifold in a phenomenon be always comfortable, because the synthesis itself can only take place according to these forms. But space and time are not merely forms of sensuous intuition, but intuitions themselves (which contain a manifold), and therefore contain à priori the determination of the unity of this manifold.[14] (See the Transcendent Æsthetic.) Therefore is unity of the synthesis of the manifold without or within us, consequently also a conjunction to which all that is to be represented as determined in space or time must correspond, given à priori along with (not in) these intuitions, as the condition of the synthesis of all apprehension of them. But this synthetical unity can be no other than that of the conjunction of the manifold of a given intuition in general, in a primitive act of consciousness, according to the categories, but applied to our sensuous intuition. Consequently all synthesis, whereby alone is even perception possible, is subject to the categories. And, as experience is cognition by means of conjoined perceptions, the categories are conditions of the possibility of experience and are therefore valid à priori for all objects of experience.

When, then, for example, I make the empirical intuition of a house by apprehension of the manifold contained therein into a perception, the necessary unity of space and of my external sensuous intuition lies at the foundation of this act, and I, as it were, draw the form of the house conformably to this synthetical unity of the manifold in space. But this very synthetical unity remains, even when I abstract the form of space, and has its seat in the understanding, and is in fact the category of the synthesis of the homogeneous in an intuition; that is to say, the category of quantity, to which the aforesaid synthesis of apprehension, that is, the perception, must be completely conformable.[15]

To take another example, when I perceive the freezing of water, I apprehend two states (fluidity and solidity), which, as such, stand toward each other mutually in a relation of time. But in the time, which I place as an internal intuition, at the foundation of this phenomenon, I represent to myself synthetical unity of the manifold, without which the aforesaid relation could not be given in an intuition as determined (in regard to the succession of time). Now this synthetical unity, as the à priori condition under which I conjoin the manifold of an intuition, is, if I make abstraction of the permanent form of my internal intuition (that is to say, of time), the category of cause, by means of which, when applied to my sensibility, I determine everything that occurs according to relations of time. Consequently apprehension in such an event, and the event itself, as far as regards the possibility of its perception, stands under the conception of the relation of cause and effect: and so in all other cases.

Categories are conceptions which prescribe laws à priori to phenomena, consequently to nature as the complex of all phenomena (natura materialiter spectata). And now the question arises—inasmuch as these categories are not derived from nature, and do not regulate themselves according to her as their model (for in that case they would be empirical)—how it is conceivable that nature must regulate herself according to them, in other words, how the categories can determine à priori the synthesis of the manifold of nature, and yet not derive their origin from her. The following is the solution of this enigma.

It is not in the least more difficult to conceive how the laws of the phenomena of nature must harmonize with the understanding and with its à priori form—that is, its faculty of conjoining the manifold—than it is to understand how the phenomena themselves must correspond with the à priori form of our sensuous intuition. For laws do not exist in the phenomena any more than the phenomena exist as things in themselves.

Laws do not exist except by relation to the subject in which the phenomena inhere, in so far as it possesses understanding, just as phenomena have no existence except by relation to the same existing subject in so far as it has senses. To things as things in themselves, conformability to law must necessarily belong independently of an understanding to cognize them. But phenomena are only representations of things which are utterly unknown in respect to what they are in themselves. But as mere representations, they stand under no law of conjunction except that which the conjoining faculty prescribes. Now that which conjoins the manifold of sensuous intuition is imagination, a mental act to which understanding contributes unity of intellectual synthesis, and sensibility, manifoldness of apprehension. Now as all possible perception depends on the synthesis of apprehension, and this empirical synthesis itself on the transcendental, consequently on the categories, it is evident that all possible perceptions, and therefore everything that can attain to empirical consciousness, that is, all phenomena of nature, must, as regards their conjunction, be subject to the categories. And nature (considered merely as nature in general) is dependent on them, as the original ground of her necessary conformability to law (as natura formaliter spectata). But the pure faculty (of the understanding) of prescribing laws à priori to phenomena by means of mere categories, is not competent to enounce other or more laws than those on which a nature in general, as a conformability to law of phenomena of space and time, depends. Particular laws, inasmuch as they concern empirically determined phenomena, cannot be entirely deduced from pure laws, although they all stand under them. Experience must be superadded in order to know these particular laws; but in regard to experience in general, and everything that can be cognized as an object thereof, these à priori laws are our only rule and guide.

RESULT OF THIS DEDUCTION OF THE CONCEPTIONS OF THE UNDERSTANDING § 23

We cannot think any object except by means of the categories; we cannot cognize any thought except by means of intuitions corresponding to these conceptions. Now all our intuitions are sensuous, and our cognition, in so far as the object of it is given, is empirical. But empirical cognition is experience; consequently no à priori cognition is possible for us, except of objects of possible experience.[16]

But this cognition, which is limited to objects of experience, is not for that reason derived entirely, from, experience, but—and this is asserted of the pure intuitions and the pure conceptions of the understanding—there are, unquestionably, elements of cognition, which exist in the mind à priori. Now there are only two ways in which a necessary harmony of experience with the conceptions of its objects can be cogitated. Either experience makes these conceptions possible, or the conceptions make experience possible. The former of these statements will not hold good with respect to the categories (nor in regard to pure sensuous intuition), for they are à priori conceptions, and therefore independent of experience. The assertion of an empirical origin would attribute to them a sort of generatio aequivoca. Consequently, nothing remains but to adopt the second alternative (which presents us with a system, as it were, of the epigenesis of pure reason), namely, that on the part of the understanding the categories do contain the grounds of the possibility of all experience. But with respect to the questions how they make experience possible, and what are the principles of the possibility thereof with which they present us in their application to phenomena, the following section on the transcendental exercise of the faculty of judgement will inform the reader.

It is quite possible that someone may propose a species of preformation-system of pure reason—a middle way between the two—to wit, that the categories are neither innate and first à priori principles of cognition, nor derived from experience, but are merely subjective aptitudes for thought implanted in us contemporaneously with our existence, which were so ordered and disposed by our Creator, that their exercise perfectly harmonizes with the laws of nature which regulate experience. Now, not to mention that with such an hypothesis it is impossible to say at what point we must stop in the employment of predetermined aptitudes, the fact that the categories would in this case entirely lose that character of necessity which is essentially involved in the very conception of them, is a conclusive objection to it. The conception of cause, for example, which expresses the necessity of an effect under a presupposed condition, would be false, if it rested only upon such an arbitrary subjective necessity of uniting certain empirical representations according to such a rule of relation. I could not then say— "The effect is connected with its cause in the object (that is, necessarily)," but only, "I am so constituted that I can think this representation as so connected, and not otherwise." Now this is just what the sceptic wants. For in this case, all our knowledge, depending on the supposed objective validity of our judgement, is nothing but mere illusion; nor would there be wanting people who would deny any such subjective necessity in respect to themselves, though they must feel it. At all events, we could not dispute with any one on that which merely depends on the manner in which his subject is organized.

SHORT VIEW OF THE ABOVE DEDUCTION.

The foregoing deduction is an exposition of the pure conceptions of the understanding (and with them of all theoretical à priori cognition), as principles of the possibility of experience, but of experience as the determination of all phenomena in space and time in general—of experience, finally, from the principle of the original synthetical unity of apperception, as the form of the understanding in relation to time and space as original forms of sensibility.

I consider the division by paragraphs to be necessary only up to this point, because we had to treat of the elementary conceptions. As we now proceed to the exposition of the employment of these, I shall not designate the chapters in this manner any further.

BOOK II. ANALYTIC OF PRINCIPLES

General logic is constructed upon a plan which coincides exactly with the division of the higher faculties of cognition. These are, understanding, judgement, and reason. This science, accordingly, treats in its analytic of conceptions, judgements, and conclusions in exact correspondence with the functions and order of those mental powers which we include generally under the generic denomination of understanding.

As this merely formal logic makes abstraction of all content of cognition, whether pure or empirical, and occupies itself with the mere form of thought (discursive cognition), it must contain in its analytic a canon for reason. For the form of reason has its law, which, without taking into consideration the particular nature of the cognition about which it is employed, can be discovered à priori, by the simple analysis of the action of reason into its momenta.

Transcendental logic, limited as it is to a determinate content, that of pure à priori cognitions, to wit, cannot imitate general logic in this division. For it is evident that the transcendental employment of reason is not objectively valid, and therefore does not belong to the logic of truth (that is, to analytic), but as a logic of illusion, occupies a particular department in the scholastic system under the name of transcendental dialectic.

Understanding and judgement accordingly possess in transcendental logic a canon of objectively valid, and therefore true exercise, and are comprehended in the analytical department of that logic. But reason, in her endeavours to arrive by à priori means at some true statement concerning objects and to extend cognition beyond the bounds of possible experience, is altogether dialectic, and her illusory assertions cannot be constructed into a canon such as an analytic ought to contain.

Accordingly, the analytic of principles will be merely a canon for the faculty of judgement, for the instruction of this faculty in its application to phenomena of the pure conceptions of the understanding, which contain the necessary condition for the establishment of à priori laws. On this account, although the subject of the following chapters is the especial principles of understanding, I shall make use of the term Doctrine of the faculty of judgement, in order to define more particularly my present purpose.

INTRODUCTION. OF THE TRANSCENDENTAL FACULTY OF JUDGEMENT IN GENERAL

If understanding in general be defined as the faculty of laws or rules, the faculty of judgement may be termed the faculty of subsumption under these rules; that is, of distinguishing whether this or that does or does not stand under a given rule (casus datae legis). General logic contains no directions or precepts for the faculty of judgement, nor can it contain any such. For as it makes abstraction of all content of cognition, no duty is left for it, except that of exposing analytically the mere form of cognition in conceptions, judgements, and conclusions, and of thereby establishing formal rules for all exercise of the understanding. Now if this logic wished to give some general direction how we should subsume under these rules, that is, how we should distinguish whether this or that did or did not stand under them, this again could not be done otherwise than by means of a rule. But this rule, precisely because it is a rule, requires for itself direction from the faculty of judgement. Thus, it is evident that the understanding is capable of being instructed by rules, but that the judgement is a peculiar talent, which does not, and cannot require tuition, but only exercise. This faculty is therefore the specific quality of the so-called mother wit, the want of which no scholastic discipline can compensate.

For although education may furnish, and, as it were, engraft upon a limited understanding rules borrowed from other minds, yet the power of employing these rules correctly must belong to the pupil himself; and no rule which we can prescribe to him with this purpose is, in the absence or deficiency of this gift of nature, secure from misuse.[17] A physician therefore, a judge or a statesman, may have in his head many admirable pathological, juridical, or political rules, in a degree that may enable him to be a profound teacher in his particular science, and yet in the application of these rules he may very possibly blunder—either because he is wanting in natural judgement (though not in understanding) and, whilst he can comprehend the general in abstracto, cannot distinguish whether a particular case in concreto ought to rank under the former; or because his faculty of judgement has not been sufficiently exercised by examples and real practice. Indeed, the grand and only use of examples, is to sharpen the judgement. For as regards the correctness and precision of the insight of the understanding, examples are commonly injurious rather than otherwise, because, as casus in terminis they seldom adequately fulfil the conditions of the rule. Besides, they often weaken the power of our understanding to apprehend rules or laws in their universality, independently of particular circumstances of experience; and hence, accustom us to employ them more as formulae than as principles. Examples are thus the go-cart of the judgement, which he who is naturally deficient in that faculty cannot afford to dispense with.

But although general logic cannot give directions to the faculty of judgement, the case is very different as regards transcendental logic, insomuch that it appears to be the especial duty of the latter to secure and direct, by means of determinate rules, the faculty of judgement in the employment of the pure understanding. For, as a doctrine, that is, as an endeavour to enlarge the sphere of the understanding in regard to pure à priori cognitions, philosophy is worse than useless, since from all the attempts hitherto made, little or no ground has been gained. But, as a critique, in order to guard against the mistakes of the faculty of judgement (lapsus judicii) in the employment of the few pure conceptions of the understanding which we possess, although its use is in this case purely negative, philosophy is called upon to apply all its acuteness and penetration.

But transcendental philosophy has this peculiarity, that besides indicating the rule, or rather the general condition for rules, which is given in the pure conception of the understanding, it can, at the same time, indicate à priori the case to which the rule must be applied. The cause of the superiority which, in this respect, transcendental philosophy possesses above all other sciences except mathematics, lies in this: it treats of conceptions which must relate à priori to their objects, whose objective validity consequently cannot be demonstrated à posteriori, and is, at the same time, under the obligation of presenting in general but sufficient tests, the conditions under which objects can be given in harmony with those conceptions; otherwise they would be mere logical forms, without content, and not pure conceptions of the understanding.

Our transcendental doctrine of the faculty of judgement will contain two chapters. The first will treat of the sensuous condition under which alone pure conceptions of the understanding can be employed—that is, of the schematism of the pure understanding. The second will treat of those synthetical judgements which are derived à priori from pure conceptions of the understanding under those conditions, and which lie à priori at the foundation of all other cognitions, that is to say, it will treat of the principles of the pure understanding.

TRANSCENDENTAL DOCTRINE OF THE FACULTY OF JUDGEMENT OR, ANALYTIC OF PRINCIPLES

CHAPTER I. OF THE SCHEMATISM AT OF THE PURE CONCEPTIONS OF THE UNDERSTANDING

In all subsumptions of an object under a conception, the representation of the object must be homogeneous with the conception; in other words, the conception must contain that which is represented in the object to be subsumed under it. For this is the meaning of the expression: "An object is contained under a conception." Thus the empirical conception of a plate is homogeneous with the pure geometrical conception of a circle, inasmuch as the roundness which is cogitated in the former is intuited in the latter.

But pure conceptions of the understanding, when compared with empirical intuitions, or even with sensuous intuitions in general, are quite heterogeneous, and never can be discovered in any intuition. How then is the subsumption of the latter under the former, and consequently the application of the categories to phenomena, possible?— For it is impossible to say, for example: "Causality can be intuited through the senses and is contained in the phenomenon."—This natural and important question forms the real cause of the necessity of a transcendental doctrine of the faculty of judgement, with the purpose, to wit, of showing how pure conceptions of the understanding can be applied to phenomena. In all other sciences, where the conceptions by which the object is thought in the general are not so different and heterogeneous from those which represent the object in concreto—as it is given, it is quite unnecessary to institute any special inquiries concerning the application of the former to the latter.

Now it is quite clear that there must be some third thing, which on the one side is homogeneous with the category, and with the phenomenon on the other, and so makes the application of the former to the latter possible. This mediating representation must be pure (without any empirical content), and yet must on the one side be intellectual, on the other sensuous. Such a representation is the transcendental schema.

The conception of the understanding contains pure synthetical unity of the manifold in general. Time, as the formal condition of the manifold of the internal sense, consequently of the conjunction of all representations, contains à priori a manifold in the pure intuition. Now a transcendental determination of time is so far homogeneous with the category, which constitutes the unity thereof, that it is universal and rests upon a rule à priori. On the other hand, it is so far homogeneous with the phenomenon, inasmuch as time is contained in every empirical representation of the manifold. Thus an application of the category to phenomena becomes possible, by means of the transcendental determination of time, which, as the schema of the conceptions of the understanding, mediates the subsumption of the latter under the former.

After what has been proved in our deduction of the categories, no one, it is to be hoped, can hesitate as to the proper decision of the question, whether the employment of these pure conceptions of the understanding ought to be merely empirical or also transcendental; in other words, whether the categories, as conditions of a possible experience, relate à priori solely to phenomena, or whether, as conditions of the possibility of things in general, their application can be extended to objects as things in themselves.

For we have there seen that conceptions are quite impossible, and utterly without signification, unless either to them, or at least to the elements of which they consist, an object be given; and that, consequently, they cannot possibly apply to objects as things in themselves without regard to the question whether and how these may be given to us; and, further, that the only manner in which objects can be given to us is by means of the modification of our sensibility; and, finally, that pure à priori conceptions, in addition to the function of the understanding in the category, must contain à priori formal conditions of sensibility (of the internal sense, namely), which again contain the general condition under which alone the category can be applied to any object. This formal and pure condition of sensibility, to which the conception of the understanding is restricted in its employment, we shall name the schema of the conception of the understanding, and the procedure of the understanding with these schemata we shall call the schematism of the pure understanding.

The schema is, in itself, always a mere product of the imagination. But, as the synthesis of imagination has for its aim no single intuition, but merely unity in the determination of sensibility, the schema is clearly distinguishable from the image. Thus, if I place five points one after another.... this is an image of the number five. On the other hand, if I only think a number in general, which may be either five or a hundred, this thought is rather the representation of a method of representing in an image a sum (e.g., a thousand) in conformity with a conception, than the image itself, an image which I should find some little difficulty in reviewing, and comparing with the conception. Now this representation of a general procedure of the imagination to present its image to a conception, I call the schema of this conception.

In truth, it is not images of objects, but schemata, which lie at the foundation of our pure sensuous conceptions. No image could ever be adequate to our conception of a triangle in general. For the generalness of the conception it never could attain to, as this includes under itself all triangles, whether right-angled, acute-angled, etc., whilst the image would always be limited to a single part of this sphere. The schema of the triangle can exist nowhere else than in thought, and it indicates a rule of the synthesis of the imagination in regard to pure figures in space. Still less is an object of experience, or an image of the object, ever to the empirical conception. On the contrary, the conception always relates immediately to the schema of the imagination, as a rule for the determination of our intuition, in conformity with a certain general conception. The conception of a dog indicates a rule, according to which my imagination can delineate the figure of a four-footed animal in general, without being limited to any particular individual form which experience presents to me, or indeed to any possible image that I can represent to myself in concreto. This schematism of our understanding in regard to phenomena and their mere form, is an art, hidden in the depths of the human soul, whose true modes of action we shall only with difficulty discover and unveil. Thus much only can we say: "The image is a product of the empirical faculty of the productive imagination—the schema of sensuous conceptions (of figures in space, for example) is a product, and, as it were, a monogram of the pure imagination à priori, whereby and according to which images first become possible, which, however, can be connected with the conception only mediately by means of the schema which they indicate, and are in themselves never fully adequate to it." On the other hand, the schema of a pure conception of the understanding is something that cannot be reduced into any image—it is nothing else than the pure synthesis expressed by the category, conformably, to a rule of unity according to conceptions. It is a transcendental product of the imagination, a product which concerns the determination of the internal sense, according to conditions of its form (time) in respect to all representations, in so far as these representations must be conjoined à priori in one conception, conformably to the unity of apperception.

Without entering upon a dry and tedious analysis of the essential requisites of transcendental schemata of the pure conceptions of the understanding, we shall rather proceed at once to give an explanation of them according to the order of the categories, and in connection therewith.

For the external sense the pure image of all quantities (quantorum) is space; the pure image of all objects of sense in general, is time. But the pure schema of quantity (quantitatis) as a conception of the understanding, is number, a representation which comprehends the successive addition of one to one (homogeneous quantities). Thus, number is nothing else than the unity of the synthesis of the manifold in a homogeneous intuition, by means of my generating time itself in my apprehension of the intuition.

Reality, in the pure conception of the understanding, is that which corresponds to a sensation in general; that, consequently, the conception of which indicates a being (in time). Negation is that the conception of which represents a not-being (in time). The opposition of these two consists therefore in the difference of one and the same time, as a time filled or a time empty. Now as time is only the form of intuition, consequently of objects as phenomena, that which in objects corresponds to sensation is the transcendental matter of all objects as things in themselves (Sachheit, reality). Now every sensation has a degree or quantity by which it can fill time, that is to say, the internal sense in respect of the representation of an object, more or less, until it vanishes into nothing (= 0 = negatio). Thus there is a relation and connection between reality and negation, or rather a transition from the former to the latter, which makes every reality representable to us as a quantum; and the schema of a reality as the quantity of something in so far as it fills time, is exactly this continuous and uniform generation of the reality in time, as we descend in time from the sensation which has a certain degree, down to the vanishing thereof, or gradually ascend from negation to the quantity thereof.

The schema of substance is the permanence of the real in time; that is, the representation of it as a substratum of the empirical determination of time; a substratum which therefore remains, whilst all else changes. (Time passes not, but in it passes the existence of the changeable. To time, therefore, which is itself unchangeable and permanent, corresponds that which in the phenomenon is unchangeable in existence, that is, substance, and it is only by it that the succession and coexistence of phenomena can be determined in regard to time.)

The schema of cause and of the causality of a thing is the real which, when posited, is always followed by something else. It consists, therefore, in the succession of the manifold, in so far as that succession is subjected to a rule.

The schema of community (reciprocity of action and reaction), or the reciprocal causality of substances in respect of their accidents, is the coexistence of the determinations of the one with those of the other, according to a general rule.

The schema of possibility is the accordance of the synthesis of different representations with the conditions of time in general (as, for example, opposites cannot exist together at the same time in the same thing, but only after each other), and is therefore the determination of the representation of a thing at any time.

The schema of reality is existence in a determined time.

The schema of necessity is the existence of an object in all time.

It is clear, from all this, that the schema of the category of quantity contains and represents the generation (synthesis) of time itself, in the successive apprehension of an object; the schema of quality the synthesis of sensation with the representation of time, or the filling up of time; the schema of relation the relation of perceptions to each other in all time (that is, according to a rule of the determination of time): and finally, the schema of modality and its categories, time itself, as the correlative of the determination of an object—whether it does belong to time, and how. The schemata, therefore, are nothing but à priori determinations of time according to rules, and these, in regard to all possible objects, following the arrangement of the categories, relate to the series in time, the content in time, the order in time, and finally, to the complex or totality in time.

Hence it is apparent that the schematism of the understanding, by means of the transcendental synthesis of the imagination, amounts to nothing else than the unity of the manifold of intuition in the internal sense, and thus indirectly to the unity of apperception, as a function corresponding to the internal sense (a receptivity). Thus, the schemata of the pure conceptions of the understanding are the true and only conditions whereby our understanding receives an application to objects, and consequently significance. Finally, therefore, the categories are only capable of empirical use, inasmuch as they serve merely to subject phenomena to the universal rules of synthesis, by means of an à priori necessary unity (on account of the necessary union of all consciousness in one original apperception); and so to render them susceptible of a complete connection in one experience. But within this whole of possible experience lie all our cognitions, and in the universal relation to this experience consists transcendental truth, which antecedes all empirical truth, and renders the latter possible.

It is, however, evident at first sight, that although the schemata of sensibility are the sole agents in realizing the categories, they do, nevertheless, also restrict them, that is, they limit the categories by conditions which lie beyond the sphere of understanding— namely, in sensibility. Hence the schema is properly only the phenomenon, or the sensuous conception of an object in harmony with the category. (Numerus est quantitas phaenomenon—sensatio realitas phaenomenon; constans et perdurabile rerum substantia phaenomenon—aeternitas, necessitas, phaenomena, etc.) Now, if we remove a restrictive condition, we thereby amplify, it appears, the formerly limited conception. In this way, the categories in their pure signification, free from all conditions of sensibility, ought to be valid of things as they are, and not, as the schemata represent them, merely as they appear; and consequently the categories must have a significance far more extended, and wholly independent of all schemata. In truth, there does always remain to the pure conceptions of the understanding, after abstracting every sensuous condition, a value and significance, which is, however, merely logical. But in this case, no object is given them, and therefore they have no meaning sufficient to afford us a conception of an object. The notion of substance, for example, if we leave out the sensuous determination of permanence, would mean nothing more than a something which can be cogitated as subject, without the possibility of becoming a predicate to anything else. Of this representation I can make nothing, inasmuch as it does not indicate to me what determinations the thing possesses which must thus be valid as premier subject. Consequently, the categories, without schemata are merely functions of the understanding for the production of conceptions, but do not represent any object. This significance they derive from sensibility, which at the same time realizes the understanding and restricts it.

CHAPTER II. SYSTEM OF ALL PRINCIPLES OF THE PURE UNDERSTANDING

In the foregoing chapter we have merely considered the general conditions under which alone the transcendental faculty of judgement is justified in using the pure conceptions of the understanding for synthetical judgements. Our duty at present is to exhibit in systematic connection those judgements which the understanding really produces à priori. For this purpose, our table of the categories will certainly afford us the natural and safe guidance. For it is precisely the categories whose application to possible experience must constitute all pure à priori cognition of the understanding; and the relation of which to sensibility will, on that very account, present us with a complete and systematic catalogue of all the transcendental principles of the use of the understanding.

Principles à priori are so called, not merely because they contain in themselves the grounds of other judgements, but also because they themselves are not grounded in higher and more general cognitions. This peculiarity, however, does not raise them altogether above the need of a proof. For although there could be found no higher cognition, and therefore no objective proof, and although such a principle rather serves as the foundation for all cognition of the object, this by no means hinders us from drawing a proof from the subjective sources of the possibility of the cognition of an object. Such a proof is necessary, moreover, because without it the principle might be liable to the imputation of being a mere gratuitous assertion.

In the second place, we shall limit our investigations to those principles which relate to the categories. For as to the principles of transcendental æsthetic, according to which space and time are the conditions of the possibility of things as phenomena, as also the restriction of these principles, namely, that they cannot be applied to objects as things in themselves—these, of course, do not fall within the scope of our present inquiry. In like manner, the principles of mathematical science form no part of this system, because they are all drawn from intuition, and not from the pure conception of the understanding. The possibility of these principles, however, will necessarily be considered here, inasmuch as they are synthetical judgements à priori, not indeed for the purpose of proving their accuracy and apodeictic certainty, which is unnecessary, but merely to render conceivable and deduce the possibility of such evident à priori cognitions.

But we shall have also to speak of the principle of analytical judgements, in opposition to synthetical judgements, which is the proper subject of our inquiries, because this very opposition will free the theory of the latter from all ambiguity, and place it clearly before our eyes in its true nature.

SYSTEM OF THE PRINCIPLES OF THE PURE UNDERSTANDING

SECTION I. OF THE SUPREME PRINCIPLE OF ALL ANALYTICAL JUDGEMENTS

Whatever may be the content of our cognition, and in whatever manner our cognition may be related to its object, the universal, although only negative conditions of all our judgements is that they do not contradict themselves; otherwise these judgements are in themselves (even without respect to the object) nothing. But although there may exist no contradiction in our judgement, it may nevertheless connect conceptions in such a manner that they do not correspond to the object, or without any grounds either à priori or à posteriori for arriving at such a judgement, and thus, without being self-contradictory, a judgement may nevertheless be either false or groundless.

Now, the proposition: "No subject can have a predicate that contradicts it," is called the principle of contradiction, and is a universal but purely negative criterion of all truth. But it belongs to logic alone, because it is valid of cognitions, merely as cognitions and without respect to their content, and declares that the contradiction entirely nullifies them. We can also, however, make a positive use of this principle, that is, not merely to banish falsehood and error (in so far as it rests upon contradiction), but also for the cognition of truth. For if the judgement is analytical, be it affirmative or negative, its truth must always be recognizable by means of the principle of contradiction. For the contrary of that which lies and is cogitated as conception in the cognition of the object will be always properly negatived, but the conception itself must always be affirmed of the object, inasmuch as the contrary thereof would be in contradiction to the object.

We must therefore hold the principle of contradiction to be the universal and fully sufficient Principle of all analytical cognition. But as a sufficient criterion of truth, it has no further utility or authority. For the fact that no cognition can be at variance with this principle without nullifying itself, constitutes this principle the sine qua non, but not the determining ground of the truth of our cognition. As our business at present is properly with the synthetical part of our knowledge only, we shall always be on our guard not to transgress this inviolable principle; but at the same time not to expect from it any direct assistance in the establishment of the truth of any synthetical proposition.

There exists, however, a formula of this celebrated principle—a principle merely formal and entirely without content—which contains a synthesis that has been inadvertently and quite unnecessarily mixed up with it. It is this: "It is impossible for a thing to be and not to be at the same time." Not to mention the superfluousness of the addition of the word impossible to indicate the apodeictic certainty, which ought to be self-evident from the proposition itself, the proposition is affected by the condition of time, and as it were says: "A thing = A, which is something = B, cannot at the same time be non-B." But both, B as well as non-B, may quite well exist in succession. For example, a man who is young cannot at the same time be old; but the same man can very well be at one time young, and at another not young, that is, old. Now the principle of contradiction as a merely logical proposition must not by any means limit its application merely to relations of time, and consequently a formula like the preceding is quite foreign to its true purpose. The misunderstanding arises in this way. We first of all separate a predicate of a thing from the conception of the thing, and afterwards connect with this predicate its opposite, and hence do not establish any contradiction with the subject, but only with its predicate, which has been conjoined with the subject synthetically—a contradiction, moreover, which obtains only when the first and second predicate are affirmed in the same time. If I say: "A man who is ignorant is not learned," the condition "at the same time" must be added, for he who is at one time ignorant, may at another be learned. But if I say: "No ignorant man is a learned man," the proposition is analytical, because the characteristic ignorance is now a constituent part of the conception of the subject; and in this case the negative proposition is evident immediately from the proposition of contradiction, without the necessity of adding the condition "the same time." This is the reason why I have altered the formula of this principle—an alteration which shows very clearly the nature of an analytical proposition.

SECTION II. OF THE SUPREME PRINCIPLE OF ALL SYNTHETICAL JUDGEMENTS

The explanation of the possibility of synthetical judgements is a task with which general logic has nothing to do; indeed she needs not even be acquainted with its name. But in transcendental logic it is the most important matter to be dealt with—indeed the only one, if the question is of the possibility of synthetical judgements à priori, the conditions and extent of their validity. For when this question is fully decided, it can reach its aim with perfect ease, the determination, to wit, of the extent and limits of the pure understanding.

In an analytical judgement I do not go beyond the given conception, in order to arrive at some decision respecting it. If the judgement is affirmative, I predicate of the conception only that which was already cogitated in it; if negative, I merely exclude from the conception its contrary. But in synthetical judgements, I must go beyond the given conception, in order to cogitate, in relation with it, something quite different from that which was cogitated in it, a relation which is consequently never one either of identity or contradiction, and by means of which the truth or error of the judgement cannot be discerned merely from the judgement itself.

Granted, then, that we must go out beyond a given conception, in order to compare it synthetically with another, a third thing is necessary, in which alone the synthesis of two conceptions can originate. Now what is this tertium quid that is to be the medium of all synthetical judgements? It is only a complex in which all our representations are contained, the internal sense to wit, and its form à priori, time.

The synthesis of our representations rests upon the imagination; their synthetical unity (which is requisite to a judgement), upon the unity of apperception. In this, therefore, is to be sought the possibility of synthetical judgements, and as all three contain the sources of à priori representations, the possibility of pure synthetical judgements also; nay, they are necessary upon these grounds, if we are to possess a knowledge of objects, which rests solely upon the synthesis of representations.

If a cognition is to have objective reality, that is, to relate to an object, and possess sense and meaning in respect to it, it is necessary that the object be given in some way or another. Without this, our conceptions are empty, and we may indeed have thought by means of them, but by such thinking we have not, in fact, cognized anything, we have merely played with representation. To give an object, if this expression be understood in the sense of "to present" the object, not mediately but immediately in intuition, means nothing else than to apply the representation of it to experience, be that experience real or only possible. Space and time themselves, pure as these conceptions are from all that is empirical, and certain as it is that they are represented fully à priori in the mind, would be completely without objective validity, and without sense and significance, if their necessary use in the objects of experience were not shown. Nay, the representation of them is a mere schema, that always relates to the reproductive imagination, which calls up the objects of experience, without which they have no meaning. And so it is with all conceptions without distinction.

The possibility of experience is, then, that which gives objective reality to all our à priori cognitions. Now experience depends upon the synthetical unity of phenomena, that is, upon a synthesis according to conceptions of the object of phenomena in general, a synthesis without which experience never could become knowledge, but would be merely a rhapsody of perceptions, never fitting together into any connected text, according to rules of a thoroughly united (possible) consciousness, and therefore never subjected to the transcendental and necessary unity of apperception. Experience has therefore for a foundation, à priori principles of its form, that is to say, general rules of unity in the synthesis of phenomena, the objective reality of which rules, as necessary conditions even of the possibility of experience can which rules, as necessary conditions —even of the possibility of experience—can always be shown in experience. But apart from this relation, à priori synthetical propositions are absolutely impossible, because they have no third term, that is, no pure object, in which the synthetical unity can exhibit the objective reality of its conceptions.

Although, then, respecting space, or the forms which productive imagination describes therein, we do cognize much à priori in synthetical judgements, and are really in no need of experience for this purpose, such knowledge would nevertheless amount to nothing but a busy trifling with a mere chimera, were not space to be considered as the condition of the phenomena which constitute the material of external experience. Hence those pure synthetical judgements do relate, though but mediately, to possible experience, or rather to the possibility of experience, and upon that alone is founded the objective validity of their synthesis.

While then, on the one hand, experience, as empirical synthesis, is the only possible mode of cognition which gives reality to all other synthesis; on the other hand, this latter synthesis, as cognition à priori, possesses truth, that is, accordance with its object, only in so far as it contains nothing more than what is necessary to the synthetical unity of experience.

Accordingly, the supreme principle of all synthetical judgements is: "Every object is subject to the necessary conditions of the synthetical unity of the manifold of intuition in a possible experience."

À priori synthetical judgements are possible when we apply the formal conditions of the à priori intuition, the synthesis of the imagination, and the necessary unity of that synthesis in a transcendental apperception, to a possible cognition of experience, and say: "The conditions of the possibility of experience in general are at the same time conditions of the possibility of the objects of experience, and have, for that reason, objective validity in an à priori synthetical judgement."

SECTION III. SYSTEMATIC REPRESENTATION OF ALL SYNTHETICAL PRINCIPLES OF THE PURE UNDERSTANDING

That principles exist at all is to be ascribed solely to the pure understanding, which is not only the faculty of rules in regard to that which happens, but is even the source of principles according to which everything that can be presented to us as an object is necessarily subject to rules, because without such rules we never could attain to cognition of an object. Even the laws of nature, if they are contemplated as principles of the empirical use of the understanding, possess also a characteristic of necessity, and we may therefore at least expect them to be determined upon grounds which are valid à priori and antecedent to all experience. But all laws of nature, without distinction, are subject to higher principles of the understanding, inasmuch as the former are merely applications of the latter to particular cases of experience. These higher principles alone therefore give the conception, which contains the necessary condition, and, as it were, the exponent of a rule; experience, on the other hand, gives the case which comes under the rule.

There is no danger of our mistaking merely empirical principles for principles of the pure understanding, or conversely; for the character of necessity, according to conceptions which distinguish the latter, and the absence of this in every empirical proposition, how extensively valid soever it may be, is a perfect safeguard against confounding them. There are, however, pure principles à priori, which nevertheless I should not ascribe to the pure understanding—for this reason, that they are not derived from pure conceptions, but (although by the mediation of the understanding) from pure intuitions. But understanding is the faculty of conceptions. Such principles mathematical science possesses, but their application to experience, consequently their objective validity, nay the possibility of such à priori synthetical cognitions (the deduction thereof) rests entirely upon the pure understanding.

On this account, I shall not reckon among my principles those of mathematics; though I shall include those upon the possibility and objective validity à priori, of principles of the mathematical science, which, consequently, are to be looked upon as the principle of these, and which proceed from conceptions to intuition, and not from intuition to conceptions.

In the application of the pure conceptions of the understanding to possible experience, the employment of their synthesis is either mathematical or dynamical, for it is directed partly on the intuition alone, partly on the existence of a phenomenon. But the à priori conditions of intuition are in relation to a possible experience absolutely necessary, those of the existence of objects of a possible empirical intuition are in themselves contingent. Hence the principles of the mathematical use of the categories will possess a character of absolute necessity, that is, will be apodeictic; those, on the other hand, of the dynamical use, the character of an à priori necessity indeed, but only under the condition of empirical thought in an experience, therefore only mediately and indirectly. Consequently they will not possess that immediate evidence which is peculiar to the former, although their application to experience does not, for that reason, lose its truth and certitude. But of this point we shall be better able to judge at the conclusion of this system of principles.

The table of the categories is naturally our guide to the table of principles, because these are nothing else than rules for the objective employment of the former. Accordingly, all principles of the pure understanding are:

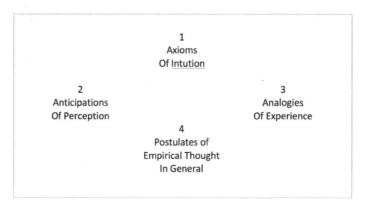

These appellations I have chosen advisedly, in order that we might not lose sight of the distinctions in respect of the evidence and the employment of these principles. It will, however, soon appear that—a fact which concerns both the evidence of these principles, and the à priori determination of phenomena—according to the categories of quantity and quality (if we attend merely to the form of these), the principles of these categories are distinguishable from those of the two others, in as much as the former are possessed of an intuitive, but the latter of a merely discursive, though in both instances a complete, certitude. I shall therefore call the former mathematical, and the latter dynamical principles.[18] It must be observed, however, that by these terms I mean just as little in the one case the principles of mathematics as those of general (physical) dynamics in the other. I have here in view merely the principles of the pure understanding, in their application to the internal sense (without distinction of the representations given therein), by means of which the sciences of mathematics and dynamics become possible. Accordingly, I have named these principles rather with reference to their application than their content; and I shall now proceed to consider them in the order in which they stand in the table.

1. AXIOMS OF INTUITION.

The principle of these is: All Intuitions are Extensive Quantities.

PROOF.

All phenomena contain, as regards their form, an intuition in space and time, which lies à priori at the foundation of all without exception. Phenomena, therefore, cannot be apprehended, that is, received into empirical consciousness otherwise than through the synthesis of a manifold, through which the representations of a determinate space or time are generated; that is to say, through the composition of the homogeneous and the consciousness of the synthetical unity of this manifold (homogeneous). Now the consciousness of a homogeneous manifold in intuition, in so far as thereby the representation of an object is rendered possible, is the conception of a quantity (quanti). Consequently, even the perception of an object as phenomenon is possible only through the same synthetical unity of the manifold of the given sensuous intuition, through which the unity of the composition of the homogeneous manifold in the conception of a quantity is cogitated; that is to say, all phenomena are quantities, and extensive quantities, because as intuitions in space or time they must be represented by means of the same synthesis through which space and time themselves are determined.

An extensive quantity I call that wherein the representation of the parts renders possible (and therefore necessarily antecedes) the representation of the whole. I cannot represent to myself any line, however small, without drawing it in thought, that is, without generating from a point all its parts one after another, and in this way alone producing this intuition. Precisely the same is the case with every, even the smallest, portion of time. I cogitate therein only the successive progress from one moment to another, and hence, by means of the different portions of time and the addition of them, a determinate quantity of time is produced. As the pure intuition in all phenomena is either time or space, so is every phenomenon in its character of intuition an extensive quantity, inasmuch as it can only be cognized in our apprehension by successive synthesis (from part to part). All phenomena are, accordingly, to be considered as aggregates, that is, as a collection of previously given parts; which is not the case with every sort of quantities, but only with those which are represented and apprehended by us as extensive.

On this successive synthesis of the productive imagination, in the generation of figures, is founded the mathematics of extension, or geometry, with its axioms, which express the conditions of sensuous intuition à priori, under which alone the schema of a pure conception of external intuition can exist; for example, "be tween two points only one straight line is possible," "two straight lines cannot enclose a space," etc. These are the axioms which properly relate only to quantities (quanta) as such.

But, as regards the quantity of a thing (quantitas), that is to say, the answer to the question: "How large is this or that object?" although, in respect to this question, we have various propositions synthetical and immediately certain (indemonstrabilia); we have, in the proper sense of the term, no axioms. For example, the propositions: "If equals be added to equals, the wholes are equal"; "If equals be taken from equals, the remainders are equal"; are analytical, because I am immediately conscious of the identity of the production of the one quantity with the production of the other; whereas axioms must be à priori synthetical propositions. On the other hand, the self-evident propositions as to the relation of numbers, are certainly synthetical but not universal, like those of geometry, and for this reason cannot be called axioms, but numerical formulae. That $7 + 5 = 12$ is not an analytical proposition. For neither in the representation of seven, nor of five, nor of the composition of the two numbers, do I cogitate the number twelve. (Whether I cogitate the number in the addition of both, is not at present the question; for in the case of an analytical proposition, the only point is whether I really cogitate the predicate in the representation of the subject.) But although the proposition is synthetical, it is nevertheless only a singular proposition. In so far as regard is here had merely to the synthesis of the homogeneous (the units), it cannot take place except in one manner, although our use of these numbers is afterwards general. If I say: "A triangle can be constructed with three lines, any two of which taken together are greater than the third," I exercise merely the pure function of the productive imagination, which may draw the lines longer or shorter and construct the angles at its pleasure. On the contrary, the number seven is possible only in one manner, and so is likewise the number twelve, which results from the synthesis of seven and five. Such propositions, then, cannot be termed axioms (for in that case we should have an infinity of these), but numerical formulae.

This transcendental principle of the mathematics of phenomena greatly enlarges our à priori cognition. For it is by this principle alone that pure mathematics is rendered applicable in all its precision to objects of experience, and without it the validity of this application would not be so self-evident; on the contrary, contradictions and confusions have often arisen on this very point. Phenomena are not things in themselves. Empirical intuition is possible only through pure intuition (of space and time); consequently, what geometry affirms of the latter, is indisputably valid of the former. All evasions, such as the statement that objects of sense do not conform to the rules of construction in space (for example, to the rule of the infinite divisibility of lines or angles), must fall to the ground. For, if these objections hold good, we deny to space, and with it to all mathematics, objective validity, and no longer know wherefore, and how far, mathematics can be applied to phenomena. The synthesis of spaces and times as the essential form of all intuition, is that which renders possible the apprehension of a phenomenon, and therefore every external experience, consequently all cognition of the objects of experience; and whatever mathematics in its pure use proves of the former, must necessarily hold good of the latter. All objections are but the chicaneries of an ill-instructed reason, which erroneously thinks to liberate the objects of sense from the formal conditions of our sensibility, and represents these, although mere phenomena, as things in themselves, presented as such to our understanding. But in this case, no à priori synthetical cognition of them could be possible, consequently not through pure conceptions of space and the science which determines these conceptions, that is to say, geometry, would itself be impossible.

2. ANTICIPATIONS OF PERCEPTION.

The principle of these is: In all phenomena the Real, that which is an object of sensation, has Intensive Quantity, that is, has a Degree.

PROOF.

Perception is empirical consciousness, that is to say, a consciousness which contains an element of sensation. Phenomena as objects of perception are not pure, that is, merely formal intuitions, like space and time, for they cannot be perceived in themselves.[19] They contain, then, over and above the intuition, the materials for an object (through which is represented something existing in space or time), that is to say, they contain the real of sensation, as a representation merely subjective, which gives us merely the consciousness that the subject is affected, and which we refer to some external object. Now, a gradual transition from empirical consciousness to pure consciousness is possible, inasmuch as the real in this consciousness entirely vanishes, and there remains a merely formal consciousness (à priori) of the manifold in time and space; consequently there is possible a synthesis also of the production of the quantity of a sensation from its commencement, that is, from the pure intuition = 0 onwards up to a certain quantity of the sensation. Now as sensation in itself is not an objective representation, and in it is to be found neither the intuition of space nor of time, it cannot possess any extensive quantity, and yet there does belong to it a quantity (and that by means of its apprehension, in which empirical consciousness can within a certain time rise from nothing = 0 up to its given amount), consequently an intensive quantity. And thus we must ascribe intensive quantity, that is, a degree of influence on sense to all objects of perception, in so far as this perception contains sensation.

All cognition, by means of which I am enabled to cognize and determine à priori what belongs to empirical cognition, may be called an anticipation; and without doubt this is the sense in which Epicurus employed his expression prholepsis. But as there is in phenomena something which is never cognized à priori, which on this account constitutes the proper difference between pure and empirical cognition, that is to say, sensation (as the matter of perception), it follows, that sensation is just that element in cognition which cannot be at all anticipated. On the other hand, we might very well term the pure determinations in space and time, as well in regard to figure as to quantity, anticipations of phenomena, because they represent à priori that which may always be given à posteriori in experience. But suppose that in every sensation, as sensation in general, without any particular sensation being thought of, there existed something which could be cognized à priori, this would deserve to be called anticipation in a special sense—special, because it may seem surprising to forestall experience, in that which concerns the matter of experience, and which we can only derive from itself. Yet such really is the case here.

Apprehension[20], by means of sensation alone, fills only one moment, that is, if I do not take into consideration a succession of many sensations. As that in the phenomenon, the apprehension of which is not a successive synthesis advancing from parts to an entire representation, sensation has therefore no extensive quantity; the want of sensation in a moment of time would represent it as empty, consequently = 0. That which in the empirical intuition corresponds to sensation is reality (realitas phaenomenon); that which corresponds to the absence of it, negation = 0. Now every sensation is capable of a diminution, so that it can decrease, and thus gradually disappear. Therefore, between reality in a phenomenon and negation, there exists a continuous concatenation of many possible intermediate sensations, the difference of which from each other is always smaller than that between the given sensation and zero, or complete negation. That is to say, the real in a phenomenon has always a quantity, which however is not discoverable in apprehension, inasmuch as apprehension take place by means of mere sensation in one instant, and not by the successive synthesis of many sensations, and therefore does not progress from parts to the whole. Consequently, it has a quantity, but not an extensive quantity.

Now that quantity which is apprehended only as unity, and in which plurality can be represented only by approximation to negation = O, I term intensive quantity. Consequently, reality in a phenomenon has intensive quantity, that is, a degree. If we consider this reality as cause (be it of sensation or of another reality in the phenomenon, for example, a change), we call the degree of reality in its character of cause a momentum, for example, the momentum of weight; and for this reason, that the degree only indicates that quantity the apprehension of which is not successive, but instantaneous. This, however, I touch upon only in passing, for with causality I have at present nothing to do.

Accordingly, every sensation, consequently every reality in phenomena, however small it may be, has a degree, that is, an intensive quantity, which may always be lessened, and between reality and negation there exists a continuous connection of possible realities, and possible smaller perceptions. Every colour—for example, red—has a degree, which, be it ever so small, is never the smallest, and so is it always with heat, the momentum of weight, etc.

This property of quantities, according to which no part of them is the smallest possible (no part simple), is called their continuity. Space and time are quanta continua, because no part of them can be given, without enclosing it within boundaries (points and moments), consequently, this given part is itself a space or a time. Space, therefore, consists only of spaces, and time of times. Points and moments are only boundaries, that is, the mere places or positions of their limitation. But places always presuppose intuitions which are to limit or determine them; and we cannot conceive either space or time composed of constituent parts which are given before space or time. Such quantities may also be called flowing, because synthesis (of the productive imagination) in the production of these quantities is a progression in time, the continuity of which we are accustomed to indicate by the expression flowing.

All phenomena, then, are continuous quantities, in respect both to intuition and mere perception (sensation, and with it reality). In the former case they are extensive quantities; in the latter, intensive. When the synthesis of the manifold of a phenomenon is interrupted, there results merely an aggregate of several phenomena, and not properly a phenomenon as a quantity, which is not produced by the mere continuation of the productive synthesis of a certain kind, but by the repetition of a synthesis always ceasing. For example, if I call thirteen dollars a sum or quantity of money, I employ the term quite correctly, inasmuch as I understand by thirteen dollars the value of a mark in standard silver, which is, to be sure, a continuous quantity, in which no part is the smallest, but every part might constitute a piece of money, which would contain material for still smaller pieces. If, however, by the words thirteen dollars I understand so many coins (be their value in silver what it may), it would be quite erroneous to use the expression a quantity of dollars; on the contrary, I must call them aggregate, that is, a number of coins. And as in every number we must have unity as the foundation, so a phenomenon taken as unity is a quantity, and as such always a continuous quantity (quantum continuum).

Now, seeing all phenomena, whether considered as extensive or intensive, are continuous quantities, the proposition: "All change (transition of a thing from one state into another) is continuous," might be proved here easily, and with mathematical evidence, were it not that the causality of a change lies, entirely beyond the bounds of a transcendental philosophy, and presupposes empirical principles. For of the possibility of a cause which changes the condition of things, that is, which determines them to the contrary to a certain given state, the understanding gives us à priori no knowledge; not merely because it has no insight into the possibility of it (for such insight is absent in several à priori cognitions), but because the notion of change concerns only certain determinations of phenomena, which experience alone can acquaint us with, while their cause lies in the unchangeable. But seeing that we have nothing which we could here employ but the pure fundamental conceptions of all possible experience, among which of course nothing empirical can be admitted, we dare not, without injuring the unity of our system, anticipate general physical science, which is built upon certain fundamental experiences.

Nevertheless, we are in no want of proofs of the great influence which the principle above developed exercises in the anticipation of perceptions, and even in supplying the want of them, so far as to shield us against the false conclusions which otherwise we might rashly draw.

If all reality in perception has a degree, between which and negation there is an endless sequence of ever smaller degrees, and if, nevertheless, every sense must have a determinate degree of receptivity for sensations; no perception, and consequently no experience is possible, which can prove, either immediately or mediately, an entire absence of all reality in a phenomenon; in other words, it is impossible ever to draw from experience a proof of the existence of empty space or of empty time. For in the first place, an entire absence of reality in a sensuous intuition cannot of course be an object of perception; secondly, such absence cannot be deduced from the contemplation of any single phenomenon, and the difference of the degrees in its reality; nor ought it ever to be admitted in explanation of any phenomenon. For if even the complete intuition of a determinate space or time is thoroughly real, that is, if no part thereof is empty, yet because every reality has its degree, which, with the extensive quantity of the phenomenon unchanged, can diminish through endless gradations down to nothing (the void), there must be infinitely graduated degrees, with which space or time is filled, and the intensive quantity in different phenomena may be smaller or greater, although the extensive quantity of the intuition remains equal and unaltered.

We shall give an example of this. Almost all natural philosophers, remarking a great difference in the quantity of the matter of different kinds in bodies with the same volume (partly on account of the momentum of gravity or weight, partly on account of the momentum of resistance to other bodies in motion), conclude unanimously that this volume (extensive quantity of the phenomenon) must be void in all bodies, although in different proportion. But who would suspect that these for the most part mathematical and mechanical inquirers into nature should ground this conclusion solely on a metaphysical hypothesis—a sort of hypothesis which they profess to disparage and avoid? Yet this they do, in assuming that the real in space (I must not here call it impenetrability or weight, because these are empirical conceptions) is always identical, and can only be distinguished according to its extensive quantity, that is, multiplicity. Now to this presupposition, for which they can have no ground in experience, and which consequently is merely metaphysical, I oppose a transcendental demonstration, which it is true will not explain the difference in the filling up of spaces, but which nevertheless completely does away with the supposed necessity of the above-mentioned presupposition that we cannot explain the said difference otherwise than by the hypothesis of empty spaces. This demonstration, moreover, has the merit of setting the understanding at liberty to conceive this distinction in a different manner, if the explanation of the fact requires any such hypothesis. For we perceive that although two equal spaces may be completely filled by matters altogether different, so that in neither of them is there left a single point wherein matter is not present, nevertheless, every reality has its degree (of resistance or of weight), which, without diminution of the extensive quantity, can become less and less ad infinitum, before it passes into nothingness and disappears. Thus an expansion which fills a space—for example, caloric, or any other reality in the phenomenal world—can decrease in its degrees to infinity, yet without leaving the smallest part of the space empty; on the contrary, filling it with those lesser degrees as completely as another phenomenon could with greater. My intention here is by no means to maintain that this is really the case with the difference of matters, in regard to their specific gravity; I wish only to prove, from a principle of the pure understanding, that the nature of our perceptions makes such a mode of explanation possible, and that it is erroneous to regard the real in a phenomenon as equal quoad its degree, and different only quoad its aggregation and extensive quantity, and this, too, on the pretended authority of an à priori principle of the understanding.

Nevertheless, this principle of the anticipation of perception must somewhat startle an inquirer whom initiation into transcendental philosophy has rendered cautious. We must naturally entertain some doubt whether or not the understanding can enounce any such synthetical proposition as that respecting the degree of all reality in phenomena, and consequently the possibility of the internal difference of sensation itself—abstraction being made of its empirical quality. Thus it is a question not unworthy of solution: "How the understanding can pronounce synthetically and à priori respecting phenomena, and thus anticipate these, even in that which is peculiarly and merely empirical, that, namely, which concerns sensation itself?"

The quality of sensation is in all cases merely empirical, and cannot be represented à priori (for example, colours, taste, etc.). But the real—that which corresponds to sensation—in opposition to negation = 0, only represents something the conception of which in itself contains a being (ein seyn), and signifies nothing but the synthesis in an empirical consciousness. That is to say, the empirical consciousness in the internal sense can be raised from 0 to every higher degree, so that the very same extensive quantity of intuition, an illuminated surface, for example, excites as great a sensation as an aggregate of many other surfaces less illuminated. We can therefore make complete abstraction of the extensive quantity of a phenomenon, and represent to ourselves in the mere sensation in a certain momentum, a synthesis of homogeneous ascension from 0 up to the given empirical consciousness, All sensations therefore as such are given only à posteriori, but this property thereof, namely, that they have a degree, can be known à priori. It is worthy of remark, that in respect to quantities in general, we can cognize à priori only a single quality, namely, continuity; but in respect to all quality (the real in phenomena), we cannot cognize à priori anything more than the intensive quantity thereof, namely, that they have a degree. All else is left to experience.

3. ANALOGIES OF EXPERIENCE.

The principle of these is: Experience is possible only through the representation of a necessary connection of Perceptions.

PROOF.

Experience is an empirical cognition; that is to say, a cognition which determines an object by means of perceptions. It is therefore a synthesis of perceptions, a synthesis which is not itself contained in perception, but which contains the synthetical unity of the manifold of perception in a consciousness; and this unity constitutes the essential of our cognition of objects of the senses, that is, of experience (not merely of intuition or sensation). Now in experience our perceptions come together contingently, so that no character of necessity in their connection appears, or can appear from the perceptions themselves, because apprehension is only a placing together of the manifold of empirical intuition, and no representation of a necessity in the connected existence of the phenomena which apprehension brings together, is to be discovered therein. But as experience is a cognition of objects by means of perceptions, it follows that the relation of the existence of the existence of the manifold must be represented in experience not as it is put together in time, but as it is objectively in time. And as time itself cannot be perceived, the determination of the existence of objects in time can only take place by means of their connection in time in general, consequently only by means of à priori connecting conceptions. Now as these conceptions always possess the character of necessity, experience is possible only by means of a representation of the necessary connection of perception.

The three modi of time are permanence, succession, and coexistence. Accordingly, there are three rules of all relations of time in phenomena, according to which the existence of every phenomenon is determined in respect of the unity of all time, and these antecede all experience and render it possible.

The general principle of all three analogies rests on the necessary unity of apperception in relation to all possible empirical consciousness (perception) at every time, consequently, as this unity lies à priori at the foundation of all mental operations, the principle rests on the synthetical unity of all phenomena according to their relation in time. For the original apperception relates to our internal sense (the complex of all representations), and indeed relates à priori to its form, that is to say, the relation of the manifold empirical consciousness in time. Now this manifold must be combined in original apperception according to relations of time—a necessity imposed by the à priori transcendental unity of apperception, to which is subjected all that can belong to my (i.e., my own) cognition, and therefore all that can become an object for me. This synthetical and à priori determined unity in relation of perceptions in time is therefore the rule: "All empirical determinations of time must be subject to rules of the general determination of time"; and the analogies of experience, of which we are now about to treat, must be rules of this nature.

These principles have this peculiarity, that they do not concern phenomena, and the synthesis of the empirical intuition thereof, but merely the existence of phenomena and their relation to each other in regard to this existence. Now the mode in which we apprehend a thing in a phenomenon can be determined à priori in such a manner that the rule of its synthesis can give, that is to say, can produce this à priori intuition in every empirical example. But the existence of phenomena cannot be known à priori, and although we could arrive by this path at a conclusion of the fact of some existence, we could not cognize that existence determinately, that is to say, we should be incapable of anticipating in what respect the empirical intuition of it would be distinguishable from that of others.

The two principles above mentioned, which I called mathematical, in consideration of the fact of their authorizing the application of mathematic phenomena, relate to these phenomena only in regard to their possibility, and instruct us how phenomena, as far as regards their intuition or the real in their perception, can be generated according to the rules of a mathematical synthesis. Consequently, numerical quantities, and with them the determination of a phenomenon as a quantity, can be employed in the one case as well as in the other. Thus, for example, out of 200,000 illuminations by the moon, I might compose and give à priori, that is construct, the degree of our sensations of the sun-light.[21] We may therefore entitle these two principles constitutive.

The case is very different with those principles whose province it is to subject the existence of phenomena to rules à priori. For as existence does not admit of being constructed, it is clear that they must only concern the relations of existence and be merely regulative principles. In this case, therefore, neither axioms nor anticipations are to be thought of. Thus, if a perception is given us, in a certain relation of time to other (although undetermined) perceptions, we cannot then say à priori, what and how great (in quantity) the other perception necessarily connected with the former is, but only how it is connected, quoad its existence, in this given modus of time. Analogies in philosophy mean something very different from that which they represent in mathematics. In the latter they are formulae, which enounce the equality of two relations of quantity, and are always constitutive, so that if two terms of the proportion are given, the third is also given, that is, can be constructed by the aid of these formulae. But in philosophy, analogy is not the equality of two quantitative but of two qualitative relations. In this case, from three given terms, I can give à priori and cognize the relation to a fourth member, but not this fourth term itself, although I certainly possess a rule to guide me in the search for this fourth term in experience, and a mark to assist me in discovering it. An analogy of experience is therefore only a rule according to which unity of experience must arise out of perceptions in respect to objects (phenomena) not as a constitutive, but merely as a regulative principle. The same holds good also of the postulates of empirical thought in general, which relate to the synthesis of mere intuition (which concerns the form of phenomena), the synthesis of perception (which concerns the matter of phenomena), and the synthesis of experience (which concerns the relation of these perceptions). For they are only regulative principles, and clearly distinguishable from the mathematical, which are constitutive, not indeed in regard to the certainty which both possess à priori, but in the mode of evidence thereof, consequently also in the manner of demonstration.

But what has been observed of all synthetical propositions, and must be particularly remarked in this place, is this, that these analogies possess significance and validity, not as principles of the transcendental, but only as principles of the empirical use of the understanding, and their truth can therefore be proved only as such, and that consequently the phenomena must not be subjoined directly under the categories, but only under their schemata. For if the objects to which those principles must be applied were things in themselves, it would be quite impossible to cognize aught concerning them synthetically à priori. But they are nothing but phenomena; a complete knowledge of which—a knowledge to which all principles à priori must at last relate—is the only possible experience. It follows that these principles can have nothing else for their aim than the conditions of the empirical cognition in the unity of synthesis of phenomena. But this synthesis is cogitated only in the schema of the pure conception of the understanding, of whose unity, as that of a synthesis in general, the category contains the function unrestricted by any sensuous condition. These principles will therefore authorize us to connect phenomena according to an analogy, with the logical and universal unity of conceptions, and consequently to employ the categories in the principles themselves; but in the application of them to experience, we shall use only their schemata, as the key to their proper application, instead of the categories, or rather the latter as restricting conditions, under the title of "formulae" of the former.

A. FIRST ANALOGY.

Principle of the Permanence of Substance.

In all changes of phenomena, substance is permanent, and the quantum thereof in nature is neither increased nor diminished.

PROOF.

All phenomena exist in time, wherein alone as substratum, that is, as the permanent form of the internal intuition, coexistence and succession can be represented. Consequently time, in which all changes of phenomena must be cogitated, remains and changes not, because it is that in which succession and coexistence can be represented only as determinations thereof. Now, time in itself cannot be an object of perception. It follows that in objects of perception, that is, in phenomena, there must be found a substratum which represents time in general, and in which all change or coexistence can be perceived by means of the relation of phenomena to it. But the substratum of all reality, that is, of all that pertains to the existence of things, is substance; all that pertains to existence can be cogitated only as a determination of substance. Consequently, the permanent, in relation to which alone can all relations of time in phenomena be determined, is substance in the world of phenomena, that is, the real in phenomena, that which, as the substratum of all change, remains ever the same. Accordingly, as this cannot change in existence, its quantity in nature can neither be increased nor diminished.

Our apprehension of the manifold in a phenomenon is always successive, is Consequently always changing. By it alone we could, therefore, never determine whether this manifold, as an object of experience, is coexistent or successive, unless it had for a foundation something fixed and permanent, of the existence of which all succession and coexistence are nothing but so many modes (modi of time). Only in the permanent, then, are relations of time possible (for simultaneity and succession are the only relations in time); that is to say, the permanent is the substratum of our empirical representation of time itself, in which alone all determination of time is possible. Permanence is, in fact, just another expression for time, as the abiding correlate of all existence of phenomena, and of all change, and of all coexistence. For change does not affect time itself, but only the phenomena in time (just as coexistence cannot be regarded as a modus of time itself, seeing that in time no parts are coexistent, but all successive). If we were to attribute succession to time itself, we should be obliged to cogitate another time, in which this succession would be possible. It is only by means of the permanent that existence in different parts of the successive series of time receives a quantity, which we entitle duration. For in mere succession, existence is perpetually vanishing and recommencing, and therefore never has even the least quantity. Without the permanent, then, no relation in time is possible. Now, time in itself is not an object of perception; consequently the permanent in phenomena must be regarded as the substratum of all determination of time, and consequently also as the condition of the possibility of all synthetical unity of perceptions, that is, of experience; and all existence and all change in time can only be regarded as a mode in the existence of that which abides unchangeably. Therefore, in all phenomena, the permanent is the object in itself, that is, the substance (phenomenon); but all that changes or can change belongs only to the mode of the existence of this substance or substances, consequently to its determinations.

I find that in all ages not only the philosopher, but even the common understanding, has preposited this permanence as a substratum of all change in phenomena; indeed, I am compelled to believe that they will always accept this as an indubitable fact. Only the philosopher expresses himself in a more precise and definite manner, when he says: "In all changes in the world, the substance remains, and the accidents alone are changeable." But of this decidedly synthetical proposition, I nowhere meet with even an attempt at proof; nay, it very rarely has the good fortune to stand, as it deserves to do, at the head of the pure and entirely à priori laws of nature. In truth, the statement that substance is permanent, is tautological. For this very permanence is the ground on which we apply the category of substance to the phenomenon; and we should have been obliged to prove that in all phenomena there is something permanent, of the existence of which the changeable is nothing but a determination. But because a proof of this nature cannot be dogmatical, that is, cannot be drawn from conceptions, inasmuch as it concerns a synthetical proposition à priori, and as philosophers never reflected that such propositions are valid only in relation to possible experience, and therefore cannot be proved except by means of a deduction of the possibility of experience, it is no wonder that while it has served as the foundation of all experience (for we feel the need of it in empirical cognition), it has never been supported by proof.

A philosopher was asked: "What is the weight of smoke?" He answered: "Subtract from the weight of the burnt wood the weight of the remaining ashes, and you will have the weight of the smoke." Thus he presumed it to be incontrovertible that even in fire the matter (substance) does not perish, but that only the form of it undergoes a change. In like manner was the saying: "From nothing comes nothing," only another inference from the principle or permanence, or rather of the ever-abiding existence of the true subject in phenomena. For if that in the phenomenon which we call substance is to be the proper substratum of all determination of time, it follows that all existence in past as well as in future time, must be determinable by means of it alone. Hence we are entitled to apply the term substance to a phenomenon, only because we suppose its existence in all time, a notion which the word permanence does not fully express, as it seems rather to be referable to future time. However, the internal necessity perpetually to be, is inseparably connected with the necessity always to have been, and so the expression may stand as it is. "Gigni de nihilo nihil; in nihilum nil posse reverti,"[22] are two propositions which the ancients never parted, and which people nowadays sometimes mistakenly disjoin, because they imagine that the propositions apply to objects as things in themselves, and that the former might be inimical to the dependence (even in respect of its substance also) of the world upon a supreme cause. But this apprehension is entirely needless, for the question in this case is only of phenomena in the sphere of experience, the unity of which never could be possible, if we admitted the possibility that new things (in respect of their substance) should arise. For in that case, we should lose altogether that which alone can represent the unity of time, to wit, the identity of the substratum, as that through which alone all change possesses complete and thorough unity. This permanence is, however, nothing but the manner in which we represent to ourselves the existence of things in the phenomenal world.

The determinations of a substance, which are only particular modes of its existence, are called accidents. They are always real, because they concern the existence of substance (negations are only determinations, which express the non-existence of something in the substance). Now, if to this real in the substance we ascribe a particular existence (for example, to motion as an accident of matter), this existence is called inherence, in contradistinction to the existence of substance, which we call subsistence.

But hence arise many misconceptions, and it would be a more accurate and just mode of expression to designate the accident only as the mode in which the existence of a substance is positively determined. Meanwhile, by reason of the conditions of the logical exercise of our understanding, it is impossible to avoid separating, as it were, that which in the existence of a substance is subject to change, whilst the substance remains, and regarding it in relation to that which is properly permanent and radical. On this account, this category of substance stands under the title of relation, rather because it is the condition thereof than because it contains in itself any relation.

Now, upon this notion of permanence rests the proper notion of the conception change. Origin and extinction are not changes of that which originates or becomes extinct. Change is but a mode of existence, which follows on another mode of existence of the same object; hence all that changes is permanent, and only the condition thereof changes. Now since this mutation affects only determinations, which can have a beginning or an end, we may say, employing an expression which seems somewhat paradoxical: "Only the permanent (substance) is subject to change; the mutable suffers no change, but rather alternation, that is, when certain determinations cease, others begin."

Change, when, cannot be perceived by us except in substances, and origin or extinction in an absolute sense, that does not concern merely a determination of the permanent, cannot be a possible perception, for it is this very notion of the permanent which renders possible the representation of a transition from one state into another, and from non-being to being, which, consequently, can be empirically cognized only as alternating determinations of that which is permanent. Grant that a thing absolutely begins to be; we must then have a point of time in which it was not. But how and by what can we fix and determine this point of time, unless by that which already exists? For a void time—preceding—is not an object of perception; but if we connect this beginning with objects which existed previously, and which continue to exist till the object in question in question begins to be, then the latter can only be a determination of the former as the permanent. The same holds good of the notion of extinction, for this presupposes the empirical representation of a time, in which a phenomenon no longer exists.

Substances (in the world of phenomena) are the substratum of all determinations of time. The beginning of some, and the ceasing to be of other substances, would utterly do away with the only condition of the empirical unity of time; and in that case phenomena would relate to two different times, in which, side by side, existence would pass; which is absurd. For there is only one time in which all different times must be placed, not as coexistent, but as successive.

Accordingly, permanence is a necessary condition under which alone phenomena, as things or objects, are determinable in a possible experience. But as regards the empirical criterion of this necessary permanence, and with it of the substantiality of phenomena, we shall find sufficient opportunity to speak in the sequel.

B. SECOND ANALOGY.

Principle of the Succession of Time According to the Law of Causality. All changes take place according to the law of the connection of Cause and Effect.

PROOF.

(That all phenomena in the succession of time are only changes, that is, a successive being and non-being of the determinations of substance, which is permanent; consequently that a being of substance itself which follows on the non-being thereof, or a non-being of substance which follows on the being thereof, in other words, that the origin or extinction of substance itself, is impossible—all this has been fully established in treating of the foregoing principle. This principle might have been expressed as follows: "All alteration (succession) of phenomena is merely change"; for the changes of substance are not origin or extinction, because the conception of change presupposes the same subject as existing with two opposite determinations, and consequently as permanent. After this premonition, we shall proceed to the proof.)

I perceive that phenomena succeed one another, that is to say, a state of things exists at one time, the opposite of which existed in a former state. In this case, then, I really connect together two perceptions in time. Now connection is not an operation of mere sense and intuition, but is the product of a synthetical faculty of imagination, which determines the internal sense in respect of a relation of time. But imagination can connect these two states in two ways, so that either the one or the other may antecede in time; for time in itself cannot be an object of perception, and what in an object precedes and what follows cannot be empirically determined in relation to it. I am only conscious, then, that my imagination places one state before and the other after; not that the one state antecedes the other in the object. In other words, the objective relation of the successive phenomena remains quite undetermined by means of mere perception. Now in order that this relation may be cognized as determined, the relation between the two states must be so cogitated that it is thereby determined as necessary, which of them must be placed before and which after, and not conversely. But the conception which carries with it a necessity of synthetical unity, can be none other than a pure conception of the understanding which does not lie in mere perception; and in this case it is the conception of "the relation of cause and effect," the former of which determines the latter in time, as its necessary consequence, and not as something which might possibly antecede (or which might in some cases not be perceived to follow). It follows that it is only because we subject the sequence of phenomena, and consequently all change, to the law of causality, that experience itself, that is, empirical cognition of phenomena, becomes possible; and consequently, that phenomena themselves, as objects of experience, are possible only by virtue of this law.

Our apprehension of the manifold of phenomena is always successive. The representations of parts succeed one another. Whether they succeed one another in the object also, is a second point for reflection, which was not contained in the former. Now we may certainly give the name of object to everything, even to every representation, so far as we are conscious thereof; but what this word may mean in the case of phenomena, not merely in so far as they (as representations) are objects, but only in so far as they indicate an object, is a question requiring deeper consideration. In so far as they, regarded merely as representations, are at the same time objects of consciousness, they are not to be distinguished from apprehension, that is, reception into the synthesis of imagination, and we must therefore say: "The manifold of phenomena is always produced successively in the mind." If phenomena were things in themselves, no man would be able to conjecture from the succession of our representations how this manifold is connected in the object; for we have to do only with our representations. How things may be in themselves, without regard to the representations through which they affect us, is utterly beyond the sphere of our cognition. Now although phenomena are not things in themselves, and are nevertheless the only thing given to us to be cognized, it is my duty to show what sort of connection in time belongs to the manifold in phenomena themselves, while the representation of this manifold in apprehension is always successive. For example, the apprehension of the manifold in the phenomenon of a house which stands before me, is successive. Now comes the question whether the manifold of this house is in itself successive—which no one will be at all willing to grant. But, so soon as I raise my conception of an object to the transcendental signification thereof, I find that the house is not a thing in itself, but only a phenomenon, that is, a representation, the transcendental object of which remains utterly unknown. What then am I to understand by the question: "How can the manifold be connected in the phenomenon itself—not considered as a thing in itself, but merely as a phenomenon?" Here that which lies in my successive apprehension is regarded as representation, whilst the phenomenon which is given me, notwithstanding that it is nothing more than a complex of these representations, is regarded as the object thereof, with which my conception, drawn from the representations of apprehension, must harmonize. It is very soon seen that, as accordance of the cognition with its object constitutes truth, the question now before us can only relate to the formal conditions of empirical truth; and that the phenomenon, in opposition to the representations of apprehension, can only be distinguished therefrom as the object of them, if it is subject to a rule which distinguishes it from every other apprehension, and which renders necessary a mode of connection of the manifold. That in the phenomenon which contains the condition of this necessary rule of apprehension, is the object.

Let us now proceed to our task. That something happens, that is to say, that something or some state exists which before was not, cannot be empirically perceived, unless a phenomenon precedes, which does not contain in itself this state. For a reality which should follow upon a void time, in other words, a beginning, which no state of things precedes, can just as little be apprehended as the void time itself. Every apprehension of an event is therefore a perception which follows upon another perception. But as this is the case with all synthesis of apprehension, as I have shown above in the example of a house, my apprehension of an event is not yet sufficiently distinguished from other apprehensions. But I remark also that if in a phenomenon which contains an occurrence, I call the antecedent state of my perception, A, and the following state, B, the perception B can only follow A in apprehension, and the perception A cannot follow B, but only precede it. For example, I see a ship float down the stream of a river. My perception of its place lower down follows upon my perception of its place higher up the course of the river, and it is impossible that, in the apprehension of this phenomenon, the vessel should be perceived first below and afterwards higher up the stream. Here, therefore, the order in the sequence of perceptions in apprehension is determined; and by this order apprehension is regulated. In the former example, my perceptions in the apprehension of a house might begin at the roof and end at the foundation, or vice versa; or I might apprehend the manifold in this empirical intuition, by going from left to right, and from right to left. Accordingly, in the series of these perceptions, there was no determined order, which necessitated my beginning at a certain point, in order empirically to connect the manifold. But this rule is always to be met with in the perception of that which happens, and it makes the order of the successive perceptions in the apprehension of such a phenomenon necessary.

I must, therefore, in the present case, deduce the subjective sequence of apprehension from the objective sequence of phenomena, for otherwise the former is quite undetermined, and one phenomenon is not distinguishable from another. The former alone proves nothing as to the connection of the manifold in an object, for it is quite arbitrary. The latter must consist in the order of the manifold in a phenomenon, according to which order the apprehension of one thing (that which happens) follows that of another thing (which precedes), in conformity with a rule. In this way alone can I be authorized to say of the phenomenon itself, and not merely of my own apprehension, that a certain order or sequence is to be found therein. That is, in other words, I cannot arrange my apprehension otherwise than in this order.

In conformity with this rule, then, it is necessary that in that which antecedes an event there be found the condition of a rule, according to which in this event follows always and necessarily; but I cannot reverse this and go back from the event, and determine (by apprehension) that which antecedes it. For no phenomenon goes back from the succeeding point of time to the preceding point, although it does certainly relate to a preceding point of time; from a given time, on the other hand, there is always a necessary progression to the determined succeeding time. Therefore, because there certainly is something that follows, I must of necessity connect it with something else, which antecedes, and upon which it follows, in conformity with a rule, that is necessarily, so that the event, as conditioned, affords certain indication of a condition, and this condition determines the event.

Let us suppose that nothing precedes an event, upon which this event must follow in conformity with a rule. All sequence of perception would then exist only in apprehension, that is to say, would be merely subjective, and it could not thereby be objectively determined what thing ought to precede, and what ought to follow in perception. In such a case, we should have nothing but a play of representations, which would possess no application to any object. That is to say, it would not be possible through perception to distinguish one phenomenon from another, as regards relations of time; because the succession in the act of apprehension would always be of the same sort, and therefore there would be nothing in the phenomenon to determine the succession, and to render a certain sequence objectively necessary. And, in this case, I cannot say that two states in a phenomenon follow one upon the other, but only that one apprehension follows upon another. But this is merely subjective, and does not determine an object, and consequently cannot be held to be cognition of an object—not even in the phenomenal world.

Accordingly, when we know in experience that something happens, we always presuppose that something precedes, whereupon it follows in conformity with a rule. For otherwise I could not say of the object that it follows; because the mere succession in my apprehension, if it be not determined by a rule in relation to something preceding, does not authorize succession in the object. Only, therefore, in reference to a rule, according to which phenomena are determined in their sequence, that is, as they happen, by the preceding state, can I make my subjective synthesis (of apprehension) objective, and it is only under this presupposition that even the experience of an event is possible.

No doubt it appears as if this were in thorough contradiction to all the notions which people have hitherto entertained in regard to the procedure of the human understanding. According to these opinions, it is by means of the perception and comparison of similar consequences following upon certain antecedent phenomena that the under-standing is led to the discovery of a rule, according to which certain events always follow certain phenomena, and it is only by this process that we attain to the conception of cause. Upon such a basis, it is clear that this conception must be merely empirical, and the rule which it furnishes us with—"Everything that happens must have a cause" —would be just as contingent as experience itself. The universality and necessity of the rule or law would be perfectly spurious attributes of it. Indeed, it could not possess universal validity, inasmuch as it would not in this case be à priori, but founded on deduction. But the same is the case with this law as with other pure à priori representa-tions (e.g., space and time), which we can draw in perfect clearness and completeness from experience, only because we had already placed them therein, and by that means, and by that alone, had rendered experience possible. Indeed, the logical clearness of this representation of a rule, determining the series of events, is possible only when we have made use thereof in experience. Nevertheless, the recognition of this rule, as a condition of the synthetical unity of phenomena in time, was the ground of experience itself and consequently preceded it à priori.

It is now our duty to show by an example that we never, even in experience, attribute to an object the notion of succession or effect (of an event—that is, the happening of something that did not exist before), and distinguish it from the subjective succession of apprehension, unless when a rule lies at the foundation, which compels us to observe this order of perception in preference to any other, and that, indeed, it is this necessity which first renders possible the representation of a succession in the object.

We have representations within us, of which also we can be conscious. But, however widely extended, however accurate and thoroughgoing this consciousness may be, these representations are still nothing more than representations, that is, internal deter-minations of the mind in this or that relation of time. Now how happens it that to these representations we should set an object, or that, in addition to their subjective reality, as modifications, we should still further attribute to them a certain unknown objective reality? It is clear that objective significancy cannot consist in a relation to another repre-sentation (of that which we desire to term object), for in that case the question again arises: "How does this other representation go out of itself, and obtain objective signifi-cancy over and above the subjective, which is proper to it, as a determination of a state of mind?" If we try to discover what sort of new property the relation to an object gives to our subjective representations, and what new importance they thereby receive, we shall find that this relation has no other effect than that of rendering necessary the connection of our representations in a certain manner, and of subjecting them to a rule; and that conversely, it is only because a certain order is necessary in the relations of time of our representations, that objective significancy is ascribed to them.

In the synthesis of phenomena, the manifold of our representations is always succes-sive. Now hereby is not represented an object, for by means of this succession, which is common to all apprehension, no one thing is distinguished from another. But so soon as I perceive or assume that in this succession there is a relation to a state antecedent, from which the representation follows in accordance with a rule, so soon do I represent some-thing as an event, or as a thing that happens; in other words, I cognize an object to which I must assign a certain determinate position in time, which cannot be altered, because of the preceding state in the object. When, therefore, I perceive that something happens, there is contained in this representation, in the first place, the fact, that something antecedes; because, it is only in relation to this that the phenomenon obtains its proper relation of time, in other words, exists after an antecedent time, in which it did not exist. But it can receive its determined place in time only by the presupposition that something existed in the foregoing state, upon which it follows inevitably and always, that is, in conformity with a rule. From all this it is evident that, in the first place, I cannot reverse the order of succession, and make that which happens precede that upon which it follows; and that, in the second place, if the antecedent state be posited, a certain determinate event inevitably and necessarily follows. Hence it follows that there exists a certain order in our representations, whereby the present gives a sure indication of some previously existing state, as a correlate, though still undetermined, of the existing event which is given—a correlate which itself relates to the event as its consequence, conditions it, and connects it necessarily with itself in the series of time.

If then it be admitted as a necessary law of sensibility, and consequently a formal condition of all perception, that the preceding necessarily determines the succeeding time (inasmuch as I cannot arrive at the succeeding except through the preceding), it must likewise be an indispensable law of empirical representation of the series of time that the phenomena of the past determine all phenomena in the succeeding time, and that the latter, as events, cannot take place, except in so far as the former determine their existence in time, that is to say, establish it according to a rule. For it is of course only in phenomena that we can empirically cognize this continuity in the connection of times.

For all experience and for the possibility of experience, understanding is indispensable, and the first step which it takes in this sphere is not to render the representation of objects clear, but to render the representation of an object in general, possible. It does this by applying the order of time to phenomena, and their existence. In other words, it assigns to each phenomenon, as a consequence, a place in relation to preceding phenomena, determined à priori in time, without which it could not harmonize with time itself, which determines a place à priori to all its parts. This determination of place cannot be derived from the relation of phenomena to absolute time (for it is not an object of perception); but, on the contrary, phenomena must reciprocally determine the places in time of one another, and render these necessary in the order of time. In other words, whatever follows or happens, must follow in conformity with a universal rule upon that which was contained in the foregoing state. Hence arises a series of phenomena, which, by means of the understanding, produces and renders necessary exactly the same order and continuous connection in the series of our possible perceptions, as is found à priori in the form of internal intuition (time), in which all our perceptions must have place.

That something happens, then, is a perception which belongs to a possible experience, which becomes real only because I look upon the phenomenon as determined in regard to its place in time, consequently as an object, which can always be found by means of a rule in the connected series of my perceptions. But this rule of the determination of a thing according to succession in time is as follows: "In what precedes may be found the condition, under which an event always (that is, necessarily) follows." From all this it is obvious that the principle of cause and effect is the principle of possible experience, that is, of objective cognition of phenomena, in regard to their relations in the succession of time.

The proof of this fundamental proposition rests entirely on the following momenta of argument. To all empirical cognition belongs the synthesis of the manifold by the imagination, a synthesis which is always successive, that is, in which the representations therein always follow one another. But the order of succession in imagination is not determined, and the series of successive representations may be taken retrogressively as well as progressively. But if this synthesis is a synthesis of apprehension (of the manifold of a given phenomenon), then the order is determined in the object, or to speak more accurately, there is therein an order of successive synthesis which determines an object, and according to which something necessarily precedes, and when this is posited, something else necessarily follows. If, then, my perception is to contain the cognition of an event, that is, of something which really happens, it must be an empirical judgement, wherein we think that the succession is determined; that is, it presupposes another phenomenon, upon which this event follows necessarily, or in conformity with a rule. If, on the contrary, when I posited the antecedent, the event did not necessarily follow, I should be obliged to consider it merely as a subjective play of my imagination, and if in this I represented to myself anything as objective, I must look upon it as a mere dream. Thus, the relation of phenomena (as possible perceptions), according to which that which happens is, as to its existence, necessarily determined in time by something which antecedes, in conformity with a rule—in other words, the relation of cause and effect—is the condition of the objective validity of our empirical judgements in regard to the sequence of perceptions, consequently of their empirical truth, and therefore of experience. The principle of the relation of causality in the succession of phenomena is therefore valid for all objects of experience, because it is itself the ground of the possibility of experience.

Here, however, a difficulty arises, which must be resolved. The principle of the connection of causality among phenomena is limited in our formula to the succession thereof, although in practice we find that the principle applies also when the phenomena exist together in the same time, and that cause and effect may be simultaneous. For example, there is heat in a room, which does not exist in the open air. I look about for the cause, and find it to be the fire, Now the fire as the cause is simultaneous with its effect, the heat of the room. In this case, then, there is no succession as regards time, between cause and effect, but they are simultaneous; and still the law holds good. The greater part of operating causes in nature are simultaneous with their effects, and the succession in time of the latter is produced only because the cause cannot achieve the total of its effect in one moment. But at the moment when the effect first arises, it is always simultaneous with the causality of its cause, because, if the cause had but a moment before ceased to be, the effect could not have arisen. Here it must be specially remembered that we must consider the order of time and not the lapse thereof. The relation remains, even though no time has elapsed. The time between the causality of the cause and its immediate effect may entirely vanish, and the cause and effect be thus simultaneous, but the relation of the one to the other remains always determinable according to time. If, for example, I consider a leaden ball, which lies upon a cushion and makes a hollow in it, as a cause, then it is simultaneous with the effect. But I distinguish the two through the relation of time of the dynamical connection of both. For if I lay the ball upon the cushion, then the hollow follows upon the before smooth surface;

but supposing the cushion has, from some cause or another, a hollow, there does not thereupon follow a leaden ball.

Thus, the law of succession of time is in all instances the only empirical criterion of effect in relation to the causality of the antecedent cause. The glass is the cause of the rising of the water above its horizontal surface, although the two phenomena are contemporaneous. For, as soon as I draw some water with the glass from a larger vessel, an effect follows thereupon, namely, the change of the horizontal state which the water had in the large vessel into a concave, which it assumes in the glass.

This conception of causality leads us to the conception of action; that of action, to the conception of force; and through it, to the conception of substance. As I do not wish this critical essay, the sole purpose of which is to treat of the sources of our synthetical cognition à priori, to be crowded with analyses which merely explain, but do not enlarge the sphere of our conceptions, I reserve the detailed explanation of the above conceptions for a future system of pure reason. Such an analysis, indeed, executed with great particularity, may already be found in well-known works on this subject. But I cannot at present refrain from making a few remarks on the empirical criterion of a substance, in so far as it seems to be more evident and more easily recognized through the conception of action than through that of the permanence of a phenomenon.

Where action (consequently activity and force) exists, substance also must exist, and in it alone must be sought the seat of that fruitful source of phenomena. Very well. But if we are called upon to explain what we mean by substance, and wish to avoid the vice of reasoning in a circle, the answer is by no means so easy. How shall we conclude immediately from the action to the permanence of that which acts, this being nevertheless an essential and peculiar criterion of substance (phenomenon)? But after what has been said above, the solution of this question becomes easy enough, although by the common mode of procedure—merely analysing our conceptions—it would be quite impossible. The conception of action indicates the relation of the subject of causality to the effect. Now because all effect consists in that which happens, therefore in the changeable, the last subject thereof is the permanent, as the substratum of all that changes, that is, substance. For according to the principle of causality, actions are always the first ground of all change in phenomena and, consequently, cannot be a property of a subject which itself changes, because if this were the case, other actions and another subject would be necessary to determine this change. From all this it results that action alone, as an empirical criterion, is a sufficient proof of the presence of substantiality, without any necessity on my part of endeavouring to discover the permanence of substance by a comparison. Besides, by this mode of induction we could not attain to the completeness which the magnitude and strict universality of the conception requires. For that the primary subject of the causality of all arising and passing away, all origin and extinction, cannot itself (in the sphere of phenomena) arise and pass away, is a sound and safe conclusion, a conclusion which leads us to the conception of empirical necessity and permanence in existence, and consequently to the conception of a substance as phenomenon.

When something happens, the mere fact of the occurrence, without regard to that which occurs, is an object requiring investigation. The transition from the non-being of a state into the existence of it, supposing that this state contains no quality which previously existed in the phenomenon, is a fact of itself demanding inquiry. Such an event, as has been shown in No. A, does not concern substance (for substance does not thus originate), but its condition or state. It is therefore only change, and not origin from nothing. If this origin be regarded as the effect of a foreign cause, it is termed creation, which cannot be admitted as an event among phenomena, because the very possibility of it would annihilate the unity of experience. If, however, I regard all things not as phenomena, but as things in themselves and objects of understanding alone, they, although substances, may be considered as dependent, in respect of their existence, on a foreign cause. But this would require a very different meaning in the words, a meaning which could not apply to phenomena as objects of possible experience.

How a thing can be changed, how it is possible that upon one state existing in one point of time, an opposite state should follow in another point of time—of this we have not the smallest conception à priori. There is requisite for this the knowledge of real powers, which can only be given empirically; for example, knowledge of moving forces, or, in other words, of certain successive phenomena (as movements) which indicate the presence of such forces. But the form of every change, the condition under which alone it can take place as the coming into existence of another state (be the content of the change, that is, the state which is changed, what it may), and consequently the succession of the states themselves can very well be considered à priori, in relation to the law of causality and the conditions of time.[23]

When a substance passes from one state, a, into another state, b, the point of time in which the latter exists is different from, and subsequent to that in which the former existed. In like manner, the second state, as reality (in the phenomenon), differs from the first, in which the reality of the second did not exist, as b from zero. That is to say, if the state, b, differs from the state, a, only in respect to quantity, the change is a coming into existence of b -a, which in the former state did not exist, and in relation to which that state is = O.

Now the question arises how a thing passes from one state = a, into another state = b. Between two moments there is always a certain time, and between two states existing in these moments there is always a difference having a certain quantity (for all parts of phenomena are in their turn quantities). Consequently, every transition from one state into another is always effected in a time contained between two moments, of which the first determines the state which leaves, and the second determines the state into the thing passes. The thing leaves, and the second determines the state into which the thing Both moments, then, are limitations of the time of a change, consequently of the intermediate state between both, and as such they belong to the total of the change. Now every change has a cause, which evidences its causality in the whole time during which the charge takes place. The cause, therefore, does not produce the change all at once or in one moment, but in a time, so that, as the time gradually increases from the commencing instant, a, to its completion at b, in like manner also, the quantity of the reality (b - a) is generated through the lesser degrees which are contained between the first and last. All change is therefore possible only through a continuous action of the causality, which, in so far as it is uniform, we call a momentum. The change does not consist of these momenta, but is generated or produced by them as their effect.

Such is the law of the continuity of all change, the ground of which is that neither time itself nor any phenomenon in time consists of parts which are the smallest possible, but that, notwithstanding, the state of a thing passes in the process of a change through all these parts, as elements, to its second state. There is no smallest degree of reality in a phenomenon, just as there is no smallest degree in the quantity of time; and so the new state of reality grows up out of the former state, through all the infinite degrees thereof, the differences of which one from another, taken all together, are less than the difference between o and a.

It is not our business to inquire here into the utility of this principle in the investigation of nature. But how such a proposition, which appears so greatly to extend our knowledge of nature, is possible completely à priori, is indeed a question which deserves investigation, although the first view seems to demonstrate the truth and reality of the principle, and the question, how it is possible, may be considered superfluous. For there are so many groundless pretensions to the enlargement of our knowledge by pure reason that we must take it as a general rule to be mistrustful of all such, and without a thoroughgoing and radical deduction, to believe nothing of the sort even on the clearest dogmatical evidence.

Every addition to our empirical knowledge, and every advance made in the exercise of our perception, is nothing more than an extension of the determination of the internal sense, that is to say, a progression in time, be objects themselves what they may, phenomena, or pure intuitions. This progression in time determines everything, and is itself determined by nothing else. That is to say, the parts of the progression exist only in time, and by means of the synthesis thereof, and are not given antecedently to it. For this reason, every transition in perception to anything which follows upon another in time, is a determination of time by means of the production of this perception. And as this determination of time is, always and in all its parts, a quantity, the perception produced is to be considered as a quantity which proceeds through all its degrees—no one of which is the smallest possible—from zero up to its determined degree. From this we perceive the possibility of cognizing à priori a law of changes—a law, however, which concerns their form merely. We merely anticipate our own apprehension, the formal condition of which, inasmuch as it is itself to be found in the mind antecedently to all given phenomena, must certainly be capable of being cognized à priori.

Thus, as time contains the sensuous condition à priori of the possibility of a continuous progression of that which exists to that which follows it, the understanding, by virtue of the unity of apperception, contains the condition à priori of the possibility of a continuous determination of the position in time of all phenomena, and this by means of the series of causes and effects, the former of which necessitate the sequence of the latter, and thereby render universally and for all time, and by consequence, objectively, valid the empirical cognition of the relations of time.

C. THIRD ANALOGY.

Principle of Coexistence, According to the Law of Reciprocity or Community.

All substances, in so far as they can be perceived in space at the same time, exist in a state of complete reciprocity of action.

PROOF.

Things are coexistent, when in empirical intuition the perception of the one can follow upon the perception of the other, and vice versa—which cannot occur in the succession of phenomena, as we have shown in the explanation of the second principle. Thus I can perceive the moon and then the earth, or conversely, first the earth and then the moon; and for the reason that my perceptions of these objects can reciprocally follow each other, I say, they exist contemporaneously. Now coexistence is the existence of the manifold in the same time. But time itself is not an object of perception; and therefore we cannot conclude from the fact that things are placed in the same time, the other fact, that the perception of these things can follow each other reciprocally. The synthesis of the imagination in apprehension would only present to us each of these perceptions as present in the subject when the other is not present, and contrariwise; but would not show that the objects are coexistent, that is to say, that, if the one exists, the other also exists in the same time, and that this is necessarily so, in order that the perceptions may be capable of following each other reciprocally. It follows that a conception of the understanding or category of the reciprocal sequence of the determinations of phenomena (existing, as they do, apart from each other, and yet contemporaneously), is requisite to justify us in saying that the reciprocal succession of perceptions has its foundation in the object, and to enable us to represent coexistence as objective. But that relation of substances in which the one contains determinations the ground of which is in the other substance, is the relation of influence. And, when this influence is reciprocal, it is the relation of community or reciprocity. Consequently the coexistence of substances in space cannot be cognized in experience otherwise than under the precondition of their reciprocal action. This is therefore the condition of the possibility of things themselves as objects of experience.

Things are coexistent, in so far as they exist in one and the same time. But how can we know that they exist in one and the same time? Only by observing that the order in the synthesis of apprehension of the manifold is arbitrary and a matter of indifference, that is to say, that it can proceed from A, through B, C, D, to E, or contrariwise from E to A. For if they were successive in time (and in the order, let us suppose, which begins with A), it is quite impossible for the apprehension in perception to begin with E and go backwards to A, inasmuch as A belongs to past time and, therefore, cannot be an object of apprehension.

Let us assume that in a number of substances considered as phenomena each is completely isolated, that is, that no one acts upon another. Then I say that the coexistence of these cannot be an object of possible perception and that the existence of one cannot, by any mode of empirical synthesis, lead us to the existence of another. For we imagine them in this case to be separated by a completely void space, and thus perception, which proceeds from the one to the other in time, would indeed determine their existence by means of a following perception, but would be quite unable to distinguish whether the one phenomenon follows objectively upon the first, or is coexistent with it.

Besides the mere fact of existence, then, there must be something by means of which A determines the position of B in time and, conversely, B the position of A; because only under this condition can substances be empirically represented as existing contemporaneously. Now that alone determines the position of another thing in time which is the cause of it or of its determinations. Consequently every substance (inasmuch as it can have succession predicated of it only in respect of its determinations) must contain the causality of certain determinations in another substance, and at the same time the effects of the causality of the other in itself. That is to say, substances must stand (mediately or immediately) in dynamical community with each other, if coexistence is to be cognized in any possible experience. But, in regard to objects of experience, that is absolutely necessary without which the experience of these objects would itself be impossible. Consequently it is absolutely necessary that all substances in the world of phenomena, in so far as they are coexistent, stand in a relation of complete community of reciprocal action to each other.

The word community has in our language[24] two meanings, and contains the two notions conveyed in the Latin communio and commercium. We employ it in this place in the latter sense—that of a dynamical community, without which even the community of place (communio spatii) could not be empirically cognized. In our experiences it is easy to observe that it is only the continuous influences in all parts of space that can conduct our senses from one object to another; that the light which plays between our eyes and the heavenly bodies produces a mediating community between them and us, and thereby evidences their coexistence with us; that we cannot empirically change our position (perceive this change), unless the existence of matter throughout the whole of space rendered possible the perception of the positions we occupy; and that this perception can prove the contemporaneous existence of these places only through their reciprocal influence, and thereby also the coexistence of even the most remote objects—although in this case the proof is only mediate. Without community, every perception (of a phenomenon in space) is separated from every other and isolated, and the chain of empirical representations, that is, of experience, must, with the appearance of a new object, begin entirely de novo, without the least connection with preceding representations, and without standing towards these even in the relation of time. My intention here is by no means to combat the notion of empty space; for it may exist where our perceptions cannot exist, inasmuch as they cannot reach thereto, and where, therefore, no empirical perception of coexistence takes place. But in this case it is not an object of possible experience.

The following remarks may be useful in the way of explanation. In the mind, all phenomena, as contents of a possible experience, must exist in community (communio) of apperception or consciousness, and in so far as it is requisite that objects be represented as coexistent and connected, in so far must they reciprocally determine the position in time of each other and thereby constitute a whole. If this subjective community is to rest upon an objective basis, or to be applied to substances as phenomena, the perception of one substance must render possible the perception of another, and conversely. For otherwise succession, which is always found in perceptions as apprehensions, would be predicated of external objects, and their representation of their coexistence be thus impossible. But this is a reciprocal influence, that is to say, a real community (commercium) of substances, without which therefore the empirical relation of coexistence would be a notion beyond the reach of our minds. By virtue of this commercium, phenomena, in so far as they are apart from, and nevertheless in connection with each other, constitute a compositum reale. Such composita are possible in many different ways. The three dynamical relations then, from which all others spring, are those of inherence, consequence, and composition.

These, then, are the three analogies of experience. They are nothing more than principles of the determination of the existence of phenomena in time, according to the three modi of this determination; to wit, the relation to time itself as a quantity (the quantity of existence, that is, duration), the relation in time as a series or succession, finally, the relation in time as the complex of all existence (simultaneity). This unity of determination in regard to time is thoroughly dynamical; that is to say, time is not considered as that in which experience determines immediately to every existence its position; for this is impossible, inasmuch as absolute time is not an object of perception, by means of which phenomena can be connected with each other. On the contrary, the rule of the understanding, through which alone the existence of phenomena can receive synthetical unity as regards relations of time, determines for every phenomenon its position in time, and consequently à priori, and with validity for all and every time.

By nature, in the empirical sense of the word, we understand the totality of phenomena connected, in respect of their existence, according to necessary rules, that is, laws. There are therefore certain laws (which are moreover à priori) which make nature possible; and all empirical laws can exist only by means of experience, and by virtue of those primitive laws through which experience itself becomes possible. The purpose of the analogies is therefore to represent to us the unity of nature in the connection of all phenomena under certain exponents, the only business of which is to express the relation of time (in so far as it contains all existence in itself) to the unity of apperception, which can exist in synthesis only according to rules. The combined expression of all is this: "All phenomena exist in one nature, and must so exist, inasmuch as without this à priori unity, no unity of experience, and consequently no determination of objects in experience, is possible."

As regards the mode of proof which we have employed in treating of these transcendental laws of nature, and the peculiar character of we must make one remark, which will at the same time be important as a guide in every other attempt to demonstrate the truth of intellectual and likewise synthetical propositions à priori. Had we endeavoured to prove these analogies dogmatically, that is, from conceptions; that is to say, had we employed this method in attempting to show that everything which exists, exists only in that which is permanent—that every thing or event presupposes the existence of something in a preceding state, upon which it follows in conformity with a rule—lastly, that in the manifold, which is coexistent, the states coexist in connection with each other according to a rule, all our labour would have been utterly in vain. For more conceptions of things, analyse them as we may, cannot enable us to conclude from the existence of one object to the existence of another. What other course was left for us to pursue? This only, to demonstrate the possibility of experience as a cognition in which at last all objects must be capable of being presented to us, if the representation of them is to possess any objective reality. Now in this third, this mediating term, the essential form of which consists in the synthetical unity of the apperception of all phenomena, we found à priori conditions of the universal and necessary determination as to time of all existences in the world of phenomena, without which the empirical determination thereof as to time would itself be impossible, and we also discovered rules of synthetical unity à priori, by means of which we could anticipate experience. For want of this method, and from the fancy that it was possible to discover a dogmatical proof of the synthetical propositions which are requisite in the empirical employment of the understanding, has it happened that a proof of the principle of sufficient reason has been so often attempted, and always in vain. The other two analogies nobody has ever thought of, although they have always been silently employed by the mind,[25] because the guiding thread furnished by the categories was wanting, the guide which alone can enable us to discover every hiatus, both in the system of conceptions and of principles.

4. THE POSTULATES OF EMPIRICAL THOUGHT.

1. That which agrees with the formal conditions (intuition and conception) of experience, is possible.

2. That which coheres with the material conditions of experience (sensation), is real.

3. That whose coherence with the real is determined according to universal conditions of experience is (exists) necessary.

Explanation.

The categories of modality possess this peculiarity, that they do not in the least determine the object, or enlarge the conception to which they are annexed as predicates, but only express its relation to the faculty of cognition. Though my conception of a thing is in itself complete, I am still entitled to ask whether the object of it is merely possible, or whether it is also real, or, if the latter, whether it is also necessary. But hereby the object itself is not more definitely determined in thought, but the question is only in what relation it, including all its determinations, stands to the understanding and its employment in experience, to the empirical faculty of judgement, and to the reason of its application to experience.

For this very reason, too, the categories of modality are nothing more than explanations of the conceptions of possibility, reality, and necessity, as employed in experience, and at the same time, restrictions of all the categories to empirical use alone, not authorizing the transcendental employment of them. For if they are to have something more than a merely logical significance, and to be something more than a mere analytical expression of the form of thought, and to have a relation to things and their possibility, reality, or necessity, they must concern possible experience and its synthetical unity, in which alone objects of cognition can be given.

The postulate of the possibility of things requires also, that the conception of the things agree with the formal conditions of our experience in general. But this, that is to say, the objective form of experience, contains all the kinds of synthesis which are requisite for the cognition of objects. A conception which contains a synthesis must be regarded as empty and, without reference to an object, if its synthesis does not belong to experience—either as borrowed from it, and in this case it is called an empirical conception, or such as is the ground and à priori condition of experience (its form), and in this case it is a pure conception, a conception which nevertheless belongs to experience, inasmuch as its object can be found in this alone. For where shall we find the criterion or character of the possibility of an object which is cogitated by means of an à priori synthetical conception, if not in the synthesis which constitutes the form of empirical cognition of objects? That in such a conception no contradiction exists is indeed a necessary logical condition, but very far from being sufficient to establish the objective reality of the conception, that is, the possibility of such an object as is thought in the conception. Thus, in the conception of a figure which is contained within two straight lines, there is no contradiction, for the conceptions of two straight lines and of their junction contain no negation of a figure. The impossibility in such a case does not rest upon the conception in itself, but upon the construction of it in space, that is to say, upon the conditions of space and its determinations. But these have themselves objective reality, that is, they apply to possible things, because they contain à priori the form of experience in general.

And now we shall proceed to point out the extensive utility and influence of this postulate of possibility. When I represent to myself a thing that is permanent, so that everything in it which changes belongs merely to its state or condition, from such a conception alone I never can cognize that such a thing is possible. Or, if I represent to myself something which is so constituted that, when it is posited, something else follows always and infallibly, my thought contains no self-contradiction; but whether such a property as causality is to be found in any possible thing, my thought alone affords no means of judging. Finally, I can represent to myself different things (substances) which are so constituted that the state or condition of one causes a change in the state of the other, and reciprocally; but whether such a relation is a property of things cannot be perceived from these conceptions, which contain a merely arbitrary synthesis. Only from the fact, therefore, that these conceptions express à priori the relations of perceptions in every experience, do we know that they possess objective reality, that is, transcendental truth; and that independent of experience, though not independent of all relation to form of an experience in general and its synthetical unity, in which alone objects can be empirically cognized.

But when we fashion to ourselves new conceptions of substances, forces, action, and reaction, from the material presented to us by perception, without following the example of experience in their connection, we create mere chimeras, of the possibility of which we cannot discover any criterion, because we have not taken experience for our instructress, though we have borrowed the conceptions from her. Such fictitious conceptions derive their character of possibility not, like the categories, à priori, as conceptions on which all experience depends, but only, à posteriori, as conceptions given by means of experience itself, and their possibility must either be cognized à posteriori and empirically, or it cannot be cognized at all. A substance which is permanently present in space, yet without filling it (like that tertium quid between matter and the thinking subject which some have tried to introduce into metaphysics), or a peculiar fundamental power of the mind of intuiting the future by anticipation (instead of merely inferring from past and present events), or, finally, a power of the mind to place itself in community of thought with other men, however distant they may be—these are conceptions the possibility of which has no ground to rest upon. For they are not based upon experience and its known laws; and, without experience, they are a merely arbitrary conjunction of thoughts, which, though containing no internal contradiction, has no claim to objective reality, neither, consequently, to the possibility of such an object as is thought in these conceptions. As far as concerns reality, it is self-evident that we cannot cogitate such a possibility in concreto without the aid of experience; because reality is concerned only with sensation, as the matter of experience, and not with the form of thought, with which we can no doubt indulge in shaping fancies.

But I pass by everything which derives its possibility from reality in experience, and I purpose treating here merely of the possibility of things by means of à priori conceptions. I maintain, then, that the possibility of things is not derived from such conceptions per se, but only when considered as formal and objective conditions of an experience in general.

It seems, indeed, as if the possibility of a triangle could be cognized from the conception of it alone (which is certainly independent of experience); for we can certainly give to the conception a corresponding object completely à priori, that is to say, we can construct it. But as a triangle is only the form of an object, it must remain a mere product of the imagination, and the possibility of the existence of an object corresponding to it must remain doubtful, unless we can discover some other ground, unless we know that the figure can be cogitated under the conditions upon which all objects of experience rest. Now, the facts that space is a formal condition à priori of external experience, that the formative synthesis, by which we construct a triangle in imagination, is the very same as that we employ in the apprehension of a phenomenon for the purpose of making an empirical conception of it, are what alone connect the notion of the possibility of such a thing, with the conception of it. In the same manner, the possibility of continuous quantities, indeed of quantities in general, for the conceptions of them are without exception synthetical, is never evident from the conceptions in themselves, but only when they are considered as the formal conditions of the determination of objects in experience. And where, indeed, should we look for objects to correspond to our conceptions, if not in experience, by which alone objects are presented to us? It is, however, true that without antecedent experience we can cognize and characterize the possibility of things, relatively to the formal conditions, under which something is determined in experience as an object, consequently, completely à priori. But still this is possible only in relation to experience and within its limits.

The postulate concerning the cognition of the reality of things requires perception, consequently conscious sensation, not indeed immediately, that is, of the object itself, whose existence is to be cognized, but still that the object have some connection with a real perception, in accordance with the analogies of experience, which exhibit all kinds of real connection in experience.

From the mere conception of a thing it is impossible to conclude its existence. For, let the conception be ever so complete, and containing a statement of all the determinations of the thing, the existence of it has nothing to do with all this, but only with thew question whether such a thing is given, so that the perception of it can in every case precede the conception. For the fact that the conception of it precedes the perception, merely indicates the possibility of its existence; it is perception which presents matter to the conception, that is the sole criterion of reality. Prior to the perception of the thing, however, and therefore comparatively à priori, we are able to cognize its existence, provided it stands in connection with some perceptions according to the principles of the empirical conjunction of these, that is, in conformity with the analogies of perception. For, in this case, the existence of the supposed thing is connected with our perception in a possible experience, and we are able, with the guidance of these analogies, to reason in the series of possible perceptions from a thing which we do really perceive to the thing we do not perceive. Thus, we cognize the existence of a magnetic matter penetrating all bodies from the perception of the attraction of the steel-filings by the magnet, although the constitution of our organs renders an immediate perception of this matter impossible for us. For, according to the laws of sensibility and the connected context of our perceptions, we should in an experience come also on an immediate empirical intuition of this matter, if our senses were more acute—but this obtuseness has no influence upon and cannot alter the form of possible experience in general. Our knowledge of the existence of things reaches as far as our perceptions, and what may be inferred from them according to empirical laws, extend. If we do not set out from experience, or do not proceed according to the laws of the empirical connection of phenomena, our pretensions to discover the existence of a thing which we do not immediately perceive are vain. Idealism, however, brings forward powerful objections to these rules for proving existence mediately. This is, therefore, the proper place for its refutation.

REFUTATION OF IDEALISM.

Idealism—I mean material idealism—is the theory which declares the existence of objects in space without us to be either () doubtful and indemonstrable, or (2) false and impossible. The first is the problematical idealism of Descartes, who admits the undoubted certainty of only one empirical assertion (assertio), to wit, "I am." The second is the dogmatical idealism of Berkeley, who maintains that space, together with all the objects of which it is the inseparable condition, is a thing which is in itself impossible, and that consequently the objects in space are mere products of the imagination. The dogmatical theory of idealism is unavoidable, if we regard space as a property of things in themselves; for in that case it is, with all to which it serves as condition, a nonentity. But the foundation for this kind of idealism we have already destroyed in the transcendental æsthetic. Problematical idealism, which makes no such assertion, but only alleges our incapacity to prove the existence of anything besides ourselves by means of immediate experience, is a theory rational and evidencing a thorough and philosophical mode of thinking, for it observes the rule not to form a decisive judgement before sufficient proof be shown. The desired proof must therefore demonstrate that we have experience of external things, and not mere fancies. For this purpose, we must prove, that our internal and, to Descartes, indubitable experience is itself possible only under the previous assumption of external experience.

THEOREM.

The simple but empirically determined consciousness of my own existence proves the existence of external objects in space.

PROOF

I am conscious of my own existence as determined in time. All determination in regard to time presupposes the existence of something permanent in perception. But this permanent something cannot be something in me, for the very reason that my existence in time is itself determined by this permanent something. It follows that the perception of this permanent existence is possible only through a thing without me and not through the mere representation of a thing without me. Consequently, the determination of my existence in time is possible only through the existence of real things external to me. Now, consciousness in time is necessarily connected with the consciousness of the possibility of this determination in time. Hence it follows that consciousness in time is necessarily connected also with the existence of things without me, inasmuch as the existence of these things is the condition of determination in time. That is to say, the consciousness of my own existence is at the same time an immediate consciousness of the existence of other things without me.

Remark I. The reader will observe, that in the foregoing proof the game which idealism plays is retorted upon itself, and with more justice. It assumed that the only immediate experience is internal and that from this we can only infer the existence of external things. But, as always happens, when we reason from given effects to determined causes, idealism has reasoned with too much haste and uncertainty, for it is quite possible that the cause of our representations may lie in ourselves, and that we ascribe it falsely to external things. But our proof shows that external experience is properly immediate,[26] that only by virtue of it—not, indeed, the consciousness of our own existence, but certainly the determination of our existence in time, that is, internal experience—is possible. It is true, that the representation "I am," which is the expression of the consciousness which can accompany all my thoughts, is that which immediately includes the existence of a subject. But in this representation we cannot find any knowledge of the subject, and therefore also no empirical knowledge, that is, experience. For experience contains, in addition to the thought of something existing, intuition, and in this case it must be internal intuition, that is, time, in relation to which the subject must be determined. But the existence of external things is absolutely requisite for this purpose, so that it follows that internal experience is itself possible only mediately and through external experience.

Remark II. Now with this view all empirical use of our faculty of cognition in the determination of time is in perfect accordance. Its truth is supported by the fact that it is possible to perceive a determination of time only by means of a change in external relations (motion) to the permanent in space (for example, we become aware of the sun's motion by observing the changes of his relation to the objects of this earth). But this is not all. We find that we possess nothing permanent that can correspond and be submitted to the conception of a substance as intuition, except matter. This idea of permanence is not itself derived from external experience, but is an à priori necessary condition of all determination of time, consequently also of the internal sense in reference to our own existence, and that through the existence of external things. In the representation "I," the consciousness of myself is not an intuition, but a merely intellectual representation produced by the spontaneous activity of a thinking subject. It follows, that this "i" has not any predicate of intuition, which, in its character of permanence, could serve as correlate to the determination of time in the internal sense—in the same way as impenetrability is the correlate of matter as an empirical intuition.

Remark III. From the fact that the existence of external things is a necessary condition of the possibility of a determined consciousness of ourselves, it does not follow that every intuitive representation of external things involves the existence of these things, for their representations may very well be the mere products of the imagination (in dreams as well as in madness); though, indeed, these are themselves created by the reproduction of previous external perceptions, which, as has been shown, are possible only through the reality of external objects. The sole aim of our remarks has, however, been to prove that internal experience in general is possible only through external experience in general. Whether this or that supposed experience be purely imaginary must be discovered from its particular determinations and by comparing these with the criteria of all real experience.

Finally, as regards the third postulate, it applies to material necessity in existence, and not to merely formal and logical necessity in the connection of conceptions. Now as we cannot cognize completely à priori the existence of any object of sense, though we can do so comparatively à priori, that is, relatively to some other previously given existence—a cognition, however, which can only be of such an existence as must be contained in the complex of experience, of which the previously given perception is a part—the necessity of existence can never be cognized from conceptions, but always, on the contrary, from its connection with that which is an object of perception. But the only existence cognized, under the condition of other given phenomena, as necessary, is the existence of effects from given causes in conformity with the laws of causality. It is consequently not the necessity of the existence of things (as substances), but the necessity of the state of things that we cognize, and that not immediately, but by means of the existence of other states given in perception, according to empirical laws of causality. Hence it follows that the criterion of necessity is to be found only in the law of possible experience—that everything which happens is determined à priori in the phenomenon by its cause. Thus we cognize only the necessity of effects in nature, the causes of which are given us. Moreover, the criterion of necessity in existence possesses no application beyond the field of possible experience, and even in this it is not valid of the existence of things as substances, because these can never be considered as empirical effects, or as something that happens and has a beginning. Necessity, therefore, regards only the relations of phenomena according to the dynamical law of causality, and the possibility grounded thereon, of reasoning from some given existence (of a cause) à priori to another existence (of an effect). "Everything that happens is hypothetically necessary," is a principle which subjects the changes that take place in the world to a law, that is, to a rule of necessary existence, without which nature herself could not possibly exist. Hence the proposition, "Nothing happens by blind chance (in mundo non datur casus)," is an à priori law of nature. The case is the same with the proposition, "Necessity in nature is not blind," that is, it is conditioned, consequently intelligible necessity (non datur fatum). Both laws subject the play of change to "a nature of things (as phenomena)," or, which is the same thing, to the unity of the understanding, and through the understanding alone can changes belong to an experience, as the synthetical unity of phenomena. Both belong to the class of dynamical principles. The former is properly a consequence of the principle of causality—one of the analogies of experience. The latter belongs to the principles of modality, which to the determination of causality adds the conception of necessity, which is itself, however, subject to a rule of the understanding. The principle of continuity forbids any leap in the series of phenomena regarded as changes (in mundo non datur saltus); and likewise, in the complex of all empirical intuitions in space, any break or hiatus between two phenomena (non datur hiatus)—for we can so express the principle, that experience can admit nothing which proves the existence of a vacuum, or which even admits it as a part of an empirical synthesis. For, as regards a vacuum or void, which we may cogitate as out and beyond the field of possible experience (the world), such a question cannot come before the tribunal of mere understanding, which decides only upon questions that concern the employment of given phenomena for the construction of empirical cognition. It is rather a problem for ideal reason, which passes beyond the sphere of a possible experience and aims at forming a judgement of that which surrounds and circumscribes it, and the proper place for the consideration of it is the transcendental dialectic. These four propositions, "In mundo non datur hiatus, non datur saltus, non datur casus, non datur fatum," as well as all principles of transcendental origin, we could very easily exhibit in their proper order, that is, in conformity with the order of the categories, and assign to each its proper place. But the already practised reader will do this for himself, or discover the clue to such an arrangement. But the combined result of all is simply this, to admit into the empirical synthesis nothing which might cause a break in or be foreign to the understanding and the continuous connection of all phenomena, that is, the unity of the conceptions of the understanding. For in the understanding alone is the unity of experience, in which all perceptions must have their assigned place, possible.

Whether the field of possibility be greater than that of reality, and whether the field of the latter be itself greater than that of necessity, are interesting enough questions, and quite capable of synthetic solution, questions, however, which come under the jurisdiction of reason alone. For they are tantamount to asking whether all things as phenomena do without exception belong to the complex and connected whole of a single experience, of which every given perception is a part which therefore cannot be conjoined with any other phenomena—or, whether my perceptions can belong to more than one possible experience? The understanding gives to experience, according to the subjective and formal conditions, of sensibility as well as of apperception, the rules which alone make this experience possible. Other forms of intuition besides those of space and time, other forms of understanding besides the discursive forms of thought, or of cognition by means of conceptions, we can neither imagine nor make intelligible to ourselves; and even if we could, they would still not belong to experience, which is the only mode of cognition by which objects are presented to us. Whether other perceptions besides those which belong to the total of our possible experience, and consequently whether some other sphere of matter exists, the understanding has no power to decide, its proper occupation being with the synthesis of that which is given. Moreover, the poverty of the usual arguments which go to prove the existence of a vast sphere of possibility, of which all that is real (every object of experience) is but a small part, is very remarkable. "All real is possible"; from this follows naturally, according to the logical laws of conversion, the particular proposition: "Some possible is real." Now this seems to be equivalent to: "Much is possible that is not real." No doubt it does seem as if we ought to consider the sum of the possible to be greater than that of the real, from the fact that something must be added to the former to constitute the latter. But this notion of adding to the possible is absurd. For that which is not in the sum of the possible, and consequently requires to be added to it, is manifestly impossible. In addition to accordance with the formal conditions of experience, the understanding requires a connection with some perception; but that which is connected with this perception is real, even although it is not immediately perceived. But that another series of phenomena, in complete coherence with that which is given in perception, consequently more than one all-embracing experience is possible, is an inference which cannot be concluded from the data given us by experience, and still less without any data at all. That which is possible only under conditions which are themselves merely possible, is not possible in any respect. And yet we can find no more certain ground on which to base the discussion of the question whether the sphere of possibility is wider than that of experience.

I have merely mentioned these questions, that in treating of the conception of the understanding, there might be no omission of anything that, in the common opinion, belongs to them. In reality, however, the notion of absolute possibility (possibility which is valid in every respect) is not a mere conception of the understanding, which can be employed empirically, but belongs to reason alone, which passes the bounds of all empirical use of the understanding. We have, therefore, contented ourselves with a merely critical remark, leaving the subject to be explained in the sequel.

Before concluding this fourth section, and at the same time the system of all principles of the pure understanding, it seems proper to mention the reasons which induced me to term the principles of modality postulates. This expression I do not here use in the sense which some more recent philosophers, contrary to its meaning with mathematicians, to whom the word properly belongs, attach to it—that of a proposition, namely, immediately certain, requiring neither deduction nor proof. For if, in the case of synthetical propositions, however evident they may be, we accord to them without deduction, and merely on the strength of their own pretensions, unqualified belief, all critique of the understanding is entirely lost; and, as there is no want of bold pretensions, which the common belief (though for the philosopher this is no credential) does not reject, the understanding lies exposed to every delusion and conceit, without the power of refusing its assent to those assertions, which, though illegitimate, demand acceptance as veritable axioms. When, therefore, to the conception of a thing an à priori determination is synthetically added, such a proposition must obtain, if not a proof, at least a deduction of the legitimacy of its assertion.

The principles of modality are, however, not objectively synthetical, for the predicates of possibility, reality, and necessity do not in the least augment the conception of that of which they are affirmed, inasmuch as they contribute nothing to the representation of the object. But as they are, nevertheless, always synthetical, they are so merely subjectively. That is to say, they have a reflective power, and apply to the conception of a thing, of which, in other respects, they affirm nothing, the faculty of cognition in which the conception originates and has its seat. So that if the conception merely agree with the formal conditions of experience, its object is called possible; if it is in connection with perception, and determined thereby, the object is real; if it is determined according to conceptions by means of the connection of perceptions, the object is called necessary. The principles of modality therefore predicate of a conception nothing more than the procedure of the faculty of cognition which generated it. Now a postulate in mathematics is a practical proposition which contains nothing but the synthesis by which we present an object to ourselves, and produce the conception of it, for example—"With a given line, to describe a circle upon a plane, from a given point"; and such a proposition does not admit of proof, because the procedure, which it requires, is exactly that by which alone it is possible to generate the conception of such a figure. With the same right, accordingly, can we postulate the principles of modality, because they do not augment[27] the conception of a thing but merely indicate the manner in which it is connected with the faculty of cognition.

GENERAL REMARK ON THE SYSTEM OF PRINCIPLES.

It is very remarkable that we cannot perceive the possibility of a thing from the category alone, but must always have an intuition, by which to make evident the objective reality of the pure conception of the understanding. Take, for example, the categories of relation. How (1) a thing can exist only as a subject, and not as a mere determination of other things, that is, can be substance; or how (2), because something exists, some other thing must exist, consequently how a thing can be a cause; or how (3), when several things exist, from the fact that one of these things exists, some consequence to the others follows, and reciprocally, and in this way a community of substances can be possible— are questions whose solution cannot be obtained from mere conceptions. The very same is the case with the other categories; for example, how a thing can be of the same sort with many others, that is, can be a quantity, and so on. So long as we have not intuition we cannot know whether we do really think an object by the categories, and where an object can anywhere be found to cohere with them, and thus the truth is established, that the categories are not in themselves cognitions, but mere forms of thought for the construction of cognitions from given intuitions. For the same reason is it true that from categories alone no synthetical proposition can be made. For example: "In every existence there is substance," that is, something that can exist only as a subject and not as mere predicate; or, "Everything is a quantity"—to construct propositions such as these, we require something to enable us to go out beyond the given conception and connect another with it. For the same reason the attempt to prove a synthetical proposition by means of mere conceptions, for example: "Everything that exists contingently has a cause," has never succeeded. We could never get further than proving that, without this relation to conceptions, we could not conceive the existence of the contingent, that is, could not à priori through the understanding cognize the existence of such a thing; but it does not hence follow that this is also the condition of the possibility of the thing itself that is said to be contingent. If, accordingly; we look back to our proof of the principle of causality, we shall find that we were able to prove it as valid only of objects of possible experience, and, indeed, only as itself the principle of the possibility of experience, Consequently of the cognition of an object given in empirical intuition, and not from mere conceptions. That, however, the proposition: "Everything that is contingent must have a cause," is evident to every one merely from conceptions, is not to be denied. But in this case the conception of the contingent is cogitated as involving not the category of modality (as that the non-existence of which can be conceived) but that of relation (as that which can exist only as the consequence of something else), and so it is really an identical proposition: "That which can exist only as a consequence, has a cause." In fact, when we have to give examples of contingent existence, we always refer to changes, and not merely to the possibility of conceiving the opposite.[28] But change is an event, which, as such, is possible only through a cause, and considered per se its non-existence is therefore possible, and we become cognizant of its contingency from the fact that it can exist only as the effect of a cause. Hence, if a thing is assumed to be contingent, it is an analytical proposition to say, it has a cause.

But it is still more remarkable that, to understand the possibility of things according to the categories and thus to demonstrate the objective reality of the latter, we require not merely intuitions, but external intuitions. If, for example, we take the pure conceptions of relation, we find that (1) for the purpose of presenting to the conception of substance something permanent in intuition corresponding thereto and thus of demonstrating the objective reality of this conception, we require an intuition (of matter) in space, because space alone is permanent and determines things as such, while time, and with it all that is in the internal sense, is in a state of continual flow; (2) in order to represent change as the intuition corresponding to the conception of causality, we require the representation of motion as change in space; in fact, it is through it alone that changes, the possibility of which no pure understanding can perceive, are capable of being intuited. Change is the connection of determinations contradictorily opposed to each other in the existence of one and the same thing. Now, how it is possible that out of a given state one quite opposite to it in the same thing should follow, reason without an example can not only not conceive, but cannot even make intelligible without intuition; and this intuition is the motion of a point in space; the existence of which in different spaces (as a consequence of opposite determinations) alone makes the intuition of change possible. For, in order to make even internal change cognitable, we require to represent time, as the form of the internal sense, figuratively by a line, and the internal change by the drawing of that line (motion), and consequently are obliged to employ external intuition to be able to represent the successive existence of ourselves in different states. The proper ground of this fact is that all change to be perceived as change presupposes something permanent in intuition, while in the internal sense no permanent intuition is to be found. Lastly, the objective possibility of the category of community cannot be conceived by mere reason, and consequently its objective reality cannot be demonstrated without an intuition, and that external in space. For how can we conceive the possibility of community, that is, when several substances exist, that some effect on the existence of the one follows from the existence of the other, and recip-rocally, and therefore that, because something exists in the latter, something else must exist in the former, which could not be understood from its own existence alone? For this is the very essence of community—which is inconceivable as a property of things which are perfectly isolated. Hence, Leibnitz, in attributing to the substances of the world—as cogitated by the understanding alone—a community, required the mediating aid of a divinity; for, from their existence, such a property seemed to him with justice inconceivable. But we can very easily conceive the possibility of community (of substances as phenomena) if we represent them to ourselves as in space, consequently in external intuition. For external intuition contains in itself à priori formal external rela-tions, as the conditions of the possibility of the real relations of action and reaction, and therefore of the possibility of community. With the same ease can it be demonstrated, that the possibility of things as quantities, and consequently the objective reality of the category of quantity, can be grounded only in external intuition, and that by its means alone is the notion of quantity appropriated by the internal sense. But I must avoid prolixity, and leave the task of illustrating this by examples to the reader's own reflection.

The above remarks are of the greatest importance, not only for the confirmation of our previous confutation of idealism, but still more when the subject of self-cognition by mere internal consciousness and the determination of our own nature without the aid of external empirical intuitions is under discussion, for the indication of the grounds of the possibility of such a cognition.

The result of the whole of this part of the analytic of principles is, therefore: "All principles of the pure understanding are nothing more than à priori principles of the possibility of experience, and to experience alone do all à priori synthetical propositions apply and relate"; indeed, their possibility itself rests entirely on this relation.

CHAPTER III OF THE GROUND OF THE DIVISION OF ALL OBJECTS INTO PHENOMENA AND NOUMENA

We have now not only traversed the region of the pure understanding and carefully surveyed every part of it, but we have also measured it, and assigned to everything therein its proper place. But this land is an island, and enclosed by nature herself within unchangeable limits. It is the land of truth (an attractive word), surrounded by a wide and stormy ocean, the region of illusion, where many a fog-bank, many an iceberg, seems to the mariner, on his voyage of discovery, a new country, and, while constantly deluding him with vain hopes, engages him in dangerous adventures, from which he never can desist, and which yet he never can bring to a termination. But before venturing upon this sea, in order to explore it in its whole extent, and to arrive at a certainty whether anything is to be discovered there, it will not be without advantage if we cast our eyes upon the chart of the land that we are about to leave, and to ask ourselves, firstly, whether we cannot rest perfectly contented with what it contains, or whether we must not of necessity be contented with it, if we can find nowhere else a solid foundation to build upon; and, secondly, by what title we possess this land itself, and how we hold it secure against all hostile claims? Although, in the course of our analytic, we have already given sufficient answers to these questions, yet a summary recapitulation of these solutions may be useful in strengthening our conviction, by uniting in one point the momenta of the arguments.

We have seen that everything which the understanding draws from itself, without borrowing from experience, it nevertheless possesses only for the behoof and use of experience. The principles of the pure understanding, whether constitutive à priori (as the mathematical principles), or merely regulative (as the dynamical), contain nothing but the pure schema, as it were, of possible experience. For experience possesses its unity from the synthetical unity which the understanding, originally and from itself, imparts to the synthesis of the imagination in relation to apperception, and in à priori relation to and agreement with which phenomena, as data for a possible cognition, must stand. But although these rules of the understanding are not only à priori true, but the very source of all truth, that is, of the accordance of our cognition with objects, and on this ground, that they contain the basis of the possibility of experience, as the ensemble of all cognition, it seems to us not enough to propound what is true—we desire also to be told what we want to know. If, then, we learn nothing more by this critical examination than what we should have practised in the merely empirical use of the understanding, without any such subtle inquiry, the presumption is that the advantage we reap from it is not worth the labour bestowed upon it. It may certainly be answered that no rash curiosity is more prejudicial to the enlargement of our knowledge than that which must know beforehand the utility of this or that piece of information which we seek, before we have entered on the needful investigations, and before one could form the least conception of its utility, even though it were placed before our eyes. But there is one advantage in such transcendental inquiries which can be made comprehensible to the dullest and most reluctant learner—this, namely, that the understanding which is occupied merely with empirical exercise, and does not reflect on the sources of its own cognition, may exercise its functions very well and very successfully, but is quite unable to do one thing, and that of very great importance, to determine, namely, the bounds that limit its employment, and to know what lies within or without its own sphere. This purpose can be obtained only by such profound investigations as we have instituted. But if it cannot distinguish whether certain questions lie within its horizon or not, it can never be sure either as to its claims or possessions, but must lay its account with many humiliating corrections, when it transgresses, as it unavoidably will, the limits of its own territory, and loses itself in fanciful opinions and blinding illusions.

That the understanding, therefore, cannot make of its à priori principles, or even of its conceptions, other than an empirical use, is a proposition which leads to the most important results. A transcendental use is made of a conception in a fundamental proposition or principle, when it is referred to things in general and considered as things in themselves; an empirical use, when it is referred merely to phenomena, that is, to objects of a possible experience. That the latter use of a conception is the only admissible one is evident from the reasons following. For every conception are requisite, firstly, the logical form of a conception (of thought) general; and, secondly, the possibility of presenting to this an object to which it may apply. Failing this latter, it has no sense, and utterly void of content, although it may contain the logical function for constructing a conception from certain data. Now, object cannot be given to a conception otherwise than by intuition, and, even if a pure intuition antecedent to the object is à priori possible, this pure intuition can itself obtain objective validity only from empirical intuition, of which it is itself but the form. All conceptions, therefore, and with them all principles, however high the degree of their à priori possibility, relate to empirical intuitions, that is, to data towards a possible experience. Without this they possess no objective validity, but are mere play of imagination or of understanding with images or notions. Let us take, for example, the conceptions of mathematics, and first in its pure intuitions. "Space has three dimensions"—"Between two points there can be only one straight line," etc. Although all these principles, and the representation of the object with which this science occupies itself, are generated in the mind entirely à priori, they would nevertheless have no significance if we were not always able to exhibit their significance in and by means of phenomena (empirical objects). Hence it is requisite that an abstract conception be made sensuous, that is, that an object corresponding to it in intuition be forthcoming, otherwise the conception remains, as we say, without sense, that is, without meaning. Mathematics fulfils this requirement by the construction of the figure, which is a phenomenon evident to the senses. The same science finds support and significance in number; this in its turn finds it in the fingers, or in counters, or in lines and points. The conception itself is always produced à priori, together with the synthetical principles or formulas from such conceptions; but the proper employment of them, and their application to objects, can exist nowhere but in experience, the possibility of which, as regards its form, they contain à priori.

That this is also the case with all of the categories and the principles based upon them is evident from the fact that we cannot render intelligible the possibility of an object corresponding to them without having recourse to the conditions of sensibility, consequently, to the form of phenomena, to which, as their only proper objects, their use must therefore be confined, inasmuch as, if this condition is removed, all significance, that is, all relation to an object, disappears, and no example can be found to make it comprehensible what sort of things we ought to think under such conceptions.

The conception of quantity cannot be explained except by saying that it is the determination of a thing whereby it can be cogitated how many times one is placed in it. But this "how many times" is based upon successive repetition, consequently upon time and the synthesis of the homogeneous therein. Reality, in contradistinction to negation, can be explained only by cogitating a time which is either filled therewith or is void. If I leave out the notion of permanence (which is existence in all time), there remains in the conception of substance nothing but the logical notion of subject, a notion of which I endeavour to realize by representing to myself something that can exist only as a subject. But not only am I perfectly ignorant of any conditions under which this logical prerogative can belong to a thing, I can make nothing out of the notion, and draw no inference from it, because no object to which to apply the conception is determined, and we consequently do not know whether it has any meaning at all. In like manner, if I leave out the notion of time, in which something follows upon some other thing in conformity with a rule, I can find nothing in the pure category, except that there is a something of such a sort that from it a conclusion may be drawn as to the existence of some other thing. But in this case it would not only be impossible to distinguish between a cause and an effect, but, as this power to draw conclusions requires conditions of which I am quite ignorant, the conception is not determined as to the mode in which it ought to apply to an object. The so-called principle: "Everything that is contingent has a cause," comes with a gravity and self-assumed authority that seems to require no support from without. But, I ask, what is meant by contingent? The answer is that the non-existence of which is possible. But I should like very well to know by what means this possibility of non-existence is to be cognized, if we do not represent to ourselves a succession in the series of phenomena, and in this succession an existence which follows a non-existence, or conversely, consequently, change. For to say, that the non-existence of a thing is not self-contradictory is a lame appeal to a logical condition, which is no doubt a necessary condition of the existence of the conception, but is far from being sufficient for the real objective possibility of non-existence. I can annihilate in thought every existing substance without self-contradiction, but I cannot infer from this their objective contingency in existence, that is to say, the possibility of their non-existence in itself. As regards the category of community, it may easily be inferred that, as the pure categories of substance and causality are incapable of a definition and explanation sufficient to determine their object without the aid of intuition, the category of reciprocal causality in the relation of substances to each other (commercium) is just as little susceptible thereof. Possibility, existence, and necessity nobody has ever yet been able to explain without being guilty of manifest tautology, when the definition has been drawn entirely from the pure understanding. For the substitution of the logical possibility of the conception—the condition of which is that it be not self-contradictory, for the transcendental possibility of things—the condition of which is that there be an object corresponding to the conception, is a trick which can only deceive the inexperienced.[29]

It follows incontestably, that the pure conceptions of the understanding are incapable of transcendental, and must always be of empirical use alone, and that the principles of the pure understanding relate only to the general conditions of a possible experience, to objects of the senses, and never to things in general, apart from the mode in which we intuite them.

Transcendental analytic has accordingly this important result, to wit, that the understanding is competent effect nothing à priori, except the anticipation of the form of a possible experience in general, and that, as that which is not phenomenon cannot be an object of experience, it can never overstep the limits of sensibility, within which alone objects are presented to us. Its principles are merely principles of the exposition of phenomena, and the proud name of an ontology, which professes to present synthetical cognitions à priori of things in general in a systematic doctrine, must give place to the modest title of analytic of the pure understanding.

Thought is the act of referring a given intuition to an object. If the mode of this intuition is unknown to us, the object is merely transcendental, and the conception of the understanding is employed only transcendentally, that is, to produce unity in the thought of a manifold in general. Now a pure category, in which all conditions of sensuous intuition—as the only intuition we possess—are abstracted, does not determine an object, but merely expresses the thought of an object in general, according to different modes. Now, to employ a conception, the function of judgement is required, by which an object is subsumed under the conception, consequently the at least formal condition, under which something can be given in intuition. Failing this condition of judgement (schema), subsumption is impossible; for there is in such a case nothing given, which may be subsumed under the conception. The merely transcendental use of the categories is therefore, in fact, no use at all and has no determined, or even, as regards its form, determinable object. Hence it follows that the pure category is incompetent to establish a synthetical à priori principle, and that the principles of the pure understanding are only of empirical and never of transcendental use, and that beyond the sphere of possible experience no synthetical à priori principles are possible.

It may be advisable, therefore, to express ourselves thus. The pure categories, apart from the formal conditions of sensibility, have a merely transcendental meaning, but are nevertheless not of transcendental use, because this is in itself impossible, inasmuch as all the conditions of any employment or use of them (in judgements) are absent, to wit, the formal conditions of the subsumption of an object under these conceptions. As, therefore, in the character of pure categories, they must be employed empirically, and cannot be employed transcendentally, they are of no use at all, when separated from sensibility, that is, they cannot be applied to an object. They are merely the pure form of the employment of the understanding in respect of objects in general and of thought, without its being at the same time possible to think or to determine any object by their means. But there lurks at the foundation of this subject an illusion which it is very difficult to avoid. The categories are not based, as regards their origin, upon sensibility, like the forms of intuition, space, and time; they seem, therefore, to be capable of an application beyond the sphere of sensuous objects. But this is not the case. They are nothing but mere forms of thought, which contain only the logical faculty of uniting à priori in consciousness the manifold given in intuition. Apart, then, from the only intuition possible for us, they have still less meaning than the pure sensuous forms, space and time, for through them an object is at least given, while a mode of connection of the manifold, when the intuition which alone gives the manifold is wanting, has no meaning at all. At the same time, when we designate certain objects as phenomena or sensuous existences, thus distinguishing our mode of intuiting them from their own nature as things in themselves, it is evident that by this very distinction we as it were place the latter, considered in this their own nature, although we do not so intuite them, in opposition to the former, or, on the other hand, we do so place other possible things, which are not objects of our senses, but are cogitated by the understanding alone, and call them intelligible existences (noumena). Now the question arises whether the pure conceptions of our understanding do possess significance in respect of these latter, and may possibly be a mode of cognizing them.

But we are met at the very commencement with an ambiguity, which may easily occasion great misapprehension. The understanding, when it terms an object in a certain relation phenomenon, at the same time forms out of this relation a representation or notion of an object in itself, and hence believes that it can form also conceptions of such objects. Now as the understanding possesses no other fundamental conceptions besides the categories, it takes for granted that an object considered as a thing in itself must be capable of being thought by means of these pure conceptions, and is thereby led to hold the perfectly undetermined conception of an intelligible existence, a something out of the sphere of our sensibility, for a determinate conception of an existence which we can cognize in some way or other by means of the understanding.

If, by the term noumenon, we understand a thing so far as it is not an object of our sensuous intuition, thus making abstraction of our mode of intuiting it, this is a noumenon in the negative sense of the word. But if we understand by it an object of a non-sensuous intuition, we in this case assume a peculiar mode of intuition, an intellectual intuition, to wit, which does not, however, belong to us, of the very possibility of which we have no notion—and this is a noumenon in the positive sense.

The doctrine of sensibility is also the doctrine of noumena in the negative sense, that is, of things which the understanding is obliged to cogitate apart from any relation to our mode of intuition, consequently not as mere phenomena, but as things in themselves. But the understanding at the same time comprehends that it cannot employ its categories for the consideration of things in themselves, because these possess significance only in relation to the unity of intuitions in space and time, and that they are competent to determine this unity by means of general à priori connecting conceptions only on account of the pure ideality of space and time. Where this unity of time is not to be met with, as is the case with noumena, the whole use, indeed the whole meaning of the categories is entirely lost, for even the possibility of things to correspond to the categories is in this case incomprehensible. On this point, I need only refer the reader to what I have said at the commencement of the General Remark appended to the foregoing chapter. Now, the possibility of a thing can never be proved from the fact that the conception of it is not self-contradictory, but only by means of an intuition corresponding to the conception. If, therefore, we wish to apply the categories to objects which cannot be regarded as phenomena, we must have an intuition different from the sensuous, and in this case the objects would be a noumena in the positive sense of the word. Now, as such an intuition, that is, an intellectual intuition, is no part of our faculty of cognition, it is absolutely impossible for the categories to possess any application beyond the limits of experience. It may be true that there are intelligible existences to which our faculty of sensuous intuition has no relation, and cannot be applied, but our conceptions of the understanding, as mere forms of thought for our sensuous intuition, do not extend to these. What, therefore, we call noumenon must be understood by us as such in a negative sense.

If I take away from an empirical intuition all thought (by means of the categories), there remains no cognition of any object; for by means of mere intuition nothing is cogitated, and, from the existence of such or such an affection of sensibility in me, it does not follow that this affection or representation has any relation to an object without me. But if I take away all intuition, there still remains the form of thought, that is, the mode of determining an object for the manifold of a possible intuition. Thus the categories do in some measure really extend further than sensuous intuition, inasmuch as they think objects in general, without regard to the mode (of sensibility) in which these objects are given. But they do not for this reason apply to and determine a wider sphere of objects, because we cannot assume that such can be given, without presupposing the possibility of another than the sensuous mode of intuition, a supposition we are not justified in making.

I call a conception problematical which contains in itself no contradiction, and which is connected with other cognitions as a limitation of given conceptions, but whose objective reality cannot be cognized in any manner. The conception of a noumenon, that is, of a thing which must be cogitated not as an object of sense, but as a thing in itself (solely through the pure understanding), is not self-contradictory, for we are not entitled to maintain that sensibility is the only possible mode of intuition. Nay, further, this conception is necessary to restrain sensuous intuition within the bounds of phenomena, and thus to limit the objective validity of sensuous cognition; for things in themselves, which lie beyond its province, are called noumena for the very purpose of indicating that this cognition does not extend its application to all that the understanding thinks. But, after all, the possibility of such noumena is quite incomprehensible, and beyond the sphere of phenomena, all is for us a mere void; that is to say, we possess an understanding whose province does problematically extend beyond this sphere, but we do not possess an intuition, indeed, not even the conception of a possible intuition, by means of which objects beyond the region of sensibility could be given us, and in reference to which the understanding might be employed assertorically. The conception of a noumenon is therefore merely a limitative conception and therefore only of negative use. But it is not an arbitrary or fictitious notion, but is connected with the limitation of sensibility, without, however, being capable of presenting us with any positive datum beyond this sphere.

The division of objects into phenomena and noumena, and of the world into a mundus sensibilis and intelligibilis is therefore quite inadmissible in a positive sense, although conceptions do certainly admit of such a division; for the class of noumena have no determinate object corresponding to them, and cannot therefore possess objective validity. If we abandon the senses, how can it be made conceivable that the categories (which are the only conceptions that could serve as conceptions for noumena) have any sense or meaning at all, inasmuch as something more than the mere unity of thought, namely, a possible intuition, is requisite for their application to an object? The conception of a noumenon, considered as merely problematical, is, however, not only admissible, but, as a limitative conception of sensibility, absolutely necessary. But, in this case, a noumenon is not a particular intelligible object for our understanding; on the contrary, the kind of understanding to which it could belong is itself a problem, for we cannot form the most distant conception of the possibility of an understanding which should cognize an object, not discursively by means of categories, but intuitively in a non-sensuous intuition. Our understanding attains in this way a sort of negative extension. That is to say, it is not limited by, but rather limits, sensibility, by giving the name of noumena to things, not considered as phenomena, but as things in themselves. But it at the same time prescribes limits to itself, for it confesses itself unable to cognize these by means of the categories, and hence is compelled to cogitate them merely as an unknown something.

I find, however, in the writings of modern authors, an entirely different use of the expressions, mundus sensibilis and intelligibilis, which quite departs from the meaning of the ancients—an acceptation in which, indeed, there is to be found no difficulty, but which at the same time depends on mere verbal quibbling. According to this meaning, some have chosen to call the complex of phenomena, in so far as it is intuited, mundus sensibilis, but in so far as the connection thereof is cogitated according to general laws of thought, mundus intelligibilis. Astronomy, in so far as we mean by the word the mere observation of the starry heaven, may represent the former; a system of astronomy, such as the Copernican or Newtonian, the latter. But such twisting of words is a mere sophistical subterfuge, to avoid a difficult question, by modifying its meaning to suit our own convenience. To be sure, understanding and reason are employed in the cognition of phenomena; but the question is, whether these can be applied when the object is not a phenomenon and in this sense we regard it if it is cogitated as given to the understanding alone, and not to the senses. The question therefore is whether, over and above the empirical use of the understanding, a transcendental use is possible, which applies to the noumenon as an object. This question we have answered in the negative.

When therefore we say, the senses represent objects as they appear, the understanding as they are, the latter statement must not be understood in a transcendental, but only in an empirical signification, that is, as they must be represented in the complete connection of phenomena, and not according to what they may be, apart from their relation to possible experience, consequently not as objects of the pure understanding. For this must ever remain unknown to us. Nay, it is also quite unknown to us whether any such transcendental or extraordinary cognition is possible under any circumstances, at least, whether it is possible by means of our categories. Understanding and sensibility, with us, can determine objects only in conjunction. If we separate them, we have intuitions without conceptions, or conceptions without intuitions; in both cases, representations, which we cannot apply to any determinate object.

If, after all our inquiries and explanations, any one still hesitates to abandon the mere transcendental use of the categories, let him attempt to construct with them a synthetical proposition. It would, of course, be unnecessary for this purpose to construct an analytical proposition, for that does not extend the sphere of the understanding, but, being concerned only about what is cogitated in the conception itself, it leaves it quite undecided whether the conception has any relation to objects, or merely indicates the unity of thought—complete abstraction being made of the modi in which an object may be given: in such a proposition, it is sufficient for the understanding to know what lies in the conception—to what it applies is to it indifferent. The attempt must therefore be made with a synthetical and so-called transcendental principle, for example: "Everything that exists, exists as substance," or, "Everything that is contingent exists as an effect of some other thing, viz., of its cause." Now I ask, whence can the understanding draw these synthetical propositions, when the conceptions contained therein do not relate to possible experience but to things in themselves (noumena)? Where is to be found the third term, which is always requisite PURE site in a synthetical proposition, which may connect in the same proposition conceptions which have no logical (analytical) connection with each other? The proposition never will be demonstrated, nay, more, the possibility of any such pure assertion never can be shown, without making reference to the empirical use of the understanding, and thus, ipso facto, completely renouncing pure and non-sensuous judgement. Thus the conception of pure and merely intelligible objects is completely void of all principles of its application, because we cannot imagine any mode in which they might be given, and the problematical thought which leaves a place open for them serves only, like a void space, to limit the use of empirical principles, without containing at the same time any other object of cognition beyond their sphere.

APPENDIX

Of the Equivocal Nature or Amphiboly of the Conceptions of Reflection from the Confusion of the Transcendental with the Empirical use of the Understanding.

Reflection (reflexio) is not occupied about objects themselves, for the purpose of directly obtaining conceptions of them, but is that state of the mind in which we set ourselves to discover the subjective conditions under which we obtain conceptions. It is the consciousness of the relation of given representations to the different sources or faculties of cognition, by which alone their relation to each other can be rightly determined. The first question which occurs in considering our representations is to what faculty of cognition do they belong? To the understanding or to the senses? Many judgements are admitted to be true from mere habit or inclination; but, because reflection neither precedes nor follows, it is held to be a judgement that has its origin in the understanding. All judgements do not require examination, that is, investigation into the grounds of their truth. For, when they are immediately certain (for example: "Between two points there can be only one straight line"), no better or less mediate test of their truth can be found than that which they themselves contain and express. But all judgement, nay, all comparisons require reflection, that is, a distinction of the faculty of cognition to which the given conceptions belong. The act whereby I compare my representations with the faculty of cognition which originates them, and whereby I distinguish whether they are compared with each other as belonging to the pure understanding or to sensuous intuition, I term transcendental reflection. Now, the relations in which conceptions can stand to each other are those of identity and difference, agreement and opposition, of the internal and external, finally, of the determinable and the determining (matter and form). The proper determination of these relations rests on the question, to what faculty of cognition they subjectively belong, whether to sensibility or understanding? For, on the manner in which we solve this question depends the manner in which we must cogitate these relations.

Before constructing any objective judgement, we compare the conceptions that are to be placed in the judgement, and observe whether there exists identity (of many representations in one conception), if a general judgement is to be constructed, or difference, if a particular; whether there is agreement when affirmative; and opposition when negative judgements are to be constructed, and so on. For this reason we ought to call these conceptions, conceptions of comparison (conceptus comparationis). But as, when the question is not as to the logical form, but as to the content of conceptions, that is to say, whether the things themselves are identical or different, in agreement or opposition, and so on, the things can have a twofold relation to our faculty of cognition, to wit, a relation either to sensibility or to the understanding, and as on this relation depends their relation to each other, transcendental reflection, that is, the relation of given representations to one or the other faculty of cognition, can alone determine this latter relation. Thus we shall not be able to discover whether the things are identical or different, in agreement or opposition, etc., from the mere conception of the things by means of comparison (comparatio), but only by distinguishing the mode of cognition to which they belong, in other words, by means of transcendental reflection. We may, therefore, with justice say, that logical reflection is mere comparison, for in it no account is taken of the faculty of cognition to which the given conceptions belong, and they are consequently, as far as regards their origin, to be treated as homogeneous; while transcendental reflection (which applies to the objects themselves) contains the ground of the possibility of objective comparison of representations with each other, and is therefore very different from the former, because the faculties of cognition to which they belong are not even the same. Transcendental reflection is a duty which no one can neglect who wishes to establish an à priori judgement upon things. We shall now proceed to fulfil this duty, and thereby throw not a little light on the question as to the determination of the proper business of the understanding.

1. Identity and Difference. When an object is presented to us several times, but always with the same internal determinations (qualitas et quantitas), it, if an object of pure understanding, is always the same, not several things, but only one thing (numerica identitas); but if a phenomenon, we do not concern ourselves with comparing the conception of the thing with the conception of some other, but, although they may be in this respect perfectly the same, the difference of place at the same time is a sufficient ground for asserting the numerical difference of these objects (of sense). Thus, in the case of two drops of water, we may make complete abstraction of all internal difference (quality and quantity), and, the fact that they are intuited at the same time in different places, is sufficient to justify us in holding them to be numerically different. Leibnitz regarded phenomena as things in themselves, consequently as intelligibilia, that is, objects of pure understanding (although, on account of the confused nature of their representations, he gave them the name of phenomena), and in this case his principle of the indiscernible (principium identatis indiscernibilium) is not to be impugned. But, as phenomena are objects of sensibility, and, as the understanding, in respect of them, must be employed empirically and not purely or transcendentally, plurality and numerical difference are given by space itself as the condition of external phenomena. For one part of space, although it may be perfectly similar and equal to another part, is still without it, and for this reason alone is different from the latter, which is added to it in order to make up a greater space. It follows that this must hold good of all things that are in the different parts of space at the same time, however similar and equal one may be to another.

2. Agreement and Opposition. When reality is represented by the pure understanding (realitas noumenon), opposition between realities is incogitable—such a relation, that is, that when these realities are connected in one subject, they annihilate the effects of each other and may be represented in the formula $3 - 3 = 0$. On the other hand, the real in a phenomenon (realitas phaenomenon) may very well be in mutual opposition, and, when united in the same subject, the one may completely or in part annihilate the effect or consequence of the other; as in the case of two moving forces in the same straight line drawing or impelling a point in opposite directions, or in the case of a pleasure counterbalancing a certain amount of pain.

3. The Internal and External. In an object of the pure understanding, only that is internal which has no relation (as regards its existence) to anything different from itself. On the other hand, the internal determinations of a substantia phaenomenon in space are nothing but relations, and it is itself nothing more than a complex of mere relations. Substance in space we are cognizant of only through forces operative in it, either drawing others towards itself (attraction), or preventing others from forcing into itself (repulsion and impenetrability). We know no other properties that make up the concep-

tion of substance phenomenal in space, and which we term matter. On the other hand, as an object of the pure understanding, every substance must have internal determination and forces. But what other internal attributes of such an object can I think than those which my internal sense presents to me? That, to wit, which in either itself thought, or something analogous to it. Hence Leibnitz, who looked upon things as noumena, after denying them everything like external relation, and therefore also composition or combination, declared that all substances, even the component parts of matter, were simple substances with powers of representation, in one word, monads.

4. Matter and Form. These two conceptions lie at the foundation of all other reflection, so inseparably are they connected with every mode of exercising the understanding. The former denotes the determinable in general, the second its determination, both in a transcendental sense, abstraction being made of every difference in that which is given, and of the mode in which it is determined. Logicians formerly termed the universal, matter, the specific difference of this or that part of the universal, form. In a judgement one may call the given conceptions logical matter (for the judgement), the relation of these to each other (by means of the copula), the form of the judgement. In an object, the composite parts thereof (essentialia) are the matter; the mode in which they are connected in the object, the form. In respect to things in general, unlimited reality was regarded as the matter of all possibility, the limitation thereof (negation) as the form, by which one thing is distinguished from another according to transcendental conceptions. The understanding demands that something be given (at least in the conception), in order to be able to determine it in a certain manner. Hence, in a conception of the pure understanding, the matter precedes the form, and for this reason Leibnitz first assumed the existence of things (monads) and of an internal power of representation in them, in order to found upon this their external relation and the community their state (that is, of their representations). Hence, with him, space and time were possible—the former through the relation of substances, the latter through the connection of their determinations with each other, as causes and effects. And so would it really be, if the pure understanding were capable of an immediate application to objects, and if space and time were determinations of things in themselves. But being merely sensuous intuitions, in which we determine all objects solely as phenomena, the form of intuition (as a subjective property of sensibility) must antecede all matter (sensations), consequently space and time must antecede all phenomena and all data of experience, and rather make experience itself possible. But the intellectual philosopher could not endure that the form should precede the things themselves and determine their possibility; an objection perfectly correct, if we assume that we intuite things as they are, although with confused representation. But as sensuous intuition is a peculiar subjective condition, which is à priori at the foundation of all perception, and the form of which is primitive, the form must be given per se, and so far from matter (or the things themselves which appear) lying at the foundation of experience (as we must conclude, if we judge by mere conceptions), the very possibility of itself presupposes, on the contrary, a given formal intuition (space and time).

REMARK ON THE AMPHIBOLY OF THE CONCEPTIONS OF REFLECTION.

Let me be allowed to term the position which we assign to a conception either in the sensibility or in the pure understanding, the transcendental place. In this manner, the appointment of the position which must be taken by each conception according to the difference in its use, and the directions for determining this place to all conceptions according to rules, would be a transcendental topic, a doctrine which would thoroughly shield us from the surreptitious devices of the pure understanding and the delusions which thence arise, as it would always distinguish to what faculty of cognition each conception properly belonged. Every conception, every title, under which many cognitions rank together, may be called a logical place. Upon this is based the logical topic of Aristotle, of which teachers and rhetoricians could avail themselves, in order, under certain titles of thought, to observe what would best suit the matter they had to treat, and thus enable themselves to quibble and talk with fluency and an appearance of profundity.

Transcendental topic, on the contrary, contains nothing more than the above-mentioned four titles of all comparison and distinction, which differ from categories in this respect, that they do not represent the object according to that which constitutes its conception (quantity, reality), but set forth merely the comparison of representations, which precedes our conceptions of things. But this comparison requires a previous reflection, that is, a determination of the place to which the representations of the things which are compared belong, whether, to wit, they are cogitated by the pure understanding, or given by sensibility.

Conceptions may be logically compared without the trouble of inquiring to what faculty their objects belong, whether as noumena, to the understanding, or as phenomena, to sensibility. If, however, we wish to employ these conceptions in respect of objects, previous transcendental reflection is necessary. Without this reflection I should make a very unsafe use of these conceptions, and construct pretended synthetical propositions which critical reason cannot acknowledge and which are based solely upon a transcendental amphiboly, that is, upon a substitution of an object of pure understanding for a phenomenon.

For want of this doctrine of transcendental topic, and consequently deceived by the amphiboly of the conceptions of reflection, the celebrated Leibnitz constructed an intellectual system of the world, or rather, believed himself competent to cognize the internal nature of things, by comparing all objects merely with the understanding and the abstract formal conceptions of thought. Our table of the conceptions of reflection gives us the unexpected advantage of being able to exhibit the distinctive peculiarities of his system in all its parts, and at the same time of exposing the fundamental principle of this peculiar mode of thought, which rested upon naught but a misconception. He compared all things with each other merely by means of conceptions, and naturally found no other differences than those by which the understanding distinguishes its pure conceptions one from another. The conditions of sensuous intuition, which contain in themselves their own means of distinction, he did not look upon as primitive, because sensibility was to him but a confused mode of representation and not any particular source of representations. A phenomenon was for him the representation of the thing in itself, although distinguished from cognition by the understanding only in respect of the logical form—the former with its usual want of analysis containing, according to him, a certain mixture of collateral representations in its conception of a thing, which it is the duty of the understanding to separate and distinguish. In one word, Leibnitz intellectualized phenomena, just as Locke, in his system of noogony (if I may be allowed to make use of such expressions), sensualized the conceptions of the understanding, that is to say, declared them to be nothing more than empirical or abstract conceptions of reflection. Instead of seeking in the understanding and sensibility two different sources of representations, which, however, can present us with objective judgements of things only in conjunction, each of these great men recognized but one of these faculties, which, in their opinion, applied immediately to things in themselves, the other having no duty but that of confusing or arranging the representations of the former.

Accordingly, the objects of sense were compared by Leibnitz as things in general merely in the understanding.

1st. He compares them in regard to their identity or difference—as judged by the understanding. As, therefore, he considered merely the conceptions of objects, and not their position in intuition, in which alone objects can be given, and left quite out of sight the transcendental locale of these conceptions—whether, that is, their object ought to be classed among phenomena, or among things in themselves, it was to be expected that he should extend the application of the principle of indiscernibles, which is valid solely of conceptions of things in general, to objects of sense (mundus phaenomenon), and that he should believe that he had thereby contributed in no small degree to extend our knowledge of nature. In truth, if I cognize in all its inner determinations a drop of water as a thing in itself, I cannot look upon one drop as different from another, if the conception of the one is completely identical with that of the other. But if it is a phenomenon in space, it has a place not merely in the understanding (among conceptions), but also in sensuous external intuition (in space), and in this case, the physical locale is a matter of indifference in regard to the internal determinations of things, and one place, B, may contain a thing which is perfectly similar and equal to another in a place, A, just as well as if the two things were in every respect different from each other. Difference of place without any other conditions, makes the plurality and distinction of objects as phenomena, not only possible in itself, but even necessary. Consequently, the above so-called law is not a law of nature. It is merely an analytical rule for the comparison of things by means of mere conceptions.

2nd. The principle: "Realities (as simple affirmations) never logically contradict each other," is a proposition perfectly true respecting the relation of conceptions, but, whether as regards nature, or things in themselves (of which we have not the slightest conception), is without any the least meaning. For real opposition, in which A -B is = 0, exists everywhere, an opposition, that is, in which one reality united with another in the same subject annihilates the effects of the other—a fact which is constantly brought before our eyes by the different antagonistic actions and operations in nature, which, nevertheless, as depending on real forces, must be called realitates phaenomena. General mechanics can even present us with the empirical condition of this opposition in an à priori rule, as it directs its attention to the opposition in the direction of forces—a condition of which the transcendental conception of reality can tell us nothing. Although M. Leibnitz did not announce this proposition with precisely the pomp of a new principle, he yet employed it for the establishment of new propositions, and his followers introduced it into their Leibnitzio-Wolfian system of philosophy. According to this principle, for example, all evils are but consequences of the limited nature of created beings, that is, negations, because these are the only opposite of reality. (In the mere conception of a thing in general this is really the case, but not in things as phenomena.) In like manner, the upholders of this system deem it not only possible, but natural also, to connect and unite all reality in one being, because they acknowledge no other sort of opposition than that of contradiction (by which the conception itself of a thing is annihilated), and find themselves unable to conceive an opposition of reciprocal destruction, so to speak, in which one real cause destroys the effect of another, and the conditions of whose representation we meet with only in sensibility.

3rd. The Leibnitzian monadology has really no better foundation than on this philosopher's mode of falsely representing the difference of the internal and external solely in relation to the understanding. Substances, in general, must have something inward, which is therefore free from external relations, consequently from that of composition also. The simple—that which can be represented by a unit—is therefore the foundation of that which is internal in things in themselves. The internal state of substances cannot therefore consist in place, shape, contact, or motion, determinations which are all external relations, and we can ascribe to them no other than that whereby we internally determine our faculty of sense itself, that is to say, the state of representation. Thus, then, were constructed the monads, which were to form the elements of the universe, the active force of which consists in representation, the effects of this force being thus entirely confined to themselves.

For the same reason, his view of the possible community of substances could not represent it but as a predetermined harmony, and by no means as a physical influence. For inasmuch as everything is occupied only internally, that is, with its own representations, the state of the representations of one substance could not stand in active and living connection with that of another, but some third cause operating on all without exception was necessary to make the different states correspond with one another. And this did not happen by means of assistance applied in each particular case (systema assistentiae), but through the unity of the idea of a cause occupied and connected with all substances, in which they necessarily receive, according to the Leibnitzian school, their existence and permanence, consequently also reciprocal correspondence, according to universal laws.

4th. This philosopher's celebrated doctrine of space and time, in which he intellectualized these forms of sensibility, originated in the same delusion of transcendental reflection. If I attempt to represent by the mere understanding, the external relations of things, I can do so only by employing the conception of their reciprocal action, and if I wish to connect one state of the same thing with another state, I must avail myself of the notion of the order of cause and effect. And thus Leibnitz regarded space as a certain order in the community of substances, and time as the dynamical sequence of their states. That which space and time possess proper to themselves and independent of things, he ascribed to a necessary confusion in our conceptions of them, whereby that which is a mere form of dynamical relations is held to be a self-existent intuition, antecedent even to things themselves. Thus space and time were the intelligible form of the connection of things (substances and their states) in themselves. But things were intelligible substances (substantiae noumena). At the same time, he made these conceptions valid of phenomena, because he did not allow to sensibility a peculiar mode of intuition, but sought all, even the empirical representation of objects, in the understanding, and left to sense naught but the despicable task of confusing and disarranging the representations of the former.

But even if we could frame any synthetical proposition concerning things in themselves by means of the pure understanding (which is impossible), it could not apply to phenomena, which do not represent things in themselves. In such a case I should be obliged in transcendental reflection to compare my conceptions only under the conditions of sensibility, and so space and time would not be determinations of things in themselves, but of phenomena. What things may be in themselves, I know not and need not know, because a thing is never presented to me otherwise than as a phenomenon.

I must adopt the same mode of procedure with the other conceptions of reflection. Matter is substantia phaenomenon. That in it which is internal I seek to discover in all parts of space which it occupies, and in all the functions and operations it performs, and which are indeed never anything but phenomena of the external sense. I cannot therefore find anything that is absolutely, but only what is comparatively internal, and which itself consists of external relations. The absolutely internal in matter, and as it should be according to the pure understanding, is a mere chimera, for matter is not an object for the pure understanding. But the transcendental object, which is the foundation of the phenomenon which we call matter, is a mere nescio quid, the nature of which we could not understand, even though someone were found able to tell us. For we can understand nothing that does not bring with it something in intuition corresponding to the expressions employed. If, by the complaint of being unable to perceive the internal nature of things, it is meant that we do not comprehend by the pure understanding what the things which appear to us may be in themselves, it is a silly and unreasonable complaint; for those who talk thus really desire that we should be able to cognize, consequently to intuite, things without senses, and therefore wish that we possessed a faculty of cognition perfectly different from the human faculty, not merely in degree, but even as regards intuition and the mode thereof, so that thus we should not be men, but belong to a class of beings, the possibility of whose existence, much less their nature and constitution, we have no means of cognizing. By observation and analysis of phenomena we penetrate into the interior of nature, and no one can say what progress this knowledge may make in time. But those transcendental questions which pass beyond the limits of nature, we could never answer, even although all nature were laid open to us, because we have not the power of observing our own mind with any other intuition than that of our internal sense. For herein lies the mystery of the origin and source of our faculty of sensibility. Its application to an object, and the transcendental ground of this unity of subjective and objective, lie too deeply concealed for us, who cognize ourselves only through the internal sense, consequently as phenomena, to be able to discover in our existence anything but phenomena, the non-sensuous cause of which we at the same time earnestly desire to penetrate to.

The great utility of this critique of conclusions arrived at by the processes of mere reflection consists in its clear demonstration of the nullity of all conclusions respecting objects which are compared with each other in the understanding alone, while it at the same time confirms what we particularly insisted on, namely, that, although phenomena are not included as things in themselves among the objects of the pure understanding, they are nevertheless the only things by which our cognition can possess objective reality, that is to say, which give us intuitions to correspond with our conceptions.

When we reflect in a purely logical manner, we do nothing more than compare conceptions in our understanding, to discover whether both have the same content, whether they are self-contradictory or not, whether anything is contained in either conception, which of the two is given, and which is merely a mode of thinking that given. But if I apply these conceptions to an object in general (in the transcendental sense), without first determining whether it is an object of sensuous or intellectual intuition, certain limitations present themselves, which forbid us to pass beyond the conceptions and render all empirical use of them impossible. And thus these limitations prove that the representation of an object as a thing in general is not only insufficient, but, without sensuous determination and independently of empirical conditions, self-contradictory; that we must therefore make abstraction of all objects, as in logic, or, admitting them, must think them under conditions of sensuous intuition; that, consequently, the intelligible requires an altogether peculiar intuition, which we do not possess, and in the absence of which it is for us nothing; while, on the other hand phenomena cannot be objects in themselves. For, when I merely think things in general, the difference in their external relations cannot constitute a difference in the things themselves; on the contrary, the former presupposes the latter, and if the conception of one of two things is not internally different from that of the other, I am merely thinking the same thing in different relations. Further, by the addition of one affirmation (reality) to the other, the positive therein is really augmented, and nothing is abstracted or withdrawn from it; hence the real in things cannot be in contradiction with or opposition to itself—and so on.

The true use of the conceptions of reflection in the employment of the understanding has, as we have shown, been so misconceived by Leibnitz, one of the most acute philosophers of either ancient or modern times, that he has been misled into the construction of a baseless system of intellectual cognition, which professes to determine its objects without the intervention of the senses. For this reason, the exposition of the cause of the amphiboly of these conceptions, as the origin of these false principles, is of great utility in determining with certainty the proper limits of the understanding.

It is right to say whatever is affirmed or denied of the whole of a conception can be affirmed or denied of any part of it (dictum de omni et nullo); but it would be absurd so to alter this logical proposition as to say whatever is not contained in a general conception is likewise not contained in the particular conceptions which rank under it; for the latter are particular conceptions, for the very reason that their content is greater than that which is cogitated in the general conception. And yet the whole intellectual system of Leibnitz is based upon this false principle, and with it must necessarily fall to the ground, together with all the ambiguous principles in reference to the employment of the understanding which have thence originated.

Leibnitz's principle of the identity of indiscernibles or indistinguishables is really based on the presupposition that, if in the conception of a thing a certain distinction is not to be found, it is also not to be met with in things themselves; that, consequently, all things are completely identical (numero eadem) which are not distinguishable from each other (as to quality or quantity) in our conceptions of them. But, as in the mere conception of anything abstraction has been made of many necessary conditions of intuition, that of which abstraction has been made is rashly held to be non-existent, and nothing is attributed to the thing but what is contained in its conception.

The conception of a cubic foot of space, however I may think it, is in itself completely identical. But two cubic feet in space are nevertheless distinct from each other from the sole fact of their being in different places (they are numero diversa); and these places are conditions of intuition, wherein the object of this conception is given, and which do not belong to the conception, but to the faculty of sensibility. In like manner, there is in the conception of a thing no contradiction when a negative is not connected with an affirmative; and merely affirmative conceptions cannot, in conjunction, produce any negation. But in sensuous intuition, wherein reality (take for example, motion) is given, we find conditions (opposite directions)—of which abstraction has been made in the conception of motion in general—which render possible a contradiction or opposition (not indeed of a logical kind)—and which from pure positives produce zero = 0. We are therefore not justified in saying that all reality is in perfect agreement and harmony, because no contradiction is discoverable among its conceptions.[30] According to mere conceptions, that which is internal is the substratum of all relations or external determinations. When, therefore, I abstract all conditions of intuition, and confine myself solely to the conception of a thing in general, I can make abstraction of all external relations, and there must nevertheless remain a conception of that which indicates no relation, but merely internal determinations. Now it seems to follow that in everything (substance) there is something which is absolutely internal and which antecedes all external determinations, inasmuch as it renders them possible; and that therefore this substratum is something which does not contain any external relations and is consequently simple (for corporeal things are never anything but relations, at least of their parts external to each other); and, inasmuch as we know of no other absolutely internal determinations than those of the internal sense, this substratum is not only simple, but also, analogously with our internal sense, determined through representations, that is to say, all things are properly monads, or simple beings endowed with the power of representation. Now all this would be perfectly correct, if the conception of a thing were the only necessary condition of the presentation of objects of external intuition. It is, on the contrary, manifest that a permanent phenomenon in space (impenetrable extension) can contain mere relations, and nothing that is absolutely internal, and yet be the primary substratum of all external perception. By mere conceptions I cannot think anything external, without, at the same time, thinking something internal, for the reason that conceptions of relations presuppose given things, and without these are impossible. But, as an intuition there is something (that is, space, which, with all it contains, consists of purely formal, or, indeed, real relations) which is not found in the mere conception of a thing in general, and this presents to us the substratum which could not be cognized through conceptions alone, I cannot say: because a thing cannot be represented by mere conceptions without something absolutely internal, there is also, in the things themselves which are contained under these conceptions, and in their intuition nothing external to which something absolutely internal does not serve as the foundation. For, when we have made abstraction of all the conditions of intuition, there certainly remains in the mere conception nothing but the internal in general, through which alone the external is possible. But this necessity, which is grounded upon abstraction alone, does not obtain in the case of things themselves, in so far as they are given in intuition with such determinations as express mere relations, without having anything internal as their foundation; for they are not things of a thing of which we can neither for they are not things in themselves, but only phenomena. What we cognize in matter is nothing but relations (what we call its internal determinations are but comparatively internal). But there are some self-subsistent and permanent, through which a determined object is given. That I, when abstraction is made of these relations, have nothing more to think, does not destroy the conception of a thing as phenomenon, nor the conception of an object in abstracto, but it does away with the possibility of an object that is determinable according to mere conceptions, that is, of a noumenon. It is certainly startling to hear that a thing consists solely of relations; but this thing is simply a phenomenon, and cannot be cogitated by means of the mere categories: it does itself consist in the mere relation of something in general to the senses. In the same way, we cannot cogitate relations of things in abstracto, if we commence with conceptions alone, in any other manner than that one is the cause of determinations in the other; for that is itself the conception of the understanding or category of relation. But, as in this case we make abstraction of all intuition, we lose altogether the mode in which the manifold determines to each of its parts its place, that is, the form of sensibility (space); and yet this mode antecedes all empirical causality.

If by intelligible objects we understand things which can be thought by means of the pure categories, without the need of the schemata of sensibility, such objects are impossible. For the condition of the objective use of all our conceptions of understanding is the mode of our sensuous intuition, whereby objects are given; and, if we make abstraction of the latter, the former can have no relation to an object. And even if we should suppose a different kind of intuition from our own, still our functions of thought would have no use or signification in respect thereof. But if we understand by the term, objects of a non-sensuous intuition, in respect of which our categories are not valid, and of which we can accordingly have no knowledge (neither intuition nor conception), in this merely negative sense noumena must be admitted. For this is no more than saying that our mode of intuition is not applicable to all things, but only to objects of our senses, that consequently its objective validity is limited, and that room is therefore left for another kind of intuition, and thus also for things that may be objects of it. But in this sense the conception of a noumenon is problematical, that is to say, it is the notion of that it that it is possible, nor that it is impossible, inasmuch as we do not know of any mode of intuition besides the sensuous, or of any other sort of conceptions than the categories—a mode of intuition and a kind of conception neither of which is applicable to a non-sensuous object. We are on this account incompetent to extend the sphere of our objects of thought beyond the conditions of our sensibility, and to assume the existence of objects of pure thought, that is, of noumena, inasmuch as these have no true positive signification. For it must be confessed of the categories that they are not of themselves sufficient for the cognition of things in themselves and, without the data of sensibility, are mere subjective forms of the unity of the understanding. Thought is certainly not a product of the senses, and in so far is not limited by them, but it does not therefore follow that it may be employed purely and without the intervention of sensibility, for it would then be without reference to an object. And we cannot call a noumenon an object of pure thought; for the representation thereof is but the problematical conception of an object for a perfectly different intuition and a perfectly different understanding from ours, both of which are consequently themselves problematical. The conception of a noumenon is therefore not the conception of an object, but merely a problematical conception inseparably connected with the limitation of our sensibility. That is to say, this conception contains the answer to the question: "Are there objects quite unconnected with, and independent of, our intuition?"—a question to which only an indeterminate answer can be given. That answer is: "Inasmuch as sensuous intuition does not apply to all things without distinction, there remains room for other and different objects." The existence of these problematical objects is therefore not absolutely denied, in the absence of a determinate conception of them, but, as no category is valid in respect of them, neither must they be admitted as objects for our understanding.

Understanding accordingly limits sensibility, without at the same time enlarging its own field. While, moreover, it forbids sensibility to apply its forms and modes to things in themselves and restricts it to the sphere of phenomena, it cogitates an object in itself, only, however, as a transcendental object, which is the cause of a phenomenon (consequently not itself a phenomenon), and which cannot be thought either as a quantity or as reality, or as substance (because these conceptions always require sensuous forms in which to determine an object)—an object, therefore, of which we are quite unable to say whether it can be met with in ourselves or out of us, whether it would be annihilated together with sensibility, or, if this were taken away, would continue to exist. If we wish to call this object a noumenon, because the representation of it is non-sensuous, we are at liberty to do so. But as we can apply to it none of the conceptions of our understanding, the representation is for us quite void, and is available only for the indication of the limits of our sensuous intuition, thereby leaving at the same time an empty space, which we are competent to fill by the aid neither of possible experience, nor of the pure understanding.

The critique of the pure understanding, accordingly, does not permit us to create for ourselves a new field of objects beyond those which are presented to us as phenomena, and to stray into intelligible worlds; nay, it does not even allow us to endeavour to form so much as a conception of them. The specious error which leads to this—and which is a perfectly excusable one—lies in the fact that the employment of the understanding, contrary to its proper purpose and destination, is made transcendental, and objects, that is, possible intuitions, are made to regulate themselves according to conceptions, instead of the conceptions arranging themselves according to the intuitions, on which alone their own objective validity rests. Now the reason of this again is that apperception, and with it thought, antecedes all possible determinate arrangement of representations. Accordingly we think something in general and determine it on the one hand sensuously, but, on the other, distinguish the general and in abstracto represented object from this particular mode of intuiting it. In this case there remains a mode of determining the object by mere thought, which is really but a logical form without content, which, however, seems to us to be a mode of the existence of the object in itself (noumenon), without regard to intuition which is limited to our senses.

Before ending this transcendental analytic, we must make an addition, which, although in itself of no particular importance, seems to be necessary to the completeness of the system. The highest conception, with which a transcendental philosophy commonly begins, is the division into possible and impossible. But as all division presupposes a divided conception, a still higher one must exist, and this is the conception of an object in general—problematically understood and without its being decided whether it is something or nothing. As the categories are the only conceptions which apply to objects in general, the distinguishing of an object, whether it is something or nothing, must proceed according to the order and direction of the categories.

1. To the categories of quantity, that is, the conceptions of all, many, and one, the conception which annihilates all, that is, the conception of none, is opposed. And thus the object of a conception, to which no intuition can be found to correspond, is = nothing. That is, it is a conception without an object (ens rationis), like noumena, which cannot be considered possible in the sphere of reality, though they must not therefore be held to be impossible—or like certain new fundamental forces in matter, the existence of which is cogitable without contradiction, though, as examples from experience are not forthcoming, they must not be regarded as possible.

2. Reality is something; negation is nothing, that is, a conception of the absence of an object, as cold, a shadow (nihil privativum).

3. The mere form of intuition, without substance, is in itself no object, but the merely formal condition of an object (as phenomenon), as pure space and pure time. These are certainly something, as forms of intuition, but are not themselves objects which are intuited (ens imaginarium).

4. The object of a conception which is self-contradictory, is nothing, because the conception is nothing—is impossible, as a figure composed of two straight lines (nihil negativum).

The table of this division of the conception of nothing (the corresponding division of the conception of something does not require special description) must therefore be arranged as follows:

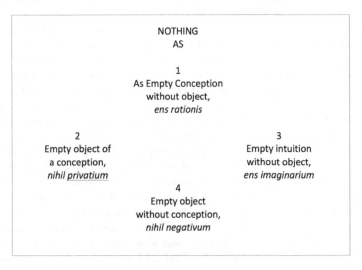

We see that the ens rationis is distinguished from the nihil negativum or pure nothing by the consideration that the former must not be reckoned among possibilities, because it is a mere fiction—though not self-contradictory, while the latter is completely opposed to all possibility, inasmuch as the conception annihilates itself. Both, however, are empty conceptions. On the other hand, the nihil privativum and ens imaginarium are empty data for conceptions. If light be not given to the senses, we cannot represent to ourselves darkness, and if extended objects are not perceived, we cannot represent space. Neither the negation, nor the mere form of intuition can, without something real, be an object.

SECOND DIVISION—TRANSCENDENTAL LOGIC

TRANSCENDENTAL DIALECTIC.

INTRODUCTION

I. OF TRANSCENDENTAL ILLUSORY APPEARANCE

We termed dialectic in general a logic of appearance. This does not signify a doctrine of probability; for probability is truth, only cognized upon insufficient grounds, and though the information it gives us is imperfect, it is not therefore deceitful. Hence it must not be separated from the analytical part of logic. Still less must phenomenon and appearance be held to be identical. For truth or illusory appearance does not reside in the object, in so far as it is intuited, but in the judgement upon the object, in so far as it is thought. It is, therefore, quite correct to say that the senses do not err, not because they always judge correctly, but because they do not judge at all. Hence truth and error, consequently also, illusory appearance as the cause of error, are only to be found in a judgement, that is, in the relation of an object to our understanding. In a cognition which completely harmonizes with the laws of the understanding, no error can exist. In a representation of the senses—as not containing any judgement—there is also no error. But no power of nature can of itself deviate from its own laws. Hence neither the understanding per se (without the influence of another cause), nor the senses per se, would fall into error; the former could not, because, if it acts only according to its own laws, the effect (the judgement) must necessarily accord with these laws. But in accordance with the laws of the understanding consists the formal element in all truth. In the senses there is no judgement—neither a true nor a false one. But, as we have no source of cognition besides these two, it follows that error is caused solely by the unobserved influence of the sensibility upon the understanding. And thus it happens that the subjective grounds of a judgement and are confounded with the objective, and cause them to deviate from their proper determination,[31] just as a body in motion would always of itself proceed in a straight line, but if another impetus gives to it a different direction, it will then start off into a curvilinear line of motion. To distinguish the peculiar action of the understanding from the power which mingles with it, it is necessary to consider an erroneous judgement as the diagonal between two forces, that determine the judgement in two different directions, which, as it were, form an angle, and to resolve this composite operation into the simple ones of the understanding and the sensibility. In pure à priori judgements this must be done by means of transcendental reflection, whereby, as has been already shown, each representation has its place appointed in the corresponding faculty of cognition, and consequently the influence of the one faculty upon the other is made apparent.

It is not at present our business to treat of empirical illusory appearance (for example, optical illusion), which occurs in the empirical application of otherwise correct rules of the understanding, and in which the judgement is misled by the influence of imagination. Our purpose is to speak of transcendental illusory appearance, which influences principles—that are not even applied to experience, for in this case we should possess a sure test of their correctness—but which leads us, in disregard of all the warnings of criticism, completely beyond the empirical employment of the categories and deludes us with the chimera of an extension of the sphere of the pure understanding. We shall term those principles the application of which is confined entirely within the limits of possible experience, immanent; those, on the other hand, which transgress these limits, we shall call transcendent principles. But by these latter I do not understand principles of the transcendental use or misuse of the categories, which is in reality a mere fault of the judgement when not under due restraint from criticism, and therefore not paying sufficient attention to the limits of the sphere in which the pure understanding is allowed to exercise its functions; but real principles which exhort us to break down all those barriers, and to lay claim to a perfectly new field of cognition, which recognizes no line of demarcation. Thus transcendental and transcendent are not identical terms. The principles of the pure understanding, which we have already propounded, ought to be of empirical and not of transcendental use, that is, they are not applicable to any object beyond the sphere of experience. A principle which removes these limits, nay, which authorizes us to overstep them, is called transcendent. If our criticism can succeed in exposing the illusion in these pretended principles, those which are limited in their employment to the sphere of experience may be called, in opposition to the others, immanent principles of the pure understanding.

Logical illusion, which consists merely in the imitation of the form of reason (the illusion in sophistical syllogisms), arises entirely from a want of due attention to logical rules. So soon as the attention is awakened to the case before us, this illusion totally disappears. Transcendental illusion, on the contrary, does not cease to exist, even after it has been exposed, and its nothingness clearly perceived by means of transcendental criticism. Take, for example, the illusion in the proposition: "The world must have a beginning in time." The cause of this is as follows. In our reason, subjectively considered as a faculty of human cognition, there exist fundamental rules and maxims of its exercise, which have completely the appearance of objective principles. Now from this cause it happens that the subjective necessity of a certain connection of our conceptions, is regarded as an objective necessity of the determination of things in themselves. This illusion it is impossible to avoid, just as we cannot avoid perceiving that the sea appears to be higher at a distance than it is near the shore, because we see the former by means of higher rays than the latter, or, which is a still stronger case, as even the astronomer cannot prevent himself from seeing the moon larger at its rising than some time afterwards, although he is not deceived by this illusion.

Transcendental dialectic will therefore content itself with exposing the illusory appearance in transcendental judgements, and guarding us against it; but to make it, as in the case of logical illusion, entirely disappear and cease to be illusion is utterly beyond its power. For we have here to do with a natural and unavoidable illusion, which rests upon subjective principles and imposes these upon us as objective, while logical dialectic, in the detection of sophisms, has to do merely with an error in the logical consequence of the propositions, or with an artificially constructed illusion, in imitation of the natural error. There is, therefore, a natural and unavoidable dialectic of pure reason—not that in which the bungler, from want of the requisite knowledge, involves himself, nor that which the sophist devises for the purpose of misleading, but that which is an inseparable adjunct of human reason, and which, even after its illusions have been exposed, does not cease to deceive, and continually to lead reason into momentary errors, which it becomes necessary continually to remove.

II. OF PURE REASON AS THE SEAT OF TRANSCENDENTAL ILLUSORY APPEARANCE

A. OF REASON IN GENERAL.

All our knowledge begins with sense, proceeds thence to understanding, and ends with reason, beyond which nothing higher can be discovered in the human mind for elaborating the matter of intuition and subjecting it to the highest unity of thought. At this stage of our inquiry it is my duty to give an explanation of this, the highest faculty of cognition, and I confess I find myself here in some difficulty. Of reason, as of the understanding, there is a merely formal, that is, logical use, in which it makes abstraction of all content of cognition; but there is also a real use, inasmuch as it contains in itself the source of certain conceptions and principles, which it does not borrow either from the senses or the understanding. The former faculty has been long defined by logicians as the faculty of mediate conclusion in contradistinction to immediate conclusions (consequentiae immediatae); but the nature of the latter, which itself generates conceptions, is not to be understood from this definition. Now as a division of reason into a logical and a transcendental faculty presents itself here, it becomes necessary to seek for a higher conception of this source of cognition which shall comprehend both conceptions. In this we may expect, according to the analogy of the conceptions of the understanding, that the logical conception will give us the key to the transcendental, and that the table of the functions of the former will present us with the clue to the conceptions of reason.

In the former part of our transcendental logic, we defined the understanding to be the faculty of rules; reason may be distinguished from understanding as the faculty of principles.

The term principle is ambiguous, and commonly signifies merely a cognition that may be employed as a principle, although it is not in itself, and as regards its proper origin, entitled to the distinction. Every general proposition, even if derived from experience by the process of induction, may serve as the major in a syllogism; but it is not for that reason a principle. Mathematical axioms (for example, there can be only one straight line between two points) are general à priori cognitions, and are therefore rightly denominated principles, relatively to the cases which can be subsumed under them. But I cannot for this reason say that I cognize this property of a straight line from principles—I cognize it only in pure intuition.

Cognition from principles, then, is that cognition in which I cognize the particular in the general by means of conceptions. Thus every syllogism is a form of the deduction of a cognition from a principle. For the major always gives a conception, through which everything that is subsumed under the condition thereof is cognized according to a principle. Now as every general cognition may serve as the major in a syllogism, and the understanding presents us with such general à priori propositions, they may be termed principles, in respect of their possible use.

But if we consider these principles of the pure understanding in relation to their origin, we shall find them to be anything rather than cognitions from conceptions. For they would not even be possible à priori, if we could not rely on the assistance of pure intuition (in mathematics), or on that of the conditions of a possible experience. That everything that happens has a cause, cannot be concluded from the general conception of that which happens; on the contrary the principle of causality instructs us as to the mode of obtaining from that which happens a determinate empirical conception.

Synthetical cognitions from conceptions the understanding cannot supply, and they alone are entitled to be called principles. At the same time, all general propositions may be termed comparative principles.

It has been a long-cherished wish—that (who knows how late), may one day, be happily accomplished—that the principles of the endless variety of civil laws should be investigated and exposed; for in this way alone can we find the secret of simplifying legislation. But in this case, laws are nothing more than limitations of our freedom upon conditions under which it subsists in perfect harmony with itself; they consequently have for their object that which is completely our own work, and of which we ourselves may be the cause by means of these conceptions. But how objects as things in themselves—how the nature of things is subordinated to principles and is to be determined, according to conceptions, is a question which it seems well nigh impossible to answer. Be this, however, as it may—for on this point our investigation is yet to be made—it is at least manifest from what we have said that cognition from principles is something very different from cognition by means of the understanding, which may indeed precede other cognitions in the form of a principle, but in itself—in so far as it is synthetical—is neither based upon mere thought, nor contains a general proposition drawn from conceptions alone.

The understanding may be a faculty for the production of unity of phenomena by virtue of rules; the reason is a faculty for the production of unity of rules (of the understanding) under principles. Reason, therefore, never applies directly to experience, or to any sensuous object; its object is, on the contrary, the understanding, to the manifold cognition of which it gives a unity à priori by means of conceptions—a unity which may be called rational unity, and which is of a nature very different from that of the unity produced by the understanding.

The above is the general conception of the faculty of reason, in so far as it has been possible to make it comprehensible in the absence of examples. These will be given in the sequel.

B. OF THE LOGICAL USE OF REASON.

A distinction is commonly made between that which is immediately cognized and that which is inferred or concluded. That in a figure which is bounded by three straight lines there are three angles, is an immediate cognition; but that these angles are together equal to two right angles, is an inference or conclusion. Now, as we are constantly employing this mode of thought and have thus become quite accustomed to it, we no longer remark the above distinction, and, as in the case of the so-called deceptions of sense, consider as immediately perceived, what has really been inferred. In every reasoning or syllogism, there is a fundamental proposition, afterwards a second drawn from it, and finally the conclusion, which connects the truth in the first with the truth in the second—and that infallibly. If the judgement concluded is so contained in the first proposition that it can be deduced from it without the meditation of a third notion, the conclusion is called immediate (consequentia immediata); I prefer the term conclusion of the understanding. But if, in addition to the fundamental cognition, a second judgement is necessary for the production of the conclusion, it is called a conclusion of the reason. In the proposition: All men are mortal, are contained the propositions: Some men are mortal, Nothing that is not mortal is a man, and these are therefore immediate conclusions from the first. On the other hand, the proposition: all the learned are mortal, is not contained in the main proposition (for the conception of a learned man does not occur in it), and it can be deduced from the main proposition only by means of a mediating judgement.

In every syllogism I first cogitate a rule (the major) by means of the understanding. In the next place I subsume a cognition under the condition of the rule (and this is the minor) by means of the judgement. And finally I determine my cognition by means of the predicate of the rule (this is the conclusio), consequently, I determine it à priori by means of the reason. The relations, therefore, which the major proposition, as the rule, represents between a cognition and its condition, constitute the different kinds of syllogisms. These are just threefold—analogously with all judgements, in so far as they differ in the mode of expressing the relation of a cognition in the understanding—namely, categorical, hypothetical, and disjunctive.

When as often happens, the conclusion is a judgement which may follow from other given judgements, through which a perfectly different object is cogitated, I endeavour to discover in the understanding whether the assertion in this conclusion does not stand under certain conditions according to a general rule. If I find such a condition, and if the object mentioned in the conclusion can be subsumed under the given condition, then this conclusion follows from a rule which is also valid for other objects of cognition. From this we see that reason endeavours to subject the great variety of the cognitions of the understanding to the smallest possible number of principles (general conditions), and thus to produce in it the highest unity.

C. OF THE PURE USE OF REASON.

Can we isolate reason, and, if so, is it in this case a peculiar source of conceptions and judgements which spring from it alone, and through which it can be applied to objects; or is it merely a subordinate faculty, whose duty it is to give a certain form to given cognitions—a form which is called logical, and through which the cognitions of the understanding are subordinated to each other, and lower rules to higher (those, to wit, whose condition comprises in its sphere the condition of the others), in so far as this can be done by comparison? This is the question which we have at present to answer. Manifold variety of rules and unity of principles is a requirement of reason, for the purpose of bringing the understanding into complete accordance with itself, just as understanding subjects the manifold content of intuition to conceptions, and thereby introduces connection into it. But this principle prescribes no law to objects, and does not contain any ground of the possibility of cognizing or of determining them as such, but is merely a subjective law for the proper arrangement of the content of the understanding. The purpose of this law is, by a comparison of the conceptions of the understanding, to reduce them to the smallest possible number, although, at the same time, it does not justify us in demanding from objects themselves such a uniformity as might contribute to the convenience and the enlargement of the sphere of the understanding, or in expecting that it will itself thus receive from them objective validity. In one word, the question is: "does reason in itself, that is, does pure reason contain à priori synthetical principles and rules, and what are those principles?"

The formal and logical procedure of reason in syllogisms gives us sufficient information in regard to the ground on which the transcendental principle of reason in its pure synthetical cognition will rest.

1. Reason, as observed in the syllogistic process, is not applicable to intuitions, for the purpose of subjecting them to rules—for this is the province of the understanding with its categories—but to conceptions and judgements. If pure reason does apply to objects and the intuition of them, it does so not immediately, but mediately—through the understanding and its judgements, which have a direct relation to the senses and their intuition, for the purpose of determining their objects. The unity of reason is therefore not the unity of a possible experience, but is essentially different from this unity, which is that of the understanding. That everything which happens has a cause, is not a principle cognized and prescribed by reason. This principle makes the unity of experience possible and borrows nothing from reason, which, without a reference to possible experience, could never have produced by means of mere conceptions any such synthetical unity.

2. Reason, in its logical use, endeavours to discover the general condition of its judgement (the conclusion), and a syllogism is itself nothing but a judgement by means of the subsumption of its condition under a general rule (the major). Now as this rule may itself be subjected to the same process of reason, and thus the condition of the condition be sought (by means of a prosyllogism) as long as the process can be continued, it is very manifest that the peculiar principle of reason in its logical use is to find for the conditioned cognition of the understanding the unconditioned whereby the unity of the former is completed.

But this logical maxim cannot be a principle of pure reason, unless we admit that, if the conditioned is given, the whole series of conditions subordinated to one another—a series which is consequently itself unconditioned—is also given, that is, contained in the object and its connection.

But this principle of pure reason is evidently synthetical; for, analytically, the conditioned certainly relates to some condition, but not to the unconditioned. From this principle also there must originate different synthetical propositions, of which the pure understanding is perfectly ignorant, for it has to do only with objects of a possible experience, the cognition and synthesis of which is always conditioned. The unconditioned, if it does really exist, must be especially considered in regard to the determinations which distinguish it from whatever is conditioned, and will thus afford us material for many à priori synthetical propositions.

The principles resulting from this highest principle of pure reason will, however, be transcendent in relation to phenomena, that is to say, it will be impossible to make any adequate empirical use of this principle. It is therefore completely different from all principles of the understanding, the use made of which is entirely immanent, their object and purpose being merely the possibility of experience. Now our duty in the transcendental dialectic is as follows. To discover whether the principle that the series of conditions (in the synthesis of phenomena, or of thought in general) extends to the unconditioned is objectively true, or not; what consequences result therefrom affecting the empirical use of the understanding, or rather whether there exists any such objectively valid proposition of reason, and whether it is not, on the contrary, a merely logical precept which directs us to ascend perpetually to still higher conditions, to approach completeness in the series of them, and thus to introduce into our cognition the highest possible unity of reason. We must ascertain, I say, whether this requirement of reason has not been regarded, by a misunderstanding, as a transcendental principle of pure reason, which postulates a thorough completeness in the series of conditions in objects themselves. We must show, moreover, the misconceptions and illusions that intrude into syllogisms, the major proposition of which pure reason has supplied—a proposition which has perhaps more of the character of a petitio than of a postulatum—and that proceed from experience upwards to its conditions. The solution of these problems is our task in transcendental dialectic, which we are about to expose even at its source, that lies deep in human reason. We shall divide it into two parts, the first of which will treat of the transcendent conceptions of pure reason, the second of transcendent and dialectical syllogisms.

TRANSCENDENTAL DIALECTIC—BOOK I—OF THE CONCEPTIONS OF PURE REASON.

The conceptions of pure reason—we do not here speak of the possibility of them—are not obtained by reflection, but by inference or conclusion. The conceptions of understanding are also cogitated à priori antecedently to experience, and render it possible; but they contain nothing but the unity of reflection upon phenomena, in so far as these must necessarily belong to a possible empirical consciousness. Through them alone are cognition and the determination of an object possible. It is from them, accordingly, that we receive material for reasoning, and antecedently to them we possess no à priori conceptions of objects from which they might be deduced, On the other hand, the sole basis of their objective reality consists in the necessity imposed on them, as containing the intellectual form of all experience, of restricting their application and influence to the sphere of experience.

But the term, conception of reason, or rational conception, itself indicates that it does not confine itself within the limits of experience, because its object-matter is a cognition, of which every empirical cognition is but a part—nay, the whole of possible experience may be itself but a part of it—a cognition to which no actual experience ever fully attains, although it does always pertain to it. The aim of rational conceptions is the comprehension, as that of the conceptions of understanding is the understanding of perceptions. If they contain the unconditioned, they relate to that to which all experience is subordinate, but which is never itself an object of experience—that towards which reason tends in all its conclusions from experience, and by the standard of which it estimates the degree of their empirical use, but which is never itself an element in an empirical synthesis. If, notwithstanding, such conceptions possess objective validity, they may be called conceptus ratiocinati (conceptions legitimately concluded); in cases where they do not, they have been admitted on account of having the appearance of being correctly concluded, and may be called conceptus ratiocinantes (sophistical conceptions). But as this can only be sufficiently demonstrated in that part of our treatise which relates to the dialectical conclusions of reason, we shall omit any consideration of it in this place. As we called the pure conceptions of the understanding categories, we shall also distinguish those of pure reason by a new name and call them transcendental ideas. These terms, however, we must in the first place explain and justify.

SECTION I. OF IDEAS IN GENERAL

Despite the great wealth of words which European languages possess, the thinker finds himself often at a loss for an expression exactly suited to his conception, for want of which he is unable to make himself intelligible either to others or to himself. To coin new words is a pretension to legislation in language which is seldom successful; and, before recourse is taken to so desperate an expedient, it is advisable to examine the dead and learned languages, with the hope and the probability that we may there meet with some adequate expression of the notion we have in our minds. In this case, even if the original meaning of the word has become somewhat uncertain, from carelessness or want of caution on the part of the authors of it, it is always better to adhere to and confirm its proper meaning—even although it may be doubtful whether it was formerly used in exactly this sense—than to make our labour vain by want of sufficient care to render ourselves intelligible.

For this reason, when it happens that there exists only a single word to express a certain conception, and this word, in its usual acceptation, is thoroughly adequate to the conception, the accurate distinction of which from related conceptions is of great importance, we ought not to employ the expression improvidently, or, for the sake of variety and elegance of style, use it as a synonym for other cognate words. It is our duty, on the contrary, carefully to preserve its peculiar signification, as otherwise it easily happens that when the attention of the reader is no longer particularly attracted to the expression, and it is lost amid the multitude of other words of very different import, the thought which it conveyed, and which it alone conveyed, is lost with it.

Plato employed the expression idea in a way that plainly showed he meant by it something which is never derived from the senses, but which far transcends even the conceptions of the understanding (with which Aristotle occupied himself), inasmuch as in experience nothing perfectly corresponding to them could be found. Ideas are, according to him, archetypes of things themselves, and not merely keys to possible experiences, like the categories. In his view they flow from the highest reason, by which they have been imparted to human reason, which, however, exists no longer in its original state, but is obliged with great labour to recall by reminiscence—which is called philosophy—the old but now sadly obscured ideas. I will not here enter upon any literary investigation of the sense which this sublime philosopher attached to this expression. I shall content myself with remarking that it is nothing unusual, in common conversation as well as in written works, by comparing the thoughts which an author has delivered upon a subject, to understand him better than he understood himself inasmuch as he may not have sufficiently determined his conception, and thus have sometimes spoken, nay even thought, in opposition to his own opinions.

Plato perceived very clearly that our faculty of cognition has the feeling of a much higher vocation than that of merely spelling out phenomena according to synthetical unity, for the purpose of being able to read them as experience, and that our reason naturally raises itself to cognitions far too elevated to admit of the possibility of an object given by experience corresponding to them—cognitions which are nevertheless real, and are not mere phantoms of the brain.

This philosopher found his ideas especially in all that is practical,[32] that is, which rests upon freedom, which in its turn ranks under cognitions that are the peculiar product of reason. He who would derive from experience the conceptions of virtue, who would make (as many have really done) that, which at best can but serve as an imperfectly illustrative example, a model for or the formation of a perfectly adequate idea on the subject, would in fact transform virtue into a nonentity changeable according to time and circumstance and utterly incapable of being employed as a rule. On the contrary, every one is conscious that, when any one is held up to him as a model of virtue, he compares this so-called model with the true original which he possesses in his own mind and values him according to this standard. But this standard is the idea of virtue, in relation to which all possible objects of experience are indeed serviceable as examples—proofs of the practicability in a certain degree of that which the conception of virtue demands—but certainly not as archetypes. That the actions of man will never be in perfect accordance with all the requirements of the pure ideas of reason, does not prove the thought to be chimerical. For only through this idea are all judgements as to moral merit or demerit possible; it consequently lies at the foundation of every approach to moral perfection, however far removed from it the obstacles in human nature—indeterminable as to degree—may keep us.

The Platonic Republic has become proverbial as an example—and a striking one—of imaginary perfection, such as can exist only in the brain of the idle thinker; and Brucker ridicules the philosopher for maintaining that a prince can never govern well, unless he is participant in the ideas. But we should do better to follow up this thought and, where this admirable thinker leaves us without assistance, employ new efforts to place it in clearer light, rather than carelessly fling it aside as useless, under the very miserable and pernicious pretext of impracticability. A constitution of the greatest possible human freedom according to laws, by which the liberty of every individual can consist with the liberty of every other (not of the greatest possible happiness, for this follows necessarily from the former), is, to say the least, a necessary idea, which must be placed at the foundation not only of the first plan of the constitution of a state, but of all its laws. And, in this, it not necessary at the outset to take account of the obstacles which lie in our way— obstacles which perhaps do not necessarily arise from the character of human nature, but rather from the previous neglect of true ideas in legislation. For there is nothing more pernicious and more unworthy of a philosopher, than the vulgar appeal to a so-called adverse experience, which indeed would not have existed, if those institutions had been established at the proper time and in accordance with ideas; while, instead of this, conceptions, crude for the very reason that they have been drawn from experience, have marred and frustrated all our better views and intentions. The more legislation and government are in harmony with this idea, the more rare do punishments become and thus it is quite reasonable to maintain, as Plato did, that in a perfect state no punishments at all would be necessary. Now although a perfect state may never exist, the idea is not on that account the less just, which holds up this maximum as the archetype or standard of a constitution, in order to bring legislative government always nearer and nearer to the greatest possible perfection. For at what precise degree human nature must stop in its progress, and how wide must be the chasm which must necessarily exist between the idea and its realization, are problems which no one can or ought to determine—and for this reason, that it is the destination of freedom to overstep all assigned limits between itself and the idea.

But not only in that wherein human reason is a real causal agent and where ideas are operative causes (of actions and their objects), that is to say, in the region of ethics, but also in regard to nature herself, Plato saw clear proofs of an origin from ideas. A plant, and animal, the regular order of nature—probably also the disposition of the whole universe—give manifest evidence that they are possible only by means of and according to ideas; that, indeed, no one creature, under the individual conditions of its existence, perfectly harmonizes with the idea of the most perfect of its kind—just as little as man with the idea of humanity, which nevertheless he bears in his soul as the archetypal standard of his actions; that, notwithstanding, these ideas are in the highest sense individually, unchangeably, and completely determined, and are the original causes of things; and that the totality of connected objects in the universe is alone fully adequate to that idea. Setting aside the exaggerations of expression in the writings of this philosopher, the mental power exhibited in this ascent from the ectypal mode of regarding the physical world to the architectonic connection thereof according to ends, that is, ideas, is an effort which deserves imitation and claims respect. But as regards the principles of ethics, of legislation, and of religion, spheres in which ideas alone render experience possible, although they never attain to full expression therein, he has vindicated for himself a position of peculiar merit, which is not appreciated only because it is judged by the very empirical rules, the validity of which as principles is destroyed by ideas. For as regards nature, experience presents us with rules and is the source of truth, but in relation to ethical laws experience is the parent of illusion, and it is in the highest degree reprehensible to limit or to deduce the laws which dictate what I ought to do, from what is done.

We must, however, omit the consideration of these important subjects, the development of which is in reality the peculiar duty and dignity of philosophy, and confine ourselves for the present to the more humble but not less useful task of preparing a firm foundation for those majestic edifices of moral science. For this foundation has been hitherto insecure from the many subterranean passages which reason in its confident but vain search for treasures has made in all directions. Our present duty is to make ourselves perfectly acquainted with the transcendental use made of pure reason, its principles and ideas, that we may be able properly to determine and value its influence and real worth. But before bringing these introductory remarks to a close, I beg those who really have philosophy at heart—and their number is but small—if they shall find themselves convinced by the considerations following as well as by those above, to exert themselves to preserve to the expression idea its original signification, and to take care that it be not lost among those other expressions by which all sorts of representations are loosely designated—that the interests of science may not thereby suffer. We are in no want of words to denominate adequately every mode of representation, without the necessity of encroaching upon terms which are proper to others. The following is a graduated list of them. The genus is representation in general (representatio). Under it stands representation with consciousness (perceptio). A perception which relates solely to the subject as a modification of its state, is a sensation (sensatio), an objective perception is a cognition (cognitio). A cognition is either an intuition or a conception (intuitus vel conceptus). The former has an immediate relation to the object and is singular and individual; the latter has but a mediate relation, by means of a characteristic mark which may be common to several things. A conception is either empirical or pure. A pure conception, in so far as it has its origin in the understanding alone, and is not the conception of a pure sensuous image, is called notio. A conception formed from notions, which transcends the possibility of experience, is an idea, or a conception of reason. To one who has accustomed himself to these distinctions, it must be quite intolerable to hear the representation of the colour red called an idea. It ought not even to be called a notion or conception of understanding.

SECTION II. OF TRANSCENDENTAL IDEAS

Transcendental analytic showed us how the mere logical form of our cognition can contain the origin of pure conceptions à priori, conceptions which represent objects antecedently to all experience, or rather, indicate the synthetical unity which alone renders possible an empirical cognition of objects. The form of judgements—converted into a conception of the synthesis of intuitions—produced the categories which direct the employment of the understanding in experience. This consideration warrants us to expect that the form of syllogisms, when applied to synthetical unity of intuitions, following the rule of the categories, will contain the origin of particular à priori conceptions, which we may call pure conceptions of reason or transcendental ideas, and which will determine the use of the understanding in the totality of experience according to principles.

The function of reason in arguments consists in the universality of a cognition according to conceptions, and the syllogism itself is a judgement which is determined à priori in the whole extent of its condition. The proposition: "Caius is mortal," is one which may be obtained from experience by the aid of the understanding alone; but my wish is to find a conception which contains the condition under which the predicate of this judgement is given—in this case, the conception of man—and after subsuming under this condition, taken in its whole extent (all men are mortal), I determine according to it the cognition of the object thought, and say: "Caius is mortal."

Hence, in the conclusion of a syllogism we restrict a predicate to a certain object, after having thought it in the major in its whole extent under a certain condition. This complete quantity of the extent in relation to such a condition is called universality (universalitas). To this corresponds totality (universitas) of conditions in the synthesis of intuitions. The transcendental conception of reason is therefore nothing else than the conception of the totality of the conditions of a given conditioned. Now as the unconditioned alone renders possible totality of conditions, and, conversely, the totality of conditions is itself always unconditioned; a pure rational conception in general can be defined and explained by means of the conception of the unconditioned, in so far as it contains a basis for the synthesis of the conditioned.

To the number of modes of relation which the understanding cogitates by means of the categories, the number of pure rational conceptions will correspond. We must therefore seek for, first, an unconditioned of the categorical synthesis in a subject; secondly, of the hypothetical synthesis of the members of a series; thirdly, of the disjunctive synthesis of parts in a system.

There are exactly the same number of modes of syllogisms, each of which proceeds through prosyllogisms to the unconditioned—one to the subject which cannot be employed as predicate, another to the presupposition which supposes nothing higher than itself, and the third to an aggregate of the members of the complete division of a conception. Hence the pure rational conceptions of totality in the synthesis of conditions have a necessary foundation in the nature of human reason—at least as modes of elevating the unity of the understanding to the unconditioned. They may have no valid application, corresponding to their transcendental employment, in concreto, and be thus of no greater utility than to direct the understanding how, while extending them as widely as possible, to maintain its exercise and application in perfect consistence and harmony.

But, while speaking here of the totality of conditions and of the unconditioned as the common title of all conceptions of reason, we again light upon an expression which we find it impossible to dispense with, and which nevertheless, owing to the ambiguity attaching to it from long abuse, we cannot employ with safety. The word absolute is one of the few words which, in its original signification, was perfectly adequate to the conception it was intended to convey—a conception which no other word in the same language exactly suits, and the loss—or, which is the same thing, the incautious and loose employment—of which must be followed by the loss of the conception itself. And, as it is a conception which occupies much of the attention of reason, its loss would be greatly to the detriment of all transcendental philosophy. The word absolute is at present frequently used to denote that something can be predicated of a thing considered in itself and intrinsically. In this sense absolutely possible would signify that which is possible in itself (interne)—which is, in fact, the least that one can predicate of an object. On the other hand, it is sometimes employed to indicate that a thing is valid in all respects—for example, absolute sovereignty. Absolutely possible would in this sense signify that which is possible in all relations and in every respect; and this is the most that can be predicated of the possibility of a thing. Now these significations do in truth frequently coincide. Thus, for example, that which is intrinsically impossible, is also impossible in all relations, that is, absolutely impossible. But in most cases they differ from each other toto caelo, and I can by no means conclude that, because a thing is in itself possible, it is also possible in all relations, and therefore absolutely. Nay, more, I shall in the sequel show that absolute necessity does not by any means depend on internal necessity, and that, therefore, it must not be considered as synonymous with it. Of an opposite which is intrinsically impossible, we may affirm that it is in all respects impossible, and that, consequently, the thing itself, of which this is the opposite, is absolutely necessary; but I cannot reason conversely and say, the opposite of that which is absolutely necessary is intrinsically impossible, that is, that the absolute necessity of things is an internal necessity. For this internal necessity is in certain cases a mere empty word with which the least conception cannot be connected, while the conception of the necessity of a thing in all relations possesses very peculiar determinations. Now as the loss of a conception of great utility in speculative science cannot be a matter of indifference to the philosopher, I trust that the proper determination and careful preservation of the expression on which the conception depends will likewise be not indifferent to him.

In this enlarged signification, then, shall I employ the word absolute, in opposition to that which is valid only in some particular respect; for the latter is restricted by conditions, the former is valid without any restriction whatever.

Now the transcendental conception of reason has for its object nothing else than absolute totality in the synthesis of conditions and does not rest satisfied till it has attained to the absolutely, that is, in all respects and relations, unconditioned. For pure reason leaves to the understanding everything that immediately relates to the object of intuition or rather to their synthesis in imagination. The former restricts itself to the absolute totality in the employment of the conceptions of the understanding and aims at carrying out the synthetical unity which is cogitated in the category, even to the unconditioned. This unity may hence be called the rational unity of phenomena, as the other, which the category expresses, may be termed the unity of the understanding. Reason, therefore, has an immediate relation to the use of the understanding, not indeed in so far as the latter contains the ground of possible experience (for the conception of the absolute totality of conditions is not a conception that can be employed in experience, because no experience is unconditioned), but solely for the purpose of directing it to a certain unity, of which the understanding has no conception, and the aim of which is to collect into an absolute whole all acts of the understanding. Hence the objective employment of the pure conceptions of reason is always transcendent, while that of the pure conceptions of the understanding must, according to their nature, be always immanent, inasmuch as they are limited to possible experience.

I understand by idea a necessary conception of reason, to which no corresponding object can be discovered in the world of sense. Accordingly, the pure conceptions of reason at present under consideration are transcendental ideas. They are conceptions of pure reason, for they regard all empirical cognition as determined by means of an absolute totality of conditions. They are not mere fictions, but natural and necessary products of reason, and have hence a necessary relation to the whole sphere of the exercise of the understanding. And, finally, they are transcendent, and overstep the limits of all experiences, in which, consequently, no object can ever be presented that would be perfectly adequate to a transcendental idea. When we use the word idea, we say, as regards its object (an object of the pure understanding), a great deal, but as regards its subject (that is, in respect of its reality under conditions of experience), exceedingly little, because the idea, as the conception of a maximum, can never be completely and adequately presented in concreto. Now, as in the merely speculative employment of reason the latter is properly the sole aim, and as in this case the approximation to a conception, which is never attained in practice, is the same thing as if the conception were non-existent—it is commonly said of the conception of this kind, "it is only an idea." So we might very well say, "the absolute totality of all phenomena is only an idea," for, as we never can present an adequate representation of it, it remains for us a problem incapable of solution. On the other hand, as in the practical use of the understanding we have only to do with action and practice according to rules, an idea of pure reason can always be given really in concreto, although only partially, nay, it is the indispensable condition of all practical employment of reason. The practice or execution of the idea is always limited and defective, but nevertheless within indeterminable boundaries, consequently always under the influence of the conception of an absolute perfection. And thus the practical idea is always in the highest degree fruitful, and in relation to real actions indispensably necessary. In the idea, pure reason possesses even causality and the power of producing that which its conception contains. Hence we cannot say of wisdom, in a disparaging way, "it is only an idea." For, for the very reason that it is the idea of the necessary unity of all possible aims, it must be for all practical exertions and endeavours the primitive condition and rule—a rule which, if not constitutive, is at least limitative.

Now, although we must say of the transcendental conceptions of reason, "they are only ideas," we must not, on this account, look upon them as superfluous and nugatory. For, although no object can be determined by them, they can be of great utility, unobserved and at the basis of the edifice of the understanding, as the canon for its extended and self-consistent exercise—a canon which, indeed, does not enable it to cognize more in an object than it would cognize by the help of its own conceptions, but which guides it more securely in its cognition. Not to mention that they perhaps render possible a transition from our conceptions of nature and the non-ego to the practical conceptions, and thus produce for even ethical ideas keeping, so to speak, and connection with the speculative cognitions of reason. The explication of all this must be looked for in the sequel.

But setting aside, in conformity with our original purpose, the consideration of the practical ideas, we proceed to contemplate reason in its speculative use alone, nay, in a still more restricted sphere, to wit, in the transcendental use; and here must strike into the same path which we followed in our deduction of the categories. That is to say, we shall consider the logical form of the cognition of reason, that we may see whether reason may not be thereby a source of conceptions which enables us to regard objects in themselves as determined synthetically à priori, in relation to one or other of the functions of reason.

Reason, considered as the faculty of a certain logical form of cognition, is the faculty of conclusion, that is, of mediate judgement—by means of the subsumption of the condition of a possible judgement under the condition of a given judgement. The given judgement is the general rule (major). The subsumption of the condition of another possible judgement under the condition of the rule is the minor. The actual judgement, which enounces the assertion of the rule in the subsumed case, is the conclusion (conclusio). The rule predicates something generally under a certain condition. The condition of the rule is satisfied in some particular case. It follows that what was valid in general under that condition must also be considered as valid in the particular case which satisfies this condition. It is very plain that reason attains to a cognition, by means of acts of the understanding which constitute a series of conditions. When I arrive at the proposition, "All bodies are changeable," by beginning with the more remote cognition (in which the conception of body does not appear, but which nevertheless contains the condition of that conception), "All compound is changeable," by proceeding from this to a less remote cognition, which stands under the condition of the former, "Bodies are compound," and hence to a third, which at length connects for me the remote cognition (changeable) with the one before me, "Consequently, bodies are changeable"—I have arrived at a cognition (conclusion) through a series of conditions (premises). Now every series, whose exponent (of the categorical or hypothetical judgement) is given, can be continued; consequently the same procedure of reason conducts us to the ratiocinatio polysyllogistica, which is a series of syllogisms, that can be continued either on the side of the conditions (per prosyllogismos) or of the conditioned (per episyllogismos) to an indefinite extent.

But we very soon perceive that the chain or series of prosyllogisms, that is, of deduced cognitions on the side of the grounds or conditions of a given cognition, in other words, the ascending series of syllogisms must have a very different relation to the faculty of reason from that of the descending series, that is, the progressive procedure of reason on the side of the conditioned by means of episyllogisms. For, as in the former case the cognition (conclusio) is given only as conditioned, reason can attain to this cognition only under the presupposition that all the members of the series on the side of the conditions are given (totality in the series of premises), because only under this supposition is the judgement we may be considering possible à priori; while on the side of the conditioned or the inferences, only an incomplete and becoming, and not a presupposed or given series, consequently only a potential progression, is cogitated. Hence, when a cognition is contemplated as conditioned, reason is compelled to consider the series of conditions in an ascending line as completed and given in their totality. But if the very same condition is considered at the same time as the condition of other cognitions, which together constitute a series of inferences or consequences in a descending line, reason may preserve a perfect indifference, as to how far this progression may extend a parte posteriori, and whether the totality of this series is possible, because it stands in no need of such a series for the purpose of arriving at the conclusion before it, inasmuch as this conclusion is sufficiently guaranteed and determined on grounds a parte priori. It may be the case, that upon the side of the conditions the series of premises has a first or highest condition, or it may not possess this, and so be a parte priori unlimited; but it must, nevertheless, contain totality of conditions, even admitting that we never could succeed in completely apprehending it; and the whole series must be unconditionally true, if the conditioned, which is considered as an inference resulting from it, is to be held as true. This is a requirement of reason, which announces its cognition as determined à priori and as necessary, either in itself—and in this case it needs no grounds to rest upon—or, if it is deduced, as a member of a series of grounds, which is itself unconditionally true.

SECTION III. SYSTEM OF TRANSCENDENTAL IDEAS

We are not at present engaged with a logical dialectic, which makes complete abstraction of the content of cognition and aims only at unveiling the illusory appearance in the form of syllogisms. Our subject is transcendental dialectic, which must contain, completely à priori, the origin of certain cognitions drawn from pure reason, and the origin of certain deduced conceptions, the object of which cannot be given empirically and which therefore lie beyond the sphere of the faculty of understanding. We have observed, from the natural relation which the transcendental use of our cognition, in syllogisms as well as in judgements, must have to the logical, that there are three kinds of dialectical arguments, corresponding to the three modes of conclusion, by which reason attains to cognitions on principles; and that in all it is the business of reason to ascend from the conditioned synthesis, beyond which the understanding never proceeds, to the unconditioned which the understanding never can reach.

Now the most general relations which can exist in our representations are: 1st, the relation to the subject; 2nd, the relation to objects, either as phenomena, or as objects of thought in general. If we connect this subdivision with the main division, all the relations of our representations, of which we can form either a conception or an idea, are threefold: 1. The relation to the subject; 2. The relation to the manifold of the object as a phenomenon; 3. The relation to all things in general.

Now all pure conceptions have to do in general with the synthetical unity of representations; conceptions of pure reason (transcendental ideas), on the other hand, with the unconditional synthetical unity of all conditions. It follows that all transcendental ideas arrange themselves in three classes, the first of which contains the absolute (unconditioned) unity of the thinking subject, the second the absolute unity of the series of the conditions of a phenomenon, the third the absolute unity of the condition of all objects of thought in general.

The thinking subject is the object-matter of Psychology; the sum total of all phenomena (the world) is the object-matter of Cosmology; and the thing which contains the highest condition of the possibility of all that is cogitable (the being of all beings) is the object-matter of all Theology. Thus pure reason presents us with the idea of a transcendental doctrine of the soul (psychologia rationalis), of a transcendental science of the world (cosmologia rationalis), and finally of a transcendental doctrine of God (theologia transcendentalis). Understanding cannot originate even the outline of any of these sciences, even when connected with the highest logical use of reason, that is, all cogitable syllogisms—for the purpose of proceeding from one object (phenomenon) to all others, even to the utmost limits of the empirical synthesis. They are, on the contrary, pure and genuine products, or problems, of pure reason.

What modi of the pure conceptions of reason these transcendental ideas are will be fully exposed in the following chapter. They follow the guiding thread of the categories. For pure reason never relates immediately to objects, but to the conceptions of these contained in the understanding. In like manner, it will be made manifest in the detailed explanation of these ideas—how reason, merely through the synthetical use of the same function which it employs in a categorical syllogism, necessarily attains to the conception of the absolute unity of the thinking subject—how the logical procedure in hypothetical ideas necessarily produces the idea of the absolutely unconditioned in a series of given conditions, and finally—how the mere form of the disjunctive syllogism involves the highest conception of a being of all beings: a thought which at first sight seems in the highest degree paradoxical.

An objective deduction, such as we were able to present in the case of the categories, is impossible as regards these transcendental ideas. For they have, in truth, no relation to any object, in experience, for the very reason that they are only ideas. But a subjective deduction of them from the nature of our reason is possible, and has been given in the present chapter.

It is easy to perceive that the sole aim of pure reason is the absolute totality of the synthesis on the side of the conditions, and that it does not concern itself with the absolute completeness on the Part of the conditioned. For of the former alone does she stand in need, in order to preposit the whole series of conditions, and thus present them to the understanding à priori. But if we once have a completely (and unconditionally) given condition, there is no further necessity, in proceeding with the series, for a conception of reason; for the understanding takes of itself every step downward, from the condition to the conditioned. Thus the transcendental ideas are available only for ascending in the series of conditions, till we reach the unconditioned, that is, principles. As regards descending to the conditioned, on the other hand, we find that there is a widely extensive logical use which reason makes of the laws of the understanding, but that a transcendental use thereof is impossible; and that when we form an idea of the absolute totality of such a synthesis, for example, of the whole series of all future changes in the world, this idea is a mere ens rationis, an arbitrary fiction of thought, and not a necessary presupposition of reason. For the possibility of the conditioned presupposes the totality of its conditions, but not of its consequences. Consequently, this conception is not a transcendental idea—and it is with these alone that we are at present occupied.

Finally, it is obvious that there exists among the transcendental ideas a certain connection and unity, and that pure reason, by means of them, collects all its cognitions into one system. From the cognition of self to the cognition of the world, and through these to the supreme being, the progression is so natural, that it seems to resemble the logical march of reason from the premises to the conclusion.[33] Now whether there lies unobserved at the foundation of these ideas an analogy of the same kind as exists between the logical and transcendental procedure of reason, is another of those questions, the answer to which we must not expect till we arrive at a more advanced stage in our inquiries. In this cursory and preliminary view, we have, meanwhile, reached our aim. For we have dispelled the ambiguity which attached to the transcendental conceptions of reason, from their being commonly mixed up with other conceptions in the systems of philosophers, and not properly distinguished from the conceptions of the understanding; we have exposed their origin and, thereby, at the same time their determinate number, and presented them in a systematic connection, and have thus marked out and enclosed a definite sphere for pure reason.

TRANSCENDENTAL DIALECTIC—BOOK II—OF THE DIALECTICAL PROCEDURE OF PURE REASON

It may be said that the object of a merely transcendental idea is something of which we have no conception, although the idea may be a necessary product of reason according to its original laws. For, in fact, a conception of an object that is adequate to the idea given by reason, is impossible. For such an object must be capable of being presented and intuited in a Possible experience. But we should express our meaning better, and with less risk of being misunderstood, if we said that we can have no knowledge of an object, which perfectly corresponds to an idea, although we may possess a problematical conception thereof.

Now the transcendental (subjective) reality at least of the pure conceptions of reason rests upon the fact that we are led to such ideas by a necessary procedure of reason. There must therefore be syllogisms which contain no empirical premisses, and by means of which we conclude from something that we do know, to something of which we do not even possess a conception, to which we, nevertheless, by an unavoidable illusion, ascribe objective reality. Such arguments are, as regards their result, rather to be termed sophisms than syllogisms, although indeed, as regards their origin, they are very well entitled to the latter name, inasmuch as they are not fictions or accidental products of reason, but are necessitated by its very nature. They are sophisms, not of men, but of pure reason herself, from which the Wisest cannot free himself. After long labour he may be able to guard against the error, but he can never be thoroughly rid of the illusion which continually mocks and misleads him.

Of these dialectical arguments there are three kinds, corresponding to the number of the ideas which their conclusions present. In the argument or syllogism of the first class, I conclude, from the transcendental conception of the subject contains no manifold, the absolute unity of the subject itself, of which I cannot in this manner attain to a conception. This dialectical argument I shall call the transcendental paralogism. The second class of sophistical arguments is occupied with the transcendental conception of the absolute totality of the series of conditions for a given phenomenon, and I conclude, from the fact that I have always a self-contradictory conception of the unconditioned synthetical unity of the series upon one side, the truth of the opposite unity, of which I have nevertheless no conception. The condition of reason in these dialectical arguments, I shall term the antinomy of pure reason. Finally, according to the third kind of sophistical argument, I conclude, from the totality of the conditions of thinking objects in general, in so far as they can be given, the absolute synthetical unity of all conditions of the possibility of things in general; that is, from things which I do not know in their mere transcendental conception, I conclude a being of all beings which I know still less by means of a transcendental conception, and of whose unconditioned necessity I can form no conception whatever. This dialectical argument I shall call the ideal of pure reason.

CHAPTER I. OF THE PARALOGISMS OF PURE REASON

The logical paralogism consists in the falsity of an argument in respect of its form, be the content what it may. But a transcendental paralogism has a transcendental foundation, and concludes falsely, while the form is correct and unexceptionable. In this manner the paralogism has its foundation in the nature of human reason, and is the parent of an unavoidable, though not insoluble, mental illusion.

We now come to a conception which was not inserted in the general list of transcendental conceptions, and yet must be reckoned with them, but at the same time without in the least altering, or indicating a deficiency in that table. This is the conception, or, if the term is preferred, the judgement, "I think." But it is readily perceived that this thought is as it were the vehicle of all conceptions in general, and consequently of transcendental conceptions also, and that it is therefore regarded as a transcendental conception, although it can have no peculiar claim to be so ranked, inasmuch as its only use is to indicate that all thought is accompanied by consciousness. At the same time, pure as this conception is from empirical content (impressions of the senses), it enables us to distinguish two different kinds of objects. "I," as thinking, am an object of the internal sense, and am called soul. That which is an object of the external senses is called body. Thus the expression, "I," as a thinking being, designates the object-matter of psychology, which may be called "the rational doctrine of the soul," inasmuch as in this science I desire to know nothing of the soul but what, independently of all experience (which determines me in concreto), may be concluded from this conception "I," in so far as it appears in all thought.

Now, the rational doctrine of the soul is really an undertaking of this kind. For if the smallest empirical element of thought, if any particular perception of my internal state, were to be introduced among the grounds of cognition of this science, it would not be a rational, but an empirical doctrine of the soul. We have thus before us a pretended science, raised upon the single proposition, "I think," whose foundation or want of foundation we may very properly, and agreeably with the nature of a transcendental philosophy, here examine. It ought not to be objected that in this proposition, which expresses the perception of one's self, an internal experience is asserted, and that consequently the rational doctrine of the soul which is founded upon it, is not pure, but partly founded upon an empirical principle. For this internal perception is nothing more than the mere apperception, "I think," which in fact renders all transcendental conceptions possible, in which we say, "I think substance, cause, etc." For internal experience in general and its possibility, or perception in general, and its relation to other perceptions, unless some particular distinction or determination thereof is empirically given, cannot be regarded as empirical cognition, but as cognition of the empirical, and belongs to the investigation of the possibility of every experience, which is certainly transcendental. The smallest object of experience (for example, only pleasure or pain), that should be included in the general representation of self-consciousness, would immediately change the rational into an empirical psychology.

"I think" is therefore the only text of rational psychology, from which it must develop its whole system. It is manifest that this thought, when applied to an object (myself), can contain nothing but transcendental predicates thereof; because the least empirical predicate would destroy the purity of the science and its independence of all experience.

But we shall have to follow here the guidance of the categories—only, as in the present case a thing, "I," as thinking being, is at first given, we shall—not indeed change the order of the categories as it stands in the table—but begin at the category of substance, by which at the a thing in itself is represented and proceeds backwards through the series. The topic of the rational doctrine of the soul, from which everything else it may contain must be deduced, is accordingly as follows:

1 The soul is SUBSTANCE	**2** As regards its quality it is SIMPLE

3
As regards the different times
in which is exists, it is numerically
identical, that is UNITY, not Plurality.

4
It is in relation to possible objects in space.

34

From these elements originate all the conceptions of pure psychology, by combination alone, without the aid of any other principle. This substance, merely as an object of the internal sense, gives the conception of Immateriality; as simple substance, that of Incorruptibility; its identity, as intellectual substance, gives the conception of Personality; all these three together, Spirituality. Its relation to objects in space gives us the conception of connection (commercium) with bodies. Thus it represents thinking substance as the principle of life in matter, that is, as a soul (anima), and as the ground of Animality; and this, limited and determined by the conception of spirituality, gives us that of Immortality.

Now to these conceptions relate four paralogisms of a transcendental psychology, which is falsely held to be a science of pure reason, touching the nature of our thinking being. We can, however, lay at the foundation of this science nothing but the simple and in itself perfectly contentless representation "i" which cannot even be called a conception, but merely a consciousness which accompanies all conceptions. By this "I," or "He," or "It," who or which thinks, nothing more is represented than a transcendental subject of thought = x, which is cognized only by means of the thoughts that are its predicates, and of which, apart from these, we cannot form the least conception. Hence in a perpetual circle, inasmuch as we must always employ it, in order to frame any judgement respecting it. And this inconvenience we find it impossible to rid ourselves of, because consciousness in itself is not so much a representation distinguishing a particular object, as a form of representation in general, in so far as it may be termed cognition; for in and by cognition alone do I think anything.

It must, however, appear extraordinary at first sight that the condition under which I think, and which is consequently a property of my subject, should be held to be likewise valid for every existence which thinks, and that we can presume to base upon a seemingly empirical proposition a judgement which is apodeictic and universal, to wit, that everything which thinks is constituted as the voice of my consciousness declares it to be, that is, as a self-conscious being. The cause of this belief is to be found in the fact that we necessarily attribute to things à priori all the properties which constitute conditions under which alone we can cogitate them. Now I cannot obtain the least representation of a thinking being by means of external experience, but solely through self-consciousness. Such objects are consequently nothing more than the transference of this consciousness of mine to other things which can only thus be represented as thinking beings. The proposition, "I think," is, in the present case, understood in a problematical sense, not in so far as it contains a perception of an existence (like the Cartesian "Cogito, ergo sum"), but in regard to its mere possibility—for the purpose of discovering what properties may be inferred from so simple a proposition and predicated of the subject of it.

If at the foundation of our pure rational cognition of thinking beings there lay more than the mere Cogito—if we could likewise call in aid observations on the play of our thoughts, and the thence derived natural laws of the thinking self, there would arise an empirical psychology which would be a kind of physiology of the internal sense and might possibly be capable of explaining the phenomena of that sense. But it could never be available for discovering those properties which do not belong to possible experience (such as the quality of simplicity), nor could it make any apodeictic enunciation on the nature of thinking beings: it would therefore not be a rational psychology.

Now, as the proposition "I think" (in the problematical sense) contains the form of every judgement in general and is the constant accompaniment of all the categories, it is manifest that conclusions are drawn from it only by a transcendental employment of the understanding. This use of the understanding excludes all empirical elements; and we cannot, as has been shown above, have any favourable conception beforehand of its procedure. We shall therefore follow with a critical eye this proposition through all the predicaments of pure psychology; but we shall, for brevity's sake, allow this examination to proceed in an uninterrupted connection.

Before entering on this task, however, the following general remark may help to quicken our attention to this mode of argument. It is not merely through my thinking that I cognize an object, but only through my determining a given intuition in relation to the unity of consciousness in which all thinking consists. It follows that I cognize myself, not through my being conscious of myself as thinking, but only when I am conscious of the intuition of myself as determined in relation to the function of thought. All the modi of self-consciousness in thought are hence not conceptions of objects (conceptions of the understanding—categories); they are mere logical functions, which do not present to thought an object to be cognized, and cannot therefore present my Self as an object. Not the consciousness of the determining, but only that of the determinable self, that is, of my internal intuition (in so far as the manifold contained in it can be connected conformably with the general condition of the unity of apperception in thought), is the object.

1. In all judgements I am the determining subject of that relation which constitutes a judgement. But that the I which thinks, must be considered as in thought always a subject, and as a thing which cannot be a predicate to thought, is an apodeictic and identical proposition. But this proposition does not signify that I, as an object, am, for myself, a self-subsistent being or substance. This latter statement—an ambitious one—requires to be supported by data which are not to be discovered in thought; and are perhaps (in so far as I consider the thinking self merely as such) not to be discovered in the thinking self at all.

2. That the I or Ego of apperception, and consequently in all thought, is singular or

simple, and cannot be resolved into a plurality of subjects, and therefore indicates a logically simple subject—this is self-evident from the very conception of an Ego, and is consequently an analytical proposition. But this is not tantamount to declaring that the thinking Ego is a simple substance—for this would be a synthetical proposition. The conception of substance always relates to intuitions, which with me cannot be other than sensuous, and which consequently lie completely out of the sphere of the understanding and its thought: but to this sphere belongs the affirmation that the Ego is simple in thought. It would indeed be surprising, if the conception of "substance," which in other cases requires so much labour to distinguish from the other elements presented by intuition—so much trouble, too, to discover whether it can be simple (as in the case of the parts of matter)—should be presented immediately to me, as if by revelation, in the poorest mental representation of all.

3. The proposition of the identity of my Self amidst all the manifold representations of which I am conscious, is likewise a proposition lying in the conceptions themselves, and is consequently analytical. But this identity of the subject, of which I am conscious in all its representations, does not relate to or concern the intuition of the subject, by which it is given as an object. This proposition cannot therefore enounce the identity of the person, by which is understood the consciousness of the identity of its own substance as a thinking being in all change and variation of circumstances. To prove this, we should require not a mere analysis of the proposition, but synthetical judgements based upon a given intuition.

4. I distinguish my own existence, as that of a thinking being, from that of other things external to me—among which my body also is reckoned. This is also an analytical proposition, for other things are exactly those which I think as different or distinguished from myself. But whether this consciousness of myself is possible without things external to me; and whether therefore I can exist merely as a thinking being (without being man)—cannot be known or inferred from this proposition.

Thus we have gained nothing as regards the cognition of myself as object, by the analysis of the consciousness of my Self in thought. The logical exposition of thought in general is mistaken for a metaphysical determination of the object.

Our Critique would be an investigation utterly superfluous, if there existed a possibility of proving à priori, that all thinking beings are in themselves simple substances, as such, therefore, possess the inseparable attribute of personality, and are conscious of their existence apart from and unconnected with matter. For we should thus have taken a step beyond the world of sense, and have penetrated into the sphere of noumena; and in this case the right could not be denied us of extending our knowledge in this sphere, of establishing ourselves, and, under a favouring star, appropriating to ourselves possessions in it. For the proposition: "Every thinking being, as such, is simple substance," is an à priori synthetical proposition; because in the first place it goes beyond the conception which is the subject of it, and adds to the mere notion of a thinking being the mode of its existence, and in the second place annexes a predicate (that of simplicity) to the latter conception—a predicate which it could not have discovered in the sphere of experience. It would follow that à priori synthetical propositions are possible and legitimate, not only, as we have maintained, in relation to objects of possible experience, and as principles of the possibility of this experience itself, but are applicable to things in themselves—an inference which makes an end of the whole of this Critique, and obliges us to fall back on the old mode of metaphysical procedure. But indeed the danger is not so great, if we look a little closer into the question.

There lurks in the procedure of rational Psychology a paralogism, which is represented in the following syllogism:

That which cannot be cogitated otherwise than as subject, does not exist otherwise than as subject, and is therefore substance.

A thinking being, considered merely as such, cannot be cogitated otherwise than as subject.

Therefore it exists also as such, that is, as substance.

In the major we speak of a being that can be cogitated generally and in every relation, consequently as it may be given in intuition. But in the minor we speak of the same being only in so far as it regards itself as subject, relatively to thought and the unity of consciousness, but not in relation to intuition, by which it is presented as an object to thought. Thus the conclusion is here arrived at by a Sophisma figurae dictionis.[35]

That this famous argument is a mere paralogism, will be plain to any one who will consider the general remark which precedes our exposition of the principles of the pure understanding, and the section on noumena. For it was there proved that the conception of a thing, which can exist per se—only as a subject and never as a predicate, possesses no objective reality; that is to say, we can never know whether there exists any object to correspond to the conception; consequently, the conception is nothing more than a conception, and from it we derive no proper knowledge. If this conception is to indicate by the term substance, an object that can be given, if it is to become a cognition, we must have at the foundation of the cognition a permanent intuition, as the indispensable condition of its objective reality. For through intuition alone can an object be given. But in internal intuition there is nothing permanent, for the Ego is but the consciousness of my thought. If then, we appeal merely to thought, we cannot discover the necessary condition of the application of the conception of substance—that is, of a subject existing per se—to the subject as a thinking being. And thus the conception of the simple nature of substance, which is connected with the objective reality of this conception, is shown to be also invalid, and to be, in fact, nothing more than the logical qualitative unity of self-consciousness in thought; whilst we remain perfectly ignorant whether the subject is composite or not.

Refutation of the Argument of Mendelssohn for the Substantiality or Permanence of the Soul.

This acute philosopher easily perceived the insufficiency of the common argument which attempts to prove that the soul—it being granted that it is a simple being—cannot perish by dissolution or decomposition; he saw it is not impossible for it to cease to be by extinction, or disappearance. He endeavoured to prove in his Phaedo, that the soul cannot be annihilated, by showing that a simple being cannot cease to exist. Inasmuch as, he said, a simple existence cannot diminish, nor gradually lose portions of its being, and thus be by degrees reduced to nothing (for it possesses no parts, and therefore no multiplicity), between the moment in which it is, and the moment in which it is not, no time can be discovered—which is impossible. But this philosopher did not consider that, granting the soul to possess this simple nature, which contains no parts external to each other and consequently no extensive quantity, we cannot refuse to it any less than to any other being, intensive quantity, that is, a degree of reality in regard to all its faculties, nay, to all that constitutes its existence. But this degree of reality can become less and less through an infinite series of smaller degrees. It follows, therefore, that this supposed substance—this thing, the permanence of which is not assured in any other way, may, if not by decomposition, by gradual loss (remissio) of its powers (consequently by elanguescence, if I may employ this expression), be changed into nothing. For consciousness itself has always a degree, which may be lessened.[36] Consequently the faculty of being conscious may be diminished; and so with all other faculties. The permanence of the soul, therefore, as an object of the internal sense, remains undemonstrated, nay, even indemonstrable. Its permanence in life is evident, per se, inasmuch as the thinking being (as man) is to itself, at the same time, an object of the external senses. But this does not authorize the rational psychologist to affirm, from mere conceptions, its permanence beyond life.[37]

If, now, we take the above propositions—as they must be accepted as valid for all thinking beings in the system of rational psychology—in synthetical connection, and proceed, from the category of relation, with the proposition: "All thinking beings are, as such, substances," backwards through the series, till the circle is completed; we come at last to their existence, of which, in this system of rational psychology, substances are held to be conscious, independently of external things; nay, it is asserted that, in relation to the permanence which is a necessary characteristic of substance, they can of themselves determine external things. It follows that idealism—at least problematical idealism, is perfectly unavoidable in this rationalistic system. And, if the existence of outward things is not held to be requisite to the determination of the existence of a substance in time, the existence of these outward things at all, is a gratuitous assumption which remains without the possibility of a proof.

But if we proceed analytically—the "I think" as a proposition containing in itself an existence as given, consequently modality being the principle—and dissect this proposition, in order to ascertain its content, and discover whether and how this Ego determines its existence in time and space without the aid of anything external; the propositions of rationalistic psychology would not begin with the conception of a thinking being, but with a reality, and the properties of a thinking being in general would be deduced from the mode in which this reality is cogitated, after everything empirical had been abstracted; as is shown in the following table:

	1 I think,	
2 as Subject		3 as simple Subject
	4 as identical Subject, in every state of my thought.	

Now, inasmuch as it is not determined in this second proposition, whether I can exist and be cogitated only as subject, and not also as a predicate of another being, the conception of a subject is here taken in a merely logical sense; and it remains undetermined, whether substance is to be cogitated under the conception or not. But in the third proposition, the absolute unity of apperception—the simple Ego in the representation to which all connection and separation, which constitute thought, relate, is of itself important; even although it presents us with no information about the constitution or subsistence of the subject. Apperception is something real, and the simplicity of its nature is given in the very fact of its possibility. Now in space there is nothing real that is at the same time simple; for points, which are the only simple things in space, are merely limits, but not constituent parts of space. From this follows the impossibility of a definition on the basis of materialism of the constitution of my Ego as a merely thinking subject. But, because my existence is considered in the first proposition as given, for it does not mean, "Every thinking being exists" (for this would be predicating of them absolute necessity), but only, "I exist thinking"; the proposition is quite empirical, and contains the determinability of my existence merely in relation to my representations in time. But as I require for this purpose something that is permanent, such as is not given in internal intuition; the mode of my existence, whether as substance or as accident, cannot be determined by means of this simple self-consciousness. Thus, if materialism is inadequate to explain the mode in which I exist, spiritualism is likewise as insufficient; and the conclusion is that we are utterly unable to attain to any knowledge of the constitution of the soul, in so far as relates to the possibility of its existence apart from external objects.

And, indeed, how should it be possible, merely by the aid of the unity of consciousness—which we cognize only for the reason that it is indispensable to the possibility of experience—to pass the bounds of experience (our existence in this life); and to extend our cognition to the nature of all thinking beings by means of the empirical—but in relation to every sort of intuition, perfectly undetermined—proposition, "I think"?

There does not then exist any rational psychology as a doctrine furnishing any addition to our knowledge of ourselves. It is nothing more than a discipline, which sets impassable limits to speculative reason in this region of thought, to prevent it, on the one hand, from throwing itself into the arms of a soulless materialism, and, on the other, from losing itself in the mazes of a baseless spiritualism. It teaches us to consider this refusal of our reason to give any satisfactory answer to questions which reach beyond the limits of this our human life, as a hint to abandon fruitless speculation; and to direct, to a practical use, our knowledge of ourselves—which, although applicable only to objects of experience, receives its principles from a higher source, and regulates its procedure as if our destiny reached far beyond the boundaries of experience and life.

From all this it is evident that rational psychology has its origin in a mere misunderstanding. The unity of consciousness, which lies at the basis of the categories, is considered to be an intuition of the subject as an object; and the category of substance is applied to the intuition. But this unity is nothing more than the unity in thought, by which no object is given; to which therefore the category of substance—which always presupposes a given intuition—cannot be applied. Consequently, the subject cannot be cognized. The subject of the categories cannot, therefore, for the very reason that it cogitates these, frame any conception of itself as an object of the categories; for, to cogitate these, it must lay at the foundation its own pure self-consciousness—the very thing that it wishes to explain and describe. In like manner, the subject, in which the representation of time has its basis, cannot determine, for this very reason, its own existence in time. Now, if the latter is impossible, the former, as an attempt to determine itself by means of the categories as a thinking being in general, is no less so.[38]

Thus, then, appears the vanity of the hope of establishing a cognition which is to extend its rule beyond the limits of experience—a cognition which is one of the highest interests of humanity; and thus is proved the futility of the attempt of speculative philosophy in this region of thought. But, in this interest of thought, the severity of criticism has rendered to reason a not unimportant service, by the demonstration of the impossibility of making any dogmatical affirmation concerning an object of experience beyond the boundaries of experience. She has thus fortified reason against all affirmations of the contrary. Now, this can be accomplished in only two ways. Either our proposition must be proved apodeictically; or, if this is unsuccessful, the sources of this inability must be sought for, and, if these are discovered to exist in the natural and necessary limitation of our reason, our opponents must submit to the same law of renunciation and refrain from advancing claims to dogmatic assertion.

But the right, say rather the necessity to admit a future life, upon principles of the practical conjoined with the speculative use of reason, has lost nothing by this renunciation; for the merely speculative proof has never had any influence upon the common reason of men. It stands upon the point of a hair, so that even the schools have been able to preserve it from falling only by incessantly discussing it and spinning it like a top; and even in their eyes it has never been able to present any safe foundation for the erection of a theory. The proofs which have been current among men, preserve their value undiminished; nay, rather gain in clearness and unsophisticated power, by the rejection of the dogmatical assumptions of speculative reason. For reason is thus confined within her own peculiar province—the arrangement of ends or aims, which is at the same time the arrangement of nature; and, as a practical faculty, without limiting itself to the latter, it is justified in extending the former, and with it our own existence, beyond the boundaries of experience and life. If we turn our attention to the analogy of the nature of living beings in this world, in the consideration of which reason is obliged to accept as a principle that no organ, no faculty, no appetite is useless, and that nothing is superfluous, nothing disproportionate to its use, nothing unsuited to its end; but that, on the contrary, everything is perfectly conformed to its destination in life—we shall find that man, who alone is the final end and aim of this order, is still the only animal that seems to be excepted from it. For his natural gifts—not merely as regards the talents and motives that may incite him to employ them, but especially the moral law in him—stretch so far beyond all mere earthly utility and advantage, that he feels himself bound to prize the mere consciousness of probity, apart from all advantageous consequences—even the shadowy gift of posthumous fame—above everything; and he is conscious of an inward call to constitute himself, by his conduct in this world—without regard to mere sublunary interests—the citizen of a better. This mighty, irresistible proof—accompanied by an ever-increasing knowledge of the conformability to a purpose in everything we see around us, by the conviction of the boundless immensity of creation, by the consciousness of a certain illimitableness in the possible extension of our knowledge, and by a desire commensurate therewith—remains to humanity, even after the theoretical cognition of ourselves has failed to establish the necessity of an existence after death.

CONCLUSION OF THE SOLUTION OF THE PSYCHOLOGICAL PARALOGISM.

The dialectical illusion in rational psychology arises from our confounding an idea of reason (of a pure intelligence) with the conception—in every respect undetermined—of a thinking being in general. I cogitate myself in behalf of a possible experience, at the same time making abstraction of all actual experience; and infer therefrom that I can be conscious of myself apart from experience and its empirical conditions. I consequently confound the possible abstraction of my empirically determined existence with the supposed consciousness of a possible separate existence of my thinking self; and I believe that I cognize what is substantial in myself as a transcendental subject, when I have nothing more in thought than the unity of consciousness, which lies at the basis of all determination of cognition.

The task of explaining the community of the soul with the body does not properly belong to the psychology of which we are here speaking; because it proposes to prove the personality of the soul apart from this communion (after death), and is therefore transcendent in the proper sense of the word, although occupying itself with an object of experience—only in so far, however, as it ceases to be an object of experience. But a sufficient answer may be found to the question in our system. The difficulty which lies in the execution of this task consists, as is well known, in the presupposed heterogeneity of the object of the internal sense (the soul) and the objects of the external senses; inasmuch as the formal condition of the intuition of the one is time, and of that of the other space also. But if we consider that both kinds of objects do not differ internally, but only in so far as the one appears externally to the other—consequently, that what lies at the basis of phenomena, as a thing in itself, may not be heterogeneous; this difficulty disappears. There then remains no other difficulty than is to be found in the question—how a community of substances is possible; a question which lies out of the region of psychology, and which the reader, after what in our analytic has been said of primitive forces and faculties, will easily judge to be also beyond the region of human cognition.

GENERAL REMARK

On the Transition from Rational Psychology to Cosmology.

The proposition, "I think," or, "I exist thinking," is an empirical proposition. But such a proposition must be based on empirical intuition, and the object cogitated as a phenomenon; and thus our theory appears to maintain that the soul, even in thought, is merely a phenomenon; and in this way our consciousness itself, in fact, abuts upon nothing.

Thought, per se, is merely the purely spontaneous logical function which operates to connect the manifold of a possible intuition; and it does not represent the subject of consciousness as a phenomenon—for this reason alone, that it pays no attention to the question whether the mode of intuiting it is sensuous or intellectual. I therefore do not represent myself in thought either as I am, or as I appear to myself; I merely cogitate myself as an object in general, of the mode of intuiting which I make abstraction. When I represent myself as the subject of thought, or as the ground of thought, these modes of representation are not related to the categories of substance or of cause; for these are functions of thought applicable only to our sensuous intuition. The application of these categories to the Ego would, however, be necessary, if I wished to make myself an object of knowledge. But I wish to be conscious of myself only as thinking; in what mode my Self is given in intuition, I do not consider, and it may be that I, who think, am a phenomenon—although not in so far as I am a thinking being; but in the consciousness of myself in mere thought I am a being, though this consciousness does not present to me any property of this being as material for thought.

But the proposition, "I think," in so far as it declares, "I exist thinking," is not the mere representation of a logical function. It determines the subject (which is in this case an object also) in relation to existence; and it cannot be given without the aid of the internal sense, whose intuition presents to us an object, not as a thing in itself, but always as a phenomenon. In this proposition there is therefore something more to be found than the mere spontaneity of thought; there is also the receptivity of intuition, that is, my thought of myself applied to the empirical intuition of myself. Now, in this intuition the thinking self must seek the conditions of the employment of its logical functions as categories of substance, cause, and so forth; not merely for the purpose of distinguishing itself as an object in itself by means of the representation "I," but also for the purpose of determining the mode of its existence, that is, of cognizing itself as noumenon. But this is impossible, for the internal empirical intuition is sensuous, and presents us with nothing but phenomenal data, which do not assist the object of pure consciousness in its attempt to cognize itself as a separate existence, but are useful only as contributions to experience.

But, let it be granted that we could discover, not in experience, but in certain firmly-established à priori laws of the use of pure reason—laws relating to our existence, authority to consider ourselves as legislating à priori in relation to our own existence and as determining this existence; we should, on this supposition, find ourselves possessed of a spontaneity, by which our actual existence would be determinable, without the aid of the conditions of empirical intuition. We should also become aware that in the consciousness of our existence there was an à priori content, which would serve to determine our own existence—an existence only sensuously determinable— relatively, however, to a certain internal faculty in relation to an intelligible world.

But this would not give the least help to the attempts of rational psychology. For this wonderful faculty, which the consciousness of the moral law in me reveals, would present me with a principle of the determination of my own existence which is purely intellectual—but by what predicates? By none other than those which are given in sensuous intuition. Thus I should find myself in the same position in rational psychology which I formerly occupied, that is to say, I should find myself still in need of sensuous intuitions, in order to give significance to my conceptions of substance and cause, by means of which alone I can possess a knowledge of myself: but these intu-itions can never raise me above the sphere of experience. I should be justified, however, in applying these conceptions, in regard to their practical use, which is always directed to objects of experience—in conformity with their analogical significance when employed theoretically—to freedom and its subject. At the same time, I should under-stand by them merely the logical functions of subject and predicate, of principle and consequence, in conformity with which all actions are so determined, that they are capable of being explained along with the laws of nature, conformably to the categories of substance and cause, although they originate from a very different principle. We have made these observations for the purpose of guarding against misunderstanding, to which the doctrine of our intuition of self as a phenomenon is exposed. We shall have occasion to perceive their utility in the sequel.

CHAPTER II. THE ANTINOMY OF PURE REASON

We showed in the introduction to this part of our work, that all transcendental illusion of pure reason arose from dialectical arguments, the schema of which logic gives us in its three formal species of syllogisms—just as the categories find their logical schema in the four functions of all judgements. The first kind of these sophistical arguments related to the unconditioned unity of the subjective conditions of all representations in general (of the subject or soul), in correspondence with the categorical syllogisms, the major of which, as the principle, enounces the relation of a predicate to a subject. The second kind of dialectical argument will therefore be concerned, following the analogy with hypothetical syllogisms, with the unconditioned unity of the objective conditions in the phenomenon; and, in this way, the theme of the third kind to be treated of in the following chapter will be the unconditioned unity of the objective conditions of the possibility of objects in general.

But it is worthy of remark that the transcendental paralogism produced in the mind only a one-third illusion, in regard to the idea of the subject of our thought; and the conceptions of reason gave no ground to maintain the contrary proposition. The advantage is completely on the side of Pneumatism; although this theory itself passes into naught, in the crucible of pure reason.

Very different is the case when we apply reason to the objective synthesis of phenomena. Here, certainly, reason establishes, with much plausibility, its principle of unconditioned unity; but it very soon falls into such contradictions that it is compelled, in relation to cosmology, to renounce its pretensions.

For here a new phenomenon of human reason meets us—a perfectly natural antithetic, which does not require to be sought for by subtle sophistry, but into which reason of itself unavoidably falls. It is thereby preserved, to be sure, from the slumber of a fancied conviction—which a merely one-sided illusion produces; but it is at the same time compelled, either, on the one hand, to abandon itself to a despairing scepticism, or, on the other, to assume a dogmatical confidence and obstinate persistence in certain assertions, without granting a fair hearing to the other side of the question. Either is the death of a sound philosophy, although the former might perhaps deserve the title of the euthanasia of pure reason.

Before entering this region of discord and confusion, which the conflict of the laws of pure reason (antinomy) produces, we shall present the reader with some considerations, in explanation and justification of the method we intend to follow in our treatment of this subject. I term all transcendental ideas, in so far as they relate to the absolute totality in the synthesis of phenomena, cosmical conceptions; partly on account of this unconditioned totality, on which the conception of the world-whole is based—a conception, which is itself an idea—partly because they relate solely to the synthesis of phenomena—the empirical synthesis; while, on the other hand, the absolute totality in the synthesis of the conditions of all possible things gives rise to an ideal of pure reason, which is quite distinct from the cosmical conception, although it stands in relation with it. Hence, as the paralogisms of pure reason laid the foundation for a dialectical psychology, the antinomy of pure reason will present us with the transcendental principles of a pretended pure (rational) cosmology—not, however, to declare it valid and to appropriate it, but—as the very term of a conflict of reason sufficiently indicates, to present it as an idea which cannot be reconciled with phenomena and experience.

SECTION I. SYSTEM OF COSMOLOGICAL IDEAS

That We may be able to enumerate with systematic precision these ideas according to a principle, we must remark, in the first place, that it is from the understanding alone that pure and transcendental conceptions take their origin; that the reason does not properly give birth to any conception, but only frees the conception of the understanding from the unavoidable limitation of a possible experience, and thus endeavours to raise it above the empirical, though it must still be in connection with it. This happens from the fact that, for a given conditioned, reason demands absolute totality on the side of the conditions (to which the understanding submits all phenomena), and thus makes of the category a transcendental idea. This it does that it may be able to give absolute completeness to the empirical synthesis, by continuing it to the unconditioned (which is not to be found in experience, but only in the idea). Reason requires this according to the principle: If the conditioned is given the whole of the conditions, and consequently the absolutely unconditioned, is also given, whereby alone the former was possible. First, then, the transcendental ideas are properly nothing but categories elevated to the unconditioned; and they may be arranged in a table according to the titles of the latter. But, secondly, all the categories are not available for this purpose, but only those in which the synthesis constitutes a series—of conditions subordinated to, not co-ordinated with, each other. Absolute totality is required of reason only in so far as concerns the ascending series of the conditions of a conditioned; not, consequently, when the question relates to the descending series of consequences, or to the aggregate of the co-ordinated conditions of these consequences. For, in relation to a given conditioned, conditions are presupposed and considered to be given along with it. On the other hand, as the consequences do not render possible their conditions, but rather presuppose them—in the consideration of the procession of consequences (or in the descent from the given condition to the conditioned), we may be quite unconcerned whether the series ceases or not; and their totality is not a necessary demand of reason.

Thus we cogitate—and necessarily—a given time completely elapsed up to a given moment, although that time is not determinable by us. But as regards time future, which is not the condition of arriving at the present, in order to conceive it; it is quite indifferent whether we consider future time as ceasing at some point, or as prolonging itself to infinity. Take, for example, the series m, n, o, in which n is given as conditioned in relation to m, but at the same time as the condition of o, and let the series proceed upwards from the conditioned n to m (l, k, i, etc.), and also downwards from the condition n to the conditioned o (p, q, r, etc.)—I must presuppose the former series, to be able to consider n as given, and n is according to reason (the totality of conditions) possible only by means of that series. But its possibility does not rest on the following series o, p, q, r, which for this reason cannot be regarded as given, but only as capable of being given (dabilis).

I shall term the synthesis of the series on the side of the conditions—from that nearest to the given phenomenon up to the more remote—regressive; that which proceeds on the side of the conditioned, from the immediate consequence to the more remote, I shall call the progressive synthesis. The former proceeds in antecedentia, the latter in consequentia. The cosmological ideas are therefore occupied with the totality of the regressive synthesis, and proceed in antecedentia, not in consequentia. When the latter takes place, it is an arbitrary and not a necessary problem of pure reason; for we require, for the complete understanding of what is given in a phenomenon, not the consequences which succeed, but the grounds or principles which precede.

In order to construct the table of ideas in correspondence with the table of categories, we take first the two primitive quanta of all our intuitions, time and space. Time is in itself a series (and the formal condition of all series), and hence, in relation to a given present, we must distinguish à priori in it the antecedentia as conditions (time past) from the consequentia (time future). Consequently, the transcendental idea of the absolute totality of the series of the conditions of a given conditioned, relates merely to all past time. According to the idea of reason, the whole past time, as the condition of the given moment, is necessarily cogitated as given. But, as regards space, there exists in it no distinction between progressus and regressus; for it is an aggregate and not a series —its parts existing together at the same time. I can consider a given point of time in relation to past time only as conditioned, because this given moment comes into existence only through the past time rather through the passing of the preceding time. But as the parts of space are not subordinated, but co-ordinated to each other, one part cannot be the condition of the possibility of the other; and space is not in itself, like time, a series. But the synthesis of the manifold parts of space—(the syntheses whereby we apprehend space)—is nevertheless successive; it takes place, therefore, in time, and contains a series. And as in this series of aggregated spaces (for example, the feet in a rood), beginning with a given portion of space, those which continue to be annexed form the condition of the limits of the former—the measurement of a space must also be regarded as a synthesis of the series of the conditions of a given conditioned. It differs, however, in this respect from that of time, that the side of the conditioned is not in itself distinguishable from the side of the condition; and, consequently, regressus and progressus in space seem to be identical. But, inasmuch as one part of space is not given, but only limited, by and through another, we must also consider every limited space as conditioned, in so far as it presupposes some other space as the condition of its limitation, and so on. As regards limitation, therefore, our procedure in space is also a regressus, and the transcendental idea of the absolute totality of the synthesis in a series of conditions applies to space also; and I am entitled to demand the absolute totality of the phenomenal synthesis in space as well as in time. Whether my demand can be satisfied is a question to be answered in the sequel.

Secondly, the real in space—that is, matter—is conditioned. Its internal conditions are its parts, and the parts of parts its remote conditions; so that in this case we find a regressive synthesis, the absolute totality of which is a demand of reason. But this cannot be obtained otherwise than by a complete division of parts, whereby the real in matter becomes either nothing or that which is not matter, that is to say, the simple.

Consequently we find here also a series of conditions and a progress to the unconditioned.

Thirdly, as regards the categories of a real relation between phenomena, the category of substance and its accidents is not suitable for the formation of a transcendental idea; that is to say, reason has no ground, in regard to it, to proceed regressively with conditions. For accidents (in so far as they inhere in a substance) are co-ordinated with each other, and do not constitute a series. And, in relation to substance, they are not properly subordinated to it, but are the mode of existence of the substance itself. The conception of the substantial might nevertheless seem to be an idea of the transcendental reason. But, as this signifies nothing more than the conception of an object in general, which subsists in so far as we cogitate in it merely a transcendental subject without any predicates; and as the question here is of an unconditioned in the series of phenomena—it is clear that the substantial can form no member thereof. The same holds good of substances in community, which are mere aggregates and do not form a series. For they are not subordinated to each other as conditions of the possibility of each other; which, however, may be affirmed of spaces, the limits of which are never determined in themselves, but always by some other space. It is, therefore, only in the category of causality that we can find a series of causes to a given effect, and in which we ascend from the latter, as the conditioned, to the former as the conditions, and thus answer the question of reason.

Fourthly, the conceptions of the possible, the actual, and the necessary do not conduct us to any series—excepting only in so far as the contingent in existence must always be regarded as conditioned, and as indicating, according to a law of the understanding, a condition, under which it is necessary to rise to a higher, till in the totality of the series, reason arrives at unconditioned necessity.

There are, accordingly, only four cosmological ideas, corresponding with the four titles of the categories. For we can select only such as necessarily furnish us with a series in the synthesis of the manifold.

1
The absolute Completeness
of the
COMPOSITION
of the given totality of all phenomena.

2
The absolute Completeness
of the
DIVISION
of given totality in a phenomenon.

3
The absolute Completeness
of the
ORIGINATION
of a phenomenon.

4

The absolute Completeness
of the DEPENDENCE of the EXISTENCE
of what is changeable in a phenomenon.

We must here remark, in the first place, that the idea of absolute totality relates to nothing but the exposition of phenomena, and therefore not to the pure conception of a totality of things. Phenomena are here, therefore, regarded as given, and reason requires the absolute completeness of the conditions of their possibility, in so far as these conditions constitute a series—consequently an absolutely (that is, in every respect) complete synthesis, whereby a phenomenon can be explained according to the laws of the understanding.

Secondly, it is properly the unconditioned alone that reason seeks in this serially and regressively conducted synthesis of conditions. It wishes, to speak in another way, to attain to completeness in the series of premises, so as to render it unnecessary to presuppose others. This unconditioned is always contained in the absolute totality of the series, when we endeavour to form a representation of it in thought. But this absolutely complete synthesis is itself but an idea; for it is impossible, at least before hand, to know whether any such synthesis is possible in the case of phenomena. When we represent all existence in thought by means of pure conceptions of the understanding, without any conditions of sensuous intuition, we may say with justice that for a given conditioned the whole series of conditions subordinated to each other is also given; for the former is only given through the latter. But we find in the case of phenomena a particular limitation of the mode in which conditions are given, that is, through the successive synthesis of the manifold of intuition, which must be complete in the regress. Now whether this completeness is sensuously possible, is a problem. But the idea of it lies in the reason—be it possible or impossible to connect with the idea adequate empirical conceptions. Therefore, as in the absolute totality of the regressive synthesis of the manifold in a phenomenon (following the guidance of the categories, which represent it as a series of conditions to a given conditioned) the unconditioned is necessarily contained—it being still left unascertained whether and how this totality exists; reason sets out from the idea of totality, although its proper and final aim is the unconditioned —of the whole series, or of a part thereof.

This unconditioned may be cogitated—either as existing only in the entire series, all the members of which therefore would be without exception conditioned and only the totality absolutely unconditioned—and in this case the regressus is called infinite; or the absolutely unconditioned is only a part of the series, to which the other members are subordinated, but which Is not itself submitted to any other condition.[39] In the former case the series is a parte priori unlimited (without beginning), that is, infinite, and nevertheless completely given. But the regress in it is never completed, and can only be called potentially infinite. In the second case there exists a first in the series. This first is called, in relation to past time, the beginning of the world; in relation to space, the limit of the world; in relation to the parts of a given limited whole, the simple; in relation to causes, absolute spontaneity (liberty); and in relation to the existence of changeable things, absolute physical necessity.

We possess two expressions, world and nature, which are generally interchanged.

The first denotes the mathematical total of all phenomena and the totality of their synthesis—in its progress by means of composition, as well as by division. And the world is termed nature,[40] when it is regarded as a dynamical whole—when our attention is not directed to the aggregation in space and time, for the purpose of cogitating it as a quantity, but to the unity in the existence of phenomena. In this case the condition of that which happens is called a cause; the unconditioned causality of the cause in a phenomenon is termed liberty; the conditioned cause is called in a more limited sense a natural cause. The conditioned in existence is termed contingent, and the unconditioned necessary. The unconditioned necessity of phenomena may be called natural necessity.

The ideas which we are at present engaged in discussing I have called cosmological ideas; partly because by the term world is understood the entire content of all phenomena, and our ideas are directed solely to the unconditioned among phenomena; partly also, because world, in the transcendental sense, signifies the absolute totality of the content of existing things, and we are directing our attention only to the completeness of the synthesis—although, properly, only in regression. In regard to the fact that these ideas are all transcendent, and, although they do not transcend phenomena as regards their mode, but are concerned solely with the world of sense (and not with noumena), nevertheless carry their synthesis to a degree far above all possible experience—it still seems to me that we can, with perfect propriety, designate them cosmical conceptions. As regards the distinction between the mathematically and the dynamically unconditioned which is the aim of the regression of the synthesis, I should call the two former, in a more limited signification, cosmical conceptions, the remaining two transcendent physical conceptions. This distinction does not at present seem to be of particular importance, but we shall afterwards find it to be of some value.

SECTION II. ANTITHETIC OF PURE REASON

Thetic is the term applied to every collection of dogmatical propositions. By antithetic I do not understand dogmatical assertions of the opposite, but the self-contradiction of seemingly dogmatical cognitions (thesis cum antithesis), in none of which we can discover any decided superiority. Antithetic is not, therefore, occupied with one-sided statements, but is engaged in considering the contradictory nature of the general cognitions of reason and its causes. Transcendental antithetic is an investigation into the antinomy of pure reason, its causes and result. If we employ our reason not merely in the application of the principles of the understanding to objects of experience, but venture with it beyond these boundaries, there arise certain sophistical propositions or theorems. These assertions have the following peculiarities: They can find neither confirmation nor confutation in experience; and each is in itself not only self-consistent, but possesses conditions of its necessity in the very nature of reason—only that, unluckily, there exist just as valid and necessary grounds for maintaining the contrary proposition.

The questions which naturally arise in the consideration of this dialectic of pure reason, are therefore: 1st. In what propositions is pure reason unavoidably subject to an antinomy? 2nd. What are the causes of this antinomy? 3rd. Whether and in what way can reason free itself from this self-contradiction?

A dialectical proposition or theorem of pure reason must, according to what has been said, be distinguishable from all sophistical propositions, by the fact that it is not an answer to an arbitrary question, which may be raised at the mere pleasure of any person, but to one which human reason must necessarily encounter in its progress. In the second place, a dialectical proposition, with its opposite, does not carry the appearance of a merely artificial illusion, which disappears as soon as it is investigated, but a natural and unavoidable illusion, which, even when we are no longer deceived by it, continues to mock us and, although rendered harmless, can never be completely removed.

This dialectical doctrine will not relate to the unity of understanding in empirical conceptions, but to the unity of reason in pure ideas. The conditions of this doctrine are —inasmuch as it must, as a synthesis according to rules, be conformable to the understanding, and at the same time as the absolute unity of the synthesis, to the reason— that, if it is adequate to the unity of reason, it is too great for the understanding, if according with the understanding, it is too small for the reason. Hence arises a mutual opposition, which cannot be avoided, do what we will.

These sophistical assertions of dialectic open, as it were, a battle-field, where that side obtains the victory which has been permitted to make the attack, and he is compelled to yield who has been unfortunately obliged to stand on the defensive. And hence, champions of ability, whether on the right or on the wrong side, are certain to carry away the crown of victory, if they only take care to have the right to make the last attack, and are not obliged to sustain another onset from their opponent. We can easily believe that this arena has been often trampled by the feet of combatants, that many victories have been obtained on both sides, but that the last victory, decisive of the affair between the contending parties, was won by him who fought for the right, only if his adversary was forbidden to continue the tourney. As impartial umpires, we must lay aside entirely the consideration whether the combatants are fighting for the right or for the wrong side, for the true or for the false, and allow the combat to be first decided. Perhaps, after they have wearied more than injured each other, they will discover the nothingness of their cause of quarrel and part good friends.

This method of watching, or rather of originating, a conflict of assertions, not for the purpose of finally deciding in favour of either side, but to discover whether the object of the struggle is not a mere illusion, which each strives in vain to reach, but which would be no gain even when reached—this procedure, I say, may be termed the sceptical method. It is thoroughly distinct from scepticism—the principle of a technical and scientific ignorance, which undermines the foundations of all knowledge, in order, if possible, to destroy our belief and confidence therein. For the sceptical method aims at certainty, by endeavouring to discover in a conflict of this kind, conducted honestly and intelligently on both sides, the point of misunderstanding; just as wise legislators derive, from the embarrassment of judges in lawsuits, information in regard to the defective and ill-defined parts of their statutes. The antinomy which reveals itself in the application of laws, is for our limited wisdom the best criterion of legislation. For the attention of reason, which in abstract speculation does not easily become conscious of its errors, is thus roused to the momenta in the determination of its principles.

But this sceptical method is essentially peculiar to transcendental philosophy, and can perhaps be dispensed with in every other field of investigation. In mathematics its use would be absurd; because in it no false assertions can long remain hidden, inasmuch as its demonstrations must always proceed under the guidance of pure intuition, and by means of an always evident synthesis. In experimental philosophy, doubt and delay may be very useful; but no misunderstanding is possible, which cannot be easily removed; and in experience means of solving the difficulty and putting an end to the dissension must at last be found, whether sooner or later. Moral philosophy can always exhibit its principles, with their practical consequences, in concreto—at least in possible experiences, and thus escape the mistakes and ambiguities of abstraction. But transcendental propositions, which lay claim to insight beyond the region of possible experience, cannot, on the one hand, exhibit their abstract synthesis in any à priori intuition, nor, on the other, expose a lurking error by the help of experience. Transcendental reason, therefore, presents us with no other criterion than that of an attempt to reconcile such assertions, and for this purpose to permit a free and unrestrained conflict between them. And this we now proceed to arrange.[41]

FIRST CONFLICT OF THE TRANSCENDENTAL IDEAS. THESIS.

The world has a beginning in time, and is also limited in regard to space.

PROOF.

Granted that the world has no beginning in time; up to every given moment of time, an eternity must have elapsed, and therewith passed away an infinite series of successive conditions or states of things in the world. Now the infinity of a series consists in the fact that it never can be completed by means of a successive synthesis. It follows that an infinite series already elapsed is impossible and that, consequently, a beginning of the world is a necessary condition of its existence. And this was the first thing to be proved.

As regards the second, let us take the opposite for granted. In this case, the world must be an infinite given total of coexistent things. Now we cannot cogitate the dimensions of a quantity, which is not given within certain limits of an intuition,[42] in any other way than by means of the synthesis of its parts, and the total of such a quantity only by means of a completed synthesis, or the repeated addition of unity to itself. Accordingly, to cogitate the world, which fills all spaces, as a whole, the successive synthesis of the parts of an infinite world must be looked upon as completed, that is to say, an infinite time must be regarded as having elapsed in the enumeration of all co-existing things; which is impossible. For this reason an infinite aggregate of actual things cannot be considered as a given whole, consequently, not as a contemporaneously given whole. The world is consequently, as regards extension in space, not infinite, but enclosed in limits. And this was the second thing to be proved.

ANTITHESIS.

The world has no beginning, and no limits in space, but is, in relation both to time and space, infinite.

PROOF.

For let it be granted that it has a beginning. A beginning is an existence which is preceded by a time in which the thing does not exist. On the above supposition, it follows that there must have been a time in which the world did not exist, that is, a void time. But in a void time the origination of a thing is impossible; because no part of any such time contains a distinctive condition of being, in preference to that of non-being (whether the supposed thing originate of itself, or by means of some other cause).

Consequently, many series of things may have a beginning in the world, but the world itself cannot have a beginning, and is, therefore, in relation to past time, infinite.

As regards the second statement, let us first take the opposite for granted—that the world is finite and limited in space; it follows that it must exist in a void space, which is not limited. We should therefore meet not only with a relation of things in space, but also a relation of things to space. Now, as the world is an absolute whole, out of and beyond which no object of intuition, and consequently no correlate to which can be discovered, this relation of the world to a void space is merely a relation to no object. But such a relation, and consequently the limitation of the world by void space, is nothing. Consequently, the world, as regards space, is not limited, that is, it is infinite in regard to extension.[43]

OBSERVATIONS ON THE FIRST ANTINOMY. ON THE THESIS.

In bringing forward these conflicting arguments, I have not been on the search for sophisms, for the purpose of availing myself of special pleading, which takes advantage of the carelessness of the opposite party, appeals to a misunderstood statute, and erects its unrighteous claims upon an unfair interpretation. Both proofs originate fairly from the nature of the case, and the advantage presented by the mistakes of the dogmatists of both parties has been completely set aside.

The thesis might also have been unfairly demonstrated, by the introduction of an erroneous conception of the infinity of a given quantity. A quantity is infinite, if a greater than itself cannot possibly exist. The quantity is measured by the number of given units—which are taken as a standard—contained in it. Now no number can be the greatest, because one or more units can always be added. It follows that an infinite given quantity, consequently an infinite world (both as regards time and extension) is impossible. It is, therefore, limited in both respects. In this manner I might have conducted my proof; but the conception given in it does not agree with the true conception of an infinite whole. In this there is no representation of its quantity, it is not said how large it is; consequently its conception is not the conception of a maximum. We cogitate in it merely its relation to an arbitrarily assumed unit, in relation to which it is greater than any number. Now, just as the unit which is taken is greater or smaller, the infinite will be greater or smaller; but the infinity, which consists merely in the relation to this given unit, must remain always the same, although the absolute quantity of the whole is not thereby cognized.

The true (transcendental) conception of infinity is: that the successive synthesis of unity in the measurement of a given quantum can never be completed.[44] Hence it follows, without possibility of mistake, that an eternity of actual successive states up to a given (the present) moment cannot have elapsed, and that the world must therefore have a beginning.

In regard to the second part of the thesis, the difficulty as to an infinite and yet elapsed series disappears; for the manifold of a world infinite in extension is contemporaneously given. But, in order to cogitate the total of this manifold, as we cannot have the aid of limits constituting by themselves this total in intuition, we are obliged to give some account of our conception, which in this case cannot proceed from the whole to the determined quantity of the parts, but must demonstrate the possibility of a whole by means of a successive synthesis of the parts. But as this synthesis must constitute a series that cannot be completed, it is impossible for us to cogitate prior to it, and consequently not by means of it, a totality. For the conception of totality itself is in the present case the representation of a completed synthesis of the parts; and this completion, and consequently its conception, is impossible.

ON THE ANTITHESIS.

The proof in favour of the infinity of the cosmical succession and the cosmical content is based upon the consideration that, in the opposite case, a void time and a void space must constitute the limits of the world. Now I am not unaware, that there are some ways of escaping this conclusion. It may, for example, be alleged, that a limit to the world, as regards both space and time, is quite possible, without at the same time holding the existence of an absolute time before the beginning of the world, or an absolute space extending beyond the actual world—which is impossible. I am quite well satisfied with the latter part of this opinion of the philosophers of the Leibnitzian school. Space is merely the form of external intuition, but not a real object which can itself be externally intuited; it is not a correlate of phenomena, it is the form of phenomena itself. Space, therefore, cannot be regarded as absolutely and in itself something determinative of the existence of things, because it is not itself an object, but only the form of possible objects. Consequently, things, as phenomena, determine space; that is to say, they render it possible that, of all the possible predicates of space (size and relation), certain may belong to reality. But we cannot affirm the converse, that space, as something self-subsistent, can determine real things in regard to size or shape, for it is in itself not a real thing. Space (filled or void)[45] may therefore be limited by phenomena, but phenomena cannot be limited by an empty space without them. This is true of time also. All this being granted, it is nevertheless indisputable, that we must assume these two nonentities, void space without and void time before the world, if we assume the existence of cosmical limits, relatively to space or time.

For, as regards the subterfuge adopted by those who endeavour to evade the consequence—that, if the world is limited as to space and time, the infinite void must determine the existence of actual things in regard to their dimensions—it arises solely from the fact that instead of a sensuous world, an intelligible world—of which nothing is known—is cogitated; instead of a real beginning (an existence, which is preceded by a period in which nothing exists), an existence which presupposes no other condition than that of time; and, instead of limits of extension, boundaries of the universe. But the question relates to the mundus phaenomenon, and its quantity; and in this case we cannot make abstraction of the conditions of sensibility, without doing away with the essential reality of this world itself. The world of sense, if it is limited, must necessarily lie in the infinite void. If this, and with it space as the à priori condition of the possibility of phenomena, is left out of view, the whole world of sense disappears. In our problem is this alone considered as given. The mundus intelligibilis is nothing but the general conception of a world, in which abstraction has been made of all conditions of intuition, and in relation to which no synthetical proposition—either affirmative or negative—is possible.

SECOND CONFLICT OF TRANSCENDENTAL IDEAS. THESIS.

Every composite substance in the world consists of simple parts; and there exists nothing that is not either itself simple, or composed of simple parts.

PROOF.

For, grant that composite substances do not consist of simple parts; in this case, if all combination or composition were annihilated in thought, no composite part, and (as, by the supposition, there do not exist simple parts) no simple part would exist. Consequently, no substance; consequently, nothing would exist. Either, then, it is impossible to annihilate composition in thought; or, after such annihilation, there must remain something that subsists without composition, that is, something that is simple. But in the former case the composite could not itself consist of substances, because with substances composition is merely a contingent relation, apart from which they must still exist as self-subsistent beings. Now, as this case contradicts the supposition, the second must contain the truth—that the substantial composite in the world consists of simple parts.

It follows, as an immediate inference, that the things in the world are all, without exception, simple beings—that composition is merely an external condition pertaining to them—and that, although we never can separate and isolate the elementary substances from the state of composition, reason must cogitate these as the primary subjects of all composition, and consequently, as prior thereto—and as simple substances.

ANTITHESIS.

No composite thing in the world consists of simple parts; and there does not exist in the world any simple substance.

PROOF.

Let it be supposed that a composite thing (as substance) consists of simple parts. Inasmuch as all external relation, consequently all composition of substances, is possible only in space; the space, occupied by that which is composite, must consist of the same number of parts as is contained in the composite. But space does not consist of simple parts, but of spaces. Therefore, every part of the composite must occupy a space. But the absolutely primary parts of what is composite are simple. It follows that what is simple occupies a space. Now, as everything real that occupies a space, contains a manifold the parts of which are external to each other, and is consequently composite—and a real composite, not of accidents (for these cannot exist external to each other apart from substance), but of substances—it follows that the simple must be a substantial composite, which is self-contradictory.

The second proposition of the antithesis—that there exists in the world nothing that is simple—is here equivalent to the following: The existence of the absolutely simple cannot be demonstrated from any experience or perception either external or internal; and the absolutely simple is a mere idea, the objective reality of which cannot be demonstrated in any possible experience; it is consequently, in the exposition of phenomena, without application and object. For, let us take for granted that an object may be found in experience for this transcendental idea; the empirical intuition of such an object must then be recognized to contain absolutely no manifold with its parts external to each other, and connected into unity. Now, as we cannot reason from the non-consciousness of such a manifold to the impossibility of its existence in the intuition of an object, and as the proof of this impossibility is necessary for the establishment and proof of absolute simplicity; it follows that this simplicity cannot be inferred from any perception whatever. As, therefore, an absolutely simple object cannot be given in any experience, and the world of sense must be considered as the sum total of all possible experiences: nothing simple exists in the world.

This second proposition in the antithesis has a more extended aim than the first. The first merely banishes the simple from the intuition of the composite; while the second drives it entirely out of nature. Hence we were unable to demonstrate it from the conception of a given object of external intuition (of the composite), but we were obliged to prove it from the relation of a given object to a possible experience in general.

OBSERVATIONS ON THE SECOND ANTINOMY. THESIS.

When I speak of a whole, which necessarily consists of simple parts, I understand thereby only a substantial whole, as the true composite; that is to say, I understand that contingent unity of the manifold which is given as perfectly isolated (at least in thought), placed in reciprocal connection, and thus constituted a unity. Space ought not to be called a compositum but a totum, for its parts are possible in the whole, and not the whole by means of the parts. It might perhaps be called a compositum ideale, but not a compositum reale. But this is of no importance. As space is not a composite of substances (and not even of real accidents), if I abstract all composition therein—nothing, not even a point, remains; for a point is possible only as the limit of a space—consequently of a composite. Space and time, therefore, do not consist of simple parts. That which belongs only to the condition or state of a substance, even although it possesses a quantity (motion or change, for example), likewise does not consist of simple parts. That is to say, a certain degree of change does not originate from the addition of many simple changes. Our inference of the simple from the composite is valid only of self-subsisting things. But the accidents of a state are not self-subsistent. The proof, then, for the necessity of the simple, as the component part of all that is substantial and composite, may prove a failure, and the whole case of this thesis be lost, if we carry the proposition too far, and wish to make it valid of everything that is composite without distinction—as indeed has really now and then happened. Besides, I am here speaking only of the simple, in so far as it is necessarily given in the composite—the latter being capable of solution into the former as its component parts. The proper signification of the word monas (as employed by Leibnitz) ought to relate to the simple, given immediately as simple substance (for example, in consciousness), and not as an element of the composite. As an element, the term atomus would be more appropriate. And as I wish to prove the existence of simple substances, only in relation to, and as the elements of, the composite, I might term the antithesis of the second Antinomy, transcendental Atomistic. But as this word has long been employed to designate a particular theory of corporeal phenomena (moleculae), and thus presupposes a basis of empirical conceptions, I prefer calling it the dialectical principle of Monadology.

ANTITHESIS.

Against the assertion of the infinite subdivisibility of matter whose ground of proof is purely mathematical, objections have been alleged by the Monadists. These objections lay themselves open, at first sight, to suspicion, from the fact that they do not recognize the clearest mathematical proofs as propositions relating to the constitution of space, in so far as it is really the formal condition of the possibility of all matter, but regard them merely as inferences from abstract but arbitrary conceptions, which cannot have any application to real things. Just as if it were possible to imagine another mode of intuition than that given in the primitive intuition of space; and just as if its à priori determinations did not apply to everything, the existence of which is possible, from the fact alone of its filling space. If we listen to them, we shall find ourselves required to cogitate, in addition to the mathematical point, which is simple—not, however, a part, but a mere limit of space—physical points, which are indeed likewise simple, but possess the peculiar property, as parts of space, of filling it merely by their aggregation. I shall not repeat here the common and clear refutations of this absurdity, which are to be found everywhere in numbers: every one knows that it is impossible to undermine the evidence of mathematics by mere discursive conceptions; I shall only remark that, if in this case philosophy endeavours to gain an advantage over mathematics by sophistical artifices, it is because it forgets that the discussion relates solely to Phenomena and their conditions. It is not sufficient to find the conception of the simple for the pure conception of the composite, but we must discover for the intuition of the composite (matter), the intuition of the simple. Now this, according to the laws of sensibility, and consequently in the case of objects of sense, is utterly impossible. In the case of a whole composed of substances, which is cogitated solely by the pure understanding, it may be necessary to be in possession of the simple before composition is possible. But this does not hold good of the Totum substantiale phaenomenon, which, as an empirical intuition in space, possesses the necessary property of containing no simple part, for the very reason that no part of space is simple. Meanwhile, the Monadists have been subtle enough to escape from this difficulty, by presupposing intuition and the dynamical relation of substances as the condition of the possibility of space, instead of regarding space as the condition of the possibility of the objects of external intuition, that is, of bodies. Now we have a conception of bodies only as phenomena, and, as such, they necessarily presuppose space as the condition of all external phenomena. The evasion is therefore in vain; as, indeed, we have sufficiently shown in our Æsthetic. If bodies were things in themselves, the proof of the Monadists would be unexceptionable.

The second dialectical assertion possesses the peculiarity of having opposed to it a dogmatical proposition, which, among all such sophistical statements, is the only one that undertakes to prove in the case of an object of experience, that which is properly a transcendental idea—the absolute simplicity of substance. The proposition is that the object of the internal sense, the thinking Ego, is an absolute simple substance. Without at present entering upon this subject—as it has been considered at length in a former chapter—I shall merely remark that, if something is cogitated merely as an object, without the addition of any synthetical determination of its intuition—as happens in the case of the bare representation, I—it is certain that no manifold and no composition can be perceived in such a representation. As, moreover, the predicates whereby I cogitate this object are merely intuitions of the internal sense, there cannot be discovered in them anything to prove the existence of a manifold whose parts are external to each other, and, consequently, nothing to prove the existence of real composition. Consciousness, therefore, is so constituted that, inasmuch as the thinking subject is at the same time its own object, it cannot divide itself—although it can divide its inhering determinations. For every object in relation to itself is absolute unity. Nevertheless, if the subject is regarded externally, as an object of intuition, it must, in its character of phenomenon, possess the property of composition. And it must always be regarded in this manner, if we wish to know whether there is or is not contained in it a manifold whose parts are external to each other.

THIRD CONFLICT OF THE TRANSCENDENTAL IDEAS. THESIS.

Causality according to the laws of nature, is not the only causality operating to originate the phenomena of the world. A causality of freedom is also necessary to account fully for these phenomena.

PROOF.

Let it be supposed, that there is no other kind of causality than that according to the laws of nature. Consequently, everything that happens presupposes a previous condition, which it follows with absolute certainty, in conformity with a rule. But this previous condition must itself be something that has happened (that has arisen in time, as it did not exist before), for, if it has always been in existence, its consequence or effect would not thus originate for the first time, but would likewise have always existed. The causality, therefore, of a cause, whereby something happens, is itself a thing that has happened. Now this again presupposes, in conformity with the law of nature, a previous condition and its causality, and this another anterior to the former, and so on. If, then, everything happens solely in accordance with the laws of nature, there cannot be any real first beginning of things, but only a subaltern or comparative beginning. There cannot, therefore, be a completeness of series on the side of the causes which originate the one from the other. But the law of nature is that nothing can happen without a sufficient à priori determined cause. The proposition therefore—if all causality is possible only in accordance with the laws of nature—is, when stated in this unlimited and general manner, self-contradictory. It follows that this cannot be the only kind of causality.

From what has been said, it follows that a causality must be admitted, by means of which something happens, without its cause being determined according to necessary laws by some other cause preceding. That is to say, there must exist an absolute spontaneity of cause, which of itself originates a series of phenomena which proceeds according to natural laws—consequently transcendental freedom, without which even in the course of nature the succession of phenomena on the side of causes is never complete.

ANTITHESIS.

There is no such thing as freedom, but everything in the world happens solely according to the laws of nature.

PROOF.

Granted, that there does exist freedom in the transcendental sense, as a peculiar kind of causality, operating to produce events in the world—a faculty, that is to say, of originating a state, and consequently a series of consequences from that state. In this case, not only the series originated by this spontaneity, but the determination of this spontaneity itself to the production of the series, that is to say, the causality itself must have an absolute commencement, such that nothing can precede to determine this action according to unvarying laws. But every beginning of action presupposes in the acting cause a state of inaction; and a dynamically primal beginning of action presupposes a state, which has no connection—as regards causality—with the preceding state of the cause—which does not, that is, in any wise result from it. Transcendental freedom is therefore opposed to the natural law of cause and effect, and such a conjunction of successive states in effective causes is destructive of the possibility of unity in experience and for that reason not to be found in experience—is consequently a mere fiction of thought.

We have, therefore, nothing but nature to which we must look for connection and order in cosmical events. Freedom—independence of the laws of nature—is certainly a deliverance from restraint, but it is also a relinquishing of the guidance of law and rule. For it cannot be alleged that, instead of the laws of nature, laws of freedom may be introduced into the causality of the course of nature. For, if freedom were determined according to laws, it would be no longer freedom, but merely nature. Nature, therefore, and transcendental freedom are distinguishable as conformity to law and lawlessness. The former imposes upon understanding the difficulty of seeking the origin of events ever higher and higher in the series of causes, inasmuch as causality is always conditioned thereby; while it compensates this labour by the guarantee of a unity complete and in conformity with law. The latter, on the contrary, holds out to the understanding the promise of a point of rest in the chain of causes, by conducting it to an unconditioned causality, which professes to have the power of spontaneous origination, but which, in its own utter blindness, deprives it of the guidance of rules, by which alone a completely connected experience is possible.

OBSERVATIONS ON THE THIRD ANTINOMY. ON THE THESIS.

The transcendental idea of freedom is far from constituting the entire content of the psychological conception so termed, which is for the most part empirical. It merely presents us with the conception of spontaneity of action, as the proper ground for imputing freedom to the cause of a certain class of objects. It is, however, the true stumbling-stone to philosophy, which meets with unconquerable difficulties in the way of its admitting this kind of unconditioned causality. That element in the question of the freedom of the will, which has for so long a time placed speculative reason in such perplexity, is properly only transcendental, and concerns the question, whether there must be held to exist a faculty of spontaneous origination of a series of successive things or states. How such a faculty is possible is not a necessary inquiry; for in the case of natural causality itself, we are obliged to content ourselves with the à priori knowledge that such a causality must be presupposed, although we are quite incapable of comprehending how the being of one thing is possible through the being of another, but must for this information look entirely to experience. Now we have demonstrated this necessity of a free first beginning of a series of phenomena, only in so far as it is required for the comprehension of an origin of the world, all following states being regarded as a succession according to laws of nature alone. But, as there has thus been proved the existence of a faculty which can of itself originate a series in time—although we are unable to explain how it can exist—we feel ourselves authorized to admit, even in the midst of the natural course of events, a beginning, as regards causality, of different successions of phenomena, and at the same time to attribute to all substances a faculty of free action. But we ought in this case not to allow ourselves to fall into a common misunderstanding, and to suppose that, because a successive series in the world can only have a comparatively first beginning—another state or condition of things always preceding—an absolutely first beginning of a series in the course of nature is impossible. For we are not speaking here of an absolutely first beginning in relation to time, but as regards causality alone. When, for example, I, completely of my own free will, and independently of the necessarily determinative influence of natural causes, rise from my chair, there commences with this event, including its material consequences in infinitum, an absolutely new series; although, in relation to time, this event is merely the continuation of a preceding series. For this resolution and act of mine do not form part of the succession of effects in nature, and are not mere continuations of it; on the contrary, the determining causes of nature cease to operate in reference to this event, which certainly succeeds the acts of nature, but does not proceed from them. For these reasons, the action of a free agent must be termed, in regard to causality, if not in relation to time, an absolutely primal beginning of a series of phenomena.

The justification of this need of reason to rest upon a free act as the first beginning of the series of natural causes is evident from the fact, that all philosophers of antiquity (with the exception of the Epicurean school) felt themselves obliged, when constructing a theory of the motions of the universe, to accept a prime mover, that is, a freely acting cause, which spontaneously and prior to all other causes evolved this series of states. They always felt the need of going beyond mere nature, for the purpose of making a first beginning comprehensible.

ON THE ANTITHESIS.

The assertor of the all-sufficiency of nature in regard to causality (transcendental Physiocracy), in opposition to the doctrine of freedom, would defend his view of the question somewhat in the following manner. He would say, in answer to the sophistical arguments of the opposite party: If you do not accept a mathematical first, in relation to time, you have no need to seek a dynamical first, in regard to causality. Who compelled you to imagine an absolutely primal condition of the world, and therewith an absolute beginning of the gradually progressing successions of phenomena—and, as some foundation for this fancy of yours, to set bounds to unlimited nature? Inasmuch as the substances in the world have always existed—at least the unity of experience renders such a supposition quite necessary—there is no difficulty in believing also, that the changes in the conditions of these substances have always existed; and, consequently, that a first beginning, mathematical or dynamical, is by no means required. The possibility of such an infinite derivation, without any initial member from which all the others result, is certainly quite incomprehensible. But, if you are rash enough to deny the enigmatical secrets of nature for this reason, you will find yourselves obliged to deny also the existence of many fundamental properties of natural objects (such as fundamental forces), which you can just as little comprehend; and even the possibility of so simple a conception as that of change must present to you insuperable difficulties. For if experience did not teach you that it was real, you never could conceive à priori the possibility of this ceaseless sequence of being and non-being.

But if the existence of a transcendental faculty of freedom is granted—a faculty of originating changes in the world—this faculty must at least exist out of and apart from the world; although it is certainly a bold assumption, that, over and above the complete content of all possible intuitions, there still exists an object which cannot be presented in any possible perception. But, to attribute to substances in the world itself such a faculty, is quite inadmissible; for, in this case; the connection of phenomena reciprocally determining and determined according to general laws, which is termed nature, and along with it the criteria of empirical truth, which enable us to distinguish experience from mere visionary dreaming, would almost entirely disappear. In proximity with such a lawless faculty of freedom, a system of nature is hardly cogitable; for the laws of the latter would be continually subject to the intrusive influences of the former, and the course of phenomena, which would otherwise proceed regularly and uniformly, would become thereby confused and disconnected.

FOURTH CONFLICT OF THE TRANSCENDENTAL IDEAS. THESIS.

There exists either in, or in connection with the world—either as a part of it, or as the cause of it—an absolutely necessary being.

PROOF.

The world of sense, as the sum total of all phenomena, contains a series of changes. For, without such a series, the mental representation of the series of time itself, as the condition of the possibility of the sensuous world, could not be presented to us.[46] But every change stands under its condition, which precedes it in time and renders it necessary. Now the existence of a given condition presupposes a complete series of conditions up to the absolutely unconditioned, which alone is absolutely necessary. It follows that something that is absolutely necessary must exist, if change exists as its consequence. But this necessary thing itself belongs to the sensuous world. For suppose it to exist out of and apart from it, the series of cosmical changes would receive from it a beginning, and yet this necessary cause would not itself belong to the world of sense. But this is impossible. For, as the beginning of a series in time is determined only by that which precedes it in time, the supreme condition of the beginning of a series of changes must exist in the time in which this series itself did not exist; for a beginning supposes a time preceding, in which the thing that begins to be was not in existence. The causality of the necessary cause of changes, and consequently the cause itself, must for these reasons belong to time—and to phenomena, time being possible only as the form of phenomena. Consequently, it cannot be cogitated as separated from the world of sense—the sum total of all phenomena. There is, therefore, contained in the world, something that is absolutely necessary—whether it be the whole cosmical series itself, or only a part of it.

ANTITHESIS.

An absolutely necessary being does not exist, either in the world, or out of it—as its cause.

PROOF.

Grant that either the world itself is necessary, or that there is contained in it a necessary existence. Two cases are possible. First, there must either be in the series of cosmical changes a beginning, which is unconditionally necessary, and therefore uncaused—which is at variance with the dynamical law of the determination of all phenomena in time; or, secondly, the series itself is without beginning, and, although contingent and conditioned in all its parts, is nevertheless absolutely necessary and unconditioned as a whole—which is self-contradictory. For the existence of an aggregate cannot be necessary, if no single part of it possesses necessary existence.

Grant, on the other hand, that an absolutely necessary cause exists out of and apart from the world. This cause, as the highest member in the series of the causes of cosmical changes, must originate or begin[47] the existence of the latter and their series. In this case it must also begin to act, and its causality would therefore belong to time, and consequently to the sum total of phenomena, that is, to the world. It follows that the cause cannot be out of the world; which is contradictory to the hypothesis. Therefore, neither in the world, nor out of it (but in causal connection with it), does there exist any absolutely necessary being.

OBSERVATIONS ON THE FOURTH ANTINOMY. ON THE THESIS.

To demonstrate the existence of a necessary being, I cannot be permitted in this place to employ any other than the cosmological argument, which ascends from the conditioned in phenomena to the unconditioned in conception—the unconditioned being considered the necessary condition of the absolute totality of the series. The proof, from the mere idea of a supreme being, belongs to another principle of reason and requires separate discussion.

The pure cosmological proof demonstrates the existence of a necessary being, but at the same time leaves it quite unsettled, whether this being is the world itself, or quite distinct from it. To establish the truth of the latter view, principles are requisite, which are not cosmological and do not proceed in the series of phenomena. We should require to introduce into our proof conceptions of contingent beings—regarded merely as objects of the understanding, and also a principle which enables us to connect these, by means of mere conceptions, with a necessary being. But the proper place for all such arguments is a transcendent philosophy, which has unhappily not yet been established.

But, if we begin our proof cosmologically, by laying at the foundation of it the series of phenomena, and the regress in it according to empirical laws of causality, we are not at liberty to break off from this mode of demonstration and to pass over to something which is not itself a member of the series. The condition must be taken in exactly the same signification as the relation of the conditioned to its condition in the series has been taken, for the series must conduct us in an unbroken regress to this supreme condition. But if this relation is sensuous, and belongs to the possible empirical employment of understanding, the supreme condition or cause must close the regressive series according to the laws of sensibility and consequently, must belong to the series of time. It follows that this necessary existence must be regarded as the highest member of the cosmical series.

Certain philosophers have, nevertheless, allowed themselves the liberty of making such a saltus (metabasis eis allo gonos). From the changes in the world they have concluded their empirical contingency, that is, their dependence on empirically-determined causes, and they thus admitted an ascending series of empirical conditions: and in this they are quite right. But as they could not find in this series any primal beginning or any highest member, they passed suddenly from the empirical conception of contingency to the pure category, which presents us with a series—not sensuous, but intellectual—whose completeness does certainly rest upon the existence of an absolutely necessary cause. Nay, more, this intellectual series is not tied to any sensuous conditions; and is therefore free from the condition of time, which requires it spontaneously to begin its causality in time. But such a procedure is perfectly inadmissible, as will be made plain from what follows.

In the pure sense of the categories, that is contingent the contradictory opposite of which is possible. Now we cannot reason from empirical contingency to intellectual. The opposite of that which is changed—the opposite of its state—is actual at another time, and is therefore possible. Consequently, it is not the contradictory opposite of the former state. To be that, it is necessary that, in the same time in which the preceding state existed, its opposite could have existed in its place; but such a cognition is not given us in the mere phenomenon of change. A body that was in motion = A, comes into a state of rest = non-A. Now it cannot be concluded from the fact that a state opposite to the state A follows it, that the contradictory opposite of A is possible; and that A is therefore contingent. To prove this, we should require to know that the state of rest could have existed in the very same time in which the motion took place. Now we know nothing more than that the state of rest was actual in the time that followed the state of motion; consequently, that it was also possible. But motion at one time, and rest at another time, are not contradictorily opposed to each other. It follows from what has been said that the succession of opposite determinations, that is, change, does not demonstrate the fact of contingency as represented in the conceptions of the pure understanding; and that it cannot, therefore, conduct us to the fact of the existence of a necessary being. Change proves merely empirical contingency, that is to say, that the new state could not have existed without a cause, which belongs to the preceding time. This cause—even although it is regarded as absolutely necessary—must be presented to us in time, and must belong to the series of phenomena.

ON THE ANTITHESIS.

The difficulties which meet us, in our attempt to rise through the series of phenomena to the existence of an absolutely necessary supreme cause, must not originate from our inability to establish the truth of our mere conceptions of the necessary existence of a thing. That is to say, our objections not be ontological, but must be directed against the causal connection with a series of phenomena of a condition which is itself unconditioned. In one word, they must be cosmological and relate to empirical laws. We must show that the regress in the series of causes (in the world of sense) cannot conclude with an empirically unconditioned condition, and that the cosmological argument from the contingency of the cosmical state—a contingency alleged to arise from change—does not justify us in accepting a first cause, that is, a prime originator of the cosmical series.

The reader will observe in this antinomy a very remarkable contrast. The very same grounds of proof which established in the thesis the existence of a supreme being, demonstrated in the antithesis—and with equal strictness—the non-existence of such a being. We found, first, that a necessary being exists, because the whole time past contains the series of all conditions, and with it, therefore, the unconditioned (the necessary); secondly, that there does not exist any necessary being, for the same reason, that the whole time past contains the series of all conditions—which are themselves, therefore, in the aggregate, conditioned. The cause of this seeming incongruity is as follows. We attend, in the first argument, solely to the absolute totality of the series of conditions, the one of which determines the other in time, and thus arrive at a necessary unconditioned. In the second, we consider, on the contrary, the contingency of everything that is determined in the series of time—for every event is preceded by a time, in which the condition itself must be determined as conditioned—and thus everything that is unconditioned or absolutely necessary disappears. In both, the mode of proof is quite in accordance with the common procedure of human reason, which often falls into discord with itself, from considering an object from two different points of view. Herr von Mairan regarded the controversy between two celebrated astronomers, which arose from a similar difficulty as to the choice of a proper standpoint, as a phenomenon of sufficient importance to warrant a separate treatise on the subject. The one concluded: the moon revolves on its own axis, because it constantly presents the same side to the earth; the other declared that the moon does not revolve on its own axis, for the same reason. Both conclusions were perfectly correct, according to the point of view from which the motions of the moon were considered.

SECTION III. OF THE INTEREST OF REASON IN THESE SELF-CONTRADICTIONS

We have thus completely before us the dialectical procedure of the cosmological ideas. No possible experience can present us with an object adequate to them in extent. Nay, more, reason itself cannot cogitate them as according with the general laws of experience. And yet they are not arbitrary fictions of thought. On the contrary, reason, in its uninterrupted progress in the empirical synthesis, is necessarily conducted to them, when it endeavours to free from all conditions and to comprehend in its unconditioned totality that which can only be determined conditionally in accordance with the laws of experience. These dialectical propositions are so many attempts to solve four natural and unavoidable problems of reason. There are neither more, nor can there be less, than this number, because there are no other series of synthetical hypotheses, limiting à priori the empirical synthesis.

The brilliant claims of reason striving to extend its dominion beyond the limits of experience, have been represented above only in dry formulae, which contain merely the grounds of its pretensions. They have, besides, in conformity with the character of a transcendental philosophy, been freed from every empirical element; although the full splendour of the promises they hold out, and the anticipations they excite, manifests itself only when in connection with empirical cognitions. In the application of them, however, and in the advancing enlargement of the employment of reason, while struggling to rise from the region of experience and to soar to those sublime ideas, philosophy discovers a value and a dignity, which, if it could but make good its assertions, would raise it far above all other departments of human knowledge—professing, as it does, to present a sure foundation for our highest hopes and the ultimate aims of all the exertions of reason. The questions: whether the world has a beginning and a limit to its extension in space; whether there exists anywhere, or perhaps, in my own thinking Self, an indivisible and indestructible unity—or whether nothing but what is divisible and transitory exists; whether I am a free agent, or, like other beings, am bound in the chains of nature and fate; whether, finally, there is a supreme cause of the world, or all our thought and speculation must end with nature and the order of external things—are questions for the solution of which the mathematician would willingly exchange his whole science; for in it there is no satisfaction for the highest aspirations and most ardent desires of humanity. Nay, it may even be said that the true value of mathematics —that pride of human reason—consists in this: that she guides reason to the knowledge of nature—in her greater as well as in her less manifestations—in her beautiful order and regularity—guides her, moreover, to an insight into the wonderful unity of the moving forces in the operations of nature, far beyond the expectations of a philosophy building only on experience; and that she thus encourages philosophy to extend the province of reason beyond all experience, and at the same time provides it with the most excellent materials for supporting its investigations, in so far as their nature admits, by adequate and accordant intuitions.

Unfortunately for speculation—but perhaps fortunately for the practical interests of humanity—reason, in the midst of her highest anticipations, finds herself hemmed in by a press of opposite and contradictory conclusions, from which neither her honour nor her safety will permit her to draw back. Nor can she regard these conflicting trains of reasoning with indifference as mere passages at arms, still less can she command peace; for in the subject of the conflict she has a deep interest. There is no other course left open to her than to reflect with herself upon the origin of this disunion in reason—whether it may not arise from a mere misunderstanding. After such an inquiry, arrogant claims would have to be given up on both sides; but the sovereignty of reason over understanding and sense would be based upon a sure foundation.

We shall at present defer this radical inquiry and, in the meantime, consider for a little what side in the controversy we should most willingly take, if we were obliged to become partisans at all. As, in this case, we leave out of sight altogether the logical criterion of truth, and merely consult our own interest in reference to the question, these considerations, although inadequate to settle the question of right in either party, will enable us to comprehend how those who have taken part in the struggle, adopt the one view rather than the other—no special insight into the subject, however, having influenced their choice. They will, at the same time, explain to us many other things by the way—for example, the fiery zeal on the one side and the cold maintenance of their cause on the other; why the one party has met with the warmest approbations, and the other has always been repulsed by irreconcilable prejudices.

There is one thing, however, that determines the proper point of view, from which alone this preliminary inquiry can be instituted and carried on with the proper completeness—and that is the comparison of the principles from which both sides, thesis and antithesis, proceed. My readers would remark in the propositions of the antithesis a complete uniformity in the mode of thought and a perfect unity of principle. Its principle was that of pure empiricism, not only in the explication of the phenomena in the world, but also in the solution of the transcendental ideas, even of that of the universe itself. The affirmations of the thesis, on the contrary, were based, in addition to the empirical mode of explanation employed in the series of phenomena, on intellectual propositions; and its principles were in so far not simple. I shall term the thesis, in view of its essential characteristic, the dogmatism of pure reason.

On the side of Dogmatism, or of the thesis, therefore, in the determination of the cosmological ideas, we find:

1. A practical interest, which must be very dear to every right-thinking man. That the word has a beginning—that the nature of my thinking self is simple, and therefore indestructible—that I am a free agent, and raised above the compulsion of nature and her laws—and, finally, that the entire order of things, which form the world, is dependent upon a Supreme Being, from whom the whole receives unity and connection—these are so many foundation-stones of morality and religion. The antithesis deprives us of all these supports—or, at least, seems so to deprive us.

2. A speculative interest of reason manifests itself on this side. For, if we take the transcendental ideas and employ them in the manner which the thesis directs, we can exhibit completely à priori the entire chain of conditions, and understand the derivation of the conditioned—beginning from the unconditioned. This the antithesis does not do; and for this reason does not meet with so welcome a reception. For it can give no answer to our question respecting the conditions of its synthesis—except such as must be supplemented by another question, and so on to infinity. According to it, we must rise from a given beginning to one still higher; every part conducts us to a still smaller one; every event is preceded by another event which is its cause; and the conditions of

existence rest always upon other and still higher conditions, and find neither end nor basis in some self-subsistent thing as the primal being.

3. This side has also the advantage of popularity; and this constitutes no small part of its claim to favour. The common understanding does not find the least difficulty in the idea of the unconditioned beginning of all synthesis—accustomed, as it is, rather to follow our consequences than to seek for a proper basis for cognition. In the conception of an absolute first, moreover—the possibility of which it does not inquire into—it is highly gratified to find a firmly-established point of departure for its attempts at theory; while in the restless and continuous ascent from the conditioned to the condition, always with one foot in the air, it can find no satisfaction.

On the side of the antithesis, or Empiricism, in the determination of the cosmological ideas:

1. We cannot discover any such practical interest arising from pure principles of reason as morality and religion present. On the contrary, pure empiricism seems to empty them of all their power and influence. If there does not exist a Supreme Being distinct from the world—if the world is without beginning, consequently without a Creator—if our wills are not free, and the soul is divisible and subject to corruption just like matter—the ideas and principles of morality lose all validity and fall with the transcendental ideas which constituted their theoretical support.

2. But empiricism, in compensation, holds out to reason, in its speculative interests, certain important advantages, far exceeding any that the dogmatist can promise us. For, when employed by the empiricist, understanding is always upon its proper ground of investigation—the field of possible experience, the laws of which it can explore, and thus extend its cognition securely and with clear intelligence without being stopped by limits in any direction. Here can it and ought it to find and present to intuition its proper object—not only in itself, but in all its relations; or, if it employ conceptions, upon this ground it can always present the corresponding images in clear and unmistakable intuitions. It is quite unnecessary for it to renounce the guidance of nature, to attach itself to ideas, the objects of which it cannot know; because, as mere intellectual entities, they cannot be presented in any intuition. On the contrary, it is not even permitted to abandon its proper occupation, under the pretence that it has been brought to a conclusion (for it never can be), and to pass into the region of idealizing reason and transcendent conceptions, which it is not required to observe and explore the laws of nature, but merely to think and to imagine—secure from being contradicted by facts, because they have not been called as witnesses, but passed by, or perhaps subordinated to the so-called higher interests and considerations of pure reason.

Hence the empiricist will never allow himself to accept any epoch of nature for the first—the absolutely primal state; he will not believe that there can be limits to his outlook into her wide domains, nor pass from the objects of nature, which he can satisfactorily explain by means of observation and mathematical thought—which he can determine synthetically in intuition, to those which neither sense nor imagination can ever present in concreto; he will not concede the existence of a faculty in nature, operating independently of the laws of nature—a concession which would introduce uncertainty into the procedure of the understanding, which is guided by necessary laws to the observation of phenomena; nor, finally, will he permit himself to seek a cause beyond nature, inasmuch as we know nothing but it, and from it alone receive an objective basis for all our conceptions and instruction in the unvarying laws of things.

In truth, if the empirical philosopher had no other purpose in the establishment of his antithesis than to check the presumption of a reason which mistakes its true destination, which boasts of its insight and its knowledge, just where all insight and knowledge cease to exist, and regards that which is valid only in relation to a practical interest, as an advancement of the speculative interests of the mind (in order, when it is convenient for itself, to break the thread of our physical investigations, and, under pretence of extending our cognition, connect them with transcendental ideas, by means of which we really know only that we know nothing)—if, I say, the empiricist rested satisfied with this benefit, the principle advanced by him would be a maxim recommending moderation in the pretensions of reason and modesty in its affirmations, and at the same time would direct us to the right mode of extending the province of the understanding, by the help of the only true teacher, experience. In obedience to this advice, intellectual hypotheses and faith would not be called in aid of our practical interests; nor should we introduce them under the pompous titles of science and insight. For speculative cognition cannot find an objective basis any other where than in experience; and, when we overstep its limits our synthesis, which requires ever new cognitions independent of experience, has no substratum of intuition upon which to build.

But if—as often happens—empiricism, in relation to ideas, becomes itself dogmatic and boldly denies that which is above the sphere of its phenomenal cognition, it falls itself into the error of intemperance—an error which is here all the more reprehensible, as thereby the practical interest of reason receives an irreparable injury.

And this constitutes the opposition between Epicureanism[48] and Platonism.

Both Epicurus and Plato assert more in their systems than they know. The former encourages and advances science—although to the prejudice of the practical; the latter presents us with excellent principles for the investigation of the practical, but, in relation to everything regarding which we can attain to speculative cognition, permits reason to append idealistic explanations of natural phenomena, to the great injury of physical investigation.

3. In regard to the third motive for the preliminary choice of a party in this war of assertions, it seems very extraordinary that empiricism should be utterly unpopular. We should be inclined to believe that the common understanding would receive it with pleasure—promising as it does to satisfy it without passing the bounds of experience and its connected order; while transcendental dogmatism obliges it to rise to conceptions which far surpass the intelligence and ability of the most practised thinkers. But in this, in truth, is to be found its real motive. For the common understanding thus finds itself in a situation where not even the most learned can have the advantage of it. If it understands little or nothing about these transcendental conceptions, no one can boast of understanding any more; and although it may not express itself in so scholastically correct a manner as others, it can busy itself with reasoning and arguments without end, wandering among mere ideas, about which one can always be very eloquent, because we know nothing about them; while, in the observation and investigation of nature, it would be forced to remain dumb and to confess its utter ignorance. Thus indolence and vanity form of themselves strong recommendations of these principles. Besides, although it is a hard thing for a philosopher to assume a principle, of which he

can give to himself no reasonable account, and still more to employ conceptions, the objective reality of which cannot be established, nothing is more usual with the common understanding. It wants something which will allow it to go to work with confidence. The difficulty of even comprehending a supposition does not disquiet it, because—not knowing what comprehending means—it never even thinks of the supposition it may be adopting as a principle; and regards as known that with which it has become familiar from constant use. And, at last, all speculative interests disappear before the practical interests which it holds dear; and it fancies that it understands and knows what its necessities and hopes incite it to assume or to believe. Thus the empiricism of transcendentally idealizing reason is robbed of all popularity; and, however prejudicial it may be to the highest practical principles, there is no fear that it will ever pass the limits of the schools, or acquire any favour or influence in society or with the multitude.

Human reason is by nature architectonic. That is to say, it regards all cognitions as parts of a possible system, and hence accepts only such principles as at least do not incapacitate a cognition to which we may have attained from being placed along with others in a general system. But the propositions of the antithesis are of a character which renders the completion of an edifice of cognitions impossible. According to these, beyond one state or epoch of the world there is always to be found one more ancient; in every part always other parts themselves divisible; preceding every event another, the origin of which must itself be sought still higher; and everything in existence is conditioned, and still not dependent on an unconditioned and primal existence. As, therefore, the antithesis will not concede the existence of a first beginning which might be available as a foundation, a complete edifice of cognition, in the presence of such hypothesis, is utterly impossible. Thus the architectonic interest of reason, which requires a unity— not empirical, but à priori and rational—forms a natural recommendation for the assertions of the thesis in our antinomy.

But if any one could free himself entirely from all considerations of interest, and weigh without partiality the assertions of reason, attending only to their content, irrespective of the consequences which follow from them; such a person, on the supposition that he knew no other way out of the confusion than to settle the truth of one or other of the conflicting doctrines, would live in a state of continual hesitation. Today, he would feel convinced that the human will is free; to-morrow, considering the indissoluble chain of nature, he would look on freedom as a mere illusion and declare nature to be all-in-all. But, if he were called to action, the play of the merely speculative reason would disappear like the shapes of a dream, and practical interest would dictate his choice of principles. But, as it well befits a reflective and inquiring being to devote certain periods of time to the examination of its own reason—to divest itself of all partiality, and frankly to communicate its observations for the judgement and opinion of others; so no one can be blamed for, much less prevented from, placing both parties on their trial, with permission to end themselves, free from intimidation, before intimidation, before a sworn jury of equal condition with themselves—the condition of weak and fallible men.

SECTION IV. OF THE NECESSITY IMPOSED UPON PURE REASON OF PRESENTING A SOLUTION OF ITS TRANSCENDENTAL PROBLEMS

To avow an ability to solve all problems and to answer all questions would be a profession certain to convict any philosopher of extravagant boasting and self-conceit, and at once to destroy the confidence that might otherwise have been reposed in him. There are, however, sciences so constituted that every question arising within their sphere must necessarily be capable of receiving an answer from the knowledge already possessed, for the answer must be received from the same sources whence the question arose. In such sciences it is not allowable to excuse ourselves on the plea of necessary and unavoidable ignorance; a solution is absolutely requisite. The rule of right and wrong must help us to the knowledge of what is right or wrong in all possible cases; otherwise, the idea of obligation or duty would be utterly null, for we cannot have any obligation to that which we cannot know. On the other hand, in our investigations of the phenomena of nature, much must remain uncertain, and many questions continue insoluble; because what we know of nature is far from being sufficient to explain all the phenomena that are presented to our observation. Now the question is: Whether there is in transcendental philosophy any question, relating to an object presented to pure reason, which is unanswerable by this reason; and whether we must regard the subject of the question as quite uncertain, so far as our knowledge extends, and must give it a place among those subjects, of which we have just so much conception as is sufficient to enable us to raise a question—faculty or materials failing us, however, when we attempt an answer.

Now I maintain that, among all speculative cognition, the peculiarity of transcendental philosophy is that there is no question, relating to an object presented to pure reason, which is insoluble by this reason; and that the profession of unavoidable ignorance—the problem being alleged to be beyond the reach of our faculties—cannot free us from the obligation to present a complete and satisfactory answer. For the very conception which enables us to raise the question must give us the power of answering it; inasmuch as the object, as in the case of right and wrong, is not to be discovered out of the conception.

But, in transcendental philosophy, it is only the cosmological questions to which we can demand a satisfactory answer in relation to the constitution of their object; and the philosopher is not permitted to avail himself of the pretext of necessary ignorance and impenetrable obscurity. These questions relate solely to the cosmological ideas. For the object must be given in experience, and the question relates to the adequateness of the object to an idea. If the object is transcendental and therefore itself unknown; if the question, for example, is whether the object—the something, the phenomenon of which (internal—in ourselves) is thought—that is to say, the soul, is in itself a simple being; or whether there is a cause of all things, which is absolutely necessary—in such cases we are seeking for our idea an object, of which we may confess that it is unknown to us, though we must not on that account assert that it is impossible.[49] The cosmological ideas alone posses the peculiarity that we can presuppose the object of them and the empirical synthesis requisite for the conception of that object to be given; and the question, which arises from these ideas, relates merely to the progress of this synthesis, in so far as it must contain absolute totality—which, however, is not empirical, as it cannot be given in any experience. Now, as the question here is solely in regard to a thing as the object of a possible experience and not as a thing in itself, the answer to the transcendental cosmological question need not be sought out of the idea, for the question does not regard an object in itself. The question in relation to a possible experience is not, "What can be given in an experience in concreto" but "what is contained in the idea, to which the empirical synthesis must approximate." The question must therefore be capable of solution from the idea alone. For the idea is a creation of reason itself, which therefore cannot disclaim the obligation to answer or refer us to the unknown object.

It is not so extraordinary, as it at first sight appears, that a science should demand and expect satisfactory answers to all the questions that may arise within its own sphere (questiones domesticae), although, up to a certain time, these answers may not have been discovered. There are, in addition to transcendental philosophy, only two pure sciences of reason; the one with a speculative, the other with a practical content—pure mathematics and pure ethics. Has any one ever heard it alleged that, from our complete and necessary ignorance of the conditions, it is uncertain what exact relation the diameter of a circle bears to the circle in rational or irrational numbers? By the former the sum cannot be given exactly, by the latter only approximately; and therefore we decide that the impossibility of a solution of the question is evident. Lambert presented us with a demonstration of this. In the general principles of morals there can be nothing uncertain, for the propositions are either utterly without meaning, or must originate solely in our rational conceptions. On the other hand, there must be in physical science an infinite number of conjectures, which can never become certainties; because the phenomena of nature are not given as objects dependent on our conceptions. The key to the solution of such questions cannot, therefore, be found in our conceptions, or in pure thought, but must lie without us and for that reason is in many cases not to be discovered; and consequently a satisfactory explanation cannot be expected. The questions of transcendental analytic, which relate to the deduction of our pure cognition, are not to be regarded as of the same kind as those mentioned above; for we are not at present treating of the certainty of judgements in relation to the origin of our conceptions, but only of that certainty in relation to objects.

We cannot, therefore, escape the responsibility of at least a critical solution of the questions of reason, by complaints of the limited nature of our faculties, and the seemingly humble confession that it is beyond the power of our reason to decide, whether the world has existed from all eternity or had a beginning—whether it is infinitely extended, or enclosed within certain limits—whether anything in the world is simple, or whether everything must be capable of infinite divisibility—whether freedom can originate phenomena, or whether everything is absolutely dependent on the laws and order of nature—and, finally, whether there exists a being that is completely unconditioned and necessary, or whether the existence of everything is conditioned and consequently dependent on something external to itself, and therefore in its own nature contingent. For all these questions relate to an object, which can be given nowhere else than in thought. This object is the absolutely unconditioned totality of the synthesis of phenomena. If the conceptions in our minds do not assist us to some certain result in regard to these problems, we must not defend ourselves on the plea that the object itself remains hidden from and unknown to us. For no such thing or object can be given—it is not to be found out of the idea in our minds. We must seek the cause of our failure in our idea itself, which is an insoluble problem and in regard to which we obstinately assume that there exists a real object corresponding and adequate to it. A clear explanation of the dialectic which lies in our conception, will very soon enable us to come to a satisfactory decision in regard to such a question.

The pretext that we are unable to arrive at certainty in regard to these problems may be met with this question, which requires at least a plain answer: "From what source do the ideas originate, the solution of which involves you in such difficulties? Are you seeking for an explanation of certain phenomena; and do you expect these ideas to give you the principles or the rules of this explanation?" Let it be granted, that all nature was laid open before you; that nothing was hid from your senses and your consciousness. Still, you could not cognize in concreto the object of your ideas in any experience. For what is demanded is not only this full and complete intuition, but also a complete synthesis and the consciousness of its absolute totality; and this is not possible by means of any empirical cognition. It follows that your question—your idea—is by no means necessary for the explanation of any phenomenon; and the idea cannot have been in any sense given by the object itself. For such an object can never be presented to us, because it cannot be given by any possible experience. Whatever perceptions you may attain to, you are still surrounded by conditions—in space, or in time—and you cannot discover anything unconditioned; nor can you decide whether this unconditioned is to be placed in an absolute beginning of the synthesis, or in an absolute totality of the series without beginning. A whole, in the empirical signification of the term, is always merely comparative. The absolute whole of quantity (the universe), of division, of derivation, of the condition of existence, with the question—whether it is to be produced by finite or infinite synthesis, no possible experience can instruct us concerning. You will not, for example, be able to explain the phenomena of a body in the least degree better, whether you believe it to consist of simple, or of composite parts; for a simple phenomenon—and just as little an infinite series of composition—can never be presented to your perception. Phenomena require and admit of explanation, only in so far as the conditions of that explanation are given in perception; but the sum total of that which is given in phenomena, considered as an absolute whole, is itself a perception—and we cannot therefore seek for explanations of this whole beyond itself, in other perceptions. The explanation of this whole is the proper object of the transcendental problems of pure reason.

Although, therefore, the solution of these problems is unattainable through experience, we must not permit ourselves to say that it is uncertain how the object of our inquiries is constituted. For the object is in our own mind and cannot be discovered in experience; and we have only to take care that our thoughts are consistent with each other, and to avoid falling into the amphiboly of regarding our idea as a representation of an object empirically given, and therefore to be cognized according to the laws of experience. A dogmatical solution is therefore not only unsatisfactory but impossible. The critical solution, which may be a perfectly certain one, does not consider the question objectively, but proceeds by inquiring into the basis of the cognition upon which the question rests.

SECTION V. SCEPTICAL EXPOSITION OF THE COSMOLOGICAL PROBLEMS PRESENTED IN THE FOUR TRANSCENDENTAL IDEAS

We should be quite willing to desist from the demand of a dogmatical answer to our questions, if we understood beforehand that, be the answer what it may, it would only serve to increase our ignorance, to throw us from one incomprehensibility into another, from one obscurity into another still greater, and perhaps lead us into irreconcilable contradictions. If a dogmatical affirmative or negative answer is demanded, is it at all prudent to set aside the probable grounds of a solution which lie before us and to take into consideration what advantage we shall gain, if the answer is to favour the one side or the other? If it happens that in both cases the answer is mere nonsense, we have in this an irresistible summons to institute a critical investigation of the question, for the purpose of discovering whether it is based on a groundless presupposition and relates to an idea, the falsity of which would be more easily exposed in its application and consequences than in the mere representation of its content. This is the great utility of the sceptical mode of treating the questions addressed by pure reason to itself. By this method we easily rid ourselves of the confusions of dogmatism, and establish in its place a temperate criticism, which, as a genuine cathartic, will successfully remove the presumptuous notions of philosophy and their consequence—the vain pretension to universal science.

If, then, I could understand the nature of a cosmological idea and perceive, before I entered on the discussion of the subject at all, that, whatever side of the question regarding the unconditioned of the regressive synthesis of phenomena it favoured—it must either be too great or too small for every conception of the understanding—I would be able to comprehend how the idea, which relates to an object of experience—an experience which must be adequate to and in accordance with a possible conception of the understanding—must be completely void and without significance, inasmuch as its object is inadequate, consider it as we may. And this is actually the case with all cosmological conceptions, which, for the reason above mentioned, involve reason, so long as it remains attached to them, in an unavoidable antinomy. For suppose:

First, that the world has no beginning—in this case it is too large for our conception; for this conception, which consists in a successive regress, cannot overtake the whole eternity that has elapsed. Grant that it has a beginning, it is then too small for the conception of the understanding. For, as a beginning presupposes a time preceding, it cannot be unconditioned; and the law of the empirical employment of the understanding imposes the necessity of looking for a higher condition of time; and the world is, therefore, evidently too small for this law.

The same is the case with the double answer to the question regarding the extent, in space, of the world. For, if it is infinite and unlimited, it must be too large for every possible empirical conception. If it is finite and limited, we have a right to ask: "What determines these limits?" Void space is not a self-subsistent correlate of things, and cannot be a final condition—and still less an empirical condition, forming a part of a possible experience. For how can we have any experience or perception of an absolute void? But the absolute totality of the empirical synthesis requires that the unconditioned be an empirical conception. Consequently, a finite world is too small for our conception.

Secondly, if every phenomenon (matter) in space consists of an infinite number of parts, the regress of the division is always too great for our conception; and if the division of space must cease with some member of the division (the simple), it is too small for the idea of the unconditioned. For the member at which we have discontinued our division still admits a regress to many more parts contained in the object.

Thirdly, suppose that every event in the world happens in accordance with the laws of nature; the causality of a cause must itself be an event and necessitates a regress to a still higher cause, and consequently the unceasing prolongation of the series of conditions a parte priori. Operative nature is therefore too large for every conception we can form in the synthesis of cosmical events.

If we admit the existence of spontaneously produced events, that is, of free agency, we are driven, in our search for sufficient reasons, on an unavoidable law of nature and are compelled to appeal to the empirical law of causality, and we find that any such totality of connection in our synthesis is too small for our necessary empirical conception.

Fourthly, if we assume the existence of an absolutely necessary being—whether it be the world or something in the world, or the cause of the world—we must place it in a time at an infinite distance from any given moment; for, otherwise, it must be dependent on some other and higher existence. Such an existence is, in this case, too large for our empirical conception, and unattainable by the continued regress of any synthesis.

But if we believe that everything in the world—be it condition or conditioned—is contingent; every given existence is too small for our conception. For in this case we are compelled to seek for some other existence upon which the former depends.

We have said that in all these cases the cosmological idea is either too great or too small for the empirical regress in a synthesis, and consequently for every possible conception of the understanding. Why did we not express ourselves in a manner exactly the reverse of this and, instead of accusing the cosmological idea of over stepping or of falling short of its true aim, possible experience, say that, in the first case, the empirical conception is always too small for the idea, and in the second too great, and thus attach the blame of these contradictions to the empirical regress? The reason is this. Possible experience can alone give reality to our conceptions; without it a conception is merely an idea, without truth or relation to an object. Hence a possible empirical conception must be the standard by which we are to judge whether an idea is anything more than an idea and fiction of thought, or whether it relates to an object in the world. If we say of a thing that in relation to some other thing it is too large or too small, the former is considered as existing for the sake of the latter, and requiring to be adapted to it. Among the trivial subjects of discussion in the old schools of dialectics was this question: "If a ball cannot pass through a hole, shall we say that the ball is too large or the hole too small?" In this case it is indifferent what expression we employ; for we do not know which exists for the sake of the other. On the other hand, we cannot say: "The man is too long for his coat"; but: "The coat is too short for the man."

We are thus led to the well-founded suspicion that the cosmological ideas, and all the conflicting sophistical assertions connected with them, are based upon a false and fictitious conception of the mode in which the object of these ideas is presented to us; and this suspicion will probably direct us how to expose the illusion that has so long led us astray from the truth.

SECTION VI. TRANSCENDENTAL IDEALISM AS THE KEY TO THE SOLUTION OF PURE COSMOLOGICAL DIALECTIC

In the transcendental æsthetic we proved that everything intuited in space and time, all objects of a possible experience, are nothing but phenomena, that is, mere representations; and that these, as presented to us—as extended bodies, or as series of changes—have no self-subsistent existence apart from human thought. This doctrine I call Transcendental Idealism.[50] The realist in the transcendental sense regards these modifications of our sensibility, these mere representations, as things subsisting in themselves.

It would be unjust to accuse us of holding the long-decried theory of empirical idealism, which, while admitting the reality of space, denies, or at least doubts, the existence of bodies extended in it, and thus leaves us without a sufficient criterion of reality and illusion. The supporters of this theory find no difficulty in admitting the reality of the phenomena of the internal sense in time; nay, they go the length of maintaining that this internal experience is of itself a sufficient proof of the real existence of its object as a thing in itself.

Transcendental idealism allows that the objects of external intuition—as intuited in space, and all changes in time—as represented by the internal sense, are real. For, as space is the form of that intuition which we call external, and, without objects in space, no empirical representation could be given us, we can and ought to regard extended bodies in it as real. The case is the same with representations in time. But time and space, with all phenomena therein, are not in themselves things. They are nothing but representations and cannot exist out of and apart from the mind. Nay, the sensuous internal intuition of the mind (as the object of consciousness), the determination of which is represented by the succession of different states in time, is not the real, proper self, as it exists in itself—not the transcendental subject—but only a phenomenon, which is presented to the sensibility of this, to us, unknown being. This internal phenomenon cannot be admitted to be a self-subsisting thing; for its condition is time, and time cannot be the condition of a thing in itself. But the empirical truth of phenomena in space and time is guaranteed beyond the possibility of doubt, and sufficiently distinguished from the illusion of dreams or fancy—although both have a proper and thorough connection in an experience according to empirical laws. The objects of experience then are not things in themselves, but are given only in experience, and have no existence apart from and independently of experience. That there may be inhabitants in the moon, although no one has ever observed them, must certainly be admitted; but this assertion means only, that we may in the possible progress of experience discover them at some future time. For that which stands in connection with a perception according to the laws of the progress of experience is real. They are therefore really existent, if they stand in empirical connection with my actual or real consciousness, although they are not in themselves real, that is, apart from the progress of experience.

There is nothing actually given—we can be conscious of nothing as real, except a perception and the empirical progression from it to other possible perceptions. For phenomena, as mere representations, are real only in perception; and perception is, in fact, nothing but the reality of an empirical representation, that is, a phenomenon. To call a phenomenon a real thing prior to perception means either that we must meet with this phenomenon in the progress of experience, or it means nothing at all. For I can say only of a thing in itself that it exists without relation to the senses and experience. But we are speaking here merely of phenomena in space and time, both of which are determinations of sensibility, and not of things in themselves. It follows that phenomena are not things in themselves, but are mere representations, which if not given in us—in perception—are non-existent.

The faculty of sensuous intuition is properly a receptivity—a capacity of being affected in a certain manner by representations, the relation of which to each other is a pure intuition of space and time—the pure forms of sensibility. These representations, in so far as they are connected and determinable in this relation (in space and time) according to laws of the unity of experience, are called objects. The non-sensuous cause of these representations is completely unknown to us and hence cannot be intuited as an object. For such an object could not be represented either in space or in time; and without these conditions intuition or representation is impossible. We may, at the same time, term the non-sensuous cause of phenomena the transcendental object—but merely as a mental correlate to sensibility, considered as a receptivity. To this transcendental object we may attribute the whole connection and extent of our possible perceptions, and say that it is given and exists in itself prior to all experience. But the phenomena, corresponding to it, are not given as things in themselves, but in experience alone. For they are mere representations, receiving from perceptions alone significance and relation to a real object, under the condition that this or that perception—indicating an object—is in complete connection with all others in accordance with the rules of the unity of experience. Thus we can say: "The things that really existed in past time are given in the transcendental object of experience." But these are to me real objects, only in so far as I can represent to my own mind, that a regressive series of possible perceptions—following the indications of history, or the footsteps of cause and effect—in accordance with empirical laws—that, in one word, the course of the world conducts us to an elapsed series of time as the condition of the present time. This series in past time is represented as real, not in itself, but only in connection with a possible experience. Thus, when I say that certain events occurred in past time, I merely assert the possibility of prolonging the chain of experience, from the present perception, upwards to the conditions that determine it according to time.

If I represent to myself all objects existing in all space and time, I do not thereby place these in space and time prior to all experience; on the contrary, such a representation is nothing more than the notion of a possible experience, in its absolute completeness. In experience alone are those objects, which are nothing but representations, given. But, when I say they existed prior to my experience, this means only that I must begin with the perception present to me and follow the track indicated until I discover them in some part or region of experience. The cause of the empirical condition of this progression—and consequently at what member therein I must stop, and at what point in the regress I am to find this member—is transcendental, and hence necessarily incognizable. But with this we have not to do; our concern is only with the law of progression in experience, in which objects, that is, phenomena, are given. It is a matter of indifference, whether I say, "I may in the progress of experience discover stars, at a hundred times greater distance than the most distant of those now visible," or, "Stars at this distance may be met in space, although no one has, or ever will discover them." For, if they are given as things in themselves, without any relation to possible experience, they are for me non-existent, consequently, are not objects, for they are not contained in the regressive series of experience. But, if these phenomena must be employed in the construction or support of the cosmological idea of an absolute whole, and when we are discussing a question that oversteps the limits of possible experience, the proper distinction of the different theories of the reality of sensuous objects is of great importance, in order to avoid the illusion which must necessarily arise from the misinterpretation of our empirical conceptions.

SECTION VII. CRITICAL SOLUTION OF THE COSMOLOGICAL PROBLEM

The antinomy of pure reason is based upon the following dialectical argument: "If that which is conditioned is given, the whole series of its conditions is also given; but sensuous objects are given as conditioned; consequently..." This syllogism, the major of which seems so natural and evident, introduces as many cosmological ideas as there are different kinds of conditions in the synthesis of phenomena, in so far as these conditions constitute a series. These ideas require absolute totality in the series, and thus place reason in inextricable embarrassment. Before proceeding to expose the fallacy in this dialectical argument, it will be necessary to have a correct understanding of certain conceptions that appear in it.

In the first place, the following proposition is evident, and indubitably certain: "If the conditioned is given, a regress in the series of all its conditions is thereby imperatively required." For the very conception of a conditioned is a conception of something related to a condition, and, if this condition is itself conditioned, to another condition—and so on through all the members of the series. This proposition is, therefore, analytical and has nothing to fear from transcendental criticism. It is a logical postulate of reason: to pursue, as far as possible, the connection of a conception with its conditions.

If, in the second place, both the conditioned and the condition are things in themselves, and if the former is given, not only is the regress to the latter requisite, but the latter is really given with the former. Now, as this is true of all the members of the series, the entire series of conditions, and with them the unconditioned, is at the same time given in the very fact of the conditioned, the existence of which is possible only in and through that series, being given. In this case, the synthesis of the conditioned with its condition, is a synthesis of the understanding merely, which represents things as they are, without regarding whether and how we can cognize them. But if I have to do with phenomena, which, in their character of mere representations, are not given, if I do not attain to a cognition of them (in other words, to themselves, for they are nothing more than empirical cognitions), I am not entitled to say: "If the conditioned is given, all its conditions (as phenomena) are also given." I cannot, therefore, from the fact of a conditioned being given, infer the absolute totality of the series of its conditions. For phenomena are nothing but an empirical synthesis in apprehension or perception, and are therefore given only in it. Now, in speaking of phenomena it does not follow that, if the conditioned is given, the synthesis which constitutes its empirical condition is also thereby given and presupposed; such a synthesis can be established only by an actual regress in the series of conditions. But we are entitled to say in this case that a regress to the conditions of a conditioned, in other words, that a continuous empirical synthesis is enjoined; that, if the conditions are not given, they are at least required; and that we are certain to discover the conditions in this regress.

We can now see that the major, in the above cosmological syllogism, takes the conditioned in the transcendental signification which it has in the pure category, while the minor speaks of it in the empirical signification which it has in the category as applied to phenomena. There is, therefore, a dialectical fallacy in the syllogism—a sophisma figurae dictionis. But this fallacy is not a consciously devised one, but a perfectly natural illusion of the common reason of man. For, when a thing is given as conditioned, we presuppose in the major its conditions and their series, unperceived, as it were, and unseen; because this is nothing more than the logical requirement of complete and satisfactory premises for a given conclusion. In this case, time is altogether left out in the connection of the conditioned with the condition; they are supposed to be given in themselves, and contemporaneously. It is, moreover, just as natural to regard phenomena (in the minor) as things in themselves and as objects presented to the pure understanding, as in the major, in which complete abstraction was made of all conditions of intuition. But it is under these conditions alone that objects are given. Now we overlooked a remarkable distinction between the conceptions. The synthesis of the conditioned with its condition, and the complete series of the latter (in the major) are not limited by time, and do not contain the conception of succession. On the contrary, the empirical synthesis and the series of conditions in the phenomenal world—subsumed in the minor—are necessarily successive and given in time alone. It follows that I cannot presuppose in the minor, as I did in the major, the absolute totality of the synthesis and of the series therein represented; for in the major all the members of the series are given as things in themselves—without any limitations or conditions of time, while in the minor they are possible only in and through a successive regress, which cannot exist, except it be actually carried into execution in the world of phenomena.

After this proof of the viciousness of the argument commonly employed in maintaining cosmological assertions, both parties may now be justly dismissed, as advancing claims without grounds or title. But the process has not been ended by convincing them that one or both were in the wrong and had maintained an assertion which was without valid grounds of proof. Nothing seems to be clearer than that, if one maintains: "The world has a beginning," and another: "The world has no beginning," one of the two must be right. But it is likewise clear that, if the evidence on both sides is equal, it is impossible to discover on what side the truth lies; and the controversy continues, although the parties have been recommended to peace before the tribunal of reason. There remains, then, no other means of settling the question than to convince the parties, who refute each other with such conclusiveness and ability, that they are disputing about nothing, and that a transcendental illusion has been mocking them with visions of reality where there is none. The mode of adjusting a dispute which cannot be decided upon its own merits, we shall now proceed to lay before our readers.

Zeno of Elea, a subtle dialectician, was severely reprimanded by Plato as a sophist, who, merely from the base motive of exhibiting his skill in discussion, maintained and subverted the same proposition by arguments as powerful and convincing on the one side as on the other. He maintained, for example, that God (who was probably nothing more, in his view, than the world) is neither finite nor infinite, neither in motion nor in rest, neither similar nor dissimilar to any other thing. It seemed to those philosophers who criticized his mode of discussion that his purpose was to deny completely both of two self-contradictory propositions—which is absurd. But I cannot believe that there is any justice in this accusation. The first of these propositions I shall presently consider in a more detailed manner. With regard to the others, if by the word of God he understood merely the Universe, his meaning must have been—that it cannot be permanently present in one place—that is, at rest—nor be capable of changing its place—that is, of moving—because all places are in the universe, and the universe itself is, therefore, in no place. Again, if the universe contains in itself everything that exists, it cannot be similar or dissimilar to any other thing, because there is, in fact, no other thing with which it can be compared. If two opposite judgements presuppose a contingent impossible, or arbitrary condition, both—in spite of their opposition (which is, however, not properly or really a contradiction)—fall away; because the condition, which ensured the validity of both, has itself disappeared.

If we say: "Everybody has either a good or a bad smell," we have omitted a third possible judgement—it has no smell at all; and thus both conflicting statements may be false. If we say: "It is either good-smelling or not good-smelling (vel suaveolens vel non-suaveolens)," both judgements are contradictorily opposed; and the contradictory opposite of the former judgement—some bodies are not good-smelling—embraces also those bodies which have no smell at all. In the preceding pair of opposed judgements (per disparata), the contingent condition of the conception of body (smell) attached to both conflicting statements, instead of having been omitted in the latter, which is consequently not the contradictory opposite of the former.

If, accordingly, we say: "The world is either infinite in extension, or it is not infinite (non est infinitus)"; and if the former proposition is false, its contradictory opposite—the world is not infinite—must be true. And thus I should deny the existence of an infinite, without, however affirming the existence of a finite world. But if we construct our proposition thus: "The world is either infinite or finite (non-infinite)," both statements may be false. For, in this case, we consider the world as per se determined in regard to quantity, and while, in the one judgement, we deny its infinite and consequently, perhaps, its independent existence; in the other, we append to the world, regarded as a thing in itself, a certain determination—that of finitude; and the latter may be false as well as the former, if the world is not given as a thing in itself, and thus neither as finite nor as infinite in quantity. This kind of opposition I may be allowed to term dialectical; that of contradictories may be called analytical opposition. Thus then, of two dialectically opposed judgements both may be false, from the fact, that the one is not a mere contradictory of the other, but actually enounces more than is requisite for a full and complete contradiction.

When we regard the two propositions—"The world is infinite in quantity," and, "The world is finite in quantity," as contradictory opposites, we are assuming that the world—the complete series of phenomena—is a thing in itself. For it remains as a permanent quantity, whether I deny the infinite or the finite regress in the series of its phenomena. But if we dismiss this assumption—this transcendental illusion—and deny that it is a thing in itself, the contradictory opposition is metamorphosed into a merely dialectical one; and the world, as not existing in itself—independently of the regressive series of my representations—exists in like manner neither as a whole which is infinite nor as a whole which is finite in itself. The universe exists for me only in the empirical regress of the series of phenomena and not per se. If, then, it is always conditioned, it is never completely or as a whole; and it is, therefore, not an unconditioned whole and does not exist as such, either with an infinite, or with a finite quantity.

What we have here said of the first cosmological idea—that of the absolute totality of quantity in phenomena—applies also to the others. The series of conditions is discoverable only in the regressive synthesis itself, and not in the phenomenon considered as a thing in itself—given prior to all regress. Hence I am compelled to say: "The aggregate of parts in a given phenomenon is in itself neither finite nor infinite; and these parts are given only in the regressive synthesis of decomposition—a synthesis which is never given in absolute completeness, either as finite, or as infinite." The same is the case with the series of subordinated causes, or of the conditioned up to the unconditioned and necessary existence, which can never be regarded as in itself, and in its totality, either as finite or as infinite; because, as a series of subordinate representations, it subsists only in the dynamical regress and cannot be regarded as existing previously to this regress, or as a self-subsistent series of things.

Thus the antinomy of pure reason in its cosmological ideas disappears. For the above demonstration has established the fact that it is merely the product of a dialectical and illusory opposition, which arises from the application of the idea of absolute totality —admissible only as a condition of things in themselves—to phenomena, which exist only in our representations, and—when constituting a series—in a successive regress. This antinomy of reason may, however, be really profitable to our speculative interests, not in the way of contributing any dogmatical addition, but as presenting to us another material support in our critical investigations. For it furnishes us with an indirect proof of the transcendental ideality of phenomena, if our minds were not completely satisfied with the direct proof set forth in the Trancendental Æsthetic. The proof would proceed in the following dilemma. If the world is a whole existing in itself, it must be either finite or infinite. But it is neither finite nor infinite—as has been shown, on the one side, by the thesis, on the other, by the antithesis. Therefore the world—the content of all phenomena—is not a whole existing in itself. It follows that phenomena are nothing, apart from our representations. And this is what we mean by transcendental ideality.

This remark is of some importance. It enables us to see that the proofs of the fourfold antinomy are not mere sophistries—are not fallacious, but grounded on the nature of reason, and valid—under the supposition that phenomena are things in themselves. The opposition of the judgements which follow makes it evident that a fallacy lay in the initial supposition, and thus helps us to discover the true constitution of objects of sense. This transcendental dialectic does not favour scepticism, although it presents us with a triumphant demonstration of the advantages of the sceptical method, the great utility of which is apparent in the antinomy, where the arguments of reason were allowed to confront each other in undiminished force. And although the result of these conflicts of reason is not what we expected—although we have obtained no positive dogmatical addition to metaphysical science—we have still reaped a great advantage in the correction of our judgements on these subjects of thought.

SECTION VIII. REGULATIVE PRINCIPLE OF PURE REASON IN RELATION TO THE COSMOLOGICAL IDEAS

The cosmological principle of totality could not give us any certain knowledge in regard to the maximum in the series of conditions in the world of sense, considered as a thing in itself. The actual regress in the series is the only means of approaching this maximum. This principle of pure reason, therefore, may still be considered as valid—not as an axiom enabling us to cogitate totality in the object as actual, but as a problem for the understanding, which requires it to institute and to continue, in conformity with the idea of totality in the mind, the regress in the series of the conditions of a given conditioned. For in the world of sense, that is, in space and time, every condition which we discover in our investigation of phenomena is itself conditioned; because sensuous objects are not things in themselves (in which case an absolutely unconditioned might be reached in the progress of cognition), but are merely empirical representations the conditions of which must always be found in intuition. The principle of reason is therefore properly a mere rule—prescribing a regress in the series of conditions for given phenomena, and prohibiting any pause or rest on an absolutely unconditioned. It is, therefore, not a principle of the possibility of experience or of the empirical cognition of sensuous objects—consequently not a principle of the understanding; for every experience is confined within certain proper limits determined by the given intuition. Still less is it a constitutive principle of reason authorizing us to extend our conception of the sensuous world beyond all possible experience. It is merely a principle for the enlargement and extension of experience as far as is possible for human faculties. It forbids us to consider any empirical limits as absolute. It is, hence, a principle of reason, which, as a rule, dictates how we ought to proceed in our empirical regress, but is unable to anticipate or indicate prior to the empirical regress what is given in the object itself. I have termed it for this reason a regulative principle of reason; while the principle of the absolute totality of the series of conditions, as existing in itself and given in the object, is a constitutive cosmological principle. This distinction will at once demonstrate the falsehood of the constitutive principle, and prevent us from attributing (by a transcendental subreptio) objective reality to an idea, which is valid only as a rule.

In order to understand the proper meaning of this rule of pure reason, we must notice first that it cannot tell us what the object is, but only how the empirical regress is to be proceeded with in order to attain to the complete conception of the object. If it gave us any information in respect to the former statement, it would be a constitutive principle—a principle impossible from the nature of pure reason. It will not therefore enable us to establish any such conclusions as: "The series of conditions for a given conditioned is in itself finite," or, "It is infinite." For, in this case, we should be cogitating in the mere idea of absolute totality, an object which is not and cannot be given in experience; inasmuch as we should be attributing a reality objective and independent of the empirical synthesis, to a series of phenomena. This idea of reason cannot then be regarded as valid—except as a rule for the regressive synthesis in the series of conditions, according to which we must proceed from the conditioned, through all intermediate and subordinate conditions, up to the unconditioned; although this goal is unattained and unattainable. For the absolutely unconditioned cannot be discovered in the sphere of experience.

We now proceed to determine clearly our notion of a synthesis which can never be complete. There are two terms commonly employed for this purpose. These terms are regarded as expressions of different and distinguishable notions, although the ground of the distinction has never been clearly exposed. The term employed by the mathematicians is progressus in infinitum. The philosophers prefer the expression progressus in indefinitum. Without detaining the reader with an examination of the reasons for such a distinction, or with remarks on the right or wrong use of the terms, I shall endeavour clearly to determine these conceptions, so far as is necessary for the purpose in this Critique.

We may, with propriety, say of a straight line, that it may be produced to infinity. In this case the distinction between a progressus in infinitum and a progressus in indefinitum is a mere piece of subtlety. For, although when we say, "Produce a straight line," it is more correct to say in indefinitum than in infinitum; because the former means, "Produce it as far as you please," the second, "You must not cease to produce it"; the expression in infinitum is, when we are speaking of the power to do it, perfectly correct, for we can always make it longer if we please—on to infinity. And this remark holds good in all cases, when we speak of a progressus, that is, an advancement from the condition to the conditioned; this possible advancement always proceeds to infinity. We may proceed from a given pair in the descending line of generation from father to son, and cogitate a never-ending line of descendants from it. For in such a case reason does not demand absolute totality in the series, because it does not presuppose it as a condition and as given (datum), but merely as conditioned, and as capable of being given (dabile).

Very different is the case with the problem: "How far the regress, which ascends from the given conditioned to the conditions, must extend"; whether I can say: "It is a regress in infinitum," or only "in indefinitum"; and whether, for example, setting out from the human beings at present alive in the world, I may ascend in the series of their ancestors, in infinitum—or whether all that can be said is, that so far as I have proceeded, I have discovered no empirical ground for considering the series limited, so that I am justified, and indeed, compelled to search for ancestors still further back, although I am not obliged by the idea of reason to presuppose them.

My answer to this question is: "If the series is given in empirical intuition as a whole, the regress in the series of its internal conditions proceeds in infinitum; but, if only one member of the series is given, from which the regress is to proceed to absolute totality, the regress is possible only in indefinitum." For example, the division of a portion of matter given within certain limits—of a body, that is—proceeds in infinitum. For, as the condition of this whole is its part, and the condition of the part a part of the part, and so on, and as in this regress of decomposition an unconditioned indivisible member of the series of conditions is not to be found; there are no reasons or grounds in experience for stopping in the division, but, on the contrary, the more remote members of the division are actually and empirically given prior to this division. That is to say, the division proceeds to infinity. On the other hand, the series of ancestors of any given human being is not given, in its absolute totality, in any experience, and yet the regress proceeds from every genealogical member of this series to one still higher, and does not meet with any empirical limit presenting an absolutely unconditioned member of the series. But as the members of such a series are not contained in the empirical intuition of the whole, prior to the regress, this regress does not proceed to infinity, but only in indefinitum, that is, we are called upon to discover other and higher members, which are themselves always conditioned.

In neither case—the regressus in infinitum, nor the regressus in indefinitum, is the series of conditions to be considered as actually infinite in the object itself. This might be true of things in themselves, but it cannot be asserted of phenomena, which, as conditions of each other, are only given in the empirical regress itself. Hence, the question no longer is, "What is the quantity of this series of conditions in itself—is it finite or infinite?" for it is nothing in itself; but, "How is the empirical regress to be commenced, and how far ought we to proceed with it?" And here a signal distinction in the application of this rule becomes apparent. If the whole is given empirically, it is possible to recede in the series of its internal conditions to infinity. But if the whole is not given, and can only be given by and through the empirical regress, I can only say: "It is possible to infinity, to proceed to still higher conditions in the series." In the first case, I am justified in asserting that more members are empirically given in the object than I attain to in the regress (of decomposition). In the second case, I am justified only in saying, that I can always proceed further in the regress, because no member of the series is given as absolutely conditioned, and thus a higher member is possible, and an inquiry with regard to it is necessary. In the one case it is necessary to find other members of the series, in the other it is necessary to inquire for others, inasmuch as experience presents no absolute limitation of the regress. For, either you do not possess a perception which absolutely limits your empirical regress, and in this case the regress cannot be regarded as complete; or, you do possess such a limitative perception, in which case it is not a part of your series (for that which limits must be distinct from that which is limited by it), and it is incumbent you to continue your regress up to this condition, and so on.

These remarks will be placed in their proper light by their application in the following section.

SECTION IX. OF THE EMPIRICAL USE OF THE REGULATIVE PRINCIPLE OF REASON WITH REGARD TO THE COSMOLOGICAL IDEAS

We have shown that no transcendental use can be made either of the conceptions of reason or of understanding. We have shown, likewise, that the demand of absolute totality in the series of conditions in the world of sense arises from a transcendental employment of reason, resting on the opinion that phenomena are to be regarded as things in themselves. It follows that we are not required to answer the question respecting the absolute quantity of a series—whether it is in itself limited or unlimited. We are only called upon to determine how far we must proceed in the empirical regress from condition to condition, in order to discover, in conformity with the rule of reason, a full and correct answer to the questions proposed by reason itself.

This principle of reason is hence valid only as a rule for the extension of a possible experience—its invalidity as a principle constitutive of phenomena in themselves having been sufficiently demonstrated. And thus, too, the antinomial conflict of reason with itself is completely put an end to; inasmuch as we have not only presented a critical solution of the fallacy lurking in the opposite statements of reason, but have shown the true meaning of the ideas which gave rise to these statements. The dialectical principle of reason has, therefore, been changed into a doctrinal principle. But in fact, if this principle, in the subjective signification which we have shown to be its only true sense, may be guaranteed as a principle of the unceasing extension of the employment of our understanding, its influence and value are just as great as if it were an axiom for the à priori determination of objects. For such an axiom could not exert a stronger influence on the extension and rectification of our knowledge, otherwise than by procuring for the principles of the understanding the most widely expanded employment in the field of experience.

I. SOLUTION OF THE COSMOLOGICAL IDEA OF THE TOTALITY OF THE COMPOSITION OF PHENOMENA IN THE UNIVERSE

Here, as well as in the case of the other cosmological problems, the ground of the regulative principle of reason is the proposition that in our empirical regress no experience of an absolute limit, and consequently no experience of a condition, which is itself absolutely unconditioned, is discoverable. And the truth of this proposition itself rests upon the consideration that such an experience must represent to us phenomena as limited by nothing or the mere void, on which our continued regress by means of perception must abut—which is impossible.

Now this proposition, which declares that every condition attained in the empirical regress must itself be considered empirically conditioned, contains the rule in terminis, which requires me, to whatever extent I may have proceeded in the ascending series, always to look for some higher member in the series—whether this member is to become known to me through experience, or not.

Nothing further is necessary, then, for the solution of the first cosmological problem, than to decide, whether, in the regress to the unconditioned quantity of the universe (as regards space and time), this never limited ascent ought to be called a regressus in infinitum or indefinitum.

The general representation which we form in our minds of the series of all past states or conditions of the world, or of all the things which at present exist in it, is itself nothing more than a possible empirical regress, which is cogitated—although in an undetermined manner—in the mind, and which gives rise to the conception of a series of conditions for a given object.[51] Now I have a conception of the universe, but not an intuition—that is, not an intuition of it as a whole. Thus I cannot infer the magnitude of the regress from the quantity or magnitude of the world, and determine the former by means of the latter; on the contrary, I must first of all form a conception of the quantity or magnitude of the world from the magnitude of the empirical regress. But of this regress I know nothing more than that I ought to proceed from every given member of the series of conditions to one still higher. But the quantity of the universe is not thereby determined, and we cannot affirm that this regress proceeds in infinitum. Such an affirmation would anticipate the members of the series which have not yet been reached, and represent the number of them as beyond the grasp of any empirical synthesis; it would consequently determine the cosmical quantity prior to the regress (although only in a negative manner)—which is impossible. For the world is not given in its totality in any intuition: consequently, its quantity cannot be given prior to the regress. It follows that we are unable to make any declaration respecting the cosmical quantity in itself—

not even that the regress in it is a regress in infinitum; we must only endeavour to attain to a conception of the quantity of the universe, in conformity with the rule which determines the empirical regress in it. But this rule merely requires us never to admit an absolute limit to our series—how far soever we may have proceeded in it, but always, on the contrary, to subordinate every phenomenon to some other as its condition, and consequently to proceed to this higher phenomenon. Such a regress is, therefore, the regressus in indefinitum, which, as not determining a quantity in the object, is clearly distinguishable from the regressus in infinitum.

It follows from what we have said that we are not justified in declaring the world to be infinite in space, or as regards past time. For this conception of an infinite given quantity is empirical; but we cannot apply the conception of an infinite quantity to the world as an object of the senses. I cannot say, "The regress from a given perception to everything limited either in space or time, proceeds in infinitum," for this presupposes an infinite cosmical quantity; neither can I say, "It is finite," for an absolute limit is likewise impossible in experience. It follows that I am not entitled to make any assertion at all respecting the whole object of experience—the world of sense; I must limit my declarations to the rule according to which experience or empirical knowledge is to be attained.

To the question, therefore, respecting the cosmical quantity, the first and negative answer is: "The world has no beginning in time, and no absolute limit in space."

For, in the contrary case, it would be limited by a void time on the one hand, and by a void space on the other. Now, since the world, as a phenomenon, cannot be thus limited in itself for a phenomenon is not a thing in itself; it must be possible for us to have a perception of this limitation by a void time and a void space. But such a perception—such an experience is impossible; because it has no content. Consequently, an absolute cosmical limit is empirically, and therefore absolutely, impossible.[52]

From this follows the affirmative answer: "The regress in the series of phenomena—as a determination of the cosmical quantity, proceeds in indefinitum." This is equivalent to saying: "The world of sense has no absolute quantity, but the empirical regress (through which alone the world of sense is presented to us on the side of its conditions) rests upon a rule, which requires it to proceed from every member of the series, as conditioned, to one still more remote (whether through personal experience, or by means of history, or the chain of cause and effect), and not to cease at any point in this extension of the possible empirical employment of the understanding." And this is the proper and only use which reason can make of its principles.

The above rule does not prescribe an unceasing regress in one kind of phenomena. It does not, for example, forbid us, in our ascent from an individual human being through the line of his ancestors, to expect that we shall discover at some point of the regress a primeval pair, or to admit, in the series of heavenly bodies, a sun at the farthest possible distance from some centre. All that it demands is a perpetual progress from phenomena to phenomena, even although an actual perception is not presented by them (as in the case of our perceptions being so weak as that we are unable to become conscious of them), since they, nevertheless, belong to possible experience.

Every beginning is in time, and all limits to extension are in space. But space and time are in the world of sense. Consequently phenomena in the world are conditionally limited, but the world itself is not limited, either conditionally or unconditionally.

For this reason, and because neither the world nor the cosmical series of conditions to a given conditioned can be completely given, our conception of the cosmical quantity is given only in and through the regress and not prior to it—in a collective intuition. But the regress itself is really nothing more than the determining of the cosmical quantity, and cannot therefore give us any determined conception of it—still less a conception of a quantity which is, in relation to a certain standard, infinite. The regress does not, therefore, proceed to infinity (an infinity given), but only to an indefinite extent, for or the of presenting to us a quantity—realized only in and through the regress itself.

II. SOLUTION OF THE COSMOLOGICAL IDEA OF THE TOTALITY OF THE DIVISION OF A WHOLE GIVEN IN INTUITION

When I divide a whole which is given in intuition, I proceed from a conditioned to its conditions. The division of the parts of the whole (subdivisio or decompositio) is a regress in the series of these conditions. The absolute totality of this series would be actually attained and given to the mind, if the regress could arrive at simple parts. But if all the parts in a continuous decomposition are themselves divisible, the division, that is to say, the regress, proceeds from the conditioned to its conditions in infinitum; because the conditions (the parts) are themselves contained in the conditioned, and, as the latter is given in a limited intuition, the former are all given along with it. This regress cannot, therefore, be called a regressus in indefinitum, as happened in the case of the preceding cosmological idea, the regress in which proceeded from the conditioned to the conditions not given contemporaneously and along with it, but discoverable only through the empirical regress. We are not, however, entitled to affirm of a whole of this kind, which is divisible in infinitum, that it consists of an infinite number of parts. For, although all the parts are contained in the intuition of the whole, the whole division is not contained therein. The division is contained only in the progressing decomposition—in the regress itself, which is the condition of the possibility and actuality of the series. Now, as this regress is infinite, all the members (parts) to which it attains must be contained in the given whole as an aggregate. But the complete series of division is not contained therein. For this series, being infinite in succession and always incomplete, cannot represent an infinite number of members, and still less a composition of these members into a whole.

To apply this remark to space. Every limited part of space presented to intuition is a whole, the parts of which are always spaces—to whatever extent subdivided. Every limited space is hence divisible to infinity.

Let us again apply the remark to an external phenomenon enclosed in limits, that is, a body. The divisibility of a body rests upon the divisibility of space, which is the condition of the possibility of the body as an extended whole. A body is consequently divisible to infinity, though it does not, for that reason, consist of an infinite number of parts.

It certainly seems that, as a body must be cogitated as substance in space, the law of divisibility would not be applicable to it as substance. For we may and ought to grant, in the case of space, that division or decomposition, to any extent, never can utterly annihilate composition (that is to say, the smallest part of space must still consist of spaces); otherwise space would entirely cease to exist—which is impossible. But, the assertion on the other hand that when all composition in matter is annihilated in thought, nothing remains, does not seem to harmonize with the conception of substance, which must be properly the subject of all composition and must remain, even after the conjunction of its attributes in space—which constituted a body—is annihilated in thought. But this is not the case with substance in the phenomenal world, which is not a thing in itself cogitated by the pure category. Phenomenal substance is not an absolute subject; it is merely a permanent sensuous image, and nothing more than an intuition, in which the unconditioned is not to be found.

But, although this rule of progress to infinity is legitimate and applicable to the subdivision of a phenomenon, as a mere occupation or filling of space, it is not applicable to a whole consisting of a number of distinct parts and constituting a quantum discretum—that is to say, an organized body. It cannot be admitted that every part in an organized whole is itself organized, and that, in analysing it to infinity, we must always meet with organized parts; although we may allow that the parts of the matter which we decompose in infinitum, may be organized. For the infinity of the division of a phenomenon in space rests altogether on the fact that the divisibility of a phenomenon is given only in and through this infinity, that is, an undetermined number of parts is given, while the parts themselves are given and determined only in and through the subdivision; in a word, the infinity of the division necessarily presupposes that the whole is not already divided in se. Hence our division determines a number of parts in the whole—a number which extends just as far as the actual regress in the division; while, on the other hand, the very notion of a body organized to infinity represents the whole as already and in itself divided. We expect, therefore, to find in it a determinate, but at the same time, infinite, number of parts—which is self-contradictory. For we should thus have a whole containing a series of members which could not be completed in any regress—which is infinite, and at the same time complete in an organized composite. Infinite divisibility is applicable only to a quantum continuum, and is based entirely on the infinite divisibility of space, But in a quantum discretum the multitude of parts or units is always determined, and hence always equal to some number. To what extent a body may be organized, experience alone can inform us; and although, so far as our experience of this or that body has extended, we may not have discovered any inorganic part, such parts must exist in possible experience. But how far the transcendental division of a phenomenon must extend, we cannot know from experience—it is a question which experience cannot answer; it is answered only by the principle of reason which forbids us to consider the empirical regress, in the analysis of extended body, as ever absolutely complete.

CONCLUDING REMARK ON THE SOLUTION OF THE TRANSCENDENTAL MATHEMATICAL IDEAS—AND INTRODUCTORY TO THE SOLUTION OF THE DYNAMICAL IDEAS.

We presented the antinomy of pure reason in a tabular form, and we endeavoured to show the ground of this self-contradiction on the part of reason, and the only means of bringing it to a conclusion—namely, by declaring both contradictory statements to be false. We represented in these antinomies the conditions of phenomena as belonging to the conditioned according to relations of space and time—which is the usual supposition of the common understanding. In this respect, all dialectical representations of totality, in the series of conditions to a given conditioned, were perfectly homogeneous. The condition was always a member of the series along with the conditioned, and thus the homogeneity of the whole series was assured. In this case the regress could never be cogitated as complete; or, if this was the case, a member really conditioned was falsely regarded as a primal member, consequently as unconditioned. In such an antinomy, therefore, we did not consider the object, that is, the conditioned, but the series of conditions belonging to the object, and the magnitude of that series. And thus arose the difficulty—a difficulty not to be settled by any decision regarding the claims of the two parties, but simply by cutting the knot—by declaring the series proposed by reason to be either too long or too short for the understanding, which could in neither case make its conceptions adequate with the ideas.

But we have overlooked, up to this point, an essential difference existing between the conceptions of the understanding which reason endeavours to raise to the rank of ideas—two of these indicating a mathematical, and two a dynamical synthesis of phenomena. Hitherto, it was necessary to signalize this distinction; for, just as in our general representation of all transcendental ideas, we considered them under phenomenal conditions, so, in the two mathematical ideas, our discussion is concerned solely with an object in the world of phenomena. But as we are now about to proceed to the consideration of the dynamical conceptions of the understanding, and their adequateness with ideas, we must not lose sight of this distinction. We shall find that it opens up to us an entirely new view of the conflict in which reason is involved. For, while in the first two antinomies, both parties were dismissed, on the ground of having advanced statements based upon false hypothesis; in the present case the hope appears of discovering a hypothesis which may be consistent with the demands of reason, and, the judge completing the statement of the grounds of claim, which both parties had left in an unsatisfactory state, the question may be settled on its own merits, not by dismissing the claimants, but by a comparison of the arguments on both sides. If we consider merely their extension, and whether they are adequate with ideas, the series of conditions may be regarded as all homogeneous. But the conception of the understanding which lies at the basis of these ideas, contains either a synthesis of the homogeneous (presupposed in every quantity—in its composition as well as in its division) or of the heterogeneous, which is the case in the dynamical synthesis of cause and effect, as well as of the necessary and the contingent.

Thus it happens that in the mathematical series of phenomena no other than a sensuous condition is admissible—a condition which is itself a member of the series; while the dynamical series of sensuous conditions admits a heterogeneous condition, which is not a member of the series, but, as purely intelligible, lies out of and beyond it. And thus reason is satisfied, and an unconditioned placed at the head of the series of phenomena, without introducing confusion into or discontinuing it, contrary to the principles of the understanding.

Now, from the fact that the dynamical ideas admit a condition of phenomena which does not form a part of the series of phenomena, arises a result which we should not have expected from an antinomy. In former cases, the result was that both contradictory dialectical statements were declared to be false. In the present case, we find the conditioned in the dynamical series connected with an empirically unconditioned, but nonsensuous condition; and thus satisfaction is done to the understanding on the one hand

and to the reason on the other.[53] While, moreover, the dialectical arguments for unconditioned totality in mere phenomena fall to the ground, both propositions of reason may be shown to be true in their proper signification. This could not happen in the case of the cosmological ideas which demanded a mathematically unconditioned unity; for no condition could be placed at the head of the series of phenomena, except one which was itself a phenomenon and consequently a member of the series.

III. SOLUTION OF THE COSMOLOGICAL IDEA OF THE TOTALITY OF THE DEDUCTION OF COSMICAL EVENTS FROM THEIR CAUSES

There are only two modes of causality cogitable—the causality of nature or of freedom. The first is the conjunction of a particular state with another preceding it in the world of sense, the former following the latter by virtue of a law. Now, as the causality of phenomena is subject to conditions of time, and the preceding state, if it had always existed, could not have produced an effect which would make its first appearance at a particular time, the causality of a cause must itself be an effect—must itself have begun to be, and therefore, according to the principle of the understanding, itself requires a cause.

We must understand, on the contrary, by the term freedom, in the cosmological sense, a faculty of the spontaneous origination of a state; the causality of which, therefore, is not subordinated to another cause determining it in time. Freedom is in this sense a pure transcendental idea, which, in the first place, contains no empirical element; the object of which, in the second place, cannot be given or determined in any experience, because it is a universal law of the very possibility of experience, that everything which happens must have a cause, that consequently the causality of a cause, being itself something that has happened, must also have a cause. In this view of the case, the whole field of experience, how far soever it may extend, contains nothing that is not subject to the laws of nature. But, as we cannot by this means attain to an absolute totality of conditions in reference to the series of causes and effects, reason creates the idea of a spontaneity, which can begin to act of itself, and without any external cause determining it to action, according to the natural law of causality.

It is especially remarkable that the practical conception of freedom is based upon the transcendental idea, and that the question of the possibility of the former is difficult only as it involves the consideration of the truth of the latter. Freedom, in the practical sense, is the independence of the will of coercion by sensuous impulses. A will is sensuous, in so far as it is pathologically affected (by sensuous impulses); it is termed animal (arbitrium brutum), when it is pathologically necessitated. The human will is certainly an arbitrium sensitivum, not brutum, but liberum; because sensuousness does not necessitate its action, a faculty existing in man of self-determination, independently of all sensuous coercion.

It is plain that, if all causality in the world of sense were natural—and natural only— every event would be determined by another according to necessary laws, and that, consequently, phenomena, in so far as they determine the will, must necessitate every action as a natural effect from themselves; and thus all practical freedom would fall to the ground with the transcendental idea. For the latter presupposes that although a certain thing has not happened, it ought to have happened, and that, consequently, its phenomenal cause was not so powerful and determinative as to exclude the causality of our will—a causality capable of producing effects independently of and even in opposition to the power of natural causes, and capable, consequently, of spontaneously originating a series of events.

Here, too, we find it to be the case, as we generally found in the self-contradictions and perplexities of a reason which strives to pass the bounds of possible experience, that the problem is properly not physiological, but transcendental. The question of the possibility of freedom does indeed concern psychology; but, as it rests upon dialectical arguments of pure reason, its solution must engage the attention of transcendental philosophy. Before attempting this solution, a task which transcendental philosophy cannot decline, it will be advisable to make a remark with regard to its procedure in the settlement of the question.

If phenomena were things in themselves, and time and space forms of the existence of things, condition and conditioned would always be members of the same series; and thus would arise in the present case the antinomy common to all transcendental ideas—that their series is either too great or too small for the understanding. The dynamical ideas, which we are about to discuss in this and the following section, possess the peculiarity of relating to an object, not considered as a quantity, but as an existence; and thus, in the discussion of the present question, we may make abstraction of the quantity of the series of conditions, and consider merely the dynamical relation of the condition to the conditioned. The question, then, suggests itself, whether freedom is possible; and, if it is, whether it can consist with the universality of the natural law of causality; and, consequently, whether we enounce a proper disjunctive proposition when we say: "Every effect must have its origin either in nature or in freedom," or whether both cannot exist together in the same event in different relations. The principle of an unbroken connection between all events in the phenomenal world, in accordance with the unchangeable laws of nature, is a well-established principle of transcendental analytic which admits of no exception. The question, therefore, is: "Whether an effect, determined according to the laws of nature, can at the same time be produced by a free agent, or whether freedom and nature mutually exclude each other?" And here, the common but fallacious hypothesis of the absolute reality of phenomena manifests its injurious influence in embarrassing the procedure of reason. For if phenomena are things in themselves, freedom is impossible. In this case, nature is the complete and all-sufficient cause of every event; and condition and conditioned, cause and effect are contained in the same series, and necessitated by the same law. If, on the contrary, phenomena are held to be, as they are in fact, nothing more than mere representations, connected with each other in accordance with empirical laws, they must have a ground which is not phenomenal. But the causality of such an intelligible cause is not determined or determinable by phenomena; although its effects, as phenomena, must be determined by other phenomenal existences. This cause and its causality exist therefore out of and apart from the series of phenomena; while its effects do exist and are discoverable in the series of empirical conditions. Such an effect may therefore be considered to be free in relation to its intelligible cause, and necessary in relation to the phenomena from which it is a necessary consequence—a distinction which, stated in this perfectly general and abstract manner, must appear in the highest degree subtle and obscure. The sequel will explain. It is sufficient, at present, to remark that, as the complete and unbroken connection of phenomena is an unalterable law of nature, freedom is impossible—on the supposition that phenomena are absolutely real. Hence those philosophers who adhere to the common opinion on this subject can never succeed in reconciling the ideas of nature and freedom.

Possibility of Freedom in Harmony with the Universal Law of Natural Necessity.

That element in a sensuous object which is not itself sensuous, I may be allowed to term intelligible. If, accordingly, an object which must be regarded as a sensuous phenomenon possesses a faculty which is not an object of sensuous intuition, but by means of which it is capable of being the cause of phenomena, the causality of an object or existence of this kind may be regarded from two different points of view. It may be considered to be intelligible, as regards its action—the action of a thing which is a thing in itself, and sensuous, as regards its effects—the effects of a phenomenon belonging to the sensuous world. We should accordingly, have to form both an empirical and an intellectual conception of the causality of such a faculty or power—both, however, having reference to the same effect. This twofold manner of cogitating a power residing in a sensuous object does not run counter to any of the conceptions which we ought to form of the world of phenomena or of a possible experience. Phenomena—not being things in themselves—must have a transcendental object as a foundation, which determines them as mere representations; and there seems to be no reason why we should not ascribe to this transcendental object, in addition to the property of self-phenomenization, a causality whose effects are to be met with in the world of phenomena, although it is not itself a phenomenon. But every effective cause must possess a character, that is to say, a law of its causality, without which it would cease to be a cause. In the above case, then, every sensuous object would possess an empirical character, which guaranteed that its actions, as phenomena, stand in complete and harmonious connection, conformably to unvarying natural laws, with all other phenomena, and can be deduced from these, as conditions, and that they do thus, in connection with these, constitute a series in the order of nature. This sensuous object must, in the second place, possess an intelligible character, which guarantees it to be the cause of those actions, as phenomena, although it is not itself a phenomenon nor subordinate to the conditions of the world of sense. The former may be termed the character of the thing as a phenomenon, the latter the character of the thing as a thing in itself.

Now this active subject would, in its character of intelligible subject, be subordinate to no conditions of time, for time is only a condition of phenomena, and not of things in themselves. No action would begin or cease to be in this subject; it would consequently be free from the law of all determination of time—the law of change, namely, that everything which happens must have a cause in the phenomena of a preceding state. In one word, the causality of the subject, in so far as it is intelligible, would not form part of the series of empirical conditions which determine and necessitate an event in the world of sense. Again, this intelligible character of a thing cannot be immediately cognized, because we can perceive nothing but phenomena, but it must be capable of being cogitated in harmony with the empirical character; for we always find ourselves compelled to place, in thought, a transcendental object at the basis of phenomena although we can never know what this object is in itself.

In virtue of its empirical character, this subject would at the same time be subordinate to all the empirical laws of causality, and, as a phenomenon and member of the sensuous world, its effects would have to be accounted for by a reference to preceding phenomena. Eternal phenomena must be capable of influencing it; and its actions, in accordance with natural laws, must explain to us how its empirical character, that is, the law of its causality, is to be cognized in and by means of experience. In a word, all requisites for a complete and necessary determination of these actions must be presented to us by experience.

In virtue of its intelligible character, on the other hand (although we possess only a general conception of this character), the subject must be regarded as free from all sensuous influences, and from all phenomenal determination. Moreover, as nothing happens in this subject—for it is a noumenon, and there does not consequently exist in it any change, demanding the dynamical determination of time, and for the same reason no connection with phenomena as causes—this active existence must in its actions be free from and independent of natural necessity, for this necessity exists only in the world of phenomena. It would be quite correct to say that it originates or begins its effects in the world of sense from itself, although the action productive of these effects does not begin in itself. We should not be in this case affirming that these sensuous effects began to exist of themselves, because they are always determined by prior empirical conditions—by virtue of the empirical character, which is the phenomenon of the intelligible character—and are possible only as constituting a continuation of the series of natural causes. And thus nature and freedom, each in the complete and absolute signification of these terms, can exist, without contradiction or disagreement, in the same action.

Exposition of the Cosmological Idea of Freedom in Harmony with the Universal Law of Natural Necessity.

I have thought it advisable to lay before the reader at first merely a sketch of the solution of this transcendental problem, in order to enable him to form with greater ease a clear conception of the course which reason must adopt in the solution. I shall now proceed to exhibit the several momenta of this solution, and to consider them in their order.

The natural law that everything which happens must have a cause, that the causality of this cause, that is, the action of the cause (which cannot always have existed, but must be itself an event, for it precedes in time some effect which it has originated), must have itself a phenomenal cause, by which it is determined and, and, consequently, all events are empirically determined in an order of nature—this law, I say, which lies at the foundation of the possibility of experience, and of a connected system of phenomena or nature is a law of the understanding, from which no departure, and to which no exception, can be admitted. For to except even a single phenomenon from its operation is to exclude it from the sphere of possible experience and thus to admit it to be a mere fiction of thought or phantom of the brain.

Thus we are obliged to acknowledge the existence of a chain of causes, in which, however, absolute totality cannot be found. But we need not detain ourselves with this question, for it has already been sufficiently answered in our discussion of the antinomies into which reason falls, when it attempts to reach the unconditioned in the series of phenomena. If we permit ourselves to be deceived by the illusion of transcendental idealism, we shall find that neither nature nor freedom exists. Now the question is: "Whether, admitting the existence of natural necessity in the world of phenomena, it is possible to consider an effect as at the same time an effect of nature and an effect of freedom—or, whether these two modes of causality are contradictory and incompatible?"

No phenomenal cause can absolutely and of itself begin a series. Every action, in so far as it is productive of an event, is itself an event or occurrence, and presupposes another preceding state, in which its cause existed. Thus everything that happens is but a continuation of a series, and an absolute beginning is impossible in the sensuous world. The actions of natural causes are, accordingly, themselves effects, and presuppose causes preceding them in time. A primal action which forms an absolute beginning, is beyond the causal power of phenomena.

Now, is it absolutely necessary that, granting that all effects are phenomena, the causality of the cause of these effects must also be a phenomenon and belong to the empirical world? Is it not rather possible that, although every effect in the phenomenal world must be connected with an empirical cause, according to the universal law of nature, this empirical causality may be itself the effect of a non-empirical and intelligible causality—its connection with natural causes remaining nevertheless intact? Such a causality would be considered, in reference to phenomena, as the primal action of a cause, which is in so far, therefore, not phenomenal, but, by reason of this faculty or power, intelligible; although it must, at the same time, as a link in the chain of nature, be regarded as belonging to the sensuous world.

A belief in the reciprocal causality of phenomena is necessary, if we are required to look for and to present the natural conditions of natural events, that is to say, their causes. This being admitted as unexceptionably valid, the requirements of the understanding, which recognizes nothing but nature in the region of phenomena, are satisfied, and our physical explanations of physical phenomena may proceed in their regular course, without hindrance and without opposition. But it is no stumbling-block in the way, even assuming the idea to be a pure fiction, to admit that there are some natural causes in the possession of a faculty which is not empirical, but intelligible, inasmuch as it is not determined to action by empirical conditions, but purely and solely upon grounds brought forward by the understanding—this action being still, when the cause is phenomenized, in perfect accordance with the laws of empirical causality. Thus the acting subject, as a causal phenomenon, would continue to preserve a complete connection with nature and natural conditions; and the phenomenon only of the subject (with all its phenomenal causality) would contain certain conditions, which, if we ascend from the empirical to the transcendental object, must necessarily be regarded as intelligible. For, if we attend, in our inquiries with regard to causes in the world of phenomena, to the directions of nature alone, we need not trouble ourselves about the relation in which the transcendental subject, which is completely unknown to us, stands to these phenomena and their connection in nature. The intelligible ground of phenomena in this subject does not concern empirical questions. It has to do only with pure thought; and, although the effects of this thought and action of the pure understanding are discoverable in phenomena, these phenomena must nevertheless be capable of a full and complete explanation, upon purely physical grounds and in accordance with natural laws. And in this case we attend solely to their empirical and omit all consideration of their intelligible character (which is the transcendental cause of the former) as completely unknown, except in so far as it is exhibited by the latter as its empirical symbol. Now let us apply this to experience. Man is a phenomenon of the sensuous world and, at the same time, therefore, a natural cause, the causality of which must be regulated by empirical laws. As such, he must possess an empirical character, like all other natural phenomena. We remark this empirical character in his actions, which reveal the presence of certain powers and faculties. If we consider inanimate or merely animal nature, we can discover no reason for ascribing to ourselves any other than a faculty which is determined in a purely sensuous manner. But man, to whom nature reveals herself only through sense, cognizes himself not only by his senses, but also through pure apperception; and this in actions and internal determinations, which he cannot regard as sensuous impressions. He is thus to himself, on the one hand, a phenomenon, but on the other hand, in respect of certain faculties, a purely intelligible object—intelligible, because its action cannot be ascribed to sensuous receptivity. These faculties are understanding and reason. The latter, especially, is in a peculiar manner distinct from all empirically-conditioned faculties, for it employs ideas alone in the consideration of its objects, and by means of these determines the understanding, which then proceeds to make an empirical use of its own conceptions, which, like the ideas of reason, are pure and non-empirical.

That reason possesses the faculty of causality, or that at least we are compelled so to represent it, is evident from the imperatives, which in the sphere of the practical we impose on many of our executive powers. The words I ought express a species of necessity, and imply a connection with grounds which nature does not and cannot present to the mind of man. Understanding knows nothing in nature but that which is, or has been, or will be. It would be absurd to say that anything in nature ought to be other than it is in the relations of time in which it stands; indeed, the ought, when we consider merely the course of nature, has neither application nor meaning. The question, "What ought to happen in the sphere of nature?" is just as absurd as the question, "What ought to be the properties of a circle?" All that we are entitled to ask is, "What takes place in nature?" or, in the latter case, "What are the properties of a circle?"

But the idea of an ought or of duty indicates a possible action, the ground of which is a pure conception; while the ground of a merely natural action is, on the contrary, always a phenomenon. This action must certainly be possible under physical conditions, if it is prescribed by the moral imperative ought; but these physical or natural conditions do not concern the determination of the will itself, they relate to its effects alone, and the consequences of the effect in the world of phenomena. Whatever number of motives nature may present to my will, whatever sensuous impulses—the moral ought it is beyond their power to produce. They may produce a volition, which, so far from being necessary, is always conditioned—a volition to which the ought enunciated by reason, sets an aim and a standard, gives permission or prohibition. Be the object what it may, purely sensuous—as pleasure, or presented by pure reason—as good, reason will not yield to grounds which have an empirical origin. Reason will not follow the order of things presented by experience, but, with perfect spontaneity, rearranges them according to ideas, with which it compels empirical conditions to agree. It declares, in the name of these ideas, certain actions to be necessary which nevertheless have not taken place and which perhaps never will take place; and yet presupposes that it possesses the faculty of causality in relation to these actions. For, in the absence of this supposition, it could not expect its ideas to produce certain effects in the world of experience.

Now, let us stop here and admit it to be at least possible that reason does stand in a really causal relation to phenomena. In this case it must—pure reason as it is—exhibit an empirical character. For every cause supposes a rule, according to which certain phenomena follow as effects from the cause, and every rule requires uniformity in these effects; and this is the proper ground of the conception of a cause—as a faculty or power. Now this conception (of a cause) may be termed the empirical character of reason; and this character is a permanent one, while the effects produced appear, in conformity with the various conditions which accompany and partly limit them, in various forms.

Thus the volition of every man has an empirical character, which is nothing more than the causality of his reason, in so far as its effects in the phenomenal world manifest the presence of a rule, according to which we are enabled to examine, in their several kinds and degrees, the actions of this causality and the rational grounds for these actions, and in this way to decide upon the subjective principles of the volition. Now we learn what this empirical character is only from phenomenal effects, and from the rule of these which is presented by experience; and for this reason all the actions of man in the world of phenomena are determined by his empirical character, and the co-operative causes of nature. If, then, we could investigate all the phenomena of human volition to their lowest foundation in the mind, there would be no action which we could not anticipate with certainty, and recognize to be absolutely necessary from its preceding conditions. So far as relates to this empirical character, therefore, there can be no freedom; and it is only in the light of this character that we can consider the human will, when we confine ourselves to simple observation and, as is the case in anthropology, institute a physiological investigation of the motive causes of human actions.

But when we consider the same actions in relation to reason—not for the purpose of explaining their origin, that is, in relation to speculative reason, but to practical reason, as the producing cause of these actions—we shall discover a rule and an order very different from those of nature and experience. For the declaration of this mental faculty may be that what has and could not but take place in the course of nature, ought not to have taken place. Sometimes, too, we discover, or believe that we discover, that the ideas of reason did actually stand in a causal relation to certain actions of man; and that these actions have taken place because they were determined, not by empirical causes, but by the act of the will upon grounds of reason.

Now, granting that reason stands in a causal relation to phenomena; can an action of reason be called free, when we know that, sensuously, in its empirical character, it is completely determined and absolutely necessary? But this empirical character is itself determined by the intelligible character. The latter we cannot cognize; we can only indicate it by means of phenomena, which enable us to have an immediate cognition only of the empirical character.[54] An action, then, in so far as it is to be ascribed to an intelligible cause, does not result from it in accordance with empirical laws. That is to say, not the conditions of pure reason, but only their effects in the internal sense, precede the act.

Pure reason, as a purely intelligible faculty, is not subject to the conditions of time. The causality of reason in its intelligible character does not begin to be; it does not make its appearance at a certain time, for the purpose of producing an effect. If this were not the case, the causality of reason would be subservient to the natural law of phenomena, which determines them according to time, and as a series of causes and effects in time; it would consequently cease to be freedom and become a part of nature. We are therefore justified in saying: "If reason stands in a causal relation to phenomena, it is a faculty which originates the sensuous condition of an empirical series of effects." For the condition, which resides in the reason, is non-sensuous, and therefore cannot be originated, or begin to be. And thus we find—what we could not discover in any empirical series— a condition of a successive series of events itself empirically unconditioned. For, in the present case, the condition stands out of and beyond the series of phenomena—it is intelligible, and it consequently cannot be subjected to any sensuous condition, or to any time-determination by a preceding cause.

But, in another respect, the same cause belongs also to the series of phenomena. Man is himself a phenomenon. His will has an empirical character, which is the empirical cause of all his actions. There is no condition—determining man and his volition in conformity with this character—which does not itself form part of the series of effects in nature, and is subject to their law—the law according to which an empirically undeter- mined cause of an event in time cannot exist. For this reason no given action can have an absolute and spontaneous origination, all actions being phenomena, and belonging to the world of experience. But it cannot be said of reason, that the state in which it determines the will is always preceded by some other state determining it. For reason is not a phenomenon, and therefore not subject to sensuous conditions; and, consequently, even in relation to its causality, the sequence or conditions of time do not influence reason, nor can the dynamical law of nature, which determines the sequence of time according to certain rules, be applied to it.

Reason is consequently the permanent condition of all actions of the human will. Each of these is determined in the empirical character of the man, even before it has taken place. The intelligible character, of which the former is but the sensuous schema, knows no before or after; and every action, irrespective of the time-relation in which it stands with other phenomena, is the immediate effect of the intelligible character of pure reason, which, consequently, enjoys freedom of action, and is not dynamically determined either by internal or external preceding conditions. This freedom must not be described, in a merely negative manner, as independence of empirical conditions, for in this case the faculty of reason would cease to be a cause of phenomena; but it must be regarded, positively, as a faculty which can spontaneously originate a series of events. At the same time, it must not be supposed that any beginning can take place in reason; on the contrary, reason, as the unconditioned condition of all action of the will, admits of no time-conditions, although its effect does really begin in a series of phenomena—a beginning which is not, however, absolutely primal.

I shall illustrate this regulative principle of reason by an example, from its employ- ment in the world of experience; proved it cannot be by any amount of experience, or by any number of facts, for such arguments cannot establish the truth of transcendental propositions. Let us take a voluntary action—for example, a falsehood—by means of which a man has introduced a certain degree of confusion into the social life of humanity, which is judged according to the motives from which it originated, and the blame of which and of the evil consequences arising from it, is imputed to the offender. We at first proceed to examine the empirical character of the offence, and for this purpose we endeavour to penetrate to the sources of that character, such as a defective education, bad company, a shameless and wicked disposition, frivolity, and want of reflection—not forgetting also the occasioning causes which prevailed at the moment of the transgression. In this the procedure is exactly the same as that pursued in the investigation of the series of causes which determine a given physical effect. Now, although we believe the action to have been determined by all these circumstances, we do not the less blame the offender. We do not blame him for his unhappy disposition, nor for the circumstances which influenced him, nay, not even for his former course of life; for we presuppose that all these considerations may be set aside, that the series of preceding conditions may be regarded as having never existed, and that the action may be considered as completely unconditioned in relation to any state preceding, just as if the agent commenced with it an entirely new series of effects. Our blame of the offender is grounded upon a law of reason, which requires us to regard this faculty as a cause, which could have and ought to have otherwise determined the behaviour of the culprit, independently of all empirical conditions. This causality of reason we do not regard as a co-operating agency, but as complete in itself. It matters not whether the sensuous impulses favoured or opposed the action of this causality, the offence is estimated according to its intelligible character —the offender is decidedly worthy of blame, the moment he utters a falsehood. It follows that we regard reason, in spite of the empirical conditions of the act, as completely free, and therefore, as in the present case, culpable.

The above judgement is complete evidence that we are accustomed to think that reason is not affected by sensuous conditions, that in it no change takes place—although its phenomena, in other words, the mode in which it appears in its effects, are subject to change—that in it no preceding state determines the following, and, consequently, that it does not form a member of the series of sensuous conditions which necessitate phenomena according to natural laws. Reason is present and the same in all human actions and at all times; but it does not itself exist in time, and therefore does not enter upon any state in which it did not formerly exist. It is, relatively to new states or conditions, determining, but not determinable. Hence we cannot ask: "Why did not reason determine itself in a different manner?" The question ought to be thus stated: "Why did not reason employ its power of causality to determine certain phenomena in a different manner?" But this is a question which admits of no answer. For a different intelligible character would have exhibited a different empirical character; and, when we say that, in spite of the course which his whole former life has taken, the offender could have refrained from uttering the falsehood, this means merely that the act was subject to the power and authority—permissive or prohibitive—of reason. Now, reason is not subject in its causality to any conditions of phenomena or of time; and a difference in time may produce a difference in the relation of phenomena to each other—for these are not things and therefore not causes in themselves—but it cannot produce any difference in the relation in which the action stands to the faculty of reason.

Thus, then, in our investigation into free actions and the causal power which produced them, we arrive at an intelligible cause, beyond which, however, we cannot go; although we can recognize that it is free, that is, independent of all sensuous conditions, and that, in this way, it may be the sensuously unconditioned condition of phenomena. But for what reason the intelligible character generates such and such phenomena and exhibits such and such an empirical character under certain circumstances, it is beyond the power of our reason to decide. The question is as much above the power and the sphere of reason as the following would be: "Why does the transcendental object of our external sensuous intuition allow of no other form than that of intuition in space?" But the problem, which we were called upon to solve, does not require us to entertain any such questions. The problem was merely this—whether freedom and natural necessity can exist without opposition in the same action. To this question we have given a sufficient answer; for we have shown that, as the former stands in a relation to a different kind of condition from those of the latter, the law of the one does not affect the law of the other and that, consequently, both can exist together in independence of and without interference with each other.

The reader must be careful to remark that my intention in the above remarks has not been to prove the actual existence of freedom, as a faculty in which resides the cause of certain sensuous phenomena. For, not to mention that such an argument would not have a transcendental character, nor have been limited to the discussion of pure conceptions—all attempts at inferring from experience what cannot be cogitated in accordance with its laws, must ever be unsuccessful. Nay, more, I have not even aimed at demonstrating the possibility of freedom; for this too would have been a vain endeavour, inasmuch as it is beyond the power of the mind to cognize the possibility of a reality or of a causal power by the aid of mere à priori conceptions. Freedom has been considered in the foregoing remarks only as a transcendental idea, by means of which reason aims at originating a series of conditions in the world of phenomena with the help of that which is sensuously unconditioned, involving itself, however, in an antinomy with the laws which itself prescribes for the conduct of the understanding. That this antinomy is based upon a mere illusion, and that nature and freedom are at least not opposed—this was the only thing in our power to prove, and the question which it was our task to solve.

IV. SOLUTION OF THE COSMOLOGICAL IDEA OF THE TOTALITY OF THE DEPENDENCE OF PHENOMENAL EXISTENCES

In the preceding remarks, we considered the changes in the world of sense as constituting a dynamical series, in which each member is subordinated to another—as its cause. Our present purpose is to avail ourselves of this series of states or conditions as a guide to an existence which may be the highest condition of all changeable phenomena, that is, to a necessary being. Our endeavour to reach, not the unconditioned causality, but the unconditioned existence, of substance. The series before us is therefore a series of conceptions, and not of intuitions (in which the one intuition is the condition of the other).

But it is evident that, as all phenomena are subject to change and conditioned in their existence, the series of dependent existences cannot embrace an unconditioned member, the existence of which would be absolutely necessary. It follows that, if phenomena were things in themselves, and—as an immediate consequence from this supposition—condition and conditioned belonged to the same series of phenomena, the existence of a necessary being, as the condition of the existence of sensuous phenomena, would be perfectly impossible.

An important distinction, however, exists between the dynamical and the mathematical regress. The latter is engaged solely with the combination of parts into a whole, or with the division of a whole into its parts; and therefore are the conditions of its series parts of the series, and to be consequently regarded as homogeneous, and for this reason, as consisting, without exception, of phenomena. If the former regress, on the contrary, the aim of which is not to establish the possibility of an unconditioned whole consisting of given parts, or of an unconditioned part of a given whole, but to demonstrate the possibility of the deduction of a certain state from its cause, or of the contingent existence of substance from that which exists necessarily, it is not requisite that the condition should form part of an empirical series along with the conditioned.

In the case of the apparent antinomy with which we are at present dealing, there exists a way of escape from the difficulty; for it is not impossible that both of the contradictory statements may be true in different relations. All sensuous phenomena may be contingent, and consequently possess only an empirically conditioned existence, and yet there may also exist a non-empirical condition of the whole series, or, in other words, a necessary being. For this necessary being, as an intelligible condition, would not form a member—not even the highest member—of the series; the whole world of sense would be left in its empirically determined existence uninterfered with and uninfluenced. This would also form a ground of distinction between the modes of solution employed for the third and fourth antinomies. For, while in the consideration of freedom in the former antinomy, the thing itself—the cause (substantia phaenomenon) —was regarded as belonging to the series of conditions, and only its causality to the intelligible world—we are obliged in the present case to cogitate this necessary being as purely intelligible and as existing entirely apart from the world of sense (as an ens extramundanum); for otherwise it would be subject to the phenomenal law of contingency and dependence.

In relation to the present problem, therefore, the regulative principle of reason is that everything in the sensuous world possesses an empirically conditioned existence—that no property of the sensuous world possesses unconditioned necessity—that we are bound to expect, and, so far as is possible, to seek for the empirical condition of every member in the series of conditions—and that there is no sufficient reason to justify us in deducing any existence from a condition which lies out of and beyond the empirical series, or in regarding any existence as independent and self-subsistent; although this should not prevent us from recognizing the possibility of the whole series being based upon a being which is intelligible, and for this reason free from all empirical conditions.

But it has been far from my intention, in these remarks, to prove the existence of this unconditioned and necessary being, or even to evidence the possibility of a purely intelligible condition of the existence of all sensuous phenomena. As bounds were set to reason, to prevent it from leaving the guiding thread of empirical conditions and losing itself in transcendent theories which are incapable of concrete presentation; so it was my purpose, on the other hand, to set bounds to the law of the purely empirical understanding, and to protest against any attempts on its part at deciding on the possibility of things, or declaring the existence of the intelligible to be impossible, merely on the ground that it is not available for the explanation and exposition of phenomena. It has been shown, at the same time, that the contingency of all the phenomena of nature and their empirical conditions is quite consistent with the arbitrary hypothesis of a necessary, although purely intelligible condition, that no real contradiction exists between them and that, consequently, both may be true. The existence of such an absolutely necessary being may be impossible; but this can never be demonstrated from the universal contingency and dependence of sensuous phenomena, nor from the principle which forbids us to discontinue the series at some member of it, or to seek for its cause in some sphere of existence beyond the world of nature. Reason goes its way in the empirical world, and follows, too, its peculiar path in the sphere of the transcendental.

The sensuous world contains nothing but phenomena, which are mere representations, and always sensuously conditioned; things in themselves are not, and cannot be, objects to us. It is not to be wondered at, therefore, that we are not justified in leaping from some member of an empirical series beyond the world of sense, as if empirical representations were things in themselves, existing apart from their transcendental ground in the human mind, and the cause of whose existence may be sought out of the empirical series. This would certainly be the case with contingent things; but it cannot be with mere representations of things, the contingency of which is itself merely a phenomenon and can relate to no other regress than that which determines phenomena, that is, the empirical. But to cogitate an intelligible ground of phenomena, as free, moreover, from the contingency of the latter, conflicts neither with the unlimited nature of the empirical regress, nor with the complete contingency of phenomena. And the demonstration of this was the only thing necessary for the solution of this apparent antinomy. For if the condition of every conditioned—as regards its existence—is sensuous, and for this reason a part of the same series, it must be itself conditioned, as was shown in the antithesis of the fourth antinomy. The embarrassments into which a reason, which postulates the unconditioned, necessarily falls, must, therefore, continue to exist; or the unconditioned must be placed in the sphere of the intelligible. In this way, its necessity does not require, nor does it even permit, the presence of an empirical condition: and it is, consequently, unconditionally necessary.

The empirical employment of reason is not affected by the assumption of a purely intelligible being; it continues its operations on the principle of the contingency of all phenomena, proceeding from empirical conditions to still higher and higher conditions, themselves empirical. Just as little does this regulative principle exclude the assumption of an intelligible cause, when the question regards merely the pure employment of reason—in relation to ends or aims. For, in this case, an intelligible cause signifies merely the transcendental and to us unknown ground of the possibility of sensuous phenomena, and its existence, necessary and independent of all sensuous conditions, is not inconsistent with the contingency of phenomena, or with the unlimited possibility of regress which exists in the series of empirical conditions.

CONCLUDING REMARKS ON THE ANTINOMY OF PURE REASON.

So long as the object of our rational conceptions is the totality of conditions in the world of phenomena, and the satisfaction, from this source, of the requirements of reason, so long are our ideas transcendental and cosmological. But when we set the unconditioned —which is the aim of all our inquiries—in a sphere which lies out of the world of sense and possible experience, our ideas become transcendent. They are then not merely serviceable towards the completion of the exercise of reason (which remains an idea, never executed, but always to be pursued); they detach themselves completely from experience and construct for themselves objects, the material of which has not been presented by experience, and the objective reality of which is not based upon the completion of the empirical series, but upon pure à priori conceptions. The intelligible object of these transcendent ideas may be conceded, as a transcendental object. But we cannot cogitate it as a thing determinable by certain distinct predicates relating to its internal nature, for it has no connection with empirical conceptions; nor are we justified in affirming the existence of any such object. It is, consequently, a mere product of the mind alone. Of all the cosmological ideas, however, it is that occasioning the fourth antinomy which compels us to venture upon this step. For the existence of phenomena, always conditioned and never self-subsistent, requires us to look for an object different from phenomena—an intelligible object, with which all contingency must cease. But, as we have allowed ourselves to assume the existence of a self-subsistent reality out of the field of experience, and are therefore obliged to regard phenomena as merely a contingent mode of representing intelligible objects employed by beings which are themselves intelligences—no other course remains for us than to follow analogy and employ the same mode in forming some conception of intelligible things, of which we have not the least knowledge, which nature taught us to use in the formation of empirical conceptions. Experience made us acquainted with the contingent. But we are at present engaged in the discussion of things which are not objects of experience; and must, therefore, deduce our knowledge of them from that which is necessary absolutely and in itself, that is, from pure conceptions. Hence the first step which we take out of the world of sense obliges us to begin our system of new cognition with the investigation of a necessary being, and to deduce from our conceptions of it all our conceptions of intelligible things. This we propose to attempt in the following chapter.

CHAPTER III. THE IDEAL OF PURE REASON

SECTION I. OF THE IDEAL IN GENERAL

We have seen that pure conceptions do not present objects to the mind, except under sensuous conditions; because the conditions of objective reality do not exist in these conceptions, which contain, in fact, nothing but the mere form of thought. They may, however, when applied to phenomena, be presented in concreto; for it is phenomena that present to them the materials for the formation of empirical conceptions, which are nothing more than concrete forms of the conceptions of the understanding. But ideas are still further removed from objective reality than categories; for no phenomenon can ever present them to the human mind in concreto. They contain a certain perfection, attainable by no possible empirical cognition; and they give to reason a systematic unity, to which the unity of experience attempts to approximate, but can never completely attain.

But still further removed than the idea from objective reality is the Ideal, by which term I understand the idea, not in concreto, but in individuo—as an individual thing, determinable or determined by the idea alone. The idea of humanity in its complete perfection supposes not only the advancement of all the powers and faculties, which constitute our conception of human nature, to a complete attainment of their final aims, but also everything which is requisite for the complete determination of the idea; for of all contradictory predicates, only one can conform with the idea of the perfect man. What I have termed an ideal was in Plato's philosophy an idea of the divine mind—an individual object present to its pure intuition, the most perfect of every kind of possible beings, and the archetype of all phenomenal existences.

Without rising to these speculative heights, we are bound to confess that human reason contains not only ideas, but ideals, which possess, not, like those of Plato, creative, but certainly practical power—as regulative principles, and form the basis of the perfectibility of certain actions. Moral conceptions are not perfectly pure conceptions of reason, because an empirical element—of pleasure or pain—lies at the foundation of them. In relation, however, to the principle, whereby reason sets bounds to a freedom which is in itself without law, and consequently when we attend merely to their form, they may be considered as pure conceptions of reason. Virtue and wisdom in their perfect purity are ideas. But the wise man of the Stoics is an ideal, that is to say, a human being existing only in thought and in complete conformity with the idea of wisdom. As the idea provides a rule, so the ideal serves as an archetype for the perfect and complete determination of the copy. Thus the conduct of this wise and divine man serves us as a standard of action, with which we may compare and judge ourselves, which may help us to reform ourselves, although the perfection it demands can never be attained by us. Although we cannot concede objective reality to these ideals, they are not to be considered as chimeras; on the contrary, they provide reason with a standard, which enables it to estimate, by comparison, the degree of incompleteness in the objects presented to it. But to aim at realizing the ideal in an example in the world of experience —to describe, for instance, the character of the perfectly wise man in a romance—is impracticable. Nay more, there is something absurd in the attempt; and the result must be little edifying, as the natural limitations, which are continually breaking in upon the perfection and completeness of the idea, destroy the illusion in the story and throw an air of suspicion even on what is good in the idea, which hence appears fictitious and unreal.

Such is the constitution of the ideal of reason, which is always based upon determinate conceptions, and serves as a rule and a model for limitation or of criticism. Very different is the nature of the ideals of the imagination. Of these it is impossible to present an intelligible conception; they are a kind of monogram, drawn according to no determinate rule, and forming rather a vague picture—the production of many diverse experiences—than a determinate image. Such are the ideals which painters and physiognomists profess to have in their minds, and which can serve neither as a model for production nor as a standard for appreciation. They may be termed, though improperly, sensuous ideals, as they are declared to be models of certain possible empirical intuitions. They cannot, however, furnish rules or standards for explanation or examination.

In its ideals, reason aims at complete and perfect determination according to à priori rules; and hence it cogitates an object, which must be completely determinable in conformity with principles, although all empirical conditions are absent, and the conception of the object is on this account transcendent.

SECTION II. OF THE TRANSCENDENTAL IDEAL (PROTOTYPON TRANCENDENTALE)

Every conception is, in relation to that which is not contained in it, undetermined and subject to the principle of determinability. This principle is that, of every two contradictorily opposed predicates, only one can belong to a conception. It is a purely logical principle, itself based upon the principle of contradiction; inasmuch as it makes complete abstraction of the content and attends merely to the logical form of the cognition.

But again, everything, as regards its possibility, is also subject to the principle of complete determination, according to which one of all the possible contradictory predicates of things must belong to it. This principle is not based merely upon that of contradiction; for, in addition to the relation between two contradictory predicates, it regards everything as standing in a relation to the sum of possibilities, as the sum total of all predicates of things, and, while presupposing this sum as an à priori condition, presents to the mind everything as receiving the possibility of its individual existence from the relation it bears to, and the share it possesses in, the aforesaid sum of possibilities.[55] The principle of complete determination relates the content and not to the logical form. It is the principle of the synthesis of all the predicates which are required to constitute the complete conception of a thing, and not a mere principle analytical representation, which enounces that one of two contradictory predicates must belong to a conception. It contains, moreover, a transcendental presupposition—that, namely, of the material for all possibility, which must contain à priori the data for this or that particular possibility.

The proposition, everything which exists is completely determined, means not only that one of every pair of given contradictory attributes, but that one of all possible attributes, is always predicable of the thing; in it the predicates are not merely compared logically with each other, but the thing itself is transcendentally compared with the sum-total of all possible predicates. The proposition is equivalent to saying: "To attain to a complete knowledge of a thing, it is necessary to possess a knowledge of everything that is possible, and to determine it thereby in a positive or negative manner." The conception of complete determination is consequently a conception which cannot be presented in its totality in concreto, and is therefore based upon an idea, which has its seat in the reason—the faculty which prescribes to the understanding the laws of its harmonious and perfect exercise.

Now, although this idea of the sum-total of all possibility, in so far as it forms the condition of the complete determination of everything, is itself undetermined in relation to the predicates which may constitute this sum-total, and we cogitate in it merely the sum-total of all possible predicates—we nevertheless find, upon closer examination, that this idea, as a primitive conception of the mind, excludes a large number of predicates—those deduced and those irreconcilable with others, and that it is evolved as a conception completely determined à priori. Thus it becomes the conception of an individual object, which is completely determined by and through the mere idea, and must consequently be termed an ideal of pure reason.

When we consider all possible predicates, not merely logically, but transcendentally, that is to say, with reference to the content which may be cogitated as existing in them à priori, we shall find that some indicate a being, others merely a non-being. The logical negation expressed in the word not does not properly belong to a conception, but only to the relation of one conception to another in a judgement, and is consequently quite insufficient to present to the mind the content of a conception. The expression not mortal does not indicate that a non-being is cogitated in the object; it does not concern the content at all. A transcendental negation, on the contrary, indicates non-being in itself, and is opposed to transcendental affirmation, the conception of which of itself expresses a being. Hence this affirmation indicates a reality, because in and through it objects are considered to be something—to be things; while the opposite negation, on the other hand, indicates a mere want, or privation, or absence, and, where such negations alone are attached to a representation, the non-existence of anything corresponding to the representation.

Now a negation cannot be cogitated as determined, without cogitating at the same time the opposite affirmation. The man born blind has not the least notion of darkness, because he has none of light; the vagabond knows nothing of poverty, because he has never known what it is to be in comfort;[56] the ignorant man has no conception of his ignorance, because he has no conception of knowledge. All conceptions of negatives are accordingly derived or deduced conceptions; and realities contain the data, and, so to speak, the material or transcendental content of the possibility and complete determination of all things.

If, therefore, a transcendental substratum lies at the foundation of the complete determination of things—a substratum which is to form the fund from which all possible predicates of things are to be supplied, this substratum cannot be anything else than the idea of a sum-total of reality (omnitudo realitatis). In this view, negations are nothing but limitations—a term which could not, with propriety, be applied to them, if the unlimited (the all) did not form the true basis of our conception.

This conception of a sum-total of reality is the conception of a thing in itself, regarded as completely determined; and the conception of an ens realissimum is the conception of an individual being, inasmuch as it is determined by that predicate of all possible contradictory predicates, which indicates and belongs to being. It is, therefore, a transcendental ideal which forms the basis of the complete determination of everything that exists, and is the highest material condition of its possibility—a condition on which must rest the cogitation of all objects with respect to their content. Nay, more, this ideal is the only proper ideal of which the human mind is capable; because in this case alone a general conception of a thing is completely determined by and through itself, and cognized as the representation of an individuum.

The logical determination of a conception is based upon a disjunctive syllogism, the major of which contains the logical division of the extent of a general conception, the minor limits this extent to a certain part, while the conclusion determines the conception by this part. The general conception of a reality cannot be divided à priori, because, without the aid of experience, we cannot know any determinate kinds of reality, standing under the former as the genus. The transcendental principle of the complete determination of all things is therefore merely the representation of the sum-total of all reality; it is not a conception which is the genus of all predicates under itself, but one which comprehends them all within itself. The complete determination of a thing is consequently based upon the limitation of this total of reality, so much being predicated of the thing, while all that remains over is excluded—a procedure which is in exact agreement with that of the disjunctive syllogism and the determination of the objects in the conclusion by one of the members of the division. It follows that reason, in laying the transcendental ideal at the foundation of its determination of all possible things, takes a course in exact analogy with that which it pursues in disjunctive syllogisms—a proposition which formed the basis of the systematic division of all transcendental ideas, according to which they are produced in complete parallelism with the three modes of syllogistic reasoning employed by the human mind.

It is self-evident that reason, in cogitating the necessary complete determination of things, does not presuppose the existence of a being corresponding to its ideal, but merely the idea of the ideal—for the purpose of deducing from the unconditional totality of complete determination, The ideal is therefore the prototype of all things, which, as defective copies (ectypa), receive from it the material of their possibility, and approximate to it more or less, though it is impossible that they can ever attain to its perfection.

The possibility of things must therefore be regarded as derived—except that of the thing which contains in itself all reality, which must be considered to be primitive and original. For all negations—and they are the only predicates by means of which all other things can be distinguished from the ens realissimum—are mere limitations of a greater and a higher—nay, the highest reality; and they consequently presuppose this reality, and are, as regards their content, derived from it. The manifold nature of things is only an infinitely various mode of limiting the conception of the highest reality, which is their common substratum; just as all figures are possible only as different modes of limiting infinite space. The object of the ideal of reason—an object existing only in reason itself—is also termed the primal being (ens originarium); as having no existence superior to him, the supreme being (ens summum); and as being the condition of all other beings, which rank under it, the being of all beings (ens entium). But none of these terms indicate the objective relation of an actually existing object to other things, but merely that of an idea to conceptions; and all our investigations into this subject still leave us in perfect uncertainty with regard to the existence of this being.

A primal being cannot be said to consist of many other beings with an existence which is derivative, for the latter presuppose the former, and therefore cannot be constitutive parts of it. It follows that the ideal of the primal being must be cogitated as simple.

The deduction of the possibility of all other things from this primal being cannot, strictly speaking, be considered as a limitation, or as a kind of division of its reality; for this would be regarding the primal being as a mere aggregate—which has been shown to be impossible, although it was so represented in our first rough sketch. The highest reality must be regarded rather as the ground than as the sum-total of the possibility of all things, and the manifold nature of things be based, not upon the limitation of the primal being itself, but upon the complete series of effects which flow from it. And thus all our powers of sense, as well as all phenomenal reality, may be with propriety regarded as belonging to this series of effects, while they could not have formed parts of the idea, considered as an aggregate. Pursuing this track, and hypostatizing this idea, we shall find ourselves authorized to determine our notion of the Supreme Being by means of the mere conception of a highest reality, as one, simple, all-sufficient, eternal, and so on—in one word, to determine it in its unconditioned completeness by the aid of every possible predicate. The conception of such a being is the conception of God in its transcendental sense, and thus the ideal of pure reason is the object-matter of a transcendental theology.

But, by such an employment of the transcendental idea, we should be over stepping the limits of its validity and purpose. For reason placed it, as the conception of all reality, at the basis of the complete determination of things, without requiring that this conception be regarded as the conception of an objective existence. Such an existence would be purely fictitious, and the hypostatizing of the content of the idea into an ideal, as an individual being, is a step perfectly unauthorized. Nay, more, we are not even called upon to assume the possibility of such an hypothesis, as none of the deductions drawn from such an ideal would affect the complete determination of things in general —for the sake of which alone is the idea necessary.

It is not sufficient to circumscribe the procedure and the dialectic of reason; we must also endeavour to discover the sources of this dialectic, that we may have it in our power to give a rational explanation of this illusion, as a phenomenon of the human mind. For the ideal, of which we are at present speaking, is based, not upon an arbitrary, but upon a natural, idea. The question hence arises: How happens it that reason regards the possibility of all things as deduced from a single possibility, that, to wit, of the highest reality, and presupposes this as existing in an individual and primal being?

The answer is ready; it is at once presented by the procedure of transcendental analytic. The possibility of sensuous objects is a relation of these objects to thought, in which something (the empirical form) may be cogitated à priori; while that which constitutes the matter—the reality of the phenomenon (that element which corresponds to sensation)—must be given from without, as otherwise it could not even be cogitated by, nor could its possibility be presentable to the mind. Now, a sensuous object is completely determined, when it has been compared with all phenomenal predicates, and represented by means of these either positively or negatively. But, as that which constitutes the thing itself—the real in a phenomenon, must be given, and that, in which the real of all phenomena is given, is experience, one, sole, and all-embracing—the material of the possibility of all sensuous objects must be presupposed as given in a whole, and it is upon the limitation of this whole that the possibility of all empirical objects, their distinction from each other and their complete determination, are based. Now, no other objects are presented to us besides sensuous objects, and these can be given only in connection with a possible experience; it follows that a thing is not an object to us, unless it presupposes the whole or sum-total of empirical reality as the condition of its possibility. Now, a natural illusion leads us to consider this principle, which is valid only of sensuous objects, as valid with regard to things in general. And thus we are induced to hold the empirical principle of our conceptions of the possibility of things, as phenomena, by leaving out this limitative condition, to be a transcendental principle of the possibility of things in general.

We proceed afterwards to hypostatize this idea of the sum-total of all reality, by changing the distributive unity of the empirical exercise of the understanding into the collective unity of an empirical whole—a dialectical illusion, and by cogitating this whole or sum of experience as an individual thing, containing in itself all empirical reality. This individual thing or being is then, by means of the above-mentioned transcendental subreption, substituted for our notion of a thing which stands at the head of the possibility of all things, the real conditions of whose complete determination it presents.[57]

SECTION III. OF THE ARGUMENTS EMPLOYED BY SPECULATIVE REASON IN PROOF OF THE EXISTENCE OF A SUPREME BEING

Notwithstanding the pressing necessity which reason feels, to form some presupposition that shall serve the understanding as a proper basis for the complete determination of its conceptions, the idealistic and factitious nature of such a presupposition is too evident to allow reason for a moment to persuade itself into a belief of the objective existence of a mere creation of its own thought. But there are other considerations which compel reason to seek out some resting place in the regress from the conditioned to the unconditioned, which is not given as an actual existence from the mere conception of it, although it alone can give completeness to the series of conditions. And this is the natural course of every human reason, even of the most uneducated, although the path at first entered it does not always continue to follow. It does not begin from conceptions, but from common experience, and requires a basis in actual existence. But this basis is insecure, unless it rests upon the immovable rock of the absolutely necessary. And this foundation is itself unworthy of trust, if it leave under and above it empty space, if it do not fill all, and leave no room for a why or a wherefore, if it be not, in one word, infinite in its reality.

If we admit the existence of some one thing, whatever it may be, we must also admit that there is something which exists necessarily. For what is contingent exists only under the condition of some other thing, which is its cause; and from this we must go on to conclude the existence of a cause which is not contingent, and which consequently exists necessarily and unconditionally. Such is the argument by which reason justifies its advances towards a primal being.

Now reason looks round for the conception of a being that may be admitted, without inconsistency, to be worthy of the attribute of absolute necessity, not for the purpose of inferring à priori, from the conception of such a being, its objective existence (for if reason allowed itself to take this course, it would not require a basis in given and actual existence, but merely the support of pure conceptions), but for the purpose of discovering, among all our conceptions of possible things, that conception which possesses no element inconsistent with the idea of absolute necessity. For that there must be some absolutely necessary existence, it regards as a truth already established. Now, if it can remove every existence incapable of supporting the attribute of absolute necessity, excepting one—this must be the absolutely necessary being, whether its necessity is comprehensible by us, that is, deducible from the conception of it alone, or not.

Now that, the conception of which contains a therefore to every wherefore, which is not defective in any respect whatever, which is all-sufficient as a condition, seems to be the being of which we can justly predicate absolute necessity—for this reason, that, possessing the conditions of all that is possible, it does not and cannot itself require any condition. And thus it satisfies, in one respect at least, the requirements of the conception of absolute necessity. In this view, it is superior to all other conceptions, which, as deficient and incomplete, do not possess the characteristic of independence of all higher conditions. It is true that we cannot infer from this that what does not contain in itself the supreme and complete condition—the condition of all other things—must possess only a conditioned existence; but as little can we assert the contrary, for this supposed being does not possess the only characteristic which can enable reason to cognize by means of an à priori conception the unconditioned and necessary nature of its existence.

The conception of an ens realissimum is that which best agrees with the conception of an unconditioned and necessary being. The former conception does not satisfy all the requirements of the latter; but we have no choice, we are obliged to adhere to it, for we find that we cannot do without the existence of a necessary being; and even although we admit it, we find it out of our power to discover in the whole sphere of possibility any being that can advance well-grounded claims to such a distinction.

The following is, therefore, the natural course of human reason. It begins by persuading itself of the existence of some necessary being. In this being it recognizes the characteristics of unconditioned existence. It then seeks the conception of that which is independent of all conditions, and finds it in that which is itself the sufficient condition of all other things—in other words, in that which contains all reality. But the unlimited all is an absolute unity, and is conceived by the mind as a being one and supreme; and thus reason concludes that the Supreme Being, as the primal basis of all things, possesses an existence which is absolutely necessary.

This conception must be regarded as in some degree satisfactory, if we admit the existence of a necessary being, and consider that there exists a necessity for a definite and final answer to these questions. In such a case, we cannot make a better choice, or rather we have no choice at all, but feel ourselves obliged to declare in favour of the absolute unity of complete reality, as the highest source of the possibility of things. But if there exists no motive for coming to a definite conclusion, and we may leave the question unanswered till we have fully weighed both sides—in other words, when we are merely called upon to decide how much we happen to know about the question, and how much we merely flatter ourselves that we know—the above conclusion does not appear to be so great advantage, but, on the contrary, seems defective in the grounds upon which it is supported.

For, admitting the truth of all that has been said, that, namely, the inference from a given existence (my own, for example) to the existence of an unconditioned and necessary being is valid and unassailable; that, in the second place, we must consider a being which contains all reality, and consequently all the conditions of other things, to be absolutely unconditioned; and admitting too, that we have thus discovered the conception of a thing to which may be attributed, without inconsistency, absolute necessity—it does not follow from all this that the conception of a limited being, in which the supreme reality does not reside, is therefore incompatible with the idea of absolute necessity. For, although I do not discover the element of the unconditioned in the conception of such a being—an element which is manifestly existent in the sum-total of all conditions—I am not entitled to conclude that its existence is therefore conditioned; just as I am not entitled to affirm, in a hypothetical syllogism, that where a certain condition does not exist (in the present, completeness, as far as pure conceptions are concerned), the conditioned does not exist either. On the contrary, we are free to consider all limited beings as likewise unconditionally necessary, although we are unable to infer this from the general conception which we have of them. Thus conducted, this argument is incapable of giving us the least notion of the properties of a necessary being, and must be in every respect without result.

This argument continues, however, to possess a weight and an authority, which, in spite of its objective insufficiency, it has never been divested of. For, granting that certain responsibilities lie upon us, which, as based on the ideas of reason, deserve to be respected and submitted to, although they are incapable of a real or practical application to our nature, or, in other words, would be responsibilities without motives, except upon the supposition of a Supreme Being to give effect and influence to the practical laws: in such a case we should be bound to obey our conceptions, which, although objectively insufficient, do, according to the standard of reason, preponderate over and are superior to any claims that may be advanced from any other quarter. The equilibrium of doubt would in this case be destroyed by a practical addition; indeed, Reason would be compelled to condemn herself, if she refused to comply with the demands of the judgement, no superior to which we know—however defective her understanding of the grounds of these demands might be.

This argument, although in fact transcendental, inasmuch as it rests upon the intrinsic insufficiency of the contingent, is so simple and natural, that the commonest understanding can appreciate its value. We see things around us change, arise, and pass away; they, or their condition, must therefore have a cause. The same demand must again be made of the cause itself—as a datum of experience. Now it is natural that we should place the highest causality just where we place supreme causality, in that being, which contains the conditions of all possible effects, and the conception of which is so simple as that of an all-embracing reality. This highest cause, then, we regard as absolutely necessary, because we find it absolutely necessary to rise to it, and do not discover any reason for proceeding beyond it. Thus, among all nations, through the darkest polytheism glimmer some faint sparks of monotheism, to which these idolaters have been led, not from reflection and profound thought, but by the study and natural progress of the common understanding.

There are only three modes of proving the existence of a Deity, on the grounds of speculative reason.

All the paths conducting to this end begin either from determinate experience and the peculiar constitution of the world of sense, and rise, according to the laws of causality, from it to the highest cause existing apart from the world—or from a purely indeterminate experience, that is, some empirical existence—or abstraction is made of all experience, and the existence of a supreme cause is concluded from à priori conceptions alone. The first is the physico-theological argument, the second the cosmological, the third the ontological. More there are not, and more there cannot be.

I shall show it is as unsuccessful on the one path—the empirical—as on the other—the transcendental, and that it stretches its wings in vain, to soar beyond the world of sense by the mere might of speculative thought. As regards the order in which we must discuss those arguments, it will be exactly the reverse of that in which reason, in the progress of its development, attains to them—the order in which they are placed above. For it will be made manifest to the reader that, although experience presents the occasion and the starting-point, it is the transcendental idea of reason which guides it in its pilgrimage and is the goal of all its struggles. I shall therefore begin with an examination of the transcendental argument, and afterwards inquire what additional strength has accrued to this mode of proof from the addition of the empirical element.

SECTION IV. OF THE IMPOSSIBILITY OF AN ONTOLOGICAL PROOF OF THE EXISTENCE OF GOD

It is evident from what has been said that the conception of an absolutely necessary being is a mere idea, the objective reality of which is far from being established by the mere fact that it is a need of reason. On the contrary, this idea serves merely to indicate a certain unattainable perfection, and rather limits the operations than, by the presentation of new objects, extends the sphere of the understanding. But a strange anomaly meets us at the very threshold; for the inference from a given existence in general to an absolutely necessary existence seems to be correct and unavoidable, while the conditions of the understanding refuse to aid us in forming any conception of such a being.

Philosophers have always talked of an absolutely necessary being, and have nevertheless declined to take the trouble of conceiving whether—and how—a being of this nature is even cogitable, not to mention that its existence is actually demonstrable. A verbal definition of the conception is certainly easy enough: it is something the non-existence of which is impossible. But does this definition throw any light upon the conditions which render it impossible to cogitate the non-existence of a thing—conditions which we wish to ascertain, that we may discover whether we think anything in the conception of such a being or not? For the mere fact that I throw away, by means of the word unconditioned, all the conditions which the understanding habitually requires in order to regard anything as necessary, is very far from making clear whether by means of the conception of the unconditionally necessary I think of something, or really of nothing at all.

Nay, more, this chance-conception, now become so current, many have endeavoured to explain by examples which seemed to render any inquiries regarding its intelligibility quite needless. Every geometrical proposition—a triangle has three angles—it was said, is absolutely necessary; and thus people talked of an object which lay out of the sphere of our understanding as if it were perfectly plain what the conception of such a being meant.

All the examples adduced have been drawn, without exception, from judgements, and not from things. But the unconditioned necessity of a judgement does not form the absolute necessity of a thing. On the contrary, the absolute necessity of a judgement is only a conditioned necessity of a thing, or of the predicate in a judgement. The proposition above-mentioned does not enounce that three angles necessarily exist, but, upon condition that a triangle exists, three angles must necessarily exist—in it. And thus this logical necessity has been the source of the greatest delusions. Having formed an à priori conception of a thing, the content of which was made to embrace existence, we believed ourselves safe in concluding that, because existence belongs necessarily to the object of the conception (that is, under the condition of my positing this thing as given), the existence of the thing is also posited necessarily, and that it is therefore absolutely necessary—merely because its existence has been cogitated in the conception.

If, in an identical judgement, I annihilate the predicate in thought, and retain the subject, a contradiction is the result; and hence I say, the former belongs necessarily to the latter. But if I suppress both subject and predicate in thought, no contradiction arises; for there is nothing at all, and therefore no means of forming a contradiction. To suppose the existence of a triangle and not that of its three angles, is self-contradictory; but to suppose the non-existence of both triangle and angles is perfectly admissible. And so is it with the conception of an absolutely necessary being. Annihilate its existence in thought, and you annihilate the thing itself with all its predicates; how then can there be any room for contradiction? Externally, there is nothing to give rise to a contradiction, for a thing cannot be necessary externally; nor internally, for, by the annihilation or suppression of the thing itself, its internal properties are also annihilated. God is omnipotent—that is a necessary judgement. His omnipotence cannot be denied, if the existence of a Deity is posited—the existence, that is, of an infinite being, the two conceptions being identical. But when you say, God does not exist, neither omnipotence nor any other predicate is affirmed; they must all disappear with the subject, and in this judgement there cannot exist the least self-contradiction.

You have thus seen that when the predicate of a judgement is annihilated in thought along with the subject, no internal contradiction can arise, be the predicate what it may. There is no possibility of evading the conclusion—you find yourselves compelled to declare: There are certain subjects which cannot be annihilated in thought. But this is nothing more than saying: There exist subjects which are absolutely necessary—the very hypothesis which you are called upon to establish. For I find myself unable to form the slightest conception of a thing which when annihilated in thought with all its predicates, leaves behind a contradiction; and contradiction is the only criterion of impossibility in the sphere of pure à priori conceptions.

Against these general considerations, the justice of which no one can dispute, one argument is adduced, which is regarded as furnishing a satisfactory demonstration from the fact. It is affirmed that there is one and only one conception, in which the non-being or annihilation of the object is self-contradictory, and this is the conception of an ens realissimum. It possesses, you say, all reality, and you feel yourselves justified in admitting the possibility of such a being. (This I am willing to grant for the present, although the existence of a conception which is not self-contradictory is far from being sufficient to prove the possibility of an object.)[58] Now the notion of all reality embraces in it that of existence; the notion of existence lies, therefore, in the conception of this possible thing. If this thing is annihilated in thought, the internal possibility of the thing is also annihilated, which is self-contradictory.

I answer: It is absurd to introduce—under whatever term disguised—into the conception of a thing, which is to be cogitated solely in reference to its possibility, the conception of its existence. If this is admitted, you will have apparently gained the day, but in reality have enounced nothing but a mere tautology. I ask, is the proposition, this or that thing (which I am admitting to be possible) exists, an analytical or a synthetical proposition? If the former, there is no addition made to the subject of your thought by the affirmation of its existence; but then the conception in your minds is identical with the thing itself, or you have supposed the existence of a thing to be possible, and then inferred its existence from its internal possibility—which is but a miserable tautology. The word reality in the conception of the thing, and the word existence in the conception of the predicate, will not help you out of the difficulty. For, supposing you were to term all positing of a thing reality, you have thereby posited the thing with all its predicates in the conception of the subject and assumed its actual existence, and this you merely repeat in the predicate. But if you confess, as every reasonable person must, that every existential proposition is synthetical, how can it be maintained that the predicate of existence cannot be denied without contradiction?—a property which is the characteristic of analytical propositions, alone.

I should have a reasonable hope of putting an end for ever to this sophistical mode of argumentation, by a strict definition of the conception of existence, did not my own experience teach me that the illusion arising from our confounding a logical with a real predicate (a predicate which aids in the determination of a thing) resists almost all the endeavours of explanation and illustration. A logical predicate may be what you please, even the subject may be predicated of itself; for logic pays no regard to the content of a judgement. But the determination of a conception is a predicate, which adds to and enlarges the conception. It must not, therefore, be contained in the conception.

Being is evidently not a real predicate, that is, a conception of something which is added to the conception of some other thing. It is merely the positing of a thing, or of certain determinations in it. Logically, it is merely the copula of a judgement. The proposition, God is omnipotent, contains two conceptions, which have a certain object or content; the word is, is no additional predicate—it merely indicates the relation of the predicate to the subject. Now, if I take the subject (God) with all its predicates (omnipotence being one), and say: God is, or, There is a God, I add no new predicate to the conception of God, I merely posit or affirm the existence of the subject with all its predicates—I posit the object in relation to my conception. The content of both is the same; and there is no addition made to the conception, which expresses merely the possibility of the object, by my cogitating the object—in the expression, it is—as absolutely given or existing. Thus the real contains no more than the possible. A hundred real dollars contain no more than a hundred possible dollars. For, as the latter indicate the conception, and the former the object, on the supposition that the content of the former was greater than that of the latter, my conception would not be an expression of the whole object, and would consequently be an inadequate conception of it. But in reckoning my wealth there may be said to be more in a hundred real dollars than in a hundred possible dollars—that is, in the mere conception of them. For the real object—the dollars —is not analytically contained in my conception, but forms a synthetical addition to my conception (which is merely a determination of my mental state), although this objective reality—this existence—apart from my conceptions, does not in the least degree increase the aforesaid hundred dollars.

By whatever and by whatever number of predicates—even to the complete determination of it—I may cogitate a thing, I do not in the least augment the object of my conception by the addition of the statement: This thing exists. Otherwise, not exactly the same, but something more than what was cogitated in my conception, would exist, and I could not affirm that the exact object of my conception had real existence. If I cogitate a thing as containing all modes of reality except one, the mode of reality which is absent is not added to the conception of the thing by the affirmation that the thing exists; on the contrary, the thing exists—if it exist at all—with the same defect as that cogitated in its conception; otherwise not that which was cogitated, but something different, exists. Now, if I cogitate a being as the highest reality, without defect or imperfection, the question still remains—whether this being exists or not? For, although no element is wanting

CRITIQUE OF PURE REASON | 241

in the possible real content of my conception, there is a defect in its relation to my mental state, that is, I am ignorant whether the cognition of the object indicated by the conception is possible à posteriori. And here the cause of the present difficulty becomes apparent. If the question regarded an object of sense merely, it would be impossible for me to confound the conception with the existence of a thing. For the conception merely enables me to cogitate an object as according with the general conditions of experience; while the existence of the object permits me to cogitate it as contained in the sphere of actual experience. At the same time, this connection with the world of experience does not in the least augment the conception, although a possible perception has been added to the experience of the mind. But if we cogitate existence by the pure category alone, it is not to be wondered at, that we should find ourselves unable to present any criterion sufficient to distinguish it from mere possibility.

Whatever be the content of our conception of an object, it is necessary to go beyond it, if we wish to predicate existence of the object. In the case of sensuous objects, this is attained by their connection according to empirical laws with some one of my perceptions; but there is no means of cognizing the existence of objects of pure thought, because it must be cognized completely à priori. But all our knowledge of existence (be it immediately by perception, or by inferences connecting some object with a perception) belongs entirely to the sphere of experience—which is in perfect unity with itself; and although an existence out of this sphere cannot be absolutely declared to be impossible, it is a hypothesis the truth of which we have no means of ascertaining.

The notion of a Supreme Being is in many respects a highly useful idea; but for the very reason that it is an idea, it is incapable of enlarging our cognition with regard to the existence of things. It is not even sufficient to instruct us as to the possibility of a being which we do not know to exist. The analytical criterion of possibility, which consists in the absence of contradiction in propositions, cannot be denied it. But the connection of real properties in a thing is a synthesis of the possibility of which an à priori judgement cannot be formed, because these realities are not presented to us specifically; and even if this were to happen, a judgement would still be impossible, because the criterion of the possibility of synthetical cognitions must be sought for in the world of experience, to which the object of an idea cannot belong. And thus the celebrated Leibnitz has utterly failed in his attempt to establish upon à priori grounds the possibility of this sublime ideal being.

The celebrated ontological or Cartesian argument for the existence of a Supreme Being is therefore insufficient; and we may as well hope to increase our stock of knowledge by the aid of mere ideas, as the merchant to augment his wealth by the addition of noughts to his cash account.

SECTION V. OF THE IMPOSSIBILITY OF A COSMOLOGICAL PROOF OF THE EXISTENCE OF GOD

It was by no means a natural course of proceeding, but, on the contrary, an invention entirely due to the subtlety of the schools, to attempt to draw from a mere idea a proof of the existence of an object corresponding to it. Such a course would never have been pursued, were it not for that need of reason which requires it to suppose the existence of a necessary being as a basis for the empirical regress, and that, as this necessity must be unconditioned and à priori, reason is bound to discover a conception which shall satisfy, if possible, this requirement, and enable us to attain to the à priori cognition of such a being. This conception was thought to be found in the idea of an ens realissimum, and thus this idea was employed for the attainment of a better defined knowledge of a necessary being, of the existence of which we were convinced, or persuaded, on other grounds. Thus reason was seduced from her natural courage; and, instead of concluding with the conception of an ens realissimum, an attempt was made to begin with it, for the purpose of inferring from it that idea of a necessary existence which it was in fact called in to complete. Thus arose that unfortunate ontological argument, which neither satisfies the healthy common sense of humanity, nor sustains the scientific examination of the philosopher.

The cosmological proof, which we are about to examine, retains the connection between absolute necessity and the highest reality; but, instead of reasoning from this highest reality to a necessary existence, like the preceding argument, it concludes from the given unconditioned necessity of some being its unlimited reality. The track it pursues, whether rational or sophistical, is at least natural, and not only goes far to persuade the common understanding, but shows itself deserving of respect from the speculative intellect; while it contains, at the same time, the outlines of all the arguments employed in natural theology—arguments which always have been, and still will be, in use and authority. These, however adorned, and hid under whatever embellishments of rhetoric and sentiment, are at bottom identical with the arguments we are at present to discuss. This proof, termed by Leibnitz the argumentum a contingentia mundi, I shall now lay before the reader, and subject to a strict examination.

It is framed in the following manner: If something exists, an absolutely necessary being must likewise exist. Now I, at least, exist. Consequently, there exists an absolutely necessary being. The minor contains an experience, the major reasons from a general experience to the existence of a necessary being.[59] Thus this argument really begins at experience, and is not completely à priori, or ontological. The object of all possible experience being the world, it is called the cosmological proof. It contains no reference to any peculiar property of sensuous objects, by which this world of sense might be distinguished from other possible worlds; and in this respect it differs from the physico-theological proof, which is based upon the consideration of the peculiar constitution of our sensuous world.

The proof proceeds thus: A necessary being can be determined only in one way, that is, it can be determined by only one of all possible opposed predicates; consequently, it must be completely determined in and by its conception. But there is only a single conception of a thing possible, which completely determines the thing à priori: that is, the conception of the ens realissimum. It follows that the conception of the ens realissimum is the only conception by and in which we can cogitate a necessary being. Consequently, a Supreme Being necessarily exists.

In this cosmological argument are assembled so many sophistical propositions that speculative reason seems to have exerted in it all her dialectical skill to produce a transcendental illusion of the most extreme character. We shall postpone an investigation of this argument for the present, and confine ourselves to exposing the stratagem by which it imposes upon us an old argument in a new dress, and appeals to the agreement of two witnesses, the one with the credentials of pure reason, and the other with those of empiricism; while, in fact, it is only the former who has changed his dress and voice, for the purpose of passing himself off for an additional witness. That it may possess a secure foundation, it bases its conclusions upon experience, and thus appears to be completely distinct from the ontological argument, which places its confidence entirely in pure à priori conceptions. But this experience merely aids reason in making one step —to the existence of a necessary being. What the properties of this being are cannot be learned from experience; and therefore reason abandons it altogether, and pursues its inquiries in the sphere of pure conception, for the purpose of discovering what the properties of an absolutely necessary being ought to be, that is, what among all possible things contain the conditions (requisita) of absolute necessity. Reason believes that it has discovered these requisites in the conception of an ens realissimum—and in it alone, and hence concludes: The ens realissimum is an absolutely necessary being. But it is evident that reason has here presupposed that the conception of an ens realissimum is perfectly adequate to the conception of a being of absolute necessity, that is, that we may infer the existence of the latter from that of the former—a proposition which formed the basis of the ontological argument, and which is now employed in the support of the cosmological argument, contrary to the wish and professions of its inventors. For the existence of an absolutely necessary being is given in conceptions alone. But if I say: "The conception of the ens realissimum is a conception of this kind, and in fact the only conception which is adequate to our idea of a necessary being," I am obliged to admit, that the latter may be inferred from the former. Thus it is properly the ontological argument which figures in the cosmological, and constitutes the whole strength of the latter; while the spurious basis of experience has been of no further use than to conduct us to the conception of absolute necessity, being utterly insufficient to demonstrate the presence of this attribute in any determinate existence or thing. For when we propose to ourselves an aim of this character, we must abandon the sphere of experience, and rise to that of pure conceptions, which we examine with the purpose of discovering whether any one contains the conditions of the possibility of an absolutely necessary being. But if the possibility of such a being is thus demonstrated, its existence is also proved; for we may then assert that, of all possible beings there is one which possesses the attribute of necessity—in other words, this being possesses an absolutely necessary existence.

All illusions in an argument are more easily detected when they are presented in the formal manner employed by the schools, which we now proceed to do.

If the proposition: "Every absolutely necessary being is likewise an ens realissimum," is correct (and it is this which constitutes the nervus probandi of the cosmological argument), it must, like all affirmative judgements, be capable of conversion—the conversio per accidens, at least. It follows, then, that some entia realissima are absolutely necessary beings. But no ens realissimum is in any respect different from another, and what is valid of some is valid of all. In this present case, therefore, I may employ simple conversion, and say: "Every ens realissimum is a necessary being." But as this proposition is determined à priori by the conceptions contained in it, the mere conception of an ens realissimum must possess the additional attribute of absolute necessity. But this is exactly what was maintained in the ontological argument, and not recognized by the cosmological, although it formed the real ground of its disguised and illusory reasoning.

Thus the second mode employed by speculative reason of demonstrating the existence of a Supreme Being, is not only, like the first, illusory and inadequate, but possesses the additional blemish of an ignoratio elenchi—professing to conduct us by a new road to the desired goal, but bringing us back, after a short circuit, to the old path which we had deserted at its call.

I mentioned above that this cosmological argument contains a perfect nest of dialectical assumptions, which transcendental criticism does not find it difficult to expose and to dissipate. I shall merely enumerate these, leaving it to the reader, who must by this time be well practised in such matters, to investigate the fallacies residing therein.

The following fallacies, for example, are discoverable in this mode of proof: 1. The transcendental principle: "Everything that is contingent must have a cause"—a principle without significance, except in the sensuous world. For the purely intellectual conception of the contingent cannot produce any synthetical proposition, like that of causality, which is itself without significance or distinguishing characteristic except in the phenomenal world. But in the present case it is employed to help us beyond the limits of its sphere. 2. "From the impossibility of an infinite ascending series of causes in the world of sense a first cause is inferred"; a conclusion which the principles of the employment of reason do not justify even in the sphere of experience, and still less when an attempt is made to pass the limits of this sphere. 3. Reason allows itself to be satisfied upon insufficient grounds, with regard to the completion of this series. It removes all conditions (without which, however, no conception of Necessity can take place); and, as after this it is beyond our power to form any other conceptions, it accepts this as a completion of the conception it wishes to form of the series. 4. The logical possibility of a conception of the total of reality (the criterion of this possibility being the absence of contradiction) is confounded with the transcendental, which requires a principle of the practicability of such a synthesis—a principle which again refers us to the world of experience. And so on.

The aim of the cosmological argument is to avoid the necessity of proving the existence of a necessary being priori from mere conceptions—a proof which must be ontological, and of which we feel ourselves quite incapable. With this purpose, we reason from an actual existence—an experience in general, to an absolutely necessary condition of that existence. It is in this case unnecessary to demonstrate its possibility. For after having proved that it exists, the question regarding its possibility is superfluous. Now, when we wish to define more strictly the nature of this necessary being, we do not look out for some being the conception of which would enable us to comprehend the necessity of its being—for if we could do this, an empirical presupposition would be unnecessary; no, we try to discover merely the negative condition (conditio sine qua non), without which a being would not be absolutely necessary. Now this would be perfectly admissible in every sort of reasoning, from a consequence to its principle; but in the present case it unfortunately happens that the condition of absolute necessity can be discovered in but a single being, the conception of which must consequently contain all that is requisite for demonstrating the presence of absolute necessity, and thus entitle me to infer this absolute necessity à priori. That is, it must be possible to reason conversely, and say: The thing, to which the conception of the highest reality belongs, is absolutely necessary. But if I cannot reason thus—and I cannot, unless I believe in the sufficiency of the ontological argument—I find insurmountable obstacles in my new path, and am really no farther than the point from which I set out. The conception of a Supreme Being satisfies all questions à priori regarding the internal determinations of a thing, and is for this reason an ideal without equal or parallel, the general conception of it indicating it as at the same time an ens individuum among all possible things. But the conception does not satisfy the question regarding its existence—which was the purpose of all our inquiries; and, although the existence of a necessary being were admitted, we should find it impossible to answer the question: What of all things in the world must be regarded as such?

It is certainly allowable to admit the existence of an all-sufficient being—a cause of all possible effects—for the purpose of enabling reason to introduce unity into its mode and grounds of explanation with regard to phenomena. But to assert that such a being necessarily exists, is no longer the modest enunciation of an admissible hypothesis, but the boldest declaration of an apodeictic certainty; for the cognition of that which is absolutely necessary must itself possess that character.

The aim of the transcendental ideal formed by the mind is either to discover a conception which shall harmonize with the idea of absolute necessity, or a conception which shall contain that idea. If the one is possible, so is the other; for reason recognizes that alone as absolutely necessary which is necessary from its conception. But both attempts are equally beyond our power—we find it impossible to satisfy the understanding upon this point, and as impossible to induce it to remain at rest in relation to this incapacity.

Unconditioned necessity, which, as the ultimate support and stay of all existing things, is an indispensable requirement of the mind, is an abyss on the verge of which human reason trembles in dismay. Even the idea of eternity, terrible and sublime as it is, as depicted by Haller, does not produce upon the mental vision such a feeling of awe and terror; for, although it measures the duration of things, it does not support them. We cannot bear, nor can we rid ourselves of the thought that a being, which we regard as the greatest of all possible existences, should say to himself: I am from eternity to eternity; beside me there is nothing, except that which exists by my will; whence then am I? Here all sinks away from under us; and the greatest, as the smallest, perfection, hovers without stay or footing in presence of the speculative reason, which finds it as easy to part with the one as with the other.

Many physical powers, which evidence their existence by their effects, are perfectly inscrutable in their nature; they elude all our powers of observation. The transcendental object which forms the basis of phenomena, and, in connection with it, the reason why our sensibility possesses this rather than that particular kind of conditions, are and must ever remain hidden from our mental vision; the fact is there, the reason of the fact we cannot see. But an ideal of pure reason cannot be termed mysterious or inscrutable, because the only credential of its reality is the need of it felt by reason, for the purpose of giving completeness to the world of synthetical unity. An ideal is not even given as a cogitable object, and therefore cannot be inscrutable; on the contrary, it must, as a mere idea, be based on the constitution of reason itself, and on this account must be capable of explanation and solution. For the very essence of reason consists in its ability to give an account, of all our conceptions, opinions, and assertions—upon objective, or, when they happen to be illusory and fallacious, upon subjective grounds.

Detection and Explanation of the Dialectical Illusion in all Transcendental Arguments for the Existence of a Necessary Being.

Both of the above arguments are transcendental; in other words, they do not proceed upon empirical principles. For, although the cosmological argument professed to lay a basis of experience for its edifice of reasoning, it did not ground its procedure upon the peculiar constitution of experience, but upon pure principles of reason—in relation to an existence given by empirical consciousness; utterly abandoning its guidance, however, for the purpose of supporting its assertions entirely upon pure conceptions. Now what is the cause, in these transcendental arguments, of the dialectical, but natural, illusion, which connects the conceptions of necessity and supreme reality, and hypostatizes that which cannot be anything but an idea? What is the cause of this unavoidable step on the part of reason, of admitting that some one among all existing things must be necessary, while it falls back from the assertion of the existence of such a being as from an abyss? And how does reason proceed to explain this anomaly to itself, and from the wavering condition of a timid and reluctant approbation—always again withdrawn—arrive at a calm and settled insight into its cause?

It is something very remarkable that, on the supposition that something exists, I cannot avoid the inference that something exists necessarily. Upon this perfectly natural—but not on that account reliable—inference does the cosmological argument rest. But, let me form any conception whatever of a thing, I find that I cannot cogitate the existence of the thing as absolutely necessary, and that nothing prevents me—be the thing or being what it may—from cogitating its non-existence. I may thus be obliged to admit that all existing things have a necessary basis, while I cannot cogitate any single or individual thing as necessary. In other words, I can never complete the regress through the conditions of existence, without admitting the existence of a necessary being; but, on the other hand, I cannot make a commencement from this being.

If I must cogitate something as existing necessarily as the basis of existing things, and yet am not permitted to cogitate any individual thing as in itself necessary, the inevitable inference is that necessity and contingency are not properties of things themselves—otherwise an internal contradiction would result; that consequently neither of these principles are objective, but merely subjective principles of reason—the one requiring us to seek for a necessary ground for everything that exists, that is, to be satisfied with no other explanation than that which is complete à priori, the other forbidding us ever to hope for the attainment of this completeness, that is, to regard no member of the empirical world as unconditioned. In this mode of viewing them, both principles, in their purely heuristic and regulative character, and as concerning merely the formal interest of reason, are quite consistent with each other. The one says: "You must philosophize upon nature," as if there existed a necessary primal basis of all existing things, solely for the purpose of introducing systematic unity into your knowledge, by pursuing an idea of this character—a foundation which is arbitrarily admitted to be ultimate; while the other warns you to consider no individual determination, concerning the existence of things, as such an ultimate foundation, that is, as absolutely necessary, but to keep the way always open for further progress in the deduction, and to treat every determination as determined by some other. But if all that we perceive must be regarded as conditionally necessary, it is impossible that anything which is empirically given should be absolutely necessary.

It follows from this that you must accept the absolutely necessary as out of and beyond the world, inasmuch as it is useful only as a principle of the highest possible unity in experience, and you cannot discover any such necessary existence in the would, the second rule requiring you to regard all empirical causes of unity as themselves deduced.

The philosophers of antiquity regarded all the forms of nature as contingent; while matter was considered by them, in accordance with the judgement of the common reason of mankind, as primal and necessary. But if they had regarded matter, not relatively—as the substratum of phenomena, but absolutely and in itself—as an independent existence, this idea of absolute necessity would have immediately disappeared. For there is nothing absolutely connecting reason with such an existence; on the contrary, it can annihilate it in thought, always and without self-contradiction. But in thought alone lay the idea of absolute necessity. A regulative principle must, therefore, have been at the foundation of this opinion. In fact, extension and impenetrability—which together constitute our conception of matter—form the supreme empirical principle of the unity of phenomena, and this principle, in so far as it is empirically unconditioned, possesses the property of a regulative principle. But, as every determination of matter which constitutes what is real in it—and consequently impenetrability—is an effect, which must have a cause, and is for this reason always derived, the notion of matter cannot harmonize with the idea of a necessary being, in its character of the principle of all derived unity. For every one of its real properties, being derived, must be only conditionally necessary, and can therefore be annihilated in thought; and thus the whole existence of matter can be so annihilated or suppressed. If this were not the case, we should have found in the world of phenomena the highest ground or condition of unity—which is impossible, according to the second regulative principle. It follows that matter, and, in general, all that forms part of the world of sense, cannot be a necessary primal being, nor even a principle of empirical unity, but that this being or principle must have its place assigned without the world. And, in this way, we can proceed in perfect confidence to deduce the phenomena of the world and their existence from other phenomena, just as if there existed no necessary being; and we can at the same time, strive without ceasing towards the attainment of completeness for our deduction, just as if such a being—the supreme condition of all existences—were presupposed by the mind.

These remarks will have made it evident to the reader that the ideal of the Supreme Being, far from being an enouncement of the existence of a being in itself necessary, is nothing more than a regulative principle of reason, requiring us to regard all connection existing between phenomena as if it had its origin from an all-sufficient necessary cause, and basing upon this the rule of a systematic and necessary unity in the explanation of phenomena. We cannot, at the same time, avoid regarding, by a transcendental subreptio, this formal principle as constitutive, and hypostatizing this unity. Precisely similar is the case with our notion of space. Space is the primal condition of all forms, which are properly just so many different limitations of it; and thus, although it is merely a principle of sensibility, we cannot help regarding it as an absolutely necessary and self-subsistent thing—as an object given à priori in itself. In the same way, it is quite natural that, as the systematic unity of nature cannot be established as a principle for the empirical employment of reason, unless it is based upon the idea of an ens realissimum, as the supreme cause, we should regard this idea as a real object, and this object, in its character of supreme condition, as absolutely necessary, and that in this way a regulative should be transformed into a constitutive principle. This interchange becomes evident when I regard this supreme being, which, relatively to the world, was absolutely (unconditionally) necessary, as a thing per se. In this case, I find it impossible to represent this necessity in or by any conception, and it exists merely in my own mind, as the formal condition of thought, but not as a material and hypostatic condition of existence.

SECTION VI. OF THE IMPOSSIBILITY OF A PHYSICO-THEOLOGICAL PROOF

If, then, neither a pure conception nor the general experience of an existing being can provide a sufficient basis for the proof of the existence of the Deity, we can make the attempt by the only other mode—that of grounding our argument upon a determinate experience of the phenomena of the present world, their constitution and disposition, and discover whether we can thus attain to a sound conviction of the existence of a Supreme Being. This argument we shall term the physico-theological argument. If it is shown to be insufficient, speculative reason cannot present us with any satisfactory proof of the existence of a being corresponding to our transcendental idea.

It is evident from the remarks that have been made in the preceding sections, that an answer to this question will be far from being difficult or unconvincing. For how can any experience be adequate with an idea? The very essence of an idea consists in the fact that no experience can ever be discovered congruent or adequate with it. The transcendental idea of a necessary and all-sufficient being is so immeasurably great, so high above all that is empirical, which is always conditioned, that we hope in vain to find materials in the sphere of experience sufficiently ample for our conception, and in vain seek the unconditioned among things that are conditioned, while examples, nay, even guidance is denied us by the laws of empirical synthesis.

If the Supreme Being forms a link in the chain of empirical conditions, it must be a member of the empirical series, and, like the lower members which it precedes, have its origin in some higher member of the series. If, on the other hand, we disengage it from the chain, and cogitate it as an intelligible being, apart from the series of natural causes —how shall reason bridge the abyss that separates the latter from the former? All laws respecting the regress from effects to causes, all synthetical additions to our knowledge relate solely to possible experience and the objects of the sensuous world, and, apart from them, are without significance.

The world around us opens before our view so magnificent a spectacle of order, variety, beauty, and conformity to ends, that whether we pursue our observations into the infinity of space in the one direction, or into its illimitable divisions in the other, whether we regard the world in its greatest or its least manifestations—even after we have attained to the highest summit of knowledge which our weak minds can reach, we find that language in the presence of wonders so inconceivable has lost its force, and number its power to reckon, nay, even thought fails to conceive adequately, and our conception of the whole dissolves into an astonishment without power of expression— all the more eloquent that it is dumb. Everywhere around us we observe a chain of causes and effects, of means and ends, of death and birth; and, as nothing has entered of itself into the condition in which we find it, we are constantly referred to some other thing, which itself suggests the same inquiry regarding its cause, and thus the universe must sink into the abyss of nothingness, unless we admit that, besides this infinite chain of contingencies, there exists something that is primal and self-subsistent—something which, as the cause of this phenomenal world, secures its continuance and preservation.

This highest cause—what magnitude shall we attribute to it? Of the content of the world we are ignorant; still less can we estimate its magnitude by comparison with the sphere of the possible. But this supreme cause being a necessity of the human mind, what is there to prevent us from attributing to it such a degree of perfection as to place it above the sphere of all that is possible? This we can easily do, although only by the aid of the faint outline of an abstract conception, by representing this being to ourselves as containing in itself, as an individual substance, all possible perfection—a conception which satisfies that requirement of reason which demands parsimony in principles, which is free from self-contradiction, which even contributes to the extension of the employment of reason in experience, by means of the guidance afforded by this idea to order and system, and which in no respect conflicts with any law of experience.

This argument always deserves to be mentioned with respect. It is the oldest, the clearest, and that most in conformity with the common reason of humanity. It animates the study of nature, as it itself derives its existence and draws ever new strength from that source. It introduces aims and ends into a sphere in which our observation could not of itself have discovered them, and extends our knowledge of nature, by directing our attention to a unity, the principle of which lies beyond nature. This knowledge of nature again reacts upon this idea—its cause; and thus our belief in a divine author of the universe rises to the power of an irresistible conviction.

For these reasons it would be utterly hopeless to attempt to rob this argument of the authority it has always enjoyed. The mind, unceasingly elevated by these considerations, which, although empirical, are so remarkably powerful, and continually adding to their force, will not suffer itself to be depressed by the doubts suggested by subtle speculation; it tears itself out of this state of uncertainty, the moment it casts a look upon the wondrous forms of nature and the majesty of the universe, and rises from height to height, from condition to condition, till it has elevated itself to the supreme and unconditioned author of all.

But although we have nothing to object to the reasonableness and utility of this procedure, but have rather to commend and encourage it, we cannot approve of the claims which this argument advances to demonstrative certainty and to a reception upon its own merits, apart from favour or support by other arguments. Nor can it injure the cause of morality to endeavour to lower the tone of the arrogant sophist, and to teach him that modesty and moderation which are the properties of a belief that brings calm and content into the mind, without prescribing to it an unworthy subjection. I maintain, then, that the physico-theological argument is insufficient of itself to prove the existence of a Supreme Being, that it must entrust this to the ontological argument—to which it serves merely as an introduction, and that, consequently, this argument contains the only possible ground of proof (possessed by speculative reason) for the existence of this being.

The chief momenta in the physico-theological argument are as follow: 1. We observe in the world manifest signs of an arrangement full of purpose, executed with great wisdom, and argument in whole of a content indescribably various, and of an extent without limits. 2. This arrangement of means and ends is entirely foreign to the things existing in the world—it belongs to them merely as a contingent attribute; in other words, the nature of different things could not of itself, whatever means were employed, harmoniously tend towards certain purposes, were they not chosen and directed for these purposes by a rational and disposing principle, in accordance with certain fundamental ideas. 3. There exists, therefore, a sublime and wise cause (or several), which is not merely a blind, all-powerful nature, producing the beings and events which fill the world in unconscious fecundity, but a free and intelligent cause of the world. 4. The unity of this cause may be inferred from the unity of the reciprocal relation existing between the parts of the world, as portions of an artistic edifice—an inference which all our observation favours, and all principles of analogy support.

In the above argument, it is inferred from the analogy of certain products of nature with those of human art, when it compels Nature to bend herself to its purposes, as in the case of a house, a ship, or a watch, that the same kind of causality—namely, understanding and will—resides in nature. It is also declared that the internal possibility of this freely-acting nature (which is the source of all art, and perhaps also of human reason) is derivable from another and superhuman art—a conclusion which would perhaps be found incapable of standing the test of subtle transcendental criticism. But to neither of these opinions shall we at present object. We shall only remark that it must be confessed that, if we are to discuss the subject of cause at all, we cannot proceed more securely than with the guidance of the analogy subsisting between nature and such products of design—these being the only products whose causes and modes of organization are completely known to us. Reason would be unable to satisfy her own requirements, if she passed from a causality which she does know, to obscure and indemonstrable principles of explanation which she does not know.

According to the physico-theological argument, the connection and harmony existing in the world evidence the contingency of the form merely, but not of the matter, that is, of the substance of the world. To establish the truth of the latter opinion, it would be necessary to prove that all things would be in themselves incapable of this harmony and order, unless they were, even as regards their substance, the product of a supreme wisdom. But this would require very different grounds of proof from those presented by the analogy with human art. This proof can at most, therefore, demonstrate the existence of an architect of the world, whose efforts are limited by the capabilities of the material with which he works, but not of a creator of the world, to whom all things are subject. Thus this argument is utterly insufficient for the task before us—a demonstration of the existence of an all-sufficient being. If we wish to prove the contingency of matter, we must have recourse to a transcendental argument, which the physico-theological was constructed expressly to avoid.

We infer, from the order and design visible in the universe, as a disposition of a thoroughly contingent character, the existence of a cause proportionate thereto. The conception of this cause must contain certain determinate qualities, and it must therefore be regarded as the conception of a being which possesses all power, wisdom, and so on, in one word, all perfection—the conception, that is, of an all-sufficient being. For the predicates of very great, astonishing, or immeasurable power and excellence, give us no determinate conception of the thing, nor do they inform us what the thing may be in itself. They merely indicate the relation existing between the magnitude of the object and the observer, who compares it with himself and with his own power of comprehension, and are mere expressions of praise and reverence, by which the object is either magnified, or the observing subject depreciated in relation to the object. Where we have to do with the magnitude (of the perfection) of a thing, we can discover no determinate conception, except that which comprehends all possible perfection or completeness, and it is only the total (omnitudo) of reality which is completely determined in and through its conception alone.

Now it cannot be expected that any one will be bold enough to declare that he has a perfect insight into the relation which the magnitude of the world he contemplates bears (in its extent as well as in its content) to omnipotence, into that of the order and design in the world to the highest wisdom, and that of the unity of the world to the absolute unity of a Supreme Being. Physico-theology is therefore incapable of presenting a determinate conception of a supreme cause of the world, and is therefore insufficient as a principle of theology—a theology which is itself to be the basis of religion.

The attainment of absolute totality is completely impossible on the path of empiricism. And yet this is the path pursued in the physico-theological argument. What means shall we employ to bridge the abyss?

After elevating ourselves to admiration of the magnitude of the power, wisdom, and other attributes of the author of the world, and finding we can advance no further, we leave the argument on empirical grounds, and proceed to infer the contingency of the world from the order and conformity to aims that are observable in it. From this contingency we infer, by the help of transcendental conceptions alone, the existence of something absolutely necessary; and, still advancing, proceed from the conception of the absolute necessity of the first cause to the completely determined or determining conception thereof—the conception of an all-embracing reality. Thus the physico-theological, failing in its undertaking, recurs in its embarrassment to the cosmological argument; and, as this is merely the ontological argument in disguise, it executes its design solely by the aid of pure reason, although it at first professed to have no connection with this faculty and to base its entire procedure upon experience alone.

The physico-theologians have therefore no reason to regard with such contempt the transcendental mode of argument, and to look down upon it, with the conceit of clear-sighted observers of nature, as the brain-cobweb of obscure speculatists. For, if they reflect upon and examine their own arguments, they will find that, after following for some time the path of nature and experience, and discovering themselves no nearer their object, they suddenly leave this path and pass into the region of pure possibility, where they hope to reach upon the wings of ideas what had eluded all their empirical investigations. Gaining, as they think, a firm footing after this immense leap, they extend their determinate conception—into the possession of which they have come, they know not how—over the whole sphere of creation, and explain their ideal, which is entirely a product of pure reason, by illustrations drawn from experience—though in a degree miserably unworthy of the grandeur of the object, while they refuse to acknowledge that they have arrived at this cognition or hypothesis by a very different road from that of experience.

Thus the physico-theological is based upon the cosmological, and this upon the ontological proof of the existence of a Supreme Being; and as besides these three there is no other path open to speculative reason, the ontological proof, on the ground of pure conceptions of reason, is the only possible one, if any proof of a proposition so far transcending the empirical exercise of the understanding is possible at all.

SECTION VII. CRITIQUE OF ALL THEOLOGY BASED UPON SPECULATIVE PRINCIPLES OF REASON

If by the term theology I understand the cognition of a primal being, that cognition is based either upon reason alone (theologia rationalis) or upon revelation (theologia revelata). The former cogitates its object either by means of pure transcendental conceptions, as an ens originarium, realissimum, ens entium, and is termed transcendental theology; or, by means of a conception derived from the nature of our own mind, as a supreme intelligence, and must then be entitled natural theology. The person who believes in a transcendental theology alone, is termed a deist; he who acknowledges the possibility of a natural theology also, a theist. The former admits that we can cognize by pure reason alone the existence of a Supreme Being, but at the same time maintains that our conception of this being is purely transcendental, and that all we can say of it is that it possesses all reality, without being able to define it more closely. The second asserts that reason is capable of presenting us, from the analogy with nature, with a more definite conception of this being, and that its operations, as the cause of all things, are the results of intelligence and free will. The former regards the Supreme Being as the cause of the world—whether by the necessity of his nature, or as a free agent, is left undetermined; the latter considers this being as the author of the world.

Transcendental theology aims either at inferring the existence of a Supreme Being from a general experience, without any closer reference to the world to which this experience belongs, and in this case it is called cosmotheology; or it endeavours to cognize the existence of such a being, through mere conceptions, without the aid of experience, and is then termed ontotheology.

Natural theology infers the attributes and the existence of an author of the world, from the constitution of, the order and unity observable in, the world, in which two modes of causality must be admitted to exist—those of nature and freedom. Thus it rises from this world to a supreme intelligence, either as the principle of all natural, or of all moral order and perfection. In the former case it is termed physico-theology, in the latter, ethical or moral-theology.[60]

As we are wont to understand by the term God not merely an eternal nature, the operations of which are insensate and blind, but a Supreme Being, who is the free and intelligent author of all things, and as it is this latter view alone that can be of interest to humanity, we might, in strict rigour, deny to the deist any belief in God at all, and regard him merely as a maintainer of the existence of a primal being or thing—the supreme cause of all other things. But, as no one ought to be blamed, merely because he does not feel himself justified in maintaining a certain opinion, as if he altogether denied its truth and asserted the opposite, it is more correct—as it is less harsh—to say, the deist believes in a God, the theist in a living God (summa intelligentia). We shall now proceed to investigate the sources of all these attempts of reason to establish the existence of a Supreme Being.

It may be sufficient in this place to define theoretical knowledge or cognition as knowledge of that which is, and practical knowledge as knowledge of that which ought to be. In this view, the theoretical employment of reason is that by which I cognize à priori (as necessary) that something is, while the practical is that by which I cognize à priori what ought to happen. Now, if it is an indubitably certain, though at the same time an entirely conditioned truth, that something is, or ought to happen, either a certain determinate condition of this truth is absolutely necessary, or such a condition may be arbitrarily presupposed. In the former case the condition is postulated (per thesin), in the latter supposed (per hypothesin). There are certain practical laws—those of morality—which are absolutely necessary. Now, if these laws necessarily presuppose the existence of some being, as the condition of the possibility of their obligatory power, this being must be postulated, because the conditioned, from which we reason to this determinate condition, is itself cognized à priori as absolutely necessary. We shall at some future time show that the moral laws not merely presuppose the existence of a Supreme Being, but also, as themselves absolutely necessary in a different relation, demand or postulate it—although only from a practical point of view. The discussion of this argument we postpone for the present.

When the question relates merely to that which is, not to that which ought to be, the conditioned which is presented in experience is always cogitated as contingent. For this reason its condition cannot be regarded as absolutely necessary, but merely as relatively necessary, or rather as needful; the condition is in itself and à priori a mere arbitrary presupposition in aid of the cognition, by reason, of the conditioned. If, then, we are to possess a theoretical cognition of the absolute necessity of a thing, we cannot attain to this cognition otherwise than à priori by means of conceptions; while it is impossible in this way to cognize the existence of a cause which bears any relation to an existence given in experience.

Theoretical cognition is speculative when it relates to an object or certain conceptions of an object which is not given and cannot be discovered by means of experience. It is opposed to the cognition of nature, which concerns only those objects or predicates which can be presented in a possible experience.

The principle that everything which happens (the empirically contingent) must have a cause, is a principle of the cognition of nature, but not of speculative cognition. For, if we change it into an abstract principle, and deprive it of its reference to experience and the empirical, we shall find that it cannot with justice be regarded any longer as a synthetical proposition, and that it is impossible to discover any mode of transition from that which exists to something entirely different—termed cause. Nay, more, the conception of a cause likewise that of the contingent—loses, in this speculative mode of employing it, all significance, for its objective reality and meaning are comprehensible from experience alone.

When from the existence of the universe and the things in it the existence of a cause of the universe is inferred, reason is proceeding not in the natural, but in the speculative method. For the principle of the former enounces, not that things themselves or substances, but only that which happens or their states—as empirically contingent, have a cause: the assertion that the existence of substance itself is contingent is not justified by experience, it is the assertion of a reason employing its principles in a speculative manner. If, again, I infer from the form of the universe, from the way in which all things are connected and act and react upon each other, the existence of a cause entirely distinct from the universe—this would again be a judgement of purely speculative reason; because the object in this case—the cause—can never be an object of possible experience. In both these cases the principle of causality, which is valid only in the field of experience—useless and even meaningless beyond this region, would be diverted from its proper destination.

Now I maintain that all attempts of reason to establish a theology by the aid of speculation alone are fruitless, that the principles of reason as applied to nature do not conduct us to any theological truths, and, consequently, that a rational theology can have no existence, unless it is founded upon the laws of morality. For all synthetical principles of the understanding are valid only as immanent in experience; while the cognition of a Supreme Being necessitates their being employed transcendentally, and of this the understanding is quite incapable. If the empirical law of causality is to conduct us to a Supreme Being, this being must belong to the chain of empirical objects—in which case it would be, like all phenomena, itself conditioned. If the possibility of passing the limits of experience be admitted, by means of the dynamical law of the relation of an effect to its cause, what kind of conception shall we obtain by this procedure? Certainly not the conception of a Supreme Being, because experience never presents us with the greatest of all possible effects, and it is only an effect of this character that could witness to the existence of a corresponding cause. If, for the purpose of fully satisfying the requirements of Reason, we recognize her right to assert the existence of a perfect and absolutely necessary being, this can be admitted only from favour, and cannot be regarded as the result of irresistible demonstration. The physico-theological proof may add weight to others—if other proofs there are—by connecting speculation with experience; but in itself it rather prepares the mind for theological cognition, and gives it a right and natural direction, than establishes a sure foundation for theology.

It is now perfectly evident that transcendental questions admit only of transcendental answers—those presented à priori by pure conceptions without the least empirical admixture. But the question in the present case is evidently synthetical—it aims at the extension of our cognition beyond the bounds of experience—it requires an assurance respecting the existence of a being corresponding with the idea in our minds, to which no experience can ever be adequate. Now it has been abundantly proved that all à priori synthetical cognition is possible only as the expression of the formal conditions of a possible experience; and that the validity of all principles depends upon their immanence in the field of experience, that is, their relation to objects of empirical cognition or phenomena. Thus all transcendental procedure in reference to speculative theology is without result.

If any one prefers doubting the conclusiveness of the proofs of our analytic to losing the persuasion of the validity of these old and time honoured arguments, he at least cannot decline answering the question—how he can pass the limits of all possible experience by the help of mere ideas. If he talks of new arguments, or of improvements upon old arguments, I request him to spare me. There is certainly no great choice in this sphere of discussion, as all speculative arguments must at last look for support to the ontological, and I have, therefore, very little to fear from the argumentative fecundity of the dogmatical defenders of a non-sensuous reason. Without looking upon myself as a remarkably combative person, I shall not decline the challenge to detect the fallacy and destroy the pretensions of every attempt of speculative theology. And yet the hope of better fortune never deserts those who are accustomed to the dogmatical mode of procedure. I shall, therefore, restrict myself to the simple and equitable demand that such reasoners will demonstrate, from the nature of the human mind as well as from that of the other sources of knowledge, how we are to proceed to extend our cognition completely à priori, and to carry it to that point where experience abandons us, and no means exist of guaranteeing the objective reality of our conceptions. In whatever way the understanding may have attained to a conception, the existence of the object of the conception cannot be discovered in it by analysis, because the cognition of the existence of the object depends upon the object's being posited and given in itself apart from the conception. But it is utterly impossible to go beyond our conception, without the aid of experience—which presents to the mind nothing but phenomena, or to attain by the help of mere conceptions to a conviction of the existence of new kinds of objects or supernatural beings.

But although pure speculative reason is far from sufficient to demonstrate the existence of a Supreme Being, it is of the highest utility in correcting our conception of this being—on the supposition that we can attain to the cognition of it by some other means —in making it consistent with itself and with all other conceptions of intelligible objects, clearing it from all that is incompatible with the conception of an ens summun, and eliminating from it all limitations or admixtures of empirical elements.

Transcendental theology is still therefore, notwithstanding its objective insufficiency, of importance in a negative respect; it is useful as a test of the procedure of reason when engaged with pure ideas, no other than a transcendental standard being in this case admissible. For if, from a practical point of view, the hypothesis of a Supreme and All-sufficient Being is to maintain its validity without opposition, it must be of the highest importance to define this conception in a correct and rigorous manner—as the transcendental conception of a necessary being, to eliminate all phenomenal elements (anthropomorphism in its most extended signification), and at the same time to overflow all contradictory assertions—be they atheistic, deistic, or anthropomorphic. This is of course very easy; as the same arguments which demonstrated the inability of human reason to affirm the existence of a Supreme Being must be alike sufficient to prove the invalidity of its denial. For it is impossible to gain from the pure speculation of reason demonstration that there exists no Supreme Being, as the ground of all that exists, or that this being possesses none of those properties which we regard as analogical with the dynamical qualities of a thinking being, or that, as the anthropomorphists would have us believe, it is subject to all the limitations which sensibility imposes upon those intelligences which exist in the world of experience.

A Supreme Being is, therefore, for the speculative reason, a mere ideal, though a faultless one—a conception which perfects and crowns the system of human cognition, but the objective reality of which can neither be proved nor disproved by pure reason. If this defect is ever supplied by a moral theology, the problematic transcendental theology which has preceded, will have been at least serviceable as demonstrating the mental necessity existing for the conception, by the complete determination of it which it has furnished, and the ceaseless testing of the conclusions of a reason often deceived by sense, and not always in harmony with its own ideas. The attributes of necessity, infinitude, unity, existence apart from the world (and not as a world soul), eternity (free from conditions of time), omnipresence (free from conditions of space), omnipotence, and others, are pure transcendental predicates; and thus the accurate conception of a Supreme Being, which every theology requires, is furnished by transcendental theology alone.

APPENDIX. OF THE REGULATIVE EMPLOYMENT OF THE IDEAS OF PURE REASON

The result of all the dialectical attempts of pure reason not only confirms the truth of what we have already proved in our Transcendental Analytic, namely, that all inferences which would lead us beyond the limits of experience are fallacious and groundless, but it at the same time teaches us this important lesson, that human reason has a natural inclination to overstep these limits, and that transcendental ideas are as much the natural property of the reason as categories are of the understanding. There exists this difference, however, that while the categories never mislead us, outward objects being always in perfect harmony therewith, ideas are the parents of irresistible illusions, the severest and most subtle criticism being required to save us from the fallacies which they induce.

Whatever is grounded in the nature of our powers will be found to be in harmony with the final purpose and proper employment of these powers, when once we have discovered their true direction and aim. We are entitled to suppose, therefore, that there exists a mode of employing transcendental ideas which is proper and immanent; although, when we mistake their meaning, and regard them as conceptions of actual things, their mode of application is transcendent and delusive. For it is not the idea itself, but only the employment of the idea in relation to possible experience, that is transcendent or immanent. An idea is employed transcendently, when it is applied to an object falsely believed to be adequate with and to correspond to it; imminently, when it is applied solely to the employment of the understanding in the sphere of experience. Thus all errors of subreptio—of misapplication, are to be ascribed to defects of judgement, and not to understanding or reason.

Reason never has an immediate relation to an object; it relates immediately to the understanding alone. It is only through the understanding that it can be employed in the field of experience. It does not form conceptions of objects, it merely arranges them and gives to them that unity which they are capable of possessing when the sphere of their application has been extended as widely as possible. Reason avails itself of the conception of the understanding for the sole purpose of producing totality in the different series. This totality the understanding does not concern itself with; its only occupation is the connection of experiences, by which series of conditions in accordance with conceptions are established. The object of reason is, therefore, the understanding and its proper destination. As the latter brings unity into the diversity of objects by means of its conceptions, so the former brings unity into the diversity of conceptions by means of ideas; as it sets the final aim of a collective unity to the operations of the understanding, which without this occupies itself with a distributive unity alone.

I accordingly maintain that transcendental ideas can never be employed as constitutive ideas, that they cannot be conceptions of objects, and that, when thus considered, they assume a fallacious and dialectical character. But, on the other hand, they are capable of an admirable and indispensably necessary application to objects—as regulative ideas, directing the understanding to a certain aim, the guiding lines towards which all its laws follow, and in which they all meet in one point. This point—though a mere idea (focus imaginarius), that is, not a point from which the conceptions of the understanding do really proceed, for it lies beyond the sphere of possible experience—serves, notwithstanding, to give to these conceptions the greatest possible unity combined with the greatest possible extension. Hence arises the natural illusion which induces us to believe that these lines proceed from an object which lies out of the sphere of empirical cognition, just as objects reflected in a mirror appear to be behind it. But this illusion—which we may hinder from imposing upon us—is necessary and unavoidable, if we desire to see, not only those objects which lie before us, but those which are at a great distance behind us; that is to say, when, in the present case, we direct the aims of the understanding, beyond every given experience, towards an extension as great as can possibly be attained.

If we review our cognitions in their entire extent, we shall find that the peculiar business of reason is to arrange them into a system, that is to say, to give them connection according to a principle. This unity presupposes an idea—the idea of the form of a whole (of cognition), preceding the determinate cognition of the parts, and containing the conditions which determine à priori to every part its place and relation to the other parts of the whole system. This idea, accordingly, demands complete unity in the cognition of the understanding—not the unity of a contingent aggregate, but that of a system connected according to necessary laws. It cannot be affirmed with propriety that this idea is a conception of an object; it is merely a conception of the complete unity of the conceptions of objects, in so far as this unity is available to the understanding as a rule. Such conceptions of reason are not derived from nature; on the contrary, we employ them for the interrogation and investigation of nature, and regard our cognition as defective so long as it is not adequate to them. We admit that such a thing as pure earth, pure water, or pure air, is not to be discovered. And yet we require these conceptions (which have their origin in the reason, so far as regards their absolute purity and completeness) for the purpose of determining the share which each of these natural causes has in every phenomenon. Thus the different kinds of matter are all referred to earths, as mere weight; to salts and inflammable bodies, as pure force; and finally, to water and air, as the vehicula of the former, or the machines employed by them in their operations—for the purpose of explaining the chemical action and reaction of bodies in accordance with the idea of a mechanism. For, although not actually so expressed, the influence of such ideas of reason is very observable in the procedure of natural philosophers.

If reason is the faculty of deducing the particular from the general, and if the general be certain in se and given, it is only necessary that the judgement should subsume the particular under the general, the particular being thus necessarily determined. I shall term this the demonstrative or apodeictic employment of reason. If, however, the general is admitted as problematical only, and is a mere idea, the particular case is certain, but the universality of the rule which applies to this particular case remains a problem. Several particular cases, the certainty of which is beyond doubt, are then taken and examined, for the purpose of discovering whether the rule is applicable to them; and if it appears that all the particular cases which can be collected follow from the rule, its universality is inferred, and at the same time, all the causes which have not, or cannot be presented to our observation, are concluded to be of the same character with those which we have observed. This I shall term the hypothetical employment of the reason.

The hypothetical exercise of reason by the aid of ideas employed as problematical conceptions is properly not constitutive. That is to say, if we consider the subject strictly, the truth of the rule, which has been employed as an hypothesis, does not follow from the use that is made of it by reason. For how can we know all the possible cases that may arise? some of which may, however, prove exceptions to the universality of the rule. This employment of reason is merely regulative, and its sole aim is the introduction of unity into the aggregate of our particular cognitions, and thereby the approximating of the rule to universality.

The object of the hypothetical employment of reason is therefore the systematic unity of cognitions; and this unity is the criterion of the truth of a rule. On the other hand, this systematic unity—as a mere idea—is in fact merely a unity projected, not to be regarded as given, but only in the light of a problem—a problem which serves, however, as a principle for the various and particular exercise of the understanding in experience, directs it with regard to those cases which are not presented to our observation, and introduces harmony and consistency into all its operations.

All that we can be certain of from the above considerations is that this systematic unity is a logical principle, whose aim is to assist the understanding, where it cannot of itself attain to rules, by means of ideas, to bring all these various rules under one principle, and thus to ensure the most complete consistency and connection that can be attained. But the assertion that objects and the understanding by which they are cognized are so constituted as to be determined to systematic unity, that this may be postulated à priori, without any reference to the interest of reason, and that we are justified in declaring all possible cognitions—empirical and others—to possess systematic unity, and to be subject to general principles from which, notwithstanding their various character, they are all derivable such an assertion can be founded only upon a transcendental principle of reason, which would render this systematic unity not subjectively and logically—in its character of a method, but objectively necessary.

We shall illustrate this by an example. The conceptions of the understanding make us acquainted, among many other kinds of unity, with that of the causality of a substance, which is termed power. The different phenomenal manifestations of the same substance appear at first view to be so very dissimilar that we are inclined to assume the existence of just as many different powers as there are different effects—as, in the case of the human mind, we have feeling, consciousness, imagination, memory, wit, analysis, pleasure, desire and so on. Now we are required by a logical maxim to reduce these differences to as small a number as possible, by comparing them and discovering the hidden identity which exists. We must inquire, for example, whether or not imagination (connected with consciousness), memory, wit, and analysis are not merely different forms of understanding and reason. The idea of a fundamental power, the existence of which no effort of logic can assure us of, is the problem to be solved, for the systematic representation of the existing variety of powers. The logical principle of reason requires us to produce as great a unity as is possible in the system of our cognitions; and the more the phenomena of this and the other power are found to be identical, the more probable does it become, that they are nothing but different manifestations of one and the same power, which may be called, relatively speaking, a fundamental power. And so with other cases.

These relatively fundamental powers must again be compared with each other, to discover, if possible, the one radical and absolutely fundamental power of which they are but the manifestations. But this unity is purely hypothetical. It is not maintained, that this unity does really exist, but that we must, in the interest of reason, that is, for the establishment of principles for the various rules presented by experience, try to discover and introduce it, so far as is practicable, into the sphere of our cognitions.

But the transcendental employment of the understanding would lead us to believe that this idea of a fundamental power is not problematical, but that it possesses objective reality, and thus the systematic unity of the various powers or forces in a substance is demanded by the understanding and erected into an apodeictic or necessary principle. For, without having attempted to discover the unity of the various powers existing in nature, nay, even after all our attempts have failed, we notwithstanding presuppose that it does exist, and may be, sooner or later, discovered. And this reason does, not only, as in the case above adduced, with regard to the unity of substance, but where many substances, although all to a certain extent homogeneous, are discoverable, as in the case of matter in general. Here also does reason presuppose the existence of the systematic unity of various powers—inasmuch as particular laws of nature are subordinate to general laws; and parsimony in principles is not merely an economical principle of reason, but an essential law of nature.

We cannot understand, in fact, how a logical principle of unity can of right exist, unless we presuppose a transcendental principle, by which such a systematic unit—as a property of objects themselves—is regarded as necessary à priori. For with what right can reason, in its logical exercise, require us to regard the variety of forces which nature displays, as in effect a disguised unity, and to deduce them from one fundamental force or power, when she is free to admit that it is just as possible that all forces should be different in kind, and that a systematic unity is not conformable to the design of nature? In this view of the case, reason would be proceeding in direct opposition to her own destination, by setting as an aim an idea which entirely conflicts with the procedure and arrangement of nature. Neither can we assert that reason has previously inferred this unity from the contingent nature of phenomena. For the law of reason which requires us to seek for this unity is a necessary law, inasmuch as without it we should not possess a faculty of reason, nor without reason a consistent and self-accordant mode of employing the understanding, nor, in the absence of this, any proper and sufficient criterion of empirical truth. In relation to this criterion, therefore, we must suppose the idea of the systematic unity of nature to possess objective validity and necessity.

We find this transcendental presupposition lurking in different forms in the principles of philosophers, although they have neither recognized it nor confessed to themselves its presence. That the diversities of individual things do not exclude identity of species, that the various species must be considered as merely different determinations of a few genera, and these again as divisions of still higher races, and so on—that, accordingly, a certain systematic unity of all possible empirical conceptions, in so far as they can be deduced from higher and more general conceptions, must be sought for, is a scholastic maxim or logical principle, without which reason could not be employed by us. For we can infer the particular from the general, only in so far as general properties of things constitute the foundation upon which the particular rest.

That the same unity exists in nature is presupposed by philosophers in the well-known scholastic maxim, which forbids us unnecessarily to augment the number of entities or principles (entia praeter necessitatem non esse multiplicanda). This maxim asserts that nature herself assists in the establishment of this unity of reason, and that the seemingly infinite diversity of phenomena should not deter us from the expectation of discovering beneath this diversity a unity of fundamental properties, of which the aforesaid variety is but a more or less determined form. This unity, although a mere idea, thinkers have found it necessary rather to moderate the desire than to encourage it. It was considered a great step when chemists were able to reduce all salts to two main genera—acids and alkalis; and they regard this difference as itself a mere variety, or different manifestation of one and the same fundamental material. The different kinds of earths (stones and even metals) chemists have endeavoured to reduce to three, and afterwards to two; but still, not content with this advance, they cannot but think that behind these diversities there lurks but one genus—nay, that even salts and earths have a common principle. It might be conjectured that this is merely an economical plan of reason, for the purpose of sparing itself trouble, and an attempt of a purely hypothetical character, which, when successful, gives an appearance of probability to the principle of explanation employed by the reason. But a selfish purpose of this kind is easily to be distinguished from the idea, according to which every one presupposes that this unity is in accordance with the laws of nature, and that reason does not in this case request, but requires, although we are quite unable to determine the proper limits of this unity.

If the diversity existing in phenomena—a diversity not of form (for in this they may be similar) but of content—were so great that the subtlest human reason could never by comparison discover in them the least similarity (which is not impossible), in this case the logical law of genera would be without foundation, the conception of a genus, nay, all general conceptions would be impossible, and the faculty of the understanding, the exercise of which is restricted to the world of conceptions, could not exist. The logical principle of genera, accordingly, if it is to be applied to nature (by which I mean objects presented to our senses), presupposes a transcendental principle. In accordance with this principle, homogeneity is necessarily presupposed in the variety of phenomena (although we are unable to determine à priori the degree of this homogeneity), because without it no empirical conceptions, and consequently no experience, would be possible.

The logical principle of genera, which demands identity in phenomena, is balanced by another principle—that of species, which requires variety and diversity in things, notwithstanding their accordance in the same genus, and directs the understanding to attend to the one no less than to the other. This principle (of the faculty of distinction) acts as a check upon the reason and reason exhibits in this respect a double and conflicting interest—on the one hand, the interest in the extent (the interest of generality) in relation to genera; on the other, that of the content (the interest of individuality) in relation to the variety of species. In the former case, the understanding cogitates more under its conceptions, in the latter it cogitates more in them. This distinction manifests itself likewise in the habits of thought peculiar to natural philosophers, some of whom

—the remarkably speculative heads—may be said to be hostile to heterogeneity in phenomena, and have their eyes always fixed on the unity of genera, while others— with a strong empirical tendency—aim unceasingly at the analysis of phenomena, and almost destroy in us the hope of ever being able to estimate the character of these according to general principles.

The latter mode of thought is evidently based upon a logical principle, the aim of which is the systematic completeness of all cognitions. This principle authorizes me, beginning at the genus, to descend to the various and diverse contained under it; and in this way extension, as in the former case unity, is assured to the system. For if we merely examine the sphere of the conception which indicates a genus, we cannot discover how far it is possible to proceed in the division of that sphere; just as it is impossible, from the consideration of the space occupied by matter, to determine how far we can proceed in the division of it. Hence every genus must contain different species, and these again different subspecies; and as each of the latter must itself contain a sphere (must be of a certain extent, as a conceptus communis), reason demands that no species or sub-species is to be considered as the lowest possible. For a species or sub-species, being always a conception, which contains only what is common to a number of different things, does not completely determine any individual thing, or relate imme-diately to it, and must consequently contain other conceptions, that is, other sub-species under it. This law of specification may be thus expressed: entium varietates non temere sunt minuendae.

But it is easy to see that this logical law would likewise be without sense or applica-tion, were it not based upon a transcendental law of specification, which certainly does not require that the differences existing phenomena should be infinite in number, for the logical principle, which merely maintains the indeterminateness of the logical sphere of a conception, in relation to its possible division, does not authorize this statement; while it does impose upon the understanding the duty of searching for subspecies to every species, and minor differences in every difference. For, were there no lower conceptions, neither could there be any higher. Now the understanding cognizes only by means of conceptions; consequently, how far soever it may proceed in division, never by mere intuition, but always by lower and lower conceptions. The cognition of phenomena in their complete determination (which is possible only by means of the understanding) requires an unceasingly continued specification of conceptions, and a progression to ever smaller differences, of which abstraction had been made in the conception of the species, and still more in that of the genus.

This law of specification cannot be deduced from experience; it can never present us with a principle of so universal an application. Empirical specification very soon stops in its distinction of diversities, and requires the guidance of the transcendental law, as a principle of the reason—a law which imposes on us the necessity of never ceasing in our search for differences, even although these may not present themselves to the senses. That absorbent earths are of different kinds could only be discovered by obeying the anticipatory law of reason, which imposes upon the understanding the task of discovering the differences existing between these earths, and supposes that nature is richer in substances than our senses would indicate. The faculty of the understanding belongs to us just as much under the presupposition of differences in the objects of nature, as under the condition that these objects are homogeneous, because we could not possess conceptions, nor make any use of our understanding, were not the phenomena included under these conceptions in some respects dissimilar, as well as similar, in their character.

Reason thus prepares the sphere of the understanding for the operations of this faculty: 1. By the principle of the homogeneity of the diverse in higher genera; 2. By the principle of the variety of the homogeneous in lower species; and, to complete the systematic unity, it adds, 3. A law of the affinity of all conceptions which prescribes a continuous transition from one species to every other by the gradual increase of diversity. We may term these the principles of the homogeneity, the specification, and the continuity of forms. The latter results from the union of the two former, inasmuch as we regard the systematic connection as complete in thought, in the ascent to higher genera, as well as in the descent to lower species. For all diversities must be related to each other, as they all spring from one highest genus, descending through the different gradations of a more and more extended determination.

We may illustrate the systematic unity produced by the three logical principles in the following manner. Every conception may be regarded as a point, which, as the standpoint of a spectator, has a certain horizon, which may be said to enclose a number of things that may be viewed, so to speak, from that centre. Within this horizon there must be an infinite number of other points, each of which has its own horizon, smaller and more circumscribed; in other words, every species contains sub-species, according to the principle of specification, and the logical horizon consists of smaller horizons (sub-species), but not of points (individuals), which possess no extent. But different horizons or genera, which include under them so many conceptions, may have one common horizon, from which, as from a mid-point, they may be surveyed; and we may proceed thus, till we arrive at the highest genus, or universal and true horizon, which is determined by the highest conception, and which contains under itself all differences and varieties, as genera, species, and subspecies.

To this highest standpoint I am conducted by the law of homogeneity, as to all lower and more variously-determined conceptions by the law of specification. Now as in this way there exists no void in the whole extent of all possible conceptions, and as out of the sphere of these the mind can discover nothing, there arises from the presupposition of the universal horizon above mentioned, and its complete division, the principle: Non datur vacuum formarum. This principle asserts that there are not different primitive and highest genera, which stand isolated, so to speak, from each other, but all the various genera are mere divisions and limitations of one highest and universal genus; and hence follows immediately the principle: Datur continuum formarum. This principle indicates that all differences of species limit each other, and do not admit of transition from one to another by a saltus, but only through smaller degrees of the difference between the one species and the other. In one word, there are no species or sub-species which (in the view of reason) are the nearest possible to each other; intermediate species or sub-species being always possible, the difference of which from each of the former is always smaller than the difference existing between these.

The first law, therefore, directs us to avoid the notion that there exist different primal genera, and enounces the fact of perfect homogeneity; the second imposes a check upon this tendency to unity and prescribes the distinction of sub-species, before proceeding to apply our general conceptions to individuals. The third unites both the former, by enouncing the fact of homogeneity as existing even in the most various diversity, by means of the gradual transition from one species to another. Thus it indicates a relationship between the different branches or species, in so far as they all spring from the same stem.

But this logical law of the continuum specierum (formarum logicarum) presupposes a transcendental principle (lex continui in natura), without which the understanding might be led into error, by following the guidance of the former, and thus perhaps pursuing a path contrary to that prescribed by nature. This law must, consequently, be based upon pure transcendental, and not upon empirical, considerations. For, in the latter case, it would come later than the system; whereas it is really itself the parent of all that is systematic in our cognition of nature. These principles are not mere hypotheses employed for the purpose of experimenting upon nature; although when any such connection is discovered, it forms a solid ground for regarding the hypothetical unity as valid in the sphere of nature—and thus they are in this respect not without their use. But we go farther, and maintain that it is manifest that these principles of parsimony in fundamental causes, variety in effects, and affinity in phenomena, are in accordance both with reason and nature, and that they are not mere methods or plans devised for the purpose of assisting us in our observation of the external world.

But it is plain that this continuity of forms is a mere idea, to which no adequate object can be discovered in experience. And this for two reasons. First, because the species in nature are really divided, and hence form quanta discreta; and, if the gradual progression through their affinity were continuous, the intermediate members lying between two given species must be infinite in number, which is impossible. Secondly, because we cannot make any determinate empirical use of this law, inasmuch as it does not present us with any criterion of affinity which could aid us in determining how far we ought to pursue the graduation of differences: it merely contains a general indication that it is our duty to seek for and, if possible, to discover them.

When we arrange these principles of systematic unity in the order conformable to their employment in experience, they will stand thus: Variety, Affinity, Unity, each of them, as ideas, being taken in the highest degree of their completeness. Reason presupposes the existence of cognitions of the understanding, which have a direct relation to experience, and aims at the ideal unity of these cognitions—a unity which far transcends all experience or empirical notions. The affinity of the diverse, notwithstanding the differences existing between its parts, has a relation to things, but a still closer one to the mere properties and powers of things. For example, imperfect experience may represent the orbits of the planets as circular. But we discover variations from this course, and we proceed to suppose that the planets revolve in a path which, if not a circle, is of a character very similar to it. That is to say, the movements of those planets which do not form a circle will approximate more or less to the properties of a circle, and probably form an ellipse. The paths of comets exhibit still greater variations, for, so far as our observation extends, they do not return upon their own course in a circle or ellipse. But we proceed to the conjecture that comets describe a parabola, a figure which is closely allied to the ellipse. In fact, a parabola is merely an ellipse, with its longer axis produced to an indefinite extent. Thus these principles conduct us to a unity in the genera of the forms of these orbits, and, proceeding farther, to a unity as regards the cause of the motions of the heavenly bodies—that is, gravitation. But we go on extending our conquests over nature, and endeavour to explain all seeming deviations from these rules, and even make additions to our system which no experience can ever substantiate—for example, the theory, in affinity with that of ellipses, of hyperbolic paths of comets, pursuing which, these bodies leave our solar system and, passing from sun to sun, unite the most distant parts of the infinite universe, which is held together by the same moving power.

The most remarkable circumstance connected with these principles is that they seem to be transcendental, and, although only containing ideas for the guidance of the empirical exercise of reason, and although this empirical employment stands to these ideas in an asymptotic relation alone (to use a mathematical term), that is, continually approximate, without ever being able to attain to them, they possess, notwithstanding, as à priori synthetical propositions, objective though undetermined validity, and are available as rules for possible experience. In the elaboration of our experience, they may also be employed with great advantage, as heuristic[61] principles. A transcendental deduction of them cannot be made; such a deduction being always impossible in the case of ideas, as has been already shown.

We distinguished, in the Transcendental Analytic, the dynamical principles of the understanding, which are regulative principles of intuition, from the mathematical, which are constitutive principles of intuition. These dynamical laws are, however, constitutive in relation to experience, inasmuch as they render the conceptions without which experience could not exist possible à priori. But the principles of pure reason cannot be constitutive even in regard to empirical conceptions, because no sensuous schema corresponding to them can be discovered, and they cannot therefore have an object in concreto. Now, if I grant that they cannot be employed in the sphere of experience, as constitutive principles, how shall I secure for them employment and objective validity as regulative principles, and in what way can they be so employed?

The understanding is the object of reason, as sensibility is the object of the understanding. The production of systematic unity in all the empirical operations of the understanding is the proper occupation of reason; just as it is the business of the understanding to connect the various content of phenomena by means of conceptions, and subject them to empirical laws. But the operations of the understanding are, without the schemata of sensibility, undetermined; and, in the same manner, the unity of reason is perfectly undetermined as regards the conditions under which, and the extent to which, the understanding ought to carry the systematic connection of its conceptions. But, although it is impossible to discover in intuition a schema for the complete systematic unity of all the conceptions of the understanding, there must be some analogon of this schema. This analogon is the idea of the maximum of the division and the connection of our cognition in one principle. For we may have a determinate notion of a maximum and an absolutely perfect, all the restrictive conditions which are connected with an indeterminate and various content having been abstracted. Thus the idea of reason is analogous with a sensuous schema, with this difference, that the application of the categories to the schema of reason does not present a cognition of any object (as is the case with the application of the categories to sensuous schemata), but merely provides us with a rule or principle for the systematic unity of the exercise of the understanding. Now, as every principle which imposes upon the exercise of the understanding à priori compliance with the rule of systematic unity also relates, although only in an indirect manner, to an object of experience, the principles of pure reason will also possess objective reality and validity in relation to experience. But they will not aim at determining our knowledge in regard to any empirical object; they will merely indicate the procedure, following which the empirical and determinate exercise of the understanding may be in complete harmony and connection with itself—a result which is produced by its being brought into harmony with the principle of systematic unity, so far as that is possible, and deduced from it.

I term all subjective principles, which are not derived from observation of the constitution of an object, but from the interest which Reason has in producing a certain completeness in her cognition of that object, maxims of reason. Thus there are maxims of speculative reason, which are based solely upon its speculative interest, although they appear to be objective principles.

When principles which are really regulative are regarded as constitutive, and employed as objective principles, contradictions must arise; but if they are considered as mere maxims, there is no room for contradictions of any kind, as they then merely indicate the different interests of reason, which occasion differences in the mode of thought. In effect, Reason has only one single interest, and the seeming contradiction existing between her maxims merely indicates a difference in, and a reciprocal limitation of, the methods by which this interest is satisfied.

This reasoner has at heart the interest of diversity—in accordance with the principle of specification; another, the interest of unity—in accordance with the principle of aggregation. Each believes that his judgement rests upon a thorough insight into the subject he is examining, and yet it has been influenced solely by a greater or less degree of adherence to some one of the two principles, neither of which are objective, but originate solely from the interest of reason, and on this account to be termed maxims rather than principles. When I observe intelligent men disputing about the distinctive characteristics of men, animals, or plants, and even of minerals, those on the one side assuming the existence of certain national characteristics, certain well-defined and hereditary distinctions of family, race, and so on, while the other side maintain that nature has endowed all races of men with the same faculties and dispositions, and that all differences are but the result of external and accidental circumstances—I have only to consider for a moment the real nature of the subject of discussion, to arrive at the conclusion that it is a subject far too deep for us to judge of, and that there is little probability of either party being able to speak from a perfect insight into and understanding of the nature of the subject itself. Both have, in reality, been struggling for the twofold interest of reason; the one maintaining the one interest, the other the other. But this difference between the maxims of diversity and unity may easily be reconciled and adjusted; although, so long as they are regarded as objective principles, they must occasion not only contradictions and polemic, but place hinderances in the way of the advancement of truth, until some means is discovered of reconciling these conflicting interests, and bringing reason into union and harmony with itself.

The same is the case with the so-called law discovered by Leibnitz, and supported with remarkable ability by Bonnet—the law of the continuous gradation of created beings, which is nothing more than an inference from the principle of affinity; for observation and study of the order of nature could never present it to the mind as an objective truth. The steps of this ladder, as they appear in experience, are too far apart from each other, and the so-called petty differences between different kinds of animals are in nature commonly so wide separations that no confidence can be placed in such views (particularly when we reflect on the great variety of things, and the ease with which we can discover resemblances), and no faith in the laws which are said to express the aims and purposes of nature. On the other hand, the method of investigating the order of nature in the light of this principle, and the maxim which requires us to regard this order—it being still undetermined how far it extends—as really existing in nature, is beyond doubt a legitimate and excellent principle of reason—a principle which extends farther than any experience or observation of ours and which, without giving us any positive knowledge of anything in the region of experience, guides us to the goal of systematic unity.

Of the Ultimate End of the Natural Dialectic of Human Reason.

The ideas of pure reason cannot be, of themselves and in their own nature, dialectical; it is from their misemployment alone that fallacies and illusions arise. For they originate in the nature of reason itself, and it is impossible that this supreme tribunal for all the rights and claims of speculation should be itself undeserving of confidence and promotive of error. It is to be expected, therefore, that these ideas have a genuine and legitimate aim. It is true, the mob of sophists raise against reason the cry of inconsistency and contradiction, and affect to despise the government of that faculty, because they cannot understand its constitution, while it is to its beneficial influences alone that they owe the position and the intelligence which enable them to criticize and to blame its procedure.

We cannot employ an à priori conception with certainty, until we have made a transcendental deduction therefore. The ideas of pure reason do not admit of the same kind of deduction as the categories. But if they are to possess the least objective validity, and to represent anything but mere creations of thought (entia rationis ratiocinantis), a deduction of them must be possible. This deduction will complete the critical task imposed upon pure reason; and it is to this part Of our labours that we now proceed.

There is a great difference between a thing's being presented to the mind as an object in an absolute sense, or merely as an ideal object. In the former case I employ my conceptions to determine the object; in the latter case nothing is present to the mind but a mere schema, which does not relate directly to an object, not even in a hypothetical sense, but which is useful only for the purpose of representing other objects to the mind, in a mediate and indirect manner, by means of their relation to the idea in the intellect. Thus I say the conception of a supreme intelligence is a mere idea; that is to say, its objective reality does not consist in the fact that it has an immediate relation to an object (for in this sense we have no means of establishing its objective validity), it is merely a schema constructed according to the necessary conditions of the unity of reason—the schema of a thing in general, which is useful towards the production of the highest degree of systematic unity in the empirical exercise of reason, in which we deduce this or that object of experience from the imaginary object of this idea, as the ground or cause of the said object of experience. In this way, the idea is properly a heuristic, and not an ostensive, conception; it does not give us any information respecting the constitution of an object, it merely indicates how, under the guidance of the idea, we ought to investigate the constitution and the relations of objects in the world of experience. Now, if it can be shown that the three kinds of transcendental ideas (psychological, cosmological, and theological), although not relating directly to any object nor determining it, do nevertheless, on the supposition of the existence of an ideal object, produce systematic unity in the laws of the empirical employment of the reason, and extend our empirical cognition, without ever being inconsistent or in opposition with it—it must be a necessary maxim of reason to regulate its procedure according to these ideas. And this forms the transcendental deduction of all speculative ideas, not as constitutive principles of the extension of our cognition beyond the limits of our experience, but as regulative principles of the systematic unity of empirical cognition, which is by the aid of these ideas arranged and emended within its own proper limits, to an extent unattainable by the operation of the principles of the understanding alone.

I shall make this plainer. Guided by the principles involved in these ideas, we must, in the first place, so connect all the phenomena, actions, and feelings of the mind, as if it were a simple substance, which, endowed with personal identity, possesses a permanent existence (in this life at least), while its states, among which those of the body are to be included as external conditions, are in continual change. Secondly, in cosmology, we must investigate the conditions of all natural phenomena, internal as well as external, as if they belonged to a chain infinite and without any prime or supreme member, while we do not, on this account, deny the existence of intelligible grounds of these phenomena, although we never employ them to explain phenomena, for the simple reason that they are not objects of our cognition. Thirdly, in the sphere of theology, we must regard the whole system of possible experience as forming an absolute, but dependent and sensuously-conditioned unity, and at the same time as based upon a sole, supreme, and all-sufficient ground existing apart from the world itself—a ground which is a self-subsistent, primeval and creative reason, in relation to which we so employ our reason in the field of experience, as if all objects drew their origin from that archetype of all reason. In other words, we ought not to deduce the internal phenomena of the mind from a simple thinking substance, but deduce them from each other under the guidance of the regulative idea of a simple being; we ought not to deduce the phenomena, order, and unity of the universe from a supreme intelligence, but merely draw from this idea of a supremely wise cause the rules which must guide reason in its connection of causes and effects.

Now there is nothing to hinder us from admitting these ideas to possess an objective and hyperbolic existence, except the cosmological ideas, which lead reason into an antinomy: the psychological and theological ideas are not antinomial. They contain no contradiction; and how, then, can any one dispute their objective reality, since he who denies it knows as little about their possibility as we who affirm? And yet, when we wish to admit the existence of a thing, it is not sufficient to convince ourselves that there is no positive obstacle in the way; for it cannot be allowable to regard mere creations of thought, which transcend, though they do not contradict, all our conceptions, as real and determinate objects, solely upon the authority of a speculative reason striving to compass its own aims. They cannot, therefore, be admitted to be real in themselves; they can only possess a comparative reality—that of a schema of the regulative principle of the systematic unity of all cognition. They are to be regarded not as actual things, but as in some measure analogous to them. We abstract from the object of the idea all the conditions which limit the exercise of our understanding, but which, on the other hand, are the sole conditions of our possessing a determinate conception of any given thing. And thus we cogitate a something, of the real nature of which we have not the least conception, but which we represent to ourselves as standing in a relation to the whole system of phenomena, analogous to that in which phenomena stand to each other.

By admitting these ideal beings, we do not really extend our cognitions beyond the objects of possible experience; we extend merely the empirical unity of our experience, by the aid of systematic unity, the schema of which is furnished by the idea, which is therefore valid—not as a constitutive, but as a regulative principle. For although we posit a thing corresponding to the idea—a something, an actual existence—we do not on that account aim at the extension of our cognition by means of transcendent conceptions. This existence is purely ideal, and not objective; it is the mere expression of the systematic unity which is to be the guide of reason in the field of experience. There are no attempts made at deciding what the ground of this unity may be, or what the real nature of this imaginary being.

Thus the transcendental and only determinate conception of God, which is presented to us by speculative reason, is in the strictest sense deistic. In other words, reason does not assure us of the objective validity of the conception; it merely gives us the idea of something, on which the supreme and necessary unity of all experience is based. This something we cannot, following the analogy of a real substance, cogitate otherwise than as the cause of all things operating in accordance with rational laws, if we regard it as an individual object; although we should rest contented with the idea alone as a regulative principle of reason, and make no attempt at completing the sum of the conditions imposed by thought. This attempt is, indeed, inconsistent with the grand aim of complete systematic unity in the sphere of cognition—a unity to which no bounds are set by reason.

Hence it happens that, admitting a divine being, I can have no conception of the internal possibility of its perfection, or of the necessity of its existence. The only advantage of this admission is that it enables me to answer all other questions relating to the contingent, and to give reason the most complete satisfaction as regards the unity which it aims at attaining in the world of experience. But I cannot satisfy reason with regard to this hypothesis itself; and this proves that it is not its intelligence and insight into the subject, but its speculative interest alone which induces it to proceed from a point lying far beyond the sphere of our cognition, for the purpose of being able to consider all objects as parts of a systematic whole.

Here a distinction presents itself, in regard to the way in which we may cogitate a presupposition—a distinction which is somewhat subtle, but of great importance in transcendental philosophy. I may have sufficient grounds to admit something, or the existence of something, in a relative point of view (suppositio relativa), without being justified in admitting it in an absolute sense (suppositio absoluta). This distinction is undoubtedly requisite, in the case of a regulative principle, the necessity of which we recognize, though we are ignorant of the source and cause of that necessity, and which we assume to be based upon some ultimate ground, for the purpose of being able to cogitate the universality of the principle in a more determinate way. For example, I cogitate the existence of a being corresponding to a pure transcendental idea. But I cannot admit that this being exists absolutely and in itself, because all of the conceptions by which I can cogitate an object in a determinate manner fall short of assuring me of its existence; nay, the conditions of the objective validity of my conceptions are excluded by the idea—by the very fact of its being an idea. The conceptions of reality, substance, causality, nay, even that of necessity in existence, have no significance out of the sphere of empirical cognition, and cannot, beyond that sphere, determine any object. They may, accordingly, be employed to explain the possibility of things in the world of sense, but they are utterly inadequate to explain the possibility of the universe itself considered as a whole; because in this case the ground of explanation must lie out of and beyond the world, and cannot, therefore, be an object of possible experience. Now, I may admit the existence of an incomprehensible being of this nature—the object of a mere idea, relatively to the world of sense; although I have no ground to admit its existence absolutely and in itself. For if an idea (that of a systematic and complete unity, of which I shall presently speak more particularly) lies at the foundation of the most extended empirical employment of reason, and if this idea cannot be adequately represented in concreto, although it is indispensably necessary for the approximation of empirical unity to the highest possible degree—I am not only authorized, but compelled, to realize this idea, that is, to posit a real object corresponding thereto. But I cannot profess to know this object; it is to me merely a something, to which, as the ground of systematic unity in cognition, I attribute such properties as are analogous to the conceptions employed by the understanding in the sphere of experience. Following the analogy of the notions of reality, substance, causality, and necessity, I cogitate a being, which possesses all these attributes in the highest degree; and, as this idea is the offspring of my reason alone, I cogitate this being as self-subsistent reason, and as the cause of the universe operating by means of ideas of the greatest possible harmony and unity. Thus I abstract all conditions that would limit my idea, solely for the purpose of rendering systematic unity possible in the world of empirical diversity, and thus securing the widest possible extension for the exercise of reason in that sphere. This I am enabled to do, by regarding all connections and relations in the world of sense, as if they were the dispositions of a supreme reason, of which our reason is but a faint image. I then proceed to cogitate this Supreme Being by conceptions which have, properly, no meaning or application, except in the world of sense. But as I am authorized to employ the transcendental hypothesis of such a being in a relative respect alone, that is, as the substratum of the greatest possible unity in experience—I may attribute to a being which I regard as distinct from the world, such properties as belong solely to the sphere of sense and experience. For I do not desire, and am not justified in desiring, to cognize this object of my idea, as it exists in itself; for I possess no conceptions sufficient for this task, those of reality, substance, causality, nay, even that of necessity in existence, losing all significance, and becoming merely the signs of conceptions, without content and without applicability, when I attempt to carry them beyond the limits of the world of sense. I cogitate merely the relation of a perfectly unknown being to the greatest possible systematic unity of experience, solely for the purpose of employing it as the schema of the regulative principle which directs reason in its empirical exercise.

It is evident, at the first view, that we cannot presuppose the reality of this transcendental object, by means of the conceptions of reality, substance, causality, and so on, because these conceptions cannot be applied to anything that is distinct from the world of sense. Thus the supposition of a Supreme Being or cause is purely relative; it is cogitated only in behalf of the systematic unity of experience; such a being is but a some-thing, of whose existence in itself we have not the least conception. Thus, too, it becomes sufficiently manifest why we required the idea of a necessary being in relation to objects given by sense, although we can never have the least conception of this being, or of its absolute necessity.

And now we can clearly perceive the result of our transcendental dialectic, and the proper aim of the ideas of pure reason—which become dialectical solely from misun-derstanding and inconsiderateness. Pure reason is, in fact, occupied with itself, and not with any object. Objects are not presented to it to be embraced in the unity of an empir-ical conception; it is only the cognitions of the understanding that are presented to it, for the purpose of receiving the unity of a rational conception, that is, of being connected according to a principle. The unity of reason is the unity of system; and this systematic unity is not an objective principle, extending its dominion over objects, but a subjective maxim, extending its authority over the empirical cognition of objects. The systematic connection which reason gives to the empirical employment of the understanding not only advances the extension of that employment, but ensures its correctness, and thus the principle of a systematic unity of this nature is also objective, although only in an indefinite respect (principium vagum). It is not, however, a constitutive principle, deter-mining an object to which it directly relates; it is merely a regulative principle or maxim, advancing and strengthening the empirical exercise of reason, by the opening up of new paths of which the understanding is ignorant, while it never conflicts with the laws of its exercise in the sphere of experience.

But reason cannot cogitate this systematic unity, without at the same time cogitating an object of the idea—an object that cannot be presented in any experience, which contains no concrete example of a complete systematic unity. This being (ens rationis ratiocinatae) is therefore a mere idea and is not assumed to be a thing which is real absolutely and in itself. On the contrary, it forms merely the problematical foundation of the connection which the mind introduces among the phenomena of the sensuous world. We look upon this connection, in the light of the above-mentioned idea, as if it drew its origin from the supposed being which corresponds to the idea. And yet all we aim at is the possession of this idea as a secure foundation for the systematic unity of experience—a unity indispensable to reason, advantageous to the understanding, and promotive of the interests of empirical cognition.

We mistake the true meaning of this idea when we regard it as an enouncement, or even as a hypothetical declaration of the existence of a real thing, which we are to regard as the origin or ground of a systematic constitution of the universe. On the contrary, it is left completely undetermined what the nature or properties of this so-called ground may be. The idea is merely to be adopted as a point of view, from which this unity, so essential to reason and so beneficial to the understanding, may be regarded as radiating. In one word, this transcendental thing is merely the schema of a regulative principle, by means of which Reason, so far as in her lies, extends the dominion of systematic unity over the whole sphere of experience.

The first object of an idea of this kind is the ego, considered merely as a thinking nature or soul. If I wish to investigate the properties of a thinking being, I must interro-gate experience. But I find that I can apply none of the categories to this object, the schema of these categories, which is the condition of their application, being given only in sensuous intuition. But I cannot thus attain to the cognition of a systematic unity of all the phenomena of the internal sense. Instead, therefore, of an empirical conception of what the soul really is, reason takes the conception of the empirical unity of all thought, and, by cogitating this unity as unconditioned and primitive, constructs the rational conception or idea of a simple substance which is in itself unchangeable, possessing personal identity, and in connection with other real things external to it; in one word, it constructs the idea of a simple self-subsistent intelligence. But the real aim of reason in this procedure is the attainment of principles of systematic unity for the explanation of the phenomena of the soul. That is, reason desires to be able to represent all the determinations of the internal sense as existing in one subject, all powers as deduced from one fundamental power, all changes as mere varieties in the condition of a being which is permanent and always the same, and all phenomena in space as entirely different in their nature from the procedure of thought. Essential simplicity (with the other attributes predicated of the ego) is regarded as the mere schema of this regulative principle; it is not assumed that it is the actual ground of the properties of the soul. For these properties may rest upon quite different grounds, of which we are completely ignorant; just as the above predicates could not give us any knowledge of the soul as it is in itself, even if we regarded them as valid in respect of it, inasmuch as they constitute a mere idea, which cannot be represented in concreto. Nothing but good can result from a psychological idea of this kind, if we only take proper care not to consider it as more than an idea; that is, if we regard it as valid merely in relation to the employment of reason, in the sphere of the phenomena of the soul. Under the guidance of this idea, or principle, no empirical laws of corporeal phenomena are called in to explain that which is a phenomenon of the internal sense alone; no windy hypotheses of the generation, annihilation, and palingenesis of souls are admitted. Thus the consideration of this object of the internal sense is kept pure, and unmixed with heterogeneous elements; while the investigation of reason aims at reducing all the grounds of explanation employed in this sphere of knowledge to a single principle. All this is best effected, nay, cannot be effected otherwise than by means of such a schema, which requires us to regard this ideal thing as an actual existence. The psychological idea is, therefore, meaningless and inapplicable, except as the schema of a regulative conception. For, if I ask whether the soul is not really of a spiritual nature—it is a question which has no meaning. From such a conception has been abstracted, not merely all corporeal nature, but all nature, that is, all the predicates of a possible experience; and consequently, all the conditions which enable us to cogitate an object to this conception have disappeared. But, if these conditions are absent, it is evident that the conception is meaningless.

The second regulative idea of speculative reason is the conception of the universe. For nature is properly the only object presented to us, in regard to which reason requires regulative principles. Nature is twofold—thinking and corporeal nature. To cogitate the latter in regard to its internal possibility, that is, to determine the application of the categories to it, no idea is required—no representation which transcends experience. In this sphere, therefore, an idea is impossible, sensuous intuition being our only guide; while, in the sphere of psychology, we require the fundamental idea (I), which contains à priori a certain form of thought namely, the unity of the ego. Pure reason has, therefore, nothing left but nature in general, and the completeness of conditions in nature in accordance with some principle. The absolute totality of the series of these conditions is an idea, which can never be fully realized in the empirical exercise of reason, while it is serviceable as a rule for the procedure of reason in relation to that totality. It requires us, in the explanation of given phenomena (in the regress or ascent in the series), to proceed as if the series were infinite in itself, that is, were prolonged in indefinitum; while on the other hand, where reason is regarded as itself the determining cause (in the region of freedom), we are required to proceed as if we had not before us an object of sense, but of the pure understanding. In this latter case, the conditions do not exist in the series of phenomena, but may be placed quite out of and beyond it, and the series of conditions may be regarded as if it had an absolute beginning from an intelligible cause. All this proves that the cosmological ideas are nothing but regulative principles, and not constitutive; and that their aim is not to realize an actual totality in such series. The full discussion of this subject will be found in its proper place in the chapter on the antinomy of pure reason.

The third idea of pure reason, containing the hypothesis of a being which is valid merely as a relative hypothesis, is that of the one and all-sufficient cause of all cosmological series, in other words, the idea of God. We have not the slightest ground absolutely to admit the existence of an object corresponding to this idea; for what can empower or authorize us to affirm the existence of a being of the highest perfection—a being whose existence is absolutely necessary—merely because we possess the conception of such a being? The answer is: It is the existence of the world which renders this hypothesis necessary. But this answer makes it perfectly evident that the idea of this being, like all other speculative ideas, is essentially nothing more than a demand upon reason that it shall regulate the connection which it and its subordinate faculties introduce into the phenomena of the world by principles of systematic unity and, consequently, that it shall regard all phenomena as originating from one all-embracing being, as the supreme and all-sufficient cause. From this it is plain that the only aim of reason in this procedure is the establishment of its own formal rule for the extension of its dominion in the world of experience; that it does not aim at an extension of its cognition beyond the limits of experience; and that, consequently, this idea does not contain any constitutive principle.

The highest formal unity, which is based upon ideas alone, is the unity of all things —a unity in accordance with an aim or purpose; and the speculative interest of reason renders it necessary to regard all order in the world as if it originated from the intention and design of a supreme reason. This principle unfolds to the view of reason in the sphere of experience new and enlarged prospects, and invites it to connect the phenomena of the world according to teleological laws, and in this way to attain to the highest possible degree of systematic unity. The hypothesis of a supreme intelligence, as the sole cause of the universe—an intelligence which has for us no more than an ideal existence—is accordingly always of the greatest service to reason. Thus, if we presuppose, in relation to the figure of the earth (which is round, but somewhat flattened at the poles),[62] or that of mountains or seas, wise designs on the part of an author of the universe, we cannot fail to make, by the light of this supposition, a great number of interesting discoveries. If we keep to this hypothesis, as a principle which is purely regulative, even error cannot be very detrimental. For, in this case, error can have no more serious consequences than that, where we expected to discover a teleological connection (nexus finalis), only a mechanical or physical connection appears. In such a case, we merely fail to find the additional form of unity we expected, but we do not lose the rational unity which the mind requires in its procedure in experience. But even a miscarriage of this sort cannot affect the law in its general and teleological relations. For although we may convict an anatomist of an error, when he connects the limb of some animal with a certain purpose, it is quite impossible to prove in a single case that any arrangement of nature, be it what it may, is entirely without aim or design. And thus medical physiology, by the aid of a principle presented to it by pure reason, extends its very limited empirical knowledge of the purposes of the different parts of an organized body so far that it may be asserted with the utmost confidence, and with the approbation of all reflecting men, that every organ or bodily part of an animal has its use and answers a certain design. Now, this is a supposition which, if regarded as of a constitutive character, goes much farther than any experience or observation of ours can justify. Hence it is evident that it is nothing more than a regulative principle of reason, which aims at the highest degree of systematic unity, by the aid of the idea of a causality according to design in a supreme cause—a cause which it regards as the highest intelligence.

If, however, we neglect this restriction of the idea to a purely regulative influence, reason is betrayed into numerous errors. For it has then left the ground of experience, in which alone are to be found the criteria of truth, and has ventured into the region of the incomprehensible and unsearchable, on the heights of which it loses its power and collectedness, because it has completely severed its connection with experience.

The first error which arises from our employing the idea of a Supreme Being as a constitutive (in repugnance to the very nature of an idea), and not as a regulative principle, is the error of inactive reason (ignava ratio).[63] We may so term every principle which requires us to regard our investigations of nature as absolutely complete, and allows reason to cease its inquiries, as if it had fully executed its task. Thus the psychological idea of the ego, when employed as a constitutive principle for the explanation of the phenomena of the soul, and for the extension of our knowledge regarding this subject beyond the limits of experience—even to the condition of the soul after death—is convenient enough for the purposes of pure reason, but detrimental and even ruinous to its interests in the sphere of nature and experience. The dogmatizing spiritualist explains the unchanging unity of our personality through all changes of condition from the unity of a thinking substance, the interest which we take in things and events that can happen only after our death, from a consciousness of the immaterial nature of our thinking subject, and so on. Thus he dispenses with all empirical investigations into the cause of these internal phenomena, and with all possible explanations of them upon purely natural grounds; while, at the dictation of a transcendent reason, he passes by the immanent sources of cognition in experience, greatly to his own ease and convenience, but to the sacrifice of all, genuine insight and intelligence. These prejudicial consequences become still more evident, in the case of the dogmatical treatment of our idea of a Supreme Intelligence, and the theological system of nature (physico-theology) which is falsely based upon it. For, in this case, the aims which we observe in nature, and often those which we merely fancy to exist, make the investigation of causes a very easy task, by directing us to refer such and such phenomena immediately to the unsearchable will and counsel of the Supreme Wisdom, while we ought to investigate their causes in the general laws of the mechanism of matter. We are thus recommended to consider the labour of reason as ended, when we have merely dispensed with its employment, which is guided surely and safely only by the order of nature and the series of changes in the world—which are arranged according to immanent and general laws. This error may be avoided, if we do not merely consider from the view-point of final aims certain parts of nature, such as the division and structure of a continent, the constitution and direction of certain mountain-chains, or even the organization existing in the vegetable and animal kingdoms, but look upon this systematic unity of nature in a perfectly general way, in relation to the idea of a Supreme Intelligence. If we pursue this advice, we lay as a foundation for all investigation the conformity to aims of all phenomena of nature in accordance with universal laws, for which no particular arrangement of nature is exempt, but only cognized by us with more or less difficulty; and we possess a regulative principle of the systematic unity of a teleological connection, which we do not attempt to anticipate or predetermine. All that we do, and ought to do, is to follow out the physico-mechanical connection in nature according to general laws, with the hope of discovering, sooner or later, the teleological connection also. Thus, and thus only, can the principle of final unity aid in the extension of the employment of reason in the sphere of experience, without being in any case detrimental to its interests.

The second error which arises from the misconception of the principle of systematic unity is that of perverted reason (perversa ratio, usteron roteron rationis). The idea of systematic unity is available as a regulative principle in the connection of phenomena according to general natural laws; and, how far soever we have to travel upon the path of experience to discover some fact or event, this idea requires us to believe that we have approached all the more nearly to the completion of its use in the sphere of nature, although that completion can never be attained. But this error reverses the procedure of reason. We begin by hypostatizing the principle of systematic unity, and by giving an anthropomorphic determination to the conception of a Supreme Intelligence, and then proceed forcibly to impose aims upon nature. Thus not only does teleology, which ought to aid in the completion of unity in accordance with general laws, operate to the destruction of its influence, but it hinders reason from attaining its proper aim, that is, the proof, upon natural grounds, of the existence of a supreme intelligent cause. For, if we cannot presuppose supreme finality in nature à priori, that is, as essentially belonging to nature, how can we be directed to endeavour to discover this unity and, rising gradually through its different degrees, to approach the supreme perfection of an author of all—a perfection which is absolutely necessary, and therefore cognizable à priori? The regulative principle directs us to presuppose systematic unity absolutely and, consequently, as following from the essential nature of things—but only as a unity of nature, not merely cognized empirically, but presupposed à priori, although only in an indeterminate manner. But if I insist on basing nature upon the foundation of a supreme ordaining Being, the unity of nature is in effect lost. For, in this case, it is quite foreign and unessential to the nature of things, and cannot be cognized from the general laws of nature. And thus arises a vicious circular argument, what ought to have been proved having been presupposed.

To take the regulative principle of systematic unity in nature for a constitutive principle, and to hypostatize and make a cause out of that which is properly the ideal ground of the consistent and harmonious exercise of reason, involves reason in inextricable embarrassments. The investigation of nature pursues its own path under the guidance of the chain of natural causes, in accordance with the general laws of nature, and ever follows the light of the idea of an author of the universe—not for the purpose of deducing the finality, which it constantly pursues, from this Supreme Being, but to attain to the cognition of his existence from the finality which it seeks in the existence of the phenomena of nature, and, if possible, in that of all things to cognize this being, consequently, as absolutely necessary. Whether this latter purpose succeed or not, the idea is and must always be a true one, and its employment, when merely regulative, must always be accompanied by truthful and beneficial results.

Complete unity, in conformity with aims, constitutes absolute perfection. But if we do not find this unity in the nature of the things which go to constitute the world of experience, that is, of objective cognition, consequently in the universal and necessary laws of nature, how can we infer from this unity the idea of the supreme and absolutely necessary perfection of a primal being, which is the origin of all causality? The greatest systematic unity, and consequently teleological unity, constitutes the very foundation of the possibility of the most extended employment of human reason. The idea of unity is therefore essentially and indissolubly connected with the nature of our reason. This idea is a legislative one; and hence it is very natural that we should assume the existence of a legislative reason corresponding to it, from which the systematic unity of nature—the object of the operations of reason—must be derived.

In the course of our discussion of the antinomies, we stated that it is always possible to answer all the questions which pure reason may raise; and that the plea of the limited nature of our cognition, which is unavoidable and proper in many questions regarding natural phenomena, cannot in this case be admitted, because the questions raised do not relate to the nature of things, but are necessarily originated by the nature of reason itself, and relate to its own internal constitution. We can now establish this assertion, which at first sight appeared so rash, in relation to the two questions in which reason takes the greatest interest, and thus complete our discussion of the dialectic of pure reason.

If, then, the question is asked, in relation to transcendental theology,[64] first, whether there is anything distinct from the world, which contains the ground of cosmical order and connection according to general laws? The answer is: Certainly. For the world is a sum of phenomena; there must, therefore, be some transcendental basis of these phenomena, that is, a basis cogitable by the pure understanding alone. If, secondly, the question is asked whether this being is substance, whether it is of the greatest reality, whether it is necessary, and so forth? I answer that this question is utterly without meaning. For all the categories which aid me in forming a conception of an object cannot be employed except in the world of sense, and are without meaning when not applied to objects of actual or possible experience. Out of this sphere, they are not properly conceptions, but the mere marks or indices of conceptions, which we may admit, although they cannot, without the help of experience, help us to understand any subject or thing. If, thirdly, the question is whether we may not cogitate this being, which is distinct from the world, in analogy with the objects of experience? The answer is: Undoubtedly, but only as an ideal, and not as a real object. That is, we must cogitate it only as an unknown substratum of the systematic unity, order, and finality of the world —a unity which reason must employ as the regulative principle of its investigation of nature. Nay, more, we may admit into the idea certain anthropomorphic elements, which are promotive of the interests of this regulative principle. For it is no more than an idea, which does not relate directly to a being distinct from the world, but to the regulative principle of the systematic unity of the world, by means, however, of a schema of this unity—the schema of a Supreme Intelligence, who is the wisely-designing author of the universe. What this basis of cosmical unity may be in itself, we know not—we cannot discover from the idea; we merely know how we ought to employ the idea of this unity, in relation to the systematic operation of reason in the sphere of experience.

But, it will be asked again, can we on these grounds, admit the existence of a wise and omnipotent author of the world? Without doubt; and not only so, but we must assume the existence of such a being. But do we thus extend the limits of our knowledge beyond the field of possible experience? By no means. For we have merely presupposed a something, of which we have no conception, which we do not know as it is in itself; but, in relation to the systematic disposition of the universe, which we must presuppose in all our observation of nature, we have cogitated this unknown being in analogy with an intelligent existence (an empirical conception), that is to say, we have endowed it with those attributes, which, judging from the nature of our own reason, may contain the ground of such a systematic unity. This idea is therefore valid only relatively to the employment in experience of our reason. But if we attribute to it absolute and objective validity, we overlook the fact that it is merely an ideal being that we cogitate; and, by setting out from a basis which is not determinable by considerations drawn from experience, we place ourselves in a position which incapacitates us from applying this principle to the empirical employment of reason.

But, it will be asked further, can I make any use of this conception and hypothesis in my investigations into the world and nature? Yes, for this very purpose was the idea established by reason as a fundamental basis. But may I regard certain arrangements, which seemed to have been made in conformity with some fixed aim, as the arrangements of design, and look upon them as proceeding from the divine will, with the intervention, however, of certain other particular arrangements disposed to that end? Yes, you may do so; but at the same time you must regard it as indifferent, whether it is asserted that divine wisdom has disposed all things in conformity with his highest aims, or that the idea of supreme wisdom is a regulative principle in the investigation of nature, and at the same time a principle of the systematic unity of nature according to general laws, even in those cases where we are unable to discover that unity. In other words, it must be perfectly indifferent to you whether you say, when you have discovered this unity: God has wisely willed it so; or: Nature has wisely arranged this. For it was nothing but the systematic unity, which reason requires as a basis for the investigation of nature, that justified you in accepting the idea of a supreme intelligence as a schema for a regulative principle; and, the farther you advance in the discovery of design and finality, the more certain the validity of your idea. But, as the whole aim of this regulative principle was the discovery of a necessary and systematic unity in nature, we have, in so far as we attain this, to attribute our success to the idea of a Supreme Being; while, at the same time, we cannot, without involving ourselves in contradictions, overlook the general laws of nature, as it was in reference to them alone that this idea was employed. We cannot, I say, overlook the general laws of nature, and regard this conformity to aims observable in nature as contingent or hyperphysical in its origin; inasmuch as there is no ground which can justify us in the admission of a being with such properties distinct from and above nature. All that we are authorized to assert is that this idea may be employed as a principle, and that the properties of the being which is assumed to correspond to it may be regarded as systematically connected in analogy with the causal determination of phenomena.

For the same reasons we are justified in introducing into the idea of the supreme cause other anthropomorphic elements (for without these we could not predicate anything of it); we may regard it as allowable to cogitate this cause as a being with understanding, the feelings of pleasure and displeasure, and faculties of desire and will corresponding to these. At the same time, we may attribute to this being infinite perfection—a perfection which necessarily transcends that which our knowledge of the order and design in the world authorize us to predicate of it. For the regulative law of systematic unity requires us to study nature on the supposition that systematic and final unity in infinitum is everywhere discoverable, even in the highest diversity. For, although we may discover little of this cosmical perfection, it belongs to the legislative prerogative of reason to require us always to seek for and to expect it; while it must always be beneficial to institute all inquiries into nature in accordance with this principle. But it is evident that, by this idea of a supreme author of all, which I place as the foundation of all inquiries into nature, I do not mean to assert the existence of such a being, or that I have any knowledge of its existence; and, consequently, I do not really deduce anything from the existence of this being, but merely from its idea, that is to say, from the nature of things in this world, in accordance with this idea. A certain dim consciousness of the true use of this idea seems to have dictated to the philosophers of all times the moderate language used by them regarding the cause of the world. We find them employing the expressions wisdom and care of nature, and divine wisdom, as synonymous—nay, in purely speculative discussions, preferring the former, because it does not carry the appearance of greater pretensions than such as we are entitled to make, and at the same time directs reason to its proper field of action—nature and her phenomena.

Thus, pure reason, which at first seemed to promise us nothing less than the extension of our cognition beyond the limits of experience, is found, when thoroughly examined, to contain nothing but regulative principles, the virtue and function of which is to introduce into our cognition a higher degree of unity than the understanding could of itself. These principles, by placing the goal of all our struggles at so great a distance, realize for us the most thorough connection between the different parts of our cognition, and the highest degree of systematic unity. But, on the other hand, if misunderstood and employed as constitutive principles of transcendent cognition, they become the parents of illusions and contradictions, while pretending to introduce us to new regions of knowledge.

Thus all human cognition begins with intuitions, proceeds from thence to conceptions, and ends with ideas. Although it possesses, in relation to all three elements, à priori sources of cognition, which seemed to transcend the limits of all experience, a thoroughgoing criticism demonstrates that speculative reason can never, by the aid of these elements, pass the bounds of possible experience, and that the proper destination of this highest faculty of cognition is to employ all methods, and all the principles of these methods, for the purpose of penetrating into the innermost secrets of nature, by the aid of the principles of unity (among all kinds of which teleological unity is the highest), while it ought not to attempt to soar above the sphere of experience, beyond which there lies nought for us but the void inane. The critical examination, in our Transcendental Analytic, of all the propositions which professed to extend cognition beyond the sphere of experience, completely demonstrated that they can only conduct us to a possible experience. If we were not distrustful even of the clearest abstract theorems, if we were not allured by specious and inviting prospects to escape from the constraining power of their evidence, we might spare ourselves the laborious examination of all the dialectical arguments which a transcendent reason adduces in support of its pretensions; for we should know with the most complete certainty that, however honest such professions might be, they are null and valueless, because they relate to a kind of knowledge to which no man can by any possibility attain. But, as there is no end to discussion, if we cannot discover the true cause of the illusions by which even the wisest are deceived, and as the analysis of all our transcendent cognition into its elements is of itself of no slight value as a psychological study, while it is a duty incumbent on every philosopher—it was found necessary to investigate the dialectical procedure of reason in its primary sources. And as the inferences of which this dialectic is the parent are not only deceitful, but naturally possess a profound interest for humanity, it was advisable at the same time, to give a full account of the momenta of this dialectical procedure, and to deposit it in the archives of human reason, as a warning to all future metaphysicians to avoid these causes of speculative error.

---

1. The Germans are the only people who at present use this word to indicate what others call the critique of taste. At the foundation of this term lies the disappointed hope, which the eminent analyst, Baumgarten, conceived, of subjecting the criticism of the beautiful to principles of reason, and so of elevating its rules into a science. But his endeavours were vain. For the said rules or criteria are, in respect to their chief sources, merely empirical, consequently never can serve as determinate laws à priori, by which our judgement in matters of taste is to be directed. It is rather our judgement which forms the proper test as to the correctness of the principles. On this account it is advisable to give up the use of the term as designating the critique of taste, and to apply it solely to that doctrine, which is true science—the science of the laws of sensibility—and thus come nearer to the language and the sense of the ancients in their well-known division of the objects of cognition into aiotheta kai noeta, or to share it with speculative philosophy, and employ it partly in a transcendental, partly in a psychological signification.
2. I can indeed say "my representations follow one another, or are successive"; but this means only that we are conscious of them as in a succession, that is, according to the form of the internal sense. Time, therefore, is not a thing in itself, nor is it any objective determination pertaining to, or inherent in things.
3. The predicates of the phenomenon can be affixed to the object itself in relation to our sensuous faculty; for example, the red colour or the perfume to the rose. But (illusory) appearance never can be attributed as a predicate to an object, for this very reason, that it attributes to this object in itself that which belongs to it only in relation to our sensuous faculty, or to the subject in general, e.g., the two handles which were formerly ascribed to Saturn. That which is never to be found in the object itself, but always in the relation of the object to the subject, and which moreover is inseparable from our representation of the object, we denominate phenomenon. Thus the predicates of space and time are rightly attributed to objects of the senses as such, and in this there is no illusion. On the contrary, if I ascribe redness of the rose as a thing in itself, or to Saturn his handles, or extension to all external objects, considered as things in themselves, without regarding the determinate relation of these objects to the subject, and without limiting my judgement to that relation—then, and then only, arises illusion.
4. Just as if thought were in the first instance a function of the understanding; in the second, of judgement; in the third, of reason. A remark which will be explained in the sequel.
5. In the "Metaphysical Principles of Natural Science."
6. Whether the representations are in themselves identical, and consequently whether one can be thought analytically by means of and through the other, is a question which we need not at present consider. Our Consciousness of the one, when we speak of the manifold, is always distinguishable from our consciousness of the other; and it is only respecting the synthesis of this (possible) consciousness that we here treat.

7. All general conceptions—as such—depend, for their existence, on the analytical unity of consciousness. For example, when I think of red in general, I thereby think to myself a property which (as a characteristic mark) can be discovered somewhere, or can be united with other representations; consequently, it is only by means of a forethought possible synthetical unity that I can think to myself the analytical. A representation which is cogitated as common to different representations, is regarded as belonging to such as, besides this common representation, contain something different; consequently it must be previously thought in synthetical unity with other although only possible representations, before I can think in it the analytical unity of consciousness which makes it a conceptas communis. And thus the synthetical unity of apperception is the highest point with which we must connect every operation of the understanding, even the whole of logic, and after it our transcendental philosophy; indeed, this faculty is the understanding itself.

8. Space and time, and all portions thereof, are intuitions; consequently are, with a manifold for their content, single representations. (See the Transcendental Æsthetic.) Consequently, they are not pure conceptions, by means of which the same consciousness is found in a great number of representations; but, on the contrary, they are many representations contained in one, the consciousness of which is, so to speak, compounded. The unity of consciousness is nevertheless synthetical and, therefore, primitive. From this peculiar character of consciousness follow many important consequences. (See § 21.)

9. The tedious doctrine of the four syllogistic figures concerns only categorical syllogisms; and although it is nothing more than an artifice by surreptitiously introducing immediate conclusions (consequentiae immediatae) among the premises of a pure syllogism, to give ism give rise to an appearance of more modes of drawing a conclusion than that in the first figure, the artifice would not have had much success, had not its authors succeeded in bringing categorical judgements into exclusive respect, as those to which all others must be referred—a doctrine, however, which, according to § 5, is utterly false.

10. The proof of this rests on the represented unity of intuition, by means of which an object is given, and which always includes in itself a synthesis of the manifold to be intuited, and also the relation of this latter to unity of apperception.

11. Motion of an object in space does not belong to a pure science, consequently not to geometry; because, that a thing is movable cannot be known à priori, but only from experience. But motion, considered as the description of a space, is a pure act of the successive synthesis of the manifold in external intuition by means of productive imagination, and belongs not only to geometry, but even to transcendental philosophy.

12. I do not see why so much difficulty should be found in admitting that our internal sense is affected by ourselves. Every act of attention exemplifies it. In such an act the understanding determines the internal sense by the synthetical conjunction which it cogitates, conformably to the internal intuition which corresponds to the manifold in the synthesis of the understanding. How much the mind is usually affected thereby every one will be able to perceive in himself.

13. The "I think" expresses the act of determining my own existence. My existence is thus already given by the act of consciousness; but the mode in which I must determine my existence, that is, the mode in which I must place the manifold belonging to my existence, is not thereby given. For this purpose intuition of self is required, and this intuition possesses a form given à priori, namely, time, which is sensuous, and belongs to our receptivity of the determinable. Now, as I do not possess another intuition of self which gives the determining in me (of the spontaneity of which I am conscious), prior to the act of determination, in the same manner as time gives the determinable, it is clear that I am unable to determine my own existence as that of a spontaneous being, but I am only able to represent to myself the spontaneity of my thought, that is, of my determination, and my existence remains ever determinable in a purely sensuous manner, that is to say, like the existence of a phenomenon. But it is because of this spontaneity that I call myself an intelligence.

14. Space represented as an object (as geometry really requires it to be) contains more than the mere form of the intuition; namely, a combination of the manifold given according to the form of sensibility into a representation that can be intuited; so that the form of the intuition gives us merely the manifold, but the formal intuition gives unity of representation. In the æsthetic, I regarded this unity as belonging entirely to sensibility, for the purpose of indicating that it antecedes all conceptions, although it presupposes a synthesis which does not belong to sense, through which alone, however, all our conceptions of space and time are possible. For as by means of this unity alone (the understanding determining the sensibility) space and time are given as intuitions, it follows that the unity of this intuition à priori belongs to space and time, and not to the conception of the understanding (§ 20).

15. In this manner it is proved, that the synthesis of apprehension, which is empirical, must necessarily be conformable to the synthesis of apperception, which is intellectual, and contained à priori in the category. It is one and the same spontaneity which at one time, under the name of imagination, at another under that of understanding, produces conjunction in the manifold of intuition.

16. Lest my readers should stumble at this assertion, and the conclusions that may be too rashly drawn from it, I must remind them that the categories in the act of thought are by no means limited by the conditions of our sensuous intuition, but have an unbounded sphere of action. It is only the cognition of the object of thought, the determining of the object, which requires intuition. In the absence of intuition, our thought of an object may still have true and useful consequences in regard to the exercise of reason by the subject. But as this exercise of reason is not always directed on the determination of the object, in other words, on cognition thereof, but also on the determination of the subject and its volition, I do not intend to treat of it in this place.

17. Deficiency in judgement is properly that which is called stupidity; and for such a failing we know no remedy. A dull or narrow-minded person, to whom nothing is wanting but a proper degree of understand-

ing, may be improved by tuition, even so far as to deserve the epithet of learned. But as such persons frequently labour under a deficiency in the faculty of judgement, it is not uncommon to find men extremely learned who in the application of their science betray a lamentable degree this irremediable want.

18. All combination (conjunctio) is either composition (compositio) or connection (nexus). The former is the synthesis of a manifold, the parts of which do not necessarily belong to each other. For example, the two triangles into which a square is divided by a diagonal, do not necessarily belong to each other, and of this kind is the synthesis of the homogeneous in everything that can be mathematically considered. This synthesis can be divided into those of aggregation and coalition, the former of which is applied to extensive, the latter to intensive quantities. The second sort of combination (nexus) is the synthesis of a manifold, in so far as its parts do belong necessarily to each other; for example, the accident to a substance, or the effect to the cause. Consequently it is a synthesis of that which though heterogeneous, is represented as connected à priori. This combination—not an arbitrary one—I entitle dynamical because it concerns the connection of the existence of the manifold. This, again, may be divided into the physical synthesis, of the phenomena divided among each other, and the metaphysical synthesis, or the connection of phenomena à priori in the faculty of cognition.

19. They can be perceived only as phenomena, and some part of them must always belong to the non-ego; whereas pure intuitions are entirely the products of the mind itself, and as such are cognized *in themselves.*
   —Tr

20. Apprehension is the Kantian word for preception, in the largest sense in which we employ that term. It is the genus which includes under i, as species, perception proper and sensation proper—Tr

21. Kant's meaning is: The two principles enunciated under the heads of "Axioms of Intuition," and "Anticipations of Perception," authorize the application to phenomena of determinations of size and number, that is of mathematic. For example, I may compute the light of the sun, and say that its quantity is a certain number of times greater than that of the moon. In the same way, heat is measured by the comparison of its different effects on water, &c., and on mercury in a thermometer.—Tr

22. Persius, Satirae, iii.83-84.

23. It must be remarked that I do not speak of the change of certain relations, but of the change of the state. Thus, when a body moves in a uniform manner, it does not change its state (of motion); but only when all motion increases or decreases.

24. German

25. The unity of the universe, in which all phenomena to be connected, is evidently a mere consequence of the admitted principle of the community of all substances which are coexistent. For were substances isolated, they could not as parts constitute a whole, and were their connection (reciprocal action of the manifold) not necessary from the very fact of coexistence, we could not conclude from the fact of the latter as a merely ideal relation to the former as a real one. We have, however, shown in its place that community is the proper ground of the possibility of an empirical cognition of coexistence, and that we may therefore properly reason from the latter to the former as its condition.

26. The immediate consciousness of the existence of external things is, in the preceding theorem, not presupposed, but proved, by the possibility of this consciousness understood by us or not. The question as to the possibility of it would stand thus: "Have we an internal sense, but no external sense, and is our belief in external perception a mere delusion?" But it is evident that, in order merely to fancy to ourselves anything as external, that is, to present it to the sense in intuition we must already possess an external sense, and must thereby distinguish immediately the mere receptivity of an external intuition from the spontaneity which characterizes every act of imagination. For merely to imagine also an external sense, would annihilate the faculty of intuition itself which is to be determined by the imagination.

27. When I think the reality of a thing, I do really think more than the possibility; but not in the thing; for that can never contain more in reality than was contained in its complete possibility. But while the notion of possibility is merely the notion of a position of thing in relation to the understanding (its empirical use), reality is the conjunction of the thing with perception.

28. We can easily conceive the non-existence of matter; but the ancients did not thence infer its contingency. But even the alternation of the existence and non-existence of a given state in a thing, in which all change consists, by no means proves the contingency of that state—the ground of proof being the reality of its opposite. For example, a body is in a state of rest after motion, but we cannot infer the contingency of the motion from the fact that the former is the opposite of the latter. For this opposite is merely a logical and not a real opposite to the other. If we wish to demonstrate the contingency of the motion, what we ought to prove is that, instead of the motion which took place in the preceding point of time, it was possible for the body to have been then in rest, not, that it is afterwards in rest; for in this case, both opposites are perfectly consistent with each other.

29. In one word, to none of these conceptions belongs a corresponding object, and consequently their real possibility cannot be demonstrated, if we take away sensuous intuition—the only intuition which we possess—and there then remains nothing but the logical possibility, that is, the fact that the conception or thought is possible—which, however, is not the question; what we want to know being, whether it relates to an object and thus possesses any meaning.

30. If any one wishes here to have recourse to the usual subterfuge, and to say, that at least realitates noumena cannot be in opposition to each other, it will be requisite for him to adduce an example of this pure and nonsensuous reality, that it may be understood whether the notion represents something or nothing. But an

example cannot be found except in experience, which never presents to us anything more than phenomena; and thus the proposition means nothing more than that the conception which contains only affirmatives does not contain anything negative—a proposition nobody ever doubted.

31. Sensibility, subjected to the understanding, as the object upon which the understanding employs its functions, is the source of real cognitions. But, in so far as it exercises an influence upon the action of the understanding and determines it to judgement, sensibility is itself the cause of error.

32. He certainly extended the application of his conception to speculative cognitions also, provided they were given pure and completely à priori, nay, even to mathematics, although this science cannot possess an object otherwhere than in Possible experience. I cannot follow him in this, and as little can I follow him in his mystical deduction of these ideas, or in his hypostatization of them; although, in truth, the elevated and exaggerated language which he employed in describing them is quite capable of an interpretation more subdued and more in accordance with fact and the nature of things.

33. The science of Metaphysics has for the proper object of its inquiries only three grand ideas: GOD, FREEDOM, and IMMORTALITY, and it aims at showing, that the second conception, conjoined with the first, must lead to the third, as a necessary conclusion. All the other subjects with which it occupies itself, are merely means for the attainment and realization of these ideas. It does not require these ideas for the construction of a science of nature, but, on the contrary, for the purpose of passing beyond the sphere of nature. A complete insight into and comprehension of them would render Theology, Ethics, and, through the conjunction of both, Religion, solely dependent on the speculative faculty of reason. In a systematic representation of these ideas the above-mentioned arrangement—the synthetical one—would be the most suitable; but in the investigation which must necessarily precede it, the analytical, which reverses this arrangement, would be better adapted to our purpose, as in it we should proceed from that which experience immediately presents to us—psychology, to cosmology, and thence to theology.

34. The reader, who may not so easily perceive the psychological sense of these expressions, taken here in their transcendental abstraction, and cannot guess why the latter attribute of the soul belongs to the category of existence, will find the expressions sufficiently explained and justified in the sequel. I have, moreover, to apologize for the Latin terms which have been employed, instead of their German synonyms, contrary to the rules of correct writing. But I judged it better to sacrifice elegance to perspicuity.

35. Thought is taken in the two premisses in two totally different senses. In the major it is considered as relating and applying to objects in general, consequently to objects of intuition also. In the minor, we understand it as relating merely to self-consciousness. In this sense, we do not cogitate an object, but merely the relation to the self-consciousness of the subject, as the form of thought. In the former premiss we speak of things which cannot be cogitated otherwise than as subjects. In the second, we do not speak of things, but of thought (all objects being abstracted), in which the Ego is always the subject of consciousness. Hence the conclusion cannot be, "I cannot exist otherwise than as subject"; but only "I can, in cogitating my existence, employ my Ego only as the subject of the judgement." But this is an identical proposition, and throws no light on the mode of my existence.

36. Clearness is not, as logicians maintain, the consciousness of a representation. For a certain degree of consciousness, which may not, however, be sufficient for recollection, is to be met with in many dim representations. For without any consciousness at all, we should not be able to recognize any difference in the obscure representations we connect; as we really can do with many conceptions, such as those of right and justice, and those of the musician, who strikes at once several notes in improvising a piece of music. But a representation is clear, in which our consciousness is sufficient for the consciousness of the difference of this representation from others. If we are only conscious that there is a difference, but are not conscious of the difference—that is, what the difference is—the representation must be termed obscure. There is, consequently, an infinite series of degrees of consciousness down to its entire disappearance.

37. There are some who think they have done enough to establish a new possibility in the mode of the existence of souls, when they have shown that there is no contradiction in their hypotheses on this subject. Such are those who affirm the possibility of thought—of which they have no other knowledge than what they derive from its use in connecting empirical intuitions presented in this our human life—after this life has ceased. But it is very easy to embarrass them by the introduction of counter-possibilities, which rest upon quite as good a foundation. Such, for example, is the possibility of the division of a simple substance into several substances; and conversely, of the coalition of several into one simple substance. For, although divisibility presupposes composition, it does not necessarily require a composition of substances, but only of the degrees (of the several faculties) of one and the same substance. Now we can cogitate all the powers and faculties of the soul—even that of consciousness—as diminished by one half, the substance still remaining. In the same way we can represent to ourselves without contradiction, this obliterated half as preserved, not in the soul, but without it; and we can believe that, as in this case every thing that is real in the soul, and has a degree—consequently its entire existence—has been halved, a particular substance would arise out of the soul. For the multiplicity, which has been divided, formerly existed, but not as a multiplicity of substances, but of every reality as the quantum of existence in it; and the unity of substance was merely a mode of existence, which by this division alone has been transformed into a plurality of subsistence. In the same manner several simple substances might coalesce into one, without anything being lost except the plurality of subsistence, inasmuch as the one substance would contain the degree of reality of all the former substances. Perhaps, indeed, the simple substances, which appear under the form of matter, might (not indeed by a mechanical or chemical influence upon each other, but by an unknown influence, of which the former would

be but the phenomenal appearance), by means of such a dynamical division of the parent-souls, as intensive quantities, produce other souls, while the former repaired the loss thus sustained with new matter of the same sort. I am far from allowing any value to such chimeras; and the principles of our analytic have clearly proved that no other than an empirical use of the categories—that of substance, for example—is possible. But if the rationalist is bold enough to construct, on the mere authority of the faculty of thought—without any intuition, whereby an object is given—a self-subsistent being, merely because the unity of apperception in thought cannot allow him to believe it a composite being, instead of declaring, as he ought to do, that he is unable to explain the possibility of a thinking nature; what ought to hinder the materialist, with as complete an independence of experience, to employ the principle of the rationalist in a directly opposite manner—still preserving the formal unity required by his opponent?

38. The "I think" is, as has been already stated, an empirical proposition, and contains the proposition, "I exist." But I cannot say, "Everything, which thinks, exists"; for in this case the property of thought would constitute all beings possessing it, necessary beings. Hence my existence cannot be considered as an inference from the proposition, "I think," as Descartes maintained—because in this case the major premiss, "Everything, which thinks, exists," must precede—but the two propositions are identical. The proposition, "I think," expresses an undetermined empirical intuition, that perception (proving consequently that sensation, which must belong to sensibility, lies at the foundation of this proposition); but it precedes experience, whose province it is to determine an object of perception by means of the categories in relation to time; and existence in this proposition is not a category, as it does not apply to an undetermined given object, but only to one of which we have a conception, and about which we wish to know whether it does or does not exist, out of, and apart from this conception. An undetermined perception signifies here merely something real that has been given, only, however, to thought in general—but not as a phenomenon, nor as a thing in itself (noumenon), but only as something that really exists, and is designated as such in the proposition, "I think." For it must be remarked that, when I call the proposition, "I think," an empirical proposition, I do not thereby mean that the Ego in the proposition is an empirical representation; on the contrary, it is purely intellectual, because it belongs to thought in general. But without some empirical representation, which presents to the mind material for thought, the mental act, "I think," would not take place; and the empirical is only the condition of the application or employment of the pure intellectual faculty.

39. The absolute totality of the series of conditions to a given conditioned is always unconditioned; because beyond it there exist no other conditions, on which it might depend. But the absolute totality of such a series is only an idea, or rather a problematical conception, the possibility of which must be investigated—particularly in relation to the mode in which the unconditioned, as the transcendental idea which is the real subject of inquiry, may be contained therein.

40. Nature, understood adjective (formaliter), signifies the complex of the determinations of a thing, connected according to an internal principle of causality. On the other hand, we understand by nature, substantive (materialiter), the sum total of phenomena, in so far as they, by virtue of an internal principle of causality, are connected with each other throughout. In the former sense we speak of the nature of liquid matter, of fire, etc., and employ the word only adjective; while, if speaking of the objects of nature, we have in our minds the idea of a subsisting whole.

41. The antinomies stand in the order of the four transcendental ideas above detailed.

42. We may consider an undetermined quantity as a whole, when it is enclosed within limits, although we cannot construct or ascertain its totality by measurement, that is, by the successive synthesis of its parts. For its limits of themselves determine its completeness as a whole.

43. Space is merely the form of external intuition (formal intuition), and not a real object which can be externally perceived. Space, prior to all things which determine it (fill or limit it), or, rather, which present an empirical intuition conformable to it, is, under the title of absolute space, nothing but the mere possibility of external phenomena, in so far as they either exist in themselves, or can annex themselves to given intuitions. Empirical intuition is therefore not a composition of phenomena and space (of perception and empty intuition). The one is not the correlate of the other in a synthesis, but they are vitally connected in the same empirical intuition, as matter and form. If we wish to set one of these two apart from the other—space from phenomena—there arise all sorts of empty determinations of external intuition, which are very far from being possible perceptions. For example, motion or rest of the world in an infinite empty space, or a determination of the mutual relation of both, cannot possibly be perceived, and is therefore merely the predicate of a notional entity.

44. The quantum in this sense contains a congeries of given units, which is greater than any number—and this is the mathematical conception of the infinite.

45. It is evident that what is meant here is, that empty space, in so far as it is limited by phenomena—space, that is, within the world—does not at least contradict transcendental principles, and may therefore, as regards them, be admitted, although its possibility cannot on that account be affirmed.

46. Objectively, time, as the formal condition of the possibility of change, precedes all changes; but subjectively, and in consciousness, the representation of time, like every other, is given solely by occasion of perception.

47. The word begin is taken in two senses. The first is active—the cause being regarded as beginning a series of conditions as its effect (infit). The second is passive—the causality in the cause itself beginning to operate (fit). I reason here from the first to the second.

48. It is, however, still a matter of doubt whether Epicurus ever propounded these principles as directions for the objective employment of the understanding. If, indeed, they were nothing more than maxims for the

speculative exercise of reason, he gives evidence therein a more genuine philosophic spirit than any of the philosophers of antiquity. That, in the explanation of phenomena, we must proceed as if the field of inquiry had neither limits in space nor commencement in time; that we must be satisfied with the teaching of experience in reference to the material of which the world is posed; that we must not look for any other mode of the origination of events than that which is determined by the unalterable laws of nature; and finally, that we not employ the hypothesis of a cause distinct from the world to account for a phenomenon or for the world itself—are principles for the extension of speculative philosophy, and the discovery of the true sources of the principles of morals, which, however little conformed to in the present day, are undoubtedly correct. At the same time, any one desirous of ignoring, in mere speculation, these dogmatical propositions, need not for that reason be accused of denying them.

49. The question, "What is the constitution of a transcendental object?" is unanswerable—we are unable to say what it is; but we can perceive that the question itself is nothing; because it does not relate to any object that can be presented to us. For this reason, we must consider all the questions raised in transcendental psychology as answerable and as really answered; for they relate to the transcendental subject of all internal phenomena, which is not itself phenomenon and consequently not given as an object, in which, moreover, none of the categories—and it is to them that the question is properly directed—find any conditions of its application. Here, therefore, is a case where no answer is the only proper answer. For a question regarding the constitution of a something which cannot be cogitated by any determined predicate, being completely beyond the sphere of objects and experience, is perfectly null and void.

50. I have elsewhere termed this theory formal idealism, to distinguish it from material idealism, which doubts or denies the existence of external things. To avoid ambiguity, it seems advisable in many cases to employ this term instead of that mentioned in the text.

51. The cosmical series can neither be greater nor smaller than the possible empirical regress, upon which its conception is based. And as this regress cannot be a determinate infinite regress, still less a determinate finite (absolutely limited), it is evident that we cannot regard the world as either finite or infinite, because the regress, which gives us the representation of the world, is neither finite nor infinite.

52. The reader will remark that the proof presented above is very different from the dogmatical demonstration given in the antithesis of the first antinomy. In that demonstration, it was taken for granted that the world is a thing in itself—given in its totality prior to all regress, and a determined position in space and time was denied to it—if it was not considered as occupying all time and all space. Hence our conclusion differed from that given above; for we inferred in the antithesis the actual infinity of the world.

53. For the understanding cannot admit among phenomena a condition which is itself empirically unconditioned. But if it is possible to cogitate an intelligible condition—one which is not a member of the series of phenomena—for a conditioned phenomenon, without breaking the series of empirical conditions, such a condition may be admissible as empirically unconditioned, and the empirical regress continue regular, unceasing, and intact.

54. The real morality of actions—their merit or demerit, and even that of our own conduct, is completely unknown to us. Our estimates can relate only to their empirical character. How much is the result of the action of free will, how much is to be ascribed to nature and to blameless error, or to a happy constitution of temperament (merito fortunae), no one can discover, nor, for this reason, determine with perfect justice.

55. Thus this principle declares everything to possess a relation to a common correlate—the sum-total of possibility, which, if discovered to exist in the idea of one individual thing, would establish the affinity of all possible things, from the identity of the ground of their complete determination. The determinability of every conception is subordinate to the universality (Allgemeinheit, universalitas) of the principle of excluded middle; the determination of a thing to the totality (Allheit, universitas) of all possible predicates.

56. The investigations and calculations of astronomers have taught us much that is wonderful; but the most important lesson we have received from them is the discovery of the abyss of our ignorance in relation to the universe—an ignorance the magnitude of which reason, without the information thus derived, could never have conceived. This discovery of our deficiencies must produce a great change in the determination of the aims of human reason.

57. This ideal of the ens realissimum—although merely a mental representation—is first objectivized, that is, has an objective existence attributed to it, then hypostatized, and finally, by the natural progress of reason to the completion of unity, personified, as we shall show presently. For the regulative unity of experience is not based upon phenomena themselves, but upon the connection of the variety of phenomena by the understanding in a consciousness, and thus the unity of the supreme reality and the complete determinability of all things, seem to reside in a supreme understanding, and, consequently, in a conscious intelligence.

58. A conception is always possible, if it is not self-contradictory. This is the logical criterion of possibility, distinguishing the object of such a conception from the nihil negativum. But it may be, notwithstanding, an empty conception, unless the objective reality of this synthesis, but which it is generated, is demonstrated; and a proof of this kind must be based upon principles of possible experience, and not upon the principle of analysis or contradiction. This remark may be serviceable as a warning against concluding, from the possibility of a conception—which is logical—the possibility of a thing—which is real.

59. This inference is too well known to require more detailed discussion. It is based upon the spurious transcendental law of causality, that everything which is contingent has a cause, which, if itself contingent, must also have a cause; and so on, till the series of subordinated causes must end with an absolutely necessary cause, without which it would not possess completeness.

60. Not theological ethics; for this science contains ethical laws, which presuppose the existence of a Supreme Governor of the world; while moral-theology, on the contrary, is the expression of a conviction of the existence of a Supreme Being, founded upon ethical laws.

61. From the Greek, eurhioko.

62. The advantages which a circular form, in the case of the earth, has over every other, are well known. But few are aware that the slight flattening at the poles, which gives it the figure of a spheroid, is the only cause which prevents the elevations of continents or even of mountains, perhaps thrown up by some internal convulsion, from continually altering the position of the axis of the earth—and that to some considerable degree in a short time. The great protuberance of the earth under the Equator serves to overbalance the impetus of all other masses of earth, and thus to preserve the axis of the earth, so far as we can observe, in its present position. And yet this wise arrangement has been unthinkingly explained from the equilibrium of the formerly fluid mass.

63. This was the term applied by the old dialecticians to a sophistical argument, which ran thus: If it is your fate to die of this disease, you will die, whether you employ a physician or not. Cicero says that this mode of reasoning has received this appellation, because, if followed, it puts an end to the employment of reason in the affairs of life. For a similar reason, I have applied this designation to the sophistical argument of pure reason.

64. After what has been said of the psychological idea of the ego and its proper employment as a regulative principle of the operations of reason, I need not enter into details regarding the transcendental illusion by which the systematic unity of all the various phenomena of the internal sense is hypostatized. The procedure is in this case very similar to that which has been discussed in our remarks on the theological ideal.

II. TRANSCENDENTAL DOCTRINE OF
METHOD

IF WE REGARD the sum of the cognition of pure speculative reason as an edifice, the idea of which, at least, exists in the human mind, it may be said that we have in the Transcendental Doctrine of Elements examined the materials and determined to what edifice these belong, and what its height and stability. We have found, indeed, that, although we had purposed to build for ourselves a tower which should reach to Heaven, the supply of materials sufficed merely for a habitation, which was spacious enough for all terrestrial purposes, and high enough to enable us to survey the level plain of experience, but that the bold undertaking designed necessarily failed for want of materials—not to mention the confusion of tongues, which gave rise to endless disputes among the labourers on the plan of the edifice, and at last scattered them over all the world, each to erect a separate building for himself, according to his own plans and his own inclinations. Our present task relates not to the materials, but to the plan of an edifice; and, as we have had sufficient warning not to venture blindly upon a design which may be found to transcend our natural powers, while, at the same time, we cannot give up the intention of erecting a secure abode for the mind, we must proportion our design to the material which is presented to us, and which is, at the same time, sufficient for all our wants.

I understand, then, by the transcendental doctrine of method, the determination of the formal conditions of a complete system of pure reason. We shall accordingly have to treat of the discipline, the canon, the architectonic, and, finally, the history of pure reason. This part of our Critique will accomplish, from the transcendental point of view, what has been usually attempted, but miserably executed, under the name of practical logic. It has been badly executed, I say, because general logic, not being limited to any particular kind of cognition (not even to the pure cognition of the understanding) nor to any particular objects, it cannot, without borrowing from other sciences, do more than present merely the titles or signs of possible methods and the technical expressions, which are employed in the systematic parts of all sciences; and thus the pupil is made acquainted with names, the meaning and application of which he is to learn only at some future time.

CHAPTER I. THE DISCIPLINE OF PURE REASON

Negative judgements—those which are so not merely as regards their logical form, but in respect of their content—are not commonly held in especial respect. They are, on the contrary, regarded as jealous enemies of our insatiable desire for knowledge; and it almost requires an apology to induce us to tolerate, much less to prize and to respect them.

All propositions, indeed, may be logically expressed in a negative form; but, in relation to the content of our cognition, the peculiar province of negative judgements is solely to prevent error. For this reason, too, negative propositions, which are framed for the purpose of correcting false cognitions where error is absolutely impossible, are undoubtedly true, but inane and senseless; that is, they are in reality purposeless and, for this reason, often very ridiculous. Such is the proposition of the schoolman that Alexander could not have subdued any countries without an army.

But where the limits of our possible cognition are very much contracted, the attraction to new fields of knowledge great, the illusions to which the mind is subject of the most deceptive character, and the evil consequences of error of no inconsiderable magnitude—the negative element in knowledge, which is useful only to guard us against error, is of far more importance than much of that positive instruction which makes additions to the sum of our knowledge. The restraint which is employed to repress, and finally to extirpate the constant inclination to depart from certain rules, is termed discipline. It is distinguished from culture, which aims at the formation of a certain degree of skill, without attempting to repress or to destroy any other mental power, already existing. In the cultivation of a talent, which has given evidence of an impulse towards self-development, discipline takes a negative,[1] culture and doctrine a positive, part.

That natural dispositions and talents (such as imagination and wit), which ask a free and unlimited development, require in many respects the corrective influence of discipline, every one will readily grant. But it may well appear strange that reason, whose proper duty it is to prescribe rules of discipline to all the other powers of the mind, should itself require this corrective. It has, in fact, hitherto escaped this humiliation, only because, in presence of its magnificent pretensions and high position, no one could readily suspect it to be capable of substituting fancies for conceptions, and words for things.

Reason, when employed in the field of experience, does not stand in need of criticism, because its principles are subjected to the continual test of empirical observations. Nor is criticism requisite in the sphere of mathematics, where the conceptions of reason must always be presented in concreto in pure intuition, and baseless or arbitrary assertions are discovered without difficulty. But where reason is not held in a plain track by the influence of empirical or of pure intuition, that is, when it is employed in the transcendental sphere of pure conceptions, it stands in great need of discipline, to restrain its propensity to overstep the limits of possible experience and to keep it from wandering into error. In fact, the utility of the philosophy of pure reason is entirely of this negative character. Particular errors may be corrected by particular animadversions, and the causes of these errors may be eradicated by criticism. But where we find, as in the case of pure reason, a complete system of illusions and fallacies, closely connected with each other and depending upon grand general principles, there seems to be required a peculiar and negative code of mental legislation, which, under the denomination of a discipline, and founded upon the nature of reason and the objects of its exercise, shall constitute a system of thorough examination and testing, which no fallacy will be able to withstand or escape from, under whatever disguise or concealment it may lurk.

But the reader must remark that, in this the second division of our transcendental Critique the discipline of pure reason is not directed to the content, but to the method of the cognition of pure reason. The former task has been completed in the doctrine of elements. But there is so much similarity in the mode of employing the faculty of reason, whatever be the object to which it is applied, while, at the same time, its employment in the transcendental sphere is so essentially different in kind from every other, that, without the warning negative influence of a discipline specially directed to that end, the errors are unavoidable which spring from the unskillful employment of the methods which are originated by reason but which are out of place in this sphere.

SECTION I. THE DISCIPLINE OF PURE REASON IN THE SPHERE OF DOGMATISM

The science of mathematics presents the most brilliant example of the extension of the sphere of pure reason without the aid of experience. Examples are always contagious; and they exert an especial influence on the same faculty, which naturally flatters itself that it will have the same good fortune in other case as fell to its lot in one fortunate instance. Hence pure reason hopes to be able to extend its empire in the transcendental sphere with equal success and security, especially when it applies the same method which was attended with such brilliant results in the science of mathematics. It is, therefore, of the highest importance for us to know whether the method of arriving at demonstrative certainty, which is termed mathematical, be identical with that by which we endeavour to attain the same degree of certainty in philosophy, and which is termed in that science dogmatical.

Philosophical cognition is the cognition of reason by means of conceptions; mathematical cognition is cognition by means of the construction of conceptions. The construction of a conception is the presentation à priori of the intuition which corresponds to the conception. For this purpose a non-empirical intuition is requisite, which, as an intuition, is an individual object; while, as the construction of a conception (a general representation), it must be seen to be universally valid for all the possible intuitions which rank under that conception. Thus I construct a triangle, by the presentation of the object which corresponds to this conception, either by mere imagination, in pure intuition, or upon paper, in empirical intuition, in both cases completely à priori, without borrowing the type of that figure from any experience. The individual figure drawn upon paper is empirical; but it serves, notwithstanding, to indicate the conception, even in its universality, because in this empirical intuition we keep our eye merely on the act of the construction of the conception, and pay no attention to the various modes of determining it, for example, its size, the length of its sides, the size of its angles, these not in the least affecting the essential character of the conception.

Philosophical cognition, accordingly, regards the particular only in the general; mathematical the general in the particular, nay, in the individual. This is done, however, entirely à priori and by means of pure reason, so that, as this individual figure is determined under certain universal conditions of construction, the object of the conception, to which this individual figure corresponds as its schema, must be cogitated as universally determined.

The essential difference of these two modes of cognition consists, therefore, in this formal quality; it does not regard the difference of the matter or objects of both. Those thinkers who aim at distinguishing philosophy from mathematics by asserting that the former has to do with quality merely, and the latter with quantity, have mistaken the effect for the cause. The reason why mathematical cognition can relate only to quantity is to be found in its form alone. For it is the conception of quantities only that is capable of being constructed, that is, presented à priori in intuition; while qualities cannot be given in any other than an empirical intuition. Hence the cognition of qualities by reason is possible only through conceptions. No one can find an intuition which shall correspond to the conception of reality, except in experience; it cannot be presented to the mind à priori and antecedently to the empirical consciousness of a reality. We can form an intuition, by means of the mere conception of it, of a cone, without the aid of experience; but the colour of the cone we cannot know except from experience. I cannot present an intuition of a cause, except in an example which experience offers to me. Besides, philosophy, as well as mathematics, treats of quantities; as, for example, of totality, infinity, and so on. Mathematics, too, treats of the difference of lines and surfaces—as spaces of different quality, of the continuity of extension—as a quality thereof. But, although in such cases they have a common object, the mode in which reason considers that object is very different in philosophy from what it is in mathematics. The former confines itself to the general conceptions; the latter can do nothing with a mere conception, it hastens to intuition. In this intuition it regards the conception in concreto, not empirically, but in an à priori intuition, which it has constructed; and in which, all the results which follow from the general conditions of the construction of the conception are in all cases valid for the object of the constructed conception.

Suppose that the conception of a triangle is given to a philosopher and that he is required to discover, by the philosophical method, what relation the sum of its angles bears to a right angle. He has nothing before him but the conception of a figure enclosed within three right lines, and, consequently, with the same number of angles. He may analyse the conception of a right line, of an angle, or of the number three as long as he pleases, but he will not discover any properties not contained in these conceptions. But, if this question is proposed to a geometrician, he at once begins by constructing a triangle. He knows that two right angles are equal to the sum of all the contiguous angles which proceed from one point in a straight line; and he goes on to produce one side of his triangle, thus forming two adjacent angles which are together equal to two right angles. He then divides the exterior of these angles, by drawing a line parallel with the opposite side of the triangle, and immediately perceives that he has thus got an exterior adjacent angle which is equal to the interior. Proceeding in this way, through a chain of inferences, and always on the ground of intuition, he arrives at a clear and universally valid solution of the question.

But mathematics does not confine itself to the construction of quantities (quanta), as in the case of geometry; it occupies itself with pure quantity also (quantitas), as in the case of algebra, where complete abstraction is made of the properties of the object indicated by the conception of quantity. In algebra, a certain method of notation by signs is adopted, and these indicate the different possible constructions of quantities, the extraction of roots, and so on. After having thus denoted the general conception of quantities, according to their different relations, the different operations by which quantity or number is increased or diminished are presented in intuition in accordance with general rules. Thus, when one quantity is to be divided by another, the signs which denote both are placed in the form peculiar to the operation of division; and thus algebra, by means of a symbolical construction of quantity, just as geometry, with its ostensive or geometrical construction (a construction of the objects themselves), arrives at results which discursive cognition cannot hope to reach by the aid of mere conceptions.

Now, what is the cause of this difference in the fortune of the philosopher and the mathematician, the former of whom follows the path of conceptions, while the latter pursues that of intuitions, which he represents, à priori, in correspondence with his conceptions? The cause is evident from what has been already demonstrated in the introduction to this Critique. We do not, in the present case, want to discover analytical propositions, which may be produced merely by analysing our conceptions—for in this the philosopher would have the advantage over his rival; we aim at the discovery of synthetical propositions—such synthetical propositions, moreover, as can be cognized à priori. I must not confine myself to that which I actually cogitate in my conception of a triangle, for this is nothing more than the mere definition; I must try to go beyond that, and to arrive at properties which are not contained in, although they belong to, the conception. Now, this is impossible, unless I determine the object present to my mind according to the conditions, either of empirical, or of pure, intuition. In the former case, I should have an empirical proposition (arrived at by actual measurement of the angles of the triangle), which would possess neither universality nor necessity; but that would be of no value. In the latter, I proceed by geometrical construction, by means of which I collect, in a pure intuition, just as I would in an empirical intuition, all the various properties which belong to the schema of a triangle in general, and consequently to its conception, and thus construct synthetical propositions which possess the attribute of universality.

It would be vain to philosophize upon the triangle, that is, to reflect on it discursively; I should get no further than the definition with which I had been obliged to set out. There are certainly transcendental synthetical propositions which are framed by means of pure conceptions, and which form the peculiar distinction of philosophy; but these do not relate to any particular thing, but to a thing in general, and enounce the conditions under which the perception of it may become a part of possible experience. But the science of mathematics has nothing to do with such questions, nor with the question of existence in any fashion; it is concerned merely with the properties of objects in themselves, only in so far as these are connected with the conception of the objects.

In the above example, we merely attempted to show the great difference which exists between the discursive employment of reason in the sphere of conceptions, and its intuitive exercise by means of the construction of conceptions. The question naturally arises: What is the cause which necessitates this twofold exercise of reason, and how are we to discover whether it is the philosophical or the mathematical method which reason is pursuing in an argument?

All our knowledge relates, finally, to possible intuitions, for it is these alone that present objects to the mind. An à priori or non-empirical conception contains either a pure intuition—and in this case it can be constructed; or it contains nothing but the synthesis of possible intuitions, which are not given à priori. In this latter case, it may help us to form synthetical à priori judgements, but only in the discursive method, by conceptions, not in the intuitive, by means of the construction of conceptions.

The only à priori intuition is that of the pure form of phenomena—space and time. A conception of space and time as quanta may be presented à priori in intuition, that is, constructed, either alone with their quality (figure), or as pure quantity (the mere synthesis of the homogeneous), by means of number. But the matter of phenomena, by which things are given in space and time, can be presented only in perception, à posteriori. The only conception which represents à priori this empirical content of phenomena is the conception of a thing in general; and the à priori synthetical cognition of this conception can give us nothing more than the rule for the synthesis of that which may be contained in the corresponding à posteriori perception; it is utterly inadequate to present an à priori intuition of the real object, which must necessarily be empirical.

Synthetical propositions, which relate to things in general, an à priori intuition of which is impossible, are transcendental. For this reason transcendental propositions cannot be framed by means of the construction of conceptions; they are à priori, and based entirely on conceptions themselves. They contain merely the rule, by which we are to seek in the world of perception or experience the synthetical unity of that which cannot be intuited à priori. But they are incompetent to present any of the conceptions which appear in them in an à priori intuition; these can be given only à posteriori, in experience, which, however, is itself possible only through these synthetical principles.

If we are to form a synthetical judgement regarding a conception, we must go beyond it, to the intuition in which it is given. If we keep to what is contained in the conception, the judgement is merely analytical—it is merely an explanation of what we have cogitated in the conception. But I can pass from the conception to the pure or empirical intuition which corresponds to it. I can proceed to examine my conception in concreto, and to cognize, either à priori or a posterio, what I find in the object of the conception. The former—à priori cognition—is rational-mathematical cognition by means of the construction of the conception; the latter—à posteriori cognition—is purely empirical cognition, which does not possess the attributes of necessity and universality. Thus I may analyse the conception I have of gold; but I gain no new information from this analysis, I merely enumerate the different properties which I had connected with the notion indicated by the word. My knowledge has gained in logical clearness and arrangement, but no addition has been made to it. But if I take the matter which is indicated by this name, and submit it to the examination of my senses, I am enabled to form several synthetical—although still empirical—propositions. The mathematical conception of a triangle I should construct, that is, present à priori in intuition, and in this way attain to rational-synthetical cognition. But when the transcendental conception of reality, or substance, or power is presented to my mind, I find that it does not relate to or indicate either an empirical or pure intuition, but that it indicates merely the synthesis of empirical intuitions, which cannot of course be given à priori. The synthesis in such a conception cannot proceed à priori—without the aid of experience—to the intuition which corresponds to the conception; and, for this reason, none of these conceptions can produce a determinative synthetical proposition, they can never present more than a principle of the synthesis[2] of possible empirical intuitions. A transcendental proposition is, therefore, a synthetical cognition of reason by means of pure conceptions and the discursive method, and it renders possible all synthetical unity in empirical cognition, though it cannot present us with any intuition à priori.

There is thus a twofold exercise of reason. Both modes have the properties of universality and an à priori origin in common, but are, in their procedure, of widely different character. The reason of this is that in the world of phenomena, in which alone objects are presented to our minds, there are two main elements—the form of intuition (space and time), which can be cognized and determined completely à priori, and the matter or content—that which is presented in space and time, and which, consequently, contains a something—an existence corresponding to our powers of sensation. As regards the latter, which can never be given in a determinate mode except by experience, there are no à priori notions which relate to it, except the undetermined conceptions of the synthesis of possible sensations, in so far as these belong (in a possible experience) to the unity of consciousness. As regards the former, we can determine our conceptions à priori in intuition, inasmuch as we are ourselves the creators of the objects of the conceptions in space and time—these objects being regarded simply as quanta. In the one case, reason proceeds according to conceptions and can do nothing more than subject phenomena to these—which can only be determined empirically, that is, à posteriori—in conformity, however, with those conceptions as the rules of all empirical synthesis. In the other case, reason proceeds by the construction of conceptions; and, as these conceptions relate to an à priori intuition, they may be given and determined in pure intuition à priori, and without the aid of empirical data. The examination and consideration of everything that exists in space or time—whether it is a quantum or not, in how far the particular something (which fills space or time) is a primary substratum, or a mere determination of some other existence, whether it relates to anything else—either as cause or effect, whether its existence is isolated or in reciprocal connection with and dependence upon others, the possibility of this existence, its reality and necessity or opposites—all these form part of the cognition of reason on the ground of conceptions, and this cognition is termed philosophical. But to determine à priori an intuition in space (its figure), to divide time into periods, or merely to cognize the quantity of an intuition in space and time, and to determine it by number—all this is an operation of reason by means of the construction of conceptions, and is called mathematical.

The success which attends the efforts of reason in the sphere of mathematics naturally fosters the expectation that the same good fortune will be its lot, if it applies the mathematical method in other regions of mental endeavour besides that of quantities. Its success is thus great, because it can support all its conceptions by à priori intuitions and, in this way, make itself a master, as it were, over nature; while pure philosophy, with its à priori discursive conceptions, bungles about in the world of nature, and cannot accredit or show any à priori evidence of the reality of these conceptions.

Masters in the science of mathematics are confident of the success of this method; indeed, it is a common persuasion that it is capable of being applied to any subject of human thought. They have hardly ever reflected or philosophized on their favourite science—a task of great difficulty; and the specific difference between the two modes of employing the faculty of reason has never entered their thoughts. Rules current in the field of common experience, and which common sense stamps everywhere with its approval, are regarded by them as axiomatic. From what source the conceptions of space and time, with which (as the only primitive quanta) they have to deal, enter their minds, is a question which they do not trouble themselves to answer; and they think it just as unnecessary to examine into the origin of the pure conceptions of the understanding and the extent of their validity. All they have to do with them is to employ them. In all this they are perfectly right, if they do not overstep the limits of the sphere of nature. But they pass, unconsciously, from the world of sense to the insecure ground of pure transcendental conceptions (instabilis tellus, innabilis unda), where they can neither stand nor swim, and where the tracks of their footsteps are obliterated by time; while the march of mathematics is pursued on a broad and magnificent highway, which the latest posterity shall frequent without fear of danger or impediment.

As we have taken upon us the task of determining, clearly and certainly, the limits of pure reason in the sphere of transcendentalism, and as the efforts of reason in this direction are persisted in, even after the plainest and most expressive warnings, hope still beckoning us past the limits of experience into the splendours of the intellectual world —it becomes necessary to cut away the last anchor of this fallacious and fantastic hope. We shall, accordingly, show that the mathematical method is unattended in the sphere of philosophy by the least advantage—except, perhaps, that it more plainly exhibits its own inadequacy—that geometry and philosophy are two quite different things, although they go hand in hand in the field of natural science, and, consequently, that the procedure of the one can never be imitated by the other.

The evidence of mathematics rests upon definitions, axioms, and demonstrations. I shall be satisfied with showing that none of these forms can be employed or imitated in philosophy in the sense in which they are understood by mathematicians; and that the geometrician, if he employs his method in philosophy, will succeed only in building card-castles, while the employment of the philosophical method in mathematics can result in nothing but mere verbiage. The essential business of philosophy, indeed, is to mark out the limits of the science; and even the mathematician, unless his talent is naturally circumscribed and limited to this particular department of knowledge, cannot turn a deaf ear to the warnings of philosophy, or set himself above its direction.

I. Of Definitions. A definition is, as the term itself indicates, the representation, upon primary grounds, of the complete conception of a thing within its own limits.[3] Accordingly, an empirical conception cannot be defined, it can only be explained. For, as there are in such a conception only a certain number of marks or signs, which denote a certain class of sensuous objects, we can never be sure that we do not cogitate under the word which indicates the same object, at one time a greater, at another a smaller number of signs. Thus, one person may cogitate in his conception of gold, in addition to its properties of weight, colour, malleability, that of resisting rust, while another person may be ignorant of this quality. We employ certain signs only so long as we require them for the sake of distinction; new observations abstract some and add new ones, so that an empirical conception never remains within permanent limits. It is, in fact, useless to define a conception of this kind. If, for example, we are speaking of water and its properties, we do not stop at what we actually think by the word water, but proceed to observation and experiment; and the word, with the few signs attached to it, is more properly a designation than a conception of the thing. A definition in this case would evidently be nothing more than a determination of the word. In the second place, no à priori conception, such as those of substance, cause, right, fitness, and so on, can be defined. For I can never be sure, that the clear representation of a given conception (which is given in a confused state) has been fully developed, until I know that the representation is adequate with its object. But, inasmuch as the conception, as it is presented to the mind, may contain a number of obscure representations, which we do not observe in our analysis, although we employ them in our application of the conception, I can never be sure that my analysis is complete, while examples may make this probable, although they can never demonstrate the fact. Instead of the word definition, I should rather employ the term exposition—a more modest expression, which the critic may accept without surrendering his doubts as to the completeness of the analysis of any such conception. As, therefore, neither empirical nor à priori conceptions are capable of definition, we have to see whether the only other kind of conceptions—arbitrary conceptions—can be subjected to this mental operation. Such a conception can always be defined; for I must know thoroughly what I wished to cogitate in it, as it was I who created it, and it was not given to my mind either by the nature of my understanding or by experience. At the same time, I cannot say that, by such a definition, I have defined a real object. If the conception is based upon empirical conditions, if, for example, I have a conception of a clock for a ship, this arbitrary conception does not assure me of the existence or even of the possibility of the object. My definition of such a conception would with more propriety be termed a declaration of a project than a definition of an object. There are no other conceptions which can bear definition, except those which contain an arbitrary synthesis, which can be constructed à priori. Consequently, the science of mathematics alone possesses definitions. For the object here thought is presented à priori in intuition; and thus it can never contain more or less than the conception, because the conception of the object has been given by the definition—and primarily, that is, without deriving the definition from any other source. Philosophical definitions are, therefore, merely expositions of given conceptions, while mathematical definitions are constructions of conceptions originally formed by the mind itself; the former are produced by analysis, the completeness of which is never demonstratively certain, the latter by a synthesis. In a mathematical definition the conception is formed, in a philosophical definition it is only explained. From this it follows:

(a) That we must not imitate, in philosophy, the mathematical usage of commencing with definitions—except by way of hypothesis or experiment. For, as all so-called philosophical definitions are merely analyses of given conceptions, these conceptions, although only in a confused form, must precede the analysis; and the incomplete exposition must precede the complete, so that we may be able to draw certain inferences from the characteristics which an incomplete analysis has enabled us to discover, before we attain to the complete exposition or definition of the conception. In one word, a full and clear definition ought, in philosophy, rather to form the conclusion than the commencement of our labours.[4] In mathematics, on the contrary, we cannot have a

294 | IMMANUEL KANT

conception prior to the definition; it is the definition which gives us the conception, and it must for this reason form the commencement of every chain of mathematical reasoning.

(b) Mathematical definitions cannot be erroneous. For the conception is given only in and through the definition, and thus it contains only what has been cogitated in the definition. But although a definition cannot be incorrect, as regards its content, an error may sometimes, although seldom, creep into the form. This error consists in a want of precision. Thus the common definition of a circle—that it is a curved line, every point in which is equally distant from another point called the centre—is faulty, from the fact that the determination indicated by the word curved is superfluous. For there ought to be a particular theorem, which may be easily proved from the definition, to the effect that every line, which has all its points at equal distances from another point, must be a curved line—that is, that not even the smallest part of it can be straight. Analytical definitions, on the other hand, may be erroneous in many respects, either by the introduction of signs which do not actually exist in the conception, or by wanting in that completeness which forms the essential of a definition. In the latter case, the definition is necessarily defective, because we can never be fully certain of the completeness of our analysis. For these reasons, the method of definition employed in mathematics cannot be imitated in philosophy.

2. Of Axioms. These, in so far as they are immediately certain, are à priori synthetical principles. Now, one conception cannot be connected synthetically and yet immediately with another; because, if we wish to proceed out of and beyond a conception, a third mediating cognition is necessary. And, as philosophy is a cognition of reason by the aid of conceptions alone, there is to be found in it no principle which deserves to be called an axiom. Mathematics, on the other hand, may possess axioms, because it can always connect the predicates of an object à priori, and without any mediating term, by means of the construction of conceptions in intuition. Such is the case with the proposition: Three points can always lie in a plane. On the other hand, no synthetical principle which is based upon conceptions, can ever be immediately certain (for example, the proposition: Everything that happens has a cause), because I require a mediating term to connect the two conceptions of event and cause—namely, the condition of time-determination in an experience, and I cannot cognize any such principle immediately and from conceptions alone. Discursive principles are, accordingly, very different from intuitive principles or axioms. The former always require deduction, which in the case of the latter may be altogether dispensed with. Axioms are, for this reason, always self-evident, while philosophical principles, whatever may be the degree of certainty they possess, cannot lay any claim to such a distinction. No synthetical proposition of pure transcendental reason can be so evident, as is often rashly enough declared, as the statement, twice two are four. It is true that in the Analytic I introduced into the list of principles of the pure understanding, certain axioms of intuition; but the principle there discussed was not itself an axiom, but served merely to present the principle of the possibility of axioms in general, while it was really nothing more than a principle based upon conceptions. For it is one part of the duty of transcendental philosophy to establish the possibility of mathematics itself. Philosophy possesses, then, no axioms, and has no right to impose its à priori principles upon thought, until it has established their authority and validity by a thoroughgoing deduction.

3. Of Demonstrations. Only an apodeictic proof, based upon intuition, can be termed a demonstration. Experience teaches us what is, but it cannot convince us that it might not have been otherwise. Hence a proof upon empirical grounds cannot be apodeictic. À priori conceptions, in discursive cognition, can never produce intuitive certainty or evidence, however certain the judgement they present may be. Mathematics alone, therefore, contains demonstrations, because it does not deduce its cognition from conceptions, but from the construction of conceptions, that is, from intuition, which can be given à priori in accordance with conceptions. The method of algebra, in equations, from which the correct answer is deduced by reduction, is a kind of construction—not geometrical, but by symbols—in which all conceptions, especially those of the relations of quantities, are represented in intuition by signs; and thus the conclusions in that science are secured from errors by the fact that every proof is submitted to ocular evidence. Philosophical cognition does not possess this advantage, it being required to consider the general always in abstracto (by means of conceptions), while mathematics can always consider it in concreto (in an individual intuition), and at the same time by means of à priori representation, whereby all errors are rendered manifest to the senses. The former—discursive proofs—ought to be termed acroamatic proofs, rather than demonstrations, as only words are employed in them, while demonstrations proper, as the term itself indicates, always require a reference to the intuition of the object.

It follows from all these considerations that it is not consonant with the nature of philosophy, especially in the sphere of pure reason, to employ the dogmatical method, and to adorn itself with the titles and insignia of mathematical science. It does not belong to that order, and can only hope for a fraternal union with that science. Its attempts at mathematical evidence are vain pretensions, which can only keep it back from its true aim, which is to detect the illusory procedure of reason when transgressing its proper limits, and by fully explaining and analysing our conceptions, to conduct us from the dim regions of speculation to the clear region of modest self-knowledge. Reason must not, therefore, in its transcendental endeavours, look forward with such confidence, as if the path it is pursuing led straight to its aim, nor reckon with such security upon its premises, as to consider it unnecessary to take a step back, or to keep a strict watch for errors, which, overlooked in the principles, may be detected in the arguments themselves—in which case it may be requisite either to determine these principles with greater strictness, or to change them entirely.

I divide all apodeictic propositions, whether demonstrable or immediately certain, into dogmata and mathemata. A direct synthetical proposition, based on conceptions, is a dogma; a proposition of the same kind, based on the construction of conceptions, is a mathema. Analytical judgements do not teach us any more about an object than what was contained in the conception we had of it; because they do not extend our cognition beyond our conception of an object, they merely elucidate the conception. They cannot therefore be with propriety termed dogmas. Of the two kinds of à priori synthetical propositions above mentioned, only those which are employed in philosophy can, according to the general mode of speech, bear this name; those of arithmetic or geometry would not be rightly so denominated. Thus the customary mode of speaking confirms the explanation given above, and the conclusion arrived at, that only those judgements which are based upon conceptions, not on the construction of conceptions, can be termed dogmatical.

Thus, pure reason, in the sphere of speculation, does not contain a single direct synthetical judgement based upon conceptions. By means of ideas, it is, as we have shown, incapable of producing synthetical judgements, which are objectively valid; by means of the conceptions of the understanding, it establishes certain indubitable principles, not, however, directly on the basis of conceptions, but only indirectly by means of the relation of these conceptions to something of a purely contingent nature, namely, possible experience. When experience is presupposed, these principles are apodeictically certain, but in themselves, and directly, they cannot even be cognized à priori. Thus the given conceptions of cause and event will not be sufficient for the demonstration of the proposition: Every event has a cause. For this reason, it is not a dogma; although from another point of view, that of experience, it is capable of being proved to demonstration. The proper term for such a proposition is principle, and not theorem (although it does require to be proved), because it possesses the remarkable peculiarity of being the condition of the possibility of its own ground of proof, that is, experience, and of forming a necessary presupposition in all empirical observation.

If then, in the speculative sphere of pure reason, no dogmata are to be found; all dogmatical methods, whether borrowed from mathematics, or invented by philosophical thinkers, are alike inappropriate and inefficient. They only serve to conceal errors and fallacies, and to deceive philosophy, whose duty it is to see that reason pursues a safe and straight path. A philosophical method may, however, be systematical. For our reason is, subjectively considered, itself a system, and, in the sphere of mere conceptions, a system of investigation according to principles of unity, the material being supplied by experience alone. But this is not the proper place for discussing the peculiar method of transcendental philosophy, as our present task is simply to examine whether our faculties are capable of erecting an edifice on the basis of pure reason, and how far they may proceed with the materials at their command.

SECTION II. THE DISCIPLINE OF PURE REASON IN POLEMICS

Reason must be subject, in all its operations, to criticism, which must always be permitted to exercise its functions without restraint; otherwise its interests are imperilled and its influence obnoxious to suspicion. There is nothing, however useful, however sacred it may be, that can claim exemption from the searching examination of this supreme tribunal, which has no respect of persons. The very existence of reason depends upon this freedom; for the voice of reason is not that of a dictatorial and despotic power, it is rather like the vote of the citizens of a free state, every member of which must have the privilege of giving free expression to his doubts, and possess even the right of veto.

But while reason can never decline to submit itself to the tribunal of criticism, it has not always cause to dread the judgement of this court. Pure reason, however, when engaged in the sphere of dogmatism, is not so thoroughly conscious of a strict observance of its highest laws, as to appear before a higher judicial reason with perfect confidence. On the contrary, it must renounce its magnificent dogmatical pretensions in philosophy.

Very different is the case when it has to defend itself, not before a judge, but against an equal. If dogmatical assertions are advanced on the negative side, in opposition to

CRITIQUE OF PURE REASON | 297

those made by reason on the positive side, its justification kat authrhopon is complete, although the proof of its propositions is kat aletheian unsatisfactory.

By the polemic of pure reason I mean the defence of its propositions made by reason, in opposition to the dogmatical counter-propositions advanced by other parties. The question here is not whether its own statements may not also be false; it merely regards the fact that reason proves that the opposite cannot be established with demonstrative certainty, nor even asserted with a higher degree of probability. Reason does not hold her possessions upon sufferance; for, although she cannot show a perfectly satisfactory title to them, no one can prove that she is not the rightful possessor.

It is a melancholy reflection that reason, in its highest exercise, falls into an antithetic; and that the supreme tribunal for the settlement of differences should not be at union with itself. It is true that we had to discuss the question of an apparent antithetic, but we found that it was based upon a misconception. In conformity with the common prejudice, phenomena were regarded as things in themselves, and thus an absolute completeness in their synthesis was required in the one mode or in the other (it was shown to be impossible in both); a demand entirely out of place in regard to phenomena. There was, then, no real self-contradiction of reason in the propositions: The series of phenomena given in themselves has an absolutely first beginning; and: This series is absolutely and in itself without beginning. The two propositions are perfectly consistent with each other, because phenomena as phenomena are in themselves nothing, and consequently the hypothesis that they are things in themselves must lead to self-contradictory inferences.

But there are cases in which a similar misunderstanding cannot be provided against, and the dispute must remain unsettled. Take, for example, the theistic proposition: There is a Supreme Being; and on the other hand, the atheistic counter-statement: There exists no Supreme Being; or, in psychology: Everything that thinks possesses the attribute of absolute and permanent unity, which is utterly different from the transitory unity of material phenomena; and the counter-proposition: The soul is not an immaterial unity, and its nature is transitory, like that of phenomena. The objects of these questions contain no heterogeneous or contradictory elements, for they relate to things in themselves, and not to phenomena. There would arise, indeed, a real contradiction, if reason came forward with a statement on the negative side of these questions alone. As regards the criticism to which the grounds of proof on the affirmative side must be subjected, it may be freely admitted, without necessitating the surrender of the affirmative propositions, which have, at least, the interest of reason in their favour—an advantage which the opposite party cannot lay claim to.

I cannot agree with the opinion of several admirable thinkers—Sulzer among the rest—that, in spite of the weakness of the arguments hitherto in use, we may hope, one day, to see sufficient demonstrations of the two cardinal propositions of pure reason—the existence of a Supreme Being, and the immortality of the soul. I am certain, on the contrary, that this will never be the case. For on what ground can reason base such synthetical propositions, which do not relate to the objects of experience and their internal possibility? But it is also demonstratively certain that no one will ever be able to maintain the contrary with the least show of probability. For, as he can attempt such a proof solely upon the basis of pure reason, he is bound to prove that a Supreme Being, and a thinking subject in the character of a pure intelligence, are impossible. But where

298 | IMMANUEL KANT

will he find the knowledge which can enable him to enounce synthetical judgements in regard to things which transcend the region of experience? We may, therefore, rest assured that the opposite never will be demonstrated. We need not, then, have recourse to scholastic arguments; we may always admit the truth of those propositions which are consistent with the speculative interests of reason in the sphere of experience, and form, moreover, the only means of uniting the speculative with the practical interest. Our opponent, who must not be considered here as a critic solely, we can be ready to meet with a non liquet which cannot fail to disconcert him; while we cannot deny his right to a similar retort, as we have on our side the advantage of the support of the subjective maxim of reason, and can therefore look upon all his sophistical arguments with calm indifference.

From this point of view, there is properly no antithetic of pure reason. For the only arena for such a struggle would be upon the field of pure theology and psychology; but on this ground there can appear no combatant whom we need to fear. Ridicule and boasting can be his only weapons; and these may be laughed at, as mere child's play. This consideration restores to Reason her courage; for what source of confidence could be found, if she, whose vocation it is to destroy error, were at variance with herself and without any reasonable hope of ever reaching a state of permanent repose?

Everything in nature is good for some purpose. Even poisons are serviceable; they destroy the evil effects of other poisons generated in our system, and must always find a place in every complete pharmacopoeia. The objections raised against the fallacies and sophistries of speculative reason, are objections given by the nature of this reason itself, and must therefore have a destination and purpose which can only be for the good of humanity. For what purpose has Providence raised many objects, in which we have the deepest interest, so far above us, that we vainly try to cognize them with certainty, and our powers of mental vision are rather excited than satisfied by the glimpses we may chance to seize? It is very doubtful whether it is for our benefit to advance bold affirmations regarding subjects involved in such obscurity; perhaps it would even be detrimental to our best interests. But it is undoubtedly always beneficial to leave the investigating, as well as the critical reason, in perfect freedom, and permit it to take charge of its own interests, which are advanced as much by its limitation, as by its extension of its views, and which always suffer by the interference of foreign powers forcing it, against its natural tendencies, to bend to certain preconceived designs.

Allow your opponent to say what he thinks reasonable, and combat him only with the weapons of reason. Have no anxiety for the practical interests of humanity—these are never imperilled in a purely speculative dispute. Such a dispute serves merely to disclose the antinomy of reason, which, as it has its source in the nature of reason, ought to be thoroughly investigated. Reason is benefited by the examination of a subject on both sides, and its judgements are corrected by being limited. It is not the matter that may give occasion to dispute, but the manner. For it is perfectly permissible to employ, in the presence of reason, the language of a firmly rooted faith, even after we have been obliged to renounce all pretensions to knowledge.

If we were to ask the dispassionate David Hume—a philosopher endowed, in a degree that few are, with a well-balanced judgement: What motive induced you to spend so much labour and thought in undermining the consoling and beneficial persuasion that reason is capable of assuring us of the existence, and presenting us with a determinate conception of a Supreme Being?—his answer would be: Nothing but the desire of teaching reason to know its own powers better, and, at the same time, a dislike of the procedure by which that faculty was compelled to support foregone conclusions, and prevented from confessing the internal weaknesses which it cannot but feel when it enters upon a rigid self-examination. If, on the other hand, we were to ask Priestley—a philosopher who had no taste for transcendental speculation, but was entirely devoted to the principles of empiricism—what his motives were for overturning those two main pillars of religion—the doctrines of the freedom of the will and the immortality of the soul (in his view the hope of a future life is but the expectation of the miracle of resur-rection)—this philosopher, himself a zealous and pious teacher of religion, could give no other answer than this: I acted in the interest of reason, which always suffers, when certain objects are explained and judged by a reference to other supposed laws than those of material nature—the only laws which we know in a determinate manner. It would be unfair to decry the latter philosopher, who endeavoured to harmonize his paradoxical opinions with the interests of religion, and to undervalue an honest and reflecting man, because he finds himself at a loss the moment he has left the field of natural science. The same grace must be accorded to Hume, a man not less well-disposed, and quite as blameless in his moral character, and who pushed his abstract speculations to an extreme length, because, as he rightly believed, the object of them lies entirely beyond the bounds of natural science, and within the sphere of pure ideas.

What is to be done to provide against the danger which seems in the present case to menace the best interests of humanity? The course to be pursued in reference to this subject is a perfectly plain and natural one. Let each thinker pursue his own path; if he shows talent, if he gives evidence of profound thought, in one word, if he shows that he possesses the power of reasoning—reason is always the gainer. If you have recourse to other means, if you attempt to coerce reason, if you raise the cry of treason to humanity, if you excite the feelings of the crowd, which can neither understand nor sympathize with such subtle speculations—you will only make yourselves ridiculous. For the ques-tion does not concern the advantage or disadvantage which we are expected to reap from such inquiries; the question is merely how far reason can advance in the field of speculation, apart from all kinds of interest, and whether we may depend upon the exertions of speculative reason, or must renounce all reliance on it. Instead of joining the combatants, it is your part to be a tranquil spectator of the struggle—a laborious struggle for the parties engaged, but attended, in its progress as well as in its result, with the most advantageous consequences for the interests of thought and knowledge. It is absurd to expect to be enlightened by Reason, and at the same time to prescribe to her what side of the question she must adopt. Moreover, reason is sufficiently held in check by its own power, the limits imposed on it by its own nature are sufficient; it is unnecessary for you to place over it additional guards, as if its power were dangerous to the constitution of the intellectual state. In the dialectic of reason there is no victory gained which need in the least disturb your tranquility.

The strife of dialectic is a necessity of reason, and we cannot but wish that it had been conducted long ere this with that perfect freedom which ought to be its essential condition. In this case, we should have had at an earlier period a matured and profound criticism, which must have put an end to all dialectical disputes, by exposing the illu-sions and prejudices in which they originated.

There is in human nature an unworthy propensity—a propensity which, like every-thing that springs from nature, must in its final purpose be conducive to the good of humanity—to conceal our real sentiments, and to give expression only to certain received opinions, which are regarded as at once safe and promotive of the common good. It is true, this tendency, not only to conceal our real sentiments, but to profess those which may gain us favour in the eyes of society, has not only civilized, but, in a certain measure, moralized us; as no one can break through the outward covering of respectability, honour, and morality, and thus the seemingly-good examples which we see around us form an excellent school for moral improvement, so long as our belief in their genuineness remains unshaken. But this disposition to represent ourselves as better than we are, and to utter opinions which are not our own, can be nothing more than a kind of provisionary arrangement of nature to lead us from the rudeness of an uncivilized state, and to teach us how to assume at least the appearance and manner of the good we see. But when true principles have been developed, and have obtained a sure foundation in our habit of thought, this conventionalism must be attacked with earnest vigour, otherwise it corrupts the heart, and checks the growth of good disposi-tions with the mischievous weed of fair appearances.

I am sorry to remark the same tendency to misrepresentation and hypocrisy in the sphere of speculative discussion, where there is less temptation to restrain the free expression of thought. For what can be more prejudicial to the interests of intelligence than to falsify our real sentiments, to conceal the doubts which we feel in regard to our statements, or to maintain the validity of grounds of proof which we well know to be insufficient? So long as mere personal vanity is the source of these unworthy artifices—and this is generally the case in speculative discussions, which are mostly destitute of practical interest, and are incapable of complete demonstration—the vanity of the oppo-site party exaggerates as much on the other side; and thus the result is the same, although it is not brought about so soon as if the dispute had been conducted in a sincere and upright spirit. But where the mass entertains the notion that the aim of certain subtle speculators is nothing less than to shake the very foundations of public welfare and morality—it seems not only prudent, but even praise worthy, to maintain the good cause by illusory arguments, rather than to give to our supposed opponents the advantage of lowering our declarations to the moderate tone of a merely practical conviction, and of compelling us to confess our inability to attain to apodeictic certainty in speculative subjects. But we ought to reflect that there is nothing, in the world more fatal to the maintenance of a good cause than deceit, misrepresentation, and falsehood. That the strictest laws of honesty should be observed in the discussion of a purely spec-ulative subject is the least requirement that can be made. If we could reckon with secu-rity even upon so little, the conflict of speculative reason regarding the important questions of God, immortality, and freedom, would have been either decided long ago, or would very soon be brought to a conclusion. But, in general, the uprightness of the defence stands in an inverse ratio to the goodness of the cause; and perhaps more honesty and fairness are shown by those who deny than by those who uphold these doctrines.

I shall persuade myself, then, that I have readers who do not wish to see a righteous cause defended by unfair arguments. Such will now recognize the fact that, according to the principles of this Critique, if we consider not what is, but what ought to be the case, there can be really no polemic of pure reason. For how can two persons dispute about a thing, the reality of which neither can present in actual or even in possible experience? Each adopts the plan of meditating on his idea for the purpose of drawing from the idea, if he can, what is more than the idea, that is, the reality of the object which it indicates. How shall they settle the dispute, since neither is able to make his assertions directly comprehensible and certain, but must restrict himself to attacking and confuting those of his opponent? All statements enounced by pure reason transcend the conditions of possible experience, beyond the sphere of which we can discover no criterion of truth, while they are at the same time framed in accordance with the laws of the understanding, which are applicable only to experience; and thus it is the fate of all such speculative discussions that while the one party attacks the weaker side of his opponent, he infallibly lays open his own weaknesses.

The critique of pure reason may be regarded as the highest tribunal for all speculative disputes; for it is not involved in these disputes, which have an immediate relation to certain objects and not to the laws of the mind, but is instituted for the purpose of determining the rights and limits of reason.

Without the control of criticism, reason is, as it were, in a state of nature, and can only establish its claims and assertions by war. Criticism, on the contrary, deciding all questions according to the fundamental laws of its own institution, secures to us the peace of law and order, and enables us to discuss all differences in the more tranquil manner of a legal process. In the former case, disputes are ended by victory, which both sides may claim and which is followed by a hollow armistice; in the latter, by a sentence, which, as it strikes at the root of all speculative differences, ensures to all concerned a lasting peace. The endless disputes of a dogmatizing reason compel us to look for some mode of arriving at a settled decision by a critical investigation of reason itself; just as Hobbes maintains that the state of nature is a state of injustice and violence, and that we must leave it and submit ourselves to the constraint of law, which indeed limits individual freedom, but only that it may consist with the freedom of others and with the common good of all.

This freedom will, among other things, permit of our openly stating the difficulties and doubts which we are ourselves unable to solve, without being decried on that account as turbulent and dangerous citizens. This privilege forms part of the native rights of human reason, which recognizes no other judge than the universal reason of humanity; and as this reason is the source of all progress and improvement, such a privilege is to be held sacred and inviolable. It is unwise, moreover, to denounce as dangerous any bold assertions against, or rash attacks upon, an opinion which is held by the largest and most moral class of the community; for that would be giving them an importance which they do not deserve. When I hear that the freedom of the will, the hope of a future life, and the existence of God have been overthrown by the arguments of some able writer, I feel a strong desire to read his book; for I expect that he will add to my knowledge and impart greater clearness and distinctness to my views by the argumentative power shown in his writings. But I am perfectly certain, even before I have opened the book, that he has not succeeded in a single point, not because I believe I am in possession of irrefutable demonstrations of these important propositions, but because this transcendental critique, which has disclosed to me the power and the limits of pure reason, has fully convinced me that, as it is insufficient to establish the affirmative, it is as powerless, and even more so, to assure us of the truth of the negative answer to these questions. From what source does this free-thinker derive his knowledge that there is, for example, no Supreme Being? This proposition lies out of the field of possible experience, and, therefore, beyond the limits of human cognition. But I would not read at, all the answer which the dogmatical maintainer of the good cause makes to his opponent, because I know well beforehand, that he will merely attack the fallacious grounds of his adversary, without being able to establish his own assertions. Besides, a new illusory argument, in the construction of which talent and acuteness are shown, is suggestive of new ideas and new trains of reasoning, and in this respect the old and everyday sophistries are quite useless. Again, the dogmatical opponent of religion gives employment to criticism, and enables us to test and correct its principles, while there is no occasion for anxiety in regard to the influence and results of his reasoning.

But, it will be said, must we not warn the youth entrusted to academical care against such writings, must we not preserve them from the knowledge of these dangerous assertions, until their judgement is ripened, or rather until the doctrines which we wish to inculcate are so firmly rooted in their minds as to withstand all attempts at instilling the contrary dogmas, from whatever quarter they may come?

If we are to confine ourselves to the dogmatical procedure in the sphere of pure reason, and find ourselves unable to settle such disputes otherwise than by becoming a party in them, and setting counter-assertions against the statements advanced by our opponents, there is certainly no plan more advisable for the moment, but, at the same time, none more absurd and inefficient for the future, than this retaining of the youthful mind under guardianship for a time, and thus preserving it—for so long at least—from seduction into error. But when, at a later period, either curiosity, or the prevalent fashion of thought places such writings in their hands, will the so-called convictions of their youth stand firm? The young thinker, who has in his armoury none but dogmatical weapons with which to resist the attacks of his opponent, and who cannot detect the latent dialectic which lies in his own opinions as well as in those of the opposite party, sees the advance of illusory arguments and grounds of proof which have the advantage of novelty, against as illusory grounds of proof destitute of this advantage, and which, perhaps, excite the suspicion that the natural credulity of his youth has been abused by his instructors. He thinks he can find no better means of showing that he has out grown the discipline of his minority than by despising those well-meant warnings, and, knowing no system of thought but that of dogmatism, he drinks deep draughts of the poison that is to sap the principles in which his early years were trained.

Exactly the opposite of the system here recommended ought to be pursued in academical instruction. This can only be effected, however, by a thorough training in the critical investigation of pure reason. For, in order to bring the principles of this critique into exercise as soon as possible, and to demonstrate their perfect even in the presence of the highest degree of dialectical illusion, the student ought to examine the assertions made on both sides of speculative questions step by step, and to test them by these principles. It cannot be a difficult task for him to show the fallacies inherent in these propositions, and thus he begins early to feel his own power of securing himself against the influence of such sophistical arguments, which must finally lose, for him, all their illusory power. And, although the same blows which overturn the edifice of his opponent are as fatal to his own speculative structures, if such he has wished to rear; he need not feel any sorrow in regard to this seeming misfortune, as he has now before him a fair prospect into the practical region in which he may reasonably hope to find a more secure foundation for a rational system.

There is, accordingly, no proper polemic in the sphere of pure reason. Both parties beat the air and fight with their own shadows, as they pass beyond the limits of nature, and can find no tangible point of attack—no firm footing for their dogmatical conflict. Fight as vigorously as they may, the shadows which they hew down, immediately start up again, like the heroes in Walhalla, and renew the bloodless and unceasing contest.

But neither can we admit that there is any proper sceptical employment of pure reason, such as might be based upon the principle of neutrality in all speculative disputes. To excite reason against itself, to place weapons in the hands of the party on the one side as well as in those of the other, and to remain an undisturbed and sarcastic spectator of the fierce struggle that ensues, seems, from the dogmatical point of view, to be a part fitting only a malevolent disposition. But, when the sophist evidences an invincible obstinacy and blindness, and a pride which no criticism can moderate, there is no other practicable course than to oppose to this pride and obstinacy similar feelings and pretensions on the other side, equally well or ill founded, so that reason, staggered by the reflections thus forced upon it, finds it necessary to moderate its confidence in such pretensions and to listen to the advice of criticism. But we cannot stop at these doubts, much less regard the conviction of our ignorance, not only as a cure for the conceit natural to dogmatism, but as the settlement of the disputes in which reason is involved with itself. On the contrary, scepticism is merely a means of awakening reason from its dogmatic dreams and exciting it to a more careful investigation into its own powers and pretensions. But, as scepticism appears to be the shortest road to a permanent peace in the domain of philosophy, and as it is the track pursued by the many who aim at giving a philosophical colouring to their contemptuous dislike of all inquiries of this kind, I think it necessary to present to my readers this mode of thought in its true light.

Scepticism not a Permanent State for Human Reason.

The consciousness of ignorance—unless this ignorance is recognized to be absolutely necessary ought, instead of forming the conclusion of my inquiries, to be the strongest motive to the pursuit of them. All ignorance is either ignorance of things or of the limits of knowledge. If my ignorance is accidental and not necessary, it must incite me, in the first case, to a dogmatical inquiry regarding the objects of which I am ignorant; in the second, to a critical investigation into the bounds of all possible knowledge. But that my ignorance is absolutely necessary and unavoidable, and that it consequently absolves from the duty of all further investigation, is a fact which cannot be made out upon empirical grounds—from observation—but upon critical grounds alone, that is, by a thoroughgoing investigation into the primary sources of cognition. It follows that the determination of the bounds of reason can be made only on à priori grounds; while the empirical limitation of reason, which is merely an indeterminate cognition of an ignorance that can never be completely removed, can take place only à posteriori. In other words, our empirical knowledge is limited by that which yet remains for us to know. The former cognition of our ignorance, which is possible only on a rational basis, is a science; the latter is merely a perception, and we cannot say how far the inferences drawn from it may extend. If I regard the earth, as it really appears to my senses, as a flat surface, I am ignorant how far this surface extends. But experience teaches me that, how far soever I go, I always see before me a space in which I can proceed farther; and thus I know the limits—merely visual—of my actual knowledge of the earth, although I am ignorant of the limits of the earth itself. But if I have got so far as to know that the earth is a sphere, and that its surface is spherical, I can cognize à priori and determine upon principles, from my knowledge of a small part of this surface—say to the extent of a degree—the diameter and circumference of the earth; and although I am ignorant of the objects which this surface contains, I have a perfect knowledge of its limits and extent.

The sum of all the possible objects of our cognition seems to us to be a level surface, with an apparent horizon—that which forms the limit of its extent, and which has been termed by us the idea of unconditioned totality. To reach this limit by empirical means is impossible, and all attempts to determine it à priori according to a principle, are alike in vain. But all the questions raised by pure reason relate to that which lies beyond this horizon, or, at least, in its boundary line.

The celebrated David Hume was one of those geographers of human reason who believe that they have given a sufficient answer to all such questions by declaring them to lie beyond the horizon of our knowledge—a horizon which, however, Hume was unable to determine. His attention especially was directed to the principle of causality; and he remarked with perfect justice that the truth of this principle, and even the objective validity of the conception of a cause, was not commonly based upon clear insight, that is, upon à priori cognition. Hence he concluded that this law does not derive its authority from its universality and necessity, but merely from its general applicability in the course of experience, and a kind of subjective necessity thence arising, which he termed habit. From the inability of reason to establish this principle as a necessary law for the acquisition of all experience, he inferred the nullity of all the attempts of reason to pass the region of the empirical.

This procedure of subjecting the facta of reason to examination, and, if necessary, to disapproval, may be termed the censura of reason. This censura must inevitably lead us to doubts regarding all transcendent employment of principles. But this is only the second step in our inquiry. The first step in regard to the subjects of pure reason, and which marks the infancy of that faculty, is that of dogmatism. The second, which we have just mentioned, is that of scepticism, and it gives evidence that our judgement has been improved by experience. But a third step is necessary—indicative of the maturity and manhood of the judgement, which now lays a firm foundation upon universal and necessary principles. This is the period of criticism, in which we do not examine the facta of reason, but reason itself, in the whole extent of its powers, and in regard to its capability of à priori cognition; and thus we determine not merely the empirical and ever-shifting bounds of our knowledge, but its necessary and eternal limits. We demonstrate from indubitable principles, not merely our ignorance in respect to this or that subject, but in regard to all possible questions of a certain class. Thus scepticism is a resting place for reason, in which it may reflect on its dogmatical wanderings and gain some knowledge of the region in which it happens to be, that it may pursue its way with greater certainty; but it cannot be its permanent dwelling-place. It must take up its abode only in the region of complete certitude, whether this relates to the cognition of objects themselves, or to the limits which bound all our cognition.

Reason is not to be considered as an indefinitely extended plane, of the bounds of which we have only a general knowledge; it ought rather to be compared to a sphere, the radius of which may be found from the curvature of its surface—that is, the nature of à priori synthetical propositions—and, consequently, its circumference and extent. Beyond the sphere of experience there are no objects which it can cognize; nay, even questions regarding such supposititious objects relate only to the subjective principles of a complete determination of the relations which exist between the understanding-conceptions which lie within this sphere.

We are actually in possession of à priori synthetical cognitions, as is proved by the existence of the principles of the understanding, which anticipate experience. If any one cannot comprehend the possibility of these principles, he may have some reason to doubt whether they are really à priori; but he cannot on this account declare them to be impossible, and affirm the nullity of the steps which reason may have taken under their guidance. He can only say: If we perceived their origin and their authenticity, we should be able to determine the extent and limits of reason; but, till we can do this, all propositions regarding the latter are mere random assertions. In this view, the doubt respecting all dogmatical philosophy, which proceeds without the guidance of criticism, is well grounded; but we cannot therefore deny to reason the ability to construct a sound philosophy, when the way has been prepared by a thorough critical investigation. All the conceptions produced, and all the questions raised, by pure reason, do not lie in the sphere of experience, but in that of reason itself, and hence they must be solved, and shown to be either valid or inadmissible, by that faculty. We have no right to decline the solution of such problems, on the ground that the solution can be discovered only from the nature of things, and under pretence of the limitation of human faculties, for reason is the sole creator of all these ideas, and is therefore bound either to establish their validity or to expose their illusory nature.

The polemic of scepticism is properly directed against the dogmatist, who erects a system of philosophy without having examined the fundamental objective principles on which it is based, for the purpose of evidencing the futility of his designs, and thus bringing him to a knowledge of his own powers. But, in itself, scepticism does not give us any certain information in regard to the bounds of our knowledge. All unsuccessful dogmatical attempts of reason are facia, which it is always useful to submit to the censure of the sceptic. But this cannot help us to any decision regarding the expectations which reason cherishes of better success in future endeavours; the investigations of scepticism cannot, therefore, settle the dispute regarding the rights and powers of human reason.

Hume is perhaps the ablest and most ingenious of all sceptical philosophers, and his writings have, undoubtedly, exerted the most powerful influence in awakening reason to a thorough investigation into its own powers. It will, therefore, well repay our labours to consider for a little the course of reasoning which he followed and the errors into which he strayed, although setting out on the path of truth and certitude.

Hume was probably aware, although he never clearly developed the notion, that we proceed in judgements of a certain class beyond our conception of the object. I have termed this kind of judgement synthetical. As regard the manner in which I pass

306 | IMMANUEL KANT

beyond my conception by the aid of experience, no doubts can be entertained. Experience is itself a synthesis of perceptions; and it employs perceptions to increment the conception, which I obtain by means of another perception. But we feel persuaded that we are able to proceed beyond a conception, and to extend our cognition à priori. We attempt this in two ways—either, through the pure understanding, in relation to that which may become an object of experience, or, through pure reason, in relation to such properties of things, or of the existence of things, as can never be presented in any experience. This sceptical philosopher did not distinguish these two kinds of judgements, as he ought to have done, but regarded this augmentation of conceptions, and, if we may so express ourselves, the spontaneous generation of understanding and reason, independently of the impregnation of experience, as altogether impossible. The so-called à priori principles of these faculties he consequently held to be invalid and imaginary, and regarded them as nothing but subjective habits of thought originating in experience, and therefore purely empirical and contingent rules, to which we attribute a spurious necessity and universality. In support of this strange assertion, he referred us to the generally acknowledged principle of the relation between cause and effect. No faculty of the mind can conduct us from the conception of a thing to the existence of something else; and hence he believed he could infer that, without experience, we possess no source from which we can augment a conception, and no ground sufficient to justify us in framing a judgement that is to extend our cognition à priori. That the light of the sun, which shines upon a piece of wax, at the same time melts it, while it hardens clay, no power of the understanding could infer from the conceptions which we previously possessed of these substances; much less is there any à priori law that could conduct us to such a conclusion, which experience alone can certify. On the other hand, we have seen in our discussion of transcendental logic, that, although we can never proceed immediately beyond the content of the conception which is given us, we can always cognize completely à priori—in relation, however, to a third term, namely, possible experience—the law of its connection with other things. For example, if I observe that a piece of wax melts, I can cognize à priori that there must have been something (the sun's heat) preceding, which this law; although, without the aid of experience, I could not cognize à priori and in a determinate manner either the cause from the effect, or the effect from the cause. Hume was, therefore, wrong in inferring, from the contingency of the determination according to law, the contingency of the law itself; and the passing beyond the conception of a thing to possible experience (which is an à priori proceeding, constituting the objective reality of the conception), he confounded with our synthesis of objects in actual experience, which is always, of course, empirical. Thus, too, he regarded the principle of affinity, which has its seat in the understanding and indicates a necessary connection, as a mere rule of association, lying in the imitative faculty of imagination, which can present only contingent, and not objective connections.

The sceptical errors of this remarkably acute thinker arose principally from a defect, which was common to him with the dogmatists, namely, that he had never made a systematic review of all the different kinds of à priori synthesis performed by the understanding. Had he done so, he would have found, to take one example among many, that the principle of permanence was of this character, and that it, as well as the principle of causality, anticipates experience. In this way he might have been able to describe the determinate limits of the à priori operations of understanding and reason. But he merely declared the understanding to be limited, instead of showing what its limits were; he created a general mistrust in the power of our faculties, without giving us any determinate knowledge of the bounds of our necessary and unavoidable ignorance; he examined and condemned some of the principles of the understanding, without investigating all its powers with the completeness necessary to criticism. He denies, with truth, certain powers to the understanding, but he goes further, and declares it to be utterly inadequate to the à priori extension of knowledge, although he has not fully examined all the powers which reside in the faculty; and thus the fate which always overtakes scepticism meets him too. That is to say, his own declarations are doubted, for his objections were based upon facta, which are contingent, and not upon principles, which can alone demonstrate the necessary invalidity of all dogmatical assertions.

As Hume makes no distinction between the well-grounded claims of the understanding and the dialectical pretensions of reason, against which, however, his attacks are mainly directed, reason does not feel itself shut out from all attempts at the extension of à priori cognition, and hence it refuses, in spite of a few checks in this or that quarter, to relinquish such efforts. For one naturally arms oneself to resist an attack, and becomes more obstinate in the resolve to establish the claims he has advanced. But a complete review of the powers of reason, and the conviction thence arising that we are in possession of a limited field of action, while we must admit the vanity of higher claims, puts an end to all doubt and dispute, and induces reason to rest satisfied with the undisturbed possession of its limited domain.

To the uncritical dogmatist, who has not surveyed the sphere of his understanding, nor determined, in accordance with principles, the limits of possible cognition, who, consequently, is ignorant of his own powers, and believes he will discover them by the attempts he makes in the field of cognition, these attacks of scepticism are not only dangerous, but destructive. For if there is one proposition in his chain of reasoning which he cannot prove, or the fallacy in which he cannot evolve in accordance with a principle, suspicion falls on all his statements, however plausible they may appear.

And thus scepticism, the bane of dogmatical philosophy, conducts us to a sound investigation into the understanding and the reason. When we are thus far advanced, we need fear no further attacks; for the limits of our domain are clearly marked out, and we can make no claims nor become involved in any disputes regarding the region that lies beyond these limits. Thus the sceptical procedure in philosophy does not present any solution of the problems of reason, but it forms an excellent exercise for its powers, awakening its circumspection, and indicating the means whereby it may most fully establish its claims to its legitimate possessions.

SECTION III. THE DISCIPLINE OF PURE REASON IN HYPOTHESIS

This critique of reason has now taught us that all its efforts to extend the bounds of knowledge, by means of pure speculation, are utterly fruitless. So much the wider field, it may appear, lies open to hypothesis; as, where we cannot know with certainty, we are at liberty to make guesses and to form suppositions.

Imagination may be allowed, under the strict surveillance of reason, to invent suppositions; but, these must be based on something that is perfectly certain—and that is the possibility of the object. If we are well assured upon this point, it is allowable to have recourse to supposition in regard to the reality of the object; but this supposition must, unless it is utterly groundless, be connected, as its ground of explanation, with that which is really given and absolutely certain. Such a supposition is termed a hypothesis.

It is beyond our power to form the least conception à priori of the possibility of dynamical connection in phenomena; and the category of the pure understanding will not enable us to excogitate any such connection, but merely helps us to understand it, when we meet with it in experience. For this reason we cannot, in accordance with the categories, imagine or invent any object or any property of an object not given, or that may not be given in experience, and employ it in a hypothesis; otherwise, we should be basing our chain of reasoning upon mere chimerical fancies, and not upon conceptions of things. Thus, we have no right to assume the existence of new powers, not existing in nature—for example, an understanding with a non-sensuous intuition, a force of attraction without contact, or some new kind of substances occupying space, and yet without the property of impenetrability—and, consequently, we cannot assume that there is any other kind of community among substances than that observable in experience, any kind of presence than that in space, or any kind of duration than that in time. In one word, the conditions of possible experience are for reason the only conditions of the possibility of things; reason cannot venture to form, independently of these conditions, any conceptions of things, because such conceptions, although not self-contradictory, are without object and without application.

The conceptions of reason are, as we have already shown, mere ideas, and do not relate to any object in any kind of experience. At the same time, they do not indicate imaginary or possible objects. They are purely problematical in their nature and, as aids to the heuristic exercise of the faculties, form the basis of the regulative principles for the systematic employment of the understanding in the field of experience. If we leave this ground of experience, they become mere fictions of thought, the possibility of which is quite indemonstrable; and they cannot, consequently, be employed as hypotheses in the explanation of real phenomena. It is quite admissible to cogitate the soul as simple, for the purpose of enabling ourselves to employ the idea of a perfect and necessary unity of all the faculties of the mind as the principle of all our inquiries into its internal phenomena, although we cannot cognize this unity in concreto. But to assume that the soul is a simple substance (a transcendental conception) would be enouncing a proposition which is not only indemonstrable—as many physical hypotheses are—but a proposition which is purely arbitrary, and in the highest degree rash. The simple is never presented in experience; and, if by substance is here meant the permanent object of sensuous intuition, the possibility of a simple phenomenon is perfectly inconceivable. Reason affords no good grounds for admitting the existence of intelligible beings, or of intelligible properties of sensuous things, although—as we have no conception either of their possibility or of their impossibility—it will always be out of our power to affirm dogmatically that they do not exist. In the explanation of given phenomena, no other things and no other grounds of explanation can be employed than those which stand in connection with the given phenomena according to the known laws of experience. A transcendental hypothesis, in which a mere idea of reason is employed to explain the phenomena of nature, would not give us any better insight into a phenomenon, as we should be trying to explain what we do not sufficiently understand from known empirical principles, by what we do not understand at all. The principles of such a hypothesis might conduce to the satisfaction of reason, but it would not assist the understanding in its application to objects. Order and conformity to aims in the sphere of nature must be themselves explained upon natural grounds and according to natural laws; and the wildest hypotheses, if they are only physical, are here more admissible than a hyperphysical hypothesis, such as that of a divine author. For such a hypothesis would introduce the principle of ignava ratio, which requires us to give up the search for causes that might be discovered in the course of experience and to rest satisfied with a mere idea. As regards the absolute totality of the grounds of explanation in the series of these causes, this can be no hindrance to the understanding in the case of phenomena; because, as they are to us nothing more than phenomena, we have no right to look for anything like completeness in the synthesis of the series of their conditions.

Transcendental hypotheses are therefore inadmissible; and we cannot use the liberty of employing, in the absence of physical, hyperphysical grounds of explanation. And this for two reasons; first, because such hypothesis do not advance reason, but rather stop it in its progress; secondly, because this licence would render fruitless all its exertions in its own proper sphere, which is that of experience. For, when the explanation of natural phenomena happens to be difficult, we have constantly at hand a transcendental ground of explanation, which lifts us above the necessity of investigating nature; and our inquiries are brought to a close, not because we have obtained all the requisite knowledge, but because we abut upon a principle which is incomprehensible and which, indeed, is so far back in the track of thought as to contain the conception of the absolutely primal being.

The next requisite for the admissibility of a hypothesis is its sufficiency. That is, it must determine à priori the consequences which are given in experience and which are supposed to follow from the hypothesis itself. If we require to employ auxiliary hypotheses, the suspicion naturally arises that they are mere fictions; because the necessity for each of them requires the same justification as in the case of the original hypothesis, and thus their testimony is invalid. If we suppose the existence of an infinitely perfect cause, we possess sufficient grounds for the explanation of the conformity to aims, the order and the greatness which we observe in the universe; but we find ourselves obliged, when we observe the evil in the world and the exceptions to these laws, to employ new hypothesis in support of the original one. We employ the idea of the simple nature of the human soul as the foundation of all the theories we may form of its phenomena; but when we meet with difficulties in our way, when we observe in the soul phenomena similar to the changes which take place in matter, we require to call in new auxiliary hypotheses. These may, indeed, not be false, but we do not know them to be true, because the only witness to their certitude is the hypothesis which they themselves have been called in to explain.

We are not discussing the above-mentioned assertions regarding the immaterial unity of the soul and the existence of a Supreme Being as dogmata, which certain philosophers profess to demonstrate à priori, but purely as hypotheses. In the former case, the dogmatist must take care that his arguments possess the apodeictic certainty of a demonstration. For the assertion that the reality of such ideas is probable is as absurd as a proof of the probability of a proposition in geometry. Pure abstract reason, apart from all experience, can either cognize nothing at all; and hence the judgements it enounces are never mere opinions, they are either apodeictic certainties, or declarations that nothing can be known on the subject. Opinions and probable judgements on the nature of things can only be employed to explain given phenomena, or they may relate to the effect, in accordance with empirical laws, of an actually existing cause. In other words, we must restrict the sphere of opinion to the world of experience and nature. Beyond this region opinion is mere invention; unless we are groping about for the truth on a path not yet fully known, and have some hopes of stumbling upon it by chance.

But, although hypotheses are inadmissible in answers to the questions of pure speculative reason, they may be employed in the defence of these answers. That is to say, hypotheses are admissible in polemic, but not in the sphere of dogmatism. By the defence of statements of this character, I do not mean an attempt at discovering new grounds for their support, but merely the refutation of the arguments of opponents. All à priori synthetical propositions possess the peculiarity that, although the philosopher who maintains the reality of the ideas contained in the proposition is not in possession of sufficient knowledge to establish the certainty of his statements, his opponent is as little able to prove the truth of the opposite. This equality of fortune does not allow the one party to be superior to the other in the sphere of speculative cognition; and it is this sphere, accordingly, that is the proper arena of these endless speculative conflicts. But we shall afterwards show that, in relation to its practical exercise, Reason has the right of admitting what, in the field of pure speculation, she would not be justified in supposing, except upon perfectly sufficient grounds; because all such suppositions destroy the necessary completeness of speculation—a condition which the practical reason, however, does not consider to be requisite. In this sphere, therefore, Reason is mistress of a possession, her title to which she does not require to prove—which, in fact, she could not do. The burden of proof accordingly rests upon the opponent. But as he has just as little knowledge regarding the subject discussed, and is as little able to prove the non-existence of the object of an idea, as the philosopher on the other side is to demonstrate its reality, it is evident that there is an advantage on the side of the philosopher who maintains his proposition as a practically necessary supposition (melior est conditio possidentis). For he is at liberty to employ, in self-defence, the same weapons as his opponent makes use of in attacking him; that is, he has a right to use hypotheses not for the purpose of supporting the arguments in favour of his own propositions, but to show that his opponent knows no more than himself regarding the subject under discussion and cannot boast of any speculative advantage.

Hypotheses are, therefore, admissible in the sphere of pure reason only as weapons for self-defence, and not as supports to dogmatical assertions. But the opposing party we must always seek for in ourselves. For speculative reason is, in the sphere of transcendentalism, dialectical in its own nature. The difficulties and objections we have to fear lie in ourselves. They are like old but never superannuated claims; and we must seek them out, and settle them once and for ever, if we are to expect a permanent peace. External tranquility is hollow and unreal. The root of these contradictions, which lies in the nature of human reason, must be destroyed; and this can only be done by giving it, in the first instance, freedom to grow, nay, by nourishing it, that it may send out shoots, and thus betray its own existence. It is our duty, therefore, to try to discover new objections, to put weapons in the bands of our opponent, and to grant him the most

CRITIQUE OF PURE REASON | 311

favourable position in the arena that he can wish. We have nothing to fear from these concessions; on the contrary, we may rather hope that we shall thus make ourselves master of a possession which no one will ever venture to dispute.

The thinker requires, to be fully equipped, the hypotheses of pure reason, which, although but leaden weapons (for they have not been steeled in the armoury of experience), are as useful as any that can be employed by his opponents. If, accordingly, we have assumed, from a non-speculative point of view, the immaterial nature of the soul, and are met by the objection that experience seems to prove that the growth and decay of our mental faculties are mere modifications of the sensuous organism—we can weaken the force of this objection by the assumption that the body is nothing but the fundamental phenomenon, to which, as a necessary condition, all sensibility, and consequently all thought, relates in the present state of our existence; and that the separation of soul and body forms the conclusion of the sensuous exercise of our power of cognition and the beginning of the intellectual. The body would, in this view of the question, be regarded, not as the cause of thought, but merely as its restrictive condition, as promotive of the sensuous and animal, but as a hindrance to the pure and spiritual life; and the dependence of the animal life on the constitution of the body, would not prove that the whole life of man was also dependent on the state of the organism. We might go still farther, and discover new objections, or carry out to their extreme consequences those which have already been adduced.

Generation, in the human race as well as among the irrational animals, depends on so many accidents—of occasion, of proper sustenance, of the laws enacted by the government of a country of vice even, that it is difficult to believe in the eternal existence of a being whose life has begun under circumstances so mean and trivial, and so entirely dependent upon our own control. As regards the continuance of the existence of the whole race, we need have no difficulties, for accident in single cases is subject to general laws; but, in the case of each individual, it would seem as if we could hardly expect so wonderful an effect from causes so insignificant. But, in answer to these objections, we may adduce the transcendental hypothesis that all life is properly intelligible, and not subject to changes of time, and that it neither began in birth, nor will end in death. We may assume that this life is nothing more than a sensuous representation of pure spiritual life; that the whole world of sense is but an image, hovering before the faculty of cognition which we exercise in this sphere, and with no more objective reality than a dream; and that if we could intuite ourselves and other things as they really are, we should see ourselves in a world of spiritual natures, our connection with which did not begin at our birth and will not cease with the destruction of the body. And so on.

We cannot be said to know what has been above asserted, nor do we seriously maintain the truth of these assertions; and the notions therein indicated are not even ideas of reason, they are purely fictitious conceptions. But this hypothetical procedure is in perfect conformity with the laws of reason. Our opponent mistakes the absence of empirical conditions for a proof of the complete impossibility of all that we have asserted; and we have to show him that he has not exhausted the whole sphere of possibility and that he can as little compass that sphere by the laws of experience and nature, as we can lay a secure foundation for the operations of reason beyond the region of experience. Such hypothetical defences against the pretensions of an opponent must not be regarded as declarations of opinion. The philosopher abandons them, so soon as the opposite party renounces its dogmatical conceit. To maintain a simply negative position in relation to propositions which rest on an insecure foundation, well befits the moderation of a true philosopher; but to uphold the objections urged against an opponent as proofs of the opposite statement is a proceeding just as unwarrantable and arrogant as it is to attack the position of a philosopher who advances affirmative propositions regarding such a subject.

It is evident, therefore, that hypotheses, in the speculative sphere, are valid, not as independent propositions, but only relatively to opposite transcendent assumptions. For, to make the principles of possible experience conditions of the possibility of things in general is just as transcendent a procedure as to maintain the objective reality of ideas which can be applied to no objects except such as lie without the limits of possible experience. The judgements enounced by pure reason must be necessary, or they must not be enounced at all. Reason cannot trouble herself with opinions. But the hypotheses we have been discussing are merely problematical judgements, which can neither be confuted nor proved; while, therefore, they are not personal opinions, they are indispensable as answers to objections which are liable to be raised. But we must take care to confine them to this function, and guard against any assumption on their part of absolute validity, a proceeding which would involve reason in inextricable difficulties and contradictions.

SECTION IV. THE DISCIPLINE OF PURE REASON IN RELATION TO PROOFS

It is a peculiarity, which distinguishes the proofs of transcendental synthetical propositions from those of all other à priori synthetical cognitions, that reason, in the case of the former, does not apply its conceptions directly to an object, but is first obliged to prove, à priori, the objective validity of these conceptions and the possibility of their syntheses. This is not merely a prudential rule, it is essential to the very possibility of the proof of a transcendental proposition. If I am required to pass, à priori, beyond the conception of an object, I find that it is utterly impossible without the guidance of something which is not contained in the conception. In mathematics, it is à priori intuition that guides my synthesis; and, in this case, all our conclusions may be drawn immediately from pure intuition. In transcendental cognition, so long as we are dealing only with conceptions of the understanding, we are guided by possible experience. That is to say, a proof in the sphere of transcendental cognition does not show that the given conception (that of an event, for example) leads directly to another conception (that of a cause)—for this would be a saltus which nothing can justify; but it shows that experience itself, and consequently the object of experience, is impossible without the connection indicated by these conceptions. It follows that such a proof must demonstrate the possibility of arriving, synthetically and à priori, at a certain knowledge of things, which was not contained in our conceptions of these things. Unless we pay particular attention to this requirement, our proofs, instead of pursuing the straight path indicated by reason, follow the tortuous road of mere subjective association. The illusory conviction, which rests upon subjective causes of association, and which is considered as resulting from the perception of a real and objective natural affinity, is always open to doubt and suspicion. For this reason, all the attempts which have been made to prove the principle of sufficient reason, have, according to the universal admission of philosophers, been quite unsuccessful; and, before the appearance of transcendental criticism, it was considered better, as this principle could not be abandoned, to appeal boldly to the common sense of mankind (a proceeding which always proves that the problem, which reason ought to solve, is one in which philosophers find great difficulties), rather than attempt to discover new dogmatical proofs.

But, if the proposition to be proved is a proposition of pure reason, and if I aim at passing beyond my empirical conceptions by the aid of mere ideas, it is necessary that the proof should first show that such a step in synthesis is possible (which it is not), before it proceeds to prove the truth of the proposition itself. The so-called proof of the simple nature of the soul from the unity of apperception, is a very plausible one. But it contains no answer to the objection, that, as the notion of absolute simplicity is not a conception which is directly applicable to a perception, but is an idea which must be inferred—if at all—from observation, it is by no means evident how the mere fact of consciousness, which is contained in all thought, although in so far a simple representation, can conduct me to the consciousness and cognition of a thing which is purely a thinking substance. When I represent to my mind the power of my body as in motion, my body in this thought is so far absolute unity, and my representation of it is a simple one; and hence I can indicate this representation by the motion of a point, because I have made abstraction of the size or volume of the body. But I cannot hence infer that, given merely the moving power of a body, the body may be cogitated as simple substance, merely because the representation in my mind takes no account of its content in space, and is consequently simple. The simple, in abstraction, is very different from the objectively simple; and hence the Ego, which is simple in the first sense, may, in the second sense, as indicating the soul itself, be a very complex conception, with a very various content. Thus it is evident that in all such arguments there lurks a paralogism. We guess (for without some such surmise our suspicion would not be excited in reference to a proof of this character) at the presence of the paralogism, by keeping ever before us a criterion of the possibility of those synthetical propositions which aim at proving more than experience can teach us. This criterion is obtained from the observation that such proofs do not lead us directly from the subject of the proposition to be proved to the required predicate, but find it necessary to presuppose the possibility of extending our cognition à priori by means of ideas. We must, accordingly, always use the greatest caution; we require, before attempting any proof, to consider how it is possible to extend the sphere of cognition by the operations of pure reason, and from what source we are to derive knowledge, which is not obtained from the analysis of conceptions, nor relates, by anticipation, to possible experience. We shall thus spare ourselves much severe and fruitless labour, by not expecting from reason what is beyond its power, or rather by subjecting it to discipline, and teaching it to moderate its vehement desires for the extension of the sphere of cognition.

The first rule for our guidance is, therefore, not to attempt a transcendental proof, before we have considered from what source we are to derive the principles upon which the proof is to be based, and what right we have to expect that our conclusions from these principles will be veracious. If they are principles of the understanding, it is vain to expect that we should attain by their means to ideas of pure reason; for these principles are valid only in regard to objects of possible experience. If they are principles of pure reason, our labour is alike in vain. For the principles of reason, if employed as objective, are without exception dialectical and possess no validity or truth, except as regulative principles of the systematic employment of reason in experience. But when such delusive proof are presented to us, it is our duty to meet them with the non liquet of a matured judgement; and, although we are unable to expose the particular sophism upon which the proof is based, we have a right to demand a deduction of the principles employed in it; and, if these principles have their origin in pure reason alone, such a deduction is absolutely impossible. And thus it is unnecessary that we should trouble ourselves with the exposure and confutation of every sophistical illusion; we may, at once, bring all dialectic, which is inexhaustible in the production of fallacies, before the bar of critical reason, which tests the principles upon which all dialectical procedure is based. The second peculiarity of transcendental proof is that a transcendental proposition cannot rest upon more than a single proof. If I am drawing conclusions, not from conceptions, but from intuition corresponding to a conception, be it pure intuition, as in mathematics, or empirical, as in natural science, the intuition which forms the basis of my inferences presents me with materials for many synthetical propositions, which I can connect in various modes, while, as it is allowable to proceed from different points in the intention, I can arrive by different paths at the same proposition.

But every transcendental proposition sets out from a conception, and posits the synthetical condition of the possibility of an object according to this conception. There must, therefore, be but one ground of proof, because it is the conception alone which determines the object; and thus the proof cannot contain anything more than the determination of the object according to the conception. In our Transcendental Analytic, for example, we inferred the principle: Every event has a cause, from the only condition of the objective possibility of our conception of an event. This is that an event cannot be determined in time, and consequently cannot form a part of experience, unless it stands under this dynamical law. This is the only possible ground of proof; for our conception of an event possesses objective validity, that is, is a true conception, only because the law of causality determines an object to which it can refer. Other arguments in support of this principle have been attempted—such as that from the contingent nature of a phenomenon; but when this argument is considered, we can discover no criterion of contingency, except the fact of an event—of something happening, that is to say, the existence which is preceded by the non-existence of an object, and thus we fall back on the very thing to be proved. If the proposition: "Every thinking being is simple," is to be proved, we keep to the conception of the ego, which is simple, and to which all thought has a relation. The same is the case with the transcendental proof of the existence of a Deity, which is based solely upon the harmony and reciprocal fitness of the conceptions of an ens realissimum and a necessary being, and cannot be attempted in any other manner.

This caution serves to simplify very much the criticism of all propositions of reason. When reason employs conceptions alone, only one proof of its thesis is possible, if any. When, therefore, the dogmatist advances with ten arguments in favour of a proposition, we may be sure that not one of them is conclusive. For if he possessed one which proved the proposition he brings forward to demonstration—as must always be the case with the propositions of pure reason—what need is there for any more? His intention can only be similar to that of the advocate who had different arguments for different judges; this availing himself of the weakness of those who examine his arguments, who, without going into any profound investigation, adopt the view of the case which seems most probable at first sight and decide according to it.

The third rule for the guidance of pure reason in the conduct of a proof is that all transcendental proofs must never be apagogic or indirect, but always ostensive or direct. The direct or ostensive proof not only establishes the truth of the proposition to be proved, but exposes the grounds of its truth; the apagogic, on the other hand, may assure us of the truth of the proposition, but it cannot enable us to comprehend the grounds of its possibility. The latter is, accordingly, rather an auxiliary to an argument, than a strictly philosophical and rational mode of procedure. In one respect, however, they have an advantage over direct proofs, from the fact that the mode of arguing by contradiction, which they employ, renders our understanding of the question more clear, and approximates the proof to the certainty of an intuitional demonstration.

The true reason why indirect proofs are employed in different sciences is this. When the grounds upon which we seek to base a cognition are too various or too profound, we try whether or not we may not discover the truth of our cognition from its consequences. The modus ponens of reasoning from the truth of its inferences to the truth of a proposition would be admissible if all the inferences that can be drawn from it are known to be true; for in this case there can be only one possible ground for these inferences, and that is the true one. But this is a quite impracticable procedure, as it surpasses all our powers to discover all the possible inferences that can be drawn from a proposition. But this mode of reasoning is employed, under favour, when we wish to prove the truth of an hypothesis; in which case we admit the truth of the conclusion—which is supported by analogy—that, if all the inferences we have drawn and examined agree with the proposition assumed, all other possible inferences will also agree with it. But, in this way, an hypothesis can never be established as a demonstrated truth. The modus tollens of reasoning from known inferences to the unknown proposition, is not only a rigorous, but a very easy mode of proof. For, if it can be shown that but one inference from a proposition is false, then the proposition must itself be false. Instead, then, of examining, in an ostensive argument, the whole series of the grounds on which the truth of a proposition rests, we need only take the opposite of this proposition, and if one inference from it be false, then must the opposite be itself false; and, consequently, the proposition which we wished to prove must be true.

The apagogic method of proof is admissible only in those sciences where it is impossible to mistake a subjective representation for an objective cognition. Where this is possible, it is plain that the opposite of a given proposition may contradict merely the subjective conditions of thought, and not the objective cognition; or it may happen that both propositions contradict each other only under a subjective condition, which is incorrectly considered to be objective, and, as the condition is itself false, both propositions may be false, and it will, consequently, be impossible to conclude the truth of the one from the falseness of the other.

In mathematics such subreptions are impossible; and it is in this science, accordingly, that the indirect mode of proof has its true place. In the science of nature, where all assertion is based upon empirical intuition, such subreptions may be guarded against by the repeated comparison of observations; but this mode of proof is of little value in this sphere of knowledge. But the transcendental efforts of pure reason are all made in the sphere of the subjective, which is the real medium of all dialectical illusion; and thus reason endeavours, in its premisses, to impose upon us subjective representations for objective cognitions. In the transcendental sphere of pure reason, then, and in the case of synthetical propositions, it is inadmissible to support a statement by disproving the counter-statement. For only two cases are possible; either, the counter-statement is nothing but the enouncement of the inconsistency of the opposite opinion with the subjective conditions of reason, which does not affect the real case (for example, we cannot comprehend the unconditioned necessity of the existence of a being, and hence every speculative proof of the existence of such a being must be opposed on subjective grounds, while the possibility of this being in itself cannot with justice be denied); or, both propositions, being dialectical in their nature, are based upon an impossible conception. In this latter case the rule applies: non entis nulla sunt predicata; that is to say, what we affirm and what we deny, respecting such an object, are equally untrue, and the apagogic mode of arriving at the truth is in this case impossible. If, for example, we presuppose that the world of sense is given in itself in its totality, it is false, either that it is infinite, or that it is finite and limited in space. Both are false, because the hypothesis is false. For the notion of phenomena (as mere representations) which are given in themselves (as objects) is self-contradictory; and the infinitude of this imaginary whole would, indeed, be unconditioned, but would be inconsistent (as everything in the phenomenal world is conditioned) with the unconditioned determination and finitude of quantities which is presupposed in our conception.

The apagogic mode of proof is the true source of those illusions which have always had so strong an attraction for the admirers of dogmatical philosophy. It may be compared to a champion who maintains the honour and claims of the party he has adopted by offering battle to all who doubt the validity of these claims and the purity of that honour; while nothing can be proved in this way, except the respective strength of the combatants, and the advantage, in this respect, is always on the side of the attacking party. Spectators, observing that each party is alternately conqueror and conquered, are led to regard the subject of dispute as beyond the power of man to decide upon. But such an opinion cannot be justified; and it is sufficient to apply to these reasoners the remark:

Non defensoribus istis
Tempus eget.

Each must try to establish his assertions by a transcendental deduction of the grounds of proof employed in his argument, and thus enable us to see in what way the claims of reason may be supported. If an opponent bases his assertions upon subjective grounds, he may be refuted with ease; not, however to the advantage of the dogmatist, who likewise depends upon subjective sources of cognition and is in like manner driven into a corner by his opponent. But, if parties employ the direct method of procedure, they will soon discover the difficulty, nay, the impossibility of proving their assertions, and will be forced to appeal to prescription and precedence; or they will, by the help of criticism, discover with ease the dogmatical illusions by which they had been mocked, and compel reason to renounce its exaggerated pretensions to speculative insight and to confine itself within the limits of its proper sphere—that of practical principles.

CHAPTER II. THE CANON OF PURE REASON

It is a humiliating consideration for human reason that it is incompetent to discover truth by means of pure speculation, but, on the contrary, stands in need of discipline to check its deviations from the straight path and to expose the illusions which it originates. But, on the other hand, this consideration ought to elevate and to give it confidence, for this discipline is exercised by itself alone, and it is subject to the censure of no other power. The bounds, moreover, which it is forced to set to its speculative exercise, form likewise a check upon the fallacious pretensions of opponents; and thus what remains of its possessions, after these exaggerated claims have been disallowed, is secure from attack or usurpation. The greatest, and perhaps the only, use of all philosophy of pure reason is, accordingly, of a purely negative character. It is not an organon for the extension, but a discipline for the determination, of the limits of its exercise; and without laying claim to the discovery of new truth, it has the modest merit of guarding against error.

At the same time, there must be some source of positive cognitions which belong to the domain of pure reason and which become the causes of error only from our mistaking their true character, while they form the goal towards which reason continually strives. How else can we account for the inextinguishable desire in the human mind to find a firm footing in some region beyond the limits of the world of experience? It hopes to attain to the possession of a knowledge in which it has the deepest interest. It enters upon the path of pure speculation; but in vain. We have some reason, however, to expect that, in the only other way that lies open to it—the path of practical reason—it may meet with better success.

I understand by a canon a list of the à priori principles of the proper employment of certain faculties of cognition. Thus general logic, in its analytical department, is a formal canon for the faculties of understanding and reason. In the same way, Transcendental Analytic was seen to be a canon of the pure understanding; for it alone is competent to enounce true à priori synthetical cognitions. But, when no proper employment of a faculty of cognition is possible, no canon can exist. But the synthetical cognition of pure speculative reason is, as has been shown, completely impossible. There cannot, therefore, exist any canon for the speculative exercise of this faculty—for its speculative exercise is entirely dialectical; and, consequently, transcendental logic, in this respect, is merely a discipline, and not a canon. If, then, there is any proper mode of employing the faculty of pure reason—in which case there must be a canon for this faculty—this canon will relate, not to the speculative, but to the practical use of reason. This canon we now proceed to investigate.

SECTION I. OF THE ULTIMATE END OF THE PURE USE OF REASON

There exists in the faculty of reason a natural desire to venture beyond the field of experience, to attempt to reach the utmost bounds of all cognition by the help of ideas alone, and not to rest satisfied until it has fulfilled its course and raised the sum of its cognitions into a self-subsistent systematic whole. Is the motive for this endeavour to be found in its speculative, or in its practical interests alone?

Setting aside, at present, the results of the labours of pure reason in its speculative exercise, I shall merely inquire regarding the problems the solution of which forms its ultimate aim, whether reached or not, and in relation to which all other aims are but partial and intermediate. These highest aims must, from the nature of reason, possess complete unity; otherwise the highest interest of humanity could not be successfully promoted.

The transcendental speculation of reason relates to three things: the freedom of the will, the immortality of the soul, and the existence of God. The speculative interest which reason has in those questions is very small; and, for its sake alone, we should not undertake the labour of transcendental investigation—a labour full of toil and ceaseless struggle. We should be loth to undertake this labour, because the discoveries we might make would not be of the smallest use in the sphere of concrete or physical investigation. We may find out that the will is free, but this knowledge only relates to the intelligible cause of our volition. As regards the phenomena or expressions of this will, that is, our actions, we are bound, in obedience to an inviolable maxim, without which reason cannot be employed in the sphere of experience, to explain these in the same way as we explain all the other phenomena of nature, that is to say, according to its unchangeable laws. We may have discovered the spirituality and immortality of the soul, but we cannot employ this knowledge to explain the phenomena of this life, nor the peculiar nature of the future, because our conception of an incorporeal nature is purely negative and does not add anything to our knowledge, and the only inferences to be drawn from it are purely fictitious. If, again, we prove the existence of a supreme intelligence, we should be able from it to make the conformity to aims existing in the arrangement of the world comprehensible; but we should not be justified in deducing from it any particular arrangement or disposition, or inferring any where it is not perceived. For it is a necessary rule of the speculative use of reason that we must not overlook natural causes, or refuse to listen to the teaching of experience, for the sake of deducing what we know and perceive from something that transcends all our knowledge. In one word, these three propositions are, for the speculative reason, always transcendent, and cannot be employed as immanent principles in relation to the objects of experience; they are, consequently, of no use to us in this sphere, being but the valueless results of the severe but unprofitable efforts of reason.

If, then, the actual cognition of these three cardinal propositions is perfectly useless, while Reason uses her utmost endeavours to induce us to admit them, it is plain that their real value and importance relate to our practical, and not to our speculative interest.

I term all that is possible through free will, practical. But if the conditions of the exercise of free volition are empirical, reason can have only a regulative, and not a constitutive, influence upon it, and is serviceable merely for the introduction of unity into its empirical laws. In the moral philosophy of prudence, for example, the sole business of reason is to bring about a union of all the ends, which are aimed at by our inclinations, into one ultimate end—that of happiness—and to show the agreement which should exist among the means of attaining that end. In this sphere, accordingly, reason cannot present to us any other than pragmatical laws of free action, for our guidance towards the aims set up by the senses, and is incompetent to give us laws which are pure and determined completely à priori. On the other hand, pure practical laws, the ends of which have been given by reason entirely à priori, and which are not empirically conditioned, but are, on the contrary, absolutely imperative in their nature, would be products of pure reason. Such are the moral laws; and these alone belong to the sphere of the practical exercise of reason, and admit of a canon.

All the powers of reason, in the sphere of what may be termed pure philosophy, are, in fact, directed to the three above-mentioned problems alone. These again have a still higher end—the answer to the question, what we ought to do, if the will is free, if there is a God and a future world. Now, as this problem relates to our in reference to the highest aim of humanity, it is evident that the ultimate intention of nature, in the constitution of our reason, has been directed to the moral alone.

We must take care, however, in turning our attention to an object which is foreign[5] to the sphere of transcendental philosophy, not to injure the unity of our system by digressions, nor, on the other hand, to fail in clearness, by saying too little on the new subject of discussion. I hope to avoid both extremes, by keeping as close as possible to the transcendental, and excluding all psychological, that is, empirical, elements.

I have to remark, in the first place, that at present I treat of the conception of freedom in the practical sense only, and set aside the corresponding transcendental conception, which cannot be employed as a ground of explanation in the phenomenal world, but is itself a problem for pure reason. A will is purely animal (arbitrium brutum) when it is determined by sensuous impulses or instincts only, that is, when it is determined in a pathological manner. A will, which can be determined independently of sensuous impulses, consequently by motives presented by reason alone, is called a free will (arbitrium liberum); and everything which is connected with this free will, either as principle or consequence, is termed practical. The existence of practical freedom can be proved from experience alone. For the human will is not determined by that alone which immediately affects the senses; on the contrary, we have the power, by calling up the notion of what is useful or hurtful in a more distant relation, of overcoming the immediate impressions on our sensuous faculty of desire. But these considerations of what is desirable in relation to our whole state, that is, is in the end good and useful, are based entirely upon reason. This faculty, accordingly, enounces laws, which are imperative or objective laws of freedom and which tell us what ought to take place, thus distinguishing themselves from the laws of nature, which relate to that which does take place. The laws of freedom or of free will are hence termed practical laws.

Whether reason is not itself, in the actual delivery of these laws, determined in its turn by other influences, and whether the action which, in relation to sensuous impulses, we call free, may not, in relation to higher and more remote operative causes, really form a part of nature—these are questions which do not here concern us. They are purely speculative questions; and all we have to do, in the practical sphere, is to inquire into the rule of conduct which reason has to present. Experience demonstrates to us the existence of practical freedom as one of the causes which exist in nature, that is, it shows the causal power of reason in the determination of the will. The idea of transcendental freedom, on the contrary, requires that reason—in relation to its causal power of commencing a series of phenomena—should be independent of all sensuous determining causes; and thus it seems to be in opposition to the law of nature and to all possible experience. It therefore remains a problem for the human mind. But this problem does not concern reason in its practical use; and we have, therefore, in a canon of pure reason, to do with only two questions, which relate to the practical interest of pure reason: Is there a God? and, Is there a future life? The question of transcendental freedom is purely speculative, and we may therefore set it entirely aside when we come to treat of practical reason. Besides, we have already discussed this subject in the antinomy of pure reason.

SECTION II. OF THE IDEAL OF THE SUMMUM BONUM AS A DETERMINING GROUND OF THE ULTIMATE END OF PURE REASON

Reason conducted us, in its speculative use, through the field of experience and, as it can never find complete satisfaction in that sphere, from thence to speculative ideas—which, however, in the end brought us back again to experience, and thus fulfilled the purpose of reason, in a manner which, though useful, was not at all in accordance with our expectations. It now remains for us to consider whether pure reason can be employed in a practical sphere, and whether it will here conduct us to those ideas which attain the highest ends of pure reason, as we have just stated them. We shall thus ascertain whether, from the point of view of its practical interest, reason may not be able to supply us with that which, on the speculative side, it wholly denies us.

The whole interest of reason, speculative as well as practical, is centred in the three following questions:

1. WHAT CAN I KNOW?
2. WHAT OUGHT I TO DO?
3. WHAT MAY I HOPE?

The first question is purely speculative. We have, as I flatter myself, exhausted all the replies of which it is susceptible, and have at last found the reply with which reason must content itself, and with which it ought to be content, so long as it pays no regard to the practical. But from the two great ends to the attainment of which all these efforts of pure reason were in fact directed, we remain just as far removed as if we had consulted our ease and declined the task at the outset. So far, then, as knowledge is concerned, thus much, at least, is established, that, in regard to those two problems, it lies beyond our reach.

The second question is purely practical. As such it may indeed fall within the province of pure reason, but still it is not transcendental, but moral, and consequently cannot in itself form the subject of our criticism.

The third question: If I act as I ought to do, what may I then hope?—is at once practical and theoretical. The practical forms a clue to the answer of the theoretical, and—in its highest form—speculative question. For all hoping has happiness for its object and stands in precisely the same relation to the practical and the law of morality as knowing to the theoretical cognition of things and the law of nature. The former arrives finally at the conclusion that something is (which determines the ultimate end), because something ought to take place; the latter, that something is (which operates as the highest cause), because something does take place.

Happiness is the satisfaction of all our desires; extensive, in regard to their multiplicity; intensive, in regard to their degree; and protensive, in regard to their duration. The practical law based on the motive of happiness I term a pragmatical law (or prudential rule); but that law, assuming such to exist, which has no other motive than the worthiness of being happy, I term a moral or ethical law. The first tells us what we have to do, if we wish to become possessed of happiness; the second dictates how we ought to act, in order to deserve happiness. The first is based upon empirical principles; for it is only by experience that I can learn either what inclinations exist which desire satisfaction, or what are the natural means of satisfying them. The second takes no account of our desires or the means of satisfying them, and regards only the freedom of a rational being, and the necessary conditions under which alone this freedom can harmonize with the distribution of happiness according to principles. This second law may therefore rest upon mere ideas of pure reason, and may be cognized à priori.

I assume that there are pure moral laws which determine, entirely à priori (without regard to empirical motives, that is, to happiness), the conduct of a rational being, or in other words, to use which it makes of its freedom, and that these laws are absolutely imperative (not merely hypothetically, on the supposition of other empirical ends), and therefore in all respects necessary. I am warranted in assuming this, not only by the arguments of the most enlightened moralists, but by the moral judgement of every man who will make the attempt to form a distinct conception of such a law.

Pure reason, then, contains, not indeed in its speculative, but in its practical, or, more strictly, its moral use, principles of the possibility of experience, of such actions, namely, as, in accordance with ethical precepts, might be met with in the history of man. For since reason commands that such actions should take place, it must be possible for them to take place; and hence a particular kind of systematic unity—the moral—must be possible. We have found, it is true, that the systematic unity of nature could not be established according to speculative principles of reason, because, while reason possesses a causal power in relation to freedom, it has none in relation to the whole sphere of nature; and, while moral principles of reason can produce free actions, they cannot produce natural laws. It is, then, in its practical, but especially in its moral use, that the principles of pure reason possess objective reality.

I call the world a moral world, in so far as it may be in accordance with all the ethical laws—which, by virtue of the freedom of reasonable beings, it can be, and according to the necessary laws of morality it ought to be. But this world must be conceived only as an intelligible world, inasmuch as abstraction is therein made of all conditions (ends), and even of all impediments to morality (the weakness or pravity of human nature). So far, then, it is a mere idea—though still a practical idea—which may have, and ought to have, an influence on the world of sense, so as to bring it as far as possible into conformity with itself. The idea of a moral world has, therefore, objective reality, not as referring to an object of intelligible intuition—for of such an object we can form no conception whatever—but to the world of sense—conceived, however, as an object of pure reason in its practical use—and to a corpus mysticum of rational beings in it, in so far as the liberum arbitrium of the individual is placed, under and by virtue of moral laws, in complete systematic unity both with itself and with the freedom of all others.

That is the answer to the first of the two questions of pure reason which relate to its practical interest: Do that which will render thee worthy of happiness. The second question is this: If I conduct myself so as not to be unworthy of happiness, may I hope thereby to obtain happiness? In order to arrive at the solution of this question, we must inquire whether the principles of pure reason, which prescribe à priori the law, necessarily also connect this hope with it.

I say, then, that just as the moral principles are necessary according to reason in its practical use, so it is equally necessary according to reason in its theoretical use to assume that every one has ground to hope for happiness in the measure in which he has made himself worthy of it in his conduct, and that therefore the system of morality is inseparably (though only in the idea of pure reason) connected with that of happiness.

Now in an intelligible, that is, in the moral world, in the conception of which we make abstraction of all the impediments to morality (sensuous desires), such a system of happiness, connected with and proportioned to morality, may be conceived as necessary, because freedom of volition—partly incited, and partly restrained by moral laws— would be itself the cause of general happiness; and thus rational beings, under the guidance of such principles, would be themselves the authors both of their own enduring welfare and that of others. But such a system of self-rewarding morality is only an idea, the carrying out of which depends upon the condition that every one acts as he ought; in other words, that all actions of reasonable beings be such as they would be if they sprung from a Supreme Will, comprehending in, or under, itself all particular wills. But since the moral law is binding on each individual in the use of his freedom of volition, even if others should not act in conformity with this law, neither the nature of things, nor the causality of actions and their relation to morality, determine how the consequences of these actions will be related to happiness; and the necessary connection of the hope of happiness with the unceasing endeavour to become worthy of happiness, cannot be cognized by reason, if we take nature alone for our guide. This connection can be hoped for only on the assumption that the cause of nature is a supreme reason, which governs according to moral laws.

I term the idea of an intelligence in which the morally most perfect will, united with supreme blessedness, is the cause of all happiness in the world, so far as happiness stands in strict relation to morality (as the worthiness of being happy), the ideal of the supreme Good. It is only, then, in the ideal of the supreme original good, that pure reason can find the ground of the practically necessary connection of both elements of the highest derivative good, and accordingly of an intelligible, that is, moral world. Now since we are necessitated by reason to conceive ourselves as belonging to such a world, while the senses present to us nothing but a world of phenomena, we must assume the former as a consequence of our conduct in the world of sense (since the world of sense gives us no hint of it), and therefore as future in relation to us. Thus God and a future life are two hypotheses which, according to the principles of pure reason, are inseparable from the obligation which this reason imposes upon us.

Morality per se constitutes a system. But we can form no system of happiness, except in so far as it is dispensed in strict proportion to morality. But this is only possible in the intelligible world, under a wise author and ruler. Such a ruler, together with life in such a world, which we must look upon as future, reason finds itself compelled to assume; or it must regard the moral laws as idle dreams, since the necessary consequence which this same reason connects with them must, without this hypothesis, fall to the ground. Hence also the moral laws are universally regarded as commands, which they could not be did they not connect à priori adequate consequences with their dictates, and thus carry with them promises and threats. But this, again, they could not do, did they not reside in a necessary being, as the Supreme Good, which alone can render such a teleological unity possible.

Leibnitz termed the world, when viewed in relation to the rational beings which it contains, and the moral relations in which they stand to each other, under the government of the Supreme Good, the kingdom of Grace, and distinguished it from the kingdom of Nature, in which these rational beings live, under moral laws, indeed, but expect no other consequences from their actions than such as follow according to the course of nature in the world of sense. To view ourselves, therefore, as in the kingdom of grace, in which all happiness awaits us, except in so far as we ourselves limit our participation in it by actions which render us unworthy of happiness, is a practically necessary idea of reason.

Practical laws, in so far as they are subjective grounds of actions, that is, subjective principles, are termed maxims. The judgements of moral according to in its purity and ultimate results are framed according ideas; the observance of its laws, according to maxims.

The whole course of our life must be subject to moral maxims; but this is impossible, unless with the moral law, which is a mere idea, reason connects an efficient cause which ordains to all conduct which is in conformity with the moral law an issue either in this or in another life, which is in exact conformity with our highest aims. Thus, without a God and without a world, invisible to us now, but hoped for, the glorious ideas of morality are, indeed, objects of approbation and of admiration, but cannot be the springs of purpose and action. For they do not satisfy all the aims which are natural to every rational being, and which are determined à priori by pure reason itself, and necessary.

Happiness alone is, in the view of reason, far from being the complete good. Reason does not approve of it (however much inclination may desire it), except as united with desert. On the other hand, morality alone, and with it, mere desert, is likewise far from being the complete good. To make it complete, he who conducts himself in a manner not unworthy of happiness, must be able to hope for the possession of happiness. Even reason, unbiased by private ends, or interested considerations, cannot judge otherwise, if it puts itself in the place of a being whose business it is to dispense all happiness to others. For in the practical idea both points are essentially combined, though in such a way that participation in happiness is rendered possible by the moral disposition, as its condition, and not conversely, the moral disposition by the prospect of happiness. For a disposition which should require the prospect of happiness as its necessary condition would not be moral, and hence also would not be worthy of complete happiness—a happiness which, in the view of reason, recognizes no limitation but such as arises from our own immoral conduct.

Happiness, therefore, in exact proportion with the morality of rational beings (whereby they are made worthy of happiness), constitutes alone the supreme good of a world into which we absolutely must transport ourselves according to the commands of pure but practical reason. This world is, it is true, only an intelligible world; for of such a systematic unity of ends as it requires, the world of sense gives us no hint. Its reality can be based on nothing else but the hypothesis of a supreme original good. In it independent reason, equipped with all the sufficiency of a supreme cause, founds, maintains, and fulfils the universal order of things, with the most perfect teleological harmony, however much this order may be hidden from us in the world of sense.

This moral theology has the peculiar advantage, in contrast with speculative theology, of leading inevitably to the conception of a sole, perfect, and rational First Cause, whereof speculative theology does not give us any indication on objective grounds, far less any convincing evidence. For we find neither in transcendental nor in natural theology, however far reason may lead us in these, any ground to warrant us in assuming the existence of one only Being, which stands at the head of all natural causes, and on which these are entirely dependent. On the other hand, if we take our stand on moral unity as a necessary law of the universe, and from this point of view consider what is necessary to give this law adequate efficiency and, for us, obligatory force, we must come to the conclusion that there is one only supreme will, which comprehends all these laws in itself. For how, under different wills, should we find complete unity of ends? This will must be omnipotent, that all nature and its relation to morality in the world may be subject to it; omniscient, that it may have knowledge of the most secret feelings and their moral worth; omnipresent, that it may be at hand to supply every necessity to which the highest weal of the world may give rise; eternal, that this harmony of nature and liberty may never fail; and so on.

But this systematic unity of ends in this world of intelligences—which, as mere nature, is only a world of sense, but, as a system of freedom of volition, may be termed an intelligible, that is, moral world (regnum gratiae)—leads inevitably also to the teleological unity of all things which constitute this great whole, according to universal natural laws—just as the unity of the former is according to universal and necessary moral laws—and unites the practical with the speculative reason. The world must be represented as having originated from an idea, if it is to harmonize with that use of reason without which we cannot even consider ourselves as worthy of reason—namely, the moral use, which rests entirely on the idea of the supreme good. Hence the investigation of nature receives a teleological direction, and becomes, in its widest extension, physico-theology. But this, taking its rise in moral order as a unity founded on the essence of freedom, and not accidentally instituted by external commands, establishes the teleological view of nature on grounds which must be inseparably connected with the internal possibility of things. This gives rise to a transcendental theology, which takes the ideal of the highest ontological perfection as a principle of systematic unity; and this principle connects all things according to universal and necessary natural laws, because all things have their origin in the absolute necessity of the one only Primal Being.

What use can we make of our understanding, even in respect of experience, if we do not propose ends to ourselves? But the highest ends are those of morality, and it is only pure reason that can give us the knowledge of these. Though supplied with these, and putting ourselves under their guidance, we can make no teleological use of the knowledge of nature, as regards cognition, unless nature itself has established teleological unity. For without this unity we should not even possess reason, because we should have no school for reason, and no cultivation through objects which afford the materials for its conceptions. But teleological unity is a necessary unity, and founded on the essence of the individual will itself. Hence this will, which is the condition of the application of this unity in concreto, must be so likewise. In this way the transcendental enlargement of our rational cognition would be, not the cause, but merely the effect of the practical teleology which pure reason imposes upon us.

Hence, also, we find in the history of human reason that, before the moral conceptions were sufficiently purified and determined, and before men had attained to a perception of the systematic unity of ends according to these conceptions and from necessary principles, the knowledge of nature, and even a considerable amount of intellectual culture in many other sciences, could produce only rude and vague conceptions of the Deity, sometimes even admitting of an astonishing indifference with regard to this question altogether. But the more enlarged treatment of moral ideas, which was rendered necessary by the extreme pure moral law of our religion, awakened the interest, and thereby quickened the perceptions of reason in relation to this object. In this way, and without the help either of an extended acquaintance with nature, or of a reliable transcendental insight (for these have been wanting in all ages), a conception of the Divine Being was arrived at, which we now hold to be the correct one, not because speculative reason convinces us of its correctness, but because it accords with the moral principles of reason. Thus it is to pure reason, but only in its practical use, that we must ascribe the merit of having connected with our highest interest a cognition, of which mere speculation was able only to form a conjecture, but the validity of which it was unable to establish—and of having thereby rendered it, not indeed a demonstrated dogma, but a hypothesis absolutely necessary to the essential ends of reason.

But if practical reason has reached this elevation, and has attained to the conception of a sole Primal Being as the supreme good, it must not, therefore, imagine that it has transcended the empirical conditions of its application, and risen to the immediate cognition of new objects; it must not presume to start from the conception which it has gained, and to deduce from it the moral laws themselves. For it was these very laws, the internal practical necessity of which led us to the hypothesis of an independent cause, or of a wise ruler of the universe, who should give them effect. Hence we are not entitled to regard them as accidental and derived from the mere will of the ruler, especially as we have no conception of such a will, except as formed in accordance with these laws. So far, then, as practical reason has the right to conduct us, we shall not look upon actions as binding on us, because they are the commands of God, but we shall regard them as divine commands, because we are internally bound by them. We shall study freedom under the teleological unity which accords with principles of reason; we shall look upon ourselves as acting in conformity with the divine will only in so far as we hold sacred the moral law which reason teaches us from the nature of actions themselves, and we shall believe that we can obey that will only by promoting the weal of the universe in ourselves and in others. Moral theology is, therefore, only of immanent use. It teaches us to fulfil our destiny here in the world, by placing ourselves in harmony with the general system of ends, and warns us against the fanaticism, nay, the crime of depriving reason of its legislative authority in the moral conduct of life, for the purpose of directly connecting this authority with the idea of the Supreme Being. For this would be, not an immanent, but a transcendent use of moral theology, and, like the transcendent use of mere speculation, would inevitably pervert and frustrate the ultimate ends of reason.

326 | IMMANUEL KANT

SECTION III. OF OPINION, KNOWLEDGE, AND BELIEF

The holding of a thing to be true is a phenomenon in our understanding which may rest on objective grounds, but requires, also, subjective causes in the mind of the person judging. If a judgement is valid for every rational being, then its ground is objectively sufficient, and it is termed a conviction. If, on the other hand, it has its ground in the particular character of the subject, it is termed a persuasion.

Persuasion is a mere illusion, the ground of the judgement, which lies solely in the subject, being regarded as objective. Hence a judgement of this kind has only private validity—is only valid for the individual who judges, and the holding of a thing to be true in this way cannot be communicated. But truth depends upon agreement with the object, and consequently the judgements of all understandings, if true, must be in agreement with each other (consentientia uni tertio consentiunt inter se). Conviction may, therefore, be distinguished, from an external point of view, from persuasion, by the possibility of communicating it and by showing its validity for the reason of every man; for in this case the presumption, at least, arises that the agreement of all judgements with each other, in spite of the different characters of individuals, rests upon the common ground of the agreement of each with the object, and thus the correctness of the judgement is established.

Persuasion, accordingly, cannot be subjectively distinguished from conviction, that is, so long as the subject views its judgement simply as a phenomenon of its own mind. But if we inquire whether the grounds of our judgement, which are valid for us, produce the same effect on the reason of others as on our own, we have then the means, though only subjective means, not, indeed, of producing conviction, but of detecting the merely private validity of the judgement; in other words, of discovering that there is in it the element of mere persuasion.

If we can, in addition to this, develop the subjective causes of the judgement, which we have taken for its objective grounds, and thus explain the deceptive judgement as a phenomenon in our mind, apart altogether from the objective character of the object, we can then expose the illusion and need be no longer deceived by it, although, if its subjective cause lies in our nature, we cannot hope altogether to escape its influence.

I can only maintain, that is, affirm as necessarily valid for every one, that which produces conviction. Persuasion I may keep for myself, if it is agreeable to me; but I cannot, and ought not, to attempt to impose it as binding upon others.

Holding for true, or the subjective validity of a judgement in relation to conviction (which is, at the same time, objectively valid), has the three following degrees: opinion, belief, and knowledge. Opinion is a consciously insufficient judgement, subjectively as well as objectively. Belief is subjectively sufficient, but is recognized as being objectively insufficient. Knowledge is both subjectively and objectively sufficient. Subjective sufficiency is termed conviction (for myself); objective sufficiency is termed certainty (for all). I need not dwell longer on the explanation of such simple conceptions.

I must never venture to be of opinion, without knowing something, at least, by which my judgement, in itself merely problematical, is brought into connection with the truth—which connection, although not perfect, is still something more than an arbitrary fiction. Moreover, the law of such a connection must be certain. For if, in relation to this law, I have nothing more than opinion, my judgement is but a play of the imagination, without the least relation to truth. In the judgements of pure reason, opinion has no place. For, as they do not rest on empirical grounds and as the sphere of pure reason is that of necessary truth and à priori cognition, the principle of connection in it requires universality and necessity, and consequently perfect certainty—otherwise we should have no guide to the truth at all. Hence it is absurd to have an opinion in pure mathematics; we must know, or abstain from forming a judgement altogether. The case is the same with the maxims of morality. For we must not hazard an action on the mere opinion that it is allowed, but we must know it to be so. In the transcendental sphere of reason, on the other hand, the term opinion is too weak, while the word knowledge is too strong. From the merely speculative point of view, therefore, we cannot form a judgement at all. For the subjective grounds of a judgement, such as produce belief, cannot be admitted in speculative inquiries, inasmuch as they cannot stand without empirical support and are incapable of being communicated to others in equal measure.

But it is only from the practical point of view that a theoretically insufficient judgement can be termed belief. Now the practical reference is either to skill or to morality; to the former, when the end proposed is arbitrary and accidental, to the latter, when it is absolutely necessary.

If we propose to ourselves any end whatever, the conditions of its attainment are hypothetically necessary. The necessity is subjectively, but still only comparatively, sufficient, if I am acquainted with no other conditions under which the end can be attained. On the other hand, it is sufficient, absolutely and for every one, if I know for certain that no one can be acquainted with any other conditions under which the attainment of the proposed end would be possible. In the former case my supposition—my judgement with regard to certain conditions—is a merely accidental belief; in the latter it is a necessary belief. The physician must pursue some course in the case of a patient who is in danger, but is ignorant of the nature of the disease. He observes the symptoms, and concludes, according to the best of his judgement, that it is a case of phthisis. His belief is, even in his own judgement, only contingent: another man might, perhaps come nearer the truth. Such a belief, contingent indeed, but still forming the ground of the actual use of means for the attainment of certain ends, I term Pragmatical belief.

The usual test, whether that which any one maintains is merely his persuasion, or his subjective conviction at least, that is, his firm belief, is a bet. It frequently happens that a man delivers his opinions with so much boldness and assurance, that he appears to be under no apprehension as to the possibility of his being in error. The offer of a bet startles him, and makes him pause. Sometimes it turns out that his persuasion may be valued at a ducat, but not at ten. For he does not hesitate, perhaps, to venture a ducat, but if it is proposed to stake ten, he immediately becomes aware of the possibility of his being mistaken—a possibility which has hitherto escaped his observation. If we imagine to ourselves that we have to stake the happiness of our whole life on the truth of any proposition, our judgement drops its air of triumph, we take the alarm, and discover the actual strength of our belief. Thus pragmatical belief has degrees, varying in proportion to the interests at stake.

Now, in cases where we cannot enter upon any course of action in reference to some object, and where, accordingly, our judgement is purely theoretical, we can still represent to ourselves, in thought, the possibility of a course of action, for which we suppose that we have sufficient grounds, if any means existed of ascertaining the truth of the matter. Thus we find in purely theoretical judgements an analogon of practical judgements, to which the word belief may properly be applied, and which we may term doctrinal belief. I should not hesitate to stake my all on the truth of the proposition—if there were any possibility of bringing it to the test of experience—that, at least, some one of the planets, which we see, is inhabited. Hence I say that I have not merely the opinion, but the strong belief, on the correctness of which I would stake even many of the advantages of life, that there are inhabitants in other worlds.

Now we must admit that the doctrine of the existence of God belongs to doctrinal belief. For, although in respect to the theoretical cognition of the universe I do not require to form any theory which necessarily involves this idea, as the condition of my explanation of the phenomena which the universe presents, but, on the contrary, am rather bound so to use my reason as if everything were mere nature, still teleological unity is so important a condition of the application of my reason to nature, that it is impossible for me to ignore it—especially since, in addition to these considerations, abundant examples of it are supplied by experience. But the sole condition, so far as my knowledge extends, under which this unity can be my guide in the investigation of nature, is the assumption that a supreme intelligence has ordered all things according to the wisest ends. Consequently, the hypothesis of a wise author of the universe is necessary for my guidance in the investigation of nature—is the condition under which alone I can fulfil an end which is contingent indeed, but by no means unimportant. Moreover, since the result of my attempts so frequently confirms the utility of this assumption, and since nothing decisive can be adduced against it, it follows that it would be saying far too little to term my judgement, in this case, a mere opinion, and that, even in this theoretical connection, I may assert that I firmly believe in God. Still, if we use words strictly, this must not be called a practical, but a doctrinal belief, which the theology of nature (physico-theology) must also produce in my mind. In the wisdom of a Supreme Being, and in the shortness of life, so inadequate to the development of the glorious powers of human nature, we may find equally sufficient grounds for a doctrinal belief in the future life of the human soul.

The expression of belief is, in such cases, an expression of modesty from the objective point of view, but, at the same time, of firm confidence, from the subjective. If I should venture to term this merely theoretical judgement even so much as a hypothesis which I am entitled to assume; a more complete conception, with regard to another world and to the cause of the world, might then be justly required of me than I am, in reality, able to give. For, if I assume anything, even as a mere hypothesis, I must, at least, know so much of the properties of such a being as will enable me, not to form the conception, but to imagine the existence of it. But the word belief refers only to the guidance which an idea gives me, and to its subjective influence on the conduct of my reason, which forces me to hold it fast, though I may not be in a position to give a speculative account of it.

But mere doctrinal belief is, to some extent, wanting in stability. We often quit our hold of it, in consequence of the difficulties which occur in speculation, though in the end we inevitably return to it again.

It is quite otherwise with moral belief. For in this sphere action is absolutely necessary, that is, I must act in obedience to the moral law in all points. The end is here incontrovertibly established, and there is only one condition possible, according to the best of my perception, under which this end can harmonize with all other ends, and so have practical validity—namely, the existence of a God and of a future world. I know also, to a certainty, that no one can be acquainted with any other conditions which conduct to the same unity of ends under the moral law. But since the moral precept is, at the same time, my maxim (as reason requires that it should be), I am irresistibly constrained to believe in the existence of God and in a future life; and I am sure that nothing can make me waver in this belief, since I should thereby overthrow my moral maxims, the renunciation of which would render me hateful in my own eyes.

Thus, while all the ambitious attempts of reason to penetrate beyond the limits of experience end in disappointment, there is still enough left to satisfy us in a practical point of view. No one, it is true, will be able to boast that he knows that there is a God and a future life; for, if he knows this, he is just the man whom I have long wished to find. All knowledge, regarding an object of mere reason, can be communicated; and I should thus be enabled to hope that my own knowledge would receive this wonderful extension, through the instrumentality of his instruction. No, my conviction is not logical, but moral certainty; and since it rests on subjective grounds (of the moral sentiment), I must not even say: It is morally certain that there is a God, etc., but: I am morally certain, that is, my belief in God and in another world is so interwoven with my moral nature that I am under as little apprehension of having the former torn from me as of losing the latter.

The only point in this argument that may appear open to suspicion is that this rational belief presupposes the existence of moral sentiments. If we give up this assumption, and take a man who is entirely indifferent with regard to moral laws, the question which reason proposes, becomes then merely a problem for speculation and may, indeed, be supported by strong grounds from analogy, but not by such as will compel the most obstinate scepticism to give way.[6] But in these questions no man is free from all interest. For though the want of good sentiments may place him beyond the influence of moral interests, still even in this case enough may be left to make him fear the existence of God and a future life. For he cannot pretend to any certainty of the nonexistence of God and of a future life, unless—since it could only be proved by mere reason, and therefore apodeictically—he is prepared to establish the impossibility of both, which certainly no reasonable man would undertake to do. This would be a negative belief, which could not, indeed, produce morality and good sentiments, but still could produce an analogon of these, by operating as a powerful restraint on the outbreak of evil dispositions.

But, it will be said, is this all that pure reason can effect, in opening up prospects beyond the limits of experience? Nothing more than two articles of belief? Common sense could have done as much as this, without taking the philosophers to counsel in the matter!

I shall not here eulogize philosophy for the benefits which the laborious efforts of its criticism have conferred on human reason—even granting that its merit should turn out in the end to be only negative—for on this point something more will be said in the next section. But, I ask, do you require that that knowledge which concerns all men, should transcend the common understanding, and should only be revealed to you by philosophers? The very circumstance which has called forth your censure, is the best confirmation of the correctness of our previous assertions, since it discloses, what could not have been foreseen, that Nature is not chargeable with any partial distribution of her gifts in those matters which concern all men without distinction and that, in respect to the essential ends of human nature, we cannot advance further with the help of the highest philosophy, than under the guidance which nature has vouchsafed to the meanest understanding.

CHAPTER III. THE ARCHITECTONIC OF PURE REASON

By the term architectonic I mean the art of constructing a system. Without systematic unity, our knowledge cannot become science; it will be an aggregate, and not a system. Thus architectonic is the doctrine of the scientific in cognition, and therefore necessarily forms part of our methodology.

Reason cannot permit our knowledge to remain in an unconnected and rhapsodistic state, but requires that the sum of our cognitions should constitute a system. It is thus alone that they can advance the ends of reason. By a system I mean the unity of various cognitions under one idea. This idea is the conception—given by reason—of the form of a whole, in so far as the conception determines à priori not only the limits of its content, but the place which each of its parts is to occupy. The scientific idea contains, therefore, the end and the form of the whole which is in accordance with that end. The unity of the end, to which all the parts of the system relate, and through which all have a relation to each other, communicates unity to the whole system, so that the absence of any part can be immediately detected from our knowledge of the rest; and it determines à priori the limits of the system, thus excluding all contingent or arbitrary additions. The whole is thus an organism (articulatio), and not an aggregate (coacervatio); it may grow from within (per intussusceptionem), but it cannot increase by external additions (per appositionem). It is, thus, like an animal body, the growth of which does not add any limb, but, without changing their proportions, makes each in its sphere stronger and more active.

We require, for the execution of the idea of a system, a schema, that is, a content and an arrangement of parts determined à priori by the principle which the aim of the system prescribes. A schema which is not projected in accordance with an idea, that is, from the standpoint of the highest aim of reason, but merely empirically, in accordance with accidental aims and purposes (the number of which cannot be predetermined), can give us nothing more than technical unity. But the schema which is originated from an idea (in which case reason presents us with aims à priori, and does not look for them to experience), forms the basis of architectonical unity. A science, in the proper acceptation of that term, cannot be formed technically, that is, from observation of the similarity existing between different objects, and the purely contingent use we make of our knowledge in concreto with reference to all kinds of arbitrary external aims; its constitution must be framed on architectonical principles, that is, its parts must be shown to possess an essential affinity, and be capable of being deduced from one supreme and internal aim or end, which forms the condition of the possibility of the scientific whole. The schema of a science must give à priori the plan of it (monogramma), and the division of the whole into parts, in conformity with the idea of the science; and it must also distinguish this whole from all others, according to certain understood principles.

No one will attempt to construct a science, unless he have some idea to rest on as a proper basis. But, in the elaboration of the science, he finds that the schema, nay, even the definition which he at first gave of the science, rarely corresponds with his idea; for this idea lies, like a germ, in our reason, its parts undeveloped and hid even from microscopical observation. For this reason, we ought to explain and define sciences, not according to the description which the originator gives of them, but according to the idea which we find based in reason itself, and which is suggested by the natural unity of the parts of the science already accumulated. For it will of ten be found that the originator of a science and even his latest successors remain attached to an erroneous idea, which they cannot render clear to themselves, and that they thus fail in determining the true content, the articulation or systematic unity, and the limits of their science.

It is unfortunate that, only after having occupied ourselves for a long time in the collection of materials, under the guidance of an idea which lies undeveloped in the mind, but not according to any definite plan of arrangement—nay, only after we have spent much time and labour in the technical disposition of our materials, does it become possible to view the idea of a science in a clear light, and to project, according to architectonical principles, a plan of the whole, in accordance with the aims of reason. Systems seem, like certain worms, to be formed by a kind of generatio aequivoca—by the mere confluence of conceptions, and to gain completeness only with the progress of time. But the schema or germ of all lies in reason; and thus is not only every system organized according to its own idea, but all are united into one grand system of human knowledge, of which they form members. For this reason, it is possible to frame an architectonic of all human cognition, the formation of which, at the present time, considering the immense materials collected or to be found in the ruins of old systems, would not indeed be very difficult. Our purpose at present is merely to sketch the plan of the architectonic of all cognition given by pure reason; and we begin from the point where the main root of human knowledge divides into two, one of which is reason. By reason I understand here the whole higher faculty of cognition, the rational being placed in contradistinction to the empirical.

If I make complete abstraction of the content of cognition, objectively considered, all cognition is, from a subjective point of view, either historical or rational. Historical cognition is cognitio ex datis, rational, cognitio ex principiis. Whatever may be the original source of a cognition, it is, in relation to the person who possesses it, merely historical, if he knows only what has been given him from another quarter, whether that knowledge was communicated by direct experience or by instruction. Thus the Person who has learned a system of philosophy—say the Wolfian—although he has a perfect knowledge of all the principles, definitions, and arguments in that philosophy, as well as of the divisions that have been made of the system, possesses really no more than an historical knowledge of the Wolfian system; he knows only what has been told him, his judgements are only those which he has received from his teachers. Dispute the validity of a definition, and he is completely at a loss to find another. He has formed his mind on another's; but the imitative faculty is not the productive. His knowledge has not been drawn from reason; and although, objectively considered, it is rational knowledge, subjectively, it is merely historical. He has learned this or that philosophy and is merely a plaster cast of a living man. Rational cognitions which are objective, that is, which have their source in reason, can be so termed from a subjective point of view, only when they have been drawn by the individual himself from the sources of reason, that is, from principles; and it is in this way alone that criticism, or even the rejection of what has been already learned, can spring up in the mind.

All rational cognition is, again, based either on conceptions, or on the construction of conceptions. The former is termed philosophical, the latter mathematical. I have already shown the essential difference of these two methods of cognition in the first chapter. A cognition may be objectively philosophical and subjectively historical—as is the case with the majority of scholars and those who cannot look beyond the limits of their system, and who remain in a state of pupilage all their lives. But it is remarkable that mathematical knowledge, when committed to memory, is valid, from the subjective point of view, as rational knowledge also, and that the same distinction cannot be drawn here as in the case of philosophical cognition. The reason is that the only way of arriving at this knowledge is through the essential principles of reason, and thus it is always certain and indisputable; because reason is employed in concreto—but at the same time à priori—that is, in pure and, therefore, infallible intuition; and thus all causes of illusion and error are excluded. Of all the à priori sciences of reason, therefore, mathematics alone can be learned. Philosophy—unless it be in an historical manner—cannot be learned; we can at most learn to philosophize.

Philosophy is the system of all philosophical cognition. We must use this term in an objective sense, if we understand by it the archetype of all attempts at philosophizing, and the standard by which all subjective philosophies are to be judged. In this sense, philosophy is merely the idea of a possible science, which does not exist in concreto, but to which we endeavour in various ways to approximate, until we have discovered the right path to pursue—a path overgrown by the errors and illusions of sense—and the image we have hitherto tried in vain to shape has become a perfect copy of the great prototype. Until that time, we cannot learn philosophy—it does not exist; if it does, where is it, who possesses it, and how shall we know it? We can only learn to philosophize; in other words, we can only exercise our powers of reasoning in accordance with general principles, retaining at the same time, the right of investigating the sources of these principles, of testing, and even of rejecting them.

Until then, our conception of philosophy is only a scholastic conception—a conception, that is, of a system of cognition which we are trying to elaborate into a science; all that we at present know being the systematic unity of this cognition, and consequently the logical completeness of the cognition for the desired end. But there is also a cosmical conception (conceptus cosmicus) of philosophy, which has always formed the true basis of this term, especially when philosophy was personified and presented to us in the ideal of a philosopher. In this view philosophy is the science of the relation of all cognition to the ultimate and essential aims of human reason (teleologia rationis humanae), and the philosopher is not merely an artist—who occupies himself with conceptions—but a lawgiver, legislating for human reason. In this sense of the word, it would be in the highest degree arrogant to assume the title of philosopher, and to pretend that we had reached the perfection of the prototype which lies in the idea alone.

The mathematician, the natural philosopher, and the logician—how far soever the first may have advanced in rational, and the two latter in philosophical knowledge—are merely artists, engaged in the arrangement and formation of conceptions; they cannot be termed philosophers. Above them all, there is the ideal teacher, who employs them as instruments for the advancement of the essential aims of human reason. Him alone can we call philosopher; but he nowhere exists. But the idea of his legislative power resides in the mind of every man, and it alone teaches us what kind of systematic unity philosophy demands in view of the ultimate aims of reason. This idea is, therefore, a cosmical conception.[7]

In view of the complete systematic unity of reason, there can only be one ultimate end of all the operations of the mind. To this all other aims are subordinate, and nothing more than means for its attainment. This ultimate end is the destination of man, and the philosophy which relates to it is termed moral philosophy. The superior position occupied by moral philosophy, above all other spheres for the operations of reason, sufficiently indicates the reason why the ancients always included the idea—and in an especial manner—of moralist in that of philosopher. Even at the present day, we call a man who appears to have the power of self-government, even although his knowledge may be very limited, by the name of philosopher.

The legislation of human reason, or philosophy, has two objects—nature and freedom—and thus contains not only the laws of nature, but also those of ethics, at first in two separate systems, which, finally, merge into one grand philosophical system of cognition. The philosophy of nature relates to that which is, that of ethics to that which ought to be.

But all philosophy is either cognition on the basis of pure reason, or the cognition of reason on the basis of empirical principles. The former is termed pure, the latter empirical philosophy.

The philosophy of pure reason is either propædeutic, that is, an inquiry into the powers of reason in regard to pure à priori cognition, and is termed critical philosophy; or it is, secondly, the system of pure reason—a science containing the systematic presentation of the whole body of philosophical knowledge, true as well as illusory, given by pure reason—and is called metaphysic. This name may, however, be also given to the whole system of pure philosophy, critical philosophy included, and may designate the investigation into the sources or possibility of à priori cognition, as well as the presentation of the à priori cognitions which form a system of pure philosophy—excluding, at the same time, all empirical and mathematical elements.

Metaphysic is divided into that of the speculative and that of the practical use of pure reason, and is, accordingly, either the metaphysic of nature, or the metaphysic of ethics. The former contains all the pure rational principles—based upon conceptions alone (and thus excluding mathematics)—of all theoretical cognition; the latter, the principles which determine and necessitate à priori all action. Now moral philosophy alone contains a code of laws—for the regulation of our actions—which are deduced from principles entirely à priori. Hence the metaphysic of ethics is the only pure moral philosophy, as it is not based upon anthropological or other empirical considerations. The metaphysic of speculative reason is what is commonly called metaphysic in the more limited sense. But as pure moral philosophy properly forms a part of this system of cognition, we must allow it to retain the name of metaphysic, although it is not requisite that we should insist on so terming it in our present discussion.

It is of the highest importance to separate those cognitions which differ from others both in kind and in origin, and to take great care that they are not confounded with those with which they are generally found connected. What the chemist does in the analysis of substances, what the mathematician in pure mathematics, is, in a still higher degree, the duty of the philosopher, that the value of each different kind of cognition, and the part it takes in the operations of the mind, may be clearly defined. Human reason has never wanted a metaphysic of some kind, since it attained the power of thought, or rather of reflection; but it has never been able to keep this sphere of thought and cognition pure from all admixture of foreign elements. The idea of a science of this kind is as old as speculation itself; and what mind does not speculate—either in the scholastic or in the popular fashion? At the same time, it must be admitted that even thinkers by profession have been unable clearly to explain the distinction between the two elements of our cognition—the one completely à priori, the other à posteriori; and hence the proper definition of a peculiar kind of cognition, and with it the just idea of a science which has so long and so deeply engaged the attention of the human mind, has never been established. When it was said: "Metaphysic is the science of the first principles of human cognition," this definition did not signalize a peculiarity in kind, but only a difference in degree; these first principles were thus declared to be more general than others, but no criterion of distinction from empirical principles was given. Of these some are more general, and therefore higher, than others; and—as we cannot distinguish what is completely à priori from that which is known to be à posteriori—where shall we draw the line which is to separate the higher and so-called first principles, from the lower and subordinate principles of cognition? What would be said if we were asked to be satisfied with a division of the epochs of the world into the earlier centuries and those following them? "Does the fifth, or the tenth century belong to the earlier centuries?" it would be asked. In the same way I ask: Does the conception of extension belong to metaphysics? You answer, "Yes." Well, that of body too? "Yes." And that of a fluid body? You stop, you are unprepared to admit this; for if you do, everything will belong to metaphysics. From this it is evident that the mere degree of subordination—of the particular to the general—cannot determine the limits of a science; and that, in the present case, we must expect to find a difference in the conceptions of metaphysics both in kind and in origin. The fundamental idea of metaphysics was obscured on another side by the fact that this kind of à priori cognition showed a certain similarity in character with the science of mathematics. Both have the property in common of possessing an à priori origin; but, in the one, our knowledge is based upon conceptions, in the other, on the construction of conceptions. Thus a decided dissimilarity between philosophical and mathematical cognition comes out—a dissimilarity which was always felt, but which could not be made distinct for want of an insight into the criteria of the difference. And thus it happened that, as philosophers themselves failed in the proper development of the idea of their science, the elaboration of the science could not proceed with a definite aim, or under trustworthy guidance. Thus, too, philosophers, ignorant of the path they ought to pursue and always disputing with each other regarding the discoveries which each asserted he had made, brought their science into disrepute with the rest of the world, and finally, even among themselves.

All pure à priori cognition forms, therefore, in view of the peculiar faculty which originates it, a peculiar and distinct unity; and metaphysic is the term applied to the philosophy which attempts to represent that cognition in this systematic unity. The speculative part of metaphysic, which has especially appropriated this appellation—that which we have called the metaphysic of nature—and which considers everything, as it is (not as it ought to be), by means of à priori conceptions, is divided in the following manner.

Metaphysic, in the more limited acceptation of the term, consists of two parts—transcendental philosophy and the physiology of pure reason. The former presents the system of all the conceptions and principles belonging to the understanding and the reason, and which relate to objects in general, but not to any particular given objects (Ontologia); the latter has nature for its subject-matter, that is, the sum of given objects —whether given to the senses, or, if we will, to some other kind of intuition—and is accordingly physiology, although only rationalis. But the use of the faculty of reason in this rational mode of regarding nature is either physical or hyperphysical, or, more properly speaking, immanent or transcendent. The former relates to nature, in so far as our knowledge regarding it may be applied in experience (in concreto); the latter to that connection of the objects of experience, which transcends all experience. Transcendent physiology has, again, an internal and an external connection with its object, both, however, transcending possible experience; the former is the physiology of nature as a whole, or transcendental cognition of the world, the latter of the connection of the whole of nature with a being above nature, or transcendental cognition of God.

Immanent physiology, on the contrary, considers nature as the sum of all sensuous objects, consequently, as it is presented to us—but still according to à priori conditions, for it is under these alone that nature can be presented to our minds at all. The objects of immanent physiology are of two kinds: 1. Those of the external senses, or corporeal nature; 2. The object of the internal sense, the soul, or, in accordance with our fundamental conceptions of it, thinking nature. The metaphysics of corporeal nature is called physics; but, as it must contain only the principles of an à priori cognition of nature, we must term it rational physics. The metaphysics of thinking nature is called psychology, and for the same reason is to be regarded as merely the rational cognition of the soul.

Thus the whole system of metaphysics consists of four principal parts: 1. Ontology; 2. Rational Physiology; 3. Rational cosmology; and 4. Rational theology. The second part —that of the rational doctrine of nature—may be subdivided into two, physica rationalis[8] and psychologia rationalis.

The fundamental idea of a philosophy of pure reason of necessity dictates this division; it is, therefore, architectonical—in accordance with the highest aims of reason, and not merely technical, or according to certain accidentally-observed similarities existing between the different parts of the whole science. For this reason, also, is the division immutable and of legislative authority. But the reader may observe in it a few points to which he ought to demur, and which may weaken his conviction of its truth and legitimacy.

In the first place, how can I desire an à priori cognition or metaphysic of objects, in so far as they are given à posteriori? and how is it possible to cognize the nature of things according to à priori principles, and to attain to a rational physiology? The answer is this. We take from experience nothing more than is requisite to present us with an object (in general) of the external or of the internal sense; in the former case, by the mere conception of matter (impenetrable and inanimate extension), in the latter, by the conception of a thinking being—given in the internal empirical representation, I think. As to the rest, we must not employ in our metaphysic of these objects any empirical principles (which add to the content of our conceptions by means of experience), for the purpose of forming by their help any judgements respecting these objects.

Secondly, what place shall we assign to empirical psychology, which has always been considered a part of metaphysics, and from which in our time such important philosophical results have been expected, after the hope of constructing an à priori system of knowledge had been abandoned? I answer: It must be placed by the side of empirical physics or physics proper; that is, must be regarded as forming a part of applied philosophy, the à priori principles of which are contained in pure philosophy, which is therefore connected, although it must not be confounded, with psychology. Empirical psychology must therefore be banished from the sphere of metaphysics, and is indeed excluded by the very idea of that science. In conformity, however, with scholastic usage, we must permit it to occupy a place in metaphysics—but only as an appendix to it. We adopt this course from motives of economy; as psychology is not as yet full enough to occupy our attention as an independent study, while it is, at the same time, of too great importance to be entirely excluded or placed where it has still less affinity than it has with the subject of metaphysics. It is a stranger who has been long a guest; and we make it welcome to stay, until it can take up a more suitable abode in a complete system of anthropology—the pendant to empirical physics.

The above is the general idea of metaphysics, which, as more was expected from it than could be looked for with justice, and as these pleasant expectations were unfortunately never realized, fell into general disrepute. Our Critique must have fully convinced the reader that, although metaphysics cannot form the foundation of religion, it must always be one of its most important bulwarks, and that human reason, which naturally pursues a dialectical course, cannot do without this science, which checks its tendencies towards dialectic and, by elevating reason to a scientific and clear self-knowledge, prevents the ravages which a lawless speculative reason would infallibly commit in the sphere of morals as well as in that of religion. We may be sure, therefore, whatever contempt may be thrown upon metaphysics by those who judge a science not by its own nature, but according to the accidental effects it may have produced, that it can never be completely abandoned, that we must always return to it as to a beloved one who has been for a time estranged, because the questions with which it is engaged relate to the highest aims of humanity, and reason must always labour either to attain to settled views in regard to these, or to destroy those which others have already established.

Metaphysic, therefore—that of nature, as well as that of ethics, but in an especial manner the criticism which forms the propædeutic to all the operations of reason—forms properly that department of knowledge which may be termed, in the truest sense of the word, philosophy. The path which it pursues is that of science, which, when it has once been discovered, is never lost, and never misleads. Mathematics, natural science, the common experience of men, have a high value as means, for the most part, to accidental ends—but at last also, to those which are necessary and essential to the existence of humanity. But to guide them to this high goal, they require the aid of rational cognition on the basis of pure conceptions, which, be it termed as it may, is properly nothing but metaphysics.

For the same reason, metaphysics forms likewise the completion of the culture of human reason. In this respect, it is indispensable, setting aside altogether the influence which it exerts as a science. For its subject-matter is the elements and highest maxims of reason, which form the basis of the possibility of some sciences and of the use of all. That, as a purely speculative science, it is more useful in preventing error than in the extension of knowledge, does not detract from its value; on the contrary, the supreme office of censor which it occupies assures to it the highest authority and importance. This office it administers for the purpose of securing order, harmony, and well-being to science, and of directing its noble and fruitful labours to the highest possible aim—the happiness of all mankind.

CHAPTER IV. THE HISTORY OF PURE REASON

This title is placed here merely for the purpose of designating a division of the system of pure reason of which I do not intend to treat at present. I shall content myself with casting a cursory glance, from a purely transcendental point of view—that of the nature of pure reason—on the labours of philosophers up to the present time. They have aimed at erecting an edifice of philosophy; but to my eye this edifice appears to be in a very ruinous condition.

It is very remarkable, although naturally it could not have been otherwise, that, in the infancy of philosophy, the study of the nature of God and the constitution of a future world formed the commencement, rather than the conclusion, as we should have it, of the speculative efforts of the human mind. However rude the religious conceptions generated by the remains of the old manners and customs of a less cultivated time, the intelligent classes were not thereby prevented from devoting themselves to free inquiry into the existence and nature of God; and they easily saw that there could be no surer way of pleasing the invisible ruler of the world, and of attaining to happiness in another world at least, than a good and honest course of life in this. Thus theology and morals formed the two chief motives, or rather the points of attraction in all abstract inquiries. But it was the former that especially occupied the attention of speculative reason, and which afterwards became so celebrated under the name of metaphysics.

I shall not at present indicate the periods of time at which the greatest changes in metaphysics took place, but shall merely give a hasty sketch of the different ideas which occasioned the most important revolutions in this sphere of thought. There are three different ends in relation to which these revolutions have taken place.

1. In relation to the object of the cognition of reason, philosophers may be divided into sensualists and intellectualists. Epicurus may be regarded as the head of the former, Plato of the latter. The distinction here signalized, subtle as it is, dates from the earliest times, and was long maintained. The former asserted that reality resides in sensuous objects alone, and that everything else is merely imaginary; the latter, that the senses are the parents of illusion and that truth is to be found in the understanding alone. The former did not deny to the conceptions of the understanding a certain kind of reality; but with them it was merely logical, with the others it was mystical. The former admitted intellectual conceptions, but declared that sensuous objects alone possessed real existence. The latter maintained that all real objects were intelligible, and believed that the pure understanding possessed a faculty of intuition apart from sense, which, in their opinion, served only to confuse the ideas of the understanding.

2. In relation to the origin of the pure cognitions of reason, we find one school main-

taining that they are derived entirely from experience, and another that they have their origin in reason alone. Aristotle may be regarded as the head of the empiricists, and Plato of the noologists. Locke, the follower of Aristotle in modern times, and Leibnitz of Plato (although he cannot be said to have imitated him in his mysticism), have not been able to bring this question to a settled conclusion. The procedure of Epicurus in his sensual system, in which he always restricted his conclusions to the sphere of experience, was much more consequent than that of Aristotle and Locke. The latter especially, after having derived all the conceptions and principles of the mind from experience, goes so far, in the employment of these conceptions and principles, as to maintain that we can prove the existence of God and the existence of God and the immortality of them objects lying beyond the soul—both of them of possible experience—with the same force of demonstration as any mathematical proposition.

3. In relation to method. Method is procedure according to principles. We may divide the methods at present employed in the field of inquiry into the naturalistic and the scientific. The naturalist of pure reason lays it down as his principle that common reason, without the aid of science—which he calls sound reason, or common sense—can give a more satisfactory answer to the most important questions of metaphysics than speculation is able to do. He must maintain, therefore, that we can determine the content and circumference of the moon more certainly by the naked eye, than by the aid of mathematical reasoning. But this system is mere misology reduced to principles; and, what is the most absurd thing in this doctrine, the neglect of all scientific means is paraded as a peculiar method of extending our cognition. As regards those who are naturalists because they know no better, they are certainly not to be blamed. They follow common sense, without parading their ignorance as a method which is to teach us the wonderful secret, how we are to find the truth which lies at the bottom of the well of Democritus.

Quod sapio satis est mihi, non ego curo Esse quod
Arcesilas aerumnosique Solones. PERSIUS

— SATIRAE, III. 78-79.

is their motto, under which they may lead a pleasant and praiseworthy life, without troubling themselves with science or troubling science with them.

As regards those who wish to pursue a scientific method, they have now the choice of following either the dogmatical or the sceptical, while they are bound never to desert the systematic mode of procedure. When I mention, in relation to the former, the celebrated Wolf, and as regards the latter, David Hume, I may leave, in accordance with my present intention, all others unnamed. The critical path alone is still open. If my reader has been kind and patient enough to accompany me on this hitherto untravelled route, he can now judge whether, if he and others will contribute their exertions towards making this narrow footpath a high road of thought, that which many centuries have failed to accomplish may not be executed before the close of the present—namely, to bring Reason to perfect contentment in regard to that which has always, but without permanent results, occupied her powers and engaged her ardent desire for knowledge.

1. I am well aware that, in the language of the schools, the term discipline is usually employed as synonymous with instruction. But there are so many cases in which it is necessary to distinguish the notion of the former, as a course of corrective training, from that of the latter, as the communication of knowledge, and the nature of things itself demands the appropriation of the most suitable expressions for this distinction, that it is my desire that the former terms should never be employed in any other than a negative signification.

2. In the case of the conception of cause, I do really go beyond the empirical conception of an event—but not to the intuition which presents this conception in concreto, but only to the time-conditions, which may be found in experience to correspond to the conception. My procedure is, therefore, strictly according to conceptions; I cannot in a case of this kind employ the construction of conceptions, because the conception is merely a rule for the synthesis of perceptions, which are not pure intuitions, and which, therefore, cannot be given à priori.

3. The definition must describe the conception completely that is, omit none of the marks or signs of which it composed; within its own limits, that is, it must be precise, and enumerate no more signs than belong to the conception; and on primary grounds, that is to say, the limitations of the bounds of the conception must not be deduced from other conceptions, as in this case a proof would be necessary, and the so-called definition would be incapable of taking its place at the head of all the judgements we have to form regarding an object.

4. Philosophy abounds in faulty definitions, especially such as contain some of the elements requisite to form a complete definition. If a conception could not be employed in reasoning before it had been defined, it would fare ill with all philosophical thought. But, as incompletely defined conceptions may always be employed without detriment to truth, so far as our analysis of the elements contained in them proceeds, imperfect definitions, that is, propositions which are properly not definitions, but merely approximations thereto, may be used with great advantage. In mathematics, definition belongs ad esse, in philosophy ad melius esse. It is a difficult task to construct a proper definition. Jurists are still without a complete definition of the idea of right.

5. All practical conceptions relate to objects of pleasure and pain, and consequently—in an indirect manner, at least—to objects of feeling. But as feeling is not a faculty of representation, but lies out of the sphere of our powers of cognition, the elements of our judgements, in so far as they relate to pleasure or pain, that is, the elements of our practical judgements, do not belong to transcendental philosophy, which has to do with pure à priori cognitions alone.

6. The human mind (as, I believe, every rational being must of necessity do) takes a natural interest in morality, although this interest is not undivided, and may not be practically in preponderance. If you strengthen and increase it, you will find the reason become docile, more enlightened, and more capable of uniting the speculative interest with the practical. But if you do not take care at the outset, or at least midway, to make men good, you will never force them into an honest belief.

7. By a cosmical conception, I mean one in which all men necessarily take an interest; the aim of a science must accordingly be determined according to scholastic conceptions, if it is regarded merely as a means to certain arbitrarily proposed ends.

8. It must not be supposed that I mean by this appellation what is generally called physica general is, and which is rather mathematics than a philosophy of nature. For the metaphysic of nature is completely different from mathematics, nor is it so rich in results, although it is of great importance as a critical test of the application of pure understanding—cognition to nature. For want of its guidance, even mathematicians, adopting certain common notions—which are, in fact, metaphysical—have unconsciously crowded their theories of nature with hypotheses, the fallacy of which becomes evident upon the application of the principles of this metaphysic, without detriment, however, to the employment of mathematics in this sphere of cognition.

CRITIQUE OF PRACTICAL REASON

TRANSLATED BY THOMAS KINGSMILL ABBOTT

IMMANUEL KANT

PREFACE

This work is called the Critique of Practical Reason, not of the pure practical reason, although its parallelism with the speculative critique would seem to require the latter term. The reason of this appears sufficiently from the treatise itself. Its business is to show that there is pure practical reason, and for this purpose it criticizes the entire practical faculty of reason. If it succeeds in this, it has no need to criticize the pure faculty itself in order to see whether reason in making such a claim does not presumptuously overstep itself (as is the case with the speculative reason). For if, as pure reason, it is actually practical, it proves its own reality and that of its concepts by fact, and all disputation against the possibility of its being real is futile.

With this faculty, transcendental freedom is also established; freedom, namely, in that absolute sense in which speculative reason required it in its use of the concept of causality in order to escape the antinomy into which it inevitably falls, when in the chain of cause and effect it tries to think the unconditioned. Speculative reason could only exhibit this concept (of freedom) problematically as not impossible to thought, without assuring it any objective reality, and merely lest the supposed impossibility of what it must at least allow to be thinkable should endanger its very being and plunge it into an abyss of scepticism.

Inasmuch as the reality of the concept of freedom is proved by an apodeictic law of practical reason, it is the keystone of the whole system of pure reason, even the speculative, and all other concepts (those of God and immortality) which, as being mere ideas, remain in it unsupported, now attach themselves to this concept, and by it obtain consistence and objective reality; that is to say, their possibility is proved by the fact that freedom actually exists, for this idea is revealed by the moral law.

Freedom, however, is the only one of all the ideas of the speculative reason of which we know the possibility a priori (without, however, understanding it), because it is the condition of the moral law which we know.[1] The ideas of God and immortality, however, are not conditions of the moral law, but only conditions of the necessary object of a will determined by this law; that is to say, conditions of the practical use of our pure reason. Hence, with respect to these ideas, we cannot affirm that we know and understand, I will not say the actuality, but even the possibility of them. However they are the conditions of the application of the morally determined will to its object, which is given to it a priori, viz., the summum bonum. Consequently in this practical point of view their possibility must be assumed, although we cannot theoretically know and understand it. To justify this assumption it is sufficient, in a practical point of view, that they contain no intrinsic impossibility (contradiction). Here we have what, as far as speculative reason is concerned, is a merely subjective principle of assent, which, however, is objectively valid for a reason equally pure but practical, and this principle, by means of the concept of freedom, assures objective reality and authority to the ideas of God and immortality. Nay, there is a subjective necessity (a need of pure reason) to assume them. Nevertheless the theoretical knowledge of reason is not hereby enlarged, but only the possibility is given, which heretofore was merely a problem and now becomes assertion, and thus the practical use of reason is connected with the elements of theoretical reason. And this need is not a merely hypothetical one for the arbitrary purposes of speculation, that we must assume something if we wish in speculation to carry reason to its utmost limits, but it is a need which has the force of law to assume something without which that cannot be which we must inevitably set before us as the aim of our action.

It would certainly be more satisfactory to our speculative reason if it could solve these problems for itself without this circuit and preserve the solution for practical use as a thing to be referred to, but in fact our faculty of speculation is not so well provided. Those who boast of such high knowledge ought not to keep it back, but to exhibit it publicly that it may be tested and appreciated. They want to prove: very good, let them prove; and the critical philosophy lays its arms at their feet as the victors. Quid statis? Nolint. Atqui licet esse beatis. As they then do not in fact choose to do so, probably because they cannot, we must take up these arms again in order to seek in the mortal use of reason, and to base on this, the notions of God, freedom, and immortality, the possibility of which speculation cannot adequately prove.

Here first is explained the enigma of the critical philosophy, viz.: how we deny objective reality to the supersensible use of the categories in speculation and yet admit this reality with respect to the objects of pure practical reason. This must at first seem inconsistent as long as this practical use is only nominally known. But when, by a thorough analysis of it, one becomes aware that the reality spoken of does not imply any theoretical determination of the categories and extension of our knowledge to the supersensible; but that what is meant is that in this respect an object belongs to them, because either they are contained in the necessary determination of the will a priori, or are inseparably connected with its object; then this inconsistency disappears, because the use we make of these concepts is different from what speculative reason requires. On the other hand, there now appears an unexpected and very satisfactory proof of the consistency of the speculative critical philosophy. For whereas it insisted that the objects of experience as such, including our own subject, have only the value of phenomena, while at the same time things in themselves must be supposed as their basis, so that not everything supersensible was to be regarded as a fiction and its concept as empty; so now practical reason itself, without any concert with the speculative, assures reality to a supersensible object of the category of causality, viz., freedom, although (as becomes a practical concept) only for practical use; and this establishes on the evidence of a fact that which in the former case could only be conceived. By this the strange but certain doctrine of the speculative critical philosophy, that the thinking subject is to itself in internal intuition only a phenomenon, obtains in the critical examination of the practical reason its full confirmation, and that so thoroughly that we should be compelled to adopt this doctrine, even if the former had never proved it at all.[2]

By this also I can understand why the most considerable objections which I have as yet met with against the Critique turn about these two points, namely, on the one side, the objective reality of the categories as applied to noumena, which is in the theoretical department of knowledge denied, in the practical affirmed; and on the other side, the paradoxical demand to regard oneself qua subject of freedom as a noumenon, and at the same time from the point of view of physical nature as a phenomenon in one's own empirical consciousness; for as long as one has formed no definite notions of morality and freedom, one could not conjecture on the one side what was intended to be the noumenon, the basis of the alleged phenomenon, and on the other side it seemed doubtful whether it was at all possible to form any notion of it, seeing that we had previously assigned all the notions of the pure understanding in its theoretical use exclusively to phenomena. Nothing but a detailed criticism of the practical reason can remove all this misapprehension and set in a clear light the consistency which constitutes its greatest merit.

So much by way of justification of the proceeding by which, in this work, the notions and principles of pure speculative reason which have already undergone their special critical examination are, now and then, again subjected to examination. This would not in other cases be in accordance with the systematic process by which a science is established, since matters which have been decided ought only to be cited and not again discussed. In this case, however, it was not only allowable but necessary, because reason is here considered in transition to a different use of these concepts from what it had made of them before. Such a transition necessitates a comparison of the old and the new usage, in order to distinguish well the new path from the old one and, at the same time, to allow their connection to be observed. Accordingly considerations of this kind, including those which are once more directed to the concept of freedom in the practical use of the pure reason, must not be regarded as an interpolation serving only to fill up the gaps in the critical system of speculative reason (for this is for its own purpose complete), or like the props and buttresses which in a hastily constructed building are often added afterwards; but as true members which make the connexion of the system plain, and show us concepts, here presented as real, which there could only be presented problematically. This remark applies especially to the concept of freedom, respecting which one cannot but observe with surprise that so many boast of being able to understand it quite well and to explain its possibility, while they regard it only psychologically, whereas if they had studied it in a transcendental point of view, they must have recognized that it is not only indispensable as a problematical concept, in the complete use of speculative reason, but also quite incomprehensible; and if they afterwards came to consider its practical use, they must needs have come to the very mode of determining the principles of this, to which they are now so loth to assent. The concept of freedom is the stone of stumbling for all empiricists, but at the same time the key to the loftiest practical principles for critical moralists, who perceive by its means that they must necessarily proceed by a rational method. For this reason I beg the reader not to pass lightly over what is said of this concept at the end of the Analytic.

I must leave it to those who are acquainted with works of this kind to judge whether such a system as that of the practical reason, which is here developed from the critical examination of it, has cost much or little trouble, especially in seeking not to miss the true point of view from which the whole can be rightly sketched. It presupposes, indeed, the Fundamental Principles of the Metaphysic of Morals, but only in so far as this gives a preliminary acquaintance with the principle of duty, and assigns and justifies a definite formula thereof; in other respects it is independent.[3] It results from the nature of this practical faculty itself that the complete classification of all practical sciences cannot be added, as in the critique of the speculative reason. For it is not possible to define duties specially, as human duties, with a view to their classification, until the subject of this definition (viz., man) is known according to his actual nature, at least so far as is necessary with respect to duty; this, however, does not belong to a critical examination of the practical reason, the business of which is only to assign in a complete manner the principles of its possibility, extent, and limits, without special reference to human nature. The classification then belongs to the system of science, not to the system of criticism.

In the second part of the Analytic I have given, as I trust, a sufficient answer to the objection of a truth-loving and acute critic[4] of the Fundamental Principles of the Metaphysic of Morals- a critic always worthy of respect- the objection, namely, that the notion of good was not established before the moral principle, as he thinks it ought to have been.[5] I have also had regard to many of the objections which have reached me from men who show that they have at heart the discovery of the truth, and I shall continue to do so (for those who have only their old system before their eyes, and who have already settled what is to be approved or disapproved, do not desire any explanation which might stand in the way of their own private opinion.)

When we have to study a particular faculty of the human mind in its sources, its content, and its limits; then from the nature of human knowledge we must begin with its parts, with an accurate and complete exposition of them; complete, namely, so far as is possible in the present state of our knowledge of its elements. But there is another thing to be attended to which is of a more philosophical and architectonic character, namely, to grasp correctly the idea of the whole, and from thence to get a view of all those parts as mutually related by the aid of pure reason, and by means of their derivation from the concept of the whole. This is only possible through the most intimate acquaintance with the system; and those who find the first inquiry too troublesome, and do not think it worth their while to attain such an acquaintance, cannot reach the second stage, namely, the general view, which is a synthetical return to that which had previously been given analytically. It is no wonder then if they find inconsistencies everywhere, although the gaps which these indicate are not in the system itself, but in their own incoherent train of thought.

I have no fear, as regards this treatise, of the reproach that I wish to introduce a new language, since the sort of knowledge here in question has itself somewhat of an everyday character. Nor even in the case of the former critique could this reproach occur to anyone who had thought it through and not merely turned over the leaves. To invent new words where the language has no lack of expressions for given notions is a childish effort to distinguish oneself from the crowd, if not by new and true thoughts, yet by new patches on the old garment. If, therefore, the readers of that work know any more familiar expressions which are as suitable to the thought as those seem to me to be, or if they think they can show the futility of these thoughts themselves and hence that of the expression, they would, in the first case, very much oblige me, for I only desire to be understood: and, in the second case, they would deserve well of philosophy. But, as long as these thoughts stand, I very much doubt that suitable and yet more common expressions for them can be found.[6]

In this manner, then, the a priori principles of two faculties of the mind, the faculty of cognition and that of desire, would be found and determined as to the conditions, extent, and limits of their use, and thus a sure foundation be paid for a scientific system of philosophy, both theoretic and practical.

Nothing worse could happen to these labours than that anyone should make the unexpected discovery that there neither is, nor can be, any a priori knowledge at all. But there is no danger of this. This would be the same thing as if one sought to prove by reason that there is no reason. For we only say that we know something by reason, when we are conscious that we could have known it, even if it had not been given to us in experience; hence rational knowledge and knowledge a priori are one and the same. It is a clear contradiction to try to extract necessity from a principle of experience (ex pumice aquam), and to try by this to give a judgement true universality (without which there is no rational inference, not even inference from analogy, which is at least a presumed universality and objective necessity). To substitute subjective necessity, that is, custom, for objective, which exists only in a priori judgements, is to deny to reason the power of judging about the object, i.e., of knowing it, and what belongs to it. It implies, for example, that we must not say of something which often or always follows a certain antecedent state that we can conclude from this to that (for this would imply objective necessity and the notion of an a priori connexion), but only that we may expect similar cases (just as animals do), that is that we reject the notion of cause altogether as false and a mere delusion. As to attempting to remedy this want of objective and consequently universal validity by saying that we can see no ground for attributing any other sort of knowledge to other rational beings, if this reasoning were valid, our ignorance would do more for the enlargement of our knowledge than all our meditation. For, then, on this very ground that we have no knowledge of any other rational beings besides man, we should have a right to suppose them to be of the same nature as we know ourselves to be: that is, we should really know them. I omit to mention that universal assent does not prove the objective validity of a judgement (i.e., its validity as a cognition), and although this universal assent should accidentally happen, it could furnish no proof of agreement with the object; on the contrary, it is the objective validity which alone constitutes the basis of a necessary universal consent.

Hume would be quite satisfied with this system of universal empiricism, for, as is well known, he desired nothing more than that, instead of ascribing any objective meaning to the necessity in the concept of cause, a merely subjective one should be assumed, viz., custom, in order to deny that reason could judge about God, freedom, and immortality; and if once his principles were granted, he was certainly well able to deduce his conclusions therefrom, with all logical coherence. But even Hume did not make his empiricism so universal as to include mathematics. He holds the principles of mathematics to be analytical; and if his were correct, they would certainly be apodeictic also: but we could not infer from this that reason has the faculty of forming apodeictic judgements in philosophy also- that is to say, those which are synthetical judgements, like the judgement of causality. But if we adopt a universal empiricism, then mathematics will be included.

Now if this science is in contradiction with a reason that admits only empirical principles, as it inevitably is in the antinomy in which mathematics prove the infinite divisibility of space, which empiricism cannot admit; then the greatest possible evidence of demonstration is in manifest contradiction with the alleged conclusions from experience, and we are driven to ask, like Cheselden's blind patient, "Which deceives me, sight or touch?" (for empiricism is based on a necessity felt, rationalism on a necessity seen). And thus universal empiricism reveals itself as absolute scepticism. It is erroneous to attribute this in such an unqualified sense to Hume,[7] since he left at least one certain touchstone (which can only be found in a priori principles), although experience consists not only of feelings, but also of judgements.

However, as in this philosophical and critical age such empiricism can scarcely be serious, and it is probably put forward only as an intellectual exercise and for the purpose of putting in a clearer light, by contrast, the necessity of rational a priori principles, we can only be grateful to those who employ themselves in this otherwise uninstructive labour.

---

1. Lest any one should imagine that he finds an inconsistency here when I call freedom the condition of the moral law, and hereafter maintain in the treatise itself that the moral law is the condition under which we can first become conscious of freedom, I will merely remark that freedom is the ratio essendi of the moral law, while the moral law is the ratio cognoscendi of freedom. For had not the moral law been previously distinctly thought in our reason, we should never consider ourselves justified in assuming such a thing as freedom, although it be not contradictory. But were there no freedom it would be impossible to trace the moral law in ourselves at all.
2. The union of causality as freedom with causality as rational mechanism, the former established by the moral law, the latter by the law of nature in the same subject, namely, man, is impossible, unless we conceive him with reference to the former as a being in himself, and with reference to the latter as a phenomenon- the former in pure consciousness, the latter in empirical consciousness. Otherwise reason inevitably contradicts itself.
3. A reviewer who wanted to find some fault with this work has hit the truth better, perhaps, than he thought, when he says that no new principle of morality is set forth in it, but only a new formula. But who would think of introducing a new principle of all morality and making himself as it were the first discoverer of it, just as if all the world before him were ignorant what duty was or had been in thorough- going error? But whoever knows of what importance to a mathematician a formula is, which defines accurately what is to be done to work a problem, will not think that a formula is insignificant and useless which does the same for all duty in general.
4. See Kant's "Das mag in der Theoric ricktig seyn," etc. Werke, vol. vii, p. 182.
5. It might also have been objected to me that I have not first defined the notion of the faculty of desire, or of the feeling of Pleasure, although this reproach would be unfair, because this definition might reasonably be presupposed as given in psychology. However, the definition there given might be such as to found the determination of the faculty of desire on the feeling of pleasure (as is commonly done), and thus the supreme principle of practical philosophy would be necessarily made empirical, which, however, remains to be proved and in this critique is altogether refuted. It will, therefore, give this definition here in such a manner as it ought to be given, in order to leave this contested point open at the beginning, as it should be. LIFE is the faculty a being has of acting according to laws of the faculty of desire. The faculty of DESIRE is the being's faculty of becoming by means of its ideas the cause of the actual existence of the objects of these ideas. PLEASURE is the idea of the agreement of the object, or the action with the subjective conditions of life, i.e., with the faculty of causality of an idea in respect of the actuality of its object (or with the determination of the forces of the subject to action which produces it). I have no further need for the purposes of this critique of notions borrowed from psychology; the critique itself supplies the rest. It is easily seen that the

question whether the faculty of desire is always based on pleasure, or whether under certain conditions pleasure only follows the determination of desire, is by this definition left undecided, for it is composed only of terms belonging to the pure understanding, i.e., of categories which contain nothing empirical. Such precaution is very desirable in all philosophy and yet is often neglected; namely, not to prejudge questions by adventuring definitions before the notion has been completely analysed, which is often very late. It may be observed through the whole course of the critical philosophy (of the theoretical as well as the practical reason) that frequent opportunity offers of supplying defects in the old dogmatic method of philosophy, and of correcting errors which are not observed until we make such rational use of these notions viewing them as a whole.

6. I am more afraid in the present treatise of occasional misconception in respect of some expressions which I have chosen with the greatest care in order that the notion to which they point may not be missed. Thus, in the table of categories of the Practical reason under the title of Modality, the Permitted, and forbidden (in a practical objective point of view, possible and impossible) have almost the same meaning in common language as the next category, duty and contrary to duty. Here, however, the former means what coincides with, or contradicts, a merely possible practical precept (for example, the solution of all problems of geometry and mechanics); the latter, what is similarly related to a law actually present in the reason; and this distinction is not quite foreign even to common language, although somewhat unusual. For example, it is forbidden to an orator, as such, to forge new words or constructions; in a certain degree this is permitted to a poet; in neither case is there any question of duty. For if anyone chooses to forfeit his reputation as an orator, no one can prevent him. We have here only to do with the distinction of imperatives into problematical, assertorial, and apodeictic. Similarly in the note in which I have pared the moral ideas of practical perfection in different philosophical schools, I have distinguished the idea of wisdom from that of holiness, although I have stated that essentially and objectively they are the same. But in that place I understand by the former only that wisdom to which man (the Stoic) lays claim; therefore I take it subjectively as an attribute alleged to belong to man. (Perhaps the expression virtue, with which also the Stoic made great show, would better mark the characteristic of his school.) The expression of a postulate of pure practical reason might give most occasion to misapprehension in case the reader confounded it with the signification of the postulates in pure mathematics, which carry apodeictic certainty with them. These, however, postulate the possibility of an action, the object of which has been previously recognized a priori in theory as possible, and that with perfect certainty. But the former postulates the possibility of an object itself (God and the immortality of the soul) from apodeictic practical laws, and therefore only for the purposes of a practical reason. This certainty of the postulated possibility then is not at all theoretic, and consequently not apodeictic; that is to say, it is not a known necessity as regards the object, but a necessary supposition as regards the subject, necessary for the obedience to its objective but practical laws. It is, therefore, merely a necessary hypothesis. I could find no better expression for this rational necessity, which is subjective, but yet true and unconditional.

7. Names that designate the followers of a sect have always been accompanied with much injustice; just as if one said, "N is an Idealist." For although he not only admits, but even insists, that our ideas of external things have actual objects of external things corresponding to them, yet he holds that the form of the intuition does not depend on them but on the human mind.

INTRODUCTION

OF THE IDEA OF A CRITIQUE OF PRACTICAL REASON.

THE THEORETICAL USE of reason was concerned with objects of the cognitive faculty only, and a critical examination of it with reference to this use applied properly only to the pure faculty of cognition; because this raised the suspicion, which was afterwards confirmed, that it might easily pass beyond its limits, and be lost among unattainable objects, or even contradictory notions. It is quite different with the practical use of reason. In this, reason is concerned with the grounds of determination of the will, which is a faculty either to produce objects corresponding to ideas, or to determine ourselves to the effecting of such objects (whether the physical power is sufficient or not); that is, to determine our causality. For here, reason can at least attain so far as to determine the will, and has always objective reality in so far as it is the volition only that is in question. The first question here then is whether pure reason of itself alone suffices to determine the will, or whether it can be a ground of determination only as dependent on empirical conditions. Now, here there comes in a notion of causality justified by the critique of the pure reason, although not capable of being presented empirically, viz., that of freedom; and if we can now discover means of proving that this property does in fact belong to the human will (and so to the will of all rational beings), then it will not only be shown that pure reason can be practical, but that it alone, and not reason empirically limited, is indubitably practical; consequently, we shall have to make a critical examination, not of pure practical reason, but only of practical reason generally. For when once pure reason is shown to exist, it needs no critical examination. For reason itself contains the standard for the critical examination of every use of it. The critique, then, of practical reason generally is bound to prevent the empirically conditioned reason from claiming exclusively to furnish the ground of determination of the will. If it is proved that there is a [practical] reason, its employment is alone immanent; the empirically conditioned use, which claims supremacy, is on the contrary transcendent and expresses itself in demands and precepts which go quite beyond its sphere. This is just the opposite of what might be said of pure reason in its speculative employment.

However, as it is still pure reason, the knowledge of which is here the foundation of its practical employment, the general outline of the classification of a critique of practical reason must be arranged in accordance with that of the speculative. We must, then, have the Elements and the Methodology of it; and in the former an Analytic as the rule of truth, and a Dialectic as the exposition and dissolution of the illusion in the judgements of practical reason. But the order in the subdivision of the Analytic will be the reverse of that in the critique of the pure speculative reason. For, in the present case, we shall commence with the principles and proceed to the concepts, and only then, if possible, to the senses; whereas in the case of the speculative reason we began with the senses and had to end with the principles. The reason of this lies again in this: that now we have to do with a will, and have to consider reason, not in its relation to objects, but to this will and its causality. We must, then, begin with the principles of a causality not empirically conditioned, after which the attempt can be made to establish our notions of the determining grounds of such a will, of their application to objects, and finally to the subject and its sense faculty. We necessarily begin with the law of causality from freedom, that is, with a pure practical principle, and this determines the objects to which alone it can be applied.

FIRST PART — ELEMENTS OF PURE PRACTICAL REASON.

BOOK I. THE ANALYTIC OF PURE PRACTICAL REASON.

CHAPTER I. OF THE PRINCIPLES OF PURE PRACTICAL REASON.

I. DEFINITION.

PRACTICAL PRINCIPLES ARE propositions which contain a general determination of the will, having under it several practical rules. They are subjective, or maxims, when the condition is regarded by the subject as valid only for his own will, but are objective, or practical laws, when the condition is recognized as objective, that is, valid for the will of every rational being.

REMARK.

Supposing that pure reason contains in itself a practical motive, that is, one adequate to determine the will, then there are practical laws; otherwise all practical principles will be mere maxims. In case the will of a rational being is pathologically affected, there may occur a conflict of the maxims with the practical laws recognized by itself. For example, one may make it his maxim to let no injury pass unrevenged, and yet he may see that this is not a practical law, but only his own maxim; that, on the contrary, regarded as being in one and the same maxim a rule for the will of every rational being, it must contradict itself. In natural philosophy the principles of what happens, (e.g., the principle of equality of action and reaction in the communication of motion) are at the same time laws of nature; for the use of reason there is theoretical and determined by the nature of the object. In practical philosophy, i.e., that which has to do only with the grounds of determination of the will, the principles which a man makes for himself are not laws by which one is inevitably bound; because reason in practical matters has to do with the subject, namely, with the faculty of desire, the special character of which may occasion variety in the rule. The practical rule is always a product of reason, because it prescribes action as a means to the effect. But in the case of a being with whom reason does not of itself determine the will, this rule is an imperative, i.e., a rule characterized by "shall," which expresses the objective necessitation of the action and signifies that, if reason completely determined the will, the action would inevitably take place according to this rule. Imperatives, therefore, are objectively valid, and are quite distinct from maxims, which are subjective principles. The former either determine the conditions of the causality of the rational being as an efficient cause, i.e., merely in reference to the effect and the means of attaining it; or they determine the will only, whether it is adequate to the effect or not. The former would be hypothetical imperatives, and contain mere precepts of skill; the latter, on the contrary, would be categorical, and would alone be practical laws. Thus maxims are principles, but not imperatives. Imperatives themselves, however, when they are conditional (i.e., do not determine the will simply as will, but only in respect to a desired effect, that is, when they are hypothetical imperatives), are practical precepts but not laws. Laws must be sufficient to determine the will as will, even before I ask whether I have power sufficient for a desired effect, or the means necessary to produce it; hence they are categorical: otherwise they are not laws at all, because the necessity is wanting, which, if it is to be practical, must be independent of conditions which are pathological and are therefore only contingently connected with the will. Tell a man, for example, that he must be industrious and thrifty in youth, in order that he may not want in old age; this is a correct and important practical precept of the will. But it is easy to see that in this case the will is directed to something else which it is presupposed that it desires; and as to this desire, we must leave it to the actor himself whether he looks forward to other resources than those of his own acquisition, or does not expect to be old, or thinks that in case of future necessity he will be able to make shift with little. Reason, from which alone can spring a rule involving necessity, does, indeed, give necessity to this precept (else it would not be an imperative), but this is a necessity dependent on subjective conditions, and cannot be supposed in the same degree in all subjects. But that reason may give laws it is necessary that it should only need to presuppose itself, because rules are objectively and universally valid only when they hold without any contingent subjective conditions, which distinguish one rational being from another. Now tell a man that he should never make a deceitful promise, this is a rule which only concerns his will, whether the purposes he may have can be attained thereby or not; it is the volition only which is to be determined a priori by that rule. If now it is found that this rule is practically right, then it is a law, because it is a categorical imperative. Thus, practical laws refer to the will only, without considering what is attained by its causality, and we may disregard this latter (as belonging to the world of sense) in order to have them quite pure.

II. THEOREM I.

All practical principles which presuppose an object (matter) of the faculty of desire as the ground of determination of the will are empirical and can furnish no practical laws.

By the matter of the faculty of desire I mean an object the realization of which is desired. Now, if the desire for this object precedes the practical rule and is the condition of our making it a principle, then I say (in the first place) this principle is in that case wholly empirical, for then what determines the choice is the idea of an object and that relation of this idea to the subject by which its faculty of desire is determined to its realization. Such a relation to the subject is called the pleasure in the realization of an object. This, then, must be presupposed as a condition of the possibility of determination of the will. But it is impossible to know a priori of any idea of an object whether it will be connected with pleasure or pain, or be indifferent. In such cases, therefore, the determining principle of the choice must be empirical and, therefore, also the practical material principle which presupposes it as a condition.

In the second place, since susceptibility to a pleasure or pain can be known only empirically and cannot hold in the same degree for all rational beings, a principle which is based on this subjective condition may serve indeed as a maxim for the subject which possesses this susceptibility, but not as a law even to him (because it is wanting in objective necessity, which must be recognized a priori); it follows, therefore, that such a principle can never furnish a practical law.

III. THEOREM II.

All material practical principles as such are of one and the same kind and come under the general principle of self-love or private happiness.

Pleasure arising from the idea of the idea of the existence of a thing, in so far as it is to determine the desire of this thing, is founded on the susceptibility of the subject, since it depends on the presence of an object; hence it belongs to sense (feeling), and not to understanding, which expresses a relation of the idea to an object according to concepts, not to the subject according to feelings. It is, then, practical only in so far as the faculty of desire is determined by the sensation of agreeableness which the subject expects from the actual existence of the object. Now, a rational being's consciousness of the pleasantness of life uninterruptedly accompanying his whole existence is happiness; and the principle which makes this the supreme ground of determination of the will is the principle of self-love. All material principles, then, which place the determining ground of the will in the pleasure or pain to be received from the existence of any object are all of the same kind, inasmuch as they all belong to the principle of self-love or private happiness.

COROLLARY.

All material practical rules place the determining principle of the will in the lower desires; and if there were no purely formal laws of the will adequate to determine it, then we could not admit any higher desire at all.

REMARK I.

It is surprising that men, otherwise acute, can think it possible to distinguish between higher and lower desires, according as the ideas which are connected with the feeling of pleasure have their origin in the senses or in the understanding; for when we inquire what are the determining grounds of desire, and place them in some expected pleasantness, it is of no consequence whence the idea of this pleasing object is derived, but only how much it pleases. Whether an idea has its seat and source in the understanding or not, if it can only determine the choice by presupposing a feeling of pleasure in the subject, it follows that its capability of determining the choice depends altogether on the nature of the inner sense, namely, that this can be agreeably affected by it. However dissimilar ideas of objects may be, though they be ideas of the understanding, or even of the reason in contrast to ideas of sense, yet the feeling of pleasure, by means of which they constitute the determining principle of the will (the expected satisfaction which impels the activity to the production of the object), is of one and the same kind, not only inasmuch as it can only be known empirically, but also inasmuch as it affects one and the same vital force which manifests itself in the faculty of desire, and in this respect can only differ in degree from every other ground of determination. Otherwise, how could we compare in respect of magnitude two principles of determination, the ideas of which depend upon different faculties, so as to prefer that which affects the faculty of desire in the highest degree. The same man may return unread an instructive book which he cannot again obtain, in order not to miss a hunt; he may depart in the midst of a fine speech, in order not to be late for dinner; he may leave a rational conversation, such as he otherwise values highly, to take his place at the gaming-table; he may even repulse a poor man whom he at other times takes pleasure in benefiting, because he has only just enough money in his pocket to pay for his admission to the theatre. If the determination of his will rests on the feeling of the agreeableness or disagreeableness that he expects from any cause, it is all the same to him by what sort of ideas he will be affected. The only thing that concerns him, in order to decide his choice, is, how great, how long continued, how easily obtained, and how often repeated, this agreeableness is. Just as to the man who wants money to spend, it is all the same whether the gold was dug out of the mountain or washed out of the sand, provided it is everywhere accepted at the same value; so the man who cares only for the enjoyment of life does not ask whether the ideas are of the understanding or the senses, but only how much and how great pleasure they will give for the longest time. It is only those that would gladly deny to pure reason the power of determining the will, without the presupposition of any feeling, who could deviate so far from their own exposition as to describe as quite heterogeneous what they have themselves previously brought under one and the same principle. Thus, for example, it is observed that we can find pleasure in the mere exercise of power, in the consciousness of our strength of mind in overcoming obstacles which are opposed to our designs, in the culture of our mental talents, etc.; and we justly call these more refined pleasures and enjoyments, because they are more in our power than others; they do not wear out, but rather increase the capacity for further enjoyment of them, and while they delight they at the same time cultivate. But to say on this account that they determine the will in a different way and not through sense, whereas the possibility of the pleasure presupposes a feeling for it implanted in us, which is the first condition of this satisfaction; this is just as when ignorant persons that like to dabble in metaphysics imagine matter so subtle, so supersubtle that they almost make themselves giddy with it, and then think that in this way they have conceived it as a spiritual and yet extended being. If with Epicurus we make virtue determine the will only by means of the pleasure it promises, we cannot afterwards blame him for holding that this pleasure is of the same kind as those of the coarsest senses. For we have no reason whatever to charge him with holding that the ideas by which this feeling is excited in us belong merely to the bodily senses. As far as can be conjectured, he sought the source of many of them in the use of the higher cognitive faculty, but this did not prevent him, and could not prevent him, from holding on the principle above stated, that the pleasure itself which those intellectual ideas give us, and by which alone they can determine the will, is just of the same kind. Consistency is the highest obligation of a philosopher, and yet the most rarely found. The ancient Greek schools give us more examples of it than we find in our syncretistic age, in which a certain shallow and dishonest system of compromise of contradictory principles is devised, because it commends itself better to a public which is content to know some-thing of everything and nothing thoroughly, so as to please every party.

The principle of private happiness, however much understanding and reason may be used in it, cannot contain any other determining principles for the will than those which belong to the lower desires; and either there are no [higher] desires at all, or pure reason must of itself alone be practical; that is, it must be able to determine the will by the mere form of the practical rule without supposing any feeling, and consequently without any idea of the pleasant or unpleasant, which is the matter of the desire, and which is always an empirical condition of the principles. Then only, when reason of itself determines the will (not as the servant of the inclination), it is really a higher desire to which that which is pathologically determined is subordinate, and is really, and even specifically, distinct from the latter, so that even the slightest admixture of the motives of the latter impairs its strength and superiority; just as in a mathematical demonstration the least empirical condition would degrade and destroy its force and value. Reason, with its practical law, determines the will immediately, not by means of an intervening feeling of pleasure or pain, not even of pleasure in the law itself, and it is only because it can, as pure reason, be practical, that it is possible for it to be legislative.

REMARK II.

To be happy is necessarily the wish of every finite rational being, and this, there-fore, is inevitably a determining principle of its faculty of desire. For we are not in possession originally of satisfaction with our whole existence- a bliss which would imply a consciousness of our own independent self-sufficiency this is a problem imposed upon us by our own finite nature, because we have wants and these wants regard the matter of our desires, that is, something that is relative to a subjective feeling of pleasure or pain, which determines what we need in order to be satisfied with our condition. But just because this material principle of determination can only be empirically known by the subject, it is impossible to regard this problem as a law; for a law being objective must contain the very same principle of determination of the will in all cases and for all rational beings. For, although the notion of happiness is in every case the foundation of practical relation of the objects to the desires, yet it is only a general name for the subjective determining principles, and determines nothing specifically; whereas this is what alone we are concerned with in this prac-tical problem, which cannot be solved at all without such specific determination. For it is every man's own special feeling of pleasure and pain that decides in what he is to place his happiness, and even in the same subject this will vary with the difference of his wants according as this feeling changes, and thus a law which is subjectively necessary (as a law of nature) is objectively a very contingent practical principle, which can and must be very different in different subjects and therefore can never furnish a law; since, in the desire for happiness it is not the form (of conformity to law) that is decisive, but simply the matter, namely, whether I am to expect pleasure in following the law, and how much. Principles of self-love may, indeed, contain universal precepts of skill (how to find means to accomplish one's purpose), but in that case they are merely theoretical principles;[1] as, for example, how he who would like to eat bread should contrive a mill; but practical precepts founded on them can never be universal, for the determining principle of the desire is based on the feeling pleasure and pain, which can never be supposed to be universally directed to the same objects.

Even supposing, however, that all finite rational beings were thoroughly agreed as to what were the objects of their feelings of pleasure and pain, and also as to the means which they must employ to attain the one and avoid the other; still, they could by no means set up the principle of self-love as a practical law, for this unanimity itself would be only contingent. The principle of determination would still be only subjectively valid and merely empirical, and would not possess the necessity which is conceived in every law, namely, an objective necessity arising from a priori grounds; unless, indeed, we hold this necessity to be not at all practical, but merely physical, viz., that our action is as inevitably determined by our inclination, as yawning when we see others yawn. It would be better to maintain that there are no practical laws at all, but only counsels for the service of our desires, than to raise merely subjective principles to the rank of practical laws, which have objective necessity, and not merely subjective, and which must be known by reason a priori, not by experience (however empirically universal this may be). Even the rules of corresponding phenomena are only called laws of nature (e.g., the mechanical laws), when we either know them really a priori, or (as in the case of chemical laws) suppose that they would be known a priori from objective grounds if our insight reached further. But in the case of merely subjective practical principles, it is expressly made a condition that they rest, not on objective, but on subjective conditions of choice, and hence that they must always be represented as mere maxims, never as practical laws. This second remark seems at first sight to be mere verbal refinement, but it defines the terms of the most important distinction which can come into consideration in practical investigations.

IV. THEOREM II.

A rational being cannot regard his maxims as practical universal laws, unless he conceives them as principles which determine the will, not by their matter, but by their form only.

By the matter of a practical principle I mean the object of the will. This object is either the determining ground of the will or it is not. In the former case the rule of the will is subjected to an empirical condition (viz., the relation of the determining idea to the feeling of pleasure and pain), consequently it can not be a practical law. Now, when we abstract from a law all matter, i.e., every object of the will (as a determining principle), nothing is left but the mere form of a universal legislation. Therefore, either a rational being cannot conceive his subjective practical principles, that is, his maxims, as being at the same time universal laws, or he must suppose that their mere form, by which they are fitted for universal legislation, is alone what makes them practical laws.

REMARK.

The commonest understanding can distinguish without instruction what form of maxim is adapted for universal legislation, and what is not. Suppose, for example, that I have made it my maxim to increase my fortune by every safe means. Now, I have a deposit in my hands, the owner of which is dead and has left no writing about it. This is just the case for my maxim. I desire then to know whether that maxim can also bold good as a universal practical law. I apply it, therefore, to the present case, and ask whether it could take the form of a law, and consequently whether I can by my maxim at the same time give such a law as this, that everyone may deny a deposit of which no one can produce a proof. I at once become aware that such a principle, viewed as a law, would annihilate itself, because the result would be that there would be no deposits. A practical law which I recognise as such must be qualified for universal legislation; this is an identical proposition and, therefore, self-evident. Now, if I say that my will is subject to a practical law, I cannot adduce my inclination (e.g., in the present case my avarice) as a principle of determination fitted to be a universal practical law; for this is so far from being fitted for a universal legislation that, if put in the form of a universal law, it would destroy itself.

It is, therefore, surprising that intelligent men could have thought of calling the desire of happiness a universal practical law on the ground that the desire is universal, and, therefore, also the maxim by which everyone makes this desire determine his will. For whereas in other cases a universal law of nature makes everything harmonious; here, on the contrary, if we attribute to the maxim the universality of a law, the extreme opposite of harmony will follow, the greatest opposition and the complete destruction of the maxim itself and its purpose. For, in that case, the will of all has not one and the same object, but everyone has his own (his private welfare), which may accidentally accord with the purposes of others which are equally selfish, but it is far from sufficing for a law; because the occasional exceptions which one is permitted to make are endless, and cannot be definitely embraced in one universal rule. In this manner, then, results a harmony like that which a certain satirical poem depicts as existing between a married couple bent on going to ruin, "O, marvellous harmony, what he wishes, she wishes also"; or like what is said of the pledge of Francis I to the Emperor Charles V, "What my brother Charles wishes that I wish also" (viz., Milan). Empirical principles of determination are not fit for any universal external legislation, but just as little for internal; for each man makes his own subject the foundation of his inclination, and in the same subject sometimes one inclination, sometimes another, has the preponderance. To discover a law which would govern them all under this condition, namely, bringing them all into harmony, is quite impossible.

V. PROBLEM I.

Supposing that the mere legislative form of maxims is alone the sufficient determining principle of a will, to find the nature of the will which can be determined by it alone.

Since the bare form of the law can only be conceived by reason, and is, therefore, not an object of the senses, and consequently does not belong to the class of phenomena, it follows that the idea of it, which determines the will, is distinct from all the principles that determine events in nature according to the law of causality, because in their case the determining principles must themselves be phenomena. Now, if no other determining principle can serve as a law for the will except that universal legislative form, such a will must be conceived as quite independent of the natural law of phenomena in their mutual relation, namely, the law of causality; such independence is called freedom in the strictest, that is, in the transcendental, sense; consequently, a will which can have its law in nothing but the mere legislative form of the maxim is a free will.

VI. PROBLEM II.

Supposing that a will is free, to find the law which alone is competent to determine it necessarily.

Since the matter of the practical law, i.e., an object of the maxim, can never be given otherwise than empirically, and the free will is independent on empirical conditions (that is, conditions belonging to the world of sense) and yet is determinable, consequently a free will must find its principle of determination in the law, and yet independently of the matter of the law. But, besides the matter of the law, nothing is contained in it except the legislative form. It is the legislative form, then, contained in the maxim, which can alone constitute a principle of determination of the [free] will.

REMARK.

Thus freedom and an unconditional practical law reciprocally imply each other. Now I do not ask here whether they are in fact distinct, or whether an unconditioned law is not rather merely the consciousness of a pure practical reason and the latter identical with the positive concept of freedom; I only ask, whence begins our knowledge of the unconditionally practical, whether it is from freedom or from the practical law? Now it cannot begin from freedom, for of this we cannot be immediately conscious, since the first concept of it is negative; nor can we infer it from experience, for experience gives us the knowledge only of the law of phenomena, and hence of the mechanism of nature, the direct opposite of freedom. It is therefore the moral law, of which we become directly conscious (as soon as we trace for ourselves maxims of the will), that first presents itself to us, and leads directly to the concept of freedom, inasmuch as reason presents it as a principle of determination not to be outweighed by any sensible conditions, nay, wholly independent of them. But how is the consciousness, of that moral law possible? We can become conscious of pure practical laws just as we are conscious of pure theoretical principles, by attending to the necessity with which reason prescribes them and to the elimination of all empirical conditions, which it directs. The concept of a pure will arises out of the former, as that of a pure understanding arises out of the latter. That this is the true subordination of our concepts, and that it is morality that first discovers to us the notion of freedom, hence that it is practical reason which, with this concept, first proposes to speculative reason the most insoluble problem, thereby placing it in the greatest perplexity, is evident from the following consideration:

Since nothing in phenomena can be explained by the concept of freedom, but the mechanism of nature must constitute the only clue; moreover, when pure reason tries to ascend in the series of causes to the unconditioned, it falls into an antinomy which is entangled in incomprehensibilities on the one side as much as the other; whilst the latter (namely, mechanism) is at least useful in the explanation of phenomena, therefore no one would ever have been so rash as to introduce freedom into science, had not the moral law, and with it practical reason, come in and forced this notion upon us. Experience, however, confirms this order of notions. Suppose some one asserts of his lustful appetite that, when the desired object and the opportunity are present, it is quite irresistible. [Ask him]- if a gallows were erected before the house where he finds this opportunity, in order that he should be hanged thereon immediately after the gratification of his lust, whether he could not then control his passion; we need not be long in doubt what he would reply. Ask him, however- if his sovereign ordered him, on pain of the same immediate execution, to bear false witness against an honourable man, whom the prince might wish to destroy under a plausible pretext, would he consider it possible in that case to overcome his love of life, however great it may be. He would perhaps not venture to affirm whether he would do so or not, but he must unhesitatingly admit that it is possible to do so. He judges, therefore, that he can do a certain thing because he is conscious that he ought, and he recognizes that he is free- a fact which but for the moral law he would never have known.

VII. FUNDAMENTAL LAW OF THE PURE PRACTICAL REASON

Act so that the maxim of thy will can always at the same time hold good as a principle of universal legislation.

REMARK.

Pure geometry has postulates which are practical propositions, but contain nothing further than the assumption that we can do something if it is required that we should do it, and these are the only geometrical propositions that concern actual existence. They are, then, practical rules under a problematical condition of the will; but here the rule says: We absolutely must proceed in a certain manner. The practical rule is, therefore, unconditional, and hence it is conceived a priori as a categorically practical proposition by which the will is objectively determined absolutely and immediately (by the practical rule itself, which thus is in this case a law); for pure reason practical of itself is here directly legislative. The will is thought as independent on empirical conditions, and, therefore, as pure will determined by the mere form of the law, and this principle of determination is regarded as the supreme condition of all maxims. The thing is strange enough, and has no parallel in all the rest of our practical knowledge. For the a priori thought of a possible universal legislation which is therefore merely problematical, is unconditionally commanded as a law without borrowing anything from experience or from any external will. This, however, is not a precept to do something by which some desired effect can be attained (for then the will would depend on physical conditions), but a rule that determines the will a priori only so far as regards the forms of its maxims; and thus it is at least not impossible to conceive that a law, which only applies to the subjective form of principles, yet serves as a principle of determination by means of the objective form of law in general. We may call the consciousness of this fundamental law a fact of reason, because we cannot reason it out from antecedent data of reason, e.g., the consciousness of freedom (for this is not antecedently given), but it forces itself on us as a synthetic a priori proposition, which is not based on any intuition, either pure or empirical. It would, indeed, be analytical if the freedom of the will were presupposed, but to presuppose freedom as a positive concept would require an intellectual intuition, which cannot here be assumed; however, when we regard this law as given, it must be observed, in order not to fall into any misconception, that it is not an empirical fact, but the sole fact of the pure reason, which thereby announces itself as originally legislative (sic volo, sic jubeo).

COROLLARY.

Pure reason is practical of itself alone and gives (to man) a universal law which we call the moral law.

REMARK.

The fact just mentioned is undeniable. It is only necessary to analyse the judgement that men pass on the lawfulness of their actions, in order to find that, whatever inclination may say to the contrary, reason, incorruptible and self-constrained, always confronts the maxim of the will in any action with the pure will, that is, with itself, considering itself as a priori practical. Now this principle of morality, just on account of the universality of the legislation which makes it the formal supreme determining principle of the will, without regard to any subjective differences, is declared by the reason to be a law for all rational beings, in so far as they have a will, that is, a power to determine their causality by the conception of rules; and, therefore, so far as they are capable of acting according to principles, and consequently also according to practical a priori principles (for these alone have the necessity that reason requires in a principle). It is, therefore, not limited to men only, but applies to all finite beings that possess reason and will; nay, it even includes the Infinite Being as the supreme intelligence. In the former case, however, the law has the form of an imperative, because in them, as rational beings, we can suppose a pure will, but being creatures affected with wants and physical motives, not a holy will, that is, one which would be incapable of any maxim conflicting with the moral law. In their case, therefore, the moral law is an imperative, which commands categorically, because the law is unconditioned; the relation of such a will to this law is dependence under the name of obligation, which implies a constraint to an action, though only by reason and its objective law; and this action is called duty, because an elective will, subject to pathological affections (though not determined by them, and, therefore, still free), implies a wish that arises from subjective causes and, therefore, may often be opposed to the pure objective determining principle; whence it requires the moral constraint of a resistance of the practical reason, which may be called an internal, but intellectual, compulsion. In the supreme intelligence the elective will is rightly conceived as incapable of any maxim which could not at the same time be objectively a law; and the notion of holiness, which on that account belongs to it, places it, not indeed above all practical laws, but above all practically restrictive laws, and consequently above obligation and duty. This holiness of will is, however, a practical idea, which must necessarily serve as a type to which finite rational beings can only approximate indefinitely, and which the pure moral law, which is itself on this account called holy, constantly and rightly holds before their eyes. The utmost that finite practical reason can effect is to be certain of this indefinite progress of one's maxims and of their steady disposition to advance. This is virtue, and virtue, at least as a naturally acquired faculty, can never be perfect, because assurance in such a case never becomes apodeictic certainty and, when it only amounts to persuasion, is very dangerous.

VIII. THEOREM IV.

The autonomy of the will is the sole principle of all moral laws and of all duties which conform to them; on the other hand, heteronomy of the elective will not only cannot be the basis of any obligation, but is, on the contrary, opposed to the principle thereof and to the morality of the will.

In fact the sole principle of morality consists in the independence on all matter of the law (namely, a desired object), and in the determination of the elective will by the mere universal legislative form of which its maxim must be capable. Now this independence is freedom in the negative sense, and this self-legislation of the pure, and therefore practical, reason is freedom in the positive sense. Thus the moral law expresses nothing else than the autonomy of the pure practical reason; that is, freedom; and this is itself the formal condition of all maxims, and on this condition only can they agree with the supreme practical law. If therefore the matter of the volition, which can be nothing else than the object of a desire that is connected with the law, enters into the practical law, as the condition of its possibility, there results heteronomy of the elective will, namely, dependence on the physical law that we should follow some impulse or inclination. In that case the will does not give itself the law, but only the precept how rationally to follow pathological law; and the maxim which, in such a case, never contains the universally legislative form, not only produces no obligation, but is itself opposed to the principle of a pure practical reason and, therefore, also to the moral disposition, even though the resulting action may be conformable to the law.

REMARK.

Hence a practical precept, which contains a material (and therefore empirical) condition, must never be reckoned a practical law. For the law of the pure will, which is free, brings the will into a sphere quite different from the empirical; and as the necessity involved in the law is not a physical necessity, it can only consist in the formal conditions of the possibility of a law in general. All the matter of practical rules rests on subjective conditions, which give them only a conditional universality (in case I desire this or that, what I must do in order to obtain it), and they all turn on the principle of private happiness. Now, it is indeed undeniable that every volition must have an object, and therefore a matter; but it does not follow that this is the determining principle and the condition of the maxim; for, if it is so, then this cannot be exhibited in a universally legislative form, since in that case the expectation of the existence of the object would be the determining cause of the choice, and the volition must presuppose the dependence of the faculty of desire on the existence of something; but this dependence can only be sought in empirical conditions and, therefore, can never furnish a foundation for a necessary and universal rule. Thus, the happiness of others may be the object of the will of a rational being. But if it were the determining principle of the maxim, we must assume that we find not only a rational satisfaction in the welfare of others, but also a want such as the sympathetic disposition in some men occasions. But I cannot assume the existence of this want in every rational being (not at all in God). The matter, then, of the maxim may remain, but it must not be the condition of it, else the maxim could not be fit for a law. Hence, the mere form of law, which limits the matter, must also be a reason for adding this matter to the will, not for presupposing it. For example, let the matter be my own happiness. This (rule), if I attribute it to everyone (as, in fact, I may, in the case of every finite being), can become an objective practical law only if I include the happiness of others. Therefore, the law that we should promote the happiness of others does not arise from the assumption that this is an object of everyone's choice, but merely from this, that the form of universality which reason requires as the condition of giving to a maxim of self-love the objective validity of a law is the principle that determines the will. Therefore it was not the object (the happiness of others) that determined the pure will, but it was the form of law only, by which I restricted my maxim, founded on inclination, so as to give it the universality of a law, and thus to adapt it to the practical reason; and it is this restriction alone, and not the addition of an external spring, that can give rise to the notion of the obligation to extend the maxim of my self-love to the happiness of others.

REMARK II.

The direct opposite of the principle of morality is, when the principle of private happiness is made the determining principle of the will, and with this is to be reckoned, as I have shown above, everything that places the determining principle which is to serve as a law, anywhere but in the legislative form of the maxim. This contradiction, however, is not merely logical, like that which would arise between rules empirically conditioned, if they were raised to the rank of necessary principles of cognition, but is practical, and would ruin morality altogether were not the voice of reason in reference to the will so clear, so irrepressible, so distinctly audible, even to the commonest men. It can only, indeed, be maintained in the perplexing speculations of the schools, which are bold enough to shut their ears against that heavenly voice, in order to support a theory that costs no trouble.

Suppose that an acquaintance whom you otherwise liked were to attempt to justify himself to you for having borne false witness, first by alleging the, in his view, sacred duty of consulting his own happiness; then by enumerating the advantages which he had gained thereby, pointing out the prudence he had shown in securing himself against detection, even by yourself, to whom he now reveals the secret, only in order that he may be able to deny it at any time; and suppose he were then to affirm, in all seriousness, that he has fulfilled a true human duty; you would either laugh in his face, or shrink back from him with disgust; and yet, if a man has regulated his principles of action solely with a view to his own advantage, you would have nothing whatever to object against this mode of proceeding. Or suppose some one recommends you a man as steward, as a man to whom you can blindly trust all your affairs; and, in order to inspire you with confidence, extols him as a prudent man who thoroughly understands his own interest, and is so indefatigably active that he lets slip no opportunity of advancing it; lastly, lest you should be afraid of finding a vulgar selfishness in him, praises the good taste with which he lives; not seeking his pleasure in money-making, or in coarse wantonness, but in the enlargement of his knowledge, in instructive intercourse with a select circle, and even in relieving the needy; while as to the means (which, of course, derive all their value from the end), he is not particular, and is ready to use other people's money for the purpose as if it were his own, provided only he knows that he can do so safely, and without discovery; you would either believe that the recommender was mocking you, or that he had lost his senses. So sharply and clearly marked are the boundaries of morality and self-love that even the commonest eye cannot fail to distinguish whether a thing belongs to the one or the other. The few remarks that follow may appear superfluous where the truth is so plain, but at least they may serve to give a little more distinctness to the judgement of common sense.

The principle of happiness may, indeed, furnish maxims, but never such as would be competent to be laws of the will, even if universal happiness were made the object. For since the knowledge of this rests on mere empirical data, since every man's judgement on it depends very much on his particular point of view, which is itself moreover very variable, it can supply only general rules, not universal; that is, it can give rules which on the average will most frequently fit, but not rules which must hold good always and necessarily; hence, no practical laws can be founded on it. Just because in this case an object of choice is the foundation of the rule and must therefore precede it, the rule can refer to nothing but what is [felt], and therefore it refers to experience and is founded on it, and then the variety of judgement must be endless. This principle, therefore, does not prescribe the same practical rules to all rational beings, although the rules are all included under a common title, namely, that of happiness. The moral law, however, is conceived as objectively necessary, only because it holds for everyone that has reason and will.

The maxim of self-love (prudence) only advises; the law of morality commands. Now there is a great difference between that which we are advised to do and that to which we are obliged.

The commonest intelligence can easily and without hesitation see what, on the principle of autonomy of the will, requires to be done; but on supposition of heteronomy of the will, it is hard and requires knowledge of the world to see what is to be done. That is to say, what duty is, is plain of itself to everyone; but what is to bring true durable advantage, such as will extend to the whole of one's existence, is always veiled in impenetrable obscurity; and much prudence is required to adapt the practical rule founded on it to the ends of life, even tolerably, by making proper exceptions. But the moral law commands the most punctual obedience from everyone; it must, therefore, not be so difficult to judge what it requires to be done, that the commonest unpractised understanding, even without worldly prudence, should fail to apply it rightly.

It is always in everyone's power to satisfy the categorical command of morality; whereas it is seldom possible, and by no means so to everyone, to satisfy the empirically conditioned precept of happiness, even with regard to a single purpose. The reason is that in the former case there is question only of the maxim, which must be genuine and pure; but in the latter case there is question also of one's capacity and physical power to realize a desired object. A command that everyone should try to make himself happy would be foolish, for one never commands anyone to do what he of himself infallibly wishes to do. We must only command the means, or rather supply them, since he cannot do everything that he wishes. But to command morality under the name of duty is quite rational; for, in the first place, not everyone is willing to obey its precepts if they oppose his inclinations; and as to the means of obeying this law, these need not in this case be taught, for in this respect whatever he wishes to do he can do.

He who has lost at play may be vexed at himself and his folly, but if he is conscious of having cheated at play (although he has gained thereby), he must despise himself as soon as he compares himself with the moral law. This must, therefore, be something different from the principle of private happiness. For a man must have a different criterion when he is compelled to say to himself: "I am a worthless fellow, though I have filled my purse"; and when he approves himself, and says: "I am a prudent man, for I have enriched my treasure."

Finally, there is something further in the idea of our practical reason, which accompanies the transgression of a moral law- namely, its ill desert. Now the notion of punishment, as such, cannot be united with that of becoming a partaker of happiness; for although he who inflicts the punishment may at the same time have the benevolent purpose of directing this punishment to this end, yet it must first be justified in itself as punishment, i.e., as mere harm, so that if it stopped there, and the person punished could get no glimpse of kindness hidden behind this harshness, he must yet admit that justice was done him, and that his reward was perfectly suitable to his conduct. In every punishment, as such, there must first be justice, and this constitutes the essence of the notion. Benevolence may, indeed, be united with it, but the man who has deserved punishment has not the least reason to reckon upon this. Punishment, then, is a physical evil, which, though it be not connected with moral evil as a natural consequence, ought to be connected with it as a consequence by the principles of a moral legislation. Now, if every crime, even without regarding the physical consequence with respect to the actor, is in itself punishable, that is, forfeits happiness (at least partially), it is obviously absurd to say that the crime consisted just in this, that he has drawn punishment on himself, thereby injuring his private happiness (which, on the principle of self-love, must be the proper notion of all crime). According to this view, the punishment would be the reason for calling anything a crime, and justice would, on the contrary, consist in omitting all punishment, and even preventing that which naturally follows; for, if this were done, there would no longer be any evil in the action, since the harm which otherwise followed it, and on account of which alone the action was called evil, would now be prevented. To look, however, on all rewards and punishments as merely the machinery in the hand of a higher power, which is to serve only to set rational creatures striving after their final end (happiness), this is to reduce the will to a mechanism destructive of freedom; this is so evident that it need not detain us.

More refined, though equally false, is the theory of those who suppose a certain special moral sense, which sense and not reason determines the moral law, and in consequence of which the consciousness of virtue is supposed to be directly connected with contentment and pleasure; that of vice, with mental dissatisfaction and pain; thus reducing the whole to the desire of private happiness. Without repeating what has been said above, I will here only remark the fallacy they fall into. In order to imagine the vicious man as tormented with mental dissatisfaction by the consciousness of his transgressions, they must first represent him as in the main basis of his character, at least in some degree, morally good; just as he who is pleased with the consciousness of right conduct must be conceived as already virtuous. The notion of morality and duty must, therefore, have preceded any regard to this satisfaction, and cannot be derived from it. A man must first appreciate the importance of what we call duty, the authority of the moral law, and the immediate dignity which the following of it gives to the person in his own eyes, in order to feel that satisfaction in the consciousness of his conformity to it and the bitter remorse that accompanies the consciousness of its transgression. It is, therefore, impossible to feel this satisfaction or dissatisfaction prior to the knowledge of obligation, or to make it the basis of the latter. A man must be at least half honest in order even to be able to form a conception of these feelings. I do not deny that as the human will is, by virtue of liberty, capable of being immediately determined by the moral law, so frequent practice in accordance with this principle of determination can, at least, produce subjectively a feeling of satisfaction; on the contrary, it is a duty to establish and to cultivate this, which alone deserves to be called properly the moral feeling; but the notion of duty cannot be derived from it, else we should have to suppose a feeling for the law as such, and thus make that an object of sensation which can only be thought by the reason; and this, if it is not to be a flat contradiction, would destroy all notion of duty and put in its place a mere mechanical play of refined inclinations sometimes contending with the coarser.

If now we compare our formal supreme principle of pure practical reason (that of autonomy of the will) with all previous material principles of morality, we can exhibit them all in a table in which all possible cases are exhausted, except the one formal principle; and thus we can show visibly that it is vain to look for any other principle than that now proposed. In fact all possible principles of determination of the will are either merely subjective, and therefore empirical, or are also objective and rational; and both are either external or internal.

Practical Material Principles of Determination taken as the Foundation of Morality, are:

SUBJECTIVE
EXTERNAL
Education (Montaigne)
The civil constitution (Mandeville)
INTERNAL
Physical Feeling (Epicurus)
Moral feeling (Hutcheson)

OBJECTIVE
INTERNAL
Perfection (Wolf and the Stoics)
EXTERNAL
Will of God (Crusius and other theological moralists)

Those of the upper table are all empirical and evidently incapable of furnishing the universal principle of morality; but those in the lower table are based on reason (for perfection as a quality of things, and the highest perfection conceived as substance, that is, God, can only be thought by means of rational concepts). But the former notion, namely, that of perfection, may either be taken in a theoretic signification, and then it means nothing but the completeness of each thing in its own kind (transcendental), or that of a thing merely as a thing (metaphysical); and with that we are not concerned here. But the notion of perfection in a practical sense is the fitness or sufficiency of a thing for all sorts of purposes. This perfection, as a quality of man and consequently internal, is nothing but talent and, what strengthens or completes this, skill. Supreme perfection conceived as substance, that is God, and consequently external (considered practically), is the sufficiency of this being for all ends. Ends then must first be given, relatively to which only can the notion of perfection (whether internal in ourselves or external in God) be the determining principle of the will. But an end- being an object which must precede the determination of the will by a practical rule and contain the ground of the possibility of this determination, and therefore contain also the matter of the will, taken as its determining principle- such an end is always empirical and, therefore, may serve for the Epicurean principle of the happiness theory, but not for the pure rational principle of morality and duty. Thus, talents and the improvement of them, because they contribute to the advantages of life; or the will of God, if agreement with it be taken as the object of the will, without any antecedent independent practical principle, can be motives only by reason of the happiness expected therefrom. Hence it follows, first, that all the principles here stated are material; secondly, that they include all possible material principles; and, finally, the conclusion, that since material principles are quite incapable of furnishing the supreme moral law (as has been shown), the formal practical principle of the pure reason (according to which the mere form of a universal legislation must constitute the supreme and immediate determining principle of the will) is the only one possible which is adequate to furnish categorical imperatives, that is, practical laws (which make actions a duty), and in general to serve as the principle of morality, both in criticizing conduct and also in its application to the human will to determine it.

I. OF THE DEDUCTION OF THE FUNDAMENTAL PRINCIPLES OF PURE PRACTICAL REASON.

This Analytic shows that pure reason can be practical, that is, can of itself determine the will independently of anything empirical; and this it proves by a fact in which pure reason in us proves itself actually practical, namely, the autonomy shown in the fundamental principle of morality, by which reason determines the will to action.

It shows at the same time that this fact is inseparably connected with the consciousness of freedom of the will, nay, is identical with it; and by this the will of a rational being, although as belonging to the world of sense it recognizes itself as necessarily subject to the laws of causality like other efficient causes; yet, at the same time, on another side, namely, as a being in itself, is conscious of existing in and being determined by an intelligible order of things; conscious not by virtue of a special intuition of itself, but by virtue of certain dynamical laws which determine its causality in the sensible world; for it has been elsewhere proved that if freedom is predicated of us, it transports us into an intelligible order of things.

Now, if we compare with this the analytical part of the critique of pure speculative reason, we shall see a remarkable contrast. There it was not fundamental principles, but pure, sensible intuition (space and time), that was the first datum that made a priori knowledge possible, though only of objects of the senses. Synthetical principles could not be derived from mere concepts without intuition; on the contrary, they could only exist with reference to this intuition, and therefore to objects of possible experience, since it is the concepts of the understanding, united with this intuition, which alone make that knowledge possible which we call experience. Beyond objects of experience, and therefore with regard to things as noumena, all positive knowledge was rightly disclaimed for speculative reason. This reason, however, went so far as to establish with certainty the concept of noumena; that is, the possibility, nay, the necessity, of thinking them; for example, it showed against all objections that the supposition of freedom, negatively considered, was quite consistent with those principles and limitations of pure theoretic reason. But it could not give us any definite enlargement of our knowledge with respect to such objects, but, on the contrary, cut off all view of them altogether.

On the other hand, the moral law, although it gives no view, yet gives us a fact absolutely inexplicable from any data of the sensible world, and the whole compass of our theoretical use of reason, a fact which points to a pure world of the understanding, nay, even defines it positively and enables us to know something of it, namely, a law.

This law (as far as rational beings are concerned) gives to the world of sense, which is a sensible system of nature, the form of a world of the understanding, that is, of a supersensible system of nature, without interfering with its mechanism. Now, a system of nature, in the most general sense, is the existence of things under laws. The sensible nature of rational beings in general is their existence under laws empirically conditioned, which, from the point of view of reason, is heteronomy. The supersensible nature of the same beings, on the other hand, is their existence according to laws which are independent of every empirical condition and, therefore, belong to the autonomy of pure reason. And, since the laws by which the existence of things depends on cognition are practical, supersensible nature, so far as we can form any notion of it, is nothing else than a system of nature under the autonomy of pure practical reason. Now, the law of this autonomy is the moral law, which, therefore, is the fundamental law of a supersensible nature, and of a pure world of understanding, whose counterpart must exist in the world of sense, but without interfering with its laws. We might call the former the archetypal world (natura archetypa), which we only know in the reason; and the latter the ectypal world (natura ectypa), because it contains the possible effect of the idea of the former which is the determining principle of the will. For the moral law, in fact, transfers us ideally into a system in which pure reason, if it were accompanied with adequate physical power, would produce the summum bonum, and it determines our will to give the sensible world the form of a system of rational beings.

The least attention to oneself proves that this idea really serves as the model for the determinations of our will.

When the maxim which I am disposed to follow in giving testimony is tested by the practical reason, I always consider what it would be if it were to hold as a universal law of nature. It is manifest that in this view it would oblige everyone to speak the truth. For it cannot hold as a universal law of nature that statements should be allowed to have the force of proof and yet to be purposely untrue. Similarly, the maxim which I adopt with respect to disposing freely of my life is at once determined, when I ask myself what it should be, in order that a system, of which it is the law, should maintain itself. It is obvious that in such a system no one could arbitrarily put an end to his own life, for such an arrangement would not be a permanent order of things. And so in all similar cases. Now, in nature, as it actually is an object of experience, the free will is not of itself determined to maxims which could of themselves be the foundation of a natural system of universal laws, or which could even be adapted to a system so constituted; on the contrary, its maxims are private inclinations which constitute, indeed, a natural whole in conformity with pathological (physical) laws, but could not form part of a system of nature, which would only be possible through our will acting in accordance with pure practical laws. Yet we are, through reason, conscious of a law to which all our maxims are subject, as though a natural order must be originated from our will. This law, there-fore, must be the idea of a natural system not given in experience, and yet possible through freedom; a system, therefore, which is supersensible, and to which we give objective reality, at least in a practical point of view, since we look on it as an object of our will as pure rational beings.

Hence the distinction between the laws of a natural system to which the will is subject, and of a natural system which is subject to a will (as far as its relation to its free actions is concerned), rests on this, that in the former the objects must be causes of the ideas which determine the will; whereas in the latter the will is the cause of the objects; so that its causality has its determining principle solely in the pure faculty of reason, which may therefore be called a pure practical reason.

There are therefore two very distinct problems: how, on the one side, pure reason can cognise objects a priori, and how on the other side it can be an immediate deter-mining principle of the will, that is, of the causality of the rational being with respect to the reality of objects (through the mere thought of the universal validity of its own maxims as laws).

The former, which belongs to the critique of the pure speculative reason, requires a previous explanation, how intuitions without which no object can be given, and, there-fore, none known synthetically, are possible a priori; and its solution turns out to be that these are all only sensible and, therefore, do not render possible any speculative knowl-edge which goes further than possible experience reaches; and that therefore all the principles of that pure speculative reason avail only to make experience possible; either experience of given objects or of those that may be given ad infinitum, but never are completely given.

The latter, which belongs to the critique of practical reason, requires no explanation how the objects of the faculty of desire are possible, for that being a problem of the theo-retical knowledge of nature is left to the critique of the speculative reason, but only how reason can determine the maxims of the will; whether this takes place only by means of empirical ideas as principles of determination, or whether pure reason can be practical and be the law of a possible order of nature, which is not empirically knowable. The possibility of such a supersensible system of nature, the conception of which can also be the ground of its reality through our own free will, does not require any a priori intuition (of an intelligible world) which, being in this case supersensible, would be impossible for us. For the question is only as to the determining principle of volition in its maxims, namely, whether it is empirical, or is a conception of the pure reason (having the legal character belonging to it in general), and how it can be the latter. It is left to the theoretic principles of reason to decide whether the causality of the will suffices for the realization of the objects or not, this being an inquiry into the possibility of the objects of the volition. Intuition of these objects is therefore of no importance to the practical problem. We are here concerned only with the determination of the will and the determining principles of its maxims as a free will, not at all with the result. For, provided only that the will conforms to the law of pure reason, then let its power in execution be what it may, whether according to these maxims of legislation of a possible system of nature any such system really results or not, this is no concern of the critique, which only inquires whether, and in what way, pure reason can be practical, that is directly determine the will.

In this inquiry criticism may and must begin with pure practical laws and their reality. But instead of intuition it takes as their foundation the conception of their existence in the intelligible world, namely, the concept of freedom. For this concept has no other meaning, and these laws are only possible in relation to freedom of the will; but freedom being supposed, they are necessary; or conversely freedom is necessary because those laws are necessary, being practical postulates. It cannot be further explained how this consciousness of the moral law, or, what is the same thing, of freedom, is possible; but that it is admissible is well established in the theoretical critique.

The exposition of the supreme principle of practical reason is now finished; that is to say, it has been shown first, what it contains, that it subsists for itself quite a priori and independent of empirical principles; and next in what it is distinguished from all other practical principles. With the deduction, that is, the justification of its objective and universal validity, and the discernment of the possibility of such a synthetical proposition a priori, we cannot expect to succeed so well as in the case of the principles of pure theoretical reason. For these referred to objects of possible experience, namely, to phenomena, and we could prove that these phenomena could be known as objects of experience only by being brought under the categories in accordance with these laws; and consequently that all possible experience must conform to these laws. But I could not proceed in this way with the deduction of the moral law. For this does not concern the knowledge of the properties of objects, which may be given to the reason from some other source; but a knowledge which can itself be the ground of the existence of the objects, and by which reason in a rational being has causality, i.e., pure reason, which can be regarded as a faculty immediately determining the will.

Now all our human insight is at an end as soon as we have arrived at fundamental powers or faculties, for the possibility of these cannot be understood by any means, and just as little should it be arbitrarily invented and assumed. Therefore, in the theoretic use of reason, it is experience alone that can justify us in assuming them. But this expedient of adducing empirical proofs, instead of a deduction from a priori sources of knowledge, is denied us here in respect to the pure practical faculty of reason. For whatever requires to draw the proof of its reality from experience must depend for the grounds of its possibility on principles of experience; and pure, yet practical, reason by its very notion cannot be regarded as such. Further, the moral law is given as a fact of pure reason of which we are a priori conscious, and which is apodeictically certain, though it be granted that in experience no example of its exact fulfilment can be found. Hence, the objective reality of the moral law cannot be proved by any deduction by any efforts of theoretical reason, whether speculative or empirically supported, and therefore, even if we renounced its apodeictic certainty, it could not be proved a posteriori by experience, and yet it is firmly established of itself.

But instead of this vainly sought deduction of the moral principle, something else is found which was quite unexpected, namely, that this moral principle serves conversely as the principle of the deduction of an inscrutable faculty which no experience could prove, but of which speculative reason was compelled at least to assume the possibility (in order to find amongst its cosmological ideas the unconditioned in the chain of causality, so as not to contradict itself)- I mean the faculty of freedom. The moral law, which itself does not require a justification, proves not merely the possibility of freedom, but that it really belongs to beings who recognize this law as binding on themselves. The moral law is in fact a law of the causality of free agents and, therefore, of the possibility of a supersensible system of nature, just as the metaphysical law of events in the world of sense was a law of causality of the sensible system of nature; and it therefore determines what speculative philosophy was compelled to leave undetermined, namely, the law for a causality, the concept of which in the latter was only negative; and therefore for the first time gives this concept objective reality.

This sort of credential of the moral law, viz., that it is set forth as a principle of the deduction of freedom, which is a causality of pure reason, is a sufficient substitute for all a priori justification, since theoretic reason was compelled to assume at least the possibility of freedom, in order to satisfy a want of its own. For the moral law proves its reality, so as even to satisfy the critique of the speculative reason, by the fact that it adds a positive definition to a causality previously conceived only negatively, the possibility of which was incomprehensible to speculative reason, which yet was compelled to suppose it. For it adds the notion of a reason that directly determines the will (by imposing on its maxims the condition of a universal legislative form); and thus it is able for the first time to give objective, though only practical, reality to reason, which always became transcendent when it sought to proceed speculatively with its ideas. It thus changes the transcendent use of reason into an immanent use (so that reason is itself, by means of ideas, an efficient cause in the field of experience).

The determination of the causality of beings in the world of sense, as such, can never be unconditioned; and yet for every series of conditions there must be something unconditioned, and therefore there must be a causality which is determined wholly by itself. Hence, the idea of freedom as a faculty of absolute spontaneity was not found to be a want but, as far as its possibility is concerned, an analytic principle of pure speculative reason. But as it is absolutely impossible to find in experience any example in accordance with this idea, because amongst the causes of things as phenomena it would be impossible to meet with any absolutely unconditioned determination of causality, we were only able to defend our supposition that a freely acting cause might be a being in the world of sense, in so far as it is considered in the other point of view as a noumenon, showing that there is no contradiction in regarding all its actions as subject to physical conditions so far as they are phenomena, and yet regarding its causality as physically unconditioned, in so far as the acting being belongs to the world of understanding, and in thus making the concept of freedom the regulative principle of reason. By this principle I do not indeed learn what the object is to which that sort of causality is attributed; but I remove the difficulty, for, on the one side, in the explanation of events in the world, and consequently also of the actions of rational beings, I leave to the mechanism of physical necessity the right of ascending from conditioned to condition ad infinitum, while on the other side I keep open for speculative reason the place which for it is vacant, namely, the intelligible, in order to transfer the unconditioned thither. But I was not able to verify this supposition; that is, to change it into the knowledge of a being so acting, not even into the knowledge of the possibility of such a being. This vacant place is now filled by pure practical reason with a definite law of causality in an intelligible world (causality with freedom), namely, the moral law. Speculative reason does not hereby gain anything as regards its insight, but only as regards the certainty of its problematical notion of freedom, which here obtains objective reality, which, though only practical, is nevertheless undoubted. Even the notion of causality- the application, and consequently the signification, of which holds properly only in relation to phenomena, so as to connect them into experiences (as is shown by the Critique of Pure Reason)- is not so enlarged as to extend its use beyond these limits. For if reason sought to do this, it would have to show how the logical relation of principle and consequence can be used synthetically in a different sort of intuition from the sensible; that is how a causa noumenon is possible. This it can never do; and, as practical reason, it does not even concern itself with it, since it only places the determining principle of causality of man as a sensible creature (which is given) in pure reason (which is therefore called practical); and therefore it employs the notion of cause, not in order to know objects, but to determine causality in relation to objects in general. It can abstract altogether from the application of this notion to objects with a view to theoretical knowledge (since this concept is always found a priori in the understanding even independently of any intuition). Reason, then, employs it only for a practical purpose, and hence we can transfer the determining principle of the will into the intelligible order of things, admitting, at the same time, that we cannot understand how the notion of cause can determine the knowledge of these things. But reason must cognise causality with respect to the actions of the will in the sensible world in a definite manner; otherwise, practical reason could not really produce any action. But as to the notion which it forms of its own causality as noumenon, it need not determine it theoretically with a view to the cognition of its supersensible existence, so as to give it significance in this way. For it acquires significance apart from this, though only for practical use, namely, through the moral law. Theoretically viewed, it remains always a pure a priori concept of the understanding, which can be applied to objects whether they have been given sensibly or not, although in the latter case it has no definite theoretical significance or application, but is only a formal, though essential, conception of the understanding relating to an object in general. The significance which reason gives it through the moral law is merely practical, inasmuch as the idea of the law of causality (of the will) has self causality, or is its determining principle.

II. OF THE RIGHT THAT PURE REASON IN ITS PRACTICAL USE HAS TO AN EXTENSION WHICH IS NOT POSSIBLE TO IT IN ITS SPECULATIVE USE.

We have in the moral principle set forth a law of causality, the determining principle of which is set above all the conditions of the sensible world; we have it conceived how the will, as belonging to the intelligible world, is determinable, and therefore have its subject (man) not merely conceived as belonging to a world of pure understanding, and in this respect unknown (which the critique of speculative reason enabled us to do), but also defined as regards his causality by means of a law which cannot be reduced to any physical law of the sensible world; and therefore our knowledge is extended beyond the limits of that world, a pretension which the Critique of Pure Reason declared to be futile in all speculation. Now, how is the practical use of pure reason here to be reconciled with the theoretical, as to the determination of the limits of its faculty?

David Hume, of whom we may say that he commenced the assault on the claims of pure reason, which made a thorough investigation of it necessary, argued thus: The notion of cause is a notion that involves the necessity of the connexion of the existence of different things (and that, in so far as they are different), so that, given A, I know that something quite distinct there from, namely B, must necessarily also exist. Now necessity can be attributed to a connection, only in so far as it is known a priori, for experience would only enable us to know of such a connection that it exists, not that it necessarily exists. Now, it is impossible, says he, to know a priori and as necessary the connection between one thing and another (or between one attribute and another quite distinct) when they have not been given in experience. Therefore the notion of a cause is fictitious and delusive and, to speak in the mildest way, is an illusion, only excusable inasmuch as the custom (a subjective necessity) of perceiving certain things, or their attributes as often associated in existence along with or in succession to one another, is insensibly taken for an objective necessity of supposing such a connection in the objects themselves; and thus the notion of a cause has been acquired surreptitiously and not legitimately; nay, it can never be so acquired or authenticated, since it demands a connection in itself vain, chimerical, and untenable in presence of reason, and to which no object can ever correspond. In this way was empiricism first introduced as the sole source of principles, as far as all knowledge of the existence of things is concerned (mathematics therefore remaining excepted); and with empiricism the most thorough scepticism, even with regard to the whole science of nature(as philosophy). For on such principles we can never conclude from given attributes of things as existing to a consequence (for this would require the notion of cause, which involves the necessity of such a connection); we can only, guided by imagination, expect similar cases- an expectation which is never certain, however often it has been fulfilled. Of no event could we say: a certain thing must have preceded it, on which it necessarily followed; that is, it must have a cause; and therefore, however frequent the cases we have known in which there was such an antecedent, so that a rule could be derived from them, yet we never could suppose it as always and necessarily so happening; we should, therefore, be obliged to leave its share to blind chance, with which all use of reason comes to an end; and this firmly establishes scepticism in reference to arguments ascending from effects to causes and makes it impregnable.

Mathematics escaped well, so far, because Hume thought that its propositions were analytical; that is, proceeded from one property to another, by virtue of identity and, consequently, according to the principle of contradiction. This, however, is not the case, since, on the contrary, they are synthetical; and although geometry, for example, has not to do with the existence of things, but only with their a priori properties in a possible intuition, yet it proceeds just as in the case of the causal notion, from one property (A) to another wholly distinct (B), as necessarily connected with the former. Nevertheless, mathematical science, so highly vaunted for its apodeictic certainty, must at last fall under this empiricism for the same reason for which Hume put custom in the place of objective necessity in the notion of cause and, in spite of all its pride, must consent to lower its bold pretension of claiming assent a priori and depend for assent to the universality of its propositions on the kindness of observers, who, when called as witnesses, would surely not hesitate to admit that what the geometer propounds as a theorem they have always perceived to be the fact, and, consequently, although it be not necessarily true, yet they would permit us to expect it to be true in the future. In this manner Hume's empiricism leads inevitably to scepticism, even with regard to mathematics, and consequently in every scientific theoretical use of reason (for this belongs either to philosophy or mathematics). Whether with such a terrible overthrow of the chief branches of knowledge, common reason will escape better, and will not rather become irrecoverably involved in this destruction of all knowledge, so that from the same principles a universal scepticism should follow (affecting, indeed, only the learned), this I will leave everyone to judge for himself.

As regards my own labours in the critical examination of pure reason, which were occasioned by Hume's sceptical teaching, but went much further and embraced the whole field of pure theoretical reason in its synthetic use and, consequently, the field of what is called metaphysics in general; I proceeded in the following manner with respect to the doubts raised by the Scottish philosopher touching the notion of causality. If Hume took the objects of experience for things in themselves (as is almost always done), he was quite right in declaring the notion of cause to be a deception and false illusion; for as to things in themselves, and their attributes as such, it is impossible to see why because A is given, B, which is different, must necessarily be also given, and therefore he could by no means admit such an a priori knowledge of things in themselves. Still less could this acute writer allow an empirical origin of this concept, since this is directly contradictory to the necessity of connection which constitutes the essence of the notion of causality, hence the notion was proscribed, and in its place was put custom in the observation of the course of perceptions.

It resulted, however, from my inquiries, that the objects with which we have to do in experience are by no means things in themselves, but merely phenomena; and that although in the case of things in themselves it is impossible to see how, if A is supposed, it should be contradictory that B, which is quite different from A, should not also be supposed (i.e., to see the necessity of the connection between A as cause and B as effect); yet it can very well be conceived that, as phenomena, they may be necessarily connected in one experience in a certain way (e.g., with regard to time-relations); so that they could not be separated without contradicting that connection, by means of which this experience is possible in which they are objects and in which alone they are cognisable by us. And so it was found to be in fact; so that I was able not only to prove the objective reality of the concept of cause in regard to objects of experience, but also to deduce it as an a priori concept by reason of the necessity of the connection it implied; that is, to show the possibility of its origin from pure understanding without any empirical sources; and thus, after removing the source of empiricism, I was able also to overthrow the inevitable consequence of this, namely, scepticism, first with regard to physical science, and then with regard to mathematics (in which empiricism has just the same grounds), both being sciences which have reference to objects of possible experience; herewith overthrowing the thorough doubt of whatever theoretic reason professes to discern.

But how is it with the application of this category of causality (and all the others; for without them there can be no knowledge of anything existing) to things which are not objects of possible experience, but lie beyond its bounds? For I was able to deduce the objective reality of these concepts only with regard to objects of possible experience. But even this very fact, that I have saved them, only in case I have proved that objects may by means of them be thought, though not determined a priori; this it is that gives them a place in the pure understanding, by which they are referred to objects in general (sensible or not sensible). If anything is still wanting, it is that which is the condition of the application of these categories, and especially that of causality, to objects, namely, intuition; for where this is not given, the application with a view to theoretic knowledge of the object, as a noumenon, is impossible and, therefore, if anyone ventures on it, is (as in the Critique of Pure Reason) absolutely forbidden. Still, the objective reality of the concept (of causality) remains, and it can be used even of noumena, but without our being able in the least to define the concept theoretically so as to produce knowledge. For that this concept, even in reference to an object, contains nothing impossible, was shown by this, that, even while applied to objects of sense, its seat was certainly fixed in the pure understanding; and although, when referred to things in themselves (which cannot be objects of experience), it is not capable of being determined so as to represent a definite object for the purpose of theoretic knowledge; yet for any other purpose (for instance, a practical) it might be capable of being determined so as to have such application. This could not be the case if, as Hume maintained, this concept of causality contained something absolutely impossible to be thought.

In order now to discover this condition of the application of the said concept to noumena, we need only recall why we are not content with its application to objects of experience, but desire also to apply it to things in themselves. It will appear, then, that it is not a theoretic but a practical purpose that makes this a necessity. In speculation, even if we were successful in it, we should not really gain anything in the knowledge of nature, or generally with regard to such objects as are given, but we should make a wide step from the sensibly conditioned (in which we have already enough to do to maintain ourselves, and to follow carefully the chain of causes) to the supersensible, in order to complete our knowledge of principles and to fix its limits; whereas there always remains an infinite chasm unfilled between those limits and what we know; and we should have hearkened to a vain curiosity rather than a solid-desire of knowledge.

But, besides the relation in which the understanding stands to objects (in theoretical knowledge), it has also a relation to the faculty of desire, which is therefore called the will, and the pure will, inasmuch as pure understanding (in this case called reason) is practical through the mere conception of a law. The objective reality of a pure will, or, what is the same thing, of a pure practical reason, is given in the moral law a priori, as it were, by a fact, for so we may name a determination of the will which is inevitable, although it does not rest on empirical principles. Now, in the notion of a will the notion of causality is already contained, and hence the notion of a pure will contains that of a causality accompanied with freedom, that is, one which is not determinable by physical laws, and consequently is not capable of any empirical intuition in proof of its reality, but, nevertheless, completely justifies its objective reality a priori in the pure practical law; not, indeed (as is easily seen) for the purposes of the theoretical, but of the practical use of reason. Now the notion of a being that has free will is the notion of a causa noumenon, and that this notion involves no contradiction, we are already assured by the fact- that inasmuch as the concept of cause has arisen wholly from pure understanding, and has its objective reality assured by the deduction, as it is moreover in its origin independent of any sensible conditions, it is, therefore, not restricted to phenomena (unless we wanted to make a definite theoretic use of it), but can be applied equally to things that are objects of the pure understanding. But, since this application cannot rest on any intuition (for intuition can only be sensible), therefore, causa noumenon, as regards the theoretic use of reason, although a possible and thinkable, is yet an empty notion. Now, I do not desire by means of this to understand theoretically the nature of a being, in so far as it has a pure will; it is enough for me to have thereby designated it as such, and hence to combine the notion of causality with that of freedom (and what is inseparable from it, the moral law, as its determining principle). Now, this right I certainly have by virtue of the pure, not-empirical origin of the notion of cause, since I do not consider myself entitled to make any use of it except in reference to the moral law which determines its reality, that is, only a practical use.

If, with Hume, I had denied to the notion of causality all objective reality in its [theoretic] use, not merely with regard to things in themselves (the supersensible), but also with regard to the objects of the senses, it would have lost all significance, and being a theoretically impossible notion would have been declared to be quite useless; and since what is nothing cannot be made any use of, the practical use of a concept theoretically null would have been absurd. But, as it is, the concept of a causality free from empirical conditions, although empty, i.e., without any appropriate intuition), is yet theoretically possible, and refers to an indeterminate object; but in compensation significance is given to it in the moral law and consequently in a practical sense. I have, indeed, no intuition which should determine its objective theoretic reality, but not the less it has a real application, which is exhibited in concreto in intentions or maxims; that is, it has a practical reality which can be specified, and this is sufficient to justify it even with a view to noumena.

Now, this objective reality of a pure concept of the understanding in the sphere of the supersensible, once brought in, gives an objective reality also to all the other categories, although only so far as they stand in necessary connexion with the determining principle of the will (the moral law); a reality only of practical application, which has not the least effect in enlarging our theoretical knowledge of these objects, or the discernment of their nature by pure reason. So we shall find also in the sequel that these categories refer only to beings as intelligences, and in them only to the relation of reason to the will; consequently, always only to the practical, and beyond this cannot pretend to any knowledge of these beings; and whatever other properties belonging to the theoretical representation of supersensible things may be brought into connexion with these categories, this is not to be reckoned as knowledge, but only as a right (in a practical point of view, however, it is a necessity) to admit and assume such beings, even in the case where we [conceive] supersensible beings (e.g., God) according to analogy, that is, a purely rational relation, of which we make a practical use with reference to what is sensible; and thus the application to the supersensible solely in a practical point of view does not give pure theoretic reason the least encouragement to run riot into the transcendent.

CHAPTER II. OF THE CONCEPT OF AN OBJECT OF PURE PRACTICAL REASON

By a concept of the practical reason I understand the idea of an object as an effect possible to be produced through freedom. To be an object of practical knowledge, as such, signifies, therefore, only the relation of the will to the action by which the object or its opposite would be realized; and to decide whether something is an object of pure practical reason or not is only to discern the possibility or impossibility of willing the action by which, if we had the required power (about which experience must decide), a certain object would be realized. If the object be taken as the determining principle of our desire, it must first be known whether it is physically possible by the free use of our powers, before we decide whether it is an object of practical reason or not. On the other hand, if the law can be considered a priori as the determining principle of the action, and the latter therefore as determined by pure practical reason, the judgement whether a thing is an object of pure practical reason or not does not depend at all on the comparison with our physical power; and the question is only whether we should will an action that is directed to the existence of an object, if the object were in our power; hence the previous question is only as the moral possibility of the action, for in this case it is not the object, but the law of the will, that is the determining principle of the action. The only objects of practical reason are therefore those of good and evil. For by the former is meant an object necessarily desired according to a principle of reason; by the latter one necessarily shunned, also according to a principle of reason.

If the notion of good is not to be derived from an antecedent practical law, but, on the contrary, is to serve as its foundation, it can only be the notion of something whose existence promises pleasure, and thus determines the causality of the subject to produce it, that is to say, determines the faculty of desire. Now, since it is impossible to discern a priori what idea will be accompanied with pleasure and what with pain, it will depend on experience alone to find out what is primarily good or evil. The property of the subject, with reference to which alone this experiment can be made, is the feeling of pleasure and pain, a receptivity belonging to the internal sense; thus that only would be primarily good with which the sensation of pleasure is immediately connected, and that simply evil which immediately excites pain. Since, however, this is opposed even to the usage of language, which distinguishes the pleasant from the good, the unpleasant from the evil, and requires that good and evil shall always be judged by reason, and, therefore, by concepts which can be communicated to everyone, and not by mere sensation, which is limited to individual [subjects] and their susceptibility; and, since nevertheless, pleasure or pain cannot be connected with any idea of an object a priori, the philosopher who thought himself obliged to make a feeling of pleasure the foundation of his practical judgements would call that good which is a means to the pleasant, and evil, what is a cause of unpleasantness and pain; for the judgement on the relation of means to ends certainly belongs to reason. But, although reason is alone capable of discerning the connexion of means with their ends (so that the will might even be defined as the faculty of ends, since these are always determining principles of the desires), yet the practical maxims which would follow from the aforesaid principle of the good being merely a means, would never contain as the object of the will anything good in itself, but only something good for something; the good would always be merely the useful, and that for which it is useful must always lie outside the will, in sensation. Now if this as a pleasant sensation were to be distinguished from the notion of good, then there would be nothing primarily good at all, but the good would have to be sought only in the means to something else, namely, some pleasantness.

It is an old formula of the schools: Nihil appetimus nisi sub ratione boni; Nihil aversamur nisi sub ratione mali, and it is used often correctly, but often also in a manner injurious to philosophy, because the expressions boni and mali are ambiguous, owing to the poverty of language, in consequence of which they admit a double sense, and, therefore, inevitably bring the practical laws into ambiguity; and philosophy, which in employing them becomes aware of the different meanings in the same word, but can find no special expressions for them, is driven to subtle distinctions about which there is subsequently no unanimity, because the distinction could not be directly marked by any suitable expression.[2]

The German language has the good fortune to possess expressions which do not allow this difference to be overlooked. It possesses two very distinct concepts and especially distinct expressions for that which the Latins express by a single word, bonum. For bonum it has das Gute [good], and das Wohl [well, weal], for malum das Bose [evil], and das Ubel [ill, bad], or das Well [woe]. So that we express two quite distinct judgements when we consider in an action the good and evil of it, or our weal and woe (ill). Hence it already follows that the above quoted psychological proposition is at least very doubtful if it is translated: "We desire nothing except with a view to our weal or woe"; on the other hand, if we render it thus: "Under the direction of reason we desire nothing except so far as we esteem it good or evil," it is indubitably certain and at the same time quite clearly expressed.

Well or ill always implies only a reference to our condition, as pleasant or unpleasant, as one of pleasure or pain, and if we desire or avoid an object on this account, it is only so far as it is referred to our sensibility and to the feeling of pleasure or pain that it produces. But good or evil always implies a reference to the will, as determined by the law of reason, to make something its object; for it is never determined directly by the object and the idea of it, but is a faculty of taking a rule of reason for or motive of an action (by which an object may be realized). Good and evil therefore are properly referred to actions, not to the sensations of the person, and if anything is to be good or evil absolutely (i.e., in every respect and without any further condition), or is to be so esteemed, it can only be the manner of acting, the maxim of the will, and consequently the acting person himself as a good or evil man that can be so called, and not a thing.

However, then, men may laugh at the Stoic, who in the severest paroxysms of gout cried out: "Pain, however thou tormentest me, I will never admit that thou art an evil (kakov, malum)": he was right. A bad thing it certainly was, and his cry betrayed that; but that any evil attached to him thereby, this he had no reason whatever to admit, for pain did not in the least diminish the worth of his person, but only that of his condition. If he had been conscious of a single lie, it would have lowered his pride, but pain served only to raise it, when he was conscious that he had not deserved it by any unrighteous action by which he had rendered himself worthy of punishment.

What we call good must be an object of desire in the judgement of every rational man, and evil an object of aversion in the eyes of everyone; therefore, in addition to sense, this judgement requires reason. So it is with truthfulness, as opposed to lying; so with justice, as opposed to violence, &c. But we may call a thing a bad [or ill] thing, which yet everyone must at the same time acknowledge to be good, sometimes directly, sometimes indirectly. The man who submits to a surgical operation feels it no doubt as a bad thing, but by their reason he and everyone acknowledge it to be good. If a man who delights in annoying and vexing peaceable people at last receives a right good beating, this is no doubt a bad thing; but everyone approves it and regards it as a good thing, even though nothing else resulted from it; nay, even the man who receives it must in his reason acknowledge that he has met justice, because he sees the proportion between good conduct and good fortune, which reason inevitably places before him, here put into practice.

No doubt our weal and woe are of very great importance in the estimation of our practical reason, and as far as our nature as sensible beings is concerned, our happiness is the only thing of consequence, provided it is estimated as reason especially requires, not by the transitory sensation, but by the influence that this has on our whole existence, and on our satisfaction therewith; but it is not absolutely the only thing of consequence. Man is a being who, as belonging to the world of sense, has wants, and so far his reason has an office which it cannot refuse, namely, to attend to the interest of his sensible nature, and to form practical maxims, even with a view to the happiness of this life, and if possible even to that of a future. But he is not so completely an animal as to be indifferent to what reason says on its own account, and to use it merely as an instrument for the satisfaction of his wants as a sensible being. For the possession of reason would not raise his worth above that of the brutes, if it is to serve him only for the same purpose that instinct serves in them; it would in that case be only a particular method which nature had employed to equip man for the same ends for which it has qualified brutes, without qualifying him for any higher purpose. No doubt once this arrangement of nature has been made for him he requires reason in order to take into consideration his weal and woe, but besides this he possesses it for a higher purpose also, namely, not only to take into consideration what is good or evil in itself, about which only pure reason, uninfluenced by any sensible interest, can judge, but also to distinguish this estimate thoroughly from the former and to make it the supreme condition thereof.

In estimating what is good or evil in itself, as distinguished from what can be so called only relatively, the following points are to be considered. Either a rational principle is already conceived, as of itself the determining principle of the will, without regard to possible objects of desire (and therefore by the more legislative form of the maxim), and in that case that principle is a practical a priori law, and pure reason is supposed to be practical of itself. The law in that case determines the will directly; the action conformed to it is good in itself; a will whose maxim always conforms to this law is good absolutely in every respect and is the supreme condition of all good. Or the maxim of the will is consequent on a determining principle of desire which presupposes an object of pleasure or pain, something therefore that pleases or displeases, and the maxim of reason that we should pursue the former and avoid the latter determines our actions as good relatively to our inclination, that is, good indirectly, (i.e., relatively to a different end to which they are means), and in that case these maxims can never be called laws, but may be called rational practical precepts. The end itself, the pleasure that we seek, is in the latter case not a good but a welfare; not a concept of reason, but an empirical concept of an object of sensation; but the use of the means thereto, that is, the action, is nevertheless called good (because rational deliberation is required for it), not however, good absolutely, but only relatively to our sensuous nature, with regard to its feelings of pleasure and displeasure; but the will whose maxim is affected thereby is not a pure will; this is directed only to that in which pure reason by itself can be practical.

This is the proper place to explain the paradox of method in a critique of practical reason, namely, that the concept of good and evil must not be determined before the moral law (of which it seems as if it must be the foundation), but only after it and by means of it. In fact, even if we did not know that the principle of morality is a pure a priori law determining the will, yet, that we may not assume principles quite gratuitously, we must, at least at first, leave it undecided, whether the will has merely empirical principles of determination, or whether it has not also pure a priori principles; for it is contrary to all rules of philosophical method to assume as decided that which is the very point in question. Supposing that we wished to begin with the concept of good, in order to deduce from it the laws of the will, then this concept of an object (as a good) would at the same time assign to us this object as the sole determining principle of the will. Now, since this concept had not any practical a priori law for its standard, the criterion of good or evil could not be placed in anything but the agreement of the object with our feeling of pleasure or pain; and the use of reason could only consist in determining in the first place this pleasure or pain in connexion with all the sensations of my existence, and in the second place the means of securing to myself the object of the pleasure. Now, as experience alone can decide what conforms to the feeling of pleasure, and by hypothesis the practical law is to be based on this as a condition, it follows that the possibility of a priori practical laws would be at once excluded, because it was imagined to be necessary first of all to find an object the concept of which, as a good, should constitute the universal though empirical principle of determination of the will. But what it was necessary to inquire first of all was whether there is not an a priori determining principle of the will (and this could never be found anywhere but in a pure practical law, in so far as this law prescribes to maxims merely their form without regard to an object). Since, however, we laid the foundation of all practical law in an object determined by our conceptions of good and evil, whereas without a previous law that object could not be conceived by empirical concepts, we have deprived ourselves beforehand of the possibility of even conceiving a pure practical law. On the other hand, if we had first investigated the latter analytically, we should have found that it is not the concept of good as an object that determines the moral law and makes it possible, but that, on the contrary, it is the moral law that first determines the concept of good and makes it possible, so far as it deserves the name of good absolutely.

384 | IMMANUEL KANT

This remark, which only concerns the method of ultimate ethical inquiries, is of importance. It explains at once the occasion of all the mistakes of philosophers with respect to the supreme principle of morals. For they sought for an object of the will which they could make the matter and principle of a law (which consequently could not determine the will directly, but by means of that object referred to the feeling of pleasure or pain; whereas they ought first to have searched for a law that would determine the will a priori and directly, and afterwards determine the object in accordance with the will). Now, whether they placed this object of pleasure, which was to supply the supreme conception of goodness, in happiness, in perfection, in moral [feeling], or in the will of God, their principle in every case implied heteronomy, and they must inevitably come upon empirical conditions of a moral law, since their object, which was to be the immediate principle of the will, could not be called good or bad except in its immediate relation to feeling, which is always empirical. It is only a formal law- that is, one which prescribes to reason nothing more than the form of its universal legislation as the supreme condition of its maxims- that can be a priori a determining principle of practical reason. The ancients avowed this error without concealment by directing all their moral inquiries to the determination of the notion of the summum bonum, which they intended afterwards to make the determining principle of the will in the moral law; whereas it is only far later, when the moral law has been first established for itself, and shown to be the direct determining principle of the will, that this object can be presented to the will, whose form is now determined a priori; and this we shall under- take in the Dialectic of the pure practical reason. The moderns, with whom the question of the summum bonum has gone out of fashion, or at least seems to have become a secondary matter, hide the same error under vague (expressions as in many other cases). It shows itself, nevertheless, in their systems, as it always produces heteronomy of practical reason; and from this can never be derived a moral law giving universal commands.

Now, since the notions of good and evil, as consequences of the a priori determina- tion of the will, imply also a pure practical principle, and therefore a causality of pure reason; hence they do not originally refer to objects (so as to be, for instance, special modes of the synthetic unity of the manifold of given intuitions in one consciousness) like the pure concepts of the understanding or categories of reason in its theoretic employment; on the contrary, they presuppose that objects are given; but they are all modes (modi) of a single category, namely, that of causality, the determining principle of which consists in the rational conception of a law, which as a law of freedom reason gives to itself, thereby a priori proving itself practical. However, as the actions on the one side come under a law which is not a physical law, but a law of freedom, and conse- quently belong to the conduct of beings in the world of intelligence, yet on the other side as events in the world of sense they belong to phenomena; hence the determina- tions of a practical reason are only possible in reference to the latter and, therefore, in accordance with the categories of the understanding; not indeed with a view to any theoretic employment of it, i.e., so as to bring the manifold of (sensible) intuition under one consciousness a priori; but only to subject the manifold of desires to the unity of consciousness of a practical reason, giving it commands in the moral law, i.e., to a pure will a priori.

These categories of freedom- for so we choose to call them in contrast to those theoretic categories which are categories of physical nature- have an obvious advantage over the latter, inasmuch as the latter are only forms of thought which designate objects in an indefinite manner by means of universal concept of every possible intuition; the former, on the contrary, refer to the determination of a free elective will (to which indeed no exactly corresponding intuition can be assigned, but which has as its foundation a pure practical a priori law, which is not the case with any concepts belonging to the theoretic use of our cognitive faculties); hence, instead of the form of intuition (space and time), which does not lie in reason itself, but has to be drawn from another source, namely, the sensibility, these being elementary practical concepts have as their foundation the form of a pure will, which is given in reason and, therefore, in the thinking faculty itself. From this it happens that as all precepts of pure practical reason have to do only with the determination of the will, not with the physical conditions (of practical ability) of the execution of one's purpose, the practical a priori principles in relation to the supreme principle of freedom are at once cognitions, and have not to wait for intuitions in order to acquire significance, and that for this remarkable reason, because they themselves produce the reality of that to which they refer (the intention of the will), which is not the case with theoretical concepts. Only we must be careful to observe that these categories only apply to the practical reason; and thus they proceed in order from those which are as yet subject to sensible conditions and morally indeterminate to those which are free from sensible conditions and determined merely by the moral law.

Table of the Categories of Freedom relatively to the Notions of Good and Evil.

I. Quantity
Subjective, according to maxims (practical opinions of the individual)
Objective, according to principles (Precepts)
A priori both objective and subjective principles of freedom (laws)

II. Quality
Practical rules of action (praeceptivae)
Practical rules of omission (prohibitivae)
Practical rules of exceptions (exceptivae)

III. Relation
To personality
To the condition of the person.
Reciprocal, of one person to the others of the others.

IV. Modality
The Permitted and the Forbidden
Duty and the contrary to duty.
Perfect and imperfect duty.

It will at once be observed that in this table freedom is considered as a sort of causality not subject to empirical principles of determination, in regard to actions possible by it, which are phenomena in the world of sense, and that consequently it is referred to the categories which concern its physical possibility, whilst yet each category is taken so universally that the determining principle of that causality can be placed outside the world of sense in freedom as a property of a being in the world of intelligence; and finally the categories of modality introduce the transition from practical principles generally to those of morality, but only problematically. These can be established dogmatically only by the moral law.

I add nothing further here in explanation of the present table, since it is intelligible enough of itself. A division of this kind based on principles is very useful in any science, both for the sake of thoroughness and intelligibility. Thus, for instance, we know from the preceding table and its first number what we must begin from in practical inquiries; namely, from the maxims which every one founds on his own inclinations; the precepts which hold for a species of rational beings so far as they agree in certain inclinations; and finally the law which holds for all without regard to their inclinations, etc. In this way we survey the whole plan of what has to be done, every question of practical philosophy that has to be answered, and also the order that is to be followed.

OF THE TYPIC OF THE PURE PRACTICAL JUDGEMENT.

It is the notions of good and evil that first determine an object of the will. They themselves, however, are subject to a practical rule of reason which, if it is pure reason, determines the will a priori relatively to its object. Now, whether an action which is possible to us in the world of sense, comes under the rule or not, is a question to be decided by the practical judgement, by which what is said in the rule universally (in abstracto) is applied to an action in concreto. But since a practical rule of pure reason in the first place as practical concerns the existence of an object, and in the second place as a practical rule of pure reason implies necessity as regards the existence of the action and, therefore, is a practical law, not a physical law depending on empirical principles of determination, but a law of freedom by which the will is to be determined independently on anything empirical (merely by the conception of a law and its form), whereas all instances that can occur of possible actions can only be empirical, that is, belong to the experience of physical nature; hence, it seems absurd to expect to find in the world of sense a case which, while as such it depends only on the law of nature, yet admits of the application to it of a law of freedom, and to which we can apply the supersensible idea of the morally good which is to be exhibited in it in concreto. Thus, the judgement of the pure practical reason is subject to the same difficulties as that of the pure theoretical reason. The latter, however, had means at hand of escaping from these difficulties, because, in regard to the theoretical employment, intuitions were required to which pure concepts of the understanding could be applied, and such intuitions (though only of objects of the senses) can be given a priori and, therefore, as far as regards the union of the manifold in them, conforming to the pure a priori concepts of the understanding as schemata. On the other hand, the morally good is something whose object is supersensible; for which, therefore, nothing corresponding can be found in any sensible intuition. Judgement depending on laws of pure practical reason seems, therefore, to be subject to special difficulties arising from this, that a law of freedom is to be applied to actions, which are events taking place in the world of sense, and which, so far, belong to physical nature.

But here again is opened a favourable prospect for the pure practical judgement. When I subsume under a pure practical law an action possible to me in the world of sense, I am not concerned with the possibility of the action as an event in the world of sense. This is a matter that belongs to the decision of reason in its theoretic use according to the law of causality, which is a pure concept of the understanding, for which reason has a schema in the sensible intuition. Physical causality, or the condition under which it takes place, belongs to the physical concepts, the schema of which is sketched by transcendental imagination. Here, however, we have to do, not with the schema of a case that occurs according to laws, but with the schema of a law itself (if the word is allowable here), since the fact that the will (not the action relatively to its effect) is determined by the law alone without any other principle, connects the notion of causality with quite different conditions from those which constitute physical connection.

The physical law being a law to which the objects of sensible intuition, as such, are subject, must have a schema corresponding to it- that is, a general procedure of the imagination (by which it exhibits a priori to the senses the pure concept of the under- standing which the law determines). But the law of freedom (that is, of a causality not subject to sensible conditions), and consequently the concept of the unconditionally good, cannot have any intuition, nor consequently any schema supplied to it for the purpose of its application in concreto. Consequently the moral law has no faculty but the understanding to aid its application to physical objects (not the imagination); and the understanding for the purposes of the judgement can provide for an idea of the reason, not a schema of the sensibility, but a law, though only as to its form as law; such a law, however, as can be exhibited in concreto in objects of the senses, and therefore a law of nature. We can therefore call this law the type of the moral law.

The rule of the judgement according to laws of pure practical reason is this: ask yourself whether, if the action you propose were to take place by a law of the system of nature of which you were yourself a part, you could regard it as possible by your own will. Everyone does, in fact, decide by this rule whether actions are morally good or evil. Thus, people say: "If everyone permitted himself to deceive, when he thought it to his advantage; or thought himself justified in shortening his life as soon as he was thor- oughly weary of it; or looked with perfect indifference on the necessity of others; and if you belonged to such an order of things, would you do so with the assent of your own will?" Now everyone knows well that if he secretly allows himself to deceive, it does not follow that everyone else does so; or if, unobserved, he is destitute of compassion, others would not necessarily be so to him; hence, this comparison of the maxim of his actions with a universal law of nature is not the determining principle of his will. Such a law is, nevertheless, a type of the estimation of the maxim on moral principles. If the maxim of the action is not such as to stand the test of the form of a universal law of nature, then it is morally impossible. This is the judgement even of common sense; for its ordinary judgements, even those of experience, are always based on the law of nature. It has it therefore always at hand, only that in cases where causality from freedom is to be criticised, it makes that law of nature only the type of a law of freedom, because, without something which it could use as an example in a case of experience, it could not give the law of a pure practical reason its proper use in practice.

It is therefore allowable to use the system of the world of sense as the type of a supersensible system of things, provided I do not transfer to the latter the intuitions, and what depends on them, but merely apply to it the form of law in general (the notion of which occurs even in the commonest use of reason, but cannot be definitely known a priori for any other purpose than the pure practical use of reason); for laws, as such, are so far identical, no matter from what they derive their determining principles.

Further, since of all the supersensible absolutely nothing [is known] except freedom (through the moral law), and this only so far as it is inseparably implied in that law, and moreover all supersensible objects to which reason might lead us, following the guidance of that law, have still no reality for us, except for the purpose of that law, and for the use of mere practical reason; and as reason is authorized and even compelled to use physical nature (in its pure form as an object of the understanding) as the type of the judgement; hence, the present remark will serve to guard against reckoning amongst concepts themselves that which belongs only to the typic of concepts. This, namely, as a typic of the judgement, guards against the empiricism of practical reason, which founds the practical notions of good and evil merely on experienced consequences (so-called happiness). No doubt happiness and the infinite advantages which would result from a will determined by self-love, if this will at the same time erected itself into a universal law of nature, may certainly serve as a perfectly suitable type of the morally good, but it is not identical with it. The same typic guards also against the mysticism of practical reason, which turns what served only as a symbol into a schema, that is, proposes to provide for the moral concepts actual intuitions, which, however, are not sensible (intuitions of an invisible Kingdom of God), and thus plunges into the transcendent. What is befitting the use of the moral concepts is only the rationalism of the judgement, which takes from the sensible system of nature only what pure reason can also conceive of itself, that is, conformity to law, and transfers into the supersensible nothing but what can conversely be actually exhibited by actions in the world of sense according to the formal rule of a law of nature. However, the caution against empiricism of practical reason is much more important; for mysticism is quite reconcilable with the purity and sublimity of the moral law, and, besides, it is not very natural or agreeable to common habits of thought to strain one's imagination to supersensible intuitions; and hence the danger on this side is not so general. Empiricism, on the contrary, cuts up at the roots the morality of intentions (in which, and not in actions only, consists the high worth that men can and ought to give to themselves), and substitutes for duty something quite different, namely, an empirical interest, with which the inclinations generally are secretly leagued; and empiricism, moreover, being on this account allied with all the inclinations which (no matter what fashion they put on) degrade humanity when they are raised to the dignity of a supreme practical principle; and as these, nevertheless, are so favourable to everyone's feelings, it is for that reason much more dangerous than mysticism, which can never constitute a lasting condition of any great number of persons.

CHAPTER III. OF THE MOTIVES OF PURE PRACTICAL REASON

What is essential in the moral worth of actions is that the moral law should directly determine the will. If the determination of the will takes place in conformity indeed to the moral law, but only by means of a feeling, no matter of what kind, which has to be presupposed in order that the law may be sufficient to determine the will, and therefore not for the sake of the law, then the action will possess legality, but not morality. Now, if we understand by motive (elater animi) the subjective ground of determination of the will of a being whose reason does not necessarily conform to the objective law, by virtue of its own nature, then it will follow, first, that no motives can be attributed to the Divine will, and that the motives of the human will (as well as that of every created rational being) can never be anything else than the moral law, and consequently that the objective principle of determination must always and alone be also the subjectively sufficient determining principle of the action, if this is not merely to fulfil the letter of the law, without containing its spirit.[3]

Since, then, for the purpose of giving the moral law influence over the will, we must not seek for any other motives that might enable us to dispense with the motive of the law itself, because that would produce mere hypocrisy, without consistency; and it is even dangerous to allow other motives (for instance, that of interest) even to co-operate along with the moral law; hence nothing is left us but to determine carefully in what way the moral law becomes a motive, and what effect this has upon the faculty of desire. For as to the question how a law can be directly and of itself a determining principle of the will (which is the essence of morality), this is, for human reason, an insoluble problem and identical with the question: how a free will is possible. Therefore what we have to show a priori is not why the moral law in itself supplies a motive, but what effect it, as such, produces (or, more correctly speaking, must produce) on the mind.

The essential point in every determination of the will by the moral law is that being a free will it is determined simply by the moral law, not only without the co-operation of sensible impulses, but even to the rejection of all such, and to the checking of all inclinations so far as they might be opposed to that law. So far, then, the effect of the moral law as a motive is only negative, and this motive can be known a priori to be such. For all inclination and every sensible impulse is founded on feeling, and the negative effect produced on feeling (by the check on the inclinations) is itself feeling; consequently, we can see a priori that the moral law, as a determining principle of the will, must by thwarting all our inclinations produce a feeling which may be called pain; and in this we have the first, perhaps the only, instance in which we are able from a priori considerations to determine the relation of a cognition (in this case of pure practical reason) to the feeling of pleasure or displeasure. All the inclinations together (which can be reduced to a tolerable system, in which case their satisfaction is called happiness) constitute self-regard (solipsismus). This is either the self-love that consists in an excessive fondness for oneself (philautia), or satisfaction with oneself (arrogantia). The former is called particularly selfishness; the latter self-conceit. Pure practical reason only checks selfishness, looking on it as natural and active in us even prior to the moral law, so far as to limit it to the condition of agreement with this law, and then it is called rational self-love. But self-conceit reason strikes down altogether, since all claims to self-esteem which precede agreement with the moral law are vain and unjustifiable, for the certainty of a state of mind that coincides with this law is the first condition of personal worth (as we shall presently show more clearly), and prior to this conformity any pretension to worth is false and unlawful. Now the propensity to self-esteem is one of the inclinations which the moral law checks, inasmuch as that esteem rests only on

390 | IMMANUEL KANT

morality. Therefore the moral law breaks down self-conceit. But as this law is something positive in itself, namely, the form of an intellectual causality, that is, of freedom, it must be an object of respect; for, by opposing the subjective antagonism of the inclinations, it weakens self-conceit; and since it even breaks down, that is, humiliates, this conceit, it is an object of the highest respect and, consequently, is the foundation of a positive feeling which is not of empirical origin, but is known a priori. Therefore respect for the moral law is a feeling which is produced by an intellectual cause, and this feeling is the only one that we know quite a priori and the necessity of which we can perceive.

In the preceding chapter we have seen that everything that presents itself as an object of the will prior to the moral law is by that law itself, which is the supreme condition of practical reason, excluded from the determining principles of the will which we have called the unconditionally good; and that the mere practical form which consists in the adaptation of the maxims to universal legislation first determines what is good in itself and absolutely, and is the basis of the maxims of a pure will, which alone is good in every respect. However, we find that our nature as sensible beings is such that the matter of desire (objects of inclination, whether of hope or fear) first presents itself to us; and our pathologically affected self, although it is in its maxims quite unfit for universal legislation; yet, just as if it constituted our entire self, strives to put its pretensions forward first, and to have them acknowledged as the first and original. This propensity to make ourselves in the subjective determining principles of our choice serve as the objective determining principle of the will generally may be called self-love; and if this pretends to be legislative as an unconditional practical principle it may be called self-conceit. Now the moral law, which alone is truly objective (namely, in every respect), entirely excludes the influence of self-love on the supreme practical principle, and indefinitely checks the self-conceit that prescribes the subjective conditions of the former as laws. Now whatever checks our self-conceit in our own judgement humiliates; therefore the moral law inevitably humbles every man when he compares with it the physical propensities of his nature. That, the idea of which as a determining principle of our will humbles us in our self-consciousness, awakes respect for itself, so far as it is itself positive and a determining principle. Therefore the moral law is even subjectively a cause of respect. Now since everything that enters into self-love belongs to inclination, and all inclination rests on feelings, and consequently whatever checks all the feelings together in self-love has necessarily, by this very circumstance, an influence on feeling; hence we comprehend how it is possible to perceive a priori that the moral law can produce an effect on feeling, in that it excludes the inclinations and the propensity to make them the supreme practical condition, i.e., self-love, from all participation in the supreme legislation. This effect is on one side merely negative, but on the other side, relatively to the restricting principle of pure practical reason, it is positive. No special kind of feeling need be assumed for this under the name of a practical or moral feeling as antecedent to the moral law and serving as its foundation.

The negative effect on feeling (unpleasantness) is pathological, like every influence on feeling and like every feeling generally. But as an effect of the consciousness of the moral law, and consequently in relation to a supersensible cause, namely, the subject of pure practical reason which is the supreme lawgiver, this feeling of a rational being affected by inclinations is called humiliation (intellectual self-depreciation); but with reference to the positive source of this humiliation, the law, it is respect for it. There is indeed no feeling for this law; but inasmuch as it removes the resistance out of the way, this removal of an obstacle is, in the judgement of reason, esteemed equivalent to a positive help to its causality. Therefore this feeling may also be called a feeling of respect for the moral law, and for both reasons together a moral feeling.

While the moral law, therefore, is a formal determining principle of action by practical pure reason, and is moreover a material though only objective determining principle of the objects of action as called good and evil, it is also a subjective determining principle, that is, a motive to this action, inasmuch as it has influence on the morality of the subject and produces a feeling conducive to the influence of the law on the will. There is here in the subject no antecedent feeling tending to morality. For this is impossible, since every feeling is sensible, and the motive of moral intention must be free from all sensible conditions. On the contrary, while the sensible feeling which is at the bottom of all our inclinations is the condition of that impression which we call respect, the cause that determines it lies in the pure practical reason; and this impression therefore, on account of its origin, must be called, not a pathological but a practical effect. For by the fact that the conception of the moral law deprives self-love of its influence, and self-conceit of its illusion, it lessens the obstacle to pure practical reason and produces the conception of the superiority of its objective law to the impulses of the sensibility; and thus, by removing the counterpoise, it gives relatively greater weight to the law in the judgement of reason (in the case of a will affected by the aforesaid impulses). Thus the respect for the law is not a motive to morality, but is morality itself subjectively considered as a motive, inasmuch as pure practical reason, by rejecting all the rival pretensions of self-love, gives authority to the law, which now alone has influence. Now it is to be observed that as respect is an effect on feeling, and therefore on the sensibility, of a rational being, it presupposes this sensibility, and therefore also the finiteness of such beings on whom the moral law imposes respect; and that respect for the law cannot be attributed to a supreme being, or to any being free from all sensibility, in whom, therefore, this sensibility cannot be an obstacle to practical reason.

This feeling (which we call the moral feeling) is therefore produced simply by reason. It does not serve for the estimation of actions nor for the foundation of the objective moral law itself, but merely as a motive to make this of itself a maxim. But what name could we more suitably apply to this singular feeling which cannot be compared to any pathological feeling? It is of such a peculiar kind that it seems to be at the disposal of reason only, and that pure practical reason.

Respect applies always to persons only- not to things. The latter may arouse inclination, and if they are animals (e.g., horses, dogs, etc.), even love or fear, like the sea, a volcano, a beast of prey; but never respect. Something that comes nearer to this feeling is admiration, and this, as an affection, astonishment, can apply to things also, e.g., lofty mountains, the magnitude, number, and distance of the heavenly bodies, the strength and swiftness of many animals, etc. But all this is not respect. A man also may be an object to me of love, fear, or admiration, even to astonishment, and yet not be an object of respect. His jocose humour, his courage and strength, his power from the rank he has amongst others, may inspire me with sentiments of this kind, but still inner respect for him is wanting. Fontenelle says, "I bow before a great man, but my mind does not bow." I would add, before an humble plain man, in whom I perceive uprightness of character in a higher degree than I am conscious of in myself,- my mind bows whether I choose it or not, and though I bear my head never so high that he may not forget my superior rank. Why is this? Because his example exhibits to me a law that humbles my self-conceit when I compare it with my conduct: a law, the practicability of obedience to which I see proved by fact before my eyes. Now, I may even be conscious of a like degree of uprightness, and yet the respect remains. For since in man all good is defective, the law made visible by an example still humbles my pride, my standard being furnished by a man whose imperfections, whatever they may be, are not known to me as my own are, and who therefore appears to me in a more favourable light. Respect is a tribute which we cannot refuse to merit, whether we will or not; we may indeed outwardly withhold it, but we cannot help feeling it inwardly.

Respect is so far from being a feeling of pleasure that we only reluctantly give way to it as regards a man. We try to find out something that may lighten the burden of it, some fault to compensate us for the humiliation which such an example causes. Even the dead are not always secure from this criticism, especially if their example appears inimitable. Even the moral law itself in its solemn majesty is exposed to this endeavour to save oneself from yielding it respect. Can it be thought that it is for any other reason that we are so ready to reduce it to the level of our familiar inclination, or that it is for any other reason that we all take such trouble to make it out to be the chosen precept of our own interest well understood, but that we want to be free from the deterrent respect which shows us our own unworthiness with such severity? Nevertheless, on the other hand, so little is there pain in it that if once one has laid aside self-conceit and allowed practical influence to that respect, he can never be satisfied with contemplating the majesty of this law, and the soul believes itself elevated in proportion as it sees the holy law elevated above it and its frail nature. No doubt great talents and activity proportioned to them may also occasion respect or an analogous feeling. It is very proper to yield it to them, and then it appears as if this sentiment were the same thing as admiration. But if we look closer we shall observe that it is always uncertain how much of the ability is due to native talent, and how much to diligence in cultivating it. Reason represents it to us as probably the fruit of cultivation, and therefore as meritorious, and this notably reduces our self-conceit, and either casts a reproach on us or urges us to follow such an example in the way that is suitable to us. This respect, then, which we show to such a person (properly speaking, to the law that his example exhibits) is not mere admiration; and this is confirmed also by the fact that when the common run of admirers think they have learned from any source the badness of such a man's character (for instance Voltaire's) they give up all respect for him; whereas the true scholar still feels it at least with regard to his talents, because he is himself engaged in a business and a vocation which make imitation of such a man in some degree a law.

Respect for the moral law is, therefore, the only and the undoubted moral motive, and this feeling is directed to no object, except on the ground of this law. The moral law first determines the will objectively and directly in the judgement of reason; and freedom, whose causality can be determined only by the law, consists just in this, that it restricts all inclinations, and consequently self-esteem, by the condition of obedience to its pure law. This restriction now has an effect on feeling, and produces the impression of displeasure which can be known a priori from the moral law. Since it is so far only a negative effect which, arising from the influence of pure practical reason, checks the activity of the subject, so far as it is determined by inclinations, and hence checks the opinion of his personal worth (which, in the absence of agreement with the moral law, is reduced to nothing); hence, the effect of this law on feeling is merely humiliation. We can, therefore, perceive this a priori, but cannot know by it the force of the pure practical law as a motive, but only the resistance to motives of the sensibility. But since the same law is objectively, that is, in the conception of pure reason, an immediate principle of determination of the will, and consequently this humiliation takes place only relatively to the purity of the law; hence, the lowering of the pretensions of moral self-esteem, that is, humiliation on the sensible side, is an elevation of the moral, i.e., practical, esteem for the law itself on the intellectual side; in a word, it is respect for the law, and therefore, as its cause is intellectual, a positive feeling which can be known a priori. For whatever diminishes the obstacles to an activity furthers this activity itself. Now the recognition of the moral law is the consciousness of an activity of practical reason from objective principles, which only fails to reveal its effect in actions because subjective (pathological) causes hinder it. Respect for the moral law then must be regarded as a positive, though indirect, effect of it on feeling, inasmuch as this respect weakens the impeding influence of inclinations by humiliating self-esteem; and hence also as a subjective principle of activity, that is, as a motive to obedience to the law, and as a principle of the maxims of a life conformable to it. From the notion of a motive arises that of an interest, which can never be attributed to any being unless it possesses reason, and which signifies a motive of the will in so far as it is conceived by the reason. Since in a morally good will the law itself must be the motive, the moral interest is a pure interest of practical reason alone, independent of sense. On the notion of an interest is based that of a maxim. This, therefore, is morally good only in case it rests simply on the interest taken in obedience to the law. All three notions, however, that of a motive, of an interest, and of a maxim, can be applied only to finite beings. For they all suppose a limitation of the nature of the being, in that the subjective character of his choice does not of itself agree with the objective law of a practical reason; they suppose that the being requires to be impelled to action by something, because an internal obstacle opposes itself. Therefore they cannot be applied to the Divine will.

There is something so singular in the unbounded esteem for the pure moral law, apart from all advantage, as it is presented for our obedience by practical reason, the voice of which makes even the boldest sinner tremble and compels him to hide himself from it, that we cannot wonder if we find this influence of a mere intellectual idea on the feelings quite incomprehensible to speculative reason and have to be satisfied with seeing so much of this a priori that such a feeling is inseparably connected with the conception of the moral law in every finite rational being. If this feeling of respect were pathological, and therefore were a feeling of pleasure based on the inner sense, it would be in vain to try to discover a connection of it with any idea a priori. But [it] is a feeling that applies merely to what is practical, and depends on the conception of a law, simply as to its form, not on account of any object, and therefore cannot be reckoned either as pleasure or pain, and yet produces an interest in obedience to the law, which we call the moral interest, just as the capacity of taking such an interest in the law (or respect for the moral law itself) is properly the moral feeling.

The consciousness of a free submission of the will to the law, yet combined with an inevitable constraint put upon all inclinations, though only by our own reason, is respect for the law. The law that demands this respect and inspires it is clearly no other than the moral (for no other precludes all inclinations from exercising any direct influence on the will). An action which is objectively practical according to this law, to the exclusion of every determining principle of inclination, is duty, and this by reason of that exclusion includes in its concept practical obligation, that is, a determination to actions, however reluctantly they may be done. The feeling that arises from the consciousness of this obligation is not pathological, as would be a feeling produced by an object of the senses, but practical only, that is, it is made possible by a preceding (objective) determination of the will and a causality of the reason. As submission to the law, therefore, that is, as a command (announcing constraint for the sensibly affected subject), it contains in it no pleasure, but on the contrary, so far, pain in the action. On the other hand, however, as this constraint is exercised merely by the legislation of our own reason, it also contains something elevating, and this subjective effect on feeling, inasmuch as pure practical reason is the sole cause of it, may be called in this respect self-approbation, since we recognize ourselves as determined thereto solely by the law without any interest, and are now conscious of a quite different interest subjectively produced thereby, and which is purely practical and free; and our taking this interest in an action of duty is not suggested by any inclination, but is commanded and actually brought about by reason through the practical law; whence this feeling obtains a special name, that of respect.

The notion of duty, therefore, requires in the action, objectively, agreement with the law, and, subjectively in its maxim, that respect for the law shall be the sole mode in which the will is determined thereby. And on this rests the distinction between the consciousness of having acted according to duty and from duty, that is, from respect for the law. The former (legality) is possible even if inclinations have been the determining principles of the will; but the latter (morality), moral worth, can be placed only in this, that the action is done from duty, that is, simply for the sake of the law.[4]

It is of the greatest importance to attend with the utmost exactness in all moral judgements to the subjective principle of all maxims, that all the morality of actions may be placed in the necessity of acting from duty and from respect for the law, not from love and inclination for that which the actions are to produce. For men and all created rational beings moral necessity is constraint, that is obligation, and every action based on it is to be conceived as a duty, not as a proceeding previously pleasing, or likely to be pleasing to us of our own accord. As if indeed we could ever bring it about that without respect for the law, which implies fear, or at least apprehension of transgression, we of ourselves, like the independent Deity, could ever come into possession of holiness of will by the coincidence of our will with the pure moral law becoming as it were part of our nature, never to be shaken (in which case the law would cease to be a command for us, as we could never be tempted to be untrue to it).

The moral law is in fact for the will of a perfect being a law of holiness, but for the will of every finite rational being a law of duty, of moral constraint, and of the determination of its actions by respect for this law and reverence for its duty. No other subjective principle must be assumed as a motive, else while the action might chance to be such as the law prescribes, yet, as does not proceed from duty, the intention, which is the thing properly in question in this legislation, is not moral.

It is a very beautiful thing to do good to men from love to them and from sympathetic good will, or to be just from love of order; but this is not yet the true moral maxim of our conduct which is suitable to our position amongst rational beings as men, when we pretend with fanciful pride to set ourselves above the thought of duty, like volunteers, and, as if we were independent on the command, to want to do of our own good pleasure what we think we need no command to do. We stand under a discipline of reason and in all our maxims must not forget our subjection to it, nor withdraw anything therefrom, or by an egotistic presumption diminish aught of the authority of the law (although our own reason gives it) so as to set the determining principle of our will, even though the law be conformed to, anywhere else but in the law itself and in respect for this law. Duty and obligation are the only names that we must give to our relation to the moral law. We are indeed legislative members of a moral kingdom rendered possible by freedom, and presented to us by reason as an object of respect; but yet we are subjects in it, not the sovereign, and to mistake our inferior position as creatures, and presumptuously to reject the authority of the moral law, is already to revolt from it in spirit, even though the letter of it is fulfilled.

With this agrees very well the possibility of such a command as: Love God above everything, and thy neighbour as thyself.[5] For as a command it requires respect for a law which commands love and does not leave it to our own arbitrary choice to make this our principle. Love to God, however, considered as an inclination (pathological love), is impossible, for He is not an object of the senses. The same affection towards men is possible no doubt, but cannot be commanded, for it is not in the power of any man to love anyone at command; therefore it is only practical love that is meant in that pith of all laws. To love God means, in this sense, to like to do His commandments; to love one's neighbour means to like to practise all duties towards him. But the command that makes this a rule cannot command us to have this disposition in actions conformed to duty, but only to endeavour after it. For a command to like to do a thing is in itself contradictory, because if we already know of ourselves what we are bound to do, and if further we are conscious of liking to do it, a command would be quite needless; and if we do it not willingly, but only out of respect for the law, a command that makes this respect the motive of our maxim would directly counteract the disposition commanded. That law of all laws, therefore, like all the moral precepts of the Gospel, exhibits the moral disposition in all its perfection, in which, viewed as an ideal of holiness, it is not attainable by any creature, but yet is the pattern which we should strive to approach, and in an uninterrupted but infinite progress become like to. In fact, if a rational creature could ever reach this point, that he thoroughly likes to do all moral laws, this would mean that there does not exist in him even the possibility of a desire that would tempt him to deviate from them; for to overcome such a desire always costs the subject some sacrifice and therefore requires self-compulsion, that is, inward constraint to something that one does not quite like to do; and no creature can ever reach this stage of moral disposition. For, being a creature, and therefore always dependent with respect to what he requires for complete satisfaction, he can never be quite free from desires and inclinations, and as these rest on physical causes, they can never of themselves coincide with the moral law, the sources of which are quite different; and therefore they make it necessary to found the mental disposition of one's maxims on moral obligation, not on ready inclination, but on respect, which demands obedience to the law, even though one may not like it; not on love, which apprehends no inward reluctance of the will towards the law. Nevertheless, this latter, namely, love to the law (which would then cease to be a command, and then morality, which would have passed subjectively into holiness, would cease to be virtue) must be the constant though unattainable goal of his endeavours. For in the case of what we highly esteem, but yet (on account of the consciousness of our weakness) dread, the increased facility of satisfying it changes the most reverential awe into inclination, and respect into love; at least this would be the perfection of a disposition devoted to the law, if it were possible for a creature to attain it.

This reflection is intended not so much to clear up the evangelical command just cited, in order to prevent religious fanaticism in regard to love of God, but to define accurately the moral disposition with regard directly to our duties towards men, and to check, or if possible prevent, a merely moral fanaticism which infects many persons. The stage of morality on which man (and, as far as we can see, every rational creature) stands is respect for the moral law. The disposition that he ought to have in obeying this is to obey it from duty, not from spontaneous inclination, or from an endeavour taken up from liking and unbidden; and this proper moral condition in which he can always be is virtue, that is, moral disposition militant, and not holiness in the fancied possession of a perfect purity of the disposition of the will. It is nothing but moral fanaticism and exaggerated self-conceit that is infused into the mind by exhortation to actions as noble, sublime, and magnanimous, by which men are led into the delusion that it is not duty, that is, respect for the law, whose yoke (an easy yoke indeed, because reason itself imposes it on us) they must bear, whether they like it or not, that constitutes the determining principle of their actions, and which always humbles them while they obey it; fancying that those actions are expected from them, not from duty, but as pure merit. For not only would they, in imitating such deeds from such a principle, not have fulfilled the spirit of the law in the least, which consists not in the legality of the action (without regard to principle), but in the subjection of the mind to the law; not only do they make the motives pathological (seated in sympathy or self-love), not moral (in the law), but they produce in this way a vain, high-flying, fantastic way of thinking, flattering themselves with a spontaneous goodness of heart that needs neither spur nor bridle, for which no command is needed, and thereby forgetting their obligation, which they ought to think of rather than merit. Indeed actions of others which are done with great sacrifice, and merely for the sake of duty, may be praised as noble and sublime, but only so far as there are traces which suggest that they were done wholly out of respect for duty and not from excited feelings. If these, however, are set before anyone as examples to be imitated, respect for duty (which is the only true moral feeling) must be employed as the motive- this severe holy precept which never allows our vain self-love to dally with pathological impulses (however analogous they may be to morality), and to take a pride in meritorious worth. Now if we search we shall find for all actions that are worthy of praise a law of duty which commands, and does not leave us to choose what may be agreeable to our inclinations. This is the only way of representing things that can give a moral training to the soul, because it alone is capable of solid and accurately defined principles.

If fanaticism in its most general sense is a deliberate over stepping of the limits of human reason, then moral fanaticism is such an over stepping of the bounds that practical pure reason sets to mankind, in that it forbids us to place the subjective determining principle of correct actions, that is, their moral motive, in anything but the law itself, or to place the disposition which is thereby brought into the maxims in anything but respect for this law, and hence commands us to take as the supreme vital principle of all morality in men the thought of duty, which strikes down all arrogance as well as vain self-love.

If this is so, it is not only writers of romance or sentimental educators (although they may be zealous opponents of sentimentalism), but sometimes even philosophers, nay, even the severest of all, the Stoics, that have brought in moral fanaticism instead of a sober but wise moral discipline, although the fanaticism of the latter was more heroic, that of the former of an insipid, effeminate character; and we may, without hypocrisy, say of the moral teaching of the Gospel, that it first, by the purity of its moral principle, and at the same time by its suitability to the limitations of finite beings, brought all the good conduct of men under the discipline of a duty plainly set before their eyes, which does not permit them to indulge in dreams of imaginary moral perfections; and that it also set the bounds of humility (that is, self-knowledge) to self-conceit as well as to self-love, both which are ready to mistake their limits.

Duty! Thou sublime and mighty name that dost embrace nothing charming or insinuating, but requirest submission, and yet seekest not to move the will by threatening aught that would arouse natural aversion or terror, but merely holdest forth a law which of itself finds entrance into the mind, and yet gains reluctant reverence (though not always obedience), a law before which all inclinations are dumb, even though they secretly counter-work it; what origin is there worthy of thee, and where is to be found the root of thy noble descent which proudly rejects all kindred with the inclinations; a root to be derived from which is the indispensable condition of the only worth which men can give themselves?

It can be nothing less than a power which elevates man above himself (as a part of the world of sense), a power which connects him with an order of things that only the understanding can conceive, with a world which at the same time commands the whole sensible world, and with it the empirically determinable existence of man in time, as well as the sum total of all ends (which totality alone suits such unconditional practical laws as the moral). This power is nothing but personality, that is, freedom and independence on the mechanism of nature, yet, regarded also as a faculty of a being which is subject to special laws, namely, pure practical laws given by its own reason; so that the person as belonging to the sensible world is subject to his own personality as belonging to the intelligible [supersensible] world. It is then not to be wondered at that man, as belonging to both worlds, must regard his own nature in reference to its second and highest characteristic only with reverence, and its laws with the highest respect.

On this origin are founded many expressions which designate the worth of objects according to moral ideas. The moral law is holy (inviolable). Man is indeed unholy enough, but he must regard humanity in his own person as holy. In all creation every thing one chooses and over which one has any power, may be used merely as means; man alone, and with him every rational creature, is an end in himself. By virtue of the autonomy of his freedom he is the subject of the moral law, which is holy. Just for this reason every will, even every person's own individual will, in relation to itself, is restricted to the condition of agreement with the autonomy of the rational being, that is to say, that it is not to be subject to any purpose which cannot accord with a law which might arise from the will of the passive subject himself; the latter is, therefore, never to be employed merely as means, but as itself also, concurrently, an end. We justly attribute this condition even to the Divine will, with regard to the rational beings in the world, which are His creatures, since it rests on their personality, by which alone they are ends in themselves.

This respect-inspiring idea of personality which sets before our eyes the sublimity of our nature (in its higher aspect), while at the same time it shows us the want of accord of our conduct with it and thereby strikes down self-conceit, is even natural to the commonest reason and easily observed. Has not every even moderately honourable man sometimes found that, where by an otherwise inoffensive lie he might either have withdrawn himself from an unpleasant business, or even have procured some advantages for a loved and well-deserving friend, he has avoided it solely lest he should despise himself secretly in his own eyes? When an upright man is in the greatest distress, which he might have avoided if he could only have disregarded duty, is he not sustained by the consciousness that he has maintained humanity in its proper dignity in his own person and honoured it, that he has no reason to be ashamed of himself in his own sight, or to dread the inward glance of self-examination? This consolation is not happiness, it is not even the smallest part of it, for no one would wish to have occasion for it, or would, perhaps, even desire a life in such circumstances. But he lives, and he cannot endure that he should be in his own eyes unworthy of life. This inward peace is therefore merely negative as regards what can make life pleasant; it is, in fact, only the escaping the danger of sinking in personal worth, after everything else that is valuable has been lost. It is the effect of a respect for something quite different from life, something in comparison and contrast with which life with all its enjoyment has no value. He still lives only because it is his duty, not because he finds anything pleasant in life.

Such is the nature of the true motive of pure practical reason; it is no other than the pure moral law itself, inasmuch as it makes us conscious of the sublimity of our own supersensible existence and subjectively produces respect for their higher nature in men who are also conscious of their sensible existence and of the consequent dependence of their pathologically very susceptible nature. Now with this motive may be combined so many charms and satisfactions of life that even on this account alone the most prudent choice of a rational Epicurean reflecting on the greatest advantage of life would declare itself on the side of moral conduct, and it may even be advisable to join this prospect of a cheerful enjoyment of life with that supreme motive which is already sufficient of itself; but only as a counterpoise to the attractions which vice does not fail to exhibit on the opposite side, and not so as, even in the smallest degree, to place in this the proper moving power when duty is in question. For that would be just the same as to wish to taint the purity of the moral disposition in its source. The majesty of duty has nothing to do with enjoyment of life; it has its special law and its special tribunal, and though the two should be never so well shaken together to be given well mixed, like medicine, to the sick soul, yet they will soon separate of themselves; and if they do not, the former will not act; and although physical life might gain somewhat in force, the moral life would fade away irrecoverably.

CRITICAL EXAMINATION OF THE ANALYTIC OF PURE PRACTICAL REASON.

By the critical examination of a science, or of a portion of it, which constitutes a system by itself, I understand the inquiry and proof why it must have this and no other systematic form, when we compare it with another system which is based on a similar faculty of knowledge. Now practical and speculative reason are based on the same faculty, so far as both are pure reason. Therefore the difference in their systematic form must be determined by the comparison of both, and the ground of this must be assigned.

The Analytic of pure theoretic reason had to do with the knowledge of such objects as may have been given to the understanding, and was obliged therefore to begin from intuition and consequently (as this is always sensible) from sensibility; and only after that could advance to concepts (of the objects of this intuition), and could only end with principles after both these had preceded. On the contrary, since practical reason has not to do with objects so as to know them, but with its own faculty of realizing them (in accordance with the knowledge of them), that is, with a will which is a causality, inasmuch as reason contains its determining principle; since, consequently, it has not to furnish an object of intuition, but as practical reason has to furnish only a law (because the notion of causality always implies the reference to a law which determines the existence of the many in relation to one another); hence a critical examination of the Analytic of reason, if this is to be practical reason (and this is properly the problem), must begin with the possibility of practical principles a priori. Only after that can it proceed to concepts of the objects of a practical reason, namely, those of absolute good and evil, in order to assign them in accordance with those principles (for prior to those principles they cannot possibly be given as good and evil by any faculty of knowledge), and only then could the section be concluded with the last chapter, that, namely, which treats of the relation of the pure practical reason to the sensibility and of its necessary influence thereon, which is a priori cognisable, that is, of the moral sentiment. Thus the Analytic of the practical pure reason has the whole extent of the conditions of its use in common with the theoretical, but in reverse order. The Analytic of pure theoretic reason was divided into transcendental Aesthetic and transcendental Logic, that of the practical reversely into Logic and Aesthetic of pure practical reason (if I may, for the sake of analogy merely, use these designations, which are not quite suitable). This logic again was there divided into the Analytic of concepts and that of principles: here into that of principles and concepts. The Aesthetic also had in the former case two parts, on account of the two kinds of sensible intuition; here the sensibility is not considered as a capacity of intuition at all, but merely as feeling (which can be a subjective ground of desire), and in regard to it pure practical reason admits no further division.

It is also easy to see the reason why this division into two parts with its subdivision was not actually adopted here (as one might have been induced to attempt by the example of the former critique). For since it is pure reason that is here considered in its practical use, and consequently as proceeding from a priori principles, and not from empirical principles of determination, hence the division of the analytic of pure practical reason must resemble that of a syllogism; namely, proceeding from the universal in the major premiss (the moral principle), through a minor premiss containing a subsumption of possible actions (as good or evil) under the former, to the conclusion, namely, the subjective determination of the will (an interest in the possible practical good, and in the maxim founded on it). He who has been able to convince himself of the truth of the positions occurring in the Analytic will take pleasure in such comparisons; for they justly suggest the expectation that we may perhaps some day be able to discern the unity of the whole faculty of reason (theoretical as well as practical) and be able to derive all from one principle, which, is what human reason inevitably demands, as it finds complete satisfaction only in a perfectly systematic unity of its knowledge.

If now we consider also the contents of the knowledge that we can have of a pure practical reason, and by means of it, as shown by the Analytic, we find, along with a remarkable analogy between it and the theoretical, no less remarkable differences. As regards the theoretical, the faculty of a pure rational cognition a priori could be easily and evidently proved by examples from sciences (in which, as they put their principles to the test in so many ways by methodical use, there is not so much reason as in common knowledge to fear a secret mixture of empirical principles of cognition). But, that pure reason without the admixture of any empirical principle is practical of itself, this could only be shown from the commonest practical use of reason, by verifying the fact, that every man's natural reason acknowledges the supreme practical principle as the supreme law of his will- a law completely a priori and not depending on any sensible data. It was necessary first to establish and verify the purity of its origin, even in the judgement of this common reason, before science could take it in hand to make use of it, as a fact, that is, prior to all disputation about its possibility, and all the consequences that may be drawn from it. But this circumstance may be readily explained from what has just been said; because practical pure reason must necessarily begin with principles, which therefore must be the first data, the foundation of all science, and cannot be derived from it. It was possible to effect this verification of moral principles as principles of a pure reason quite well, and with sufficient certainty, by a single appeal to the judgement of common sense, for this reason, that anything empirical which might slip into our maxims as a determining principle of the will can be detected at once by the feeling of pleasure or pain which necessarily attaches to it as exciting desire; whereas pure practical reason positively refuses to admit this feeling into its principle as a condition. The heterogeneity of the determining principles (the empirical and rational) is clearly detected by this resistance of a practically legislating reason against every admixture of inclination, and by a peculiar kind of sentiment, which, however, does not precede the legislation of the practical reason, but, on the contrary, is produced by this as a constraint, namely, by the feeling of a respect such as no man has for inclinations of whatever kind but for the law only; and it is detected in so marked and prominent a manner that even the most uninstructed cannot fail to see at once in an example presented to him, that empirical principles of volition may indeed urge him to follow their attractions, but that he can never be expected to obey anything but the pure practical law of reason alone.

The distinction between the doctrine of happiness and the doctrine of morality, in the former of which empirical principles constitute the entire foundation, while in the second they do not form the smallest part of it, is the first and most important office of the Analytic of pure practical reason; and it must proceed in it with as much exactness and, so to speak, scrupulousness, as any geometer in his work. The philosopher, however, has greater difficulties to contend with here (as always in rational cognition by means of concepts merely without construction), because he cannot take any intuition as a foundation (for a pure noumenon). He has, however, this advantage that, like the chemist, he can at any time make an experiment with every man's practical reason for the purpose of distinguishing the moral (pure) principle of determination from the empirical; namely, by adding the moral law (as a determining principle) to the empirically affected will (e.g., that of the man who would be ready to lie because he can gain something thereby). It is as if the analyst added alkali to a solution of lime in hydrochloric acid, the acid at once forsakes the lime, combines with the alkali, and the lime is precipitated. Just in the same way, if to a man who is otherwise honest (or who for this occasion places himself only in thought in the position of an honest man), we present the moral law by which he recognises the worthlessness of the liar, his practical reason (in forming a judgement of what ought to be done) at once forsakes the advantage, combines with that which maintains in him respect for his own person (truthfulness), and the advantage after it has been separated and washed from every particle of reason (which is altogether on the side of duty) is easily weighed by everyone, so that it can enter into combination with reason in other cases, only not where it could be opposed to the moral law, which reason never forsakes, but most closely unites itself with.

But it does not follow that this distinction between the principle of happiness and that of morality is an opposition between them, and pure practical reason does not require that we should renounce all claim to happiness, but only that the moment duty is in question we should take no account of happiness. It may even in certain respects be a duty to provide for happiness; partly, because (including skill, wealth, riches) it contains means for the fulfilment of our duty; partly, because the absence of it (e.g., poverty) implies temptations to transgress our duty. But it can never be an immediate duty to promote our happiness, still less can it be the principle of all duty. Now, as all determining principles of the will, except the law of pure practical reason alone (the moral law), are all empirical and, therefore, as such, belong to the principle of happiness, they must all be kept apart from the supreme principle of morality and never be incorporated with it as a condition; since this would be to destroy all moral worth just as much as any empirical admixture with geometrical principles would destroy the certainty of mathematical evidence, which in Plato's opinion is the most excellent thing in mathematics, even surpassing their utility.

Instead, however, of the deduction of the supreme principle of pure practical reason, that is, the explanation of the possibility of such a knowledge a priori, the utmost we were able to do was to show that if we saw the possibility of the freedom of an efficient cause, we should also see not merely the possibility, but even the necessity, of the moral law as the supreme practical law of rational beings, to whom we attribute freedom of causality of their will; because both concepts are so inseparably united that we might define practical freedom as independence of the will on anything but the moral law. But we cannot perceive the possibility of the freedom of an efficient cause, especially in the world of sense; we are fortunate if only we can be sufficiently assured that there is no proof of its impossibility, and are now, by the moral law which postulates it, compelled and therefore authorized to assume it. However, there are still many who think that they can explain this freedom on empirical principles, like any other physical faculty, and treat it as a psychological property, the explanation of which only requires a more exact study of the nature of the soul and of the motives of the will, and not as a transcendental predicate of the causality of a being that belongs to the world of sense (which is really the point). They thus deprive us of the grand revelation which we obtain through practical reason by means of the moral law, the revelation, namely, of a supersensible world by the realization of the otherwise transcendent concept of freedom, and by this deprive us also of the moral law itself, which admits no empirical principle of determination. Therefore it will be necessary to add something here as a protection against this delusion and to exhibit empiricism in its naked superficiality.

The notion of causality as physical necessity, in opposition to the same notion as freedom, concerns only the existence of things so far as it is determinable in time, and, consequently, as phenomena, in opposition to their causality as things in themselves. Now if we take the attributes of existence of things in time for attributes of things in themselves (which is the common view), then it is impossible to reconcile the necessity of the causal relation with freedom; they are contradictory. For from the former it follows that every event, and consequently every action that takes place at a certain point of time, is a necessary result of what existed in time preceding. Now as time past is no longer in my power, hence every action that I perform must be the necessary result of certain determining grounds which are not in my power, that is, at the moment in which I am acting I am never free. Nay, even if I assume that my whole existence is independent on any foreign cause (for instance, God), so that the determining principles of my causality, and even of my whole existence, were not outside myself, yet this would not in the least transform that physical necessity into freedom. For at every moment of time I am still under the necessity of being determined to action by that which is not in my power, and the series of events infinite a parte priori, which I only continue according to a pre-determined order and could never begin of myself, would be a continuous physical chain, and therefore my causality would never be freedom.

If, then, we would attribute freedom to a being whose existence is determined in time, we cannot except him from the law of necessity as to all events in his existence and, consequently, as to his actions also; for that would be to hand him over to blind chance. Now as this law inevitably applies to all the causality of things, so far as their existence is determinable in time, it follows that if this were the mode in which we had also to conceive the existence of these things in themselves, freedom must be rejected as a vain and impossible conception. Consequently, if we would still save it, no other way remains but to consider that the existence of a thing, so far as it is determinable in time, and therefore its causality, according to the law of physical necessity, belong to appearance, and to attribute freedom to the same being as a thing in itself. This is certainly inevitable, if we would retain both these contradictory concepts together; but in application, when we try to explain their combination in one and the same action, great difficulties present themselves which seem to render such a combination impracticable.

When I say of a man who commits a theft that, by the law of causality, this deed is a necessary result of the determining causes in preceding time, then it was impossible that it could not have happened; how then can the judgement, according to the moral law, make any change, and suppose that it could have been omitted, because the law says that it ought to have been omitted; that is, how can a man be called quite free at the same moment, and with respect to the same action in which he is subject to an inevitable physical necessity? Some try to evade this by saying that the causes that

determine his causality are of such a kind as to agree with a comparative notion of freedom. According to this, that is sometimes called a free effect, the determining physical
cause of which lies within the acting thing itself, e.g., that which a projectile performs
when it is in free motion, in which case we use the word freedom, because while it is in
flight it is not urged by anything external; or as we call the motion of a clock a free
motion, because it moves its hands itself, which therefore do not require to be pushed
by external force; so although the actions of man are necessarily determined by causes
which precede in time, we yet call them free, because these causes are ideas produced
by our own faculties, whereby desires are evoked on occasion of circumstances, and
hence actions are wrought according to our own pleasure. This is a wretched subterfuge
with which some persons still let themselves be put off, and so think they have solved,
with a petty word- jugglery, that difficult problem, at the solution of which centuries
have laboured in vain, and which can therefore scarcely be found so completely on the
surface. In fact, in the question about the freedom which must be the foundation of all
moral laws and the consequent responsibility, it does not matter whether the principles
which necessarily determine causality by a physical law reside within the subject or
without him, or in the former case whether these principles are instinctive or are
conceived by reason, if, as is admitted by these men themselves, these determining
ideas have the ground of their existence in time and in the antecedent state, and this
again in an antecedent, etc. Then it matters not that these are internal; it matters not that
they have a psychological and not a mechanical causality, that is, produce actions by
means of ideas and not by bodily movements; they are still determining principles of
the causality of a being whose existence is determinable in time, and therefore under the
necessitation of conditions of past time, which therefore, when the subject has to act, are
no longer in his power. This may imply psychological freedom (if we choose to apply
this term to a merely internal chain of ideas in the mind), but it involves physical necessity and, therefore, leaves no room for transcendental freedom, which must be
conceived as independence on everything empirical, and, consequently, on nature
generally, whether it is an object of the internal sense considered in time only, or of the
external in time and space. Without this freedom (in the latter and true sense), which
alone is practical a priori, no moral law and no moral imputation are possible. Just for
this reason the necessity of events in time, according to the physical law of causality,
may be called the mechanism of nature, although we do not mean by this that things
which are subject to it must be really material machines. We look here only to the necessity of the connection of events in a time-series as it is developed according to the physical law, whether the subject in which this development takes place is called automaton
materiale when the mechanical being is moved by matter, or with Leibnitz spirituale
when it is impelled by ideas; and if the freedom of our will were no other than the latter
(say the psychological and comparative, not also transcendental, that is, absolute), then
it would at bottom be nothing better than the freedom of a turnspit, which, when once it
is wound up, accomplishes its motions of itself.

Now, in order to remove in the supposed case the apparent contradiction between
freedom and the mechanism of nature in one and the same action, we must remember
what was said in the Critique of Pure Reason, or what follows therefrom; viz., that the
necessity of nature, which cannot co-exist with the freedom of the subject, appertains
only to the attributes of the thing that is subject to time-conditions, consequently only to

those of the acting subject as a phenomenon; that therefore in this respect the determining principles of every action of the same reside in what belongs to past time and is no longer in his power (in which must be included his own past actions and the character that these may determine for him in his own eyes as a phenomenon). But the very same subject, being on the other side conscious of himself as a thing in himself, considers his existence also in so far as it is not subject to time-conditions, and regards himself as only determinable by laws which he gives himself through reason; and in this his existence nothing is antecedent to the determination of his will, but every action, and in general every modification of his existence, varying according to his internal sense, even the whole series of his existence as a sensible being is in the consciousness of his supersensible existence nothing but the result, and never to be regarded as the determining principle, of his causality as a noumenon. In this view now the rational being can justly say of every unlawful action that he performs, that he could very well have left it undone; although as appearance it is sufficiently determined in the past, and in this respect is absolutely necessary; for it, with all the past which determines it, belongs to the one single phenomenon of his character which he makes for himself, in consequence of which he imputes the causality of those appearances to himself as a cause independent on sensibility.

With this agree perfectly the judicial sentences of that wonderful faculty in us which we call conscience. A man may use as much art as he likes in order to paint to himself an unlawful act, that he remembers, as an unintentional error, a mere oversight, such as one can never altogether avoid, and therefore as something in which he was carried away by the stream of physical necessity, and thus to make himself out innocent, yet he finds that the advocate who speaks in his favour can by no means silence the accuser within, if only he is conscious that at the time when he did this wrong he was in his senses, that is, in possession of his freedom; and, nevertheless, he accounts for his error from some bad habits, which by gradual neglect of attention he has allowed to grow upon him to such a degree that he can regard his error as its natural consequence, although this cannot protect him from the blame and reproach which he casts upon himself. This is also the ground of repentance for a long past action at every recollection of it; a painful feeling produced by the moral sentiment, and which is practically void in so far as it cannot serve to undo what has been done. (Hence Priestley, as a true and consistent fatalist, declares it absurd, and he deserves to be commended for this candour more than those who, while they maintain the mechanism of the will in fact, and its freedom in words only, yet wish it to be thought that they include it in their system of compromise, although they do not explain the possibility of such moral imputation.) But the pain is quite legitimate, because when the law of our intelligible [supersensible] existence (the moral law) is in question, reason recognizes no distinction of time, and only asks whether the event belongs to me, as my act, and then always morally connects the same feeling with it, whether it has happened just now or long ago. For in reference to the supersensible consciousness of its existence (i.e., freedom) the life of sense is but a single phenomenon, which, inasmuch as it contains merely manifestations of the mental disposition with regard to the moral law (i.e., of the character), must be judged not according to the physical necessity that belongs to it as phenomenon, but according to the absolute spontaneity of freedom. It may therefore be admitted that, if it were possible to have so profound an insight into a man's mental

CRITIQUE OF PRACTICAL REASON | 405

character as shown by internal as well as external actions as to know all its motives, even the smallest, and likewise all the external occasions that can influence them, we could calculate a man's conduct for the future with as great certainty as a lunar or solar eclipse; and nevertheless we may maintain that the man is free. In fact, if we were capable of a further glance, namely, an intellectual intuition of the same subject (which indeed is not granted to us, and instead of it we have only the rational concept), then we should perceive that this whole chain of appearances in regard to all that concerns the moral laws depends on the spontaneity of the subject as a thing in itself, of the determination of which no physical explanation can be given. In default of this intuition, the moral law assures us of this distinction between the relation of our actions as appearance to our sensible nature, and the relation of this sensible nature to the supersensible substratum in us. In this view, which is natural to our reason, though inexplicable, we can also justify some judgements which we passed with all conscientiousness, and which yet at first sight seem quite opposed to all equity. There are cases in which men, even with the same education which has been profitable to others, yet show such early depravity, and so continue to progress in it to years of manhood, that they are thought to be born villains, and their character altogether incapable of improvement; and nevertheless they are judged for what they do or leave undone, they are reproached for their faults as guilty; nay, they themselves (the children) regard these reproaches as well founded, exactly as if in spite of the hopeless natural quality of mind ascribed to them, they remained just as responsible as any other man. This could not happen if we did not suppose that whatever springs from a man's choice (as every action intentionally performed undoubtedly does) has as its foundation a free causality, which from early youth expresses its character in its manifestations (i.e., actions). These, on account of the uniformity of conduct, exhibit a natural connection, which however does not make the vicious quality of the will necessary, but on the contrary, is the consequence of the evil principles voluntarily adopted and unchangeable, which only make it so much the more culpable and deserving of punishment. There still remains a difficulty in the combination of freedom with the mechanism of nature in a being belonging to the world of sense; a difficulty which, even after all the foregoing is admitted, threatens freedom with complete destruction. But with this danger there is also a circumstance that offers hope of an issue still favourable to freedom; namely, that the same difficulty presses much more strongly (in fact as we shall presently see, presses only) on the system that holds the existence determinable in time and space to be the existence of things in themselves; it does not therefore oblige us to give up our capital supposition of the ideality of time as a mere form of sensible intuition, and consequently as a mere manner of representation which is proper to the subject as belonging to the world of sense; and therefore it only requires that this view be reconciled with this idea.

The difficulty is as follows: Even if it is admitted that the supersensible subject can be free with respect to a given action, although, as a subject also belonging to the world of sense, he is under mechanical conditions with respect to the same action, still, as soon as we allow that God as universal first cause is also the cause of the existence of substance (a proposition which can never be given up without at the same time giving up the notion of God as the Being of all beings, and therewith giving up his all sufficiency, on which everything in theology depends), it seems as if we must admit that a man's actions have their determining principle in something which is wholly out of his power- namely, in the causality of a Supreme Being distinct from himself and on whom his own existence and the whole determination of his causality are absolutely depen- dent. In point of fact, if a man's actions as belonging to his modifications in time were not merely modifications of him as appearance, but as a thing in itself, freedom could not be saved. Man would be a marionette or an automaton, like Vaucanson's, prepared and wound up by the Supreme Artist. Self-consciousness would indeed make him a thinking automaton; but the consciousness of his own spontaneity would be mere delu- sion if this were mistaken for freedom, and it would deserve this name only in a comparative sense, since, although the proximate determining causes of its motion and a long series of their determining causes are internal, yet the last and highest is found in a foreign hand. Therefore I do not see how those who still insist on regarding time and space as attributes belonging to the existence of things in themselves, can avoid admit- ting the fatality of actions; or if (like the otherwise acute Mendelssohn) they allow them to be conditions necessarily belonging to the existence of finite and derived beings, but not to that of the infinite Supreme Being, I do not see on what ground they can justify such a distinction, or, indeed, how they can avoid the contradiction that meets them, when they hold that existence in time is an attribute necessarily belonging to finite things in themselves, whereas God is the cause of this existence, but cannot be the cause of time (or space) itself (since this must be presupposed as a necessary a priori condition of the existence of things); and consequently as regards the existence of these things. His causality must be subject to conditions and even to the condition of time; and this would inevitably bring in everything contradictory to the notions of His infinity and independence. On the other hand, it is quite easy for us to draw the distinction between the attribute of the divine existence of being independent on all time-conditions, and that of a being of the world of sense, the distinction being that between the existence of a being in itself and that of a thing in appearance. Hence, if this ideality of time and space is not adopted, nothing remains but Spinozism, in which space and time are essential attributes of the Supreme Being Himself, and the things dependent on Him (ourselves, therefore, included) are not substances, but merely accidents inhering in Him; since, if these things as His effects exist in time only, this being the condition of their existence in themselves, then the actions of these beings must be simply His actions which He performs in some place and time. Thus, Spinozism, in spite of the absurdity of its fundamental idea, argues more consistently than the creation theory can, when beings assumed to be substances, and beings in themselves existing in time, are regarded as effects of a Supreme Cause, and yet as not [belonging] to Him and His action, but as separate substances.

The above-mentioned difficulty is resolved briefly and clearly as follows: If existence in time is a mere sensible mode of representation belonging to thinking beings in the world and consequently does not apply to them as things in themselves, then the creation of these beings is a creation of things in themselves, since the notion of creation does not belong to the sensible form of representation of existence or to causality, but can only be referred to noumena. Consequently, when I say of beings in the world of sense that they are created, I so far regard them as noumena. As it would be a contradic- tion, therefore, to say that God is a creator of appearances, so also it is a contradiction to say that as creator He is the cause of actions in the world of sense, and therefore as appearances, although He is the cause of the existence of the acting beings (which are noumena). If now it is possible to affirm freedom in spite of the natural mechanism of actions as appearances (by regarding existence in time as something that belongs only to appearances, not to things in themselves), then the circumstance that the acting beings are creatures cannot make the slightest difference, since creation concerns their supersensible and not their sensible existence, and, therefore, cannot be regarded as the determining principle of the appearances. It would be quite different if the beings in the world as things in themselves existed in time, since in that case the creator of substance would be at the same time the author of the whole mechanism of this substance.

Of so great importance is the separation of time (as well as space) from the existence of things in themselves which was effected in the Critique of the Pure Speculative Reason.

It may be said that the solution here proposed involves great difficulty in itself and is scarcely susceptible of a lucid exposition. But is any other solution that has been attempted, or that may be attempted, easier and more intelligible? Rather might we say that the dogmatic teachers of metaphysics have shown more shrewdness than candour in keeping this difficult point out of sight as much as possible, in the hope that if they said nothing about it, probably no one would think of it. If science is to be advanced, all difficulties must be laid open, and we must even search for those that are hidden, for every difficulty calls forth a remedy, which cannot be discovered without science gaining either in extent or in exactness; and thus even obstacles become means of increasing the thoroughness of science. On the other hand, if the difficulties are intentionally concealed, or merely removed by palliatives, then sooner or later they burst out into incurable mischiefs, which bring science to ruin in an absolute scepticism.

Since it is, properly speaking, the notion of freedom alone amongst all the ideas of pure speculative reason that so greatly enlarges our knowledge in the sphere of the supersensible, though only of our practical knowledge, I ask myself why it exclusively possesses so great fertility, whereas the others only designate the vacant space for possible beings of the pure understanding, but are unable by any means to define the concept of them. I presently find that as I cannot think anything without a category, I must first look for a category for the rational idea of freedom with which I am now concerned; and this is the category of causality; and although freedom, a concept of the reason, being a transcendent concept, cannot have any intuition corresponding to it, yet the concept of the understanding- for the synthesis of which the former demands the unconditioned- (namely, the concept of causality) must have a sensible intuition given, by which first its objective reality is assured. Now, the categories are all divided into two classes- the mathematical, which concern the unity of synthesis in the conception of objects, and the dynamical, which refer to the unity of synthesis in the conception of the existence of objects. The former (those of magnitude and quality) always contain a synthesis of the homogeneous, and it is not possible to find in this the unconditioned antecedent to what is given in sensible intuition as conditioned in space and time, as this would itself have to belong to space and time, and therefore be again still conditioned. Whence it resulted in the Dialectic of Pure Theoretic Reason that the opposite methods of attaining the unconditioned and the totality of the conditions were both wrong. The categories of the second class (those of causality and of the necessity of a thing) did not require this homogeneity (of the conditioned and the condition in synthesis), since here what we have to explain is not how the intuition is compounded from a manifold in it, but only how the existence of the conditioned object corresponding to it is added to the existence of the condition (added, namely, in the understanding as connected therewith); and in that case it was allowable to suppose in the supersensible world the unconditioned antecedent to the altogether conditioned in the world of sense (both as regards the causal connection and the contingent existence of things themselves), although this unconditioned remained indeterminate, and to make the synthesis transcendent. Hence, it was found in the Dialectic of the Pure Speculative Reason that the two apparently opposite methods of obtaining for the conditioned the unconditioned were not really contradictory, e.g., in the synthesis of causality to conceive for the conditioned in the series of causes and effects of the sensible world, a causality which has no sensible condition, and that the same action which, as belonging to the world of sense, is always sensibly conditioned, that is, mechanically necessary, yet at the same time may be derived from a causality not sensibly conditioned- being the causality of the acting being as belonging to the supersensible world- and may consequently be conceived as free. Now, the only point in question was to change this may be into is; that is, that we should be able to show in an actual case, as it were by a fact, that certain actions imply such a causality (namely, the intellectual, sensibly unconditioned), whether they are actual or only commanded, that is, objectively necessary in a practical sense. We could not hope to find this connexion in actions actually given in experience as events of the sensible world, since causality with freedom must always be sought outside the world of sense in the world of intelligence. But things of sense are the only things offered to our perception and observation. Hence, nothing remained but to find an incontestable objective principle of causality which excludes all sensible conditions: that is, a principle in which reason does not appeal further to something else as a determining ground of its causality, but contains this determining ground itself by means of that principle, and in which therefore it is itself as pure reason practical. Now, this principle had not to be searched for or discovered; it had long been in the reason of all men, and incorporated in their nature, and is the principle of morality. Therefore, that unconditioned causality, with the faculty of it, namely, freedom, is no longer merely indefinitely and problematically thought (this speculative reason could prove to be feasible), but is even as regards the law of its causality definitely and assertorially known; and with it the fact that a being (I myself), belonging to the world of sense, belongs also to the supersensible world, this is also positively known, and thus the reality of the supersensible world is established and in practical respects definitely given, and this definiteness, which for theoretical purposes would be transcendent, is for practical purposes immanent. We could not, however, make a similar step as regards the second dynamical idea, namely, that of a necessary being. We could not rise to it from the sensible world without the aid of the first dynamical idea. For if we attempted to do so, we should have ventured to leave at a bound all that is given to us, and to leap to that of which nothing is given us that can help us to effect the connection of such a supersensible being with the world of sense (since the necessary being would have to be known as given outside ourselves). On the other hand, it is now obvious that this connection is quite possible in relation to our own subject, inasmuch as I know myself to be on the one side as an intelligible [supersensible] being determined by the moral law (by means of freedom), and on the other side as acting in the world of sense. It is the concept of freedom alone that enables us to find the unconditioned and intelligible for the conditioned and sensible without going out of ourselves. For it is our own reason that by means of the supreme and unconditional practical law knows that itself and the being that is conscious of this law (our own person) belong to the pure world of understanding, and moreover defines the manner in which, as such, it can be active. In this way it can be understood why in the whole faculty of reason it is the practical reason only that can help us to pass beyond the world of sense and give us knowledge of a supersensible order and connection, which, however, for this very reason cannot be extended further than is necessary for pure practical purposes.

Let me be permitted on this occasion to make one more remark, namely, that every step that we make with pure reason, even in the practical sphere where no attention is paid to subtle speculation, nevertheless accords with all the material points of the Critique of the Theoretical Reason as closely and directly as if each step had been thought out with deliberate purpose to establish this confirmation. Such a thorough agreement, wholly unsought for and quite obvious (as anyone can convince himself, if he will only carry moral inquiries up to their principles), between the most important proposition of practical reason and the often seemingly too subtle and needless remarks of the Critique of the Speculative Reason, occasions surprise and astonishment, and confirms the maxim already recognized and praised by others, namely, that in every scientific inquiry we should pursue our way steadily with all possible exactness and frankness, without caring for any objections that may be raised from outside its sphere, but, as far as we can, to carry out our inquiry truthfully and completely by itself. Frequent observation has convinced me that, when such researches are concluded, that which in one part of them appeared to me very questionable, considered in relation to other extraneous doctrines, when I left this doubtfulness out of sight for a time and only attended to the business in hand until it was completed, at last was unexpectedly found to agree perfectly with what had been discovered separately without the least regard to those doctrines, and without any partiality or prejudice for them. Authors would save themselves many errors and much labour lost (because spent on a delusion) if they could only resolve to go to work with more frankness.

---

1. Propositions which in mathematics or physics are called practical ought properly to be called technical. For they have nothing to do with the determination of the will; they only point out how a certain effect is to be produced and are, therefore, just as theoretical as any propositions which express the connection of a cause with an effect. Now whoever chooses the effect must also choose the cause.
2. Besides this, the expression sub ratione boni is also ambiguous. For it may mean: "We represent something to ourselves as good, when and because we desire (will) it"; or "We desire something because we represent it to ourselves as good," so that either the desire determines the notion of the object as a good, or the notion of good determines the desire (the will); so that in the first case sub ratione boni would mean, "We will something under the idea of the good"; in the second, "In consequence of this idea," which, as determining the volition, must precede it.
3. We may say of every action that conforms to the law, but is not done for the sake of the law, that it is morally good in the letter, not in the spirit (the intention).
4. If we examine accurately the notion of respect for persons as it has been already laid down, we shall perceive that it always rests on the consciousness of a duty which an example shows us, and that respect, therefore, can never have any but a moral ground, and that it is very good and even, in a psychological point of view, very useful for the knowledge of mankind, that whenever we use this expression we should attend to this secret and marvellous, yet often recurring, regard which men in their judgement pay to the moral law.
5. This law is in striking contrast with the principle of private happiness which some make the supreme principle of morality. This would be expressed thus: Love thyself above everything, and God and thy neighbour for thine own sake.

BOOK II. DIALECTIC OF PURE PRACTICAL REASON.

CHAPTER I. OF A DIALECTIC OF PURE PRACTICAL REASON GENERALLY

PURE REASON always has its dialectic, whether it is considered in its speculative or its practical employment; for it requires the absolute totality of the 'conditions of what is given conditioned, and this can only be found in things in themselves. But as all conceptions of things in themselves must be referred to intuitions, and with us men these can never be other than sensible and hence can never enable us to know objects as things in themselves but only as appearances, and since the unconditioned can never be found in this chain of appearances which consists only of conditioned and conditions; thus from applying this rational idea of the totality of the conditions (in other words of the unconditioned) to appearances, there arises an inevitable illusion, as if these latter were things in themselves (for in the absence of a warning critique they are always regarded as such). This illusion would never be noticed as delusive if it did not betray itself by a conflict of reason with itself, when it applies to appearances its fundamental principle of presupposing the unconditioned to everything conditioned. By this, however, reason is compelled to trace this illusion to its source, and search how it can be removed, and this can only be done by a complete critical examination of the whole pure faculty of reason; so that the antinomy of the pure reason which is manifest in its dialectic is in fact the most beneficial error into which human reason could ever have fallen, since it at last drives us to search for the key to escape from this labyrinth; and when this key is found, it further discovers that which we did not seek but yet had need of, namely, a view into a higher and an immutable order of things, in which we even now are, and in which we are thereby enabled by definite precepts to continue to live according to the highest dictates of reason.

It may be seen in detail in the Critique of Pure Reason how in its speculative employment this natural dialectic is to be solved, and how the error which arises from a very natural illusion may be guarded against. But reason in its practical use is not a whit better off. As pure practical reason, it likewise seeks to find the unconditioned for the practically conditioned (which rests on inclinations and natural wants), and this is not as the determining principle of the will, but even when this is given (in the moral law) it seeks the unconditioned totality of the object of pure practical reason under the name of the summum bonum.

To define this idea practically, i.e., sufficiently for the maxims of our rational conduct, is the business of practical wisdom, and this again as a science is philosophy, in the sense in which the word was understood by the ancients, with whom it meant instruction in the conception in which the summum bonum was to be placed, and the conduct by which it was to be obtained. It would be well to leave this word in its ancient signification as a doctrine of the summum bonum, so far as reason endeavours to make this into a science. For on the one hand the restriction annexed would suit the Greek expression (which signifies the love of wisdom), and yet at the same time would be sufficient to embrace under the name of philosophy the love of science: that is to say, of all speculative rational knowledge, so far as it is serviceable to reason, both for that conception and also for the practical principle determining our conduct, without letting out of sight the main end, on account of which alone it can be called a doctrine of practical wisdom. On the other hand, it would be no harm to deter the self-conceit of one who ventures to claim the title of philosopher by holding before him in the very definition a standard of self-estimation which would very much lower his pretensions. For a teacher of wisdom would mean something more than a scholar who has not come so far as to guide himself, much less to guide others, with certain expectation of attaining so high an end: it would mean a master in the knowledge of wisdom, which implies more than a modest man would claim for himself. Thus philosophy as well as wisdom would always remain an ideal, which objectively is presented complete in reason alone, while subjectively for the person it is only the goal of his unceasing endeavours; and no one would be justified in professing to be in possession of it so as to assume the name of philosopher who could not also show its infallible effects in his own person as an example (in his self-mastery and the unquestioned interest that he takes pre-eminently in the general good), and this the ancients also required as a condition of deserving that honourable title.

We have another preliminary remark to make respecting the dialectic of the pure practical reason, on the point of the definition of the summum bonum (a successful solution of which dialectic would lead us to expect, as in case of that of the theoretical reason, the most beneficial effects, inasmuch as the self-contradictions of pure practical reason honestly stated, and not concealed, force us to undertake a complete critique of this faculty).

The moral law is the sole determining principle of a pure will. But since this is merely formal (viz., as prescribing only the form of the maxim as universally legislative), it abstracts as a determining principle from all matter that is to say, from every object of volition. Hence, though the summum bonum may be the whole object of a pure practical reason, i.e., a pure will, yet it is not on that account to be regarded as its determining principle; and the moral law alone must be regarded as the principle on which that and its realization or promotion are aimed at. This remark is important in so delicate a case as the determination of moral principles, where the slightest misinterpretation perverts men's minds. For it will have been seen from the Analytic that, if we assume any object under the name of a good as a determining principle of the will prior to the moral law and then deduce from it the supreme practical principle, this would always introduce heteronomy and crush out the moral principle.

It is, however, evident that if the notion of the summum bonum includes that of the moral law as its supreme condition, then the summum bonum would not merely be an object, but the notion of it and the conception of its existence as possible by our own practical reason would likewise be the determining principle of the will, since in that case the will is in fact determined by the moral law which is already included in this conception, and by no other object, as the principle of autonomy requires. This order of the conceptions of determination of the will must not be lost sight of, as otherwise we should misunderstand ourselves and think we had fallen into a contradiction, while everything remains in perfect harmony.

CHAPTER II. OF THE DIALECTIC OF PURE REASON IN DEFINING THE CONCEPTION OF THE "SUMMUM BONUM"

The conception of the summum itself contains an ambiguity which might occasion needless disputes if we did not attend to it. The summum may mean either the supreme (supremum) or the perfect (consummatum). The former is that condition which is itself unconditioned, i.e., is not subordinate to any other (originarium); the second is that whole which is not a part of a greater whole of the same kind (perfectissimum). It has been shown in the Analytic that virtue (as worthiness to be happy) is the supreme condition of all that can appear to us desirable, and consequently of all our pursuit of happiness, and is therefore the supreme good. But it does not follow that it is the whole and perfect good as the object of the desires of rational finite beings; for this requires happiness also, and that not merely in the partial eyes of the person who makes himself an end, but even in the judgement of an impartial reason, which regards persons in general as ends in themselves. For to need happiness, to deserve it, and yet at the same time not to participate in it, cannot be consistent with the perfect volition of a rational being possessed at the same time of all power, if, for the sake of experiment, we conceive such a being. Now inasmuch as virtue and happiness together constitute the possession of the summum bonum in a person, and the distribution of happiness in exact proportion to morality (which is the worth of the person, and his worthiness to be happy) constitutes the summum bonum of a possible world; hence this summum bonum expresses the whole, the perfect good, in which, however, virtue as the condition is always the supreme good, since it has no condition above it; whereas happiness, while it is pleasant to the possessor of it, is not of itself absolutely and in all respects good, but always presupposes morally right behaviour as its condition.

When two elements are necessarily united in one concept, they must be connected as reason and consequence, and this either so that their unity is considered as analytical (logical connection), or as synthetical (real connection) the former following the law of identity, the latter that of causality. The connection of virtue and happiness may therefore be understood in two ways: either the endeavour to be virtuous and the rational pursuit of happiness are not two distinct actions, but absolutely identical, in which case no maxim need be made the principle of the former, other than what serves for the latter; or the connection consists in this, that virtue produces happiness as something distinct from the consciousness of virtue, as a cause produces an effect.

The ancient Greek schools were, properly speaking, only two, and in determining the conception of the summum bonum these followed in fact one and the same method, inasmuch as they did not allow virtue and happiness to be regarded as two distinct elements of the summum bonum, and consequently sought the unity of the principle by the rule of identity; but they differed as to which of the two was to be taken as the fundamental notion. The Epicurean said: "To be conscious that one's maxims lead to happiness is virtue"; the Stoic said: "To be conscious of one's virtue is happiness." With the former, Prudence was equivalent to morality; with the latter, who chose a higher designation for virtue, morality alone was true wisdom.

While we must admire the men who in such early times tried all imaginable ways of extending the domain of philosophy, we must at the same time lament that their acuteness was unfortunately misapplied in trying to trace out identity between two extremely heterogeneous notions, those of happiness and virtue. But it agrees with the dialectical spirit of their times (and subtle minds are even now sometimes misled in the same way) to get rid of irreconcilable differences in principle by seeking to change them into a mere contest about words, and thus apparently working out the identity of the notion under different names, and this usually occurs in cases where the combination of heterogeneous principles lies so deep or so high, or would require so complete a transformation of the doctrines assumed in the rest of the philosophical system, that men are afraid to penetrate deeply into the real difference and prefer treating it as a difference in questions of form.

While both schools sought to trace out the identity of the practical principles of virtue and happiness, they were not agreed as to the way in which they tried to force this identity, but were separated infinitely from one another, the one placing its principle on the side of sense, the other on that of reason; the one in the consciousness of sensible wants, the other in the independence of practical reason on all sensible grounds of determination. According to the Epicurean, the notion of virtue was already involved in the maxim: "To promote one's own happiness"; according to the Stoics, on the other hand, the feeling of happiness was already contained in the consciousness of virtue. Now whatever is contained in another notion is identical with part of the containing notion, but not with the whole, and moreover two wholes may be specifically distinct, although they consist of the same parts; namely if the parts are united into a whole in totally different ways. The Stoic maintained that the virtue was the whole summum bonum, and happiness only the consciousness of possessing it, as making part of the state of the subject. The Epicurean maintained that happiness was the whole summum bonum, and virtue only the form of the maxim for its pursuit; viz., the rational use of the means for attaining it.

Now it is clear from the Analytic that the maxims of virtue and those of private happiness are quite heterogeneous as to their supreme practical principle, and, although they belong to one summum bonum which together they make possible, yet they are so far from coinciding that they restrict and check one another very much in the same subject. Thus the question: "How is the summum bonum practically possible?" still remains an unsolved problem, notwithstanding all the attempts at coalition that have hitherto been made. The Analytic has, however, shown what it is that makes the problem difficult to solve; namely, that happiness and morality are two specifically distinct elements of the summum bonum and, therefore, their combination cannot be analytically cognised (as if the man that seeks his own happiness should find by mere analysis of his conception that in so acting he is virtuous, or as if the man that follows virtue should in the consciousness of such conduct find that he is already happy ipso facto), but must be a synthesis of concepts. Now since this combination is recognised as a priori, and therefore as practically necessary, and consequently not as derived from experience, so that the possibility of the summum bonum does not rest on any empirical principle, it follows that the deduction [legitimation] of this concept must be transcendental. It is a priori (morally) necessary to produce the summum bonum by freedom of will: therefore the condition of its possibility must rest solely on a priori principles of cognition.

I. THE ANTINOMY OF PRACTICAL REASON.

In the summum bonum which is practical for us, i.e., to be realized by our will, virtue and happiness are thought as necessarily combined, so that the one cannot be assumed by pure practical reason without the other also being attached to it. Now this combination (like every other) is either analytical or synthetical. It has been shown that it cannot be analytical; it must then be synthetical and, more particularly, must be conceived as the connection of cause and effect, since it concerns a practical good, i.e., one that is possible by means of action; consequently either the desire of happiness must be the motive to maxims of virtue, or the maxim of virtue must be the efficient cause of happiness. The first is absolutely impossible, because (as was proved in the Analytic) maxims which place the determining principle of the will in the desire of personal happiness are not moral at all, and no virtue can be founded on them. But the second is also impossible, because the practical connection of causes and effects in the world, as the result of the determination of the will, does not depend upon the moral dispositions of the will, but on the knowledge of the laws of nature and the physical power to use them for one's purposes; consequently we cannot expect in the world by the most punctilious observance of the moral laws any necessary connection of happiness with virtue adequate to the summum bonum. Now, as the promotion of this summum bonum, the conception of which contains this connection, is a priori a necessary object of our will and inseparably attached to the moral law, the impossibility of the former must prove the falsity of the latter. If then the supreme good is not possible by practical rules, then the moral law also which commands us to promote it is directed to vain imaginary ends and must consequently be false.

II. CRITICAL SOLUTION OF THE ANTINOMY OF PRACTICAL REASON.

The antinomy of pure speculative reason exhibits a similar conflict between freedom and physical necessity in the causality of events in the world. It was solved by showing that there is no real contradiction when the events and even the world in which they occur are regarded (as they ought to be) merely as appearances; since one and the same acting being, as an appearance (even to his own inner sense), has a causality in the world of sense that always conforms to the mechanism of nature, but with respect to the same events, so far as the acting person regards himself at the same time as a noumenon (as pure intelligence in an existence not dependent on the condition of time), he can contain a principle by which that causality acting according to laws of nature is determined, but which is itself free from all laws of nature.

It is just the same with the foregoing antinomy of pure practical reason. The first of the two propositions, "That the endeavour after happiness produces a virtuous mind," is absolutely false; but the second, "That a virtuous mind necessarily produces happiness," is not absolutely false, but only in so far as virtue is considered as a form of causality in the sensible world, and consequently only if I suppose existence in it to be the only sort of existence of a rational being; it is then only conditionally false. But as I am not only justified in thinking that I exist also as a noumenon in a world of the understanding, but even have in the moral law a purely intellectual determining principle of my causality (in the sensible world), it is not impossible that morality of mind should have a connection as cause with happiness (as an effect in the sensible world) if not immediate yet mediate (viz., through an intelligent author of nature), and moreover necessary; while in a system of nature which is merely an object of the senses, this combination could never occur except contingently and, therefore, could not suffice for the summum bonum.

Thus, notwithstanding this seeming conflict of practical reason with itself, the summum bonum, which is the necessary supreme end of a will morally determined, is a true object thereof; for it is practically possible, and the maxims of the will which as regards their matter refer to it have objective reality, which at first was threatened by the antinomy that appeared in the connection of morality with happiness by a general law; but this was merely from a misconception, because the relation between appearances was taken for a relation of the things in themselves to these appearances.

When we find ourselves obliged to go so far, namely, to the connection with an intelligible world, to find the possibility of the summum bonum, which reason points out to all rational beings as the goal of all their moral wishes, it must seem strange that, nevertheless, the philosophers both of ancient and modern times have been able to find happiness in accurate proportion to virtue even in this life (in the sensible world), or have persuaded themselves that they were conscious thereof. For Epicurus as well as the Stoics extolled above everything the happiness that springs from the consciousness of living virtuously; and the former was not so base in his practical precepts as one might infer from the principles of his theory, which he used for explanation and not for action, or as they were interpreted by many who were misled by his using the term pleasure for contentment; on the contrary, he reckoned the most disinterested practice of good amongst the ways of enjoying the most intimate delight, and his scheme of pleasure (by which he meant constant cheerfulness of mind) included the moderation and control of the inclinations, such as the strictest moral philosopher might require. He differed from the Stoics chiefly in making this pleasure the motive, which they very rightly refused to do. For, on the one hand, the virtuous Epicurus, like many well-intentioned men of this day who do not reflect deeply enough on their principles, fell into the error of presupposing the virtuous disposition in the persons for whom he wished to provide the springs to virtue (and indeed the upright man cannot be happy if he is not first conscious of his uprightness; since with such a character the reproach that his habit of thought would oblige him to make against himself in case of transgression and his moral self-condemnation would rob him of all enjoyment of the pleasantness which his condition might otherwise contain). But the question is: How is such a disposition possible in the first instance, and such a habit of thought in estimating the worth of one's existence, since prior to it there can be in the subject no feeling at all for moral worth? If a man is virtuous without being conscious of his integrity in every action, he will certainly not enjoy life, however favourable fortune may be to him in its physical circumstances; but can we make him virtuous in the first instance, in other words, before he esteems the moral worth of his existence so highly, by praising to him the peace of mind that would result from the consciousness of an integrity for which he has no sense?

On the other hand, however, there is here an occasion of a vitium subreptionis, and as it were of an optical illusion, in the self-consciousness of what one does as distinguished from what one feels- an illusion which even the most experienced cannot altogether avoid. The moral disposition of mind is necessarily combined with a consciousness that the will is determined directly by the law. Now the consciousness of a determination of the faculty of desire is always the source of a satisfaction in the resulting action; but this pleasure, this satisfaction in oneself, is not the determining principle of the action; on the contrary, the determination of the will directly by reason is the source of the feeling of pleasure, and this remains a pure practical not sensible determination of the faculty of desire. Now as this determination has exactly the same effect within in impelling to activity, that a feeling of the pleasure to be expected from the desired action would have had, we easily look on what we ourselves do as something which we merely passively feel, and take the moral spring for a sensible impulse, just as it happens in the so-called illusion of the senses (in this case the inner sense). It is a sublime thing in human nature to be determined to actions immediately by a purely rational law; sublime even is the illusion that regards the subjective side of this capacity of intellectual determination as something sensible and the effect of a special sensible feeling (for an intellectual feeling would be a contradiction). It is also of great importance to attend to this property of our personality and as much as possible to cultivate the effect of reason on this feeling. But we must beware lest by falsely extolling this moral determining principle as a spring, making its source lie in particular feelings of pleasure (which are in fact only results), we degrade and disfigure the true genuine spring, the law itself, by putting as it were a false foil upon it. Respect, not pleasure or enjoyment of happiness, is something for which it is not possible that reason should have any antecedent feeling as its foundation (for this would always be sensible and pathological); and consciousness of immediate obligation of the will by the law is by no means analogous to the feeling of pleasure, although in relation to the faculty of desire it produces the same effect, but from different sources: it is only by this mode of conception, however, that we can attain what we are seeking, namely, that actions be done not merely in accordance with duty (as a result of pleasant feelings) but from duty, which must be the true end of all moral cultivation.

Have we not, however, a word which does not express enjoyment, as happiness does, but indicates a satisfaction in one's existence, an analogue of the happiness which must necessarily accompany the consciousness of virtue? Yes this word is self-contentment which in its proper signification always designates only a negative satisfaction in one's existence, in which one is conscious of needing nothing. Freedom and the consciousness of it as a faculty of following the moral law with unyielding resolution is independence of inclinations, at least as motives determining (though not as affecting) our desire, and so far as I am conscious of this freedom in following my moral maxims, it is the only source of an unaltered contentment which is necessarily connected with it and rests on no special feeling. This may be called intellectual contentment. The sensible contentment (improperly so-called) which rests on the satisfaction of the inclinations, however delicate they may be imagined to be, can never be adequate to the conception of it. For the inclinations change, they grow with the indulgence shown them, and always leave behind a still greater void than we had thought to fill. Hence they are always burdensome to a rational being, and, although he cannot lay them aside, they wrest from him the wish to be rid of them. Even an inclination to what is right (e.g., to beneficence), though it may much facilitate the efficacy of the moral maxims, cannot produce any. For in these all must be directed to the conception of the law as a determining principle, if the action is to contain morality and not merely legality. Inclination is blind and slavish, whether it be of a good sort or not, and, when morality is in question, reason must not play the part merely of guardian to inclination, but disregarding it altogether must attend simply to its own interest as pure practical reason. This very feeling of compassion and tender sympathy, if it precedes the deliberation on the question of duty and becomes a determining principle, is even annoying to right thinking persons, brings their deliberate maxims into confusion, and makes them wish to be delivered from it and to be subject to lawgiving reason alone.

From this we can understand how the consciousness of this faculty of a pure practical reason produces by action (virtue) a consciousness of mastery over one's inclinations, and therefore of independence of them, and consequently also of the discontent that always accompanies them, and thus a negative satisfaction with one's state, i.e., contentment, which is primarily contentment with one's own person. Freedom itself becomes in this way (namely, indirectly) capable of an enjoyment which cannot be called happiness, because it does not depend on the positive concurrence of a feeling, nor is it, strictly speaking, bliss, since it does not include complete independence of inclinations and wants, but it resembles bliss in so far as the determination of one's will at least can hold itself free from their influence; and thus, at least in its origin, this enjoyment is analogous to the self-sufficiency which we can ascribe only to the Supreme Being.

From this solution of the antinomy of practical pure reason, it follows that in practical principles we may at least conceive as possible a natural and necessary connection between the consciousness of morality and the expectation of a proportionate happiness as its result, though it does not follow that we can know or perceive this connection; that, on the other hand, principles of the pursuit of happiness cannot possibly produce morality; that, therefore, morality is the supreme good (as the first condition of the summum bonum), while happiness constitutes its second element, but only in such a way that it is the morally conditioned, but necessary consequence of the former. Only with this subordination is the summum bonum the whole object of pure practical reason, which must necessarily conceive it as possible, since it commands us to contribute to the utmost of our power to its realization. But since the possibility of such connection of the conditioned with its condition belongs wholly to the supersensual relation of things and cannot be given according to the laws of the world of sense, although the practical consequences of the idea belong to the world of sense, namely, the actions that aim at realizing the summum bonum; we will therefore endeavour to set forth the grounds of that possibility, first, in respect of what is immediately in our power, and then, secondly, in that which is not in our power, but which reason presents to us as the supplement of our impotence, for the realization of the summum bonum (which by practical principles is necessary).

III. OF THE PRIMACY OF PURE PRACTICAL REASON IN ITS UNION WITH THE SPECULATIVE REASON.

By primacy between two or more things connected by reason, I understand the prerogative, belonging to one, of being the first determining principle in the connection with all the rest. In a narrower practical sense it means the prerogative of the interest of one in so far as the interest of the other is subordinated to it, while it is not postponed to any other. To every faculty of the mind we can attribute an interest, that is, a principle, that contains the condition on which alone the former is called into exercise. Reason, as the faculty of principles, determines the interest of all the powers of the mind and is determined by its own. The interest of its speculative employment consists in the cognition of the object pushed to the highest a priori principles: that of its practical employment, in the determination of the will in respect of the final and complete end. As to what is necessary for the possibility of any employment of reason at all, namely, that its principles and affirmations should not contradict one another, this constitutes no part of its interest, but is the condition of having reason at all; it is only its development, not mere consistency with itself, that is reckoned as its interest.

If practical reason could not assume or think as given anything further than what speculative reason of itself could offer it from its own insight, the latter would have the primacy. But supposing that it had of itself original a priori principles with which certain theoretical positions were inseparably connected, while these were withdrawn from any possible insight of speculative reason (which, however, they must not contradict); then the question is: Which interest is the superior (not which must give way, for they are not necessarily conflicting), whether speculative reason, which knows nothing of all that the practical offers for its acceptance, should take up these propositions and (although they transcend it) try to unite them with its own concepts as a foreign possession handed over to it, or whether it is justified in obstinately following its own separate interest and, according to the canon of Epicurus, rejecting as vain subtlety everything that cannot accredit its objective reality by manifest examples to be shown in experience, even though it should be never so much interwoven with the interest of the practical (pure) use of reason, and in itself not contradictory to the theoretical, merely because it infringes on the interest of the speculative reason to this extent, that it removes the bounds which this latter had set to itself, and gives it up to every nonsense or delusion of imagination?

In fact, so far as practical reason is taken as dependent on pathological conditions, that is, as merely regulating the inclinations under the sensible principle of happiness, we could not require speculative reason to take its principles from such a source. Mohammed's paradise, or the absorption into the Deity of the theosophists and mystics would press their monstrosities on the reason according to the taste of each, and one might as well have no reason as surrender it in such fashion to all sorts of dreams. But if pure reason of itself can be practical and is actually so, as the consciousness of the moral law proves, then it is still only one and the same reason which, whether in a theoretical or a practical point of view, judges according to a priori principles; and then it is clear that although it is in the first point of view incompetent to establish certain propositions positively, which, however, do not contradict it, then, as soon as these propositions are inseparably attached to the practical interest of pure reason, it must accept them, though it be as something offered to it from a foreign source, something that has not grown on its own ground, but yet is sufficiently authenticated; and it must try to compare and connect them with everything that it has in its power as speculative reason. It must remember, however, that these are not additions to its insight, but yet are extensions of its employment in another, namely, a practical aspect; and this is not in the least opposed to its interest, which consists in the restriction of wild speculation.

Thus, when pure speculative and pure practical reason are combined in one cognition, the latter has the primacy, provided, namely, that this combination is not contingent and arbitrary, but founded a priori on reason itself and therefore necessary. For without this subordination there would arise a conflict of reason with itself; since, if they were merely co-ordinate, the former would close its boundaries strictly and admit nothing from the latter into its domain, while the latter would extend its bounds over everything and when its needs required would seek to embrace the former within them. Nor could we reverse the order and require pure practical reason to be subordinate to the speculative, since all interest is ultimately practical, and even that of speculative reason is conditional, and it is only in the practical employment of reason that it is complete.

IV. THE IMMORTALITY OF THE SOUL AS A POSTULATE OF PURE PRACTICAL REASON.

The realization of the summum bonum in the world is the necessary object of a will determinable by the moral law. But in this will the perfect accordance of the mind with the moral law is the supreme condition of the summum bonum. This then must be possible, as well as its object, since it is contained in the command to promote the latter. Now, the perfect accordance of the will with the moral law is holiness, a perfection of which no rational being of the sensible world is capable at any moment of his existence. Since, nevertheless, it is required as practically necessary, it can only be found in a progress in infinitum towards that perfect accordance, and on the principles of pure practical reason it is necessary to assume such a practical progress as the real object of our will.

Now, this endless progress is only possible on the supposition of an endless duration of the existence and personality of the same rational being (which is called the immortality of the soul). The summum bonum, then, practically is only possible on the supposition of the immortality of the soul; consequently this immortality, being inseparably connected with the moral law, is a postulate of pure practical reason (by which I mean a theoretical proposition, not demonstrable as such, but which is an inseparable result of an unconditional a priori practical law.

This principle of the moral destination of our nature, namely, that it is only in an endless progress that we can attain perfect accordance with the moral law, is of the greatest use, not merely for the present purpose of supplementing the impotence of speculative reason, but also with respect to religion. In default of it, either the moral law is quite degraded from its holiness, being made out to be indulgent and conformable to our convenience, or else men strain their notions of their vocation and their expectation to an unattainable goal, hoping to acquire complete holiness of will, and so they lose themselves in fanatical theosophic dreams, which wholly contradict self-knowledge. In both cases the unceasing effort to obey punctually and thoroughly a strict and inflexible command of reason, which yet is not ideal but real, is only hindered. For a rational but finite being, the only thing possible is an endless progress from the lower to higher degrees of moral perfection. The Infinite Being, to whom the condition of time is nothing, sees in this to us endless succession a whole of accordance with the moral law; and the holiness which his command inexorably requires, in order to be true to his justice in the share which He assigns to each in the summum bonum, is to be found in a single intellectual intuition of the whole existence of rational beings. All that can be expected of the creature in respect of the hope of this participation would be the consciousness of his tried character, by which from the progress he has hitherto made from the worse to the morally better, and the immutability of purpose which has thus become known to him, he may hope for a further unbroken continuance of the same, however long his existence may last, even beyond this life,[1] and thus he may hope, not indeed here, nor in any imaginable point of his future existence, but only in the endlessness of his duration (which God alone can survey) to be perfectly adequate to his will (without indulgence or excuse, which do not harmonize with justice).

V. THE EXISTENCE OF GOD AS A POSTULATE OF PURE PRACTICAL REASON.

In the foregoing analysis the moral law led to a practical problem which is prescribed by pure reason alone, without the aid of any sensible motives, namely, that of the necessary completeness of the first and principle element of the summum bonum, viz., morality; and, as this can be perfectly solved only in eternity, to the postulate of immortality. The same law must also lead us to affirm the possibility of the second element of the summum bonum, viz., happiness proportioned to that morality, and this on grounds as disinterested as before, and solely from impartial reason; that is, it must lead to the supposition of the existence of a cause adequate to this effect; in other words, it must postulate the existence of God, as the necessary condition of the possibility of the summum bonum (an object of the will which is necessarily connected with the moral legislation of pure reason). We proceed to exhibit this connection in a convincing manner.

Happiness is the condition of a rational being in the world with whom everything goes according to his wish and will; it rests, therefore, on the harmony of physical nature with his whole end and likewise with the essential determining principle of his will. Now the moral law as a law of freedom commands by determining principles, which ought to be quite independent of nature and of its harmony with our faculty of desire (as springs). But the acting rational being in the world is not the cause of the world and of nature itself. There is not the least ground, therefore, in the moral law for a necessary connection between morality and proportionate happiness in a being that belongs to the world as part of it, and therefore dependent on it, and which for that reason cannot by his will be a cause of this nature, nor by his own power make it thoroughly harmonize, as far as his happiness is concerned, with his practical principles. Nevertheless, in the practical problem of pure reason, i.e., the necessary pursuit of the summum bonum, such a connection is postulated as necessary: we ought to endeavour to promote the summum bonum, which, therefore, must be possible. Accordingly, the existence of a cause of all nature, distinct from nature itself and containing the principle of this connection, namely, of the exact harmony of happiness with morality, is also postulated. Now this supreme cause must contain the principle of the harmony of nature, not merely with a law of the will of rational beings, but with the conception of this law, in so far as they make it the supreme determining principle of the will, and consequently not merely with the form of morals, but with their morality as their motive, that is, with their moral character. Therefore, the summum bonum is possible in the world only on the supposition of a Supreme Being having a causality corresponding to moral character. Now a being that is capable of acting on the conception of laws is an intelligence (a rational being), and the causality of such a being according to this conception of laws is his will; therefore the supreme cause of nature, which must be presupposed as a condition of the summum bonum is a being which is the cause of nature by intelligence and will, consequently its author, that is God. It follows that the postulate of the possibility of the highest derived good (the best world) is likewise the postulate of the reality of a highest original good, that is to say, of the existence of God. Now it was seen to be a duty for us to promote the summum bonum; consequently it is not merely allowable, but it is a necessity connected with duty as a requisite, that we should presuppose the possibility of this summum bonum; and as this is possible only on condition of the existence of God, it inseparably connects the supposition of this with duty; that is, it is morally necessary to assume the existence of God.

It must be remarked here that this moral necessity is subjective, that is, it is a want, and not objective, that is, itself a duty, for there cannot be a duty to suppose the existence of anything (since this concerns only the theoretical employment of reason). Moreover, it is not meant by this that it is necessary to suppose the existence of God as a basis of all obligation in general (for this rests, as has been sufficiently proved, simply on the autonomy of reason itself). What belongs to duty here is only the endeavour to realize and promote the summum bonum in the world, the possibility of which can therefore be postulated; and as our reason finds it not conceivable except on the supposition of a supreme intelligence, the admission of this existence is therefore connected with the consciousness of our duty, although the admission itself belongs to the domain of speculative reason. Considered in respect of this alone, as a principle of explanation, it may be called a hypothesis, but in reference to the intelligibility of an object given us by the moral law (the summum bonum), and consequently of a requirement for practical purposes, it may be called faith, that is to say a pure rational faith, since pure reason (both in its theoretical and practical use) is the sole source from which it springs.

From this deduction it is now intelligible why the Greek schools could never attain the solution of their problem of the practical possibility of the summum bonum, because they made the rule of the use which the will of man makes of his freedom the sole and sufficient ground of this possibility, thinking that they had no need for that purpose of the existence of God. No doubt they were so far right that they established the principle of morals of itself independently of this postulate, from the relation of reason only to the will, and consequently made it the supreme practical condition of the summum bonum; but it was not therefore the whole condition of its possibility. The Epicureans had indeed assumed as the supreme principle of morality a wholly false one, namely that of happiness, and had substituted for a law a maxim of arbitrary choice according to every man's inclination; they proceeded, however, consistently enough in this, that they degraded their summum bonum likewise, just in proportion to the meanness of their fundamental principle, and looked for no greater happiness than can be attained by human prudence (including temperance and moderation of the inclinations), and this as we know would be scanty enough and would be very different according to circumstances; not to mention the exceptions that their maxims must perpetually admit and which make them incapable of being laws. The Stoics, on the contrary, had chosen their supreme practical principle quite rightly, making virtue the condition of the summum bonum; but when they represented the degree of virtue required by its pure law as fully attainable in this life, they not only strained the moral powers of the man whom they called the wise beyond all the limits of his nature, and assumed a thing that contradicts all our knowledge of men, but also and principally they would not allow the second element of the summum bonum, namely, happiness, to be properly a special object of human desire, but made their wise man, like a divinity in his consciousness of the excellence of his person, wholly independent of nature (as regards his own contentment); they exposed him indeed to the evils of life, but made him not subject to them (at the same time representing him also as free from moral evil). They thus, in fact, left out the second element of the summum bonum namely, personal happiness, placing it solely in action and satisfaction with one's own personal worth, thus including it in the consciousness of being morally minded, in which they might have been sufficiently refuted by the voice of their own nature.

The doctrine of Christianity,[2] even if we do not yet consider it as a religious doctrine, gives, touching this point, a conception of the summum bonum (the kingdom of God), which alone satisfies the strictest demand of practical reason. The moral law is holy (unyielding) and demands holiness of morals, although all the moral perfection to which man can attain is still only virtue, that is, a rightful disposition arising from respect for the law, implying consciousness of a constant propensity to transgression, or at least a want of purity, that is, a mixture of many spurious (not moral) motives of obedience to the law, consequently a self-esteem combined with humility. In respect, then, of the holiness which the Christian law requires, this leaves the creature nothing but a progress in infinitum, but for that very reason it justifies him in hoping for an endless duration of his existence. The worth of a character perfectly accordant with the moral law is infinite, since the only restriction on all possible happiness in the judgement of a wise and all powerful distributor of it is the absence of conformity of rational beings to their duty. But the moral law of itself does not promise any happiness, for according to our conceptions of an order of nature in general, this is not necessarily connected with obedience to the law. Now Christian morality supplies this defect (of the second indispensable element of the summum bonum) by representing the world in which rational beings devote themselves with all their soul to the moral law, as a kingdom of God, in which nature and morality are brought into a harmony foreign to each of itself, by a holy Author who makes the derived summum bonum possible. Holiness of life is prescribed to them as a rule even in this life, while the welfare proportioned to it, namely, bliss, is represented as attainable only in an eternity; because the former must always be the pattern of their conduct in every state, and progress towards it is already possible and necessary in this life; while the latter, under the name of happiness, cannot be attained at all in this world (so far as our own power is concerned), and therefore is made simply an object of hope. Nevertheless, the Christian principle of morality itself is not theological (so as to be heteronomy), but is autonomy of pure practical reason, since it does not make the knowledge of God and His will the foundation of these laws, but only of the attainment of the summum bonum, on condition of following these laws, and it does not even place the proper spring of this obedience in the desired results, but solely in the conception of duty, as that of which the faithful observance alone constitutes the worthiness to obtain those happy consequences.

In this manner, the moral laws lead through the conception of the summum bonum as the object and final end of pure practical reason to religion, that is, to the recognition of all duties as divine commands, not as sanctions, that is to say, arbitrary ordinances of a foreign and contingent in themselves, but as essential laws of every free will in itself, which, nevertheless, must be regarded as commands of the Supreme Being, because it is only from a morally perfect (holy and good) and at the same time all-powerful will, and consequently only through harmony with this will, that we can hope to attain the summum bonum which the moral law makes it our duty to take as the object of our endeavours. Here again, then, all remains disinterested and founded merely on duty; neither fear nor hope being made the fundamental springs, which if taken as principles would destroy the whole moral worth of actions. The moral law commands me to make the highest possible good in a world the ultimate object of all my conduct. But I cannot hope to effect this otherwise than by the harmony of my will with that of a holy and good Author of the world; and although the conception of the summum bonum as a whole, in which the greatest happiness is conceived as combined in the most exact proportion with the highest degree of moral perfection (possible in creatures), includes my own happiness, yet it is not this that is the determining principle of the will which is enjoined to promote the summum bonum, but the moral law, which, on the contrary, limits by strict conditions my unbounded desire of happiness.

Hence also morality is not properly the doctrine how we should make ourselves happy, but how we should become worthy of happiness. It is only when religion is added that there also comes in the hope of participating some day in happiness in proportion as we have endeavoured to be not unworthy of it.

A man is worthy to possess a thing or a state when his possession of it is in harmony with the summum bonum. We can now easily see that all worthiness depends on moral conduct, since in the conception of the summum bonum this constitutes the condition of the rest (which belongs to one's state), namely, the participation of happiness. Now it follows from this that morality should never be treated as a doctrine of happiness, that is, an instruction how to become happy; for it has to do simply with the rational condition (conditio sine qua non) of happiness, not with the means of attaining it. But when morality has been completely expounded (which merely imposes duties instead of providing rules for selfish desires), then first, after the moral desire to promote the summum bonum (to bring the kingdom of God to us) has been awakened, a desire founded on a law, and which could not previously arise in any selfish mind, and when for the behoof of this desire the step to religion has been taken, then this ethical doctrine may be also called a doctrine of happiness because the hope of happiness first begins with religion only.

We can also see from this that, when we ask what is God's ultimate end in creating the world, we must not name the happiness of the rational beings in it, but the summum bonum, which adds a further condition to that wish of such beings, namely, the condition of being worthy of happiness, that is, the morality of these same rational beings, a condition which alone contains the rule by which only they can hope to share in the former at the hand of a wise Author. For as wisdom, theoretically considered, signifies the knowledge of the summum bonum and, practically, the accordance of the will with the summum bonum, we cannot attribute to a supreme independent wisdom an end based merely on goodness. For we cannot conceive the action of this goodness (in respect of the happiness of rational beings) as suitable to the highest original good, except under the restrictive conditions of harmony with the holiness[3] of his will. Therefore, those who placed the end of creation in the glory of God (provided that this is not conceived anthropomorphically as a desire to be praised) have perhaps hit upon the best expression. For nothing glorifies God more than that which is the most estimable thing in the world, respect for his command, the observance of the holy duty that his law imposes on us, when there is added thereto his glorious plan of crowning such a beautiful order of things with corresponding happiness. If the latter (to speak humanly) makes Him worthy of love, by the former He is an object of adoration. Even men can never acquire respect by benevolence alone, though they may gain love, so that the greatest beneficence only procures them honour when it is regulated by worthiness.

That in the order of ends, man (and with him every rational being) is an end in himself, that is, that he can never be used merely as a means by any (not even by God) without being at the same time an end also himself, that therefore humanity in our person must be holy to ourselves, this follows now of itself because he is the subject of the moral law, in other words, of that which is holy in itself, and on account of which and in agreement with which alone can anything be termed holy. For this moral law is founded on the autonomy of his will, as a free will which by its universal laws must necessarily be able to agree with that to which it is to submit itself.

VI. OF THE POSTULATES OF PURE PRACTICAL REASON GENERALLY.

They all proceed from the principle of morality, which is not a postulate but a law, by which reason determines the will directly, which will, because it is so determined as a pure will, requires these necessary conditions of obedience to its precept. These postulates are not theoretical dogmas but, suppositions practically necessary; while then they do [not] extend our speculative knowledge, they give objective reality to the ideas of speculative reason in general (by means of their reference to what is practical), and give it a right to concepts, the possibility even of which it could not otherwise venture to affirm.

These postulates are those of immortality, freedom positively considered (as the causality of a being so far as he belongs to the intelligible world), and the existence of

God. The first results from the practically necessary condition of a duration adequate to the complete fulfilment of the moral law; the second from the necessary supposition of independence of the sensible world, and of the faculty of determining one's will according to the law of an intelligible world, that is, of freedom; the third from the necessary condition of the existence of the summum bonum in such an intelligible world, by the supposition of the supreme independent good, that is, the existence of God.

Thus the fact that respect for the moral law necessarily makes the summum bonum an object of our endeavours, and the supposition thence resulting of its objective reality, lead through the postulates of practical reason to conceptions which speculative reason might indeed present as problems, but could never solve. Thus it leads: 1. To that one in the solution of which the latter could do nothing but commit paralogisms (namely, that of immortality), because it could not lay hold of the character of permanence, by which to complete the psychological conception of an ultimate subject necessarily ascribed to the soul in self-consciousness, so as to make it the real conception of a substance, a character which practical reason furnishes by the postulate of a duration required for accordance with the moral law in the summum bonum, which is the whole end of practical reason. 2. It leads to that of which speculative reason contained nothing but antinomy, the solution of which it could only found on a notion problematically conceivable indeed, but whose objective reality it could not prove or determine, namely, the cosmological idea of an intelligible world and the consciousness of our existence in it, by means of the postulate of freedom (the reality of which it lays down by virtue of the moral law), and with it likewise the law of an intelligible world, to which speculative reason could only point, but could not define its conception. 3. What speculative reason was able to think, but was obliged to leave undetermined as a mere transcendental ideal, viz., the theological conception of the first Being, to this it gives significance (in a practical view, that is, as a condition of the possibility of the object of a will determined by that law), namely, as the supreme principle of the summum bonum in an intelligible world, by means of moral legislation in it invested with sovereign power.

Is our knowledge, however, actually extended in this way by pure practical reason, and is that immanent in practical reason which for the speculative was only transcendent? Certainly, but only in a practical point of view. For we do not thereby take knowledge of the nature of our souls, nor of the intelligible world, nor of the Supreme Being, with respect to what they are in themselves, but we have merely combined the conceptions of them in the practical concept of the summum bonum as the object of our will, and this altogether a priori, but only by means of the moral law, and merely in reference to it, in respect of the object which it commands. But how freedom is possible, and how we are to conceive this kind of causality theoretically and positively, is not thereby discovered; but only that there is such a causality is postulated by the moral law and in its behoof. It is the same with the remaining ideas, the possibility of which no human intelligence will ever fathom, but the truth of which, on the other hand, no sophistry will ever wrest from the conviction even of the commonest man.

VII. HOW IS IT POSSIBLE TO CONCEIVE AN EXTENSION OF PURE REASON IN A PRACTICAL POINT OF VIEW, WITHOUT ITS KNOWLEDGE AS SPECULATIVE BEING ENLARGED AT THE SAME TIME?

In order not to be too abstract, we will answer this question at once in its application to the present case. In order to extend a pure cognition practically, there must be an a priori purpose given, that is, an end as object (of the will), which independently of all theological principle is presented as practically necessary by an imperative which determines the will directly (a categorical imperative), and in this case that is the summum bonum. This, however, is not possible without presupposing three theoretical conceptions (for which, because they are mere conceptions of pure reason, no corresponding intuition can be found, nor consequently by the path of theory any objective reality); namely, freedom, immortality, and God. Thus by the practical law which commands the existence of the highest good possible in a world, the possibility of those objects of pure speculative reason is postulated, and the objective reality which the latter could not assure them. By this the theoretical knowledge of pure reason does indeed obtain an accession; but it consists only in this, that those concepts which otherwise it had to look upon as problematical (merely thinkable) concepts, are now shown assertorially to be such as actually have objects; because practical reason indispensably requires their existence for the possibility of its object, the summum bonum, which practically is absolutely necessary, and this justifies theoretical reason in assuming them. But this extension of theoretical reason is no extension of speculative, that is, we cannot make any positive use of it in a theoretical point of view. For as nothing is accomplished in this by practical reason, further than that these concepts are real and actually have their (possible) objects, and nothing in the way of intuition of them is given thereby (which indeed could not be demanded), hence the admission of this reality does not render any synthetical proposition possible. Consequently, this discovery does not in the least help us to extend this knowledge of ours in a speculative point of view, although it does in respect of the practical employment of pure reason. The above three ideas of speculative reason are still in themselves not cognitions; they are however (transcendent) thoughts, in which there is nothing impossible. Now, by help of an apodeictic practical law, being necessary conditions of that which it commands to be made an object, they acquire objective reality; that is, we learn from it that they have objects, without being able to point out how the conception of them is related to an object, and this, too, is still not a cognition of these objects; for we cannot thereby form any synthetical judgement about them, nor determine their application theoretically; consequently, we can make no theoretical rational use of them at all, in which use all speculative knowledge of reason consists. Nevertheless, the theoretical knowledge, not indeed of these objects, but of reason generally, is so far enlarged by this, that by the practical postulates objects were given to those ideas, a merely problematical thought having by this means first acquired objective reality. There is therefore no extension of the knowledge of given supersensible objects, but an extension of theoretical reason and of its knowledge in respect of the supersensible generally; inasmuch as it is compelled to admit that there are such objects, although it is not able to define them more closely, so as itself to extend this knowledge of the objects (which have now been given it on practical grounds, and only for practical use). For this accession, then, pure theoretical reason, for which all those

428 | IMMANUEL KANT

ideas are transcendent and without object, has simply to thank its practical faculty. In this they become immanent and constitutive, being the source of the possibility of realizing the necessary object of pure practical reason (the summum bonum); whereas apart from this they are transcendent, and merely regulative principles of speculative reason, which do not require it to assume a new object beyond experience, but only to bring its use in experience nearer to completeness. But when once reason is in possession of this accession, it will go to work with these ideas as speculative reason (properly only to assure the certainty of its practical use) in a negative manner: that is, not extending but clearing up its knowledge so as on one side to keep off anthropomorphism, as the source of superstition, or seeming extension of these conceptions by supposed experience; and on the other side fanaticism, which promises the same by means of supersensible intuition or feelings of the like kind. All these are hindrances to the practical use of pure reason, so that the removal of them may certainly be considered an extension of our knowledge in a practical point of view, without contradicting the admission that for speculative purposes reason has not in the least gained by this.

Every employment of reason in respect of an object requires pure concepts of the understanding (categories), without which no object can be conceived. These can be applied to the theoretical employment of reason, i.e., to that kind of knowledge, only in case an intuition (which is always sensible) is taken as a basis, and therefore merely in order to conceive by means of- them an object of possible experience. Now here what have to be thought by means of the categories in order to be known are ideas of reason, which cannot be given in any experience. Only we are not here concerned with the theoretical knowledge of the objects of these ideas, but only with this, whether they have objects at all. This reality is supplied by pure practical reason, and theoretical reason has nothing further to do in this but to think those objects by means of categories. This, as we have elsewhere clearly shown, can be done well enough without needing any intuition (either sensible or supersensible) because the categories have their seat and origin in the pure understanding, simply as the faculty of thought, before and independently of any intuition, and they always only signify an object in general, no matter in what way it may be given to us. Now when the categories are to be applied to these ideas, it is not possible to give them any object in intuition; but that such an object actually exists, and consequently that the category as a mere form of thought is here not empty but has significance, this is sufficiently assured them by an object which practical reason presents beyond doubt in the concept of the summum bonum, the reality of the conceptions which are required for the possibility of the summum bonum; without, however, effecting by this accession the least extension of our knowledge on theoretical principles.

When these ideas of God, of an intelligible world (the kingdom of God), and of immortality are further determined by predicates taken from our own nature, we must not regard this determination as a sensualizing of those pure rational ideas (anthropomorphism), nor as a transcendent knowledge of supersensible objects; for these predicates are no others than understanding and will, considered too in the relation to each other in which they must be conceived in the moral law, and therefore, only so far as a pure practical use is made of them. As to all the rest that belongs to these conceptions psychologically, that is, so far as we observe these faculties of ours empirically in their exercise (e.g., that the understanding of man is discursive, and its notions therefore not intuitions but thoughts, that these follow one another in time, that his will has its satis-faction always dependent on the existence of its object, etc., which cannot be the case in the Supreme Being), from all this we abstract in that case, and then there remains of the notions by which we conceive a pure intelligence nothing more than just what is required for the possibility of conceiving a moral law. There is then a knowledge of God indeed, but only for practical purposes, and, if we attempt to extend it to a theoretical knowledge, we find an understanding that has intuitions, not thoughts, a will that is directed to objects on the existence of which its satisfaction does not in the least depend (not to mention the transcendental predicates, as, for example, a magnitude of existence, that is duration, which, however, is not in time, the only possible means we have of conceiving existence as magnitude). Now these are all attributes of which we can form no conception that would help to the knowledge of the object, and we learn from this that they can never be used for a theory of supersensible beings, so that on this side they are quite incapable of being the foundation of a speculative knowledge, and their use is limited simply to the practice of the moral law.

This last is so obvious, and can be proved so clearly by fact, that we may confidently challenge all pretended natural theologians (a singular name)[4] to specify (over and above the merely ontological predicates) one single attribute, whether of the under-standing or of the will, determining this object of theirs, of which we could not show incontrovertibly that, if we abstract from it everything anthropomorphic, nothing would remain to us but the mere word, without our being able to connect with it the smallest notion by which we could hope for an extension of theoretical knowledge. But as to the practical, there still remains to us of the attributes of understanding and will the conception of a relation to which objective reality is given by the practical law (which determines a priori precisely this relation of the understanding to the will). When once this is done, then reality is given to the conception of the object of a will morally determined (the conception of the summum bonum), and with it to the condi-tions of its possibility, the ideas of God, freedom, and immortality, but always only rela-tively to the practice of the moral law (and not for any speculative purpose).

According to these remarks it is now easy to find the answer to the weighty question whether the notion of God is one belonging to physics (and therefore also to meta-physics, which contains the pure a priori principles of the former in their universal import) or to morals. If we have recourse to God as the Author of all things, in order to explain the arrangements of nature or its changes, this is at least not a physical explana-tion, and is a complete confession that our philosophy has come to an end, since we are obliged to assume something of which in itself we have otherwise no conception, in order to be able to frame a conception of the possibility of what we see before our eyes. Metaphysics, however, cannot enable us to attain by certain inference from the knowl-edge of this world to the conception of God and to the proof of His existence, for this reason, that in order to say that this world could be produced only by a God (according to the conception implied by this word) we should know this world as the most perfect whole possible; and for this purpose should also know all possible worlds (in order to be able to compare them with this); in other words, we should be omniscient. It is abso-lutely impossible, however, to know the existence of this Being from mere concepts, because every existential proposition, that is, every proposition that affirms the exis-tence of a being of which I frame a concept, is a synthetic proposition, that is, one by which I go beyond that conception and affirm of it more than was thought in the conception itself; namely, that this concept in the understanding has an object corresponding to it outside the understanding, and this it is obviously impossible to elicit by any reasoning. There remains, therefore, only one single process possible for reason to attain this knowledge, namely, to start from the supreme principle of its pure practical use (which in every case is directed simply to the existence of something as a consequence of reason) and thus determine its object. Then its inevitable problem, namely, the necessary direction of the will to the summum bonum, discovers to us not only the necessity of assuming such a First Being in reference to the possibility of this good in the world, but, what is most remarkable, something which reason in its progress on the path of physical nature altogether failed to find, namely, an accurately defined conception of this First Being. As we can know only a small part of this world, and can still less compare it with all possible worlds, we may indeed from its order, design, and greatness, infer a wise, good, powerful, etc., Author of it, but not that He is all-wise, all-good, all-powerful, etc. It may indeed very well be granted that we should be justified in supplying this inevitable defect by a legitimate and reasonable hypothesis; namely, that when wisdom, goodness, etc, are displayed in all the parts that offer themselves to our nearer knowledge, it is just the same in all the rest, and that it would therefore be reasonable to ascribe all possible perfections to the Author of the world, but these are not strict logical inferences in which we can pride ourselves on our insight, but only permitted conclusions in which we may be indulged and which require further recommendation before we can make use of them. On the path of empirical inquiry then (physics), the conception of God remains always a conception of the perfection of the First Being not accurately enough determined to be held adequate to the conception of Deity. (With metaphysic in its transcendental part nothing whatever can be accomplished.)

When I now try to test this conception by reference to the object of practical reason, I find that the moral principle admits as possible only the conception of an Author of the world possessed of the highest perfection. He must be omniscient, in order to know my conduct up to the inmost root of my mental state in all possible cases and into all future time; omnipotent, in order to allot to it its fitting consequences; similarly He must be omnipresent, eternal, etc. Thus the moral law, by means of the conception of the summum bonum as the object of a pure practical reason, determines the concept of the First Being as the Supreme Being; a thing which the physical (and in its higher development the metaphysical), in other words, the whole speculative course of reason, was unable to effect. The conception of God, then, is one that belongs originally not to physics, i.e., to speculative reason, but to morals. The same may be said of the other conceptions of reason of which we have treated above as postulates of it in its practical use.

In the history of Grecian philosophy we find no distinct traces of a pure rational theology earlier than Anaxagoras; but this is not because the older philosophers had not intelligence or penetration enough to raise themselves to it by the path of speculation, at least with the aid of a thoroughly reasonable hypothesis. What could have been easier, what more natural, than the thought which of itself occurs to everyone, to assume instead of several causes of the world, instead of an indeterminate degree of perfection, a single rational cause having all perfection? But the evils in the world seemed to them to be much too serious objections to allow them to feel themselves justified in such a hypothesis. They showed intelligence and penetration then in this very point, that they did not allow themselves to adopt it, but on the contrary looked about amongst natural causes to see if they could not find in them the qualities and power required for a First Being. But when this acute people had advanced so far in their investigations of nature as to treat even moral questions philosophically, on which other nations had never done anything but talk, then first they found a new and practical want, which did not fail to give definiteness to their conception of the First Being: and in this the speculative reason played the part of spectator, or at best had the merit of embellishing a conception that had not grown on its own ground, and of applying a series of confirmations from the study of nature now brought forward for the first time, not indeed to strengthen the authority of this conception (which was already established), but rather to make a show with a supposed discovery of theoretical reason.

From these remarks, the reader of the Critique of Pure Speculative Reason will be thoroughly convinced how highly necessary that laborious deduction of the categories was, and how fruitful for theology and morals. For if, on the one hand, we place them in pure understanding, it is by this deduction alone that we can be prevented from regarding them, with Plato, as innate, and founding on them extravagant pretensions to theories of the supersensible, to which we can see no end, and by which we should make theology a magic lantern of chimeras; on the other hand, if we regard them as acquired, this deduction saves us from restricting, with Epicurus, all and every use of them, even for practical purposes, to the objects and motives of the senses. But now that the Critique has shown by that deduction, first, that they are not of empirical origin, but have their seat and source a priori in the pure understanding; secondly, that as they refer to objects in general independently of the intuition of them, hence, although they cannot effect theoretical knowledge, except in application to empirical objects, yet when applied to an object given by pure practical reason they enable us to conceive the supersensible definitely, only so far, however, as it is defined by such predicates as are necessarily connected with the pure practical purpose given a priori and with its possibility. The speculative restriction of pure reason and its practical extension bring it into that relation of equality in which reason in general can be employed suitably to its end, and this example proves better than any other that the path to wisdom, if it is to be made sure and not to be impassable or misleading, must with us men inevitably pass through science; but it is not till this is complete that we can be convinced that it leads to this goal.

VIII. OF BELIEF FROM A REQUIREMENT OF PURE REASON.

A want or requirement of pure reason in its speculative use leads only to a hypothesis; that of pure practical reason to a postulate; for in the former case I ascend from the result as high as I please in the series of causes, not in order to give objective reality to the result (e.g., the causal connection of things and changes in the world), but in order thoroughly to satisfy my inquiring reason in respect of it. Thus I see before me order and design in nature, and need not resort to speculation to assure myself of their reality, but to explain them I have to presuppose a Deity as their cause; and then since the inference from an effect to a definite cause is always uncertain and doubtful, especially to a cause so precise and so perfectly defined as we have to conceive in God, hence the highest degree of certainty to which this pre-supposition can be brought is that it is the most rational opinion for us men.[5] On the other hand, a requirement of pure practical reason is based on a duty, that of making something (the summum bonum) the object of my will so as to promote it with all my powers; in which case I must suppose its possibility and, consequently, also the conditions necessary thereto, namely, God, freedom, and immortality; since I cannot prove these by my speculative reason, although neither can I refute them. This duty is founded on something that is indeed quite independent of these suppositions and is of itself apodeictically certain, namely, the moral law; and so far it needs no further support by theoretical views as to the inner constitution of things, the secret final aim of the order of the world, or a presiding ruler thereof, in order to bind me in the most perfect manner to act in unconditional conformity to the law. But the subjective effect of this law, namely, the mental disposition conformed to it and made necessary by it, to promote the practically possible summum bonum, this pre-supposes at least that the latter is possible, for it would be practically impossible to strive after the object of a conception which at bottom was empty and had no object. Now the above-mentioned postulates concern only the physical or metaphysical conditions of the possibility of the summum bonum; in a word, those which lie in the nature of things; not, however, for the sake of an arbitrary speculative purpose, but of a practically necessary end of a pure rational will, which in this case does not choose, but obeys an inexorable command of reason, the foundation of which is objective, in the constitution of things as they must be universally judged by pure reason, and is not based on inclination; for we are in nowise justified in assuming, on account of what we wish on merely subjective grounds, that the means thereto are possible or that its object is real. This, then, is an absolutely necessary requirement, and what it pre-supposes is not merely justified as an allowable hypothesis, but as a postulate in a practical point of view; and admitting that the pure moral law inexorably binds every man as a command (not as a rule of prudence), the righteous man may say: "I will that there be a God, that my existence in this world be also an existence outside the chain of physical causes and in a pure world of the understanding, and lastly, that my duration be endless; I firmly abide by this, and will not let this faith be taken from me; for in this instance alone my interest, because I must not relax anything of it, inevitably determines my judgement, without regarding sophistries, however unable I may be to answer them or to oppose them with others more plausible.[6]

In order to prevent misconception in the use of a notion as yet so unusual as that of a faith of pure practical reason, let me be permitted to add one more remark. It might almost seem as if this rational faith were here announced as itself a command, namely, that we should assume the summum bonum as possible. But a faith that is commanded is nonsense. Let the preceding analysis, however, be remembered of what is required to be supposed in the conception of the summum bonum, and it will be seen that it cannot be commanded to assume this possibility, and no practical disposition of mind is required to admit it; but that speculative reason must concede it without being asked, for no one can affirm that it is impossible in itself that rational beings in the world should at the same time be worthy of happiness in conformity with the moral law and also possess this happiness proportionately. Now in respect of the first element of the summum bonum, namely, that which concerns morality, the moral law gives merely a command, and to doubt the possibility of that element would be the same as to call in question the moral law itself. But as regards the second element of that object, namely, happiness perfectly proportioned to that worthiness, it is true that there is no need of a command to admit its possibility in general, for theoretical reason has nothing to say against it; but the manner in which we have to conceive this harmony of the laws of nature with those of freedom has in it something in respect of which we have a choice, because theoretical reason decides nothing with apodeictic certainty about it, and in respect of this there may be a moral interest which turns the scale.

I had said above that in a mere course of nature in the world an accurate correspondence between happiness and moral worth is not to be expected and must be regarded as impossible, and that therefore the possibility of the summum bonum cannot be admitted from this side except on the supposition of a moral Author of the world. I purposely reserved the restriction of this judgement to the subjective conditions of our reason, in order not to make use of it until the manner of this belief should be defined more precisely. The fact is that the impossibility referred to is merely subjective, that is, our reason finds it impossible for it to render conceivable in the way of a mere course of nature a connection so exactly proportioned and so thoroughly adapted to an end, between two sets of events happening according to such distinct laws; although, as with everything else in nature that is adapted to an end, it cannot prove, that is, show by sufficient objective reason, that it is not possible by universal laws of nature.

Now, however, a deciding principle of a different kind comes into play to turn the scale in this uncertainty of speculative reason. The command to promote the summum bonum is established on an objective basis (in practical reason); the possibility of the same in general is likewise established on an objective basis (in theoretical reason, which has nothing to say against it). But reason cannot decide objectively in what way we are to conceive this possibility; whether by universal laws of nature without a wise Author presiding over nature, or only on supposition of such an Author. Now here there comes in a subjective condition of reason, the only way theoretically possible for it, of conceiving the exact harmony of the kingdom of nature with the kingdom of morals, which is the condition of the possibility of the summum bonum; and at the same time the only one conducive to morality (which depends on an objective law of reason). Now since the promotion of this summum bonum, and therefore the supposition of its possibility, are objectively necessary (though only as a result of practical reason), while at the same time the manner in which we would conceive it rests with our own choice, and in this choice a free interest of pure practical reason decides for the assumption of a wise Author of the world; it is clear that the principle that herein determines our judgement, though as a want it is subjective, yet at the same time being the means of promoting what is objectively (practically) necessary, is the foundation of a maxim of belief in a moral point of view, that is, a faith of pure practical reason. This, then, is not commanded, but being a voluntary determination of our judgement, conducive to the moral (commanded) purpose, and moreover harmonizing with the theoretical requirement of reason, to assume that existence and to make it the foundation of our further employment of reason, it has itself sprung from the moral disposition of mind; it may therefore at times waver even in the well-disposed, but can never be reduced to unbelief.

IX. OF THE WISE ADAPTATION OF MAN'S COGNITIVE FACULTIES TO HIS PRACTICAL DESTINATION.

If human nature is destined to endeavour after the summum bonum, we must suppose also that the measure of its cognitive faculties, and particularly their relation to one another, is suitable to this end. Now the Critique of Pure Speculative Reason proves that this is incapable of solving satisfactorily the most weighty problems that are proposed to it, although it does not ignore the natural and important hints received from the same reason, nor the great steps that it can make to approach to this great goal that is set before it, which, however, it can never reach of itself, even with the help of the greatest knowledge of nature. Nature then seems here to have provided us only in a step-motherly fashion with the faculty required for our end.

Suppose, now, that in this matter nature had conformed to our wish and had given us that capacity of discernment or that enlightenment which we would gladly possess, or which some imagine they actually possess, what would in all probability be the consequence? Unless our whole nature were at the same time changed, our inclinations, which always have the first word, would first of all demand their own satisfaction, and, joined with rational reflection, the greatest possible and most lasting satisfaction, under the name of happiness; the moral law would afterwards speak, in order to keep them within their proper bounds, and even to subject them all to a higher end, which has no regard to inclination. But instead of the conflict that the moral disposition has now to carry on with the inclinations, in which, though after some defeats, moral strength of mind may be gradually acquired, God and eternity with their awful majesty would stand unceasingly before our eyes (for what we can prove perfectly is to us as certain as that of which we are assured by the sight of our eyes). Transgression of the law, would, no doubt, be avoided; what is commanded would be done; but the mental disposition, from which actions ought to proceed, cannot be infused by any command, and in this case the spur of action is ever active and external, so that reason has no need to exert itself in order to gather strength to resist the inclinations by a lively representation of the dignity of the law: hence most of the actions that conformed to the law would be done from fear, a few only from hope, and none at all from duty, and the moral worth of actions, on which alone in the eyes of supreme wisdom the worth of the person and even that of the world depends, would cease to exist. As long as the nature of man remains what it is, his conduct would thus be changed into mere mechanism, in which, as in a puppet-show, everything would gesticulate well, but there would be no life in the figures. Now, when it is quite otherwise with us, when with all the effort of our reason we have only a very obscure and doubtful view into the future, when the Governor of the world allows us only to conjecture his existence and his majesty, not to behold them or prove them clearly; and on the other hand, the moral law within us, without promising or threatening anything with certainty, demands of us disinterested respect; and only when this respect has become active and dominant, does it allow us by means of it a prospect into the world of the supersensible, and then only with weak glances: all this being so, there is room for true moral disposition, immediately devoted to the law, and a rational creature can become worthy of sharing in the summum bonum that corresponds to the worth of his person and not merely to his actions. Thus what the study of nature and of man teaches us sufficiently elsewhere may well be true here also; that the unsearchable wisdom by which we exist is not less worthy of admiration in what it has denied than in what it has granted.

---

1. It seems, nevertheless, impossible for a creature to have the conviction of his unwavering firmness of mind in the progress towards goodness. On this account the Christian religion makes it come only from the same Spirit that works sanctification, that is, this firm purpose, and with it the consciousness of steadfastness in the moral progress. But naturally one who is conscious that he has persevered through a long portion of his life up to the end in the progress to the better, and this genuine moral motives, may well have the comforting hope, though not the certainty, that even in an existence prolonged beyond this life he will continue in these principles; and although he is never justified here in his own eyes, nor can ever hope to be so in the increased perfection of his nature, to which he looks forward, together with an increase of duties, nevertheless in this progress which, though it is directed to a goal infinitely remote, yet is in God's sight regarded as equivalent to possession, he may have a prospect of a blessed future; for this is the word that reason employs to designate perfect well-being independent of all contingent causes of the world, and which, like holiness, is an idea that can be contained only in an endless progress and its totality, and consequently is never fully attained by a creature.
2. It is commonly held that the Christian precept of morality has no advantage in respect of purity over the moral conceptions of the Stoics; the distinction between them is, however, very obvious. The Stoic system made the consciousness of strength of mind the pivot on which all moral dispositions should turn; and although its disciples spoke of duties and even defined them very well, yet they placed the spring and proper determining principle of the will in an elevation of the mind above the lower springs of the senses, which owe their power only to weakness of mind. With them therefore, virtue was a sort of heroism in the wise man raising himself above the animal nature of man, is sufficient for Himself, and, while he prescribes duties to others, is himself raised above them, and is not subject to any temptation to transgress the moral law. All this, however, they could not have done if they had conceived this law in all its purity and strictness, as the precept of the Gospel does. When I give the name idea to a perfection to which nothing adequate can be given in experience, it does not follow that the moral ideas are thing transcendent, that is something of which we could not even determine the concept adequately, or of which it is uncertain whether there is any object corresponding to it at all, as is the case with the ideas of speculative reason; on the contrary, being types of practical perfection, they serve as the indispensable rule of conduct and likewise as the standard of comparison. Now if I consider Christian morals on their philosophical side, then compared with the ideas of the Greek schools, they would appear as follows: the ideas of the Cynics, the Epicureans, the Stoics, and the Christians are: simplicity of nature, prudence, wisdom, and holiness. In respect of the way of attaining them, the Greek schools were distinguished from one another thus that the Cynics only required common sense, the others the path of science, but both found the mere use of natural powers sufficient for the purpose. Christian morality, because its precept is framed (as a moral precept must be) so pure and unyielding, takes from man all confidence that he can be fully adequate to it, at least in this life, but again sets it up by enabling us to hope that if we act as well as it is in our power to do, then what is not in our power will come in to our aid from another source, whether we know how this may be or not. Aristotle and Plato differed only as to the origin of our moral conceptions.
3. In order to make these characteristics of these conceptions clear, I add the remark that whilst we ascribe to God various attributes, the quality of which we also find applicable to creatures, only that in Him they are raised to the highest degree, e.g., power, knowledge, presence, goodness, etc., under the designations of omnipotence, omniscience, omnipresence, etc., there are three that are ascribed to God exclusively, and yet without the addition of greatness, and which are all moral He is the only holy, the only blessed, the only wise, because these conceptions already imply the absence of limitation. In the order of these attributes He is also the holy lawgiver (and creator), the good governor (and preserver) and the just judge, three attributes which include everything by which God is the object of religion, and in conformity with which the metaphysical perfections are added of themselves in the reason.
4. Learning is properly only the whole content of the historical sciences. Consequently it is only the teacher of revealed theology that can be called a learned theologian. If, however, we choose to call a man learned who is in possession of the rational sciences (mathematics and philosophy), although even this would be contrary to the signification of the word (which always counts as learning only that which one must be "learned" and which, therefore, he cannot discover of himself by reason), even in that case the philosopher would make too poor a figure with his knowledge of God as a positive science to let himself be called on that account a learned man.
5. But even here we should not be able to allege a requirement of reason, if we had not before our eyes a problematical, but yet inevitable, conception of reason, namely, that of an absolutely necessary being. This conception now seeks to be defined, and this, in addition to the tendency to extend itself, is the objective ground of a requirement of speculative reason, namely, to have a more precise definition of the conception of a necessary being which is to serve as the first cause of other beings, so as to make these latter knowable by some means. Without such antecedent necessary problems there are no requirements- at least not of pure reason- the rest are requirements of inclination.

6. In the Deutsches Museum, February, 1787, there is a dissertation by a very subtle and clear-headed man, the late Wizenmann, whose early death is to be lamented, in which he disputes the right to argue from a want to the objective reality of its object, and illustrates the point by the example of a man in love, who having fooled himself into an idea of beauty, which is merely a chimera of his own brain, would fain conclude that such an object really exists somewhere. I quite agree with him in this, in all cases where the want is founded on inclination, which cannot necessarily postulate the existence of its object even for the man that is affected by it, much less can it contain a demand valid for everyone, and therefore it is merely a subjective ground of the wish. But in the present case we have a want of reason springing from an objective determining principle of the will, namely, the moral law, which necessarily binds every rational being, and therefore justifies him in assuming a priori in nature the conditions proper for it, and makes the latter inseparable from the complete practical use of reason. It is a duty to realize the summum bonum to the utmost of our power, therefore it must be possible, consequently it is unavoidable for every rational being in the world to assume what is necessary for its objective possibility. The assumption is as necessary as the moral law, in connection with which alone it is valid.

SECOND PART —
METHODOLOGY OF PURE
PRACTICAL REASON

METHODOLOGY OF PURE PRACTICAL
REASON

By THE METHODOLOGY of pure practical reason we are not to understand the mode of proceeding with pure practical principles (whether in study or in exposition), with a view to a scientific knowledge of them, which alone is what is properly called method elsewhere in theoretical philosophy (for popular knowledge requires a manner, science a method, i.e., a process according to principles of reason by which alone the manifold of any branch of knowledge can become a system). On the contrary, by this methodology is understood the mode in which we can give the laws of pure practical reason access to the human mind and influence on its maxims, that is, by which we can make the objectively practical reason subjectively practical also.

Now it is clear enough that those determining principles of the will which alone make maxims properly moral and give them a moral worth, namely, the direct conception of the law and the objective necessity of obeying it as our duty, must be regarded as the proper springs of actions, since otherwise legality of actions might be produced, but not morality of character. But it is not so clear; on the contrary, it must at first sight seem to every one very improbable that even subjectively that exhibition of pure virtue can have more power over the human mind, and supply a far stronger spring even for effecting that legality of actions, and can produce more powerful resolutions to prefer the law, from pure respect for it, to every other consideration, than all the deceptive allurements of pleasure or of all that may be reckoned as happiness, or even than all threatenings of pain and misfortune. Nevertheless, this is actually the case, and if human nature were not so constituted, no mode of presenting the law by roundabout ways and indirect recommendations would ever produce morality of character. All would be simple hypocrisy; the law would be hated, or at least despised, while it was followed for the sake of one's own advantage. The letter of the law (legality) would be found in our actions, but not the spirit of it in our minds (morality); and as with all our efforts we could not quite free ourselves from reason in our judgement, we must inevitably appear in our own eyes worthless, depraved men, even though we should seek to compensate ourselves for this mortification before the inner tribunal, by enjoying the pleasure that a supposed natural or divine law might be imagined to have connected with it a sort of police machinery, regulating its operations by what was done without troubling itself about the motives for doing it.

It cannot indeed be denied that in order to bring an uncultivated or degraded mind into the track of moral goodness some preparatory guidance is necessary, to attract it by a view of its own advantage, or to alarm it by fear of loss; but as soon as this mechanical work, these leading-strings have produced some effect, then we must bring before the mind the pure moral motive, which, not only because it is the only one that can be the foundation of a character (a practically consistent habit of mind with unchangeable maxims), but also because it teaches a man to feel his own dignity, gives the mind a power unexpected even by himself, to tear himself from all sensible attachments so far as they would fain have the rule, and to find a rich compensation for the sacrifice he offers, in the independence of his rational nature and the greatness of soul to which he sees that he is destined. We will therefore show, by such observations as every one can make, that this property of our minds, this receptivity for a pure moral interest, and consequently the moving force of the pure conception of virtue, when it is properly applied to the human heart, is the most powerful spring and, when a continued and punctual observance of moral maxims is in question, the only spring of good conduct. It must, however, be remembered that if these observations only prove the reality of such a feeling, but do not show any moral improvement brought about by it, this is no argument against the only method that exists of making the objectively practical laws of pure reason subjectively practical, through the mere force of the conception of duty; nor does it prove that this method is a vain delusion. For as it has never yet come into vogue, experience can say nothing of its results; one can only ask for proofs of the receptivity for such springs, and these I will now briefly present, and then sketch the method of founding and cultivating genuine moral dispositions.

When we attend to the course of conversation in mixed companies, consisting not merely of learned persons and subtle reasoners, but also of men of business or of women, we observe that, besides story-telling and jesting, another kind of entertainment finds a place in them, namely, argument; for stories, if they are to have novelty and interest, are soon exhausted, and jesting is likely to become insipid. Now of all argument there is none in which persons are more ready to join who find any other subtle discussion tedious, none that brings more liveliness into the company, than that which concerns the moral worth of this or that action by which the character of some person is to be made out. Persons, to whom in other cases anything subtle and speculative in theoretical questions is dry and irksome, presently join in when the question is to make out the moral import of a good or bad action that has been related, and they display an exactness, a refinement, a subtlety, in excogitating everything that can lessen the purity of purpose, and consequently the degree of virtue in it, which we do not expect from them in any other kind of speculation. In these criticisms, persons who are passing judgement on others often reveal their own character: some, in exercising their judicial office, especially upon the dead, seem inclined chiefly to defend the goodness that is related of this or that deed against all injurious charges of insincerity, and ultimately to defend the whole moral worth of the person against the reproach of dissimulation and secret wickedness; others, on the contrary, turn their thoughts more upon attacking this worth by accusation and fault finding. We cannot always, however, attribute to these latter the intention of arguing away virtue altogether out of all human examples in order to make it an empty name; often, on the contrary, it is only well-meant strictness in determining the true moral import of actions according to an uncompromising law. Comparison with such a law, instead of with examples, lowers self-conceit in moral matters very much, and not merely teaches humility, but makes every one feel it when he examines himself closely. Nevertheless, we can for the most part observe, in those who defend the purity of purpose in giving examples that where there is the presumption of uprightness they are anxious to remove even the least spot, lest, if all examples had their truthfulness disputed, and if the purity of all human virtue were denied, it might in the end be regarded as a mere phantom, and so all effort to attain it be made light of as vain affectation and delusive conceit.

I do not know why the educators of youth have not long since made use of this propensity of reason to enter with pleasure upon the most subtle examination of the practical questions that are thrown up; and why they have not, after first laying the foundation of a purely moral catechism, searched through the biographies of ancient and modern times with the view of having at hand instances of the duties laid down, in which, especially by comparison of similar actions under different circumstances, they might exercise the critical judgement of their scholars in remarking their greater or less moral significance. This is a thing in which they would find that even early youth, which is still unripe for speculation of other kinds, would soon Become very acute and not a little interested, because it feels the progress of its faculty of judgement; and, what is most important, they could hope with confidence that the frequent practice of knowing and approving good conduct in all its purity, and on the other hand of remarking with regret or contempt the least deviation from it, although it may be pursued only as a sport in which children may compete with one another, yet will leave a lasting impression of esteem on the one hand and disgust on the other; and so, by the mere habit of looking on such actions as deserving approval or blame, a good foundation would be laid for uprightness in the future course of life. Only I wish they would spare them the example of so-called noble (super-meritorious) actions, in which our sentimental books so much abound, and would refer all to duty merely, and to the worth that a man can and must give himself in his own eyes by the consciousness of not having transgressed it, since whatever runs up into empty wishes and longings after inaccessible perfection produces mere heroes of romance, who, while they pique themselves on their feeling for transcendent greatness, release themselves in return from the observance of common and every-day obligations, which then seem to them petty and insignificant.[1]

But if it is asked: "What, then, is really pure morality, by which as a touchstone we must test the moral significance of every action," then I must admit that it is only philosophers that can make the decision of this question doubtful, for to common sense it has been decided long ago, not indeed by abstract general formulae, but by habitual use, like the distinction between the right and left hand. We will then point out the criterion of pure virtue in an example first, and, imagining that it is set before a boy, of say ten years old, for his judgement, we will see whether he would necessarily judge so of himself without being guided by his teacher. Tell him the history of an honest man whom men want to persuade to join the calumniators of an innocent and powerless person (say Anne Boleyn, accused by Henry VIII of England). He is offered advantages, great gifts, or high rank; he rejects them. This will excite mere approbation and applause in the mind of the hearer. Now begins the threatening of loss. Amongst these traducers are his best friends, who now renounce his friendship; near kinsfolk, who threaten to disinherit him (he being without fortune); powerful persons, who can persecute and harass him in all places and circumstances; a prince, who threatens him with loss of freedom, yea, loss of life. Then to fill the measure of suffering, and that he may feel the pain that only the morally good heart can feel very deeply, let us conceive his family threatened with extreme distress and want, entreating him to yield; conceive himself, though upright, yet with feelings not hard or insensible either to compassion or to his own distress; conceive him, I say, at the moment when he wishes that he had never lived to see the day that exposed him to such unutterable anguish, yet remaining true to his uprightness of purpose, without wavering or even doubting; then will my youthful hearer be raised gradually from mere approval to admiration, from that to amazement, and finally to the greatest veneration, and a lively wish that he himself could be such a man (though certainly not in such circumstances). Yet virtue is here worth so much only because it costs so much, not because it brings any profit. All the admiration, and even the endeavour to resemble this character, rest wholly on the purity of the moral principle, which can only be strikingly shown by removing from the springs of action everything that men may regard as part of happiness. Morality, then, must have the more power over the human heart the more purely it is exhibited. Whence it follows that, if the law of morality and the image of holiness and virtue are to exercise any influence at all on our souls, they can do so only so far as they are laid to heart in their purity as motives, unmixed with any view to prosperity, for it is in suffering that they display themselves most nobly. Now that whose removal strengthens the effect of a moving force must have been a hindrance, consequently every admixture of motives taken from our own happiness is a hindrance to the influence of the moral law on the heart. I affirm further that even in that admired action, if the motive from which it was done was a high regard for duty, then it is just this respect for the law that has the greatest influence on the mind of the spectator, not any pretension to a supposed inward greatness of mind or noble meritorious sentiments; consequently duty, not merit, must have not only the most definite, but, when it is represented in the true light of its inviolability, the most penetrating, influence on the mind.

It is more necessary than ever to direct attention to this method in our times, when men hope to produce more effect on the mind with soft, tender feelings, or high-flown, puffing-up pretensions, which rather wither the heart than strengthen it, than by a plain and earnest representation of duty, which is more suited to human imperfection and to progress in goodness. To set before children, as a pattern, actions that are called noble, magnanimous, meritorious, with the notion of captivating them by infusing enthusiasm for such actions, is to defeat our end. For as they are still so backward in the observance of the commonest duty, and even in the correct estimation of it, this means simply to make them fantastical romancers betimes. But, even with the instructed and experienced part of mankind, this supposed spring has, if not an injurious, at least no genuine, moral effect on the heart, which, however, is what it was desired to produce.

All feelings, especially those that are to produce unwonted exertions, must accomplish their effect at the moment they are at their height and before the calm down;

otherwise they effect nothing; for as there was nothing to strengthen the heart, but only to excite it, it naturally returns to its normal moderate tone and, thus, falls back into its previous languor. Principles must be built on conceptions; on any other basis there can only be paroxysms, which can give the person no moral worth, nay, not even confidence in himself, without which the highest good in man, consciousness of the morality of his mind and character, cannot exist. Now if these conceptions are to become subjectively practical, we must not rest satisfied with admiring the objective law of morality, and esteeming it highly in reference to humanity, but we must consider the conception of it in relation to man as an individual, and then this law appears in a form indeed that is highly deserving of respect, but not so pleasant as if it belonged to the element to which he is naturally accustomed; but on the contrary as often compelling him to quit this element, not without self-denial, and to betake himself to a higher, in which he can only maintain himself with trouble and with unceasing apprehension of a relapse. In a word, the moral law demands obedience, from duty not from predilection, which cannot and ought not to be presupposed at all.

Let us now see, in an example, whether the conception of an action, as a noble and magnanimous one, has more subjective moving power than if the action is conceived merely as duty in relation to the solemn law of morality. The action by which a man endeavours at the greatest peril of life to rescue people from shipwreck, at last losing his life in the attempt, is reckoned on one side as duty, but on the other and for the most part as a meritorious action, but our esteem for it is much weakened by the notion of duty to himself which seems in this case to be somewhat infringed. More decisive is the magnanimous sacrifice of life for the safety of one's country; and yet there still remains some scruple whether it is a perfect duty to devote one's self to this purpose spontaneously and unbidden, and the action has not in itself the full force of a pattern and impulse to imitation. But if an indispensable duty be in question, the transgression of which violates the moral law itself, and without regard to the welfare of mankind, and as it were tramples on its holiness (such as are usually called duties to God, because in Him we conceive the ideal of holiness in substance), then we give our most perfect esteem to the pursuit of it at the sacrifice of all that can have any value for the dearest inclinations, and we find our soul strengthened and elevated by such an example, when we convince ourselves by contemplation of it that human nature is capable of so great an elevation above every motive that nature can oppose to it. Juvenal describes such an example in a climax which makes the reader feel vividly the force of the spring that is contained in the pure law of duty, as duty:

Esto bonus miles, tutor bonus, arbiter idem
Integer; ambiguae si quando citabere testis
Incertaeque rei, Phalaris licet imperet ut sis
Falsus, et admoto dictet periuria tauro,
Summum crede nefas animam praeferre pudori,
Et propter vitam vivendi perdere causas.[2]

When we can bring any flattering thought of merit into our action, then the motive is already somewhat alloyed with self-love and has therefore some assistance from the side of the sensibility. But to postpone everything to the holiness of duty alone, and to be conscious that we can because our own reason recognises this as its command and says that we ought to do it, this is, as it were, to raise ourselves altogether above the world of sense, and there is inseparably involved in the same a consciousness of the law, as a spring of a faculty that controls the sensibility; and although this is not always attended with effect, yet frequent engagement with this spring, and the at first minor attempts at using it, give hope that this effect may be wrought, and that by degrees the greatest, and that a purely moral interest in it may be produced in us.

The method then takes the following course. At first we are only concerned to make the judging of actions by moral laws a natural employment accompanying all our own free actions, as well as the observation of those of others, and to make it as it were a habit, and to sharpen this judgement, asking first whether the action conforms objectively to the moral law, and to what law; and we distinguish the law that merely furnishes a principle of obligation from that which is really obligatory (leges obligandi a legibus obligantibus); as, for instance, the law of what men's wants require from me, as contrasted with that which their rights demand, the latter of which prescribes essential, the former only non-essential duties; and thus we teach how to distinguish different kinds of duties which meet in the same action. The other point to which attention must be directed is the question whether the action was also (subjectively) done for the sake of the moral law, so that it not only is morally correct as a deed, but also, by the maxim from which it is done, has moral worth as a disposition. Now there is no doubt that this practice, and the resulting culture of our reason in judging merely of the practical, must gradually produce a certain interest even in the law of reason, and consequently in morally good actions. For we ultimately take a liking for a thing, the contemplation of which makes us feel that the use of our cognitive faculties is extended; and this extension is especially furthered by that in which we find moral correctness, since it is only in such an order of things that reason, with its faculty of determining a priori on principle what ought to be done, can find satisfaction. An observer of nature takes liking at last to objects that at first offended his senses, when he discovers in them the great adaptation of their organization to design, so that his reason finds food in its contemplation. So Leibnitz spared an insect that he had carefully examined with the microscope, and replaced it on its leaf, because he had found himself instructed by the view of it and had, as it were, received a benefit from it.

But this employment of the faculty of judgement, which makes us feel our own cognitive powers, is not yet the interest in actions and in their morality itself. It merely causes us to take pleasure in engaging in such criticism, and it gives to virtue or the disposition that conforms to moral laws a form of beauty, which is admired, but not on that account sought after (laudatur et alget); as everything the contemplation of which produces a consciousness of the harmony of our powers of conception, and in which we feel the whole of our faculty of knowledge (understanding and imagination) strengthened, produces a satisfaction, which may also be communicated to others, while nevertheless the existence of the object remains indifferent to us, being only regarded as the occasion of our becoming aware of the capacities in us which are elevated above mere animal nature. Now, however, the second exercise comes in, the living exhibition of morality of character by examples, in which attention is directed to purity of will, first only as a negative perfection, in so far as in an action done from duty no motives of inclination have any influence in determining it. By this the pupil's attention is fixed upon the consciousness of his freedom, and although this renunciation at first excites a feeling of pain, nevertheless, by its withdrawing the pupil from the constraint of even real wants, there is proclaimed to him at the same time a deliverance from the manifold dissatisfaction in which all these wants entangle him, and the mind is made capable of receiving the sensation of satisfaction from other sources. The heart is freed and light-ened of a burden that always secretly presses on it, when instances of pure moral reso-lutions reveal to the man an inner faculty of which otherwise he has no right knowledge, the inward freedom to release himself from the boisterous importunity of inclinations, to such a degree that none of them, not even the dearest, shall have any influence on a resolution, for which we are now to employ our reason. Suppose a case where I alone know that the wrong is on my side, and although a free confession of it and the offer of satisfaction are so strongly opposed by vanity, selfishness, and even an otherwise not illegitimate antipathy to the man whose rights are impaired by me, I am nevertheless able to discard all these considerations; in this there is implied a conscious-ness of independence on inclinations and circumstances, and of the possibility of being sufficient for myself, which is salutary to me in general for other purposes also. And now the law of duty, in consequence of the positive worth which obedience to it makes us feel, finds easier access through the respect for ourselves in the consciousness of our freedom. When this is well established, when a man dreads nothing more than to find himself, on self-examination, worthless and contemptible in his own eyes, then every good moral disposition can be grafted on it, because this is the best, nay, the only guard that can keep off from the mind the pressure of ignoble and corrupting motives.

I have only intended to point out the most general maxims of the methodology of moral cultivation and exercise. As the manifold variety of duties requires special rules for each kind, and this would be a prolix affair, I shall be readily excused if in a work like this, which is only preliminary, I content myself with these outlines.

---

1. It is quite proper to extol actions that display a great, unselfish, sympathizing mind or humanity. But, in this case, we must fix attention not so much on the elevation of soul, which is very fleeting and transitory, as on the subjection of the heart to duty, from which a more enduring impression may be expected, because this implies principle (whereas the former only implies ebullitions). One need only reflect a little and he will always find a debt that he has by some means incurred towards the human race (even if it were only this, by the inequality of men in the civil constitution, enjoys advantages on account of which others must be the more in want), which will prevent the thought of duty from being repressed by the self-complacent imagina-tion of merit.
2. Juvenal, Satirae, "Be you a good soldier, a faithful tutor, an uncorrupted umpire also; if you are summoned as a witness in a doubtful and uncertain thing, though Phalaris should command that you should be false, and should dictate perjuries with the bull brought to you, believe it the highest impiety to prefer life to repu-tation, and for the sake of life, to lose the causes of living."

CONCLUSION

Two things fill the mind with ever new and increasing admiration and awe, the oftener and the more steadily we reflect on them: the starry heavens above and the moral law within. I have not to search for them and conjecture them as though they were veiled in darkness or were in the transcendent region beyond my horizon; I see them before me and connect them directly with the consciousness of my existence. The former begins from the place I occupy in the external world of sense, and enlarges my connection therein to an unbounded extent with worlds upon worlds and systems of systems, and moreover into limitless times of their periodic motion, its beginning and continuance. The second begins from my invisible self, my personality, and exhibits me in a world which has true infinity, but which is traceable only by the understanding, and with which I discern that I am not in a merely contingent but in a universal and necessary connection, as I am also thereby with all those visible worlds. The former view of a countless multitude of worlds annihilates as it were my importance as an animal creature, which after it has been for a short time provided with vital power, one knows not how, must again give back the matter of which it was formed to the planet it inhabits (a mere speck in the universe). The second, on the contrary, infinitely elevates my worth as an intelligence by my personality, in which the moral law reveals to me a life independent of animality and even of the whole sensible world, at least so far as may be inferred from the destination assigned to my existence by this law, a destination not restricted to conditions and limits of this life, but reaching into the infinite.

But though admiration and respect may excite to inquiry, they cannot supply the want of it. What, then, is to be done in order to enter on this in a useful manner and one adapted to the loftiness of the subject? Examples may serve in this as a warning and also for imitation. The contemplation of the world began from the noblest spectacle that the human senses present to us, and that our understanding can bear to follow in their vast reach; and it ended- in astrology. Morality began with the noblest attribute of human nature, the development and cultivation of which give a prospect of infinite utility; and ended- in fanaticism or superstition. So it is with all crude attempts where the principal part of the business depends on the use of reason, a use which does not come of itself, like the use of the feet, by frequent exercise, especially when attributes are in question which cannot be directly exhibited in common experience. But after the maxim had come into vogue, though late, to examine carefully beforehand all the steps that reason purposes to take, and not to let it proceed otherwise than in the track of a previously well considered method, then the study of the structure of the universe took quite a different direction, and thereby attained an incomparably happier result. The fall of a stone, the motion of a sling, resolved into their elements and the forces that are manifested in them, and treated mathematically, produced at last that clear and henceforward unchangeable insight into the system of the world which, as observation is continued, may hope always to extend itself, but need never fear to be compelled to retreat.

This example may suggest to us to enter on the same path in treating of the moral capacities of our nature, and may give us hope of a like good result. We have at hand the instances of the moral judgement of reason. By analysing these into their elementary conceptions, and in default of mathematics adopting a process similar to that of chemistry, the separation of the empirical from the rational elements that may be found in them, by repeated experiments on common sense, we may exhibit both pure, and learn with certainty what each part can accomplish of itself, so as to prevent on the one hand the errors of a still crude untrained judgement, and on the other hand (what is far more necessary) the extravagances of genius, by which, as by the adepts of the philosopher's stone, without any methodical study or knowledge of nature, visionary treasures are promised and the true are thrown away. In one word, science (critically undertaken and methodically directed) is the narrow gate that leads to the true doctrine of practical wisdom, if we understand by this not merely what one ought to do, but what ought to serve teachers as a guide to construct well and clearly the road to wisdom which everyone should travel, and to secure others from going astray. Philosophy must always continue to be the guardian of this science; and although the public does not take any interest in its subtle investigations, it must take an interest in the resulting doctrines, which such an examination first puts in a clear light.

CRITIQUE OF JUDGEMENT

TRANSLATED BY J.H. BERNARD

IMMANUEL KANT

PREFACE

We may call the faculty of cognition from principles *a priori*, *pure Reason*, and the inquiry into its possibility and bounds generally the Critique of pure Reason, although by this faculty we only understand Reason in its theoretical employment, as it appears under that name in the former work; without wishing to inquire into its faculty, as practical Reason, according to its special principles. That [Critique] goes merely into our faculty of knowing things *a priori*, and busies itself therefore only with the *cognitive faculty* to the exclusion of the feeling of pleasure and pain and the faculty of desire; and of the cognitive faculties it only concerns itself with *Understanding*, according to its principles *a priori*, to the exclusion of *Judgement* and *Reason* (as faculties alike belonging to theoretical cognition), because it is found in the sequel that no other cognitive faculty but the Understanding can furnish constitutive principles of cognition *a priori*. The Critique, then, which sifts them all, as regards the share which each of the other faculties might pretend to have in the clear possession of knowledge from its own peculiar root, leaves nothing but what the *Understanding* prescribes *a priori* as law for nature as the complex of phenomena (whose form also is given *a priori*). It relegates all other pure concepts under Ideas, which are transcendent for our theoretical faculty of cognition, but are not therefore useless or to be dispensed with. For they serve as regulative principles; partly to check the dangerous pretensions of Understanding, as if (because it can furnish *a priori* the conditions of the possibility of all things which it can know) it had thereby confined within these bounds the possibility of all things in general; and partly to lead it to the consideration of nature according to a principle of completeness, although it can never attain to this, and thus to further the final design of all knowledge.

It was then properly the *Understanding* which has its special realm in the *cognitive faculty*, so far as it contains constitutive principles of cognition *a priori*, which by the Critique, comprehensively called the Critique of pure Reason, was to be placed in certain and sole possession8 against all other competitors. And so also to *Reason*, which contains constitutive principles *a priori* nowhere except simply in respect of the *faculty of desire*, should be assigned its place in the Critique of practical Reason.

Whether now the *Judgement*, which in the order of our cognitive faculties forms a mediating link between Understanding and Reason, has also principles *a priori* for itself; whether these are constitutive or merely regulative (thus indicating no special realm); and whether they give a rule *a priori* to the feeling of pleasure and pain, as the mediating link between the cognitive faculty and the faculty of desire (just as the Understanding prescribes laws *a priori* to the first, Reason to the second); these are the questions with which the present Critique of Judgement is concerned.

A Critique of pure Reason, *i.e.* of our faculty of judging *a priori* according to principles, would be incomplete, if the Judgement, which as a cognitive faculty also makes claim to such principles, were not treated as a particular part of it; although its principles in a system of pure Philosophy need form no particular part between the theoretical and the practical, but can be annexed when needful to one or both as occasion requires. For if such a system is one day to be completed under the general name of Metaphysic (which it is possible to achieve quite completely, and which is supremely important for the use of Reason in every reference), the soil for the edifice must be explored by Criticism as deep down as the foundation of the faculty of principles independent of experience, in order that it may sink in no part, for this would inevitably bring about the downfall of the whole.

We can easily infer from the nature of the Judgement (whose right use is so necessarily and so universally requisite, that by the name of sound Understanding nothing else but this faculty is meant), that it must be attended with great difficulties to find a principle peculiar to it; (some such it must contain *a priori* in itself, for otherwise it would not be set apart by the commonest Criticism as a special cognitive faculty). This principle must not be derived *a priori* from concepts, for these belong to the Understanding, and Judgement is only concerned with their application. It must, therefore, furnish of itself a concept, through which, properly speaking, no thing is cognised, but which only serves as a rule, though not an objective one to which it can adapt its judgement; because for this latter another faculty of Judgement would be requisite, in order to be able to distinguish whether [any given case] is or is not the case for the rule.

This perplexity about a principle (whether it is subjective or objective) presents itself mainly in those judgements that we call aesthetical, which concern the Beautiful and the Sublime of Nature or of Art. And, nevertheless, the critical investigation of a principle of Judgement in these is the most important part in a Critique of this faculty. For although they do not by themselves contribute to the knowledge of things, yet they belong to the cognitive faculty alone, and point to an immediate reference of this faculty to the feeling of pleasure or pain according to some principle *a priori*; without confusing this with what may be the determining ground of the faculty of desire, which has its principles *a priori* in concepts of Reason.—In the logical judging of nature, experience exhibits a conformity to law in things, to the understanding or to the explanation of which the general concept of the sensible does not attain; here the Judgement can only derive from itself a principle of the reference of the natural thing to the unknowable supersensible (a principle which it must only use from its own point of view for the cognition of nature). And so, though in this case such a principle *a priori* can and must be applied to the *cognition* of the beings of the world, and opens out at the same time prospects which are advantageous for the practical Reason, yet it has no immediate reference to the feeling of pleasure and pain. But this reference is precisely the puzzle in the principle of Judgement, which renders a special section for this faculty necessary in the Critique; since the logical judging according to concepts (from which an immediate inference can never be drawn to the feeling of pleasure and pain) along with their critical limitation, has at all events been capable of being appended to the theoretical part of Philosophy.

The examination of the faculty of taste, as the aesthetical Judgement, is not here planned in reference to the formation or the culture of taste (for this will take its course in the future as in the past without any such investigations), but merely in a transcendental point of view. Hence, I trust that as regards the deficiency of the former purpose it will be judged with indulgence, though in the latter point of view it must be prepared for the severest scrutiny. But I hope that the great difficulty of solving a problem so involved by nature may serve as excuse for some hardly avoidable obscurity in its solution, if only it be clearly established that the principle is correctly stated. I grant that the mode of deriving the phenomena of the Judgement from it has not all the clearness which might be rightly demanded elsewhere, viz. in the case of cognition according to concepts; but I believe that I have attained to it in the second part of this work.

Here then I end my whole critical undertaking. I shall proceed without delay to the doctrinal [part] in order to profit, as far as is possible, by the more favourable moments of my increasing years. It is obvious that in this [part] there will be no special section for the Judgement, because in respect of this faculty Criticism serves instead of Theory; but, according to the division of Philosophy (and also of pure Philosophy) into theoretical and practical, the Metaphysic of Nature and of Morals will complete the undertaking.

INTRODUCTION

I. OF THE DIVISION OF PHILOSOPHY

WE PROCEED QUITE CORRECTLY IF, as usual, we divide Philosophy, as containing the principles of the rational cognition of things by means of concepts (not merely, as logic does, principles of the form of thought in general without distinction of Objects), into *theoretical* and *practical*. But then the concepts, which furnish their Object to the principles of this rational cognition, must be specifically distinct; otherwise they would not justify a division, which always presupposes a contrast between the principles of the rational cognition belonging to the different parts of a science.

Now there are only two kinds of concepts, and these admit as many distinct principles of the possibility of their objects, viz. *natural concepts* and the *concept of freedom*. The former render possible *theoretical* cognition according to principles a priori; the latter in respect of this theoretical cognition only supplies in itself a negative principle (that of mere contrast), but on the other hand it furnishes fundamental propositions which extend the sphere of the determination of the will and are therefore called practical. Thus Philosophy is correctly divided into two parts, quite distinct in their principles; the theoretical part or *Natural Philosophy*, and the practical part or *Moral Philosophy* (for that is the name given to the practical legislation of Reason in accordance with the concept of freedom). But up to the present a gross misuse of these expressions has prevailed, both in the division of the different principles and consequently also of Philosophy itself. For what is practical according to natural concepts has been identified with the practical according to the concept of freedom; and so with the like titles, 'theoretical' and 'practical' Philosophy, a division has been made, by which in fact nothing has been divided (for both parts might in such case have principles of the same kind).

The will, regarded as the faculty of desire, is (in this view) one of the many natural causes in the world, viz. that cause which acts in accordance with concepts. All that is represented as possible (or necessary) by means of a will is called practically possible (or necessary); as distinguished from the physical possibility or necessity of an effect, whose cause is not determined to causality by concepts (but in lifeless matter by mechanism and in animals by instinct). Here, in respect of the practical, it is left undetermined whether the concept which gives the rule to the causality of the will, is a natural concept or a concept of freedom.

But the last distinction is essential. For if the concept which determines the causality is a natural concept, then the principles are *technically practical*; whereas, if it is a concept of freedom they are *morally practical*. And as the division of a rational science depends on the distinction between objects whose cognition needs distinct principles, the former will belong to theoretical Philosophy (doctrine of Nature), but the latter alone will constitute the second part, viz. practical Philosophy (doctrine of Morals).

All technically practical rules (*i.e.* the rules of art and skill generally, or of prudence regarded as skill in exercising an influence over men and their wills), so far as their principles rest on concepts, must be reckoned only as corollaries to theoretical Philosophy. For they concern only the possibility of things according to natural concepts, to which belong not only the means which are to be met with in nature, but also the will itself (as a faculty of desire and consequently a natural faculty), so far as it can be determined conformably to these rules by natural motives. However, practical rules of this kind are not called laws (like physical laws), but only precepts; because the will does not stand merely under the natural concept, but also under the concept of freedom, in relation to which its principles are called laws. These with their consequences alone constitute the second or practical part of Philosophy.

The solution of the problems of pure geometry does not belong to a particular part of the science; mensuration does not deserve the name of practical, in contrast to pure, geometry, as a second part of geometry in general; and just as little ought the mechanical or chemical art of experiment or observation to be reckoned as a practical part of the doctrine of Nature. Just as little, in fine, ought housekeeping, farming, statesmanship, the art of conversation, the prescribing of diet, the universal doctrine of happiness itself, or the curbing of the inclinations and checking of the affections for the sake of happiness, to be reckoned as practical Philosophy, or taken to constitute the second part of Philosophy in general. For all these contain only rules of skill (and are consequently only technically practical) for bringing about an effect that is possible according to the natural concepts of causes and effects, which, since they belong to theoretical Philosophy, are subject to those precepts as mere corollaries from it (viz. natural science), and can therefore claim no place in a special Philosophy called practical. On the other hand, the morally practical precepts, which are altogether based on the concept of freedom to the complete exclusion of the natural determining grounds of the will, constitute a quite special class. These, like the rules which nature obeys, are called simply laws, but they do not, like them, rest on sensuous conditions but on a supersensible principle; and accordingly they require for themselves a quite different part of Philosophy, called practical, corresponding to its theoretical part.

We hence see that a complex of practical precepts given by Philosophy does not constitute a distinct part of Philosophy, as opposed to the theoretical part, because these precepts are practical; for they might be that, even if their principles were derived altogether from the theoretical cognition of nature (as technically practical rules). [A distinct branch of Philosophy is constituted only] if their principle, as it is not borrowed from the natural concept, which is always sensuously conditioned, rests on the supersensible, which alone makes the concept of freedom cognisable by formal laws. These precepts are then morally practical, *i.e.* not merely precepts or rules in this or that aspect, but, without any preceding reference to purposes and designs, are laws.

II. OF THE REALM OF PHILOSOPHY IN GENERAL

So far as our concepts have *a priori* application, so far extends the use of our cognitive faculty according to principles, and with it Philosophy.

But the complex of all objects, to which those concepts are referred, in order to bring about a knowledge of them where it is possible, may be subdivided according to the adequacy or inadequacy of our [cognitive] faculty to this design.

Concepts, so far as they are referred to objects, independently of the possibility or impossibility of the cognition of these objects, have their field which is determined merely according to the relation that their Object has to our cognitive faculty in general. The part of this field in which knowledge is possible for us is a ground or territory (*territorium*) for these concepts and the requisite cognitive faculty. The part of this territory, where they are legislative, is the realm (*ditio*) of these concepts and of the corresponding cognitive faculties. Empirical concepts have, therefore, their territory in nature, as the complex of all objects of sense, but no realm, only a dwelling-place (*domicilium*); for though they are produced in conformity to law they are not legislative, but the rules based on them are empirical and consequently contingent.

Our whole cognitive faculty has two realms, that of natural concepts and that of the concept of freedom; for through both it is legislative a priori. In accordance with this, Philosophy is divided into theoretical and practical. But the territory to which its realm extends and in which its legislation is *exercised*, is always only the complex of objects of all possible experience, so long as they are taken for nothing more than mere phenomena; for otherwise no legislation of the Understanding in respect of them is conceivable.

Legislation through natural concepts is carried on by means of the Understanding and is theoretical. Legislation through the concept of freedom is carried on by the Reason and is merely practical. It is only in the practical [sphere] that the Reason can be legislative; in respect of theoretical cognition (of nature) it can merely (as acquainted with law by the Understanding) deduce from given laws consequences which always remain within [the limits of] nature. But on the other hand, Reason is not always therefore *legislative*, where there are practical rules, for they may be only technically practical.

Understanding and Reason exercise, therefore, two distinct legislations in regard to one and the same territory of experience, without prejudice to each other. The concept of freedom as little disturbs the legislation of nature, as the natural concept influences the legislation through the former.—The possibility of at least thinking without contradiction the co-existence of both legislations, and of the corresponding faculties in the same subject, has been shown in the Critique of pure Reason; for it annulled the objections on the other side by exposing the dialectical illusion which they contain.

These two different realms then do not limit each other in their legislation, though they perpetually do so in the world of sense. That they do not constitute *one* realm, arises from this, that the natural concept represents its objects in intuition, not as things in themselves, but as mere phenomena; the concept of freedom, on the other hand, represents in its Object a thing in itself, but not in intuition. Hence, neither of them can furnish a theoretical knowledge of its Object (or even of the thinking subject) as a thing in itself; this would be the supersensible, the Idea of which we must indeed make the basis of the possibility of all these objects of experience, but which we can never extend or elevate into a cognition.

There is, then, an unbounded but also inaccessible field for our whole cognitive faculty—the field of the supersensible—wherein we find no territory, and, therefore, can have in it, for theoretical cognition, no realm either for concepts of Understanding or Reason. This field we must indeed occupy with Ideas on behalf of the theoretical as well as the practical use of Reason, but we can supply to them in reference to the laws [arising] from the concept of freedom no other than practical reality, by which our theoretical cognition is not extended in the slightest degree towards the supersensible.

Now even if an immeasurable gulf is fixed between the sensible realm of the concept of nature and the supersensible realm of the concept of freedom, so that no transition is possible from the first to the second (by means of the theoretical use of Reason), just as if they were two different worlds of which the first could have no influence upon the second, yet the second is *meant* to have an influence upon the first. The concept of freedom is meant to actualise in the world of sense the purpose proposed by its laws, and consequently nature must be so thought that the conformity to law of its form, at least harmonises with the possibility of the purposes to be effected in it according to laws of freedom.—There must, therefore, be a ground of the *unity* of the supersensible, which lies at the basis of nature, with that which the concept of freedom practically contains; and the concept of this ground, although it does not attain either theoretically or practically to a knowledge of the same, and hence has no peculiar realm, nevertheless makes possible the transition from the mode of thought according to the principles of the one to that according to the principles of the other.

III. OF THE CRITIQUE OF JUDGEMENT AS A MEANS OF COMBINING THE TWO PARTS OF PHILOSOPHY INTO A WHOLE.

The Critique of the cognitive faculties, as regards what they can furnish a priori, has properly speaking no realm in respect of Objects, because it is not a doctrine, but only has to investigate whether and how, in accordance with the state of these faculties, a doctrine is possible by their means. Its field extends to all their pretensions, in order to confine them within their legitimate bounds. But what cannot enter into the division of Philosophy may yet enter, as a chief part, into the Critique of the pure faculty of cognition in general, viz. if it contains principles which are available neither for theoretical nor for practical use.

The natural concepts, which contain the ground of all theoretical knowledge a priori, rest on the legislation of the Understanding.—The concept of freedom, which contains the ground of all sensuously-unconditioned practical precepts a priori, rests on the legislation of the Reason. Both faculties, therefore, besides being capable of application as regards their logical form to principles of whatever origin, have also as regards their content, their special legislations above which there is no other (a priori); and hence the division of Philosophy into theoretical and practical is justified.

But in the family of the higher cognitive faculties there is a middle term between the

Understanding and the Reason. This is the *Judgement*, of which we have cause for supposing according to analogy that it may contain in itself, if not a special legislation, yet a special principle of its own to be sought according to laws, though merely subjective *a priori*. This principle, even if it have no field of objects as its realm, yet may have somewhere a territory with a certain character, for which no other principle can be valid.

But besides (to judge by analogy) there is a new ground for bringing the Judgement into connexion with another arrangement of our representative faculties, which seems to be of even greater importance than that of its relationship with the family of the cognitive faculties. For all faculties or capacities of the soul can be reduced to three, which cannot be any further derived from one common ground: the *faculty of knowledge*, the *feeling of pleasure and pain*, and the *faculty of desire*.[1] For the faculty of knowledge the Understanding is alone legislative, if (as must happen when it is considered by itself without confusion with the faculty of desire) this faculty is referred to nature as the faculty of *theoretical knowledge*; for in respect of nature (as phenomenon) it is alone possible for us to give laws by means of natural concepts *a priori*, *i.e.* by pure concepts of Understanding.—For the faculty of desire, as a higher faculty according to the concept of freedom, the Reason (in which alone this concept has a place) is alone *a priori* legislative.—Now between the faculties of knowledge and desire there is the feeling of pleasure, just as the Judgement is intermediate between the Understanding and the Reason. We may therefore suppose provisionally that the Judgement likewise contains in itself an *a priori* principle. And as pleasure or pain is necessarily combined with the faculty of desire (either preceding this principle as in the lower desires, or following it as in the higher, when the desire is determined by the moral law), we may also suppose that the Judgement will bring about a transition from the pure faculty of knowledge, the realm of natural concepts, to the realm of the concept of freedom, just as in its logical use it makes possible the transition from Understanding to Reason.

Although, then, Philosophy can be divided only into two main parts, the theoretical and the practical, and although all that we may be able to say of the special principles of Judgement must be counted as belonging in it to the theoretical part, *i.e.* to rational cognition in accordance with natural concepts; yet the Critique of pure Reason, which must decide all this, as regards the possibility of the system before undertaking it, consists of three parts; the Critique of pure Understanding, of pure Judgement, and of pure Reason, which faculties are called pure because they are legislative *a priori*.

IV. OF JUDGEMENT AS A FACULTY LEGISLATING *A PRIORI*

Judgement in general is the faculty of thinking the particular as contained under the Universal. If the universal (the rule, the principle, the law) be given, the Judgement which subsumes the particular under it (even if, as transcendental Judgement, it furnishes *a priori*, the conditions in conformity with which subsumption under that universal is alone possible) is *determinant*. But if only the particular be given for which the universal has to be found, the Judgement is merely *reflective*.

The determinant Judgement only subsumes under universal transcendental laws given by the Understanding; the law is marked out for it, *a priori*, and it has therefore no need to seek a law for itself in order to be able to subordinate the particular in nature to the universal.—But the forms of nature are so manifold, and there are so many modifications of the universal transcendental natural concepts left undetermined by the laws given, *a priori*, by the pure Understanding,—because these only concern the possibility of a nature in general (as an object of sense),—that there must be laws for these [forms] also. These, as empirical, may be contingent from the point of view of *our* Understanding, and yet, if they are to be called laws (as the concept of a nature requires), they must be regarded as necessary in virtue of a principle of the unity of the manifold, though it be unknown to us.—The reflective Judgement, which is obliged to ascend from the particular in nature to the universal, requires on that account a principle that it cannot borrow from experience, because its function is to establish the unity of all empirical principles under higher ones, and hence to establish the possibility of their systematic subordination. Such a transcendental principle, then, the reflective Judgement can only give as a law from and to itself. It cannot derive it from outside (because then it would be the determinant Judgement); nor can it prescribe it to nature, because reflection upon the laws of nature adjusts itself by nature, and not nature by the conditions according to which we attempt to arrive at a concept of it which is quite contingent in respect of these.

This principle can be no other than the following: As universal laws of nature have their ground in our Understanding, which prescribes them to nature (although only according to the universal concept of it as nature); so particular empirical laws, in respect of what is in them left undetermined by these universal laws, must be considered in accordance with such a unity as they would have if an Understanding (although not our Understanding) had furnished them to our cognitive faculties, so as to make possible a system of experience according to particular laws of nature. Not as if, in this way, such an Understanding must be assumed as actual (for it is only our reflective Judgement to which this Idea serves as a principle—for reflecting, not for determining); but this faculty thus gives a law only to itself and not to nature.

Now the concept of an Object, so far as it contains the ground of the actuality of this Object, is the *purpose*; and the agreement of a thing with that constitution of things, which is only possible according to purposes, is called the *purposiveness* of its form. Thus the principle of Judgement, in respect of the form of things of nature under empirical laws generally, is the *purposiveness of nature* in its manifoldness. That is, nature is represented by means of this concept, as if an Understanding contained the ground of the unity of the manifold of its empirical laws.

The purposiveness of nature is therefore a particular concept, *a priori*, which has its origin solely in the reflective Judgement. For we cannot ascribe to natural products anything like a reference of nature in them to purposes; we can only use this concept to reflect upon such products in respect of the connexion of phenomena which is given in nature according to empirical laws. This concept is also quite different from practical purposiveness (in human art or in morals), though it is certainly thought according to the analogy of these last.

V. THE PRINCIPLE OF THE FORMAL PURPOSIVENESS OF NATURE IS A TRANSCENDENTAL PRINCIPLE OF JUDGEMENT.

A transcendental principle is one by means of which is represented, *a priori*, the universal condition under which alone things can be in general Objects of our cognition. On the other hand, a principle is called metaphysical if it represents the *a priori* condition under which alone Objects, whose concept must be empirically given, can be further determined *a priori*. Thus the principle of the cognition of bodies as substances, and as changeable substances, is transcendental, if thereby it is asserted that their changes must have a cause; it is metaphysical if it asserts that their changes must have an *external* cause. For in the former case bodies need only be thought by means of ontological predicates (pure concepts of Understanding), *e.g.* substance, in order to cognise the proposition *a priori*; but in the latter case the empirical concept of a body (as a movable thing in space) must lie at the basis of the proposition, although once this basis has been laid down, it may be seen completely *a priori* that this latter predicate (motion only by external causes) belongs to body.—Thus, as I shall presently show, the principle of the purposiveness of nature (in the manifoldness of its empirical laws) is a transcendental principle. For the concept of Objects, so far as they are thought as standing under this principle, is only the pure concept of objects of possible empirical cognition in general and contains nothing empirical. On the other hand, the principle of practical purposiveness, which must be thought in the Idea of the *determination* of a free *will*, is a metaphysical principle; because the concept of a faculty of desire as a will must be given empirically (*i.e.* does not belong to transcendental predicates). Both principles are, however, not empirical, but *a priori*; because for the combination of the predicate with the empirical concept of the subject of their judgements no further experience is needed, but it can be apprehended completely *a priori*.

That the concept of a purposiveness of nature belongs to transcendental principles can be sufficiently seen from the maxims of the Judgement, which lie at the basis of the investigation of nature *a priori*, and yet do not go further than the possibility of experience, and consequently of the cognition of nature—not indeed nature in general, but nature as determined through a variety of particular laws. These maxims present themselves in the course of this science often enough, though in a scattered way, as sentences of metaphysical wisdom, whose necessity we cannot demonstrate from concepts. "Nature takes the shortest way (*lex parsimoniae*); at the same time it makes no leaps, either in the course of its changes or in the juxtaposition of specifically different forms (*lex continui in natura*); its great variety in empirical laws is yet unity under a few principles (*principia praeter necessitatem non sunt multiplicanda*)," etc.

If we propose to set forth the origin of these fundamental propositions and try to do so by the psychological method, we violate their sense. For they do not tell us what happens, *i.e.* by what rule our cognitive powers actually operate, and how we judge, but how we ought to judge; and this logical objective necessity does not emerge if the principles are merely empirical. Hence that purposiveness of nature for our cognitive faculties and their use, which is plainly apparent from them, is a transcendental principle of judgements, and needs therefore also a Transcendental Deduction, by means of which the ground for so judging must be sought in the sources of cognition *a priori*.

We find in the grounds of the possibility of an experience in the very first place something necessary, viz. the universal laws without which nature in general (as an object of sense) cannot be thought; and these rest upon the Categories, applied to the formal conditions of all intuition possible for us, so far as it is also given *a priori*. Now under these laws the Judgement is determinant, for it has nothing to do but to subsume under given laws. For example, the Understanding says that every change has its cause (universal law of nature); the transcendental Judgement has nothing further to do than to supply *a priori* the condition of subsumption under the concept of the Understanding placed before it, *i.e.* the succession [in time] of the determinations of one and the same thing. For nature in general (as an object of possible experience) that law is cognised as absolutely necessary.—But now the objects of empirical cognition are determined in many other ways than by that formal time-condition, or, at least as far as we can judge *a priori*, are determinable. Hence specifically different natures can be causes in an infinite variety of ways, as well as in virtue of what they have in common as belonging to nature in general; and each of these modes must (in accordance with the concept of a cause in general) have its rule, which is a law and therefore brings necessity with it, although we do not at all comprehend this necessity, in virtue of the constitution and the limitations of our cognitive faculties. We must therefore think in nature, in respect of its merely empirical laws, a possibility of infinitely various empirical laws, which are, as far as our insight goes, contingent (cannot be cognised *a priori*), and in respect of which we judge nature, according to empirical laws and the possibility of the unity of experience (as a system according to empirical laws), to be contingent. But such a unity must be necessarily presupposed and assumed, for otherwise there would be no thorough-going connexion of empirical cognitions in a whole of experience. The universal laws of nature no doubt furnish such a connexion of things according to their kind as things of nature in general, but not specifically, as such particular beings of nature. Hence the Judgement must assume for its special use this principle *a priori*, that what in the particular (empirical) laws of nature is from the human point of view contingent, yet contains a unity of law in the combination of its manifold into an experience possible in itself—a unity not indeed to be fathomed by us, but yet thinkable. Consequently as the unity of law in a combination, which we cognise as contingent in itself, although in conformity with a necessary design (a need) of Understanding, is represented as the purposiveness of Objects (here of nature); so must the Judgement, which in respect of things under possible (not yet discovered) empirical laws is merely reflection, think of nature in respect of the latter according to *a principle of purposiveness* for our cognitive faculty, which then is expressed in the above maxims of the Judgement. This transcendental concept of a purposiveness of nature is neither a natural concept nor a concept of freedom, because it ascribes nothing to the Object (of nature), but only represents the peculiar way in which we must proceed in reflection upon the objects of nature in reference to a thoroughly connected experience, and is consequently a subjective principle (maxim) of the Judgement. Hence, as if it were a lucky chance favouring our design, we are rejoiced (properly speaking, relieved of a want), if we meet with such systematic unity under merely empirical laws; although we must necessarily assume that there is such a unity without our comprehending it or being able to prove it.

In order to convince ourselves of the correctness of this Deduction of the concept before us, and the necessity of assuming it as a transcendental principle of cognition, just consider the magnitude of the problem. The problem, which lies *a priori* in our

Understanding, is to make a connected experience out of given perceptions of a nature containing at all events an infinite variety of empirical laws. The Understanding is, no doubt, in possession *a priori* of universal laws of nature, without which nature could not be an object of experience; but it needs in addition a certain order of nature in its particular rules, which can only be empirically known and which are, as regards the Understanding, contingent. These rules, without which we could not proceed from the universal analogy of a possible experience in general to the particular, must be thought by it as laws (*i.e.* as necessary), for otherwise they would not constitute an order of nature; although their necessity can never be cognised or comprehended by it. Although, therefore, the Understanding can determine nothing *a priori* in respect of Objects, it must, in order to trace out these empirical so-called laws, place at the basis of all reflection upon Objects an *a priori* principle, viz. that a cognisable order of nature is possible in accordance with these laws. The following propositions express some such principle. There is in nature a subordination of genera and species comprehensible by us. Each one approximates to some other according to a common principle, so that a transition from one to another and so on to a higher genus may be possible. Though it seems at the outset unavoidable for our Understanding to assume different kinds of causality for the specific differences of natural operations, yet these different kinds may stand under a small number of principles, with the investigation of which we have to busy ourselves. This harmony of nature with our cognitive faculty is presupposed *a priori* by the Judgement, on behalf of its reflection upon nature in accordance with its empirical laws; whilst the Understanding at the same time cognises it objectively as contingent, and it is only the Judgement that ascribes it to nature as a trancendental purposiveness (in relation to the cognitive faculty of the subject). For without this presupposition we should have no order of nature in accordance with empirical laws, and consequently no guiding thread for an experience ordered by these in all their variety, or for an investigation of them.

For it might easily be thought that, in spite of all the uniformity of natural things according to the universal laws, without which we should not have the form of an empirical cognition in general, the specific variety of the empirical laws of nature including their effects might yet be so great, that it would be impossible for our Understanding, to detect in nature a comprehensible order; to divide its products into genera and species, so as to use the principles which explain and make intelligible one for the explanation and comprehension of another; or out of such confused material (strictly we should say, so infinitely various and not to be measured by our faculty of comprehension) to make a connected experience.

The Judgement has therefore also in itself a principle *a priori* of the possibility of nature, but only in a subjective aspect; by which it prescribes, not to nature (autonomy), but to itself (heautonomy) a law for its reflection upon nature. This we might call the *law of the specification of nature* in respect of its empirical laws. The Judgement does not cognise this *a priori* in nature, but assumes it on behalf of a natural order cognisable by our Understanding in the division which it makes of the universal laws of nature when it wishes to subordinate to these the variety of particular laws. If then we say that nature specifies its universal laws according to the principles of purposiveness for our cognitive faculty, *i.e.* in accordance with the necessary business of the human Understanding of finding the universal for the particular which perception offers it, and again

464 | IMMANUEL KANT

of finding connexion for the diverse (which however is a universal for each species) in the unity of a principle,—we thus neither prescribe to nature a law, nor do we learn one from it by observation (although such a principle may be confirmed by this means). For it is not a principle of the determinant but merely of the reflective Judgement. We only require that, be nature disposed as it may as regards its universal laws, investigation into its empirical laws may be carried on in accordance with that principle and the maxims founded thereon, because it is only so far as that holds that we can make any progress with the use of our Understanding in experience, or gain knowledge.

VI. OF THE COMBINATION OF THE FEELING OF PLEASURE WITH THE CONCEPT OF THE PURPOSIVENESS OF NATURE.

The thought harmony of nature in the variety of its particular laws with our need of finding universality of principles for it, must be judged as contingent in respect of our insight, but yet at the same time as indispensable for the needs of our Understanding, and consequently as a purposiveness by which nature is harmonised with our design, which, however, has only knowledge for its aim. The universal laws of the Understanding, which are at the same time laws of nature, are just as necessary (although arising from spontaneity) as the material laws of motion. Their production presupposes no design on the part of our cognitive faculty, because it is only by means of them that we, in the first place, attain a concept of what the cognition of things (of nature) is, and attribute them necessarily to nature as Object of our cognition in general. But, so far as we can see, it is contingent that the order of nature according to its particular laws, in all its variety and heterogeneity possibly at least transcending our comprehension, should be actually conformable to these [laws]. The discovery of this [order] is the business of the Understanding which is designedly borne towards a necessary purpose, viz. the bringing of unity of principles into nature, which purpose then the Judgement must ascribe to nature, because the Understanding cannot here prescribe any law to it.

The attainment of that design is bound up with the feeling of pleasure, and since the condition of this attainment is a representation *a priori*,—as here a principle for the reflective Judgement in general,—therefore the feeling of pleasure is determined by a ground *a priori* and valid for every man, and that merely by the reference of the Object to the cognitive faculty, the concept of purposiveness here not having the least reference to the faculty of desire. It is thus quite distinguished from all practical purposiveness of nature.

In fact, although from the agreement of perceptions with laws in accordance with universal natural concepts (the categories), we do not and cannot find in ourselves the slightest effect upon the feeling of pleasure, because the Understanding necessarily proceeds according to its nature without any design; yet, on the other hand, the discovery that two or more empirical heterogeneous laws of nature may be combined under one principle comprehending them both, is the ground of a very marked pleasure, often even of an admiration, which does not cease, though we may be already quite familiar with the objects of it. We no longer find, it is true, any marked pleasure in the comprehensibility of nature and in the unity of its divisions into genera and species, whereby are possible all empirical concepts, through which we cognise it according to its particular laws. But this pleasure has certainly been present at one time, and it is only because the commonest experience would be impossible without it that it is gradually confounded with mere cognition and no longer arrests particular attention. There is then something in our judgements upon nature which makes us attentive to its purposiveness for our Understanding—an endeavour to bring, where possible, its dissimilar laws under higher ones, though still always empirical—and thus, if successful, makes us feel pleasure in that harmony of these with our cognitive faculty, which harmony we regard as merely contingent. On the other hand, a representation of nature would altogether displease, by which it should be foretold to us that in the smallest investigation beyond the commonest experience we should meet with a heterogeneity of its laws, which would make the union of its particular laws under universal empirical laws impossible for our Understanding. For this would contradict the principle of the subjectively-purposive specification of nature in its genera, and also of our reflective Judgement in respect of such principle.

This presupposition of the Judgement is, however, at the same time so indeterminate as to how far that ideal purposiveness of nature for our cognitive faculty should be extended, that if we were told that a deeper or wider knowledge of nature derived from observation must lead at last to a variety of laws, which no human Understanding could reduce to a principle, we should at once acquiesce. But still we more gladly listen to one who offers hope that the more we know nature internally, and can compare it with external members now unknown to us, the more simple shall we find it in its principles, and that the further our experience reaches the more uniform shall we find it amid the apparent heterogeneity of its empirical laws. For it is a mandate of our Judgement to proceed according to the principle of the harmony of nature with our cognitive faculty so far as that reaches, without deciding (because it is not the determinant Judgement which gives us this rule) whether or not it is bounded anywhere. For although in respect of the rational use of our cognitive faculty we can determine such bounds, this is not possible in the empirical field.

VII. OF THE AESTHETICAL REPRESENTATION OF THE PURPOSIVENESS OF NATURE.

That which in the representation of an Object is merely subjective, *i.e.* which decides its reference to the subject, not to the object, is its aesthetical character; but that which serves or can be used for the determination of the object (for cognition), is its logical validity. In the cognition of an object of sense both references present themselves. In the sense-representation of external things the quality of space wherein we intuite them is the merely subjective [element] of my representation (by which it remains undecided what they may be in themselves as Objects), on account of which reference the object is thought thereby merely as phenomenon. But space, notwithstanding its merely subjective quality, is at the same time an ingredient in the cognition of things as phenomena. *Sensation*, again (*i.e.* external sensation), expresses the merely subjective [element] of our representations of external things, but it is also the proper material (reale) of them (by which something existing is given), just as space is the mere form *a priori* of the possibility of their intuition. Nevertheless, however, sensation is also employed in the cognition of external Objects.

But the subjective [element] in a representation *which cannot be an ingredient of cogni-*

tion, is the *pleasure* or *pain* which is bound up with it; for through it I cognise nothing in the object of the representation, although it may be the effect of some cognition. Now the purposiveness of a thing, so far as it is represented in perception, is no characteristic of the Object itself (for such cannot be perceived), although it may be inferred from a cognition of things. The purposiveness, therefore, which precedes the cognition of an Object, and which, even without our wishing to use the representation of it for cognition, is, at the same time, immediately bound up with it, is that subjective [element] which cannot be an ingredient in cognition. Hence the object is only called purposive, when its representation is immediately combined with the feeling of pleasure; and this very representation is an aesthetical representation of purposiveness.—The only question is whether there is, in general, such a representation of purposiveness.

If pleasure is bound up with the mere apprehension (*apprehensio*) of the form of an object of intuition, without reference to a concept for a definite cognition, then the representation is thereby not referred to the Object, but simply to the subject; and the pleasure can express nothing else than its harmony with the cognitive faculties which come into play in the reflective Judgement, and so far as they are in play; and hence can only express a subjective formal purposiveness of the Object. For that apprehension of forms in the Imagination can never take place without the reflective Judgement, though undesignedly, at least comparing them with its faculty of referring intuitions to concepts. If now in this comparison the Imagination (as the faculty of *a priori* intuitions) is placed by means of a given representation undesignedly in agreement with the Understanding, as the faculty of concepts, and thus a feeling of pleasure is aroused, the object must then be regarded as purposive for the reflective Judgement. Such a judgement is an aesthetical judgement upon the purposiveness of the Object, which does not base itself upon any present concept of the object, nor does it furnish any such. In the case of an object whose form (not the matter of its representation, as sensation), in the mere reflection upon it (without reference to any concept to be obtained of it), is judged as the ground of a pleasure in the representation of such an Object, this pleasure is judged as bound up with the representation necessarily; and, consequently, not only for the subject which apprehends this form, but for every judging being in general. The object is then called beautiful; and the faculty of judging by means of such a pleasure (and, consequently, with universal validity) is called Taste. For since the ground of the pleasure is placed merely in the form of the object for reflection in general—and, consequently, in no sensation of the object, and also without reference to any concept which anywhere involves design— it is only the conformity to law in the empirical use of the Judgement in general (unity of the Imagination with the Understanding) in the subject, with which the representation of the Object in reflection, whose conditions are universally valid *a priori,* harmonises. And since this harmony of the object with the faculties of the subject is contingent, it brings about the representation of its purposiveness in respect of the cognitive faculties of the subject.

Here now is a pleasure, which, like all pleasure or pain that is not produced through the concept of freedom (*i.e.* through the preceding determination of the higher faculties of desire by pure Reason), can never be comprehended from concepts, as necessarily bound up with the representation of an object. It must always be cognised as combined with this only by means of reflective perception; and, consequently, like all empirical judgements, it can declare no objective necessity and lay claim to no *a priori* validity. But the judgement of taste also claims, as every other empirical judgement does, to be valid for every one; and in spite of its inner contingency this is always possible. The strange and irregular thing is that it is not an empirical concept, but a feeling of pleasure (consequently not a concept at all), which by the judgement of taste is attributed to every one, —just as if it were a predicate bound up with the cognition of the Object—and which is connected with the representation thereof.

A singular judgement of experience, *e.g.*, when we perceive a moveable drop of water in an ice-crystal, may justly claim that every one else should find it the same; because we have formed this judgement, according to the universal conditions of the determinant faculty of Judgement, under the laws of a possible experience in general. Just in the same way he who feels pleasure in the mere reflection upon the form of an object without respect to any concept, although this judgement be empirical and singular, justly claims the agreement of every one; because the ground of this pleasure is found in the universal, although subjective, condition of reflective judgements, viz., the purposive harmony of an object (whether a product of nature or of art) with the mutual relations of the cognitive faculties (the Imagination and the Understanding), a harmony which is requisite for every empirical cognition. The pleasure, therefore, in the judgement of taste is dependent on an empirical representation, and cannot be bound up *a priori* with any concept (we cannot determine *a priori* what object is or is not according to taste; that we must find out by experiment). But the pleasure is the determining ground of this judgement only because we are conscious that it rests merely on reflection and on the universal though only subjective conditions of the harmony of that reflection with the cognition of Objects in general, for which the form of the Object is purposive.

Thus the reason why judgements of taste according to their possibility are subjected to a Critique is that they presuppose a principle *a priori*, although this principle is neither one of cognition for the Understanding nor of practice for the Will, and therefore is not in any way determinant *a priori*.

Susceptibility to pleasure from reflection upon the forms of things (of Nature as well as of Art), indicates not only a purposiveness of the Objects in relation to the reflective Judgement, conformably to the concept of nature in the subject; but also conversely a purposiveness of the subject in respect of the objects according to their form or even their formlessness, in virtue of the concept of freedom. Hence the aesthetical judgement is not only related as a judgement of taste to the beautiful, but also as springing from a spiritual feeling is related to the *sublime*; and thus the Critique of the aesthetical Judgement must be divided into two corresponding sections.

VIII. OF THE LOGICAL REPRESENTATION OF THE PURPOSIVENESS OF NATURE

Purposiveness may be represented in an object given in experience on a merely subjective ground, as the harmony of its form,—in the *apprehension* (*apprehensio*) of it prior to any concept,—with the cognitive faculties, in order to unite the intuition with concepts for a cognition generally. Or it may be represented objectively as the harmony of the form of the object with the possibility of the thing itself, according to a concept of it which precedes and contains the ground of this form. We have seen that the representation of purposiveness of the first kind rests on the immediate pleasure in the form of the object in the mere reflection upon it. But the representation of purposiveness of the second kind, since it refers the form of the Object, not to the cognitive faculties of the subject in the apprehension of it, but to a definite cognition of the object under a given concept, has nothing to do with a feeling of pleasure in things, but only with the Understanding in its judgement upon them. If the concept of an object is given, the business of the Judgement in the use of the concept for cognition consists in *presentation* (*exhibitio*), *i.e.* in setting a corresponding intuition beside the concept. This may take place either through our own Imagination, as in Art when we realise a preconceived concept of an object which is a purpose of ours; or through Nature in its Technic (as in organised bodies) when we supply to it our concept of its purpose in order to judge of its products. In the latter case it is not merely the *purposiveness* of nature in the form of the thing that is represented, but this its product is represented as a *natural purpose*.—Although our concept of a subjective purposiveness of nature in its forms according to empirical laws is not a concept of the Object, but only a principle of the Judgement for furnishing itself with concepts amid the immense variety of nature (and thus being able to ascertain its own position), yet we thus ascribe to nature as it were a regard to our cognitive faculty according to the analogy of purpose. Thus we can regard *natural beauty* as the *presentation* of the concept of the formal (merely subjective) purposiveness, and *natural purposes* as the presentation of the concept of a real (objective) purposiveness. The former of these we judge of by Taste (aesthetically, by the medium of the feeling of pleasure), the latter by Understanding and Reason (logically, according to concepts).

On this is based the division of the Critique of Judgement into the Critique of *aesthetical* and of *teleological* Judgement. By the first we understand the faculty of judging of the formal purposiveness (otherwise called subjective) of Nature by means of the feeling of pleasure or pain; by the second the faculty of judging its real (objective) purposiveness by means of Understanding and Reason.

In a Critique of Judgement the part containing the aesthetical Judgement is essential, because this alone contains a principle which the Judgement places quite *a priori* at the basis of its reflection upon nature; viz., the principle of a formal purposiveness of nature, according to its particular (empirical) laws, for our cognitive faculty, without which the Understanding could not find itself in nature. On the other hand no reason *a priori* could be specified,—and even the possibility of a reason would not be apparent from the concept of nature as an object of experience whether general or particular,— why there should be objective purposes of nature, *i.e.* things which are only possible as natural purposes; but the Judgement, without containing such a principle *a priori* in itself, in given cases (of certain products), in order to make use of the concept of purposes on behalf of Reason, would only contain the rule according to which that transcendental principle has already prepared the Understanding to apply to nature the concept of a purpose (at least as regards its form).

But the transcendental principle which represents a purposiveness of nature (in subjective reference to our cognitive faculty) in the form of a thing as a principle by which we judge of nature, leaves it quite undetermined where and in what cases I have to judge of a product according to a principle of purposiveness, and not rather according to universal natural laws. It leaves it to the *aesthetical* Judgement to decide by taste the harmony of this product (of its form) with our cognitive faculty (so far as this decision rests not on any agreement with concepts but on feeling). On the other hand, the Judgement teleologically employed furnishes conditions determinately under which something (*e.g.* an organised body) is to be judged according to the Idea of a purpose of nature; but it can adduce no fundamental proposition from the concept of nature as an object of experience authorising it to ascribe to nature *a priori* a reference to purposes, or even indeterminately to assume this of such products in actual experience. The reason of this is that we must have many particular experiences, and consider them under the unity of their principle, in order to be able to cognise, even empirically, objective purposiveness in a certain object.—The aesthetical Judgement is therefore a special faculty for judging of things according to a rule, but not according to concepts. The teleological Judgement is not a special faculty, but only the reflective Judgement in general, so far as it proceeds, as it always does in theoretical cognition, according to concepts; but in respect of certain objects of nature according to special principles, viz., of a merely reflective Judgement, and not of a Judgement that determines Objects. Thus as regards its application it belongs to the theoretical part of Philosophy; and on account of its special principles which are not determinant, as they must be in Doctrine, it must constitute a special part of the Critique. On the other hand, the aesthetical Judgement contributes nothing towards the knowledge of its objects, and thus must be reckoned as belonging to the criticism of the judging subject and its cognitive faculties, *only* so far as they are susceptible of *a priori* principles, of whatever other use (theoretical or practical) they may be. This is the propaedeutic of all Philosophy.

IX. OF THE CONNEXION OF THE LEGISLATION OF UNDERSTANDING WITH THAT OF REASON BY MEANS OF THE JUDGEMENT

The Understanding legislates *a priori* for nature as an Object of sense—for a theoretical knowledge of it in a possible experience. Reason legislates *a priori* for freedom and its peculiar causality; as the supersensible in the subject, for an unconditioned practical knowledge. The realm of the natural concept under the one legislation and that of the concept of freedom under the other are entirely removed from all mutual influence which they might have on one another (each according to its fundamental laws) by the great gulf that separates the supersensible from phenomena. The concept of freedom determines nothing in respect of the theoretical cognition of nature; and the natural concept determines nothing in respect of the practical laws of freedom. So far then it is not possible to throw a bridge from the one realm to the other. But although the determining grounds of causality according to the concept of freedom (and the practical rules which it contains) are not resident in nature, and the sensible cannot determine the supersensible in the subject, yet this is possible conversely (not, to be sure, in respect of the cognition of nature, but as regards the effects of the supersensible upon the sensible). This in fact is involved in the concept of a causality through freedom, the *effect* of which is to take place in the world according to its formal laws. The word *cause*, of course, when used of the supersensible only signifies the *ground* which determines the causality of natural things to an effect in accordance with their proper natural laws, although harmoniously with the formal principle of the laws of Reason. Although the possibility of this cannot be comprehended, yet the objection of a contradiction alleged to be found in it can be sufficiently answered.[2]—The effect in accordance with the concept of freedom is the final purpose which (or its phenomenon in the world of sense) ought to exist; and the condition of the possibility of this is presupposed in nature (in the nature of the subject as a sensible being, that is, as man). The Judgement presupposes this *a priori* and without reference to the practical; and thus furnishes the mediating concept between the concepts of nature and that of freedom. It makes possible the transition from the conformity to law in accordance with the former to the final purpose in accordance with the latter, and this by the concept of a *purposiveness* of nature. For thus is cognised the possibility of the final purpose which alone can be actualised in nature in harmony with its laws.

The Understanding by the possibility of its *a priori* laws for nature, gives a proof that nature is only cognised by us as phenomenon; and implies at the same time that it has a supersensible substrate, though it leaves this quite *undetermined*. The Judgement by its *a priori* principle for the judging of nature according to its possible particular laws, makes the supersensible substrate (both in us and without us) *determinable by means of the intellectual faculty*. But the Reason by its practical *a priori* law *determines* it; and thus the Judgement makes possible the transition from the realm of the concept of nature to that of the concept of freedom.

As regards the faculties of the soul in general, in their higher aspect, as containing an autonomy; the Understanding is that which contains the *constitutive* principles *a priori* for the *cognitive faculty* (the theoretical cognition of nature). For the *feeling of pleasure and pain* there is the Judgement, independently of concepts and sensations which relate to the determination of the faculty of desire and can thus be immediately practical. For the *faculty of desire* there is the Reason which is practical without the mediation of any pleasure whatever. It determines for the faculty of desire, as a superior faculty, the final purpose which carries with it the pure intellectual satisfaction in the Object.—The concept formed by Judgement of a purposiveness of nature belongs to natural concepts, but only as a regulative principle of the cognitive faculty; although the aesthetical judgement upon certain objects (of Nature or Art) which occasions it is, in respect of the feeling of pleasure or pain, a constitutive principle. The spontaneity in the play of the cognitive faculties, the harmony of which contains the ground of this pleasure, makes the above concept [of the purposiveness of nature] fit to be the mediating link between the realm of the natural concept and that of the concept of freedom in its effects; whilst at the same time it promotes the sensibility of the mind for moral feeling.—The following table may facilitate the review of all the higher faculties according to their systematic unity.[3]

All the faculties of the mind
Cognitive faculties.
Faculties of desire.
Feeling of pleasure and pain.

Cognitive faculties
Understanding.
Judgement.
Reason.

A priori principles
Conformity to law.
Purposiveness.
Final purpose.

Application to
Nature.
Art.
Freedom.

1. If we have cause for supposing that concepts which we use as empirical principles stand in relationship with the pure cognitive faculty *a priori*, it is profitable, because of this reference, to seek for them a transcendental definition; *i.e.* a definition through pure categories, so far as these by themselves adequately furnish the distinction of the concept in question from others. We here follow the example of the mathematician who leaves undetermined the empirical data of his problem, and only brings their relation in their pure synthesis under the concepts of pure Arithmetic, and thus generalises the solution. Objection has been brought against a similar procedure of mine (cf. the Preface to the Critique of Practical Reason, *Abbott's Translation*, p. 94), and my definition of the faculty of desire has been found fault with, viz. that it is [the being's] *faculty of becoming by means of its representations the cause of the actuality of the objects of these representations*; for the desires might be mere *cravings*, and by means of these alone every one is convinced the Object cannot be produced.—But this proves nothing more than that there are desires in man, by which he is in contradiction with himself. For here he strives for the production of the Object by means of the representation *alone*, from which he can expect no result, because he is conscious that his mechanical powers (if I may so call those which are not psychological) which must be determined by that representation to bring about the Object (mediately) are either not competent, or even tend towards what is impossible; e.g. to reverse the past (*O mihi praeteritos ...* etc.), or to annihilate in the impatience of expectation the interval before the wished for moment.—Although in such fantastic desires we are conscious of the inadequacy (or even the unsuitability) of our representations for being *causes* of their objects, yet their reference as causes, and consequently the representation of their *causality*, is contained in every *wish*; and this is specially evident if the wish is an affection or *longing*. For these [longings] by their dilatation and contraction of the heart and consequent exhaustion of its powers, prove that these powers are continually kept on the stretch by representations, but that they perpetually let the mind, having regard to the impossibility [of the desire], fall back in exhaustion. Even prayers for the aversion of great and (as far as one can see) unavoidable evils, and many superstitious means for attaining in a natural way impossible purposes, point to the causal reference of representations to their Objects; a reference which cannot at all be checked by the consciousness of the inadequacy of the effort to produce the effect.—As to why there should be in our nature this propensity to desires which are consciously vain, that is an anthropologico-teleological problem. It seems that if we were not determined to the application of our powers before we were assured of the adequacy of our faculties to produce an Object, these powers would remain in great part unused. For we commonly learn to know our powers only by first making trial of them. This deception in the case of vain wishes is then only the consequence of a benevolent ordinance in our nature. [This note was added by Kant in the Second Edition.]
2. One of the various pretended contradictions in this whole distinction of the causality of nature from that of freedom is this. It is objected that if I speak of *obstacles* which nature opposes to causality according to (moral) laws of freedom or of the *assistance* it affords, I am admitting an *influence* of the former upon the latter. But if we try to understand what has been said, this misinterpretation is very easy to avoid. The opposition or assistance is not between nature and freedom, but between the former as phenomenon and the *effects* of the latter as phenomena in the world of sense. The causality of freedom itself (of pure and practical Reason) is the causality of a natural cause subordinated to freedom (*i.e.* of the subject considered as man and therefore as phenomenon). The intelligible, which is thought under freedom, contains the ground of the *determination* of this [natural cause] in a way not explicable any further (just as that intelligible does which constitutes the supersensible substrate of nature).
3. It has been thought a doubtful point that my divisions in pure Philosophy should always be threefold. But that lies in the nature of the thing. If there is to be an *a priori* division it must be either *analytical*, according to the law of contradiction, which is always twofold (*quodlibet ens est aut A aut non A*); or it is *synthetical*. And if in this latter case it is to be derived from *a priori concepts* (not as in Mathematic from the intuition corresponding to the concept), the division must necessarily be trichotomy. For according to what is requisite for synthetical unity in general there must be (1) a condition, (2) a conditioned, and (3) the concept which arises from the union of the conditioned with its condition.

FIRST PART — CRITIQUE OF THE AESTHETICAL JUDGEMENT

FIRST DIVISION—ANALYTIC OF THE AESTHETICAL JUDGEMENT

FIRST BOOK—ANALYTIC OF THE BEAUTIFUL

FIRST MOMENT—OF THE JUDGEMENT OF TASTE ACCORDING TO QUALITY

1

§ 1. THE JUDGEMENT OF TASTE IS AESTHETICAL

In order to decide whether anything is beautiful or not, we refer the representation, not by the Understanding to the Object for cognition but, by the Imagination (perhaps in conjunction with the Understanding) to the subject, and its feeling of pleasure or pain. The judgement of taste is therefore not a judgement of cognition, and is consequently not logical but aesthetical, by which we understand that whose determining ground can be *no other than subjective*. Every reference of representations, even that of sensations, may be objective (and then it signifies the real in an empirical representation); save only the reference to the feeling of pleasure and pain, by which nothing in the Object is signified, but through which there is a feeling in the subject, as it is affected by the representation.

To apprehend a regular, purposive building by means of one's cognitive faculty (whether in a clear or a confused way of representation) is something quite different from being conscious of this representation as connected with the sensation of satisfaction. Here the representation is altogether referred to the subject and to its feeling of life, under the name of the feeling of pleasure or pain. This establishes a quite separate faculty of distinction and of judgement, adding nothing to cognition, but only comparing the given representation in the subject with the whole faculty of representations, of which the mind is conscious in the feeling of its state. Given representations in a judgement can be empirical (consequently, aesthetical); but the judgement which is formed by means of them is logical, provided they are referred in the judgement to the Object. Conversely, if the given representations are rational, but are referred in a judgement simply to the subject (to its feeling), the judgement is so far always aesthetical.

§ 2. THE SATISFACTION WHICH DETERMINES THE JUDGEMENT OF TASTE IS DISINTERESTED

The satisfaction which we combine with the representation of the existence of an object is called interest. Such satisfaction always has reference to the faculty of desire, either as its determining ground or as necessarily connected with its determining ground. Now when the question is if a thing is beautiful, we do not want to know whether anything depends or can depend on the existence of the thing either for myself or for any one else, but how we judge it by mere observation (intuition or reflection). If any one asks me if I find that palace beautiful which I see before me, I may answer: I do not like things of that kind which are made merely to be stared at. Or I can answer like that Iroquois *sachem* who was pleased in Paris by nothing more than by the cook-shops. Or again after the manner of *Rousseau* I may rebuke the vanity of the great who waste the sweat of the people on such superfluous things. In fine I could easily convince myself that if I found myself on an uninhabited island without the hope of ever again coming among men, and could conjure up just such a splendid building by my mere wish, I should not even give myself the trouble if I had a sufficiently comfortable hut. This may all be admitted and approved; but we are not now talking of this. We wish only to know if this mere representation of the object is accompanied in me with satisfaction, however indifferent I may be as regards the existence of the object of this representation. We easily see that in saying it is *beautiful* and in showing that I have taste, I am concerned, not with that in which I depend on the existence of the object, but with that which I make out of this representation in myself. Every one must admit that a judgement about beauty, in which the least interest mingles, is very partial and is not a pure judgement of taste. We must not be in the least prejudiced in favour of the existence of the things, but be quite indifferent in this respect, in order to play the judge in things of taste.

We cannot, however, better elucidate this proposition, which is of capital importance, than by contrasting the pure disinterested[2] satisfaction in judgements of taste, with that which is bound up with an interest, especially if we can at the same time be certain that there are no other kinds of interest than those which are now to be specified.

§ 3. THE SATISFACTION IN THE PLEASANT IS BOUND UP WITH INTEREST

That which pleases the senses in sensation is PLEASANT. Here the opportunity presents itself of censuring a very common confusion of the double sense which the word sensation can have, and of calling attention to it. All satisfaction (it is said or thought) is itself sensation (of a pleasure). Consequently everything that pleases is pleasant because it pleases (and according to its different degrees or its relations to other pleasant sensations it is *agreeable, lovely, delightful, enjoyable,* etc.). But if this be admitted, then impressions of Sense which determine the inclination, fundamental propositions of Reason which determine the Will, mere reflective forms of intuition which determine the Judgement, are quite the same, as regards the effect upon the feeling of pleasure. For this would be pleasantness in the sensation of one's state, and since in the end all the operations of our faculties must issue in the practical and unite in it as their goal, we could suppose no other way of estimating things and their worth than that which consists in the gratification that they promise. It is of no consequence at all how this is attained, and since then the choice of means alone could make a difference, men could indeed blame one another for stupidity and indiscretion, but never for baseness and wickedness. For all, each according to his own way of seeing things, seek one goal, that is, gratification.

If a determination of the feeling of pleasure or pain is called sensation, this expression signifies something quite different from what I mean when I call the representation of a thing (by sense, as a receptivity belonging to the cognitive faculty) sensation. For in the latter case the representation is referred to the Object, in the former simply to the subject, and is available for no cognition whatever, not even for that by which the subject *cognises* itself.

In the above elucidation we understand by the word sensation, an objective representation of sense; and in order to avoid misinterpretation, we shall call that, which must always remain merely subjective and can constitute absolutely no representation of an object, by the ordinary term "feeling." The green colour of the meadows belongs to *objective* sensation, as a perception of an object of sense; the pleasantness of this belongs to *subjective* sensation by which no object is represented, *i.e.* to feeling, by which the object is considered as an Object of satisfaction (which does not furnish a cognition of it).

Now that a judgement about an object, by which I describe it as pleasant, expresses an interest in it, is plain from the fact that by sensation it excites a desire for objects of that kind; consequently the satisfaction presupposes not the mere judgement about it, but the relation of its existence to my state, so far as this is affected by such an Object. Hence we do not merely say of the pleasant, *it pleases*; but, *it gratifies*. I give to it no mere approval, but inclination is aroused by it; and in the case of what is pleasant in the most lively fashion, there is no judgement at all upon the character of the Object, for those who always lay themselves out only for enjoyment (for that is the word describing intense gratification) would fain dispense with all judgement.

§ 4. THE SATISFACTION IN THE GOOD IS BOUND UP WITH INTEREST

Whatever by means of Reason pleases through the mere concept is GOOD. That which pleases only as a means we call *good for something* (the useful); but that which pleases for itself is *good in itself*. In both there is always involved the concept of a purpose, and consequently the relation of Reason to the (at least possible) volition, and thus a satisfaction in the *presence* of an Object or an action, *i.e.* some kind of interest.

In order to find anything good, I must always know what sort of a thing the object ought to be, *i.e.* I must have a concept of it. But there is no need of this, to find a thing beautiful. Flowers, free delineations, outlines intertwined with one another without design and called foliage, have no meaning, depend on no definite concept, and yet they please. The satisfaction in the beautiful must depend on the reflection upon an object, leading to any concept (however indefinite); and it is thus distinguished from the pleasant which rests entirely upon sensation.

It is true, the Pleasant seems in many cases to be the same as the Good. Thus people are accustomed to say that all gratification (especially if it lasts) is good in itself; which is very much the same as to say that lasting pleasure and the good are the same. But we can soon see that this is merely a confusion of words; for the concepts which properly belong to these expressions can in no way be interchanged. The pleasant, which, as such, represents the object simply in relation to Sense, must first be brought by the concept of a purpose under principles of Reason, in order to call it good, as an object of the Will. But that there is [involved] a quite different relation to satisfaction in calling that which gratifies at the same time *good*, may be seen from the fact that in the case of the good the question always is, whether it is mediately or immediately good (useful or good in itself); but on the contrary in the case of the pleasant there can be no question about this at all, for the word always signifies something which pleases immediately. (The same is applicable to what I call beautiful.)

Even in common speech men distinguish the Pleasant from the Good. Of a dish which stimulates the taste by spices and other condiments we say unhesitatingly that it is pleasant, though it is at the same time admitted not to be good; for though it immediately *delights* the senses, yet mediately, *i.e.* considered by Reason which looks to the after results, it displeases. Even in the judging of health we may notice this distinction. It is immediately pleasant to every one possessing it (at least negatively, *i.e.* as the absence of all bodily pains). But in order to say that it is good, it must be considered by Reason with reference to purposes; viz. that it is a state which makes us fit for all our business. Finally in respect of happiness every one believes himself entitled to describe the greatest sum of the pleasantnesses of life (as regards both their number and their duration) as a true, even as the highest, good. However Reason is opposed to this. Pleasantness is enjoyment. And if we were concerned with this alone, it would be foolish to be scrupulous as regards the means which procure it for us, or [to care] whether it is obtained passively by the bounty of nature or by our own activity and work. But Reason can never be persuaded that the existence of a man who merely lives for *enjoyment* (however busy he may be in this point of view), has a worth in itself; even if he at the same time is conducive as a means to the best enjoyment of others, and shares in all their gratifications by sympathy. Only what he does, without reference to enjoyment, in full freedom and independently of what nature can procure for him passively, gives an [absolute³] worth to his being, as the existence of a person; and happiness, with the whole abundance of its pleasures, is far from being an unconditioned good.⁴

However, notwithstanding all this difference between the pleasant and the good, they both agree in this that they are always bound up with an interest in their object. [This is true] not only of the pleasant(§ 3), and the mediate good (the useful) which is pleasing as a means towards pleasantness somewhere, but also of that which is good absolutely and in every aspect, viz. moral good, which brings with it the highest interest. For the good is the Object of will (*i.e.* of a faculty of desire determined by Reason).

But to will something, and to have a satisfaction in its existence, *i.e.* to take an interest in it, are identical.

§ 5. COMPARISON OF THE THREE SPECIFICALLY DIFFERENT KINDS OF SATISFACTION

The pleasant and the good have both a reference to the faculty of desire; and they bring with them—the former a satisfaction pathologically conditioned (by impulses, *stimuli*)—the latter a pure practical satisfaction, which is determined not merely by the representation of the object, but also by the represented connexion of the subject with the existence of the object. [It is not merely the object that pleases, but also its existence.[5]] On the other hand, the judgement of taste is merely *contemplative*; *i.e.* it is a judgement which, indifferent as regards the being of an object, compares its character with the feeling of pleasure and pain. But this contemplation itself is not directed to concepts; for the judgement of taste is not a cognitive judgement (either theoretical or practical), and thus is not *based* on concepts, nor has it concepts as its *purpose*.

The Pleasant, the Beautiful, and the Good, designate then, three different relations of representations to the feeling of pleasure and pain, in reference to which we distinguish from each other objects or methods of representing them. And the expressions corresponding to each, by which we mark our complacency in them, are not the same. That which GRATIFIES a man is called *pleasant*; that which merely PLEASES him is *beautiful*; that which is ESTEEMED [or *approved*[6]] by him, *i.e.* that to which he accords an objective worth, is *good*. Pleasantness concerns irrational animals also; but Beauty only concerns men, *i.e.* animal, but still rational, beings—not merely *quâ* rational (*e.g.* spirits), but *quâ* animal also; and the Good concerns every rational being in general. This is a proposition which can only be completely established and explained in the sequel. We may say that of all these three kinds of satisfaction, that of taste in the Beautiful is alone a disinterested and *free* satisfaction; for no interest, either of Sense or of Reason, here forces our assent. Hence we may say of satisfaction that it is related in the three aforesaid cases to *inclination*, to *favour*, or to *respect*. Now *favour* is the only free satisfaction. An object of inclination, and one that is proposed to our desire by a law of Reason, leave us no freedom in forming for ourselves anywhere an object of pleasure. All interest presupposes or generates a want; and, as the determining ground of assent, it leaves the judgement about the object no longer free.

As regards the interest of inclination in the case of the Pleasant, every one says that hunger is the best sauce, and everything that is eatable is relished by people with a healthy appetite; and thus a satisfaction of this sort does not indicate choice directed by taste. It is only when the want is appeased that we can distinguish which of many men has or has not taste. In the same way there may be manners (conduct) without virtue, politeness without goodwill, decorum without modesty, etc. For where the moral law speaks there is no longer, objectively, a free choice as regards what is to be done; and to display taste in its fulfilment (or in judging of another's fulfilment of it) is something quite different from manifesting the moral attitude of thought. For this involves a command and generates a want, whilst moral taste only plays with the objects of satisfaction, without attaching itself to one of them.

Explanation of the Beautiful Resulting from the First Moment

Taste is the faculty of judging of an object or a method of representing it by an *entirely disinterested* satisfaction or dissatisfaction. The object of such satisfaction is called *beautiful*.[7]

SECOND MOMENT—OF THE JUDGEMENT OF TASTE, VIZ. ACCORDING TO QUANTITYT

§ 6. THE BEAUTIFUL IS THAT WHICH APART FROM CONCEPTS IS REPRESENTED AS THE OBJECT OF A UNIVERSAL SATISFACTION

This explanation of the beautiful can be derived from the preceding explanation of it as the object of an entirely disinterested satisfaction. For the fact of which every one is conscious, that the satisfaction is for him quite disinterested, implies in his judgement a ground of satisfaction for every one. For since it does not rest on any inclination of the subject (nor upon any other premeditated interest), but since he who judges feels himself quite *free* as regards the satisfaction which he attaches to the object, he cannot find the ground of this satisfaction in any private conditions connected with his own subject; and hence it must be regarded as grounded on what he can presuppose in every other man. Consequently he must believe that he has reason for attributing a similar satisfaction to every one. He will therefore speak of the beautiful, as if beauty were a characteristic of the object and the judgement logical (constituting a cognition of the Object by means of concepts of it); although it is only aesthetical and involves merely a reference of the representation of the object to the subject. For it has this similarity to a logical judgement that we can presuppose its validity for every one. But this universality cannot arise from concepts; for from concepts there is no transition to the feeling of pleasure or pain (except in pure practical laws, which bring an interest with them such as is not bound up with the pure judgement of taste). Consequently the judgement of taste, accompanied with the consciousness of separation from all interest, must claim validity for every one, without this universality depending on Objects. That is, there must be bound up with it a title to subjective universality.

§ 7. COMPARISON OF THE BEAUTIFUL WITH THE PLEASANT AND THE GOOD BY MEANS OF THE ABOVE CHARACTERISTIC

As regards the Pleasant every one is content that his judgement, which he bases upon private feeling, and by which he says of an object that it pleases him, should be limited merely to his own person. Thus he is quite contented that if he says "Canary wine is pleasant," another man may correct his expression and remind him that he ought to say "It is pleasant *to me*." And this is the case not only as regards the taste of the tongue, the palate, and the throat, but for whatever is pleasant to any one's eyes and ears. To one violet colour is soft and lovely, to another it is faded and dead. One man likes the tone of wind instruments, another that of strings. To strive here with the design of reproving as incorrect another man's judgement which is different from our own, as if the judgements were logically opposed, would be folly. As regards the pleasant therefore the fundamental proposition is valid, *every one has his own taste* (the taste of Sense).

The case is quite different with the Beautiful. It would (on the contrary) be laughable if a man who imagined anything to his own taste, thought to justify himself by saying: "This object (the house we see, the coat that person wears, the concert we hear, the poem submitted to our judgement) is beautiful *for me*." For he must not call it *beautiful* if it merely pleases himself. Many things may have for him charm and pleasantness; no one troubles himself at that; but if he gives out anything as beautiful, he supposes in others the same satisfaction—he judges not merely for himself, but for every one, and speaks of beauty as if it were a property of things. Hence he says "the *thing* is beautiful"; and he does not count on the agreement of others with this his judgement of satisfaction, because he has found this agreement several times before, but he *demands* it of them. He blames them if they judge otherwise and he denies them taste, which he nevertheless requires from them. Here then we cannot say that each man has his own particular taste. For this would be as much as to say that there is no taste whatever; *i.e.* no aesthetical judgement, which can make a rightful claim upon every one's assent.

At the same time we find as regards the Pleasant that there is an agreement among men in their judgements upon it, in regard to which we deny Taste to some and attribute it to others; by this not meaning one of our organic senses, but a faculty of judging in respect of the pleasant generally. Thus we say of a man who knows how to entertain his guests with pleasures (of enjoyment for all the senses), so that they are all pleased, "he has taste." But here the universality is only taken comparatively; and there emerge rules which are only *general* (like all empirical ones), and not *universal*; which latter the judgement of Taste upon the beautiful undertakes or lays claim to. It is a judgement in reference to sociability, so far as this rests on empirical rules. In respect of the Good it is true that judgements make rightful claim to validity for every one; but the Good is represented only *by means of a concept* as the Object of a universal satisfaction, which is the case neither with the Pleasant nor with the Beautiful.

§ 8. THE UNIVERSALITY OF THE SATISFACTION IS REPRESENTED IN A JUDGEMENT OF TASTE ONLY AS SUBJECTIVE

This particular determination of the universality of an aesthetical judgement, which is to be met with in a judgement of taste, is noteworthy, not indeed for the logician, but for the transcendental philosopher. It requires no small trouble to discover its origin, but we thus detect a property of our cognitive faculty which without this analysis would remain unknown.

First, we must be fully convinced of the fact that in a judgement of taste (about the Beautiful) the satisfaction in the object is imputed to *every one*, without being based on a concept (for then it would be the Good). Further, this claim to universal validity so essentially belongs to a judgement by which we describe anything as *beautiful*, that if this were not thought in it, it would never come into our thoughts to use the expression at all, but everything which pleases without a concept would be counted as pleasant. In respect of the latter every one has his own opinion; and no one assumes, in another, agreement with his judgement of taste, which is always the case in a judgement of taste about beauty. I may call the first the taste of Sense, the second the taste of Reflection; so far as the first lays down mere private judgements, and the second judgements supposed to be generally valid (public), but in both cases aesthetical (not practical) judgements about an object merely in respect of the relation of its representation to the feeling of pleasure and pain. Now here is something strange. As regards the taste of Sense not only does experience show that its judgement (of pleasure or pain connected with anything) is not valid universally, but every one is content not to impute agreement with it to others (although actually there is often found a very extended concurrence in these judgements). On the other hand, the taste of Reflection has its claim to the universal validity of its judgements (about the beautiful) rejected often enough, as experience teaches; although it may find it possible (as it actually does) to represent judgements which can demand this universal agreement. In fact for each of its judgements of taste it imputes this to every one, without the persons that judge disputing as to the possibility of such a claim; although in particular cases they cannot agree as to the correct application of this faculty.

Here we must, in the first place, remark that a universality which does not rest on concepts of Objects (not even on empirical ones) is not logical but aesthetical, *i.e.* it involves no objective quantity of the judgement but only that which is subjective. For this I use the expression *general validity* which signifies the validity of the reference of a representation, not to the cognitive faculty but, to the feeling of pleasure and pain for every subject. (We can avail ourselves also of the same expression for the logical quantity of the judgement, if only we prefix *objective* to "universal validity," to distinguish it from that which is merely subjective and aesthetical.)

A judgement with *objective universal validity* is also always valid subjectively; *i.e.* if the judgement holds for everything contained under a given concept, it holds also for every one who represents an object by means of this concept. But from a *subjective universal validity, i.e.* aesthetical and resting on no concept, we cannot infer that which is logical; because that kind of judgement does not extend to the Object. Hence the aesthetical universality which is ascribed to a judgement must be of a particular kind, because it does not unite the predicate of beauty with the concept of the *Object*, considered in its whole logical sphere, and yet extends it to the whole sphere of judging persons.

In respect of logical quantity all judgements of taste are *singular* judgements. For because I must refer the object immediately to my feeling of pleasure and pain, and that not by means of concepts, they cannot have the quantity of objective generally valid judgements. Nevertheless if the singular representation of the Object of the judgement of taste in accordance with the conditions determining the latter, were transformed by comparison into a concept, a logically universal judgement could result therefrom. *E.g.* I describe by a judgement of taste the rose, that I see, as beautiful. But the judgement which results from the comparison of several singular judgements, "Roses in general are beautiful" is no longer described simply as aesthetical, but as a logical judgement based on an aesthetical one. Again the judgement "The rose is pleasant" (to smell) is, although aesthetical and singular, not a judgement of Taste but of Sense. It is distinguished from the former by the fact that the judgement of Taste carries with it an *aesthetical quantity* of universality, *i.e.* of validity for every one; which cannot be found in a judgement about the Pleasant. It is only judgements about the Good which—although they also determine satisfaction in an object,—have logical and not merely aesthetical universality; for they are valid of the Object, as cognitive of it, and thus are valid for every one.

If we judge Objects merely according to concepts, then all representation of beauty is lost. Thus there can be no rule according to which any one is to be forced to recognise anything as beautiful. We cannot press [upon others] by the aid of any reasons or fundamental propositions our judgement that a coat, a house, or a flower is beautiful. We wish to submit the Object to our own eyes, as if the satisfaction in it depended on sensation; and yet if we then call the object beautiful, we believe that we speak with a universal voice, and we claim the assent of every one, although on the contrary all private sensation can only decide for the observer himself and his satisfaction.

We may see now that in the judgement of taste nothing is postulated but such a *universal voice*, in respect of the satisfaction without the intervention of concepts; and thus the *possibility* of an aesthetical judgement that can, at the same time, be regarded as valid for every one. The judgement of taste itself does not *postulate* the agreement of every one (for that can only be done by a logically universal judgement because it can adduce reasons); it only *imputes* this agreement to every one, as a case of the rule in respect of which it expects, not confirmation by concepts, but assent from others. The universal voice is, therefore, only an Idea (we do not yet inquire upon what it rests). It may be uncertain whether or not the man, who believes that he is laying down a judgement of taste, is, as a matter of fact, judging in conformity with that Idea; but that he refers his judgement thereto, and, consequently, that it is intended to be a judgement of taste, he announces by the expression "beauty." He can be quite certain of this for himself by the mere consciousness of the separation of everything belonging to the Pleasant and the Good from the satisfaction which is left; and this is all for which he promises himself the agreement of every one—a claim which would be justifiable under these conditions, provided only he did not often make mistakes, and thus lay down an erroneous judgement of taste.

§ 9. INVESTIGATION OF THE QUESTION WHETHER IN THE JUDGEMENT OF TASTE THE FEELING OF PLEASURE PRECEDES OR FOLLOWS THE JUDGING OF THE OBJECT

The solution of this question is the key to the Critique of Taste, and so is worthy of all attention.

If the pleasure in the given object precedes, and it is only its universal communicability that is to be acknowledged in the judgement of taste about the representation of the object, there would be a contradiction. For such pleasure would be nothing different from the mere pleasantness in the sensation, and so in accordance with its nature could have only private validity, because it is immediately dependent on the representation through which the object *is given*.

Hence, it is the universal capability of communication of the mental state in the given representation which, as the subjective condition of the judgement of taste, must be fundamental, and must have the pleasure in the object as its consequent. But nothing can be universally communicated except cognition and representation, so far as it belongs to cognition. For it is only thus that this latter can be objective; and only through this has it a universal point of reference, with which the representative power of every one is compelled to harmonise. If the determining ground of our judgement as to this universal communicability of the representation is to be merely subjective, *i.e.* is conceived independently of any concept of the object, it can be nothing else than the state of mind, which is to be met with in the relation of our representative powers to each other, so far as they refer a given representation to *cognition in general*.

The cognitive powers, which are involved by this representation, are here in free play, because no definite concept limits them to a particular[8] rule of cognition. Hence, the state of mind in this representation must be a feeling of the free play of the representative powers in a given representation with reference to a cognition in general. Now a representation by which an object is given, that is to become a cognition in general, requires *Imagination*, for the gathering together the manifold of intuition, and *Understanding*, for the unity of the concept uniting the representations. This state of *free play* of the cognitive faculties in a representation by which an object is given, must be universally communicable; because cognition, as the determination of the Object with which given representations (in whatever subject) are to agree, is the only kind of representation which is valid for every one.

The subjective universal communicability of the mode of representation in a judgement of taste, since it is to be possible without presupposing a definite concept, can refer to nothing else than the state of mind in the free play of the Imagination and the Understanding (so far as they agree with each other, as is requisite for *cognition in general*). We are conscious that this subjective relation, suitable for cognition in general, must be valid for every one, and thus must be universally communicable, just as if it were a definite cognition, resting always on that relation as its subjective condition.

This merely subjective (aesthetical) judging of the object, or of the representation by which it is given, precedes the pleasure in it, and is the ground of this pleasure in the harmony of the cognitive faculties; but on the universality of the subjective conditions for judging of objects is alone based the universal subjective validity of the satisfaction bound up by us with the representation of the object that we call beautiful.

The power of communicating one's state of mind, even though only in respect of the cognitive faculties, carries a pleasure with it, as we can easily show from the natural propension of man towards sociability (empirical and psychological). But this is not enough for our design. The pleasure that we feel is, in a judgement of taste, necessarily imputed by us to every one else; as if, when we call a thing beautiful, it is to be regarded as a characteristic of the object which is determined in it according to concepts; though beauty, without a reference to the feeling of the subject, is nothing by itself. But we must reserve the examination of this question until we have answered another, viz. "If and how aesthetical judgements are possible *a priori*?"

We now occupy ourselves with the easier question, in what way we are conscious of a mutual subjective harmony of the cognitive powers with one another in the judgement of taste; is it aesthetically by mere internal sense and sensation? or is it intellectually by the consciousness of our designed activity, by which we bring them into play?

If the given representation, which occasions the judgement of taste, were a concept uniting Understanding and Imagination in the judging of the object, into a cognition of the Object, the consciousness of this relation would be intellectual (as in the objective schematism of the Judgement of which the Critique[9] treats). But then the judgement would not be laid down in reference to pleasure and pain, and consequently would not be a judgement of taste. But the judgement of taste, independently of concepts, deter-mines the Object in respect of satisfaction and of the predicate of beauty. Therefore that subjective unity of relation can only make itself known by means of sensation. The excitement of both faculties (Imagination and Understanding) to indeterminate, but yet, through the stimulus of the given sensation, harmonious activity, viz. that which belongs to cognition in general, is the sensation whose universal communicability is postulated by the judgement of taste. An objective relation can only be thought, but yet, so far as it is subjective according to its conditions, can be felt in its effect on the mind; and, of a relation based on no concept (like the relation of the representative powers to a cognitive faculty in general), no other consciousness is possible than that through the sensation of the effect, which consists in the more lively play of both mental powers (the Imagination and the Understanding) when animated by mutual agreement. A represen-tation which, as singular and apart from comparison with others, yet has an agreement with the conditions of universality which it is the business of the Understanding to supply, brings the cognitive faculties into that proportionate accord which we require for all cognition, and so regard as holding for every one who is determined to judge by means of Understanding and Sense in combination (*i.e.* for every man).

Explanation of the Beautiful Resulting from the Second Moment

The *beautiful* is that which pleases universally, without a concept.

THIRD MOMENT—OF JUDGEMENTS OF TASTE, ACCORDING TO THE RELATION OF THE PURPOSES WHICH ARE BROUGHT INTO CONSIDERATION THEREIN.

§ 10. OF PURPOSIVENESS IN GENERAL

If we wish to explain what a purpose is according to its transcendental determinations (without presupposing anything empirical like the feeling of pleasure) [we say that] the purpose is the object of a concept, in so far as the concept is regarded as the cause of the object (the real ground of its possibility); and the causality of a *concept* in respect of its *Object* is its purposiveness (*forma finalis*). Where then not merely the cognition of an object, but the object itself (its form and existence) is thought as an effect only possible by means of the concept of this latter, there we think a purpose. The representation of the effect is here the determining ground of its cause and precedes it. The consciousness of the causality of a representation, for *maintaining* the subject in the same state, may here generally denote what we call pleasure; while on the other hand pain is that repre-sentation which contains the ground of the determination of the state of representations into their opposite [of restraining or removing them[10]].

The faculty of desire, so far as it is determinable only through concepts, *i.e.* to act in conformity with the representation of a purpose, would be the Will. But an Object, or a state of mind, or even an action, is called purposive, although its possibility does not necessarily presuppose the representation of a purpose, merely because its possibility can be explained and conceived by us only so far as we assume for its ground a

484 | IMMANUEL KANT

causality according to purposes, *i.e.* a will which would have so disposed it according to the representation of a certain rule. There can be, then, purposiveness without[11] purpose, so far as we do not place the causes of this form in a will, but yet can only make the explanation of its possibility intelligible to ourselves by deriving it from a will. Again, we are not always forced to regard what we observe (in respect of its possibility) from the point of view of Reason. Thus we can at least observe a purposiveness according to form, without basing it on a purpose (as the material of the *nexus finalis*), and we can notice it in objects, although only by reflection.

§ 11. THE JUDGEMENT OF TASTE HAS NOTHING AT ITS BASIS BUT THE FORM OF THE PURPOSIVENESS OF AN OBJECT (OR OF ITS MODE OF REPRESENTATION)

Every purpose, if it be regarded as a ground of satisfaction, always carries with it an interest—as the determining ground of the judgement—about the object of pleasure. Therefore no subjective purpose can lie at the basis of the judgement of taste. But neither can the judgement of taste be determined by any representation of an objective purpose, *i.e.* of the possibility of the object itself in accordance with principles of purposive combination, and consequently it can be determined by no concept of the good; because it is an aesthetical and not a cognitive judgement. It therefore has to do with no *concept* of the character and internal or external possibility of the object by means of this or that cause, but merely with the relation of the representative powers to one another, so far as they are determined by a representation.

Now this relation in the determination of an object as beautiful is bound up with the feeling of pleasure, which is declared by the judgement of taste to be valid for every one; hence a pleasantness, accompanying the representation, can as little contain the determining ground [of the judgement] as the representation of the perfection of the object and the concept of the good can. Therefore it can be nothing else than the subjective purposiveness in the representation of an object without any purpose (either objective or subjective); and thus it is the mere form of purposiveness in the representation by which an object is *given* to us, so far as we are conscious of it, which constitutes the satisfaction that we without a concept judge to be universally communicable; and, consequently, this is the determining ground of the judgement of taste.

§ 12. THE JUDGEMENT OF TASTE RESTS ON A PRIORI GROUNDS

To establish *a priori* the connexion of the feeling of a pleasure or pain as an effect, with any representation whatever (sensation or concept) as its cause, is absolutely impossible; for that would be a [particular][12] causal relation which (with objects of experience) can always only be cognised *a posteriori*, and through the medium of experience itself. We actually have, indeed, in the Critique of practical Reason, derived from universal moral concepts *a priori* the feeling of respect (as a special and peculiar modification of feeling which will not strictly correspond either to the pleasure or the pain that we get from empirical objects). But there we could go beyond the bounds of experience and call in a causality which rested on a supersensible attribute of the subject, viz. freedom. And even there, properly speaking, it was not this *feeling* which we derived from the Idea of the moral as cause, but merely the determination of the will. But the state of mind which accompanies any determination of the will is in itself a feeling of pleasure and identical with it, and therefore does not follow from it as its effect. This last must only be assumed if the concept of the moral as a good precede the determination of the will by the law; for in that case the pleasure that is bound up with the concept could not be derived from it as from a mere cognition.

Now the case is similar with the pleasure in aesthetical judgements, only that here it is merely contemplative and does not bring about an interest in the Object, which on the other hand in the moral judgement it is practical.[13] The consciousness of the mere formal purposiveness in the play of the subject's cognitive powers, in a representation through which an object is given, is the pleasure itself; because it contains a determining ground of the activity of the subject in respect of the excitement of its cognitive powers, and therefore an inner causality (which is purposive) in respect of cognition in general without however being limited to any definite cognition; and consequently contains a mere form of the subjective purposiveness of a representation in an aesthetical judgement. This pleasure is in no way practical, neither like that arising from the pathological ground of pleasantness, nor that from the intellectual ground of the represented good. But yet it involves causality, viz. of *maintaining* the state of the representation itself, and the exercise of the cognitive powers without further design. We *linger* over the contemplation of the beautiful, because this contemplation strengthens and reproduces itself, which is analogous to (though not of the same kind as) that lingering which takes place when a [physical] charm in the representation of the object repeatedly arouses the attention, the mind being passive.

§ 13. THE PURE JUDGEMENT OF TASTE IS INDEPENDENT OF CHARM AND EMOTION

Every interest spoils the judgement of taste and takes from its impartiality, especially if the purposiveness is not, as with the interest of Reason, placed before the feeling of pleasure but grounded on it. This last always happens in an aesthetical judgement upon anything so far as it gratifies or grieves us. Hence judgements so affected can lay no claim at all to a universally valid satisfaction, or at least so much the less claim, in proportion as there are sensations of this sort among the determining grounds of taste. That taste is still barbaric which needs a mixture of *charms* and *emotions* in order that there may be satisfaction, and still more so if it make these the measure of its assent.

Nevertheless charms are often not only taken account of in the case of beauty (which properly speaking ought merely to be concerned with form) as contributory to the aesthetical universal satisfaction; but they are passed off as in themselves beauties, and thus the matter of satisfaction is substituted for the form. This misconception, however, like so many others which have something true at their basis, may be removed by a careful definition of these concepts.

A judgement of taste on which charm and emotion have no influence (although they may be bound up with the satisfaction in the beautiful),—which therefore has as its determining ground merely the purposiveness of the form,—is a *pure judgement of taste*.

§ 14. ELUCIDATION BY MEANS OF EXAMPLES

Aesthetical judgements can be divided just like theoretical (logical) judgements into empirical and pure. The first assert pleasantness or unpleasantness; the second assert the beauty of an object or of the manner of representing it. The former are judgements of Sense (material aesthetical judgements); the latter [as formal[14]] are alone strictly judgements of Taste.

A judgement of taste is therefore pure, only so far as no merely empirical satisfaction is mingled with its determining ground. But this always happens if charm or emotion have any share in the judgement by which anything is to be described as beautiful.

Now here many objections present themselves, which fallaciously put forward charm not merely as a necessary ingredient of beauty, but as alone sufficient [to justify] a thing's being called beautiful. A mere colour, *e.g.* the green of a grass plot, a mere tone (as distinguished from sound and noise) like that of a violin, are by most people described as beautiful in themselves; although both seem to have at their basis merely the matter of representations, viz. simply sensation, and therefore only deserve to be called pleasant. But we must at the same time remark that the sensations of colours and of tone have a right to be regarded as beautiful only in so far as they are *pure*. This is a determination which concerns their form, and is the only [element] of these representations which admits with certainty of universal communicability; for we cannot assume that the quality of sensations is the same in all subjects, and we can hardly say that the pleasantness of one colour or the tone of one musical instrument is judged preferable to that of another in the same[15] way by every one.

If we assume with *Euler* that colours are isochronous vibrations (*pulsus*) of the aether, as sounds are of the air in a state of disturbance, and,—what is most important, —that the mind not only perceives by sense the effect of these in exciting the organ, but also perceives by reflection the regular play of impressions (and thus the form of the combination of different representations) which I still do not doubt[16]—then colours and tone cannot be reckoned as mere sensations, but as the formal determination of the unity of a manifold of sensations, and thus as beauties in themselves.

But "pure" in a simple mode of sensation means that its uniformity is troubled and interrupted by no foreign sensation, and it belongs merely to the form; because here we can abstract from the quality of that mode of sensation (abstract from the colours and tone, if any, which it represents). Hence all simple colours, so far as they are pure, are regarded as beautiful; composite colours have not this advantage, because, as they are not simple, we have no standard for judging whether they should be called pure or not.

But as regards the beauty attributed to the object on account of its form, to suppose it to be capable of augmentation through the charm of the object is a common error, and one very prejudicial to genuine, uncorrupted, well-founded taste. We can doubtless add these charms to beauty, in order to interest the mind by the representation of the object, apart from the bare satisfaction [received]; and thus they may serve as a recommendation of taste and its cultivation, especially when it is yet crude and unexercised. But they actually do injury to the judgement of taste if they draw attention to themselves as the grounds for judging of beauty. So far are they from adding to beauty that they must only be admitted by indulgence as aliens; and provided always that they do not disturb the beautiful form, in cases when taste is yet weak and untrained.

In painting, sculpture, and in all the formative arts—in architecture, and horticulture, so far as they are beautiful arts—the *delineation* is the essential thing; and here it is not what gratifies in sensation but what pleases by means of its form that is fundamental for taste. The colours which light up the sketch belong to the charm; they may indeed enliven[17] the object for sensation, but they cannot make it worthy of contemplation and beautiful. In most cases they are rather limited by the requirements of the beautiful form; and even where charm is permissible it is ennobled solely by this.

Every form of the objects of sense (both of external sense and also mediately of internal) is either *figure* or *play*. In the latter case it is either play of figures (in space, viz. pantomime and dancing), or the mere play of sensations (in time). The *charm* of colours or of the pleasant tones of an instrument may be added; but the *delineation* in the first case and the composition in the second constitute the proper object of the pure judgement of taste. To say that the purity of colours and of tones, or their variety and contrast, seems to add to beauty, does not mean that they supply a homogeneous addition to our satisfaction in the form because they are pleasant in themselves; but they do so, because they make the form more exactly, definitely, and completely, intuitible, and besides by their charm [excite the representation, whilst they[18]] awaken and fix our attention on the object itself.

Even what we call *ornaments* [parerga29], *i.e.* those things which do not belong to the complete representation of the object internally as elements but only externally as complements, and which augment the satisfaction of taste, do so only by their form; as for example [the frames of pictures,29 or] the draperies of statues or the colonnades of palaces. But if the ornament does not itself consist in beautiful form, and if it is used as a golden frame is used, merely to recommend the painting by its *charm*, it is then called *finery* and injures genuine beauty.

Emotion, i.e. a sensation in which pleasantness is produced by means of a momentary checking and a consequent more powerful outflow of the vital force, does not belong at all to beauty. But sublimity [with which the feeling of emotion is bound up29] requires a different standard of judgement from that which is at the foundation of taste; and thus a pure judgement of taste has for its determining ground neither charm nor emotion, in a word, no sensation as the material of the aesthetical judgement.

§ 15. *THE JUDGEMENT OF TASTE IS QUITE INDEPENDENT OF THE CONCEPT OF PERFECTION*

Objective purposiveness can only be cognised by means of the reference of the manifold to a definite purpose, and therefore only through a concept. From this alone it is plain that the Beautiful, the judging of which has at its basis a merely formal purposiveness, *i.e.* a purposiveness without purpose, is quite independent of the concept of the Good; because the latter presupposes an objective purposiveness, *i.e.* the reference of the object to a definite purpose.

Objective purposiveness is either external, *i.e.* the *utility*, or internal, *i.e.* the *perfection* of the object. That the satisfaction in an object, on account of which we call it beautiful, cannot rest on the representation of its utility, is sufficiently obvious from the two preceding sections; because in that case it would not be an immediate satisfaction in the object, which is the essential condition of a judgement about beauty. But objective internal purposiveness, *i.e.* perfection, comes nearer to the predicate of beauty; and it has been regarded by celebrated philosophers[19] as the same as beauty, with the proviso, *if it is thought in a confused way.* It is of the greatest importance in a Critique of Taste to decide whether beauty can thus actually be resolved into the concept of perfection.

To judge of objective purposiveness we always need not only the concept of a purpose, but (if that purposiveness is not to be external utility but internal) the concept of an internal purpose which shall contain the ground of the internal possibility of the object. Now as a purpose in general is that whose *concept* can be regarded as the ground of the possibility of the object itself; so, in order to represent objective purposiveness in a thing, the concept of *what sort of thing it is to be* must come first. The agreement of the manifold in it with this concept (which furnishes the rule for combining the manifold) is the *qualitative perfection* of the thing. Quite different from this is *quantitative* perfection, the completeness of a thing after its kind, which is a mere concept of magnitude (of totality).[20] In this *what the thing ought to be* is conceived as already determined, and it is only asked if it has *all* its requisites. The formal [element] in the representation of a thing, *i.e.* the agreement of the manifold with a unity (it being undetermined what this ought to be), gives to cognition no objective purposiveness whatever. For since abstraction is made of this unity as *purpose* (what the thing ought to be), nothing remains but the subjective purposiveness of the representations in the mind of the intuiting subject. And this, although it furnishes a certain purposiveness of the representative state of the subject, and so a facility of apprehending a given form by the Imagination, yet furnishes no perfection of an Object, since the Object is not here conceived by means of the concept of a purpose. For example, if in a forest I come across a plot of sward, round which trees stand in a circle, and do not then represent to myself a purpose, viz. that it is intended to serve for country dances, not the least concept of perfection is furnished by the mere form. But to represent to oneself a formal *objective* purposiveness without purpose, *i.e.* the mere form of a *perfection* (without any matter and without the *concept* of that with which it is accordant, even if it were merely the Idea of conformity to law in general[21]) is a veritable contradiction.

Now the judgement of taste is an aesthetical judgement, *i.e.* such as rests on subjective grounds, the determining ground of which cannot be a concept, and consequently cannot be the concept of a definite purpose. Therefore in beauty, regarded as a formal subjective purposiveness, there is in no way thought a perfection of the object, as a would-be formal purposiveness, which yet is objective. And thus to distinguish between the concepts of the Beautiful and the Good, as if they were only different in logical form, the first being a confused, the second a clear concept of perfection, but identical in content and origin, is quite fallacious. For then there would be no *specific* difference between them, but a judgement of taste would be as much a cognitive judgement as the judgement by which a thing is described as good; just as when the ordinary man says that fraud is unjust he bases his judgement on confused grounds, whilst the philosopher bases it on clear grounds, but both on identical principles of Reason. I have already, however, said that an aesthetical judgement is unique of its kind, and gives absolutely no cognition (not even a confused cognition) of the Object; this is only supplied by a logical judgement. On the contrary, it simply refers the representation, by which an Object is given, to the subject; and brings to our notice no characteristic of the object, but only the purposive form in the determination of the representative powers which are occupying themselves therewith. The judgement is called aesthetical just because its determining ground is not a concept, but the feeling (of internal sense) of that harmony in the play of the mental powers, so far as it can be felt in sensation. On the other hand, if we wish to call confused concepts and the objective judgement based on them, aesthetical, we shall have an Understanding judging sensibly or a Sense representing its Objects by means of concepts [both of which are contradictory.[22]] The faculty of concepts, be they confused or clear, is the Understanding; and although Understanding has to do with the judgement of taste, as an aesthetical judgement (as it has with all judgements), yet it has to do with it not as a faculty by which an object is cognised, but as the faculty which determines the judgement and its representation (without any concept) in accordance with its relation to the subject and the subject's internal feeling, in so far as this judgement may be possible in accordance with a universal rule.

§ 16. THE JUDGEMENT OF TASTE, BY WHICH AN OBJECT IS DECLARED TO BE BEAUTIFUL UNDER THE CONDITION OF A DEFINITE CONCEPT, IS NOT PURE

There are two kinds of beauty; free beauty (*pulchritudo vaga*) or merely dependent beauty (*pulchritudo adhaerens*). The first presupposes no concept of what the object ought to be; the second does presuppose such a concept and the perfection of the object in accordance therewith. The first is called the (self-subsistent) beauty of this or that thing; the second, as dependent upon a concept (conditioned beauty), is ascribed to Objects which come under the concept of a particular purpose.

Flowers are free natural beauties. Hardly any one but a botanist knows what sort of a thing a flower ought to be; and even he, though recognising in the flower the reproductive organ of the plant, pays no regard to this natural purpose if he is passing judgement on the flower by Taste. There is then at the basis of this judgement no perfection of any kind, no internal purposiveness, to which the collection of the manifold is referred. Many birds (such as the parrot, the humming bird, the bird of paradise), and many sea shells are beauties in themselves, which do not belong to any object determined in respect of its purpose by concepts, but please freely and in themselves. So also delineations à la grecque, foliage for borders or wall-papers, mean nothing in themselves; they represent nothing—no Object under a definite concept,—and are free beauties. We can refer to the same class what are called in music phantasies (*i.e.* pieces without any theme), and in fact all music without words.

In the judging of a free beauty (according to the mere form) the judgement of taste is pure. There is presupposed no concept of any purpose, for which the manifold should serve the given Object, and which therefore is to be represented therein. By such a concept the freedom of the Imagination which disports itself in the contemplation of the figure would be only limited.

But human beauty (*i.e.* of a man, a woman, or a child), the beauty of a horse, or a building (be it church, palace, arsenal, or summer-house) presupposes a concept of the purpose which determines what the thing is to be, and consequently a concept of its perfection; it is therefore adherent beauty. Now as the combination of the Pleasant (in sensation) with Beauty, which properly is only concerned with form, is a hindrance to the purity of the judgement of taste; so also is its purity injured by the combination with Beauty of the Good (viz. that manifold which is good for the thing itself in accordance with its purpose).

We could add much to a building which would immediately please the eye, if only it were not to be a church. We could adorn a figure with all kinds of spirals and light but regular lines, as the New Zealanders do with their tattooing, if only it were not the figure of a human being. And again this could have much finer features and a more pleasing and gentle cast of countenance provided it were not intended to represent a man, much less a warrior.

Now the satisfaction in the manifold of a thing in reference to the internal purpose which determines its possibility is a satisfaction grounded on a concept; but the satisfaction in beauty is such as presupposes no concept, but is immediately bound up with the representation through which the object is given (not through which it is thought). If now the judgement of Taste in respect of the beauty of a thing is made dependent on the purpose in its manifold, like a judgement of Reason, and thus limited, it is no longer a free and pure judgement of Taste.

It is true that taste gains by this combination of aesthetical with intellectual satisfaction, inasmuch as it becomes fixed; and though it is not universal, yet in respect to certain purposively determined Objects it becomes possible to prescribe rules for it. These, however, are not rules of taste, but merely rules for the unification of Taste with Reason, i.e. of the Beautiful with the Good, by which the former becomes available as an instrument of design in respect of the latter. Thus the tone of mind which is self-maintaining and of subjective universal validity is subordinated to the way of thinking which can be maintained only by painful resolve, but is of objective universal validity. Properly speaking, however, perfection gains nothing by beauty or beauty by perfection; but, when we compare the representation by which an object is given to us with the Object (as regards what it ought to be) by means of a concept, we cannot avoid considering along with it the sensation in the subject. And thus when both states of mind are in harmony our *whole faculty* of representative power gains.

A judgement of taste, then, in respect of an object with a definite internal purpose, can only be pure, if either the person judging has no concept of this purpose, or else abstracts from it in his judgement. Such a person, although forming an accurate judgement of taste in judging of the object as free beauty, would yet by another who considers the beauty in it only as a dependent attribute (who looks to the purpose of the object) be blamed, and accused of false taste; although both are right in their own way, the one in reference to what he has before his eyes, the other in reference to what he has in his thought. By means of this distinction we can settle many disputes about beauty between judges of taste; by showing that the one is speaking of free, the other of dependent, beauty,—that the first is making a pure, the second an applied, judgement of taste.

§ 17. OF THE IDEAL OF BEAUTY

There can be no objective rule of taste which shall determine by means of concepts what is beautiful. For every judgement from this source is aesthetical; i.e. the feeling of the subject, and not a concept of the Object, is its determining ground. To seek for a principle of taste which shall furnish, by means of definite concepts, a universal criterion of the beautiful, is fruitless trouble; because what is sought is impossible and self-contradictory. The universal communicability of sensation (satisfaction or dissatisfaction) without the aid of a concept—the agreement, as far as is possible, of all times and peoples as regards this feeling in the representation of certain objects—this is the empirical criterion, although weak and hardly sufficing for probability, of the derivation of a taste, thus confirmed by examples, from the deep-lying grounds of agreement common to all men, in judging of the forms under which objects are given to them.

Hence, we consider some products of taste as *exemplary.* Not that taste can be acquired by imitating others; for it must be an original faculty. He who imitates a model shows, no doubt, in so far as he attains to it, skill; but only shows taste in so far as he can judge of this model itself.[23] It follows from hence that the highest model, the archetype of taste, is a mere Idea, which every one must produce in himself; and according to which he must judge every Object of taste, every example of judgement by taste, and even the taste of every one. *Idea* properly means a rational concept, and *Ideal* the representation of an individual being, regarded as adequate to an Idea.[24] Hence that archetype of taste, which certainly rests on the indeterminate Idea that Reason has of a maximum, but which cannot be represented by concepts, but only in an individual presentation, is better called the Ideal of the beautiful. Although we are not in possession of this, we yet strive to produce it in ourselves. But it can only be an Ideal of the Imagination, because it rests on a presentation and not on concepts, and the Imagination is the faculty of presentation.—How do we arrive at such an Ideal of beauty? *A priori*, or empirically? Moreover, what species of the beautiful is susceptible of an Ideal?

First, it is well to remark that the beauty for which an Ideal is to be sought cannot be *vague* beauty, but is *fixed* by a concept of objective purposiveness; and thus it cannot appertain to the Object of a quite pure judgement of taste, but to that of a judgement of taste which is in part intellectual. That is, in whatever grounds of judgement an Ideal is to be found, an Idea of Reason in accordance with definite concepts must lie at its basis; which determines *a priori* the purpose on which the internal possibility of the object rests. An Ideal of beautiful flowers, of a beautiful piece of furniture, of a beautiful view, is inconceivable. But neither can an Ideal be represented of a beauty dependent on definite purposes, *e.g.* of a beautiful dwelling-house, a beautiful tree, a beautiful garden, etc.; presumably because their purpose is not sufficiently determined and fixed by the concept, and thus the purposiveness is nearly as free as in the case of *vague* beauty. The only being which has the purpose of its existence in itself is *man*, who can determine his purposes by Reason; or, where he must receive them from external perception, yet can compare them with essential and universal purposes, and can judge this their accordance aesthetically. This *man* is, then, alone of all objects in the world, susceptible of an Ideal of *beauty*; as it is only *humanity* in his person, as an intelligence, that is susceptible of the Ideal of *perfection*.

But there are here two elements. *First*, there is the aesthetical *normal Idea*, which is an individual intuition (of the Imagination), representing the standard of our judgement [upon man] as a thing belonging to a particular animal species. *Secondly*, there is the *rational Idea* which makes the purposes of humanity, so far as they cannot be sensibly represented, the principle for judging of a figure through which, as their phenomenal effect, those purposes are revealed. The normal Idea of the figure of an animal of a particular race must take its elements from experience. But the greatest purposiveness in the construction of the figure, that would be available for the universal standard of aesthetical judgement upon each individual of this species—the image which is as it were designedly at the basis of nature's Technic, to which only the whole race and not any isolated individual is adequate—this lies merely in the Idea of the judging [subject]. And this, with its proportions, as an aesthetical Idea, can be completely presented *in concreto* in a model. In order to make intelligible in some measure (for who can extract her whole secret from nature?) how this comes to pass, we shall attempt a psychological explanation.

We must remark that, in a way quite incomprehensible by us, the Imagination can not only recall, on occasion, the signs for concepts long past, but can also reproduce the image of the figure of the object out of an unspeakable number of objects of different kinds or even of the same kind. Further, if the mind is concerned with comparisons, the Imagination can, in all probability, actually though unconsciously let one image glide into another, and thus by the concurrence of several of the same kind come by an average, which serves as the common measure of all. Every one has seen a thousand full-grown men. Now if you wish to judge of their normal size, estimating it by means of comparison, the Imagination (as I think) allows a great number of images (perhaps the whole thousand) to fall on one another. If I am allowed to apply here the analogy of optical presentation, it is in the space where most of them are combined and inside the contour, where the place is illuminated with the most vivid colours, that the *average size* is cognisable; which, both in height and breadth, is equally far removed from the extreme bounds of the greatest and smallest stature. And this is the stature of a beautiful man. (We could arrive at the same thing mechanically, by adding together all thousand magnitudes, heights, breadths, and thicknesses, and dividing the sum by a thousand. But the Imagination does this by means of a dynamical effect, which arises from the various impressions of such figures on the organ of internal sense.) If now in a similar way for this average man we seek the average head, for this head the average nose, etc., such figure is at the basis of the normal Idea in the country where the comparison is instituted. Thus necessarily under these empirical conditions a negro must have a different normal Idea of the beauty of the [human figure] from a white man, a Chinaman a different normal Idea from a European, etc. And the same is the case with the model of a beautiful horse or dog (of a certain breed).—This *normal Idea* is not derived from proportions got from experience [and regarded] as *definite rules*; but in accordance with it rules for judging become in the first instance possible. It is the image for the whole race, which floats among all the variously different intuitions of individuals, which nature takes as archetype in her productions of the same species, but which seems not to be fully reached in any individual case. It is by no means the whole *archetype of beauty* in the race, but only the form constituting the indispensable condition of all beauty, and thus merely *correctness* in the [mental] presentation of the race. It is, like the celebrated *Doryphorus* of *Polycletus*,[25] the *rule* (*Myron's*[26] Cow might also be used thus for its kind). It can therefore contain nothing specifically characteristic, for otherwise it would not be the *normal Idea* for the race. Its presentation pleases, not by its beauty, but merely because it contradicts no condition, under which alone a thing of this kind can be beautiful. The presentation is merely correct.[27]

We must yet distinguish the *normal Idea* of the beautiful from the *Ideal*, which latter, on grounds already alleged, we can only expect in the *human* figure. In this the Ideal consists in the expression of the *moral*, without which the object would not please universally and thus positively (not merely negatively in a correct presentation). The visible expression of moral Ideas that rule men inwardly, can indeed only be got from experience; but to make its connexion with all which our Reason unites with the morally good in the Idea of the highest purposiveness,—goodness of heart, purity, strength, peace, etc.,—visible as it were in bodily manifestation (as the effect of that which is internal), requires a union of pure Ideas of Reason with great imaginative power, even in him who wishes to judge of it, still more in him who wishes to present it. The correctness of such an Ideal of beauty is shown by its permitting no sensible charm to mingle with the satisfaction in the Object and yet allowing us to take a great interest therein. This shows that a judgement in accordance with such a standard can never be purely aesthetical, and that a judgement in accordance with an Ideal of beauty is not a mere judgement of taste.

Explanation of the Beautiful Derived from this Third Moment

Beauty is the form of the *purposiveness* of an object, so far as this is perceived in it *without any representation of a purpose.*[28]

FOURTH MOMENT—OF THE JUDGEMENT OF TASTE, ACCORDING TO THE MODALITY OF THE SATISFACTION IN THE OBJECT

§ 18. WHAT THE MODALITY IN A JUDGEMENT OF TASTE IS

I can say of every representation that it is at least *possible* that (as a cognition) it should be bound up with a pleasure. Of a representation that I call *pleasant* I say that it *actually* excites pleasure in me. But the *beautiful* we think as having a *necessary* reference to satisfaction. Now this necessity is of a peculiar kind. It is not a theoretical objective necessity; in which case it would be cognised *a priori* that every one *will feel* this satisfaction in the object called beautiful by me. It is not a practical necessity; in which case, by concepts of a pure rational will serving as a rule for freely acting beings, the satisfaction is the necessary result of an objective law and only indicates that we absolutely (without any further design) ought to act in a certain way. But the necessity which is thought in an aesthetical judgement can only be called *exemplary; i.e.* a necessity of the assent of *all* to a judgement which is regarded as the example of a universal rule that we cannot state. Since an aesthetical judgement is not an objective cognitive judgement, this necessity cannot be derived from definite concepts, and is therefore not apodictic. Still less can it be inferred from the universality of experience (of a complete agreement of judgements as to the beauty of a certain object). For not only would experience hardly furnish sufficiently numerous vouchers for this; but also, on empirical judgements we can base no concept of the necessity of these judgements.

§ 19. THE SUBJECTIVE NECESSITY, WHICH WE ASCRIBE TO THE JUDGEMENT OF TASTE, IS CONDITIONED

The judgement of taste requires the agreement of every one; and he who describes anything as beautiful claims that every one *ought* to give his approval to the object in question and also describe it as beautiful. The *ought* in the aesthetical judgement is therefore pronounced in accordance with all the data which are required for judging and yet is only conditioned. We ask for the agreement of every one else, because we have for it a ground that is common to all; and we could count on this agreement, provided we were always sure that the case was correctly subsumed under that ground as rule of assent.

§ 20. THE CONDITION OF NECESSITY WHICH A JUDGEMENT OF TASTE ASSERTS IS THE IDEA OF A COMMON SENSE

If judgements of taste (like cognitive judgements) had a definite objective principle, then the person who lays them down in accordance with this latter would claim an unconditioned necessity for his judgement. If they were devoid of all principle, like those of the mere taste of sense, we would not allow them in thought any necessity whatever. Hence they must have a subjective principle which determines what pleases or displeases only by feeling and not by concepts, but yet with universal validity. But such a principle could only be regarded as a *common sense*, which is essentially different from common Understanding which people sometimes call common Sense (*sensus communis*); for the latter does not judge by feeling but always by concepts, although ordinarily only as by obscurely represented principles.

Hence it is only under the presupposition that there is a common sense (by which we do not understand an external sense, but the effect resulting from the free play of our cognitive powers)—it is only under this presupposition, I say, that the judgement of taste can be laid down.

§ 21. HAVE WE GROUND FOR PRESUPPOSING A COMMON SENSE?

Cognitions and judgements must, along with the conviction that accompanies them, admit of universal communicability; for otherwise there would be no harmony between them and the Object, and they would be collectively a mere subjective play of the representative powers, exactly as scepticism would have it. But if cognitions are to admit of communicability, so must also the state of mind,—*i.e.* the accordance of the cognitive powers with a cognition generally, and that proportion of them which is suitable for a representation (by which an object is given to us) in order that a cognition may be made out of it—admit of universal communicability. For without this as the subjective condition of cognition, knowledge as an effect could not arise. This actually always takes place when a given object by means of Sense excites the Imagination to collect the manifold, and the Imagination in its turn excites the Understanding to bring about a unity of this collective process in concepts. But this accordance of the cognitive powers has a different proportion according to the variety of the Objects which are given. However, it must be such that this internal relation, by which one mental faculty is excited by another, shall be generally the most beneficial for both faculties in respect of cognition (of given objects); and this accordance can only be determined by feeling (not according to concepts). Since now this accordance itself must admit of universal communicability, and consequently also our feeling of it (in a given representation), and since the universal communicability of a feeling presupposes a common sense, we have grounds for assuming this latter. And this common sense is assumed without relying on psychological observations, but simply as the necessary condition of the universal communicability of our knowledge, which is presupposed in every Logic and in every principle of knowledge that is not sceptical.

§ 22. THE NECESSITY OF THE UNIVERSAL AGREEMENT THAT IS THOUGHT IN A JUDGEMENT OF TASTE IS A SUBJECTIVE NECESSITY, WHICH IS REPRESENTED AS OBJECTIVE UNDER THE PRESUPPOSITION OF A COMMON SENSE

In all judgements by which we describe anything as beautiful, we allow no one to be of another opinion; without however grounding our judgement on concepts but only on our feeling, which we therefore place at its basis not as a private, but as a communal feeling.[29] Now this common sense cannot be grounded on experience; for it aims at justifying judgements which contain an *ought*. It does not say that every one *will* agree with my judgement, but that he *ought*. And so common sense, as an example of whose judgement I here put forward my judgement of taste and on account of which I attribute to the latter an *exemplary* validity, is a mere ideal norm, under the supposition of which I have a right to make into a rule for every one a judgement that accords therewith, as well as the satisfaction in an Object expressed in such judgement. For the principle, which concerns the agreement of different judging persons, although only subjective, is yet assumed as subjectively universal (an Idea necessary for every one); and thus can claim universal assent (as if it were objective) provided we are sure that we have correctly subsumed [the particulars] under it.

This indeterminate norm of a common sense is actually presupposed by us; as is shown by our claim to lay down judgements of taste. Whether there is in fact such a common sense, as a constitutive principle of the possibility of experience, or whether a yet higher principle of Reason makes it only into a regulative principle for producing in us a common sense for higher purposes: whether therefore Taste is an original and natural faculty, or only the Idea of an artificial one yet to be acquired, so that a judgement of taste with its assumption of a universal assent in fact, is only a requirement of Reason for producing such harmony of sentiment; whether the "ought," *i.e.* the objective necessity of the confluence of the feeling of any one man with that of every other, only signifies the possibility of arriving at this accord, and the judgement of taste only affords an example of the application of this principle: these questions we have neither the wish nor the power to investigate as yet; we have now only to resolve the faculty of taste into its elements in order to unite them at last in the Idea of a common sense.

Explanation of the Beautiful Resulting from the Fourth Moment

The *beautiful* is that which without any concept is cognised as the object of a *necessary* satisfaction.

GENERAL REMARK ON THE FIRST SECTION OF THE ANALYTIC

If we seek the result of the preceding analysis we find that everything runs up into this concept of Taste, that it is a faculty for judging an object in reference to the Imagination's *free conformity to law*. Now if in the judgement of taste the Imagination must be considered in its freedom, it is in the first place not regarded as reproductive, as it is subject to the laws of association, but as productive and spontaneous (as the author of arbitrary forms of possible intuition). And although in the apprehension of a given object of sense it is tied to a definite form of this Object, and so far has no free play (such as that of poetry) yet it may readily be conceived that the object can furnish it with such a form containing a collection of the manifold, as the Imagination itself, if it were left free, would project in accordance with the *conformity to law of the Understanding* in general. But that the *imaginative power* should be *free* and yet *of itself conformed to law, i.e.* bringing autonomy with it, is a contradiction. The Understanding alone gives the law. If, however, the Imagination is compelled to proceed according to a definite law, its product in respect of form is determined by concepts as to what it ought to be. But then, as is above shown, the satisfaction is not that in the Beautiful, but in the Good (in perfection, at any rate in mere formal perfection); and the judgement is not a judgement of taste. Hence it is a conformity to law without a law; and a subjective agreement of the Imagination and Understanding,—without such an objective agreement as there is when the representation is referred to a definite concept of an object,—can subsist along with the free conformity to law of the Understanding (which is also called purposiveness without purpose) and with the peculiar feature of a judgement of taste.

Now geometrically regular figures, such as a circle, a square, a cube, etc., are commonly adduced by critics of taste as the simplest and most indisputable examples of beauty; and yet they are called regular, because we can only represent them by regarding them as mere presentations of a definite concept which prescribes the rule for the figure (according to which alone it is possible). One of these two must be wrong, either that judgement of the critic which ascribes beauty to the said figures, or ours, which regards purposiveness apart from a concept as requisite for beauty.

Hardly any one will say that a man must have taste in order that he should find more satisfaction in a circle than in a scrawled outline, in an equilateral and equiangular quadrilateral than in one which is oblique, irregular, and as it were deformed, for this belongs to the ordinary Understanding and is not Taste at all. Where, *e.g.* our design is to judge of the size of an area, or to make intelligible the relation of the parts of it, when divided, to one another and to the whole, then regular figures and those of the simplest kind are needed, and the satisfaction does not rest immediately on the aspect of the figure, but on its availability for all kinds of possible designs. A room whose walls form oblique angles, or a parterre of this kind, even every violation of symmetry in the figure of animals (*e.g.* being one-eyed), of buildings, or of flower beds, displeases, because it contradicts the purpose of the thing, not only practically in respect of a definite use of it, but also when we pass judgement on it as regards any possible design. This is not the case in the judgement of taste, which when pure combines satisfaction or dissatisfaction,—without any reference to its use or to a purpose,—with the mere *consideration* of the object.

The regularity which leads to the concept of an object is indeed the indispensable condition (*conditio sine qua non*) for grasping the object in a single representation and determining the manifold in its form. This determination is a purpose in respect of cognition, and in reference to this it is always bound up with satisfaction (which accompanies the execution of every, even problematical, design). There is here, however, merely the approval of the solution satisfying a problem, and not a free and indefinite purposive entertainment of the mental powers with what we call beautiful, where the Understanding is at the service of Imagination and not *vice versa*.

In a thing that is only possible by means of design,—a building, or even an animal, —the regularity consisting in symmetry must express the unity of the intuition that accompanies the concept of purpose, and this regularity belongs to cognition. But where only a free play of the representative powers (under the condition, however, that the Understanding is to suffer no shock thereby) is to be kept up, in pleasure gardens, room decorations, all kinds of tasteful furniture, etc., regularity that shows constraint is avoided as much as possible. Thus in the English taste in gardens, or in bizarre taste in furniture, the freedom of the Imagination is pushed almost near to the grotesque, and in this separation from every constraint of rule we have the case, where taste can display its greatest perfection in the enterprises of the Imagination.

All stiff regularity (such as approximates to mathematical regularity) has something in it repugnant to taste; for our entertainment in the contemplation of it lasts for no length of time, but it rather, in so far as it has not expressly in view cognition or a definite practical purpose, produces weariness. On the other hand that with which Imagination can play in an unstudied and purposive manner is always new to us, and one does not get tired of looking at it. *Marsden* in his description of Sumatra makes the remark that the free beauties of nature surround the spectator everywhere and thus lose their attraction for him.[30] On the other hand a pepper-garden, where the stakes on which this plant twines itself form parallel rows, had much attractiveness for him, if he met with it in the middle of a forest. And hence he infers that wild beauty, apparently irregular, only pleases as a variation from the regular beauty of which one has seen enough. But he need only have made the experiment of spending one day in a pepper-garden, to have been convinced that, once the Understanding, by the aid of this regularity, has put itself in accord with the order that it always needs, the object will not entertain for long, —nay rather it will impose a burdensome constraint upon the Imagination. On the other hand, nature, which there is prodigal in its variety even to luxuriance, that is subjected to no constraint of artificial rules, can supply constant food for taste.—Even the song of birds, which we can bring under no musical rule, seems to have more freedom, and therefore more for taste, than a song of a human being which is produced in accordance with all the rules of music; for we very much sooner weary of the latter, if it is repeated often and at length. Here, however, we probably confuse our participation in the mirth of a little creature that we love, with the beauty of its song; for if this were exactly imitated by man (as sometimes the notes of the nightingale are)[31] it would seem to our ear quite devoid of taste.

Again, beautiful objects are to be distinguished from beautiful views of objects (which often on account of their distance cannot be clearly recognised). In the latter case taste appears not so much in what the Imagination *apprehends* in this field, as in the impulse it thus gets to *fiction*, *i.e.* in the peculiar fancies with which the mind entertains itself, whilst it is continually being aroused by the variety which strikes the eye. An illustration is afforded, *e.g.* by the sight of the changing shapes of a fire on the hearth or of a rippling brook; neither of these has beauty, but they bring with them a charm for the Imagination, because they entertain it in free play.

SECOND BOOK—ANALYTIC OF THE SUBLIME

§ 23. TRANSITION FROM THE FACULTY WHICH JUDGES OF THE BEAUTIFUL TO THAT WHICH JUDGES OF THE SUBLIME

The Beautiful and the Sublime agree in this, that both please in themselves. Further, neither presupposes a judgement of sense nor a judgement logically determined, but a judgement of reflection. Consequently the satisfaction [belonging to them] does not depend on a sensation, as in the case of the Pleasant, nor on a definite concept, as in the case of the Good; but it is nevertheless referred to concepts although indeterminate ones. And so the satisfaction is connected with the mere presentation [of the object] or with the faculty of presentation; so that in the case of a given intuition this faculty or the Imagination is considered as in agreement with the *faculty of concepts* of Understanding or Reason (in its furtherance of these latter). Hence both kinds of judgements are *singular*, and yet announce themselves as universally valid for every subject; although they lay claim merely to the feeling of pleasure and not to any knowledge of the object.

But there are also remarkable differences between the two. The Beautiful in nature is connected with the form of the object, which consists in having boundaries. The Sublime, on the other hand, is to be found in a formless object, so far as in it or by occasion of it *boundlessness* is represented, and yet its totality is also present to thought. Thus the Beautiful seems to be regarded as the presentation of an indefinite concept of Understanding; the Sublime as that of a like concept of Reason. Therefore the satisfaction in the one case is bound up with the representation of *quality*, in the other with that of *quantity*. And the latter satisfaction is quite different in kind from the former, for this [the Beautiful[32]] directly brings with it a feeling of the furtherance of life, and thus is compatible with charms and with the play of the Imagination. But the other [the feeling of the Sublime[43]] is a pleasure that arises only indirectly; viz. it is produced by the feeling of a momentary checking of the vital powers and a consequent stronger outflow of them, so that it seems to be regarded as emotion,—not play, but earnest in the exercise of the Imagination.—Hence it is incompatible with charms; and as the mind is not merely attracted by the object but is ever being alternately repelled, the satisfaction in the sublime does not so much involve a positive pleasure as admiration or respect, which rather deserves to be called negative pleasure.

But the inner and most important distinction between the Sublime and Beautiful is, certainly, as follows. (Here, as we are entitled to do, we only bring under consideration in the first instance the sublime in natural Objects; for the sublime of Art is always limited by the conditions of agreement with Nature.) Natural beauty (which is self-subsisting) brings with it a purposiveness in its form by which the object seems to be, as it were, pre-adapted to our Judgement, and thus constitutes in itself an object of satis-faction. On the other hand, that which excites in us, without any reasoning about it, but in the mere apprehension of it, the feeling of the sublime, may appear as regards its form to violate purpose in respect of the Judgement, to be unsuited to our presentative faculty, and, as it were, to do violence to the Imagination; and yet it is judged to be only the more sublime.

Now from this we may see that in general we express ourselves incorrectly if we call any *object of nature* sublime, although we can quite correctly call many objects of nature beautiful. For how can that be marked by an expression of approval, which is appre-hended in itself as being a violation of purpose? All that we can say is that the object is fit for the presentation of a sublimity which can be found in the mind; for no sensible form can contain the sublime properly so-called. This concerns only Ideas of the Reason, which, although no adequate presentation is possible for them, by this inadequacy that admits of sensible presentation, are aroused and summoned into the mind. Thus the wide ocean, agitated by the storm, cannot be called sublime. Its aspect is horrible; and the mind must be already filled with manifold Ideas if it is to be determined by such an intuition to a feeling itself sublime, as it is incited to abandon sensibility and to busy itself with Ideas that involve higher purposiveness.

Self-subsisting natural beauty discovers to us a Technic of nature, which represents it as a system in accordance with laws, the principle of which we do not find in the whole of our faculty of Understanding. That principle is the principle of purposiveness, in respect of the use of our Judgement in regard to phenomena; [which requires] that these must not be judged as merely belonging to nature in its purposeless mechanism, but also as belonging to something analogous to art. It, therefore, actually extends, not indeed our cognition of natural Objects, but our concept of nature; [which is now not regarded] as mere mechanism but as art. This leads to profound investigations as to the possibility of such a form. But in what we are accustomed to call sublime there is nothing at all that leads to particular objective principles and forms of nature corre-sponding to them; so far from it that for the most part nature excites the Ideas of the sublime in its chaos or in its wildest and most irregular disorder and desolation, provided size and might are perceived. Hence, we see that the concept of the Sublime is not nearly so important or rich in consequences as the concept of the Beautiful; and that in general it displays nothing purposive in nature itself, but only in that possible use of our intuitions of it by which there is produced in us a feeling of a purposiveness quite independent of nature. We must seek a ground external to ourselves for the Beautiful of nature; but seek it for the Sublime merely in ourselves and in our attitude of thought which introduces sublimity into the representation of nature. This is a very needful preliminary remark, which quite separates the Ideas of the sublime from that of a purposiveness of *nature*, and makes the theory of the sublime a mere appendix to the aesthetical judging of that purposiveness; because by means of it no particular form is represented in nature, but there is only developed a purposive use which the Imagina-tion makes of its representation.

§ 24. OF THE DIVISIONS OF AN INVESTIGATION INTO THE FEELING OF THE SUBLIME

As regards the division of the moments of the aesthetical judging of objects in reference to the feeling of the sublime, the Analytic can proceed according to the same principle as was adapted in the analysis of judgements of taste. For as an act of the aesthetical reflective Judgement, the satisfaction in the Sublime must be represented just as in the case of the Beautiful,—according to *quantity* as universally valid, according to *quality* as devoid of *interest*, according to *relation* as subjective purposiveness, and according to *modality* as necessary. And so the method here will not diverge from that of the preceding section; unless, indeed, we count it a difference that in the case where the aesthetical Judgement is concerned with the form of the Object we began with the investigation of its quality, but here, in view of the formlessness which may belong to what we call sublime, we shall begin with quantity, as the first moment of the aesthetical judgement as to the sublime. The reason for this may be seen from the preceding paragraph.

But the analysis of the Sublime involves a division not needed in the case of the Beautiful, viz. a division into the *mathematically* and the *dynamically sublime.*

For the feeling of the Sublime brings with it as its characteristic feature a *movement* of the mind bound up with the judging of the object, while in the case of the Beautiful taste presupposes and maintains the mind in *restful* contemplation. Now this movement ought to be judged as subjectively purposive (because the sublime pleases us), and thus it is referred through the Imagination either to the *faculty of cognition* or of *desire*. In either reference the purposiveness of the given representation ought to be judged only in respect of this *faculty* (without purpose or interest); but in the first case it is ascribed to the Object as a *mathematical* determination of the Imagination, in the second as *dynamical.* And hence we have this twofold way of representing the sublime.

A.—OF THE MATHEMATICALLY SUBLIME

§ 25. EXPLANATION OF THE TERM "SUBLIME"

We call that *sublime* which is *absolutely great.* But to be great, and to be a great something are quite different concepts (*magnitudo* and *quantitas*). In like manner to *say simply* (*simpliciter*) that anything is *great* is quite different from saying that it is *absolutely great* (*absolute, non comparative magnum*). The latter is *what is great beyond all comparison.*— What now is meant by the expression that anything is great or small or of medium size? It is not a pure concept of Understanding that is thus signified; still less is it an intuition of Sense, and just as little is it a concept of Reason, because it brings with it no principle of cognition. It must therefore be a concept of Judgement or derived from one; and a subjective purposiveness of the representation in reference to the Judgement must lie at its basis. That anything is a magnitude (*quantum*) may be cognised from the thing itself, without any comparison of it with other things; viz. if there is a multiplicity of the homogeneous constituting one thing. But to cognise *how great* it is always requires some other magnitude as a measure. But because the judging of magnitude depends not merely on multiplicity (number), but also on the magnitude of the unit (the measure), and since, to judge of the magnitude of this latter again requires another as measure with which it may be compared, we see that the determination of the magnitude of phenomena can supply no absolute concept whatever of magnitude, but only a comparative one.

If now I say simply that anything is great, it appears that I have no comparison in view, at least none with an objective measure; because it is thus not determined at all how great the object is. But although the standard of comparison is merely subjective, yet the judgement none the less claims universal assent; "this man is beautiful," and "he is tall," are judgements not limited merely to the judging subject, but, like theoretical judgements, demanding the assent of every one.

In a judgement by which anything is designated simply as great, it is not merely meant that the object has a magnitude, but that this magnitude is superior to that of many other objects of the same kind, without, however, any exact determination of this superiority. Thus there is always at the basis of our judgement a standard which we assume as the same for every one; this, however, is not available for any logical (mathematically definite) judging of magnitude, but only for aesthetical judging of the same, because it is a merely subjective standard lying at the basis of the reflective judgement upon magnitude. It may be empirical, as, *e.g.* the average size of the men known to us, of animals of a certain kind, trees, houses, mountains, etc. Or it may be a standard given *a priori*, which through the defects of the judging subject is limited by the subjective conditions of presentation *in concreto*; as, *e.g.* in the practical sphere, the greatness of a certain virtue, or of the public liberty and justice in a country; or, in the theoretical sphere, the greatness of the accuracy or the inaccuracy of an observation or measurement that has been made, etc.

Here it is remarkable that, although we have no interest whatever in an Object,—*i.e.* its existence is indifferent to us,—yet its mere size, even if it is considered as formless, may bring a satisfaction with it that is universally communicable, and that consequently involves the consciousness of a subjective purposiveness in the use of our cognitive faculty. This is not indeed a satisfaction in the Object (because it may be formless), as in the case of the Beautiful, in which the reflective Judgement finds itself purposively determined in reference to cognition in general; but [a satisfaction] in the extension of the Imagination by itself.

If (under the above limitation) we say simply of an object "it is great," this is no mathematically definite judgement but a mere judgement of reflection upon the representation of it, which is subjectively purposive for a certain use of our cognitive powers in the estimation of magnitude; and we always then bind up with the representation a kind of respect, as also a kind of contempt for what we simply call "small." Further, the judging of things as great or small extends to everything, even to all their characteristics; thus we describe beauty as great or small. The reason of this is to be sought in the fact that whatever we present in intuition according to the precept of the Judgement (and thus represent aesthetically) is always a phenomenon and thus a quantum.

But if we call anything not only great, but absolutely great in every point of view (great beyond all comparison), *i.e.* sublime, we soon see that it is not permissible to seek for an adequate standard of this outside itself, but merely in itself. It is a magnitude which is like itself alone. It follows hence that the sublime is not to be sought in the things of nature, but only in our Ideas; but in which of them it lies must be reserved for the Deduction.

The foregoing explanation can be thus expressed: *the sublime is that in comparison with which everything else is small.* Here we easily see that nothing can be given in nature, however great it is judged by us to be, which could not if considered in another relation be reduced to the infinitely small; and conversely there is nothing so small, which does not admit of extension by our Imagination to the greatness of a world, if compared with still smaller standards. Telescopes have furnished us with abundant material for making the first remark, microscopes for the second. Nothing, therefore, which can be an object of the senses, is, considered on this basis, to be called sublime. But because there is in our Imagination a striving towards infinite progress, and in our Reason a claim for absolute totality, regarded as a real Idea, therefore this very inadequateness for that Idea in our faculty for estimating the magnitude of things of sense, excites in us the feeling of a supersensible faculty. And it is not the object of sense, but the use which the Judgement naturally makes of certain objects on behalf of this latter feeling, that is absolutely great; and in comparison every other use is small. Consequently it is the state of mind produced by a certain representation with which the reflective Judgement is occupied, and not the Object, that is to be called sublime.

We may therefore append to the preceding formulas explaining the sublime this other: *the sublime is that, the mere ability to think which, shows a faculty of the mind surpassing every standard of Sense.*

§ 26. OF THAT ESTIMATION OF THE MAGNITUDE OF NATURAL THINGS WHICH IS REQUISITE FOR THE IDEA OF THE SUBLIME

The estimation of magnitude by means of concepts of number (or their signs in Algebra) is mathematical; but that in mere intuition (by the measurement of the eye) is aesthetical. Now we can come by definite concepts of *how great* a thing is, [only][33] by numbers, of which the unit is the measure (at all events by series of numbers progressing to infinity); and so far all logical estimation of magnitude is mathematical. But since the magnitude of the measure must then be assumed known, and this again is only to be estimated mathematically by means of numbers,—the unit of which must be another [smaller] measure,—we can never have a first or fundamental measure, and therefore can never have a definite concept of a given magnitude. So the estimation of the magnitude of the fundamental measure must consist in this, that we can immediately apprehend it in intuition and use it by the Imagination for the presentation of concepts of number. That is, all estimation of the magnitude of the objects of nature is in the end aesthetical (*i.e.* subjectively and not objectively determined).

Now for the mathematical estimation of magnitude there is, indeed, no maximum (for the power of numbers extends to infinity); but for its aesthetical estimation there is always a maximum, and of this I say that if it is judged as the absolute measure than which no greater is possible subjectively (for the judging subject), it brings with it the Idea of the sublime and produces that emotion which no mathematical estimation of its magnitude by means of numbers can bring about (except so far as the aesthetical fundamental measure remains vividly in the Imagination). For the former only presents relative magnitude by means of comparison with others of the same kind; but the latter presents magnitude absolutely, so far as the mind can grasp it in an intuition.

In receiving a quantum into the Imagination by intuition, in order to be able to use it for a measure or as a unit for the estimation of magnitude by means of numbers, there are two operations of the Imagination involved: *apprehension* (*apprehensio*) and *comprehension* (*comprehensio aesthetica*). As to apprehension there is no difficulty, for it can go on *ad infinitum*; but comprehension becomes harder the further apprehension advances, and soon attains to its maximum, viz. the aesthetically greatest fundamental measure for the estimation of magnitude. For when apprehension has gone so far that the partial representations of sensuous intuition at first apprehended begin to vanish in the Imagination, whilst this ever proceeds to the apprehension of others, then it loses as much on the one side as it gains on the other; and in comprehension there is a maximum beyond which it cannot go.

Hence can be explained what *Savary*[34] remarks in his account of Egypt, viz. that we must keep from going very near the Pyramids just as much as we keep from going too far from them, in order to get the full emotional effect from their size. For if we are too far away, the parts to be apprehended (the stones lying one over the other) are only obscurely represented, and the representation of them produces no effect upon the aesthetical judgement of the subject. But if we are very near, the eye requires some time to complete the apprehension of the tiers from the bottom up to the apex; and then the first tiers are always partly forgotten before the Imagination has taken in the last, and so the comprehension of them is never complete.—The same thing may sufficiently explain the bewilderment or, as it were, perplexity which, it is said, seizes the spectator on his first entrance into St. Peter's at Rome. For there is here a feeling of the inadequacy of his Imagination for presenting the Ideas of a whole, wherein the Imagination reaches its maximum, and, in striving to surpass it, sinks back into itself, by which, however, a kind of emotional satisfaction is produced.

I do not wish to speak as yet of the ground of this satisfaction, which is bound up with a representation from which we should least of all expect it, viz. a representation which lets us remark its inadequacy and consequently its subjective want of purposiveness for the Judgement in the estimation of magnitude. I only remark that if the aesthetical judgement is pure (i.e. *mingled with no teleological judgement* or judgement of Reason) and is to be given as a completely suitable example of the Critique of the *aesthetical* Judgement, we must not exhibit the sublime in products of art (*e.g.* buildings, pillars, etc.) where human purpose determines the form as well as the size; nor yet in things of nature *the concepts of which bring with them a definite purpose* (*e.g.* animals with a known natural destination); but in rude nature (and in this only in so far as it does not bring with it any charm or emotion produced by actual danger) merely as containing magnitude. For in this kind of representation nature contains nothing monstrous (either magnificent or horrible); the magnitude that is apprehended may be increased as much as you wish provided it can be comprehended in a whole by the Imagination. An object is *monstrous* if by its size it destroys the purpose which constitutes the concept of it. But the mere presentation of a concept is called *colossal*, which is almost too great for any presentation (bordering on the relatively monstrous); because the purpose of the presentation of a concept is made harder [to realise] by the intuition of the object being almost too great for our faculty of apprehension.—A pure judgement upon the sublime must, however, have no purpose of the Object as its determining ground, if it is to be aesthetical and not mixed up with any judgement of Understanding or Reason.

BECAUSE EVERYTHING which is to give disinterested pleasure to the merely reflective Judgement must bring with the representation of it, subjective and, as subjective, universally valid purposiveness—although no purposiveness of the *form* of the object lies (as in the case of the Beautiful) at the ground of the judgement—the question arises "what is this subjective purposiveness?" And how does it come to be prescribed as the norm by which a ground for universally valid satisfaction is supplied in the mere estimation of magnitude, even in that which is forced up to the point where our faculty of Imagination is inadequate for the presentation of the concept of magnitude?

In the process of combination requisite for the estimation of magnitude, the Imagination proceeds of itself to infinity without anything hindering it; but the Understanding guides it by means of concepts of number, for which the Imagination must furnish the schema. And in this procedure, as belonging to the logical estimation of magnitude, there is indeed something objectively purposive,—in accordance with the concept of a purpose (as all measurement is),—but nothing purposive and pleasing for the aesthetical Judgement. There is also in this designed purposiveness nothing which would force us to push the magnitude of the measure, and consequently the *comprehension* of the manifold in an intuition, to the bounds of the faculty of Imagination, or as far as ever this can reach in its presentations. For in the estimation of magnitude by the Understanding (Arithmetic) we only go to a certain point whether we push the comprehension of the units up to the number 10 (as in the decimal scale) or only up to 4 (as in the quaternary scale); the further production of magnitude proceeds by combination or, if the quantum is given in intuition, by apprehension, but merely by way of progression (not of comprehension) in accordance with an assumed principle of progression. In this mathematical estimation of magnitude the Understanding is equally served and contented whether the Imagination chooses for unit a magnitude that we can take in in a glance, *e.g.* a foot or rod, or a German mile or even the earth's diameter,—of which the apprehension is indeed possible, but not the comprehension in an intuition of the Imagination (not possible by *comprehensio aesthetica*, although quite possible by *comprehensio logica* in a concept of number). In both cases the logical estimation of magnitude goes on without hindrance to infinity.

But now the mind listens to the voice of Reason which, for every given magnitude, —even for those that can never be entirely apprehended, although (in sensible representation) they are judged as entirely given,—requires totality. Reason consequently desires comprehension in *one* intuition, and so the *presentation* of all these members of a progressively increasing series. It does not even exempt the infinite (space and past time) from this requirement; it rather renders it unavoidable to think the infinite (in the judgement of common Reason) as *entirely given* (according to its totality).

But the infinite is absolutely (not merely comparatively) great. Compared with it everything else (of the same kind of magnitudes) is small. And what is most important is that to be able only to think it as *a whole* indicates a faculty of mind which surpasses every standard of Sense. For [to represent it sensibly] would require a comprehension having for unit a standard bearing a definite relation, expressible in numbers, to the infinite; which is impossible. Nevertheless, *the bare capability of thinking* this infinite without contradiction requires in the human mind a faculty itself supersensible. For it is only by means of this faculty and its Idea of a noumenon,—which admits of no intuition, but which yet serves as the substrate for the intuition of the world, as a mere phenomenon, —that the infinite of the world of sense, in the pure intellectual estimation of magnitude, can be *completely* comprehended *under* a concept, although in the mathematical estimation of magnitude by means of *concepts of number* it can never be completely thought. The faculty of being able to think the infinite of supersensible intuition as given (in its intelligible substrate), surpasses every standard of sensibility, and is great beyond all comparison even with the faculty of mathematical estimation; not of course in a theoretical point of view and on behalf of the cognitive faculty, but as an extension of the mind which feels itself able in another (practical) point of view to go beyond the limit of sensibility.

Nature is therefore sublime in those of its phenomena, whose intuition brings with it the Idea of their infinity. This last can only come by the inadequacy of the greatest effort of our Imagination to estimate the magnitude of an object. But now in mathematical estimation of magnitude the Imagination is equal to providing a sufficient measure for every object; because the numerical concepts of the Understanding, by means of progression, can make any measure adequate to any given magnitude. Therefore it must be the *aesthetical* estimation of magnitude in which it is felt that the effort towards comprehension surpasses the power of the Imagination to grasp in a whole of intuition the progressive apprehension; and at the same time is perceived the inadequacy of this faculty, unbounded in its progress, for grasping and using, for the estimation of magnitude, a fundamental measure which could be made available by the Understanding with little trouble. Now the proper unchangeable fundamental measure of nature is its absolute whole; which, regarding nature as a phenomenon, would be infinity comprehended. But since this fundamental measure is a self-contradictory concept (on account of the impossibility of the absolute totality of an endless progress), that magnitude of a natural Object, on which the Imagination fruitlessly spends its whole faculty of comprehension, must carry our concept of nature to a supersensible substrate (which lies at its basis and also at the basis of our faculty of thought). As this, however, is great beyond all standards of sense, it makes us judge as *sublime*, not so much the object, as our own state of mind in the estimation of it.

Therefore, just as the aesthetical Judgement in judging the Beautiful refers the Imagination in its free play to the *Understanding*, in order to harmonise it with the *concepts* of the latter in general (without any determination of them); so does the same faculty when judging a thing as Sublime refer itself to the *Reason* in order that it may subjectively be in accordance with its *Ideas* (no matter what they are):—*i.e.* that it may produce a state of mind conformable to them and compatible with that brought about by the influence of definite (practical) Ideas upon feeling.

We hence see also that true sublimity must be sought only in the mind of the [subject] judging, not in the natural Object, the judgement upon which occasions this state. Who would call sublime, *e.g.* shapeless mountain masses piled in wild disorder upon each other with their pyramids of ice, or the gloomy raging sea? But the mind feels itself elevated in its own judgement if, while contemplating them without any reference to

506 | IMMANUEL KANT

their form, and abandoning itself to the Imagination and to the Reason—which although placed in combination with the Imagination without any definite purpose, merely extends it—it yet finds the whole power of the Imagination inadequate to its Ideas.

Examples of the mathematically Sublime of nature in mere intuition are all the cases in which we are given, not so much a larger numerical concept as a large unit for the measure of the Imagination (for shortening the numerical series). A tree, [the height of] which we estimate with reference to the height of a man, at all events gives a standard for a mountain; and if this were a mile high, it would serve as unit for the number expressive of the earth's diameter, so that the latter might be made intuitible. The earth's diameter [would supply a unit] for the known planetary system; this again for the Milky Way; and the immeasurable number of milky way systems called nebulae,—which presumably constitute a system of the same kind among themselves—lets us expect no bounds here. Now the Sublime in the aesthetical judging of an immeasurable whole like this lies not so much in the greatness of the number [of units], as in the fact that in our progress we ever arrive at yet greater units. To this the systematic division of the universe contributes, which represents every magnitude in nature as small in its turn; and represents our Imagination with its entire freedom from bounds, and with it Nature, as a mere nothing in comparison with the Ideas of Reason, if it is sought to furnish a presentation which shall be adequate to them.

§ 27. OF THE QUALITY OF THE SATISFACTION IN OUR JUDGEMENTS UPON THE SUBLIME

The feeling of our incapacity to attain to an Idea, *which is a law for us*, is RESPECT. Now the Idea of the comprehension of every phenomenon that can be given us in the intuition of a whole, is an Idea prescribed to us by a law of Reason, which recognises no other measure, definite, valid for every one, and invariable, than the absolute whole. But our Imagination, even in its greatest efforts, in respect of that comprehension, which we expect from it, of a given object in a whole of intuition (and thus with reference to the presentation of the Idea of Reason), exhibits its own limits and inadequacy; although at the same time it shows that its destination is to make itself adequate to this Idea regarded as a law. Therefore the feeling of the Sublime in nature is respect for our own destination, which by a certain subreption we attribute to an Object of nature (conversion of respect for the Idea of humanity in our own subject into respect for the Object). This makes intuitively evident the superiority of the rational determination of our cognitive faculties to the greatest faculty of our Sensibility.

The feeling of the Sublime is therefore a feeling of pain, arising from the want of accordance between the aesthetical estimation of magnitude formed by the Imagination and the estimation of the same formed by Reason. There is at the same time a pleasure thus excited, arising from the correspondence with rational Ideas of this very judgement of the inadequacy of our greatest faculty of Sense; in so far as it is a law for us to strive after these Ideas. In fact it is for us a law (of Reason), and belongs to our destination, to estimate as small, in comparison with Ideas of Reason, everything which nature, regarded as an object of Sense, contains that is great for us; and that which arouses in us the feeling of this supersensible destination agrees with that law. Now the greatest effort of the Imagination in the presentation of the unit for the estimation of magnitude indicates a reference to something *absolutely great*; and consequently a reference to the law of Reason, which bids us take this alone as the supreme measure of magnitude. Therefore the inner perception of the inadequacy of all sensible standards for rational estimation of magnitude indicates a correspondence with rational laws; it involves a pain, which arouses in us the feeling of our supersensible destination, according to which it is purposive and therefore pleasurable to find every standard of Sensibility inadequate to the Ideas of Understanding.

The mind feels itself *moved* in the representation of the Sublime in nature; whilst in aesthetical judgements about the Beautiful it is in *restful* contemplation. This movement may (especially in its beginnings) be compared to a vibration, *i.e.* to a quickly alternating attraction towards, and repulsion from, the same Object. The transcendent (towards which the Imagination is impelled in its apprehension of intuition) is for the Imagination like an abyss in which it fears to lose itself; but for the rational Idea of the supersensible it is not transcendent but in conformity with law to bring about such an effort of the Imagination, and consequently here there is the same amount of attraction as there was of repulsion for the mere Sensibility. But the judgement itself always remains in this case only aesthetical, because—without having any determinate concept of the Object at its basis—it merely represents the subjective play of the mental powers (Imagination and Reason) as harmonious through their very contrast. For just as Imagination and *Understanding*, in judging of the Beautiful, generate a subjective purposiveness of the mental powers by means of their harmony, so [here[35]] Imagination and *Reason* do so by means of their conflict. That is, they bring about a feeling that we possess pure self-subsistent Reason, or a faculty for the estimation of magnitude, whose pre-eminence can be made intuitively evident only by the inadequacy of that faculty [Imagination] which is itself unbounded in the presentation of magnitudes (of sensible objects).

The measurement of a space (regarded as apprehension) is at the same time a description of it, and thus an objective movement in the act of Imagination and a progress. On the other hand, the comprehension of the manifold in the unity,—not of thought but of intuition,—and consequently the comprehension of the successively apprehended [elements] in one glance, is a regress, which annihilates the condition of time in this progress of the Imagination and makes *coexistence* intuitible.[36] It is therefore (since the time-series is a condition of the internal sense and of an intuition) a subjective movement of the Imagination, by which it does violence to the internal sense; this must be the more noticeable, the greater the quantum is which the Imagination comprehends in one intuition. The effort, therefore, to receive in one single intuition a measure for magnitudes that requires an appreciable time to apprehend, is a kind of representation, which, subjectively considered, is contrary to purpose: but objectively, as requisite for the estimation of magnitude, it is purposive. Thus that very violence which is done to the subject through the Imagination is judged as purposive *in reference to the whole determination* of the mind.

The *quality* of the feeling of the Sublime is that it is a feeling of pain in reference to the faculty by which we judge aesthetically of an object, which pain, however, is represented at the same time as purposive. This is possible through the fact that the very incapacity in question discovers the consciousness of an unlimited faculty of the same subject, and that the mind can only judge of the latter aesthetically by means of the former.

In the logical estimation of magnitude the impossibility of ever arriving at absolute totality, by means of the progress of the measurement of things of the sensible world in time and space, was cognised as objective, *i.e.* as an impossibility of *thinking* the infinite as entirely given; and not as merely subjective or that there was only an incapacity to *grasp* it. For there we have not to do with the degree of comprehension in an intuition, regarded as a measure, but everything depends on a concept of number. But in aesthetical estimation of magnitude the concept of number must disappear or be changed, and the comprehension of the Imagination in reference to the unit of measure (thus avoiding the concepts of a law of the successive production of concepts of magnitude) is alone purposive for it.—If now a magnitude almost reaches the limit of our faculty of comprehension in an intuition, and yet the Imagination is invited by means of numerical magnitudes (in respect of which we are conscious that our faculty is unbounded) to aesthetical comprehension in a greater unit, then we mentally feel ourselves confined aesthetically within bounds. But nevertheless the pain in regard to the necessary extension of the Imagination for accordance with that which is unbounded in our faculty of Reason, viz. the Idea of the absolute whole, and consequently the very unpurposiveness of the faculty of Imagination for rational Ideas and the arousing of them, are represented as purposive. Thus it is that the aesthetical judgement itself is subjectively purposive for the Reason as the source of Ideas, *i.e.* as the source of an intellectual comprehension for which all aesthetical comprehension is small; and there accompanies the reception of an object as sublime a pleasure, which is only possible through the medium of a pain.

B.—OF THE DYNAMICALLY SUBLIME IN NATURE

§ 28. OF NATURE REGARDED AS MIGHT

Might is that which is superior to great hindrances. It is called *dominion* if it is superior to the resistance of that which itself possesses might. Nature considered in an aesthetical judgement as might that has no dominion over us, is *dynamically sublime*.

If nature is to be judged by us as dynamically sublime, it must be represented as exciting fear (although it is not true conversely that every object which excites fear is regarded in our aesthetical judgement as sublime). For in aesthetical judgements (without the aid of concepts) superiority to hindrances can only be judged according to the greatness of the resistance. Now that which we are driven to resist is an evil, and, if we do not find our faculties a match for it, is an object of fear. Hence nature can be regarded by the aesthetical Judgement as might, and consequently as dynamically sublime, only so far as it is considered an object of fear.

But we can regard an object as *fearful*, without being afraid *of* it; viz. if we judge of it in such a way that we merely *think* a case in which we would wish to resist it, and yet in which all resistance would be altogether vain. Thus the virtuous man fears God without being afraid of Him; because to wish to resist Him and His commandments, he thinks is a case as to which *he* need not be anxious. But in every such case that he thinks as not impossible, he cognises Him as fearful.

He who fears can form no judgement about the Sublime in nature; just as he who is seduced by inclination and appetite can form no judgement about the Beautiful. The former flies from the sight of an object which inspires him with awe; and it is impossible to find satisfaction in a terror that is seriously felt. Hence the pleasurableness arising from the cessation of an uneasiness is *a state of joy*. But this, on account of the deliverance from danger [which is involved], is a state of joy conjoined with the resolve not to expose ourselves to the danger again; we cannot willingly look back upon our sensations [of danger], much less seek the occasion for them again.

Bold, overhanging, and as it were threatening, rocks; clouds piled up in the sky, moving with lightning flashes and thunder peals; volcanoes in all their violence of destruction; hurricanes with their track of devastation; the boundless ocean in a state of tumult; the lofty waterfall of a mighty river, and such like; these exhibit our faculty of resistance as insignificantly small in comparison with their might. But the sight of them is the more attractive, the more fearful it is, provided only that we are in security; and we readily call these objects sublime, because they raise the energies of the soul above their accustomed height, and discover in us a faculty of resistance of a quite different kind, which gives us courage to measure ourselves against the apparent almightiness of nature.

Now, in the immensity of nature, and in the inadequacy of our faculties for adopting a standard proportionate to the aesthetical estimation of the magnitude of its *realm*, we find our own limitation; although at the same time in our rational faculty we find a different, non-sensuous standard, which has that infinity itself under it as a unit, and in comparison with which everything in nature is small. Thus in our mind we find a superiority to nature even in its immensity. And so also the irresistibility of its might, while making us recognise our own [physical[37]] impotence, considered as beings of nature, discloses to us a faculty of judging independently of, and a superiority over, nature; on which is based a kind of self-preservation, entirely different from that which can be attacked and brought into danger by external nature. Thus, humanity in our person remains unhumiliated, though the individual might have to submit to this dominion. In this way nature is not judged to be sublime in our aesthetical judgements, in so far as it excites fear; but because it calls up that power in us (which is not nature) of regarding as small the things about which we are solicitous (goods, health, and life), and of regarding its might (to which we are no doubt subjected in respect of these things), as nevertheless without any dominion over us and our personality to which we must bow where our highest fundamental propositions, and their assertion or abandonment, are concerned. Therefore nature is here called sublime merely because it elevates the Imagination to a presentation of those cases in which the mind can make felt the proper sublimity of its destination, in comparison with nature itself.

This estimation of ourselves loses nothing through the fact that we must regard ourselves as safe in order to feel this inspiriting satisfaction; and that hence, as there is no seriousness in the danger, there might be also (as might seem to be the case) just as little seriousness in the sublimity of our spiritual faculty. For the satisfaction here concerns only the *destination* of our faculty which discloses itself in such a case, so far as the tendency to this destination lies in our nature, whilst its development and exercise remain incumbent and obligatory. And in this there is truth, however conscious the man may be of his present actual powerlessness, when he stretches his reflection so far.

No doubt this principle seems to be too far-fetched and too subtly reasoned, and consequently seems to go beyond the scope of an aesthetical judgement; but observation of men proves the opposite, and shows that it may lie at the root of the most ordinary judgements, although we are not always conscious of it. For what is that which is, even to the savage, an object of the greatest admiration? It is a man who shrinks from nothing, who fears nothing, and therefore does not yield to danger, but rather goes to face it vigorously with the fullest deliberation. Even in the most highly civilised state this peculiar veneration for the soldier remains, though only under the condition that he exhibit all the virtues of peace, gentleness, compassion, and even a becoming care for his own person; because even by these it is recognised that his mind is unsubdued by danger. Hence whatever disputes there may be about the superiority of the respect which is to be accorded them, in the comparison of a statesman and a general, the aesthetical judgement decides for the latter. War itself, if it is carried on with order and with a sacred respect for the rights of citizens, has something sublime in it, and makes the disposition of the people who carry it on thus, only the more sublime, the more numerous are the dangers to which they are exposed, and in respect of which they behave with courage. On the other hand, a long peace generally brings about a predominant commercial spirit, and along with it, low selfishness, cowardice, and effeminacy, and debases the disposition of the people.[38]

It appears to conflict with this solution of the concept of the sublime, so far as sublimity is ascribed to might, that we are accustomed to represent God as presenting Himself in His wrath and yet in His sublimity, in the tempest, the storm, the earthquake, etc.; and that it would be foolish and criminal to imagine a superiority of our minds over these works of His, and, as it seems, even over the designs of such might. Hence it would appear that no feeling of the sublimity of our own nature, but rather subjection, abasement, and a feeling of complete powerlessness, is a fitting state of mind before the manifestation of such an object, and this is generally bound up with the Idea of it during natural phenomena of this kind. Generally in religion, prostration, adoration with bent head, with contrite, anxious demeanour and voice, seems to be the only fitting behaviour in presence of the Godhead; and hence most peoples have adopted and still observe it. But this state of mind is far from being necessarily bound up with the Idea of the *sublimity* of a religion and its object. The man who is actually afraid, because he finds reasons for fear in himself, whilst conscious by his culpable disposition of offending against a Might whose will is irresistible and at the same time just, is not in the frame of mind for admiring the divine greatness. For this a mood of calm contemplation and a quite free judgement are needed. Only if he is conscious of an upright disposition pleasing to God do those operations of might serve to awaken in him the Idea of the sublimity of this Being, for then he recognises in himself a sublimity of disposition conformable to His will; and thus he is raised above the fear of such operations of nature, which he no longer regards as outbursts of His wrath. Even humility, in the shape of a stern judgement upon his own faults,—which otherwise, with a consciousness of good intentions, could be easily palliated from the frailty of human nature,—is a sublime state of mind, consisting in a voluntary subjection of himself to the pain of remorse, in order that its causes may be gradually removed. In this way religion is essentially distinguished from superstition. The latter establishes in the mind, not reverence for the Sublime, but fear and apprehension of the all-powerful Being to whose will the terrified man sees himself subject, without according Him any high esteem. From this nothing can arise but a seeking of favour, and flattery, instead of a religion which consists in a good life.[39]

Sublimity, therefore, does not reside in anything of nature, but only in our mind, in so far as we can become conscious that we are superior to nature within, and therefore also to nature without us (so far as it influences us). Everything that excites this feeling in us, *e.g.* the *might* of nature which calls forth our forces, is called then (although improperly) sublime. Only by supposing this Idea in ourselves, and in reference to it, are we capable of attaining to the Idea of the sublimity of that Being, which produces respect in us, not merely by the might that it displays in nature, but rather by means of the faculty which resides in us of judging it fearlessly and of regarding our destination as sublime in respect of it.

§ 29. OF THE MODALITY OF THE JUDGEMENT UPON THE SUBLIME IN NATURE

There are numberless beautiful things in nature about which we can assume and even expect, without being far mistaken, the harmony of every one's judgement with our own. But in respect of our judgement upon the sublime in nature, we cannot promise ourselves so easily the accordance of others. For a far greater culture, as well of the aesthetical Judgement as of the cognitive faculties which lie at its basis, seems requisite in order to be able to pass judgement on this pre-eminent quality of natural objects.

That the mind be attuned to feel the sublime postulates a susceptibility of the mind for Ideas. For in the very inadequacy of nature to these latter, and thus only by presupposing them and by straining the Imagination to use nature as a schema for them, is to be found that which is terrible to sensibility and yet is attractive. [It is attractive] because Reason exerts a dominion over sensibility in order to extend it in conformity with its own realm (the practical) and to make it look out into the Infinite, which is for it an abyss. In fact, without development of moral Ideas, that which we, prepared by culture, call sublime, presents itself to the uneducated man merely as terrible. In the indications of the dominion of nature in destruction, and in the great scale of its might, in comparison with which his own is a vanishing quantity, he will only see the misery, danger, and distress which surround the man who is exposed to it. So the good, and indeed intelligent, Savoyard peasant (as Herr von *Saussure*[40] relates) unhesitatingly called all lovers of snow-mountains fools. And who knows, whether he would have been so completely wrong, if Saussure had undertaken the danger to which he exposed himself merely, as most travellers do, from amateur curiosity, or that he might be able to give a pathetic account of them? But his design was the instruction of men; and this excellent man gave the readers of his Travels, soul-stirring sensations such as he himself had, into the bargain.

But although the judgement upon the Sublime in nature needs culture (more than the judgement upon the Beautiful), it is not therefore primarily produced by culture and introduced in a merely conventional way into society. Rather has it root in human nature, even in that which, alike with common Understanding, we can impute to and expect of every one, viz. in the tendency to the feeling for (practical) Ideas, *i.e.* to the moral feeling.

Hereon is based the necessity of that agreement of the judgement of others about the sublime with our own which we include in the latter. For just as we charge with want of *taste* the man who is indifferent when passing judgement upon an object of nature that we regard as beautiful; so we say of him who remains unmoved in the presence of that which we judge to be sublime, he has no *feeling*. But we claim both from every man, and we presuppose them in him if he has any culture at all; only with the difference, that we expect the former directly of every one, because in it the Judgement refers the Imagination merely to the Understanding, the faculty of concepts; but the latter, because in it the Imagination is related to the Reason, the faculty of Ideas, only under a subjective presupposition (which, however, we believe we are authorised in imputing to every one), viz. the presupposition of the moral feeling [in man.[41]] Thus it is that we ascribe necessity to this aesthetical judgement also.

In this modality of aesthetical judgements, viz. in the necessity claimed for them, lies an important moment of the Critique of Judgement. For it enables us to recognise in them an *a priori* principle, and raises them out of empirical psychology, in which otherwise they would remain buried amongst the feelings of gratification and grief (only with the unmeaning addition of being called *finer* feelings). Thus it enables us too to place the Judgement among those faculties that have *a priori* principles at their basis, and so to bring it into Transcendental Philosophy.

GENERAL REMARK UPON THE EXPOSITION OF THE AESTHETICAL REFLECTIVE JUDGEMENT

In reference to the feeling of pleasure an object is to be classified as either *pleasant*, or *beautiful*, or *sublime*, or *good* (absolutely), (*jucundum, pulchrum, sublime, honestum*).

The *pleasant*, as motive of desire, is always of one and the same kind, no matter whence it comes and however specifically different the representation (of sense, and sensation objectively considered) may be. Hence in judging its influence on the mind, account is taken only of the number of its charms (simultaneous and successive), and so only of the mass, as it were, of the pleasant sensation; and this can be made intelligible only by *quantity*. It has no reference to culture, but belongs to mere enjoyment.—On the other hand, the *beautiful* requires the representation of a certain *quality* of the Object, that can be made intelligible and reduced to concepts (although it is not so reduced in an aesthetical judgement); and it cultivates us, in that it teaches us to attend to the purposiveness in the feeling of pleasure.—The *sublime* consists merely in the *relation* by which the sensible in the representation of nature is judged available for a possible supersensible use.—The *absolutely good*, subjectively judged according to the feeling that it inspires (the Object of the moral feeling), as capable of determining the powers of the subject through the representation of an *absolutely compelling* law, is specially distinguished by the *modality* of a necessity that rests *a priori* upon concepts. This necessity involves not merely a *claim*, but a *command* for the assent of every one, and belongs in itself to the pure intellectual, rather than to the aesthetical Judgement; and is by a determinant and not a mere reflective judgement ascribed not to Nature but to Freedom. But the *determinability of the subject* by means of this Idea, and especially of a subject that can feel *hindrances* in sensibility, and at the same time its superiority to them by their subjugation involving a *modification of its state*—*i.e.* the moral feeling,—is yet so far cognate to the aesthetical Judgement and its formal conditions that it can serve to represent the conformity to law of action from duty as aesthetical, *i.e.* as sublime or even as beautiful, without losing its purity. This would not be so, if we were to put it in natural combination with the feeling of the pleasant.

If we take the result of the foregoing exposition of the two kinds of aesthetical judgements, there arise therefrom the following short explanations:

The *Beautiful* is what pleases in the mere judgement (and therefore not by the medium of sensation in accordance with a concept of the Understanding). It follows at once from this that it must please apart from all interest.

The *Sublime* is what pleases immediately through its opposition to the interest of sense.

Both, as explanations of aesthetical universally valid judging, are referred to subjective grounds; in the one case to grounds of sensibility, in favour of the contemplative Understanding; in the other case *in opposition to* sensibility, but on behalf of the purposes of practical Reason. Both, however, united in the same subject, are purposive in reference to the moral feeling. The Beautiful prepares us to love disinterestedly something, even nature itself; the Sublime prepares us to esteem something highly even in opposition to our own (sensible) interest.

We may describe the Sublime thus: it is an object (of nature) the representation of which determines the mind to think the unattainability of nature regarded as a presentation of Ideas.

Literally taken and logically considered, Ideas cannot be presented. But if we extend our empirical representative faculty (mathematically or dynamically) to the intuition of nature, Reason inevitably intervenes, as the faculty expressing the independence of absolute totality,[42] and generates the effort of the mind, vain though it be, to make the representation of the senses adequate to this. This effort,—and the feeling of the unattainability of the Idea by means of the Imagination,—is itself a presentation of the subjective purposiveness of our mind in the employment of the Imagination for its supersensible destination; and forces us, subjectively, to *think* nature itself in its totality as a presentation of something supersensible, without being able *objectively* to arrive at this presentation.

For we soon see that nature in space and time entirely lacks the unconditioned, and, consequently, that absolute magnitude, which yet is desired by the most ordinary Reason. It is by this that we are reminded that we only have to do with nature as phenomenon, and that it must be regarded as the mere presentation of a nature in itself (of which Reason has the Idea). But this Idea of the supersensible, which we can no further determine,—so that we cannot *know* but only *think* nature as its presentation,—is awakened in us by means of an object, whose aesthetical appreciation strains the Imagination to its utmost bounds, whether of extension (mathematical) or of its might over the mind (dynamical). And this judgement is based upon a feeling of the mind's destination, which entirely surpasses the realm of the former (*i.e.* upon the moral feeling), in respect of which the representation of the object is judged as subjectively purposive.

In fact, a feeling for the Sublime in nature cannot well be thought without combining therewith a mental disposition which is akin to the Moral. And although the immediate pleasure in the Beautiful of nature likewise presupposes and cultivates a certain *liber-*

ality in our mental attitude, *i.e.* a satisfaction independent of mere sensible enjoyment, yet freedom is thus represented as in *play* rather than in that law-directed *occupation* which is the genuine characteristic of human morality, in which Reason must exercise dominion over Sensibility. But in aesthetical judgements upon the Sublime this dominion is represented as exercised by the Imagination, regarded as an instrument of Reason.

The satisfaction in the Sublime of nature is then only *negative* (whilst that in the Beautiful is *positive*); viz. a feeling that the Imagination is depriving itself of its freedom, while it is purposively determined according to a different law from that of its empirical employment. It thus acquires an extension and a might greater than it sacrifices,—the ground of which, however, is concealed from itself; whilst yet it *feels* the sacrifice or the deprivation and, at the same time, the cause to which it is subjected. *Astonishment*, that borders upon terror, the dread and the holy awe which seizes the observer at the sight of mountain peaks rearing themselves to heaven, deep chasms and streams raging therein, deep-shadowed solitudes that dispose one to melancholy meditations—this, in the safety in which we know ourselves to be, is not actual fear, but only an attempt to feel fear by the aid of the Imagination; that we may feel the might of this faculty in combining with the mind's repose the mental movement thereby excited, and being thus superior to internal nature,—and therefore to external,—so far as this can have any influence on our feeling of well-being. For the Imagination by the laws of Association makes our state of contentment dependent on physical [causes]; but it also, by the principles of the Schematism of the Judgement (being so far, therefore, ranked under freedom), is the instrument of Reason and its Ideas, and, as such, has might to maintain our independence of natural influences, to regard as small what in reference to them is great, and so to place the absolutely great only in the proper destination of the subject. The raising of this reflection of the aesthetical Judgement so as to be adequate to Reason (though without a definite concept of Reason) represents the object as subjectively purposive, even by the objective want of accordance between the Imagination in its greatest extension and the Reason (as the faculty of Ideas).

We must here, generally, attend to what has been already noted, that in the Transcendental Aesthetic of Judgement we must speak solely of pure aesthetical judgements; consequently our examples are not to be taken from such beautiful or sublime objects of Nature as presuppose the concept of a purpose. For, if so, the purposiveness would be either teleological, or would be based on mere sensations of an object (gratification or grief); and thus would be in the former case not aesthetical, in the latter not merely formal. If then we call the sight of the starry heaven *sublime*, we must not place at the basis of our judgement concepts of worlds inhabited by rational beings, and regard the bright points, with which we see the space above us filled, as their suns moving in circles purposively fixed with reference to them; but we must regard it, just as we see it, as a distant, all-embracing vault. Only under such a representation can we range that sublimity which a pure aesthetical judgement ascribes to this object. And in the same way, if we are to call the sight of the ocean sublime, we must not *think* of it as we [ordinarily] do, endowed as we are with all kinds of knowledge (not contained, however, in the immediate intuition). For example, we sometimes think of the ocean as a vast kingdom of aquatic creatures; or as the great source of those vapours that fill the air with clouds for the benefit of the land; or again as an element which, though dividing continents from each other, yet promotes the greatest communication between them: but these furnish merely teleological judgements. To call the ocean sublime we must regard it as poets do, merely by what strikes the eye; if it is at rest, as a clear mirror of water only bounded by the heaven; if it is restless, as an abyss threatening to overwhelm everything. The like is to be said of the Sublime and Beautiful in the human figure. We must not regard as the determining grounds of our judgement the concepts of the purposes which all our limbs serve, and we must not allow this coincidence to *influence* our aesthetical judgement (for then it would no longer be pure); although it is certainly a necessary condition of aesthetical satisfaction that there should be no conflict between them. Aesthetical purposiveness is the conformity to law of the Judgement in its *freedom*. The satisfaction in the object depends on the relation in which we wish to place the Imagination; always provided that it by itself entertains the mind in free occupation. If, on the other hand, the judgement be determined by anything else,—whether sensation or concept,—although it may be conformable to law, it cannot be the act of a *free* Judgement.

If then we speak of intellectual beauty or sublimity, these expressions are, *first*, not quite accurate, because beauty and sublimity are aesthetical modes of representation, which would not be found in us at all if we were pure intelligences (or even regarded ourselves as such in thought). *Secondly*, although both, as objects of an intellectual (moral) satisfaction, are so far compatible with aesthetical satisfaction that they *rest* upon no interest, yet they are difficult to unite with it, because they are meant to *produce* an interest. This, if its presentation is to harmonise with the satisfaction in the aesthetical judgement, could only arise by means of a sensible interest that we combine with it in the presentation; and thus damage would be done to the intellectual purposiveness, and it would lose its purity.

The object of a pure and unconditioned intellectual satisfaction is the Moral Law in that might which it exercises in us over all mental motives *that precede it*. This might only makes itself aesthetically known to us through sacrifices (which causing a feeling of deprivation, though on behalf of internal freedom, in return discloses in us an unfathomable depth of this supersensible faculty, with consequences extending beyond our ken); thus the satisfaction on the aesthetical side (in relation to sensibility) is negative, *i.e.* against this interest, but regarded from the intellectual side it is positive and combined with an interest. Hence it follows that the intellectual, in itself purposive, (moral) good, aesthetically judged, must be represented as sublime rather than beautiful, so that it rather awakens the feeling of respect (which disdains charm) than that of love and familiar inclination; for human nature does not attach itself to this good spontaneously, but only by the authority which Reason exercises over Sensibility. Conversely also, that which we call sublime in nature, whether external or internal (*e.g.* certain affections), is only represented as a might in the mind to overcome [*certain*][43] hindrances of the Sensibility by means of moral fundamental propositions, and only thus does it interest.

I will dwell a moment on this latter point. The Idea of the Good conjoined with affection is called *enthusiasm*. This state of mind seems to be sublime, to the extent that we commonly assert that nothing great could be done without it. Now every affection[44] is blind, either in the choice of its purpose, or, if this be supplied by Reason, in its accomplishment; for it is a mental movement which makes it impossible to exercise a free deliberation about fundamental propositions so as to determine ourselves thereby. It can therefore in no way deserve the approval of the Reason. Nevertheless, aesthetically, enthusiasm is sublime, because it is a tension of forces produced by Ideas, which give an impulse to the mind, that operates far more powerfully and lastingly than the impulse arising from sensible representations. But (which seems strange) the *absence of affection* (*apatheia, phlegma in significatu bono*) in a mind that vigorously follows its unalterable principles is sublime, and in a far preferable way, because it has also on its side the satisfaction of pure Reason.[45] It is only a mental state of this kind that is called noble; and this expression is subsequently applied to things, *e.g.* a building, a garment, literary style, bodily presence, etc., when these do not so much arouse *astonishment* (the affection produced by the representation of novelty exceeding our expectations), as *admiration* (astonishment that does not cease when the novelty disappears); and this is the case when Ideas agree in their presentation undesignedly and artlessly with the aesthetical satisfaction.

Every affection of the STRENUOUS kind (viz. that excites the consciousness of our power to overcome every obstacle—*animi strenui*) is *aesthetically sublime, e.g.* wrath, even despair (*i.e.* the despair of *indignation*, not of *faintheartedness*). But affections of the LANGUID kind (which make the very effort of resistance an object of pain—*animum languidum*) have nothing *noble* in themselves, but they may be reckoned under the sensuously beautiful. *Emotions*, which may rise to the strength of affections, are very different. We have both *spirited* and *tender* emotions. The latter, if they rise to the height of affections, are worthless; the propensity to them is called *sentimentality*. A sympathetic grief that will not admit of consolation, or one referring to imaginary evils to which we deliberately surrender ourselves—being deceived by fancy—as if they were actual, indicates and produces a tender,[46] though weak, soul—which shows a beautiful side and which can be called fanciful, though not enthusiastic. Romances, lacrymose plays, shallow moral precepts, which toy with (falsely) so-called moral dispositions, but in fact make the heart languid, insensible to the severe precept of duty, and incapable of all respect for the worth of humanity in our own person, and for the rights of men (a very different thing from their happiness), and in general incapable of all steady principle; even a religious discourse,[47] which recommends a cringing, abject seeking of favour and ingratiation of ourselves, which proposes the abandonment of all confidence in our own faculties in opposition to the evil within us, instead of a sturdy resolution to endeavour to overcome our inclinations by means of those powers which with all our frailty yet remain to us; that false humility which sets the only way of pleasing the Supreme Being in self-depreciation, in whining hypocritical repentance and in a mere passive state of mind—these are not compatible with any frame of mind that can be counted beautiful, still less with one which is to be counted sublime.

But even stormy movements of mind which may be connected under the name of edification with Ideas of religion, or—as merely belonging to culture—with Ideas containing a social interest, can in no way, however they strain the Imagination, lay claim to the honour of being *sublime* presentations, unless they leave after them a mental mood which, although only indirectly, has influence upon the mind's consciousness of its strength, and its resolution in reference to that which involves pure intellectual purposiveness (the supersensible). For otherwise all these emotions belong only to *motion*, which one would fain enjoy for the sake of health. The pleasant exhaustion, consequent upon such disturbance produced by the play of the affections, is an enjoyment of our well-being arising from the restored equilibrium of the various vital forces. This in the end amounts to the same thing as that state which Eastern voluptuaries find so delightful, when they get their bodies as it were kneaded and all their muscles and joints softly pressed and bent; only that in this case the motive principle is for the most part external, in the other case it is altogether internal. Many a man believes himself to be edified by a sermon, when indeed there is no edification at all (no system of good maxims); or to be improved by a tragedy, when he is only glad at his ennui being happily dispelled. So the Sublime must always have reference to the *disposition,* i.e. to the maxims which furnish to the intellectual [part] and to the Ideas of Reason a superiority over sensibility.

We need not fear that the feeling of the sublime will lose by so abstract a mode of presentation,—which is quite negative in respect of what is sensible,—for the Imagination, although it finds nothing beyond the sensible to which it can attach itself, yet feels itself unbounded by this removal of its limitations; and thus that very abstraction is a presentation of the Infinite, which can be nothing but a mere negative presentation, but which yet expands the soul. Perhaps there is no sublimer passage in the Jewish Law than the command, *Thou shalt not make to thyself any graven image, nor the likeness of anything which is in heaven or on the earth or under the earth,* etc. This command alone can explain the enthusiasm that the Jewish people in their moral period felt for their religion, when they compared themselves with other peoples; or explain the pride which Mahommedanism inspires. The same is true of the moral law and of the tendency to morality in us. It is quite erroneous to fear that if we deprive this [tendency] of all that can recommend it to sense it will only involve a cold lifeless assent and no moving force or emotion. It is quite the other way, for where the senses see nothing more before them, and the unmistakable and indelible Idea of morality remains, it would be rather necessary to moderate the impetus of an unbounded Imagination, to prevent it from rising to enthusiasm, than through fear of the powerlessness of these Ideas to seek aid for them in images and childish ritual. Thus governments have willingly allowed religion to be abundantly provided with the latter accessories; and seeking thereby to relieve their subjects of trouble, they have also sought to deprive them of the faculty of extending their spiritual powers beyond the limits that are arbitrarily assigned to them, and by means of which they can be the more easily treated as mere passive[48] beings.

This pure, elevating, merely negative presentation of morality brings with it, on the other hand, no danger of *fanaticism,* which is *a delusion that we can will ourselves to see something beyond all bounds of sensibility,* i.e. to dream in accordance with fundamental propositions (or to go mad with Reason); and this is so just because this presentation is merely negative. For the *inscrutableness of the Idea of Freedom* quite cuts it off from any positive presentation; but the moral law is in itself sufficiently and originally determinant in us, so that it does not permit us to cast a glance at any ground of determination external to itself. If enthusiasm is comparable to *madness,* fanaticism is comparable to *monomania;* of which the latter is least of all compatible with the sublime, because in its detail it is ridiculous. In enthusiasm, regarded as an affection, the Imagination is without bridle; in fanaticism, regarded as an inveterate, brooding passion, it is without rule. The first is a transitory accident which sometimes befalls the soundest Understanding; the second is a disease which unsettles it.

Simplicity (purposiveness without art) is as it were the style of Nature in the sublime, and so also of Morality which is a second (supersensible) nature; of which we only know the laws without being able to reach by intuition that supersensible faculty in ourselves which contains the ground of the legislation.

Now the satisfaction in the Beautiful, like that in the Sublime, is not alone distinguishable from other aesthetical judgements by its universal *communicability*, but also because, through this very property, it acquires an interest in reference to society (in which this communication is possible). We must, however, remark that *separation from all society* is regarded as sublime, if it rests upon Ideas that overlook all sensible interest. To be sufficient for oneself, and consequently to have no need of society, without at the same time being unsociable, *i.e.* without flying from it, is something bordering on the sublime; as is any dispensing with wants. On the other hand, to fly from men from *misanthropy*, because we bear ill-will to them, or from *anthropophoby* (shyness), because we fear them as foes, is partly hateful, partly contemptible. There is indeed a misanthropy (very improperly so-called), the tendency to which frequently appears with old age in many right-thinking men; which is philanthropic enough as far as *goodwill* to men is concerned, but which through long and sad experience is far removed from *satisfaction* with men. Evidence of this is afforded by the propensity to solitude, the fantastic wish for a secluded country seat, or (in the case of young persons) by the dream of the happiness of passing one's life with a little family upon some island unknown to the rest of the world; a dream of which story-tellers or writers of Robinsonades know how to make good use. Falsehood, ingratitude, injustice, the childishness of the purposes regarded by ourselves as important and great, in the pursuit of which men inflict upon each other all imaginable evils, are so contradictory to the Idea of what men might be if they would, and conflict so with our lively wish to see them better, that, in order that we may not hate them (since we cannot love them), the renunciation of all social joys seems but a small sacrifice. This sadness—not the sadness (of which sympathy is the cause) for the evils which fate brings upon others,—but for those things which men do to one another (which depends upon an antipathy in fundamental propositions), is sublime, because it rests upon Ideas, whilst the former can only count as beautiful.—The brilliant and thorough *Saussure*,[49] in his account of his Alpine travels, says of one of the Savoy mountains, called *Bonhomme*, "There reigns there a certain *insipid sadness*." He therefore recognised an *interesting* sadness, that the sight of a solitude might inspire, to which men might wish to transport themselves that they might neither hear nor experience any more of the world; which, however, would not be quite so inhospitable that it would offer only an extremely painful retreat.—I make this remark solely with the design of indicating again that even depression (not dejected sadness) may be counted among the *sturdy* affections, if it has its ground in moral Ideas. But if it is grounded on sympathy and, as such, is amiable, it belongs merely to the *languid* affections. [I make this remark] to call attention to the state of mind which is *sublime* only in the first case.

––––––

WE CAN NOW COMPARE the above Transcendental Exposition of aesthetical judgements with the Physiological worked out by *Burke* and by many clear-headed men among us, in order to see whither a merely empirical exposition of the Sublime and Beautiful leads. *Burke*, who deserves to be regarded as the most important author who adopts this mode of treatment, infers by this method "that the feeling of the Sublime rests on the impulse towards self-preservation and on *fear*, *i.e.* on a pain, which not going so far as actually to derange the parts of the body, produces movements which, since they purify the finer or grosser vessels of dangerous or troublesome stoppages, are capable of exciting pleasant sensations; not indeed pleasure, but a kind of satisfying horror, a certain tranquillity tinged with terror."[50] The Beautiful, which he founded on love (which he wishes to keep quite separate from desire), he reduces to "the relaxing, slackening, and enervating of the fibres of the body, and a consequent weakening, languor, and exhaustion, a fainting, dissolving, and melting away for enjoyment."[51] And he confirms this explanation not only by cases in which the Imagination in combination with the Understanding can excite in us the feeling of the Beautiful or of the Sublime, but by cases in which it is combined with sensation.—As psychological observations, these analyses of the phenomena of our mind are exceedingly beautiful, and afford rich material for the favourite investigations of empirical anthropology. It is also not to be denied that all representations in us, whether, objectively viewed, they are merely sensible or are quite intellectual, may yet subjectively be united to gratification or grief, however imperceptible either may be; because they all affect the feeling of life, and none of them, so far as it is a modification of the subject, can be indifferent. And so, as Epicurus maintained, all *gratification* or *grief* may ultimately be corporeal, whether it arises from the representations of the Imagination or the Understanding; because life without a feeling of bodily organs would be merely a consciousness of existence, without any feeling of well-being or the reverse, *i.e.* of the furthering or the checking of the vital powers. For the mind is by itself alone life (the principle of life), and hindrances or furtherances must be sought outside it and yet in the man, consequently in union with his body.

If, however, we place the satisfaction in the object altogether in the fact that it gratifies us by charm or emotion, we must not assume that any *other* man agrees with the aesthetical judgement which *we* pass; for as to these each one rightly consults his own individual sensibility. But in that case all censorship of taste would disappear, except indeed the example afforded by the accidental agreement of others in their judgements were regarded as *commanding* our assent; and this principle we should probably resist, and should appeal to the natural right of subjecting the judgement, which rests on the immediate feeling of our own well-being, to our own sense and not to that of any other man.

If then the judgement of taste is not to be valid merely *egoistically*, but according to its inner nature,—*i.e.* on account of itself and not on account of the examples that others give of their taste,—to be necessarily valid *pluralistically*, if we regard it as a judgement which may exact the adhesion of every one; then there must lie at its basis some *a priori* principle (whether objective or subjective) to which we can never attain by seeking out the empirical laws of mental changes. For these only enable us to know how we judge, but do not prescribe to us how we ought to judge. They do not supply an *unconditioned* command,[52] such as judgements of taste presuppose, inasmuch as they require that the satisfaction be *immediately* connected with the representation. Thus the empirical exposition of aesthetical judgements may be a beginning of a collection of materials for a higher investigation; but a transcendental discussion of this faculty is also possible, and is an essential part of the Critique of Taste. For if it had not *a priori* principles, it could not possibly pass sentence on the judgements of others, and it could not approve or blame them with any appearance of right.

The remaining part of the Analytic of the Aesthetical Judgement contains first the

DEDUCTION OF PURE AESTHETICAL JUDGEMENTS

§ 30. THE DEDUCTION OF AESTHETICAL JUDGEMENTS ON THE OBJECTS OF NATURE MUST NOT BE DIRECTED TO WHAT WE CALL SUBLIME IN NATURE, BUT ONLY TO THE BEAUTIFUL.

The claim of an aesthetical judgement to universal validity for every subject requires, as a judgement resting on some *a priori* principle, a Deduction (or legitimatising of its pretensions) in addition to its Exposition; if it is concerned with satisfaction or dissatisfaction in the *form of the Object*. Of this kind are judgements of taste about the Beautiful in Nature. For in that case the purposiveness has its ground in the Object and in its figure, although it does not indicate the reference of this to other objects according to concepts (for a cognitive judgement), but merely has to do in general with the apprehension of this form, so far as it shows itself conformable in the mind to the *faculty* of concepts and to that of their presentation (which is identical with that of apprehension). We can thus, in respect of the Beautiful in nature, suggest many questions touching the cause of this purposiveness of their forms, *e.g.* to explain why nature has scattered abroad beauty with such profusion, even in the depth of the ocean, where the human eye (for which alone that purposiveness exists) but seldom penetrates.

But the Sublime in nature—if we are passing upon it a pure aesthetical judgement, not mixed up with any concepts of perfection or objective purposiveness, in which case it would be a teleological judgement—may be regarded as quite formless or devoid of figure, and yet as the object of a pure satisfaction; and it may display a subjective purposiveness in the given representation. And we ask if, for an aesthetical judgement of this kind,—over and above the Exposition of what is thought in it,—a Deduction also of its claim to any (subjective) *a priori* principle may be demanded?

To which we may answer that the Sublime in nature is improperly so called, and that properly speaking the word should only be applied to a state of mind, or rather to its foundation in human nature. The apprehension of an otherwise formless and unpurposive object gives merely the occasion, through which we become conscious of such a state; the object is thus *employed* as subjectively purposive, but is not judged as such *in itself* and on account of its form (it is, as it were, a *species finalis accepta, non data*). Hence our Exposition of judgements concerning the Sublime in nature was at the same time their Deduction. For when we analysed the reflection of the Judgement in such acts, we found in them a purposive relation of the cognitive faculties, which must be ascribed ultimately to the faculty of purposes (the will), and hence is itself purposive *a priori*. This then immediately involves the Deduction, *i.e.* the justification of the claim of such a judgement to universal and necessary validity.

We shall therefore only have to seek for the deduction of judgements of Taste, *i.e.* of judgements about the Beauty of natural things; we shall thus treat satisfactorily the problem with which the whole faculty of aesthetical Judgement is concerned.

§ 31. OF THE METHOD OF DEDUCTION OF JUDGEMENTS OF TASTE

A Deduction, *i.e.* the guarantee of the legitimacy of a class of judgements, is only obligatory if the judgement lays claim to necessity. This it does, if it demands even subjective universality or the agreement of every one, although it is not a judgement of cognition but only one of pleasure or pain in a given object; *i.e.* it assumes a subjective purposiveness thoroughly valid for every one, which must not be based on any concept of the thing, because the judgement is one of taste.

We have before us in the latter case no cognitive judgement—neither a theoretical one based on the concept of a *Nature* in general formed by the Understanding, nor a (pure) practical one based on the Idea of *Freedom*, as given *a priori* by Reason. Therefore we have to justify *a priori* the validity neither of a judgement which represents what a thing is, nor of one which prescribes that I ought to do something in order to produce it. We have merely to prove for the Judgement generally the *universal validity* of a singular judgement that expresses the subjective purposiveness of an empirical representation of the form of an object; in order to explain how it is possible that a thing can please in the mere act of judging it (without sensation or concept), and how the satisfaction of one man can be proclaimed as a rule for every other; just as the act of judging of an object for the sake of a *cognition* in general has universal rules.

If now this universal validity is not to be based on any collecting of the suffrages of others, or on any questioning of them as to the kind of sensations they have, but is to rest, as it were, on an autonomy of the judging subject in respect of the feeling of pleasure (in the given representation), *i.e.* on his own taste, and yet is not to be derived from concepts; then a judgement like this—such as the judgement of taste is, in fact—has a twofold logical peculiarity. *First*, there is its *a priori* universal validity, which is not a logical universality in accordance with concepts, but the universality of a singular judgement. *Secondly*, it has a necessity (which must always rest on *a priori* grounds), which however does not depend on any *a priori* grounds of proof, through the representation of which the assent that every one concedes to the judgement of taste could be exacted.

The solution of these logical peculiarities, wherein a judgement of taste is different from all cognitive judgements—if we at the outset abstract from all content, viz. from the feeling of pleasure, and merely compare the aesthetical form with the form of objective judgements as logic prescribes it—is sufficient by itself for the deduction of this singular faculty. We shall then represent and elucidate by examples these characteristic properties of taste.

§ 32. FIRST PECULIARITY OF THE JUDGEMENT OF TASTE

The judgement of taste determines its object in respect of satisfaction (in its beauty) with an accompanying claim for the assent of *every one*, just as if it were objective.

To say that "this flower is beautiful" is the same as to assert its proper claim to satisfy every one. By the pleasantness of its smell it has no such claim. A smell which one man enjoys gives another a headache. Now what are we to presume from this except that beauty is to be regarded as a property of the flower itself, which does not accommodate itself to any diversity of persons or of their sensitive organs, but to which these must accommodate themselves if they are to pass any judgement upon it? And yet this is not so. For a judgement of taste consists in calling a thing beautiful just because of that characteristic in respect of which it accommodates itself to our mode of apprehension.

Moreover, it is required of every judgement which is to prove the taste of the subject, that the subject shall judge by himself, without needing to grope about empirically among the judgements of others, and acquaint himself previously as to their satisfaction or dissatisfaction with the same object; thus his judgement should be pronounced *a priori*, and not be a mere imitation because the thing actually gives universal pleasure. One would think, however, that an *a priori* judgement must contain a concept of the Object, for the cognition of which it contains the principle; but the judgement of taste is not based upon concepts at all, and is in general not a cognitive but an aesthetical judgement.

Thus a young poet does not permit himself to be dissuaded from his conviction that his poem is beautiful, by the judgement of the public or of his friends; and if he gives ear to them he does so, not because he now judges differently, but because, although (in regard to him) the whole public has false taste, in his desire for applause he finds reason for accommodating himself to the common error (even against his judgement). It is only at a later time, when his Judgement has been sharpened by exercise, that he voluntarily departs from his former judgements; just as he proceeds with those of his judgements which rest upon Reason. Taste [merely]⁵³ claims autonomy. To make the judgements of others the determining grounds of his own would be heteronomy.

That we, and rightly, recommend the works of the ancients as models and call their authors classical, thus forming among writers a kind of noble class who give laws to the people by their example, seems to indicate *a posteriori* sources of taste, and to contradict the autonomy of taste in every subject. But we might just as well say that the old mathematicians,—who are regarded up to the present day as supplying models not easily to be dispensed with for the supreme profundity and elegance of their synthetical methods,—prove that our Reason is only imitative, and that we have not the faculty of producing from it in combination with intuition rigid proofs by means of the construction of concepts.⁵⁴ There is no use of our powers, however free, no use of Reason itself (which must create all its judgements *a priori* from common sources) which would not give rise to faulty attempts, if every subject had always to begin anew from the rude basis of his natural state, and if others had not preceded him with their attempts. Not that these make mere imitators of those who come after them, but rather by their procedure they put others on the track of seeking in themselves principles and so of pursuing their own course, often a better one. Even in religion—where certainly every one has to derive the rule of his conduct from himself, because he remains responsible for it and cannot shift the blame of his transgressions upon others, whether his teachers or his predecessors—there is never as much accomplished by means of universal precepts, either obtained from priests or philosophers or got from oneself, as by means of an example of virtue or holiness which, exhibited in history, does not dispense with the autonomy of virtue based on the proper and original Idea of morality (*a priori*), or change it into a mechanical imitation. *Following*, involving something precedent, not "imitation," is the right expression for all influence that the products of an exemplary author may have upon others. And this only means that we draw from the same sources as our predecessor did, and learn from him only the way to avail ourselves of them. But of all faculties and talents Taste, because its judgement is not determinable by concepts and precepts, is just that one which most needs examples of what has in the progress of culture received the longest approval; that it may not become again uncivilised and return to the crudeness of its first essays.

§ 33. SECOND PECULIARITY OF THE JUDGEMENT OF TASTE

The judgement of taste is not determinable by grounds of proof, just as if it were merely *subjective*.

If a man, *in the first place*, does not find a building, a prospect, or a poem beautiful, a hundred voices all highly praising it will not force his inmost agreement. He may indeed feign that it pleases him in order that he may not be regarded as devoid of taste; he may even begin to doubt whether he has formed his taste on a knowledge of a sufficient number of objects of a certain kind (just as one, who believes that he recognises in the distance as a forest, something which all others regard as a town, doubts the judgement of his own sight). But he clearly sees that the agreement of others gives no valid proof of the judgement about beauty. Others might perhaps see and observe for him; and what many have seen in one way, although he believes that he has seen it differently, might serve him as an adequate ground of proof of a theoretical and consequently logical judgement. But that a thing has pleased others could never serve as the basis of an aesthetical judgement. A judgement of others which is unfavourable to ours may indeed rightly make us scrutinise our own with care, but it can never convince us of its incorrectness. There is therefore no empirical *ground of proof* which would force a judgement of taste upon any one.

Still less, *in the second place*, can an *a priori* proof determine according to definite rules a judgement about beauty. If a man reads me a poem of his or brings me to a play, which does not after all suit my taste, he may bring forward in proof of the beauty of his poem Batteux[55] or *Lessing* or still more ancient and famous critics of taste, and all the rules laid down by them; certain passages which displease me may agree very well with rules of beauty (as they have been put forth by these writers and are universally recognised): but I stop my ears, I will listen to no arguments and no reasoning; and I will rather assume that these rules of the critics are false, or at least that they do not apply to the case in question, than admit that my judgement should be determined by grounds of proof *a priori*. For it is to be a judgement of Taste and not of Understanding or Reason.

It seems that this is one of the chief reasons why this aesthetical faculty of judgement has been given the name of Taste. For though a man enumerate to me all the ingredients of a dish, and remark that each is separately pleasant to me and further extol with justice the wholesomeness of this particular food—yet am I deaf to all these reasons; I try the dish with *my* tongue and my palate, and thereafter (and not according to universal principles) do I pass my judgement.

In fact the judgement of Taste always takes the form of a singular judgement about an Object. The Understanding can form a universal judgement by comparing the Object in point of the satisfaction it affords with the judgement of others upon it: *e.g.* "all tulips are beautiful." But then this is not a judgement of taste but a logical judgement, which takes the relation of an Object to taste as the predicate of things of a certain species. That judgement, however, in which I find an individual given tulip beautiful, *i.e.* in which I find my satisfaction in it to be universally valid, is alone a judgement of taste. Its peculiarity consists in the fact that, although it has merely subjective validity, it claims the assent of *all* subjects, exactly as it would do if it were an objective judgement resting on grounds of knowledge, that could be established by a proof.

§ 34. *THERE IS NO OBJECTIVE PRINCIPLE OF TASTE POSSIBLE*

By a principle of taste I mean a principle under the condition of which we could subsume the concept of an object and thus infer by means of a syllogism that the object is beautiful. But that is absolutely impossible. For I must feel the pleasure immediately in the representation of the object, and of that I can be persuaded by no grounds of proof whatever. Although, as *Hume* says,[56] all critics can reason more plausibly than cooks, yet the same fate awaits them. They cannot expect the determining ground of their judgement [to be derived] from the force of the proofs, but only from the reflection of the subject upon its own proper state (of pleasure or pain), all precepts and rules being rejected.

But although critics can and ought to pursue their reasonings so that our judgements of taste may be corrected and extended, it is not with a view to set forth the determining ground of this kind of aesthetical judgements in a universally applicable formula, which is impossible; but rather to investigate the cognitive faculties and their exercise in these judgements, and to explain by examples the reciprocal subjective purposiveness, the form of which, as has been shown above, in a given representation, constitutes the beauty of the object. Therefore the Critique of Taste is only subjective as regards the representation through which an Object is given to us; viz. it is the art or science of reducing to rules the reciprocal relation between the Understanding and the Imagination in the given representation (without reference to any preceding sensation or concept). That is, it is the art or science of reducing to rules their accordance or discordance, and of determining them with regard to their conditions. It is an *art*, if it only shows this by examples; it is a *science* if it derives the possibility of such judgements from the nature of these faculties, as cognitive faculties in general. We have here, in Transcendental Criticism, only to do with the latter. It should develop and justify the subjective principle of taste, as an *a priori* principle of the Judgement. This Critique, as an art, merely seeks to apply, in the judging of objects, the physiological (here psychological), and therefore empirical rules, according to which taste actually proceeds (without taking any account of their possibility); and it criticises the products of beautiful art just as, regarded as a science, it criticises the faculty by which they are judged.

§ 35. THE PRINCIPLE OF TASTE IS THE SUBJECTIVE PRINCIPLE OF JUDGEMENT IN GENERAL

The judgement of taste is distinguished from a logical judgement in this, that the latter subsumes a representation under the concept of the Object, while the former does not subsume it under any concept; because otherwise the necessary universal agreement [in these judgements] would be capable of being enforced by proofs. Nevertheless it is like the latter in this, that it claims universality and necessity, though not according to concepts of the Object, and consequently a merely subjective necessity. Now, because the concepts in a judgement constitute its content (what belongs to the cognition of the Object), but the judgement of taste is not determinable by concepts, it is based only on the subjective formal condition of a judgement in general. The subjective condition of all judgements is the faculty of Judgement itself. This when used with reference to a representation by which an object is given, requires the accordance of two representative powers: viz. Imagination (for the intuition and comprehension of the manifold) and Understanding (for the concept as a representation of the unity of this comprehension). Now because no concept of the Object lies here at the basis of the judgement, it can only consist in the subsumption of the Imagination itself (in the case of a representation by which an object is given) under the conditions that the Understanding requires to pass from intuition to concepts. That is, because the freedom of the Imagination consists in the fact that it schematises without any concept, the judgement of taste must rest on a mere sensation of the reciprocal activity of the Imagination in its *freedom* and the Understanding with its *conformity to law*. It must therefore rest on a feeling, which makes us judge the object by the purposiveness of the representation (by which an object is given) in respect of the furtherance of the cognitive faculty in its free play. Taste, then, as subjective Judgement, contains a principle of subsumption, not of intuitions under concepts, but of the *faculty* of intuitions or presentations (*i.e.* the Imagination) under the *faculty* of the concepts (*i.e.* the Understanding); so far as the former *in its freedom* harmonises with the latter *in its conformity to law*.

In order to discover this ground of legitimacy by a Deduction of the judgements of taste we can only take as a clue the formal peculiarities of this kind of judgements, and consequently can only consider their logical form.

§ 36. OF THE PROBLEM OF A DEDUCTION OF JUDGEMENTS OF TASTE

The concept of an Object in general can immediately be combined with the perception of an object, containing its empirical predicates, so as to form a cognitive judgement; and it is thus that a judgement of experience is produced.[57] At the basis of this lie *a priori* concepts of the synthetical unity of the manifold of intuition, by which the manifold is thought as the determination of an Object. These concepts (the Categories) require a Deduction, which is given in the Critique of pure Reason; and by it we can get the solution of the problem, how are synthetical *a priori* cognitive judgements possible? This problem concerns then the *a priori* principles of the pure Understanding and its theoretical judgements.

But with a perception there can also be combined a feeling of pleasure (or pain) and a satisfaction, that accompanies the representation of the Object and serves instead of its predicate; thus there can result an aesthetical non-cognitive judgement. At the basis of such a judgement—if it is not a mere judgement of sensation but a formal judgement of reflection, which imputes the same satisfaction necessarily to every one,—must lie some *a priori* principle; which may be merely subjective (if an objective one should prove impossible for judgements of this kind), but also as such may need a Deduction, that we may thereby comprehend how an aesthetical judgement can lay claim to necessity. On this is founded the problem with which we are now occupied, how are judgements of taste possible? This problem then has to do with the *a priori* principles of the pure faculty of Judgement in *aesthetical* judgements; *i.e.* judgements in which it has not (as in theoretical ones) merely to subsume under objective concepts of Understanding, and in which it is subject to a law, but in which it is, itself, subjectively, both object and law.

This problem then may be thus represented: how is a judgement possible, in which merely from *our own* feeling of pleasure in an object, independently of its concept, we judge that this pleasure attaches to the representation of the same Object *in every other subject*, and that *a priori* without waiting for the accordance of others?

It is easy to see that judgements of taste are synthetical, because they go beyond the concept and even beyond the intuition of the Object, and add to that intuition as predicate something that is not a cognition, viz. a feeling of pleasure (or pain). Although the predicate (of the *personal* pleasure bound up with the representation) is empirical, nevertheless, as concerns the required assent of *every one* the judgements are *a priori*, or desire to be regarded as such; and this is already involved in the expressions of this claim. Thus this problem of the Critique of Judgement belongs to the general problem of transcendental philosophy, how are synthetical *a priori* judgements possible?

§ 37. WHAT IS PROPERLY ASSERTED A PRIORI OF AN OBJECT IN A JUDGEMENT OF TASTE

That the representation of an object is immediately bound up with pleasure can only be internally perceived, and if we did not wish to indicate anything more than this it would give a merely empirical judgement. For I cannot combine a definite feeling (of pleasure or pain) with any representation except where there is at bottom an *a priori* principle in the Reason determining the Will. In that case the pleasure (in the moral feeling) is the consequence of the principle, but cannot be compared with the pleasure in taste, because it requires a definite concept of a law; and the latter pleasure, on the contrary, must be bound up with the mere act of judging, prior to all concepts. Hence also all judgements of taste are singular judgements, because they do not combine their predicate of satisfaction with a concept, but with a given individual empirical representation.

And so it is not the pleasure, but the *universal validity of this pleasure*, perceived as mentally bound up with the mere judgement upon an object, which is represented *a priori* in a judgement of taste as a universal rule for the Judgement and valid for every one. It is an empirical judgement [to say] that I perceive and judge an object with pleasure. But it is an *a priori* judgement [to say] that I find it beautiful, *i.e.* I attribute this satisfaction necessarily to every one.

§ 38. DEDUCTION OF JUDGEMENTS OF TASTE

If it be admitted that in a pure judgement of taste the satisfaction in the object is combined with the mere act of judging its form, it is nothing else than its subjective purposiveness for the Judgement which we feel to be mentally combined with the representation of the object. The Judgement, as regards the formal rules of its action, apart from all matter (whether sensation or concept), can only be directed to the subjective conditions of its employment in general (it is applied[58] neither to a particular mode of sense nor to a particular concept of the Understanding); and consequently to that subjective [element] which we can presuppose in all men (as requisite for possible cognition in general). Thus the agreement of a representation with these conditions of the Judgement must be capable of being assumed as valid *a priori* for every one. *I.e.* we may rightly impute to every one the pleasure or the subjective purposiveness of the representation for the relation between the cognitive faculties in the act of judging a sensible object in general.[59]

Remark

This Deduction is thus easy, because it has no need to justify the objective reality of any concept, for Beauty is not a concept of the Object and the judgement of taste is not cognitive. It only maintains that we are justified in presupposing universally in every man those subjective conditions of the Judgement which we find in ourselves; and further, that we have rightly subsumed the given Object under these conditions. The latter has indeed unavoidable difficulties which do not beset the logical Judgement. There we subsume under concepts, but in the aesthetical Judgement under a merely sensible relation between the Imagination and Understanding mutually harmonising in the representation of the form of the Object,—in which case the subsumption may easily be fallacious. Yet the legitimacy of the claim of the Judgement in counting upon universal assent is not thus annulled; it reduces itself merely to the correctness of the principle of judging validly for every one from subjective grounds. For as to the difficulty or doubt concerning the correctness of the subsumption under that principle, it makes the legitimacy of the claim of an aesthetical judgement in general to such validity and the principle of the same, as little doubtful, as the like faulty (though neither so commonly nor readily faulty) subsumption of the logical Judgement under its principle can make the latter, an objective principle, doubtful. But if the question were to be, how is it possible to assume nature *a priori* to be a complex of objects of taste? this problem has reference to Teleology, because it must be regarded as a purpose of nature essentially belonging to its concept to exhibit forms that are purposive for our Judgement. But the correctness of this latter assumption is very doubtful, whereas the efficacy of natural beauties is patent to experience.

§ 39. OF THE COMMUNICABILITY OF A SENSATION

If sensation, as the real in perception, is related to knowledge, it is called sensation of the senses; and its specific quality may be represented as generally communicable in a uniform way, if we assume that every one has senses like our own. But this cannot at all be presupposed of any single sensation. To a man who is deficient in the sense of smell, this kind of sensation cannot be communicated; and even if it is not wholly deficient, we cannot be certain that he gets exactly the same sensation from a flower that we have. But even more must we represent men as differing in respect of the *pleasantness* or *unpleasantness* involved in the sensation from the same object of sense; and it is absolutely not to be required that every man should take pleasure in the same objects. Pleasure of this kind, because it comes into the mind through the senses, in respect of which therefore we are passive, we may call the pleasure of *enjoyment*.

Satisfaction in an action because of its moral character is on the other hand not the pleasure of enjoyment, but of spontaneity and its accordance with the Idea of its destination. But this feeling, called moral, requires concepts, and presents not free purposiveness, but purposiveness that is conformable to law; it therefore admits of being universally communicated only by means of Reason, and, if the pleasure is to be homogeneous for every one, by very definite practical concepts of Reason.

Pleasure in the Sublime in nature, regarded as a pleasure of rational contemplation, also makes claim to universal participation; but it presupposes, besides, a different feeling, viz. that of our supersensible destination, which, however obscurely, has a moral foundation. But that other men will take account of it, and will find a satisfaction in the consideration of the wild greatness of nature (that certainly cannot be ascribed to its aspect, which is rather terrifying), I am not absolutely justified in supposing. Nevertheless, in consideration of the fact that on every suitable occasion regard should be had to these moral dispositions, I can impute such satisfaction to every man, but only by means of the moral law which on its side again is based on concepts of Reason.

On the contrary, pleasure in the Beautiful is neither a pleasure of enjoyment nor of a law-abiding activity, nor even of rational contemplation in accordance with Ideas, but of mere reflection. Without having as rule any purpose or fundamental proposition, this pleasure accompanies the ordinary apprehension of an object by the Imagination, as faculty of intuition, in relation with the Understanding, as faculty of concepts, by means of a procedure of the Judgement which it must also exercise on behalf of the commonest experience; only that in the latter case it is in order to perceive an empirical objective concept, in the former case (in aesthetical judgements) merely to perceive the accordance of the representation with the harmonious (subjectively purposive) activity of both cognitive faculties in their freedom, *i.e.* to feel with pleasure the mental state produced by the representation. This pleasure must necessarily depend for every one on the same conditions, for they are subjective conditions of the possibility of a cognition in general; and the proportion between these cognitive faculties requisite for Taste is also requisite for that ordinary sound Understanding which we have to presuppose in every one. Therefore he who judges with taste (if only he does not go astray in this act of consciousness and mistake matter for form or charm for beauty) may impute to every one subjective purposiveness, *i.e.* his satisfaction in the Object, and may assume his feeling to be universally communicable and that without the mediation of concepts.

§ 40. *OF TASTE AS A KIND OF* SENSUS COMMUNIS

We often give to the Judgement, if we are considering the result rather than the act of its reflection, the name of a sense, and we speak of a sense of truth, or of a sense of decorum, of justice, etc. And yet we know, or at least we ought to know, that these concepts cannot have their place in Sense, and further, that Sense has not the least capacity for expressing universal rules; but that no representation of truth, fitness, beauty, or justice, and so forth, could come into our thoughts if we could not rise beyond Sense to higher faculties of cognition. *The common Understanding of men*, which, as the mere sound (not yet cultivated) Understanding, we regard as the least to be expected from any one claiming the name of man, has therefore the doubtful honour of being given the name of common sense (*sensus communis*); and in such a way that by the name *common* (not merely in our language, where the word actually has a double signification, but in many others) we understand *vulgar*, that which is everywhere met with, the possession of which indicates absolutely no merit or superiority.

But under the *sensus communis* we must include the Idea of a *communal* sense, *i.e.* of a faculty of judgement, which in its reflection takes account (*a priori*) of the mode of representation of all other men in thought; in order *as it were* to compare its judgement with the collective Reason of humanity, and thus to escape the illusion arising from the private conditions that could be so easily taken for objective, which would injuriously affect the judgement. This is done by comparing our judgement with the possible rather than the actual judgements of others, and by putting ourselves in the place of any other man, by abstracting from the limitations which contingently attach to our own judgement. This, again, is brought about by leaving aside as much as possible the matter of our representative state, *i.e.* sensation, and simply having respect to the formal peculiarities of our representation or representative state. Now this operation of reflection seems perhaps too artificial to be attributed to the faculty called *common* sense; but it only appears so, when expressed in abstract formulae. In itself there is nothing more natural than to abstract from charm or emotion if we are seeking a judgement that is to serve as a universal rule.

The following Maxims of common human Understanding do not properly come in here, as parts of the Critique of Taste; but yet they may serve to elucidate its fundamental propositions. They are: 1° to think for oneself; 2° to put ourselves in thought in the place of every one else; 3° always to think consistently. The first is the maxim of *unprejudiced* thought; the second of *enlarged* thought; the third of *consecutive* thought.[60] The first is the maxim of a Reason never *passive*. The tendency to such passivity, and therefore to heteronomy of the Reason, is called *prejudice*; and the greatest prejudice of all is to represent nature as not subject to the rules that the Understanding places at its basis by means of its own essential law, *i.e.* is *superstition*. Deliverance from superstition is called *enlightenment*;[61] because although this name belongs to deliverance from prejudices in general, yet superstition specially (*in sensu eminenti*) deserves to be called a prejudice. For the blindness in which superstition places us, which it even imposes on us as an obligation, makes the need of being guided by others, and the consequent passive state of our Reason, peculiarly noticeable. As regards the second maxim of the mind, we are otherwise wont to call him limited (*borné*, the opposite of *enlarged*) whose talents attain to no great use (especially as regards intensity). But here we are not speaking of the faculty of cognition, but of the *mode of thought* which makes a purposive use thereof. However small may be the area or the degree to which a man's natural gifts reach, yet it indicates a man of *enlarged thought* if he disregards the subjective private conditions of his own judgement, by which so many others are confined, and reflects upon it from a *universal standpoint* (which he can only determine by placing himself at the standpoint of others). The third maxim, viz. that of *consecutive* thought, is the most difficult to attain, and can only be attained by the combination of both the former, and after the constant observance of them has grown into a habit. We may say that the first of these maxims is the maxim of Understanding, the second of Judgement, and the third of Reason.

I take up again the threads interrupted by this digression, and I say that Taste can be called *sensus communis* with more justice than sound Understanding can; and that the aesthetical Judgement rather than the intellectual may bear the name of a communal sense,[62] if we are willing to use the word "sense" of an effect of mere reflection upon the mind: for then we understand by sense the feeling of pleasure. We could even define Taste as the faculty of judging of that which makes *universally communicable*, without the mediation of a concept, our feeling in a given representation.

The skill that men have in communicating their thoughts requires also a relation between the Imagination and the Understanding in order to associate intuitions with concepts, and concepts again with those concepts, which then combine in a cognition. But in that case the agreement of the two mental powers is *according to law*, under the constraint of definite concepts. Only where the Imagination in its freedom awakens the Understanding, and is put by it into regular play without the aid of concepts, does the representation communicate itself not as a thought but as an internal feeling of a purposive state of the mind.

Taste is then the faculty of judging *a priori* of the communicability of feelings that are bound up with a given representation (without the mediation of a concept).

If we could assume that the mere universal communicability of a feeling must carry in itself an interest for us with it (which, however, we are not justified in concluding from the character of a merely reflective Judgement), we should be able to explain why the feeling in the judgement of taste comes to be imputed to every one, so to speak, as a duty.

§ 41. OF THE EMPIRICAL INTEREST IN THE BEAUTIFUL

That the judgement of taste by which something is declared beautiful must have no interest *as its determining ground* has been sufficiently established above. But it does not follow that after it has been given as a pure aesthetical judgement, no interest can be combined with it. This combination, however, can only be indirect, *i.e.* taste must first of all be represented as combined with something else, in order that we may unite with the satisfaction of mere reflection upon an object a *pleasure in its existence* (as that wherein all interest consists). For here also in aesthetical judgements what we say in cognitive judgements (of things in general) is valid; *a posse ad esse non valet consequentia*. This something else may be empirical, viz. an inclination proper to human nature, or intellectual, as the property of the Will of being capable of *a priori* determination by Reason. Both these involve a satisfaction in the presence of an Object, and so can lay the foundation for an interest in what has by itself pleased without reference to any interest whatever.

Empirically the Beautiful interests only in *society*. If we admit the impulse to society as natural to man, and his fitness for it, and his propension towards it, *i.e. sociability*, as a requisite for man as a being destined for society, and so as a property belonging to *humanity*, we cannot escape from regarding taste as a faculty for judging everything in respect of which we can communicate our *feeling* to all other men, and so as a means of furthering that which every one's natural inclination desires.

A man abandoned by himself on a desert island would adorn neither his hut nor his person; nor would he seek for flowers, still less would he plant them, in order to adorn himself therewith. It is only in society that it occurs to him to be not merely a man, but a refined man after his kind (the beginning of civilisation). For such do we judge him to be who is both inclined and apt to communicate his pleasure to others, and who is not contented with an Object if he cannot feel satisfaction in it in common with others. Again, every one expects and requires from every one else this reference to universal communication [of pleasure], as it were from an original compact dictated by humanity itself. Thus, doubtless, in the beginning only those things which attracted the senses, *e.g.* colours for painting oneself (roucou among the Carabs and cinnabar among the Iroquois), flowers, mussel shells, beautiful feathers, etc.,—but in time beautiful forms also (*e.g.* in their canoes, and clothes, etc.), which bring with them no gratification, or satisfaction of enjoyment—were important in society, and were combined with great interest. Until at last civilisation, having reached its highest point, makes out of this almost the main business of refined inclination; and sensations are only regarded as of worth in so far as they can be universally communicated. Here, although the pleasure which every one has in such an object is inconsiderable and in itself without any marked interest, yet the Idea of its universal communicability increases its worth in an almost infinite degree.

But this interest that indirectly attaches to the Beautiful through our inclination to society, and consequently is empirical, is of no importance for us here; because we have only to look to what may have a reference, although only indirectly, to the judgement of taste *a priori*. For if even in this form an interest bound up therewith should discover itself, taste would discover a transition of our judging faculty from sense-enjoyment to moral feeling; and so not only would we be the better guided in employing taste purposively, but there would be thus presented a link in the chain of the human faculties *a priori*, on which all legislation must depend. We can only say thus much about the empirical interest in objects of taste and in taste itself. Since it is subservient to inclination, however refined the latter may be, it may easily be confounded with all the inclinations and passions, which attain their greatest variety and highest degree in society; and the interest in the Beautiful, if it is grounded thereon, can only furnish a very ambiguous transition from the Pleasant to the Good. But whether this can or cannot be furthered by taste, taken in its purity, is what we now have to investigate.

§ 42. OF THE INTELLECTUAL INTEREST IN THE BEAUTIFUL

With the best intentions those persons who refer all activities, to which their inner natural dispositions impel men, to the final purpose of humanity, viz. the morally good, have regarded the taking an interest in the Beautiful in general as a mark of good moral character. But it is not without reason that they have been contradicted by others who rely on experience; for this shows that connoisseurs in taste, not only often but generally, are given up to idle, capricious, and mischievous passions, and that they could perhaps make less claim than others to any pre-eminent attachment to moral principles. Thus it would seem that the feeling for the Beautiful is not only (as actually is the case) specifically different from the Moral feeling; but that the interest which can be bound up with it is hardly compatible with moral interest, and certainly has no inner affinity therewith.

Now I admit at once that the interest in the *Beautiful of Art* (under which I include the artificial use of natural beauties for adornment and so for vanity) furnishes no proof whatever of a disposition attached to the morally good or even inclined thereto. But on the other hand, I maintain that to take an *immediate interest* in the Beauty of Nature (not merely to have taste in judging it) is always a mark of a good soul; and that when this interest is habitual it at least indicates a frame of mind favourable to the moral feeling, if it is voluntarily bound up with the *contemplation of nature*. It is to be remembered, however, that I here speak strictly of the beautiful *forms* of Nature, and I set aside the *charms*, that she is wont to combine so abundantly with them; because, though the interest in the latter is indeed immediate, it is only empirical.

He who by himself (and without any design of communicating his observations to others) regards the beautiful figure of a wild flower, a bird, an insect, etc., with admiration and love—who would not willingly miss it in Nature, although it may bring him some hurt, who still less wants any advantage from it—*he* takes an immediate and also an intellectual interest in the beauty of Nature. *I.e.* it is not merely the form of the product of nature which pleases him, but its very presence pleases him, the charms of sense having no share in this pleasure and no purpose whatever being combined with it.

But it is noteworthy that if we secretly deceived this lover of the beautiful by planting in the ground artificial flowers (which can be manufactured exactly like natural ones), or by placing artificially carved birds on the boughs of trees, and he discovered the deceit, the immediate interest that he previously took in them would disappear at once; though, perhaps, a different interest, viz. the interest of vanity in adorning his chamber with them for the eyes of others, would take its place. This thought then must accompany our intuition and reflection on beauty, viz. that nature has produced it; and on this alone is based the immediate interest that we take in it. Otherwise, there remains a mere judgement of taste, either devoid of all interest, or bound up with a mediate interest, viz. in that it has reference to society; which latter [interest] furnishes no certain indications of a morally good disposition.

This superiority of natural to artificial beauty in that it alone arouses an immediate interest, although as regards form the first may be surpassed by the second, harmonises with the refined and well-grounded habit of thought of all men who have cultivated their moral feeling. If a man who has taste enough to judge of the products of beautiful Art with the greatest accuracy and refinement willingly leaves a chamber where are to be found those beauties that minister to vanity or to any social joys, and turns to the beautiful in Nature in order to find, as it were, delight for his spirit in a train of thought that he can never completely evolve, we will regard this choice of his with veneration, and attribute to him a beautiful soul, to which no connoisseur or lover [of Art] can lay claim on account of the interest he takes in his [artistic] objects.—What now is the difference in our estimation of these two different kinds of Objects, which in the judgement of mere taste it is hard to compare in point of superiority?

We have a faculty of mere aesthetical Judgement by which we judge forms without the aid of concepts, and find a satisfaction in this mere act of judgement; this we make into a rule for every one, without this judgement either being based on or producing any interest.—On the other hand, we have also a faculty of intellectual Judgement which determines an *a priori* satisfaction for the mere forms of practical maxims (so far as they are in themselves qualified for universal legislation); this we make into a law for every one, without our judgement being based on any interest whatever, *though in this case it produces such an interest*. The pleasure or pain in the former judgement is called that of taste, in the latter, that of moral feeling.

But it also interests Reason that the Ideas (for which in moral feeling it arouses an immediate interest) should have objective reality; *i.e.* that nature should at least show a trace or give an indication that it contains in itself some ground for assuming a regular agreement of its products with our entirely disinterested satisfaction (which we recognise *a priori* as a law for every one, without being able to base it upon proofs). Hence Reason must take an interest in every expression on the part of nature of an agreement of this kind. Consequently, the mind cannot ponder upon the beauty of *Nature* without finding itself at the same time interested therein. But this interest is akin to moral, and he who takes such an interest in the beauties of nature can do so only in so far as he previously has firmly established his interest in the morally good. If, therefore, the beauty of Nature interests a man immediately we have reason for attributing to him, at least, a basis for a good moral disposition.

It will be said that this account of aesthetical judgements, as akin to the moral feeling, seems far too studied to be regarded as the true interpretation of that cipher through which Nature speaks to us figuratively in her beautiful forms. However, in the first place, this immediate interest in the beautiful is actually not common; but is peculiar to those whose mental disposition either has already been cultivated in the direction of the good or is eminently susceptible of such cultivation. In that case the analogy between the pure judgement of taste which, independently of any interest, causes us to feel a satisfaction, and also represents it *a priori* as suitable to humanity in general, and the moral judgement that does the same thing from concepts without any clear, subtle, and premeditated reflection—this analogy leads to a similar immediate interest in the objects of the former as in those of the latter; only that in the one case the interest is free, in the other it is based on objective laws. To this is to be added our admiration for Nature, which displays itself in its beautiful products as Art, not merely by chance, but as it were designedly, in accordance with a regular arrangement, and as purposiveness without purpose. This latter, as we never meet with it outside ourselves, we naturally seek in ourselves; and, in fact, in that which constitutes the ultimate purpose of our being, viz. our moral destination. (Of this question as to the ground of the possibility of such natural purposiveness we shall first speak in the Teleology.)

It is easy to explain why the satisfaction in the pure aesthetical judgement in the case of beautiful Art is not combined with an immediate interest as it is in the case of beautiful Nature. For the former is either such an imitation of the latter that it reaches the point of deception and then produces the same effect as natural beauty (for which it is taken); or it is an art obviously directed designedly to our satisfaction. In the latter case the satisfaction in the product would, it is true, be brought about immediately by taste, but it would be only a mediate interest in the cause lying at its root, viz. an art that can only interest by means of its purpose and never in itself. It will, perhaps, be said that this is also the case, if an Object of nature interests us by its beauty only so far as it is associated with a moral Idea. But it is not the Object itself which immediately interests us, but its character in virtue of which it is qualified for such association, which therefore essentially belongs to it.

The charms in beautiful Nature, which are so often found, as it were, blended with beautiful forms, may be referred to modifications either of light (colours) or of sound (tones). For these are the only sensations that imply not merely a sensible feeling but also reflection upon the form of these modifications of Sense; and thus they involve in themselves as it were a language by which nature speaks to us, which thus seems to have a higher sense. Thus the white colour of lilies seems to determine the mind to Ideas of innocence; and the seven colours in order from the red to the violet seem to suggest the Ideas of (1) Sublimity, (2) Intrepidity, (3) Candour, (4) Friendliness, (5) Modesty, (6) Constancy, (7) Tenderness. The song of birds proclaims gladsomeness and contentment with existence. At least so we interpret nature, whether it have this design or not. But the interest which we here take in beauty has only to do with the beauty of Nature; it vanishes altogether as soon as we notice that we are deceived and that it is only Art—vanishes so completely that taste can no longer find the thing beautiful or sight find it charming. What is more highly praised by poets than the bewitching and beautiful note of the nightingale in a lonely copse on a still summer evening by the soft light of the moon? And yet we have instances of a merry host, where no such songster was to be found, deceiving to their great contentment the guests who were staying with him to enjoy the country air, by hiding in a bush a mischievous boy who knew how to produce this sound exactly like nature (by means of a reed or a tube in his mouth). But as soon as we are aware that it is a cheat, no one will remain long listening to the song which before was counted so charming. And it is just the same with the songs of all other birds. It must be Nature or be regarded as Nature, if we are to take an immediate *interest* in the Beautiful as such; and still more is this the case if we can require that others should take an interest in it too. This happens as a matter of fact when we regard as coarse and ignoble the mental attitude of those persons who have no *feeling* for beautiful Nature (for thus we describe a susceptibility to interest in its contemplation), and who confine themselves to eating and drinking—to the mere enjoyments of sense.

§ 43. OF ART IN GENERAL

(1). *Art* is distinguished from Nature, as doing (*facere*) is distinguished from acting or working generally (*agere*), and as the product or result of the former is distinguished as *work* (*opus*) from the working (*effectus*) of the latter.

By right we ought only to describe as Art, production through freedom, *i.e.* through a will that places Reason at the basis of its actions. For although we like to call the product of bees (regularly built cells of wax) a work of art, this is only by way of analogy: as soon as we feel that this work of theirs is based on no proper rational deliberation, we say that it is a product of Nature (of instinct), and as Art only ascribe it to their Creator.

If, as sometimes happens, in searching through a bog we come upon a bit of shaped wood, we do not say: this is a product of Nature, but, of Art. Its producing cause has conceived a purpose to which the bit of wood owes its form. Elsewhere too we should see art in everything which is made so that a representation of it in its cause must have preceded its actuality (as even in the case of the bees), though the effect could not have been *thought* by the cause. But if we call anything absolutely a work of art in order to distinguish it from a natural effect, we always understand by that a work of man.

(2). *Art* regarded as human skill differs from *science* (as *can* from *know*) as a practical faculty does from a theoretical, as Technic does from Theory (as mensuration from geometry). And so what we *can* do, as soon as we merely *know* what ought to be done and therefore are sufficiently cognisant of the desired effect, is not called Art. Only that which a man, even if he knows it completely, may not therefore have the skill to accomplish, belongs to Art. *Camper*[63] describes very exactly how the best shoes must be made, but he certainly could not make one.[64]

(3). *Art* also differs from *handicraft*; the first is called *free*, the other may be called mercenary. We regard the first as if it could only prove purposive as play, *i.e.* as occupation that is pleasant in itself. But the second is regarded as if it could only be compulsorily imposed upon one as work, *i.e.* as occupation which is unpleasant (a trouble) in itself, and which is only attractive on account of its effect (*e.g.* the wage). Whether or not in the graded list of the professions we ought to count watchmakers as artists, but smiths only as handicraftsmen, would require another point of view from which to judge than that which we are here taking up; viz. [we should have to consider] the proportion of talents which must be assumed requisite in these several occupations. Whether or not, again, under the so-called seven free arts some may be included which ought to be classed as sciences, and many that are akin rather to handicraft, I shall not here discuss. But it is not inexpedient to recall that in all free arts there is yet requisite something compulsory, or, as it is called, *mechanism*, without which the *spirit*, which must be free in art and which alone inspires the work, would have no body and would evaporate altogether; *e.g.* in poetry there must be an accuracy and wealth of language, and also prosody and metre. [It is not inexpedient, I say, to recall this], for many modern educators believe that the best way to produce a free art is to remove it from all constraint, and thus to change it from work into mere play.

§ 44. OF BEAUTIFUL ART

There is no Science of the Beautiful, but only a Critique of it; and there is no such thing as beautiful Science, but only beautiful Art. For as regards the first point, if it could be decided scientifically, *i.e.* by proofs, whether a thing was to be regarded as beautiful or not, the judgement upon beauty would belong to science and would not be a judgement of taste. And as far as the second point is concerned, a science which should be beautiful as such is a nonentity. For if in such a science we were to ask for grounds and proofs, we would be put off with tasteful phrases (bon-mots).—The source of the common expression, *beautiful science*, is without doubt nothing else than this, as it has been rightly remarked, that for beautiful art in its entire completeness much science is requisite; *e.g.* a knowledge of ancient languages, a learned familiarity with classical authors, history, a knowledge of antiquities, etc. And hence these historical sciences, because they form the necessary preparation and basis for beautiful art, and also partly because under them is included the knowledge of the products of beautiful art (rhetoric and poetry), have come to be called beautiful sciences by a confusion of words.

If art which is adequate to the *cognition* of a possible object performs the actions requisite therefore merely in order to make it actual, it is *mechanical* art; but if it has for its immediate design the feeling of pleasure, it is called *aesthetical* art. This is again either *pleasant* or *beautiful*. It is the first, if its purpose is that the pleasure should accompany the representations [of the object] regarded as mere *sensations*; it is the second if they are regarded as *modes of cognition*.

Pleasant arts are those that are directed merely to enjoyment. Of this class are all those charming arts that can gratify a company at table; *e.g.* the art of telling stories in an entertaining way, of starting the company in frank and lively conversation, of raising them by jest and laugh to a certain pitch of merriment;[65] when, as people say, there may be a great deal of gossip at the feast, but no one will be answerable for what he says, because they are only concerned with momentary entertainment, and not with any permanent material for reflection or subsequent discussion. (Among these are also to be reckoned the way of arranging the table for enjoyment, and, at great feasts, the manage-ment of the music. This latter is a wonderful thing. It is meant to dispose to gaiety the minds of the guests, regarded solely as a pleasant noise, without any one paying the least attention to its composition; and it favours the free conversation of each with his neighbour.) Again, to this class belong all games which bring with them no further interest than that of making the time pass imperceptibly.

On the other hand, beautiful art is a mode of representation which is purposive for itself, and which, although devoid of [definite] purpose, yet furthers the culture of the mental powers in reference to social communication.

The universal communicability of a pleasure carries with it in its very concept that the pleasure is not one of enjoyment, from mere sensation, but must be derived from reflection; and thus aesthetical art, as the art of beauty, has for standard the reflective Judgement and not sensation.

§ 45. BEAUTIFUL ART IS AN ART, IN SO FAR AS IT SEEMS LIKE NATURE

In a product of beautiful art we must become conscious that it is Art and not Nature; but yet the purposiveness in its form must seem to be as free from all constraint of arbi-trary rules as if it were a product of mere nature. On this feeling of freedom in the play of our cognitive faculties, which must at the same time be purposive, rests that pleasure which alone is universally communicable, without being based on concepts. Nature is beautiful because it looks like Art; and Art can only be called beautiful if we are conscious of it as Art while yet it looks like Nature.

For whether we are dealing with natural or with artificial beauty we can say gener-ally: *That is beautiful which pleases in the mere act of judging it* (not in the sensation of it, or by means of a concept). Now art has always a definite design of producing something. But if this something were bare sensation (something merely subjective), which is to be accompanied with pleasure, the product would please in the act of judgement only by mediation of sensible feeling. And again, if the design were directed towards the production of a definite Object, then, if this were attained by art, the Object would only please by means of concepts. But in both cases the art would not please *in the mere act of judging; i.e.* it would not please as beautiful, but as mechanical.

Hence the purposiveness in the product of beautiful art, although it is designed, must not seem to be designed; *i.e.* beautiful art must *look* like nature, although we are conscious of it as art. But a product of art appears like nature when, although its agreement with the rules, according to which alone the product can become what it ought to be, is *punctiliously* observed, yet this is not *painfully* apparent; [the form of the schools does not obtrude itself][66]—it shows no trace of the rule having been before the eyes of the artist and having fettered his mental powers.

§ 46. BEAUTIFUL ART IS THE ART OF GENIUS

Genius is the talent (or natural gift) which gives the rule to Art. Since talent, as the innate productive faculty of the artist, belongs itself to Nature, we may express the matter thus: *Genius* is the innate mental disposition (*ingenium*) *through which* Nature gives the rule to Art.

Whatever may be thought of this definition, whether it is merely arbitrary or whether it is adequate to the concept that we are accustomed to combine with the word *genius* (which is to be examined in the following paragraphs), we can prove already beforehand that according to the signification of the word here adopted, beautiful arts must necessarily be considered as arts of *genius*.

For every art presupposes rules by means of which in the first instance a product, if it is to be called artistic, is represented as possible. But the concept of beautiful art does not permit the judgement upon the beauty of a product to be derived from any rule, which has a *concept* as its determining ground, and therefore has at its basis a concept of the way in which the product is possible. Therefore, beautiful art cannot itself devise the rule according to which it can bring about its product. But since at the same time a product can never be called Art without some precedent rule, Nature in the subject must (by the harmony of its faculties) give the rule to Art; *i.e.* beautiful Art is only possible as a product of Genius.

We thus see (1) that genius is a *talent* for producing that for which no definite rule can be given; it is not a mere aptitude for what can be learnt by a rule. Hence *originality* must be its first property. (2) But since it also can produce original nonsense, its products must be models, *i.e. exemplary*; and they consequently ought not to spring from imitation, but must serve as a standard or rule of judgement for others. (3) It cannot describe or indicate scientifically how it brings about its products, but it gives the rule just as nature does. Hence the author of a product for which he is indebted to his genius does not himself know how he has come by his Ideas; and he has not the power to devise the like at pleasure or in accordance with a plan, and to communicate it to others in precepts that will enable them to produce similar products. (Hence it is probable that the word genius is derived from *genius*, that peculiar guiding and guardian spirit given to a man at his birth, from whose suggestion these original Ideas proceed.) (4) Nature by the medium of genius does not prescribe rules to Science, but to Art; and to it only in so far as it is to be beautiful Art.

538 | IMMANUEL KANT

§ 47. ELUCIDATION AND CONFIRMATION OF THE ABOVE EXPLANATION OF GENIUS

Every one is agreed that genius is entirely opposed to the *spirit of imitation*. Now since learning is nothing but imitation, it follows that the greatest ability and teachableness (capacity) regarded *quâ* teachableness, cannot avail for genius. Even if a man thinks or invents for himself, and does not merely take in what others have taught, even if he discovers many things in art and science, this is not the right ground for calling such a (perhaps great) *head*, a genius (as opposed to him who because he can only learn and imitate is called a *shallow-pate*). For even these things could be learned, they lie in the natural path of him who investigates and reflects according to rules; and they do not differ specifically from what can be acquired by industry through imitation. Thus we can readily learn all that *Newton* has set forth in his immortal work on the Principles of Natural Philosophy, however great a head was required to discover it; but we cannot learn to write spirited poetry, however express may be the precepts of the art and however excellent its models. The reason is that *Newton* could make all his steps, from the first elements of geometry to his own great and profound discoveries, intuitively plain and definite as regards consequence, not only to himself but to every one else. But a *Homer* or a *Wieland* cannot show how his Ideas, so rich in fancy and yet so full of thought, come together in his head, simply because he does not know and therefore cannot teach others. In Science then the greatest discoverer only differs in degree from his laborious imitator and pupil; but he differs specifically from him whom Nature has gifted for beautiful Art. And in this there is no depreciation of those great men to whom the human race owes so much gratitude, as compared with nature's favourites in respect of the talent for beautiful art. For in the fact that the former talent is directed to the ever-advancing greater perfection of knowledge and every advantage depending on it, and at the same time to the imparting this same knowledge to others—in this it has a great superiority over [the talent of] those who deserve the honour of being called geniuses. For art stands still at a certain point; a boundary is set to it beyond which it cannot go, which presumably has been reached long ago and cannot be extended further. Again, artistic skill cannot be communicated; it is imparted to every artist immediately by the hand of nature; and so it dies with him, until nature endows another in the same way, so that he only needs an example in order to put in operation in a similar fashion the talent of which he is conscious.

If now it is a natural gift which must prescribe its rule to art (as beautiful art), of what kind is this rule? It cannot be reduced to a formula and serve as a precept, for then the judgement upon the beautiful would be determinable according to concepts; but the rule must be abstracted from the fact, *i.e.* from the product, on which others may try their own talent by using it as a model, not to be *copied* but to be *imitated*. How this is possible is hard to explain. The Ideas of the artist excite like Ideas in his pupils if nature has endowed them with a like proportion of their mental powers. Hence models of beautiful art are the only means of handing down these Ideas to posterity. This cannot be done by mere descriptions, especially not in the case of the arts of speech, and in this latter classical models are only to be had in the old dead languages, now preserved only as "the learned languages."

Although mechanical and beautiful art are very different, the first being a mere art of industry and learning and the second of genius, yet there is no beautiful art in which there is not a mechanical element that can be comprehended by rules and followed accordingly, and in which therefore there must be something *scholastic* as an essential condition. For [in every art] some purpose must be conceived; otherwise we could not ascribe the product to art at all, and it would be a mere product of chance. But in order to accomplish a purpose, definite rules from which we cannot dispense ourselves are requisite. Now since the originality of the talent constitutes an essential (though not the only) element in the character of genius, shallow heads believe that they cannot better show themselves to be full-blown geniuses than by throwing off the constraint of all rules; they believe, in effect, that one could make a braver show on the back of a wild horse than on the back of a trained animal. Genius can only furnish rich *material* for products of beautiful art; its execution and its *form* require talent cultivated in the schools, in order to make such a use of this material as will stand examination by the Judgement. But it is quite ridiculous for a man to speak and decide like a genius in things which require the most careful investigation by Reason. One does not know whether to laugh more at the impostor who spreads such a mist round him that we cannot clearly use our Judgement and so use our Imagination the more, or at the public which naïvely imagines that his inability to cognise clearly and to comprehend the masterpiece before him arises from new truths crowding in on him in such abundance that details (duly weighed definitions and accurate examination of fundamental propositions) seem but clumsy work.

§ 48. OF THE RELATION OF GENIUS TO TASTE

For *judging* of beautiful objects as such, *taste* is requisite; but for beautiful art, *i.e.* for the *production* of such objects, *genius* is requisite.

If we consider genius as the talent for beautiful art (which the special meaning of the word implies) and in this point of view analyse it into the faculties which must concur to constitute such a talent, it is necessary in the first instance to determine exactly the difference between natural beauty, the judging of which requires only Taste, and artificial beauty, whose possibility (to which reference must be made in judging such an object) requires Genius.

A natural beauty is a *beautiful thing*; artificial beauty is a *beautiful representation* of a thing.

In order to judge of a natural beauty as such I need not have beforehand a concept of what sort of thing the object is to be; *i.e.* I need not know its material purposiveness (the purpose), but its mere form pleases by itself in the act of judging it without any knowledge of the purpose. But if the object is given as a product of art, and as such is to be declared beautiful, then, because art always supposes a purpose in the cause (and its causality), there must be at bottom in the first instance a concept of what the thing is to be. And as the agreement of the manifold in a thing with its inner destination, its purpose, constitutes the perfection of the thing, it follows that in judging of artificial beauty the perfection of the thing must be taken into account; but in judging of natural beauty (as *such*) there is no question at all about this.—It is true that in judging of objects of nature, especially objects endowed with life, *e.g.* a man or a horse, their objective purposiveness also is commonly taken into consideration in judging of their beauty; but then the judgement is no longer purely aesthetical, *i.e.* a mere judgement of taste. Nature is no longer judged inasmuch as it appears like art, but in so far as it *is* actual (although superhuman) art; and the teleological judgement serves as the basis and condition of the aesthetical, as a condition to which the latter must have respect. In such a case, *e.g.* if it is said "that is a beautiful woman," we think nothing else than this: nature represents in her figure the purposes in view in the shape of a woman's figure. For we must look beyond the mere form to a concept, if the object is to be thought in such a way by means of a logically conditioned aesthetical judgement.

Beautiful art shows its superiority in this, that it describes as beautiful things which may be in nature ugly or displeasing.[67] The Furies, diseases, the devastations of war, etc., may [even regarded as calamitous],[68] be described as very beautiful, and even represented in a picture. There is only one kind of ugliness which cannot be represented in accordance with nature, without destroying all aesthetical satisfaction and consequently artificial beauty; viz. that which excites *disgust*. For in this peculiar sensation, which rests on mere imagination, the object is represented as it were obtruding itself for our enjoyment while we strive against it with all our might. And the artistic representation of the object is no longer distinguished from the nature of the object itself in our sensation, and thus it is impossible that it can be regarded as beautiful. The art of sculpture again, because in its products art is almost interchangeable with nature, excludes from its creations the immediate representation of ugly objects; *e.g.* it represents death by a beautiful genius, the warlike spirit by Mars, and permits [all such things] to be represented only by an allegory or attribute[69] that has a pleasing effect, and thus only indirectly by the aid of the interpretation of Reason, and not for the mere aesthetical Judgement.

So much for the beautiful representation of an object, which is properly only the form of the presentation of a concept, and the means by which the latter is communicated universally.—But to give this form to the product of beautiful art, mere taste is requisite. By taste, after he has exercised and corrected it by manifold examples from art or nature, the artist checks his work; and after many, often toilsome, attempts to content taste he finds the form which satisfies him. Hence this form is not, as it were, a thing of inspiration or the result of a free swing of the mental powers, but of a slow and even painful process of improvement, by which he seeks to render it adequate to his thought, without detriment to the freedom of the play of his powers.

But taste is merely a judging and not a productive faculty; and what is appropriate to it is not therefore a work of beautiful art. It may be only a product belonging to useful and mechanical art or even to science, produced according to definite rules that can be learned and must be exactly followed. But the pleasing form that is given to it is only the vehicle of communication, and a mode, as it were, of presenting it, in respect of which we remain free to a certain extent, although it is combined with a definite purpose. Thus we desire that table appointments, a moral treatise, even a sermon, should have in themselves this form of beautiful art, without it seeming to be *sought*: but we do not therefore call these things works of beautiful art. Under the latter class are reckoned a poem, a piece of music, a picture gallery, etc.; and in some would-be works of beautiful art we find genius without taste, while in others we find taste without genius.

§ 49. OF THE FACULTIES OF THE MIND THAT CONSTITUTE GENIUS

We say of certain products of which we expect that they should at least in part appear as beautiful art, they are without *spirit*[70]; although we find nothing to blame in them on the score of taste. A poem may be very neat and elegant, but without spirit. A history may be exact and well arranged, but without spirit. A festal discourse may be solid and at the same time elaborate, but without spirit. Conversation is often not devoid of entertainment, but yet without spirit: even of a woman we say that she is pretty, an agreeable talker, and courteous, but without spirit. What then do we mean by spirit?

Spirit, in an aesthetical sense, is the name given to the animating principle of the mind. But that whereby this principle animates the soul, the material which it applies to that [purpose], is that which puts the mental powers purposively into swing, *i.e.* into such a play as maintains itself and strengthens the [mental] powers in their exercise.

Now I maintain that this principle is no other than the faculty of presenting *aesthetical Ideas*. And by an aesthetical Idea I understand that representation of the Imagination which occasions much thought, without, however, any definite thought, *i.e.* any *concept*, being capable of being adequate to it; it consequently cannot be completely compassed and made intelligible by language.—We easily see that it is the counterpart (pendant) of a *rational Idea*, which conversely is a concept to which no *intuition* (or representation of the Imagination) can be adequate.

The Imagination (as a productive faculty of cognition) is very powerful in creating another nature, as it were, out of the material that actual nature gives it. We entertain ourselves with it when experience proves too commonplace, and by it we remould experience, always indeed in accordance with analogical laws, but yet also in accordance with principles which occupy a higher place in Reason (laws too which are just as natural to us as those by which Understanding comprehends empirical nature). Thus we feel our freedom from the law of association (which attaches to the empirical employment of Imagination), so that the material which we borrow from nature in accordance with this law can be worked up into something different which surpasses nature.

Such representations of the Imagination we may call *Ideas*, partly because they at least strive after something which lies beyond the bounds of experience, and so seek to approximate to a presentation of concepts of Reason (intellectual Ideas), thus giving to the latter the appearance of objective reality,—but especially because no concept can be fully adequate to them as internal intuitions. The poet ventures to realise to sense, rational Ideas of invisible beings, the kingdom of the blessed, hell, eternity, creation, etc.; or even if he deals with things of which there are examples in experience,—*e.g.* death, envy and all vices, also love, fame, and the like,—he tries, by means of Imagination, which emulates the play of Reason in its quest after a maximum, to go beyond the limits of experience and to present them to Sense with a completeness of which there is no example in nature. It is, properly speaking, in the art of the poet, that the faculty of aesthetical Ideas can manifest itself in its full measure. But this faculty, considered in itself, is properly only a talent (of the Imagination).

If now we place under a concept a representation of the Imagination belonging to its presentation, but which occasions solely by itself more thought than can ever be comprehended in a definite concept, and which therefore enlarges aesthetically the concept itself in an unbounded fashion,—the Imagination is here creative, and it brings the faculty of intellectual Ideas (the Reason) into movement; *i.e.* a movement, occasioned by a representation, towards more thought (though belonging, no doubt, to the concept of the object) than can be grasped in the representation or made clear.

Those forms which do not constitute the presentation of a given concept itself but only, as approximate representations of the Imagination, express the consequences bound up with it and its relationship to other concepts, are called (aesthetical) *attributes* of an object, whose concept as a rational Idea cannot be adequately presented. Thus Jupiter's eagle with the lightning in its claws is an attribute of the mighty king of heaven, as the peacock is of its magnificent queen. They do not, like *logical attributes*, represent what lies in our concepts of the sublimity and majesty of creation, but something different, which gives occasion to the Imagination to spread itself over a number of kindred representations, that arouse more thought than can be expressed in a concept determined by words. They furnish an *aesthetical Idea*, which for that rational Idea takes the place of logical presentation; and thus as their proper office they enliven the mind by opening out to it the prospect into an illimitable field of kindred representations. But beautiful art does this not only in the case of painting or sculpture (in which the term "attribute" is commonly employed): poetry and rhetoric also get the spirit that animates their works simply from the aesthetical attributes of the object, which accompany the logical and stimulate the Imagination, so that it thinks more by their aid, although in an undeveloped way, than could be comprehended in a concept and therefore in a definite form of words.— For the sake of brevity I must limit myself to a few examples only.

When the great King[71] in one of his poems expresses himself as follows:

"Oui, finissons sans trouble et mourons sans regrets,
En laissant l'univers comblé de nos bienfaits.
Ainsi l'astre du jour au bout de sa carrière,
Répand sur l'horizon une douce lumière;
Et les derniers rayons qu'il darde dans les airs,
Sont les derniers soupirs qu'il donne à l'univers;"

he quickens his rational Idea of a cosmopolitan disposition at the end of life by an attribute which the Imagination (in remembering all the pleasures of a beautiful summer day that are recalled at its close by a serene evening) associates with that representation, and which excites a number of sensations and secondary representations for which no expression is found. On the other hand, an intellectual concept may serve conversely as an attribute for a representation of sense and so can quicken this latter by means of the Idea of the supersensible; but only by the aesthetical [element], that subjectively attaches to the concept of the latter, being here employed. Thus, for example, a certain poet[72] says, in his description of a beautiful morning:

"The sun arose
As calm from virtue springs."

The consciousness of virtue, even if one only places oneself in thought in the position of a virtuous man, diffuses in the mind a multitude of sublime and restful feelings and a boundless prospect of a joyful future, to which no expression measured by a definite concept completely attains.[73]

In a word the aesthetical Idea is a representation of the Imagination associated with a given concept, which is bound up with such a multiplicity of partial representations in its free employment, that for it no expression marking a definite concept can be found; and such a representation, therefore, adds to a concept much ineffable thought, the feeling of which quickens the cognitive faculties, and with language, which is the mere letter, binds up spirit also.

The mental powers, therefore, whose union (in a certain relation) constitutes *genius* are Imagination and Understanding. In the employment of the Imagination for cognition it submits to the constraint of the Understanding and is subject to the limitation of being conformable to the concept of the latter. On the other hand, in an aesthetical point of view it is free to furnish unsought, over and above that agreement with a concept, abundance of undeveloped material for the Understanding; to which the Understanding paid no regard in its concept, but which it applies, though not objectively for cognition, yet subjectively to quicken the cognitive powers and therefore also indirectly to cognitions. Thus genius properly consists in the happy relation [between these faculties], which no science can teach and no industry can learn, by which Ideas are found for a given concept; and on the other hand, we thus find for these Ideas the *expression*, by means of which the subjective state of mind brought about by them, as an accompaniment of the concept, can be communicated to others. The latter talent is properly speaking what is called spirit; for to express the ineffable element in the state of mind implied by a certain representation and to make it universally communicable—whether the expression be in speech or painting or statuary—this requires a faculty of seizing the quickly passing play of Imagination and of unifying it in a concept (which is even on that account original and discloses a new rule that could not have been inferred from any preceding principles or examples), that can be communicated without any constraint [of rules].[74]

———

IF AFTER THIS analysis we look back to the explanation given above of what is called *genius*, we find: *first*, that it is a talent for Art, not for Science, in which clearly known rules must go beforehand and determine the procedure. *Secondly*, as an artistic talent it presupposes a definite concept of the product, as the purpose, and therefore Understanding; but it also presupposes a representation (although an indeterminate one) of the material, *i.e.* of the intuition, for the presentment of this concept; and, therefore, a relation between the Imagination and the Understanding. *Thirdly*, it shows itself not so much in the accomplishment of the proposed purpose in a presentment of a definite *concept*, as in the enunciation or expression of *aesthetical Ideas*, which contain abundant material for that very design; and consequently it represents the Imagination as free from all guidance of rules and yet as purposive in reference to the presentment of the given concept. Finally, in the *fourth* place, the unsought undesigned subjective purposiveness in the free accordance of the Imagination with the legality of the Understanding presupposes such a proportion and disposition of these faculties as no following of rules, whether of science or of mechanical imitation, can bring about, but which only the nature of the subject can produce.

In accordance with these suppositions genius is the exemplary originality of the natural gifts of a subject in the *free* employment of his cognitive faculties. In this way the product of a genius (as regards what is to be ascribed to genius and not to possible learning or schooling) is an example, not to be imitated (for then that which in it is genius and constitutes the spirit of the work would be lost), but to be followed, by another genius; whom it awakens to a feeling of his own originality and whom it stirs so to exercise his art in freedom from the constraint of rules, that thereby a new rule is gained for art, and thus his talent shows itself to be exemplary. But because a genius is a favourite of nature and must be regarded by us as a rare phenomenon, his example produces for other good heads a school, *i.e.* a methodical system of teaching according to rules, so far as these can be derived from the peculiarities of the products of his spirit. For such persons beautiful art is so far imitation, to which nature through the medium of a genius supplied the rule.

But this imitation becomes a mere *aping*, if the scholar *copies* everything down to the deformities, which the genius must have let pass only because he could not well remove them without weakening his Idea. This mental characteristic is meritorious only in the case of a genius. A certain *audacity* in expression—and in general many a departure from common rules—becomes him well, but it is in no way worthy of imitation; it always remains a fault in itself which we must seek to remove, though the genius is as it were privileged to commit it, because the inimitable rush of his spirit would suffer from over-anxious carefulness. *Mannerism* is another kind of aping, viz. of mere *peculiarity* (originality) in general; by which a man separates himself as far as possible from imitators, without however possessing the talent to be at the same time *exemplary*.—There are indeed in general two ways (*modi*) in which such a man may put together his notions of expressing himself; the one is called a *manner* (*modus aestheticus*), the other a *method* (*modus logicus*). They differ in this, that the former has no other standard than the *feeling* of unity in the presentment, but the latter follows definite *principles*; hence the former alone avails for beautiful art. But an artistic product is said to show *mannerism* only when the exposition of the artist's Idea is *founded* on its very singularity, and is not made appropriate to the Idea itself. The ostentatious (*précieux*), contorted, and affected [manner, adopted] to differentiate oneself from ordinary persons (though devoid of spirit) is like the behaviour of a man of whom we say, that he hears himself talk, or who stands and moves about as if he were on a stage in order to be stared at; this always betrays a bungler.

§ 50. OF THE COMBINATION OF TASTE WITH GENIUS IN THE PRODUCTS OF BEAUTIFUL ART

To ask whether it is more important for the things of beautiful art that Genius or Taste should be displayed, is the same as to ask whether in it more depends on Imagination or on Judgement. Now, since in respect of the first an art is rather said to be *full of spirit*, but only deserves to be called a *beautiful* art on account of the second; this latter is at least, as its indispensable condition (*conditio sine qua non*), the most important thing to which one has to look in the judging of art as beautiful art. Abundance and originality of Ideas are less necessary to beauty than the accordance of the Imagination in its freedom with the conformity to law of the Understanding. For all the abundance of the former produces in lawless freedom nothing but nonsense; on the other hand, the Judgement is the faculty by which it is adjusted to the Understanding.

Taste, like the Judgement in general, is the discipline (or training) of Genius; it clips its wings closely, and makes it cultured and polished; but, at the same time, it gives guidance as to where and how far it may extend itself, if it is to remain purposive. And while it brings clearness and order into the multitude of the thoughts, it makes the Ideas susceptible of being permanently and, at the same time, universally assented to, and capable of being followed by others, and of an ever-progressive culture. If, then, in the conflict of these two properties in a product something must be sacrificed, it should be rather on the side of genius; and the Judgement, which in the things of beautiful art gives its decision from its own proper principles, will rather sacrifice the freedom and wealth of the Imagination than permit anything prejudicial to the Understanding.

For beautiful art, therefore, *Imagination*, *Understanding*, *Spirit*, and *Taste* are requisite.[75]

§ 51. OF THE DIVISION OF THE BEAUTIFUL ARTS

We may describe beauty in general (whether natural or artificial) as the *expression* of aesthetical Ideas; only that in beautiful Art this Idea must be occasioned by a concept of the Object; whilst in beautiful Nature the mere reflection upon a given intuition, without any concept of what the object is to be, is sufficient for the awakening and communicating of the Idea of which that Object is regarded as the *expression*.

If, then, we wish to make a division of the beautiful arts, we cannot choose a more convenient principle, at least tentatively, than the analogy of art with the mode of expression of which men avail themselves in speech, in order to communicate to one another as perfectly as possible not merely their concepts but also their sensations.[76]— This is done by *word*, *deportment*, and *tone* (articulation, gesticulation, and modulation). It is only by the combination of these three kinds of expression that communication between the speaker [and his hearers] can be complete. For thus thought, intuition, and sensation are transmitted to others simultaneously and conjointly.

There are, therefore, only three kinds of beautiful arts; the arts of *speech*, the *formative* arts, and the art of the *play of sensations* (as external sensible impressions). We may also arrange a division by dichotomy; thus beautiful art may be divided into the art of expression of thoughts and of intuitions; and these further subdivided in accordance with their form or their matter (sensation). But this would appear to be too abstract, and not so accordant with ordinary concepts.

(1) The arts of SPEECH are *rhetoric* and *poetry*. *Rhetoric* is the art of carrying on a serious business of the Understanding as if it were a free play of the Imagination; *poetry*, the art of conducting a free play of the Imagination as if it were a serious business of the Understanding.

The *orator*, then, promises a serious business, and in order to entertain his audience conducts it as if it were a mere *play* with Ideas. The *poet* merely promises an entertaining play with Ideas, and yet it has the same effect upon the Understanding as if he had only intended to carry on its business. The combination and harmony of both cognitive faculties, Sensibility and Understanding, which cannot dispense with one another, but which yet cannot well be united without constraint and mutual prejudice, must appear to be undesigned and so to be brought about by themselves: otherwise it is not *beautiful* art. Hence, all that is studied and anxious must be avoided in it, for beautiful art must be free art in a double sense. It is not a work like that of a tradesman, the magnitude of which can be judged, exacted, or paid for, according to a definite standard; and again, though the mind is occupied, still it feels itself contented and stimulated, without looking to any other purpose (independently of reward.)

The orator therefore gives something which he does not promise, viz. an entertaining play of the Imagination; but he also fails to supply what he did promise, which is indeed his announced business, viz. the purposive occupation of the Understanding. On the other hand, the poet promises little and announces a mere play with Ideas; but he supplies something which is worth occupying ourselves with, because he provides in this play food for the Understanding, and by the aid of Imagination gives life to his concepts. [Thus the orator on the whole gives less, the poet more, than he promises.][77]

(2) The FORMATIVE arts, or those by which expression is found for Ideas in *sensible intuition* (not by representations of mere Imagination that are aroused by words), are either arts of *sensible truth* or of *sensible illusion*. The former is called *Plastic*, the latter *Painting*. Both express Ideas by figures in space; the former makes figures cognisable by two senses, sight and touch (although not by the latter as far as beauty is concerned); the latter only by one, the first of these. The aesthetical Idea (the archetype or original image) is fundamental for both in the Imagination, but the figure which expresses this (the ectype or copy) is either given in its bodily extension (as the object itself exists), or as it paints itself on the eye (according to its appearance when projected on a flat surface). In the first case[78] the condition given to reflection may be either the reference to an actual purpose or only the semblance of it.

To *Plastic*, the first kind of beautiful formative Art, belong *Sculpture* and *Architecture*. The *first* presents corporeally concepts of things, *as they might have existed in nature* (though as beautiful art it has regard to aesthetical purposiveness). The *second* is the art of presenting concepts of things that are possible *only through Art*, and whose form has for its determining ground not nature but an arbitrary purpose, with the view of presenting them with aesthetical purposiveness. In the latter the chief point is a certain *use* of the artistic object, by which condition the aesthetical Ideas are limited. In the former the main design is the mere *expression* of aesthetical Ideas. Thus statues of men, gods, animals, etc., are of the first kind; but temples, splendid buildings for public assemblies, even dwelling-houses, triumphal arches, columns, mausoleums, and the like, erected in honourable remembrance, belong to Architecture. Indeed all house furniture (upholsterer's work and such like things which are for use) may be reckoned under this art; because the suitability of a product for a certain use is the essential thing in an *architectural work*. On the other hand, a mere *piece of sculpture*, which is simply made for show and which is to please in itself, is as a corporeal presentation a mere imitation of nature, though with a reference to aesthetical Ideas; in it *sensible truth* is not to be carried so far that the product ceases to look like art and looks like a product of the elective will.

Painting, as the second kind of formative art, which presents a *sensible illusion* artificially combined with Ideas, I would divide into the art of the beautiful *depicting of nature* and that of the beautiful *arrangement of its products*. The first is *painting proper*, the second is the art of *landscape gardening*. The first gives only the illusory appearance of corporeal extension; the second gives this in accordance with truth, but only the appearance of utility and availableness for other purposes than the mere play of the Imagination in the contemplation of its forms.[79] This latter is nothing else than the ornamentation of the soil with a variety of those things (grasses, flowers, shrubs, trees, even ponds, hillocks, and dells) which nature presents to an observer, only arranged differently and in conformity with certain Ideas. But, again, the beautiful arrangement of corporeal things is only apparent to the eye, like painting; the sense of touch cannot supply any intuitive presentation of such a form. Under painting in the wide sense I would reckon the decoration of rooms by the aid of tapestry, bric-a-brac, and all beautiful furniture which is merely available to be *looked* at; and the same may be said of the art of tasteful dressing (with rings, snuff-boxes, etc.). For a bed of various flowers, a room filled with various ornaments (including under this head even ladies' finery), make at a fête a kind of picture; which, like pictures properly so-called (that are not intended to *teach* either history or natural science), has in view merely the entertainment of the Imagination in free play with Ideas, and the occupation of the aesthetical Judgement without any definite purpose. The detailed work in all this decoration may be quite distinct in the different cases and may require very different artists; but the judgement of taste upon whatever is beautiful in these various arts is always determined in the same way: viz. it only judges the forms (without any reference to a purpose) as they present themselves to the eye either singly or in combination, according to the effect they produce upon the Imagination.—But that formative art may be compared (by analogy) with deportment in speech is justified by the fact that the spirit of the artist supplies by these figures a bodily expression to his thought and its mode, and makes the thing itself as it were speak in mimic language. This is a very common play of our fancy, which attributes to lifeless things a spirit suitable to their form by which they speak to us.

(3) The art of the BEAUTIFUL PLAY OF SENSATIONS (externally stimulated), which admits at the same time of universal communication, can be concerned with nothing else than the proportion of the different degrees of the disposition (tension) of the sense, to which the sensation belongs, *i.e.* with its tone. In this far-reaching signification of the word it may be divided into the artistic play of the sensations of hearing and sight, *i.e.* into *Music* and the *Art of colour*.—It is noteworthy that these two senses, besides their susceptibility for impressions so far as these are needed to gain concepts of external objects, are also capable of a peculiar sensation bound up therewith, of which we cannot strictly decide whether it is based on sense or reflection. This susceptibility may sometimes be wanting, although in other respects the sense, as regards its use for the cognition of Objects, is not at all deficient but is peculiarly fine. That is, we cannot say with certainty whether colours or tones (sounds) are merely pleasant sensations or whether they form in themselves a beautiful play of sensations, and as such bring with them in aesthetical judgement a satisfaction in their form. If we think of the velocity of the vibrations of light, or in the second case of the air, which probably far surpasses all our faculty of judging immediately in perception the time interval between them, we must believe that it is only the *effect* of these vibrations upon the elastic parts of our body that is felt, but that the *time interval* between them is not remarked or brought into judgement; and thus that only pleasantness and not beauty of composition is bound up

with colours and tones. But on the other hand, *first,* we think of the mathematical [element] which enables us to pronounce on the proportion between these oscillations in music and thus to judge of them; and by analogy with which we easily may judge of the distinctions between colours. *Secondly,* we recall instances (although they are rare) of men who with the best sight in the world cannot distinguish colours, and with the sharpest hearing cannot distinguish tones; whilst for those who can do this the perception of an altered quality (not merely of the degree of sensation) in the different intensities in the scale of colours and tones is definite; and further, the very number of these is fixed by *intelligible* differences. Thus we may be compelled to see that both kinds of sensations are to be regarded not as mere sensible impressions, but as the effects of a judgement passed upon the form in the play of divers sensations. The difference in our definition, according as we adopt the one or the other opinion in judging of the grounds of Music, would be just this: either, as we have done, we must explain it as the beautiful play of sensations (of hearing), or else as a play of *pleasant* sensations. According to the former mode of explanation music is represented altogether as a *beautiful* art; according to the latter, as a *pleasant* art (at least in part).

§ 52. OF THE COMBINATION OF BEAUTIFUL ARTS IN ONE AND THE SAME PRODUCT

Rhetoric may be combined with a pictorial presentation of its subjects and objects in a *theatrical piece;* poetry may be combined with music in a *song,* and this again with pictorial (theatrical) presentation in an *opera;* the play of sensations in music may be combined with the play of figures in the *dance,* and so on. Even the presentation of the sublime, so far as it belongs to beautiful art, may combine with beauty in a *tragedy in verse,* in a *didactic poem,* in an *oratorio;* and in these combinations beautiful art is yet more artistic. Whether it is also more beautiful may in some of these cases be doubted (since so many different kinds of satisfaction cross one another). Yet in all beautiful art the essential thing is the form, which is purposive as regards our observation and judgement, where the pleasure is at the same time cultivation and disposes the spirit to Ideas, and consequently makes it susceptible of still more of such pleasure and entertainment. The essential element is not the matter of sensation (charm or emotion), which has only to do with enjoyment; this leaves behind nothing in the Idea, and it makes the spirit dull, the object gradually distasteful, and the mind, on account of its consciousness of a disposition that conflicts with purpose in the judgement of Reason, discontented with itself and peevish.

If the beautiful arts are not brought into more or less close combination with moral Ideas, which alone bring with them a self-sufficing satisfaction, this latter fate must ultimately be theirs. They then serve only as a distraction, of which we are the more in need the more we avail ourselves of them to disperse the discontent of the mind with itself; so that we thus render ourselves ever more useless and ever more discontented. The beauties of nature are generally of most benefit in this point of view, if we are early accustomed to observe, appreciate, and admire them.

§ 53. COMPARISON OF THE RESPECTIVE AESTHETICAL WORTH OF THE BEAUTIFUL ARTS

Of all the arts *poetry* (which owes its origin almost entirely to genius and will least be guided by precept or example) maintains the first rank. It expands the mind by setting the Imagination at liberty; and by offering within the limits of a given concept amid the unbounded variety of possible forms accordant therewith, that which unites the presentment of this concept with a wealth of thought, to which no verbal expression is completely adequate; and so rising aesthetically to Ideas. It strengthens the mind by making it feel its faculty—free, spontaneous and independent of natural determination —of considering and judging nature as a phenomenon in accordance with aspects which it does not present in experience either for Sense or Understanding, and therefore of using it on behalf of, and as a sort of schema for, the supersensible. It plays with illusion, which it produces at pleasure, but without deceiving by it; for it declares its exercise to be mere play, which however can be purposively used by the Understanding.— Rhetoric, in so far as this means the art of persuasion, *i.e.* of deceiving by a beautiful show (*ars oratoria*), and not mere elegance of speech (eloquence and style), is a Dialectic, which borrows from poetry only so much as is needful to win minds to the side of the orator before they have formed a judgement, and to deprive them of their freedom; it cannot therefore be recommended either for the law courts or for the pulpit. For if we are dealing with civil law, with the rights of individual persons, or with lasting instruction and determination of people's minds to an accurate knowledge and a conscientious observance of their duty, it is unworthy of so important a business to allow a trace of any exuberance of wit and imagination to appear, and still less any trace of the art of talking people over and of captivating them for the advantage of any chance person. For although this art may sometimes be directed to legitimate and praiseworthy designs, it becomes objectionable, when in this way maxims and dispositions are spoiled in a subjective point of view, though the action may objectively be lawful. It is not enough to do what is right; we should practise it solely on the ground that it is right. Again, the mere concept of this species of matters of human concern, when clear and combined with a lively presentation of it in examples, without any offence against the rules of euphony of speech or propriety of expression, has by itself for Ideas of Reason (which collectively constitute eloquence), sufficient influence upon human minds; so that it is not needful to add the machinery of persuasion, which, since it can be used equally well to beautify or to hide vice and error, cannot quite lull the secret suspicion that one is being artfully overreached. In poetry everything proceeds with honesty and candour. It declares itself to be a mere entertaining play of the Imagination, which wishes to proceed as regards form in harmony with the laws of the Understanding; and it does not desire to steal upon and ensnare the Understanding by the aid of sensible presentation.[80]

After poetry, *if we are to deal with charm and mental movement*, I would place that art which comes nearest to the art of speech and can very naturally be united with it, viz. *the art of tone*. For although it speaks by means of mere sensations without concepts, and so does not, like poetry, leave anything over for reflection, it yet moves the mind in a greater variety of ways and more intensely, although only transitorily. It is, however, rather enjoyment than culture (the play of thought that is incidentally excited by its means is merely the effect of a kind of mechanical association); and in the judgement of Reason it has less worth than any other of the beautiful arts. Hence, like all enjoyment, it desires constant change, and does not bear frequent repetition without producing weariness. Its charm, which admits of universal communication, appears to rest on this, that every expression of speech has in its context a tone appropriate to the sense. This tone indicates more or less an affection of the speaker, and produces it also in the hearer; which affection excites in its turn in the hearer the Idea that is expressed in speech by the tone in question. Thus as modulation is as it were a universal language of sensations intelligible to every man, the art of tone employs it by itself alone in its full force, viz. as a language of the affections, and thus communicates universally according to the laws of association the aesthetical Ideas naturally combined therewith. Now these aesthetical Ideas are not concepts or determinate thoughts. Hence the form of the composition of these sensations (harmony and melody) only serves instead of the form of language, by means of their proportionate accordance, to express the aesthetical Idea of a connected whole of an unspeakable wealth of thought, corresponding to a certain theme which produces the dominating affection in the piece. This can be brought mathematically under certain rules, because it rests in the case of tones on the relation between the number of vibrations of the air in the same time, so far as these tones are combined simultaneously or successively. To this mathematical form, although not represented by determinate concepts, alone attaches the satisfaction that unites the mere reflection upon such a number of concomitant or consecutive sensations with this their play, as a condition of its beauty valid for every man. It is this alone which permits Taste to claim in advance a rightful authority over every one's judgement.

But in the charm and mental movement produced by Music, Mathematic has certainly not the slightest share. It is only the indispensable condition (*conditio sine qua non*) of that proportion of the impressions in their combination and in their alternation by which it becomes possible to gather them together and prevent them from destroying one another, and to harmonise them so as to produce a continual movement and animation of the mind, by means of affections consonant therewith, and thus a delightful personal enjoyment.

If, on the other hand, we estimate the worth of the Beautiful Arts by the culture they supply to the mind, and take as a standard the expansion of the faculties which must concur in the Judgement for cognition, Music will have the lowest place among them (as it has perhaps the highest among those arts which are valued for their pleasantness), because it merely plays with sensations. The formative arts are far before it in this point of view; for in putting the Imagination in a free play, which is also accordant with the Understanding, they at the same time carry on a serious business. This they do by producing a product that serves for concepts as a permanent self-commendatory vehicle for promoting their union with sensibility and thus, as it were, the urbanity of the higher cognitive powers. These two species of art take quite different courses; the first proceeds from sensations to indeterminate Ideas, the second from determinate Ideas to sensations. The latter produce *permanent*, the former only *transitory* impressions. The Imagination can recall the one and entertain itself pleasantly therewith; but the other either vanish entirely, or if they are recalled involuntarily by the Imagination they are rather wearisome than pleasant.[81] Besides, there attaches to Music a certain want of urbanity from the fact that, chiefly from the character of its instruments, it extends its influence further than is desired (in the neighbourhood), and so as it were obtrudes itself, and does violence to the freedom of others who are not of the musical company. The Arts which appeal to the eyes do not do this; for we need only turn our eyes away, if we wish to avoid being impressed. The case of music is almost like that of the delight derived from a smell that diffuses itself widely. The man who pulls his perfumed hand-kerchief out of his pocket attracts the attention of all round him, even against their will, and he forces them, if they are to breathe at all, to enjoy the scent; hence this habit has gone out of fashion.[82]

Among the formative arts I would give the palm to painting; partly because as the art of delineation it lies at the root of all the other formative arts, and partly because it can penetrate much further into the region of Ideas, and can extend the field of intuition in conformity with them further than the others can.

§ 54. REMARK

As we have often shown, there is an essential difference between *what satisfies simply in the act of judging it*, and that which *gratifies* (pleases in sensation). We cannot ascribe the latter to every one, as we can the former. Gratification (the causes of which may even be situate in Ideas) appears always to consist in a feeling of the furtherance of the whole life of the man, and consequently, also of his bodily well-being, *i.e.* his health; so that *Epicurus*, who gave out that all gratification was at bottom bodily sensation, may, perhaps, not have been wrong, but only misunderstood himself when he reckoned intellectual and even practical satisfaction under gratification. If we have this distinction in view we can explain how a gratification may dissatisfy the man who sensibly feels it (*e.g.* the joy of a needy but well-meaning man at becoming the heir of an affectionate but penurious father); or how a deep grief may satisfy the person experiencing it (the sorrow of a widow at the death of her excellent husband); or how a gratification can in addition satisfy (as in the sciences that we pursue); or how a grief (*e.g.* hatred, envy, revenge) can moreover dissatisfy. The satisfaction or dissatisfaction here depends on Reason, and is the same as *approbation* or *disapprobation*; but gratification and grief can only rest on the feeling or prospect of a possible (on whatever grounds) *well-being* or *its opposite*.

All changing free play of sensations (that have no design at their basis) gratifies, because it promotes the feeling of health. In the judgement of Reason we may or may not have any satisfaction in its object or even in this gratification; and this latter may rise to the height of an affection, although we take no interest in the object, at least none that is proportionate to the degree of the affection. We may subdivide this free play of sensations into the *play of fortune* [games of chance], the *play of tone* [music], and the *play of thought* [wit]. The *first* requires an *interest*, whether of vanity or of selfishness; which, however, is not nearly so great as the interest that attaches to the way in which we are striving to procure it. The *second* requires merely the change of *sensations*, all of which have a relation to affection, though they have not the degree of affection, and excite aesthetical Ideas. The *third* springs merely from the change of representations in the Judgement; by it, indeed, no thought that brings an interest with it is produced, but yet the mind is animated thereby.

How much gratification games must afford, without any necessity of placing at their basis an interested design, all our evening parties show; for hardly any of them can be carried on without a game. But the affections of hope, fear, joy, wrath, scorn, are put in play by them, alternating every moment; and they are so vivid that by them, as by a kind of internal motion, all the vital processes of the body seem to be promoted, as is shown by the mental vivacity excited by them, although nothing is gained or learnt thereby. But as the beautiful does not enter into games of chance, we will here set them aside. On the other hand, music and that which excites laughter are two different kinds of play with aesthetical Ideas, or with representations of the Understanding through which ultimately nothing is thought; and yet they can give lively gratification merely by their changes. Thus we recognise pretty clearly that the animation in both cases is merely bodily, although it is excited by Ideas of the mind; and that the feeling of health produced by a motion of the intestines corresponding to the play in question makes up that whole gratification of a gay party, which is regarded as so refined and so spiritual. It is not the judging the harmony in tones or sallies of wit,—which serves only in combination with their beauty as a necessary vehicle,—but the furtherance of the vital bodily processes, the affection that moves the intestines and the diaphragm, in a word, the feeling of health (which without such inducements one does not feel) that makes up the gratification felt by us; so that we can thus reach the body through the soul and use the latter as the physician of the former.

In music this play proceeds from bodily sensations to aesthetical Ideas (the Objects of our affections), and then from these back again to the body with redoubled force. In the case of jokes (the art of which, just like music, should rather be reckoned as pleasant than beautiful) the play begins with the thoughts which together occupy the body, so far as they admit of sensible expression; and as the Understanding stops suddenly short at this presentment, in which it does not find what it expected, we feel the effect of this slackening in the body by the oscillation of the organs, which promotes the restoration of equilibrium and has a favourable influence upon health.

In everything that is to excite a lively convulsive laugh there must be something absurd (in which the Understanding, therefore, can find no satisfaction). *Laughter is an affection arising from the sudden transformation of a strained expectation into nothing.*[83] This transformation, which is certainly not enjoyable by the Understanding, yet indirectly gives it very active enjoyment for a moment. Therefore its cause must consist in the influence of the representation upon the body, and the reflex effect of this upon the mind; not, indeed, through the representation being objectively an object of gratification[84] (for how could a delusive expectation gratify?), but simply through it as a mere play of representations bringing about an equilibrium of the vital powers in the body.

Suppose this story to be told: An Indian at the table of an Englishman in Surat, when he saw a bottle of ale opened and all the beer turned into froth and overflowing, testified his great astonishment with many exclamations. When the Englishman asked him, "What is there in this to astonish you so much?" he answered, "I am not at all astonished that it should flow out, but I do wonder how you ever got it in." At this story we laugh, and it gives us hearty pleasure; not because we deem ourselves cleverer than this ignorant man, or because of anything else in it that we note as satisfactory to the Understanding, but because our expectation was strained [for a time] and then was suddenly dissipated into nothing. Again: The heir of a rich relative wished to arrange for an imposing funeral, but he lamented that he could not properly succeed; "for" (said he) "the more money I give my mourners to look sad, the more cheerful they look!"[85] When we hear this story we laugh loud, and the reason is that an expectation is suddenly transformed into nothing. We must note well that it does not transform itself into the positive opposite of an expected object—for then there would still be something, which might even be a cause of grief—but it must be transformed into nothing. For if a man arouses great expectations in us when telling a story, and at the end we see its falsehood immediately, it displeases us; *e.g.* the story of the people whose hair in consequence of great grief turned gray in one night. But if a wag, to repair the effect of this story, describes very circumstantially the grief of the merchant returning from India to Europe with all his wealth in merchandise who was forced to throw it overboard in a heavy storm, and who grieved thereat so much that his *wig* turned gray the same night—we laugh and it gives us gratification. For we treat our own mistake in the case of an object otherwise indifferent to us, or rather the Idea which we are following out, as we treat a ball which we knock to and fro for a time, though our only serious intention is to seize it and hold it fast. It is not the mere rebuff of a liar or a simpleton that arouses our gratification; for the latter story told with assumed seriousness would set a whole company in a roar of laughter, while the former would ordinarily not be regarded as worth attending to.

It is remarkable that in all such cases the jest must contain something that is capable of deceiving for a moment. Hence, when the illusion is dissipated, the mind turns back to try it once again, and thus through a rapidly alternating tension and relaxation it is jerked back and put into a state of oscillation. This, because the strain on the cord as it were is suddenly (and not gradually) relaxed, must occasion a mental movement, and an inner bodily movement harmonising therewith, which continues involuntarily and fatigues, even while cheering us (the effects of a motion conducive to health).

For if we admit that with all our thoughts is harmonically combined a movement in the organs of the body, we shall easily comprehend how to this sudden transposition of the mind, now to one now to another standpoint in order to contemplate its object, may correspond an alternating tension and relaxation of the elastic portions of our intestines, which communicates itself to the diaphragm (like that which ticklish people feel). In connexion with this the lungs expel the air at rapidly succeeding intervals, and thus bring about a movement beneficial to health; which alone, and not what precedes it in the mind, is the proper cause of the gratification in a thought that at bottom represents nothing.—*Voltaire* said that heaven had given us two things to counterbalance the many miseries of life, *hope* and *sleep*.[86] He could have added *laughter*, if the means of exciting it in reasonable men were only as easily attainable, and the requisite wit or originality of humour were not so rare, as the talent is common of imagining things which *break one's head*, as mystic dreamers do, or which *break one's neck*, as your genius does, or which *break one's heart*, as sentimental romance-writers (and even moralists of the same kidney) do.

We may therefore, as it seems to me, readily concede to *Epicurus* that all gratification, even that which is occasioned through concepts, excited by aesthetical Ideas, is *animal*, *i.e.* bodily sensation; without the least prejudice to the *spiritual* feeling of respect for moral Ideas, which is not gratification at all but an esteem for self (for humanity in us), that raises us above the need of gratification, and even without the slightest prejudice to the less noble [feeling] of *taste*.

We find a combination of these two last in *naiveté*, which is the breaking out of the sincerity originally natural to humanity in opposition to that art of dissimulation which has become a second nature. We laugh at the simplicity that does not understand how to dissemble; and yet we are delighted with the simplicity of the nature which thwarts that art. We look for the commonplace manner of artificial utterance devised with foresight to make a fair show; and behold! it is the unspoiled innocent nature which we do not expect to find, and which he who displays it did not think of disclosing. That the fair but false show which generally has so much influence upon our judgement is here suddenly transformed into nothing, so that, as it were, the rogue in us is laid bare, produces a movement of the mind in two opposite directions, which gives a wholesome shock to the body. But the fact that something infinitely better than all assumed manner, viz. purity of disposition (or at least the tendency thereto), is not quite extinguished yet in human nature, blends seriousness and high esteem with this play of the Judgement. But because it is only a transitory phenomenon and the veil of dissimulation is soon drawn over it again, there is mingled therewith a compassion which is an emotion of tenderness; this, as play, readily admits of combination with a good-hearted laugh, and ordinarily is actually so combined, and withal is wont to compensate him who supplies its material for the embarrassment which results from not yet being wise after the manner of men.—An art that is to be *naive* is thus a contradiction; but the representation of naiveté in a fictitious personage is quite possible, and is a beautiful though a rare art. Naiveté must not be confounded with open-hearted simplicity, which does not artificially spoil nature solely because it does not understand the art of social intercourse.

The *humorous* manner again may be classified as that which, as exhilarating us, is near akin to the gratification that proceeds from laughter; and belongs to the originality of spirit, but not to the talent of beautiful art. *Humour* in the good sense means the talent of being able voluntarily to put oneself into a certain mental disposition, in which everything is judged quite differently from the ordinary method (reversed, in fact), and yet in accordance with certain rational principles in such a frame of mind. He who is involuntarily subject to such mutations is called *a man of humours* [launisch]; but he who can assume them voluntarily and purposively (on behalf of a lively presentment brought about by the aid of a contrast that excites a laugh)—he and his manner of speech are called *humorous* [launigt]. This manner, however, belongs rather to pleasant than to beautiful art, because the object of the latter must always exhibit intrinsic worth, and hence requires a certain seriousness in the presentation, as taste does in the act of judgement.

SECOND DIVISION—DIALECTIC OF THE AESTHETICAL JUDGEMENT

§ 55

A faculty of Judgement that is to be dialectical must in the first place be rationalising, *i.e.* its judgements must claim universality[87] and that *a priori*; for it is in the opposition of such judgements that Dialectic consists. Hence the incompatibility of aesthetical judgements of Sense (about the pleasant and the unpleasant) is not dialectical. And again, the conflict between judgements of Taste, so far as each man depends merely on his own taste, forms no Dialectic of taste; because no one proposes to make his own judgement a universal rule. There remains therefore no other concept of a Dialectic which has to do with taste than that of a Dialectic of the *Critique* of taste (not of taste itself) in respect of its *principles*; for here concepts that contradict one another (as to the ground of the possibility of judgements of taste in general) naturally and unavoidably present themselves. The transcendental Critique of taste will therefore contain a part which can bear the name of a Dialectic of the aesthetical Judgement, only if and so far as there is found an antinomy of the principles of this faculty which renders its conformity to law, and consequently also its internal possibility, doubtful.

§ 56. REPRESENTATION OF THE ANTINOMY OF TASTE

The first commonplace of taste is contained in the proposition, with which every tasteless person proposes to avoid blame: *every one has his own taste*. That is as much as to say that the determining ground of this judgement is merely subjective (gratification or grief), and that the judgement has no right to the necessary assent of others.

The second commonplace invoked even by those who admit for judgements of taste the right to speak with validity for every one is: *there is no disputing about taste*. That is as much as to say that the determining ground of a judgement of taste may indeed be objective, but that it cannot be reduced to definite concepts, and that consequently about the judgement itself nothing can be *decided* by proofs, although much may rightly be *contested*. For *contesting* [quarrelling] and *disputing* [controversy] are doubtless the same in this, that by means of the mutual opposition of judgements they seek to produce their accordance; but different in that the latter hopes to bring this about according to definite concepts as determining grounds, and consequently assumes *objective concepts* as grounds of the judgement. But where this is regarded as impracticable, controversy is regarded as alike impracticable.

We easily see that between these two commonplaces there is a proposition wanting, which, though it has not passed into a proverb, is yet familiar to every one, viz. *there may be a quarrel about taste* (although there can be no controversy). But this proposition involves the contradictory of the former one. For wherever quarrelling is permissible, there must be a hope of mutual reconciliation; and consequently we can count on grounds of our judgement that have not merely private validity, and therefore are not merely subjective. And to this the proposition, *every one has his own taste*, is directly opposed.

There emerges therefore in respect of the principle of taste the following Antinomy:
—

(1) *Thesis*. The judgement of taste is not based upon concepts; for otherwise it would admit of controversy (would be determinable by proofs).

(2) *Antithesis*. The judgement of taste is based on concepts; for otherwise, despite its diversity, we could not quarrel about it (we could not claim for our judgement the necessary assent of others).

§ 57. SOLUTION OF THE ANTINOMY OF TASTE

There is no possibility of removing the conflict between these principles that underlie every judgement of taste (which are nothing else than the two peculiarities of the judgement of taste exhibited above in the Analytic), except by showing that the concept to which we refer the Object in this kind of judgement is not taken in the same sense in both maxims of the aesthetical Judgement. This twofold sense or twofold point of view is necessary to our transcendental Judgement; but also the illusion which arises from the confusion of one with the other is natural and unavoidable.

The judgement of taste must refer to some concept; otherwise it could make absolutely no claim to be necessarily valid for every one. But it is not therefore capable of being proved *from* a concept; because a concept may be either determinable or in itself undetermined and undeterminable. The concepts of the Understanding are of the former kind; they are determinable through predicates of sensible intuition which can correspond to them. But the transcendental rational concept of the supersensible, which lies at the basis of all sensible intuition, is of the latter kind, and therefore cannot be theoretically determined further.

Now the judgement of taste is applied to objects of Sense, but not with a view of determining a *concept* of them for the Understanding; for it is not a cognitive judgement. It is thus only a private judgement, in which a singular representation intuitively perceived is referred to the feeling of pleasure; and so far would be limited as regards its validity to the individual judging. The object is *for me* an object of satisfaction; by others it may be regarded quite differently—every one has his own taste.

Nevertheless there is undoubtedly contained in the judgement of taste a wider reference of the representation of the Object (as well as of the subject), whereon we base an extension of judgements of this kind as necessary for every one. At the basis of this there must necessarily be a concept somewhere; though a concept which cannot be determined through intuition. But through a concept of this sort we know nothing, and consequently it can *supply no proof* for the judgement of taste. Such a concept is the mere pure rational concept of the supersensible which underlies the object (and also the subject judging it), regarded as an Object of sense and thus as phenomenon.[88] For if we do not admit such a reference, the claim of the judgement of taste to universal validity would not hold good. If the concept on which it is based were only a mere confused concept of the Understanding, like that of perfection, with which we could bring the sensible intuition of the Beautiful into correspondence, it would be at least possible in itself to base the judgement of taste on proofs; which contradicts the thesis.

But all contradiction disappears if I say: the judgement of taste is based on a concept (viz. the concept of the general ground of the subjective purposiveness of nature for the Judgement); from which, however, nothing can be known and proved in respect of the Object, because it is in itself undeterminable and useless for knowledge. Yet at the same time and on that very account the judgement has validity for every one (though of course for each only as a singular judgement immediately accompanying his intuition); because its determining ground lies perhaps in the concept of that which may be regarded as the supersensible substrate of humanity.

The solution of an antinomy only depends on the possibility of showing that two apparently contradictory propositions do not contradict one another in fact, but that they may be consistent; although the explanation of the possibility of their concept may transcend our cognitive faculties. That this illusion is natural and unavoidable by human Reason, and also why it is so, and remains so, although it ceases to deceive after the analysis of the apparent contradiction, may be thus explained.

In the two contradictory judgements we take the concept, on which the universal validity of a judgement must be based, in the same sense; and yet we apply to it two opposite predicates. In the Thesis we mean that the judgement of taste is not based upon *determinate* concepts; and in the Antithesis that the judgement of taste is based upon a concept, but an *indeterminate* one (viz. of the supersensible substrate of phenomena). Between these two there is no contradiction.

We can do nothing more than remove this conflict between the claims and counterclaims of taste. It is absolutely impossible to give a definite objective principle of taste, in accordance with which its judgements could be derived, examined, and established; for then the judgement would not be one of taste at all. The subjective principle, viz. the indefinite Idea of the supersensible in us, can only be put forward as the sole key to the puzzle of this faculty whose sources are hidden from us: it can be made no further intelligible.

The proper concept of taste, that is of a merely reflective aesthetical Judgement, lies at the basis of the antinomy here exhibited and adjusted. Thus the two apparently contradictory principles are reconciled—*both can be true*; which is sufficient. If, on the other hand, we assume, as some do, *pleasantness* as the determining ground of taste (on account of the singularity of the representation which lies at the basis of the judgement of taste), or, as others will have it, the principle of perfection (on account of the universality of the same), and settle the definition of taste accordingly; then there arises an antinomy which it is absolutely impossible to adjust except by showing that *both* the contrary (though not contradictory) *propositions are false*. And this would prove that the concept on which they are based is self-contradictory. Hence we see that the removal of the antinomy of the aesthetical Judgement takes a course similar to that pursued by the Critique in the solution of the antinomies of pure theoretical Reason. And thus here, as also in the Critique of practical Reason, the antinomies force us against our will to look beyond the sensible and to seek in the supersensible the point of union for all our *a priori* faculties; because no other expedient is left to make our Reason harmonious with itself.

Remark I

As we so often find occasion in Transcendental Philosophy for distinguishing Ideas from concepts of the Understanding, it may be of use to introduce technical terms to correspond to this distinction. I believe that no one will object if I propose some.—In the most universal signification of the word, Ideas are representations referred to an object, according to a certain (subjective or objective) principle, but so that they can never become a cognition of it. They are either referred to an intuition, according to a merely subjective principle of the mutual harmony of the cognitive powers (the Imagination and the Understanding), and they are then called *aesthetical*; or they are referred to a concept according to an objective principle, although they can never furnish a cognition of the object and are called *rational Ideas*. In the latter case the concept is a *transcendent* one, which is different from a concept of the Understanding, to which an adequately corresponding experience can always be supplied, and which therefore is called *immanent*.

An *aesthetical Idea* cannot become a cognition, because it is an *intuition* (of the Imagination) for which an adequate concept can never be found. A *rational Idea* can never become a cognition, because it involves a concept (of the supersensible), corresponding to which an intuition can never be given.

Now I believe we might call the aesthetical Idea an *inexponible* representation of the Imagination, and a rational Idea an *indemonstrable* concept of Reason. It is assumed of both that they are not generated without grounds, but (according to the above explanation of an Idea in general) in conformity with certain principles of the cognitive faculties to which they belong (subjective principles in the one case, objective in the other).

Concepts of the Understanding must, as such, always be demonstrable [if by demonstration we understand, as in anatomy, merely *presentation*];[89] *i.e.* the object corresponding to them must always be capable of being given in intuition (pure or empirical); for thus alone could they become cognitions. The concept of *magnitude* can be given *a priori* in the intuition of space, *e.g.* of a right line, etc.; the concept of *cause* in impenetrability, in the collision of bodies, etc. Consequently both can be authenticated by means of an empirical intuition, *i.e.* the thought of them can be proved (demonstrated, verified) by an example; and this must be possible, for otherwise we should not be certain that the concept was not empty, *i.e.* devoid of any *Object*.

In Logic we ordinarily use the expressions demonstrable or indemonstrable only in respect of *propositions*, but these might be better designated by the titles respectively of *mediately and immediately certain* propositions; for pure Philosophy has also propositions of both kinds, *i.e.* true propositions, some of which are susceptible of proof and others not. It can, as philosophy, prove them on *a priori* grounds, but it cannot demonstrate them; unless we wish to depart entirely from the proper meaning of this word, according to which *to demonstrate* (*ostendere, exhibere*) is equivalent to presenting a concept in intuition (whether in proof or merely in definition). If the intuition is *a priori* this is called construction; but if it is empirical, then the Object is displayed by means of which objective reality is assured to the concept. Thus we say of an anatomist that he demonstrates the human eye, if by a dissection of this organ he makes intuitively evident the concept which he has previously treated discursively.

It hence follows that the rational concept of the supersensible substrate of all phenomena in general, or even of that which must be placed at the basis of our arbitrary will in respect of the moral law, viz. of transcendental freedom, is already, in kind, an indemonstrable concept and a rational Idea; while virtue is so, in degree. For there can be given in experience, as regards its quality, absolutely nothing corresponding to the former; whereas in the latter case no empirical product attains to the degree of that causality, which the rational Idea prescribes as the rule.

As in a rational Idea the *Imagination* with its intuitions does not attain to the given concept, so in an aesthetical Idea the *Understanding* by its concepts never attains completely to that internal intuition which the Imagination binds up with a given representation. Since, now, to reduce a representation of the Imagination to concepts is the same thing as to *expound* it, the aesthetical Idea may be called an *inexponible* representation of the Imagination (in its free play). I shall have occasion in the sequel to say something more of Ideas of this kind; now I only note that both kinds of Ideas, rational and aesthetical, must have their principles; and must have them in Reason—the one in the objective, the other in the subjective principles of its employment.

We can consequently explain *genius* as the faculty of *aesthetical Ideas*; by which at the same time is shown the reason why in the products of genius it is the nature (of the subject) and not a premeditated purpose that gives the rule to the art (of the production of the beautiful). For since the beautiful must not be judged by concepts, but by the purposive attuning of the Imagination to agreement with the faculty of concepts in general, it cannot be rule and precept which can serve as the subjective standard of that aesthetical but unconditioned purposiveness in beautiful art, that can rightly claim to please every one. It can only be that in the subject which is nature and cannot be brought under rules or concepts, *i.e.* the supersensible substrate of all his faculties (to which no concept of the Understanding extends), and consequently that with respect to which it is the final purpose given by the intelligible [part] of our nature to harmonise all our cognitive faculties. Thus alone is it possible that there should be *a priori* at the basis of this purposiveness, for which we can prescribe no objective principle, a principle subjective and yet of universal validity.

Remark II

The following important remark occurs here: There are *three kinds of Antinomies* of pure Reason, which, however, all agree in this, that they compel us to give up the otherwise very natural hypothesis that objects of sense are things in themselves, and force us to regard them merely as phenomena, and to supply to them an intelligible substrate (something supersensible of which the concept is only an Idea, and supplies no proper knowledge). Without such antinomies Reason could never decide upon accepting a principle narrowing so much the field of its speculation, and could never bring itself to sacrifices by which so many otherwise brilliant hopes must disappear. For even now when, by way of compensation for these losses, a greater field in a practical aspect opens out before it, it appears not to be able without grief to part from those hopes, and disengage itself from its old attachment.

That there are three kinds of antinomies has its ground in this, that there are three cognitive faculties,—Understanding, Judgement, and Reason; of which each (as a superior cognitive faculty) must have its *a priori* principles. For Reason, in so far as it judges of these principles and their use, inexorably requires, in respect of them all, the unconditioned for the given conditioned; and this can never be found if we consider the sensible as belonging to things in themselves, and do not rather supply to it, as mere phenomenon, something supersensible (the intelligible substrate of nature both external and internal) as the reality in itself [Sache an sich selbst]. There are then: (1) *For the cognitive faculty* an antinomy of Reason in respect of the theoretical employment of the Understanding extended to the unconditioned; (2) *for the feeling of pleasure and pain* an antinomy of Reason in respect of the aesthetical employment of the Judgement; and (3) *for the faculty of desire* an antinomy in respect of the practical employment of the self-legislative Reason; so far as all these faculties have their superior principles *a priori*, and, in conformity with an inevitable requirement of Reason, must judge and be able to determine their Object, *unconditionally* according to those principles.

As for the two antinomies of the theoretical and practical employment of the superior cognitive faculties, we have already shown their *unavoidableness*, if judgements of this kind are not referred to a supersensible substrate of the given Objects, as phenomena; and also the *possibility of their solution*, as soon as this is done. And as for the antinomies in the employment of the Judgement, in conformity with the requirements of Reason, and their solution which is here given, there are only two ways of avoiding them. *Either*: we must deny that any *a priori* principle lies at the basis of the aesthetical judgement of taste; we must maintain that all claim to necessary universal agreement is a groundless and vain fancy, and that a judgement of taste only deserves to be regarded as correct because *it happens* that many people agree about it; and this, not because we *assume* an *a priori* principle behind this agreement, but because (as in the taste of the palate) of the contingent similar organisation of the different subjects. *Or*: we must assume that the judgement of taste is really a disguised judgement of Reason upon the perfection discovered in a thing and the reference of the manifold in it to a purpose, and is consequently only called aesthetical on account of the confusion here attaching to our reflection, although it is at bottom teleological. In the latter case we could declare the solution of the antinomies by means of transcendental Ideas to be needless and without point, and thus could harmonise these laws of taste with Objects of sense, not as mere phenomena but as things in themselves. But we have shown in several places in the exposition of judgements of taste how little either of these expedients will satisfy.

However, if it be granted that our deduction at least proceeds by the right method, although it be not yet plain enough in all its parts, three Ideas manifest themselves. *First*, there is the Idea of the supersensible in general, without any further determination of it, as the substrate of nature. *Secondly*, there is the Idea of the same as the principle of the subjective purposiveness of nature for our cognitive faculty. And *thirdly*, there is the Idea of the same as the principle of the purposes of freedom, and of the agreement of freedom with its purposes in the moral sphere.

§ 58. OF THE IDEALISM OF THE PURPOSIVENESS OF BOTH NATURE AND ART AS THE UNIQUE PRINCIPLE OF THE AESTHETICAL JUDGEMENT

To begin with, we can either place the principle of taste in the fact that it always judges in accordance with grounds which are empirical and therefore are only given *a posteriori* by sense, or concede that it judges on *a priori* grounds. The former would be the *empiricism* of the Critique of Taste; the latter its *rationalism*. According to the *former* the Object of our satisfaction would not differ from the *pleasant*; according to the latter, if the judgement rests on definite concepts, it would not differ from the *good*. Thus all *beauty* would be banished from the world, and only a particular name, expressing perhaps a certain mingling of the two above-named kinds of satisfaction, would remain in its place. But we have shown that there are also *a priori* grounds of satisfaction which can subsist along with the principle of rationalism, although they cannot be comprehended in *definite concepts*.

On the other hand, the rationalism of the principle of taste is either that of the *realism* of the purposiveness, or of its *idealism*. Because a judgement of taste is not a cognitive judgement, and beauty is not a characteristic of the Object, considered in itself, the rationalism of the principle of taste can never be placed in the fact that the purposiveness in this judgement is thought as objective, *i.e.* that the judgement theoretically, and therefore also logically (although only in a confused way), refers to the perfection of the Object. It only refers *aesthetically* to the agreement of the representation of the Object in the Imagination with the essential principles of Judgement in general in the subject. Consequently, even according to the principle of rationalism, the judgement of taste and the distinction between its realism and idealism can only be settled thus. Either in the first case, this subjective purposiveness is assumed as an actual (designed) *purpose* of nature (or art) harmonising with our Judgement; or, in the second case, as a purposive harmony with the needs of Judgement, in respect of nature and its forms produced according to particular laws, which shows itself, without purpose, spontaneously, and contingently.

The beautiful formations in the kingdom of organised nature speak loudly for the realism of the aesthetical purposiveness of nature; since we might assume that behind the production of the beautiful there is an Idea of the beautiful in the producing cause, viz. a *purpose* in respect of our Imagination. Flowers, blossoms, even the shapes of entire plants; the elegance of animal formations of all kinds, unneeded for their proper use, but, as it were, selected for our taste; especially the charming variety so satisfying to the eye and the harmonious arrangement of colours (in the pheasant, in shell-fish, in insects, even in the commonest flowers), which, as it only concerns the surface and not the figure of these creations (though perhaps requisite in regard of their internal purposes), seems to be entirely designed for external inspection; these things give great weight to that mode of explanation which assumes actual purposes of nature for our aesthetical Judgement.

On the other hand, not only is Reason opposed to this assumption in its maxims, which bid us always avoid as far as possible unnecessary multiplication of principles; but nature everywhere shows in its free formations much mechanical tendency to the productions of forms which seem, as it were, to be made for the aesthetical exercise of our Judgement, without affording the least ground for the supposition that there is need of anything more than its mechanism, merely as nature, according to which, without any Idea lying at their root, they can be purposive for our judgement. But I understand by *free formations* of nature *those* whereby from a *fluid at rest*, through the volatilisation or separation of a portion of its constituents (sometimes merely of caloric), the remainder in becoming solid assumes a definite shape or tissue (figure or texture), which is different according to the specific difference of the material, but in the same material is constant. Here it is always presupposed that we are speaking of a perfect fluid, *i.e.* that the material in it is completely dissolved, and that it is not a mere medley of solid particles in a state of suspension.

Formation, then, takes place by a *shooting together, i.e.* by a sudden solidification, not by a gradual transition from the fluid to the solid state, but all at once by a *saltus*; which transition is also called *crystallisation*. The commonest example of this kind of formation is the freezing of water, where first icicles are produced, which combine at angles of 60°, while others attach themselves to each vertex, until it all becomes ice; and so that, while this is going on, the water does not gradually become viscous, but is as perfectly fluid as if its temperature were far higher, although it is absolutely ice-cold. The matter that disengages itself, which is dissipated suddenly at the moment of solidification, is a considerable quantum of caloric, the disappearance of which, as it was only required for preserving fluidity, leaves the new ice not in the least colder than the water which shortly before was fluid.

Many salts, and also rocks, of a crystalline figure, are produced thus from a species of earth dissolved in water, we do not exactly know how. Thus are formed the glandular configurations of many minerals, the cubical sulphide of lead, the ruby silver ore, etc., in all probability in water and by the shooting together of particles, as they become forced by some cause to dispense with this vehicle and to unite in definite external shapes.

But also all kinds of matter, which have been kept in a fluid state by heat, and have become solid by cooling, show internally, when fractured, a definite texture. This makes us judge that if their own weight or the disturbance of the air had not prevented it, they would also have exhibited on the outer surface their specifically peculiar shapes. This has been observed in some metals on their inner surface, which have been hardened externally by fusion but are fluid in the interior, by the drawing off the internal fluid and the consequent undisturbed crystallisation of the remainder. Many of these mineral crystallisations, such as spars, hematite, arragonite, etc., often present beautiful shapes, the like of which art can only conceive; and the halo in the cavern of Antiparos[90] is merely produced by water trickling down strata of gypsum.

The fluid state is, to all appearance, older than the solid state, and plants as well as animal bodies are fashioned out of fluid nutritive matter, so far as this forms itself in a state of rest. This last of course primarily combines and forms itself in freedom according to a certain original disposition directed towards purposes (which, as will be shown in Part II., must not be judged aesthetically but teleologically according to the principle of realism), but also perhaps in conformity with the universal law of the affinity of materials. Again, the watery fluids dissolved in an atmosphere that is a mixture of different gases, if they separate from the latter on account of cooling, produce snow figures, which in correspondence with the character of the special mixture of gases, often seem very artistic and are extremely beautiful. So, without detracting from the teleological principle by which we judge of organisation, we may well think that the beauty of flowers, of the plumage of birds, or of shell-fish, both in shape and colour, may be ascribed to nature and its faculty of producing forms in an aesthetically purposive way, in its freedom, without particular purposes adapted thereto, according to chemical laws by the arrangement of the material requisite for the organisation in question.

But what shows the principle of the *Ideality* of the purposiveness in the beauty of nature, as that which we always place at the basis of an aesthetical judgement, and which allows us to employ, as a ground of explanation for our representative faculty, no realism of purpose, is the fact that in judging beauty we invariably seek its gauge in ourselves *a priori*, and that our aesthetical Judgement is itself legislative in respect of the judgement whether anything is beautiful or not. This could not be, on the assumption of the Realism of the purposiveness of nature; because in that case we must have learned from nature what we ought to find beautiful, and the aesthetical judgement would be subjected to empirical principles. For in such an act of judging the important point is not, what nature is, or even, as a purpose, is in relation to us, but how we take it. There would be an objective purposiveness in nature if it had fashioned its forms for our satisfaction; and not a subjective purposiveness which depended upon the play of the Imagination in its freedom, where it is we who receive nature with favour, not nature which shows us favour. The property of nature that gives us occasion to perceive the inner purposiveness in the relation of our mental faculties in judging certain of its products— a purposiveness which is to be explained on supersensible grounds as necessary and universal—cannot be a natural purpose or be judged by us as such; for otherwise the judgement hereby determined would not be free, and would have at its basis heteronomy, and not, as beseems a judgement of taste, autonomy.

In beautiful Art the principle of the Idealism of purposiveness is still clearer. As in the case of the beautiful in Nature, an aesthetical Realism of this purposiveness cannot be perceived by sensations (for then the art would be only pleasant, not beautiful). But that the satisfaction produced by aesthetical Ideas must not depend on the attainment of definite purposes (as in mechanically designed art), and that consequently, in the very rationalism of the principle, the ideality of the purposes and not their reality must be fundamental, appears from the fact that beautiful Art, as such, must not be considered as a product of Understanding and Science, but of Genius, and therefore must get its rule through *aesthetical* Ideas, which are essentially different from rational Ideas of definite purposes.

Just as the *ideality* of the objects of sense as phenomena is the only way of explaining the possibility of their forms being susceptible of *a priori* determination, so the *idealism* of purposiveness, in judging the beautiful in nature and art, is the only hypothesis under which Criticism can explain the possibility of a judgement of taste which demands *a priori* validity for every one (without grounding on concepts the purposiveness that is represented in the Object).

§ 59. OF BEAUTY AS THE SYMBOL OF MORALITY

Intuitions are always required to establish the reality of our concepts. If the concepts are empirical, the intuitions are called *examples*. If they are pure concepts of Understanding, the intuitions are called *schemata*. If we desire to establish the objective reality of rational concepts, *i.e.* of Ideas, on behalf of theoretical cognition, then we are asking for something impossible, because absolutely no intuition can be given which shall be adequate to them.

All *hypotyposis* (presentation, *subjectio sub adspectum*), or sensible illustration, is twofold. It is either *schematical*, when to a concept comprehended by the Understanding the corresponding intuition is given *a priori*; or it is *symbolical*. In the latter case to a concept only thinkable by the Reason, to which no sensible intuition can be adequate, an intuition is supplied with which accords a procedure of the Judgement analogous to what it observes in schematism: it accords with it, that is, in respect of the rule of this procedure merely, not of the intuition itself; consequently in respect of the form of reflection merely, and not of its content.

There is a use of the word *symbolical* that has been adopted by modern logicians, which is misleading and incorrect, *i.e.* to speak of the *symbolical* mode of representation as if it were opposed to the *intuitive*; for the symbolical is only a mode of the intuitive. The latter (the intuitive), that is, may be divided into the *schematical* and the *symbolical* modes of representation. Both are hypotyposes, *i.e.* presentations (*exhibitiones*); not mere *characterisations*, or designations of concepts by accompanying sensible signs which contain nothing belonging to the intuition of the Object, and only serve as a means for reproducing the concepts, according to the law of association of the Imagination, and consequently in a subjective point of view. These are either words, or visible (algebraical, even mimetical) signs, as mere expressions for concepts.[91]

All intuitions, which we supply to concepts *a priori*, are therefore either *schemata* or *symbols*, of which the former contain direct, the latter indirect, presentations of the concept. The former do this demonstratively; the latter by means of an analogy (for which we avail ourselves even of empirical intuitions) in which the Judgement exercises a double function; first applying the concept to the object of a sensible intuition, and then applying the mere rule of the reflection made upon that intuition to a quite different object of which the first is only the symbol. Thus a monarchical state is represented by a living body, if it is governed by national laws, and by a mere machine (like a hand-mill) if governed by an individual absolute will; but in both cases only *symbolically*. For between a despotic state and a hand-mill there is, to be sure, no similarity; but there is a similarity in the rules according to which we reflect upon these two things and their causality. This matter has not been sufficiently analysed hitherto, for it deserves a deeper investigation; but this is not the place to linger over it. Our language [*i.e.* German] is full of indirect presentations of this sort, in which the expression does not contain the proper schema for the concept, but merely a symbol for reflection. Thus the words *ground* (support, basis), *to depend* (to be held up from above), to *flow* from something (instead of, to follow), *substance* (as *Locke* expresses it, the support of accidents), and countless others, are not schematical but symbolical hypotyposes and expressions for concepts, not by means of a direct intuition, but only by analogy with it, *i.e.* by the transference of reflection upon an object of intuition to a quite different concept to which perhaps an intuition can never directly correspond. If we are to give the name of cognition to a mere mode of representation (which is quite permissible if the latter is not a principle of the theoretical determination of what an object is in itself, but of the practical determination of what the Idea of it should be for us and for its purposive use), then all our knowledge of God is merely symbolical; and he who regards it as schematical, along with the properties of Understanding, Will, etc., which only establish their objective reality in beings of this world, falls into Anthropomorphism, just as he who gives up every intuitive element falls into Deism, by which nothing at all is cognised, not even in a practical point of view.

Now I say the Beautiful is the symbol of the morally Good, and that it is only in this respect (a reference which is natural to every man and which every man postulates in others as a duty) that it gives pleasure with a claim for the agreement of every one else. By this the mind is made conscious of a certain ennoblement and elevation above the mere sensibility to pleasure received through sense, and the worth of others is estimated in accordance with a like maxim of their Judgement. That is the *intelligible*, to which, as pointed out in the preceding paragraph, Taste looks; with which our higher cognitive faculties are in accord; and without which a downright contradiction would arise between their nature and the claims made by taste. In this faculty the Judgement does not see itself, as in empirical judging, subjected to a heteronomy of empirical laws; it gives the law to itself in respect of the objects of so pure a satisfaction, just as the Reason does in respect of the faculty of desire. Hence, both on account of this inner possibility in the subject and of the external possibility of a nature that agrees with it, it finds itself to be referred to something within the subject as well as without him, something which is neither nature nor freedom, but which yet is connected with the supersensible ground of the latter. In this supersensible ground, therefore, the theoretical faculty is bound together in unity with the practical, in a way which though common is yet unknown. We shall indicate some points of this analogy, while at the same time we shall note the differences.

(1) The beautiful pleases *immediately* (but only in reflective intuition, not, like morality, in its concept). (2) It pleases *apart from any interest* (the morally good is indeed necessarily bound up with an interest, though not with one which precedes the judgement upon the satisfaction, but with one which is first of all produced by it). (3) The *freedom* of the Imagination (and therefore of the sensibility of our faculty) is represented in judging the beautiful as harmonious with the conformity to law of the Understanding (in the moral judgement the freedom of the will is thought as the harmony of the latter with itself according to universal laws of Reason). (4) The subjective principle in judging the beautiful is represented as *universal*, *i.e.* as valid for every man, though not cognisable through any universal concept. (The objective principle of morality is also expounded as universal, *i.e.* for every subject and for every action of the same subject, and thus as cognisable by means of a universal concept). Hence the moral judgement is not only susceptible of definite constitutive principles, but is possible *only* by grounding its maxims on these in their universality.

A reference to this analogy is usual even with the common Understanding [of men], and we often describe beautiful objects of nature or art by names that seem to put a moral appreciation at their basis. We call buildings or trees majestic and magnificent, landscapes laughing and gay; even colours are called innocent, modest, tender, because they excite sensations which have something analogous to the consciousness of the state of mind brought about by moral judgements. Taste makes possible the transition, without any violent leap, from the charm of Sense to habitual moral interest; for it represents the Imagination in its freedom as capable of purposive determination for the Understanding, and so teaches us to find even in objects of sense a free satisfaction apart from any charm of sense.

APPENDIX

§ 60. OF THE METHOD OF TASTE

The division of a Critique into Elementology and Methodology, as preparatory to science, is not applicable to the Critique of taste, because there neither is nor can be a science of the Beautiful, and the judgement of taste is not determinable by means of principles. As for the scientific element in every art, which regards *truth* in the presentation of its Object, this is indeed the indispensable condition (*conditio sine qua non*) of beautiful art, but not beautiful art itself. There is therefore for beautiful art only a *manner* (*modus*), not a *method of teaching* (*methodus*). The master must show what the pupil is to do and how he is to do it; and the universal rules, under which at last he brings his procedure, serve rather for bringing the main points back to his remembrance when occasion requires, than for prescribing them to him. Nevertheless regard must be had here to a certain ideal, which art must have before its eyes, although it cannot be completely attained in practice. It is only through exciting the Imagination of the pupil to accordance with a given concept, by making him note the inadequacy of the expression for the Idea, to which the concept itself does not attain because it is an aesthetical Idea, and by severe criticism, that he can be prevented from taking the examples set before him as types and models for imitation, to be subjected to no higher standard or independent judgement. It is thus that genius, and with it the freedom of the Imagination, is stifled by its very conformity to law; and without these no beautiful art, and not even an accurately judging individual taste, is possible.

The propaedeutic to all beautiful art, regarded in the highest degree of its perfection, seems to lie, not in precepts, but in the culture of the mental powers by means of those elements of knowledge called *humaniora*, probably because *humanity* on the one side indicates the universal *feeling of sympathy*, and on the other the faculty of being able to *communicate* universally our inmost [feelings]. For these properties taken together constitute the characteristic social spirit[92] of humanity by which it is distinguished from the limitations of animal life. The age and peoples, in which the impulse towards a *law-abiding* social life, by which a people becomes a permanent community, contended with the great difficulties presented by the difficult problem of uniting freedom (and therefore equality also) with compulsion (rather of respect and submission from a sense of duty than of fear)—such an age and such a people naturally first found out the art of reciprocal communication of Ideas between the cultivated and uncultivated classes and thus discovered how to harmonise the large-mindedness and refinement of the former with the natural simplicity and originality of the latter. In this way they first found that mean between the higher culture and simple nature which furnishes that true standard for taste as a sense common to all men which no universal rules can supply.

With difficulty will a later age dispense with those models, because it will be always farther from nature; and in fine, without having permanent examples before it, a concept will hardly be possible, in one and the same people, of the happy union of the law-abiding constraint of the highest culture with the force and truth of free nature which feels its own proper worth.

Now taste is at bottom a faculty for judging of the sensible illustration of moral Ideas (by means of a certain analogy involved in our reflection upon both these); and it is from this faculty also and from the greater susceptibility grounded thereon for the feeling arising from the latter (called moral feeling), that the pleasure is derived which taste regards as valid for mankind in general and not merely for the private feeling of each. Hence it appears plain that the true propaedeutic for the foundation of taste is the development of moral Ideas and the culture of the moral feeling; because it is only when sensibility is brought into agreement with this that genuine taste can assume a definite invariable form.

---

1. The definition of taste which is laid down here is that it is the faculty of judging of the beautiful. But the analysis of judgements of taste must show what is required in order to call an object beautiful. The moments, to which this Judgement has regard in its reflection, I have sought in accordance with the guidance of the logical functions of judgement (for in a judgement of taste a reference to the Understanding is always involved). I have considered the moment of quality first, because the aesthetical judgement upon the beautiful first pays attention to it.

2. A judgement upon an object of satisfaction may be quite *disinterested*, but yet very *interesting, i.e.* not based upon an interest, but bringing an interest with it; of this kind are all pure moral judgements. Judgements of taste, however, do not in themselves establish any interest. Only in society is it *interesting* to have taste: the reason of this will be shown in the sequel.
3. [Second Edition.]
4. An obligation to enjoyment is a manifest absurdity. Thus the obligation to all actions which have merely enjoyment for their aim can only be a pretended one; however spiritually it may be conceived (or decked out), even if it is a mystical, or so-called heavenly, enjoyment.
5. [Second Edition.]
6. [Second Edition.]
7. Ueberweg points out (*Hist. of Phil.*, ii. 528, Eng. Trans.) that Mendelssohn had already called attention to the disinterestedness of our satisfaction in the Beautiful. "It appears," says Mendelssohn, "to be a particular mark of the beautiful, that it is contemplated with quiet satisfaction, that it pleases, even though it be not in our possession, and even though we be never so far removed from the desire to put it to our use." But, of course, as Ueberweg remarks, Kant's conception of disinterestedness extends far beyond the absence of a desire to possess the object.
8. Reading *besondere* with Windelband; Hartenstein reads *bestimmte*.
9. I.e. *The Critique of Pure Reason*, Analytic, bk. ii. c. i.
10. Second Edition. Spencer expresses much more concisely what Kant has in his mind here. "Pleasure ... is a feeling which we seek to bring into consciousness and retain there; pain is ... a feeling which we seek to get out of consciousness and to keep out." *Principles of Psychology*, § 125.
11. The editions of Hartenstein and Kirchmann omit *ohne* before *zweck*, which makes havoc of the sentence. It is correctly printed by Rosenkranz and Windelband.
12. First Edition.
13. Cf. *Metaphysic of Morals*, Introd. I. "The pleasure which is necessarily bound up with the desire (of the object whose representation affects feeling) may be called *practical* pleasure, whether it be cause or effect of the desire. On the contrary, the pleasure which is not necessarily bound up with the desire of the object, and which, therefore, is at bottom not a pleasure in the existence of the Object of the representation, but clings to the representation only, may be called mere contemplative pleasure or *passive satisfaction*. The feeling of the latter kind of pleasure we call *taste*."
14. Second Edition.
15. First Edition has *gleiche*; Second Edition has *solche*.
16. First and Second Editions have *sehr zweifle*; but this was corrected to *nicht zweifle* in the Third Edition of 1799.
17. *Belebt machen*; First Edition had *beliebt*.
18. Second Edition.
19. Kant probably alludes here to Baumgarten (1714–1762), who was the first writer to give the name of Aesthetics to the Philosophy of Taste. He defined beauty as "perfection apprehended through the senses." Kant is said to have used as a text-book at lectures a work by Meier, a pupil of Baumgarten's, on this subject.
20. Cf. Preface to the *Metaphysical Elements of Ethics*, v.: "The word *perfection* is liable to many misconceptions. It is sometimes understood as a concept belonging to Transcendental Philosophy; viz. the concept of the *totality* of the manifold, which, taken together, constitutes a Thing; sometimes, again, it is understood as belonging to *Teleology*, so that it signifies the agreement of the characteristics of a thing with a *purpose*. Perfection in the former sense might be called *quantitative* (material), in the latter *qualitative* (formal) perfection."
21. The words *even if ... general* were added in the Second Edition.
22. Second Edition.
23. Models of taste as regards the arts of speech must be composed in a dead and learned language. The first, in order that they may not suffer that change which inevitably comes over living languages, in which noble expressions become flat, common ones antiquated, and newly created ones have only a short currency. The second, because learned languages have a grammar which is subject to no wanton change of fashion, but the rules of which are preserved unchanged.
24. This distinction between an *Idea* and an *Ideal*, as also the further contrast between Ideals of the Reason and Ideals of the Imagination, had already been given by Kant in the *Critique of Pure Reason*, Dialectic, bk. ii. c. iii. § 1.
25. Polycletus of Argos flourished about 430 B.C. His statue of the *Spearbearer* (*Doryphorus*), afterwards became known as the *Canon*; because in it the artist was supposed to have embodied a perfect representation of the ideal of the human figure.
26. This was a celebrated statue executed by Myron, a Greek sculptor, contemporary with Polycletus. It is frequently mentioned in the Greek Anthology.
27. It will be found that a perfectly regular countenance, such as a painter might wish to have for a model, ordinarily tells us nothing; because it contains nothing characteristic, and therefore rather expresses the Idea of the race than the specific [traits] of a person. The exaggeration of a characteristic of this kind, *i.e.* such as does violence to the normal Idea (the purposiveness of the race) is called *caricature*. Experience also shows that these quite regular countenances commonly indicate internally only a mediocre man; presumably (if it may be assumed that external nature expresses the proportions of internal) because, if no mental disposition exceeds that proportion which is requisite in order to constitute a man free from faults, nothing can be

expected of what is called *genius*, in which nature seems to depart from the ordinary relations of the mental powers on behalf of some special one.

28. It might be objected to this explanation that there are things, in which we see a purposive form without cognising any [definite] purpose in them, like the stone implements often got from old sepulchral tumuli with a hole in them as if for a handle. These, although they plainly indicate by their shape a purposiveness of which we do not know the purpose, are nevertheless not described as beautiful. But if we regard a thing as a work of art, that is enough to make us admit that its shape has reference to some design and definite purpose. And hence there is no immediate satisfaction in the contemplation of it. On the other hand a flower, *e.g.* a tulip, is regarded as beautiful; because in perceiving it we find a certain purposiveness which, in our judgement, is referred to no purpose at all.

29. Cf. p. 170, *infra*.
30. See *The History of Sumatra*, by W. Marsden (London, 1783), p. 113.
31. Cf. § 42, *infra*.
32. Second Edition.
33. Second Edition.
34. *Lettres sur l'Égypte*, par M. Savary, Amsterdam, 1787.
35. Second Edition.
36. With this should be compared the similar discussion in the *Critique of Pure Reason*, Dialectic, bk. ii. c. ii. § 1, *On the System of Cosmological Ideas*.
37. Second Edition.
38. Cf. § 83, *infra*.
39. In the *Philosophical Theory of Religion*, pt. i. *sub fin.* (Abbott's Translation, p. 360), Kant, as here, divides "all religions into two classes—*favour-seeking* religion (mere worship) and *moral* religion, that is, the religion *of a good life*;" and he concludes that "amongst all the public religions that have ever existed the Christian alone is moral."
40. *Voyages dans les Alpes*, par H. B. de Saussure; vol. i. was published at Neuchatel in 1779; vol. ii. at Geneva in 1786.
41. Second Edition.
42. *Als Vermögen der Independenz der absoluten Totalität*, a curious phrase.
43. Second Edition.
44. *Affections* are specifically different from *passions*. The former are related merely to feeling; the latter belong to the faculty of desire, and are inclinations which render difficult or impossible all determination of the [elective] will by principles. The former are stormy and unpremeditated; the latter are steady and deliberate; thus indignation in the form of wrath is an affection, but in the form of hatred (revenge) is a passion. The latter can never and in no reference be called sublime; because while in an affection the freedom of the mind is *hindered*, in a passion it is abolished. [Cf. Preface to the *Metaphysical Elements of Ethics*, § xvi., where this distinction is more fully drawn out. Affection is described as *hasty*; and passion is defined as the sensible *appetite* grown into a permanent inclination.]
45. In the Preface to the *Metaphysical Elements of Ethics*, § xvii., Kant gives the term *moral apathy* to that freedom from the sway of the affections, which is distinguished from indifference to them.
46. Reading *weiche* with Rosenkranz and Windelband; Hartenstein and Kirchmann have *weise*, which yields no sense.
47. Cf. p. 129, *supra*.
48. Kirchmann has *positiv*; but this is probably a mere misprint.
49. L.c. vol. ii. p. 181.
50. See Burke, *On the Sublime and Beautiful*, Part IV., Sect. vii. "If the pain and terror are so modified as not to be actually noxious; if the pain is not carried to violence, and the terror is not conversant about the present destruction of the person, as these emotions clear the parts, whether fine or gross, of a dangerous and troublesome incumbrance, they are capable of producing delight; not pleasure, but a sort of delightful horror, a sort of tranquillity tinged with terror; which, as it belongs to self-preservation, is one of the strongest of all the passions." Kant quotes from the German version published at Riga in 1773. This was a free translation made from Burke's fifth edition.
51. See Burke, l.c., Part IV., Sect. xix. "Beauty acts by relaxing the solids of the whole system. There are all the appearances of such a relaxation; and a relaxation somewhat below the natural tone seems to me to be the cause of all positive pleasure. Who is a stranger to that manner of expression so common in all times and in all countries, of being softened, relaxed, enervated, dissolved, melted away by pleasure?"
52. Reading *Gebot*; Kirchmann has *Gesetz*.
53. Second Edition.
54. Cf. *Critique of Pure Reason*, Methodology, c. 1, § 1. "The construction of a concept is the *a priori* presentation of the corresponding intuition."
55. Charles Batteux (1713–1780), author of *Les Beaux Arts reduits à un même principe*.
56. Essay XVIII, *The Sceptic*. "Critics can reason and dispute more plausibly than cooks or perfumers. We may observe, however, that this uniformity among human kind, hinders not, but that there is a considerable diversity in the sentiments of beauty and worth, and that education, custom, prejudice, caprice, and humour, frequently vary our taste of this kind.... Beauty and worth are merely of a relative nature, and consist in an

agreeable sentiment, produced by an object in a particular mind, according to the peculiar structure and constitution of that mind."

57. For the distinction, an important one in Kant, between judgements of experience and judgements of perception, see his *Prolegomena*, § 18. Cf. *Kant's Critical Philosophy for English Readers*, vol. i. p. 116.

58. First Edition has "limited."

59. In order to be justified in claiming universal assent for an aesthetical judgement that rests merely on subjective grounds, it is sufficient to assume, (1) that the subjective conditions of the Judgement, as regards the relation of the cognitive powers thus put into activity to a cognition in general, are the same in all men. This must be true, because otherwise men would not be able to communicate their representations or even their knowledge. (2) The judgement must merely have reference to this relation (consequently to the *formal condition* of the Judgement) and be pure, *i.e.* not mingled either with concepts of the Object or with sensations, as determining grounds. If there has been any mistake as regards this latter condition, then there is only an inaccurate application of the privilege, which a law gives us, to a particular case; but that does not destroy the privilege itself in general.

60. Kant lays down these three maxims in his *Introduction to Logic*, § vii., as "general rules and conditions of the avoidance of error."

61. We soon see that although enlightenment is easy *in thesi*, yet *in hypothesi* it is difficult and slow of accomplishment. For not to be passive as regards Reason, but to be always self-legislative, is indeed quite easy for the man who wishes only to be in accordance with his essential purpose, and does not desire to know what is beyond his Understanding. But since we can hardly avoid seeking this, and there are never wanting others who promise with much confidence that they are able to satisfy our curiosity, it must be very hard to maintain in or restore to the mind (especially the mind of the public) that bare negative which properly constitutes enlightenment.

62. We may designate Taste as *sensus communis aestheticus*, common Understanding as *sensus communis logicus*.

63. Peter Camper (1722–1789), a celebrated naturalist and comparative anatomist; for some years professor at Groningen.

64. In my country a common man, if you propose to him such a problem as that of Columbus with his egg, says, *that is not art, it is only science*. *I.e.* if we *know* how, we can *do* it; and he says the same of all the pretended arts of jugglers. On the other hand, he will not refuse to apply the term art to the performance of a rope-dancer.

65. Kant was accustomed to say that the talk at a dinner table should always pass through these three stages— narrative, discussion, and jest; and punctilious in this, as in all else, he is said to have directed the conversation at his own table accordingly (Wallace's *Kant*, p. 39).

66. Second Edition.

67. Cf. Aristotle's *Poetics*, c. iv. p. 1448 b: ἃ γὰρ αὐτὰ λυπηρῶς ὁρῶμεν, τούτων τὰς εἰκόνας τὰς μάλιστα ἠκριβωμένας χαίρομεν θεωροῦντες οἷον θηρίων τε μορφὰς τῶν ἀτιμοτάτων καὶ νεκρῶν. Cf. also *Rhetoric*, I. 11, p. 1371 b; and Burke on the *Sublime and Beautiful*, Part I. § 16. Boileau (*L'art poétique*, chant 3), makes a similar observation:

> "Il n'est point de serpent ni de monstre odieux
> Qui, par l'art imité, ne puisse plaire aux yeux.
> D'un pinceau délicat l'artifice agréable
> Du plus affreux objet fait un objet aimable."

68. Second Edition.

69. Cf. p. 199, *infra*.

70. In English we would rather say "without *soul*"; but I prefer to translate *Geist* consistently by *spirit*, to avoid the confusion of it with *Seele*.

71. These lines occur in one of Frederick the Great's French poems: Épître au maréchal Keith XVIII., "sur les vaines terreurs de la mort et les frayeurs d'une autre vie." Kant here translates them into German.

72. Withof, whose "Moral Poems" appeared in 1755. This reference was supplied by H. Krebs in *Notes and Queries* 5th January 1895.

73. Perhaps nothing more sublime was ever said and no sublimer thought ever expressed than the famous inscription on the Temple of *Isis* (Mother *Nature*): "I am all that is and that was and that shall be, and no mortal hath lifted my veil." Segner availed himself of this Idea in a *suggestive* vignette prefixed to his Natural Philosophy, in order to inspire beforehand the pupil whom he was about to lead into that temple with a holy awe, which should dispose his mind to serious attention. [J. A. de Segner (1704–1777) was Professor of Natural Philosophy at Göttingen, and the author of several scientific works of repute.]

74. Second Edition.

75. The three former faculties are *united* in the first instance by means of the fourth. Hume gives us to understand in his *History of England* that although the English are inferior in their productions to no people in the world as regards the evidences they display of the three former properties, *separately* considered, yet they must be put after their neighbours the French as regards that which unites these properties. [In his *Observations on the Beautiful and Sublime*, § iv. *sub init.*, Kant remarks that the English have the keener sense of the *sublime*, the French of the *beautiful*.]

76. The reader is not to judge this scheme for a possible division of the beautiful arts as a deliberate theory. It is only one of various attempts which we may and ought to devise.

77. Second Edition.

78. *I.e.* the case of Plastic art, with its subdivisions of Architecture and Sculpture, as is explained in the next paragraph.

79. That landscape gardening may be regarded as a species of the art of painting, although it presents its forms corporeally, seems strange. But since it actually takes its forms from nature (trees, shrubs, grasses, and flowers from forest and field—at least in the first instance), and so far is not an art like Plastic; and since it also has no concept of the object and its purpose (as in Architecture) conditioning its arrangements, but involves merely the free play of the Imagination in contemplation, it so far agrees with mere aesthetical painting which has no definite theme (which arranges sky, land, and water, so as to entertain us by means of light and shade only).—In general the reader is only to judge of this as an attempt to combine the beautiful arts under one principle, viz. that of the expression of aesthetical Ideas (according to the analogy of speech), and not to regard it as a definitive analysis of them.

80. I must admit that a beautiful poem has always given me a pure gratification; whilst the reading of the best discourse, whether of a Roman orator or of a modern parliamentary speaker or of a preacher, has always been mingled with an unpleasant feeling of disapprobation of a treacherous art, which means to move men in important matters like machines to a judgement that must lose all weight for them on quiet reflection. Readiness and accuracy in speaking (which taken together constitute Rhetoric) belong to beautiful art; but the art of the orator (*ars oratoria*), the art of availing oneself of the weaknesses of men for one's own designs (whether these be well meant or even actually good does not matter) is worthy of no *respect*. Again, this art only reached its highest point, both at Athens and at Rome, at a time when the state was hastening to its ruin and true patriotic sentiment had disappeared. The man who along with a clear insight into things has in his power a wealth of pure speech, and who with a fruitful Imagination capable of presenting his Ideas unites a lively sympathy with what is truly good, is the *vir bonus discendi peritus*, the orator without art but of great impressiveness, as *Cicero* has it; though he may not always remain true to this ideal

81. From this to the end of the paragraph, and the next note, were added in the Second Edition.

82. Those who recommend the singing of spiritual songs at family prayers do not consider that they inflict a great hardship upon the public by such *noisy* (and therefore in general pharisaical) devotions; for they force the neighbours either to sing with them or to abandon their meditations. [Kant suffered himself from such annoyances, which may account for the asperity of this note. At one period he was disturbed by the devotional exercises of the prisoners in the adjoining jail. In a letter to the burgomaster "he suggested the advantage of closing the windows during these hymn-singings, and added that the warders of the prison might probably be directed to accept less sonorous and neighbour-annoying chants as evidence of the penitent spirit of their captives" (Wallace's *Kant*, p. 42).]

83. Cf. "Parturiunt montes, nascitur *ridiculus* mus."

84. The First Edition adds "as in the case of a man who gets the news of a great commercial success."

85. The jest may have been taken from Steele's play, "The Funeral or Grief *à la mode*," where it occurs verbatim. This play was published in 1702.

86. *Henriade, Chant 7*, sub init.
     "Du Dieu qui nous créa la clémence infinie,
     Pour adoucir les maux de cette courte vie,
     A placé parmi nous deux êtres bienfaisants,
     De la terre à jamais aimables habitants,
     Soutiens dans les travaux, trésors dans l'indigence:
     L'un est le doux sommeil, et l'autre est l'espérance."

87. We may describe as a rationalising judgement (*judicium ratiocinans*) one which proclaims itself as universal, for as such it can serve as the major premise of a syllogism. On the other hand, we can only speak of a judgement as rational (*judicium ratiocinatum*) which is thought as the conclusion of a syllogism, and consequently as grounded *a priori*.

88. Cf. p. 241, *infra*.

89. Second Edition.

90. Antiparos is a small island in the Cyclades, remarkable for a splendid stalactite cavern near the southern coast.

91. The intuitive in cognition must be opposed to the discursive (not to the symbolical). The former is either *schematical*, by *demonstration*; or *symbolical* as a representation in accordance with a mere *analogy*.

92. I read *Geselligkeit* with Rosenkranz and Windelband; Hartenstein and Kirchmann have *Glückseligkeit*.

SECOND PART — CRITIQUE OF THE
TELEOLOGICAL JUDGEMENT

§ 61. OF THE OBJECTIVE PURPOSIVENESS OF NATURE

WE HAVE on transcendental principles good ground to assume a subjective purposiveness in nature, in its particular laws, in reference to its comprehensibility by human Judgement and to the possibility of the connexion of particular experiences in a system. This may be expected as possible in many products of nature, which, as if they were devised quite specially for our Judgement, contain a specific form conformable thereto; which through their manifoldness and unity serve at once to strengthen and to sustain the mental powers (that come into play in the employment of this faculty); and to which therefore we give the name of *beautiful* forms.

But that the things of nature serve one another as means to purposes, and that their possibility is only completely intelligible through this kind of causality—for this we have absolutely no ground in the universal Idea of nature, as the complex of the objects of sense. In the above-mentioned case, the representation of things, because it is something in ourselves, can be quite well thought *a priori* as suitable and useful for the internally purposive determination of our cognitive faculties; but that purposes, which neither are our own nor belong to nature (for we do not regard nature as an intelligent being), could or should constitute a particular kind of causality, at least a quite special conformity to law,—this we have absolutely no *a priori* reason for presuming. Yet more, experience itself cannot prove to us the actuality of this; there must then have preceded a rationalising subtlety which only sportively introduces the concept of purpose into the nature of things, but which does not derive it from Objects or from their empirical cognition. To this latter it is of more service to make nature comprehensible according to analogy with the subjective ground of the connexion of our representations, than to cognise it from objective grounds.

Further, objective purposiveness, as a principle of the possibility of things of nature, is so far removed from *necessary* connexion with the concept of nature, that it is much oftener precisely that upon which one relies to prove the contingency of nature and of its form. When, *e.g.* we adduce the structure of a bird, the hollowness of its bones, the disposition of its wings for motion and of its tail for steering, *etc.*, we say that all this is contingent in the highest degree according to the mere *nexus effectivus* of nature, without calling in the aid of a particular kind of causality, namely that of purpose (*nexus finalis*). In other words, nature, considered as mere mechanism, could have produced its forms in a thousand other ways without stumbling upon the unity which is in accordance with such a principle. It is not in the concept of nature but quite apart from it that we can hope to find the least ground *a priori* for this.

Nevertheless the teleological act of judgement is rightly brought to bear, at least problematically, upon the investigation of nature; but only in order to bring it under principles of observation and inquiry according to the *analogy* with the causality of purpose, without any pretence to *explain* it thereby. It belongs therefore to the reflective and not to the determinant judgement. The concept of combinations and forms of nature in accordance with purposes is then at least *one principle more* for bringing its phenomena under rules where the laws of simply mechanical causality do not suffice. For we bring in a teleological ground, where we attribute causality in respect of an Object to the concept of an Object, as if it were to be found in nature (not in ourselves); or rather when we represent to ourselves the possibility of the Object after the analogy of that causality which we experience in ourselves, and consequently think nature technically as through a special faculty. If we did not ascribe to it such a method of action, its causality would have to be represented as blind mechanism. If, on the contrary, we supply to nature causes acting *designedly*, and consequently place at its basis teleology, not merely as a *regulative* principle for the mere *judging* of phenomena, to which nature can be thought as subject in its particular laws, but as a *constitutive* principle of the *derivation* of its products from their causes; then would the concept of a natural purpose no longer belong to the reflective but to the determinant Judgement. Then, in fact, it would not belong specially to the Judgement (like the concept of beauty regarded as formal subjective purposiveness), but as a rational concept it would introduce into natural science a new causality, which we only borrow from ourselves and ascribe to other beings, without meaning to assume them to be of the same kind with ourselves.

FIRST DIVISION—ANALYTIC OF THE TELEOLOGICAL JUDGEMENT

§ 62. OF THE OBJECTIVE PURPOSIVENESS WHICH IS MERELY FORMAL AS DISTINGUISHED FROM THAT WHICH IS MATERIAL

All geometrical figures drawn on a principle display a manifold, oft admired, objective purposiveness; *i.e.* in reference to their usefulness for the solution of several problems by a single principle, or of the same problem in an infinite variety of ways. The purposiveness is here obviously objective and intellectual, not merely subjective and aesthetical. For it expresses the suitability of the figure for the production of many intended figures, and is cognised through Reason. But this purposiveness does not make the concept of the object itself possible, *i.e.* it is not regarded as possible merely with reference to this use.

In so simple a figure as the circle lies the key to the solution of a multitude of problems, each of which would demand various appliances; whereas the solution results of itself, as it were, as one of the infinite number of elegant properties of this figure. Are we, for example, asked to construct a triangle, being given the base and vertical angle? The problem is indeterminate, *i.e.* it can be solved in an infinite number of ways. But the circle embraces them altogether as the geometrical locus of the vertices of triangles satisfying the given conditions. Again, suppose that two lines are to cut one another so that the rectangle under the segments of the one should be equal to the rectangle under the segments of the other; the solution of the problem from this point of view presents much difficulty. But all chords intersecting inside a circle divide one another in this *proportion*. Other curved lines suggest other purposive solutions of which nothing was thought in the rule that furnished their construction. All conic sections in themselves and when compared with one another are fruitful in principles for the solution of a number of possible problems, however simple is the definition which determines their concept.—It is a true joy to see the zeal with which the old geometers investigated the properties of lines of this class, without allowing themselves to be led astray by the questions of narrow-minded persons, as to what use this knowledge would be. Thus they worked out the properties of the parabola without knowing the law of gravitation, which would have suggested to them its application to the trajectory of heavy bodies (for the motion of a heavy body can be seen to be parallel to the curve of a parabola). Again, they found out the properties of an ellipse without surmising that any of the heavenly bodies had weight, and without knowing the law of force at different distances from the point of attraction, which causes it to describe this curve in free motion. While they thus unconsciously worked for the science of the future, they delighted themselves with a purposiveness in the [essential] being of things which yet they were able to present completely *a priori* in its necessity. *Plato*, himself master of this science, hinted at such an original constitution of things in the discovery of which we can dispense with all experience, and at the power of the mind to produce from its supersensible principle the harmony of beings (where the properties of number come in, with which the mind plays in music). This [he touches upon] in the inspiration that raised him above the concepts of experience to Ideas, which seem to him to be explicable only through an intellectual affinity with the origin of all beings. No wonder that he banished from his school the man who was ignorant of geometry, since he thought he could derive from pure intuition, which has its home in the human spirit, that which *Anaxagoras* drew from empirical objects and their purposive combination. For in the very necessity of that which is purposive, and is constituted just as if it were designedly intended for our use,—but at the same time seems to belong originally to the being of things without any reference to our use—lies the ground of our great admiration of nature, and that not so much external as in our own Reason. It is surely excusable that this admiration should through misunderstanding gradually rise to the height of fanaticism.

But this intellectual purposiveness, although no doubt objective (not subjective like aesthetical purposiveness), is in reference to its possibility merely formal (not real). It can only be conceived as purposiveness in general without any [definite] purpose being assumed as its basis, and consequently without teleology being needed for it. The figure of a circle is an intuition which is determined by means of the Understanding according to a principle. The unity of this principle which I arbitrarily assume and use as fundamental concept, applied to a form of intuition (space) which is met with in myself as a representation and yet *a priori*, renders intelligible the unity of many rules resulting from the construction of that concept, which are purposive for many possible designs. But this purposiveness does not imply a *purpose* or any other ground whatever. It is quite different if I meet with order and regularity in complexes of *things*, external to myself, enclosed within certain boundaries; as, *e.g.* in a garden, the order and regularity of the trees, flower-beds, and walks. These I cannot expect to derive *a priori* from my bounding of space made after a rule of my own; for this order and regularity are existing things which must be given empirically in order to be known, and not a mere representation in myself determined *a priori* according to a principle. So then the latter (empirical) purposiveness, as *real*, is dependent on the concept of a purpose.

But the ground of admiration for a perceived purposiveness, although it be in the being of things (so far as their concepts can be constructed), may very well be seen, and seen to be legitimate. The manifold rules whose unity (derived from a principle) excites admiration, are all synthetical and do not follow from the *concept* of the Object, *e.g.* of a circle; but require this Object to be given in intuition. Hence this unity gets the appearance of having empirically an external basis of rules distinct from our representative faculty; as if therefore the correspondence of the Object to that need of rules which is proper to the Understanding were contingent in itself, and therefore only possible by means of a purpose expressly directed thereto. Now because this harmony, notwithstanding all this purposiveness, is not cognised empirically but *a priori*, it should bring us of itself to this point—that space, through whose determination (by means of the Imagination, in accordance with a concept) the Object is alone possible, is not a characteristic of things external to me, but a mere mode of representation in myself. Hence, in the figure which I draw *in conformity with a concept, i.e.* in my own mode of representing that which is given to me externally, whatever it may be in itself, *it is I that introduce the purposiveness*; I get no empirical instruction from the Object about the purposiveness, and so I require in it no particular purpose external to myself. But because this consideration already calls for a critical employment of Reason, and consequently cannot be involved in the judging of the Object according to its properties; so this latter [judging] suggests to me immediately nothing but the unification of heterogeneous rules (even according to their very diversity) in a principle. This principle, without requiring any particular *a priori* basis external to my concept, or indeed, generally speaking, to my representation, is yet cognised *a priori* by me as true. Now *wonder* is a shock of the mind arising from the incompatibility of a representation, and the rule given by its means, with the principles already lying at its basis; which provokes a doubt as to whether we have rightly seen or rightly judged. *Admiration*, however, is wonder which ever recurs, despite the disappearance of this doubt. Consequently the latter is a quite natural effect of that observed purposiveness in the being of things (as phenomena). It cannot indeed be censured, whilst the unification of the form of sensible intuition (space)—with the faculty of concepts (the Understanding)—is inexplicable to us; and that not only on account of the union being just of the kind that it is, but because it is enlarging for the mind to surmise [the existence of] something lying outside our sensible representations in which, although unknown to us, the ultimate ground of that agreement may be met with. We are, it is true, not necessitated to cognise this if we have only to do *a priori* with the formal purposiveness of our representations; but the fact that we are compelled to look out beyond it inspires at the same time an admiration for the object that impels us thereto.

We are accustomed to speak of the above-mentioned properties of geometrical figures or of numbers as *beautiful*, on account of a certain *a priori* purposiveness they have for all kinds of cognitive uses, this purposiveness being quite unexpected on account of the simplicity of the construction. We speak, *e.g.* of this or that *beautiful* property of the circle, which was discovered in this or that way. But there is no aesthetical act of judgement through which we find it purposive, no act of judgement without a concept which renders noticeable a mere *subjective* purposiveness in the free play of our cognitive faculties; but an intellectual act according to concepts which enables us clearly to cognise an objective purposiveness, *i.e.* availableness for all kinds of (infinitely manifold) purposes. We must rather call this *relative perfection* than a beauty of the mathematical figure. To speak thus of an *intellectual beauty* cannot in general be permissible; for otherwise the word beauty would lose all determinate significance, or the intellectual satisfaction all superiority over the sensible. We should rather call a *demonstration* of such properties beautiful, because through it the Understanding as the faculty of concepts, and the Imagination as the faculty of presenting them, feel themselves strengthened *a priori*. (This, when viewed in connexion with the precision introduced by Reason, is spoken of as elegant.) Here, however, the satisfaction, although it is based on concepts, is subjective; while perfection brings with itself an objective satisfaction.

§ 63. OF THE RELATIVE, AS DISTINGUISHED FROM THE INNER, PURPOSIVENESS OF NATURE

Experience leads our Judgement to the concept of an objective and material purposiveness, *i.e.* to the concept of a purpose of nature, only when[1] we have to judge of a relation of cause to effect which we find ourselves able to apprehend as legitimate only by presupposing the Idea of the effect of the causality of the cause as the fundamental condition, in the cause, of the possibility of the effect. This can take place in two ways. We may regard the effect directly as an art product, or only as material for the art of other possible natural beings; in other words, either as a purpose or as a means towards the purposive employment of other causes. This latter purposiveness is called utility (for man) or mere advantage (for other creatures), and is merely relative; while the former is an inner purposiveness of the natural being.

For example, rivers bring down with them all kinds of earth serviceable for the growth of plants which sometimes is deposited inland, often also at their mouths. The tide brings this mud to many coasts over the land or deposits it on the shore; and so, more especially if men give their aid so that the ebb shall not carry it back again, the fruit-bearing land increases in area, and the vegetable kingdom gains the place which formerly was the habitation of fish and shells. In this way has nature itself brought about most of the extensions of the land, and still continues to do so, although very slowly.—Now the question is whether this is to be judged a purpose of nature, because it contains utility for men. We cannot put it down to the account of the vegetable kingdom, because just as much is subtracted from sea-life as is added to land-life.

Or, to give an example of the advantageousness of certain natural things as means for other creatures (if we suppose them to be means), no soil is more suitable to pine trees than a sandy soil. Now the deep sea, before it withdrew from the land, left behind large tracts of sand in our northern regions, so that on this soil, so unfavourable for all cultivation, widely extended pine forests were enabled to grow, for the unreasoning destruction of which we frequently blame our ancestors. We may ask if this original deposit of tracts of sand was a purpose of nature for the benefit of the possible pine forests? So much is clear, that if we regard this as a purpose of nature, we must also regard the sand as a relative purpose, in reference to which the ocean strand and its withdrawal were means: for in the series of the mutually subordinated members of a purposive combination, every member must be regarded as a purpose (though not as a final purpose), to which its proximate cause is the means. So too if cattle, sheep, horses, etc., are to exist, there must be grass on the earth, but there must also be saline plants in the desert if camels are to thrive; and again these and other herbivorous animals must be met with in numbers if there are to be wolves, tigers, and lions. Consequently the objective purposiveness, which is based upon advantage, is not an objective purposiveness of things in themselves; as if the sand could not be conceived for itself as an effect of a cause, viz. the sea, without attributing to the latter a purpose, and regarding the effect, namely, the sand, as a work of art. It is a merely relative purposiveness contingent upon the thing to which it is ascribed; and although in the examples we have cited, the different kinds of grass are to be judged as in themselves organised products of nature, and consequently as artificial, yet are they to be regarded, in reference to the beasts which feed upon them, as mere raw material.

But above all, though man, through the freedom of his causality, finds certain natural things of advantage for his designs—designs often foolish, such as using the variegated plumage of birds to adorn his clothes, or coloured earths and the juices of plants for painting his face; often again reasonable as when the horse is used for riding, the ox or (as in Minorca) the ass or pig for ploughing—yet we cannot even here assume a relative natural purpose. For his Reason knows how to give things a conformity with his own arbitrary fancies for which he was not at all predestined by nature. Only, *if* we assume that men are to live upon the earth, then the means must be there without which they could not exist as animals, and even as rational animals (in however low a degree of rationality); and thereupon those natural things, which are indispensable in this regard, must be considered as natural purposes.

We can hence easily see that external purposiveness (advantage of one thing in respect of others) can be regarded as an external natural purpose only under the condition, that the existence of that [being], to which it is immediately or distantly advantageous, is in itself a purpose of nature. Since that can never be completely determined by mere contemplation of nature, it follows that relative purposiveness, although it hypothetically gives indications of natural purposes, yet justifies no absolute teleological judgement.

Snow in cold countries protects the crops from the frost; it makes human intercourse easier (by means of sleighs). The Laplander finds in his country animals by whose aid this intercourse is brought about, *i.e.* reindeer, who find sufficient sustenance in a dry moss which they have to scratch out for themselves from under the snow, and who are easily tamed and readily permit themselves to be deprived of that freedom in which they could have remained if they chose. For other people in the same frozen regions marine animals afford rich stores; in addition to the food and clothing which are thus supplied, and the wood which is floated in by the sea to their dwellings, these marine animals provide material for fuel by which their huts are warmed. Here is a wonderful concurrence of many references of nature to one purpose; and all this applies to the cases of the Greenlander, the Lapp, the Samoyede, the inhabitant of Yakutsk, etc. But then we do not see why, generally, men must live there at all. Therefore to say that vapour falls out of the atmosphere in the form of snow, that the sea has its currents which float down wood that has grown in warmer lands, and that there are in it great sea monsters filled with oil, *because* the idea of advantage for certain poor creatures is fundamental for the cause which collects all these natural products, would be a very venturesome and arbitrary judgement. For even if there were none of this natural utility, we should miss nothing as regards the adequateness of natural causes to nature's constitution; much more even to desire such a tendency in, and to attribute such a purpose to, nature would be the part of a presumptuous and inconsiderate fancy. For indeed it might be observed that it could only have been the greatest unsociability among men which thus scattered them into such inhospitable regions.

§ 64. OF THE PECULIAR CHARACTER OF THINGS AS NATURAL PURPOSES

In order to see that a thing is only possible as a purpose, that is, to be forced to seek the causality of its origin not in the mechanism of nature but in a cause whose faculty of action is determined through concepts, it is requisite that its form be not possible according to mere natural laws, *i.e.* laws which can be cognised by us through the Understanding alone when applied to objects of Sense; but that even the empirical knowledge of it as regards its cause and effect presupposes concepts of Reason. This *contingency* of its form in all empirical natural laws in reference to Reason affords a ground for regarding its causality as possible only through Reason. For Reason, which must cognise the necessity of every form of a natural product in order to comprehend even the conditions of its genesis, cannot assume such [natural] necessity in that particular given form. The causality of its origin is then referred to the faculty of acting in accordance with purposes (a will); and the Object which can only thus be represented as possible is represented as a purpose.

If in a seemingly uninhabited country a man perceived a geometrical figure, say a regular hexagon, inscribed on the sand, his reflection busied with such a concept would attribute, although obscurely, the unity in the principle of its genesis to Reason, and consequently would not regard as a ground of the possibility of such a shape the sand, or the neighbouring sea, or the winds, or beasts with familiar footprints, or any other irrational cause. For the chance against meeting with such a concept, which is only possible through Reason, would seem so infinitely great, that it would be just as if there were no natural law, no cause in the mere mechanical working of nature capable of producing it; but as if only the concept of such an Object, as a concept which Reason alone can supply and with which it can compare the thing, could contain the causality for such an effect. This then would be regarded as a purpose, but as a product of *art*, not as a natural purpose (*vestigium hominis video*).[2]

But in order to regard a thing cognised as a natural product as a purpose also—

consequently as a *natural purpose*, if this is not a contradiction—something more is required. I would say provisionally: a thing exists as a natural purpose, if it is [although in a double sense]³ both *cause and effect of itself*. For herein lies a causality the like of which cannot be combined with the mere concept of a nature without attributing to it a purpose; it can certainly be thought without contradiction, but cannot be comprehended. We shall elucidate the determination of this Idea of a natural purpose by an example, before we analyse it completely.

In the first place, a tree generates another tree according to a known natural law. But the tree produced is of the same genus; and so it produces itself *generically*. On the one hand, as effect it is continually self-produced; on the other hand, as cause it continually produces itself, and so perpetuates itself generically.

Secondly, a tree produces itself as an *individual*. This kind of effect no doubt we call growth; but it is quite different from any increase according to mechanical laws, and is to be reckoned as generation, though under another name. The matter that the tree incorporates it previously works up into a specifically peculiar quality, which natural mechanism external to it cannot supply; and thus it develops itself by aid of a material which, as compounded, is its own product. No doubt, as regards the constituents got from nature without, it must only be regarded as an educt; but yet in the separation and recombination of this raw material we see such an originality in the separating and formative faculty of this kind of natural being, as is infinitely beyond the reach of art, if the attempt is made to reconstruct such vegetable products out of elements obtained by their dissection or material supplied by nature for their sustenance.

Thirdly, each part of a tree generates itself in such a way that the maintenance of any one part depends reciprocally on the maintenance of the rest. A bud of one tree engrafted on the twig of another produces in the alien stock a plant of its own kind, and so also a scion engrafted on a foreign stem. Hence we may regard each twig or leaf of the same tree as merely engrafted or inoculated into it, and so as an independent tree attached to another and parasitically nourished by it. At the same time, while the leaves are products of the tree they also in turn give support to it; for the repeated defoliation of a tree kills it, and its growth thus depends on the action of the leaves upon the stem. The self-help of nature in case of injury in the vegetable creation, when the want of a part that is necessary for the maintenance of its neighbours is supplied by the remaining parts; and the abortions or malformations in growth, in which certain parts, on account of casual defects or hindrances, form themselves in a new way to maintain what exists, and so produce an anomalous creature, I shall only mention in passing, though they are among the most wonderful properties of organised creatures.

§ 65. THINGS REGARDED AS NATURAL PURPOSES ARE ORGANISED BEINGS

According to the character alleged in the preceding section, a thing, which, though a natural product, is to be cognised as only possible as a natural purpose, must bear itself alternately as cause and as effect. This, however, is a somewhat inexact and indeterminate expression which needs derivation from a determinate concept.

Causal combination as thought merely by the Understanding is a connexion constituting an ever-progressive series (of causes and effects); and things which as effects presuppose others as causes cannot be reciprocally at the same time causes of these. This sort of causal combination we call that of effective causes (*nexus effectivus*). But on the other hand, a causal combination according to a concept of Reason (of purposes) can also be thought, which regarded as a series would lead either forwards or backwards; in this the thing that has been called the effect may with equal propriety be termed the cause of that of which it is the effect. In the practical department of human art we easily find connexions such as this; *e.g.* a house, no doubt, is the cause of the money received for rent, but also conversely the representation of this possible income was the cause of building the house. Such a causal connexion we call that of final causes (*nexus finalis*). We may perhaps suitably name the first the connexion of real causes, the second of those which are ideal; because from this nomenclature it is at once comprehended that there can be no more than these two kinds of causality.

For a thing to be a natural purpose in the *first* place it is requisite that its parts (as regards their being and their form) are only possible through their reference to the whole. For the thing itself is a purpose and so is comprehended under a concept or an Idea which must determine *a priori* all that is to be contained in it. But so far as a thing is only thought as possible in this way, it is a mere work of art; *i.e.* a product of one rational cause distinct from the matter (of the parts), whose causality (in the collection and combination of the parts) is determined through its Idea of a whole possible by their means (and consequently not through external nature).

But if a thing as a natural product is to involve in itself and in its internal possibility a reference to purposes,—*i.e.* to be possible only as a natural purpose, and without the causality of the concepts of rational beings external to itself,—then it is requisite *secondly* that its parts should so combine in the unity of a whole that they are reciprocally cause and effect of each other's form. Only in this way can the Idea of the whole conversely (reciprocally) determine the form and combination of all the parts; not indeed as cause —for then it would be an artificial product—but as the ground of cognition, for him who is judging it, of the systematic unity and combination of all the manifold contained in the given material.

For a body then which is to be judged in itself and its internal possibility as a natural purpose, it is requisite that its parts mutually depend upon each other both as to their form and their combination, and so produce a whole by their own causality; while conversely the concept of the whole may be regarded as its cause according to a prin- ciple (in a being possessing a causality according to concepts adequate to such a prod- uct). In this case then the connexion of *effective causes* may be judged as an *effect through final causes*.

In such a product of nature every part not only exists *by means of* the other parts, but is thought as existing *for the sake of* the others and the whole, that is as an (organic) instrument. Thus, however, it might be an artificial instrument, and so might be repre- sented only as a purpose that is possible in general; but also its parts are all organs reci- procally *producing* each other. This can never be the case with artificial instruments, but only with nature which supplies all the material for instruments (even for those of art). Only a product of such a kind can be called a *natural purpose*, and this because it is an *organised* and *self-organising being*.

In a watch one part is the instrument for moving the other parts, but the wheel is not the effective cause of the production of the others; no doubt one part is for the sake of the others, but it does not exist by their means. In this case the producing cause of the parts and of their form is not contained in the nature (of the material), but is external to it in a being which can produce effects according to Ideas of a whole possible by means of its causality. Hence a watch wheel does not produce other wheels, still less does one watch produce other watches, utilising (organising) foreign material for that purpose; hence it does not replace of itself parts of which it has been deprived, nor does it make good what is lacking in a first formation by the addition of the missing parts, nor if it has gone out of order does it repair itself—all of which, on the contrary, we may expect from organised nature.—An organised being is then not a mere machine, for that has merely *moving* power, but it possesses in itself *formative* power of a self-propagating kind which it communicates to its materials though they have it not of themselves; it organises them, in fact, and this cannot be explained by the mere mechanical faculty of motion.

We say of nature and its faculty in organised products far too little if we describe it as an *analogon of art*; for this suggests an artificer (a rational being) external to it. Much rather does it organise itself and its organised products in every species, no doubt after one general pattern but yet with suitable deviations, which self-preservation demands according to circumstances. We perhaps approach nearer to this inscrutable property, if we describe it as an *analogon of life*; but then we must either endow matter, as mere matter, with a property which contradicts its very being (hylozoism), or associate therewith an alien principle *standing in communion* with it (a soul). But in the latter case we must, if such a product is to be a natural product, either presuppose organised matter as the instrument of that soul, which does not make the soul a whit more comprehensible; or regard the soul as artificer of this structure and so remove the product from (corporeal) nature. To speak strictly, then, the organisation of nature has in it nothing analogous to any causality we know.[4] Beauty in nature can be rightly described as an analogon of art, because it is ascribed to objects only in reference to reflection upon their *external* aspect, and consequently only on account of the form of their external surface. But *internal natural perfection*, as it belongs to those things which are only possible as *natural purposes*, and are therefore called organised beings, is not analogous to any physical, *i.e.* natural, faculty known to us; nay even, regarding ourselves as, in the widest sense, belonging to nature, it is not even thinkable or explicable by means of any exactly fitting analogy to human art.

The concept of a thing as in itself a natural purpose is therefore no constitutive concept of Understanding or of Reason, but it can serve as a regulative concept for the reflective Judgement, to guide our investigation about objects of this kind by a distant analogy with our own causality according to purposes generally, and in our meditations upon their ultimate ground. This latter use, however, is not in reference to the knowledge of nature or of its original ground, but rather to our own practical faculty of Reason, in analogy with which we considered the cause of that purposiveness.

Organised beings are then the only beings in nature which, considered in themselves and apart from any relation to other things, can be thought as possible only as purposes of nature. Hence they first afford objective reality to the concept of a *purpose of nature*, as distinguished from a practical purpose; and so they give to the science of nature the basis for a teleology, *i.e.* a mode of judgement about natural Objects according to a special principle which otherwise we should in no way be justified in introducing (because we cannot see *a priori* the possibility of this kind of causality).

§ 66. OF THE PRINCIPLE OF JUDGING OF INTERNAL PURPOSIVENESS IN ORGANISED BEINGS

This principle, which is at the same time a definition, is as follows: *An organised product of nature is one in which every part is reciprocally purpose, [end] and means.* In it nothing is vain, without purpose, or to be ascribed to a blind mechanism of nature.

This principle, as regards its occasion, is doubtless derived from experience, viz. from that methodised experience called observation; but on account of the universality and necessity which it ascribes to such purposiveness it cannot rest solely on empirical grounds, but must have at its basis an *a priori* principle, although it be merely regulative and these purposes lie only in the idea of the judging [subject] and not in an effective cause. We may therefore describe the aforesaid principle as a *maxim* for judging of the internal purposiveness of organised beings.

It is an acknowledged fact that the dissectors of plants and animals, in order to investigate their structure and to find out the reasons, why and for what end such parts, such a disposition and combination of parts, and just such an internal form have been given them, assume as indisputably necessary the maxim that nothing in such a creature is *vain*; just as they lay down as the fundamental proposition of the universal science of nature, that *nothing* happens *by chance*. In fact, they can as little free themselves from this teleological proposition as from the universal physical proposition; for as without the latter we should have no experience at all, so without the former we should have no guiding thread for the observation of a species of natural things which we have thought teleologically under the concept of natural purposes.

Now this concept brings the Reason into a quite different order of things from that of a mere mechanism of nature, which is no longer satisfying here. An Idea is to be the ground of the possibility of the natural product. But because this is an absolute unity of representation, instead of the material being a plurality of things that can supply by itself no definite unity of composition,—if that unity of the Idea is to serve at all as the *a priori* ground of determination of a natural law of the causality of such a form of composition,—the purpose of nature must be extended to *everything* included in its product. For if we once refer action of this sort *on the whole* to any supersensible ground of determination beyond the blind mechanism of nature, we must judge of it altogether according to this principle; and we have then no reason to regard the form of such a thing as partly dependent on mechanism—for by such mixing up of disparate principles no certain rule of judging would be left.

For example, it may be that in an animal body many parts can be conceived as concretions according to mere mechanical laws (as the hide, the bones, the hair). And yet the cause which brings together the required matter, modifies it, forms it, and puts it in its appropriate place, must always be judged of teleologically; so that here everything must be considered as organised, and everything again in a certain relation to the thing itself is an organ.

§ 67. OF THE PRINCIPLE OF THE TELEOLOGICAL JUDGING OF NATURE IN GENERAL AS A SYSTEM OF PURPOSES

We have already said above that the *external* purposiveness of natural things affords no sufficient warrant for using them as purposes of nature in order to explain their presence, and for regarding their contingently purposive effects as the grounds of their presence according to the principle of final causes. Thus we cannot take for natural purposes, *rivers* because they promote intercourse among inland peoples, *mountains* because they contain the sources of the rivers and for their maintenance in rainless seasons have a store of snow, or the *slope* of the land which carries away the water and leaves the country dry; because although this shape of the earth's surface be very necessary for the origin and maintenance of the vegetable and animal kingdoms, it has nothing in itself for the possibility of which we are forced to assume a causality according to purposes. The same is true of plants which man uses for his needs or his pleasures; of beasts, the camel, the ox, the horse, dog, etc., which are indispensable to him as well for food as because they are used in his service in many different ways. In the case of things which we have no reason for regarding in themselves as purposes, such external relation can only be hypothetically judged as purposive.

To judge of a thing as a natural purpose on account of its internal form is something very different from taking the existence of that thing to be a purpose of nature. For the latter assertion we require not merely the concept of a possible purpose, but the knowledge of the final purpose (*scopus*) of nature. But this requires a reference of such knowledge to something supersensible far transcending all our teleological knowledge of nature, for the purpose of [the existence of]⁵ nature must itself be sought beyond nature. The internal form of a mere blade of grass is sufficient to show that for our human faculty of judgement its origin is possible only according to the rule of purposes. But if we change our point of view and look to the use which other natural beings make of it, abandon the consideration of its internal organisation and only look to its externally purposive references, we shall arrive at no categorical purpose; all this purposive reference rests on an ever more distant condition, which, as unconditioned (the presence of a thing as final purpose), lies quite outside the physico-teleological view of the world. For example, grass is needful for the ox, which again is needful for man as a means of existence, but then we do not see why it is necessary that men should exist (a question this, which we shall not find so easy to answer if we sometimes cast our thoughts on the New Hollanders or the inhabitants of Tierra del Fuego). So conceived, the thing is not even a natural purpose, for neither it (nor its whole genus) is to be regarded as a natural product.

Hence it is only so far as matter is organised that it necessarily carries with it the concept of a natural purpose, because this its specific form is at the same time a product of nature. But this concept leads necessarily to the Idea of collective nature as a system in accordance with the rule of purposes, to which Idea all the mechanism of nature must be subordinated according to principles of Reason (at least in order to investigate natural phenomena therein). The principle of Reason belongs to it only as a subjective principle or a maxim: viz. everything in the World is some way good for something; nothing is vain in it. By the example that nature gives us in its organic products we are justified, nay called upon, to expect of it and of its laws nothing that is not purposive on the whole.

It is plain that this is not a principle for the determinant but only for the reflective Judgement; that it is regulative and not constitutive; and that we derive from it a clue by which we consider natural things in reference to an already given ground of determination according to a new law-abiding order; and extend our natural science according to a different principle, viz. that of final causes, but yet without prejudice to the principle of mechanical causality. Furthermore, it is in no wise thus decided, whether anything of which we judge by this principle, is a *designed* purpose of nature; whether the grass is for the ox or the sheep, or whether these and the other things of nature are here for men. It is well also from this side to consider the things which are unpleasant to us and are contrary to purpose in particular references. Thus, for example, we can say: The vermin that torment men in their clothes, their hair, or their beds, may be, according to a wise appointment of nature, a motive to cleanliness which is in itself an important means for the preservation of health. Or again the mosquitoes and other stinging insects that make the wildernesses of America so oppressive to the savages, may be so many goads to activity for these primitive men, [inducing them] to drain the marshes and bring light into the forests which intercept every breath of air, and in this way, as well as by cultivating the soil, to make their habitations more healthy. The same thing, which appears to men contradictory to nature in its inner organisation, if viewed in this light gives an entertaining, sometimes an instructive, outlook into a teleological order of things, to which, without such a principle, mere physical observation would not lead us by itself. Thus some persons regard the tapeworm as given to the men or animals in whom it resides, as a kind of set-off for some defect in their vital organs; now I would ask if dreams (without which we never sleep, though we seldom remember them) may not be a purposive ordinance of nature? For during the relaxation of all the moving powers of the body, they serve to excite internally the vital organs by the medium of the Imagination and its great activity (which in this state generally rises to the height of affection). During sleep the Imagination commonly is more actively at play when the stomach is overloaded, in which case this excitement is the more necessary. Consequently, then, without this internal power of motion and this fatiguing unrest, on account of which we complain about our dreams (though in fact they are rather remedial), sleep even in a sound state of health would be a complete extinction of life.

Also the beauty of nature, *i.e.* its connexion with the free play of our cognitive faculties in apprehending and judging of its appearance, can be regarded as a kind of objective purposiveness of nature in its whole [content] as a system of which man is a member; if once the teleological judging of the same by means of the natural purposes which organised beings suggest to us, has justified for us the Idea of a great system of purposes of nature. We can regard it as a favour[6] which nature has felt for us, that in addition to what is useful it has so profusely dispensed beauty and charm; and we can therefore love it, as well as regard it with respect on account of its immensity, and feel ourselves ennobled by such regard; just as if nature had established and adorned its splendid theatre precisely with this view.

We shall say only one thing more in this paragraph. If we have once discovered in nature a faculty of bringing forth products that can only be thought by us in accordance with the concept of final causes, we go further still. We venture to judge that things belong to a system of purposes, which yet do not (either in themselves or in their purposive relations) necessitate our seeking for any principle of their possibility beyond the mechanism of causes working blindly. For the first Idea, as concerns its ground, already brings us beyond the world of sense; since the unity of the supersensible principle must be regarded as valid in this way not merely for certain species of natural beings, but for the whole of nature as a system.

§ 68. OF THE PRINCIPLE OF TELEOLOGY AS INTERNAL PRINCIPLE OF NATURAL SCIENCE

The principles of a science are either internal to it and are then called domestic (*principia domestica*), or are based on concepts that can only find their place outside it and so are *foreign* principles (*peregrina*). Sciences that contain the latter, place at the basis of their doctrines auxiliary propositions (*lemmata*), *i.e.* they borrow some concept, and with it a ground of arrangement, from another science.

Every science is in itself a system, and it is not enough in it to build in accordance with principles and thus to employ a technical procedure, but we must go to work with it architectonically, as a building subsisting for itself; we must not treat it as an additional wing or part of another building, but as a whole in itself, although we may subsequently make a passage from it into that other or conversely.

If then we introduce into the context of natural science the concept of God in order to explain the purposiveness in nature, and subsequently use this purposiveness to prove that there is a God, there is no internal consistency in either science [*i.e.* either in natural science or theology]; and a delusive circle brings them both into uncertainty, because they have allowed their boundaries to overlap.

The expression, a purpose of nature, already sufficiently prevents the confusion of mixing up natural science and the occasion that it gives for judging *teleologically* of its objects, with the consideration of God, and so of a *theological* derivation of them. We must not regard it as insignificant, if one interchanges this expression with that of a divine purpose in the ordering of nature, or gives out the latter as more suitable and proper for a pious soul, because it must come in the end to deriving these purposive forms in nature from a wise author of the world. On the contrary, we must carefully and modestly limit ourselves to the expression, a purpose of nature, which asserts exactly as much as we know. Before we ask after the cause of nature itself, we find in nature, and in the course of its development, products of the same kind which are developed in it according to known empirical laws, in accordance with which natural science must judge of its objects, and, consequently, must seek in nature their causality according to the rule of purposes. So then it must not transgress its bounds in order to introduce into itself as a domestic principle that, to whose concept no experience can be commensurate, upon which we are only entitled to venture after the completion of natural science.

Natural characteristics which demonstrate themselves *a priori*, and consequently admit of insight into their possibility from universal principles without any admixture of experience, although they carry with them a technical purposiveness, yet cannot, because they are absolutely necessary, be referred to the Teleology of nature, as to a method belonging to Physic for solving its problems. Arithmetical or geometrical analogies, as well as universal mechanical laws,—however strange and admirable may seem to us the union of different rules, quite independent of one another according to all appearance, in a single principle,—possess on that account no claim to be teleological grounds of explanation in Physic. Even if they deserve to be brought into consideration in the universal theory of the purposiveness of things of nature, yet they belong to another [science], *i.e.* Metaphysic, and constitute no internal principle of natural science; as with the empirical laws of natural purposes in organised beings, it is not only permissible but unavoidable to use the teleological *mode of judging* as a principle of the doctrine of nature in regard to a particular class of its objects.

So to the end that Physic may keep within its own bounds, it abstracts itself entirely from the question, whether natural purposes are *designed* or *undesigned*; for that would be to meddle in an extraneous business, in Metaphysic. It is enough that there are objects, alone *explicable* according to natural laws which we can only think by means of the Idea of purposes as principle, and also alone internally *cognisable* as concerns their internal form, in this way. In order, therefore, to remove the suspicion of the slightest assumption,—as if we wished to mix with our grounds of cognition something not belonging to Physic at all, viz. a supernatural cause,—we speak in Teleology, indeed, of nature as if the purposiveness therein were designed, but in such a way that this design is ascribed to nature, *i.e.* to matter. Now in this way there can be no misunderstanding, because no design in the proper meaning of the word can possibly be ascribed to inanimate matter; we thus give notice that this word here only expresses a principle of the reflective not of the determinant Judgement, and so is to introduce no particular ground of causality; but only adds for the use of the Reason a different kind of investigation from that according to mechanical laws, in order to supplement the inadequacy of the latter even for empirical research into all particular laws of nature. Hence we speak quite correctly in Teleology, so far as it is referred to Physic, of the wisdom, the economy, the forethought, the beneficence of Nature, without either making an intelligent being of it, for that would be preposterous; or even without presuming to place another intelligent Being above it as its Architect, for that would be presumptuous.[7] But there should be only signified thereby a kind of causality of nature after the analogy of our own in the technical use of Reason, in order to have before us the rule according to which certain products of nature must be investigated.

But now why is it that Teleology usually forms no proper part of theoretical natural science, but is regarded as a propaedeutic or transition to Theology? This is done in order to restrict the study of nature, mechanically considered, to that which we can so subject to observation or experiment that we are able to produce it ourselves as nature does, or at least by similar laws. For we see into a thing completely only so far as we can make it in accordance with our concepts and bring it to completion. But organisation, as an inner purpose of nature, infinitely surpasses all our faculty of presenting the like by means of art. And as concerns the external contrivances of nature regarded as purposive (wind, rain, etc.), Physic, indeed, considers their mechanism, but it cannot at all present their reference to purposes, so far as this is a condition necessarily belonging to cause; for this necessity of connexion has to do altogether with the combination of our concepts and not with the constitution of things.

SECOND DIVISION—DIALECTIC OF THE TELEOLOGICAL JUDGEMENT

§ 69. WHAT IS AN ANTINOMY OF THE JUDGEMENT?

The *determinant* Judgement has for itself no principles which are the foundation of *concepts of Objects*. It has no autonomy, for it *subsumes* only under given laws or concepts as principles. Hence it is exposed to no danger of an antinomy of its own or to a conflict of its principles. So [we saw that] the transcendental Judgement which contains the conditions of subsuming under categories was for itself not *nomothetic*, but that it only indicated the conditions of sensuous intuition, under which reality (application) can be supplied to a given concept, as law of the Understanding, whereby the Judgement could never fall into discord with itself (at least as far as its principles are concerned).

But the *reflective* Judgement must subsume under a law, which is not yet given, and is therefore in fact only a principle of reflection upon objects, for which we are objectively quite in want of a law or of a concept of an Object that would be adequate as a principle for the cases that occur. Since now no use of the cognitive faculties can be permitted without principles, the reflective Judgement must in such cases serve as a principle for itself. This, because it is not objective and can supply no ground of cognition of the Object adequate for design, must serve as a mere subjective principle, for the purposive employment of our cognitive faculties, *i.e.* for reflecting upon a class of objects. Therefore in reference to such cases the reflective Judgement has its maxims— necessary maxims—on behalf of the cognition of natural laws in experience, in order to attain by their means to concepts, even concepts of Reason; since it has absolute need of such in order to learn merely to cognise nature according to its empirical laws.— Between these necessary maxims of the reflective Judgement there may be a conflict and consequently an antinomy, upon which a Dialectic bases itself. If each of two conflicting maxims has its ground in the nature of the cognitive faculties, this may be called a natural Dialectic, and an unavoidable illusion which we must expose and resolve in our Critique, to the end that it may not deceive us.

§ 70. REPRESENTATION OF THIS ANTINOMY

So far as Reason has to do with nature, as the complex of objects of external sense, it can base itself partly upon laws which the Understanding itself prescribes a priori to nature, partly upon laws which it can extend indefinitely by means of the empirical determinations occurring in experience. To apply the former kind of laws, *i.e.* the *universal* laws of material nature in general, the Judgement needs no special principle of reflection, since it is there determinant because an objective principle is given to it through Understanding. But as regards the particular laws that can only be made known to us through experience, there can be under them such great manifoldness and diversity, that the Judgement must serve as its own principle in order to investigate and search into the phenomena of nature in accordance with a law. Such a guiding thread is needed, if we are only to hope for a connected empirical cognition according to a thoroughgoing conformity of nature to law, even its unity according to empirical laws. In this contingent unity of particular laws it may very well happen that the Judgement in its reflection proceeds from two maxims. One of these is suggested to it *a priori* by the mere Understanding; but the other is prompted by particular experiences, which bring the Reason into play in order to form a judgement upon corporeal nature and its laws in accordance with a particular principle. Hence it comes about that these two kinds of maxims seem to be incapable of existing together, and consequently a Dialectic arises which leads the Judgement into error in the principle of its reflection.

The *first maxim* of Judgement is the *proposition*: all production of material things and their forms must be judged to be possible according to merely mechanical laws.

The *second maxim* is the *counter-proposition*: some products of material nature cannot be judged to be possible according to merely mechanical laws. (To judge them requires quite a different law of causality, namely, that of final causes.)

If these regulative principles of investigation be converted into constitutive principles of the possibility of Objects, they will run thus:

Proposition: All production of material things is possible according to merely mechanical laws.

Counter-proposition: Some production of material things is not possible according to merely mechanical laws.

In this latter aspect, as objective principles for the determinant Judgement, they would contradict each other; and consequently one of the two propositions must necessarily be false. We shall then, it is true, have an antinomy, but not of Judgement; there will be a conflict in the legislation of Reason. Reason, however, can prove neither the one nor the other of these fundamental propositions, because we can have *a priori* no determinant principle of the possibility of things according to mere empirical laws of nature.

On the other hand, as regards the first-mentioned maxims of a reflective Judgement, they involve no contradiction in fact. For if I say, I must *judge*, according to merely mechanical laws, of the possibility of all events in material nature, and consequently of all forms regarded as its products, I do not therefore say: *They are possible in this way alone* (apart from any other kind of causality). All that is implied is: I *must* always *reflect* upon them *according to the principle* of the mere mechanism of nature, and consequently investigate this as far as I can; because unless this lies at the basis of investigation, there can be no proper knowledge of nature at all. But this does not prevent us, if occasion offers, from following out the second maxim in the case of certain natural forms (and even by occasion of these in the whole of nature), in order to reflect upon them according to the principle of final causes, which is quite a different thing from explaining them according to the mechanism of nature. Reflection in accordance with the first maxim is thus not abrogated; on the contrary, we are told to follow it as far as we can. Nor is it said that these forms would not be possible in accordance with the mechanism of nature. It is only asserted that *human Reason* in following up this maxim and in this way could never find the least ground for that which constitutes the specific [character] of a natural purpose, although it would increase its knowledge of natural laws. Thus it is left undecided whether or not in the unknown inner ground of nature, physico-mechanical and purposive combination may be united in the same things in one principle. We only say that our Reason is not in a position so to unite them; and that therefore the Judgement (as *reflective*—from subjective grounds, not as determinant, in consequence of an objective principle of the possibility of things in themselves) is compelled to think a different principle from that of natural mechanism as the ground of the possibility of certain forms in nature.

§ 71. PRELIMINARY TO THE SOLUTION OF THE ABOVE ANTINOMY

We can in no way prove the impossibility of the production of organised natural products by the mere mechanism of nature, because we cannot see into the first inner ground of the infinite multiplicity of the particular laws of nature, which are contingent for us since they are only empirically known; and so we cannot arrive at the inner all-sufficient principle of the possibility of a nature (a principle which lies in the supersensible). Whether therefore the productive faculty of nature is sufficient for that which we judge to be formed or combined in accordance with the Idea of purposes, as well as for that which we believe to require merely a mechanical system [Maschinenwesen] of nature; or whether there lies at the basis of things which we must necessarily judge as properly natural purposes, a quite different kind of original causality, which cannot be contained in material nature or in its intelligible substrate, viz. an architectonic Understanding— this is a question to which our Reason, very narrowly limited in respect of the concept of causality if it is to be specified *a priori,* can give no answer whatever.—But it is just as certain and beyond doubt that, in regard to our cognitive faculties, the mere mechanism of nature can furnish no ground of explanation of the production of organised beings. *For the reflective Judgement* it is therefore a quite correct fundamental proposition, that for that connexion of things according to final causes which is so plain, there must be thought a causality distinct from that of mechanism, viz. that of an (intelligent) cause of the world acting in accordance with purposes; but *for the determinant Judgement* this would be a hasty and unprovable proposition. In the first case it is a mere maxim of the Judgement, wherein the concept of that causality is a mere Idea, to which we by no means undertake to concede reality, but which we use as a guide to reflection, which remains thereby always open to all mechanical grounds of explanation and does not withdraw out of the world of Sense. In the second case the proposition would be an objective principle prescribed by Reason, to which the determinant Judgement must subject itself, whereby however it withdraws beyond the world of Sense into the transcendent and perhaps is led into error.

All appearance of an antinomy between the maxims of the proper physical (mechanical) and the teleological (technical) methods of explanation rests therefore on this; that we confuse a fundamental proposition of the reflective with one of the determinant Judgement, and the *autonomy* of the first (which has mere subjective validity for our use of Reason in respect of particular empirical laws) with the *heteronomy* of the second, which must regulate itself according to laws (universal or particular) given to it by the Understanding.

§ 72. OF THE DIFFERENT SYSTEMS WHICH DEAL WITH THE PURPOSIVENESS OF NATURE

No one has ever doubted the correctness of the proposition that judgement must be passed upon certain things of nature (organised beings) and their possibility in accordance with the concept of final causes, even if we only desire a *guiding thread* to learn how to cognise their constitution through observation, without aspiring to an investigation into their first origin. The question therefore can only be: whether this fundamental proposition is merely subjectively valid, *i.e.* is a mere maxim of our Judgement; or whether it is an objective principle of nature, in accordance with which, apart from its mechanism (according to the mere laws of motion), quite a different kind of causality attaches to it, viz. that of final causes, under which these laws (of moving forces) stand only as intermediate causes.

We could leave this question or problem quite undecided and unsolved speculatively; because if we content ourselves with speculation within the bounds of mere natural knowledge, we have enough in these maxims for the study of nature and for the tracking out of its hidden secrets, as far as human powers reach. There is then indeed a certain presentiment of our Reason or a hint as it were given us by nature, that, by means of this concept of final causes, we go beyond nature, and could unite it to the highest point in the series of causes, if we were to abandon or at least to lay aside for a time the investigation of nature (although we may not have advanced far in it), and seek thenceforth to find out whither this stranger in natural science, viz. the concept of natural purposes, would lead us.

But here these undisputed maxims pass over into problems opening out a wide field for difficulties. Does purposive connexion in nature *prove* a particular kind of causality? Or is it not rather, considered in itself and in accordance with objective principles, similar to the mechanism of nature, resting on one and the same ground? Only, as this ground in many natural products is often hidden too deep for our investigation, we make trial of a subjective principle, that of art, *i.e.* of causality according to Ideas, and we ascribe it to nature by analogy. This expedient succeeds in many cases, but seems in some to mislead, and in no case does it justify us in introducing into natural science a particular kind of operation quite distinct from the causality according to the mere mechanical laws of nature. We give the name of *Technic* to the procedure (the causality) of nature, on account of the appearance of purpose that we find in its products; and we shall divide this into *designed* (*technica intentionalis*) and *undesigned* (*technica naturalis*). The first is meant to signify that the productive faculty of nature according to final causes must be taken for a particular kind of causality; the second that it is at bottom quite similar to the mechanism of nature, and that its contingent agreement with our artistic concepts and their rules should be explained as a mere subjective condition of judging it, and not, falsely, as a particular kind of natural production.

If we now speak of systems explanatory of nature in regard of final causes, it must be remarked that they all controvert each other dogmatically, *i.e.* as to objective principles of the possibility of things, whether there are causes which act designedly or whether they are quite without design. They do not dispute as to the subjective maxims, by which we merely judge of the causes of such purposive products. In this latter case *disparate* principles could very well be unified; but in the former, contradictorily opposed laws annul each other and cannot subsist together.

There are two sorts of systems as to the Technic of nature, *i.e.* its productive power in accordance with the rule of purposes; viz. *Idealism* or *Realism* of natural purposes. The first maintains that all purposiveness of nature is *undesigned*; the second that some (in organised beings) is *designed*. From this latter the hypothetical consequence can be deduced that the Technic of Nature, as concerns all its other products in reference to the whole of nature, is also designed, *i.e.* is a purpose.

(1) The *Idealism* of purposiveness (I always understand here by this, objective purposiveness) is either that of the *causality* or the *fatality* of the determination of nature in the purposive form of its products. The former principle treats of the reference of matter to the physical basis of its form, viz. the laws of motion; the second, its reference to the *hyperphysical* basis of itself and of the whole of nature. The system of *causality* that is ascribed to *Epicurus* or *Democritus* is, taken literally, so plainly absurd that it need not detain us. Opposed to this is the system of fatality, of which *Spinoza* is taken as the author, although it is much older according to all appearance. This, as it appeals to something supersensible to which our insight does not extend, is not so easy to controvert; but that is because its concept of the original Being is not possible to understand. But so much is clear, that on this theory the purposive combination in the world must be taken as undesigned; for although derived from an original Being, it is not derived from its Understanding or from any design on its part, but rather from the necessity of its nature and of the world-unity which emanates therefrom. Consequently the Fatalism of purposiveness is at the same time an Idealism.

(2) The *Realism* of the purposiveness of nature is also either physical or hyperphysical. The *former* bases the purposes in nature, by the analogy of a faculty acting with design, on the *life of matter* (either its own or the life of an inner principle in it, a world-soul) and is called *Hylozoism*. The *latter* derives them from the original ground of the universe, as from an intelligent Being (originally living), who produces them with design, and is *Theism*.[8]

§ 73. NONE OF THE ABOVE SYSTEMS GIVE WHAT THEY PRETEND

What do all these systems desire? They desire to explain our teleological judgements about nature, and they go so to work therewith that some deny their truth and, consequently, explain them as an Idealism of Nature (represented as Art); others recognise them as true, and promise to establish the possibility of a nature in accordance with the Idea of final causes.

(1) The systems which defend the Idealism of final causes in nature grant, it is true, on the one hand to their principle a causality in accordance with the laws of motion (through which [causality] natural things exist purposively); but they deny to it *intentionality, i.e.* that it designedly determines itself to this its purposive production; in other words, they deny that the cause is a purpose. This is *Epicurus's* method of explanation, according to which the distinction between a Technic of nature and mere mechanism is altogether denied. Blind chance is taken as the explanatory ground not only of the agreement of the developed products with our concepts of the purpose, and consequently of [nature's] Technic; but also of the determination of the causes of this production in accordance with the laws of motion, and consequently of their mechanism. Thus nothing is explained, not even the illusion in our teleological judgements, and consequently, the would-be Idealism of these in no way established.

On the other hand, *Spinoza* wishes to dispense with all inquiries into the ground of the possibility of purposes of nature, and to take away all reality from this Idea. He allows their validity in general not as products but as accidents inhering in an original

Being; and to this Being, as substrate of those natural things, he ascribes not causality in regard to them but mere subsistence. On account of its unconditioned necessity, and also that of all natural things as accidents inhering in it, he secures, it is true, to the forms of nature that unity of ground which is requisite for all purposiveness; but at the same time he tears away their contingence, without which no *unity of purpose* can be thought, and with it all *design*, inasmuch as he takes away all intelligence from the original ground of natural things.

But Spinozism does not furnish what it desires. It desires to afford an explanatory ground of the purposive connexion (which it does not deny) of the things of nature, and it merely speaks of the unity of the subject in which they all inhere. But even if we concede to it that the beings of the world exist in this way, such ontological unity is not therefore a *unity of purpose*, and does not make this in any way comprehensible. For this latter is a quite particular kind of unity which does not follow from the connexion of things (the beings of the world) in a subject (the original Being), but implies in itself reference to a *cause* which has Understanding; and even if we unite all these things in a simple subject, this never exhibits a purposive reference. For we do not think of them, first, as the inner *effects* of the substance, as if it were a *cause*; nor, secondly, of this cause as a cause producing effects *by means of its Understanding*. Without these formal conditions all unity is mere natural necessity; and, if it is ascribed as well to things which we represent as external to one another, blind necessity. But if we wish to give the name of purposiveness of nature to that which the schoolmen call the transcendental perfection of things (in reference to their proper being), according to which everything has in itself that which is requisite to make it one thing and not another, then we are only like children playing with words instead of concepts. For if all things must be thought as purposes, then to be a thing is the same as to be a purpose, and there is at bottom nothing which specially deserves to be represented as a purpose.

We hence see at once that Spinoza by his reducing our concepts of the purposive in nature to our own consciousness of existing in an all-embracing (though simple) Being, and by his seeking that form merely in the unity of this Being, must have intended to maintain not the realism, but the idealism of its purposiveness. Even this he was not able to accomplish, because the mere representation of the unity of the substrate cannot bring about the Idea of a purposiveness, even that which is only undesigned.

(2) Those who not only maintain the *Realism* of natural purposes, but also set about explaining it, believe that they can comprehend, at least as regards its possibility, a practical kind of causality, viz. that of causes working designedly; otherwise they could not undertake to supply this explanation. For to authorise even the most daring of hypotheses, at least the *possibility* of what we assume as basis must be *certain*, and we must be able to assure objective reality to its concept.

But the possibility of living matter cannot even be thought; its concept involves a contradiction because lifelessness, *inertia*, constitutes the essential character of matter. The possibility of matter endowed with life, and of collective nature regarded as an animal, can only be used in an inadequate way (in the interests of the hypothesis of purposiveness in the whole of nature), so far as it is manifested by experience in the organisation of nature on a small scale; but in no way can we have insight into its possibility a priori. There must then be a circle in the explanation, if we wish to derive the purposiveness of nature in organised beings from the life of matter, and yet only know this life in organised beings, and can form no concept of its possibility without experience of this kind. Hylozoism, therefore, does not furnish what it promises.

Finally, *Theism* can just as little establish dogmatically the possibility of natural purposes as a key to Teleology; although it certainly is superior to all other grounds of explanation in that, through the Understanding which it ascribes to the original Being, it rescues in the best way the purposiveness of nature from Idealism, and introduces a causality acting with design for its production.

But we must first prove satisfactorily to the determinant Judgement the impossibility of the unity of purpose in matter resulting from its mere mechanism, before we are justified in placing the ground of this beyond nature in a determinate way. We can, however, advance no further than this. In accordance with the constitution and limits of our cognitive faculties (whilst we do not comprehend even the first inner ground of this mechanism) we must in no wise seek in matter a principle of determinate purposive references; but no other way of judging of the origination of its products as natural purposes remains to us than that by means of a supreme Understanding as cause of the world. But this is only a ground for the reflective, not for the determinant Judgement, and can justify absolutely no objective assertion.

§ 74. THE REASON THAT WE CANNOT TREAT THE CONCEPT OF A TECHNIC OF NATURE DOGMATICALLY IS THE FACT THAT A NATURAL PURPOSE IS INEXPLICABLE

We deal with a concept dogmatically (even though it should be empirically conditioned) if we consider it as contained under another concept of the Object which constitutes a principle[9] of Reason, and determine it in conformity with this. But we deal with it merely critically, if we consider it only in reference to our cognitive faculties and consequently to the subjective conditions of thinking it, without undertaking to decide anything about its Object. Dogmatic procedure with a concept is then that which is conformable to law for the determinant Judgement, critical procedure for the reflective Judgement.

Now the concept of a thing as a natural purpose is a concept which subsumes nature under a causality only thinkable through Reason, in order to judge in accordance with this principle about that which is given of the Object in experience. But in order to use it dogmatically for the determinant Judgement, we must be assured first of the objective reality of this concept, because otherwise we could subsume no natural thing under it. Again, the concept of a thing as a natural purpose is, no doubt, empirically conditioned, *i.e.* only possible under certain conditions given in experience, though not to be abstracted therefrom; but it is a concept only possible in accordance with a rational principle in the judgement about the object. Its objective reality, therefore (*i.e.* that an object in conformity with it is possible), cannot be comprehended and dogmatically established as such a principle; and we do not know whether it is merely a sophistical and objectively empty concept (*conceptus ratiocinans*), or a rational concept, establishing a cognition and confirmed by Reason (*conceptus ratiocinatus*).[10] Therefore it cannot be dogmatically treated for the determinant Judgement, *i.e.* it is not only impossible to decide whether or not things of nature considered as natural purposes require for their production a causality of a quite peculiar kind (that acting on design); but the question cannot even be put, because the concept of a natural purpose is simply not susceptible of proof through Reason as regards its objective reality. That is, it is not constitutive for the determinant Judgement, but merely regulative for the reflective.

That it is not susceptible of proof is clear because (as concept of a *natural product*) it embraces in itself natural necessity, and at the same time (as purpose) a contingency of the form of the Object (in reference to the mere laws of nature) in the very same thing. Hence, if there is to be no contradiction here it must contain a ground for the possibility of the thing in nature, and also a ground of the possibility of this nature itself and of its reference to something which, not being empirically cognisable nature (supersensible), is therefore for us not cognisable at all. [This is requisite] if it is to be judged according to a different kind of causality from that of natural mechanism when we wish to establish its possibility. The concept of a thing, then, as a natural purpose, is transcendent *for the determinant Judgement*, if we consider the Object through Reason (although for the reflective Judgement it certainly may be immanent in respect of the objects of experience). Hence for determinant judgements objective reality cannot be supplied to it; and so it is intelligible how all systems that one may project for the dogmatic treatment of the concept of natural purposes and of nature itself [considered] as a whole connected together by means of final causes, can decide nothing either by objective affirmation or by objective denial. For if things be subsumed under a concept that is merely problematical, its synthetical predicates (*e.g.* in the question whether the purpose of nature which we conceive for the production of things is designed or undesigned) can furnish only problematical judgements of the Object, whether affirmative or negative; and we do not know whether we are judging about something or about nothing. The concept of a causality through purposes (of art) has at all events objective reality, and also the concept of a causality according to the mechanism of nature. But the concept of a causality of nature according to the rule of purposes,—still more of a Being such as cannot be given us in experience, a Being who is the original cause of nature,—though it can be thought without contradiction, yet is of no avail for dogmatic determinations. For, since it cannot be derived from experience, and also is not requisite for the possibility thereof, its objective reality can in no way be assured. But even if this could be done, how can I number among the products of nature things which are definitely accounted products of divine art, when it is just the incapacity of nature to produce such things according to its own laws that made it necessary to invoke a cause different from it?

§ 75. THE CONCEPT OF AN OBJECTIVE PURPOSIVENESS OF NATURE IS A CRITICAL PRINCIPLE OF REASON FOR THE REFLECTIVE JUDGEMENT

It is then one thing to say, "the production of certain things of nature or that of collective nature is only possible through a cause which determines itself to action according to design"; and quite another to say, "I can *according to the peculiar constitution of my cognitive faculties* judge concerning the possibility of these things and their production, in no other fashion than by conceiving for this a cause working according to design, *i.e.* a Being which is productive in a way analogous to the causality of an intelligence." In the former case I wish to establish something concerning the Object, and am bound to establish the objective reality of an assumed concept; in the latter, Reason only determines the use of my cognitive faculties, conformably to their peculiarities and to the essential conditions of their range and their limits. Thus the former principle is an objective proposition for the determinant Judgement, the latter merely a subjective proposition for the reflective Judgement, *i.e.* a maxim which Reason prescribes to it.

We are in fact indispensably obliged to ascribe the concept of design to nature if we wish to investigate it, though only in its organised products, by continuous observation; and this concept is therefore an absolutely necessary maxim for the empirical use of our Reason. It is plain that once such a guiding thread for the study of nature is admitted and verified, we must at least try the said maxim of Judgement in nature as a whole; because thereby many of nature's laws might discover themselves, which otherwise, on account of the limitation of our insight into its inner mechanism, would remain hidden. But though in regard to this latter employment that maxim of Judgement is certainly useful, it is not indispensable, for nature as a whole is not given as organised (in the narrow sense of the word above indicated). On the other hand, in regard to those natural products, which must be judged of as designed and not formed otherwise (if we are to have empirical knowledge of their inner constitution), this maxim of the reflective Judgement is essentially necessary; because the very thought of them as organised beings is impossible without combining therewith the thought of their designed production.

Now the concept of a thing whose existence or form we represent to ourselves as possible under the condition of a purpose is inseparably bound up with the concept of its contingency (according to natural laws). Hence the natural things that we find possible only as purposes supply the best proof of the contingency of the world-whole; to the common Understanding and to the philosopher alike they are the only valid ground of proof for its dependence on and origin from a Being existing outside the world—a Being who must also be intelligent on account of that purposive form. Teleology then finds the consummation of its investigations only in Theology.

But what now in the end does the most complete Teleology prove? Does it prove that there is such an intelligent Being? No. It only proves that according to the constitution of our cognitive faculties and in the consequent combination of experience with the highest principles of Reason, we can form absolutely no concept of the possibility of such a world [as this] save by thinking a *designedly-working* supreme cause thereof. Objectively we cannot therefore lay down the proposition, there is an intelligent original Being; but only subjectively, for the use of our Judgement in its reflection upon the purposes in nature, which can be thought according to no other principle than that of a designing causality of a highest cause.

If we wished to establish on teleological grounds the above proposition dogmatically we should be beset with difficulties from which we could not extricate ourselves. For then the proposition must at bottom be reduced to the conclusion, that the organised beings in the world are no otherwise possible than by a designedly-working cause. And we should unavoidably have to assert that, because we can follow up these things in their causal combination only under the Idea of purposes, and cognise them only according to their conformity to law, we are thereby justified in assuming this as a condition necessary for every thinking and cognising being—a condition consequently attaching to the Object and not merely to our subject. But such an assertion we do not succeed in sustaining. For, since we do not, properly speaking, *observe* the purposes in nature as designed, but only in our reflection upon its products *think* this concept as a guiding thread for our Judgement, they are not given to us through the Object. It is quite impossible for us *a priori* to vindicate, as capable of assumption, such a concept according to its objective reality. It remains therefore a proposition absolutely resting upon subjective conditions alone, viz. of the Judgement reflecting in conformity with our cognitive faculties. If we expressed this proposition dogmatically as objectively valid, it would be: "There is a God." But for us men there is only permissible the limited formula: "We cannot otherwise think and make comprehensible the purposiveness which must lie at the bottom of our cognition of the internal possibility of many natural things, than by representing it and the world in general as a product of an intelligent cause, [a God]."[11]

Now if this proposition, based on an inevitably necessary maxim of our Judgement, is completely satisfactory from every *human* point of view for both the speculative and practical use of our Reason, I should like to know what we lose by not being able to prove it as also valid for higher beings, from objective grounds (which unfortunately are beyond our faculties). It is indeed quite certain that we cannot adequately cognise, much less explain, organised beings and their internal possibility, according to mere mechanical principles of nature; and we can say boldly it is alike certain that it is absurd for men to make any such attempt or to hope that another *Newton* will arise in the future, who shall make comprehensible by us the production of a blade of grass according to natural laws which no design has ordered.[12] We must absolutely deny this insight to men. But then how do we know that in nature, if we could penetrate to the principle by which it specifies the universal laws known to us, there *cannot* lie hidden (in its mere mechanism) a sufficient ground of the possibility of organised beings without supposing any design in their production? would it not be judged by us presumptuous to say this? Probabilities here are of no account when we have to do with judgements of pure Reason.—We cannot therefore judge objectively, either affirmatively or negatively, concerning the proposition: "Does a Being acting according to design lie at the basis of what we rightly call natural purposes, as the cause of the world (and consequently as its author)?" So much only is sure, that if we are to judge according to what is permitted us to see by our own proper nature (the conditions and limitations of our Reason), we can place at the basis of the possibility of these natural purposes nothing else than an intelligent Being. This alone is in conformity with the maxim of our reflective Judgement and therefore with a ground which, though subjective, is inseparably attached to the human race.

§ 76. REMARK

This consideration, which very well deserves to be worked out in detail in Transcendental Philosophy, can come in here only in passing, by way of elucidation (not as a proof of what is here proposed).

Reason is a faculty of principles and proceeds in its extremest advance to the unconditioned; on the other hand, the Understanding stands at its service always only under a certain condition which must be given. But without concepts of Understanding, to which objective reality must be given, the Reason cannot form any objective (synthetical) judgement; and contains in itself, as theoretical Reason, absolutely no constitutive but merely regulative principles. We soon see that where the Understanding cannot follow, the Reason is transcendent, and shows itself in Ideas formerly established (as regulative principles), but not in objectively valid concepts. But the Understanding which cannot keep pace with Reason but yet is requisite for the validity of Objects, limits the validity of these Ideas to the subject, although [extending it] generally to all [subjects] of this kind. That is, the Understanding limits their validity to the condition, that according to the nature of our (human) cognitive faculties, or, generally, according to the concept which we *ourselves* can *make* of the faculty of a finite intelligent being, nothing else can or must be thought; though this is not to assert that the ground of such a judgement lies in the Object. We shall adduce some examples which, though they are too important and difficult to impose them on the reader as proved propositions, yet will give him material for thought and may serve to elucidate what we are here specially concerned with.

It is indispensably necessary for the human Understanding to distinguish between the possibility and the actuality of things. The ground for this lies in the subject and in the nature of our cognitive faculties. Such a distinction (between the possible and the actual) would not be given were there not requisite for knowledge two quite different elements, Understanding for concepts and sensible intuition for Objects corresponding to them. If our Understanding were intuitive it would have no objects but those which are actual. Concepts (which merely extend to the possibility of an object) and sensible intuitions (which give us something without allowing us to cognise it thus as an object) would both disappear. But now the whole of our distinction between the merely possible and the actual rests on this, that the former only signifies the positing of the representation of a thing in respect of our concept, and, in general, in respect of the faculty of thought; while the latter signifies the positing of the thing in itself [outside this concept].[13] The distinction, then, of possible things from actual is one which has merely subjective validity for the human Understanding, because we can always have a thing in our thoughts although it is [really] nothing, or we can represent a thing as given although we have no concept of it. The propositions therefore—that things can be possible without being actual, and that consequently no conclusion can be drawn as to actuality from mere possibility—are quite valid for human Reason, without thereby proving that this distinction lies in things themselves. That this does not follow, and that consequently these propositions, though valid of Objects (in so far as our cognitive faculty, as sensuously conditioned, busies itself with Objects of sense), do not hold for things in general, appears from the irrepressible demand of Reason to assume something (the original ground) necessarily existing as unconditioned, in which possibility and actuality should no longer be distinguished, and for which Idea our Understanding has absolutely no concept; *i.e.* it can find no way of representing such a thing and its manner of existence. For if the Understanding *thinks* such a thing (which it may do at pleasure), the thing is merely represented as possible. If it is conscious of it as given in intuition, then is it actual; but nothing as to its possibility is thus thought. Hence the concept of an absolutely necessary Being is no doubt an indispensable Idea of Reason, but yet it is a problematical concept unattainable by the human Understanding. It is indeed valid for the employment of our cognitive faculties in accordance with their peculiar constitution, but not valid of the Object. Nor is it valid for every knowing being, because I cannot presuppose in every such being thought and intuition as two distinct conditions of the exercise of its cognitive faculties, and consequently as conditions of the possibility and actuality of things. An Understanding into which this distinction did not enter, might say: All Objects that I know *are*, *i.e.* exist; and the possibility of some, which yet do not exist (*i.e.* the contingency or the contrasted necessity of those which do exist), might never come into the representation of such a being at all. But what makes it difficult for our Understanding to treat its concepts here as Reason does, is merely that for it, as human Understanding, that is transcendent (*i.e.* impossible for the subjective conditions of its cognition) which Reason makes into a principle appertaining to the Object.—Here the maxim always holds, that all Objects whose cognition surpasses the faculty of the Understanding are thought by us according to the subjective conditions of the exercise of that faculty which necessarily attach to our (human) nature. If judgements laid down in this way (and there is no other alternative in regard to transcendent concepts) cannot be constitutive principles determining the Object as it is, they will remain regulative principles adapted to the human point of view, immanent in their exercise and sure.

Just as Reason in the theoretical consideration of nature must assume the Idea of an unconditioned necessity of its original ground, so also it presupposes in the practical [sphere] its own (in respect of nature) unconditioned causality, or freedom, in that it is conscious of its own moral command. Here the objective necessity of the act, as a duty, is opposed to that necessity which it would have as an event, if its ground lay in nature and not in freedom (*i.e.* in the causality of Reason). The morally absolutely necessary act is regarded as physically quite contingent, since that which *ought* necessarily to happen often does not happen. It is clear then that it is owing to the subjective constitution of our practical faculty that the moral laws must be represented as commands, and the actions conforming to them as duties; and that Reason expresses this necessity not by an "*is*" (happens), but by an "ought to be." This would not be the case were Reason considered as in its causality independent of sensibility (as the subjective condition of its application to objects of nature), and so as cause in an intelligible world entirely in agreement with the moral law. For in such a world there would be no distinction between "ought to do" and "does," between a practical law of that which is possible through us, and the theoretical law of that which is actual through us. Though, therefore, an intelligible world in which everything would be actual merely because (as something good) it is possible, together with freedom as its formal condition, is for us a transcendent concept, not available as a constitutive principle to determine an Object and its objective reality; yet, because of the constitution of our (in part sensuous) nature and faculty it is, so far as we can represent it in accordance with the constitution of our Reason, for us and for all rational beings that have a connexion with the world of sense, a universal *regulative principle*. This principle does not objectively determine the constitution of freedom, as a form of causality, but it makes the rule of actions according to that Idea a command for every one, with no less validity than if it did so determine it.

In the same way we may concede thus much as regards the case in hand. Between natural mechanism and the Technic of nature, *i.e.* its purposive connexion, we should find no distinction, were it not that our Understanding is of the kind that must proceed from the universal to the particular. The Judgement then in respect of the particular can cognise no purposiveness and, consequently, can form no determinant judgements, without having a universal law under which to subsume that particular. Now the particular, as such, contains something contingent in respect of the universal, while yet Reason requires unity and conformity to law in the combination of particular laws of nature. This conformity of the contingent to law is called purposiveness; and the derivation of particular laws from the universal, as regards their contingent element, is impossible *a priori* through a determination of the concept of the Object. Hence, the concept of the purposiveness of nature in its products is necessary for human Judgement in respect of nature, but has not to do with the determination of Objects. It is, therefore, a subjective principle of Reason for the Judgement, which as regulative (not constitutive) is just as necessarily valid for our *human Judgement* as if it were an objective principle.

§ 77. OF THE PECULIARITY OF THE HUMAN UNDERSTANDING, BY MEANS OF WHICH THE CONCEPT OF A NATURAL PURPOSE IS POSSIBLE

We have brought forward in the *Remark* peculiarities of our cognitive faculties (even the higher ones) which we are easily led to transfer as objective predicates to the things themselves. But they concern Ideas, no object adequate to which can be given in experience, and they could only serve as regulative principles in the pursuit of experience. This is the case with the concept of a natural purpose, which concerns the cause of the possibility of such a predicate, which cause can only lie in the Idea. But the result corresponding to it (*i.e.* the product) is given in nature; and the concept of a causality of nature as of a being acting according to purposes seems to make the Idea of a natural purpose into a constitutive principle, which Idea has thus something different from all other Ideas.

This difference consists, however, in the fact that the Idea in question is not a rational principle for the Understanding but for the Judgement. It is, therefore, merely the application of an Understanding in general to possible objects of experience, in cases where the judgement can only be reflective, not determinant, and where, consequently, the object, although given in experience, cannot be *determinately judged* in conformity with the Idea (not to say with complete adequacy), but can only be reflected on.

There emerges, therefore, a peculiarity of *our* (human) Understanding in respect of the Judgement in its reflection upon things of nature. But if this be so, the Idea of a possible Understanding different from the human must be fundamental here. (Just so in the Critique of Pure Reason we must have in our thoughts another possible [kind of] intuition, if ours is to be regarded as a particular species for which objects are only valid as phenomena.) And so we are able to say: Certain natural products, from the special constitution of our Understanding, *must be considered by us*, in regard to their possibility, as if produced designedly and as purposes. But we do not, therefore, demand that there should be actually given a particular cause which has the representation of a purpose as its determining ground; and we do not deny that an Understanding, different from (*i.e.* higher than) the human, might find the ground of the possibility of such products of nature in the mechanism of nature, *i.e.* in a causal combination for which an Understanding is not explicitly assumed as cause.

We have now to do with the relation of *our* Understanding to the Judgement; viz. we seek for a certain contingency in the constitution of our Understanding, to which we may point as a peculiarity distinguishing it from other possible Understandings.

This contingency is found, naturally enough, in the *particular*, which the Judgement is to bring under the *universal* of the concepts of Understanding. For the universal of *our* (human) Understanding does not determine the particular, and it is contingent in how many ways different things which agree in a common characteristic may come before our perception. Our Understanding is a faculty of concepts, *i.e.* a discursive Understanding, for which it obviously must be contingent of what kind and how very different the particular may be that can be given to it in nature and brought under its concepts. But now intuition also belongs to knowledge, and a faculty of a *complete spontaneity of intuition* would be a cognitive faculty distinct from sensibility, and quite independent of it, in other words, an Understanding in the most general sense. Thus we can think an *intuitive* Understanding [negatively, merely as not discursive[14]], which does not proceed from the universal to the particular, and so to the individual (through concepts). For it that contingency of the accordance of nature in its products according to *particular* laws with the Understanding would not be met with; and it is this contingency that makes it so hard for our Understanding to reduce the manifold of nature to the unity of knowledge. This reduction our Understanding can only accomplish by bringing natural characteristics into a very contingent correspondence with our faculty of concepts, of which an intuitive Understanding would have no need.

Our Understanding has then this peculiarity as concerns the Judgement, that in cognition by it the particular is not determined by the universal and cannot therefore be derived from it; but at the same time this particular in the manifold of nature must accord with the universal (by means of concepts and laws) so that it may be capable of being subsumed under it. This accordance under such circumstances must be very contingent and without definite principle as concerns the Judgement.

In order now to be able at least to think the possibility of such an accordance of things of nature with our Judgement (which accordance we represent as contingent and consequently as only possible by means of a purpose directed thereto), we must at the same time think of another Understanding, by reference to which and apart from any purpose ascribed to it, we may represent as *necessary* that accordance of natural laws with our Judgement, which for our Understanding is only thinkable through the medium of purposes.

In fact our Understanding has the property of proceeding in its cognition, *e.g.* of the cause of a product, from the *analytical-universal* (concepts) to the particular (the given empirical intuition). Thus as regards the manifold of the latter it determines nothing, but must await this determination by the Judgement, which subsumes the empirical intuition (if the object is a natural product) under the concept. We can however think an Understanding which, being, not like ours, discursive, but intuitive, proceeds from the *synthetical-universal* (the intuition of a whole as such) to the particular, *i.e.* from the whole to the parts. The *contingency* of the combination of the parts, in order that a definite form of the whole shall be possible, is not implied by such an Understanding and its representation of the whole. Our Understanding requires this because it must proceed from the parts as universally conceived grounds to different forms possible to be subsumed under them, as consequences. According to the constitution of our Understanding a real whole of nature is regarded only as the effect of the concurrent motive powers of the parts. Suppose then that we wish not to represent the possibility of the whole as dependent on that of the parts (after the manner of our discursive Understanding), but according to the standard of the intuitive (original) Understanding to represent the possibility of the parts (according to their constitution and combination) as dependent on that of the whole. In accordance with the above peculiarity of our Understanding it cannot happen that the whole shall contain the ground of the possibility of the connexion of the parts (which would be a contradiction in discursive cognition), but only that the *representation* of a whole may contain the ground of the possibility of its form and the connexion of the parts belonging to it. Now such a whole would be an effect (*product*) the *representation* of which is regarded as the *cause* of its possibility; but the product of a cause whose determining ground is merely the representation of its effect is called a purpose. Hence it is merely a consequence of the particular constitution of our Understanding, that it represents products of nature as possible, according to a different kind of causality from that of the natural laws of matter, namely, that of purposes and final causes. Hence also this principle has not to do with the possibility of such things themselves (even when considered as phenomena) according to the manner of their production, but merely with the judgement upon them which is possible to our Understanding. Here we see at once why it is that in natural science we are not long contented with an explanation of the products of nature by a causality according to purposes. For there we desire to judge of natural production merely in a manner conformable to our faculty of judging, *i.e.* to the reflective Judgement, and not in reference to things themselves on behalf of the determinant Judgement. It is here not at all requisite to prove that such an *intellectus archetypus* is possible, but only that we are led to the Idea of it,—which contains no contradiction,—in contrast to our discursive Understanding which has need of images (*intellectus ectypus*) and to the contingency of its constitution.

If we consider a material whole, according to its form, as a product of the parts with their powers and faculties of combining with one another (as well as of bringing in foreign materials), we represent to ourselves a mechanical mode of producing it. But in this way no concept emerges of a whole as purpose, whose internal possibility presupposes throughout the Idea of a whole on which depend the constitution and mode of action of the parts, as we must represent to ourselves an organised body. It does not follow indeed, as has been shown, that the mechanical production of such a body is impossible; for to say so would be to say that it would be impossible (contradictory) for *any Understanding* to represent to itself such a unity in the connexion of the manifold, without the Idea of the unity being at the same time its producing cause, *i.e.* without designed production. This, however, would follow in fact if we were justified in regarding material beings as things in themselves. For then the unity that constitutes the ground of the possibility of natural formations would be simply the unity of space. But space is no real ground of the products, but only their formal condition, although it has this similarity to the real ground which we seek that in it no part can be determined except in relation to the whole (the representation of which therefore lies at the ground of the possibility of the parts). But now it is at least possible to consider the material world as mere phenomenon, and to think as its substrate something like a thing in itself (which is not phenomenon), and to attach to this a corresponding intellectual intuition (even though it is not ours). Thus there would be, although incognisable by us, a supersensible real ground for nature, to which we ourselves belong. In this we consider according to mechanical laws what is necessary in nature regarded as an object of Sense; but we consider according to teleological laws the agreement and unity of its particular laws and its forms—which in regard to mechanism we must judge contingent—regarded as objects of Reason (in fact the whole of nature as a system). Thus we should judge nature according to two different kinds of principles without the mechanical way of explanation being shut out by the teleological, as if they contradicted one another.

From this we are enabled to see what otherwise, though we could easily surmise it, could with difficulty be maintained with certainty and proved, viz. that the principle of a mechanical derivation of purposive natural products is consistent with the teleological, but in no way enables us to dispense with it. In a thing that we must judge as a natural purpose (an organised being) we can no doubt try all the known and yet to be discovered laws of mechanical production, and even hope to make good progress therewith; but we can never get rid of the call for a quite different ground of production for the possibility of such a product, viz. causality by means of purposes. Absolutely no human Reason (in fact no finite Reason like ours in quality, however much it may surpass it in degree) can hope to understand the production of even a blade of grass by mere mechanical causes. As regards the possibility of such an object, the teleological connexion of causes and effects is quite indispensable for the Judgement, even for studying it by the clue of experience. For external objects as phenomena an adequate ground related to purposes cannot be met with; this, although it lies in nature, must only be sought in the supersensible substrate of nature, from all possible insight into which we are cut off. Hence it is absolutely impossible for us to produce from nature itself grounds of explanation for purposive combinations; and it is necessary by the constitution of the human cognitive faculties to seek the supreme ground of these purposive combinations in an original Understanding as the cause of the world.

§ 78. OF THE UNION OF THE PRINCIPLE OF THE UNIVERSAL MECHANISM OF MATTER WITH THE TELEOLOGICAL PRINCIPLE IN THE TECHNIC OF NATURE

It is infinitely important for Reason not to let slip the mechanism of nature in its products, and in their explanation not to pass it by, because without it no insight into the nature of things can be attained. Suppose it admitted that a supreme Architect immediately created the forms of nature as they have been from the beginning, or that He predetermined those which in the course of nature continually form themselves on the same model. Our knowledge of nature is not thus in the least furthered, because we cannot know the mode of action of that Being and the Ideas which are to contain the principles of the possibility of natural beings, and we cannot by them explain nature as from above downwards (*a priori*). And if, starting from the forms of the objects of experience, from below upwards (*a posteriori*), we wish to explain the purposiveness, which we believe is met with in experience, by appealing to a cause working in accordance with purposes, then is our explanation quite tautological and we are only mocking Reason with words. Indeed when we lose ourselves with this way of explanation in the transcendent, whither natural knowledge cannot follow, Reason is seduced into poetical extravagance, which it is its peculiar destination to avoid.

602 | IMMANUEL KANT

On the other hand, it is just as necessary a maxim of Reason not to pass by the principle of purposes in the products of nature. For, although it does not make their mode of origination any more comprehensible, yet it is a heuristic principle for investigating the particular laws of nature; supposing even that we wish to make no use of it for explaining nature itself,—in which we still always speak only of natural purposes, although it apparently exhibits a designed unity of purpose,—*i.e.* without seeking beyond nature the ground of the possibility of these particular laws. But since we must come in the end to this latter question, it is just as necessary to think for nature a particular kind of causality which does not present itself in it, as the mechanism of natural causes which does. To the receptivity of several forms, different from those of which matter is susceptible by mechanism, must be added a spontaneity of a cause (which therefore cannot be matter), without which no ground can be assigned for those forms. No doubt Reason, before it takes this step, must proceed with caution, and not try to explain teleologically every Technic of nature, *i.e.* every productive faculty of nature which displays in itself (as in regular bodies) purposiveness of figure to our mere apprehension; but must always regard such as so far mechanically possible. But on that account to wish entirely to exclude the teleological principle, and to follow simple mechanism only—in cases where, in the rational investigation of the possibility of natural forms through their causes, purposiveness shows itself quite undeniably as the reference to a different kind of causality—to do this must make Reason fantastic, and send it wandering among chimeras of unthinkable natural faculties; just as a mere teleological mode of explanation which takes no account of natural mechanism makes it visionary.

In the same natural thing both principles cannot be connected as fundamental propositions of explanation (deduction) of one by the other, *i.e.* they do not unite for the determinant Judgement as dogmatical and constitutive principles of insight into nature. If I choose, *e.g.* to regard a maggot as the product of the mere mechanism of nature (of the new formation that it produces of itself, when its elements are set free by corruption), I cannot derive the same product from the same matter as from a causality that acts according to purposes. Conversely, if I regard the same product as a natural purpose, I cannot count on any mechanical mode of its production and regard this as the constitutive principle of my judgement upon its possibility, and so unite both principles. One method of explanation excludes the other; even supposing that objectively both grounds of the possibility of such a product rested on a single ground, to which we did not pay attention. The principle which should render possible the compatibility of both in judging of nature must be placed in that which lies outside both (and consequently outside the possible empirical representation of nature), but yet contains their ground, *i.e.* in the supersensible; and each of the two methods of explanation must be referred thereto. Now of this we can have no concept but the indeterminate concept of a ground, which makes the judging of nature by empirical laws possible, but which we cannot determine more nearly by any predicate. Hence the union of both principles cannot rest upon a ground of *explanation* of the possibility of a product according to given laws, for the *determinant* Judgement, but only upon a ground of its *exposition* for the *reflective* Judgement.—To explain is to derive from a principle, which therefore we must clearly know and of which we can give an account. No doubt the principle of the mechanism of nature and that of its causality in one and the same natural product must coalesce in a single higher principle, which is their common source, because otherwise they could not subsist side by side in the observation of nature. But if this principle, objectively common to the two, which therefore warrants the association of the maxims of natural investigation depending on both, be such that, though it can be pointed to, it cannot be determinately known nor clearly put forward for use in cases which arise, then from such a principle we can draw no explanation, *i.e.* no clear and determinate derivation of the possibility of a natural product in accordance with those two heterogeneous principles. But now the principle common to the mechanical and teleological derivations is the *supersensible*, which we must place at the basis of nature, regarded as phenomenon. And of this, in a theoretical point of view, we cannot form the smallest positive determinate concept. It cannot, therefore, in any way be explained how, according to it as principle, nature (in its particular laws) constitutes for us one system, which can be cognised as possible either by the principle of physical development or by that of final causes. If it happens that objects of nature present themselves which cannot be thought by us, as regards their possibility, according to the principle of mechanism (which always has a claim on a natural being), without relying on teleological propositions, we can only make an hypothesis. Namely, we suppose that we may hopefully investigate natural laws with reference to both (according as the possibility of its product is cognisable by our Understanding by one or the other principle), without stumbling at the apparent contradiction which comes into view between the principles by which they are judged. For at least the possibility is assured that both may be united objectively in one principle, since they concern phenomena that presuppose a supersensible ground.

Mechanism, then, and the teleological (designed) Technic of nature, in respect of the same product and its possibility, may stand under a common supreme principle of nature in particular laws. But since this principle is *transcendent* we cannot, because of the limitation of our Understanding, unite both principles *in the explanation* of the same production of nature even if the inner possibility of this product is only *intelligible* [verständlich] through a causality according to purposes (as is the case with organised matter). We revert then to the above fundamental proposition of Teleology. According to the constitution of the human Understanding, no other than designedly-working causes can be assumed for the possibility of organised beings in nature; and the mere mechanism of nature cannot be adequate to the explanation of these its products. But we do not attempt to decide anything by this fundamental proposition as to the possibility of such things themselves.

This is only a maxim of the reflective, not of the determinant Judgement; consequently only subjectively valid for us, not objectively for the possibility of things themselves of this kind (in which both kinds of production may well cohere in one and the same ground). Further, without any concept,—besides the teleologically conceived method of production,—of a simultaneously presented mechanism of nature, no judgement can be passed on this kind of production as a natural product. Hence the above maxim leads to the necessity of an unification of both principles in judging of things as natural purposes in themselves, but does not lead us to substitute one for the other either altogether or in certain parts. For in the place of what is thought (at least by us) as possible only by design we cannot set mechanism, and in the place of what is cognised as mechanically necessary we cannot set contingency, which would need a purpose as its determining ground; but we can only subordinate the one (Mechanism) to the other (designed Technic), which may quite well be the case according to the transcendental principle of the purposiveness of nature.

For where purposes are thought as grounds of the possibility of certain things, we must assume also means, whose law of working requires *for itself* nothing presupposing a purpose,—a mechanical law—and yet can be a subordinate cause of designed effects. Thus—in the organic products of nature, and specially when prompted by their infinite number, we assume (at least as a permissible hypothesis) design in the combination of natural causes by particular laws as a *universal principle* of the reflective Judgement for the whole of nature (the world),—we can think a great and indeed universal combination of mechanical with teleological laws in the productions of nature, without interchanging the principles by which they are judged or putting one in the place of the other. For, in a teleological judgement, the matter, even if the form that it assumes be judged possible only by design, can also, conformably to the mechanical laws of its nature, be subordinated as a means to the represented purpose. But, since the ground of this compatibility lies in that which is neither one nor the other (neither mechanism nor purposive combination), but is the supersensible substrate of nature of which we know nothing, the two ways of representing the possibility of such Objects are not to be blended together by our (human) Reason. However, we cannot judge of their possibility otherwise than by judging them as ultimately resting on a supreme Understanding by the connexion of final causes; and thus the teleological method of explanation is not eliminated.

Now it is quite indeterminate, and for our Understanding always indeterminable, how much the mechanism of nature does as a means towards each final design in nature. However, on account of the above-mentioned intelligible principle of the possibility of a nature in general, it may be assumed that it is possible throughout according to the two kinds of universally accordant laws (the physical and those of final causes), although we cannot see into the way how this takes place. Hence we do not know how far the mechanical method of explanation which is possible for us may extend. So much only is certain that, so far as we can go in this direction, it must always be inadequate for things that we once recognise as natural purposes; and therefore we must, by the constitution of our Understanding, subordinate these grounds collectively to a teleological principle.

Hereon is based a privilege, and on account of the importance which the study of nature by the principle of mechanism has for the theoretical use of our Reason, also an appeal. We should explain all products and occurrences in nature, even the most purposive, by mechanism as far as is in our power (the limits of which we cannot specify in this kind of investigation). But at the same time we are not to lose sight of the fact that those things which we cannot even state for investigation except under the concept of a purpose of Reason, must, in conformity with the essential constitution of our Reason, mechanical causes notwithstanding, be subordinated by us finally to causality in accordance with purposes.

---

1. As in pure mathematics we can never talk of the existence, but only of the possibility of things, viz. of an intuition corresponding to a concept, and so never of cause and effect, it follows that all purposiveness observed there must be considered merely as formal and never as a natural purpose.

2. The allusion is to *Vitruvius de Architectura*, Bk. vi. Praef. "Aristippus philosophus Socraticus, naufragio cum eiectus ad Rhodiensium litus animadvertisset geometrica schemata descripta, exclamavisse ad comites ita dicitur, Bene speremus, hominum enim vestigia video."

3. Second Edition.

4. We can conversely throw light upon a certain combination, much more often met with in Idea than in actuality, by means of an analogy to the so-called immediate natural purposes. In a recent complete transformation of a great people into a state the word *organisation* for the regulation of magistracies, etc., and even of the whole body politic, has often been fitly used. For in such a whole every member should surely be purpose as well as means, and, whilst all work together towards the possibility of the whole, each should be determined as regards place and function by means of the Idea of the whole. [Kant probably alludes here to the organisation of the United States of America.]

5. These words are inserted by Rosenkranz and Windelband, but omitted by Hartenstein and Kirchmann.

6. In the aesthetical part [§ 58, p. 247] it was said: *We view beautiful nature with favour*, whilst we have a quite free (disinterested) satisfaction in its form. For in this mere judgement of taste no consideration is given to the purpose for which these natural beauties exist; whether to excite pleasure in us, or as purposes without any reference to us at all. But in a teleological judgement we pay attention to this reference, and here we can *regard it as a favour of nature* that it has been willing to minister to our culture by the exhibition of so many beautiful figures.

7. The German word *vermessen* is a good word and full of meaning. A judgement in which we forget to consider the extent of our powers (our Understanding) may sometimes sound very humble, and yet make great pretensions, and so be very presumptuous. Of this kind are most of those by which we pretend to extol the divine wisdom by ascribing to it designs in the works of creation and preservation which are really meant to do honour to the private wisdom of the reasoner.

8. We thus see that in most speculative things of pure Reason, as regards dogmatic assertions, the philosophical schools have commonly tried all possible solutions of a given question. To explain the purposiveness of nature men have tried either *lifeless matter* or a *lifeless God*, or again, *living matter* or a *living God*. It only remains for us, if the need should arise, to abandon all these objective *assertions* and to examine critically our judgement merely in reference to our cognitive faculties, in order to supply to their principle a validity which, if not dogmatic, shall at least be that of a maxim sufficient for the sure employment of Reason.

9. That is, the wider concept serves as a universal, under which the particular may be brought; cognition from principles, in Kant's phrase, is the process of knowing the particular in the universal by means of concepts.

10. This distinction will be familiar to the student of the *Critique of Pure Reason*. See Dialectic, bk. i., *Of the Concepts of Pure Reason*.

11. Second Edition.

12. This principle, that for our intellect, the conception of an organised body is impossible except by the aid of the Idea of design, is frequently insisted on by Kant. Professor Wallace points out (*Kant*, p. 110) that as far back as 1755, in his *General Physiogony and Theory of the Heavens*, Kant classed the origin of animals and plants with the secrets of Providence and the mystical number 666 "as one of the topics on which ingenuity and thought are occasionally wasted."

13. Second Edition.

14. Second Edition.

APPENDIX—METHODOLOGY OF THE
TELEOLOGICAL JUDGEMENT.119

§ 79. WHETHER TELEOLOGY MUST BE TREATED AS IF IT BELONGED TO THE DOCTRINE OF NATURE

EVERY SCIENCE MUST HAVE its definite position in the encyclopaedia of all the sciences. If it is a philosophical science its position must be either in the theoretical or practical part. If again it has its place in the former of these, it must be either in the doctrine of nature, so far as it concerns that which can be an object of experience (in the doctrine of bodies, the doctrine of the soul, or the universal science of the world), or in the doctrine of God (the original ground of the world as the complex of all objects of experience).

Now the question is, what place is due to Teleology? Does it belong to Natural Science (properly so called) or to Theology? One of the two it must be; for no science belongs to the transition from one to the other, because this transition only marks the articulation or organisation of the system, and not a place in it.

That it does not belong to Theology as a part thereof, although it may be made of the most important use therein, is self-evident. For it has as its objects, natural productions, and their cause, and although it refers at the same time to the latter as to a ground lying outside of and beyond nature (a Divine Author), yet it does not do this for the determinant but only for the reflective Judgement in the consideration of nature (in order to guide our judgement on things in the world by means of such an Idea as a regulative principle, in conformity with the human Understanding).

But it appears to belong just as little to Natural Science, which needs determinant and not merely reflective principles in order to supply objective grounds for natural effects. In fact, nothing is gained for the theory of nature or the mechanical explanation of its phenomena by means of its effective causes, by considering them as connected according to the relation of purposes. The exhibition of the purposes of nature in its products, so far as they constitute a system according to teleological concepts, properly belongs only to a description of nature which is drawn up in accordance with a particular guiding thread. Here Reason, no doubt, accomplishes a noble work, instructive and practically purposive in many points of view; but it gives no information as to the origin and the inner possibility of these forms, which is the special business of theoretical Natural Science. Teleology, therefore, as science, belongs to no Doctrine, but only to Criticism; and to the criticism of a special cognitive faculty, viz. Judgement. But so far as it contains principles *a priori*, it can and must furnish the method by which nature must be judged according to the principle of final causes. Hence its Methodology has at least negative influence upon the procedure in theoretical Natural Science, and also upon the relation which this can have in Metaphysic to Theology as its propaedeutic.

§ 80. OF THE NECESSARY SUBORDINATION OF THE MECHANICAL TO THE TELEOLOGICAL PRINCIPLE IN THE EXPLANATION OF A THING AS A NATURAL PURPOSE

The *privilege of aiming at* a merely mechanical method of explanation of all natural products is in itself quite unlimited; but the *faculty of attaining* thereto is by the constitution of our Understanding, so far as it has to do with things as natural purposes, not only very much limited but also clearly bounded. For, according to a principle of the Judgement, by this process alone nothing can be accomplished towards an explanation of these things; and consequently the judgement upon such products must always be at the same time subordinated by us to a teleological principle.

It is therefore rational, even meritorious, to pursue natural mechanism, in respect of the explanation of natural products, so far as can be done with probability; and if we give up the attempt it is not because it is impossible *in itself* to meet in this path with the purposiveness of nature, but only because it is impossible *for us* as men. For there would be required for that an intuition other than sensuous, and a determinate knowledge of the intelligible substrate of nature from which a ground could be assigned for the mechanism of phenomena according to particular laws, which quite surpasses our faculties.

Hence if the naturalist would not waste his labour he must in judging of things, the concept of any of which is indubitably established as a natural purpose (organised beings), always lay down as basis an original organisation, which uses that very mechanism in order to produce fresh organised forms or to develop the existing ones into new shapes (which, however, always result from that purpose and conformably to it).

It is praiseworthy by the aid of comparative anatomy to go through the great creation of organised natures, in order to see whether there may not be in it something similar to a system and also in accordance with the principle of production. For otherwise we should have to be content with the mere principle of judgement (which gives no insight into their production) and, discouraged, to give up all claim to *natural insight* in this field. The agreement of so many genera of animals in a certain common schema, which appears to be fundamental not only in the structure of their bones but also in the disposition of their remaining parts,—so that with an admirable simplicity of original outline, a great variety of species has been produced by the shortening of one member and the lengthening of another, the involution of this part and the evolution of that,— allows a ray of hope, however faint, to penetrate into our minds, that here something may be accomplished by the aid of the principle of the mechanism of nature (without which there can be no natural science in general). This analogy of forms, which with all their differences seem to have been produced according to a common original type, strengthens our suspicions of an actual relationship between them in their production from a common parent, through the gradual approximation of one animal-genus to another—from those in which the principle of purposes seems to be best authenticated, *i.e.* from man, down to the polype, and again from this down to mosses and lichens, and finally to the lowest stage of nature noticeable by us, viz. to crude matter. And so the whole Technic of nature, which is so incomprehensible to us in organised beings that we believe ourselves compelled to think a different principle for it, seems to be derived from matter and its powers according to mechanical laws (like those by which it works in the formation of crystals).

Here it is permissible for the *archaeologist* of nature to derive from the surviving traces of its oldest revolutions, according to all its mechanism known or supposed by him, that great family of creatures (for so we must represent them if the said thorough-going relationship is to have any ground). He can suppose the bosom of mother earth, as she passed out of her chaotic state (like a great animal), to have given birth in the beginning to creatures of less purposive form, that these again gave birth to others which formed themselves with greater adaptation to their place of birth and their relations to each other; until this womb becoming torpid and ossified, limited its births to definite species not further modifiable, and the manifoldness remained as it was at the end of the operation of that fruitful formative power.—Only he must still in the end ascribe to this universal mother an organisation purposive in respect of all these creatures; otherwise it would not be possible to think the possibility of the purposive form of the products of the animal and vegetable kingdoms.[1] He has then only pushed further back the ground of explanation and cannot pretend to have made the development of those two kingdoms independent of the condition of final causes.

Even as concerns the variation to which certain individuals of organised genera are accidentally subjected, if we find that the character so changed is hereditary and is taken up into the generative power, then we cannot pertinently judge the variation to be anything else than an occasional development of purposive capacities originally present in the species with a view to the preservation of the race. For in the complete inner purposiveness of an organised being, the generation of its like is closely bound up with the condition of taking nothing up into the generative power which does not belong, in such a system of purposes, to one of its undeveloped original capacities. Indeed, if we depart from this principle, we cannot know with certainty whether several parts of the form which is now apparent in a species have not a contingent and unpurposive origin; and the principle of Teleology, to judge nothing in an organised being as unpurposive which maintains it in its propagation, would be very unreliable in its application and would be valid solely for the original stock (of which we have no further knowledge).

Hume[2] takes exception to those who find it requisite to assume for all such natural purposes a teleological principle of judgement, *i.e.* an architectonic Understanding. He says that it may fairly be asked: how is such an Understanding possible? How can the manifold faculties and properties that constitute the possibility of an Understanding, which has at the same time executive force, be found so purposively together in one Being? But this objection is without weight. For the whole difficulty which surrounds the question concerning the first production of a thing containing in itself purposes and only comprehensible by means of them, rests on the further question as to the unity of the ground of the combination in this product of the various elements [des Mannich-faltigen] which are *external to one another*. For if this ground be placed in the Under-standing of a producing cause as simple substance, the question, so far as it is teleological, is sufficiently answered; but if the cause be sought merely in matter as an aggregate of many substances external to one another, the unity of the principle is quite wanting for the internally purposive form of its formation, and the *autocracy* of matter in productions which can only be conceived by our Understanding as purposes is a word without meaning.

Hence it comes to pass that those who seek a supreme ground of possibility for the objectively-purposive forms of matter, without attributing to it Understanding, either make the world-whole into a single all-embracing substance (Pantheism), or (which is only a more determinate explanation of the former) into a complex of many determina-tions inhering in a single *simple substance* (Spinozism); merely in order to satisfy that condition of all purposiveness—the *unity* of ground. Thus they do justice indeed to *one* condition of the problem, viz. the unity in the purposive combination, by means of the mere ontological concept of a simple substance; but they adduce nothing for the *other* condition, viz. the relation of this substance to its result as *purpose*, through which rela-tion that ontological ground is to be more closely determined in respect of the question at issue. Hence they answer *the whole* question in no way. It remains absolutely unan-swerable (for our Reason) if we do not represent that original ground of things, as simple *substance*; its property which has reference to the specific constitution of the forms of nature grounded thereon, viz. its purposive unity, as the property of an intelli-gent substance; and the relation of these forms to this intelligence (on account of the contingency which we ascribe to everything that we think possible only as a purpose) as that of *causality*.

§ 81. OF THE ASSOCIATION OF MECHANISM WITH THE TELEOLOGICAL PRINCIPLE IN THE EXPLANATION OF A NATURAL PURPOSE AS A NATURAL PRODUCT

According to the preceding paragraphs the mechanism of nature alone does not enable us to think the possibility of an organised being; but (at least according to the constitu-tion of our cognitive faculty) it must be originally subordinated to a cause working designedly. But, just as little is the mere teleological ground of such a being sufficient for considering it and judging it as a product of nature, if the mechanism of the latter be not associated with the former, like the instrument of a cause working designedly, to whose purposes nature is subordinated in its mechanical laws. The possibility of such a unifi-cation of two quite different kinds of causality,—of nature in its universal conformity to law with an Idea which limits it to a particular form, for which it contains no ground in itself—is not comprehended by our Reason. It lies in the supersensible substrate of nature, of which we can determine nothing positively, except that it is the being in itself of which we merely know the phenomenon. But the principle, "all that we assume as belonging to this nature (*phenomenon*) and as its product, must be thought as connected therewith according to mechanical laws," has none the less force, because without this kind of causality organised beings (as purposes of nature) would not be natural products.

Now if the teleological principle of the production of these beings be assumed (as is inevitable), we can place at the basis of the cause of their internally purposive form either *Occasionalism* or *Pre-established Harmony*. According to the former the Supreme Cause of the world would, conformably to its Idea, furnish immediately the organic formation on the occasion of every union of intermingling materials. According to the latter it would, in the original products of its wisdom, only have supplied the capacity by means of which an organic being produces another of like kind, and the species perpetually maintains itself; whilst the loss of individuals is continually replaced by that nature which at the same time works towards their destruction. If we assume the Occasionalism of the production of organised beings, all nature is quite lost, and with it all employment of Reason in judging of the possibility of such products; hence we may suppose that no one will adopt this system, who has anything to do with philosophy.

[The theory of] *Pre-established Harmony* may proceed in two different ways. It regards every organised being as generated by one of like kind, either as an *educt* or a *product*. The system which regards generations as mere educts is called the theory of *individual preformation* or the theory of *evolution*: that which regards them as products is entitled the system of *epigenesis*. This latter may also be entitled the system of *generic preformation*, because the productive faculty of the generator and consequently the specific form would be *virtually* performed according to the inner purposive capacities which are part of its stock. In correspondence with this the opposite theory of individual preformations would be better entitled the *theory of involution*.

The advocates of the *theory of evolution*, who remove every individual from the formative power of nature, in order to make it come immediately from the hand of the Creator, would, however, not venture to regard this as happening according to the hypothesis of Occasionalism. For according to this the copulation is a mere formality, *à propos* of which a supreme intelligent Cause of the world has concluded to form a fruit immediately by his hand, and only to leave to the mother its development and nourishment. They declare themselves for preformation; as if it were not all the same, whether a supernatural origin is assigned to these forms in the beginning or in the course of the world. On the contrary, a great number of supernatural arrangements would be spared by occasional creation, which would be requisite, in order that the embryo formed in the beginning of the world might not be injured throughout the long period of its development by the destructive powers of nature, and might keep itself unharmed; and there would also be requisite an incalculably greater number of such preformed beings than would ever be developed, and with them many creations would be made without need and without purpose. They would, however, be willing to leave at least something to nature, so as not to fall into a complete Hyperphysic which can dispense with all natural explanations. It is true, they hold so fast by their Hyperphysic that they find even in abortions (which it is quite impossible to take for purposes of nature) an admirable purposiveness; though it be only directed to the fact that an anatomist would take exception to it as a purposeless purposiveness, and would feel a disheartened wonder thereat. But the production of hybrids could absolutely not be accommodated with the system of preformation; and to the seeds of the male creature, to which they had attributed nothing but the mechanical property of serving as the first means of nourishment for the embryo, they must attribute in addition a purposive formative power, which in the case of the product of two creatures of the same genus they would concede to neither parent.

On the other hand, even if we do not recognise the great superiority which the theory of *Epigenesis* has over the former as regards the empirical grounds of its proof, still prior to proof Reason views this way of explanation with peculiar favour. For in respect of the things which we can only represent as possible originally according to the causality of purposes, at least as concerns their propagation, this theory regards nature as self-producing, not merely as self-evolving: and so with the least expenditure of the supernatural leaves to nature all that follows after the first beginning (though without determining anything about this first beginning by which Physic generally is thwarted, however it may essay its explanation by a chain of causes).

As regards this theory of Epigenesis, no one has contributed more either to its proof or to the establishment of the legitimate principles of its application,—partly by the limitation of a too presumptuous employment of it,—than Herr Hofr. *Blumenbach*.[3] In all physical explanations of these formations he starts from organised matter. That crude matter should have originally formed itself according to mechanical laws, that life should have sprung from the nature of what is lifeless, that matter should have been able to dispose itself into the form of a self-maintaining purposiveness—this he rightly declares to be contradictory to Reason. But at the same time he leaves to natural mechanism under this to us indispensable *principle* of an original *organisation*, an undeterminable but yet unmistakeable element, in reference to which the faculty of matter in an organised body is called by him a *formative impulse* (in contrast to, and yet standing under the higher guidance and direction of, that merely mechanical *formative power* universally resident in matter).

§ 82. OF THE TELEOLOGICAL SYSTEM IN THE EXTERNAL RELATIONS OF ORGANISED BEINGS

By external purposiveness I mean that by which one thing of nature serves another as means to a purpose. Now things which have no internal purposiveness and which presuppose none for their possibility, *e.g.* earth, air, water, etc., may at the same time be very purposive externally, *i.e.* in relation to other beings. But these latter must be organised beings, *i.e.* natural purposes, for otherwise the former could not be judged as means to them. Thus water, air, and earth cannot be regarded as means to the raising of mountains, because mountains contain nothing in themselves that requires a ground of their possibility according to purposes, in reference to which therefore their cause can never be represented under the predicate of a means (as useful therefor).

External purposiveness is a quite different concept from that of internal purposiveness, which is bound up with the possibility of an object irrespective of its actuality being itself a purpose. We can ask about an organised being the question: What is it for? But we cannot easily ask this about things in which we recognise merely the working of nature's mechanism. For in the former, as regards their internal possibility, we represent a causality according to purposes, a creative Understanding, and we refer this active faculty to its determining ground, viz. design. There is only one external purposiveness which is connected with the internal purposiveness of organisation, and yet serves in the external relation of a means to a purpose, without the question necessarily arising, as to what end this being so organised must have existed for. This is the organisation of both sexes in their mutual relation for the propagation of their kind; since here we can always ask, as in the case of an individual, why must such a pair exist? The answer is: This pair first constitutes an *organising* whole, though not an organised whole in a single body.

If we now ask, wherefore anything is, the answer is either: Its presence and its production have no reference at all to a cause working according to design, and so we always refer its origin to the mechanism of nature, or: There is somewhere a designed ground of its presence (as a contingent natural being). This thought we can hardly separate from the concept of an organised thing; for, since we must place at the basis of its internal possibility a causality of final causes and an Idea lying at the ground of this, we cannot think the existence of this product except as a purpose. For the represented effect, the representation of which is at the same time the determining ground of the intelligent cause working towards its production, is called a *purpose*. In this case therefore we can either say: The purpose of the existence of such a natural being is in itself; *i.e.* it is not merely a purpose but a *final purpose*, or: This is external to it in another natural being, *i.e.* it exists purposively not as a final purpose, but necessarily as a means.

But if we go through the whole of nature we find in it, as nature, no being which could make claim to the eminence of being the final purpose of creation; and we can even prove *a priori* that what might be for nature an *ultimate purpose*, according to all the thinkable determinations and properties wherewith one could endow it, could yet as a natural thing never be a *final purpose*.

If we consider the vegetable kingdom we might at first sight, on account of the immeasurable fertility with which it spreads itself almost on every soil, be led to take it for a mere product of that mechanism which nature displays in the formations of the mineral kingdom. But a more intimate knowledge of its indescribably wise organisation does not permit us to hold to this thought, but prompts the question: What are these things created for? If it is answered: For the animal kingdom, which is thereby nourished and has thus been able to spread over the earth in genera so various, then the further question comes: What are these plant-devouring animals for? The answer would be something like this: For beasts of prey, which can only be nourished by that which has life. Finally we have the question: What are these last, as well as the first-mentioned natural kingdoms, good for? For man, in reference to the manifold use which his Understanding teaches him to make of all these creatures. He is the ultimate purpose of creation here on earth, because he is the only being upon it who can form a concept of purposes, and who can by his Reason make out of an aggregate of purposively formed things a system of purposes.

We might also with the chevalier *Linnaeus*[4] go the apparently opposite way and say: The herbivorous animals are there to moderate the luxurious growth of the vegetable kingdom, by which many of its species are choked. The carnivora are to set bounds to the voracity of the herbivora. Finally man, by his pursuit of these and his diminution of their numbers, preserves a certain equilibrium between the producing and the destructive powers of nature. And so man, although in a certain reference he might be esteemed a purpose, yet in another has only the rank of a means.

If an objective purposiveness in the variety of the genera of creatures and their

external relations to one another, as purposively constructed beings, be made a principle, then it is conformable to Reason to conceive in these relations a certain organisation
and a system of all natural kingdoms according to final causes. Only here experience
seems flatly to contradict the maxims of Reason, especially as concerns an ultimate
purpose of nature, which is indispensable for the possibility of such a system and which
we can put nowhere else but in man. For regarding him as one of the many animal
genera, nature has not in the least excepted him from its destructive or its productive
powers, but has subjected everything to a mechanism thereof without any purpose.

The first thing that must be designedly prepared in an arrangement for a purposive
complex of natural beings on the earth would be their place of habitation, the soil and
the element on and in which they are to thrive. But a more exact knowledge of the
constitution of this basis of all organic production indicates no other causes than those
working quite undesignedly, causes which rather destroy than favour production,
order, and purposes. Land and sea not only contain in themselves memorials of ancient
mighty desolations which have confounded them and all creatures that are in them; but
their whole structure, the strata of the one and the boundaries of the other, have quite
the appearance of being the product of the wild and violent forces of a nature working
in a state of chaos. Although the figure, the structure, and the slope of the land might
seem to be purposively ordered for the reception of water from the air, for the welling
up of streams between strata of different kinds (for many kinds of products), and for the
course of rivers—yet a closer investigation shows that they are merely the effects of
volcanic eruptions or of inundations of the ocean, as regards not only the first production of this figure, but, above all, its subsequent transformation, as well as the disappearance of its first organic productions.[5] Now if the place of habitation of all these
creatures, the soil (of the land) or the bosom (of the sea), indicates nothing but a quite
undesigned mechanism of its production, how and with what right can we demand and
maintain a different origin for these latter products? The closest examination, indeed (in
Camper's judgement), of the remains of the aforesaid devastations of nature seems to
show that man was not comprehended in these revolutions; but yet he is so dependent
on the remaining creatures that, if a universally directing mechanism of nature be
admitted in the case of the others, he must also be regarded as comprehended under it;
even though his Understanding (for the most part at least) has been able to deliver him
from these devastations.

But this argument seems to prove more than was intended by it. It seems to prove
not merely that man cannot be the ultimate purpose of nature, and that on the same
grounds the aggregate of the organised things of nature on the earth cannot be a system
of purposes; but also that the natural products formerly held to be natural purposes
have no other origin than the mechanism of nature.

But in the solution given above of the Antinomy of the principles of the mechanical
and teleological methods of production of organic beings of nature, we have seen that
they are merely principles of the reflective Judgement in respect of nature as it produces
forms in accordance with particular laws (for the systematic connexion of which we
have no key). They do not determine the origin of these beings in themselves; but only
say that we, by the constitution of our Understanding and our Reason, cannot conceive
it in this kind of being except according to final causes. The greatest possible effort, even
audacity, in the attempt to explain them mechanically is not only permitted, but we are

invited to it by Reason; notwithstanding that we know from the subjective grounds of the particular species and limitations of our Understanding (not *e.g.* because the mechanism of production would contradict in itself an origin according to purposes) that we can never attain thereto. Finally, the compatibility of both ways of representing the possibility of nature may lie in the supersensible principle of nature (external to us, as well as in us); whilst the method of representation according to final causes may be only a subjective condition of the use of our Reason, when it not merely wishes to form a judgement upon objects as phenomena, but desires to refer these phenomena together with their principles to their supersensible substrate, in order to find certain laws of their unity possible, which it cannot represent to itself except through purposes (of which the Reason also has such as are supersensible).

§ 83. OF THE ULTIMATE PURPOSE OF NATURE AS A TELEOLOGICAL SYSTEM

We have shown in the preceding that, though not for the determinant but for the reflective Judgement, we have sufficient cause for judging man to be, not merely like all organised beings a *natural purpose*, but also the *ultimate purpose* of nature here on earth; in reference to whom all other natural things constitute a system of purposes according to fundamental propositions of Reason. If now that must be found in man himself, which is to be furthered as a purpose by means of his connexion with nature, this purpose must either be of a kind that can be satisfied by nature in its beneficence; or it is the aptitude and skill for all kinds of purposes for which nature (external and internal) can be used by him. The first purpose of nature would be man's *happiness*, the second his *culture*.

The concept of happiness is not one that man derives by abstraction from his instincts and so deduces from his animal nature; but it is a mere *Idea* of a state, that he wishes to make adequate to the Idea under merely empirical conditions (which is impossible). This Idea he projects in such different ways on account of the complication of his Understanding with Imagination and Sense, and changes so often, that nature, even if it were entirely subjected to his elective will, could receive absolutely no determinate, universal and fixed law, so as to harmonise with this vacillating concept and thus with the purpose which each man arbitrarily sets before himself. And even if we reduce this to the true natural wants as to which our race is thoroughly agreed, or on the other hand, raise ever so high man's skill to accomplish his imagined purposes; yet, even thus, what man understands by happiness, and what is in fact his proper, ultimate, natural purpose (not purpose of freedom), would never be attained by him. For it is not his nature to rest and be contented with the possession and enjoyment of anything whatever. On the other side, too, there is something wanting. Nature has not taken him for her special darling and favoured him with benefit above all animals. Rather, in her destructive operations,—plague, hunger, perils of waters, frost, assaults of other animals great and small, etc.,—in these things has she spared him as little as any other animal. Further, the inconsistency of his own *natural dispositions* drives him into self-devised torments, and also reduces others of his own race to misery, by the oppression of lordship, the barbarism of war, and so forth; he, himself, as far as in him lies, works for the destruction of his own race; so that even with the most beneficent external

616 | IMMANUEL KANT

nature, its purpose, if it were directed to the happiness of our species, would not be attained in an earthly system, because our nature is not susceptible of it. Man is then always only a link in the chain of natural purposes; a principle certainly in respect of many purposes, for which nature seems to have destined him in her disposition, and towards which he sets himself, but also a means for the maintenance of purposiveness in the mechanism of the remaining links. As the only being on earth which has an Understanding and, consequently, a faculty of setting arbitrary purposes before itself, he is certainly entitled to be the lord of nature; and if it be regarded as a teleological system he is, by his destination, the ultimate purpose of nature. But this is subject to the condition of his having an Understanding and the Will to give to it and to himself such a reference to purposes, as can be self-sufficient independently of nature, and, conse-quently, can be a final purpose; which, however, must not be sought in nature itself.

But in order to find out where in man we have to place that *ultimate purpose* of nature, we must seek out what nature can supply to prepare him for what he must do himself in order to be a final purpose, and we must separate it from all those purposes whose possibility depends upon things that one can expect only from nature. Of the latter kind is earthly happiness, by which is understood the complex of all man's purposes possible through nature, whether external nature or man's nature; *i.e.* the matter of all his earthly purposes, which, if he makes it his whole purpose, renders him incapable of positing his own existence as a final purpose, and being in harmony there-with. There remains therefore of all his purposes in nature only the formal subjective condition; viz. the aptitude of setting purposes in general before himself, and (indepen-dent of nature in his purposive determination) of using nature, conformably to the maxims of his free purposes in general, as a means. This nature can do in regard to the final purpose that lies outside it, and it therefore may be regarded as its ultimate purpose. The production of the aptitude of a rational being for arbitrary purposes in general (consequently in his freedom) is *culture*. Therefore, culture alone can be the ulti-mate purpose which we have cause for ascribing to nature in respect to the human race (not man's earthly happiness or the fact that he is the chief instrument of instituting order and harmony in irrational nature external to himself).

But all culture is not adequate to this ultimate purpose of nature. The culture of *skill* is indeed the chief subjective condition of aptitude for furthering one's purposes in general; but it is not adequate to furthering the *will*[6] in the determination and choice of purposes, which yet essentially belongs to the whole extent of an aptitude for purposes. The latter condition of aptitude, which we might call the culture of training (discipline), is negative, and consists in the freeing of the will from the despotism of desires. By these, tied as we are to certain natural things, we are rendered incapable even of choos-ing, while we allow those impulses to serve as fetters, which Nature has given us as guiding threads that we should not neglect or violate the destination of our animal nature—we being all the time free enough to strain or relax, to extend or diminish them, according as the purposes of Reason require.

Skill cannot be developed in the human race except by means of inequality among men; for the great majority provide the necessities of life, as it were, mechanically, without requiring any art in particular, for the convenience and leisure of others who work at the less necessary elements of culture, science and art. In an oppressed condi-tion they have hard work and little enjoyment, although much of the culture of the higher classes gradually spreads to them. Yet with the progress of this culture (the height of which is called luxury, reached when the propensity to what can be done without begins to be injurious to what is indispensable), their calamities increase equally in two directions, on the one hand through violence from without, on the other hand through internal discontent; but still this splendid misery is bound up with the development of the natural capacities of the human race, and the purpose of nature itself, although not our purpose, is thus attained. The formal condition under which nature can alone attain this its final design, is that arrangement of men's relations to one another, by which lawful authority in a whole, which we call a *civil community*, is opposed to the abuse of their conflicting freedoms; only in this can the greatest development of natural capacities take place. For this also there would be requisite,—if men were clever enough to find it out and wise enough to submit themselves voluntarily to its constraint,—a *cosmopolitan* whole, *i.e.* a system of all states that are in danger of acting injuriously upon each other.[7] Failing this, and with the obstacles which ambition, lust of dominion, and avarice, especially in those who have the authority in their hands, oppose even to the possibility of such a scheme, there is, inevitably, *war* (by which sometimes states subdivide and resolve themselves into smaller states, sometimes a state annexes other smaller states and strives to form a greater whole). Though war is an undesigned enterprise of men (stirred up by their unbridled passions), yet is it [perhaps][8] a deep-hidden and designed enterprise of supreme wisdom for preparing, if not for establishing, conformity to law amid the freedom of states, and with this a unity of a morally grounded system of those states. In spite of the dreadful afflictions with which it visits the human race, and the perhaps greater afflictions with which the constant preparation for it in time of peace oppresses them, yet is it (although the hope for a restful state of popular happiness is ever further off) a motive for developing all talents serviceable for culture, to the highest possible pitch.[9]

As concerns the discipline of the inclinations,—for which our natural capacity in regard of our destination as an animal race is quite purposive, but which render the development of humanity very difficult,—there is manifest in respect of this second requirement for culture a purposive striving of nature to a cultivation which makes us receptive of higher purposes than nature itself can supply. We cannot strive against the preponderance of evil, which is poured out upon us by the refinement of taste pushed to idealisation, and even by the luxury of science as affording food for pride, through the insatiable number of inclinations thus aroused. But yet we cannot mistake the purpose of nature—ever aiming to win us away from the rudeness and violence of those inclinations (inclinations to enjoyment) which belong rather to our animality, and for the most part are opposed to the cultivation of our higher destiny, and to make way for the development of our humanity. The beautiful arts and the sciences which, by their universally-communicable pleasure, and by the polish and refinement of society, make man more civilised, if not morally better, win us in large measure from the tyranny of sense-propensions, and thus prepare men for a lordship, in which Reason alone shall have authority; whilst the evils with which we are visited, partly by nature, partly by the intolerant selfishness of men, summon, strengthen, and harden the powers of the soul not to submit to them, and so make us feel an aptitude for higher purposes, which lies hidden in us.[10]

§ 84. OF THE FINAL PURPOSE OF THE EXISTENCE OF A WORLD, I.E. OF CREATION ITSELF

A *final purpose* is that purpose which needs no other as condition of its possibility.

If the mere mechanism of nature be assumed as the ground of explanation of its purposiveness, we cannot ask: what are things in the world there for? For according to such an idealistic system it is only the physical possibility of things (to think which as purposes would be mere subtlety without any Object) that is under discussion; whether we refer this form of things to chance or to blind necessity, in either case the question would be vain. If, however, we assume the purposive combination in the world to be real and to be [brought about] by a particular kind of causality, viz. that of a *designedly-working* cause, we cannot stop at the question: why have things of the world (organised beings) this or that form? why are they placed by nature in this or that relation to one another? But once an Understanding is thought that must be regarded as the cause of the possibility of such forms as are actually found in things, it must be also asked on objective grounds: Who could have determined this productive Understanding to an operation of this kind? This being is then the final purpose in reference to which such things are there.

I have said above that the final purpose is not a purpose which nature would be competent to bring about and to produce in conformity with its Idea, because it is unconditioned. For there is nothing in nature (regarded as a sensible being) for which the determining ground present in itself would not be always conditioned; and this holds not merely of external (material) nature, but also of internal (thinking) nature—it being of course understood that I only am considering that in myself which is nature. But a thing that is to exist necessarily, on account of its objective constitution, as the final purpose of an intelligent cause, must be of the kind that in the order of purposes it is dependent on no further condition than merely its Idea.

Now we have in the world only one kind of beings whose causality is teleological, *i.e.* is directed to purposes and is at the same time so constituted that the law according to which they have to determine purposes for themselves is represented as unconditioned and independent of natural conditions, and yet as in itself necessary. The being of this kind is man, but man considered as noumenon; the only natural being in which we can recognise, on the side of its peculiar constitution, a supersensible faculty (*freedom*) and also the law of causality, together with its Object, which this faculty may propose to itself as highest purpose (the highest good in the world).

Now of man (and so of every rational creature in the World) as a moral being it can no longer be asked: why (*quem in finem*) he exists? His existence involves the highest purpose to which, as far as is in his power, he can subject the whole of nature; contrary to which at least he cannot regard himself as subject to any influence of nature.—If now things of the world, as beings dependent in their existence, need a supreme cause acting according to purposes, man is the final purpose of creation; since without him the chain of mutually subordinated purposes would not be complete as regards its ground. Only in man, and only in him as subject of morality, do we meet with unconditioned legislation in respect of purposes, which therefore alone renders him capable of being a final purpose, to which the whole of nature is teleologically subordinated.[11]

§ 85. OF PHYSICO-THEOLOGY

Physico-theology is the endeavour of Reason to infer the Supreme Cause of nature and its properties from the *purposes* of nature (which can only be empirically known). *Moral theology* (ethico-theology) would be the endeavour to infer that Cause and its properties from the moral purpose of rational beings in nature (which can be known *a priori*).

The former naturally precedes the latter. For if we wish to infer a World Cause *teleologically* from the things in the world, purposes of nature must first be given, for which we afterwards have to seek a final purpose, and for this the principle of the causality of this Supreme Cause.

Many investigations of nature can and must be conducted according to the teleological principle, without our having cause to inquire into the ground of the possibility of purposive working with which we meet in various products of nature. But if we wish to have a concept of this we have absolutely no further insight into it than the maxim of the reflective Judgement affords: viz. if only a single organic product of nature were given to us, by the constitution of our cognitive faculty we could think no other ground for it than that of a cause of nature itself (whether the whole of nature or only this bit of it) which contains the causality for it through Understanding. This principle of judging, though it does not bring us any further in the explanation of natural things and their origin, yet discloses to us an outlook over nature, by which perhaps we may be able to determine more closely the concept, otherwise so unfruitful, of an Original Being.

Now I say that Physico-theology, however far it may be pursued, can disclose to us nothing of a *final purpose* of creation; for it does not even extend to the question as to this. It can, it is true, justify the concept of an intelligent World Cause, as a subjective concept (only available for the constitution of our cognitive faculty) of the possibility of things that we can make intelligible to ourselves according to purposes; but it cannot determine this concept further, either in a theoretical or a practical point of view. Its endeavour does not come up to its design of being the basis of a Theology, but it always remains only a physical Teleology; because the purposive reference therein is and must be always considered only as conditioned in nature, and it consequently cannot inquire into the purpose for which nature itself exists (for which the ground must be sought outside nature),—notwithstanding that it is upon the determinate Idea of this that the determinate concept of that Supreme Intelligent World Cause, and the consequent possibility of a Theology, depend.

What the things in the world are mutually useful for; what good the manifold in a thing does for the thing; how we have ground to assume that nothing in the world is in vain, but that everything *in nature* is good for something,—the condition being granted that certain things are to exist (as purposes), whence our Reason has in its power for the Judgement no other principle of the possibility of the Object, which it inevitably judges teleologically, than that of subordinating the mechanism of nature to the Architectonic of an intelligent Author of the world—all this the teleological consideration of the world supplies us with excellently and to our extreme admiration. But because the data, and so the principles, for *determining* that concept of an intelligent World Cause (as highest artist) are merely empirical, they do not enable us to infer any of its properties beyond those which experience reveals in its effects. Now experience, since it can never embrace collective nature as a system, must often (apparently) happen upon this concept (and by mutually conflicting grounds of proof); but it can never, even if we had the power of surveying empirically the whole system as far as it concerns mere nature, raise us above nature to the purpose of its existence, and so to the determinate concept of that supreme Intelligence.

If we lessen the problem with the solution of which Physico-theology has to do, its solution appears easy. If we reduce the concept of a *Deity* to that of an intelligent being thought by us, of which there may be one or more, which possesses many and very great properties, but not all the properties which are requisite for the foundation of a nature in harmony with the greatest possible purpose; or if we do not scruple in a theory to supply by arbitrary additions what is deficient in the grounds of proof, and so, where we have only ground for assuming *much* perfection (and what is "much" for us?), consider ourselves entitled to presuppose *all possible* perfection; thus indeed physical Teleology may make weighty claims to the distinction of being the basis of a Theology. But if we are desired to point out what impels and moreover authorises us to add these supplements, then we shall seek in vain for a ground of justification in the principles of the theoretical use of Reason, which is ever desirous in the explanation of an Object of experience to ascribe to it no more properties than those for which empirical data of possibility are to be found. On closer examination we should see that properly speaking an Idea of a Supreme Being, which rests on a quite different use of Reason (the practical use), lies in us fundamentally *a priori*, impelling us to supplement, by the concept of a Deity, the defective representation, supplied by a physical Teleology, of the original ground of the purposes in nature; and we should not falsely imagine that we had worked out this Idea, and with it a Theology by means of the theoretical use of Reason in the physical cognition of the world—much less that we had proved its reality.

One cannot blame the ancients much, if they thought of their gods as differing much from each other both as regards their faculties and as regards their designs and volitions, but yet thought of all of them, the Supreme One not excepted, as always limited after human fashion. For if they considered the arrangement and the course of things in nature, they certainly found ground enough for assuming something more than mechanism as its cause, and for conjecturing behind the machinery of this world designs of certain higher causes, which they could not think otherwise than superhuman. But because they met with good and evil, the purposive and the unpurposive, mingled together (at least as far as our insight goes), and could not permit themselves to assume nevertheless that wise and benevolent purposes of which they saw no proof lay hidden at bottom, on behalf of the arbitrary Idea of a supremely perfect original Author, their judgement upon the supreme World Cause could hardly have been other than it was, so long as they proceeded consistently according to maxims of the mere theoretical use of Reason. Others, who wished to be theologians as well as physicists, thought to find contentment for the Reason by providing for the absolute unity of the principle of natural things which Reason demands, the Idea of a Being of which as sole Substance the things would be all only inherent determinations. This Substance would not be Cause of the World by means of intelligence, but in it all the intelligences of the beings in the world would be comprised. This Being consequently would produce nothing according to purposes; but in it all things, on account of the unity of the subject of which they are mere determinations, must necessarily relate themselves purposively to one another, though without purpose and design. Thus they introduced the Idealism of final causes, by changing the unity (so difficult to explain) of a number of purposively combined substances, from being the unity of causal dependence *on one* Substance to be the unity of inherence *in one*. This system—which in the sequel, considered on the side of the inherent world beings, becomes *Pantheism*, and (later) on the side of the Subject subsisting by itself as Original Being, becomes *Spinozism*,—does not so much resolve as explain away into nothing the question of the first ground of the purposiveness of nature; because this latter concept, bereft of all reality, must be taken for a mere misinterpretation of a universal ontological concept of a thing in general.

Hence the concept of a Deity, which would be adequate for our teleological judging of nature, can never be derived from mere theoretical principles of the use of Reason (on which Physico-theology alone is based). For as one alternative we may explain all Teleology as a mere deception of the Judgement in its judging of the causal combination of things, and fly to the sole principle of a mere mechanism of nature, which merely seems to us, on account of the unity of the Substance of whose determinations nature is but the manifold, to contain a universal reference to purposes. Or if, instead of this Idealism of final causes, we wish to remain attached to the principle of the Realism of this particular kind of causality, we may set beneath natural purposes many intelligent original beings or only a single one. But so far as we have for the basis of this concept [of Realism] only empirical principles derived from the actual purposive combination in the world, we cannot on the one hand find any remedy for the discordance that nature presents in many examples in respect of unity of purpose; and on the other hand, as to the concept of a single intelligent Cause, so far as we are authorised by mere experience, we can never draw it therefrom in a manner sufficiently determined for any serviceable Theology whatever (whether theoretical or practical).

Physical Teleology impels us, it is true, to seek a Theology; but it cannot produce one, however far we may investigate nature by means of experience and, in reference to the purposive combination apparent in it, call in Ideas of Reason (which must be theoretical for physical problems). What is the use, one might well complain, of placing at the basis of all these arrangements a great Understanding incommensurable by us, and supposing it to govern the world according to design, if nature does not and cannot tell us anything of the final design? For without this we cannot refer all these natural purposes to any common point, nor can we form any teleological principle, sufficient either for cognising the purposes collected in a system, or for forming a concept of the Supreme Understanding, as Cause of such a nature, that could serve as a standard for our Judgement reflecting teleologically thereon. I should thus have an *artistic Understanding* for scattered purposes, but no *Wisdom* for a final purpose, in which final purpose nevertheless must be contained the determining ground of the said Understanding. But in the absence of a final purpose which pure Reason alone can supply (because all purposes in the world are empirically conditioned, and can contain nothing absolutely good but only what is good for this or that regarded as a contingent design), and which alone would teach me what properties, what degree, and what relation of the Supreme Cause to nature I have to think in order to judge of nature as a teleological system; how and with what right do I dare to extend at pleasure my very limited concept of that original Understanding (which I can base on my limited knowledge of the world), of the Might of that original Being in actualising its Ideas, and of its Will to do so, and complete this into the Idea of an Allwise, Infinite Being? If this is to be done theoretically, it would presuppose omniscience in me, in order to see into the purposes of nature in their whole connexion, and in addition the power of conceiving all possible plans, in comparison with which the present plan would be judged on [sufficient] grounds as the best. For without this complete knowledge of the effect I can arrive at no determinate concept of the Supreme Cause, which can only be found in the concept of an Intelligence infinite in every respect, *i.e.* the concept of a Deity, and so I can supply no foundation for Theology.

Hence, with every possible extension of physical Teleology, according to the propositions above laid down we may say: By the constitution and the principles of our cognitive faculty we can think of nature, in its purposive arrangements which have become known to us, in no other way than as the product of an Understanding to which it is subject. But the theoretical investigation of nature can never reveal to us whether this Understanding may not also, with the whole of nature and its production, have had a final design (which would not lie in the nature of the sensible world). On the contrary, with all our knowledge of nature it remains undecided whether that Supreme Cause is its original ground according to a final purpose, or not rather by means of an Understanding determined by the mere necessity of its nature to produce certain forms (according to the analogy of what we call the art-instinct in animals); without it being necessary to ascribe to it even wisdom, much less the highest wisdom combined with all other properties requisite for the perfection of its product.

Hence Physico-theology is a misunderstood physical Teleology, only serviceable as a preparation (propaedeutic) for Theology; and it is only adequate to this design by the aid of a foreign principle on which it can rely, and not in itself, as its name would intimate.

§ 86. OF ETHICO-THEOLOGY

The commonest Understanding, if it thinks over the presence of things in the world, and the existence of the world itself, cannot forbear from the judgement that all the various creatures, no matter how great the art displayed in their arrangement, and how various their purposive mutual connexion,—even the complex of their numerous systems (which we incorrectly call worlds),—would be for nothing, if there were not also men (rational beings in general). Without men the whole creation would be a mere waste, in vain, and without final purpose. But it is not in reference to man's cognitive faculty (theoretical Reason) that the being of everything else in the world gets its worth; he is not there merely that there may be some one to *contemplate* the world. For if the contemplation of the world only afforded a representation of things without any final purpose, no worth could accrue to its being from the mere fact that it is known; we must presuppose for it a final purpose, in reference to which its contemplation itself has worth. Again it is not in reference to the feeling of pleasure, or to the sum of pleasures, that we think a final purpose of creation as given; *i.e.* we do not estimate that absolute worth by well-being or by enjoyment (whether bodily or mental), or in a word, by happiness. For the fact that man, if he exists, takes this for his final design, gives us no concept as to why in general he should exist, and as to what worth he has in himself to make his existence pleasant. He must, therefore, be supposed to be the final purpose of creation, in order to have a rational ground for holding that nature must harmonise with his happiness, if it is considered as an absolute whole according to principles of purposes.—Hence there remains only the faculty of desire; not, however, that which makes man dependent (through sensuous impulses) upon nature, nor that in respect of which the worth of his being depends upon what he receives and enjoys. But the worth which he alone can give to himself, and which consists in what he does, how and according to what principles he acts, and that not as a link in nature's chain but in the *freedom* of his faculty of desire—*i.e.* a good will—is that whereby alone his being can have an absolute worth, and in reference to which the being of the world can have a *final purpose*.

The commonest judgement of healthy human Reason completely accords with this, that it is only as a moral being that man can be a final purpose of creation; if we but direct men's attention to the question and incite them to investigate it. What does it avail, one will say, that this man has so much talent, that he is so active therewith, and that he exerts thereby a useful influence over the community, thus having a great worth both in relation to his own happy condition and to the benefit of others, if he does not possess a good will? He is a contemptible Object considered in respect of his inner self; and if the creation is not to be without any final purpose at all, he, who as man belongs to it, must, in a world under moral laws, inasmuch as he is a bad man, forfeit his subjective purpose (happiness). This is the only condition under which his existence can accord with the final purpose.

If now we meet with purposive arrangements in the world and, as Reason inevitably requires, subordinate the purposes that are only conditioned to an unconditioned, supreme, *i.e.* final, purpose; then we easily see in the first place that we are thus concerned not with a purpose of nature (internal to itself), so far as it exists, but with the purpose of its existence along with all its ordinances, and, consequently, with the ultimate *purpose of creation*, and specially with the supreme condition under which can be posited a final purpose (*i.e.* the ground which determines a supreme Understanding to produce the beings of the world).

Since now it is only as a moral being that we recognise man as the purpose of creation, we have in the first place a ground (at least, the chief condition) for regarding the world as a whole connected according to purposes, and as a *system* of final causes. And, more especially, as regards the reference (necessary for us by the constitution of our Reason) of natural purposes to an intelligent World Cause, we have *one principle* enabling us to think the nature and properties of this First Cause as supreme ground in the kingdom of purposes, and to determine its concept. This physical Teleology could not do; it could only lead to indeterminate concepts thereof, unserviceable alike in theoretical and in practical use.

From the principle, thus determined, of the causality of the Original Being we must not think Him merely as Intelligence and as legislative for nature, but also as legislating supremely in a moral kingdom of purposes. In reference to the *highest good*, alone possible under His sovereignty, viz. the existence of rational beings under moral laws, we shall think this Original Being as *all-knowing*: thus our inmost dispositions (which constitute the proper moral worth of the actions of rational beings of the world) will not be hid from Him. We shall think Him as *all-mighty*: thus He will be able to make the whole of nature accord with this highest purpose. We shall think Him as *all-good*, and at the same time as *just*: because these two properties (which when united constitute

Wisdom) are the conditions of the causality of a supreme Cause of the world, as highest good, under moral laws. So also all the other transcendental properties, such as *Eternity*, *Omnipresence*, etc. [for goodness and justice are moral properties[12]], which are presupposed in reference to such a final purpose, must be thought in Him.—In this way *moral Teleology* supplies the deficiency in *physical Teleology*, and first establishes a *Theology*; because the latter, if it did not borrow from the former without being observed, but were to proceed consistently, could only found a *Demonology*, which is incapable of any definite concept.

But the principle of the reference of the world to a supreme Cause, as Deity, on account of the moral purposive destination of certain beings in it, does not accomplish this by completing the physico-teleological ground of proof and so taking this necessarily as its basis. It is sufficient *in itself* and directs attention to the purposes of nature and the investigation of that incomprehensible great art lying hidden behind its forms, in order to confirm incidentally by means of natural purposes the Ideas that pure practical Reason furnishes. For the concept of beings of the world under moral laws is a principle (*a priori*) according to which man must of necessity judge himself. Further, if there is in general a World Cause acting designedly and directed towards a purpose, this moral relation must be just as necessarily the condition of the possibility of a creation, as that in accordance with physical laws (if, that is, this intelligent Cause has also a final purpose). This is regarded *a priori* by Reason as a necessary fundamental proposition for it in its teleological judging of the existence of things. It now only comes to this, whether we have sufficient ground for Reason (either speculative or practical) to ascribe to the supreme Cause, acting in accordance with purposes, a *final purpose*. For it may *a priori* be taken by us as certain that this, by the subjective constitution of our Reason and even of the Reason of other beings as far as we can think it, can be nothing else than *man under moral laws*: since otherwise the purposes of nature in the physical order could not be known *a priori*, especially as it can in no way be seen that nature could not exist without such purposes.

Remark

Suppose the case of a man at the moment when his mind is disposed to a moral sensation. If surrounded by the beauties of nature, he is in a state of restful, serene enjoyment of his being, he feels a want, viz. to be grateful for this to some being or other. Or if another time he finds himself in the same state of mind when pressed by duties that he can and will only adequately discharge by a voluntary sacrifice, he again feels in himself a want, viz. to have thus executed a command and obeyed a Supreme Lord. Or, again; if he has in some heedless way transgressed his duty, but without becoming answerable to men, his severe self-reproach will speak to him with the voice of a judge to whom he has to give account. In a word, he needs a moral Intelligence, in order to have a Being for the purpose of his existence, which may be, conformably to this purpose, the cause of himself and of the world. It is vain to assign motives behind these feelings, for they are immediately connected with the purest moral sentiment, because *gratitude*, *obedience*, and *humiliation* (submission to deserved chastisement) are mental dispositions that make for duty; and the mind which is inclined towards a widening of its moral sentiment here only voluntarily conceives an object that is not in the world in order where possible to render its duty before such an one. It is therefore at least possible and grounded too in our moral disposition to represent a pure moral need of the existence of a Being, by which our morality gains strength or even (at least according to our representation) more scope, viz. a new object for its exercise. That is, [there is a need] to assume a morally-legislating Being outside the world, without any reference to theoretical proofs, still less to self-interest, from pure moral grounds free from all foreign influence (and consequently only subjective), on the mere recommendation of a pure practical Reason legislating by itself alone. And although such a mental disposition might seldom occur or might not last long, but be transient and without permanent effect, or might even pass away without any meditation on the object represented in such shadowy outline, or without care to bring it under clear concepts—there is yet here unmistakably the ground why our moral capacity, as a subjective principle, should not be contented in its contemplation of the world with its purposiveness by means of natural causes, but should ascribe to it a supreme Cause governing nature according to moral principles.—In addition, we feel ourselves constrained by the moral law to strive for a universal highest purpose which yet we, in common with the rest of nature, are incapable of attaining; and it is only so far as we strive for it that we can judge ourselves to be in harmony with the final purpose of an intelligent World Cause (if such there be). Thus is found a pure moral ground of practical Reason for assuming this Cause (since it can be done without contradiction), in order that we may no more regard that effort of Reason as quite idle, and so run the risk of abandoning it from weariness.

With all this, so much only is to be said, that though *fear* first produces *gods* (demons), it is *Reason* by means of its moral principles that can first produce the concept of *God* (even when, as commonly is the case, one is unskilled in the Teleology of nature, or is very doubtful on account of the difficulty of adjusting by a sufficiently established principle its mutually contradictory phenomena). Also, the inner *moral* purposive destination of man's being supplies that in which natural knowledge is deficient, by directing us to think, for the final purpose of the being of all things (for which no other principle than an *ethical* one is satisfactory to Reason), the supreme Cause [as endowed] with properties, whereby it is able to subject the whole of nature to that single design (for which nature is merely the instrument),—*i.e.* to think it as a *Deity*.

§ 87. OF THE MORAL PROOF OF THE BEING OF GOD

There is a *physical Teleology*, which gives sufficient ground of proof to our theoretical reflective Judgement to assume the being of an intelligent World-Cause. But we find also in ourselves and still more in the concept of a rational being in general endowed with freedom (of his causality) a *moral Teleology*. However, as the purposive reference, together with its law, is determined *a priori* in ourselves and therefore can be cognised as necessary, this internal conformity to law requires no intelligent cause external to us; any more than we need look to a highest Understanding as the source of the purposiveness (for every possible exercise of art) that we find in the geometrical properties of figures. But this moral Teleology concerns us as beings of the world, and therefore as beings bound up with other things in the world; upon which latter, whether as purposes or as objects in respect of which we ourselves are final purpose, the same moral laws require us to pass judgement. This moral Teleology, then, has to do with the reference of our own causality to purposes and even to a final purpose that we must aim at in the world, as well as with the reciprocal reference of the world to that moral purpose, and the external possibility of its accomplishment (to which no physical Teleology can lead us). Hence the question necessarily arises, whether it compels our rational judgement to go beyond the world and seek an intelligent supreme principle for that reference of nature to the moral in us; in order to represent nature as purposive even in reference to our inner moral legislation and its possible accomplishment. There is therefore certainly a moral Teleology, which is connected on the one hand with the *nomothetic* of freedom and on the other with that of nature; just as necessarily as civil legislation is connected with the question where the executive authority is to be sought, and in general in every case [with the question] wherein Reason is to furnish a principle of the actuality of a certain regular order of things only possible according to Ideas.— We shall first set forth the progress of Reason from that moral Teleology and its reference to physical, to *Theology*; and then make some observations upon the possibility and the validity of this way of reasoning.

If we assume the being of certain things (or even only certain forms of things) to be contingent and so to be possible only through something else which is their cause, we may seek for the unconditioned ground of this causality of the supreme (and so of the conditioned) either in the physical or the teleological order (either according to the *nexus effectivus* or the *nexus finalis*). That is, we may either ask, what is the supreme productive cause of these things; or what is their supreme (absolutely unconditioned) purpose, *i.e.* the final purpose of that cause in its production of this or all its products generally? In the second case it is plainly presupposed that this cause is capable of representing purposes to itself, and consequently is an intelligent Being; at least it must be thought as acting in accordance with the laws of such a being.

If we follow the latter order, it is a FUNDAMENTAL PROPOSITION to which even the commonest human Reason is compelled to give immediate assent, that if there is to be in general a *final purpose* furnished *a priori* by Reason, this can be no other than *man* (every rational being of the world) *under moral laws*.[13] For (and so every one judges) if the world consisted of mere lifeless, or even in part of living but irrational, beings, its existence would have no worth because in it there would be no being who would have the least concept of what worth is. Again, if there were intelligent beings, whose Reason were only able to place the worth of the existence of things in the relation of nature to themselves (their well-being), but not to furnish of itself an original worth (in freedom), then there would certainly be (relative) purposes in the world, but no (absolute) final purpose, because the existence of such rational beings would be always purposeless. But the moral laws have this peculiar characteristic that they prescribe to Reason something as a purpose without any condition, and consequently exactly as the concept of a final purpose requires. The existence of a Reason that can be for itself the supreme law in the purposive reference, in other words the existence of rational beings under moral laws, can therefore alone be thought as the final purpose of the being of a world. If on the contrary this be not so, there would be either no purpose at all in the cause of its being, or there would be purposes, but no final purpose.

The moral law as the formal rational condition of the use of our freedom obliges us by itself alone, without depending on any purpose as material condition; but it nevertheless determines for us, and indeed *a priori*, a final purpose towards which it obliges us to strive; and this purpose is the *highest good in the world* possible through freedom.

The subjective condition under which man (and, according to all our concepts, every rational finite being) can set a final purpose before himself under the above law is happiness. Consequently, the highest physical good possible in the world, to be furthered as a final purpose as far as in us lies, is *happiness*, under the objective condition of the harmony of man with the law of *morality* as worthiness to be happy.

But it is impossible for us in accordance with all our rational faculties to represent these two requirements of the final purpose proposed to us by the moral law, as *connected* by merely natural causes, and yet as conformable to the Idea of that final purpose. Hence the concept of the *practical necessity* of such a purpose through the application of our powers does not harmonise with the theoretical concept of the *physical possibility* of working it out, if we connect with our freedom no other causality (as a means) than that of nature.

Consequently, we must assume a moral World-Cause (an Author of the world), in order to set before ourselves a final purpose consistently with the moral law; and in so far as the latter is necessary, so far (*i.e.* in the same degree and on the same ground) the former also must be necessarily assumed; *i.e.* we must admit that there is a God.[14]

This proof, to which we can easily give the form of logical precision, does not say: it is as necessary to assume the Being of God as to recognise the validity of the moral law; and consequently he who cannot convince himself of the first, can judge himself free from the obligations of the second. No! there must in such case only be given up the *aiming at* the final purpose in the world, to be brought about by the pursuit of the second (viz. a happiness of rational beings in harmony with the pursuit of moral laws, regarded as the highest good). Every rational being would yet have to cognise himself as straitly bound by the precepts of morality, for its laws are formal and command unconditionally without respect to purposes (as the matter of volition). But the one requisite of the final purpose, as practical Reason prescribes it to beings of the world, is an irresistible purpose imposed on them by their nature (as finite beings), which Reason wishes to know as subject only to the moral law as inviolable *condition*, or even as universally set up in accordance with it. Thus Reason takes for final purpose the furthering of happiness in harmony with morality. To further this so far as is in our power (*i.e.* in respect of happiness) is commanded us by the moral law; be the issue of this endeavour what it may. The fulfilling of duty consists in the form of the earnest will, not in the intermediate causes of success.

Suppose then that partly through the weakness of all the speculative arguments so highly extolled, and partly through many irregularities in nature and the world of sense which come before him, a man is persuaded of the proposition, There is no God; he would nevertheless be contemptible in his own eyes if on that account he were to imagine the laws of duty as empty, invalid and inobligatory, and wished to resolve to transgress them boldly. Such an one, even if he could be convinced in the sequel of that which he had doubted at the first, would always be contemptible while having such a disposition, although he should fulfil his duty as regards its [external] effect as punctiliously as could be desired, for [he would be acting] from fear or from the aim at recompense, without the sentiment of reverence for duty. If, conversely, as a believer [in God] he performs his duty according to his conscience, uprightly and disinterestedly, and nevertheless believes that he is free from all moral obligation so soon as he is convinced that there is no God, this could accord but badly with an inner moral disposition.

We may then suppose the case of a righteous man [*e.g. Spinoza*],[15] who holds himself firmly persuaded that there is no God, and also (because in respect of the Object of morality a similar consequence results) no future life; how is he to judge of his own inner purposive destination, by means of the moral law, which he reveres in practice? He desires no advantage to himself from following it, either in this or another world; he wishes, rather, disinterestedly to establish the good to which that holy law directs all his powers. But his effort is bounded; and from nature, although he may expect here and there a contingent accordance, he can never expect a regular harmony agreeing according to constant rules (such as his maxims are and must be, internally), with the purpose that he yet feels himself obliged and impelled to accomplish. Deceit, violence, and envy will always surround him, although he himself be honest, peaceable, and kindly; and the righteous men with whom he meets will, notwithstanding all their worthiness of happiness, be yet subjected by nature which regards not this, to all the evils of want, disease, and untimely death, just like the beasts of the earth. So it will be until one wide grave engulfs them together (honest or not, it makes no difference), and throws them back—who were able to believe themselves the final purpose of creation—into the abyss of the purposeless chaos of matter from which they were drawn.— The purpose, then, which this well-intentioned person had and ought to have before him in his pursuit of moral laws, he must certainly give up as impossible. Or else, if he wishes to remain dependent upon the call of his moral internal destination, and not to weaken the respect with which the moral law immediately inspires him, by assuming the nothingness of the single, ideal, final purpose adequate to its high demand (which cannot be brought about without a violation of moral sentiment), he must, as he well can—since there is at least no contradiction from a practical point of view in forming a concept of the possibility of a morally prescribed final purpose—assume the being of a *moral* author of the world, that is, a God.

§ 88. LIMITATION OF THE VALIDITY OF THE MORAL PROOF

Pure Reason, as a practical faculty, *i.e.* as the faculty of determining the free use of our causality by Ideas (pure rational concepts), not only comprises in the moral law a regulative principle of our actions, but supplies us at the same time with a subjective constitutive principle in the concept of an Object which Reason alone can think, and which is to be actualised by our actions in the world according to that law. The Idea of a final purpose in the employment of freedom according to moral laws has therefore subjective *practical* reality. We are *a priori* determined by Reason to promote with all our powers the *summum bonum* [Weltbeste] which consists in the combination of the greatest welfare of rational beings with the highest condition of the good in itself, *i.e.* in universal happiness conjoined with morality most accordant to law. In this final purpose the possibility of one part, happiness, is empirically conditioned, *i.e.* dependent on the constitution of nature (which may or may not agree with this purpose) and is in a theoretical aspect problematical; whilst the other part, morality, in respect of which we are free from the effects of nature, stands fast *a priori* as to its possibility, and is dogmatically certain. It is then requisite for the objective theoretical reality of the concept of the final purpose of rational beings, that we should not only have *a priori* presupposed a final purpose for ourselves, but also that the creation, *i.e.* the world itself, should have as regards its existence a final purpose, which if it could be proved *a priori* would add objectivity to the subjective reality of the final purpose [of rational beings]. For if the creation has on the whole a final purpose, we cannot think it otherwise than as harmonising with the moral purpose (which alone makes the concept of a purpose possible). Now we find without doubt purposes in the world, and physical Teleology exhibits them in such abundance, that if we judge in accordance with Reason, we have ground for assuming as a principle in the investigation of nature that nothing in nature is without a purpose; but the final purpose of nature we seek there in vain. This can and must therefore, as its Idea only lies in Reason, be sought as regards its objective possibility only in rational beings. And the practical Reason of these latter not only supplies this final purpose; it also determines this concept in respect of the conditions under which alone a final purpose of creation can be thought by us.

The question is now, whether the objective reality of the concept of a final purpose of creation cannot be exhibited adequately to the theoretical requirements of pure Reason —if not apodictically for the determinant Judgement yet adequately for the maxims of the theoretical reflective Judgement? This is the least one could expect from theoretical philosophy, which undertakes to combine the moral purpose with natural purposes by means of the Idea of one single purpose; but yet this little is far more than it can accomplish.

According to the principle of the theoretical reflective Judgement we should say: if we have ground for assuming for the purposive products of nature a supreme Cause of nature—whose causality in respect of the actuality of creation is of a different kind from that required for the mechanism of nature, *i.e.* must be thought as the causality of an Understanding—we have also sufficient ground for thinking in this original Being not merely the purposes everywhere in nature but also a final purpose. This is not indeed a final purpose by which we can explain the presence of such a Being, but one of which we may at least convince ourselves (as was the case in physical Teleology) that we can make the possibility of such a world conceivable, not merely according to purposes, but only through the fact that we ascribe to its existence a final purpose.

But a final purpose is merely a concept of our practical Reason, and can be inferred from no data of experience for the theoretical judging of nature, nor can it be applied to the cognition of nature. No use of this concept is possible except its use for practical Reason according to moral laws; and the final purpose of creation is that constitution of the world which harmonises with that which alone we can put forward definitely according to laws, viz. the final purpose of our pure practical Reason, in so far as it is to be practical.— Now we have in the moral law, which enjoins on us in a practical point of view the application of our powers to the accomplishment of this final purpose, a ground for assuming its possibility and practicability, and consequently too (because without the concurrence of nature with a condition not in our power, its accomplishment would be impossible) a nature of things harmonious with it. Hence we have a moral ground for thinking in a world also a final purpose of creation.

We have not yet advanced from moral Teleology to a Theology, *i.e.* to the being of a moral Author of the world, but only to a final purpose of creation which is determined in this way. But in order to account for this creation, *i.e.* the existence of things, in accordance with a *final purpose*, we must assume not only first an intelligent Being (for the possibility of things of nature which we are compelled to judge of as *purposes*), but also a *moral* Being, as author of the world, *i.e.* a *God*. This second conclusion is of such a character that we see it holds merely for the Judgement according to concepts of practical Reason, and as such for the reflective and not the determinant Judgement. It is true that in us morally practical Reason is essentially different in its principles from technically practical Reason. But we cannot assume that it must be so likewise in the supreme World-Cause, regarded as Intelligence, and that a peculiar mode of its causality is requisite for the final purpose, different from that which is requisite merely for purposes of nature. We cannot therefore assume that in our final purpose we have not merely a *moral ground* for admitting a final purpose of creation (as an effect), but also for admitting a *moral Being* as the original ground of creation. But we may well say, that, *according to the constitution of our rational faculty*, we cannot comprehend the possibility of such a purposiveness *in respect of the moral law*, and its Object, as there is in this final purpose, apart from an Author and Governor of the world, who is at the same time its moral Lawgiver.

The actuality of a highest morally-legislating Author is therefore sufficiently established merely *for the practical use* of our Reason, without determining anything theoretically as regards its being. For Reason requires, in respect of the possibility of its purpose, which is given to us independently by its own legislation, an Idea through which the inability to follow up this purpose, according to the mere natural concepts of the world, is removed (sufficiently for the reflective Judgement). Thus this Idea gains practical reality, although all means of creating such for it in a theoretical point of view, for the explanation of nature and determination of the supreme Cause, are entirely wanting for speculative cognition. For the theoretical reflective Judgement physical Teleology sufficiently proves from the purposes of nature an intelligent World-Cause; for the practical Judgement moral Teleology establishes it by the concept of a final purpose, which it is forced to ascribe to creation in a practical point of view. The objective reality of the Idea of God, as moral Author of the world, cannot, it is true, be established by physical purposes *alone*. But nevertheless, if the cognition of these purposes is combined with that of the moral purpose, they are, by virtue of the maxim of pure Reason which bids us seek unity of principles so far as is possible, of great importance for the practical reality of that Idea, by bringing in the reality which it has for the Judgement in a theoretical point of view.

To prevent a misunderstanding which may easily arise, it is in the highest degree needful to remark that, in the first place, we can *think* these properties of the highest Being only according to analogy. How indeed could we explore the nature of that, to which experience can show us nothing similar? Secondly, in this way we only think the supreme Being; we cannot thereby *cognise* Him and ascribe anything theoretically to Him. It would be needful for the determinant Judgement in the speculative aspect of our Reason, to consider what the supreme World-Cause is in Himself. But here we are only concerned with the question what concept we can form of Him, according to the constitution of our cognitive faculties; and whether we have to assume His existence in order merely to furnish practical reality to a purpose, which pure Reason without any such presupposition enjoins upon us *a priori* to bring about with all our powers, *i.e.* in order to be able to think as possible a designed effect. Although that concept may be transcendent for the speculative Reason, and the properties which we ascribe to the Being thereby thought may, objectively used, conceal an anthropomorphism in themselves; yet the design of its use is not to determine the nature of that Being which is unattainable by us, but to determine ourselves and our will accordingly. We may call a cause after the concept which we have of its effect (though only in reference to this relation), without thereby meaning to determine internally its inner constitution, by means of the properties which can be made known to us solely by similar causes and must be given in experience. For example, amongst other properties we ascribe to the soul a *vis locomotiva* because bodily movements actually arise whose cause lies in the representation of them; without therefore meaning to ascribe to it the only mode [of action] that we know in moving forces (viz. by attraction, pressure, impulse, and consequently motion, which always presuppose an extended being). Just so we must assume *something*, which contains the ground of the possibility and practical reality, *i.e.* the practicability, of a necessary moral final purpose; but we can think of this, in accordance with the character of the effect expected of it, as a wise Being governing the world according to moral laws, and, conformably to the constitution of our cognitive faculties, as a cause of things distinct from nature, only in order to express the *relation* of this Being (which transcends all our cognitive faculties) to the Objects of *our* practical Reason. We do not pretend thus to ascribe to it theoretically the only causality of this kind known to us, viz. an Understanding and a Will: we do not even pretend to distinguish objectively the causality thought in this Being, as regards what is *for us* final purpose, from the causality thought in it as regards nature (and its purposive determinations in general). We can only assume this distinction as subjectively necessary by the constitution of our cognitive faculties, and as valid for the reflective, not for the objectively determinant Judgement. But if we come to practice, then such a *regulative* principle (of prudence or wisdom) [commanding us] to act conformably to that as purpose, which by the constitution of our cognitive faculties can only be thought as possible in a certain way, is at the same *constitutive, i.e.* practically determinant. Nevertheless, as a principle for judging of the objective possibility of things, it is no way theoretically determinant (*i.e.* it does not say that the only kind of possibility which belongs to the Object is that which belongs to our thinking faculty), but is a mere *regulative* principle for the reflective Judgement.

Remark

This moral proof is not one newly discovered, although perhaps its basis is newly set forth; since it has lain in man's rational faculty from its earliest germ, and is only continually developed with its advancing cultivation. So soon as men begin to reflect upon right and wrong—at a time when, quite indifferent as to the purposiveness of nature, they avail themselves of it without thinking anything more of it than that it is the accustomed course of nature—this judgement is inevitable, viz. that the issue cannot be the same, whether a man has behaved candidly or falsely, fairly or violently, even though up to his life's end, as far as can be seen, he has met with no happiness for his virtues, no punishment for his vices. It is as if they perceived a voice within [saying] that the issue must be different. And so there must lie hidden in them a representation, however obscure, of something after which they feel themselves bound to strive; with which such a result would not agree,—with which, if they looked upon the course of the world as the only order of things, they could not harmonise that inner purposive determination of their minds. Now they might represent in various rude fashions the way in which such an irregularity could be adjusted (an irregularity which must be far more revolting to the human mind than the blind chance that we are sometimes willing to use as a principle for judging of nature). But they could never think any other principle of the possibility of the unification of nature with its inner ethical laws, than a supreme Cause governing the world according to moral laws; because a final purpose in them proposed as duty, and a nature without any final purpose beyond them in which that purpose might be actualised, would involve a contradiction. As to the [inner]¹⁶ constitution of that World-Cause they could contrive much nonsense. But that moral relation in the government of the world would remain always the same, which by the uncultivated Reason, considered as practical, is universally comprehensible, but with which the speculative Reason can make far from the like advance.—And in all probability attention would be directed first by this moral interest to the beauty and the purposes in nature, which would serve excellently to strengthen this Idea though they could not be the foundation of it. Still less could that moral interest be dispensed with, because it is only in reference to the final purpose that the investigation of the purposes of nature acquires that immediate interest which displays itself in such a great degree in the admiration of them without any reference to the advantage to be derived from them.

§ 89. OF THE USE OF THE MORAL ARGUMENT

The limitation of Reason in respect of all our Ideas of the supersensible to the conditions of its practical employment has, as far as the Idea of God is concerned, undeniable uses. For it prevents *Theology* from rising into THEOSOPHY (into transcendent concepts which confound Reason), or from sinking into DEMONOLOGY (an anthropomorphic way of representing the highest Being). And it also prevents *Religion* from turning into *Theurgy* (a fanatical belief that we can have a feeling of other supersensible beings and can reciprocally influence them), or into *Idolatry* (a superstitious belief that we can please the Supreme Being by other means than by a moral sentiment).¹⁷

For if we permit the vanity or the presumption of sophistry to determine the least thing theoretically (in a way that extends our knowledge) in respect of what lies beyond the world of sense, or if we allow any pretence to be made of insight into the being and constitution of the nature of God, of His Understanding and Will, of the laws of both and of His properties which thus affect the world, I should like to know where and at what point we will bound these assumptions of Reason. For wherever such insight can be derived, there may yet more be expected (if we only strain our reflection, as we have a mind to do). Bounds must then be put to such claims according to a certain principle, and not merely because we find that all attempts of the sort have hitherto failed, for that proves nothing against the possibility of a better result. But here no principle is possible, except either to assume that in respect of the supersensible absolutely nothing can be theoretically determined (except mere negations); or else that our Reason contains in itself a yet unused mine of cognitions, reaching no one knows how far, stored up for ourselves and our posterity.—But as concerns Religion, *i.e.* morals in reference to God as legislator, if the theoretical cognition of Him is to come first, morals must be adjusted in accordance with Theology; and not only is an external arbitrary legislation of a Supreme Being introduced in place of an internal necessary legislation of Reason, but also whatever is defective in our insight into the nature of this Being must extend to ethical precepts, and thus make Religion immoral and perverted.

As regards the hope of a future life, if instead of the final purpose we have to accomplish in conformity with the precept of the moral law, we ask of our theoretical faculty of cognition a clue for the judgement of Reason upon our destination (which clue is only considered as necessary or worthy of acceptance in a practical reference), then in this aspect Psychology, like Theology, gives no more than a negative concept of our thinking being. That is, none of its actions or of the phenomena of the internal sense can be explained materialistically; and hence of its separate nature and of the continuance or non-continuance of its personality after death absolutely no ampliative determinant judgement is possible on speculative grounds by means of our whole theoretical cognitive faculty. Here then everything is handed over to the teleological judging of our existence in a practically necessary aspect, and to the assumption of our continuance as a condition requisite for the final purpose absolutely furnished by Reason. And so this advantage (which indeed at first glance seems to be a loss) is apparent; that, as Theology for us can never be Theosophy, or rational *Psychology* become *Pneumatology*—an ampliative science—so on the other hand this latter is assured of never falling into *Materialism*. Psychology, rather, is a mere anthropology of the internal sense, *i.e.* is the knowledge of our thinking self *in life*; and, as theoretical cognition, remains merely empirical. On the other hand, rational Psychology, as far as it is concerned with questions as to our eternal existence, is not a theoretical science at all, but rests on a single conclusion of moral Teleology; as also its whole use is necessary merely on account of the latter, *i.e.* on account of our practical destination.

§ 90. OF THE KIND OF BELIEF IN A TELEOLOGICAL PROOF OF THE BEING OF GOD

The first requisite for every proof, whether it be derived from the immediate empirical presentation (as in the proof from observation of the object or from experiment) of that which is to be proved, or by Reason *a priori* from principles, is this. It should not *persuade*, but *convince*,[18] or at least should tend to conviction. *I.e.* the ground of proof or the conclusion should not be merely a subjective (aesthetical) determining ground of assent (mere illusion), but objectively valid and a logical ground of cognition; for otherwise the Understanding is ensnared, but not convinced. Such an illusory proof is that which, perhaps with good intent but yet with wilful concealment of its weaknesses, is adduced in Natural Theology. In this we bring in the great number of indications of the origin of natural things according to the principle of purposes, and take advantage of the merely subjective basis of human Reason, viz. its special propensity to think only one principle instead of several, whenever this can be done without contradiction; and, when in this principle only one or more requisites for determining a concept are furnished, to add in our thought these additional [features] so as to complete the concept of the thing by arbitrarily supplementing it. For, in truth, when we meet with so many products in nature which are to us marks of an intelligent cause, why should we not think One cause rather than many; and in this One, not merely great intelligence, power, etc., but rather Omniscience, and Omnipotence—in a word, think it as a Cause that contains the sufficient ground of such properties in all possible things? Further, why should we not ascribe to this unique, all-powerful, original Being not only intelligence for natural laws and products, but also, as to a moral Cause of the world, supreme, ethical, practical Reason? For by this completion of the concept a sufficient principle is furnished both for insight into nature and for moral wisdom; and no objection grounded in any way can be made against the possibility of such an Idea. If now at the same time the moral motives of the mind are aroused, and a lively interest in the latter is added by the force of eloquence (of which they are indeed very worthy), then there arises therefrom a persuasion of the objective adequacy of the proof; and also (in most cases of its use) a wholesome illusion which quite dispenses with all examination of its logical strictness, and even on the contrary regards this with abhorrence and dislike as if an impious doubt lay at its basis.—Now against this there is indeed nothing to say, so long as we only have regard to its popular usefulness. But then the division of the proof into the two dissimilar parts involved in the argument—belonging to physical and moral Teleology respectively—cannot and must not be prevented. For the blending of these makes it impossible to discern where the proper force of the proof lies, and in what part and how it must be elaborated in order that its validity may be able to stand the strictest examination (even if we should be compelled to admit in one part the weakness of our rational insight). Thus it is the duty of the philosopher (supposing even that he counts as nothing the claims of sincerity) to expose the above illusion, however wholesome it is, which such a confusion can produce; and to distinguish what merely belongs to persuasion from that which leads to conviction (for these are determinations of assent which differ not merely in degree but in kind), in order to present plainly the state of the mind in this proof in its whole clearness, and to be able to subject it frankly to the closest examination.

But a proof which is intended to convince, can again be of two kinds; either deciding what the object is *in itself,* or what it is *for us* (for men in general) according to our necessary rational principles of judgement (proof κατ' ἀλήθειαν or κατ' ἄνθρωπον, the last word being taken in its universal signification of man in general). In the first case it is based on adequate principles for the determinant Judgement, in the second for the reflective Judgement. In the latter case it can never, when resting on merely theoretical principles, tend to conviction; but if a practical principle of Reason (which is therefore universally and necessarily valid) lies at its basis, it may certainly lay claim to conviction adequate in a pure practical point of view, *i.e.* to moral conviction. But a proof *tends to conviction,* though without convincing, if it is [merely][19] brought on the way thereto; *i.e.* if it contains in itself only objective grounds, which although not attaining to certainty are yet of such a kind that they do not serve merely for persuasion as subjective grounds of the judgement.[20]

All theoretical grounds of proof resolve themselves either into: (1) Proofs by logically strict *Syllogisms of Reason;* or where this is not the case, (2) *Conclusions* according to *analogy;* or where this also has no place, (3) *Probable opinion;* or finally, which has the least weight, (4) Assumption of a merely possible ground of explanation, *i.e. Hypothesis.* —Now I say that all grounds of proof in general, which aim at theoretical conviction, can bring about no belief of this kind from the highest to the lowest degree, if there is to be proved the proposition of the *existence* of an original Being, as a God, in the signification adequate to the whole content of this concept; viz. a *moral* Author of the world, by whom the final purpose of creation is at the same time supplied.

(1.) As to the *logically accurate* proof proceeding from universal to particular, we have sufficiently established in the Critique the following: Since no intuition possible for us corresponds to the concept of a Being that is to be sought beyond nature—whose concept therefore, so far as it is to be theoretically determined by synthetical predicates, remains always problematical for us—there is absolutely no cognition of it to be had (by which the extent of our theoretical knowledge is in the least enlarged). The particular concept of a supersensible Being cannot be subsumed under the universal principles of the nature of things, in order to conclude from them to it, because those principles are valid simply for nature, as an object of sense.

(2.) We can indeed *think* one of two dissimilar things, even in the very point of their dissimilarity, in accordance with the *analogy*[21] of the other; but we cannot, from that wherein they are dissimilar, *conclude* from the one to the other by analogy, *i.e.* transfer from the one to the other this sign of specific distinction. Thus I can, according to the analogy of the law of the equality of action and reaction in the mutual attraction and repulsion of bodies, also conceive of the association of the members of a commonwealth according to rules of right; but I cannot transfer to it those specific determinations (material attraction or repulsion), and ascribe them to the citizens in order to constitute a system called a state.—Just so we can indeed conceive of the causality of the original Being in respect of the things of the world, as natural purposes, according to the analogy of an Understanding, as ground of the forms of certain products which we call works of art (for this only takes place on behalf of the theoretical or practical use that we have to make by our cognitive faculty of this concept in respect of the natural things in the world according to a certain principle). But we can in no way conclude according to analogy, because in the case of beings of the world Understanding must be ascribed to the cause of an effect which is judged artificial, that in respect of nature the same causality which we perceive in men attaches also to the Being which is quite distinct from nature. For this concerns the very point of dissimilarity which is thought between a cause sensibly conditioned in respect of its effects and the supersensible original Being itself in our concept of it, and which therefore cannot be transferred from one to the other.— In the very fact that I must conceive the divine causality only according to the analogy of an Understanding (which faculty we know in no other being than in sensibly-conditioned man) lies the prohibition to ascribe to it this Understanding in its peculiar signification.[22]

(3.) *Opinion* finds in *a priori* judgements no place whatever, for by them we either cognise something as quite certain or else cognise nothing at all. But if the given grounds of proof from which we start (as here from the purposes in the world) are empirical, then we cannot even with their aid form any opinion as to anything beyond the world of sense, nor can we concede to such venturesome judgements the smallest claim to probability. For probability is part of a certainty possible in a certain series of grounds (its grounds compare with the sufficient ground as parts with a whole), the insufficient ground of which must be susceptible of completion. But since, as determining grounds of one and the same judgement, they must be of the same kind, for otherwise they would not together constitute a whole (such as certainty is), one part of them cannot lie within the bounds of possible experience and another outside all possible experience. Consequently, since merely empirical grounds of proof lead to nothing supersensible, and since what is lacking in the series of them cannot in any way be completed, we do not approach in the least nearer in our attempt to attain by their means to the supersensible and to a cognition thereof. Thus in any judgement about the latter by means of arguments derived from experience, probability has no place.

(4.) If an *hypothesis* is to serve for the explanation of the possibility of a given phenomenon, at least its possibility must be completely certain.[23] It is sufficient that in an hypothesis I disclaim any cognition of actuality (which is claimed in an opinion given out as probable); more than this I cannot give up. The possibility of that which I place at the basis of my explanation, must at least be exposed to no doubt; otherwise there would be no end of empty chimeras. But to assume the possibility of a supersensible Being determined according to certain concepts would be a completely groundless supposition. For here none of the conditions requisite for cognition, as regards that in it which rests upon intuition, is given, and so the sole criterion of possibility remaining is the mere principle of Contradiction (which can only prove the possibility of the thought, not of the object thought).

The result then is this. For the existence [Dasein] of the original Being, as a Godhead, or of the soul as an immortal spirit, absolutely no proof in a theoretical point of view is possible for the human Reason, which can bring about even the least degree of belief. The ground of this is quite easy to comprehend. For determining our Ideas of the supersensible we have no material whatever, and we must derive this latter from things in the world of sense, which is absolutely inadequate for such an Object. Thus, in the absence of all determination of it, nothing remains but the concept of a non-sensible something which contains the ultimate ground of the world of sense, but which does not furnish any knowledge (any amplification of the concept) of its inner constitution.

§ 91. OF THE KIND OF BELIEF PRODUCED BY A PRACTICAL FAITH

If we look merely to the way in which anything can be *for us* (according to the subjective constitution of our representative powers) an Object of knowledge (*res cognoscibilis*), then our concepts will not cohere with Objects, but merely with our cognitive faculties and the use which they can make of a given representation (in a theoretical or practical point of view). Thus the question whether anything is or is not a cognisable being is not a question concerning the possibility of things but of our knowledge of them.

Cognisable things are of three kinds: things of opinion (opinabile); things of fact (scibile); and things of faith (mere credibile).

(1.) Objects of mere rational Ideas, which for theoretical knowledge cannot be presented in any possible experience, are so far not *cognisable* things, and consequently in respect of them we can form no *opinion*; for to form an opinion a priori is absurd in itself and the straight road to mere chimeras. Either then our proposition is certain *a priori* or it contains nothing for belief. Therefore *things of opinion* are always Objects of an empirical cognition at least possible in itself (objects of the world of sense); but, which, on account merely of the [low] degree of this faculty that we possess, is *for us* impossible. Thus the ether of the new physicists,[24] an elastic fluid pervading all other matter (mingled intimately with it) is a mere thing of opinion, yet is such that, if our external senses were sharpened to the highest degree, it could be perceived; though it can never be presented in any observation or experiment. To assume [the existence of] rational inhabitants of other planets is a thing of opinion; for if we could come closer to them, which is in itself possible, we should decide by experience whether they did or did not exist; but as we shall never come so near, it remains in the region of opinion. But to hold the opinion that there are in the material universe pure thinking spirits without bodies (viz. if we dismiss as unworthy of our notice certain phenomena which have been published as actual[25]) is to be called poetic fiction. This is no thing of opinion, but a mere Idea which remains over, when we remove from a thinking being everything material, and only leave thought to it. Whether then the latter (which we know only in man, that is, in combination with a body) does survive, we cannot decide. Such a thing is a *sophistical being* (*ens rationis ratiocinantis*), not a *rational being* (*ens rationis ratiocinatae*)[26]; of which latter it is possible to show conclusively, the objective reality of its concept; at least for the practical use of Reason, because this which has its peculiar and apodictically certain principles *a priori*, demands (postulates) it.

(2.) Objects for concepts, whose objective reality can be proved (whether through pure Reason or through experience, and, in the first case, from its theoretical or practical data, in all cases by means of a corresponding intuition) are *things of fact* (*res facti*).[27] Of this kind are the mathematical properties of magnitudes (in geometry), because they are susceptible of a *presentation a priori* for the theoretical use of Reason. Further, things or their characteristics, which can be exhibited in experience (either our own or that of others through the medium of testimony) are likewise things of fact.—And, what is very remarkable, there is one rational Idea (susceptible in itself of no presentation in intuition, and consequently, of no theoretical proof of its possibility) which also comes under things of fact. This is the Idea of *freedom*, whose reality, regarded as that of a particular kind of causality (of which the concept, theoretically considered, would be transcendent), may be exhibited by means of practical laws of pure Reason, and conformably to this, in actual actions, and, consequently, in experience.—This is the only one of all the Ideas of pure Reason, whose object is a thing of fact, and to be reckoned under the *scibilia*.

(3.) Objects, which in reference to the use of pure practical Reason that is in conformity with duty must be thought *a priori* (whether as consequences or as grounds), but which are transcendent for its theoretical use, are mere *things of faith*. Of this kind is the *highest good* in the world, to be brought about by freedom.[28] The concept of this cannot be established as regards its objective reality in any experience possible for us and thus adequately for the theoretical use of Reason; but its use is commanded by practical pure Reason [in reference to the best possible working out of that purpose],[29] and it consequently must be assumed possible. This commanded effect, *together with the only conditions of its possibility thinkable by us*, viz. the Being of God and the immortality of the soul, are *things of faith* (*res fidei*), and of all objects are the only ones which can be so called.[30] For though what we learn by *testimony* from the experience of others must be believed by us, yet it is not therefore a thing of faith; for it was the proper experience of some *one* witness and so a thing of fact, or is presupposed as such. Again it must be possible by this path (that of historical faith) to arrive at knowledge; and the Objects of history and geography, like everything in general which it is at least possible to know by the constitution of our cognitive faculties, belong not to things of faith but to things of fact. It is only objects of pure Reason which can be things of faith at all, though not as objects of the mere pure speculative Reason: for then they could not be reckoned with certainty among things, *i.e.* Objects of that cognition which is possible for us. They are Ideas, *i.e.* concepts of the objective reality of which we cannot theoretically be certain. On the other hand, the highest final purpose to be worked out by us, by which alone we can become worthy of being ourselves the final purpose of creation, is an Idea which has in a practical reference objective reality for us, and is also a thing. But because we cannot furnish such reality to this concept in a theoretical point of view, it is a mere thing of faith of the pure Reason, along with God and Immortality, as the conditions under which alone we, in accordance with the constitution of our (human) Reason, can conceive the possibility of that effect of the use of our freedom in conformity with law. But belief in things of faith is a belief in a pure practical point of view, *i.e.* a moral faith, which proves nothing for theoretical pure rational cognition, but only for that which is practical and directed to the fulfilment of its duties; it in no way extends speculation or the practical rules of prudence in accordance with the principle of self-love. If the supreme principle of all moral laws is a postulate, so is also the possibility of its highest Object; and consequently, too, the condition under which we can think this possibility is postulated along with it and by it. Thus the cognition of the latter is neither knowledge nor opinion of the being and character of these conditions, regarded as theoretical cognition; but is a mere assumption in a reference which is practical and commanded for the moral use of our Reason.

If we were able also plausibly to base upon the purposes of nature, which physical Teleology presents to us in such rich abundance, a *determinate* concept of an intelligent World-Cause, then the existence [Dasein] of this Being would not be a thing of faith. For since this would not be assumed on behalf of the performance of my duty, but only in reference to the explanation of nature, it would be merely the opinion and hypothesis most conformable to our Reason. Now such Teleology leads in no way to a determinate concept of God; on the contrary, this can only be found in the concept of a moral Author of the World, because this alone furnishes the final purpose to which we can only reckon ourselves [as attached] if we behave conformably to what the moral law prescribes as final purpose and consequently obliges us [to do]. Hence it is only by its reference to the Object of our duty, as the condition of the possibility of attaining the final purpose of the same, that the concept of God attains the privilege of counting as a thing of faith, in our belief; but on the other hand, this same concept cannot make its Object valid as a thing of fact. For, although the necessity of duty is very plain for prac-tical Reason, yet the attainment of its final purpose, so far as it is not altogether in our own power, is only assumed on behalf of the practical use of Reason, and therefore is not so practically necessary as duty itself.[31]

Faith (as *habitus*, not as *actus*) is the moral attitude of Reason as to belief in that which is unattainable by theoretical cognition. It is therefore the constant principle of the mind, to assume as true, on account of the obligation in reference to it, that which it is neces-sary to presuppose as condition of the possibility of the highest moral final purpose[32]; although its possibility or impossibility be alike impossible for us to see into. Faith (absolutely so called) is trust in the attainment of a design, the promotion of which is a duty, but the possibility of the fulfilment of which (and consequently also that of the only conditions of it thinkable by us) is not to be *comprehended* by us. Faith, then, that refers to particular objects, which are not objects of possible knowledge or opinion (in which latter case it ought to be called, especially in historical matters, credulity and not faith), is quite moral. It is a free belief, not in that for which dogmatical proofs for the theoretically determinant Judgement are to be found, or in that to which we hold ourselves bound, but in that which we assume on behalf of a design in accordance with laws of freedom. This, however, is not, like opinion, without any adequate ground; but, is grounded as in Reason (although only in respect of its practical employment), and *adequately for its design*. For without this, the moral attitude of thought in its repudiation of the claim of the theoretical Reason for proofs (of the possibility of the Objects of morality) has no permanence; but wavers between practical commands and theoretical doubts. To be *incredulous* means to cling to maxims, and not to believe testimony in general; but he is *unbelieving*, who denies all validity to rational Ideas, because there is wanting a *theoretical* ground of their reality.[33] He judges therefore dogmatically. A dogmatical *unbelief* cannot subsist together with a moral maxim dominant in the mental attitude (for Reason cannot command one to follow a purpose, which is cognised as nothing more than a chimera); but a *doubtful faith* can. To this the absence of conviction by grounds of speculative Reason is only a hindrance, the influence of which upon conduct a critical insight into the limits of this faculty can remove, while it substitutes by way of compensation a paramount practical belief.

IF, in place of certain mistaken attempts, we wish to introduce a different principle into philosophy and to promote its influence, it makes us highly contented to see how and why those attempts must have disappointed us.

God, freedom, and *immortality,* are the problems at the solution of which all the equipments of Metaphysic aim, as their ultimate and unique purpose. Now it was believed that the doctrine of freedom is needed for practical philosophy only as its negative condition; but that on the other hand the doctrine of God and of the constitution of the soul, as belonging to theoretical philosophy, must be established for themselves and separately, in order afterwards to unite both with that which the moral law (possible only under the condition of freedom) commands, and so to constitute a religion. But we can easily see that these attempts must fail. For from mere ontological concepts of things in general, or of the existence of a necessary Being, it is possible to form absolutely no determinate concept of an original Being by means of predicates which can be given in experience and can therefore serve for cognition. Again a concept based on experience of the physical purposiveness of nature could furnish no adequate proof for morality, or consequently for cognition of a Deity. Just as little could the cognition of the soul by means of experience (which we only apply in this life) supply us with a concept of its spiritual immortal nature, a concept which would be adequate for morality. *Theology* and *Pneumatology,* regarded as problems of the sciences of a speculative Reason, can be established by no empirical data and predicates, because the concept of them is transcendent for our whole cognitive faculty.—The determination of both concepts, God and the soul (in respect of its immortality) alike, can only take place by means of predicates, which, although they are only possible from a supersensible ground, must yet prove their reality in experience; for thus alone can they make possible a cognition of a quite supersensible Being.—The only concept of this kind to be met with in human

Reason is that of the freedom of men under moral laws, along with the final purpose which Reason prescribes by these laws. Of these two [the moral laws and the final purpose] the first are useful for ascribing to the Author of Nature, the second for ascribing to man, those properties which contain the necessary condition of the possibility of both [God and the soul]; so that from this Idea a conclusion can be drawn as to the existence and constitution of these beings which are otherwise quite hidden from us.

Thus the ground of the failure of the attempt to prove God and immortality by the merely theoretical path lies in this, that no cognition whatever is possible of the supersensible in this way (of natural concepts). The ground of its success by the moral way (of the concept of freedom) is as follows. Here the supersensible (freedom), which in this case is fundamental, by a determinate law of causality that springs from it, not only supplies material for cognition of other supersensibles (the moral final purpose and the conditions of its attainability), but also establishes its reality in actions as a fact; though at the same time it can furnish a valid ground of proof in no other than a practical point of view (the only one, however, of which Religion has need).

It is thus very remarkable that of the three pure rational Ideas, *God, freedom,* and *immortality,* that of freedom is the only concept of the supersensible which (by means of the causality that is thought in it) proves its objective reality in nature by means of the effects it can produce there; and thus renders possible the connexion of both the others with nature, and of all three together with Religion. We have therefore in us a principle capable of determining the Idea of the supersensible within us, and thus also that of the supersensible without us, for knowledge, although only in a practical point of view; a principle this of which mere speculative philosophy (which could give a merely negative concept of freedom) must despair. Consequently the concept of freedom (as fundamental concept of all unconditioned practical laws) can extend Reason beyond those bounds, within which every natural (theoretical) concept must remain hopelessly limited.

---

1. We may call a hypothesis of this kind a daring venture of reason, and there may be few even of the most acute naturalists through whose head it has not sometimes passed. For it is not absurd, like that *generatio aequivoca* by which is understood the production of an organised being through the mechanics of crude unorganised matter. It would always remain *generatio univoca* in the most universal sense of the word, for it only considers one organic being as derived from another organic being, although from one which is specifically different; *e.g.* certain water-animals transform themselves gradually into marsh-animals and from these, after some generations, into land-animals. *A priori,* in the judgement of Reason alone, there is no contradiction here. Only experience gives no example of it; according to experience all generation that we know is *generatio homonyma.* This is not merely *univoca* in contrast to the generation out of unorganised material, but in the organisation the product is of like kind to that which produced it; and *generation heteronyma,* so far as our empirical knowledge of nature extends, is nowhere found.
2. It is probable that Kant alludes here to Hume's Essay *On a Providence and a Future State,* § xi of the *Inquiry.* Hume argues that though the inference from an effect to an intelligent cause may be valid in the case of human contrivance, it is not legitimate to rise by a like argument to Supreme Intelligence. "In human nature there is a certain experienced coherence of designs and inclinations; so that when from any fact we have discovered one intention of any man, it may often be reasonable from experience to infer another, and draw a long chain of conclusions concerning his past or future conduct. But this method of reasoning can never have place with regard to a being so remote and incomprehensible, who bears much less analogy to any other being in the universe than the sun to a waxen taper, and who discovers himself only by some faint traces or outlines, beyond which we have no authority to ascribe to him any attribute or perfection."
3. J. F. Blumenbach (1752–1840), a German naturalist and professor at Göttingen; the author of *Institutiones Physiologicae* (1787) and other works. An interesting account of him is given in Lever's novel *Adventures of Arthur O'Leary,* ch. xix.
4. Carl von Linné (1707–1778), Knight of the Polar Star, the celebrated Swedish botanist.

5. If the once adopted name *Natural history* is to continue for the description of nature, we may in contrast with art, give the title of *Archaeology of nature* to that which the former literally indicates, viz. a representation of the *old* condition of the earth, about which, although we cannot hope for certainty, we have good ground for conjecture. As sculptured stones, etc., belong to the province of art, so petrefactions belong to the archaeology of nature. And since work is actually being done in this [science] (under the name of the Theory of the Earth), constantly, although of course slowly, this name is not given to a merely imaginary investigation of nature, but to one to which nature itself leads and invites us.

6. First Edition has *freedom*.

7. These views are set forth by Kant more fully in the essay *Zum ewigen Frieden* (1795).

8. Second Edition.

9. Cf. *The Philosophical Theory of Religion*, Part i., *On the bad principle in Human Nature*, III., where Kant remarks that although war "is not so incurably bad as the deadness of a universal monarchy ... yet, as an ancient observed, it makes more bad men than it takes away."

10. The value of life for us, if it is estimated by that *which we enjoy* (by the natural purpose of the sum of all inclinations, *i.e.* happiness), is easy to decide. It sinks below zero; for who would be willing to enter upon life anew under the same conditions? who would do so even according to a new, self-chosen plan (yet in conformity with the course of nature), if it were merely directed to enjoyment? We have shown above what value life has in virtue of what it contains in itself, when lived in accordance with the purpose that nature has along with us, and which consists in what we do (not merely what we enjoy), in which, however, we are always but means towards an undetermined final purpose. There remains then nothing but the value which we ourselves give our life, through what we can not only do, but do purposively in such independence of nature that the existence of nature itself can only be a purpose under this condition.

11. It would be possible that the happiness of rational beings in the world should be a purpose of nature, and then also this would be its *ultimate* purpose. At least we cannot see *a priori* why nature should not be so ordered, because by means of its mechanism this effect would be certainly possible, at least so far as we see. But morality, with a causality according to purposes subordinated thereto, is absolutely impossible by means of natural causes; for the principle by which it determines to action is supersensible, and is therefore the only possible principle in the order of purposes that in respect of nature is absolutely unconditioned. Its subject consequently alone is qualified to be the *final purpose* of creation to which the whole of nature is subordinated.—*Happiness*, on the contrary, as has been shown in the preceding paragraphs by the testimony of experience, is not even a *purpose of nature* in respect of man in preference to other creatures; much less a *final purpose of creation*. Men may of course make it their ultimate subjective purpose. But if I ask, in reference to the final purpose of creation, why must men exist? then we are speaking of an objective supreme purpose, such as the highest Reason would require for creation. If we answer: These beings exist to afford objects for the benevolence of that Supreme Cause; then we contradict the condition to which the Reason of man subjects even his inmost wish for happiness (viz. the harmony with his own internal moral legislation). This proves that happiness can only be a conditioned purpose, and that it is only as a moral being that man can be the final purpose of creation; but that as concerns his state happiness is only connected with it as a consequence, according to the measure of his harmony with that purpose regarded as the purpose of his being.

12. Second Edition.

13. I say deliberately under moral laws. It is not man *in accordance with* moral laws, *i.e.* a being who behaves himself in conformity with them, who is the final purpose of creation. For by using the latter expression we should be asserting more than we know; viz. that it is in the power of an Author of the world to cause man always to behave himself in accordance with moral laws. But this presupposes a concept of freedom and of nature (of which latter we can only think an external author), which would imply an insight into the supersensible substrate of nature and its identity with that which causality through freedom makes possible in the world. And this far surpasses the insight of our Reason. Only of *man under moral laws* can we say, without transgressing the limits of our insight: his being constitutes the final purpose of the world. This harmonises completely with the judgement of human Reason reflecting morally upon the course of the world. We believe that we perceive in the case of the wicked the traces of a wise purposive reference, if we only see that the wanton criminal does not die before he has undergone the deserved punishment of his misdeeds. According to our concepts of free causality, our good or bad behaviour depends on ourselves; we regard it the highest wisdom in the government of the world to ordain for the first, opportunity, and for both, their consequence, in accordance with moral laws. In the latter properly consists the glory of God, which is hence not unsuitably described by theologians as the ultimate purpose of creation.— It is further to be remarked that when we use the word creation, we understand nothing more than we have said here, viz. the cause of the *being* of the world or of the things in it (substances). This is what the concept properly belonging to this word involves (*actuatio substantiae est creatio*); and consequently there is not implied in it the supposition of a freely working, and therefore intelligent, cause (whose being we first of all want to prove).

14. [Note added in Second Edition.] This moral argument does not supply any *objectively-valid* proof of the Being of God; it does not prove to the sceptic that there is a God, but proves that if he wishes to think in a way consonant with morality, he must admit the *assumption* of this proposition under the maxims of his practical Reason.— We should therefore not say: it is necessary *for morals* [Sittlichkeit], to assume the happiness of all rational beings of the world in proportion to their morality [Moralität]; but rather, this is necessitated *by* morality. Accordingly, this is a *subjective* argument sufficient for moral beings.

15. Second Edition.

16. Second Edition.
17. In a practical sense that religion is always idolatry which conceives the Supreme Being with properties, according to which something else besides morality can be a fit condition for that which man can do being in accordance with His Will. For however pure and free from sensible images the concept that we have formed may be in a theoretical point of view, yet it will be in a practical point of view still represented as an *idol*, *i.e.* in regard to the character of His Will, anthropomorphically.
18. Cf. *Introd. to Logic*, ix. p. 63, "Conviction is opposed to Persuasion, which is a belief from inadequate reasons, of which we do not know whether they are only subjective or are also objective."
19. Second Edition.
20. *I.e. Urtheils*. First Edition had *Urtheilens*, the judging subject.
21. *Analogy* (in a qualitative signification) is the identity of the relation between reasons and consequences (causes and effects), so far as it is to be found, notwithstanding the specific difference of the things or those properties in them which contain the reason for like consequences (*i.e.* considered apart from this relation). Thus we conceive of the artificial constructions of beasts by comparing them with those of men; by comparing the ground of those effects brought about by the former, which we do not know, with the ground of similar effects brought about by men (reason), which we do know; *i.e.* we regard the ground of the former as an analogon of reason. We then try at the same time to show that the ground of the artisan faculty of beasts, which we call instinct, specifically different as it is in fact from reason, has yet a similar relation to its effect (the buildings of the beaver as compared with those of men).—But then I cannot therefore conclude that because man uses *reason* for his building, the beaver must have the like, and call this a *conclusion* according to analogy. But from the similarity of the mode of operation of beasts (of which we cannot immediately perceive the ground) to that of men (of which we are immediately conscious), we can quite rightly conclude *according to analogy*, that beasts too act in accordance with *representations* (not as *Descartes* has it, that they are machines), and that despite their specific distinction they are yet (as living beings) of the same genus as man. The principle of our right so to conclude consists in the sameness of the ground for reckoning beasts in respect of the said determination in the same genus with men, regarded as men, so far as we can externally compare them with one another in accordance with their actions. There is *par ratio*. Just so I can conceive, according to the analogy of an Understanding, the causality of the supreme World-Cause, by comparing its purposive products in the world with the artificial works of men; but I cannot conclude according to analogy to those properties in it [which are in man], because here the principle of the possibility of such a method of reasoning entirely fails, viz. the *paritas rationis* for counting the Supreme Being in one and the same genus with man (in respect of the causality of both). The causality of the beings of the world, which is always sensibly conditioned (as is causality through Understanding) cannot be transferred to a Being which has in common with them no generic concept save that of Thing in general.
22. We thus miss nothing in the representation of the relations of this Being to the world, as far as the consequences, theoretical or practical, of this concept are concerned. To wish to investigate what it is in itself, is a curiosity as purposeless as it is vain.
23. Cf. *Introd. to Logic*, p. 76, where the conditions of a legitimate hypothesis are laid down. See also *Critique of Pure Reason*, Methodology, c. i. § 3.
24. This illustration is also given in the *Logic* (p. 57); where the three *modi* of belief, Opinion, Faith, and Knowledge, are distinguished from each other. Cf. *Critique of Pure Reason*, Methodology, c. ii. § 3.
25. The speculations of Swedenborg seem to have always had a strange fascination for Kant. He says of two reported cases of Swedenborg's clairvoyance that he knows not how to disprove them (Rosenkranz vii. 5); but in his *Anthropology* §§ 35, 37, he attacks Swedenborgianism as folly. So in an early essay, *Dreams of a Visionary explained by Dreams of Metaphysics*, he avows his scepticism as to the value of the information which "psychical research" can supply about the spirit-world, though he is careful not to commit himself to any dogmatic statement on the subject of ghosts. In the *Critique of Pure Reason* (when discussing the Postulates of Empirical Thought) he gives, as an instance of a concept inconsistent with the canons of possibility, "a power of being in a community of thought with other men, however distant from us."
26. Cf. *supra*, p. 229.
27. I here extend, correctly as it seems to me, the concept of a thing of fact beyond the usual signification of this word. For it is not needful, not even feasible, to limit this expression merely to actual experience, if we are talking of the relation of things to our cognitive faculties; for an experience merely possible is quite sufficient in order that we may speak of them merely as objects of a definite kind of cognition.
28. Cf. *introduction to Logic*, p. 59 note.
29. Second Edition.
30. Things of fact are not therefore *articles of faith*; if we understand by the latter things of faith to the *confession* of which (internal or external) we can be bound. Natural theology contains nothing like this. For since they, as things of faith (like things of fact) cannot be based on theoretical proofs, [they are accepted by] a belief which is free and which only as such is compatible with the morality of the subject.
31. The final purpose which the moral law enjoins upon us to further, is not the ground of duty; since this lies in the moral law, which, as formal practical principle, leads categorically, independently of the Objects of the faculty of desire (the material of the will) and consequently of any purpose whatever. This formal characteristic of my actions (their subordination under the principle of universal validity), wherein alone consists their inner moral worth, is quite in our power; and I can quite well abstract from the possibility or the unattainableness of purposes which I am obliged to promote in conformity with that law (because in them

consists only the external worth of my actions) as something which is never completely in my power, in order only to look to that which is of my doing. But then the design of promoting the final purpose of all rational beings (happiness so far as it is possible for it to be accordant with duty) is even yet prescribed by the law of duty. The speculative Reason, however, does not see at all the attainableness of this (neither on the side of our own physical faculty nor on that of the co-operation of nature). It must rather, so far as we can judge in a rational way, hold the derivation, by the aid of such causes, of such a consequence of our good conduct from mere nature (internal and external) without God and immortality, to be an ungrounded and vain, though well-meant, expectation; and if it could have complete certainty of this judgement, it would regard the moral law itself as the mere deception of our Reason in a practical aspect. But since the speculative Reason fully convinces itself that the latter can never take place, but that on the other hand those Ideas whose object lies outside nature can be thought without contradiction, it must for its own practical law and the problem prescribed thereby, and therefore in a moral aspect, recognise those Ideas as real in order not to come into contradiction with itself.

32. It is a trust in the promise of the moral law; [not however such as is contained in it, but such as I put into it and that on morally adequate grounds. For a final purpose cannot be commanded by any law of Reason without this latter at the same time promising, however uncertainly, its attainableness; and thus justifying our belief in the special conditions under which alone our Reason can think it as attainable. The word *fides* expresses this; and it can only appear doubtful, how this expression and this particular Idea came into moral philosophy, since it first was introduced with Christianity, and the adoption of it perhaps might seem to be only a flattering imitation of Christian terminology. But this is not the only case in which this wonderful religion with its great simplicity of statement has enriched philosophy with far more definite and purer concepts of morality, than it had been able to furnish before; but which, once they are there, are *freely* assented to by Reason and are assumed as concepts to which it could well have come of itself and which it could and should have introduced.] [Second Edition.]

33. Cf. *Introd. to Logic*, ix. p. 60, "That man is morally *unbelieving* who does not accept that which though *impossible* to know is *morally necessary* to suppose."

GENERAL REMARK ON TELEOLOGY

IF THE QUESTION IS, what rank the moral argument, which proves the Being of God only as a thing of faith for the practical pure Reason, maintains among the other arguments in philosophy, it is easy to set aside the whole achievement of this last; by which it appears that there is no choice, but that our theoretical faculty must give up all its pretensions before an impartial criticism.

All belief must in the first place be grounded upon facts, if it is not to be completely groundless; and therefore the only distinction in proofs that there can be is that belief in the consequence derived therefrom can either be grounded on this fact as *knowledge* for theoretical cognition, or merely as *faith* for practical. All facts belong either to the *natural concept* which proves its reality in the objects of sense, given (or which may possibly be given) before all natural concepts; or to the *concept of freedom*, which sufficiently establishes its reality through the causality of Reason in regard of certain effects in the world of sense, possible through it, which it incontrovertibly postulates in the moral law. The natural concept (merely belonging to theoretical cognition) is now either metaphysical and thinkable completely *a priori*, or physical, *i.e.* thinkable *a posteriori* and as necessary only through determinate experience. The metaphysical natural concept (which presupposes no determinate experience) is therefore ontological.

The *ontological* proof of the being of God from the concept of an original Being is either that which from ontological predicates, by which alone it can be thought as completely determined, infers absolutely necessary being; or that which, from the absolute necessity of the being somewhere of some thing, whatever it be, infers the predicates of the original Being. For there belongs to the concept of an original Being, inasmuch as it is not derived from anything, the unconditioned necessity of its presence, and (in order to represent this) its complete determination by its [mere][1] concept. It was believed that both requirements were found in the concept of the ontological Idea of a *Being the most real of all*; and thus two metaphysical proofs originated.

The proof (properly called ontological) resting upon a merely metaphysical natural concept concludes from the concept of the Being the most real of all, its absolutely necessary existence; for (it is said), if it did not exist, a reality would be wanting to it, viz. existence.—The other (which is also called the metaphysico-*cosmological* proof) concludes from the necessity of the existence somewhere of a thing (which must be conceded, for a being is given to us in self-consciousness), its complete determination as that of a Being the most real of all; for everything existing must be completely determined, but the absolutely necessary (*i.e.* that which *we* ought to cognise as such and consequently *a priori*) must be completely determined *by means of its own concept*. But this is only the case with the concept of a thing the most real of all. It is not needful to expose here the sophistry in both arguments, which has been already done elsewhere;[2] it is only needful to remark that neither proof, even if they could be defended by all manner of dialectical subtlety, could ever pass from the schools into the world, or have the slightest influence on the mere sound Understanding.

The proof, which rests on a natural concept that can only be empirical and yet is to lead us beyond the bounds of nature regarded as the complex of the objects of sense, can be no other than that derived from the *purposes* of nature. The concept of these cannot, it is true, be given *a priori* but only through experience; but yet it promises such a concept of the original ground of nature as alone, among all those which we can conceive, is suited to the supersensible, viz. that of a highest Understanding as Cause of the world. This, in fact, it completely performs in accordance with principles of the reflective Judgement, *i.e.* in accordance with the constitution of our (human) faculty of cognition.—But whether or not it is in a position to supply from the same data this concept of a *supreme, i.e.* independent intelligent Being, in short of a God or Author of a world under moral laws, and consequently as sufficiently determined for the Idea of a final purpose of the being of the world—this is the question upon which everything depends, whether we desire a theoretically adequate concept of the Original Being on behalf of our whole knowledge of nature, or a practical concept for religion.

This argument derived from physical Teleology is worthy of respect. It produces a similar effect in the way of conviction upon the common Understanding as upon the subtlest thinker; and a *Reimarus*[3] has acquired immortal honour in his work (not yet superseded), in which he abundantly develops this ground of proof with his peculiar thoroughness and lucidity.—But how does this proof acquire such mighty influence upon the mind? How does a judgement by cold reason (for we might refer to persuasion the emotion and elevation of reason produced by the wonders of nature) issue thus in a calm and unreserved assent? It is not the physical purposes, which all indicate in the World Cause an unfathomable intelligence; these are inadequate thereto, because they do not satisfy the need of the inquiring Reason. For, wherefore (it asks) are all those natural things that exhibit art? Wherefore is man himself, whom we must regard as the ultimate purpose of nature thinkable by us? Wherefore is this collective Nature here, and what is the final purpose of such great and manifold art? Reason cannot be contented with enjoyment or with contemplation, observation, and admiration (which, if it stops there, is only enjoyment of a particular kind) as the ultimate final purpose for the creation of the world and of man himself; for this presupposes a personal worth, which man alone can give himself, as the condition under which alone he and his being can be the final purpose. Failing this (which alone is susceptible of a definite concept), the purposes of nature do not satisfactorily answer our questions; especially because they cannot furnish any *determinate* concept of the highest Being as an all-sufficient (and therefore unique and so properly called *highest*) being, and of the laws according to which an Understanding is Cause of the world.

Hence that the physico-teleological proof convinces, just as if it were a theological proof, does not arise from our availing ourselves of the Ideas of purposes of nature as so many empirical grounds of proof of a *highest* Understanding. But it mingles itself unnoticed with that moral ground of proof, which dwells in every man and influences him secretly, in the conclusion by which we ascribe to the Being, which manifests itself with such incomprehensible art in the purposes of nature, a final purpose and consequently wisdom (without however being justified in doing so by the perception of the former); and by which therefore we arbitrarily fill up the lacunas of the [design] argument. In fact it is only the moral ground of proof which produces conviction, and that only in a moral reference with which every man feels inwardly his agreement. But the physico-teleological proof has only the merit of leading the mind, in its consideration of the world, by the way of purposes and through them to an *intelligent* Author of the world. The moral reference to purposes and the Idea of a moral legislator and Author of the world, as a theological concept, seem to be developed of themselves out of that ground of proof, although they are in truth pure additions.

Henceforward we may allow the customary statement to stand. For it is generally difficult (if the distinction requires much reflection) for ordinary sound Understanding to distinguish from one another as heterogeneous the different principles which it confuses, and from one of which alone it actually draws conclusions with correctness. The moral ground of proof of the Being of God, properly speaking, does not merely *complete* and render perfect the physico-teleological proof; but it is a special proof that *supplies* the conviction which is wanting in the latter. This latter in fact can do nothing more than guide Reason, in its judgements upon the ground of nature and that contingent but admirable order of nature only known to us by experience, to the causality of a Cause containing the ground of the same in accordance with purposes (which we by the constitution of our cognitive faculties must think as an intelligent cause); and thus by arresting the attention of Reason it makes it more susceptible of the moral proof. For what is requisite to the latter concept is so essentially different from everything which natural concepts contain and can teach, that there is need of a particular ground of proof quite independent of the former, in order to supply the concept of the original Being adequately for Theology and to infer its existence.—The moral proof (which it is true only proves the Being of God in a practical though indispensable aspect of Reason) would preserve all its force, if we found in the world no material, or only that which is doubtful, for physical Teleology. It is possible to conceive rational beings surrounded by a nature which displayed no clear trace of organisation but only the effects of a mere mechanism of crude matter; on behalf of which and amid the changeability of some merely contingent purposive forms and relations there would appear to be no ground for inferring an intelligent Author. In such case there would be no occasion for a physical Teleology; and yet Reason, which here gets no guidance from natural concepts, would find in the concept of freedom and in the moral Ideas founded thereon a practically sufficient ground for postulating the concept of the original Being in conformity with these, *i.e.* as a Deity, and for postulating nature (even the nature of our own being) as a final purpose in accordance with freedom and its laws—and all this in reference to the indispensable command of practical Reason.—However the fact that there is in the actual world for the rational beings in it abundant material for physical Teleology (even though this is not necessary) serves as a desirable confirmation of the moral argument, as far as nature can exhibit anything analogous to the (moral) rational Ideas. For the concept of a supreme Cause possessing intelligence (though not reaching far enough for a Theology) thus acquires sufficient reality for the reflective Judgement, but it is not required as the basis of the moral proof; nor does this latter serve to complete as a proof the former, which does not by itself point to morality at all, by means of an argument developed according to a single principle. Two such heterogeneous principles as nature and freedom can only furnish two different kinds of proof; and the attempt to derive one from the other is found unavailing as regards that which is to be proved.

If the physico-teleological ground of proof sufficed for the proof which is sought, it would be very satisfactory for the speculative Reason; for it would furnish the hope of founding a Theosophy (for so we must call the theoretical cognition of the divine nature and its existence which would suffice at once for the explanation of the constitution of the world and for the determination of moral laws). In the same way if Psychology enabled us to arrive at a cognition of the immortality of the soul it would make Pneumatology possible, which would be just as welcome to the speculative Reason. But neither, agreeable as they would be to the arrogance of our curiosity, would satisfy the wish of Reason in respect of a theory which must be based on a cognition of the nature of things. Whether the first, as Theology, and the second, as Anthropology, when founded on the moral principle, *i.e.* the principle of freedom, and consequently in accordance with the practical use [of Reason] do not better fulfil their objective final design, is another question which we need not here pursue.

The physico-teleological ground of proof does not reach to Theology, because it does not and cannot give any determinate concept, sufficient for this design, of the original Being; but we must derive this from quite another quarter, or must supply its lacuna by an arbitrary addition. You infer, from the great purposiveness of natural forms and their relations, a world-cause endowed with Understanding; but what is the degree of this Understanding? Without doubt you cannot assume that it is the highest possible Understanding; because for that it would be requisite that you should see that a greater Understanding than that of which you perceive proofs in the world, is not thinkable; and this would be to ascribe Omniscience to yourself.[4] In the same way, if you infer from the magnitude of the world the very great might of its Author, you must be content with this having only a comparative significance for your faculty of comprehension; for since you do not know all that is possible, so as to compare it with the magnitude of the world as far as you know it, you cannot infer the Almightiness of its Author from so small a standard, and so on. Now you arrive in this way at no definite concept of an original Being available for a Theology; for this can only be found in the concept of the totality of perfections compatible with intelligence, and you cannot help yourself to this by merely *empirical* data. But without such a definite concept you cannot infer a *unique* intelligent original Being; you can only assume it (with whatever motive).—Now it may certainly be conceded that you should arbitrarily add (for Reason has nothing fundamental to say to the contrary): Where so much perfection is found, we may well assume that all perfection is united in a unique Cause of the world, because Reason succeeds better both theoretically and practically with a principle thus definite. But then you cannot regard this concept of the original Being as proved by you, for you have only assumed it on behalf of a better employment of Reason. Hence all lamentation or impotent anger on account of the alleged mischief of rendering doubtful the coherency of your chain of reasoning, is vain pretentiousness, which would fain have us believe that the doubt here freely expressed as to your argument is a doubting of sacred truth, in order that under this cover the shallowness of your argument may pass unnoticed.

Moral Teleology, on the other hand, which is not less firmly based than physical,—which, indeed, rather deserves the preference because it rests *a priori* on principles inseparable from our Reason—leads to that which is requisite for the possibility of a Theology, viz. to a determinate *concept* of the supreme Cause, as Cause of the world according to moral laws, and, consequently, to the concept of such a cause as satisfies our moral final purpose. For this are required, as natural properties belonging to it, nothing less than Omniscience, Omnipotence, Omnipresence, and the like, which must be thought as bound up with the moral final purpose which is infinite and thus as adequate to it. Hence moral Teleology alone can furnish the concept of a *unique* Author of the world, which is available for a Theology.

In this way Theology leads immediately to *Religion, i.e. the recognition of our duties as divine commands*[5]; because it is only the recognition of our duty and of the final purpose enjoined upon us by Reason which brings out with definiteness the concept of God. This concept, therefore, is inseparable in its origin from obligation to that Being. On the other hand, even if the concept of the original Being could be also found determinately by the merely theoretical path (viz. the concept of it as mere Cause of nature), it would afterwards be very difficult—perhaps impossible without arbitrary interpolation [of elements]—to ascribe to this Being by well-grounded proofs a causality in accordance with moral laws; and yet without this that quasi-theological concept could furnish no foundation for religion. Even if a religion could be established by this theoretical path, it would actually, as regards sentiment (wherein its essence lies) be different from that in which the concept of God and the (practical) conviction of His Being originate from the fundamental Ideas of morality. For if we must suppose the Omnipotence, Omniscience, etc., of an Author of the world as concepts given to us from another quarter, in order afterwards only to apply our concepts of duties to our relation to Him, then these latter concepts must bear very markedly the appearance of compulsion and forced submission. If, instead of this, the respect for the moral law, quite freely, in virtue of the precept of our own Reason, represents to us the final purpose of our destination, we admit among our moral views a Cause harmonising with this and with its accomplishment, with the sincerest reverence, which is quite distinct from pathological fear; and we willingly submit ourselves thereto.[6]

If it be asked why it is incumbent upon us to have any Theology at all, it appears clear that it is not needed for the extension or correction of our cognition of nature or in general for any theory, but simply in a subjective point of view for Religion, *i.e.* the practical or moral use of our Reason. If it is found that the only argument which leads to a definite concept of the object of Theology is itself moral, it is not only not strange, but we miss nothing in respect of its final purpose as regards the sufficiency of belief from this ground of proof, provided that it be admitted that such an argument only establishes the Being of God sufficiently for our moral destination, *i.e.* in a practical point of view, and that here speculation neither shows its strength in any way, nor extends by means of it the sphere of its domain. Our surprise and the alleged contradiction between the possibility of a Theology asserted here and that which the Critique of speculative Reason said of the Categories—viz. that they can only produce knowledge when applied to objects of sense, but in no way when applied to the supersensible—vanish, if we see that they are here used for a cognition of God not in a theoretical point of view (in accordance with what His own nature, inscrutable to us, may be) but simply in a practical.—In order then at this opportunity to make an end of the misinterpretation of that very necessary doctrine of the Critique, which, to the chagrin of the blind dogmatist, refers Reason to its bounds, I add here the following elucidation.

If I ascribe to a body *motive force* and thus think it by means of the category of *causality*, then I at the same time *cognise* it by that [category]; *i.e.* I determine the concept of it, as of an Object in general, by means of what belongs to it by itself (as the condition of the possibility of that relation) as an object of sense. If the motive force ascribed to it is repulsive, then there belongs to it (although I do not place near it any other body upon which it may exert force) a place in space, and moreover extension, *i.e.* space in itself, besides the filling up of this by means of the repulsive forces of its parts. In addition there is the law of this filling up (that the ground of the repulsion of the parts must decrease in the same proportion as the extension of the body increases, and as the space, which it fills with the same parts by means of this force, is augmented).—On the contrary, if I think a supersensible Being as the first *mover*, and thus by the category of causality as regards its determination of the world (motion of matter), I must not think it as existing in any place in space nor as extended; I must not even think it as existing in time or simultaneously with other beings. Hence I have no determinations whatever, which could make intelligible to me the condition of the possibility of motion by means of this Being as its ground. Consequently, I do not in the very least cognise it by means of the predicate of Cause (as first mover), for itself; but I have only the representation of a something containing the ground of the motions in the world; and the relation of the latter to it as their cause, since it does not besides furnish me with anything belonging to the constitution of the thing which is cause, leaves its concept quite empty. The reason of this is, that by predicates which only find their Object in the world of sense I can indeed proceed to the being of something which must contain their ground, but not to the determination of its concept as a supersensible being, which excludes all these predicates. By the category of causality, then, if I determine it by the concept of a *first mover*, I do not in the very least cognise what God is. Perhaps, however, I shall have better success if I start from the order of the world, not merely to *think* its causality as that of a supreme *Understanding*, but to *cognise* it by means of this determination of the said concept; because here the troublesome condition of space and of extension disappears.—At all events the great purposiveness in the world compels us to *think* a supreme cause of it, and to *think* its causality as that of an Understanding; but we are not therefore entitled to *ascribe* this to it. (*E.g.* we think of the eternity of God as presence in all time, because we can form no other concept of mere being as a quantum, *i.e.* as duration; or we think of the divine Omnipresence as presence in all places in order to make comprehensible to ourselves His immediate presence in things which are external to one another; without daring to ascribe to God any of these determinations, as something cognised in Him.) If I determine the causality of a man, in respect of certain products which are only explicable by designed purposiveness, by thinking it as that of Understanding, I need not stop here, but I can ascribe to him this predicate as a well-known property and cognise him accordingly. For I know that intuitions are given to the senses of men and are brought by the Understanding under a concept and thus under a rule; that this concept only contains the common characteristic (with omission of the particular ones) and is thus discursive; and that the rules for bringing given representations under a consciousness in general are given by Understanding before those intuitions, etc. I therefore ascribe this property to man as a property by means of which I *cognise* him. However, if I wish to *think* a supersensible Being (God) as an intelligence, this is not only permissible in a certain aspect of my employment of Reason—it is unavoidable; but to ascribe to Him Understanding and to flatter ourselves that we can *cognise* Him by means of it as a property of His, is in no way permissible. For I must omit all those conditions under which alone I know an Understanding, and thus the predicate which only serves for determining man cannot be applied at all to a supersensible Object; and therefore by a causality thus determined, I cannot cognise what God is. And so it is with all Categories, which can have no significance for cognition in a theoretical aspect, if they are not applied to objects of possible experience.—However, according to the analogy of an Understanding I can in a certain other aspect think a supersensible being, without at the same time meaning thereby to cognise it theoretically; viz. if this determination of its causality concerns an effect in the world, which contains a design morally necessary but unattainable by a sensible being. For then a cognition of God and of His Being (Theology) is possible by means of properties and determinations of His causality merely thought in Him according to analogy, which has all requisite reality in a practical reference though *only in respect of this* (as moral).—An Ethical Theology is therefore possible; for though morality can subsist without theology as regards its rule, it cannot do so as regards the final design which this proposes, unless Reason in respect of it is to be renounced. But a Theological Ethic (of pure Reason) is impossible; for laws which Reason itself does not give and whose observance it does not bring about as a pure practical faculty, can not be moral. In the same way a Theological Physic would be a nonentity, for it would propose no laws of nature but ordinances of a Highest Will; while on the other hand a physical (properly speaking a physico-teleological) Theology can serve at least as a propaedeutic to Theology proper, by giving occasion for the Idea of a final purpose which nature cannot present by the observation of natural purposes of which it offers abundant material. It thus makes felt the need of a Theology which shall determine the concept of God adequately for the highest practical use of Reason, but it cannot develop this and base it satisfactorily on its proofs.

---

1. First Edition.
2. In the *Critique of Pure Reason*, Dialectic, bk. II. c. iii. §§ 4, 5.
3. H. S. Reimarus (1694–1768), the author of the famous *Wolfenbüttel Fragments*, published after the death of Reimarus by Lessing. The book alluded to by Kant is probably the *Abhandlungen von den vornehmsten Wahrheiten der natürlichen Religion* (1754), which had great popularity in its day.
4. These arguments are advanced by Hume, *Inquiry*, § vii. Cf. also *Pure Reason*, Dialectic, bk. II. c. iii. § 6, and *Practical Reason*, Dialectic, c. ii. § vii.
5. Cf. *Practical Reason*, Dialectic, c. ii. § v.

6. The admiration for beauty, and also the emotion aroused by the manifold purposes of nature, which a reflective mind is able to feel even prior to a clear representation of a rational Author of the world, have something in themselves like *religious* feeling. They seem in the first place by a method of judging analogous to moral to produce an effect upon the moral feeling (gratitude to, and veneration for, the unknown cause); and thus by exciting moral Ideas to produce an effect upon the mind, when they inspire that admiration which is bound up with far more interest than mere theoretical observation can bring about.